NINETY-FOURTH EDITION
SINCE 1912

WHO'S WHO
IN BASEBALL
2009

Official Lifetime Records
Of Major League Players

Editor
Pete Palmer

Associate Editor
Stuart Shea

Managing Editor
Rory S. Slifkin

ABREU, BOB KELLY (BOBBY)
Born, Maracay, Venezuela, March 11, 1974.
Bats Left. Throws Right. Height, 6 feet. Weight, 210 pounds.

Year Club	Lea	Pos	G	AB	R	H	2B	3B	HR	RBI	SB	Avg
1991 Astros	Gulf Coast	OF-SS	56	183	21	55	7	3	0	20	10	.301
1992 Asheville	So. Atl.	OF	135	480	81	140	21	4	8	48	15	.292
1993 Osceola	Fla. St.	OF	129	474	62	134	21	17	5	55	10	.283
1994 Jackson	Texas	OF	118	400	61	121	25	9	16	73	12	.303
1995 Tucson	P.C.	OF-2B	114	415	72	126	24	17	10	75	16	.304
1996 Tucson	P.C.	OF	132	484	86	138	14	16	13	68	24	.285
1996 Houston	N.L.	OF	15	22	1	5	1	0	0	1	0	.227
1997 Jackson	Texas	OF	3	12	2	2	1	0	0	0	0	.167
1997 New Orleans	A.A.	OF	47	194	25	52	9	4	2	22	7	.268
1997 Houston a-b-c	N.L.	OF	59	188	22	47	10	2	3	26	7	.250
1998 Philadelphia	N.L.	OF	151	497	68	155	29	6	17	74	19	.312
1999 Philadelphia	N.L.	OF	152	546	118	183	35	*11	20	93	27	.335
2000 Philadelphia	N.L.	OF	154	576	103	182	42	10	25	79	28	.316
2001 Philadelphia	N.L.	OF *162	588	118	170	48	4	31	110	36		.289
2002 Philadelphia	N.L.	OF	157	572	102	176	*50	6	20	85	31	.308
2003 Philadelphia	N.L.	OF	158	577	99	173	35	1	20	101	22	.300
2004 Philadelphia	N.L.	OF	159	574	118	173	47	1	30	105	40	.301
2005 Philadelphia	N.L.	OF *162	588	104	168	37	1	24	102	31		.286
2006 Philadelphia	N.L.	OF	98	339	61	94	25	2	8	65	20	.277
2006 New York d	A.L.	OF	58	209	37	69	16	0	7	42	10	.330
2007 New York	A.L.	OF	158	605	123	171	40	5	16	101	25	.283
2008 New York e	A.L.	OF	156	609	100	180	39	4	20	100	22	.296
Major League Totals		13 Yrs.	1799	6490	1174	1946	454	53	241	1084	318	.300
Division Series												
1997 Houston	N.L.	PH	3	3	0	1	0	0	0	0	1	.333
2006 New York	A.L.	OF	4	15	2	5	1	0	0	4	0	.333
2007 New York	A.L.	OF	4	15	1	4	1	0	1	2	1	.267
Division Series Totals			11	33	3	10	2	0	1	6	2	.303

a On disabled list from May 25 to July 1, 1997.
b Selected in expansion draft by Tampa Bay Devil Rays, November 18, 1997.
c Traded to Philadelphia Phillies for infielder Kevin Stocker, November 19, 1997.
d Traded to New York Yankees with pitcher Cory Lidle for infielder C.J. Henry, pitcher Matt Smith, catcher Jesus Sanchez and pitcher Carlos Monasterios, July 30, 2006.
e Filed for free agency, October 30, 2008.

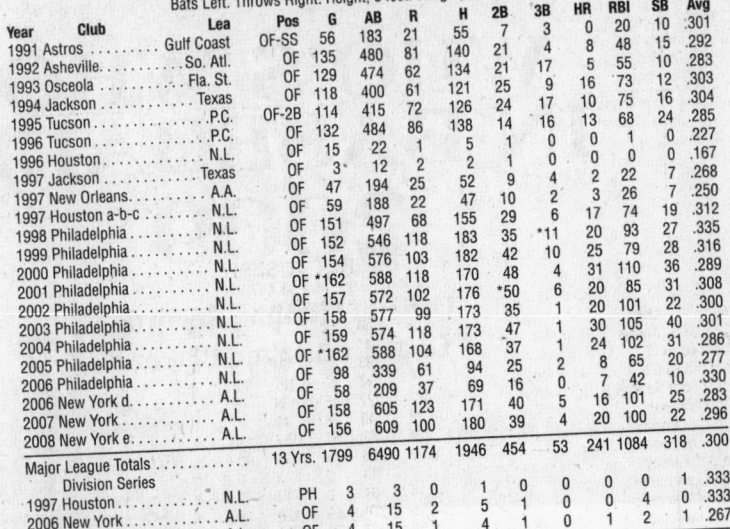

AMEZAGA (DELGADO), ALFREDO
Born, Ciudad Obregon, Mexico, January 16, 1978.
Bats Both. Throws Right. Height, 5 feet, 10 inches. Weight, 190 pounds.

Year Club	Lea	Pos	G	AB	R	H	2B	3B	HR	RBI	SB	Avg
1999 Boise	Northwest	2B-SS	48	205	52	66	6	4	2	29	14	.322
1999 Butte	Pioneer	2B-SS	8	34	11	10	2	0	0	5	6	.294
2000 Lake Elsinore	Calif.	2B-SS	108	420	90	117	13	4	4	44	73	.279
2001 Salt Lake	P.C.	SS	49	200	28	50	5	4	1	16	9	.250
2001 Arkansas	Texas	SS	70	285	50	89	10	5	4	21	24	.312
2002 Salt Lake	P.C.	SS-2B	128	518	77	130	25	7	6	51	23	.251
2002 Anaheim	A.L.	SS	12	13	3	7	2	0	0	2	1	.538
2003 Salt Lake	P.C.	SS-2B	75	317	55	110	20	5	3	45	14	.347
2003 Anaheim	A.L.	SS-3B	37	105	15	22	3	2	2	7	2	.210
2004 Salt Lake	P.C.	SS	32	135	15	35	5	2	2	14	7	.259
2004 Anaheim a	A.L.	SS-3B-2B	73	93	12	15	2	0	2	11	3	.161
2005 Indianapolis	Int.	SS-2B-OF-3B	64	185	28	63	12	2	1	12	14	.341
2005 Colorado-Pitt. b-c	N.L.	3B-SS	5	6	2	1	0	0	0	0	1	.167
2006 Florida	N.L.	OF-2B-SS-3B	132	334	42	87	9	3	3	19	20	.260
2007 Florida	N.L.	OF-SS-3B-2B	133	400	46	105	14	9	3	30	13	.262
2008 Florida	N.L.	OF-SS-3B-2B	125	311	41	82	13	5	3	32	8	.264
Major League Totals		7 Yrs.	517	1262	161	319	43	19	12	101	48	.253
Division Series												
2004 Anaheim a	A.L.	2B	2	2	0	0	0	0	0	0	0	.000

a Claimed on waivers by Colorado Rockies, December 17, 2004.
b Claimed on waivers by Pittsburgh Pirates, April 20, 2005.
c Filed for free agency, October 15, 2005. Signed with Florida Marlins, November 22, 2005.

Year Club	Lea	Pos	G	AB	R	H	2B	3B	HR	RBI	SB	Avg
2003 Great Falls	Pioneer	OF	13	49	6	19	2	1	2	13	3	.388
2004 Winston-Salem	Carolina	OF	69	254	43	81	22	4	8	46	10	.319
2004 Birmingham	Southern	OF	48	185	26	50	9	3	4	27	3	.270
2005 Charlotte	Int.	OF	118	448	71	132	24	3	16	57	4	.295
2005 Chicago	A.L.	OF	13	34	3	6	1	0	2	3	1	.176
2006 Chicago	A.L.	OF	134	365	46	82	23	1	8	33	4	.225
2007 Chicago	A.L.	OF	13	17	3	2	1	0	0	0	0	.118
2007 Charlotte	Int.	OF	57	200	29	51	8	2	8	31	3	.255
2008 Chicago	A.L.	OF	109	181	24	42	13	0	8	26	5	.232
Major League Totals	4 Yrs.		269	597	76	132	38	1	18	62	10	.221
Division Series												
2008 Chicago	A.L.	OF	3	5	1	0	0	0	0	0	1	.000

Year Club	Lea	Pos	G	AB	R	H	2B	3B	HR	RBI	SB	Avg
1990 Mesa Angels	Arizona	OF	32	127	5	27	2	0	0	14	3	.213
1990 Boise	Northwest	OF	25	83	11	21	3	1	1	8	0	.253
1991 Quad City	Midwest	OF	105	392	40	102	22	2	2	42	5	.260
1992 Palm Springs	California	OF	81	322	46	104	15	2	1	62	1	.323
1992 Midland	Texas	OF	39	146	16	40	5	0	2	19	2	.274
1993 Vancouver	P.C.	OF-1B	124	467	57	137	34	4	4	71	3	.293
1994 Vancouver	P.C.	OF-1B	123	505	75	162	42	6	12	102	3	.321
1994 California	A.L.	OF	5	13	0	5	0	0	0	1	0	.385
1995 Vancouver	P.C.	OF	14	61	9	19	7	0	0	12	0	.311
1995 California	A.L.	OF	106	374	50	120	19	1	16	69	6	.321
1996 California	A.L.	OF	150	607	79	173	33	2	12	72	7	.285
1997 Anaheim	A.L.	OF	154	624	76	189	36	3	8	92	10	.303
1998 Anaheim	A.L.	OF	156	622	62	183	41	7	15	79	8	.294
1999 Anaheim	A.L.	OF	157	620	88	188	36	2	21	80	3	.303
2000 Anaheim	A.L.	OF	159	647	92	185	40	3	35	117	7	.286
2001 Anaheim	A.L.	OF	161	672	83	194	39	2	28	123	13	.289
2002 Anaheim	A.L.	OF	158	638	93	195	*56	3	29	123	6	.306
2003 Anaheim	A.L.	OF	159	638	80	201	*49	4	29	116	6	.315
2004 Rancho Cucamonga	Calif.	OF	3	9	1	4	0	0	1	1	0	.444
2004 Anaheim a	A.L.	OF	112	442	57	133	20	1	14	75	2	.301
2005 Los Angeles	A.L.	OF	142	575	68	163	34	1	17	96	1	.283
2006 Los Angeles	A.L.	OF	141	543	63	152	28	2	17	85	1	.280
2007 Rancho Cucamonga	Calif.	OF	6	18	3	4	1	0	0	2	1	.222
2007 Los Angeles b	A.L.	OF	108	417	67	124	31	1	16	80	1	.297
2008 Los Angeles c	A.L.	OF	145	557	66	163	27	3	15	84	7	.293
Major League Totals	15 Yrs.		2013	7989	1024	2368	489	35	272	1292	78	.296
Division Series												
2002 Anaheim	A.L.	OF	4	18	5	7	2	0	1	4	0	.389
2004 Anaheim	A.L.	OF	3	13	1	2	0	0	0	0	0	.154
2005 Los Angeles	A.L.	OF	5	19	2	5	0	1	2	7	0	.263
2007 Los Angeles	A.L.	OF	3	9	0	2	1	0	0	0	0	.222
2008 Los Angeles	A.L.	OF	4	19	1	3	0	0	0	0	0	.158
Division Series Totals			19	78	9	19	3	1	3	11	0	.244
Championship Series												
2002 Anaheim	A.L.	OF	5	20	3	5	1	0	1	3	0	.250
2005 Los Angeles	A.L.	OF	5	17	2	3	0	0	1	2	0	.176
Championship Series Totals			10	37	5	8	1	0	2	5	0	.216
World Series Record												
2002 Anaheim	A.L.	OF	7	32	3	9	1	0	0	6	0	.281

a On disabled list from April 22 to June 10, 2004.
b On disabled list from April 28 to June 3 and June 17 to July 3, 2007.
c Not offered contract, October 28, 2008.

ANDERSON, JOSHUA AARON (JOSH)
Born, Somerset, Kentucky, August 10, 1982.
Bats Left. Throws Right. Height, 6 feet, 2 inches. Weight, 195 pounds.

Year Club	Lea	Pos	G	AB	R	H	2B	3B	HR	RBI	SB	Avg
2003 Tri-City	N.Y.-Penn.	OF	74	297	44	85	11	4	3	30	26	.286
2004 Salem	Carolina	OF	66	280	45	75	13	6	2	21	31	.268
2004 Lexington	So.Atl.	OF	73	298	69	97	12	3	4	31	48	.326
2005 Corpus Christi	Texas	OF	127	524	67	148	16	9	1	26	50	.282
2006 Corpus Christi	Texas	OF	130	561	83	173	26	4	3	50	43	.308
2007 Round Rock	P.C.	OF-1B	132	513	64	140	17	6	2	43	40	.273
2007 Houston a	N.L.	OF	21	67	10	24	3	0	0	11	1	.358
2008 Richmond	Int.	OF	121	494	77	155	25	4	4	40	42	.314
2008 Atlanta	N.L.	OF	40	136	21	40	7	1	3	12	10	.294
Major League Totals		2 Yrs.	61	203	31	64	10	1	3	23	11	.315

a Traded by Houston Astros to Atlanta Braves for pitcher Oscar Villareal, November 16, 2007.

ANDERSON, MARLON ORDELL
Born, Montgomery, Alabama, January 6, 1974.
Bats Left. Throws Right. Height, 5 feet, 11 inches. Weight, 200 pounds.

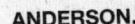

Year Club	Lea	Pos	G	AB	R	H	2B	3B	HR	RBI	SB	Avg
1995 Batavia a	N.Y.-Penn.	2B	74	312	52	92	13	4	3	40	22	.295
1996 Clearwater	Fla.St.	2B	60	257	37	70	10	3	2	22	26	.272
1996 Reading	Eastern	2B	75	314	38	86	14	3	3	28	17	.274
1997 Reading	Eastern	2B	137	553	88	147	18	6	10	62	27	.266
1998 Scranton-W.B.	Int.	2B	136	575	104	176	32	14	16	86	24	.306
1998 Philadelphia	N.L.	2B	17	43	4	14	3	0	1	4	2	.326
1999 Philadelphia	N.L.	2B	129	452	48	114	26	4	5	54	13	.252
2000 Scranton-W.B.	Int.	2B	103	397	57	121	18	8	8	53	24	.305
2000 Philadelphia	N.L.	2B	41	162	10	37	8	1	1	15	2	.228
2001 Philadelphia	N.L.	2B	147	522	69	153	30	2	11	61	8	.293
2002 Philadelphia b-c	N.L.	2B	145	539	64	139	30	6	8	48	5	.258
2003 Tampa Bay d	A.L.	2B-OF	145	482	59	130	27	3	6	67	19	.270
2004 St. Louis e	N.L.	2B-OF-1B	113	253	31	60	12	0	8	28	6	.237
2005 New York f	N.L.	1B-OF-2B	123	235	31	62	9	0	7	19	6	.264
2006 Washington-L.A. g	N.L.	2B-OF-1B	134	279	43	83	16	4	12	38	4	.297
2007 Las Vegas	P.C.	OF-2B-1B	11	29	6	7	2	1	1	11	2	.241
2007 New Orleans	P.C.	OF-2B	6	23	1	4	1	0	0	1	0	.174
2007 Los Angeles-New York h-i-j.	N.L.	OF-1B-2B	66	95	17	28	7	0	3	27	4	.295
2008 St. Lucie	Fla.St.	OF	4	13	0	3	0	0	0	0	0	.231
2008 New York k	N.L.	OF-1B-2B	87	138	16	29	6	0	1	10	2	.210
Major League Totals		11 Yrs.	1147	3200	392	849	174	20	63	371	71	.265
Division Series												
2004 St. Louis	N.L.	PH	3	3	0	0	0	0	0	0	0	.000
2006 Los Angeles	N.L.	OF	3	13	2	4	1	0	0	1	0	.308
Division Series Totals			6	16	2	4	1	0	0	1	0	.250
Championship Series												
2004 St. Louis	N.L.	2B	5	3	1	1	1	0	0	0	0	.333
World Series Record												
2004 St. Louis	N.L.	2B-DH	4	6	0	1	1	0	0	0	0	.167

a Drafted by Philadelphia Phillies with choice received for St. Louis Cardinals signing of Danny Jackson, June 1, 1995.
b Not offered 2003 contract, December 21, 2002.
c Signed with Tampa Bay Devil Rays, January 16, 2003.
d Not offered contract, December 21, 2003. Signed with St. Louis Cardinals, January 9, 2004.
e Released by St. Louis Cardinals, November 19, 2004. Signed with New York Mets organization, December 23, 2004.
f Filed for free agency, October 27, 2005. Signed with Washington Nationals, November 18, 2005.
g Traded to Los Angeles Dodgers for pitcher Jhonny Nunez, August 31, 2006.
h On disabled list from May 5 to June 18, 2007.
i Released by Los Angeles Dodgers, July 11, 2007. Signed with New York Mets organization, July 12, 2007.
j Filed for free agency, October 29, 2007, re-signed with New York Mets, November 9, 2007.
k On disabled list from May 24 to June 10 and August 2 to September 1, 2008.

ANKIEL, RICHARD ALEXANDER (RICK)
Born, Fort Pierce, Florida, July 19, 1979.
Bats Left. Throws Left. Height, 6 feet, 1 inch. Weight, 210 pounds.

Year Club	Lea	Pos	G	AB	R	H	2B	3B	HR	RBI	SB	Avg
1998 Peoria	Midwest	P	3	0	0	0	0	0	0	0	0	000
1998 Pr William	Carolina	P	9	0	0	0	0	0	0	0	0	000

Year	Club	Lea	Pos	G	AB	R	H	2B	3B	HR	RBI	SB	Avg
1999 Arkansas	Texas		P	8	10	1	4	0	0	1	1	0	.400
1999 Memphis	P.C.		P	16	21	3	6	2	0	0	4	0	.286
1999 St. Louis	N.L.		P	9	10	0	1	0	0	0	0	0	.100
2000 St. Louis	N.L.		P	35	68	8	17	1	1	2	9	0	.250
2001 Memphis	P.C.		P	3	0	0	0	0	0	0	0	0	.000
2001 Johnson City	Appal.		P	41	105	21	30	7	0	10	35	0	.286
2001 St. Louis	N.L.		P	6	8	1	0	0	0	0	0	0	.000
2002 St. Louis a	N.L.					INJURED—Did Not Play							
2003 Tennessee	Southern		P	30	25	2	6	1	0	1	5	0	.240
2004 Tennessee	Southern		P	2	4	0	0	0	0	0	0	0	.000
2004 St. Louis b	N.L.		P	5	1	0	0	0	0	0	0	0	.000
2005 Quad Cities	Midwest		OF	51	185	33	50	10	1	11	45	0	.270
2005 Springfield	Texas		OF	34	136	18	33	7	0	10	30	0	.243
2006 St. Louis c	N.L.					INJURED—Did Not Play							
2007 Memphis	P.C.		OF	102	389	62	104	15	3	32	89	4	.267
2007 St. Louis	N.L.		OF	47	172	31	49	8	1	11	39	1	.285
2008 St. Louis	N.L.		OF	120	413	65	109	21	2	25	71	2	.264
Major League Totals			6 Yrs.	222	672	105	176	30	4	38	119	3	.262
Division Series													
2000 St. Louis	N.L.		P	1	1	0	0	0	0	0	0	0	.000
Championship Series													
2000 St. Louis	N.L.		P	2	0	0	0	0	0	0	0	0	.000

a On disabled list from March 26 to June 5, 2002.
b On disabled list from March 25 to September 1, 2004.
c On disabled list from March 24 to November 2, 2006.

ATKINS, GARRETT BERNARD

Born, Orange, California, December 12, 1979.
Bats Right. Throws Right. Height, 6 feet, 3 inches. Weight, 215 pounds.

Year	Club	Lea	Pos	G	AB	R	H	2B	3B	HR	RBI	SB	Avg
2000 Portland	Northwest		1B-3B	69	251	34	76	12	0	7	47	2	.303
2001 Salem	Carolina		1B-3B	135	465	70	151	43	5	5	67	6	.325
2002 Carolina	Southern		3B-1B	128	510	71	138	27	3	12	61	6	.271
2003 Colorado Springs	P.C.		3B-1B	118	439	80	140	30	1	13	67	4	.319
2003 Colorado	N.L.		3B	25	69	6	11	2	0	0	4	0	.159
2004 Colorado Springs	P.C.		3B-1B	122	445	88	163	43	3	15	94	0	.366
2004 Colorado	N.L.		3B-1B-OF	15	28	3	10	2	0	1	8	0	.357
2005 Colorado Springs	P.C.		3B	5	21	4	7	1	0	1	3	0	.333
2005 Colorado a	N.L.		3B	138	519	62	149	31	1	13	89	0	.287
2006 Colorado	N.L.		3B-1B	157	602	117	198	48	1	29	120	4	.329
2007 Colorado	N.L.		3B-1B	157	605	83	182	35	1	25	111	3	.301
2008 Colorado	N.L.		3B-1B-2B	155	611	86	175	32	3	21	99	1	.286
Major League Totals			6 Yrs.	647	2434	357	725	150	6	89	431	8	.298
Division Series													
2007 Colorado	N.L.		3B	3	13	3	3	2	0	1	1	0	.231
Championship Series													
2007 Colorado	N.L.		3B	4	14	0	2	0	0	0	0	0	.143
World Series Record													
2007 Colorado	N.L.		3B	4	13	3	2	1	0	1	2	0	.154

a On disabled list from April 3 to April 26, 2005.

AURILIA, RICHARD SANTO (RICH)

Born, Brooklyn, New York, September 2, 1971.
Bats Right. Throws Right. Height, 6 feet. Weight, 190 pounds.

Year	Club	Lea	Pos	G	AB	R	H	2B	3B	HR	RBI	SB	Avg
1992 Butte	Pioneer		SS	59	202	37	68	11	3	3	30	13	.337
1993 Charlotte	Fla. St.		SS	122	440	80	136	16	5	5	56	15	.309
1994 Tulsa	Texas		SS	129	458	67	107	18	6	12	57	10	.234
1995 Shreveport	Texas		SS	64	226	29	74	17	1	4	42	10	.327
1995 Phoenix	P.C.		SS	71	258	42	72	12	0	5	34	2	.279
1995 San Francisco	N.L.		SS	9	19	4	9	3	0	2	4	1	.474
1996 Phoenix	P.C.		SS-2B	7	30	9	13	7	1	0	4	1	.433
1996 San Francisco a	N.L.		SS-2B	105	318	27	76	7	1	3	26	4	.239
1997 Phoenix	P.C.		SS	8	34	9	10	2	0	1	5	2	.294
1997 San Francisco	N.L.		SS	46	102	16	28	8	0	5	19	1	.275
1998 San Francisco b	N.L.		SS	122	413	54	110	27	2	9	49	3	.266
1999 San Francisco	N.L.		SS	152	558	68	157	23	1	22	80	2	.281

5

Year	Club	Lea	Pos	G	AB	R	H	2B	3B	HR	RBI	SB	Avg
2000 San Francisco		N.L.	SS	141	509	67	138	24	2	20	79	1	.271
2001 San Francisco		N.L.	SS	156	636	114	*206	37	5	37	97	1	.324
2002 San Francisco c		N.L.	SS	133	538	76	138	35	2	15	61	1	.257
2003 San Francisco d-e		N.L.	SS	129	505	65	140	26	1	13	58	2	.277
2004 Seattle		A.L.	SS	73	261	27	63	13	0	4	28	1	.241
2004 San Diego f-g		N.L.	3B-2B-SS-1B	51	138	22	35	8	2	2	16	0	.254
2005 Louisville		Int.	SS	1	3	2	1	1	0	0	1	0	.333
2005 Cincinnati h-i		N.L.	2B-SS-3B	114	426	61	120	23	2	14	68	2	.282
2006 Cincinnati j-k		N.L.	3B-1B-SS-2B	122	440	61	132	25	1	23	70	3	.300
2007 Fresno		P.C.	1B-3B-SS	2	6	1	2	0	0	0	2	0	.333
2007 San Francisco l		N.L.	1B-3B-SS-2B	99	329	40	83	19	2	5	33	0	.252
2008 San Francisco m		N.L.	1B-3B-2B	140	407	33	115	21	1	10	52	1	.283
Major League Totals			14 Yrs.	1592	5599	735	1550	299	22	184	740	23	.277
Division Series													
2000 San Francisco		N.L.	SS	4	15	0	2	1	0	0	0	0	.133
2002 San Francisco		N.L.	SS	5	21	4	5	1	0	2	7	0	.238
2003 San Francisco		N.L.	SS	4	15	4	2	1	0	0	1	0	.133
Division Series Totals				13	51	8	9	3	0	2	8	0	.176
Championship Series													
2002 San Francisco		N.L.	SS	5	15	4	5	1	0	2	5	0	.333
World Series Record													
2002 San Francisco		N.L.	SS	7	32	5	8	2	0	2	5	0	.250

a On disabled list from September 24 to September 30, 1996.
b On disabled list from July 4 to July 20, 1998.
c On disabled list from May 20 to June 4, 2002.
d On disabled list from August 4 to August 19, 2003.
e Filed for free agency, October 27, 2003. Signed with Seattle Mariners, January 8, 2004.
f Traded to San Diego Padres for player to be named later, July 19, 2004.
g Filed for free agency, October 28, 2004. Signed with Cincinnati Reds organization, January 24, 2005.
h On disabled list from May 11 to May 29, 2005.
i Filed for free agency, November 2, 2005, re-signed with Cincinnati Reds, January 9, 2006.
j On disabled list from May 4 to May 19, 2006.
k Filed for free agency, October 31, 2006. Signed with San Francisco Giants, December 4, 2006.
l On disabled list from June 17 to July 2 and August 2 to August 17, 2007.
m Filed for free agency, October 31, 2008.

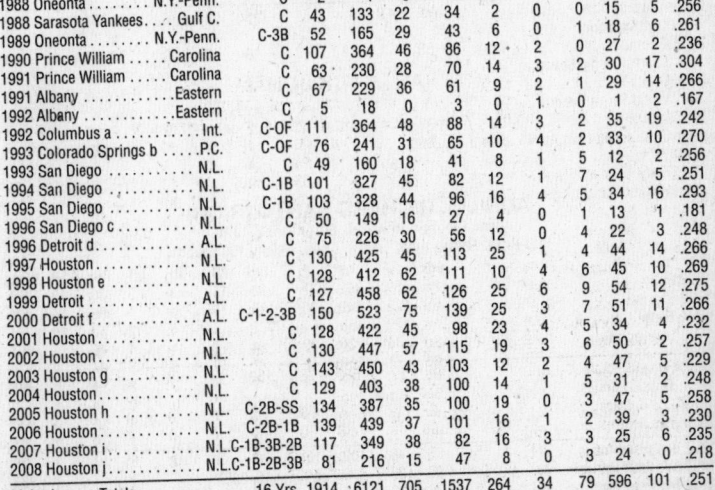

AUSMUS, BRADLEY DAVID (BRAD)

Born, New Haven, Connecticut, April 14, 1969.
Bats Right. Throws Right. Height, 5 feet, 11 inches. Weight, 190 pounds.

Year	Club	Lea	Pos	G	AB	R	H	2B	3B	HR	RBI	SB	Avg
1988 Oneonta		N.Y.-Penn.	C	2	4	0	1	0	0	0	0	0	.250
1988 Sarasota Yankees		Gulf C.	C	43	133	22	34	2	0	0	15	5	.256
1989 Oneonta		N.Y.-Penn.	C-3B	52	165	29	43	6	0	1	18	6	.261
1990 Prince William		Carolina	C	107	364	46	86	12	2	0	27	2	.236
1991 Prince William		Carolina	C	63	230	28	70	14	3	2	30	17	.304
1991 Albany		Eastern	C	67	229	36	61	9	2	1	29	14	.266
1992 Albany		Eastern	C	5	18	0	3	0	1	0	1	2	.167
1992 Columbus a		Int.	C-OF	111	364	48	88	14	3	2	35	19	.242
1993 Colorado Springs b		P.C.	C-OF	76	241	31	65	10	4	2	33	10	.270
1993 San Diego		N.L.	C	49	160	18	41	8	1	5	12	2	.256
1994 San Diego		N.L.	C-1B	101	327	45	82	12	1	7	24	5	.251
1995 San Diego		N.L.	C-1B	103	328	44	96	16	4	5	34	16	.293
1996 San Diego c		N.L.	C	50	149	16	27	4	0	1	13	1	.181
1996 Detroit d		A.L.	C	75	226	30	56	12	0	4	22	3	.248
1997 Houston		N.L.	C	130	425	45	113	25	1	4	44	14	.266
1998 Houston e		N.L.	C	128	412	62	111	10	4	6	45	10	.269
1999 Detroit		A.L.	C	127	458	62	126	25	6	9	54	12	.275
2000 Detroit f		A.L.	C-1-2-3B	150	523	75	139	25	3	7	51	11	.266
2001 Houston		N.L.	C	128	422	45	98	23	4	5	34	4	.232
2002 Houston		N.L.	C	130	447	57	115	19	3	6	50	2	.257
2003 Houston g		N.L.	C	143	450	43	103	12	2	4	47	5	.229
2004 Houston		N.L.	C	129	403	38	100	14	1	5	31	2	.248
2005 Houston h		N.L.	C-2B-SS	134	387	35	100	19	0	3	47	5	.258
2006 Houston		N.L.	C-2B-1B	139	439	37	101	16	1	2	39	3	.230
2007 Houston i		N.L.	C-1B-3B-2B	117	349	38	82	16	3	3	25	6	.235
2008 Houston j		N.L.	C-1B-2B-3B	81	216	15	47	8	0	3	24	0	.218
Major League Totals			16 Yrs.	1914	6121	705	1537	264	34	79	596	101	.251

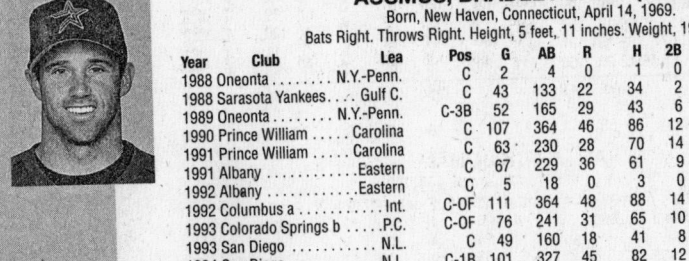

Year	Club	Lea	Pos	G	AB	R	H	2B	3B	HR	RBI	SB	Avg
Division Series													
1997 Houston	N.L.		C	2	5	1	2	1	0	0	0	0	.400
1998 Houston	N.L.		C	4	9	0	2	0	0	0	0	0	.222
2001 Houston	N.L.		C	3	8	1	2	0	0	0	2	0	.250
2004 Houston	N.L.		C	5	9	3	3	0	0	1	1	0	.333
2005 Houston	N.L.		C-1B	4	18	3	4	1	0	1	1	0	.222
Division Series Totals				18	49	8	13	2	0	3	6	0	.265
Championship Series													
2004 Houston	N.L.		C	7	19	0	2	0	0	0	0	0	.105
2005 Houston	N.L.		C	6	22	3	7	2	0	0	1	1	.318
Championship Series Totals ..				13	41	3	9	2	0	0	1	1	.220
World Series Record													
2005 Houston	N.L.		C	4	16	1	4	1	0	0	0	0	.250

a Selected by Colorado Rockies from New York Yankees organization in expansion draft, November 17, 1992.
b Traded by Colorado Rockies to San Diego Padres with pitcher Doug Bochtler and player to be named for pitchers Greg W. Harris and Bruce Hurst, July 26; San Diego Padres acquired pitcher Andy Ashby to complete trade, July 28, 1993.
c Traded to Detroit Tigers with infielder Andujar Cedeno for catcher John Flaherty and infielder Chris Gomez, June 18, 1996.
d Traded to Houston Astros with pitcher C.J. Nitkowski, pitcher Jose Lima, pitcher Trever Miller and infielder Daryle Ward for outfielder Brian Hunter, infielder Orlando Miller, pitcher Todd Jones and pitcher Doug Brocail, December 10, 1996.
e Traded to Detroit Tigers with pitcher C.J. Nitkowski for pitcher Dean Crow, pitcher Mark Persails, pitcher Brian Powell, catcher Paul Bako and infielder Carlos Villalobos, January 14, 1999.
f Traded to Houston Astros with pitcher Doug Brocail and pitcher Nelson Cruz for pitcher Chris Holt, outfielder Roger Cedeno and catcher Mitch Meluskey, December 11, 2000.
g Filed for free agency, October 27, 2003, re-signed with Houston Astros, November 19, 2003.
h Filed for free agency, November 1, 2005, re-signed with Houston Astros, December 13, 2005.
i Filed for free agency, October 29, 2007, re-signed with Houston Astros, November 2, 2007.
j Filed for free agency, October 31, 2008.

AVILES, MICHAEL ANTHONY (MIKE)
Born, New York, New York, March 13, 1981.
Bats Right. Throws Right. Height, 5 feet, 9 inches. Weight, 195 pounds.

Year	Club	Lea	Pos	G	AB	R	H	2B	3B	HR	RBI	SB	Avg
2003 Roy 1	Arizona		SS	52	212	51	77	19	5	6	39	11	.363
2004 Wilmington ...	Carolina		SS	126	463	66	139	40	4	6	68	2	.300
2005 Wichita	Texas		SS-3B-2B	133	521	79	146	33	6	14	80	11	.280
2006 Omaha	P.C.		3B-SS-2B	129	469	52	124	21	3	8	47	14	.264
2007 Omaha	P.C.		SS-3B-2B	133	538	78	159	27	6	17	75	5	.296
2008 Omaha	P.C.		2B-SS	51	214	42	72	21	6	10	42	3	.336
2008 Kansas City	A.L.		SS-2B-3B	102	419	68	136	27	4	10	51	8	.325

AYBAR, ERICK JOHAN
Born, Bani, Dominican Republic, January 14, 1984.
Bats Both. Throws Right. Height, 5 feet, 10 inches. Weight, 170 pounds.

Year	Club	Lea	Pos	G	AB	R	H	2B	3B	HR	RBI	SB	Avg
2002 Provo	Pioneer		SS	67	273	64	89	15	6	4	29	15	.326
2003 Cedar Rapids	Midwest		SS	125	496	83	153	30	10	6	57	32	.308
2004 Rancho Cucamonga....	Calif.		SS-2B	136	573	102	189	25	11	14	65	51	.330
2005 Arkansas	Texas		SS	134	535	101	162	29	10	9	54	49	.303
2006 Salt Lake	P.C.		SS	81	339	63	96	20	3	6	45	32	.283
2006 Los Angeles	A.L.		SS-2B	34	40	5	10	1	1	0	2	1	.250
2007 Rancho Cucamonga....	Calif.		SS	2	5	3	2	0	0	0	0	3	.400
2007 Salt Lake	P.C.		SS-2B	3	12	2	4	0	0	0	2	2	.333
2007 Los Angeles a	A.L.		2B-SS-OF-3B	79	194	18	46	5	1	1	19	4	.237
2008 Rancho Cucamonga....	Calif.		SS	3	10	2	4	1	0	0	3	2	.400
2008 Los Angeles b	A.L.		SS-2B	98	346	53	96	18	5	3	39	7	.277
Major League Totals		3 Yrs.		211	580	76	152	24	7	4	60	12	.262
Division Series													
2007 Los Angeles	A.L.		OF	1	1	0	0	0	0	0	0	0	.000
2008 Los Angeles	A.L.		SS	4	18	0	2	0	0	0	1	0	.111
Division Series Totals				5	19	0	2	0	0	0	1	0	.105

a On disabled list from July 2 to August 6 and August 20 to September 5, 2007.
b On disabled list from May 21 to June 18, 2008.

AYBAR, WILLY DEL JESUS

Born, Bani, Dominican Republic, March 9, 1983.
Bats Both. Throws Right. Height, 6 feet. Weight, 200 pounds.

Year Club	Lea	Pos	G	AB	R	H	2B	3B	HR	RBI	SB	Avg
2000 Great Falls	Pioneer	3B	70	266	39	70	15	1	4	49	5	.263
2001 Vero Beach	Fla.St.	3B	2	7	0	2	0	0	0	0	0	.286
2001 Wilmington	So.Atl.	3B	120	431	45	102	25	2	4	48	7	.237
2002 Vero Beach	Fla.St.	3B	108	372	56	80	18	2	11	65	15	.215
2003 Vero Beach	Fla.St.	3B-2B-SS	119	445	47	122	29	3	11	74	9	.274
2004 Jacksonville	Southern	2B	126	482	56	133	27	0	15	77	8	.276
2005 Las Vegas	P.C.	3B-2B	108	401	47	119	26	4	5	60	1	.297
2005 Los Angeles	N.L.	3B-2B	26	86	12	28	8	0	1	10	3	.326
2006 Las Vegas	P.C.	3B-2B	50	197	30	62	12	1	10	41	1	.315
2006 Richmond	Int.	3B-2B	3	10	2	3	1	0	0	1	0	.300
2006 Los Angeles-Atlanta a-b	N.L.	3B-2B	79	243	32	68	18	0	4	30	1	.280
2007 Atlanta c	N.L.					INJURED—Did Not Play						
2008 Vero Beach	Fla.St.	2B-3B	3	12	1	3	0	0	0	0	1	.250
2008 Durham	Int.	2B-3B-1B	5	20	3	6	3	0	0	3	0	.300
2008 Tampa Bay d-e	A.L.	3B-1B-2B	95	324	33	82	17	2	10	33	2	.253
Major League Totals		3 Yrs.	200	653	77	178	43	2	15	73	6	.273
Division Series												
2008 Tampa Bay	N.L.	1B-DH	4	11	2	3	1	0	0	1	0	.273
Championship Series												
2008 Tampa Bay	N.L.	DH	6	19	3	8	1	0	2	6	0	.421†
World Series Record												
2008 Tampa Bay	N.L.	1B-DH	4	4	0	1	0	0	0	0	0	.250

a Traded to Atlanta Braves with pitcher Danys Baez and cash for outfielder Wilson Betemit, July 28, 2006.
b On disabled list from August 12 to September 1, 2006.
c On disabled list from March 25 to November 13, 2007.
d Traded with infielder Chase Fontaine to Tampa Bay Rays for pitcher Jeff Ridgway, January 8, 2008.
e On disabled list from April 10 to May 29, 2008.

BAKER, JEFFREY GLEN (JEFF)

Born, Bad Kissingen, West Germany, June 21, 1981.
Bats Right. Throws Right. Height, 6 feet, 2 inches. Weight, 210 pounds.

Year Club	Lea	Pos	G	AB	R	H	2B	3B	HR	RBI	SB	Avg
2003 Asheville	So.Atl.	3B	70	263	44	76	17	0	11	44	4	.289
2004 Visalia	Calif.	3B-SS	73	271	60	88	23	1	11	64	1	.325
2004 Tulsa	Texas	3B	24	91	10	27	5	1	4	20	1	.297
2005 Colorado	N.L.	3B	12	38	6	8	4	0	1	4	0	.211
2005 Colorado Springs	P.C.	3B	61	228	40	69	16	1	10	41	3	.303
2006 Colorado Springs	P.C.	OF-3B	128	482	71	147	30	4	20	108	7	.305
2006 Colorado	N.L.	OF-1B	18	57	13	21	7	2	5	21	2	.368
2007 Colorado Springs	P.C.	1B-OF	7	26	3	6	1	0	1	2	0	.231
2007 Colorado a	N.L.	1B-OF-3B	85	144	17	32	2	2	4	12	0	.222
2008 Colorado	N.L.	2B-1B-3B-OF	104	299	55	80	22	1	12	48	4	.268
Major League Totals		4 Yrs.	219	538	91	141	35	5	22	85	6	.262
Division Series												
2007 Colorado	N.L.	PH	1	1	0	1	0	0	0	1	0	1.000
Championship Series												
2007 Colorado	N.L.	PH	2	2	0	1	0	0	0	0	0	.500
World Series Record												
2007 Colorado	N.L.	PH	1	1	0	0	0	0	0	0	0	.000

a On disabled list from August 12 to September 1, 2007.

BAKER, JOHN DAVID

Born, Alameda, California, January 20, 1981.
Bats Left. Throws Right. Height, 6 feet, 1 inch. Weight, 210 pounds.

Year Club	Lea	Pos	G	AB	R	H	2B	3B	HR	RBI	SB	Avg
2002 Vancouver	Northwest	C	39	115	15	27	5	0	1	13	2	.235
2003 Kane County	Midwest	C	82	304	42	94	23	2	6	49	0	.309
2003 Midland	Texas	C	43	150	16	36	3	0	1	21	0	.240
2004 Sacramento	P.C.	C	14	49	11	17	3	0	0	10	0	.347
2004 Midland	Texas	C-1B	117	439	67	123	32	5	15	78	0	.280
2005 Sacramento a	P.C.	C	103	346	43	81	24	3	5	41	1	.234
2006 Sacramento b	P.C.	C	83	293	49	80	19	1	4	38	6	.273
2007 Albuquerque c	P.C.	C-1B	89	270	35	77	15	0	8	41	2	.285

Year Club	Lea	Pos	G	AB	R	H	2B	3B	HR	RBI	SB	Avg
2008 Albuquerque..........P.C.		C-1B	59	193	35	62	14	1	6	31	1	.321
2008 Florida ..............N.L.		C	61	197	32	59	14	0	5	32	0	.299

a Claimed on waivers by Florida Marlins from Oakland Athletics, December 15, 2005.
b Claimed on waivers by Oakland Athletics, January 5, 2006.
c Traded to Florida Marlins for infielder Jason Stokes, March 30, 2007.

BAKO, GABOR PAUL (PAUL)

Born, Lafayette, Louisiana, June 20, 1972.
Bats Left. Throws Right. Height, 6 feet, 2 inches. Weight, 205 pounds.

Year Club	Lea	Pos	G	AB	R	H	2B	3B	HR	RBI	SB	Avg
1993 Billings................Pioneer		C-1B	57	194	34	61	11	0	4	30	5	.314
1994 Winston-Sal........Carolina		C	90	289	29	59	9	1	3	26	2	.204
1995 Winston-Sal........Carolina		C	82	249	29	71	11	2	7	27	3	.285
1996 Chattanooga.......Southern		C	110	360	53	106	27	0	8	48	1	.294
1997 Indianapolis a.........A.A.		C	104	321	34	78	14	1	8	43	0	.243
1998 Toledo ....Int.		C	13	48	5	14	3	1	1	6	0	.292
1998 Detroit ..............A.L.		C	96	305	23	83	12	1	3	30	1	.272
1999 New Orleans........P.C.		C	12	47	2	9	3	1	1	4	0	.191
1999 Houston b ..........N.L.		C	73	215	16	55	14	1	2	17	1	.256
2000 Houston-Florida-Atlanta c-d.. N.L.		C-1B	81	221	18	50	10	1	2	20	0	.226
2001 Atlanta..............N.L.		C	61	137	19	29	10	1	2	15	1	.212
2002 Milwaukee e-f-g.......N.L.		C	87	234	24	55	8	1	4	20	0	.235
2003 Chicago .............N.L.		C	70	188	19	43	13	3	0	17	0	.229
2004 Chicago .............N.L.		C	49	138	13	28	8	0	1	10	1	.203
2005 Los Angeles h-i-j......N.L.		C	13	40	1	10	2	0	0	4	0	.250
2006 Wichita..............Texas		C	3	12	3	2	0	0	0	2	0	.167
2006 Kansas City k-l.......A.L.		C	56	153	7	32	3	0	0	10	0	.209
2007 Baltimore m.........A.L.		C	60	156	13	32	3	1	1	8	0	.205
2008 Cincinnati n.........N.L.		C	99	299	30	65	11	2	6	35	0	.217
Major League Totals	11 Yrs.		745	2086	183	482	94	11	21	186	4	.231
Division Series												
2000 Atlanta..............N.L.		C	2	1	0	0	0	0	0	0	0	.000
2001 Atlanta..............N.L.		C	3	7	1	2	1	0	1	3	0	.286
2003 Chicago .............N.L.		C	3	4	0	0	0	0	0	1	0	.000
Division Series Totals			8	12	1	2	1	0	1	4	0	.167
Championship Series												
2001 Atlanta..............N.L.		C	3	3	0	0	0	0	0	0	0	.000
2003 Chicago .............N.L.		C	6	16	4	4	1	0	0	1	0	.250
Championship Series Totals			9	19	4	4	1	0	0	1	0	.211

a Traded to Detroit Tigers by Cincinnati Reds with pitcher Donne Wall for outfielder Melvin Nieves, November 11, 1997.
b Traded to Houston Astros with pitcher Dean Crow, pitcher Mark Persails, pitcher Brian Powell and infielder Carlos Villalobos for pitcher C.J. Nitkowski and catcher Brad Ausmus, January 14, 1999.
c Traded to Florida Marlins for player to be named later, April 11, 2000. Houston Astros received cash to complete trade, October 10, 2000.
d Claimed on waivers by Atlanta Braves, July 21, 2000.
e On disabled list from June 9 to June 24, 2002.
f Traded to Milwaukee Brewers with pitcher Jose Cabrera for catcher Henry Blanco, March 19, 2002.
g Traded to Chicago Cubs for player to be named later, November 26, 2002. Milwaukee Brewers received infielder Ryan Gipp to complete trade, December 16, 2002.
h Filed for free agency, October 29, 2004. Signed with Los Angeles Dodgers, January 13, 2005.
i On disabled list from May 27 to October 28, 2005.
j Filed for free agency, October 31, 2005. Signed with Kansas City Royals, December 16, 2005.
k On disabled list from July 2 to August 2, 2006.
l Filed for free agency, October 30, 2006. Signed with Baltimore Orioles, December 6, 2006.
m Filed for free agency, October 30, 2007. Signed with Cincinnati Reds organization, February 1, 2008.
n Filed for free agency, November 3, 2008.

BALDELLI, ROCCO DANIEL

Born, Woonsocket, Rhode Island, September 25, 1981.
Bats Right. Throws Right. Height, 6 feet, 4 inches. Weight, 200 pounds.

Year Club	Lea	Pos	G	AB	R	H	2B	3B	HR	RBI	SB	Avg
2000 Princeton ....Appal.		OF-3B	60	232	33	50	9	2	3	25	11	.216
2001 Charleston-SC ......So.Atl.		OF	113	406	58	101	23	6	8	55	25	.249
2002 Bakersfield ....California		OF	77	312	63	104	19	1	14	51	21	.333
2002 Orlando ....Southern		OF	17	70	10	26	3	1	2	13	3	.371
2002 Durham ....Int.		OF	23	96	13	28	6	1	3	7	2	.292

9

Year Club	Lea	Pos	G	AB	R	H	2B	3B	HR	RBI	SB	Avg
2003 Tampa Bay	A.L.	OF	156	637	89	184	32	8	11	78	27	.289
2004 Tampa Bay a	A.L.	OF	136	518	79	145	27	3	16	74	17	.280
2005 Tampa Bay b				INJURED — Did Not Play								
2006 Durham	Int.	OF	12	47	7	19	5	0	0	4	0	.404
2006 Tampa Bay c	A.L.	OF	92	364	59	110	24	6	16	57	10	.302
2007 Vero Beach	Fla.St.	DH	2	5	1	0	0	0	0	0	0	.000
2007 Durham	Int.	OF	2	8	2	1	0	0	1	1	0	.125
2007 Tampa Bay d	A.L.	OF	35	137	16	28	6	0	5	12	4	.204
2008 Vero Beach	Fla.St.	DH	11	37	3	8	1	0	2	8	2	.216
2008 Montgomery	Southern	OF	13	37	6	11	1	0	3	8	0	.297
2008 Tampa Bay e-f	A.L.	DH-OF	28	80	12	21	5	0	4	13	0	.262
Major League Totals	5 Yrs.		447	1736	255	488	94	17	52	234	58	.281
Division Series												
2008 Tampa Bay	N.L.	OF-DH	3	8	2	1	0	0	0	1	0	.125
Championship Series												
2008 Tampa Bay	N.L.	OF	2	6	1	2	0	0	1	4	0	.333
World Series Record												
2008 Tampa Bay	N.L.	OF	3	6	1	1	0	0	1	1	0	.16

a On disabled list from August 14 to September 1, 2004.
b On disabled list from March 25 to November 4, 2005.
c On disabled list from March 24 to June 7, 2006.
d On disabled list from May 16 to November 12, 2007.
e On disabled list from March 28 to August 10, 2008.
f Filed for free agency, October 31, 2008. Signed with Boston Red Sox, January 8, 2009.

BALENTIEN, WLADIMIR RAMON
Born, Willemstad, Curacao, Netherlands Antilles, July 2, 1984.
Bats Right. Throws Right. Height, 6 feet, 2 inches. Weight, 215 pounds.

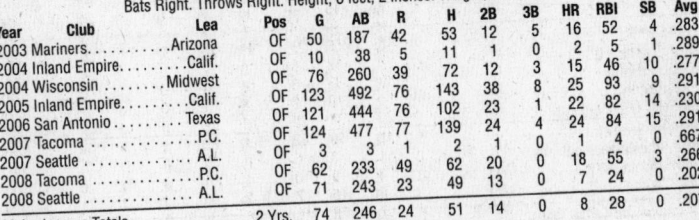

Year Club	Lea	Pos	G	AB	R	H	2B	3B	HR	RBI	SB	Avg
2003 Mariners..........	Arizona	OF	50	187	42	53	12	5	16	52	4	.283
2004 Inland Empire....	Calif.	OF	10	38	5	11	1	0	2	5	1	.289
2004 Wisconsin	Midwest	OF	76	260	39	72	12	3	15	46	10	.277
2005 Inland Empire....	Calif.	OF	123	492	76	143	38	8	25	93	9	.291
2006 San Antonio	Texas	OF	121	444	76	102	23	1	22	82	14	.230
2007 Tacoma	P.C.	OF	124	477	77	139	24	4	24	84	15	.291
2007 Seattle	A.L.	OF	3	3	1	2	1	0	1	4	0	.667
2008 Tacoma	P.C.	OF	62	233	49	62	20	0	18	55	3	.266
2008 Seattle	A.L.	OF	71	243	23	49	13	0	7	24	0	.202
Major League Totals	2 Yrs.		74	246	24	51	14	0	8	28	0	.207

BARAJAS, RODRIGO RICHARD (ROD)
Born, Ontario, California, September 5, 1975.
Bats Right. Throws Right. Height, 6 feet, 2 inches. Weight, 245 pounds.

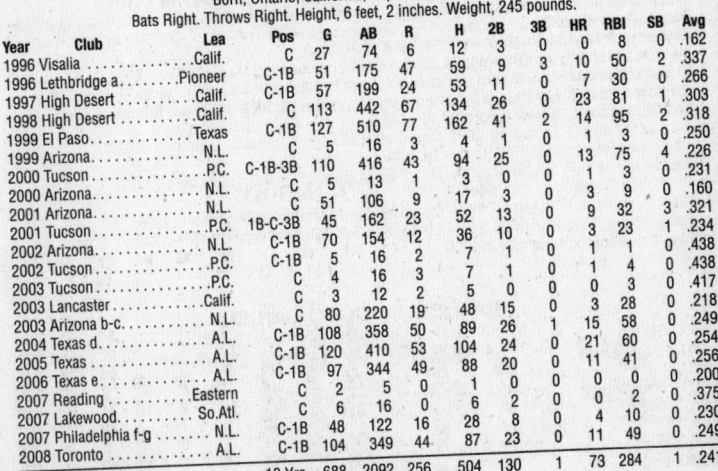

Year Club	Lea	Pos	G	AB	R	H	2B	3B	HR	RBI	SB	Avg
1996 Visalia............	Calif.	C	27	74	6	12	3	0	0	8	0	.162
1996 Lethbridge a.......	Pioneer	C-1B	51	175	47	59	9	3	10	50	2	.337
1997 High Desert	Calif.	C-1B	57	199	24	53	11	0	7	30	1	.266
1998 High Desert	Calif.	C	113	442	67	134	26	0	23	81	2	.303
1999 El Paso............	Texas	C-1B	127	510	77	162	41	2	14	95	2	.318
1999 Arizona...........	N.L.	C	5	16	3	4	1	0	1	3	0	.250
2000 Tucson............	P.C.	C-1B-3B	110	416	43	94	25	0	13	75	4	.226
2000 Arizona...........	N.L.	C	5	13	1	3	0	0	1	3	0	.231
2001 Arizona...........	N.L.	C	51	106	9	17	3	0	3	9	0	.160
2001 Tucson............	P.C.	1B-C-3B	45	162	23	52	13	0	9	32	3	.321
2002 Arizona...........	N.L.	C-1B	70	154	12	36	10	0	3	23	1	.234
2002 Tucson............	P.C.	C-1B	5	16	2	7	1	0	1	1	0	.438
2003 Tucson............	P.C.	C	4	16	3	7	1	0	1	4	0	.417
2003 Lancaster.........	Calif.	C	3	12	2	5	0	0	0	1	0	.218
2003 Arizona b-c.......	N.L.	C	80	220	19	48	15	1	15	58	0	.249
2004 Texas d...........	A.L.	C-1B	108	358	50	89	26	0	21	60	0	.254
2005 Texas.............	A.L.	C-1B	120	410	53	104	24	0	11	41	0	.256
2006 Texas e...........	A.L.	C-1B	97	344	49	88	20	0	0	0	0	.200
2007 Reading...........	Eastern	C	2	5	0	1	0	0	0	0	0	.375
2007 Lakewood.........	So.Atl.	C	6	16	0	6	2	0	4	10	0	.230
2007 Philadelphia f-g...	N.L.	C-1B	48	122	16	28	8	0	11	49	0	.249
2008 Toronto	A.L.	C-1B	104	349	44	87	23	0	11	49	0	.241
Major League Totals	10 Yrs.		688	2092	256	504	130	1	73	284	1	.241

Year Club	Lea	Pos	G	AB	R	H	2B	3B	HR	RBI	SB	Avg
Division Series												
2001 Arizona.............	N.L.	C	1	0	0	0	0	0	0	0	0	.000
2002 Arizona.............	N.L.	C	2	4	1	1	0	0	0	1	0	.250
Division Series Totals			3	4	1	1	0	0	1	1	0	.250
World Series Record												
2001 Arizona.............	N.L.	C	2	5	1	2	0	0	1	1	0	.400

a Loaned to Oakland A's organization, April 5 to June 16, 1996.
b On disabled list from April 7 to April 28, 2003.
c On disabled list from July 5 to July 23, 2003.
d Not offered contract, December 21, 2003. Signed with Texas Rangers organization, January 12, 2004.
e Filed for free agency, October 28, 2006. Signed with Philadelphia Phillies organization, December 21, 2006.
f On disabled list from August 3 to September 1, 2007.
g Filed for free agency, October 30, 2007. Signed with Toronto Blue Jays, January 24, 2008.

BARD, JOSHUA DAVID (JOSH)

Born, Ithaca, New York, March 30, 1978.
Bats Both. Throws Right. Height, 6 feet, 3 inches. Weight, 225 pounds.

Year Club	Lea	Pos	G	AB	R	H	2B	3B	HR	RBI	SB	Avg
2000 Salem...........	Carolina	C	93	309	40	88	17	0	2	25	3	.285
2000 Colorado Springs......	P.C.	C	4	17	0	4	0	0	0	1	0	.235
2001 Akron.............	Eastern	C	51	194	26	54	11	0	4	25	0	.278
2001 Buffalo.............	Int.	DH	1	4	0	0	0	0	0	0	0	.000
2001 Mahoning Valley..	N.Y.-Penn.	C	13	44	7	12	4	0	2	8	0	.273
2001 Carolina a.......	Southern	C	35	124	14	32	13	0	1	24	0	.258
2002 Buffalo.............	Int.	C	94	344	36	102	26	2	6	53	0	.297
2002 Cleveland...........	A.L.	C	24	90	9	20	5	0	3	12	0	.222
2003 Cleveland...........	A.L.	C	91	303	25	74	13	1	8	36	0	.244
2003 Buffalo.............	Int.	C	35	115	14	38	7	0	5	21	1	.330
2004 Akron.............	Eastern	C	10	30	5	5	1	0	0	5	0	.167
2004 Buffalo.............	Int.	C	40	156	25	41	10	0	4	18	0	.263
2004 Cleveland b........	A.L.	C	7	19	5	8	2	0	1	4	0	.421
2005 Cleveland..........	A.L.	C	34	83	6	16	4	0	1	9	0	.193
2006 Boston.............	A.L.	C	7	18	2	5	1	0	0	0	0	.278
2006 San Diego c-d........	N.L.	C	93	231	28	78	19	0	9	40	1	.338
2007 San Diego e..........	N.L.	C	118	389	42	111	27	2	5	51	0	.285
2008 Azl Padres...........	Arizona	C	1	3	0	0	0	0	0	0	0	.000
2008 Lake Elsinore........	Calif.	C	3	9	0	1	0	0	0	0	0	.111
2008 Portland.............	P.C.	C	6	15	2	2	0	0	1	1	0	.133
2008 San Diego f-g........	N.L.	C	57	178	11	36	9	0	1	16	0	.202
Major League Totals	7 Yrs.		431	1311	128	348	80	3	28	168	1	.265
Division Series												
2006 San Diego	N.L.	C	3	7	0	1	0	0	0	0	0	.143

a Traded to Cleveland Indians with outfielder Jody Gerut for outfielder Jacob Cruz, June 1, 2001.
b On disabled list from March 28 to July 5, 2004.
c Traded to Boston Red Sox with outfielder Coco Crisp and pitcher David Riske for infielder Andy Marte, catcher Kelly Shoppach and pitcher Guillermo Mota, January 27, 2006.
d Traded to San Diego Padres with pitcher Cla Meredith for catcher Doug Mirabelli, May 1, 2006.
e On disabled list from April 12 to April 27, 2007.
f On disabled list from May 22 to July 24 and August 7 to August 22, 2008.
g Filed for free agency, October 6, 2008. Signed with Boston Red Sox, January 2, 2009.

BARMES, CLINT HAROLD

Born, Vincennes, Indiana, March 6, 1979.
Bats Right. Throws Right. Height, 6 feet. Weight, 210 pounds.

Year Club	Lea	Pos	G	AB	R	H	2B	3B	HR	RBI	SB	Avg
2000 Portland.....	Northwest	SS-OF	45	181	37	51	6	4	2	16	12	.282
2000 Asheville........	So.Atl.	2B-SS-3B-OF	19	81	11	14	4	0	0	4	4	.173
2001 Salem........	Carolina	SS	38	121	17	30	3	3	0	9	4	.248
2001 Asheville........	So.Atl.	SS	74	285	40	74	14	1	5	24	21	.260
2002 Carolina......	Southern	SS	103	438	62	119	23	2	15	60	15	.272
2003 Colorado Springs...	P.C.	SS-2B	136	493	63	136	35	1	7	54	12	.276
2003 Colorado........	N.L.	SS	12	25	2	8	2	0	0	2	0	.320
2004 Colorado Springs..	P.C.	SS-2B	125	533	104	175	42	2	16	51	20	.328
2004 Colorado........	N.L.	2B-SS	20	71	14	20	3	1	2	10	0	.282
2005 Tulsa........	Texas	SS	8	34	6	11	1	0	0	1	0	.324
2005 Colorado a........	N.L.	SS	81	350	55	101	19	1	10	46	6	.289
2006 Colorado	N.L.	SS-2B	131	478	57	105	26	4	7	56	5	.220

11

Year	Club	Lea	Pos	G	AB	R	H	2B	3B	HR	RBI	SB	Avg
2007	Colorado Springs...P.C.		SS-OF-2B-3B	108	428	68	128	20	6	11	44	8	.299
2007	Colorado .........N.L.		SS-2B-OF-3B	27	37	5	8	3	0	0	1	0	.216
2008	Colorado Springs...P.C.		2B-SS	5	18	2	5	0	0	0	0	0	.278
2008	Colorado b........N.L.		2B-SS-3B-OF	107	393	47	114	25	6	11	44	13	.290
Major League Totals			6 Yrs.	378	1354	180	356	78	12	30	159	24	.263

a On disabled list from June 6 to September 2, 2005.
b On disabled list from May 24 to June 23, 2008.

BARTLETT, JASON ALAN
Born, Mountain View, California, October 30, 1979.
Bats Right. Throws Right. Height, 6 feet. Weight, 180 pounds.

Year	Club	Lea	Pos	G	AB	R	H	2B	3B	HR	RBI	SB	Avg
2001	Eugene.........	Northwest	SS	68	267	49	80	12	4	3	37	12	.300
2002	Lake Elsinore	California	SS	75	308	57	77	14	4	1	33	24	.250
2002	Fort Myers a.......	.Fla.St.	SS-3B-2B	39	145	24	38	7	0	2	9	11	.262
2003	New Britain	.Eastern	SS	139	548	96	162	31	8	8	48	41	.296
2004	Rochester............	Int.	SS-2B	67	269	54	89	15	7	3	29	7	.331
2004	Twins	Gulf Coast	SS	5	14	1	5	1	0	0	1	0	.357
2004	Minnesota	.A.L.	SS-2B	8	12	2	1	0	0	0	1	2	.083
2005	Rochester...........	.Int.	SS	61	229	41	76	10	2	5	33	2	.332
2005	Minnesota	.A.L.	SS	74	224	33	54	10	1	3	16	4	.241
2006	Rochester...........	.Int.	SS	58	235	42	72	23	3	1	20	6	.306
2006	Minnesota	.A.L.	SS	99	333	44	103	18	2	2	32	10	.309
2007	Minnesota b........	.A.L.	SS	140	510	75	135	20	7	5	43	23	.265
2008	Tampa Bay c........	.A.L.	SS	128	454	48	130	25	3	1	37	20	.286
Major League Totals			5 Yrs.	449	1533	202	423	73	13	11	129	59	.276
Division Series													
2006	Minnesota	.A.L.	SS	3	11	0	3	1	0	0	0	0	.273
2008	Tampa Bay	.N.L.	SS	4	14	3	4	1	0	0	0	0	.286
Division Series Totals				7	25	3	7	2	0	0	0	0	.280
Championship Series													
2008	Tampa Bay	.N.L.	SS	7	23	4	5	0	1	1	1	1	.217
World Series Record													
2008	Tampa Bay	.N.L.	SS	5	14	1	3	0	0	0	2	1	.214

a Traded by San Diego Padres to Minnesota Twins for outfielder Brian Buchanan, July 12, 2002.
b Traded to Tampa Bay Devil Rays with pitcher Matt Garza and pitcher Eduardo Morlan for infielder Brendan Harris, outfielder Jason Pridie and outfielder Delmon Young, November 28, 2007.
c On disabled list from July 3 to July 24, 2008.

BARTON, BRIAN DEON
Born, Los Angeles, California, April 25, 1982.
Bats Right. Throws Right. Height, 6 feet, 3 inches. Weight, 190 pounds.

Year	Club	Lea	Pos	G	AB	R	H	2B	3B	HR	RBI	SB	Avg
2005	Kinston...........	Carolina	OF	64	223	42	61	15	6	3	32	13	.274
2005	Lake County........	So.Atl.	OF	35	133	31	55	14	1	4	32	7	.414
2006	Kinston...........	Carolina	OF	82	295	56	91	16	3	13	57	26	.308
2006	Akron............	.Eastern	OF	42	151	32	53	5	0	6	26	15	.351
2007	Akron............	.Eastern	OF	106	389	56	122	18	2	9	59	20	.314
2007	Buffalo a..........	.Int.	OF	25	87	9	23	3	0	1	7	1	.264
2008	Memphis	.P.C.	OF	19	73	12	19	2	2	3	11	1	.260
2008	St. Louis b	.N.L.	OF	82	153	23	41	9	2	2	13	3	.268

a Selected by St. Louis Cardinals from Cleveland Indians in Rule V draft, December 6, 2007.
b On disabled list from July 6 to August 15 and August 25 to September 9, 2008.

BARTON, DARIC WILLIAM
Born, Springfield, Vermont, August 16, 1985.
Bats Left. Throws Right. Height, 6 feet. Weight, 225 pounds.

Year	Club	Lea	Pos	G	AB	R	H	2B	3B	HR	RBI	SB	Avg
2003	Johnson City	Appal.	C-3B	54	172	29	50	10	0	4	29	0	.291
2004	Peoria a	Midwest	C	90	313	63	98	23	0	13	77	4	.313
2005	Stockton........	Calif.	1B-3B-OF-C	79	292	60	93	16	2	8	52	0	.318
2005	Midland	Texas	1B-OF	56	212	38	67	20	1	5	37	1	.316
2006	Athletics.......	Arizona	1B	2	5	1	1	0	0	0	2	0	.200
2006	Sacramento	.P.C.	1B	43	147	25	38	6	4	2	22	1	.259
2007	Sacramento	.P.C.	1B-3B	136	516	84	151	38	5	9	70	3	.293

Year	Club	Lea	Pos	G	AB	R	H	2B	3B	HR	RBI	SB	Avg
2007 Oakland		A.L.	1B	18	72	16	25	9	0	4	8	1	.347
2008 Sacramento		P.C.	1B	8	31	4	6	0	0	1	3	0	.194
2008 Oakland b		A.L.	1B-3B	140	446	59	101	17	5	9	47	2	.226
Major League Totals			2 Yrs.	158	518	75	126	26	5	13	55	3	.243

a Traded by St. Louis Cardinals to Oakland Athletics with pitcher Danny Haren and pitcher Kiko Calero for pitcher Mark Mulder, December 18, 2004.
b On disabled list from July 14 to August 1, 2008.

BAUTISTA, JOSE ANTONIO

Born, Santo Domingo, Dominican Republic, October 19, 1980.
Bats Right. Throws Right. Height, 6 feet. Weight, 190 pounds.

Year	Club	Lea	Pos	G	AB	R	H	2B	3B	HR	RBI	SB	Avg
2001 Williamsport	N.Y.-Penn.		3B-OF	62	220	43	63	10	3	5	30	8	.286
2002 Hickory	So.Atl.		3B-SS	129	438	72	132	26	3	14	57	3	.301
2003 Lynchburg	Carolina		3B-2B	51	165	28	40	14	2	4	20	1	.242
2003 Pirates a	Gulf Coast		3B	7	23	5	8	1	0	1	3	0	.348
2004 Pittsburgh	N.L.		OF	23	40	1	8	2	0	0	0	0	.200
2004 Balt.-Tam. Bay-K.C. b-c-d-e.	A.L.		3B-OF	41	48	5	10	1	0	0	2	0	.208
2005 Altoona	Eastern		3B	117	445	63	126	27	1	23	90	7	.283
2005 Indianapolis	Int.		3B	13	51	6	13	3	0	1	4	1	.255
2005 Pittsburgh	N.L.		3B	11	28	3	4	1	0	0	1	1	.143
2006 Indianapolis	Int.		3B-OF-2B	29	101	12	28	9	0	2	9	2	.277
2006 Pittsburgh	N.L.		OF-3B-2B	117	400	58	94	20	3	16	51	2	.235
2007 Pirates	Gulf Coast		3B	2	8	1	3	2	0	0	1	0	.375
2007 Pittsburgh f	N.L.		3B-OF	142	532	75	135	36	2	15	63	6	.254
2008 Indianapolis	Int.		OF-2B	5	20	6	6	2	0	0	2	1	.300
2008 Pittsburgh	N.L.		3B	107	314	38	76	15	0	12	44	1	.242
2008 Toronto g	A.L.		3B-1B-2B	21	56	7	12	2	0	3	10	0	.214
Major League Totals			5 Yrs.	462	1418	187	339	77	5	46	171	10	.239

a Selected by Baltimore Orioles from Pittsburgh in Rule V draft, December 15, 2003.
b Claimed on waivers by Tampa Bay Devil Rays, June 3, 2004.
c Sold to Kansas City Royals, June 28, 2004.
d Traded to New York Mets for catcher Justin Huber, July 30, 2004.
e Traded to Pittsburgh Pirates with infielder Ty Wigginton and pitcher Matt Peterson for pitcher Kris Benson and infielder Jeff Keppinger, July 30, 2004.
f On disabled list from July 15 to August 1, 2007.
g Traded to Toronto Blue Jays for player to be named later, August 21, 2008. Pittsburgh Pirates received infielder Robinzon Diaz to complete trade, August 25, 2008.

BAY, JASON RAYMOND

Born, Trail, British Columbia, Canada, September 20, 1978.
Bats Right. Throws Right. Height, 6 feet, 2 inches. Weight, 205 pounds.

Year	Club	Lea	Pos	G	AB	R	H	2B	3B	HR	RBI	SB	Avg
2000 Vermont	N.Y.-Penn.		OF	35	135	17	41	5	0	2	12	17	.304
2001 Jupiter	Fla.St.		OF-2B	38	123	12	24	4	1	1	10	10	.195
2001 Clinton	Midwest		OF	87	318	67	115	20	4	13	61	15	.362
2002 St. Lucie	Fla.St.		OF	69	261	48	71	12	2	9	54	22	.272
2002 Binghamton	Eastern		OF	34	107	17	31	4	2	4	19	13	.290
2002 Mobile a-b	Southern		OF	23	81	16	25	5	2	4	12	4	.309
2003 Portland	P.C.		OF	91	307	64	93	11	1	20	59	23	.303
2003 San Diego-Pittsburgh c-d-e.	N.L.		OF	30	87	15	25	7	1	4	14	3	.287
2004 Nashville	P.C.		OF	4	10	3	4	2	0	1	3	0	.400
2004 Pittsburgh f-g.	N.L.		OF	120	411	61	116	24	4	26	82	4	.282
2005 Pittsburgh	N.L.		OF	*162	599	110	183	44	6	32	101	21	.306
2006 Pittsburgh	N.L.		OF	159	570	101	163	29	3	35	109	11	.286
2007 Pittsburgh	N.L.		OF	145	538	78	133	25	2	21	84	4	.247
2008 Pittsburgh	N.L.		OF	106	393	72	111	23	2	22	64	7	.282
2008 Boston h	A.L.		OF	49	184	39	54	12	2	9	37	3	.293
Major League Totals			6 Yrs.	771	2782	476	785	164	20	149	491	53	.282
Division Series													
2008 Boston	A.L.		OF	4	17	3	7	2	0	2	5	0	.412
Championship Series													
2008 Boston	A.L.		OF	7	24	3	7	1	0	1	4	0	.292

a Traded by Montreal Expos to New York Mets with pitcher Jim Serrano for infielder Lou Collier, March 26, 2002.
b Traded to San Diego Padres with pitcher Bobby M. Jones and pitcher Josh Reynolds for pitcher Jason Middlebrook and pitcher Steve Reed, July 31, 2002.
c On disabled list from May 26 to July 8, 2003.

d Traded to Pittsburgh Pirates with pitcher Oliver Perez and player to be named later for outfielder Brian Giles, August 26, 2003.
e Pittsburgh Pirates received pitcher Cory Stewart to complete trade, October 2, 2003.
f On disabled list from March 26 to May 7, 2004.
g Selected Rookie of the Year in National League for 2004.
h Traded to Boston Red Sox for outfielder Manny Ramirez, outfielder Brandon Moss and pitcher Craig Hansen, July 31, 2008.

BELLIARD, RONALD (RONNIE)
Born, Bronx, New York, April 7, 1975.
Bats Right. Throws Right. Height, 5 feet, 8 inches. Weight, 215 pounds.

Year	Club	Lea	Pos	G	AB	R	H	2B	3B	HR	RBI	SB	Avg
1994	Brewers	Arizona	2B-3B-SS	39	143	32	42	7	3	0	27	7	.294
1995	Beloit	Midwest	2B-3B	130	461	76	137	28	5	13	76	16	.297
1996	El Paso	Texas	2B	109	416	73	116	20	8	3	57	26	.279
1997	Tucson	P.C.	2B-SS	118	443	80	125	35	4	4	55	10	.282
1998	Louisville	Int.	2B-SS	133	507	114	163	36	7	14	73	32	.321
1998	Milwaukee	N.L.	2B	8	5	0	1	0	0	0	0	0	.200
1999	Louisville	Int.	2B	29	108	14	26	4	0	1	8	12	.241
1999	Milwaukee	N.L.	2B-3B-SS	124	457	60	135	29	4	8	58	4	.295
2000	Milwaukee	N.L.	2B	152	571	83	150	30	9	8	54	7	.263
2001	Milwaukee a	N.L.	2B	101	364	69	96	30	3	11	36	5	.264
2002	Milwaukee b	N.L.	2B-3B	104	289	30	61	13	0	3	26	2	.211
2003	Colorado Springs	P.C.	2B	6	19	2	5	1	0	0	0	0	.263
2003	Colorado c-d	N.L.	2B	116	447	73	124	31	2	8	50	7	.277
2004	Cleveland	A.L.	2B	152	599	78	169	48	1	12	70	3	.282
2005	Cleveland	A.L.	2B	145	536	71	152	36	1	17	78	2	.284
2006	Cleveland	A.L.	2B-3B	93	350	43	102	21	0	8	44	2	.291
2006	St. Louis e-f	N.L.	2B	54	194	20	46	9	1	5	23	0	.237
2007	Washington	N.L.	2B-1B-SS-3B	147	511	57	148	35	1	11	58	0	.290
2008	Potomac	Carolina	3B	1	3	0	0	0	0	0	0	0	.000
2008	Harrisburg	Eastern	2B-3B	3	12	0	0	0	0	0	0	0	.000
2008	Washington g	N.L.	1B-3B-2B-SS	96	296	37	85	22	0	11	46	3	.287
Major League Totals			11 Yrs.	1292	4619	622	1269	304	22	102	543	38	.275

Division Series
2006	St. Louis	N.L.	2B	4	13	2	6	1	0	0	2	1	.462

Championship Series
2006	St. Louis	N.L.	2B	7	25	0	6	0	0	0	2	1	.240

World Series Record
2006	St. Louis	N.L.	2B	3	12	0	0	0	0	0	0	0	.000

a On disabled list from August 9 to September 30, 2001.
b Not offered 2003 contract, December 21, 2002. Signed with Colorado Rockies organization, January 17, 2003.
c On disabled list from June 2 to June 23, 2003.
d Waived by Colorado Rockies, November 20, 2003. Signed with Cleveland Indians, December 26, 2003.
e Traded to St. Louis Cardinals for infielder Hector Luna, July 30, 2006.
f Filed for free agency, October 30, 2006. Signed with Washington Nationals organization, February 19, 2007.
g On disabled list from May 16 to June 10 and September 15 to October 3, 2008.

BELTRAN, CARLOS IVAN
Born, Manati, Puerto Rico, April 24, 1977.
Bats Both. Throws Right. Height, 6 feet. Weight, 200 pounds.

Year	Club	Lea	Pos	G	AB	R	H	2B	3B	HR	RBI	SB	Avg
1995	Royals	Gulf Coast	OF	52	180	29	50	9	0	0	23	5	.278
1996	Lansing	Midwest	OF	11	42	3	6	2	0	0	0	1	.143
1996	Spokane	Northwest	OF	59	215	29	58	8	3	7	29	10	.270
1997	Wilmington	Carolina	OF	120	419	57	96	15	4	11	46	17	.229
1998	Wilmington	Carolina	OF	52	192	32	53	14	0	5	32	11	.276
1998	Wichita	Texas	OF	47	182	50	64	13	3	14	44	7	.352
1998	Kansas City	A.L.	OF	14	58	12	16	5	3	0	7	3	.276
1999	Kansas City a	A.L.	OF	156	663	112	194	27	7	22	108	27	.293
2000	GC Royals	Gulf Coast	PH	1	4	3	2	1	0	1	1	0	.500
2000	Wilmington	Carolina	OF	3	13	2	4	0	1	2	6	0	.308
2000	Omaha	P.C.	OF	5	18	4	6	1	0	2	2	1	.333
2000	Kansas City b	A.L.	OF	98	372	49	92	15	4	7	44	13	.247
2001	Kansas City	A.L.	OF	155	617	106	189	32	12	24	101	31	.306
2002	Kansas City	A.L.	OF	*162	637	114	174	44	7	29	105	35	.273
2003	Wichita	Texas	OF	3	9	3	3	2	0	0	1	1	.333
2003	Kansas City c	A.L.	OF	141	521	102	160	14	10	26	100	41	.307
2004	Kansas City	A.L.	OF	69	266	51	74	19	2	15	51	14	.278

14

Year Club	Lea	Pos	G	AB	R	H	2B	3B	HR	RBI	SB	Avg
2004 Houston d-e.........	N.L.	OF	90	333	70	86	17	7	23	53	28	.258
2005 New York............	N.L.	OF	151	582	83	155	34	2	16	78	17	.266
2006 New York...........	N.L.	OF	140	510	127	140	38	1	41	116	18	.275
2007 New York f.........	N.L.	OF	144	554	93	153	33	3	33	112	23	.275
2008 New York...........	N.L.	OF	161	606	116	172	40	5	27	112	25	.276
Major League Totals...........	11 Yrs.	1481	5719	1035	1605	318	63	263	987	275	.281	.284
Division Series												
2004 Houston.............	N.L.	OF	5	22	9	10	2	0	4	9	2	.455
2006 New York............	N.L.	OF	3	9	2	2	0	0	0	1	1	.222
Division Series Totals...........		8	31	11	12	2	0	4	10	3	.387	
Championship Series												
2004 Houston.............	N.L.	OF	7	24	12	10	1	0	4	5	4	.417
2006 New York............	N.L.	OF	7	27	8	8	1	0	3	4	1	.296
Championship Series Totals.....		14	51	20	18	2	0	7	9	5	.353	

a Selected Rookie of the Year in American League for 1999.
b On disabled list from July 4 to September 3, 2000.
c On disabled list from March 21 to April 18, 2003.
d Traded to Houston Astros for pitcher Octavio Dotel and catcher John Buck, June 24, 2004.
e Filed for free agency, October 28, 2004. Signed with New York Mets, January 11, 2005.
f On disabled list from July 25 to August 10, 2007.

BELTRE, ADRIAN

Born, Santo Domingo, Dominican Republic, April 7, 1979.
Bats Right. Throws Right. Height, 5 feet, 11 inches. Weight, 220 pounds.

Year Club	Lea	Pos	G	AB	R	H	2B	3B	HR	RBI	SB	Avg
1995 LA-S.Domingo.....Dominican		3B	62	218	56	67	15	3	8	40	2	.307
1996 Savannah..........	So.Atl.	3B-2B	68	244	48	75	14	3	16	59	4	.307
1996 San Berndno a....	California	3B	63	238	40	62	13	1	10	40	3	.261
1997 Vero Beach........	Fla.St.	3B-OF	123	435	95	138	24	2	26	104	25	.317
1998 San Antonio........	Texas	3B	64	246	49	79	21	2	13	56	20	.321
1998 Los Angeles.......	N.L.	3B-SS	77	195	18	42	9	0	7	22	3	.215
1999 Los Angeles.......	N.L.	3B	152	538	84	148	27	5	15	67	18	.275
2000 Los Angeles b.....	N.L.	3B-SS	138	510	71	148	30	2	20	85	12	.290
2001 Vero Beach.........	Fla.St.	3B	3	9	0	4	1	0	0	1	0	.444
2001 Las Vegas.........	P.C.	3B	2	5	2	3	1	0	1	2	0	.600
2001 Los Angeles c.......	N.L.	3B-SS	126	475	59	126	22	4	13	60	13	.265
2002 Los Angeles.......	N.L.	3B	159	587	70	151	26	5	21	75	7	.257
2003 Los Angeles.......	N.L.	3B-SS	158	559	50	134	30	2	23	80	2	.240
2004 Los Angeles d.......	N.L.	3B-SS	156	598	104	200	32	0	*48	121	7	.334
2005 Seattle.............	A.L.	3B	156	603	69	154	36	1	19	87	3	.255
2006 Seattle.............	A.L.	3B-2B	156	620	88	166	39	4	25	89	11	.268
2007 Seattle.............	A.L.	3B	149	595	87	164	41	2	26	99	14	.276
2008 Seattle.............	A.L.	3B	143	556	74	148	29	1	25	77	8	.266
Major League Totals...........	11 Yrs.	1570	5836	774	1581	321	26	242	862	98	.271	
Division Series												
2004 Los Angeles.........	N.L.	3B	4	15	1	4	0	0	0	1	0	.267

a On disabled list from June 25 to July 2, 1996.
b On disabled list from May 28 to June 16, 2000.
c On disabled list from March 23 to May 12, 2001.
d Filed for free agency, October 29, 2004. Signed with Seattle Mariners, December 17, 2004.

BERKMAN, WILLIAM LANCE (LANCE)

Born, Waco, Texas, February 10, 1976.
Bats Both. Throws Left. Height, 6 feet, 1 inch. Weight, 220 pounds.

Year Club	Lea	Pos	G	AB	R	H	2B	3B	HR	RBI	SB	Avg
1997 Kissimmee.........	Fla.St.	OF	53	184	31	54	10	0	12	35	2	.293
1998 Jackson............	Texas	OF	122	425	82	130	34	0	24	89	6	.306
1998 New Orleans.......	P.C.	OF	17	59	14	16	4	0	6	13	0	.271
1999 New Orleans.......	P.C.	OF	64	226	42	73	20	0	8	49	7	.323
1999 Houston a..........	N.L.	OF-1B	34	93	10	22	2	0	4	15	5	.237
2000 New Orleans.......	P.C.	OF	31	112	18	37	4	2	6	27	4	.330
2000 Houston...........	N.L.	OF-1B	114	353	76	105	28	1	21	67	6	.297
2001 Houston...........	N.L.	OF	156	577	110	191	*55	5	34	126	7	.331
2002 Houston...........	N.L.	OF	158	578	106	169	35	2	42	*128	8	.292
2003 Houston...........	N.L.	OF	153	538	110	155	35	6	25	93	5	.288
2004 Houston...........	N.L.	OF-1B	160	544	104	172	40	3	30	106	9	.316

15

Year Club	Lea	Pos	G	AB	R	H	2B	3B	HR	RBI	SB	Avg
2005 Round Rock.........P.C.		OF	4	14	2	4	1	0	0	1	0	.286
2005 Houston b ..........N.L.		1B-OF	132	468	76	137	34	1	24	82	4	.293
2006 Houston .............N.L.		1B-OF	152	536	95	169	29	0	45	136	3	.315
2007 Houston .............N.L.		1B-OF	153	561	95	156	24	2	34	102	7	.278
2008 Houston .............N.L.		1B	159	554	114	173	*46	4	29	106	18	.312
Major League Totals		10 Yrs.	1371	4802	896	1449	328	24	288	961	72	.302
Division Series												
2001 Houston .............N.L.		OF	3	12	0	2	0	0	0	0	0	.167
2004 Houston .............N.L.		OF	5	22	5	9	1	1	1	3	0	.409
2005 Houston .............N.L.		1B-OF	4	14	4	5	1	0	1	5	0	.357
Division Series Totals			12	48	9	16	2	0	2	8	0	.333
Championship Series												
2004 Houston .............N.L.		OF	7	24	7	7	2	0	3	9	1	.292
2005 Houston .............N.L.		1B-OF	6	21	2	6	2	0	1	3	0	.286
Championship Series Totals			13	45	9	13	4	0	4	12	1	.289
World Series Record												
2005 Houston .............N.L.		OF-1B	4	13	0	5	2	0	0	6	1	.385

a On disabled list from April 13 to May 14, 1999.
b On disabled list from March 25 to May 6, 2005.

BERROA (SELMO), ANGEL MARIA

Born, Santo Domingo, Dominican Republic, January 27, 1978.
Bats Right. Throws Right. Height, 6 feet. Weight, 195 pounds.

Year Club	Lea	Pos	G	AB	R	H	2B	3B	HR	RBI	SB	Avg
1998 Oaklnd West.	Dominican	3B	58	196	51	48	7	4	8	37	4	.245
1999 Athletics.......	Arizona	SS-2B-3B-OF	46	169	42	49	11	4	2	24	11	.290
1999 Midland	Texas	SS	4	17	3	1	1	0	0	0	0	.059
2000 Visalia	Calif.	SS	129	429	61	119	25	6	10	63	11	.277
2001 Wilmington ...	Carolina	SS	51	199	43	63	18	4	6	25	10	.317
2001 Wichita........	Texas	SS	80	304	63	90	20	4	8	42	15	.296
2001 Kansas City a ...A.L.		SS	15	53	8	16	2	0	0	4	2	.302
2002 Omaha...........P.C.		SS	77	297	37	64	11	4	8	35	6	.215
2002 Kansas City b ... A.L.		SS	20	75	8	17	7	1	0	5	3	.227
2003 Kansas City .......A.L.		SS	158	567	92	163	28	3	17	73	21	.287
2004 Wichita	Texas	SS	11	51	8	16	1	0	3	10	3	.314
2004 Kansas City c ...A.L.		SS	134	512	72	134	27	6	8	43	14	.262
2005 Kansas City ..,...A.L.		SS	159	608	68	164	21	5	11	55	7	.270
2006 Kansas City .....A.L.		SS	132	474	45	111	18	1	9	54	3	.234
2007 Kansas City .....A.L.		SS-2B-3B	9	11	0	1	0	0	0	1	0	.091
2007 Omaha...........P.C.		SS-2B-3B	81	307	47	92	17	0	8	40	2	.300
2008 Omaha...........P.C.		SS-2B	51	189	34	55	13	0	10	27	4	.291
2008 Los Angeles d-e...N.L.		SS-2B	84	226	26	52	13	1	1	16	0	.230
Major League Totals		8 Yrs.	711	2526	319	658	116	21	46	251	50	.260
Division Series												
2008 Los Angeles .......N.L.		2B	3	1	0	1	0	0	0	0	0	1.000
Championship Series												
2008 Los Angeles .......N.L.		2B	2	1	0	0	0	0	0	0	0	.000

a Traded by Oakland Athletics to Kansas City Royals with pitcher Roberto Hernandez, catcher A.J. Hinch and cash for outfielder Johnny Damon, infielder Mark Ellis and player to be named later, January 8, 2001.
b On disabled list from April 15 to June 9, 2002.
c On disabled list from April 16 to May 1, 2004.
d Traded to Los Angeles Dodgers for infielder Juan Rivera, June 6, 2008.
e Not offered contract, December 12, 2008. Signed with New York Yankees organization, January 14, 2009.

BETANCOURT, YUNIESKY (PEREZ)

Born, Santa Clara, Cuba, January 31, 1982.
Bats Right. Throws Right. Height, 5 feet, 10 inches. Weight, 190 pounds.

Year Club	Lea	Pos	G	AB	R	H	2B	3B	HR	RBI	SB	Avg
2005 San Antonio. .'........	Texas	SS-2B	52	227	25	62	10	3	5	20	12	.273
2005 Tacoma..............	P.C.	SS-2B	49	183	13	54	9	6	2	30	7	.295
2005 Seattle a.............	A.L.	SS-2B	60	211	24	54	11	5	1	15	1	.256
2006 Seattle	A.L.	SS	157	558	68	161	28	6	8	47	11	.289
2007 Seattle	A.L.	SS	155	536	72	155	38	2	9	67	5	.289
2008 Seattle	A.L.	SS	153	559	66	156	36	3	7	51	4	.279
Major League Totals		4 Yrs.	525	1864	230	526	113	16	25	180	21	.282

a Played in Cuba 2000-2004. Signed with Seattle Mariners, January 26, 2005.

BETEMIT, WILSON

Born, Santo Domingo, Dominican Republic, November 2, 1981.
Bats Both. Throws Right. Height, 6 feet, 3 inches. Weight, 230 pounds.

Year	Club	Lea	Pos	G	AB	R	H	2B	3B	HR	RBI	SB	Avg
1997	Braves	Gulf Coast	SS	32	113	12	24	6	1	0	15	0	.212
1998	Braves	Gulf Coast	SS	51	173	23	38	8	4	5	16	6	.220
1999	Danville	Appal.	SS	67	259	39	83	18	2	5	53	6	.320
2000	Jamestown	N.Y.-Penn.	SS	69	269	54	89	15	2	5	37	3	.331
2001	Myrtle Beach	Carolina	SS	84	318	38	88	20	1	7	43	8	.277
2001	Greenville	Southern	SS	47	183	22	65	14	0	5	19	6	.355
2001	Atlanta	N.L.	SS	8	3	1	0	0	0	0	0	1	.000
2002	Braves	Gulf Coast	SS	7	19	2	5	4	0	0	2	1	.263
2002	Richmond	Int.	SS	93	343	43	84	17	1	8	34	8	.245
2003	Richmond	Int.	3B-SS	127	478	55	125	23	13	8	65	8	.262
2004	Richmond	Int.	3B-SS	105	356	48	99	24	2	13	59	3	.278
2004	Atlanta	N.L.	SS-3B	22	47	2	8	0	0	0	3	0	.170
2005	Atlanta	N.L.	3B-SS-2B	115	246	36	75	12	4	4	20	1	.305
2006	Atlanta-Los Angeles a	N.L.	3B-SS-2B	143	373	49	98	23	0	18	53	3	.263
2007	Los Angeles	N.L.	3B-SS-2B-OF	84	156	22	36	8	0	10	26	0	.231
2007	New York b	A.L.	1B-3B-SS-2B	37	84	11	19	4	0	4	24	0	.226
2008	Scranton-WB	Int.	1B-3B-2B-SS	8	27	5	9	4	0	1	5	0	.333
2008	New York c-d	A.L.	1B-3B-SS-2B	87	189	24	50	13	0	6	25	0	.265
Major League Totals			6 Yrs.	496	1098	145	286	60	4	42	151	5	.260
Division Series													
2004	Atlanta	N.L.	PH	1	0	0	0	0	0	0	0	0	.000
2005	Atlanta	N.L.	PH	2	2	0	1	0	0	0	0	0	.500
2006	Los Angeles	N.L.	3B	3	8	3	4	1	0	1	1	0	.500
Division Series Totals				6	10	3	5	1	0	1	1	0	.500

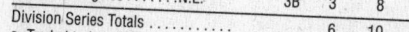

a Traded to Los Angeles Dodgers for pitcher Danys Baez, infielder Willy Aybar and cash, July 28, 2006.
b Traded to New York Yankees for pitcher Scott Proctor, July 31, 2007.
c On disabled list from April 14 to May 6 and May 11 to May 26, 2008.
d Traded to Chicago White Sox with pitcher Jeff Marquez and pitcher Jhonny Nunez for infielder Nick Swisher and pitcher Kaneoka Texeira, November 13, 2008.

BLAKE, WILLIAM CASEY (CASEY)

Born, Des Moines, Iowa, August 23, 1973.
Bats Right. Throws Right. Height, 6 feet, 2 inches. Weight, 210 pounds.

Year	Club	Lea	Pos	G	AB	R	H	2B	3B	HR	RBI	SB	Avg
1996	Hagerstown	So.Atl.	3B-1B-OF	48	172	29	43	13	1	2	18	5	.250
1997	Dunedin	Fla.St.	3B-SS	129	449	56	107	21	0	7	39	19	.238
1998	Dunedin	Fla.St.	3B	88	340	62	119	28	3	11	65	9	.350
1998	Knoxville	Southern	3B	45	172	41	64	15	4	7	38	10	.372
1999	Syracuse	Int.	3B	110	387	69	95	16	2	22	75	9	.245
1999	St. Catharines	N.Y.-Penn.	3B	1	3	0	2	0	0	0	0	0	.667
1999	Toronto	A.L.	3B	14	39	6	10	2	0	0	0	0	.256
2000	Syracuse	Int.	3B-SS	30	106	10	23	6	1	2	7	0	.217
2000	Salt Lake	P.C.	3B-SS-1B	80	293	59	93	22	2	12	52	7	.317
2000	Minnesota a-b	A.L.	3B-1B	7	16	1	3	2	0	0	1	0	.188
2001	Edmonton	P.C.	3B-1B-2B-SS	94	375	64	116	24	6	10	49	14	.309
2001	Minn.-Baltimore c-d	A.L.	1B-3B	19	37	3	9	1	0	1	4	3	.243
2002	Edmonton	P.C.	3B-2B-1B-OF	126	482	87	149	25	3	19	58	24	.309
2002	Minnesota e	A.L.	3B-1B	9	20	2	4	1	0	0	1	0	.200
2003	Cleveland	A.L.	3B-1B	152	557	80	143	35	0	17	67	7	.257
2004	Cleveland	A.L.	3B-1B	152	587	93	159	36	3	28	88	5	.271
2005	Cleveland	A.L.	OF-3B-1B	147	523	72	126	32	1	23	58	4	.241
2006	Lake County	So.Atl.	OF	1	2	1	1	0	0	1	2	0	.500
2006	Akron	Eastern	OF	1	3	0	1	1	0	0	1	0	.333
2006	Cleveland f	A.L.	OF-1B	109	401	63	113	20	1	19	68	6	.282
2007	Cleveland	A.L.	3B-1B-OF	156	588	81	159	36	4	18	78	4	.270
2008	Cleveland	A.L.	3B-1B-SS	94	325	46	94	24	0	11	58	2	.289
2008	Los Angeles g-h	N.L.	3B-1B-2B	58	211	25	53	12	1	10	23	1	.251
Major League Totals			10 Yrs.	917	3304	472	873	201	10	128	447	32	.264
Division Series													
2007	Cleveland	A.L.	3B	4	17	1	2	1	0	0	2	0	.118
2008	Los Angeles	N.L.	3B	3	11	2	3	0	0	0	2	0	.273
Division Series Totals				7	28	3	5	1	0	0	4	0	.179
Championship Series													
2007	Cleveland	A.L.	3B	7	26	4	9	2	0	1	2	0	.346

Year	Club	Lea	Pos	G	AB	R	H	2B	3B	HR	RBI	SB	Avg
2008 Los Angeles	N.L.		3B-2B	5	19	2	5	0	0	1	2	0	.263
Championship Series Totals				12	45	6	14	2	0	2	4	0	.311

a Claimed on waivers from Toronto Blue Jays by Minnesota Twins, May 23, 2000.
b On disabled list from June 28 to July 7, 2000.
c Claimed on waivers by Baltimore Orioles, September 21, 2001.
d Claimed on waivers by Minnesota Twins, October 12, 2001.
e Filed for free agency, October 14, 2002. Signed with Cleveland Indians, December 18, 2002.
f On disabled list from June 14 to July 13 and August 6 to August 25, 2006.
g Traded to Los Angeles Dodgers for pitcher Jonathan Meloan and catcher Carlos Santana, July 26, 2008.
h Filed for free agency, October 30, 2008, re-signed with Los Angeles Dodgers, December 9, 2008.

BLALOCK, HANK JOE

Born, San Diego, California, November 21, 1980.
Bats Left. Throws Right. Height, 6 feet, 1 inch. Weight, 200 pounds.

Year	Club	Lea	Pos	G	AB	R	H	2B	3B	HR	RBI	SB	Avg
1999 Rangers	Gulf Coast		3B	51	191	34	69	17	6	3	38	3	.361
1999 Savannah	So.Atl.		3B	6	25	3	6	1	0	1	2	0	.240
2000 Savannah	So.Atl.		3B	139	512	66	153	32	2	10	77	31	.299
2001 Charlotte	Fla.St.		3B	63	237	46	90	19	1	7	47	7	.380
2001 Tulsa	Texas		3B	68	272	50	89	18	4	11	61	3	.327
2002 Oklahoma	P.C.		3B-2B	95	387	63	119	32	1	8	62	2	.307
2002 Texas	A.L.		3B	49	147	16	31	8	0	3	17	0	.211
2003 Texas	A.L.		3B-2B	143	567	89	170	33	3	29	90	2	.300
2004 Texas	A.L.		3B	159	624	107	172	38	3	32	110	2	.276
2005 Texas	A.L.		3B	161	647	80	170	34	0	25	92	1	.263
2006 Texas	A.L.		3B	152	591	76	157	26	3	16	89	1	.266
2007 Texas a	A.L.		3B	58	208	32	61	16	3	10	33	4	.293
2008 Frisco	Texas		1B	6	19	5	8	3	0	0	4	1	.421
2008 Oklahoma	P.C.		1B	2	5	1	2	0	0	0	0	0	.400
2008 Texas b-c	A.L.		1B-3B	65	258	37	74	19	1	12	38	1	.287
Major League Totals		7 Yrs.		787	3042	437	835	174	13	127	469	11	.274

a On disabled list from May 17 to September 1, 2007.
b On disabled list from April 26 to July 18 and July 28 to August 22, 2008.
c Filed for free agency, October 30, 2008. Club accepted option for contract next year, November 8, 2008.

BLANCO (PEDRAZA), GREGOR MIGUEL

Born, Caracas, Venezuela, December 12, 1983.
Bats Left. Throws Left. Height, 5 feet, 11 inches. Weight, 170 pounds.

Year	Club	Lea	Pos	G	AB	R	H	2B	3B	HR	RBI	SB	Avg
2002 Macon	So.Atl.		OF	132	468	87	127	14	9	7	36	40	.271
2003 Myrtle Beach	Carolina		OF	126	461	66	125	19	7	5	36	34	.271
2004 Myrtle Beach	Carolina		OF	119	435	73	117	17	9	8	41	25	.269
2005 Mississippi	Southern		OF	123	401	64	101	11	12	6	37	28	.252
2006 Richmond	Int.		OF	73	269	43	79	12	1	0	19	14	.294
2006 Mississippi	Southern		OF	66	251	45	72	16	3	0	9	17	.287
2007 Richmond	Int.		OF	124	464	81	131	18	5	3	35	23	.282
2008 Atlanta	N.L.		OF	144	430	52	108	14	4	1	38	13	.251

BLOOMQUIST, WILLIAM PAUL (WILLIE)

Born, Bremerton, Washington, November 27, 1977.
Bats Right. Throws Right. Height, 5 feet, 11 inches. Weight, 195 pounds.

Year	Club	Lea	Pos	G	AB	R	H	2B	3B	HR	RBI	SB	Avg
1999 Everett	Northwest		2B	41	178	35	51	10	3	2	27	17	.287
2000 Lancaster	California		2B-SS	64	256	63	97	19	6	2	51	22	.379
2000 Tacoma a	P.C.		2B	51	191	17	43	5	1	1	23	5	.225
2001 San Antonio	Texas		SS-2B	123	491	59	125	23	2	0	47	34	.255
2002 Tacoma	P.C.		OF-2B-3B-SS	104	337	47	91	14	3	6	47	20	.270
2002 Seattle b	A.L.		OF-2B	12	33	11	15	4	0	0	7	3	.455
2003 Seattle	A.L.		3B-SS-OF	89	196	30	49	7	2	1	14	4	.250
2004 Tacoma	P.C.		SS-OF	3	12	2	5	0	0	1	3	1	.417
2004 Seattle c	A.L.		3B-SS-1B-OF	93	188	27	46	10	0	2	18	13	.245
2005 Seattle d	A.L.		2B-SS-OF-3B	82	249	27	64	15	2	0	22	14	.257
2006 Seattle	A.L.		OF-SS-2B-3B	102	251	36	62	6	2	1	15	16	.247
2007 Seattle	A.L.		OF-2B-3B-SS	91	173	28	48	3	0	0	9	7	.277
2008 Seattle e-f.	A.L.		OF-SS-2B-3B	71	165	32	46	1	0	0	14	14	.279
Major League Totals		7 Yrs.		540	1255	191	330	46	6	6	98	71	.263

18

a On disabled list from August 6 to September 29, 2000.
b On disabled list from April 22 to May 3 and June 6 to.18, 2002.
c On disabled list from May 2 to May 21, 2004.
d On disabled list from August 30 to October 31, 2005.
e On disabled list from August 10 to September 29, 2008.
f Filed for free agency, October 30, 2008. Signed with Kansas City Royals, January 9, 2009.

BLUM, GEOFFREY EDWARD (GEOFF)

Born, Redwood City, California, April 26, 1973.
Bats Both. Throws Right. Height, 6 feet, 3 inches. Weight, 205 pounds.

Year Club	Lea	Pos	G	AB	R	H	2B	3B	HR	RBI	SB	Avg
1994 Vermont	N.Y.-Penn.	SS	63	241	48	83	15	1	3	38	5	.344
1995 Wst Plm Bch	Fla.St.	2B-SS-3B	125	457	54	120	20	2	1	62	6	.263
1996 Harrisburg	Eastern	2B-SS-1B-OF	120	396	47	95	22	2	1	41	6	.240
1997 Ottawa	Int.	2B-SS-3B	118	407	59	101	21	2	3	35	14	.248
1998 Ottawa	Int.	2B-SS	8	23	1	4	0	0	0	1	0	.174
1998 Expos	Gulf Coast	2B	5	18	0	3	1	1	0	1	0	.167
1998 Jupiter	Fla.St.	2B-3B-SS	17	58	13	16	6	0	0	5	1	.276
1998 Harrisburg	Eastern	3B-SS-2B	39	139	25	43	12	3	6	21	2	.309
1999 Ottawa	Int.	SS	77	268	43	71	14	1	10	37	6	.265
1999 Montreal a	N.L.	SS-2B	45	133	21	32	7	2	8	18	1	.241
2000 Montreal	N.L.	3B-SS-2B-1B	124	343	40	97	20	2	11	45	1	.283
2001 Montreal	N.L.	3B-OF-2B-1B	148	453	57	107	25	0	9	50	9	.236
2002 Houston b	N.L.	3B-OF-SS-1B	130	368	45	104	20	4	10	52	2	.283
2003 Houston c	N.L.	3B-2B-SS	123	420	51	110	19	0	10	52	0	.262
2004 Tampa Bay d	A.L.	3B-2B-OF-1B	112	339	38	73	21	0	8	35	2	.215
2005 Lake Elsinore	California	3B-OF	2	8	3	2	0	0	0	2	0	.250
2005 San Diego	N.L.	3B-2B-SS-1B	78	224	26	54	13	1	5	22	3	.241
2005 Chicago e-f-g	A.L.	1B-3B-SS-2B	31	95	6	19	2	1	1	3	0	.200
2006 San Diego h	N.L.	SS-3B-1B-2B	109	276	27	70	17	1	4	34	0	.254
2007 San Diego i	N.L.	2B-3B-SS-OF	122	330	34	83	21	1	5	33	0	.252
2008 Houston	N.L.	3B-2B-1B-SS	114	325	36	78	14	1	14	53	1	.240
Major League Totals		10 Yrs.	1136	3306	381	827	179	13	85	397	19	.250
Division Series												
2005 Chicago	A.L.	1B	1	1	0	0	0	0	0	0	0	.000
2006 San Diego	N.L.	SS-3B	4	8	0	1	1	0	0	1	0	.125
Division Series Totals			5	9	0	1	1	0	0	1	0	.111
World Series Record												
2005 Chicago	A.L.	2B	1	1	1	1	0	0	1	1	0	1.000

a On disabled list from May 21 to June 15, 1999.
b Traded to Houston Astros for infielder Chris Truby, March 12, 2002.
c Traded to Tampa Bay Devil Rays for pitcher Brandon Backe, December 14, 2003.
d Released by Tampa Bay Devil Rays, November 19, 2004. Signed with San Diego Padres, December 8, 2004.
e On disabled list from April 30 to May 18, 2005.
f Traded to Chicago White Sox for pitcher Ryan Meaux, July 31, 2005.
g Filed for free agency, October 31, 2005. Signed with San Diego Padres, November 16, 2005.
h Filed for free agency, October 28, 2006, re-signed with San Diego Padres, December 1, 2006.
i Filed for free agency, October 30, 2007. Signed with Houston Astros, November 20, 2007.

BOGGS, BRANDON KYLE

Born, St.Louis, Missouri, January 9, 1983.
Bats Both. Throws Right. Height, 5 feet, 11 inches. Weight, 205 pounds.

Year Club	Lea	Pos	G	AB	R	H	2B	3B	HR	RBI	SB	Avg
2004 Spokane	Northwest	OF	45	149	27	35	11	0	3	19	6	.235
2005 Clinton	Midwest	OF	85	309	54	76	16	2	13	51	14	.246
2006 Bakersfield	Calif.	OF	78	284	48	74	20	4	8	37	13	.261
2007 Bakersfield	Calif.	OF	26	92	17	23	9	1	4	17	5	.250
2007 Frisco	Texas	OF	104	354	69	94	21	4	19	55	10	.266
2008 Oklahoma	P.C.	OF	18	68	12	21	4	3	0	6	1	.309
2008 Texas	A.L.	OF	101	283	30	64	17	4	8	41	3	.226

BOONE, AARON JOHN

Born, LaMesa, California, March 9, 1973.
Bats Right. Throws Right. Height, 6 feet, 2 inches. Weight, 200 pounds.

Year Club	Lea	Pos	G	AB	R	H	2B	3B	HR	RBI	SB	Avg
1994 Billings	Pioneer	3B-1B-SS	67	256	48	70	15	5	7	55	6	.273
1995 Chattanooga	Southern	3B	23	66	6	15	3	0	0	3	2	.227

Year Club Lea	Pos	G	AB	R	H	2B	3B	HR	RBI	SB	Avg
1995 Winston-Sal ... Carolina	3B	108	395	61	103	19	1	14	50	11	.261
1996 Chattanooga...Southern	3B-SS	136	548	86	158	44	7	17	95	21	.288
1997 Indianapolis .......A.A.	3B-SS-2B	131	476	79	138	30	4	22	75	12	.290
1997 Cincinnati ........N.L.	3B-2B	16	49	5	12	1	0	0	5	1	.245
1998 Indianapolis .... Int.	3B-2B-SS	87	332	56	80	18	1	7	38	17	.241
1998 Cincinnati........N.L.	3B-2B-SS	58	181	24	51	13	2	2	28	6	.282
1999 Indianapolis .... Int.	3B	11	41	6	14	2	1	0	7	2	.341
1999 Cincinnati........N.L.	3B-SS	139	472	56	132	26	5	14	72	17	.280
2000 Cincinnati a ......N.L.	3B-SS	84	291	44	83	18	0	12	43	6	.285
2001 Louisville .... Int.	3B	1	4	0	1	0	0	0	0	0	.250
2001 Cincinnati b ......N.L.	3B	103	381	54	112	26	2	14	62	6	.294
2002 Cincinnati........N.L.	3B-SS	*162	606	83	146	38	2	26	87	32	.241
2003 Cincinnati........N.L.	3B-2B-SS	106	403	61	110	19	3	18	65	15	.273
2003 New York c......A.L.	3B	54	189	31	48	13	0	6	31	8	.254
2004 Cleveland d-e ......A.L.				INJURED—Did Not Play							
2005 Cleveland ........A.L.	3B	143	511	61	124	19	1	16	60	9	.243
2006 Cleveland f ...... A.L.	3B-2B	104	354	50	89	19	1	7	46	5	.251
2007 Jupiter .... Fla.St.	1B	1	3	1	0	0	0	0	1	0	.000
2007 Florida g-h ........N.L.	1B-3B	69	189	27	54	11	0	5	28	2	.286
2008 Nationals ....Gulf Coast	1B	1	3	0	2	1	0	0	0	0	.667
2008 Columbus........ Int.	1B	3	8	0	0	0	0	0	0	0	.000
2008 Washington i-j .....N.L.	1B-3B-2B	104	232	23	56	13	1	6	28	0	.241
Major League Totals	11 Yrs.	1142	3858	519	1017	216	17	126	555	107	.264
Division Series											
2003 New York .........A.L.	3B	4	15	1	3	1	0	0	0	1	.200
Championship Series											
2003 New York .........A.L.	3B	7	17	2	3	0	0	1	2	1	.176
World Series Record											
2003 New York .........A.L.	3B	6	21	1	3	0	0	1	2	0	.143

a On disabled list from July 10 to October 3, 2000.
b On disabled list from May 15 to June 15 and August 15 to September 1 and September 24 to October 11, 2001.
c Traded to New York Yankees for pitcher Brandon Claussen, pitcher Charlie Manning and cash, July 31, 2003.
d Released by New York Yankees, March 1, 2004. Signed with Cleveland Indians, June 26, 2004.
e On disabled list from June 26 to November 15, 2004.
f Filed for free agency, October 30, 2006. Signed with Florida Marlins, December 29, 2006.
g On disabled list from June 25 to October 30, 2007.
h Filed for free agency, October 30, 2007. Signed with Washington Nationals, December 6, 2007.
i On disabled list from July 7 to August 14, 2008.
j Filed for free agency, November 3, 2008. Signed with Houston Astros, December 18, 2008.

BOURN, MICHAEL RAY

Born, Houston, Texas, December 27, 1982.
Bats Left. Throws Right. Height, 5 feet, 11 inches. Weight, 180 pounds.

Year Club Lea	Pos	G	AB	R	H	2B	3B	HR	RBI	SB	Avg
2003 Batavia .... N.Y.-Penn.	OF	35	125	12	35	0	1	0	4	23	.280
2004 Lakewood...........So.Atl.	OF	109	413	92	130	20	14	5	53	58	.315
2005 Reading ....Eastern	OF	135	544	80	146	18	8	6	44	38	.268
2006 Reading ....Eastern	OF	80	318	62	87	5	6	4	26	30	.274
2006 Scranton-WB ....Int.	OF	38	152	34	43	5	5	0	15	15	.283
2006 Philadelphia ...........N.L.	OF	17	8	2	1	0	0	0	1	1	.125
2007 Philadelphia a-b ...... N.L.	OF	105	119	29	33	3	3	1	6	18	.277
2008 Houston ..............N.L.	OF	138	467	57	107	10	4	5	29	41	.229
Major League Totals	3 Yrs.	260	594	88	141	13	7	6	35	60	.237
Division Series											
2007 Philadelphia ...........N.L.	PH	2	1	0	0	0	0	0	0	0	.000

a On disabled list from July 31 to September 10, 2007.
b Traded to Houston Astros with pitcher Geoff Geary and infielder Mike Costanzo for infielder Eric Bruntlett and pitcher Brad Lidge, November 12, 2007.

BOWKER, JOHN BRITE

Born, Sacramento, California, July 8, 1983.
Bats Left. Throws Left. Height, 6 feet, 2 inches. Weight, 200 pounds.

Year Club Lea	Pos	G	AB	R	H	2B	3B	HR	RBI	SB	Avg
2004 Giants............Arizona	OF	10	43	14	22	7	1	2	11	1	.512
2004 Salem-Keizer .... Northwest	OF	31	127	23	41	9	2	4	16	1	.323
2005 San Jose ....Calif.	OF	121	464	66	124	27	1	13	67	3	.267
2006 San Jose ....Calif.	OF	112	462	61	131	32	6	7	66	6	.284

Year	Club	Lea	Pos	G	AB	R	H	2B	3B	HR	RBI	SB	Avg
2006 Fresno	P.C.		OF	2	4	0	2	0	0	0	0	0	.500
2007 Connecticut	Eastern		OF	139	522	79	160	35	6	22	90	3	.307
2008 Fresno	P.C.		1B-OF	23	93	13	22	3	1	2	9	2	.237
2008 San Francisco	N.L.		1B-OF	111	326	31	83	14	3	10	43	1	.255

BRADLEY, MILTON OBELLE

Born, Harbor City, Florida, April 15, 1978.
Bats Both. Throws Right. Height, 6 feet. Weight, 225 pounds.

Year	Club	Lea	Pos	G	AB	R	H	2B	3B	HR	RBI	SB	Avg
1996 Expos	Gulf Coast		OF	32	112	18	27	7	1	1	12	7	.241
1997 Expos	Gulf Coast		OF	9	25	6	5	2	0	1	2	2	.200
1997 Vermont	N.Y.-Penn.		OF	50	200	29	60	7	5	3	30	7	.300
1998 Jupiter	Fla.St.		OF	67	261	55	75	14	1	5	34	17	.287
1998 Cape Fear	So.Atl.		OF	75	281	54	85	21	4	6	50	13	.302
1999 Harrisburg	Eastern		OF	86	346	62	114	22	5	12	50	14	.329
2000 Ottawa	Int.		OF	88	342	58	104	20	1	6	29	10	.304
2000 Montreal	N.L.		OF	42	154	20	34	8	1	2	15	2	.221
2001 Montreal	N.L.		OF	67	220	19	49	16	3	1	19	7	.223
2001 Ottawa	Int.		OF	35	136	21	37	7	2	2	13	14	.272
2001 Buffalo	Int.		OF	30	114	18	29	3	0	5	15	9	.254
2001 Cleveland a	A.L.		OF	10	18	3	4	1	0	0	0	1	.222
2002 Buffalo	Int.		OF	6	23	3	6	0	0	0	3	2	.261
2002 Akron	Eastern		OF	3	11	1	3	1	0	0	1	0	.273
2002 Cleveland b	A.L.		OF	98	325	48	81	18	3	9	38	6	.249
2003 Cleveland c	A.L.		OF	101	377	61	121	34	2	10	56	17	.321
2004 Los Angeles d-e	N.L.		OF	141	516	72	138	24	0	19	67	15	.267
2005 Las Vegas	P.C.		OF	5	13	2	4	0	0	0	1	1	.308
2005 Los Angeles f-g	N.L.		OF	75	283	49	82	14	1	13	38	6	.290
2006 Stockton	Calif.		OF	2	7	1	1	0	0	0	0	0	.143
2006 Sacramento	P.C.		OF	6	24	3	5	0	0	0	2	6	.208
2006 Oakland h	A.L.		OF	96	351	53	97	14	2	14	52	1	.276
2007 Sacramento	P.C.		OF	2	5	1	0	0	0	0	0	0	.000
2007 Oakland	A.L.		OF	19	65	6	19	4	0	2	7	2	.292
2007 San Diego i-j-k-l	N.L.		OF	42	144	31	45	5	1	11	30	3	.313
2008 Texas m	A.L.		DH-OF	126	414	78	133	32	1	22	77	5	.321
Major League Totals		9 Yrs.		817	2867	440	803	170	14	103	399	74	.280
Division Series													
2004 Los Angeles	N.L.		OF	4	11	1	3	1	0	1	1	2	.273
2006 Oakland	A.L.		OF	3	13	1	1	0	0	0	1	0	.077
Division Series Totals				7	24	2	4	1	0	1	2	2	.167
Championship Series													
2006 Oakland	A.L.		OF	4	18	4	9	2	0	2	5	0	.500

a Traded to Cleveland Indians for pitcher Zach Day, July 31, 2001.
b On disabled list from May 2 to June 4 and August 12 to August 30, 2002.
c On disabled list from April 23 to May 8 and August 10 to October 3, 2003.
d Traded to Los Angeles Dodgers for outfielder Franklin Gutierrez and player to be named later, April 4, 2004.
e Cleveland Indians received pitcher Andrew Brown to complete trade, May 19, 2004.
f On disabled list from May 30 to July 23 and August 23 to October 28, 2005.
g Traded to Oakland Athletics with infielder Antonio Perez for outfielder Andre Ethier, December 13, 2005.
h On disabled list from April 27 to June 6 and June 15 to July 14, 2006.
i On disabled list from April 23 to May 11 and May 15 to May 30 and June 3 to June 20, 2007.
j Traded to San Diego Padres for pitcher Andrew Brown, June 29, 2007.
k On disabled list from June 21 to July 7, 2007.
l Filed for free agency, October 29, 2007. Signed with Texas Rangers, December 12, 2007.
m Filed for free agency, October 30, 2008. Signed with Chicago Cubs, January 6, 2009.

BRAUN, RYAN JOSEPH

Born, Mission Hills, California, November 17, 1983.
Bats Right. Throws Right. Height, 6 feet, 2 inches. Weight, 200 pounds.

Year	Club	Lea	Pos	G	AB	R	H	2B	3B	HR	RBI	SB	Avg
2005 Helena	Pioneer		3B	10	41	6	14	2	1	2	10	2	.341
2005 West Tenn	So.Atl.		3B	37	152	21	54	16	2	8	35	2	.355
2006 Brevard County	Fla.St.		3B	59	226	34	62	12	2	7	37	14	.274
2006 Huntsville	Southern		3B	59	231	42	70	19	1	15	40	12	.303
2007 Nashville	P.C.		3B	34	117	28	40	12	0	10	22	4	.342
2007 Milwaukee a	N.L.		3B	113	451	91	146	26	6	34	97	15	.324

Year Club	Lea	Pos	G	AB	R	H	2B	3B	HR	RBI	SB	Avg
2008 Milwaukee	N.L.	OF	151	611	92	174	39	7	37	106	14	.285
Major League Totals	2 Yrs.		264	1062	183	320	65	13	71	203	29	.301
Division Series												
2008 Milwaukee	N.L.	OF	4	16	0	5	2	0	0	2	0	.313

a Selected Rookie of the Year in National League for 2007.

BROWN, EMIL QUINCY

Born, Chicago, Illinois, December 29, 1974.
Bats Right. Throws Right. Height, 6 feet, 2 inches. Weight, 210 pounds.

Year Club	Lea	Pos	G	AB	R	H	2B	3B	HR	RBI	SB	Avg
1994 Athletics...........	Arizona	OF	32	86	13	19	1	1	3	12	5	.221
1995 W Michigan	Midwest	OF	124	459	63	115	17	3	3	67	1	.251
1996 Athletics..........	Arizona	OF	4	15	5	4	3	0	0	2	1	.267
1996 Modesto a-b	California	OF	57	211	50	64	10	1	10	47	13	.303
1997 Pittsburgh	N.L.	OF	66	95	16	17	2	1	2	6	5	.179
1998 Carolina	Southern	OF	123	466	89	154	31	2	14	67	24	.330
1998 Pittsburgh	N.L.	OF	13	39	2	10	1	0	0	3	0	.256
1999 Nashville	P.C.	OF	110	430	97	132	20	5	18	60	16	.307
1999 Pittsburgh c	N.L.	OF	6	14	0	2	1	0	0	0	0	.143
2000 Nashville	P.C.	OF	70	237	44	74	20	1	5	25	26	.312
2000 Pittsburgh d	N.L.	OF	50	119	13	26	5	0	3	16	3	.218
2001 Portland	P.C.	OF	22	78	10	25	8	2	3	8	3	.321
2001 Pittsburgh-San Diego e	N.L.	OF	74	137	21	26	4	1	3	13	12	.190
2002 Durham f-g	Int.	OF	116	422	58	120	24	3	12	58	10	.284
2003 Louisville	Int.	OF	97	369	58	109	20	3	12	63	18	.295
2004 Campeche	Mexican	OF	28	101	23	32	8	0	8	24	0	.317
2004 Memphis	P.C.	OF	19	57	7	16	3	0	0	4	1	.281
2004 New Orleans h-i-j-k ...	P.C.	OF	26	92	12	31	10	1	2	17	4	.337
2005 Kansas City	A.L.	OF	150	545	75	156	31	5	17	86	10	.286
2006 Kansas City	A.L.	OF	147	527	77	151	41	2	15	81	6	.287
2007 Kansas City l	A.L.	OF	113	366	44	94	13	1	6	62	12	.257
2008 Oakland m	A.L.	OF-1B	117	402	48	98	14	2	13	59	4	.244
Major League Totals		9 Yrs.	736	2244	296	580	112	12	59	326	52	.258

a On disabled list from April 10 to July 1, 1996.
b Selected by Pittsburgh Pirates from Oakland A's in Rule V draft, December 9, 1996.
c On disabled list from April 24 to May 2, 1999.
d On disabled list from June 19 to July 3, 2000.
e Traded to San Diego Padres for pitcher Shawn Camp, July 10, 2001.
f Filed for free agency, October 15, 2001. Signed with Tampa Bay Devil Rays organization, January 9, 2002.
g Filed for free agency, October 15, 2002. Signed with Cincinnati Reds organization, December 10, 2002.
h Filed for free agency, October 15, 2003. Signed with St. Louis Cardinals organization, January 18, 2004.
i Released by St. Louis Cardinals organization, May 2, 2004. Signed with Campeche, Mexico, May 2004.
j Signed with Houston Astros organization, August 17, 2004.
k Filed for free agency, October 15, 2004. Signed with Kansas City Royals organization, December 15, 2004.
l Not offered contract, December 12, 2007. Signed with Oakland Athletics, January 11, 2008.
m Filed for free agency, October 30, 2008.

BRUCE, JAY ALLEN

Born, Beaumont, Texas, April 3, 1987.
Bats Left. Throws Left. Height, 6 feet, 3 inches. Weight, 205 pounds.

Year Club	Lea	Pos	G	AB	R	H	2B	3B	HR	RBI	SB	Avg
2005 Reds...........	Gulf Coast	OF	37	122	29	33	9	2	5	25	4	.270
2005 Billings...........	Pioneer	OF	17	70	16	18	2	0	4	13	2	.257
2006 Dayton	Midwest	OF	117	444	69	129	42	5	16	81	19	.291
2007 Sarasota...........	Fla.St.	OF	67	268	49	87	27	5	11	49	4	.325
2007 Louisville	Int.	OF	50	187	28	57	12	2	11	25	2	.305
2007 Chattanooga	Southern	OF	16	66	10	22	7	1	4	15	2	.333
2008 Louisville	Int.	OF	49	184	34	67	9	5	10	37	8	.364
2008 Cincinnati...........	N.L.	OF	108	413	63	105	17	1	21	52	4	.254

BRUNTLETT, ERIC KEVIN

Born, Lafayette, Indiana, March 29, 1978.
Bats Right. Throws Right. Height, 6 feet. Weight, 190 pounds.

Year Club	Lea	Pos	G	AB	R	H	2B	3B	HR	RBI	SB	Avg
2000 Martinsville	Appal.	SS-OF	50	172	40	47	11	4	1	21	14	.273
2001 New Orleans	P.C.	SS	5	16	3	2	0	0	0	1	0	.125

Year Club	Lea	Pos	G	AB	R	H	2B	3B	HR	RBI	SB	Avg
2001 Round Rock.....	Texas	SS	123	503	84	134	23	3	3	40	23	.266
2002 New Orleans.......	P.C.	SS-2B	18	68	9	14	2	0	0	1	1	.206
2002 Round Rock.......	Texas	SS-2B	116	464	81	123	21	2	2	48	35	.265
2003 New Orleans.......	P.C.	SS-2B-OF	84	324	48	84	10	0	2	27	9	.259
2003 Houston..........	N.L.	SS-2B-OF-3B	31	54	3	14	3	0	1	4	0	.259
2004 Houston..........	N.L.	SS-2B-OF	45	52	14	13	2	0	4	8	4	.250
2004 New Orleans.......	P.C.	SS-OF-2B	86	332	50	83	12	4	6	37	14	.250
2005 Houston..........	N.L.	2B-OF-SS-3B	91	109	19	24	5	2	4	14	7	.220
2006 Round Rock.......	P.C.	OF-SS-2B-3B	22	73	11	16	3	1	1	7	3	.219
2006 Houston..........	N.L.	2B-SS-OF-3B	73	119	11	33	8	0	0	10	3	.277
2007 Round Rock.......	P.C.	OF-SS-1B	61	227	31	63	10	4	1	21	13	.278
2007 Houston a.......	N.L.	SS-OF-3B	80	138	16	34	5	0	0	14	6	.246
2008 Philadelphia.......	N.L.	OF-SS-3B-2B	120	212	37	46	9	1	2	15	9	.217
Major League Totals		6 Yrs.	440	684	100	164	32	3	11	65	29	.240
Division Series												
2004 Houston..........	N.L.	SS	2	1	0	0	0	0	0	0	0	.000
2005 Houston..........	N.L.	OF-2B-SS	3	6	1	1	0	0	0	0	0	.167
2008 Philadelphia.......	N.L.	OF	3	1	0	1	0	0	0	0	1	1.000
Division Series Totals			8	8	1	2	0	0	0	0	1	.250
Championship Series												
2004 Houston..........	N.L.	SS	4	2	0	0	0	0	0	0	0	.000
2005 Houston..........	N.L.	2B-SS	5	1	0	0	0	0	0	0	0	.000
2008 Philadelphia.......	N.L.	OF	4	2	0	0	0	0	0	0	0	.000
Championship Series Totals			13	5	0	0	0	0	0	0	0	.000
World Series Record												
2005 Houston..........	N.L.	OF-2B	2	0	0	0	0	0	0	0	0	.000
2008 Philadelphia.......	N.L.	OF	5	3	3	1	0	0	1	1	0	.333
World Series Totals			7	3	3	1	0	0	1	1	0	.333

a Traded to Philadelphia Phillies with pitcher Brad Lidge for pitcher Geoff Geary, outfielder Michael Bourn and infielder Mike Costanzo, November 12, 2007.

BUCK, JOHNATHAN RICHARD (JOHN)

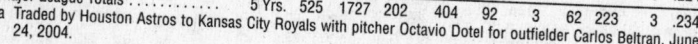

Born, Kemmerer, Wyoming, July 7, 1980.
Bats Right. Throws Right. Height, 6 feet, 3 inches. Weight, 220 pounds.

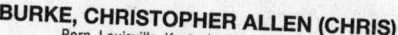

Year Club	Lea	Pos	G	AB	R	H	2B	3B	HR	RBI	SB	Avg
1998 Astros.........	Gulf Coast	C	36	126	24	36	9	0	3	15	2	.286
1999 Auburn.........	N.Y.-Penn.	C	63	233	36	57	17	0	3	29	7	.245
1999 Michigan	Midwest	C	4	10	1	1	1	0	0	0	0	.100
2000 Michigan	Midwest	C	109	390	57	110	33	0	10	71	2	.282
2001 Lexington..........	So.Atl.	C	122	443	72	122	24	1	22	73	4	.275
2002 Round Rock........	Texas	C	120	448	48	118	29	3	12	89	2	.263
2003 New Orleans..........	P.C.	C	78	274	32	70	18	2	3	39	1	.255
2004 New Orleans.........	P.C.	C	65	227	31	68	11	0	12	35	0	.300
2004 Kansas City a	A.L.	C	71	238	36	56	9	0	12	30	1	.235
2005 Kansas City	A.L.	C	118	401	40	97	21	1	12	47	2	.242
2006 Kansas City	A.L.	C	114	371	37	91	21	1	11	50	2	.245
2007 Kansas City	A.L.	C	113	347	41	77	18	0	18	48	0	.222
2008 Kansas City	A.L.	C	109	370	48	83	23	1	9	48	0	.224
Major League Totals			5 Yrs.	525	1727	202	404	92	3	62	223	3	.234

a Traded by Houston Astros to Kansas City Royals with pitcher Octavio Dotel for outfielder Carlos Beltran, June 24, 2004.

BURKE, CHRISTOPHER ALLEN (CHRIS)

Born, Louisville, Kentucky, March 11, 1980.
Bats Right. Throws Right. Height, 5 feet, 11 inches. Weight, 195 pounds.

Year Club	Lea	Pos	G	AB	R	H	2B	3B	HR	RBI	SB	Avg
2001 Michigan	Midwest	SS	56	233	47	70	11	6	3	17	21	.300
2002 Round Rock.....	Texas	2B-SS	136	481	66	127	19	8	3	37	16	.264
2003 Round Rock.....	Texas	2B-SS-OF	137	549	88	165	23	8	3	41	34	.301
2004 New Orleans.......	P.C.	2B	123	483	93	152	33	6	16	52	37	.315
2004 Houston..........	N.L.	2B	17	17	2	1	0	0	0	0	0	.059
2005 Round Rock.......	P.C.	2B-OF	22	90	15	28	6	2	2	11	9	.311
2005 Houston..........	N.L.	OF-2B	108	318	49	79	19	2	5	26	11	.248
2006 Round Rock.......	P.C.	2B-OF	2	8	2	4	1	0	1	2	1	.500
2006 Houston a	N.L.	2B-OF-SS	123	366	58	101	23	1	9	40	11	.276
2007 Round Rock.......	P.C.	2B-OF	18	66	14	16	1	0	2	7	5	.242

Year Club	Lea	Pos	G	AB	R	H	2B	3B	HR	RBI	SB	Avg
2007 Houston b .......N.L.		2B-OF-SS	111	319	39	73	19	2	6	28	9	.229
2008 Arizona c .......N.L.		OF-2B-1B-3B	86	165	20	32	5	1	2	12	5	.194
Major League Totals		5 Yrs.	445	1185	168	286	66	6	22	106	36	.241
Division Series												
2005 Houston ........N.L.		OF	3	3	1	2	1	0	1	1	0	.667
Championship Series												
2005 Houston .........N.L.		OF	6	20	5	6	0	1	1	3	0	.300
World Series Record												
2005 Houston .........N.L.		OF-2B	4	5	1	0	0	0	0	0	2	.000

a On disabled list from May 7 to May 22, 2006.
b Traded to Arizona Diamondbacks with pitcher Chad Qualls and pitcher Juan Gutierrez for pitcher Jose Valverde, December 14, 2007.
c Not offered contract, December 12, 2008. Signed with Arizona Diamondbacks organization, January 13, 2009.

BURRELL, PATRICK BRIAN (PAT)

Born, Eureka Springs, Arkansas, October 10, 1976.
Bats Right. Throws Right. Height, 6 feet, 4 inches. Weight, 235 pounds.

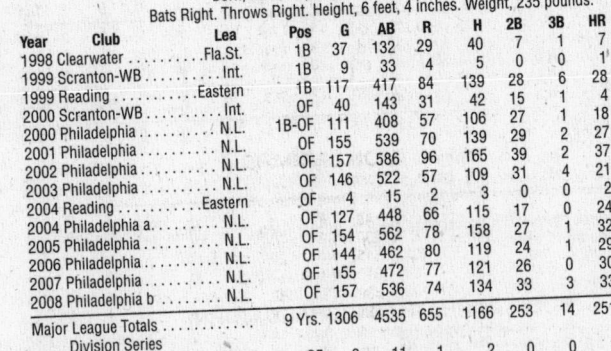

Year Club	Lea	Pos	G	AB	R	H	2B	3B	HR	RBI	SB	Avg
1998 Clearwater ....Fla.St.		1B	37	132	29	40	7	1	7	30	2	.303
1999 Scranton-WB ....Int.		1B	9	33	4	5	0	0	1	4	0	.152
1999 Reading ....Eastern		1B	117	417	84	139	28	6	28	90	3	.333
2000 Scranton-WB ....Int.		OF	40	143	31	42	15	1	4	25	1	.294
2000 Philadelphia ..........N.L.		1B-OF	111	408	57	106	27	1	18	79	0	.260
2001 Philadelphia ..........N.L.		OF	155	539	70	139	29	2	27	89	2	.258
2002 Philadelphia ..........N.L.		OF	157	586	96	165	39	2	37	116	1	.282
2003 Philadelphia ..........N.L.		OF	146	522	57	109	31	4	21	64	0	.209
2004 Reading ....Eastern		OF	4	15	2	3	0	0	2	4	0	.200
2004 Philadelphia a .......N.L.		OF	127	448	66	115	17	0	24	84	2	.257
2005 Philadelphia ..........N.L.		OF	154	562	78	158	27	1	32	117	0	.281
2006 Philadelphia ..........N.L.		OF	144	462	80	119	24	1	29	95	0	.258
2007 Philadelphia ..........N.L.		OF	155	472	77	121	26	0	30	97	0	.256
2008 Philadelphia b .......N.L.		OF	157	536	74	134	33	3	33	86	0	.250
Major League Totals		9 Yrs.	1306	4535	655	1166	253	14	251	827	5	.257
Division Series												
2007 Philadelphia .........N.L.		OF	3	11	1	2	0	0	1	1	0	.182
2008 Philadelphia .........N.L.		OF	4	12	2	3	0	0	2	4	0	.250
Division Series Totals			7	23	3	5	0	0	3	5	0	.217
Championship Series												
2008 Philadelphia .........N.L.		OF	5	18	1	6	0	0	1	3	0	.333
World Series Record												
2008 Philadelphia .........N.L.		OF	5	14	0	1	1	0	0	1	0	.071

a On disabled list from August 4 to September 3, 2004.
b Filed for free agency, November 6, 2008. Signed with Tampa Bay Rays, January 5, 2009.

BURRISS, EMMANUEL ALLEN

Born, Washington, District of Columbia, January 17, 1985.
Bats Both. Throws Right. Height, 6 feet. Weight, 190 pounds.

Year Club	Lea	Pos	G	AB	R	H	2B	3B	HR	RBI	SB	Avg
2006 Salem-Keizer .Northwest		SS	65	254	50	78	8	2	1	27	35	.307
2007 San Jose ....Calif.		SS	36	139	23	23	2	0	0	8	17	.165
2007 Augusta ....So.Atl.		SS	89	365	64	117	14	4	0	38	51	.321
2008 Fresno ...........P.C.		2B-SS	14	62	6	16	1	1	0	6	2	.258
2008 San Francisco .....N.L.		SS-2B-OF	95	240	37	68	6	1	1	18	13	.283

BUSCHER, BRIAN PHILLIP

Born, Jacksonville, Florida, April 18, 1981.
Bats Left. Throws Right. Height, 6 feet. Weight, 220 pounds.

Year Club	Lea	Pos	G	AB	R	H	2B	3B	HR	RBI	SB	Avg
2003 Hagerstown ....So.Atl.		3B	54	200	19	55	7	1	0	26	0	.275
2004 San Jose ....Calif.		3B	88	343	50	100	14	7	4	56	5	.292
2005 San Jose ....Calif.		3B	55	206	37	58	12	1	5	29	0	.282
2005 Norwich ....Eastern		3B	64	215	19	49	8	1	1	23	5	.228
2006 Connecticut a ...Eastern		3B	130	467	43	121	23	3	7	49	5	.259
2007 New Britain ....Eastern		3B-1B	63	247	37	76	19	1	7	37	2	.308
2007 Rochester ....Int.		3B	40	132	21	41	7	0	7	22	1	.311

Year	Club	Lea	Pos	G	AB	R	H	2B	3B	HR	RBI	SB	Avg
2007 Minnesota b	A.L.	3B	33	82	8	20	1	0	2	10	1	.244
2008 Rochester	Int.	3B-1B	53	185	27	59	12	0	8	30	1	.319
2008 Minnesota	A.L.	3B-1B-2B	70	218	29	64	9	0	4	47	0	.319
Major League Totals			2 Yrs.	103	300	37	84	10	0	6	57	1	.280

a Selected by Minnesota Twins from San Francisco Giants in Rule V draft, December 7, 2006.
b On disabled list from August 7 to August 23, 2007.

BUTLER, BILLY RAY

Born, Orange Park, Florida, April 18, 1986.
Bats Right. Throws Right. Height, 6 feet, 1 inch. Weight, 240 pounds.

Year	Club	Lea	Pos	G	AB	R	H	2B	3B	HR	RBI	SB	Avg
2004 Idaho Falls	Pioneer	3B	72	260	74	97	22	3	10	68	5	.373
2005 High Desert	Calif.	3B-OF	92	379	70	132	30	2	25	91	0	.348
2005 Wichita	Texas	OF	29	112	14	35	9	0	5	19	0	.313
2006 Wichita	Texas	OF	119	477	82	158	33	1	15	96	1	.331
2007 Omaha	P.C.	OF-1B	57	203	40	59	10	1	13	46	1	.291
2007 Kansas City	A.L.	DH-1B-OF	92	329	38	96	23	2	8	52	0	.292
2008 Omaha	P.C.	1B	26	101	18	34	6	1	5	13	0	.337
2008 Kansas City	A.L.	DH-1B	124	443	44	122	22	0	11	55	0	.275
Major League Totals			2 Yrs.	216	772	82	218	45	2	19	107	0	.282

BYRD, MARLON JERRARD

Born, Boynton Beach, Florida, August 30, 1977.
Bats Right. Throws Right. Height, 6 feet. Weight, 235 pounds.

Year	Club	Lea	Pos	G	AB	R	H	2B	3B	HR	RBI	SB	Avg
1999 Batavia	N.Y.-Penn.	OF	65	239	39	70	7	6	13	49	8	.293
2000 Piedmont	So.Atl.	OF	133	515	104	159	29	13	17	93	41	.309
2001 Reading	Eastern	OF	137	510	108	161	22	8	28	89	32	.316
2002 Scranton-WB	Int.	OF	136	538	103	160	37	7	15	63	15	.297
2002 Philadelphia	N.L.	OF	10	35	2	8	2	0	1	1	0	.229
2003 Scranton-WB	Int.	OF	1	4	1	3	1	0	0	1	0	.750
2003 Reading	Eastern	OF	3	16	3	5	0	0	1	3	0	.313
2003 Philadelphia a	N.L.	OF	135	495	86	150	28	4	7	45	11	.303
2004 Scranton/WB	Int.	OF	37	152	13	40	11	1	2	17	2	.263
2004 Philadelphia	N.L.	OF	106	346	48	79	13	2	5	33	2	.228
2005 New Orleans	P.C.	OF	21	81	19	33	6	0	5	11	4	.407
2005 Scranton/WB	Int.	OF	5	19	4	7	1	0	0	5	0	.368
2005 Washington-Philadelphia b-c	N.L.	OF	79	229	20	61	15	2	2	26	5	.266
2006 New Orleans	P.C.	OF	46	155	20	42	9	0	7	29	3	.271
2006 Washington d	N.L.	OF	78	197	28	44	8	1	5	18	3	.223
2007 Oklahoma	P.C.	OF	44	176	29	63	15	2	6	32	3	.358
2007 Texas	A.L.	OF	109	414	60	127	17	8	10	70	5	.307
2008 Oklahoma	P.C.	OF	4	16	3	5	0	0	0	3	0	.313
2008 Texas e	A.L.	OF	122	403	70	120	28	4	10	53	7	.298
Major League Totals			7 Yrs.	639	2119	314	589	111	21	40	246	33	.278

a On disabled list from April 14 to April 29, 2003.
b On disabled list from March 29 to May 3, 2005.
c Traded to Washington Nationals for outfielder Endy Chavez, May 14, 2005.
d Filed for free agency, October 2, 2006. Signed with Texas Rangers, December 8, 2006.
e On disabled list from April 17 to May 14, 2008.

BYRNES, ERIC JAMES

Born, Redwood City, California, February 16, 1976.
Bats Right. Throws Right. Height, 6 feet, 2 inches. Weight, 210 pounds.

Year	Club	Lea	Pos	G	AB	R	H	2B	3B	HR	RBI	SB	Avg
1998 Sou Oregon	Northwest	OF	42	169	36	53	10	2	7	31	6	.314
1998 Visalia	California	OF	29	108	26	46	9	2	4	21	11	.426
1999 Modesto	California	OF	95	365	86	123	28	1	6	66	28	.337
1999 Midland	Texas	OF	43	164	25	39	14	0	1	22	6	.238
2000 Midland	Texas	OF	67	259	49	78	25	2	5	37	21	.301
2000 Oakland	A.L.	OF	10	10	5	3	0	0	0	2	0	.300
2000 Sacramento	P.C.	OF	67	243	55	81	23	1	9	47	12	.333
2001 Sacramento	P.C.	OF	100	415	81	120	23	2	20	51	25	.289
2001 Oakland	A.L.	OF	19	38	9	9	1	0	3	5	1	.237
2002 Sacramento	P.C.	OF	31	119	16	31	7	0	4	16	5	.261

Year	Club	Lea	Pos	G	AB	R	H	2B	3B	HR	RBI	SB	Avg
2002 Oakland	A.L.	OF	90	94	24	23	4	2	3	11	3	.245
2003 Oakland	A.L.	OF	121	414	64	109	27	9	12	51	10	.263
2004 Oakland	A.L.	OF	143	569	91	161	39	3	20	73	17	.283
2005 Colorado a	N.L.	OF	15	53	2	10	2	0	0	5	2	.189
2005 Oakland-Baltimore b-c	A.L.	OF	111	359	47	83	22	3	10	35	5	.231
2006 Arizona	N.L.	OF	143	562	82	150	37	3	26	79	25	.267
2007 Arizona	N.L.	OF	160	626	103	179	30	8	21	83	50	.286
2008 Visalia	Calif.	OF	3	12	1	1	0	0	0	0	0	.083
2008 Arizona d	N.L.	OF	52	206	28	43	13	1	6	23	4	.209
Major League Totals			9 Yrs.	864	2931	455	770	175	29	101	365	119	.263
Division Series													
2001 Oakland	A.L.	DH	2	2	0	0	0	0	0	0	0	.000
2002 Oakland	A.L.	OF	2	1	0	0	0	0	0	0	0	.000
2003 Oakland	A.L.	OF	5	13	2	6	1	0	0	2	1	.462
2007 Arizona	N.L.	OF	3	12	1	3	0	1	1	3	1	.250
Division Series Totals			12	28	3	9	1	1	1	5	2	.321
Championship Series													
2007 Arizona	N.L.	OF	4	17	0	3	1	0	0	2	0	.176

a Traded to Colorado Rockies with infielder Omar Quintanilla for pitcher Jay Witasick and pitcher Joe Kennedy, July 13, 2005.
b Traded to Baltimore Orioles for outfielder Larry Bigbie, July 30, 2005.
c Not offered contract, December 21, 2005. Signed with Arizona Diamondbacks, December 30, 2005.
d On disabled list from May 27 to June 23 and July 1 to November 14, 2008.

CABRERA, ASDRUBAL JOSE
Born, Puerto La Cruz, Venezuela, November 13, 1985.
Bats Both. Throws Right. Height, 6 feet. Weight, 170 pounds.

Year	Club	Lea	Pos	G	AB	R	H	2B	3B	HR	RBI	SB	Avg
2004 Everett	Northwest	SS-2B-3B	63	239	44	65	16	3	5	41	7	.272
2005 Inland Empire	Calif.	SS	55	225	31	64	15	6	1	26	3	.284
2005 Wisconsin	Midwest	2B-SS-3B	51	192	26	61	12	3	4	30	2	.318
2005 Tacoma	P.C.	SS	6	23	4	5	0	1	0	3	0	.217
2006 Buffalo	Int.	SS	52	190	26	50	11	0	1	14	5	.263
2006 Tacoma a	P.C.	SS	60	203	27	48	12	2	3	22	7	.236
2007 Akron	Eastern	SS-2B	96	368	78	114	23	3	8	54	23	.310
2007 Buffalo	Int.	SS-2B	9	38	6	12	3	0	0	3	2	.316
2007 Cleveland	A.L.	2B-SS-3B	45	159	30	45	9	1	3	22	0	.283
2008 Buffalo	Int.	SS-2B	34	141	25	46	7	1	4	13	2	.326
2008 Cleveland	A.L.	2B-SS	114	352	48	91	20	1	6	47	4	.259
Major League Totals			2 Yrs.	159	511	78	136	29	2	9	69	4	.266
Division Series													
2007 Cleveland	A.L.	2B	4	17	3	3	0	0	1	2	0	.176
Championship Series													
2007 Cleveland	A.L.	2B	7	29	2	7	0	0	0	4	0	.241

a Traded to Cleveland Indians by Seattle Mariners for outfielder Eduardo Perez, June 30, 2006.

CABRERA, JOSE MIGUEL (MIGUEL)
Born, Maracay, Venezuela, April 18, 1983.
Bats Right. Throws Right. Height, 6 feet, 2 inches. Weight, 240 pounds.

Year	Club	Lea	Pos	G	AB	R	H	2B	3B	HR	RBI	SB	Avg
2000 Marlins	Gulf Coast	SS	57	219	38	57	10	2	2	22	1	.260
2000 Utica	N.Y.-Penn	SS	8	32	3	8	2	0	0	6	0	.250
2001 Kane County	Midwest	SS	110	422	61	134	19	4	7	66	3	.318
2002 Jupiter	Fla.St.	3B	124	478	77	134	43	1	9	75	10	.274
2003 Carolina	Southern	3B-OF	69	266	46	97	29	3	10	59	9	.365
2003 Florida	N.L.	OF-3B	87	314	39	84	21	3	12	62	0	.268
2004 Florida	N.L.	OF	160	603	101	177	31	1	33	112	5	.294
2005 Florida	N.L.	OF-3B	158	613	106	198	43	2	33	116	1	.323
2006 Florida	N.L.	3B	158	576	112	195	50	2	26	114	9	.339
2007 Florida a	N.L.	3B	157	588	91	188	38	2	34	119	2	.320
2008 Detroit	A.L.	1B-3B	160	616	85	180	36	2	*37	127	1	.292
Major League Totals			6 Yrs.	880	3310	534	1022	219	12	175	650	18	.309
Division Series													
2003 Florida	N.L.	3B	4	14	1	4	2	0	0	3	0	.286
Championship Series													
2003 Florida	N.L.	OF-3B-SS	7	30	9	10	0	0	3	6	0	.333

Year	Club	Lea	Pos	G	AB	R	H	2B	3B	HR	RBI	SB	Avg
World Series Record													
2003 Florida	N.L.		OF	6	24	1	4	0	0	0	3	0	.167

a Traded to Detroit Tigers with pitcher Dontrelle Willis for pitcher Burke Badenhop, pitcher Eulogio De La Cruz, pitcher Andrew Miller, catcher Mike Rabelo and outfielder Cameron Maybin, December 5, 2007.

CABRERA, MELKY

Born, Santo Domingo, Dominican Republic, August 11, 1984.
Bats Both. Throws Left. Height, 5 feet, 11 inches. Weight, 200 pounds.

Year	Club	Lea	Pos	G	AB	R	H	2B	3B	HR	RBI	SB	Avg
2003 Staten Island	N.Y.-Penn.		OF	67	279	34	79	10	2	2	31	13	.283
2004 Tampa	Fla.St.		OF	85	333	48	96	20	3	8	51	3	.288
2004 Battle	Midwest		OF	42	171	35	57	16	3	0	16	7	.333
2005 New York	A.L.		OF	6	19	1	4	0	0	0	0	0	.211
2005 Columbus.........	Int.		OF	26	101	15	25	3	0	3	17	2	.248
2005 Trenton.........	Eastern		OF	106	426	57	117	22	3	10	60	11	.275
2006 Columbus..........	Int.		OF	31	122	19	47	6	2	4	24	3	.385
2006 New York	A.L.		OF	130	460	75	129	26	2	7	50	12	.280
2007 New York	A.L.		OF	150	545	66	149	24	8	8	73	13	.273
2008 Scranton-WB	Int.		OF	15	57	8	19	2	0	0	5	1	.333
2008 New York	A.L.		OF	129	414	42	103	12	1	8	37	9	.249
Major League Totals			4 Yrs.	415	1438	184	385	62	11	23	160	34	.268
Division Series													
2006 New York	A.L.		OF	2	3	0	0	0	0	0	0	0	.000
2007 New York	A.L.		OF	4	16	2	3	0	0	1	2	0	.188
Division Series Totals				6	19	2	3	0	0	1	2	0	.158

CABRERA, ORLANDO LUIS

Born, Cartagena, Colombia, November 2, 1974.
Bats Right. Throws Right. Height, 5 feet, 9 inches. Weight, 180 pounds.

Year	Club	Lea	Pos	G	AB	R	H	2B	3B	HR	RBI	SB	Avg
1994 Expos..........	Gulf Coast		2B-SS-OF	22	73	13	23	4	1	0	11	6	.315
1995 Wst Plm Bch	Fla. St.		SS	3	5	0	1	0	0	0	0	0	.200
1995 Vermont........	N.Y.-Penn.		2B-SS	65	248	37	70	12	5	3	33	15	.282
1996 Delmarva........	So. Atl.		SS-2B	134	512	86	129	28	4	14	65	51	.252
1997 Wst Plm Bch	Fla. St.		SS-2B	69	279	56	77	19	2	5	26	32	.276
1997 Harrisburg	Eastern		SS-2B	35	133	34	41	13	2	5	20	7	.308
1997 Ottawa	Int.		SS-2B	31	122	17	32	5	2	2	14	8	.262
1997 Montreal............	N.L.		SS-2B	16	18	4	4	0	0	0	2	1	.222
1998 Ottawa	Int.		SS-2B	66	272	31	63	9	4	0	26	19	.232
1998 Montreal............	N.L.		SS-2B	79	261	44	73	16	5	3	22	6	.280
1999 Montreal a	N.L.		SS	104	382	48	97	23	5	8	39	2	.254
2000 Ottawa	Int.		SS	2	6	1	4	0	0	0	0	1	.667
2000 Montreal b	N.L.		SS-2B	125	422	47	100	25	1	13	55	4	.237
2001 Montreal............	N.L.		SS	*162	626	64	173	41	6	14	96	19	.276
2002 Montreal............	N.L.		SS	153	563	64	148	43	1	7	56	25	.263
2003 Montreal............	N.L.		SS	*162	626	95	186	47	2	17	80	24	.297
2004 Montreal............	N.L.		SS	103	390	41	96	19	2	4	31	12	.246
2004 Boston c-d-e	A.L.		SS	58	228	33	67	19	1	6	31	4	.294
2005 Los Angeles f	A.L.		SS	141	540	70	139	28	3	8	57	21	.257
2006 Los Angeles	A.L.		SS	153	607	95	171	45	1	9	72	27	.282
2007 Los Angeles g	A.L.		SS	155	638	101	192	35	1	8	86	20	.301
2008 Chicago h	A.L.		SS	161	661	93	186	33	1	8	57	19	.281
Major League Totals			12 Yrs.	1572	5962	799	1632	374	29	105	684	184	.274
Division Series													
2004 Boston	A.L.		SS	3	13	1	2	1	0	0	3	0	.154
2005 Los Angeles	A.L.		SS	5	21	3	5	2	0	0	3	0	.238
2007 Los Angeles	A.L.		SS	3	12	0	3	1	0	0	1	0	.250
2008 Chicago	A.L.		SS	4	16	1	2	0	0	0	0	0	.125
Division Series Totals				15	62	5	12	4	0	0	7	0	.194
Championship Series													
2004 Boston	A.L.		SS	7	29	5	11	2	0	0	5	1	.379
2005 Los Angeles	A.L.		SS	5	20	1	4	1	0	1	3	0	.200
Championship Series Totals				12	49	6	15	3	0	1	8	1	.306
World Series Record													
2004 Boston	A.L.		SS	4	17	3	4	1	0	0	3	0	.235

a On disabled list from August 9 to October 13, 1999.

b On disabled list from July 15 to August 14, 2000.
c Traded to Chicago Cubs for infielder Alex Gonzalez, infielder Brendan Harris and pitcher Francis Beltran, July 31, 2004.
d Traded to Boston Red Sox with infielder Doug Mientkiewicz for infielder Nomar Garciaparra and outfielder Matt Murton, July 31, 2004.
e Filed for free agency, November 1, 2004. Signed with Anaheim Angels, December 20, 2004.
f On disabled list from June 27 to July 16, 2005.
g Traded to Chicago White Sox for pitcher Jon Garland, November 19, 2007.
h Filed for free agency, November 1, 2008.

CAIRO, MIGUEL JESUS

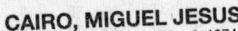

Born, Anaco, Venezuela, May 4, 1974.
Bats Right. Throws Right. Height, 6 feet, 1 inch. Weight, 210 pounds.

Year	Club	Lea	Pos	G	AB	R	H	2B	3B	HR	RBI	SB	Avg
1992	Dodgers	Gulf Coast	SS-3B	21	76	10	23	5	2	0	9	1	.303
1992	Vero Beach	Fla. St.	2B-SS	36	125	7	28	0	0	0	7	5	.224
1993	Vero Beach	Fla. St.	2B-SS-3B	90	346	50	109	10	1	1	23	23	.315
1994	Bakersfield	California	2B-SS	133	533	76	155	23	4	2	48	44	.291
1995	San Antonio a-b	Texas	2B-SS	107	435	53	121	20	1	1	41	33	.278
1996	Syracuse	Int.	2B-3B-SS	120	465	71	129	14	4	3	48	27	.277
1996	Toronto c	A.L.	2B	9	27	5	6	2	0	0	1	0	.222
1997	Iowa	A.A.	2B-SS	135	569	82	159	35	4	5	46	40	.279
1997	Chicago d	N.L.	2B-SS	16	29	7	7	1	0	0	1	0	.241
1998	Tampa Bay	A.L.	2B	150	515	49	138	26	5	5	46	19	.268
1999	St.Petersburg	Fla.St.	2B	3	13	2	5	0	0	0	0	1	.385
1999	Orlando	Southern	2B	3	13	1	5	2	0	0	1	0	.385
1999	Tampa Bay e	A.L.	2B	120	465	61	137	15	5	3	36	22	.295
2000	Tampa Bay f	A.L.	2B	119	375	49	98	18	2	1	34	28	.261
2001	Iowa	P.C.	2B-SS-3B	34	123	22	37	7	1	3	14	3	.301
2001	Chicago-St. Louis g-h	N.L.	3B-2B-OF-SS	93	156	25	46	8	1	3	16	2	.295
2002	St. Louis	N.L.	OF-2B-3B-SS	108	184	28	46	9	2	2	23	1	.250
2003	Memphis	P.C.	2B	3	13	2	3	1	0	0	0	0	.231
2003	St. Louis i-j	N.L.	2B-OF-3B-SS	92	261	41	64	15	2	5	32	4	.245
2004	New York k	A.L.	2B-3B-SS-1B	122	360	48	105	17	5	6	42	11	.292
2005	Mets	Gulf Coast	2B	3	13	3	4	1	0	0	0	0	.308
2005	St. Lucie	Fla.St.	DH	1	4	0	1	0	0	0	0	0	.250
2005	New York l-m	N.L.	2B-1B-3B-OF	100	327	31	82	18	0	2	19	13	.251
2006	New York n-o	A.L.	2B-1B-SS-3B	81	222	28	53	12	3	0	30	13	.239
2007	Memphis	P.C.	3B-SS-OF-1B	9	31	8	9	2	0	0	3	2	.290
2007	New York	A.L.	1B-SS-3B-2B	54	107	12	27	7	0	0	10	8	.252
2007	St. Louis p-q	N.L.	3B-2B-1B-OF	28	67	8	17	2	2	0	5	2	.254
2008	Seattle r	A.L.	1B-3B-2B-OF	108	221	34	55	14	2	0	23	5	.249
Major League Totals			13 Yrs.	1200	3316	426	881	164	29	27	318	128	.266
Division Series													
2001	St. Louis	N.L.	OF	3	5	0	1	0	0	0	0	1	.200
2002	St. Louis	N.L.	3B	2	4	2	4	1	0	0	3	0	1.000
2004	New York	A.L.	2B	4	14	3	3	1	0	0	1	0	.214
Division Series Totals				9	23	5	8	2	0	0	4	1	.348
Championship Series													
2002	St. Louis	N.L.	3B	3	13	2	5	0	0	1	2	0	.385
2004	New York	A.L.	2B	7	25	4	7	3	0	0	0	1	.280
Championship Series Totals				10	38	6	12	3	0	1	2	1	.316

a Traded to Seattle Mariners with infielder Willie Otanez for third baseman Mike Blowers, November 29, 1995.
b Traded to Toronto Blue Jays with pitcher Bill Risley for pitchers Edwin Hurtado and Paul Menhart, December 18, 1995.
c On disabled list, May 27 to June 5, 1996.
d Selected in expansion draft by Tampa Bay Devil Rays, November 18, 1997.
e On disabled list from April 24 to May 17 and July 26 to August 11, 1999.
d Released by Tampa Bay Devil Rays, November 27, 2000. Signed by Oakland A's organization, January 8, 2001.
e Traded to Chicago Cubs for infielder Eric Hinske, March 28, 2001.
f Released by Tampa Bay Devil Rays, November 27, 2000. Signed by Oakland A's organization, January 8, 2001.
g Traded to Chicago Cubs for infielder Eric Hinske, March 28, 2001.
h Claimed on waivers by St. Louis Cardinals, August 10, 2001.
i On disabled list from June 19 to July 29, 2003.
j Filed for free agency, October 26, 2003. Signed with New York Yankees, December 19, 2003.
k Filed for free agency, October 28, 2004. Signed with New York Mets, January 10, 2005.
l On disabled list from June 15 to July 2, 2005.
m Filed for free agency, October 28, 2005. Signed with New York Yankees, January 5, 2006.
n On disabled list from August 6 to September 11, 2006.
o Filed for free agency, October 28, 2006, re-signed with New York Yankees, January 6, 2007.

p Released by New York Yankees, August 15, 2007. Signed with St. Louis Cardinals organization, August 19, 2007.
q Filed for free agency, October 29, 2007. Signed with Seattle Mariner, January 8, 2008.
r Filed for free agency, October 30, 2008.

CALLASPO, ALBERTO JOSE

Born, Maracay, Venezuela, April 19, 1983.
Bats Both. Throws Right. Height, 5 feet, 10 inches. Weight, 180 pounds.

Year Club	Lea	Pos	G	AB	R	H	2B	3B	HR	RBI	SB	Avg
2002 Provo	Pioneer	2B-SS	70	299	70	101	16	10	3	60	13	.338
2003 Cedar Rapids ..	Midwest	2B-SS	133	514	86	168	38	4	2	67	20	.327
2004 Arkansas	Texas	SS-2B	136	550	76	156	29	2	6	48	15	.284
2005 Salt Lake	P.C.	2B	50	212	28	67	21	2	1	31	2	.316
2005 Arkansas	Texas	2B	89	350	53	104	8	0	10	49	9	.297
2006 Tucson	P.C.	2B-SS-3B-OF	114	490	93	165	24	12	7	68	8	.337
2006 Arizona a	N.L.	SS-2B-3B	23	42	2	10	1	1	0	6	0	.238
2007 Tucson	P.C.	SS-2B-3B	59	226	48	77	15	2	5	30	1	.341
2007 Arizona b	N.L.	3B-2B-OF-SS	56	144	10	31	8	0	0	7	1	.215
2008 Omaha	P.C.	2B	4	16	5	3	0	0	0	0	1	.188
2008 Kansas City c	A.L.	2B-SS-OF-3B	74	213	21	65	8	3	0	16	2	.305
Major League Totals	3 Yrs.		153	399	33	106	17	4	0	29	3	.266
Championship Series												
2007 Arizona	N.L.	PH	2	2	0	0	0	0	0	0	0	.000

a Traded to Los Angeles Angels for pitcher Jason Bulger, February 28, 2006.
b Traded to Kansas City Royals for pitcher Billy Buckner, December 14, 2007.
c On disabled list from June 28 to August 23, 2008.

CAMERON, MICHAEL TERRANCE (MIKE)

Born, La Grange, Georgia, January 8, 1973.
Bats Right, Throws Right. Height, 6 feet, 2 inches. Weight, 200 pounds.

Year Club	Lea	Pos	G	AB	R	H	2B	3B	HR	RBI	SB	Avg
1991 White Sox	Gulf Coast	OF	44	136	20	30	3	0	0	11	13	.221
1992 Utica	N.Y.-Penn.	OF	28	87	15	24	1	4	2	12	3	.276
1992 South Bend	Midwest	OF	35	114	19	26	8	1	1	9	2	.228
1993 South Bend	Midwest	OF	122	411	52	98	14	5	0	30	19	.238
1994 Pr William	Carolina	OF	131	468	86	116	15	17	6	48	22	.248
1995 Birmingham	Southern	OF	107	350	64	87	20	5	11	60	21	.249
1995 Chicago	A.L.	OF	28	38	4	7	2	0	1	2	0	.184
1996 Birmingham	Southern	OF	123	473	120	142	34	12	28	77	39	.300
1996 Chicago	A.L.	OF	11	11	1	1	0	0	0	0	0	.091
1997 Nashville	A.A.	OF	30	120	21	33	7	3	6	17	4	.275
1997 Chicago	A.L.	OF	116	379	63	98	18	3	14	55	23	.259
1998 Chicago a	A.L.	OF	141	396	53	83	16	5	8	43	27	.210
1999 Cincinnati	N.L.	OF	146	542	93	139	34	9	21	66	38	.256
2000 Seattle b	A.L.	OF	155	543	96	145	28	4	19	78	24	.267
2001 Seattle	A.L.	OF	150	540	99	144	30	5	25	110	34	.267
2002 Seattle	A.L.	OF	158	545	84	130	26	5	25	80	31	.239
2003 Seattle c	A.L.	OF	147	534	74	135	31	5	18	76	17	.253
2004 New York	N.L.	OF	140	493	76	114	30	1	30	76	22	.231
2005 St. Lucie	Fla.St.	OF	4	10	3	3	2	0	0	0	0	.300
2005 Norfolk	Int.	OF	2	7	2	2	0	1	0	2	0	.286
2005 New York d-e	N.L.	OF	76	308	47	84	23	2	12	39	13	.273
2006 Lake Elsinore	Calif.	OF	2	6	1	2	1	0	1	0	0	.333
2006 San Diego f	N.L.	OF	141	552	88	148	34	9	22	83	25	.268
2007 San Diego g	N.L.	OF	151	571	88	138	33	6	21	78	18	.242
2008 Nashville	P.C.	OF	4	15	4	3	0	0	1	2	0	.200
2008 Milwaukee	N.L.	OF	120	444	69	108	25	2	25	70	17	.243
Major League Totals	14 Yrs.		1680	5896	935	1474	330	56	241	856	289	.250
Division Series												
2000 Seattle	A.L.	OF	3	12	2	3	0	0	0	2	1	.250
2001 Seattle	A.L.	OF	5	18	2	4	3	0	1	3	0	.222
2006 San Diego	N.L.	OF	4	14	1	2	1	0	0	1	1	.143
2008 Milwaukee	N.L.	OF	4	13	2	2	0	0	0	0	0	.154
Division Series Totals			16	57	8	11	4	0	1	6	2	.193
Championship Series												
2000 Seattle	A.L.	OF	6	18	3	2	0	0		1	1	.111
2001 Seattle	A.L.	OF	5	17	3	3	2	0		0	0	.176
Championship Series Totals			11	35	6	5	2	0		1	1	.143

29

a Traded to Cincinnati Reds for infielder Paul Konerko, November 11, 1998.
b Traded to Seattle Mariners with pitcher Brett Tomko, infielder Antonio Perez and pitcher Jake Meyer for outfielder Ken Griffey, February 10, 2000.
c Filed for free agency, October 27, 2003. Signed with New York Mets, December 14, 2003.
d On disabled list from April 1 to May 5 and August 12 to October 31, 2005.
e Traded to San Diego Padres for infielder Xavier Nady, November 18, 2005.
f On disabled list from March 31 to April 23, 2006.
g Filed for free agency, October 31, 2007. Signed with Milwaukee Brewers, January 14, 2008.

CANO (MERCEDES), ROBINSON JOSE

Born, San Pedro de Macoris, Dominican Republic, October 22, 1982.
Bats Left. Throws Right. Height, 6 feet. Weight, 200 pounds.

Year	Club	Lea	Pos	G	AB	R	H	2B	3B	HR	RBI	SB	Avg
2001	Yankees	Gulf Coast	2B-SS-3B	57	200	37	46	14	2	3	34	11	.230
2001	Staten Island	N.Y.-Penn.	3B-SS	2	8	0	2	0	0	0	2	0	.250
2002	Staten Island	N.Y.-Penn.	2B-SS	22	87	11	24	5	1	1	15	6	.276
2002	Greensboro	So.Atl.	SS-2B	113	474	67	131	20	9	14	66	2	.280
2003	Trenton	Eastern	2B-SS-C	46	164	21	46	9	1	1	13	0	.276
2003	Tampa	Fla.St.	2B	90	366	50	101	16	3	5	50	1	.276
2004	Trenton	Eastern	2B-3B	74	292	43	88	20	8	7	44	2	.301
2004	Columbus	Int.	2B	61	216	22	56	9	2	6	30	0	.259
2005	Columbus	Int.	2B-3B	24	108	19	36	8	3	4	24	0	.333
2005	New York	A.L.	2B	132	522	78	155	34	4	14	62	1	.297
2006	Yankees	Gulf Coast	DH	1	5	0	2	0	0	0	1	0	.400
2006	Trenton	Eastern	2B	3	10	1	5	2	0	0	2	0	.500
2006	New York a	A.L.	2B	122	482	62	165	41	1	15	78	5	.342
2007	New York	A.L.	2B	160	617	93	189	41	7	19	97	4	.306
2008	New York	A.L.	2B	159	597	70	162	35	3	14	72	2	.271
Major League Totals			4 Yrs.	573	2218	303	671	151	15	62	309	12	.303
Division Series													
2005	New York	A.L.	2B	5	19	3	5	3	0	0	5	0	.263
2006	New York	A.L.	2B	4	15	0	2	0	0	0	0	0	.133
2007	New York	A.L.	2B	4	15	3	5	1	0	2	3	0	.333
Division Series Totals				13	49	6	12	4	0	2	8	0	.245

a On disabled list from June 26 to August 8, 2006.

CANTU (GUZMAN), JORGE LUIS

Born, McAllen, Texas, January 30, 1982.
Bats Right. Throws Right. Height, 6 feet, 3 inches. Weight, 200 pounds.

Year	Club	Lea	Pos	G	AB	R	H	2B	3B	HR	RBI	SB	Avg
1999	Hudson Valley	N.Y.-Penn.	SS	72	281	33	73	17	2	1	33	3	.260
2000	St. Petersburg	Fla.St.	SS	36	130	18	38	5	2	1	14	4	.292
2000	Charleston-Sc	So.Atl.	SS-2B	46	186	25	56	13	2	2	24	3	.301
2001	Orlando	Southern	SS	130	512	58	131	26	3	4	45	4	.256
2002	Orlando	Southern	SS-3B-2B	131	512	50	124	31	1	3	43	2	.242
2003	Durham	Int.	SS-3B	60	200	26	59	16	1	4	30	2	.295
2003	Orlando	Southern	3B-SS-2B	43	158	15	34	10	0	3	17	0	.215
2004	Durham	Int.	2B-SS-3B	95	368	57	111	33	1	22	80	3	.302
2004	Tampa Bay	A.L.	2B-3B-SS	50	173	25	52	20	1	2	17	0	.301
2005	Tampa Bay	A.L.	2B-3B	150	598	73	171	40	1	28	117	1	.286
2006	Montgomery	Southern	2B	8	31	4	6	0	0	2	8	0	.194
2006	Tampa Bay a	A.L.	2B	107	413	40	103	18	2	14	62	1	.249
2007	Tampa Bay	A.L.	1B-2B	25	58	4	12	1	0	0	10	0	.207
2007	Durham	Int.	1B-2B-3B	24	91	12	22	5	1	1	10	0	.242
2007	Louisville	Int.	2B-1B	24	94	12	29	9	0	2	13	0	.309
2007	Cincinnati b	N.L.	1B-2B-3B	27	57	8	17	8	0	1	9	0	.298
2008	Florida c	N.L.	3B-1B	155	628	92	174	41	0	29	95	6	.277
Major League Totals			5 Yrs.	514	1927	242	529	128	4	74	304	8	.275

a On disabled list from April 24 to June 6, 2006.
b Traded to Cincinnati Reds with outfielder Shaun Cumberland and cash for pitcher Calvin Medlock, pitcher Brian Shackelford and player to be named later, July 28, 2007.
c Released by Cincinnati Reds, December 5, 2007. Signed with Florida Marlins organization, January 5, 2008.

CARROLL, JAMEY BLAKE

Born, Evansville, Indiana, February 18, 1974.
Bats Right. Throws Right. Height, 5 feet, 9 inches. Weight, 170 pounds.

Year	Club	Lea	Pos	G	AB	R	H	2B	3B	HR	RBI	SB	Avg
1996	Vermont	N.Y.-Penn.	SS-2B-3B	54	203	40	56	6	1	0	17	16	.276
1997	Wst Plm Bch	Fla.St.	SS-2B-3B	121	407	56	99	19	1	0	38	17	.243
1998	Jupiter	Fla.St.	2B-SS	55	222	40	58	5	0	0	14	11	.261
1998	Harrisburg	Eastern	2B-SS	75	261	43	66	11	3	0	20	11	.253
1999	Harrisburg	Eastern	2B	141	561	78	164	34	5	5	63	21	.292
2000	Harrisburg	Eastern	3B-SS-2B	45	169	23	49	5	3	0	18	8	.290
2000	Ottawa	Int.	2B-3B-SS	91	349	53	97	17	2	2	23	6	.278
2001	Ottawa	Int.	2B-SS-3B	83	267	26	64	8	2	0	16	5	.240
2002	Harrisburg	Eastern	2B	3	9	1	4	0	0	0	1	0	.444
2002	Ottawa	Int.	3B-2B-SS	117	421	57	118	19	2	8	49	6	.280
2002	Montreal	N.L.	3B-SS-2B	16	71	16	22	5	3	1	6	1	.310
2003	Montreal	N.L.	3B-SS	105	227	31	59	10	1	1	10	5	.260
2004	Montreal	N.L.	2B-3B-SS-OF	102	218	36	63	14	2	0	16	5	.289
2005	Washington	N.L.	2B-SS-3B	113	303	44	76	8	1	0	22	3	.251
2006	Colorado a	N.L.	3B-SS	136	463	84	139	23	5	5	36	10	.300
2007	Colorado b	N.L.	2B-3B-SS-OF	108	227	45	51	9	1	2	22	6	.225
2008	Cleveland	A.L.	2B-3B-OF	113	347	60	96	13	4	1	36	7	.277
Major League Totals			7 Yrs.	693	1856	316	506	82	17	10	148	37	.273

Division Series

Year	Club	Lea	Pos	G	AB	R	H	2B	3B	HR	RBI	SB	Avg
2007	Colorado	N.L.	2B	1	0	0	0	0	0	0	0	0	.000

Championship Series

Year	Club	Lea	Pos	G	AB	R	H	2B	3B	HR	RBI	SB	Avg
2007	Colorado	N.L.	3B	2	1	0	0	0	0	0	0	0	.000

World Series Record

Year	Club	Lea	Pos	G	AB	R	H	2B	3B	HR	RBI	SB	Avg
2007	Colorado	N.L.	2B	1	1	0	0	0	0	0	0	0	.000

a Sold to Colorado Rockies, February 11, 2006.
b Traded to Cleveland Indians for player to be named later, December 8, 2007. Colorado Rockies received pitcher Sean Smith to complete trade, April 22, 2008

CARTER, WILLIAM CHRIS (CHRIS)

Born, Fremont, California, September 16, 1982.
Bats Left. Throws Left. Height, 6 feet. Weight, 230 pounds.

Year	Club	Lea	Pos	G	AB	R	H	2B	3B	HR	RBI	SB	Avg
2004	Yakima	Northwest	OF-1B	70	257	47	86	15	1	15	63	2	.335
2005	Lancaster	Calif.	1B-OF	103	412	71	122	26	2	21	85	0	.296
2005	Tennessee	Southern	1B-OF	36	128	21	38	4	0	10	30	0	.297
2006	Tucson	P.C.	1B	136	509	87	153	30	3	19	97	10	.301
2007	Pawtucket	Int.	1B	12	47	6	11	1	0	1	4	0	.234
2007	Tucson a	P.C.	1B-OF	126	503	74	163	39	3	18	84	2	.324
2008	Pawtucket	Int.	OF	121	470	65	141	25	2	24	81	0	.300
2008	Boston	A.L.	OF	9	18	5	6	0	0	0	3	0	.333

a Traded by Arizona Diamondbacks to Boston Red Sox in three-team trade, August 17, 2008. Outfielder Wily Mo Pena went from Boston Red Sox to Washington Nationals and pitch Emiliano Fruto went from Washington Nationals to Arizona Damondbacks.

CASEY, SEAN THOMAS

Born, Willingboro, New Jersey, July 2, 1974.
Bats Left. Throws Right. Height, 6 feet, 4 inches. Weight, 235 pounds.

Year	Club	Lea	Pos	G	AB	R	H	2B	3B	HR	RBI	SB	Avg
1995	Watertown	N.Y.-Penn.	1B	55	207	26	68	18	0	2	37	3	.329
1996	Kinston	Carolina	1B	92	344	62	114	31	3	12	57	1	.331
1997	Akron	Eastern	1B	62	241	38	93	19	1	10	66	0	.386
1997	Buffalo	A.A.	DH-1B	20	72	12	26	7	0	5	18	0	.361
1997	Cleveland a	A.L.	1B	6	10	1	2	0	0	0	1	0	.200
1998	Indianapolis	Int.	1B	27	95	14	31	8	1	1	13	0	.326
1998	Cincinnati b-c	N.L.	1B	96	302	44	82	21	1	7	52	1	.272
1999	Cincinnati d	N.L.	1B	151	594	103	197	42	3	25	99	0	.332
2000	Cincinnati	N.L.	1B	133	480	69	151	33	2	20	85	1	.315
2001	Cincinnati	N.L.	1B	145	533	69	165	40	0	13	89	3	.310
2002	Louisville	Int.	DH	2	8	2	4	0	0	1	3	0	.500
2002	Cincinnati e	N.L.	1B	120	425	56	111	25	0	6	42	2	.261
2003	Cincinnati	N.L.	1B	147	573	71	167	19	3	14	80	4	.291
2004	Cincinnati f	N.L.	1B	146	571	101	185	44	2	24	99	2	.324
2005	Cincinnati g	N.L.	1B	137	529	75	165	32	0	9	58	2	.312
2006	Altoona	Eastern	1B	3	11	1	3	0	0	1	2	0	.273
2006	Pittsburgh	N.L.	1B	59	213	30	63	15	0	3	29	0	.296

Year	Club	Lea	Pos	G	AB	R	H	2B	3B	HR	RBI	SB	Avg
2006 Detroit h-i-j	A.L.	1B	53	184	17	45	7	0	5	30	0	.245
2007 Detroit k	A.L.	1B	143	453	40	134	30	1	4	54	2	.296
2008 Pawtucket	Int.	1B	2	6	3	3	1	0	0	0	0	.500
2008 Boston l-m	A.L.	1B	69	199	14	64	14	0	0	17	1	.322
Major League Totals			**12 Yrs.**	**1405**	**5066**	**690**	**1531**	**322**	**12**	**130**	**735**	**18**	**.302**
Division Series													
2006 Detroit	A.L.	1B	4	17	1	6	3	0	0	4	0	.353
Championship Series													
2006 Detroit	A.L.	1B	1	3	0	1	0	0	0	0	0	.333
2008 Boston	A.L.	PH	2	2	0	0	0	0	0	0	0	.000
Championship Series Totals				3	5	0	1	0	0	0	0	0	.200
World Series Record													
2006 Detroit	A.L.	1B-DH	5	17	2	9	2	0	2	5	0	.529

a On disabled list from April 4 to June 8, 1997.
b Traded to Cincinnati Reds for pitcher Dave Burba, March 30, 1998.
c On disabled list from April 3 to May 5, 1998.
d On disabled list from April 2 to April 18, 2000.
e On disabled list from July 23 to August 9 and September 10 to September 30, 2002.
f On disabled list from June 28 to July 14, 2004.
g Traded to Pittsburgh Pirates for pitcher Dave Williams, December 8, 2005.
h On disabled list from April 15 to May 29, 2006.
i Traded to Detroit Tigers for pitcher Brian Rogers, July 31, 2006.
j Filed for free agency, October 31, 2006, re-signed with Detroit Tigers, November 16, 2006.
k Filed for free agency, October 29, 2007. Signed with Boston Red Sox, February 5, 2008.
l On disabled list from April 26 to May 12 and August 20 to September 5, 2008.
m Filed for free agency, October 31, 2008.

CASH, KEVIN FORREST

Born, Tampa, Florida, December 6, 1977.
Bats Right. Throws Right. Height, 6 feet. Weight, 200 pounds.

Year	Club	Lea	Pos	G	AB	R	H	2B	3B	HR	RBI	SB	Avg
2000 Hagerstown	So.Atl.	C	59	196	28	48	10	1	10	27	5	.245
2001 Dunedin	Fla.St.	C	105	371	55	105	27	0	12	66	4	.283
2002 Tennessee	Southern	C-3B	55	213	38	59	15	1	8	44	5	.277
2002 Syracuse	Int.	C	67	236	27	52	18	0	10	26	0	.220
2002 Toronto	A.L.	C	7	14	1	2	0	0	0	0	0	.143
2003 Syracuse	Int.	C-3B	93	326	37	88	28	2	8	37	1	.270
2003 Toronto	A.L.	C	34	106	10	15	3	0	1	8	0	.142
2004 Toronto a-b	A.L.	C	60	181	18	35	9	0	4	21	0	.193
2005 Tampa Bay	A.L.	C	13	31	4	5	1	0	2	2	0	.161
2005 Durham c	Int.	C-1B-OF	42	147	25	43	10	0	9	27	0	.293
2006 Durham	Int.	C-3B-1B-OF	78	240	17	44	10	1	2	21	1	.183
2007 Pawtucket	Int.	C-3B	59	176	22	31	7	0	7	25	0	.176
2007 Boston d-e	A.L.	C	12	27	2	3	1	0	0	4	0	.111
2008 Boston f	A.L.	C-3B	61	142	11	32	7	0	3	15	0	.225
Major League Totals			**6 Yrs.**	**187**	**501**	**46**	**92**	**21**	**0**	**10**	**50**	**0**	**.184**
Division Series													
2008 Boston	A.L.	C	1	0	0	0	0	0	0	0	0	.000
Championship Series													
2008 Boston	A.L.	C	3	3	1	1	0	0	1	1	0	.333

a On disabled list from May 24 to June 10, 2004.
b Traded to Tampa Bay Devil Rays for pitcher Chad Gaudin, December 13, 2004.
c On disabled list from March 26 to May 7, 2005.
d Released by Tampa Bay Devil Rays, October 30, 2006. Signed with Boston Red Sox organization, January 24, 2007.
e Filed for free agency, November 1, 2007, re-signed with Boston Red Sox organization, December 12, 2007.
f Not offered contract, December 12, 2008. Signed with New York Yankees organization, January 14, 2009.

CASILLA (LORA), ALEXI

Born, San Cristobal, Dominican Republic, July 20, 1984.
Bats Both. Throws Right. Height, 5 feet, 9 inches. Weight, 180 pounds.

Year	Club	Lea	Pos	G	AB	R	H	2B	3B	HR	RBI	SB	Avg
2004 Angels	Arizona	2B-SS	45	163	29	42	1	4	0	10	24	.258
2004 Cedar Rapids	Midwest	2B	9	29	6	9	2	1	0	1	1	.310
2004 Provo	Pioneer	2B-3B	4	12	4	4	1	1	0	1	1	.333
2005 Cedar Rapids	Midwest	SS-2B	78	308	62	100	11	3	3	17	47	.325
2005 Salt Lake	P.C.	2B-SS	13	39	3	10	0	0	0	1	1	.256
2005 Arkansas a	Texas	SS-2B	7	19	4	4	0	0	0	4	1	.211
2006 Fort Myers	Fla.St.	2B-SS	78	323	56	107	12	6	0	33	31	.331

32

Year Club	Lea	Pos	G	AB	R	H	2B	3B	HR	RBI	SB	Avg
2006 New Britain .... Eastern		SS	45	170	28	50	10	1	1	13	19	.294
2006 Minnesota .... A.L.		2B-SS	9	4	1	1	0	0	0	0	0	.250
2007 Rochester............ Int.		2B-SS	84	320	53	86	13	1	3	20	24	.269
2007 Minnesota .... A.L.		2B-SS	56	189	15	42	5	1	0	9	11	.222
2008 Beloit .... Midwest		2B	2	7	2	4	0	0	0	1	0	.571
2008 Rochester............. Int.		SS-2B	32	96	11	21	3	0	0	2	0	.219
2008 Minnesota b .... A.L.		2B-SS	98	385	58	108	15	0	7	50	7	.281
Major League Totals	3 Yrs.		163	578	74	151	20	1	7	59	18	.261

a Traded to Minnesota Twins for pitcher J.C. Romero, December 9, 2005.
b On disabled list from July 29 to August 21, 2008.

CASTILLO (RONDON), JOSE
Born, Las Mercedes, Venezuela, March 19, 1981.
Bats Right. Throws Right. Height, 6 feet. Weight, 210 pounds.

Year Club	Lea	Pos	G	AB	R	H	2B	3B	HR	RBI	SB	Avg
1998 Montalban ... Venzuelan		SS	55	179	31	52	9	1	1	13	23	.291
1999 Pirates ...... Gulf Coast		SS-2B	47	173	27	46	9	0	4	30	8	.266
2000 Hickory.......... So.Atl.		SS	125	529	95	158	32	8	16	72	16	.299
2001 Lynchburg .... Carolina		SS	125	485	57	119	20	7	7	49	23	.245
2002 Lynchburg .... Carolina		SS	134	503	82	151	25	2	16	81	27	.300
2003 Altoona........ Eastern		2B-SS	126	498	68	143	24	6	5	66	19	.287
2004 Pittsburgh .... N.L.		2B-SS	129	383	44	98	15	2	8	39	3	.256
2005 Indianapolis .... Int.		2B	4	13	2	5	1	0	2	2	0	.385
2005 Pittsburgh a ...... N.L.		2B	101	370	49	99	16	3	11	53	2	.268
2006 Pittsburgh .... N.L.		2B	148	518	54	131	25	0	14	65	6	.253
2007 Pittsburgh b .... N.L.		3B-2B-SS-OF	87	221	18	54	18	1	0	24	0	.244
2008 San Fran.-Houston c-d-e N.L.		3B-2B-SS	127	426	46	105	29	4	6	37	2	.246
Major League Totals	5 Yrs.		592	1918	211	487	103	10	39	218	13	.254

a On disabled list from April 7 to May 5 and August 23 to October 3, 2005.
b Released by Pittsburgh Pirates, December 6, 2007. Signed with Florida Marlins, December 24, 2007.
c Claimed on waivers by San Francisco Giants, March 22, 2008.
d Claimed on waivers by Houston Astros, August 20, 2008.
e Filed for free agency, October 9, 2008. Signed with Washington Nationals organization, December 23, 2008.

CASTILLO, LUIS ANTONIO
Born, San Pedro de Macoris, Dominican Republic, September 12, 1975.
Bats Both. Throws Right. Height, 5 feet, 11 inches. Weight, 190 pounds.

Year Club	Lea	Pos	G	AB	R	H	2B	3B	HR	RBI	SB	Avg
1993 Florida .... Dominican		2B	69	266	48	75	7	1	4	31	9	.282
1994 Marlins .... Gulf Coast		2B-SS	57	216	49	57	8	0	0	16	31	.264
1995 Kane County....... Midwest		2B	89	340	71	111	4	4	0	23	41	.326
1996 Portland .... Eastern		2B	109	420	83	133	15	7	1	35	51	.317
1996 Florida .... N.L.		2B	41	164	26	43	2	1	1	8	17	.262
1997 Florida .... N.L.		2B	75	263	27	63	8	0	0	8	16	.240
1997 Charlotte .... Int.		2B	37	130	25	46	5	0	0	5	8	.354
1998 Charlotte .... Int.		2B	100	381	74	109	11	2	0	15	41	.286
1998 Florida .... N.L.		2B	44	153	21	31	3	2	1	10	3	.203
1999 Florida .... N.L.		2B	128	487	76	147	23	4	0	28	50	.302
2000 Calgary................ P.C.		2B	4	13	4	4	1	1	0	0	1	.308
2000 Florida a .... N.L.		2B	136	539	101	180	17	3	2	17	*62	.334
2001 Florida .... N.L.		2B	134	537	76	141	16	10	2	45	33	.263
2002 Florida .... N.L.		2B	146	606	86	185	18	5	2	39	48	.305
2003 Florida b .... N.L.		2B	152	595	99	187	19	6	6	39	21	.314
2004 Florida .... N.L.		2B	150	564	91	164	12	7	2	47	21	.291
2005 Florida c .... N.L.		2B	122	439	72	132	12	4	4	30	10	.301
2006 Minnesota .... A.L.		2B	142	584	84	173	22	6	3	49	25	.296
2007 Minnesota .... A.L.		2B	85	349	54	106	11	3	0	18	9	.304
2007 New York d-e ... N.L.		2B	50	199	37	59	8	2	1	20	10	.296
2008 Mets........... Gulf Coast		2B	3	5	0	0	0	0	0	0	0	.000
2008 St. Lucie............. Fla.St.		2B	5	15	1	1	0	0	0	0	0	.067
2008 Binghamton ...... Eastern		2B	5	16	1	4	0	0	0	2	0	.250
2008 New York f .... N.L.		2B	87	298	46	73	7	1	3	28	17	.245
Major League Totals	13 Yrs.		1492	5777	896	1684	178	54	27	386	342	.292
Division Series												
2003 Florida .... N.L.		2B	4	17	2	5	3	0	0	1	0	.294
2006 Minnesota .... A.L.		2B	3	11	0	3	0	0	0	0	0	.273
Division Series Totals			7	28	2	8	3	0	0	1	0	.286

Year	Club	Lea	Pos	G	AB	R	H	2B	3B	HR	RBI	SB	Avg
	Championship Series												
2003	Florida	N.L.	2B	7	28	3	6	1	0	0	2	2	.214
	World Series Record												
2003	Florida	N.L.	2B	6	26	1	4	0	0	0	1	1	.154

a On disabled list from April 16 to May 5, 2000.
b Filed for free agency, November 6, 2003, re-signed with Florida Marlins, December 2, 2003.
c Traded to Minnesota Twins for pitcher Travis Bowyer and pitcher Scott Tyler, December 2, 2005.
d Traded to New York Mets for catcher Drew Butera and outfielder Dustin Martin, July 30, 2007.
e Filed for free agency, October 29, 2007, re-signed with New York Mets, November 19, 2007.
f On disabled list from July 3 to August 25, 2008.

CASTO, KORY CHRISTOPHER

Born, Salem, Oregon, December 8, 1981.
Bats Left. Throws Right. Height, 6 feet, 1 inch. Weight, 205 pounds.

Year	Club	Lea	Pos	G	AB	R	H	2B	3B	HR	RBI	SB	Avg
2003	Vermont	N.Y.-Penn.	OF	71	259	26	62	14	2	4	28	1	.239
2004	Savannah	So.Atl.	3B-1B	124	483	67	138	35	4	16	88	1	.286
2005	Potomac......	Carolina	3B-2B-OF	135	500	86	145	36	4	22	90	6	.290
2006	Harrisburg	Eastern	3B-OF	140	489	84	133	24	6	20	80	6	.272
2007	Washington	N.L.	OF-1B	16	54	1	7	2	0	0	3	0	.130
2007	Columbus.........	Int.	3B-OF-1B	114	411	56	101	20	2	11	55	4	.246
2008	Columbus........	Int.	OF-1B-2B-3B	33	130	19	40	5	0	6	26	1	.308
2008	Washington	N.L.	1B-3B-OF	66	163	15	35	10	0	2	16	1	.215
Major League Totals			2 Yrs.	82	217	16	42	12	0	2	19	1	.194

CASTRO, JUAN GABRIEL

Born, Los Mochis, Mexico, June 20, 1972.
Bats Right. Throws Right. Height, 5 feet, 10 inches. Weight, 190 pounds.

Year	Club	Lea	Pos	G	AB	R	H	2B	3B	HR	RBI	SB	Avg
1991	Great Falls	Pioneer	SS-2B	60	217	36	60	4	2	1	27	7	.276
1992	Bakersfield	Calif.	SS	113	446	56	116	15	4	4	42	14	.260
1993	San Antonio	Texas	SS-2B	118	424	55	117	23	8	7	41	12	.276
1994	San Antonio	Texas	SS	123	445	55	128	25	4	4	44	4	.288
1995	Albuquerque......	P.C.	SS-2B	104	341	55	91	18	4	3	43	4	.267
1995	Los Angeles	N.L.	3B-SS	11	4	0	1	0	0	0	0	0	.250
1996	Albuquerque......	P.C.	3B-SS-2B	17	56	12	21	4	2	1	8	1	.375
1996	Los Angeles	N.L.	SS-3B-2B-OF	70	132	16	26	5	3	0	5	1	.197
1997	Los Angeles	P.C.	SS-2B	27	101	11	31	5	2	2	11	1	.307
1997	Los Angeles a.....	N.L.	SS-2B-3B	40	75	3	11	3	1	0	4	0	.147
1998	Los Angeles	N.L.	SS-2B-3B	89	220	25	43	7	0	2	14	0	.195
1999	Albuquerque......	P.C.	SS-3B-2B	116	423	52	116	25	4	7	51	2	.274
1999	Los Angeles	N.L.	2B-SS	2	1	0	0	0	0	0	0	0	.000
2000	Louisville	Int.	SS-2B-3B	19	60	9	19	5	1	2	10	0	.317
2000	Cincinnati b	N.L.	SS-2B-3B	82	224	20	54	12	2	4	23	0	.241
2001	Cincinnati	N.L.	SS-2B-3B-1B	96	242	27	54	10	0	3	13	0	.223
2002	Louisville	Int.	SS-2B	5	17	2	3	0	0	0	2	0	.176
2002	Cincinnati c	N.L.	SS-2B-1B-3B	54	82	5	18	3	0	2	11	0	.220
2003	Louisville	Int.	SS	9	32	3	7	0	0	1	5	0	.219
2003	Cincinnati d	N.L.	2B-3B-SS-1B	113	320	28	81	14	1	9	33	2	.253
2004	Cincinnati	N.L.	3B-SS-2B-1B	111	299	36	73	21	2	5	26	1	.244
2004	Louisville e-f	Int.	SS-2B-3B	5	18	1	3	1	0	0	3	0	.167
2005	Minnesota g	A.L.	SS-3B-2B	97	272	27	70	18	1	5	33	0	.257
2006	Minnesota	A.L.	SS	50	156	10	36	5	2	1	14	1	.231
2006	Cincinnati h	N.L.	SS-3B-2B	54	95	8	27	5	1	2	14	0	.284
2007	Cincinnati i-j......	N.L.	3B-SS-2B	54	89	5	16	5	0	0	5	0	.180
2008	Colorado Springs ...	P.C.	SS-2B	18	50	8	15	2	0	1	3	0	.300
2008	Cincinnati	N.L.	SS-2B-3B	7	10	1	0	0	0	0	0	0	.000
2008	Baltimore k-l-m-n ..	A.L.	SS-3B	54	151	15	31	6	0	2	16	0	.205
Major League Totals			14 Yrs.	984	2372	226	541	114	13	35	211	5	.228
	Division Series												
1996	Los Angeles	N.L.	2B	2	5	0	1	1	0	0	1	0	.200

a On disabled list from June 5 to August 2, 1997.
b Traded to Cincinnati Reds for player to be named later, April 1, 2000. Los Angeles Dodgers received pitcher Kenny Kutz to complete trade, June 7, 2000.
c On disabled list from March 27 to June 1, 2002.
d On disabled list from March 25 to April 14, 2003.
e On disabled list from June 1 to June 22, 2004.
f Filed for free agency, October 29, 2004. Signed with Minnesota Twins, November 23, 2004.

h Traded to Cincinnati Reds for outfielder Brandon Roberts, June 15, 2006.
i On disabled list from July 6 to July 26, 2007.
j On disabled list from July 29 to November 2, 2007.
k Released by Cincinnati Reds, April 29, 2008.
l Signed with Colorado Rockies organization, May 2, 2008.
m Traded to Baltimore Orioles for infielder Mike McCoy, July 19, 2008.
n Filed for free agency, November 4, 2008. Signed with Los Angeles Dodgers organization, January 8, 2009.

CATALANOTTO, FRANK JOHN
Born, Smithtown, New York, April 27, 1974.
Bats Left. Throws Right. Height, 6 feet. Weight, 195 pounds.

Year Club	Lea	Pos	G	AB	R	H	2B	3B	HR	RBI	SB	Avg
1992 Bristol	Appal.	2B-1B	21	50	6	10	2	0	0	4	0	.200
1993 Bristol	Appal.	2B	55	199	37	61	9	5	3	22	3	.307
1994 Fayettevlle	So. Atl.	2B	119	458	72	149	24	8	3	56	4	.325
1995 Jacksnville	Southern	2B	134	491	66	111	19	5	8	48	13	.226
1996 Jacksnville	Southern	2B	132	497	105	148	34	6	17	67	15	.298
1997 Toledo	Int.	2B-3B-OF	134	500	75	150	32	3	16	68	12	.300
1997 Detroit	A.L.	2B	13	26	2	8	2	0	0	3	0	.308
1998 Toledo	Int.	1B-2B	28	105	20	35	6	3	4	28	0	.333
1998 Detroit	A.L.	2B-1B-3B	89	213	23	60	13	2	6	25	3	.282
1999 Detroit a	A.L.	1B-2B-3B	100	286	41	79	19	0	11	35	3	.276
2000 Oklahoma........	P.C.	2B	3	11	2	3	0	0	0	1	0	.273
2000 Texas b.........	A.L.	2B-1B-OF	103	282	55	82	13	2	10	42	6	.291
2001 Texas	A.L.	OF-2B-3B-1B	133	463	77	153	31	5	11	54	15	.330
2002 Tulsa	Texas	1B-2B-OF	4	16	1	2	0	1	0	3	0	.125
2002 Texas c-d	A.L.	OF-2B-1B	68	212	42	57	16	6	3	23	9	.269
2003 Toronto	A.L.	OF-1B	133	489	83	146	34	6	13	59	2	.299
2004 Toronto e	A.L.	OF	75	249	27	73	19	1	1	26	1	.293
2005 Toronto	A.L.	OF	130	419	56	126	29	5	8	59	1	.301
2006 Toronto f	A.L.	OF	128	437	56	131	36	2	7	56	1	.300
2007 Frisco..........	Texas	DH	1	4	1	0	0	0	0	0	0	.000
2007 Oklahoma........	P.C.	DH	4	13	5	5	2	0	0	0	0	.385
2007 Texas g........	A.L.	OF-1B	103	331	52	86	20	4	11	44	2	.260
2008 Texas	A.L.	1B-OF	88	248	28	68	23	1	2	21	1	.274
Major League Totals		12 Yrs.	1163	3655	542	1069	255	34	83	447	43	.292

a Traded to Texas Rangers with pitcher Justin Thompson, pitcher Francisco Cordero, pitcher Alan Webb, outfielder Gabe Kapler and catcher Bill Haselman for outfielder Juan Gonzalez, pitcher Danny Patterson and catcher Gregg Zaun, November 2, 1999.
b On disabled list from April 22 to May 14, 2000.
c On disabled list from May 11 to June 28 and August 17 to November 19, 2002.
d Not offered 2003 contract, December 20, 2002. Signed with Toronto Blue Jays, December 30, 2002.
e On disabled list from May 20 to June 8 and from June 18 to July 20 and from August 21 to October 29, 2004.
f Filed for free agency, October 28, 2006. Signed with Texas Rangers, November 21, 2006.
g On disabled list from April 30 to May 21, 2007.

CEDENO, RONNY ALEXANDER
Born, Puerto Cabello, Venezuela, February 2, 1983.
Bats Right. Throws Right. Height, 6 feet. Weight, 180 pounds.

Year Club	Lea	Pos	G	AB	R	H	2B	3B	HR	RBI	SB	Avg
2001 Cubs..........	Arizona	SS-2B-OF	52	206	36	72	13	4	1	17	17	.350
2001 Lansing	Midwest	2B-SS-3B	17	56	9	11	4	1	1	2	0	.196
2002 Lansing	Midwest	SS-2B	98	376	44	80	17	4	2	31	14	.213
2002 Boise	Northwest	SS-2B	29	110	17	24	5	2	0	6	8	.218
2003 Daytona	Fla.St.	SS-2B	107	380	43	80	18	1	4	36	19	.211
2004 West Tenn	Southern	SS	116	384	39	107	19	5	6	48	10	.279
2005 Iowa...........	P.C.	SS	65	245	42	87	14	1	8	36	11	.355
2005 Chicago	N.L.	SS-2B	41	80	13	24	3	0	1	6	1	.300
2006 Chicago	N.L.	SS-2B	151	534	51	131	18	7	6	41	8	.245
2007 Iowa...........	P.C.	SS	75	287	52	103	15	3	10	37	6	.359
2007 Chicago	N.L.	SS-2B-3B	38	74	6	15	2	0	4	13	2	.203
2008 Chicago	N.L.	2B-SS-3B-OF	99	216	36	58	12	0	2	28	4	.269
Major League Totals		4 Yrs.	329	904	106	228	35	7	13	88	15	.252
Division Series												
2007 Chicago	N.L.	PH	2	0	0	0	0	0	0	0	0	.000
2008 Chicago	N.L.	PH	1	0	0	0	0	0	0	0	1	.000
Division Series Totals			3	0	0	0	0	0	0	0	1	.00

CHAVEZ, ENDY DE JESUS

Born, Valencia, Venezuela, February 7, 1978.
Bats Left. Throws Left. Height, 6 feet. Weight, 165 pounds.

Year Club	Lea	Pos	G	AB	R	H	2B	3B	HR	RBI	SB	Avg
1996 N.Y. Mets	Dominican	OF	48	164	42	58	11	1	7	29	3	.354
1997 Mets	Gulf Coast	OF	33	119	26	33	6	3	0	15	1	.277
1997 Kingsport	Appal.	OF	19	73	16	22	4	0	0	4	5	.301
1998 Kingsport	Appal.	OF	33	114	26	33	8	4	0	16	10	.289
1999 St. Lucie	Fla.St.	OF	45	183	33	57	8	3	2	18	9	.311
1999 Columbia	So.Atl.	OF	73	253	40	64	8	1	0	15	20	.253
2000 St. Lucie	Fla.St.	OF	111	433	84	129	20	2	1	43	38	.298
2001 Wichita	Texas	OF	43	168	27	50	6	1	1	13	11	.298
2001 Kansas City	A.L.	OF	29	77	4	16	2	0	0	5	0	.208
2001 Omaha a-b	P.C.	OF	23	104	18	35	6	0	0	4	4	.337
2002 Ottawa	Int.	OF	103	405	67	139	28	5	4	41	21	.343
2002 Montreal c-d	N.L.	OF	36	125	20	37	8	5	1	9	3	.296
2003 Montreal	N.L.	OF	141	483	66	121	25	5	5	47	18	.251
2004 Edmonton	P.C.	OF	14	61	9	21	3	2	0	7	5	.344
2004 Montreal	N.L.	OF	132	502	65	139	20	6	5	34	32	.277
2005 New Orleans	P.C.	OF	23	87	11	22	4	0	1	4	6	.253
2005 Wash.-Philadelphia e-f	N.L.	OF	98	116	19	25	4	3	0	11	2	.216
2006 New York	N.L.	OF	133	353	48	108	22	5	4	42	12	.306
2007 Mets	Gulf Coast	OF	2	8	2	5	0	0	0	4	0	.625
2007 St. Lucie	Fla.St.	OF	4	16	3	8	1	0	0	2	0	.500
2007 Binghamton	Eastern	OF	1	3	0	0	0	0	0	0	0	.000
2007 New York g.	N.L.	OF	71	150	20	43	7	2	1	17	5	.287
2008 New York h.	N.L.	OF	133	270	30	72	10	2	1	12	6	.267
Major League Totals	8 Yrs.		773	2076	272	561	98	28	17	177	78	.270
Division Series												
2006 New York	N.L.	OF	3	8	1	3	0	0	0	0	0	.375
Championship Series												
2006 New York	N.L.	OF	7	27	1	5	2	0	0	0	0	.185

a Traded by New York Mets to Kansas City Royals for outfielder Michael Curry, March 30, 2001.
b Claimed on waivers by Detroit Tigers, December 20, 2001.
c Claimed on waivers by New York Mets, February 1, 2002.
d Claimed on waivers by Montreal Expos, February 22, 2002.
e Traded to Philadelphia Phillies for outfielder Marlon Byrd, May 14, 2005.
f Not offered contract, December 21, 2005. Signed with New York Mets, December 23, 2005.
g On disabled list from June 7 to August 28, 2007.
h Traded to Seattle Mariners with pitcher Aaron Heilman, pitcher Jason Vargas, infielder Mike Carp, outfielder Ezequiel Carrera, pitcher Maikel Cleto and pitcher Joe Smith for pitcher J.J. Putz, pitcher Sean Green and infielder Jeremy Reed, December 10, 2008.

CHAVEZ, ERIC CESAR

Born, Los Angeles, California, December 7, 1977.
Bats Left. Throws Right. Height, 6 feet, 1 inch. Weight, 210 pounds.

Year Club	Lea	Pos	G	AB	R	H	2B	3B	HR	RBI	SB	Avg
1997 Visalia	California	3B	134	520	67	141	30	3	18	100	13	.271
1998 Huntsville	Southern	3B	88	335	66	110	27	1	22	86	12	.328
1998 Edmonton	P.C.	3B	47	194	38	63	18	0	11	40	2	.325
1998 Oakland	A.L.	3B	16	45	6	14	4	1	0	6	1	.311
1999 Oakland a	A.L.	3B-SS	115	356	47	88	21	2	13	50	1	.247
2000 Oakland	A.L.	3B-SS	153	501	89	139	23	4	26	86	2	.277
2001 Oakland	A.L.	3B-1B-SS	151	552	91	159	43	0	32	114	8	.288
2002 Oakland	A.L.	3B-OF	153	585	87	161	31	3	34	109	8	.275
2003 Oakland	A.L.	3B	156	588	94	166	39	1	29	101	8	.282
2004 Sacramento	P.C.	3B	3	13	2	4	1	0	0	0	0	.308
2004 Oakland b	A.L.	3B-OF	125	475	87	131	20	0	29	77	6	.276
2005 Oakland	A.L.	3B	160	625	92	168	40	1	27	101	6	.269
2006 Oakland	A.L.	3B	137	485	74	117	24	2	22	72	3	.241
2007 Oakland c	A.L.	3B	90	341	43	82	21	2	15	46	4	.240
2008 Sacramento	P.C.	3B	9	30	7	11	3	0	2	3	0	.367
2008 Oakland d	A.L.	3B	23	89	10	22	7	0	2	14	0	.247
Major League Totals	11 Yrs.		1279	4642	720	1247	273	20	229	776	47	.269
Division Series												
2000 Oakland	A.L.	3B	5	21	4	7	3	0	0	4	0	.333
2001 Oakland	A.L.	3B	5	21	0	3	1	0	0	0	0	.143
2002 Oakland	A.L.	3B	5	21	3	8	0	0	1	5	0	.381
2003 Oakland	A.L.	3B	5	22	1	1	1	0	0	0	1	.045

Year Club	Lea	Pos	G	AB	R	H	2B	3B	HR	RBI	SB	Avg
2006 Oakland	A.L.	3B	3	10	2	2	1	0	1	1	0	.200
Division Series Totals			23	95	10	21	6	0	2	10	1	.221
Championship Series												
2006 Oakland	A.L.	3B	4	13	1	3	1	0	1	2	0	.231

a On disabled list from August 21 to September 19, 1999.
b On disabled list from June 2 to July 9, 2004.
c On disabled list from July 27 to October 8, 2007.
d On disabled list from March 19 to May 29 and July 2 to November 14, 2008.

CHOO, SHIN-SOO

Born, Pusan, South Korea, July 13, 1982.
Bats Left. Throws Left. Height, 5 feet, 11 inches. Weight, 200 pounds.

Year Club	Lea	Pos	G	AB	R	H	2B	3B	HR	RBI	SB	Avg
2001 Mariners	Arizona	OF	51	199	51	60	10	10	4	35	12	.302
2001 Wisconsin	Midwest	OF	3	13	1	6	0	0	0	3	2	.462
2002 San Bernardino	Calif.	OF	11	39	14	12	5	1	1	9	3	.308
2002 Wisconsin	Midwest	OF	119	420	69	127	24	8	6	48	34	.302
2003 Inland Empire	Calif.	OF	110	412	62	118	18	13	9	55	18	.286
2004 San Antonio	Texas	OF	132	517	89	163	17	7	15	84	40	.315
2005 Tacoma	P.C.	OF	115	429	73	121	21	5	11	54	20	.282
2005 Seattle	A.L.	OF	10	18	1	1	0	0	0	1	0	.056
2006 Tacoma	P.C.	OF	94	375	71	121	21	3	13	48	26	.323
2006 Seattle-Cleveland a	A.L.	OF	49	157	23	44	12	3	3	22	5	.280
2007 Cleveland	A.L.	OF	6	17	5	5	0	0	0	5	0	.294
2007 Indians . . . . J	Gulf Coast	OF	2	5	0	1	1	0	0	2	0	.200
2007 Buffalo	Int.	OF	59	208	34	54	11	2	3	26	10	.260
2008 Buffalo	Int.	OF	12	42	1	11	2	0	1	3	1	.262
2008 Cleveland b	A.L.	OF	94	317	68	98	28	3	14	66	4	.309
Major League Totals			4 Yrs. 159	509	97	148	40	6	17	94	9	.291

a Traded to Cleveland Indians with player to be named later for infielder Ben Broussard and cash, July 27, 2006. Cleveland Indians received pitcher Shawn Nottingham to complete trade, August 24, 2006.
b On disabled list from March 21 to May 30, 2008.

CHURCH, RYAN MATTHEW

Born, Santa Barbara, California, October 14, 1978.
Bats Left. Throws Left. Height, 6 feet, 1 inch. Weight, 190 pounds.

Year Club	Lea	Pos	G	AB	R	H	2B	3B	HR	RBI	SB	Avg
2000 Mahoning Valley . .	N.Y.-Penn.	OF	73	272	51	81	16	5	10	65	11	.298
2001 Kinston	Carolina	OF	24	83	16	20	7	0	5	15	1	.241
2001 Columbus	So.Atl.	OF	101	363	64	104	23	3	17	76	4	.287
2002 Kinston	Carolina	OF	53	181	30	59	12	1	10	30	4	.326
2002 Akron	Eastern	OF	71	291	39	86	17	4	12	51	4	.296
2003 Akron	Eastern	OF	99	371	47	97	17	3	13	52	4	.261
2004 Edmonton	P.C.	OF	98	347	74	120	29	8	17	79	0	.346
2004 Montreal a	N.L.	OF	30	63	6	11	1	0	1	6	0	.175
2005 Harrisburg b	Eastern	OF	4	18	2	5	1	0	0	0	0	.278
2005 Washington b	N.L.	OF	102	268	41	77	15	3	9	42	3	.287
2006 Harrisburg	Eastern	OF	5	19	3	4	0	0	2	3	1	.211
2006 New Orleans	P.C.	OF	53	175	29	43	6	0	7	29	5	.246
2006 Washington	N.L.	OF	71	196	22	54	17	1	10	35	6	.276
2007 Washington c	N.L.	OF	144	470	57	128	43	1	15	70	3	.272
2008 Mets	Gulf Coast	DH	2	6	0	1	0	0	0	1	0	.167
2008 Brooklyn	N.Y.-Penn.	OF	2	6	1	3	1	0	0	1	0	.500
2008 Binghamton	Eastern	OF	2	8	0	0	0	0	0	0	0	.000
2008 New Orleans	P.C.	OF	2	5	0	1	0	0	0	1	0	.200
2008 New York d	N.L.	OF	90	319	54	88	14	1	12	49	2	.276
Major League Totals			5 Yrs. 437	1316	180	358	90	6	47	202	14	.272

a Traded by Cleveland Indians to Montreal Expos with infielder Maicer Izturis for pitcher Scott Stewart, January 5, 2004.
b On disabled list from June 23 to July 13 and August 25 to September 9, 2005.
c Traded to New York Mets with catcher Brian Schneider for outfielder Lastings Milledge, November 30, 2007.
d On disabled list from June 6 to June 29 and July 6 to August 22, 2008.

CINTRON, ALEXANDER (ALEX)

Born, Humacao, Puerto Rico, December 17, 1978.
Bats Both. Throws Right. Height, 6 feet, 1 inch. Weight, 205 pounds.

Year	Club	Lea	Pos	G	AB	R	H	2B	3B	HR	RBI	SB	Avg
1997 Diamondbcks	Arizona		SS	43	152	23	30	6	1	0	20	1	.197
1997 Lethbridge	Pioneer		SS	1	3	0	1	0	0	0	0	0	.333
1998 Lethbridge	Pioneer		SS-2B	67	258	41	68	11	4	3	34	8	.264
1999 High Desert	California		SS	128	499	78	153	25	4	3	64	15	.307
2000 El Paso	Texas		SS	125	522	83	157	30	6	4	59	9	.301
2001 Tucson	P.C.		SS-2B	107	425	53	124	24	3	3	35	9	.292
2001 Arizona a	N.L.		SS	8	7	0	2	0	1	0	0	0	.286
2002 Tucson	P.C.		SS-2B	85	351	53	113	22	3	4	26	9	.322
2002 Arizona	N.L.		2B-3B-SS	38	75	11	16	6	0	0	4	0	.213
2003 Tucson	P.C.		SS-2B	26	107	21	42	11	2	2	21	1	.393
2003 Arizona	N.L.		SS-3B-2B	117	448	70	142	26	6	13	51	2	.317
2004 Arizona	N.L.		SS-2B-3B	154	564	56	148	31	7	4	49	3	.262
2005 Arizona	N.L.		SS-3B-2B	122	330	36	90	19	2	8	48	10	.273
2006 Chicago b	A.L.		SS-2B-3B	91	288	35	82	10	3	5	41	2	.285
2007 Chicago c	A.L.		3B-SS-2B	68	185	23	45	7	1	2	19	0	.243
2008 Frederick	Carolina		SS	2	5	2	3	0	0	1	2	0	.600
2008 Bowie	Eastern		SS	3	9	0	3	0	0	0	0	0	.333
2008 Norfolk	Int.		SS-2B	16	66	9	19	1	0	2	10	0	.288
2008 Baltimore d-e	A.L.		SS-3B-2B-1B	61	133	12	38	5	1	1	10	0	.286
Major League Totals			8 Yrs.	659	2030	243	563	104	21	33	222	18	.277
Division Series													
2002 Arizona	N.L.		3B	2	0	0	0	0	0	0	0	0	.000

a On disabled list from April 30 to May 8, 2001.
b Traded to Chicago White Sox for pitcher Jeff Bajenaru, March 8, 2006.
c Released by Chicago White Sox, November 28, 2007. Signed with Chicago Cubs organization, February 18, 2008.
d Released by Chicago Cubs, March 26, 2008. Signed with Baltimore Orioles organization, March 31, 2008.
e On disabled list from July 1 to August 1, 2008.

CLARK, ANTHONY CHRISTOPHER (TONY)

Born, Newton, Kansas, June 15, 1972.
Bats Both. Throws Right. Height, 6 feet, 7 inches. Weight, 245 pounds.

Year	Club	Lea	Pos	G	AB	R	H	2B	3B	HR	RBI	SB	Avg
1990 Bristol	Appal.		OF	25	73	2	12	2	0	1	8	0	.164
1991 Niagara Falls a	N.Y.-Penn.		INJURED—Did Not Play										
1992 Niagara Falls b	N.Y.-Penn.		OF	27	85	12	26	9	0	5	17	1	.306
1993 Lakeland c	Fla. St.		OF	36	117	14	31	4	14	1	22	0	.265
1994 Trenton	Eastern		1B	107	394	50	110	25	0	21	86	2	.279
1994 Toledo	Int.		1B	25	92	10	24	4	0	2	13	2	.261
1995 Toledo	Int.		1B	110	405	50	98	17	2	14	63	0	.242
1995 Detroit	A.L.		1B	27	101	10	24	5	1	3	11	0	.238
1996 Toledo	Int.		1B	55	194	42	58	7	1	14	36	1	.299
1996 Detroit	A.L.		1B	100	376	56	94	14	0	27	72	0	.250
1997 Detroit	A.L.		1B	159	580	105	160	28	3	32	117	1	.276
1998 Detroit	A.L.		1B	157	602	84	175	37	4	34	103	3	.291
1999 Toledo	Int.		1B	1	3	0	0	0	0	0	0	0	.000
1999 Detroit d	A.L.		1B	143	536	74	150	29	3	31	99	2	.280
2000 Toledo	Int.		1B	6	22	1	2	1	0	1	2	0	.091
2000 Detroit e	A.L.		1B	60	208	32	57	14	0	13	37	0	.274
2001 Detroit f	A.L.		1B	126	428	67	123	29	3	16	75	0	.287
2002 Boston g	A.L.		1B	90	275	25	57	12	1	3	29	0	.207
2003 St. Lucie	Fla.St.		1B	1	4	0	1	0	0	0	0	0	.250
2003 New York h	N.L.		1B-OF	125	254	29	59	13	0	16	43	0	.232
2004 New York i	A.L.		1B	106	253	37	56	12	0	16	49	0	.221
2005 Arizona	N.L.		1B	130	349	47	106	22	2	30	87	0	.304
2006 Tucson	P.C.		1B	2	6	2	2	0	0	1	1	0	.333
2006 Arizona j	N.L.		1B	79	132	13	26	4	0	6	16	0	.197
2007 Arizona k	N.L.		1B	113	221	31	55	5	1	17	51	0	.249
2008 San Diego-Arizona l-m	N.L.		1B	108	151	12	34	5	0	3	24	0	.225
Major League Totals			14 Yrs.	1523	4466	622	1176	229	11	247	813	6	.263
Division Series													
2004 New York	A.L.		1B	1	1	0	0	0	0	0	0	0	.000
2007 Arizona	N.L.		1B	3	6	0	0	0	0	0	0	0	.000
Division Series Totals				4	7	0	0	0	0	0	0	0	.000
Championship Series													
2004 New York	A.L.		1B	5	21	0	3	1	0	0	1	0	.143

Year Club	Lea	Pos	G	AB	R	H	2B	3B	HR	RBI	SB	Avg
2007 Arizona.............	N.L.	1B	3	9	0	2	1	0	0	0	0	.222
Championship Series Totals			8	30	0	5	2	0	0	1	0	.167

a On disabled list from May 30 to June 17; transferred to temporary inactive list from June 17 to end of 1991 season.
b On temporary inactive list from August 17 to end of 1992 season.
c On disabled list from August 24 to end of 1993 season.
d On disabled list from May 26 to June 10, 1999.
e On disabled list from May 13 to June 11 and July 15 to August 31 and September 17 to November 6, 2000.
f Claimed on waivers by Boston Red Sox, November 20, 2001.
g Filed for free agency, October 30, 2002. Signed with New York Mets organization, February 20, 2003.
h Filed for free agency, October 27, 2003. Signed with New York Yankees, January 12, 2004.
i Filed for free agency, October 29, 2004. Signed with Arizona Diamondbacks, January 24, 2005.
j On disabled list from July 17 to August 25, 2006.
k Filed for free agency, October 30, 2007. Signed with San Diego Padres, February 10, 2008.
l Traded to Arizona Diamondbacks for pitcher Evan Scribner, July 17, 2008.
m Filed for free agency, October 31, 2008, re-signed with Arizona Diamondbacks, January 2, 2009.

CLEMENT, JEFFREY BURTON (JEFF)
Born, Marshalltown, Iowa, August 21, 1983.
Bats Left. Throws Right. Height, 6 feet, 1 inch. Weight, 215 pounds.

Year Club	Lea	Pos	G	AB	R	H	2B	3B	HR	RBI	SB	Avg
2005 Wisconsin	Midwest	C	30	113	17	36	5	0	6	20	1	.319
2005 Everett	Northwest	C	4	11	4	3	1	0	0	1	0	.273
2006 Tacoma	P.C.	C	67	245	23	63	10	0	4	32	0	.257
2006 San Antonio	Texas	C	15	59	7	17	6	1	2	10	0	.288
2007 Tacoma	P.C.	C	125	455	76	125	35	3	20	80	0	.275
2007 Seattle	A.L.	DH	9	16	4	6	1	0	2	3	0	.375
2008 Tacoma	P.C.	C	48	173	40	58	17	0	14	43	0	.335
2008 Seattle	A.L.	C	66	203	17	46	10	1	5	23	0	.227
Major League Totals	2 Yrs.		75	219	21	52	11	1	7	26	0	.237

CORA, JOSE ALEXANDER (ALEX)
Born, Caguas, Puerto Rico, October 18, 1975.
Bats Left. Throws Right. Height, 6 feet. Weight, 200 pounds.

Year Club	Lea	Pos	G	AB	R	H	2B	3B	HR	RBI	SB	Avg
1996 Vero Beach......	Fla.St.	SS-OF	61	214	26	55	5	4	0	26	5	.257
1997 San Antonio	Texas	SS	127	448	52	105	20	4	3	48	12	.234
1998 Albuquerque......	P.C.	SS-2B	81	299	42	79	16	6	5	45	10	.264
1998 Los Angeles.......	N.L.	SS-2B	29	33	1	4	0	1	0	0	0	.121
1999 Albuquerque.......	P.C.	SS	80	302	51	93	11	7	4	37	9	.308
1999 Los Angeles a......	N.L.	SS-2B	11	30	2	5	1	0	0	3	0	.167
2000 Albuquerque.......	P.C.	SS	30	110	18	41	8	3	0	20	5	.373
2000 Los Angeles	N.L.	SS-2B	109	353	39	84	18	6	4	32	4	.238
2001 Los Angeles	N.L.	SS-2B	134	405	38	88	18	3	4	29	0	.217
2002 Los Angeles	N.L.	SS-2B	115	258	37	75	14	4	5	28	7	.291
2003 Los Angeles	N.L.	2B-SS	148	477	39	119	24	3	4	34	4	.249
2004 Los Angeles b	N.L.	2B	138	405	47	107	9	4	10	47	3	.264
2005 Cleveland-Boston c ..	A.L.	2B-SS-3B-OF	96	250	25	58	8	4	3	24	7	.232
2006 Boston d	A.L.	SS-2B-3B	96	235	31	56	7	2	1	18	6	.238
2007 Boston	A.L.	2B-SS-1B	83	207	30	51	10	5	3	18	1	.246
2008 Pawtucket	Int.	2B-SS	3	11	2	3	0	0	0	0	0	.273
2008 Boston e-f	A.L.	SS-2B	75	152	14	41	8	2	0	9	1	.270
Major League Totals	11 Yrs.		1034	2805	303	688	117	34	34	242	33	.245
Division Series												
2004 Los Angeles .......N.L.		2B	4	15	1	2	0	1	0	1	0	.133
2005 Boston ...........A.L.		SS	1	0	0	0	0	0	0	0	0	.000
2008 Boston ...........A.L.		SS	2	4	1	1	1	0	0	0	0	.250
Division Series Totals			7	19	2	3	1	1	0	1	0	.158
Championship Series												
2007 Boston ...........A.L.		2B-SS	2	0	0	0	0	0	0	0	0	.000
2008 Boston ...........A.L.		SS	2	7	0	1	0	0	0	0	0	.143
Championship Series Totals......			4	7	0	1	0	0	0	0	0	.143
World Series Record												
2007 Boston ...........A.L.		2B-SS	2	0	0	0	0	0	0	0	0	.000

a On disabled list from March 25 to June 27, 1999.
b Not offered contract, December 21, 2004. Signed with Cleveland Indians, January 18, 2005.
c Traded to Boston Red Sox for infielder Ramon Vazquez, July 7, 2005.

d Filed for free agency, October 31, 2006, re-signed with Boston Red Sox, November 17, 2006.
e On disabled list from April 10 to May 11, 2008.
f Filed for free agency, October 30, 2008.

COSTE, CHRISTOPHER ROBERT (CHRIS)

Born, Fargo, North Dakota, February 4, 1973.
Bats Right. Throws Right. Height, 6 feet, 1 inch. Weight, 215 pounds.

Year Club	Lea	Pos	G	AB	R	H	2B	3B	HR	RBI	SB	Avg
1995 Brandon........	Prairie	C	24	94	12	24	7	0	0	13	2	.255
1996 Fargo-Moorhead ..	Northern	C-2B-3B	81	315	40	99	30	0	6	56	2	.314
1997 Fargo-Moorhead ..	Northern	C-3B	84	337	45	105	22	0	12	50	7	.312
1998 Fargo-Moorhead ..	Northern	C-1B-3B	85	326	59	107	17	2	10	55	6	.328
1999 Fargo-Moorhead a	Northern	C-1B-3B	85	352	67	118	18	2	16	60	4	.335
2000 Akron........	Eastern	1B-3B-C	65	240	32	80	20	4	2	31	1	.333
2000 Buffalo..........	Int.	C-3B-1B-OF	31	96	15	29	2	0	4	8	0	.302
2001 Akron..........	Eastern	C	6	24	1	3	0	0	0	0	0	.125
2001 Buffalo b.........	Int.	C-1B-OF-3B	75	271	31	78	16	2	7	50	0	.288
2002 Buffalo c.........	Int.	1B-C-3B	124	478	59	152	32	1	8	67	0	.318
2003 Red Sox.....	Gulf Coast	C-1B	11	30	3	7	2	1	1	6	0	.233
2003 Pawtucket d	Int.	C-1B	29	96	5	18	5	0	1	8	0	.188
2004 Indianapolis e......	Int.	3B-C-1B	78	262	34	77	21	1	2	26	2	.294
2005 Scranton-WB f.....	Int.	3B-1B-C	134	506	73	148	26	1	20	89	3	.292
2006 Scranton-WB......	Int.	1B-C	39	147	12	26	8	0	2	14	1	.177
2006 Philadelphia.......	N.L.	C-1B	65	198	25	65	14	0	7	32	0	.328
2007 Clearwater......	Fla.St.	C-1B-3B	3	10	3	4	1	0	0	1	0	.400
2007 Ottawa..........	Int.	1B-C-3B	26	90	8	21	5	0	0	10	0	.233
2007 Reading.......	Eastern	C-1B	27	108	14	31	5	0	5	31	0	.287
2007 Philadelphia g.....	N.L.	C-1B	48	129	15	36	3	0	5	22	0	.279
2008 Philadelphia.......	N.L.	C-1B	98	274	28	72	17	0	9	36	0	.263
Major League Totals............		3 Yrs.	211	601	68	173	34	0	21	90	0	.288
Division Series												
2007 Philadelphia.......N.L.		PH	1	1	0	0	0	0	0	0	0	.000
Championship Series												
2008 Philadelphia.......N.L.		C	1	1	0	1	0	0	0	0	0	1.000
World Series Record												
2008 Philadelphia.......N.L.		DH	1	4	0	0	0	0	0	0	0	.000

a Played independent ball 1995-1999. Signed with Cleveland Indians organization, November 16, 1999.
b Filed for free agency, October 15, 2001, re-signed with Cleveland Indians organization, November 7, 2001.
c Filed for free agency, October 15, 2002. Signed with Boston Red Sox organization, November 8, 2002.
d Filed for free agency, October 15, 2003. Signed with Milwaukee Brewers organization, November 13, 2003.
e Filed for free agency, October 15, 2004. Signed with Philadelphia Phillies organization, October 29, 2004.
f Filed for free agency, October 15, 2005, re-signed with Philadelphia Phillies organization, November 15, 2005.
g On disabled list from March 23 to April 8, 2007.

COUNSELL, CRAIG JOHN

Born, South Bend, Indiana, August 21, 1970.
Bats Left. Throws Right. Height, 6 feet. Weight, 185 pounds.

Year Club	Lea	Pos	G	AB	R	H	2B	3B	HR	RBI	SB	Avg
1992 Bend........	Northwest	2B-SS	18	61	11	15	6	1	0	8	1	.246
1993 Central Val ..	California	SS	131	471	79	132	26	3	5	59	14	.280
1994 New Haven ..	Eastern	SS-2B	83	300	47	84	20	1	5	37	4	.280
1995 Colo Sprngs.......	P.C.	SS	118	399	60	112	22	6	5	53	10	.281
1995 Colorado.........	N.L.	SS	3	1	0	0	0	0	0	0	0	.000
1996 Colo Sprngs.......	P.C.	2B-3B-SS	25	75	17	18	3	0	2	10	4	.240
1997 Colo Sprngs.......	P.C.	2B-SS	96	376	77	126	31	6	5	63	12	.335
1997 Colorado-Florida a..	N.L.	2B	52	164	20	49	9	2	1	16	1	.299
1998 Florida b..........	N.L.	2B	107	335	43	84	19	5	4	40	3	.251
1999 Florida-Los Angeles c-d	N.L.	2B-SS	87	174	24	38	7	0	0	11	1	.218
2000 Tucson...........	P.C.	2B	50	198	45	69	14	3	3	27	4	.348
2000 Arizona e..........	N.L.	2B-3B-SS	67	152	23	48	8	1	2	11	3	.316
2001 Arizona...........	N.L.	SS-2B-3B-1B	141	458	76	126	22	3	4	38	6	.275
2002 Arizona e..........	N.L.	3B-SS-2B	112	436	63	123	22	1	2	51	7	.282
2003 Tucson...........	P.C.	2B-SS-3B	5	23	8	10	2	0	0	2	0	.435
2003 Arizona f-g.......	N.L.	3B-SS-2B-1B	89	303	40	71	6	3	3	21	11	.234
2004 Milwaukee h....	N.L.	SS-3B	140	473	59	114	19	5	2	23	17	.241
2005 Arizona..........	N.L.	2B-SS	150	578	85	148	34	4	9	42	26	.256
2006 Lancaster........	Calif.	DH	1	3	1	3	1	0	0	0	0	1.000
2006 Tucson...........	P.C.	DH	2	11	2	2	0	0	0	0	0	.182
2006 Arizona i-j.......	N.L.	SS-3B-2B	105	372	56	95	14	4	4	30	15	.255

Year Club	Lea	Pos	G	AB	R	H	2B	3B	HR	RBI	SB	Avg
2007 Milwaukee	N.L.	3B-SS-2B	122	282	31	62	12	2	3	24	4	.220
2008 Milwaukee k.......	N.L.	3B-SS-2B	110	248	31	56	14	1	1	14	3	.226
Major League Totals	13 Yrs.		1285	3976	551	1014	186	31	35	321	97	.255
Division Series												
1997 Florida ..........N.L.		2B	3	5	0	2	1	0	0	1	0	.400
2001 Arizona..........N.L.		2B	5	16	2	3	0	0	1	3	0	.187
2008 Milwaukee ........N.L.		2B-3B	4	12	0	2	0	0	0	1	0	.167
Division Series Totals			12	33	2	7	1	0	1	5	0	.212
Championship Series												
1997 Florida ..........N.L.		2B	5	14	0	6	0	0	0	2	0	.429
2001 Arizona..........N.L.		2B-SS	5	21	5	8	3	0	0	4	1	.381
Championship Series Totals			10	35	5	14	3	0	0	6	1	.400
World Series Record												
1997 Florida ..........N.L.		2B	7	22	4	4	1	0	0	2	1	.182
2001 Arizona..........N.L.		2B	6	24	1	2	0	0	1	1	0	.083
World Series Totals			13	46	5	6	1	0	1	3	1	.130

a Traded to Florida Marlins for pitcher Mark Hutton, July 27, 1997.
b On disabled list from August 4 to September 28, 1998.
c Traded to Los Angeles Dodgers for player to be named later, June 15, 1999. Florida Marlins received pitcher Ryan Moskau to complete trade, July 15, 1999.
d Released by Los Angeles Dodgers, March 17, 2000. Signed with Arizona Diamondbacks organization, March 20, 2000.
e On disabled list from August 9 to October 14, 2002.
f On disabled list from May 7 to July 7, 2003.
g Traded to Milwaukee Brewers with infielder Junior Spivey, infielder Lyle Overbay, catcher Chad Moeller, pitcher Chris Capuano and pitcher Jorge DeRosa for infielder Richie Sexson, pitcher Shane Nance and player to be named later. Arizona Diamondbacks received outfielder Gary Varner to complete trade, December 15, 2003.
h Filed for free agency, October 29, 2004. Signed with Arizona Diamondbacks December 15, 2004.
i On disabled list from July 15 to August 22, 2006.
j Filed for free agency, October 30, 2006. Signed with Milwaukee Brewers, November 29, 2006.
k Not offered contract, October 31, 2008.

CRAWFORD, CARL DEMONTE

Born, Houston, Texas, August 5, 1981.
Bats Left. Throws Left. Height, 6 feet, 2 inches. Weight, 220 pounds.

Year Club	Lea	Pos	G	AB	R	H	2B	3B	HR	RBI	SB	Avg
1999 Princeton ....Appal.		OF	60	260	62	83	14	4	0	25	17	.319
2000 Charleston-SC ...... So.Atl.		OF	135	564	99	170	21	11	6	57	55	.301
2001 Orlando .... Southern		OF	132	537	64	147	24	3	4	51	36	.274
2002 Durham ....Int.		OF	85	353	59	105	17	9	7	52	36	.297
2002 Tampa Bay .........A.L.		OF	63	259	23	67	11	6	2	30	9	.259
2003 Tampa Bay .........A.L.		OF	151	630	80	177	18	9	5	54	*55	.281
2004 Tampa Bay .........A.L.		OF	152	626	104	185	26	*19	11	55	*59	.296
2005 Tampa Bay .........A.L.		OF	156	644	101	194	33	*15	15	81	46	.301
2006 Tampa Bay .........A.L.		OF	151	600	89	183	29	*16	18	77	*58	.305
2007 Tampa Bay .........A.L.		OF	143	584	93	184	37	9	11	80	*50	.315
2008 Tampa Bay a.......A.L.		OF	109	443	69	121	12	10	8	57	25	.273
Major League Totals	7 Yrs.		925	3786	559	1111	157	84	70	434	302	.293
Division Series												
2008 Tampa Bay ..........N.L.		OF	4	14	2	3	0	0	0	2	3	.214
Championship Series												
2008 Tampa Bay ...........N.L.		OF	7	29	3	10	2	1	0	4	3	.345
World Series Record												
2008 Tampa Bay ..........N.L.		OF	5	19	4	5	1	0	2	2	1	.263

a On disabled list from August 10 to September 26, 2008.

CREDE, JOSEPH (JOE)

Born, Jefferson City, Missouri, April 26, 1978.
Bats Right. Throws Right. Height, 6 feet, 2 inches. Weight, 220 pounds.

Year Club	Lea	Pos	G	AB	R	H	2B	3B	HR	RBI	SB	Avg
1996 White Sox ...... Gulf Coast		3B	56	221	30	66	17	1	4	32	1	.299
1997 Hickory............ So.Atl.		3B	113	402	45	109	25	0	5	62	3	.271
1998 Winston-Sal...... Carolina		3B	137	492	92	155	32	3	20	88	9	.315
1999 Birmingham a .... Southern		3B	74	291	37	73	14	1	4	42	2	.251
2000 Birmingham...... Southern		3B	138	533	84	163	35	0	21	94	3	.306
2000 Chicago .... A.L.		3B	7	14	2	5	1	0	0	3	0	.357
2001 Charlotte .... Int.		3B	124	463	67	128	34	1	17	65	2	.276

Year Club	Lea	Pos	G	AB	R	H	2B	3B	HR	RBI	SB	Avg
2001 Chicago	A.L.	3B	17	50	1	11	1	1	0	7	1	.220
2002 Charlotte	Int.	3B	95	359	57	112	21	0	24	65	0	.312
2002 Chicago	A.L.	3B	53	200	28	57	10	0	12	35	0	.285
2003 Chicago	A.L.	3B	151	536	68	140	31	2	19	75	1	.261
2004 Chicago	A.L.	3B	144	490	67	117	25	0	21	69	1	.239
2005 Chicago b	A.L.	3B-SS	132	432	54	109	21	0	22	62	1	.252
2006 Chicago	A.L.	3B	150	544	76	154	31	0	30	94	0	.283
2007 Chicago c	A.L.	3B	47	167	13	36	5	0	4	22	0	.216
2008 Charlotte	Int.	3B	5	16	0	2	0	0	0	0	0	.125
2008 Chicago d-e	A.L.	3B	97	335	41	83	18	1	17	55	0	.248
Major League Totals		9 Yrs.	798	2768	350	712	143	4	125	422	4	.257
Division Series												
2005 Chicago	A.L.	3B	3	9	2	1	0	0	0	1	0	.111
Championship Series												
2005 Chicago	A.L.	3B	5	19	2	7	2	0	2	7	0	.368
World Series Record												
2005 Chicago	A.L.	3B	4	17	2	5	1	0	2	3	0	.294

a On disabled list from July 2 to September 30, 1999.
b On disabled list from August 26 to September 10, 2005.
c On disabled list from June 5 to October 26, 2007.
d On disabled list from July 22 to August 25, 2008.
e Filed for free agency, October 30, 2008.

CRISP, COVELLI LOYCE (COCO)

Born, Los Angeles, California, November 1, 1979.
Bats Both. Throws Right. Height, 6 feet. Weight, 180 pounds.

Year Club	Lea	Pos	G	AB	R	H	2B	3B	HR	RBI	SB	Avg
1999 Johnson City	Appal.	2B	65	229	55	59	5	4	3	22	27	.258
2000 New Jersey	N.Y.-Penn.	OF-2B	36	134	18	32	5	0	0	14	25	.239
2000 Peoria	Midwest	OF	27	98	14	27	9	0	0	7	7	.276
2001 Potomac	Carolina	OF	139	530	80	162	23	3	11	47	39	.306
2002 New Haven	Eastern	OF	89	355	61	107	16	1	9	47	26	.301
2002 Akron	Eastern	OF	7	32	9	13	1	0	1	4	4	.406
2002 Buffalo	Int.	OF	4	21	3	5	1	0	0	2	1	.238
2002 Cleveland a	A.L.	OF	32	127	16	33	9	2	1	9	4	.260
2003 Buffalo	Int.	OF	56	225	42	81	19	6	1	24	20	.360
2003 Cleveland	A.L.	OF	99	414	55	110	15	6	3	27	15	.266
2004 Cleveland	A.L.	OF	139	491	78	146	24	2	15	71	20	.297
2005 Cleveland b	A.L.	OF	145	594	86	178	42	4	16	69	15	.300
2006 Pawtucket	Int.	OF	1	3	0	1	0	0	0	0	2	.333
2006 Boston c-d	A.L.	OF	105	413	58	109	22	2	8	36	22	.264
2007 Boston	A.L.	OF	145	526	85	141	28	7	6	60	28	.268
2008 Boston e	A.L.	OF	118	361	55	102	18	3	7	41	20	.283
Major League Totals		7 Yrs.	783	2926	433	819	158	26	56	313	124	.280
Division Series												
2007 Boston	A.L.	OF	3	10	0	2	0	0	0	2	1	.200
2008 Boston	A.L.	OF	2	4	2	1	0	0	0	0	1	.250
Division Series Totals			5	14	2	3	0	0	0	2	2	.214
Championship Series												
2007 Boston	A.L.	OF	7	21	2	3	1	0	0	0	1	.143
2008 Boston	A.L.	OF	5	20	2	9	2	0	0	1	0	.450
Championship Series Totals			12	41	4	12	3	0	0	1	1	.293
World Series Record												
2007 Boston	A.L.	OF	3	2	1	1	0	0	0	0	0	.500

a Sent to Cleveland Indians as player to be named later for pitcher Chuck Finley, August 6, 2002.
b On disabled list from May 18 to June 2, 2005.
c Traded to Boston Red Sox with pitcher David Riske and catcher Josh Bard for infielder Andy Marte, catcher Kelly Shoppach and pitcher Guillermo Mota, January 27, 2006.
d On disabled list from April 9 to May 28, 2006.
e Traded to Kansas City Royals for pitcher Ramon Ramirez, November 19, 2008.

CROSBY, ROBERT EDWARD (BOBBY)

Born, Lakewood, California, January 12, 1980.
Bats Right. Throws Right. Height, 6 feet, 3 inches. Weight, 215 pounds.

Year Club	Lea	Pos	G	AB	R	H	2B	3B	HR	RBI	SB	Avg
2001 Modesto	California	SS	11	38	7	15	5	0	1	3	0	.395
2002 Modesto	California	SS	73	280	47	86	17	2	2	38	5	.307

Year	Club	Lea	Pos	G	AB	R	H	2B	3B	HR	RBI	SB	Avg
2002 Midland	Texas		SS	59	228	31	64	16	0	7	31	9	.281
2003 Sacramento	.P.C.		SS	127	465	86	143	32	6	22	90	24	.308
2003 Oakland	A.L.		SS	11	12	1	0	0	0	0	0	0	.000
2004 Oakland a	A.L.		SS	151	545	70	130	34	1	22	64	7	.239
2005 Stockton	California		SS	3	9	1	3	1	0	0	1	0	.333
2005 Sacramento	.P.C.		SS	3	12	0	1	0	0	0	1	0	.083
2005 Oakland b	A.L.		SS	84	333	66	92	25	4	9	38	0	.276
2006 Oakland c	A.L.		SS	96	358	42	82	12	0	9	40	8	.229
2007 Oakland d	A.L.		SS	93	349	40	79	16	0	8	31	10	.226
2008 Oakland e	A.L.		SS	145	556	66	132	39	1	7	61	7	.237
Major League Totals		6 Yrs.		580	2153	285	515	126	6	55	234	32	.239

a Selected Rookie of the Year in American League for 2004.
b On disabled list from April 5 to May 30 and August 28 to September 19, 2005.
c On disabled list from July 31 to August 18 and August 22 to October 25, 2006.
d On disabled list from July 15 to October 8, 2007.
e On disabled list from July 3 to July 18, 2008.

CUDDYER, MICHAEL BRENT

Born, Norfolk, Virginia, March 27, 1979.
Bats Right. Throws Right. Height, 6 feet, 2 inches. Weight, 220 pounds.

Year	Club	Lea	Pos	G	AB	R	H	2B	3B	HR	RBI	SB	Avg
1998 Fort Wayne	Midwest		SS-2B	129	497	82	137	37	7	12	81	16	.276
1999 Fort Myers	Fla.St.		3B	130	466	87	139	24	4	16	82	14	.298
2000 New Britain	Eastern		3B	138	490	72	129	30	8	6	61	5	.263
2001 New Britain	Eastern		3B-1B-OF	141	509	95	153	36	3	30	87	5	.301
2001 Minnesota	A.L.		1B-3B	8	18	1	4	2	0	0	1	1	.222
2002 Edmonton	P.C.		OF-1B-3B	86	330	70	102	16	9	20	53	12	.309
2002 Minnesota	A.L.		OF-3B-1B	41	112	12	29	7	0	4	13	2	.259
2003 Twins	Gulf Coast		OF	2	5	1	4	0	0	1	3	0	.800
2003 Rochester.	Int.		OF-2B-3B-1B	53	186	25	57	17	0	3	34	0	.306
2003 Minnesota	A.L.		OF-3B-1B-2B	35	102	14	25	1	3	4	8	1	.245
2004 Minnesota	A.L.		2B-3B-OF-1B	115	339	49	89	22	1	12	45	5	.263
2005 Rochester.	Int.		3B-1B	3	9	1	1	0	0	0	0	2	.111
2005 Minnesota a	A.L.		3B-OF-2B-1B	126	422	55	111	25	3	12	42	3	.263
2006 Minnesota b	A.L.		OF-1B	150	557	102	158	41	5	24	109	6	.284
2007 Minnesota	A.L.		OF-1B	144	547	87	151	28	5	16	81	5	.276
2008 Rochester.	Int.		OF	4	10	3	3	2	0	0	1	0	.300
2008 Minnesota c	A.L.		OF-1B	71	249	30	62	13	4	3	36	5	.249
Major League Totals		8 Yrs.		690	2346	350	629	139	21	75	335	28	.268
Division Series													
2002 Minnesota	A.L.		OF	5	13	1	5	1	0	0	1	0	.385
2003 Minnesota	A.L.		PH	1	4	0	1	0	0	0	1	0	.250
2004 Minnesota	A.L.		2B-1B	4	15	1	7	0	0	0	2	0	.467
2006 Minnesota	A.L.		OF	3	12	2	3	0	1	1	1	0	.250
Division Series Totals				13	44	4	16	1	1	1	5	0	.364
Championship Series													
2002 Minnesota	A.L.		OF	3	5	0	1	0	0	0	0	0	.200

a On disabled list from June 30 to July 17, 2005.
b On disabled list from July 19 to August 3, 2007.
c On disabled list from April 5 to April 25 and June 28 to September 13, 2008.

CUST, JOHN JOSEPH (JACK)

Born, Flemington, New Jersey, January 16, 1979.
Bats Left. Throws Right. Height, 6 feet, 2 inches. Weight, 235 pounds.

Year	Club	Lea	Pos	G	AB	R	H	2B	3B	HR	RBI	SB	Avg
1997 Diamondbcks	Arizona		OF	35	121	26	37	11	1	3	33	2	.306
1998 South Bend	Midwest		1B	16	62	5	15	3	0	0	4	0	.242
1998 Lethbridge	Pioneer		OF-1B	73	223	75	77	20	2	11	56	15	.345
1999 High Desert	Calif.		OF	125	455	107	152	42	3	32	112	1	.334
2000 El Paso	Texas		OF	129	447	100	131	32	6	20	75	12	.293
2001 Tucson	P.C.		OF	135	442	81	123	24	2	27	79	6	.278
2001 Arizona	N.L.		OF	3	2	0	1	0	0	0	0	0	.500
2002 Colorado Springs	.P.C.		OF	105	359	74	95	24	0	23	55	6	.265
2002 Colorado a	N.L.		OF	35	65	8	11	2	0	1	8	0	.169
2003 Ottawa	Int.		OF	97	333	55	95	18	1	9	58	5	.285
2003 Baltimore b	A.L.		DH-OF	27	73	7	19	7	0	4	11	0	.260
2004 Baltimore	A.L.		DH	1	1	0	0	0	0	0	0	0	.000
2004 Ottawa c	Int.		OF	102	344	55	81	15	1	17	55	4	.235

43

Year	Club	Lea	Pos	G	AB	R	H	2B	3B	HR	RBI	SB	Avg
2005 Sacramento d........	P.C.	OF	134	479	95	123	28	1	19	75	2	.257
2006 Portland..............	P.C.	OF	138	441	97	129	23	0	30	77	0	.293
2006 San Diego	N.L.	OF	4	3	1	1	0	0	0	0	0	.333
2007 Portland.............	P.C.	OF	25	80	17	24	7	0	9	20	0	.300
2007 Oakland e............	A.L.	OF	124	395	61	101	18	1	26	82	0	.256
2008 Oakland	A.L.	OF	148	481	77	111	19	0	33	77	0	.231
Major League Totals	7 Yrs.		342	1020	154	244	46	1	64	178	0	.239

a Traded to Colorado Rockies with catcher JD Closser for pitcher Mike Myers, January 7, 2002.
b Traded to Baltimore Orioles for outfielder Chris Richard and cash, March 11, 2003.
c Filed for free agency, October 27, 2004. Signed by Oakland Athletics organization, November 19, 2004.
d Filed for free agency, October 28, 2005. Signed by San Diego Padres organization, December 6, 2005.
e Traded to Oakland Athletics for player to be named later, May 3, 2007.

DAMON, JOHNNY DAVID

Born, Fort Riley, Kansas, November 5, 1973.
Bats Left. Throws Left. Height, 6 feet, 2 inches. Weight, 205 pounds.

Year	Club	Lea	Pos	G	AB	R	H	2B	3B	HR	RBI	SB	Avg
1992 Royals	Gulf Coast	OF	50	192	58	67	12	9	4	24	23	.349
1992 Baseball City	Fla. St.	OF	1	1	0	0	0	0	0	0	0	.000
1993 Rockford	Midwest	OF	127	511	82	148	25	13	5	50	59	.290
1994 Wilmington	Carolina	OF	119	472	96	149	25	13	6	75	44	.316
1995 Wichita.............	Texas	OF	111	423	83	145	15	9	16	54	26	.343
1995 Kansas City	A.L.	OF	47	188	32	53	11	5	3	23	7	.282
1996 Kansas City	A.L.	OF	145	517	61	140	22	5	6	50	25	.271
1997 Kansas City	A.L.	OF	146	472	70	130	12	8	8	48	16	.275
1998 Kansas City	A.L.	OF	161	642	104	178	30	10	18	66	26	.277
1999 Kansas City	A.L.	OF	145	583	101	179	39	9	14	77	36	.307
2000 Kansas City a	A.L.	OF	159	655	*136	214	42	10	16	88	*46	.327
2001 Oakland b..........	A.L.	OF	155	644	108	165	34	4	9	49	27	.256
2002 Boston..............	A.L.	OF	154	623	118	178	34	*11	14	63	31	.286
2003 Boston..............	A.L.	OF	145	608	103	166	32	6	12	67	30	.273
2004 Boston c...........	A.L.	OF	150	621	123	189	35	6	20	94	19	.304
2005 Boston.............	A.L.	OF	148	624	117	197	35	6	10	75	18	.316
2006 New York	A.L.	OF-1B	149	593	115	169	35	5	24	80	25	.285
2007 New York	A.L.	OF-1B	141	533	93	144	27	2	12	63	27	.270
2008 New York d..........	A.L.	OF-1B	143	555	95	168	27	5	17	71	29	.303
Major League Totals	14 Yrs.		1988	7858	1376	2270	415	92	183	914	362	.289

Division Series

Year	Club	Lea	Pos	G	AB	R	H	2B	3B	HR	RBI	SB	Avg
2001 Oakland	A.L.	OF	5	22	3	9	2	1	0	0	2	.409
2003 Boston	A.L.	OF	5	19	2	6	2	0	1	3	2	.316
2004 Boston	A.L.	OF	3	15	4	7	1	0	0	0	0	.467
2005 Boston	A.L.	OF	3	13	2	3	1	0	0	0	0	.231
2006 New York	A.L.	OF	4	17	3	4	0	0	1	3	0	.235
2007 New York	A.L.	OF	4	18	2	5	0	0	2	5	0	.278
Division Series Totals..........			24	104	16	34	6	1	4	11	7	.327

Championship Series

Year	Club	Lea	Pos	G	AB	R	H	2B	3B	HR	RBI	SB	Avg
2003 Boston...............	A.L.	OF	5	20	1	4	1	0	0	1	1	.200
2004 Boston..............	A.L.	OF	7	35	5	6	0	0	2	7	2	.171
Championship Series Totals			12	55	6	10	1	0	2	8	3	.182

World Series Record

Year	Club	Lea	Pos	G	AB	R	H	2B	3B	HR	RBI	SB	Avg
2004 Boston...............	A.L.	OF	4	21	4	6	2	1	1	2	0	.286

a Traded to Oakland Athletics with infielder Mark Ellis for pitcher Roberto Hernandez, catcher A.J. Hinch, infielder Angel Berroa and cash, January 8, 2001.
b Filed for free agency, November 5, 2001. Signed with Boston Red Sox, December 21, 2001.
c Filed for free agency, October 28, 2005. Signed with New York Yankees, December 23, 2005.
d On disabled list from July 5 to July 21, 2008.

DAVIS, CHRISTOPHER LYN (CHRIS)

Born, Longview, Texas, March 17, 1986.
Bats Left. Throws Right. Height, 6 feet, 4 inches. Weight, 235 pounds.

Year	Club	Lea	Pos	G	AB	R	H	2B	3B	HR	RBI	SB	Avg
2006 Spokane........	Northwest	OF-1B	69	253	38	70	18	1	15	42	2	.277
2007 Bakersfield..........	Calif.	3B	99	386	69	115	28	3	24	93	3	.298
2007 Frisco..............	Texas	3B	30	109	21	32	7	0	12	25	0	.294
2008 Frisco..............	Texas	1B	46	186	43	62	14	0	13	42	5	.333
2008 Oklahoma............	P.C.	1B	31	111	25	37	7	1	10	31	2	.333
2008 Texas	A.L.	1B-3B	80	295	51	84	23	2	17	55	1	.285

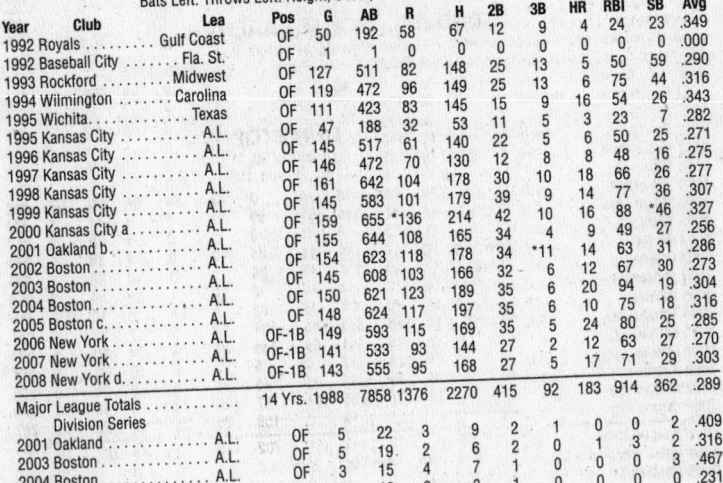

DAVIS, RAJAI LAVAE

Born, Norwich, Connecticut, October 19, 1980.
Bats Right. Throws Right. Height, 5 feet, 11 inches. Weight, 195 pounds.

Year Club	Lea	Pos	G	AB	R	H	2B	3B	HR	RBI	SB	Avg
2001 Pirates	Gulf Coast	OF	26	84	19	22	1	0	0	4	11	.262
2001 Williamsport.....	N.Y.-Penn.	OF-2B	6	12	1	1	0	0	0	0	0	.083
2002 Pirates	Gulf Coast	OF	58	224	38	86	16	5	4	35	24	.384
2002 Williamsport.....	N.Y.-Penn.	OF	1	4	0	0	0	0	0	0	0	.000
2002 Hickory..........	So.Atl.	OF	6	14	4	6	0	0	0	3	2	.429
2003 Hickory..........	So.Atl.	OF	125	478	84	146	21	7	6	54	40	.305
2004 Lynchburg	Carolina	OF	127	509	91	160	27	7	5	38	57	.314
2005 Altoona..........	Eastern	OF	123	499	82	140	22	5	4	34	45	.281
2006 Indianapolis.....	Int.	OF	100	385	53	109	17	1	2	21	45	.283
2006 Pittsburgh	N.L.	OF	20	14	1	2	1	0	0	0	1	.143 *
2007 Indianapolis.....	Int.	OF	53	211	31	67	12	4	4	30	27	.318
2007 Pittsburgh-San Francisco a	N.L.	OF	75	190	32	53	11	2	1	9	22	.279
2008 San Francisco ...	N.L.	OF	12	18	2	1	0	0	0	0	4	.056
2008 Oakland b........	A.L.	OF-2B	101	196	28	51	5	4	3	19	25	.260
Major League Totals	3 Yrs.		208	418	63	107	17	6	4	28	52	.256

a Traded to San Francisco Giants with player to be named later for pitcher Matt Morris, July 31, 2007. San Francisco Giants received pitcher Steve MacFarland to complete trade, August 27, 2007.
b Claimed on waivers by Oakland Athletics, April 23, 2008.

DE JESUS, DAVID CHRISTOPHER

Born, Brooklyn, New York, December 20, 1979.
Bats Left. Throws Left. Height, 6 feet. Weight, 190 pounds.

Year Club	Lea	Pos	G	AB	R	H	2B	3B	HR	RBI	SB	Avg
2002 Wilmington	Carolina	OF	87	334	69	99	22	6	4	41	15	.296
2002 Wichita a.........	Texas	OF	25	79	7	20	5	2	2	15	3	.253
2003 Wichita..........	Texas	OF	17	71	14	24	4	0	2	10	1	.338
2003 Omaha............	P.C.	OF	59	215	49	64	16	3	5	23	8	.298
2003 Kansas City......	A.L.	OF	12	7	0	2	0	1	0	0	0	.286
2004 Omaha............	P.C.	OF	50	197	38	62	14	4	6	16	7	.315
2004 Kansas City......	A.L.	OF	96	363	58	104	15	3	7	39	8	.287
2005 Kansas City......	A.L.	OF	122	461	69	135	31	6	9	56	5	.293
2006 Omaha............	P.C.	OF	3	13	0	5	0	0	0	2	0	.385
2006 Kansas City b....	A.L.	OF	119	491	83	145	36	7	8	56	6	.295
2007 Kansas City......	A.L.	OF	157	605	101	157	29	9	7	58	10	.260
2008 Kansas City......	A.L.	OF	135	518	70	159	25	7	12	73	11	.307
Major League Totals	6 Yrs.		641	2445	381	702	136	33	43	282	40	.287

a On minor league disabled list from June 19 to September 17, 2001.
b On disabled list from April 19 to May 29, 2006.

DELGADO (HERNANDEZ), CARLOS JUAN

Born, Aguadilla, Puerto Rico, June 25, 1972.
Bats Left. Throws Right. Height, 6 feet, 3 inches. Weight, 240 pounds.

Year Club	Lea	Pos	G	AB	R	H	2B	3B	HR	RBI	SB	Avg
1989 St. Catharines....	N.Y.-Penn.	DH-C	31	89	9	16	5	0	0	11	0	.180
1990 St. Catharines....	N.Y.-Penn.	C	67*	228	30	64	13	0	6	39	2	.281
1991 Myrtle Beach	So. Atl.	C	132	441	72	126	18	2	18	70	9	.286
1991 Syracuse	Int.	C	1	3	0	0	0	0	0	0	0	.000
1992 Dunedin	Fla. St.	C	133	485	83	*157	*30	2	*30	*100	2	.324
1993 Knoxville	Southern	C	140	468	91	142	28	0	*25	*102	10	.303
1993 Toronto	A.L.	C	2	1	0	0	0	0	0	0	0	.000
1994 Toronto	A.L.	OF-C	43	130	17	28	2	0	9	24	1	.215
1994 Syracuse	Int.	DH-C-1B	85	307	52	98	11	0	19	58	1	.319
1995 Syracuse	Int.	1B-OF	91	333	59	106	23	4	22	74	0	.318
1995 Toronto	A.L.	OF-1B	37	91	7	15	3	0	3	11	0	.165
1996 Toronto	A.L.	DH-1B	138	488	68	132	28	2	25	92	0	.270
1997 Toronto	A.L.	1B	153	519	79	136	42	3	30	91	0	.262
1998 Dunedin	Fla.St.	1B	4	16	4	5	1	0	2	7	0	.313
1998 Syracuse	Int.	1B	2	7	4	4	2	0	1	6	0	.571
1998 Toronto a	A.L.	1B	142	530	94	155	43	1	38	115	3	.292
1999 Toronto	A.L.	1B	152	573	113	156	39	0	44	134	1	.272
2000 Toronto	A.L.	1B	*162	569	115	196	*57	1	41	137	0	.344
2001 Toronto	A.L.	1B	*162	574	102	160	31	1	39	102	1	.279
2002 Toronto b	A.L.	1B	143	505	103	140	34	2	33	108	1	.277
2003 Toronto	A.L.	1B	161	570	117	172	38	1	42	*145	0	.302

Year	Club	Lea	Pos	G	AB	R	H	2B	3B	HR	RBI	SB	Avg
2004 Dunedin	Fla.St.	1B	2	8	1	2	0	0	1	2	0	.250
2004 Syracuse	Int.	1B	2	9	2	5	2	0	1	4	0	.556
2004 Toronto c-d	A.L.	1B	128	458	74	123	26	0	32	99	0	.269
2005 Florida e-f-g	N.L.	1B	144	521	81	157	41	3	33	115	0	.301
2006 New York	N.L.	1B	144	524	89	139	30	2	38	114	0	.265
2007 New York	N.L.	1B	139	538	71	139	30	0	24	87	4	.258
2008 New York	N.L.	1B	159	598	96	162	32	1	38	115	1	.271
Major League Totals	16 Yrs.	2009	7189	1226	2010	476	17	469	1489	14	.280
Division Series													
2006 New York	N.L.	1B	3	14	3	6	0	0	1	2	0	.429
Championship Series													
2006 New York	N.L.	1B	7	23	5	7	3	0	3	9	0	.304

a On disabled list from March 31 to April 24, 1998.
b On disabled list from August 9 to August 25, 2002.
c On disabled list from May 30 to July 6, 2004.
d Filed for free agency, October 28, 2004. Signed with Florida Marlins, January 26, 2005.
e Signed with Florida Marlins, January 27, 2005.
f On disabled list from July 28 to August 13, 2005.
g Traded to New York Mets with cash for infielder Mike Jacobs, pitcher Yusmeiro Petit and infielder Grant Psomas, November 23, 2005.

DELLUCCI, DAVID MICHAEL
Born, Baton Rouge, Louisiana, October 31, 1973.
Bats Left. Throws Left. Height, 5 feet, 11 inches. Weight, 195 pounds.

Year	Club	Lea	Pos	G	AB	R	H	2B	3B	HR	RBI	SB	Avg
1995 Bluefield	Appal.	OF	20	69	11	23	5	1	2	12	3	.333
1995 Frederick	Carolina	OF	28	96	16	27	3	0	1	10	1	.281
1996 Frederick	Carolina	OF	59	185	33	60	11	1	4	28	5	.324
1996 Bowie	Eastern	OF	66	251	27	73	14	1	2	33	2	.291
1997 Bowie	Eastern	OF	107	385	71	126	29	3	20	55	11	.327
1997 Baltimore a	A.L.	OF	17	27	3	6	1	0	1	3	0	.222
1998 Tucson	P.C.	OF	17	72	17	22	4	3	1	11	4	.306
1998 Arizona	N.L.	OF	124	416	43	108	19	12	5	51	3	.260
1999 Arizona b	N.L.	OF	63	109	27	43	7	1	1	15	2	.394
2000 Arizona	N.L.	OF	34	50	2	15	3	0	0	2	0	.300
2000 Tucson	P.C.	OF	33	122	16	28	6	3	3	17	4	.230
2000 Diamondbacks	Arizona	OF	2	6	0	2	1	0	0	1	0	.333
2000 South Bend c	Midwest	OF	2	5	3	1	1	0	0	0	0	.200
2001 Arizona	N.L.	OF	115	217	28	60	10	2	10	40	2	.276
2002 Tucson	P.C.	OF	4	15	2	2	1	0	0	1	0	.133
2002 Arizona d	N.L.	OF	97	229	34	56	11	2	7	29	2	.245
2003 Arizona e	N.L.	OF	70	165	18	40	11	3	2	19	9	.242
2003 New York f-g-h	A.L.	OF	21	51	8	9	1	0	1	4	3	.176
2004 Texas i	A.L.	OF	107	331	59	80	13	1	17	61	9	.242
2005 Texas	A.L.	DH-OF	128	435	97	109	17	5	29	65	5	.251
2006 Philadelphia j-k	N.L.	OF	132	264	41	77	14	5	13	39	1	.292
2007 Cleveland l	A.L.	OF	56	178	25	41	11	2	4	20	2	.230
2008 Cleveland	A.L.	OF	113	336	41	80	19	2	11	47	3	.238
Major League Totals	12 Yrs.	1077	2808	426	724	137	35	101	395	41	.258
Division Series													
2001 Arizona	N.L.	PH	2	0	0	0	0	0	0	0	0	.000
2002 Arizona	N.L.	OF	3	7	1	2	0	0	1	2	0	.286
2003 New York	A.L.	PH	1	0	0	0	0	0	0	0	0	.000
Division Series Totals				6	7	1	2	0	0	1	2	0	.286
Championship Series													
2001 Arizona	N.L.	PH	2	2	1	1	0	0	0	0	0	.500
2003 New York	A.L.	OF	3	3	2	1	0	0	0	0	1	.333
Championship Series Totals				5	5	3	2	0	0	0	0	1	.400
World Series Record													
2001 Arizona	N.L.	OF	2	2	0	1	0	0	0	0	0	.500
2003 New York	A.L.	OF	4	2	1	0	0	0	0	0	0	.000
World Series Totals				6	4	1	1	0	0	0	0	0	.250

a Selected in expansion draft by Arizona Diamondbacks, November 18, 1997.
b On disabled list from July 25 to November 18, 1999.
c On disabled list from May 8 to July 26, 2000.
d On disabled list from May 2 to May 24, 2002.
e On disabled list from June 2 to June 17, 2003.

f Traded to New York Yankees with pitcher Bret Prinz and catcher Jon-Mark Sprowl for outfielder Raul Mondesi, July 29, 2003.
g On disabled list from August 28 to September 27, 2003.
h Not offered contract, December 21, 2003. Signed with Texas Rangers, December 29, 2003.
i Filed for free agency, November 1, 2004, re-signed with Texas Rangers, December 20, 2004.
j Traded to Philadelphia Phillies for pitcher Robinson Tejeda and outfielder Jake Blalock, April 1, 2006.
k Filed for free agency, November 2, 2006. Signed with Cleveland Indians, December 6, 2006.
l On disabled list from June 20 to September 6, 2007.

DE ROSA, MARK THOMAS

Born, Passaic, New Jersey, February 26, 1975.
Bats Right. Throws Right. Height, 6 feet, 1 inch. Weight, 205 pounds.

Year	Club	Lea	Pos	G	AB	R	H	2B	3B	HR	RBI	SB	Avg
1996	Eugene	Northwest	SS	70	255	43	66	13	1	2	28	3	.259
1997	Durham	Carolina	SS	92	346	51	93	11	3	8	37	6	.269
1998	Greenville	Southern	SS	125	461	67	123	26	2	8	49	7	.267
1998	Atlanta	N.L.	SS	5	3	2	1	0	0	0	0	0	.333
1999	Richmond	Int.	SS	105	364	41	99	16	2	1	40	7	.272
1999	Atlanta	N.L.	SS	7	8	0	0	0	0	0	0	0	.000
2000	Richmond	Int.	SS-2B-3B	101	370	62	108	22	3	3	35	13	.292
2000	Atlanta	N.L.	SS	22	13	9	4	1	0	0	3	0	.308
2001	Richmond	Int.	SS-3B-2B	49	186	31	55	18	0	2	17	7	.296
2001	Atlanta	N.L.	SS-2B-3B-OF	66	164	27	47	8	0	3	20	2	.287
2002	Myrtle Beach	Car.	2B	2	7	0	0	0	0	0	0	0	.000
2002	Richmond	Int.	2B-SS	16	55	9	14	3	0	0	6	2	.255
2002	Atlanta a	N.L.	2B-SS-OF-3B	72	212	24	63	9	2	5	23	2	.297
2003	Atlanta	N.L.	2B-3B-SS-OF	103	266	40	70	14	0	6	22	2	.263
2004	Atlanta b	N.L.	3B-SS-2B-OF	118	309	33	74	16	0	3	31	1	.239
2005	Texas	A.L.	OF-2B-SS-3B	66	148	26	36	5	0	8	20	1	.243
2006	Oklahoma	P.C.	3B	3	12	2	6	1	0	0	0	0	.500
2006	Texas c-d	A.L.	OF-3B-2B-SS	136	520	78	154	40	2	13	74	4	.296
2007	Chicago	N.L.	2B-3B-OF-1B	149	502	64	147	28	3	10	72	1	.293
2008	Chicago e	N.L.	2B-OF-3B-1B	149	505	103	144	30	3	21	87	6	.285
Major League Totals			11 Yrs.	893	2650	406	740	151	10	69	352	18	.279
Division Series													
2001	Atlanta	N.L.	SS	1	1	0	1	0	0	0	0	0	1.000
2002	Atlanta	N.L.	2B	4	7	2	3	1	1	0	3	0	.429
2003	Atlanta	N.L.	2B-3B	4	7	1	3	2	0	0	2	0	.429
2007	Chicago	N.L.	2B	3	9	2	3	0	0	0	0	0	.333
2008	Chicago	N.L.	2B-OF	3	12	2	4	2	0	1	4	0	.333
Division Series Totals				15	36	7	14	5	1	1	9	0	.389
Championship Series													
2001	Atlanta	N.L.	SS	4	4	0	0	0	0	0	0	0	.000

a On disabled list from May 18 to July 17, 2002.
b Not offered contract, December 20, 2004. Signed with Texas Rangers organization, January 19, 2005.
c On disabled list from April 15 to April 30, 2006.
d Filed for free agency, October 28, 2006. Signed with Chicago Cubs, November 15, 2006.
e Traded to Cleveland Indians for pitcher Jeff Stevens, pitcher Chris Archer and pitcher John Gaub, December 31, 2008.

DEWITT, BLAKE ROBERT

Born, Sarasota, Florida, August 8, 1985.
Bats Left. Throws Right. Height, 5 feet, 11 inches. Weight, 175 pounds.

Year	Club	Lea	Pos	G	AB	R	H	2B	3B	HR	RBI	SB	Avg
2004	Ogden	Pioneer	3B	70	299	61	85	19	3	12	47	1	.284
2005	Vero Beach	Fla.St.	3B	8	31	4	13	3	0	1	7	0	.419
2005	Columbus	So.Atl.	3B	120	481	61	136	31	3	11	65	0	.283
2006	Vero Beach	Fla.St.	2B-3B	106	425	61	114	18	1	18	61	8	.268
2006	Jacksonville	Southern	3B-2B	26	104	6	19	1	0	1	6	0	.183
2007	Inland Empire	Calif.	3B	83	339	48	101	29	2	8	46	2	.298
2007	Jacksonville	Southern	3B	45	178	20	50	13	1	6	20	0	.281
2008	Las Vegas	P.C.	2B-3B-1B	27	111	16	34	4	2	4	18	1	.306
2008	Los Angeles	N.L.	3B-2B	117	368	45	97	13	2	9	52	3	.264
Division Series													
2008	Los Angeles	N.L.	2B	3	11	2	3	2	0	0	0	0	.273
Championship Series													
2008	Los Angeles	N.L.	2B	5	13	0	1	0	1	0	5	0	.077

DIAZ, MATTHEW EDWARD (MATT)
Born, Portland, Oregon, March 3, 1978.
Bats Right. Throws Right. Height, 6 feet, 1 inch. Weight, 205 pounds.

Year	Club	Lea	Pos	G	AB	R	H	2B	3B	HR	RBI	SB	Avg
1999 Hudson Valley	... N.Y.-Penn.		OF	54	208	22	51	15	2	1	20	6	.245
2000 St. Petersburg	...Fla.St.		OF	106	392	37	106	21	3	6	53	2	.270
2001 Bakersfield	...........Calif.		OF	131	524	79	172	40	2	17	81	11	.328
2002 Orlando	.... Southern		OF-1B	122	449	71	123	28	1	10	50	31	.274
2003 Orlando	.... Southern		OF	60	227	32	87	21	0	5	41	9	.383
2003 Durham	..............Int.		OF	67	253	35	83	18	3	8	45	6	.328
2003 Tampa Bay	..............A.L.		OF	4	9	2	1	0	0	0	0	0	.111
2004 Durham	..............Int.		OF	134	503	81	167	47	5	21	93	15	.332
2004 Tampa Bay	.... A.L.		OF	10	21	3	4	1	1	1	3	0	.190
2005 Royals	...........Arizona		OF	3	13	2	6	2	0	0	2	0	.462
2005 Wichita	.... Texas		OF	7	26	6	7	0	0	1	6	1	.269
2005 Omaha	..............P.C.		OF	65	259	48	96	22	4	14	56	10	.371
2005 Kansas City a-b-c	.. A.L.		OF	34	89	7	25	4	2	1	9	0	.281
2006 Atlanta	..............N.L.		OF	124	297	37	97	15	4	7	32	5	.327
2007 Atlanta	.... N.L.		OF-1B	135	358	44	121	21	0	12	45	4	.338
2008 Mississippi	...... Southern		OF	7	26	5	6	0	0	1	4	1	.231
2008 Richmond	............Int.		OF	4	12	0	2	0	0	0	0	1	.167
2008 Atlanta d.	............N.L.		OF	43	135	9	33	2	0	2	14	4	.244
Major League Totals	....	6 Yrs.		350	909	102	281	43	7	23	103	13	.309

a Released by Tampa Bay Devil Rays, February 18, 2005. Signed with Kansas City Royals organization, February 24, 2005.
b On disabled list from June 11 to July 18, 2005.
c Traded to Atlanta Braves for pitcher Ricardo Rodriguez, December 20, 2005.
d On disabled list from May 28 to September 24, 2008.

DICKERSON, CHRISTOPHER CHARLES (CHRIS)
Born, Hollywood, California, April 10, 1982.
Bats Left. Throws Left. Height, 6 feet, 3 inches. Weight, 225 pounds.

Year	Club	Lea	Pos	G	AB	R	H	2B	3B	HR	RBI	SB	Avg
2003 Billings	.............Pioneer		OF	58	201	36	49	6	4	6	38	9	.244
2004 Potomac	.... Carolina		OF	15	45	5	9	2	0	0	5	3	.200
2004 Dayton	.... Midwest		OF	84	314	50	95	15	3	4	34	27	.303
2005 Sarasota	.........Fla.St.		OF	119	436	68	103	17	7	11	43	19	.236
2006 Chattanooga	...... Southern		OF	115	389	65	94	21	7	12	48	21	.242
2007 Louisville	.............Int.		OF	104	354	58	92	11	6	13	44	23	.260
2007 Chattanooga	...... Southern		OF	30	114	11	31	4	1	1	11	7	.272
2008 Louisville	.............Int.		OF	97	349	65	100	16	9	11	53	26	.287
2008 Cincinnati	............N.L.		OF	31	102	20	31	9	2	6	15	5	.304

DOBBS, GREGORY STUART (GREG)
Born, Los Angeles, California, July 2, 1978.
Bats Left. Throws Right. Height, 6 feet, 1 inch. Weight, 205 pounds.

Year	Club	Lea	Pos	G	AB	R	H	2B	3B	HR	RBI	SB	Avg
2001 San Bernardino	.. Calif.		OF	3	13	2	5	1	0	1	3	0	.385
2001 Everett	....Northwest		1B-OF-3B	65	249	37	80	17	2	6	41	5	.321
2002 Wisconsin	.... Midwest		3B	86	320	43	88	16	2	10	48	13	.275
2002 San Antonio	..... Texas		OF-1B	27	96	13	35	2	0	5	15	1	.365
2003 San Antonio	..... Texas		3B	2	6	0	2	2	0	0	0	0	.333
2004 San Antonio	..... Texas		3B	51	203	25	66	14	4	5	34	5	.325
2004 Tacoma	.........P.C.		3B	67	255	28	69	9	2	8	31	4	.271
2004 Seattle	..........A.L.		3B	18	53	4	12	1	0	1	9	0	.226
2005 Tacoma	.........P.C.		1B-3B-OF	50	190	27	61	9	0	3	22	5	.321
2005 Seattle	...........A.L.		DH-1B-OF-3B	59	142	8	35	7	1	1	20	1	.246
2006 Tacoma	.........P.C.		3B-1B-OF	99	379	60	119	19	3	9	55	14	.314
2006 Seattle	..........A.L.		1B-OF-3B	23	27	4	10	3	1	0	3	0	.370
2007 Philadelphia a	...N.L.		3B-OF-1B-2B	142	324	45	88	20	4	10	55	3	.272
2008 Philadelphia	........N.L.		3B-OF-1B	128	226	30	68	14	1	9	40	3	.301
Major League Totals	....	5 Yrs.		370	772	91	213	45	7	21	127	7	.276
Division Series													
2007 Philadelphia	........N.L.		3B	3	3	0	0	0	0	0	0	0	.000
2008 Philadelphia	........N.L.		3B	3	5	0	3	0	0	0	0	0	.600
Division Series Totals	....			6	8	0	3	0	0	0	0	0	.375
Championship Series													
2008 Philadelphia	......N.L.		3B	3	6	2	3	1	0	0	0	0	.500

Year Club	Lea	Pos	G	AB	R	H	2B	3B	HR	RBI	SB	Avg
2008 Philadelphia	N.L.	DH	2	3	0	1	0	0	0	0	0	.333

a Claimed by Philadelphia Phillies on waivers, January 16, 2007.

DOUMIT, RYAN MATTHEW

Born, Moses Lake, Washington, April 3, 1981.
Bats Both. Throws Right. Height, 6 feet. Weight, 200 pounds.

Year Club	Lea	Pos	G	AB	R	H	2B	3B	HR	RBI	SB	Avg
1999 Pirates .... Gulf Coast		C	29	85	17	24	5	0	1	7	4	.282
2000 Williamsport..... N.Y.-Penn.		C	66	246	25	77	15	.5	2	40	2	.313
2001 Altoona...........	Eastern	C	2	4	0	1	0	0	0	2	0	.250
2001 Pirates	Gulf Coast	C	7	17	2	4	2	0	0	3	0	.235
2001 Hickory............	So.Atl.	C	39	148	14	40	6	0	2	14	2	.270
2002 Hickory............	So.Atl.	C	68	258	46	83	14	1	6	47	3	.322
2003 Lynchburg	Carolina	C	127	458	75	.126	38	1	11	77	4	.275
2004 Altoona...........	Eastern	C	67	221	31	58	20	0	10	34	0	.262
2005 Indianapolis	Int.	C-OF	51	165	41	57	11	0	12	35	1	.345
2005 Pittsburgh	N.L.	C-OF	75	231	25	59	13	1	6	35	2	.255
2006 Pirates	Gulf Coast	C-1B	5	14	1	0	0	0	0	0	0	.000
2006 Altoona...........	Eastern	C-1B	4	15	4	5	3	0	0	4	0	.333
2006 Indianapolis	Int.	C	6	22	3	7	1	1	0	7	0	.318
2006 Pittsburgh a	N.L.	1B-C	61	149	15	31	9	0	6	17	0	.208
2007 Indianapolis	Int.	C	16	53	15	22	4	0	4	20	3	.415
2007 Pittsburgh b	N.L.	OF-C-1B	83	252	33	69	19	2	9	32	1	.274
2008 Altoona...........	Eastern	C	3	7	0	3	0	0	0	0	0	.429
2008 Pittsburgh c	N.L.	C-1B	116	431	71	137	34	0	15	69	2	.318
Major League Totals	4 Yrs.		335	1063	144	296	75	3	36	153	5	.278

a On disabled list from April 12 to May 3 and June 5 to August 23, 2006.
b On disabled list from August 13 to September 8 and September 9 to November 13, 2007.
c On disabled list from May 14 to June 6, 2008.

DREW, DAVID JONATHAN (J.D.)

Born, Tallahassee, Florida, November 20, 1975.
Bats Left. Throws Right. Height, 6 feet, 1 inch. Weight, 200 pounds.

Year Club	Lea	Pos	G	AB	R	H	2B	3B	HR	RBI	SB	Avg
1997 St. Paul	Northern	OF	44	170	51	58	6	1	18	50	5	.341
1998 St. Paul	Northern	OF	30	114	27	44	11	2	9	33	8	.386
1998 Arkansas	Texas	OF	19	67	18	22	3	1	5	11	2	.328
1998 Memphis	P.C.	OF	26	79	15	25	8	1	2	13	1	.316
1998 St. Louis..........	N.L.	OF	14	36	9	15	3	1	5	13	0	.417
1999 St. Louis a	N.L.	OF	104	368	72	89	16	6	13	39	19	.242
2000 St. Louis b	N.L.	OF	135	407	73	120	17	2	18	57	17	.295
2001 Peoria..........	Midwest	OF	3	11	3	6	2	0	0	0	0	.545
2001 St. Louis c	N.L.	OF	109	375	80	121	18	5	27	73	13	.323
2002 St. Louis d	N.L.	OF	135	424	61	107	19	1	18	56	8	.252
2003 Palm Beach	Fla.St.	OF	8	19	4	7	0	0	1	3	0	.368
2003 St. Louis e-f	N.L.	OF	100	287	60	83	13	3	15	42	2	.289
2004 Atlanta g	N.L.	OF	145	518	118	158	28	8	31	93	12	.305
2005 Los Angeles h	N.L.	OF.	72	252	48	72	12	1	15	36	1	.286
2006 Los Angeles i	N.L.	OF	146	494	84	140	34	6	20	100	2	.283
2007 Boston	A.L.	OF	140	466	84	126	30	4	11	64	4	.270
2008 Boston j	A.L.	OF	109	368	79	103	23	4	19	64	4	.280
Major League Totals	11 Yrs.		1209	3995	768	1134	213	41	192	637	82	.284
Division Series												
2000 St. Louis..............	N.L.	OF	2	6	1	1	0	0	0	0	2	.167
2001 St. Louis..............	N.L.	OF	5	13	1	2	0	0	1	2	0	.154
2002 St. Louis..............	N.L.	OF	2	9	1	2	0	0	1	1	0	.222
2004 Atlanta	N.L.	OF	5	20	1	4	0	0	0	1	1	.200
2006 Los Angeles	N.L.	OF	3	13	1	2	0	0	0	0	1	.154
2007 Boston	A.L.	OF	3	11	1	2	0	0	0	3	0	.182
2008 Boston	A.L.	OF	4	14	2	4	1	0	1	3	0	.286
Division Series Totals			24	86	8	17	1	0	3	10	3	.198
Championship Series												
2000 St. Louis..............	N.L.	OF	5	12	2	4	1	0	0	1	0	.333
2002 St. Louis..............	N.L.	OF	5	13	1	5	0	0	1	1	0	.385
2007 Boston	A.L.	OF	7	25	5	9	1	0	1	6	0	.360
2008 Boston	A.L.	OF	7	24	1	6	1	0	1	3	0	.250
Championship Series Totals			24	74	9	24	3	0	3	11	0	.324

Year	Club	Lea	Pos	G	AB	R	H	2B	3B	HR	RBI	SB	Avg
World Series Record													
2007 Boston	A.L.		OF	4	15	1	5	2	0	0	2	0	.333

a On disabled list from May 16 to June 17, 1999.
b On disabled list from July 8 to July 26, 2000.
c On disabled list from June 18 to July 31, 2001.
d On disabled list from June 28 to July 13, 2002.
e On disabled list from March 21 to April 20 and August 9 to September 1, 2003.
f Traded to Atlanta Braves with catcher Eli Marrero for pitcher Jason Marquis, pitcher Ray King and pitcher Adam Wainwright, December 13, 2003.
g Filed for free agency, October 28, 2004. Signed with Los Angeles Dodgers, December 23, 2004.
h On disabled list from July 4 to October 7, 2005.
i Filed for free agency, November 10, 2006. Signed with Boston Red Sox, December 5, 2006.
j On disabled list from August 18 to September 8, 2008.

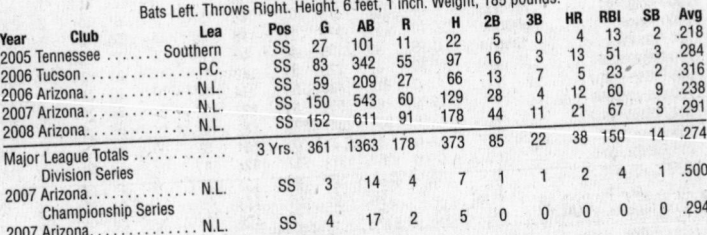

DREW, STEPHEN ORIS
Born, Hahira, Georgia, March 16, 1983.
Bats Left. Throws Right. Height, 6 feet, 1 inch. Weight, 185 pounds.

Year	Club	Lea	Pos	G	AB	R	H	2B	3B	HR	RBI	SB	Avg
2005 Tennessee	Southern		SS	27	101	11	22	5	0	4	13	2	.218
2006 Tucson	P.C.		SS	83	342	55	97	16	3	13	51	3	.284
2006 Arizona...........	N.L.		SS	59	209	27	66	13	7	5	23	2	.316
2007 Arizona...........	N.L.		SS	150	543	60	129	28	4	12	60	9	.238
2008 Arizona...........	N.L.		SS	152	611	91	178	44	11	21	67	3	.291
Major League Totals			3 Yrs.	361	1363	178	373	85	22	38	150	14	.274
Division Series													
2007 Arizona...........	N.L.		SS	3	14	4	7	1	1	2	4	1	.500
Championship Series													
2007 Arizona...........	N.L.		SS	4	17	2	5	0	0	0	0	0	.294

DUKES, ELIJAH DAVID
Born, Homestead, Florida, June 26, 1984.
Bats Right. Throws Right. Height, 6 feet, 2 inches. Weight, 240 pounds.

Year	Club	Lea	Pos	G	AB	R	H	2B	3B	HR	RBI	SB	Avg
2003 Charleston	So.Atl.		OF	117	383	51	94	17	4	7	53	33	.245
2004 Bakersfield..........	Calif.		OF	58	211	44	70	16	2	8	34	16	.332
2004 Charleston	So.Atl.		OF	43	163	26	47	12	2	2	15	14	.288
2005 Montgomery	Southern		OF	120	446	73	128	21	5	18	73	19	.287
2006 Durham	Int.		OF	80	283	58	83	15	5	10	50	9	.293
2007 Tampa Bay a.......	A.L.		OF	52	184	27	35	3	2	10	21	2	.190
2008 Nationals	Gulf Coast		OF	2	5	0	0	0	0	0	0	0	.000
2008 Potomac..........	Carolina		OF	6	17	1	3	1	0	0	1	0	.176
2008 Columbus.........	Int.		OF	17	47	8	11	3	1	1	6	2	.234
2008 Washington b.........	N.L.		OF	81	276	48	73	16	2	13	44	13	.264
Major League Totals			2 Yrs.	133	460	75	108	19	4	23	65	15	.235

a Traded to Washington Nationals for pitcher Glenn Gibson, December 3, 2007.
b On disabled list from March 31 to May 9 and July 6 to August 1 and August 3 to August 27, 2008.

DUNCAN, CHRISTOPHER EDWARD (CHRIS)
Born, Tucson, Arizona, May 5, 1981.
Bats Left. Throws Right. Height, 6 feet, 5 inches. Weight, 230 pounds.

Year	Club	Lea	Pos	G	AB	R	H	2B	3B	HR	RBI	SB	Avg
1999 Johnson City	Appal.		1B	55	201	23	43	8	1	6	34	3	.214
1999 Piedmont...........	So.Atl.		3B-SS	73	276	41	60	15	3	11	40	15	.217
2000 Clearwater.........	Fla.St.		OF	107	390	49	103	25	3	8	47	13	.264
2000 Peoria.............	Midwest		1B	122	450	52	115	34	0	8	57	1	.256
2001 Potomac...........	Carolina		1B	49	168	12	30	6	0	3	16	4	.179
2001 Peoria.............	Midwest		1B	80	297	44	91	23	2	13	59	13	.306
2002 Peoria.............	Midwest		1B	129	487	58	132	25	4	16	75	5	.271
2003 Palm Beach	Fla.St.		1B	121	425	26	108	20	0	2	42	4	.254
2003 Tennessee	Southern		OF	10	25	1	5	1	0	1	3	0	.200
2004 Tennessee	Southern		1B-OF	120	387	57	112	23	0	16	65	8	.289
2005 Memphis	P.C.		1B-OF	128	431	57	114	21	2	21	73	4	.265
2005 St. Louis..........	N.L.		1B-OF	9	10	2	2	1	0	1	3	0	.200
2006 Memphis	P.C.		OF	52	181	23	49	11	0	7	31	1	.271
2006 St. Louis..........	N.L.		OF-1B	90	280	60	82	11	3	22	43	0	.293
2007 St. Louis..........	N.L.		OF-1B	127	375	51	97	20	0	21	70	2	.259

Year Club	Lea	Pos	G	AB	R	H	2B	3B	HR	RBI	SB	Avg
2008 Memphis ............P.C.		OF	7	25	5	4	2	0	0	3	0	.160
2008 St. Louis a ...........N.L.		OF-1B	76	222	26	55	8	0	6	27	2	.248
Major League Totals		4 Yrs.	302	887	139	236	40	3	50	143	2	.266
Division Series												
2006 St. Louis............ N.L.		OF	2	6	1	1	0	0	0	0	0	.167
Championship Series												
2006 St. Louis............ N.L.		OF	5	8	1	1	0	0	1	1	0	.125
World Series Record												
2006 St. Louis............. N.L.		OF-DH	3	8	1	1	1	0	0	1	0	.125

a On disabled list from July 21 to November 7, 2008.

DUNN, ADAM TROY

Born, Houston, Texas, November 9, 1979.
Bats Left. Throws Right. Height, 6 feet, 6 inches. Weight, 275 pounds.

Year Club	Lea	Pos	G	AB	R	H	2B	3B	HR	RBI	SB	Avg
1998 Billings...........Pioneer		OF	34	125	26	36	3	1	4	13	4	.288
1999 Rockford ....Midwest		OF	92	313	62	96	16	2	11	44	21	.307
2000 Dayton ....Midwest		OF	122	420	101	118	29	1	16	79	24	.281
2001 Chattanooga......Southern		OF	39	140	30	48	9	0	12	31	6	.343
2001 Louisville ....Int.		OF	55	210	44	69	13	0	20	53	5	.329
2001 Cincinnati...........N.L.		OF	66	244	54	64	18	1	19	43	4	.262
2002 Cincinnati...........N.L.		OF-1B	158	535	84	133	28	2	26	71	19	.249
2003 Cincinnati a .........N.L.		OF-1B	116	381	70	82	12	1	27	57	8	.215
2004 Cincinnati...........N.L.		OF-1B	161	568	105	151	34	0	46	102	6	.266
2005 Cincinnati...........N.L.		OF-1B	160	543	107	134	35	2	40	101	4	.247
2006 Cincinnati...........N.L.		OF-1B	160	561	99	131	24	0	40	92	7	.234
2007 Cincinnati...........N.L.		OF	152	522	101	138	27	2	40	106	9	.264
2008 Cincinnati-Arizona b-c.. N.L.		OF-1B	158	517	79	122	23	0	40	100	2	.236
Major League Totals		8 Yrs.	1131	3871	699	955	201	8	278	672	59	.247

a On disabled list from August 16 to October 2, 2003.
b Traded to Arizona Diamondbacks for pitcher Dallas Buck and two players to be named later, August 12, 2008 To complete trade, Cincinnati Reds received catcher Wilkin Castillo on August 14, 2008 and pitcher Micah Owings on September 10, 2008.
c Filed for free agency, November 1, 2008.

DURAN, GERMAN

Born, Zacatecas, Mexico, August 3, 1984.
Bats Right. Throws Right. Height, 5 feet, 10 inches. Weight, 185 pounds.

Year Club	Lea	Pos	G	AB	R	H	2B	3B	HR	RBI	SB	Avg
2005 Spokane.....Northwest		SS	62	252	36	66	17	2	4	33	6	.262
2006 Bakersfield.......Calif.		SS-2B-3B	114	457	81	130	31	2	13	72	15	.284
2007 Frisco ....Texas		2B-SS	130	480	81	144	32	5	22	84	11	.300
2008 Oklahoma.........P.C.		2B-3B-SS	21	77	12	20	3	2	1	6	0	.260
2008 Texas ............A.L.		3B-2B-OF-SS	60	143	22	33	6	1	3	16	1	.231

DURHAM, RAY

Born, Charlotte, North Carolina, November 30, 1971.
Bats Both. Throws Right. Height, 5 feet, 8 inches. Weight, 205 pounds.

Year Club	Lea	Pos	G	AB	R	H	2B	3B	HR	RBI	SB	Avg
1990 White Sox ....Gulf C.		2B	35	116	18	32	3	3	0	13	23	.276
1991 White Sox ....Gulf C.		2B	6	23	3	7	1	0	0	4	5	.304
1991 Utica............N.Y.-Penn.		2B	39	142	29	36	2	7	0	17	12	.254
1992 White Sox ....Gulf C.		DH	5	13	3	7	2	0	0	2	1	.538
1992 Sarasota a ....Fla. St.		2B	57	202	37	55	6	3	0	7	28	.272
1993 Birmingham......Southern		2B	137	528	83	143	22	10	3	37	39	.271
1994 Nashville ............A.A.		2B	133	527	89	156	33	*12	16	66	34	.296
1995 Chicago ............A.L.		2B	125	471	68	121	27	6	7	51	18	.257
1996 Chicago ............A.L.		2B	156	557	79	153	33	5	10	65	30	.275
1997 Chicago ............A.L.		2B	155	634	106	172	27	5	11	53	33	.271
1998 Chicago ............A.L.		2B	158	635	126	181	35	8	19	67	36	.285
1999 Chicago ............A.L.		2B	153	612	109	181	30	8	13	60	34	.296
2000 Chicago ............A.L.		2B	151	614	121	172	35	9	17	75	25	.280
2001 Chicago ............A.L.		2B	152	611	104	163	42	10	20	65	23	.267
2002 Chicago-Oakland b-c... A.L.		2B	150	564	114	163	34	6	15	70	26	.289
2003 San Francisco d .....N.L.		2B	110	410	61	117	30	5	8	33	7	.285
2004 San Jose ....California		2B	1	3	0	1	0	0	0	0	0	.333
2004 Fresno ............P.C.		2B	5	14	4	8	0	1	1	5	0	.571

Year	Club	Lea	Pos	G	AB	R	H	2B	3B	HR	RBI	SB	Avg
2004 San Francisco e	N.L.	2B	120	471	95	133	28	8	17	65	10	.282
2005 San Francisco	N.L.	2B-OF	142	497	67	144	33	0	12	62	6	.290
2006 San Francisco f-g ...	N.L.	2B	137	498	79	146	30	7	26	93	7	.293
2007 San Francisco	N.L.	2B	138	464	56	101	21	2	11	71	10	.218
2008 San Fran.-Milwaukee h-i	N.L.	2B	128	370	64	107	35	0	6	45	8	.289
Major League Totals	14 Yrs.		1975	7408	1249	2054	440	79	192	875	273	.277
Division Series												
2000 Chicago	A.L.	2B	3	10	2	2	1	0	1	1	0	.200
2002 Oakland	A.L.	DH	5	21	7	7	3	0	2	2	1	.333
2003 San Francisco	N.L.	2B	4	17	2	4	0	0	0	0	0	.235
2008 Milwaukee	N.L.	2B	3	8	2	1	0	0	0	0	0	.125
Division Series Totals			15	56	13	14	4	0	3	3	1	.250

a On disabled list from June 16 to July 9, 1992.
b Traded to Oakland Athletics for pitcher Jon Adkins, July 25, 2002.
c Filed for free agency, November 1, 2002. Signed with San Francisco Giants, December 7, 2002.
d On disabled list from May 11 to May 26 and August 7 to September 1, 2003.
e On disabled list from April 28 to May 13 and from May 23 to June 15, 2004.
f On disabled list from April 27 to May 12, 2006.
g Filed for free agency, October 30, 2006, re-signed with San Francisco Giants, December 1, 2006.
h Traded to Milwaukee Brewers for outfielder Darren Ford and pitcher Steve Hamilton, July 20, 2008.
i Filed for free agency, November 1, 2008.

DYE, JERMAINE TERRELL

Born, Oakland, California, January 28, 1974.
Bats Right. Throws Right. Height, 6 feet, 5 inches. Weight, 235 pounds.

Year	Club	Lea	Pos	G	AB	R	H	2B	3B	HR	RBI	SB	Avg
1993 Braves	Gulf Coast	OF-3B	31	124	17	43	14	0	0	27	5	.347
1993 Danville	Appal.	OF	25	94	6	26	6	1	2	12	4	.277
1994 Macon	So.Atl.	OF	135	506	73	151	41	1	15	98	19	.298
1995 Greenville	Southern	OF	104	403	50	115	26	4	15	71	4	.285
1996 Richmond	Int.	OF	36	142	25	33	7	1	6	19	3	.232
1996 Atlanta	N.L.	OF	98	292	32	82	16	0	12	37	1	.281
1997 Omaha	A.A.	OF	39	144	21	44	6	0	10	25	0	.306
1997 Kansas City a-b	A.L.	OF	75	263	26	62	14	0	7	22	2	.236
1998 Omaha	P.C.	OF-1B	41	157	29	47	6	0	12	35	7	.299
1998 Kansas City c	A.L.	OF	60	214	24	50	5	1	5	23	2	.234
1999 Kansas City	A.L.	OF	158	608	96	179	44	8	27	119	2	.294
2000 Kansas City	A.L.	OF	157	601	107	193	41	2	33	118	0	.321
2001 Kansas City-Oakland d ..	A.L.	OF	158	599	91	169	31	1	26	106	9	.282
2002 Sacramento	P.C.	DH	4	16	3	3	2	0	0	0	0	.188
2002 Modesto	California	OF	2	8	1	4	3	0	0	2	0	.500
2002 Oakland e	A.L.	OF	131	488	74	123	27	1	24	86	2	.252
2003 Sacramento	P.C.	OF	13	49	9	14	2	0	2	9	0	.286
2003 Oakland f	A.L.	OF	65	221	28	38	6	0	4	20	1	.172
2004 Oakland g	A.L.	OF	137	532	87	141	29	4	23	80	4	.265
2005 Chicago	A.L.	OF-1B-SS	145	529	74	145	29	2	31	86	11	.274
2006 Chicago	A.L.	OF	146	539	103	170	27	3	44	120	7	.315
2007 Chicago	A.L.	OF	138	508	68	129	34	0	28	78	2	.254
2008 Chicago	A.L.	OF	154	590	96	172	41	2	34	96	3	.292
Major League Totals	13 Yrs.		1622	5984	906	1653	344	24	298	991	46	.276
Division Series												
1996 Atlanta	N.L.	OF	3	11	1	2	0	0	1	1	1	.182
2001 Oakland	A.L.	OF	4	13	0	3	2	0	0	0	0	.231
2002 Oakland	A.L.	OF	5	20	3	8	2	0	1	1	0	.400
2003 Oakland	A.L.	OF	4	13	2	3	0	0	1	3	0	.231
2005 Chicago	A.L.	OF	3	10	1	2	0	0	0	0	0	.200
2008 Chicago	A.L.	OF	4	16	1	6	1	0	1	1	0	.375
Division Series Totals			23	83	8	24	5	0	4	6	1	.289
Championship Series												
1996 Atlanta	N.L.	OF	7	28	2	6	1	0	0	4	0	.214
2005 Chicago	A.L.	OF	5	19	3	5	2	0	0	3	1	.263
Championship Series Totals			12	47	5	11	3	0	0	7	1	.234
World Series Record												
1996 Atlanta	N.L.	OF	5	17	0	2	0	0	0	1	0	.118
2005 Chicago	A.L.	OF	4	16	3	7	1	0	1	3	0	.438
World Series Totals			9	33	3	9	1	0	1	4	0	.273

a Traded to Kansas City Royals with pitcher Jamie Walker for infielder Keith Lockhart and outfielder Michael Tucker, March 27, 1997.

b On disabled list from April 17 to May 3 and July 3 to August 13, 1997.
c On disabled list from March 31 to May 8 and September 1 to September 28, 1998.
d Traded to Oakland Athletics for infielder Neifi Perez, July 25, 2001.
e On disabled list from March 22 to April 26, 2002.
f On disabled list from April 25 to May 30 and July 7 to September 1, 2003.
g Filed for free agency, October 28, 2004. Signed with Chicago White Sox, December 9, 2004.

EASLEY, JACINTO DAMION (DAMION)

Born, New York, New York, November 11, 1969.
Bats Right. Throws Right. Height, 5 feet, 11 inches. Weight, 190 pounds.

Year	Club	Lea	Pos	G	AB	R	H	2B	3B	HR	RBI	SB	Avg
1989 Bend	Northwest		SS	36	131	34	39	5	1	4	21	9	.298
1990 Quad City	Midwest		SS	103	365	59	100	19	3	10	56	25	.274
1991 Midland	Texas		SS	127	452	73	115	24	5	6	57	23	.254
1992 Edmonton	P.C.		SS-3B	108	429	61	124	18	3	3	44	26	.289
1992 California	A.L.		3B-SS	47	151	14	39	5	0	1	12	9	.258
1993 California	A.L.		2B-3B	73	230	33	72	13	2	2	22	6	.313
1994 California	A.L.		3B-2B	88	316	41	68	16	1	6	30	4	.215
1995 California	A.L.		2B-SS	114	357	35	77	14	2	4	35	5	.216
1996 Midland	Texas		3B-SS	4	14	1	6	2	0	0	2	1	.429
1996 Vancouver	P.C.		SS-2B-3B	12	48	13	15	2	1	2	8	4	.313
1996 California-Detroit a-b	A.L.		SS-2B-3B-OF	49	112	14	30	2	0	4	17	3	.268
1997 Detroit	A.L.		2B-SS	151	527	97	139	37	3	22	72	28	.264
1998 Detroit	A.L.		2B-SS	153	594	84	161	38	2	27	100	15	.271
1999 Detroit	A.L.		2B-SS	151	549	83	146	30	1	20	65	11	.266
2000 Detroit	A.L.		2B	126	464	76	120	27	2	14	58	13	.259
2000 Toledo c	Int.		2B	4	13	3	3	1	0	1	4	0	.231
2001 Detroit	A.L.		2B	154	585	77	146	27	7	11	65	10	.250
2002 Detroit	A.L.		2B	85	304	29	68	14	1	8	30	1	.224
2002 Toledo d	Int.		2B	8	26	5	3	1	0	0	0	0	.115
2003 Tampa Bay e-f	A.L.		3B-2B	36	107	8	20	3	1	1	7	0	.187
2004 Florida g	N.L.		2B-1B-SS-3B	98	223	26	53	20	1	9	43	4	.238
2005 Florida h	N.L.		2B-SS-3B	102	267	37	64	19	1	9	30	4	.240
2006 Arizona i	N.L.		SS-3B-2B-1B	90	189	24	44	6	1	9	28	1	.233
2007 New York j-k	N.L.		2B-OF-1B-3B	76	193	24	54	6	0	10	26	0	.280
2008 New York l	N.L.		2B-SS-OF-1B	113	316	33	85	10	2	6	44	0	.269
Major League Totals			17 Yrs.	1706	5484	735	1386	287	27	163	684	114	.2532

a On disabled list from April 1 to May 10, 1996.
b Traded to Detroit Tigers for pitcher Greg Gohr, July 31, 1996.
c On disabled list from April 10 to April 24 and May 9 to June 1, 2000.
d On disabled list from April 17 to June 1, 2002.
e Released by Detroit Tigers, March 28, 2003. Signed with Tampa Bay Devil Rays, April 2, 2003.
f Released by Tampa Bay Devil Rays, June 4, 2003. Signed with Florida Marlins, December 19, 2003.
g Filed for free agency, October 28, 2004, re-signed with Florida Marlins, November 22, 2004.
h Filed for free agency, October 28, 2005. Signed with Arizona Diamondbacks, December 12, 2005.
i Filed for free agency, October 30, 2006. Signed with New York Mets, November 17, 2006.
j On disabled list from August 19 to October 29, 2007.
k Filed for free agency, October 29, 2007, re-signed with New York Mets, November 6, 2007.
l Filed for free agency, October 30, 2008.

ECKSTEIN, DAVID MARK

Born, Sanford, Florida, January 20, 1975.
Bats Right. Throws Right. Height, 5 feet, 7 inches. Weight, 165 pounds.

Year	Club	Lea	Pos	G	AB	R	H	2B	3B	HR	RBI	SB	Avg
1997 Lowell	N.Y.-Penn.		2B	68	249	43	75	11	4	4	39	21	.301
1998 Sarasota	Fla.St.		2B-SS	135	503	99	154	29	4	3	58	45	.306
1999 Trenton	Eastern		2B	131	483	109	151	22	5	6	52	32	.313
2000 Pawtucket	Int.		2B-SS	119	422	77	104	20	0	1	31	11	.246
2000 Edmonton a	P.C.		2B	15	52	17	18	8	0	3	8	5	.346
2001 Anaheim	A.L.		SS-2B	153	582	82	166	26	2	4	41	29	.285
2002 Anaheim b	A.L.		SS	152	608	107	178	22	6	8	63	21	.293
2003 Anaheim	A.L.		SS	120	452	59	114	22	1	3	31	16	.252
2004 Anaheim c	A.L.		SS	142	566	92	156	24	1	2	35	16	.276
2005 St. Louis	N.L.		SS	158	630	90	185	26	7	8	61	11	.294
2006 St. Louis d	N.L.		SS	123	500	68	146	18	1	2	23	7	.292
2007 St. Louis e-f	A.L.		SS	117	434	58	134	23	0	3	31	10	.309
2008 Dunedin	Fla.St.		SS	5	14	4	2	1	0	0	0	0	.143
2008 Toronto	A.L.		SS-2B	76	260	27	72	18	0	1	23	2	.277

Year	Club	Lea	Pos	G	AB	R	H	2B	3B	HR	RBI	SB	Avg
2008 Arizona g-h-i	N.L.	2B	18	64	5	14	3	0	1	4	0	.219
Major League Totals			8 Yrs.	1059	4096	588	1165	182	18	32	312	112	.284
Division Series													
2002 Anaheim..............	A.L.	SS	4	18	2	5	0	0	0	1	1	.278
2004 Anaheim..............	A.L.	SS	3	12	2	4	0	0	0	0	0	.333
2005 St. Louis..........	N.L.	SS	3	13	3	5	0	0	1	4	0	.385
2006 St. Louis............	N.L.	SS	4	15	1	2	0	0	0	1	1	.133
Division Series Totals			14	58	8	16	0	0	1	6	2	.276
Championship Series													
2002 Anaheim..............	A.L.	SS	5	21	1	6	0	0	0	2	0	.286
2005 St. Louis............	N.L.	SS	6	20	5	4	0	0	0	2	1	.200
2006 St. Louis............	N.L.	SS	7	26	3	6	1	0	1	1	3	.231
Championship Series Totals ..			18	67	9	16	1	0	1	5	4	.239
World Series Record													
2002 Anaheim..............	A.L.	SS	7	29	6	9	0	0	0	3	1	.310
2006 St. Louis............	N.L.	SS	5	22	3	8	3	0	0	4	0	.364
World Series Totals........			12	51	9	17	3	0	0	7	1	.333

a Claimed on waivers by Anaheim Angels from Boston Red Sox, August 16, 2000.
b On disabled list from August 18 to September 9, 2003.
c Not offered contract, December 20, 2004. Signed with St. Louis Cardinals, December 23, 2004.
d On disabled list from August 19 to September 15, 2006.
e On disabled list from June 14 to July 13, 2007.
f Filed for free agency, October 29, 2007. Signed with Texas Rangers, December 14, 2007.
g On disabled list from May 7 to May 27, 2008.
h Traded to Arizona Diamondbacks for pitcher Chad Beck, August 31, 2008.
i Filed for free agency, October 30, 2008. Signed with San Diego Padres, January 15, 2009.

EDMONDS, JAMES PATRICK (JIM)

Born, Fullerton, California, June 27, 1970.
Bats Left. Throws Left. Height, 6 feet, 1 inch. Weight, 210 pounds.

Year	Club	Lea	Pos	G	AB	R	H	2B	3B	HR	RBI	SB	Avg
1988 Bend.............	Northwest	OF	35	122	23	27	4	0	0	13	4	.221
1989 Quad City a.........	Midwest	OF	31	92	11	24	4	0	1	4	1	.261
1990 Palm Springs	California	OF	91	314	36	92	18	6	3	56	5	.293
1991 Palm Springs b-c..	California	OF-1B-P	60	187	28	55	15	1	2	27	2	.294
1992 Midland	Texas	OF	70	246	42	77	15	2	6	36	3	.313
1992 Edmonton	P.C.	OF	50	194	37	58	15	2	6	36	6	.299
1993 Vancouver d.........	P.C.	OF	95	356	59	112	28	4	9	74	6	.315
1993 California	A.L.	OF	18	61	5	15	4	1	0	4	0	.246
1994 California	A.L.	OF-1B	94	289	35	79	13	1	5	37	4	.273
1995 California	A.L.	OF	141	558	120	162	30	4	33	107	1	.290
1996 Lk Elsinore e	California	OF	5	15	4	6	2	0	1	4	0	.400
1996 California	A.L.	OF	114	431	73	131	28	3	27	66	4	.304
1997 Anaheim f...........	A.L.	OF-1B	133	502	82	146	27	0	26	80	5	.291
1998 Anaheim	A.L.	OF	154	599	115	184	42	1	25	91	7	.307
1999 Lake Elsinore	California	DH	5	19	4	8	2	0	0	3	2	.421
1999 Anaheim g...........	A.L.	OF-1B	55	204	34	51	17	2	5	23	5	.250
2000 St. Louis h.........	N.L.	OF-1B	152	525	129	155	25	0	42	108	10	.295
2001 St. Louis............	N.L.	OF-1B	150	500	95	152	38	1	30	110	5	.304
2002 St. Louis i..........	N.L.	OF	144	476	96	148	31	2	28	83	4	.311
2003 St. Louis............	N.L.	OF	137	447	89	123	32	2	39	89	1	.275
2004 St. Louis............	N.L.	OF-1B	153	498	102	150	38	3	42	111	8	.301
2005 St. Louis............	N.L.	OF	142	467	88	123	37	1	29	89	5	.263
2006 St. Louis j.........	N.L.	OF-1B	110	350	52	90	18	0	19	70	4	.257
2007 St. Louis k-l.........	N.L.	OF-1B	117	365	39	92	15	2	12	53	0	.252
2008 Lake Elsinore	Calif.	OF	2	6	0	2	0	0	0	0	0	.333
2008 San Diego-Chicago m-n-o ..	N.L.	OF	111	340	53	80	19	2	20	55	2	.235
Major League Totals			16 Yrs.	1925	6612	1207	1881	414	25	382	1176	65	.284
Division Series													
2000 St. Louis..............	N.L.	OF	3	14	5	8	4	0	2	7	1	.571
2001 St. Louis..............	N.L.	OF	5	17	3	4	1	0	2	3	0	.235
2002 St. Louis..............	N.L.	OF	3	11	1	3	0	0	1	2	0	.273
2004 St. Louis..............	N.L.	OF	4	15	1	4	0	0	1	1	0	.267
2005 St. Louis..............	N.L.	OF	3	11	5	4	2	0	1	1	0	.364
2006 St. Louis..............	N.L.	OF	4	13	2	4	0	0	0	1	0	.308
2008 Chicago	N.L.	OF	3	10	1	2	1	0	0	3	0	.200
Division Series Totals			25	91	18	29	8	0	7	18	1	.319

Year	Club	Lea	Pos	G	AB	R	H	2B	3B	HR	RBI	SB	Avg
Championship Series													
2000 St. Louis.............	N.L.		OF	5	22	1	5	1	0	1	5	0	.227
2002 St. Louis.............	N.L.		OF	5	20	2	8	2	0	1	4	0	.400
2004 St. Louis.............	N.L.		OF	7	24	2	7	2	0	2	7	0	.292
2005 St. Louis.............	N.L.		OF	6	19	2	4	1	0	0	0	1	.211
2006 St. Louis.............	N.L.		OF	7	22	5	5	0	0	2	4	0	.227
Championship Series Totals......				30	107	12	29	6	0	6	20	1	.271
World Series Record													
2004 St. Louis.............	N.L.		OF	4	15	2	1	0	0	0	0	0	.067
2006 St. Louis.............	N.L.		OF	5	17	1	4	2	0	0	4	0	.235
World Series Totals............				9	32	3	5	2	0	0	4	0	.156

a On disabled list from June 19 to end of 1989 season.
b Record of 0-0 in one game as pitcher.
c On disabled list from April 10 to May 7 and July 23 to end of 1991 season.
d On disabled list from June 29 to July 19, 1993.
e On disabled list from May 26 to June 10 and June 12 to July 18, 1996.
f On disabled list from July 31 to August 16, 1997.
g On disabled list from March 30 to August 2, 1999.
h Traded to St. Louis Cardinals for pitcher Kent Bottenfield and infielder Adam Kennedy, March 23, 2000.
i On disabled list from June 1 to June 16, 2002.
j Filed for free agency, November 2, 2006, re-signed with St. Louis Cardinals, November 10, 2006.
k On disabled list from June 16 to July 19, 2007.
l Traded to San Diego Padres for infielder David Freese, December 15, 2007.
m On disabled list from March 21 to April 5, 2008.
n Released by San Diego Padres, May 9, 2008. Signed with Chicago Cubs May 14, 2008.
o Filed for free agency, October 30, 2008.

ELLIS, MARK WILLIAM

Born, Rapid City, South Dakota, June 6, 1977.
Bats Right. Throws Right. Height, 5 feet, 11 inches. Weight, 195 pounds.

Year	Club	Lea	Pos	G	AB	R	H	2B	3B	HR	RBI	SB	Avg
1999 Spokane.....	Northwest		SS	71	281	67	92	14	0	7	47	21	.327
2000 Wilmington ...	Carolina		SS-2B	132	484	83	146	27	4	6	62	25	.302
2000 Wichita	Texas		2B	7	22	4	7	1	0	0	4	1	.318
2001 Sacramento a......	P.C.		SS	132	472	71	129	38	0	10	53	21	.273
2002 Sacramento	P.C.		SS	21	84	14	25	10	1	0	5	4	.298
2002 Oakland	A.L.		2B-SS-3B	98	345	58	94	16	4	6	35	4	.272
2003 Oakland	A.L.		2B	154	553	78	137	31	5	9	52	6	.248
2004 Oakland b........	A.L.		INJURED—Did Not Play										
2005 Oakland	A.L.		2B-SS-1B	122	434	76	137	21	5	13	52	1	.316
2006 Sacramento	P.C.		2B	4	12	1	2	0	0	0	2	0	.167
2006 Oakland c........	A.L.		2B-1B	124	441	64	110	25	1	11	52	4	.249
2007 Oakland	A.L.		2B	150	583	84	161	33	3	19	76	9	.276
2008 Oakland d.......	A.L.		2B	117	442	55	103	20	3	12	41	14	.233
Major League Totals...........			6 Yrs.	765	2798	415	742	146	21	70	308	38	.265
Division Series													
2002 Oakland .........A.L.			2B	5	19	1	7	2	0	1	4	0	.368
2003 Oakland .........A.L.			2B	5	17	2	2	0	0	0	0	0	.118
2006 Oakland .........A.L.			2B	2	7	0	2	0	0	0	0	0	.286
Division Series Totals............				12	43	3	11	2	0	1	4	0	.256

a Traded to Oakland Athletics by Kansas City Royals with outfielder Johnny Damon and player to be named later for pitcher Roberto Hernandez, catcher A.J. Hinch, infielder Angel Berroa and cash, January 8, 2001.
b On disabled list from March 26 to October 20, 2004.
c On disabled list from June 1 to June 30, 2006.
d On disabled list from September 21 to November 14, 2008.

ELLSBURY, JACOBY MCCABE

Born, Madras, Oregon, September 11, 1983.
Bats Left. Throws Left. Height, 6 feet, 1 inch. Weight, 185 pounds.

Year	Club	Lea	Pos	G	AB	R	H	2B	3B	HR	RBI	SB	Avg
2005 Lowell	N.Y.-Penn.		OF	35	139	28	44	3	5	1	19	23	.317
2006 Wilmington	Carolina		OF	61	244	35	73	7	5	4	32	25	.299
2006 Portland..........	Eastern		OF	50	198	29	61	10	3	3	19	16	.308
2007 Portland.........	Eastern		OF	17	73	16	33	10	2	0	13	8	.452
2007 Pawtucket	Int.		OF	87	363	66	108	14	5	2	28	33	.298
2007 Boston	A.L.		OF	33	116	20	41	7	1	3	18	9	.353

Year	Club	Lea	Pos	G	AB	R	H	2B	3B	HR	RBI	SB	Avg
2008 Boston	A.L.	OF	145	554	98	155	22	7	9	47	*50	.280
Major League Totals		2 Yrs.	178	670	118	196	29	8	12	65	59	.293
Division Series													
2007 Boston	A.L.	OF	2	1	1	0	0	0	0	0	0	.000
2008 Boston	A.L.	OF	4	18	2	6	3	0	0	6	3	.333
Division Series Totals			6	19	3	6	3	0	0	6	3	.316
Championship Series													
2007 Boston	A.L.	OF	5	8	3	2	0	0	0	1	1	.250
2008 Boston	A.L.	OF	4	14	0	0	0	0	0	1	0	.000
Championship Series Totals			9	22	3	2	0	0	0	2	1	.091
World Series Record													
2007 Boston	A.L.	OF	4	16	4	7	4	0	0	3	1	.438

ENCARNACION, EDWIN ELPIDIO

Born, La Romana, Dominican Republic, January 7, 1983.
Bats Right. Throws Right. Height, 6 feet, 1 inch. Weight, 215 pounds.

Year	Club	Lea	Pos	G	AB	R	H	2B	3B	HR	RBI	SB	Avg
2000 Rangers	Gulf Coast	3B	51	177	31	55	6	3	0	36	3	.311
2001 Dayton	Midwest	3B	9	37	2	6	2	0	1	6	0	.162
2001 Billings	Pioneer	3B	52	211	27	55	8	2	5	26	8	.261
2001 Savannah a	So.Atl.	3B	45	170	23	52	9	2	4	25	3	.306
2002 Dayton	Midwest	3B-SS	136	517	80	146	32	4	17	73	25	.282
2003 Potomac	Carolina	3B	58	215	40	69	15	1	6	29	7	.321
2003 Chattanooga	Southern	3B-SS	67	254	40	69	13	1	5	36	8	.272
2004 Chattanooga	Southern	3B	120	469	73	132	35	1	13	76	17	.281
2005 Louisville	Int.	3B	78	290	44	91	23	0	15	54	7	.314
2005 Cincinnati	N.L.	3B	69	211	25	49	16	0	9	31	3	.232
2006 Louisville	Int.	3B-1B	10	36	6	11	3	0	1	1	0	.306
2006 Cincinnati b	N.L.	3B-1B	117	406	60	112	33	1	15	72	6	.276
2007 Louisville	Int.	3B	11	46	12	19	3	0	3	7	1	.413
2007 Cincinnati	N.L.	3B	139	502	66	145	25	1	16	76	8	.289
2008 Cincinnati	N.L.	3B	146	506	75	127	29	1	26	68	1	.251
Major League Totals		4 Yrs.	471	1625	226	433	103	3	66	247	18	.266

a Traded by Texas Rangers to Cincinnati Reds with outfielder Ruben Mateo for pitcher Rob Bell, June 15, 2001.
b On disabled list from June 7 to July 6, 2006.

ERSTAD, DARIN CHARLES

Born, Jamestown, North Dakota, June 4, 1974.
Bats Left. Throws Left. Height, 6 feet, 2 inches. Weight, 215 pounds.

Year	Club	Lea	Pos	G	AB	R	H	2B	3B	HR	RBI	SB	Avg
1995 Angels	Arizona	OF	4	18	2	10	1	0	0	1	1	.556
1995 Lk Elsinore	California	OF	25	113	24	41	7	3	5	24	3	.363
1996 Vancouver	P.C.	OF-1B	85	351	63	107	22	5	6	41	11	.305
1996 California	A.L.	OF	57	208	34	59	5	1	4	20	3	.284
1997 Anaheim	A.L.	1B-OF	139	539	99	161	34	4	16	77	23	.299
1998 Anaheim a	A.L.	OF-1B	133	537	84	159	39	3	19	82	20	.296
1999 Anaheim b	A.L.	1B-OF	142	585	84	148	22	5	13	53	13	.253
2000 Anaheim	A.L.	OF-1B	157	*676	121	*240	39	6	25	100	28	.355
2001 Anaheim	A.L.	OF-1B	157	631	89	163	35	1	9	63	24	.258
2002 Anaheim	A.L.	OF-1B	150	625	99	177	28	4	10	73	23	.283
2003 Salt Lake	P.C.	OF	7	27	6	11	0	0	0	4	1	.407
2003 Anaheim c	A.L.	OF	67	258	35	65	7	1	4	17	9	.252
2004 Salt Lake	P.C.	1B	4	16	2	2	0	0	0	3	0	.125
2004 Anaheim d	A.L.	1B	125	495	79	146	29	1	7	69	16	.295
2005 Los Angeles	A.L.	1B	153	609	86	166	33	3	7	66	10	.273
2006 Rancho Cucamonga	Calif.	1B	7	14	4	3	0	0	0	0	0	.214
2006 Salt Lake	P.C.	OF	7	30	0	3	0	0	0	3	1	.100
2006 Los Angeles e-f	A.L.	OF-1B	40	95	8	21	8	1	0	5	1	.221
2007 Charlotte	Int.	OF-1B	12	47	3	6	0	0	2	0	.128
2007 Chicago g-h	A.L.	OF-1B	87	310	33	77	13	1	4	32	7	.248
2008 Houston	N.L.	OF-1B	140	322	49	89	16	0	4	31	2	.276
Major League Totals		13 Yrs.	1547	5890	900	1671	308	31	122	688	179	.284
Division Series													
2002 Anaheim	A.L.	OF	4	19	4	8	2	0	0	2	1	.421
2004 Anaheim	A.L.	1B	3	10	2	5	1	0	1	2	0	.500
2005 Los Angeles	A.L.	1B	5	20	1	6	2	0	0	3	0	.300
Division Series Totals			12	49	7	19	5	0	1	7	1	.388

56

Year Club	Lea	Pos	G	AB	R	H	2B	3B	HR	RBI	SB	Avg
Championship Series												
2002 Anaheim............	A.L.	OF	5	22	4	8	0	0	1	2	1	.364
2005 Los Angeles..........	A.L.	1B	5	17	1	4	1	0	0	0	1	.235
Championship Series Totals......			10	39	5	12	1	0	1	2		.308
World Series Record												
2002 Anaheim............	A.L.	OF	7	30	6	9	3	0	1	3	1	.300

a On disabled list from August 4 to August 19, 1998.
b On disabled list from August 11 to August 26, 1999.
c On disabled list from April 20 to June 9 and August 7 to October 6, 2003.
d On disabled list from May 9 to June 14, 2004.
e On disabled list from May 1 to June 12 and June 18 to September 1, 2006.
f Filed for free agency, October 28, 2006. Signed with Chicago White Sox, January 25, 2007.
g On disabled list from June 1 to June 22 and June 23 to July 31, 2007.
h Filed for free agency, October 31, 2007. Signed with Houston Astros, December 28, 2007.

ESCOBAR, YUNEL

Born, Havana, Cuba, November 2, 1982.
Bats Right. Throws Right. Height, 6 feet, 2 inches. Weight, 200 pounds.

Year Club	Lea	Pos	G	AB	R	H	2B	3B	HR	RBI	SB	Avg
2005 Danville........	Appal.	SS	8	30	9	12	2	1	2	8	0	.400
2005 Rome...........	So.Atl.	SS	48	198	30	62	13	3	4	19	0	.313
2006 Mississippi....	Southern	SS-3B-2B	121	428	55	113	21	4	2	45	7	.264
2007 Richmond........	Int.	SS	46	180	20	60	10	3	2	29	7	.333
2007 Atlanta...........	N.L.	SS-3B-2B	94	319	54	104	25	0	5	28	5	.326
2008 Atlanta...........	N.L.	SS	136	514	71	148	24	2	10	60	2	.288
Major League Totals...........		2 Yrs.	230	833	125	252	49	2	15	88	7	.303

ETHIER, ANDRE EVERETT

Born, Phoenix, Arizona, April 10, 1982.
Bats Left. Throws Left. Height, 6 feet, 1 inch. Weight, 210 pounds.

Year Club	Lea	Pos	G	AB	R	H	2B	3B	HR	RBI	SB	Avg
2003 Kane County.......	Midwest	OF	40	162	23	44	10	0	0	11	2	.272
2003 Vancouver......	Northwest	OF	10	41	7	16	4	1	1	7	2	.390
2004 Modesto.............	Calif.	OF	99	419	72	131	23	5	7	53	2	.313
2005 Sacramento...........	P.C.	OF	4	15	0	4	1	0	0	2	0	.267
2005 Midland a...........	Texas	OF	131	505	104	161	30	3	18	80	1	.319
2006 Las Vegas...........	P.C.	OF	25	86	15	30	4	3	1	12	2	.349
2006 Los Angeles...........	N.L.	OF	126	396	50	122	20	7	11	55	5	.308
2007 Los Angeles...........	N.L.	OF	153	447	50	127	32	2	13	64	0	.284
2008 Los Angeles...........	N.L.	OF	141	525	90	160	38	5	20	77	6	.305
Major League Totals............		3 Yrs.	420	1368	190	409	90	14	44	196	11	.299
Division Series												
2006 Los Angeles...........	N.L.	OF	2	1	0	0	0	0	0	0	0	.000
2008 Los Angeles...........	N.L.	OF	3	10	2	1	0	0	0	0	0	.100
Division Series Totals......			5	11	2	1	0	0	0	0	0	.091
Championship Series												
2008 Los Angeles...........	N.L.	OF	5	22	4	5	1	0	0	0	0	.227

a Traded by Oakland Athletics to Los Angeles for outfielder Milton Bradley and infielder Antonio Perez, December 13, 2005.

FELIZ, PEDRO JULIO

Born, Azua, Dominican Republic, April 27, 1975.
Bats Right. Throws Right. Height, 6 feet, 1 inch. Weight, 210 pounds.

Year Club	Lea	Pos	G	AB	R	H	2B	3B	HR	RBI	SB	Avg
1994 Giants.........	Arizona	3B	38	119	7	23	0	0	0	3	2	.193
1995 Bellingham...	Northwest	3B-1B	43	113	14	31	2	1	0	16	1	.274
1996 Burlington....	Midwest	3B-1B	93	321	36	85	12	2	5	36	5	.265
1997 Bakersfield...	California	3B	135	515	59	140	25	4	14	56	5	.272
1998 Shreveport......	Texas	3B	100	364	39	96	23	2	12	50	5	.264
1998 Fresno...........	P.C.	3B	3	7	1	3	1	0	1	3	0	.429
1999 Shreveport......	Texas	3B	131	491	52	124	24	6	13	77	4	.253
2000 Fresno...........	P.C.	3B	128	503	85	150	34	2	33	105	1	.298
2000 San Francisco.....	N.L.	3B	8	7	1	2	0	0	0	0	0	.286
2001 San Francisco.....	N.L.	3B	94	220	23	50	9	1	7	22	0	.227
2002 San Francisco.....	N.L.	3B-SS-OF	67	146	14	37	4	1	2	13	0	.253

Year	Club	Lea	Pos	G	AB	R	H	2B	3B	HR	RBI	SB	Avg
2003 San Francisco	N.L.		3B-OF-1B	95	235	31	58	9	3	16	48	2	.247
2004 San Francisco	N.L.		1B-3B-SS-OF	144	503	72	139	33	3	22	84	5	.276
2005 San Francisco	N.L.		3B-OF-1B	156	569	69	142	30	4	20	81	0	.250
2006 San Francisco a	N.L.		3B-OF-SS	160	603	75	147	35	5	22	98	1	.244
2007 San Francisco b	N.L.		3B-1B-OF-C	150	557	61	141	28	2	20	72	2	.253
2008 Clearwater	Fla.St.		3B	1	3	0	0	0	0	0	0	0	.000
2008 Reading	Eastern		3B	2	8	2	4	0	0	2	2	0	.500
2008 Philadelphia c	N.L.		3B-SS	133	425	43	106	19	2	14	58	0	.249
Major League Totals	9 Yrs.			1007	3265	389	822	167	21	123	476	12	.252
Division Series													
2002 San Francisco	N.L.		PH	1	1	0	0	0	0	0	0	0	.000
2003 San Francisco	N.L.		PH	3	3	1	2	0	1	0	1	0	.667
2008 Philadelphia	N.L.		3B	4	13	1	3	1	0	0	1	0	.231
Division Series Totals				8	17	2	5	1	1	0	2	0	.294
Championship Series													
2002 San Francisco	N.L.		PH	1	1	0	0	0	0	0	0	0	.000
2008 Philadelphia	N.L.		3B	5	13	0	2	0	0	0	1	0	.154
Championship Series Totals				6	14	0	2	0	0	0	1	0	.143
World Series Record													
2002 San Francisco	N.L.		DH	3	5	0	0	0	0	0	0	0	.000
2008 Philadelphia	N.L.		3B	5	18	0	6	0	0	0	2	0	.333
World Series Totals...........				8	23	0	6	0	0	0	2	0	.261

a Filed for free agency, November 1, 2006, re-signed with San Francisco Giants, December 4, 2006.
b Filed for free agency, October 29, 2007. Signed with Philadelphia Phillies, January 31, 2008.
c On disabled list from July 25 to August 20, 2008.

FIELDER, PRINCE SEMIEN

Born, Ontario, California, May 9, 1984.
Bats Left. Throws Right. Height, 6 feet. Weight, 260 pounds.

Year	Club	Lea	Pos	G	AB	R	H	2B	3B	HR	RBI	SB	Avg
2002 Beloit	Midwest		1B	32	112	15	27	7	0	3	11	0	.241
2002 Ogden	Pioneer		1B	41	146	35	57	12	0	10	40	3	.390
2003 Beloit	Midwest		1B	137	502	81	157	22	2	27	112	2	.313
2004 Huntsville	Southern		1B-OF	136	497	70	135	29	1	23	78	11	.272
2005 Nashville	P.C.		1B	103	378	68	110	21	0	28	86	8	.291
2005 Milwaukee	N.L.		1B	39	59	2	17	4	0	2	10	0	.288
2006 Milwaukee	N.L.		1B	157	569	82	154	35	1	28	81	7	.271
2007 Milwaukee	N.L.		1B	158	573	109	165	35	2	*50	119	2	.288
2008 Milwaukee	N.L.		1B	159	588	86	162	30	2	34	102	3	.276
Major League Totals	4 Yrs.			513	1789	279	498	104	5	114	312	12	.278
Division Series													
2008 Milwaukee	N.L.		1B	4	14	1	1	0		1	2	0	.071

FIGGINS, DESMOND DECHONE (CHONE)

Born, Leary, Georgia, January 22, 1978.
Bats Both. Throws Right. Height, 5 feet, 7 inches. Weight, 180 pounds.

Year	Club	Lea	Pos	G	AB	R	H	2B	3B	HR	RBI	SB	Avg
1997 Rockies	Arizona		SS	54	214	41	60	5	6	1	23	30	.280
1998 Portland	Northwest		SS	69	269	41	76	9	3	1	26	25	.283
1999 Salem	Carolina		SS	123	444	65	106	12	3	0	22	27	.239
2000 Salem	Carolina		2B	134	522	92	145	26	14	3	48	37	.278
2001 Carolina	Southern		2B-SS	86	332	41	73	14	5	2	25	27	.220
2001 Arkansas a	Texas		2B-SS-3B	39	138	21	37	12	2	0	12	7	.268
2002 Salt Lake	P.C.		2B-SS	125	511	100	156	25	18	7	62	39	.305
2002 Anaheim	A.L.		2B	15	12	6	2	1	0	0	1	2	.167
2003 Salt Lake	P.C.		2B-SS-OF-3B	68	285	55	89	14	15	4	30	16	.312
2003 Anaheim	A.L.		OF-2B-SS	71	240	34	71	9	4	0	27	13	.296
2004 Anaheim	A.L.		3B-OF-2B-SS	148	577	83	171	22	17	5	60	34	.296
2005 Los Angeles	A.L.		OF-3B-2B-SS	158	642	113	186	25	10	8	57	*62	.290
2006 Los Angeles	A.L.		OF-3B-2B-SS	155	604	93	161	23	8	9	62	52	.267
2007 Salt Lake	P.C.		3B	4	14	3	5	1	0	0	1	0	.357
2007 Los Angeles b	A.L.		3B-OF-2B	115	442	81	146	24	6	3	58	41	.330
2008 Salt Lake	P.C.		3B	3	10	2	2	0	0	0	0	0	.200
2008 Los Angeles c	A.L.		3B-2B	116	453	72	125	14	1	1	22	34	.276
Major League Totals	7 Yrs.			778	2970	482	862	118	46	26	287	238	.290

Year	Club	Lea	Pos	G	AB	R	H	2B	3B	HR	RBI	SB	Avg
	Division Series												
2002 Anaheim..........A.L.			DH	1	0	1	0	0	0	0	0	1	.000
2004 Anaheim..........A.L.			2B-3B	3	14	0	2	0	0	0	0	1	.143
2005 Los Angeles......A.L.			3B-OF	5	21	2	3	1	1	0	2	0	.143
2007 Los Angeles......A.L.			OF	3	13	1	3	2	0	0	1	0	.231
2008 Los Angeles......A.L.			3B	4	21	2	7	1	1	0	1	1	.333
Division Series Totals				16	69	6	15	4	2	0	4	3	.217
	Championship Series												
2002 Anaheim..........A.L.			PH	3	1	2	1	0	0	0	0	0	1.000
2005 Los Angeles......A.L.			3B-OF	5	17	1	2	1	0	0	1		.118
Championship Series Totals ..				8	18	3	3	1	0	0	1	1	.167
	World Series Record												
2002 Anaheim..........A.L.			PH	2	0	1	0	0	0	0	0	0	.000

a Traded by Colorado Rockies to Anaheim Angels for outfielder Kimera Bartee, July 13, 2001.
b On disabled list from March 23 to April 30, 2007.
c On disabled list from May 4 to May 21 and May 22 to June 12, 2008.

FLORES, JESUS MIGUEL

Born, Carupano, Venezuela, October 26, 1984.
Bats Right. Throws Right. Height, 6 feet, 1 inch. Weight, 230 pounds.

Year	Club	Lea	Pos	G	AB	R	H	2B	3B	HR	RBI	SB	Avg
2004 Mets..........	Gulf Coast		C	45	141	16	45	12	3	4	25	1	.319
2004 Brooklyn.......	N.Y.-Penn.		C	3	6	1	2	0	1	0	3	0	.333
2005 Hagerstown.....	So.Atl.		C	82	319	34	69	18	0	7	42	2	.216
2006 St. Lucie a.........	Fla.St.		C	120	429	66	114	32	0	21	70	2	.266
2007 Washington..........	N.L.		C	79	180	21	44	9	0	4	25	0	.244
2008 Columbus.........	Int.		C-1B	17	59	8	9	3	0	1	7	0	.153
2008 Washington b........	N.L.		C	90	301	23	77	18	1	8	59	0	.256
Major League Totals			2 Yrs.	169	481	44	121	27	1	12	84	0	.252

a Selected by Washington Nationals from New York Mets in Rule V draft, December 7, 2006.
b On disabled list from September 15 to October 3, 2008.

FLOYD, CORNELIUS CLIFFORD (CLIFF)

Born, Chicago, Illinois, December 5, 1972.
Bats Left. Throws Left. Height, 6 feet, 4 inches. Weight, 230 pounds.

Year	Club	Lea	Pos	G	AB	R	H	2B	3B	HR	RBI	SB	Avg
1991 Bradenton Expos	Gulf C.		1B	56	214	35	56	9	3	6	30	13	.262
1992 Albany	So. Atl.		OF-1B	134	516	83	157	24	*16	16	*97	32	.304
1992 West Palm Beach....	Fla. St.		OF	1	4	0	0	0	0	0	1	0	.000
1993 Harrisburg.........	Eastern		1B-OF	101	380	82	125	17	4	*26	*101	31	.329
1993 Ottawa..............	Int.		1B	32	125	12	30	2	2	2	18	2	.240
1993 Montreal...........	N.L.		1B	10	31	3	7	0	0	1	2	0	.226
1994 Montreal.........	N.L.		1B-OF	100	334	43	94	19	4	4	41	10	.281
1995 Montreal a........	N.L.		1B-OF	29	69	6	9	1	0	1	8	3	.130
1996 Ottawa.............	Int.		OF-3B	20	76	7	23	3	1	1	8	2	.303
1996 Montreal...........	N.L.		OF-1B	117	227	29	55	15	4	6	26	7	.242
1997 Charlotte	Int.		OF-1B	39	131	27	48	10	0	9	33	7	.366
1997 Florida b-c...........	N.L.		OF-1B	61	137	23	32	9	1	6	19	6	.234
1998 Florida	N.L.		OF	153	588	85	166	45	3	22	90	27	.282
1999 Calgary.............	P.C.		OF	9	31	6	12	1	0	3	8	0	.387
1999 Florida d...........	N.L.		OF	69	251	37	76	19	4	11	49	5	.303
2000 Florida	N.L.		OF	121	420	75	126	30	4	22	91	24	.300
2001 Florida	N.L.		OF	149	555	123	176	44	4	31	103	18	.317
2002 Florida-Montreal f ...	N.L.		OF	99	349	56	96	22	0	21	61	11	.275
2002 Boston g-h...........	A.L.		OF	47	171	30	54	21	0	7	18	4	.316
2003 New York i	N.L.		OF	108	365	57	106	25	2	18	68	3	.290
2004 St. Lucie..........	Fla.St.		OF	1	4	2	2	0	0	0	1	0	.500
2004 New York j.........	N.L.		OF	113	396	55	103	26	0	18	63	11	.260
2005 New York	N.L.		OF	150	550	85	150	22	2	34	98	12	.273
2006 Mets.........	Gulf Coast		OF	2	6	2	3	0	0	1	4	0	.500
2006 Brooklyn......	N.Y.-Penn.		OF	1	2	0	0	0	0	0	0	0	.000
2006 St. Lucie..........	Fla.St.		OF	3	10	2	4	0	0	2	4	0	.400
2006 New York k-l........	N.L.		OF	97	332	45	81	19	1	11	44	6	.244
2007 Chicago m.........	N.L.		OF	108	282	40	80	10	1	9	45	0	.284
2008 Tampa Bay n-o	A.L.		DH	80	246	32	66	13	0	11	39	1	.268
Major League Totals			16 Yrs.	1611	5303	824	1477	340	23	233	865	148	.279

Year Club	Lea	Pos	G	AB	R	H	2B	3B	HR	RBI	SB	Avg
Division Series												
2006 New York	N.L.	OF	3	9	3	4	0	0	1	2	0	.444
2007 Chicago	N.L.	OF	2	5	0	0	0	0	0	0	0	.000
2008 Tampa Bay	N.L.	DH	2	5	1	1	1	0	0	1	0	.200
Division Series Totals			7	19	4	5	1	0	1	3	0	.263
Championship Series												
2006 New York	N.L.	OF	3	3	0	0	0	0	0	0	0	.000
2008 Tampa Bay	N.L.	DH	4	10	1	2	0	0	1	1	0	.200
Championship Series Totals			7	13	1	2	0	0	1	1	0	.154
World Series Record												
1997 Florida	N.L.	DH	4	2	1	0	0	0	0	0	0	.000
2008 Tampa Bay	N.L.	DH	1	3	1	1	0	0	0	0	0	.333
World Series Totals			5	5	2	1	0	0	0	0	0	.200

a On disabled list from May 16 to September 11, 1995.
b Traded to Florida Marlins for pitcher Dustin Hermanson and outfielder Joe Orsulak, March 26, 1997.
c On disabled list from May 9 to May 24 and June 21 to September 1, 1997.
d On disabled list from March 30 to April 27 and June 20 to September 7, 1999.
e On disabled list from July 29 to August 28, 2000.
f Traded to Montreal Expos with infielder Wilton Guerrero and cash for pitcher Carl Pavano, pitcher Graeme Lloyd, infielder Mike Mordecai and pitcher Justin Wayne, July 11, 2002.
g Traded to Boston Red Sox for pitcher Sun-Woo Kim, pitcher Seung Song and player to be named later, July 30, 2002.
h Filed for free agency, October 28, 2002. Signed with New York Mets, December 20, 2002.
i On disabled list from August 19 to November 6, 2003.
j On disabled list from April 12 to May 13, 2004.
k On disabled list from June 7 to June 30 and August 9 to September 2, 2006.
l Filed for free agency, October 28, 2006. Signed with Chicago Cubs, January 24, 2007.
m Filed for free agency, October 31, 2007. Signed with Tampa Bay Devil Rays, December 14, 2007.
n On disabled list from April 7 to May 10, 2008.
o Not offered contract, November 3, 2008.

FONTENOT, MICHAEL EUGENE (MIKE)

Born, Slidell, Louisiana, June 9, 1980.
Bats Left. Throws Right. Height, 5 feet, 8 inches. Weight, 165 pounds.

Year Club	Lea	Pos	G	AB	R	H	2B	3B	HR	RBI	SB	Avg
2002 Frederick	Carolina	2B	122	481	61	127	16	4	8	53	13	.264
2003 Bowie	Eastern	2B	126	449	63	146	24	5	12	66	16	.325
2004 Ottawa	Int.	2B	136	524	73	146	30	10	8	49	14	.279
2005 Iowa.............	P.C.	2B-3B-SS-OF	111	379	60	103	22	10	6	39	3	.272
2005 Chicago a.........	N.L.	DH	7	2	0	0	0	0	0	0	0	.000
2006 Iowa.............	P.C.	2B-3B-SS	111	362	54	107	28	2	8	36	5	.296
2007 Iowa.............	P.C.	SS-2B-3B-OF	55	211	46	71	17	4	6	34	3	.336
2007 Chicago	N.L.	2B-SS	86	234	32	65	12	4	3	29	5	.278
2008 Chicago	N.L.	2B-SS	119	243	42	74	22	1	9	40	2	.305
Major League Totals		3 Yrs.	212	479	78	139	34	5	12	69	7	.290
Division Series												
2007 Chicago	N.L.	PH	2	2	0	0	0	0	0	0	0	.000
2008 Chicago	N.L.	2B	3	6	0	2	0	0	0	0	0	.333
Division Series Totals			5	8	0	2	0	0	0	0	0	.250

a Traded to Chicago Cubs by Baltimore Orioles with infielder Jerry Hairston and pitcher Dave Crouthers for outfielder Sammy Sosa, February 2, 2005.

FRANCISCO, LOUIS BEN (BEN)

Born, Santa Ana, California, October 23, 1981.
Bats Right. Throws Right. Height, 6 feet, 1 inch. Weight, 190 pounds.

Year Club	Lea	Pos	G	AB	R	H	2B	3B	HR	RBI	SB	Avg
2002 Mahoning Valley..	N.Y.-Penn.	OF	58	235	55	82	23	2	3	23	22	.349
2003 Lake County........	So.Atl.	OF	80	289	57	83	21	1	11	48	15	.287
2004 Akron	Eastern	OF	133	497	72	126	29	3	15	71	21	.254
2005 Akron	Eastern	OF	83	323	45	99	19	7	7	46	15	.307
2005 Buffalo	Int.	OF	4	16	4	8	1	0	0	3	1	.500
2006 Buffalo	Int.	OF	134	515	80	143	32	4	17	59	25	.278
2007 Buffalo	Int.	OF	95	377	60	120	27	2	12	51	22	.318
2007 Cleveland	A.L.	OF	25	62	10	17	5	0	3	12	0	.274
2008 Buffalo	Int.	OF	24	92	9	21	3	1	1	6	3	.228
2008 Cleveland	A.L.	OF	121	447	65	119	32	0	15	54	4	.266
Major League Totals		2 Yrs.	146	509	75	136	37	0	18	66	4	.267

FRANCOEUR, JEFFREY BRADEN (JEFF)

Born, Atlanta, Georgia, January 8, 1984.
Bats Right. Throws Right. Height, 6 feet, 4 inches. Weight, 220 pounds.

Year Club	Lea	Pos	G	AB	R	H	2B	3B	HR	RBI	SB	Avg
2002 Danville	Appal.	OF	38	147	31	48	12	1	8	31	8	.327
2003 Rome	So.Atl.	OF	134	524	78	147	26	9	14	68	14	.281
2004 Myrtle Beach	Carolina	OF	88	334	56	98	26	0	15	52	10	.293
2004 Greenville	Southern	OF	18	76	8	15	2	0	3	9	1	.197
2005 Mississippi	Southern	OF	84	335	40	92	28	2	13	62	13	.275
2005 Atlanta	N.L.	OF	70	257	41	77	20	1	14	45	3	.300
2006 Atlanta	N.L.	OF	*162	651	83	169	24	6	29	103	1	.260
2007 Atlanta	N.L.	OF	*162	642	84	188	40	0	19	105	5	.293
2008 Mississippi	Southern	OF	3	13	3	7	0	1	0	2	0	.538
2008 Atlanta	N.L.	OF	155	599	70	143	33	3	11	71	0	.239
Major League Totals	4 Yrs.		549	2149	278	577	117	10	73	324	9	.268
Division Series												
2005 Atlanta	N.L.	OF	4	17	2	4	1	1	0	1	0	.235

FRANDSEN, KEVIN VINCENT

Born, San Jose, California, May 24, 1982.
Bats Right. Throws Right. Height, 6 feet. Weight, 175 pounds.

Year Club	Lea	Pos	G	AB	R	H	2B	3B	HR	RBI	SB	Avg
2004 Salem-Keizer	Northwest	2B-SS	25	98	22	29	5	0	3	14	0	.296
2005 San Jose	Calif.	2B-SS	75	291	57	102	22	3	2	40	13	.351
2005 Norwich	Eastern	2B-SS-3B	33	129	22	37	8	0	2	20	7	.287
2005 Fresno	P.C.	2B	20	94	18	33	10	1	2	16	1	.351
2006 Fresno	P.C.	2B-3B-SS	71	293	46	89	25	3	3	30	7	.304
2006 San Jose	Calif.	SS	2	7	1	3	0	0	0	1	0	.429
2006 San Francisco a	N.L.	2B-SS	41	93	12	20	4	0	2	7	0	.215
2007 Fresno	P.C.	SS	19	67	13	27	5	0	1	7	0	.403
2007 San Francisco	N.L.	2B-SS-OF-3B	109	264	26	71	12	1	5	31	4	.269
2008 San Francisco b	N.L.	PH	1	1	0	0	0	0	0	0	0	.000
Major League Totals	3 Yrs.		151	358	38	91	16	1	7	38	4	.254

a On disabled list from August 18 to September 2, 2006.
b On disabled list from March 21 to September 27, 2008.

FREEL, RYAN PAUL

Born, Jacksonville, Florida, March 8, 1976.
Bats Right. Throws Right. Height, 5 feet, 10 inches. Weight, 180 pounds.

Year Club	Lea	Pos	G	AB	R	H	2B	3B	HR	RBI	SB	Avg
1995 St.Cathrnes	N.Y.-Penn.	2B	65	243	30	68	10	5	3	29	12	.280
1996 Dunedin	Fla.St.	2B-3B	104	381	64	97	23	3	4	41	19	.255
1997 Knoxville	Southern	SS	33	94	18	19	1	1	0	4	5	.202
1997 Dunedin	Fla.St.	SS-OF-2B	61	181	42	51	8	2	3	17	24	.282
1998 Knoxville	Southern	OF-2B-SS	66	252	47	72	17	3	4	36	18	.286
1998 Syracuse	Int.	OF-2B	37	118	19	27	4	0	2	12	9	.229
1999 Syracuse	Int.	OF	20	77	15	23	3	2	1	11	10	.299
1999 Knoxville	Southern	OF	11	46	9	13	5	1	1	9	4	.283
2000 Dunedin	Fla.St.	OF	4	18	7	9	1	0	3	6	4	.500
2000 Syracuse	Int.	2B-OF-3B-SS	80	283	62	81	14	5	10	30	30	.286
2000 Tennessee	Southern	OF-2B	12	44	11	13	3	1	0	8	2	.295
2001 Toronto	A.L.	2B-OF	9	22	1	6	1	0	0	3	2	.273
2001 Syracuse a	Int.	OF-2B-3B-SS	85	319	60	83	21	3	5	33	22	.260
2002 Durham b	Int.	2B-OF	119	448	65	117	27	4	8	48	37	.261
2003 Louisville	Int.	2B-OF-3B	54	215	38	59	11	1	3	12	25	.274
2003 Cincinnati c	N.L.	OF-2B-3B	43	137	23	39	6	1	4	12	9	.285
2004 Cincinnati	N.L.	OF-3B-2B	143	505	74	140	21	8	3	28	37	.277
2005 Chattanooga	Southern	2B-OF-3B	5	17	3	3	0	0	0	1	0	.176
2005 Cincinnati d	N.L.	OF-2B-3B	103	369	69	100	19	3	4	21	36	.271
2006 Cincinnati	N.L.	OF-2B-3B	132	454	67	123	30	2	8	27	37	.271
2007 Louisville	Int.	OF-3B	8	33	6	11	2	0	0	3	2	.333
2007 Cincinnati e	N.L.	OF-3B-2B	75	277	44	68	13	3	3	16	15	.245
2008 Cincinnati f-g	N.L.	OF-3B-2B	48	131	17	39	8	0	0	10	6	.298
Major League Totals	7 Yrs.		553	1895	295	515	98	17	22	117	142	.272

a Filed for free agency, October 19, 2001. Signed with Tampa Bay Devil Rays organization, November 8, 2001.
b Filed for free agency, October 15, 2002. Signed with Cincinnati Reds organization, November 19, 2002.
c On disabled list from May 29 to July 4, 2003.

61

d On disabled list from June 19 to July 20 and August 16 to September 5, 2005.
e On disabled list from May 29 to July 3 and August 3 to November 2, 2007.
f On disabled list from June 4 to November 6, 2008.
g Traded to Baltimore Orioles with infielder Brandon Waring and infielder Justin Turner for catcher Ramon Hernandez and cash, December 9, 2008.

FUKUDOME, KOSUKE

Born, Kagoshima, Japan, April 26, 1977.
Bats Left. Throws Right. Height, 6 feet. Weight, 185 pounds.

Year Club	Lea	Pos	G	AB	R	H	2B	3B	HR	RBI	SB	Avg
1999 Chunichi	Japan Cent.	OF	132	461	76	131	25	2	16	52	4	.284
2000 Chunichi	Japan Cent.	OF	97	316	50	80	18	2	13	42	8	.253
2001 Chunichi	Japan Cent.	OF	120	375	51	94	22	2	15	56	8	.251
2002 Chunichi	Japan Cent.	OF	140	542	85	186	42	3	19	65	4	.343
2003 Chunichi	Japan Cent.	OF	140	528	107	165	30	11	34	96	10	.313
2004 Chunichi	Japan Cent.	OF	92	350	61	97	19	7	23	81	8	.277
2005 Chunichi	Japan Cent.	OF	142	515	102	169	39	6	28	103	1	.328
2006 Chunichi	Japan Cent.	OF	130	496	117	174	47	5	31	104	1	.351
2007 Chunichi a	Japan Cent.	OF	81	269	64	79	22	0	13	48	1	.294
2008 Chicago	N.L.	OF	150	501	79	129	25	3	10	58	12	.257
Division Series												
2008 Chicago	N.L.	OF	3	10	0	1	0	0	0	0	0	.100

a Signed with Chicago Cubs, December 12, 2007.

FURCAL, RAFAEL

Born, Loma de Cabrera, Dominican Republic, August 24, 1977.
Bats Both. Throws Right. Height, 5 feet, 8 inches. Weight, 195 pounds.

Year Club	Lea	Pos	G	AB	R	H	2B	3B	HR	RBI	SB	Avg
1997 Braves	Gulf Coast	2B-OF	50	190	31	49	5	4	1	9	15	.258
1998 Danville	Appal.	2B	66	268	56	88	15	4	0	23	60	.328
1999 Myrtle Beach	Carolina	SS	43	184	32	54	9	3	0	12	23	.293
1999 Macon	So.Atl.	SS	83	335	73	113	15	1	1	29	73	.337
2000 Greenville	Southern	SS	3	10	1	2	0	0	1	3	0	.200
2000 Atlanta a-b	N.L.	SS-2B	131	455	87	134	20	4	4	37	40	.295
2001 Atlanta c	N.L.	SS	79	324	39	89	19	0	4	30	22	.275
2002 Atlanta	N.L.	SS-2B	154	636	95	175	31	8	8	47	27	.275
2003 Atlanta	N.L.	SS	156	664	130	194	35	*10	15	61	25	.292
2004 Atlanta	N.L.	SS-2B	143	563	103	157	24	5	14	59	29	.279
2005 Atlanta d	N.L.	SS	154	616	100	175	31	11	12	58	46	.284
2006 Los Angeles	N.L.	SS	159	654	113	196	32	9	15	63	37	.300
2007 Inland Empire	Calif.	SS	2	6	0	1	0	0	0	0	1	.167
2007 Los Angeles e	N.L.	SS	138	581	87	157	23	4	6	47	25	.270
2008 Las Vegas	P.C.	SS	1	3	0	1	1	0	0	1	0	.333
2008 Los Angeles f-g	N.L.	SS	36	143	34	51	12	2	5	16	8	.357
Major League Totals	9 Yrs.		1150	4636	788	1328	227	53	83	418	259	.286
Division Series												
2000 Atlanta	N.L.	SS	3	11	2	1	0	0	0	0	1	.091
2002 Atlanta	N.L.	SS	5	24	2	6	1	1	0	2	1	.250
2003 Atlanta	N.L.	SS	5	19	3	4	0	0	0	0	1	.211
2004 Atlanta	N.L.	SS	5	21	5	8	0	1	2	4	3	.381
2005 Atlanta	N.L.	SS	4	20	1	3	0	0	0	0	3	.150
2006 Los Angeles	N.L.	SS	3	11	1	2	0	0	0	1	2	.182
2008 Los Angeles	N.L.	SS	3	12	4	4	0	0	0	2	0	.333
Division Series Totals			28	118	18	28	1	2	2	9	11	.237
Championship Series												
2008 Los Angeles	N.L.	SS	5	19	5	4	0	0	1	1	0	.211

a On disabled list from June 13 to June 28, 2000.
b Selected Rookie of the Year in National League for 2000.
c On disabled list from July 7 to November 6, 2001.
d Filed for free agency, October 31, 2005. Signed with Los Angeles Dodgers, December 7, 2005.
e On disabled list from March 23 to April 13, 2007.
f On disabled list from May 6 to September 24, 2008.
g Filed for free agency, November 3, 2008, re-signed with Los Angeles Dodgers, December 19, 2008.

GARCIAPARRA, ANTHONY NOMAR (NOMAR)

Born, Whittier, Calif., July 23, 1973.
Bats Right. Throws Right. Height, 6 feet. Weight, 190 pounds.

Year Club	Lea	Pos	G	AB	R	H	2B	3B	HR	RBI	SB	Avg
1994 Sarasota	Fla.St.	SS	28	105	20	31	8	1	1	16	5	.295
1995 Trenton	Eastern	SS	125	513	77	137	20	8	8	47	35	.267
1996 Red Sox	Gulf Coast	SS	5	14	4	4	2	1	0	5	0	.286
1996 Pawtucket	Int.	SS	43	172	40	59	15	2	16	46	3	.343
1996 Boston	A.L.	SS-2B	24	87	11	21	2	3	4	16	5	.241
1997 Boston a	A.L.	SS	153	*684	122	*209	44	*11	30	98	22	.306
1998 Boston b	A.L.	SS	143	604	111	195	37	8	35	122	12	.323
1999 Boston	A.L.	SS	135	532	103	190	42	4	27	104	14	*.357
2000 Boston c	A.L.	SS	140	529	104	197	51	3	21	96	5	*.372
2001 Pawtucket	Int.	SS	4	16	3	7	2	0	1	4	0	.438
2001 Boston d	A.L.	SS	21	83	13	24	3	0	4	8	0	.289
2002 Boston	A.L.	SS	156	635	101	197	56	5	24	120	5	.310
2003 Boston	A.L.	SS	156	658	120	198	37	13	28	105	19	.301
2004 Pawtucket	Int.	SS	6	21	1	5	1	0	1	3	0	.238
2004 Boston	A.L.	SS	38	156	24	50	7	3	5	21	2	.321
2004 Chicago e-f-g	N.L.	SS	43	165	28	49	14	0	4	20	2	.297
2005 Cubs	Arizona	SS	2	5	0	1	0	0	0	0	0	.200
2005 Peoria	Midwest	SS	2	5	1	1	0	0	0	2	0	.200
2005 West Tenn	Southern	SS	4	13	2	3	0	0	0	2	0	.231
2005 Chicago h-i	N.L.	3B-SS	62	230	28	65	12	0	9	30	0	.283
2006 Las Vegas	P.C.	1B	2	8	3	4	2	0	0	1	0	.500
2006 Los Angeles j-k	N.L.	1B	122	469	82	142	31	2	20	93	3	.303
2007 Los Angeles l	N.L.	1B-3B	121	431	39	122	17	0	7	59	3	.283
2008 Las Vegas	P.C.	3B-SS	7	20	4	9	1	0	1	4	0	.450
2008 Los Angeles m-n	N.L.	SS-3B-1B	55	163	24	43	9	0	8	28	1	.264
Major League Totals		13 Yrs.	1369	5426	910	1702	362	52	226	920	93	.314
Division Series												
1998 Boston	A.L.	SS	4	15	4	5	1	0	3	11	0	.333
1999 Boston	A.L.	SS	4	12	6	5	2	0	2	4	0	.417
2003 Boston	A.L.	SS	5	20	2	6	1	0	0	0	1	.300
2006 Los Angeles	N.L.	1B	3	9	0	2	1	0	0	2	0	.222
Division Series Totals			16	56	12	18	5	0	5	17	1	.321
Championship Series												
1999 Boston	A.L.	SS	5	20	2	8	2	0	2	5	1	.400
2003 Boston	A.L.	SS	7	29	2	7	0	1	0	1	0	.241
2008 Los Angeles	N.L.	3B-1B	4	7	0	3	0	0	0	1	0	.429
Championship Series Totals			16	56	4	18	2	1	2	7	1	.321

a Selected Rookie of the Year in American League for 1997.
b On disabled list from May 9 to May 28, 1998.
c On disabled list from May 12 to May 26, 2000.
d On disabled list from March 21 to July 29 and August 27 to November 7, 2001.
e On disabled list from March 26 to June 9, 2004.
f Traded to Chicago Cubs with outfielder Matt Murton for infielder Orlando Cabrera and infielder Doug Mientkiewicz, July 31, 2004.
g Filed for free agency, October 29, 2004, re-signed with Chicago Cubs, December 7, 2004.
h On disabled list from April 21 to August 5, 2005.
i Filed for free agency, October 28, 2005. Signed with Los Angeles Dodgers December 19, 2005.
j On disabled list from April 3 to April 22 and July 30 to August 9, 2006.
k Filed for free agency, October 28, 2006, re-signed with Los Angeles Dodgers, November 20, 2006.
l On disabled list from August 14 to September 4, 2007.
m On disabled list from March 21 to April 16 and April 26 to July 4 and July 28 to August 12, 2008.
n Filed for free agency, October 31, 2008.

GARKO, RYAN F.

Born, Pittsburgh, Pennsylvania, January 2, 1981.
Bats Right. Throws Right. Height, 6 feet, 2 inches. Weight, 225 pounds.

Year Club	Lea	Pos	G	AB	R	H	2B	3B	HR	RBI	SB	Avg
2003 Mahoning Valley	N.Y.-Penn.	C	45	165	23	45	8	1	4	16	1	.273
2004 Kinston	Carolina	1B-C	65	238	44	78	17	1	16	57	4	.328
2004 Akron	Eastern	C-1B	43	172	29	57	15	0	6	38	1	.331
2004 Buffalo	Int.	1B-C	5	20	2	7	1	0	0	4	0	.350
2005 Buffalo	Int.	1B-C	127	452	75	137	25	3	19	77	1	.303
2005 Cleveland	A.L.	DH	1	1	0	0	0	0	0	0	0	.000
2006 Buffalo	Int.	1B-C	103	364	43	90	18	0	15	59	4	.247
2006 Cleveland	A.L.	1B	50	185	28	54	12	0	7	45	0	.292

Year	Club	Lea	Pos	G	AB	R	H	2B	3B	HR	RBI	SB	Avg
2007 Cleveland	A.L.	1B	138	484	62	140	29	1	21	61	0	.289
2008 Cleveland	A.L.	1B	141	495	61	135	21	1	14	90	0	.273
Major League Totals		4 Yrs.	330	1165	151	329	62	2	42	196	0	.282
Division Series												
2007 Cleveland	A.L.	1B	3	11	3	4	0	0	1	3	0	.364
Championship Series												
2007 Cleveland	A.L.	1B	6	24	4	7	2	1	0	2	0	.292

GATHRIGHT, JOEY RENARD

Born, Hattiesburg, Mississippi, April 22, 1981.
Bats Left. Throws Right. Height, 5 feet, 10 inches. Weight, 185 pounds.

Year	Club	Lea	Pos	G	AB	R	H	2B	3B	HR	RBI	SB	Avg
2002 Charleston-SC	So.Atl.	OF	59	208	30	55	1	0	0	14	22	.264
2003 Bakersfield ...	California	OF	89	340	65	110	6	3	0	23	57	.324
2003 Orlando	Southern	OF	22	85	12	32	1	0	0	5	12	.376
2004 Montgomery	Southern	OF	32	126	23	43	5	1	0	8	10	.341
2004 Durham	Int.	OF	60	236	34	77	9	1	0	8	33	.326
2004 Tampa Bay	A.L.	OF	19	52	11	13	0	0	0	1	6	.250
2005 Durham	Int.	OF	58	226	46	69	10	5	1	18	31	.305
2005 Tampa Bay	A.L.	OF	76	203	29	56	7	3	0	13	20	.276
2006 Durham	Int.	OF	10	31	5	8	2	0	0	1	6	.258
2006 Tampa Bay-Kansas City a.	A.L.	OF	134	383	59	91	12	3	1	41	22	.238
2007 Omaha	P.C.	OF	60	223	44	76	10	4	0	25	25	.341
2007 Kansas City	A.L.	OF	74	228	28	70	8	0	0	19	9	.307
2008 Omaha	P.C.	OF	9	33	3	5	0	0	0	0	1	.152
2008 Kansas City b-c	A.L.	OF	105	279	41	71	3	1	0	22	21	.254
Major League Totals		5 Yrs.	408	1145	168	301	30	7	1	96	78	.263

a Traded to Kansas City Royals with infielder Fernando Cortez for pitcher J.P. Howell, June 20, 2006.
b On disabled list from July 24 to August 21, 2008.
c Not offered contract, December 12, 2008. Signed with Chicago Cubs, December 16, 2008.

GERMAN, ESTEBAN (GURIDI)

Born, Haina, Dominican Republic, January 26, 1978.
Bats Right. Throws Right. Height, 5 feet, 10 inches. Weight, 180 pounds.

Year	Club	Lea	Pos	G	AB	R	H	2B	3B	HR	RBI	SB	Avg
1997 Oaklnd-East .	Dominican	2B	69	249	69	79	17	1	2	29	58	.317
1998 Athletics.......	Arizona	2B	55	202	52	62	3	10	2	28	40	.307
1998 Oaklnd West.	Dominican	2B	10	32	9	10	1	1	0	4	1	.313
1999 Modesto........	Calif.	2B	128	501	107	156	16	12	4	52	40	.311
2000 Visalia	Calif.	2B-SS	109	428	82	113	14	10	2	35	78	.264
2000 Midland	Texas	2B	24	75	13	16	1	0	1	6	5	.213
2001 Sacramento	P.C.	2B	38	150	40	56	8	0	4	14	17	.373
2001 Midland	Texas	2B	92	335	79	95	20	3	6	30	31	.284
2002 Sacramento	P.C.	2B	121	458	72	126	16	4	2	43	26	.275
2002 Oakland	A.L.	2B	9	35	4	7	0	0	0	0	1	.200
2003 Sacramento	P.C.	2B	115	467	86	143	20	8	3	51	32	.306
2003 Oakland	A.L.	2B	5	4	0	1	0	0	0	1	0	.250
2004 Oakland	A.L.	3B-2B	31	60	9	15	1	1	0	7	0	.250
2004 Sacramento a-b	P.C.	2B-SS	55	231	33	76	8	4	2	29	18	.329
2005 Oklahoma........	P.C.	3B-SS-2B-OF	117	489	103	153	27	6	5	68	43	.313
2005 Texas c........	A.L.	2B-3B	5	4	3	3	1	0	0	1	2	.750
2006 Kansas City	A.L.	2B-OF-3B	106	279	44	91	18	5	3	34	7	.326
2007 Kansas City	A.L.	2B-3B-OF-SS	121	348	49	92	15	6	4	37	11	.264
2008 Kansas City	A.L.	OF-2B-3B-SS	89	216	30	53	14	3	0	22	7	.245
Major League Totals		7 Yrs.	366	946	139	262	49	15	7	102	28	.277

a On disabled list from July 4 to July 31, 2004.
b Filed for free agency, October 15, 2004. Signed with Texas Rangers organization, November 19, 2004.
c Traded to Kansas City Royals for pitcher Fabio Castro, December 8, 2005.

GERUT, JOSEPH DIEGO (JODY)

Born, Elmhurst, Illinois, September 18, 1977.
Bats Left. Throws Left. Height, 6 feet. Weight, 210 pounds.

Year	Club	Lea	Pos	G	AB	R	H	2B	3B	HR	RBI	SB	Avg
1999 Salem...........	Carolina	OF	133	499	80	144	33	11	11	63	25	.289
2000 Carolina	Southern	OF	109	362	48	103	32	3	3	57	18	.285
2002 Akron...........	Eastern	OF	65	256	44	72	15	2	9	39	17	.281

Year Club	Lea	Pos	G	AB	R	H	2B	3B	HR	RBI	SB	Avg
2002 Buffalo a-b	Int.	OF	55	183	31	59	7	2	1	21	3	.322
2003 Buffalo	Int.	OF	17	65	13	18	5	0	5	19	4	.277
2003 Cleveland	A.L.	OF	127	480	66	134	33	2	22	75	4	.279
2004 Cleveland c	A.L.	OF	134	481	72	121	31	5	11	51	13	.252
2005 Buffalo	Int.	OF	12	48	12	21	5	0	3	8	0	.438
2005 Cleveland d-e	A.L.	OF	44	138	12	38	9	1	1	12	1	.275
2005 Chicago-Pittsburgh f-g	N.L.	OF	15	32	3	5	2	0	0	2	0	.156
2006 Pittsburgh h	N.L.	INJURED—Did Not Play										
2007		Did Not Play										
2008 Portland i	P.C.	OF	27	107	22	33	9	2	5	18	4	.308
2008 San Diego	N.L.	OF	100	328	46	97	15	4	14	43	6	.296
Major League Totals	4 Yrs.		420	1459	199	395	90	12	48	183	24	.271

a Traded by Colorado Rockies with catcher Josh Bard to Cleveland Indians for outfielder Jacob Cruz, June 2, 2001.
b On disabled list from April 5 to September 4, 2001.
c On disabled list from September 18 to November 15, 2004.
d On disabled list from March 20 to May 13, 2005.
e Traded to Chicago Cubs for outfielder Jason Dubois, July 18, 2005.
f On disabled list from August 11 to October 3, 2005.
g Traded to Pittsburgh Pirates for outfielder Matt Lawton and cash, July 31, 2005.
h On disabled list from May 21 to November 7, 2006.
i Released by Pittsburgh Pirates, March 8, 2007. Signed with San Diego Padres organization, January 21, 2008.

GIAMBI, JASON GILBERT

Born, West Covina, California, January 8, 1971.
Bats Left. Throws Right. Height, 6 feet, 3 inches. Weight, 230 pounds.

Year Club	Lea	Pos	G	AB	R	H	2B	3B	HR	RBI	SB	Avg
1992 South Oregon	Northwest	3B	13	41	9	13	3	0	3	13	1	.317
1993 Modesto	California	3B	89	313	72	91	16	2	12	60	2	.291
1994 Huntsville	Southern	3B-1B	56	193	31	43	9	0	6	30	0	.223
1994 Tacoma	P.C.	3B-1B-SS	52	176	28	56	20	0	4	38	1	.318
1995 Edmonton	P.C.	3B-1B	55	190	34	65	26	1	3	41	0	.342
1995 Oakland	A.L.	3B-1B	54	176	27	45	7	0	6	25	2	.256
1996 Oakland	A.L.	1B-OF-3B	140	536	84	156	40	1	20	79	0	.291
1997 Oakland	A.L.	OF-1B	142	519	66	152	41	2	20	81	0	.293
1998 Oakland	A.L.	1B	153	562	92	166	28	0	27	110	2	.295
1999 Oakland	A.L.	1B-3B	158	575	115	181	36	1	33	123	1	.315
2000 Oakland a	A.L.	1B	152	510	108	170	29	1	43	137	2	.333
2001 Oakland b	A.L.	1B	154	520	109	178	*47	2	38	120	2	.342
2002 New York	A.L.	1B	155	560	120	176	34	1	41	122	2	.314
2003 New York	A.L.	1B	156	535	97	134	25	0	41	107	2	.250
2004 Tampa	Fla.St.	1B	2	6	0	1	0	0	0	0	0	.167
2004 New York c	A.L.	1B	.80	264	33	55	9	0	12	40	0	.208
2005 New York	A.L.	1B	139	417	74	113	14	0	32	87	0	.271
2006 New York	A.L.	DH-1B	139	446	92	113	25	0	37	113	2	.253
2007 Tampa	Fla.St.	DH	5	13	0	4	1	0	0	1	0	.308
2007 Scranton-WB	Int.	1B	4	9	1	1	0	0	1	1	0	.111
2007 New York d	A.L.	DH-1B	83	254	31	60	8	0	14	39	1	.236
2008 New York e	A.L.	1B	145	458	68	113	19	1	32	96	2	.247
Major League Totals	14 Yrs.		1850	6332	1116	1812	362	9	396	1279	18	.286
Division Series												
2000 Oakland	A.L.	1B	5	14	2	4	0	0	0	1	1	.286
2001 Oakland	A.L.	1B	5	17	2	6	0	0	1	4	0	.353
2002 New York	A.L.	1B-DH	4	14	5	5	0	0	1	3	0	.357
2003 New York	A.L.	DH	4	16	1	4	2	0	0	2	0	.250
2005 New York	A.L.	1B-DH	5	19	1	8	3	0	0	2	0	.421
2006 New York	A.L.	DH-1B	3	8	1	1	0	0	1	2	1	.125
2007 New York	A.L.	1B	3	4	0	1	0	0	0	0	0	.250
Division Series Totals			29	92	12	29	5	0	3	14	2	.315
Championship Series												
2003 New York	A.L.	DH	7	26	4	6	0	0	3	3	0	.231
World Series Record												
2003 New York	A.L.	1B	6	17	2	4	1	0	1	1	0	.235

a Selected Most Valuable Player in American League for 2000.
b Filed for free agency, November 5, 2001. Signed with New York Yankees, December 13, 2001.
c On disabled list from May 22 to June 6 and from July 26 to September 14, 2004.
d On disabled list from May 31 to August 7, 2007.
e Not offered contract, November 4, 2008. Signed with Oakland A's, January 7, 2009.

GILES, BRIAN STEPHEN
Born, El Cajon, California, January 20, 1971.
Bats Left. Throws Left. Height, 5 feet, 10 inches. Weight, 205 pounds.

Year Club	Lea	Pos	G	AB	R	H	2B	3B	HR	RBI	SB	Avg
1989 Burlington	Appal.	OF	36	129	18	40	7	0	0	20	6	.310
1990 Watertown	N.Y.-Penn.	OF	70	246	44	71	15	2	1	23	11	.289
1991 Kinston	Carolina	OF	125	394	71	122	14	0	4	47	19	.310
1992 Canton-Akrn.	Eastern	OF	23	74	6	16	4	0	0	3	3	.216
1992 Kinston	Carolina	OF	42	140	28	37	5	1	3	18	3	.264
1993 Canton-Akrn.	Eastern	OF	123	425	64	139	17	6	8	64	18	.327
1994 Charlotte	Int.	OF	128	434	74	136	18	3	16	58	8	.313
1995 Buffalo	A.A.	OF	123	413	67	128	18	8	15	67	7	.310
1995 Cleveland	A.L.	OF	6	9	6	5	0	0	1	3	0	.556
1996 Buffalo	A.A.	OF	83	318	65	100	17	6	20	64	1	.314
1996 Cleveland	A.L.	DH-OF	51	121	26	43	14	1	5	27	3	.355
1997 Cleveland	A.L.	OF	130	377	62	101	15	3	17	61	13	.268
1998 Buffalo	Int.	OF	13	46	5	11	2	0	2	7	0	.239
1998 Cleveland a-b	A.L.	OF	112	350	56	94	19	0	16	66	10	.269
1999 Pittsburgh	N.L.	OF	141	521	109	164	33	3	39	115	6	.315
2000 Pittsburgh	N.L.	OF	156	559	111	176	37	7	35	123	6	.315
2001 Pittsburgh	N.L.	OF	160	576	116	178	37	7	37	95	13	.309
2002 Pittsburgh	N.L.	OF	153	497	95	148	37	5	38	103	15	.298
2003 Pittsburgh-San Diego c-d-e	N.L.	OF	134	492	93	147	34	6	20	88	4	.299
2004 San Diego	N.L.	OF	159	609	97	173	33	7	23	94	10	.284
2005 San Diego f	N.L.	OF	158	545	92	164	38	8	15	83	13	.301
2006 San Diego	N.L.	OF	158	604	87	159	37	1	14	83	9	.263
2007 Lake Elsinore	Calif.	OF	3	10	2	4	0	0	1	3	0	.400
2007 San Diego g	N.L.	OF	121	483	72	131	27	2	13	51	4	.271
2008 San Diego	N.L.	OF	147	559	81	171	40	4	12	63	2	.306
Major League Totals		14 Yrs.	1786	6302	1103	1854	401	54	285	1055	108	.294
Division Series												
1996 Cleveland	A.L.	PH	1	1	0	0	0	0	0	0	0	.000
1997 Cleveland	A.L.	OF	3	7	0	1	0	0	0	0	0	.143
1998 Cleveland	A.L.	OF-DH	3	10	1	2	1	0	0	0	0	.200
2005 San Diego	N.L.	OF	3	13	0	3	0	0	0	1	1	.231
2006 San Diego	N.L.	OF	4	14	1	4	1	0	0	1	0	.286
Division Series Totals			14	45	2	10	2	0	0	2	1	.222
Championship Series												
1997 Cleveland	A.L.	OF	6	16	1	3	3	0	0	0	0	.188
1998 Cleveland	A.L.	OF	4	12	0	1	0	0	0	0	0	.083
Championship Series Totals			10	28	1	4	3	0	0	0	0	.143
World Series Record												
1997 Cleveland	A.L.	OF	5	4	1	2	1	0	0	2	0	.400

a On disabled list from June 1 to July 7, 1998.
b Traded to Pittsburgh Pirates for pitcher Ricardo Rincon, November 18, 1998.
c On disabled list from April 11 to May 7, 2003.
d Traded to San Diego Padres for pitcher Oliver Perez, outfielder Jason Bay and player to be named later, August 26, 2003.
e Pittsburgh Pirates received pitcher Cory Stewart to complete trade, October 2, 2003.
f Filed for free agency, October 27, 2005, re-signed with San Diego Padres, December 1, 2005.
g On disabled list from May 20 to June 28, 2007.

GLAUS, TROY EDWARD
Born, Tarzana, California, August 3, 1976.
Bats Right. Throws Right. Height, 6 feet, 5 inches. Weight, 240 pounds.

Year Club	Lea	Pos	G	AB	R	H	2B	3B	HR	RBI	SB	Avg
1998 Midland	Texas	3B	50	188	51	58	11	2	19	51	4	.309
1998 Vancouver	P.C.	3B	59	219	33	67	16	0	16	42	3	.306
1998 Anaheim	A.L.	3B	48	165	19	36	9	0	1	23	1	.218
1999 Anaheim	A.L.	3B	154	551	85	132	29	0	29	79	5	.240
2000 Anaheim	A.L.	3B-SS	159	563	120	160	37	1	*47	102	14	.284
2001 Anaheim	A.L.	3B-SS	161	588	100	147	38	2	41	108	10	.250
2002 Anaheim	A.L.	3B-SS	156	569	99	142	24	1	30	111	10	.250
2003 Rancho Cucamonga	Calif.	DH	2	6	1	2	0	0	0	1	0	.333
2003 Anaheim a	A.L.	3B	91	319	53	79	17	2	16	50	7	.248
2004 Rancho Cucamonga	Calif.	DH	5	15	4	3	0	0	2	4	0	.200
2004 Anaheim b-c	A.L.	DH-3B	58	207	47	52	11	1	18	42	2	.251
2005 Arizona d	N.L.	3B	149	538	78	139	29	1	37	97	4	.258
2006 Toronto	A.L.	3B-SS	153	540	105	136	27	0	38	104	3	.252

Year Club	Lea	Pos	G	AB	R	H	2B	3B	HR	RBI	SB	Avg
2007 Toronto e-f...........	A.L.	3B	115	385	60	101	19	1	20	62	0	.262
2008 St. Louis.............	N.L.	3B-1B	151	544	69	147	33	1	27	99	0	.270
Major League Totals...........		11 Yrs.	1395	4969	835	1271	273	10	304	877	56	.256
Division Series												
2002 Anaheim.............	A.L.	3B	4	16	4	5	0	0	3	3	0	.313
2004 Anaheim.............	A.L.	DH	3	11	3	4	2	0	2	3	0	.364
Division Series Totals..........			7	27	7	9	2	0	5	6	0	.333
Championship Series												
2002 Anaheim.............	A.L.	3B	5	19	4	6	0	1	1	2	0	.316
World Series Record												
2002 Anaheim.............	A.L.	3B	7	26	7	10	3	0	3	8	0	.385

a On disabled list from July 22 to October 6, 2003.
b On disabled list from May 12 to August 29, 2004.
c Filed for free agency, October 28, 2004. Signed with Arizona Diamondbacks, December 9, 2004.
d Traded to Toronto Blue Jays with infielder Sergio Santos for infielder Orlando Hudson and pitcher Miguel Batista, December 27, 2005.
e On disabled list from April 13 to April 28 and September 14 to November 13, 2007.
f Traded to St. Louis Cardinals for infielder Scott Rolen, January 14, 2008.

GLOAD, ROSS PETER
Born, Brooklyn, New York, April 5, 1976.
Bats Left. Throws Left. Height, 6 feet, 1 inches. Weight, 190 pounds.

Year Club	Lea	Pos	G	AB	R	H	2B	3B	HR	RBI	SB	Avg
1997 Utica..........	N.Y.-Penn.	1B	68	245	28	64	15	2	3	43	1	.261
1998 Kane County......	Midwest	1B	132	501	77	157	41	3	12	92	7	.313
1999 Brevard County......	Fla.St.	1B	133	490	80	146	26	3	10	74	3	.298
2000 Portland...........	Eastern	OF-1B	100	401	60	114	28	4	16	65	4	.284
2000 Iowa.............	P.C.	OF	28	104	24	42	10	2	14	39	1	.404
2000 Chicago a.........	N.L.	OF-1B	18	31	4	6	0	1	1	3	0	.194
2001 Iowa b...........	P.C.	OF-1B	133	475	70	141	32	10	15	93	9	.297
2002 Colorado Springs......	P.C.	1B-OF	104	442	69	139	28	6	16	71	9	.314
2002 Colorado c-d.......	N.L.	1B-OF	26	31	4	8	1	0	1	4	0	.258
2003 Charlotte e...........	Int.	1B-OF	133	508	72	160	40	6	18	70	6	.315
2004 Chicago..........	A.L.	1B-OF	110	234	28	75	16	0	7	44	0	.321
2005 Charlotte.........	Int.	1B-OF	60	236	45	86	22	1	15	45	0	.364
2005 Chicago f.........	A.L.	1B-OF	28	42	2	7	2	0	0	5	0	.167
2006 Chicago g.........	A.L.	1B-OF	77	156	22	51	8	2	3	18	6	.327
2007 Omaha...........	P.C.	DH	1	4	1	2	0	0	1	1	0	.500
2007 Kansas City h........	A.L.	1B-OF	102	320	37	92	22	3	7	51	2	.287
2008 Kansas City...........	A.L.	1B-OF	122	388	46	106	18	1	3	37	3	.273
Major League Totals...........		7 Yrs.	483	1202	143	345	67	7	22	162	11	.287

a Traded to Chicago Cubs with pitcher David Noyce for outfielder Henry Rodriguez and cash, July 31, 2000.
b Claimed on waivers by Colorado Rockies, September 12, 2001.
c Traded to New York Mets with pitcher Craig House and outfielder Alex Ochoa for outfielder Benny Agbayani and infielder Todd Zeile, January 21, 2002.
d Sold to Colorado Rockies, January 26, 2002.
e Traded to Chicago White Sox for pitcher Wade Parrish, March 31, 2003.
f On disabled list from April 25 to July 17, 2005.
g Traded to Kansas City Royals for pitcher Andy Sisco, December 16, 2006.
h On disabled list from May 14 to June 30, 2007.

GOMES, JONNY JOHNSON
Born, Petaluma, California, November 22, 1980.
Bats Right. Throws Right. Height, 6 feet, 1 inch. Weight, 225 pounds.

Year Club	Lea	Pos	G	AB	R	H	2B	3B	HR	RBI	SB	Avg
2001 Princeton..........	Appal.	OF	62	206	58	60	11	2	16	44	15	.291
2002 Bakersfield........	California	OF	133	446	102	123	24	9	30	72	15	.276
2003 Orlando.........	Southern	OF	120	442	68	110	28	3	17	56	23	.249
2003 Durham...............	Int.	OF	5	19	2	6	2	1	0	1	0	.316
2003 Tampa Bay...........	A.L.	DH	8	15	1	2	1	0	0	0	0	.133
2004 Durham...............	Int.	OF	114	389	73	100	27	1	26	78	8	.257
2004 Tampa Bay...........	A.L.	DH	5	14	0	1	0	0	0	1	0	.071
2005 Durham...............	Int.	OF	45	162	34	52	13	0	14	46	7	.321
2005 Tampa Bay...........	A.L.	OF	101	348	61	98	13	6	21	54	9	.282
2006 Tampa Bay a.........	A.L.	DH-OF	117	385	53	83	21	1	20	59	1	.216
2007 Durham...............	Int.	OF	13	43	6	13	2	0	1	7	0	.302
2007 Tampa Bay...........	A.L.	OF	107	348	48	85	20	2	17	49	12	.244

Year	Club	Lea	Pos	G	AB	R	H	2B	3B	HR	RBI	SB	Avg
2008 Durham	Int.	OF	26	107	19	27	11	0	2	14	0	.252
2008 Tampa Bay b	A.L.	DH-OF	77	154	23	28	5	1	8	21	8	.182
Major League Totals		6 Yrs.	415	1264	186	297	60	10	66	184	30	.235

a On disabled list from August 22 to October 2, 2006.
b Not offered contract, December 12, 2008.

GOMEZ (PENA), CARLOS ARGELIS

Born, Santiago, Dominican Republic, December 4, 1985.
Bats Right. Throws Right. Height, 6 feet, 4 inches. Weight, 195 pounds.

Year	Club	Lea	Pos	G	AB	R	H	2B	3B	HR	RBI	SB	Avg
2004 Kingsport	Appal.	OF	38	150	24	43	10	4	1	20	8	.287
2004 Mets	Gulf Coast	OF	19	71	10	19	7	0	0	11	9	.268
2005 Hagerstown	So.Atl.	OF	120	487	75	134	13	6	8	48	64	.275
2006 Binghamton	Eastern	OF	120	430	53	121	24	8	7	48	41	.281
2007 New Orleans	P.C.	OF	36	140	24	40	8	2	2	13	17	.286
2007 St. Lucie	Fla.St.	OF	5	13	1	2	0	0	0	0	2	.154
2007 New York a	N.L.	OF	58	125	14	29	3	0	2	12	12	.232
2008 Minnesota b	A.L.	OF	153	577	79	149	24	7	7	59	33	.258
Major League Totals		2 Yrs.	211	702	93	178	27	7	9	71	45	.254

a On disabled list from July 5 to September 7, 2007.
b Traded to Minnesota Twins with pitcher Philip Humber, pitcher Kevin Mulvey and pitcher Deolis Garcia for pitcher Johan Santana, February 2, 2008.

GOMEZ, CHRISTOPHER CORY (CHRIS)

Born, Los Angeles, California, June 16, 1971.
Bats Right. Throws Right. Height, 6 feet, 1 inch. Weight, 195 pounds.

Year	Club	Lea	Pos	G	AB	R	H	2B	3B	HR	RBI	SB	Avg
1992 London	Eastern	SS-3B	64	220	20	59	13	2	1	19	1	.268
1993 Toledo	Int.	SS	87	277	29	68	12	2	0	20	6	.245
1993 Detroit	A.L.	SS-2B	46	128	11	32	7	1	0	11	2	.250
1994 Detroit	A.L.	SS-2B	84	296	32	76	19	0	8	53	5	.257
1995 Detroit	A.L.	SS-2B	123	431	49	96	20	2	11	50	4	.223
1996 Detroit	A.L.	SS	48	128	21	31	5	0	1	16	1	.242
1996 San Diego a	N.L.	SS	89	328	32	86	16	1	3	29	2	.262
1997 San Diego	N.L.	SS	150	522	62	132	19	2	5	54	5	.253
1998 San Diego	N.L.	SS	145	449	55	120	32	3	4	39	1	.267
1999 San Diego	N.L.	SS	76	234	20	59	8	1	1	15	1	.252
1999 Las Vegas b	P.C.	SS	10	27	3	9	1	0	0	4	0	.333
2000 San Diego c	N.L.	SS-2B	33	54	4	12	0	0	0	3	0	.222
2001 San Diego	N.L.	SS-2B	40	112	6	21	3	0	0	7	1	.188
2001 Portland	P.C.	SS-2B	11	40	5	12	3	0	1	5	1	.300
2001 Durham	Int.	SS	23	93	16	28	5	1	4	17	1	.301
2001 Tampa Bay d-e	A.L.	SS	58	189	31	57	16	0	8	36	3	.302
2002 Tampa Bay	A.L.	SS	130	461	51	122	31	3	10	46	1	.265
2003 Minnesota f-g	A.L.	2B-3B-SS	58	175	14	44	9	3	1	15	2	.251
2004 Toronto h-i-j	A.L.	SS-1B-3B-2B	109	341	41	96	11	1	3	37	3	.282
2005 Baltimore	A.L.	1B-2B-3B-SS	89	219	27	61	11	0	1	18	2	.279
2006 Bowie	Eastern	SS-3B	4	16	4	4	1	0	0	1	0	.250
2006 Aberdeen	N.Y.-Penn.	3B	1	3	0	1	0	0	0	0	0	.333
2006 Baltimore k-l	A.L.	1B-2B-SS-3B	55	132	14	45	7	0	2	17	1	.341
2007 Baltimore-Cleveland m-n	A.L.	1B-3B-2B-SS	92	222	21	66	12	1	1	21	1	.297
2008 Pittsburgh o	N.L.	3B-2B-SS-1B	90	183	26	50	8	0	1	20	0	.273
Major League Totals		16 Yrs.	1515	4604	517	1206	234	18	60	487	35	.262
Division Series												
1996 San Diego	N.L.	SS	3	12	0	2	0	0	0	1	0	.167
1998 San Diego	N.L.	SS	4	11	1	3	0	0	0	0	0	.273
2003 Minnesota	A.L.	2B	1	0	0	0	0	0	0	0	0	.000
Division Series Totals			8	23	1	5	0	0	0	1	0	.217
Championship Series												
1998 San Diego	N.L.	SS	6	20	2	3	1	0	0	0	0	.150
2007 Cleveland	A.L.	PH	1	1	0	0	0	0	0	0	0	.000
Championship Series Totals			7	21	2	3	1	0	0	0	0	.143
World Series Record												
1998 San Diego	N.L.	SS	4	11	2	4	0	1	0	0	0	.364

a Traded to San Diego Padres with catcher John Flaherty for catcher Brad Ausmus and infielder Andujar Cedeno, June 18, 1996.
b On disabled list from June 2 to July 31, 1999.

68

c On disabled list from June 22 to October 12, 2000.
d Waived by San Diego Padres, June 22, 2001. Signed with Tampa Bay Devil Rays organization, June 27, 2001.
e Filed for free agency, November 5, 2001, re-signed with Tampa Bay Devil Rays, December 7, 2001.
f Released by Tampa Bay Devil Rays, September 30, 2002. Signed with Minnesota Twins organization, January 2, 2003.
g On disabled list from June 7 to July 5, 2003.
h Filed for free agency, October 28, 2003. Signed with Toronto Blue Jays, January 7, 2004.
i Filed for free agency, October 28, 2004. Signed with Baltimore Orioles organization, December 8, 2004.
j Selected by Philadelphia Phillies in Rule V minor league draft, December 14, 2004. Sold to Baltimore Orioles, December 20, 2004.
k On disabled list from May 11 to July 11, 2006.
l Filed for free agency, October 31, 2006, re-signed with Baltimore Orioles, December 18, 2006.
m Claimed on waivers by Cleveland Indians, August 9, 2007.
n Filed for free agency, October 30, 2007. Signed with Pittsburgh Pirates, December 12, 2007.
o Filed for free agency, October 30, 2008. Signed with Baltimore Orioles organization, January 9, 2009.

GONZALEZ, ADRIAN

Born, San Diego, California, May 8, 1982.
Bats Left. Throws Left. Height, 6 feet, 2 inches. Weight, 220 pounds.

Year Club	Lea	Pos	G	AB	R	H	2B	3B	HR	RBI	SB	Avg
2000 Marlins.........	Gulf Coast	1B	53	193	24	57	10	1	0	30	0	.295
2000 Utica..........	N.Y.-Penn.	1B	8	29	7	9	3	0	0	3	0	.310
2001 Kane County......	Midwest	1B	127	516	86	161	37	1	17	103	5	.312
2002 Portland..........	Eastern	1B	138	508	70	135	34	1	17	96	6	.266
2003 Albuquerque..........	P.C.	1B	39	139	17	30	5	1	1	18	1	.216
2003 Carolina.........	Southern	1B	36	137	15	42	9	1	1	16	1	.307
2003 Frisco a.........	Texas	1B	45	173	16	49	6	2	3	17	0	.283
2004 Oklahoma............	P.C.	1B	123	457	61	139	28	3	12	88	1	.304
2004 Texas..............	A.L.	1B	16	42	7	10	3	0	1	7	0	.238
2005 Oklahoma.........	P.C.	1B	84	328	61	111	17	1	18	65	0	.338
2005 Texas............	A.L.	DH-1B-OF	43	150	17	34	7	1	6	17	0	.227
2006 San Diego b.........	N.L.	1B	156	570	83	173	38	1	24	82	0	.304
2007 San Diego.........	N.L.	1B	161	646	101	182	46	3	30	100	0	.282
2008 San Diego.........	N.L.	1B	*162	616	103	172	32	1	36	119	0	.279
Major League Totals............		5 Yrs.	538	2024	311	571	126	6	97	325	0	.282
Division Series												
2006 San Diego	N.L.	1B	4	14	2	5	0	0	0	0	0	.357

a Traded to Texas Rangers with pitcher Ryan Snare and outfielder Will Smith for pitcher Ugueth Urbina, July 11, 2003.
b Traded to San Diego Padres with pitcher Chris Young and outfielder Terrmel Sledge for pitcher Adam Eaton, pitcher Akinori Otsuka and catcher Billy Killian, January 4, 2006.

GONZALEZ, ALEXANDER (ALEX)

Born, Cagua, Venezuela, February 15, 1977.
Bats Right. Throws Right. Height, 6 feet. Weight, 200 pounds.

Year Club	Lea	Pos	G	AB	R	H	2B	3B	HR	RBI	SB	Avg
1994 Florida	Dominican	SS	66	282	39	67	9	5	4	39	5	.238
1995 Brevard Cty	Fla.St.	SS	17	59	6	12	2	1	0	8	1	.203
1995 Marlins.........	Gulf Coast	SS	53	187	30	55	7	4	2	30	11	.294
1996 Marlins.........	Gulf Coast	SS	10	41	6	16	3	0	0	6	1	.390
1996 Kane County......	Midwest	SS	4	10	2	2	0	0	0	0	0	.200
1996 Portland..........	Eastern	SS	11	34	4	8	0	1	0	1	0	.235
1997 Portland..........	Eastern	SS	133	449	69	114	16	4	19	65	4	.254
1998 Charlotte	Int.	SS	108	422	71	117	20	10	10	51	4	.277
1998 Florida	N.L.	SS	25	86	11	13	2	0	3	7	0	.151
1999 Florida	N.L.	SS	136	560	81	155	28	8	14	59	3	.277
2000 Brevard County	Fla.St.	SS	4	17	1	2	0	0	0	2	1	.118
2000 Florida a.............	N.L.	SS	109	385	35	77	17	4	7	42	7	.200
2001 Florida	N.L.	SS	145	515	57	129	36	1	9	48	2	.250
2002 Florida b.............	N.L.	SS	42	151	15	34	7	1	2	18	3	.225
2002 Marlins.........	Gulf Coast	SS	5	12	0	2	1	0	0	1	0	.167
2003 Florida	N.L.	SS	150	528	52	135	33	6	18	77	0	.256
2004 Florida	N.L.	SS	159	561	67	130	30	3	23	79	3	.232
2005 Florida c.............	N.L.	SS	130	435	45	115	30	0	5	45	5	.264
2006 Pawtucket	Int.	SS	1	3	0	1	0	0	0	0	0	.333
2006 Boston d-e.............	A.L.	SS	111	388	48	99	24	2	9	50	1	.255
2007 Cincinnati.............	N.L.	SS	110	393	55	107	27	1	16	55	0	.272
2008 Cincinnati f.............	N.L.		INJURED—Did Not Play									
Major League Totals		10 Yrs.	1117	4002	466	994	234	26	106	480	24	.248

69

Year	Club	Lea	Pos	G	AB	R	H	2B	3B	HR	RBI	SB	Avg
	Division Series												
2003 Florida		N.L.	SS	4	16	2	1	0	0	0	0	0	.063
	Championship Series												
2003 Florida		N.L.	SS	7	24	1	3	2	0	0	4	0	.125
	World Series Record												
2003 Florida		N.L.	SS	6	22	3	6	2	0	1	2	0	.273

a On disabled list from July 28 to August 31, 2000.
b On disabled list from May 19 to November 6, 2002.
c Filed for free agency, October 27, 2005. Signed with Boston Red Sox, February 6, 2006.
d On disabled list from August 19 to September 3, 2006.
e Filed for free agency, October 30, 2006. Signed with Cincinnati Reds, November 20, 2006.
f On disabled list from March 21 to November 6, 2008.

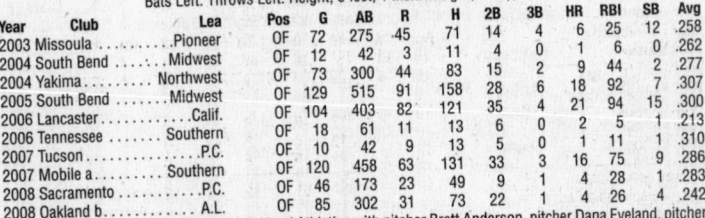

GONZALEZ, CARLOS EDUARDO
Born, Maracaibo, Venezuela, October 17, 1985.
Bats Left. Throws Left. Height, 6 feet, 1 inch. Weight, 200 pounds.

Year	Club	Lea	Pos	G	AB	R	H	2B	3B	HR	RBI	SB	Avg
2003 Missoula		Pioneer	OF	72	275	45	71	14	4	6	25	12	.258
2004 South Bend		Midwest	OF	12	42	3	11	4	0	1	6	0	.262
2004 Yakima		Northwest	OF	73	300	44	83	15	2	9	44	2	.277
2005 South Bend		Midwest	OF	129	515	91	158	28	6	18	92	7	.307
2006 Lancaster		Calif.	OF	104	403	82	121	35	4	21	94	15	.300
2006 Tennessee		Southern	OF	18	61	11	13	6	0	2	5	1	.213
2007 Tucson		P.C.	OF	10	42	9	13	5	0	1	11	1	.310
2007 Mobile a		Southern	OF	120	458	63	131	33	3	16	75	9	.286
2008 Sacramento		P.C.	OF	46	173	23	49	9	1	4	28	1	.283
2008 Oakland b		A.L.	OF	85	302	31	73	22	1	4	26	4	.242

a Traded by Arizona Diamondbacks to Oakland Athletics with pitcher Brett Anderson, pitcher Dana Eveland, pitcher Greg Smith, infielder Chris Carter and outfielder Aaron Cunningham for pitcher Danny Haren and pitcher Connor Robertson, December 14, 2007.
b Traded to Colorado Rockies with pitcher Greg Smith and pitcher Huston Street for outfielder Matt Holliday, November 12, 2008.

GONZALEZ, EDGAR
Born, San Diego, California, June 14, 1978.
Bats Right. Throws Right. Height, 6 feet. Weight, 180 pounds.

Year	Club	Lea	Pos	G	AB	R	H	2B	3B	HR	RBI	SB	Avg
2000 Princeton		Appal.	SS-OF-2B	20	63	6	17	3	3	0	8	4	.270
2000 Hudson Valley	N.Y.-Penn.	3B-SS-OF-2B	41	145	17	32	4	4	0	8	5	.221
2001 Hudson Valley	N.Y.-Penn.	3B-2B-OF-SS	73	277	49	92	19	4	9	34	6	.332
2002 Charleston-SC	So.Atl.	3B-2B	134	447	68	123	28	1	8	62	21	.275
2003 Bakersfield a	Calif.	3B-2B	100	349	51	104	34	3	6	62	8	.298
2004 Frisco b	Texas	3B-2B-OF	106	394	58	114	25	4	8	55	6	.279
2005 Harrisburg	Eastern	2B-3B-1B-OF	101	340	41	95	25	3	8	50	5	.354
2005 New Orleans	P.C.	3B-2B-SS-OF	23	48	12	17	4	0	0	4	0	.293
2006 Jupiter	Fla.St.	2B-SS	21	75	10	22	8	0	2	10	1	.293
2006 Albuquerque	P.C.	2B	46	143	29	56	10	1	5	36	1	.392
2006 Carolina c	Southern	2B-SS-3B	64	210	19	62	10	3	6	25	9	.295
2007 Memphis d-e	P.C.	2B-3B-OF	126	461	64	142	34	3	8	53	15	.308
2008 Portland	P.C.	OF-3B-1B-2B	27	82	10	24	1	0	4	12	0	.293
2008 San Diego f	N.L.	2B-OF-3B-SS	111	325	38	89	15	0	7	33	1	.274

a Selected by Texas Rangers from Tampa Bay Devil Rays in Rule V draft, December 15, 2003.
b Selected by Washington Nationals in Rule V draft, December 13, 2004.
c Released by Washington Nationals, March 31, 2006. Signed with Florida Marlins organization, April 4, 2006.
d Filed for free agency, October 15, 2006. Signed with St. Louis Cardinals organization, January 30, 2007.
e Released by St. Louis Cardinals, September 4, 2007. Signed with San Diego Padres organization, November 25, 2007.
f Filed for free agency, November 7, 2008.

GONZALEZ, LUIS EMILIO
Born, Tampa, Florida, September 3, 1967.
Bats Left. Throws Right. Height, 6 feet, 2 inches. Weight, 210 pounds.

Year	Club	Lea	Pos	G	AB	R	H	2B	3B	HR	RBI	SB	Avg
1988 Asheville		So. Atl.	3B	31	115	13	29	7	1	2	14	2	.252
1988 Auburn		N.Y.-Penn.	3B	39	157	32	49	10	3	5	27	2	.312
1989 Osceola a		Fla. St.	DH	86	287	46	82	16	7	6	38	2	.286

Year Club	Lea	Pos	G	AB	R	H	2B	3B	HR	RBI	SB	Avg
1990 Columbus........ Southern		1B-3B	138	495	86	131	30	6	*24	89	27	.265
1990 Houston.............	N.L.	3B-1B	12	21	1	4	2	0	0	0	0	.190
1991 Houston b	N.L.	OF	137	473	51	120	28	9	13	69	10	.254
1992 Tucson..............	P.C.	OF	13	44	11	19	4	2	1	9	4	.432
1992 Houston c	N.L.	OF	122	387	40	94	19	3	10	55	7	.243
1993 Houston.............	N.L.	OF	154	540	82	162	34	3	15	72	20	.300
1994 Houston.............	N.L.	OF	112	392	57	107	29	4	8	67	15	.273
1995 Houston-Chicago d-e...	N.L.	OF	133	471	69	130	29	8	13	69	6	.276
1996 Chicago f-g	N.L.	OF-1B	146	483	70	131	30	4	15	79	9	.271
1997 Houston h-i	N.L.	OF-1B	152	550	78	142	31	2	10	68	10	.258
1998 Detroit j.............	A.L.	OF	154	547	84	146	35	5	23	71	12	.267
1999 Arizona..............	N.L.	OF	153	614	112	*206	45	4	26	111	9	.336
2000 Arizona..............	N.L.	OF	*162	618	106	192	47	2	31	114	2	.311
2001 Arizona..............	N.L.	OF	*162	609	128	198	36	7	57	142	1	.325
2002 Arizona..............	N.L.	OF	148	524	90	151	19	3	28	103	9	.288
2003 Arizona..............	N.L.	OF	156	579	92	176	46	4	26	104	5	.304
2004 Arizona k	N.L.	OF	105	379	69	98	28	5	17	48	2	.259
2005 Arizona..............	N.L.	OF	155	579	90	157	37	0	24	79	4	.271
2006 Arizona l............	N.L.	OF	153	586	93	159	52	2	15	73	0	.271
2007 Los Angeles m........	N.L.	OF	139	464	70	129	23	2	15	68	6	.278
2008 Florida n............	N.L.	OF	136	341	30	89	26	1	8	47	1	.261
Major League Totals		19 Yrs.	2591	9157	1412	2591	596	68	354	1439	128	.283
Division Series												
1997 Houston.............	N.L.	OF	3	12	0	4	0	0	0	0	0	.333
1999 Arizona.............	N.L.	OF	4	10	3	2	1	0	1	2	0	.200
2001 Arizona.............	N.L.	OF	5	19	1	5	0	0	1	1	0	.263
Division Series Totals			12	41	4	11	1	0	2	3	0	.268
Championship Series												
2001 Arizona.............	N.L.	OF	5	19	4	4	0	0	1	4	0	.211
World Series Record												
2001 Arizona.............	N.L.	OF	7	27	4	7	2	0	1	5	0	.259

a On minor league disabled list from May 26 to July 5, 1989.
b On disabled list from August 29 to September 13, 1991.
c On disabled list from July 21 to August 5, 1992.
d Traded to Chicago Cubs with catcher Scott Servais for catcher Rick Wilkins, June 28, 1995.
e Not offered contract by Chicago Cubs, December 20, 1995, re-signed with Chicago Cubs December 20, 1995.
f Filed for free agency, October 28, 1996.
g Signed with Houston Astros, December 19, 1996.
h Filed for free agency, October 28, 1997.
i Signed with Detroit Tigers, December 9, 1997.
j Traded to Arizona Diamondbacks for outfielder Karim Garcia, December 28, 1998.
k On disabled list from August 2 to October 4, 2004.
l Filed for free agency, October 28, 2006. Signed with Los Angeles Dodgers, December 12, 2006.
m Filed for free agency, October 31, 2007. Signed with Florida Marlins, February 7, 2008.
n Filed for free agency, November 4, 2008.

GORDON, ALEX JONATHAN

Born, Lincoln, Nebraska, February 10, 1984.
Bats Left. Throws Right. Height, 6 feet, 1 inch. Weight, 220 pounds.

Year Club	Lea	Pos	G	AB	R	H	2B	3B	HR	RBI	SB	Avg
2006 Wichita........	Texas	3B-1B	130	486	111	158	39	1	29	101	22	.325
2007 Kansas City	A.L.	3B-1B-SS	151	543	60	134	36	4	15	60	14	.247
2008 Kansas City a	A.L.	3B	134	493	72	128	35	1	16	59	9	.260
Major League Totals		2 Yrs.	285	1036	132	262	71	5	31	119	23	.253

a On disabled list from August 22 to September 12, 2008.

GOTAY, RUBEN BRUCE

Born, Rio Piedras, Puerto Rico, December 25, 1982.
Bats Both. Throws Right. Height, 5 feet, 11 inches. Weight, 190 pounds.

Year Club	Lea	Pos	G	AB	R	H	2B	3B	HR	RBI	SB	Avg
2001 Royals	Gulf Coast	2B-3B	52	184	29	58	15	1	3	19	5	.315
2002 Burlington	Midwest	2B-3B	133	509	87	145	42	9	9	83	5	.285
2003 Wilmington ...	Carolina	2B	134	502	68	131	31	2	9	72	8	.261
2004 Wichita........	Texas	2B	106	405	71	117	22	6	9	68	9	.289
2004 Kansas City	A.L.	2B	44	152	17	41	7	3	1	16	0	.270
2005 Kansas City	A.L.	2B	86	282	32	64	14	2	5	29	2	.227
2005 Wichita........	Texas	2B	28	110	22	27	8	0	3	15	0	.245

Year Club	Lea	Pos	G	AB	R	H	2B	3B	HR	RBI	SB	Avg
2006 Norfolk	Int.	2B-3B-SS	42	154	19	41	12	1	3	21	4	.266
2006 Omaha a	P.C.	2B	87	337	45	89	16	2	9	43	7	.264
2007 New Orleans	P.C.	2B-SS-3B	23	82	12	21	7	1	2	13	1	.256
2007 New York	N.L.	2B-SS-3B	98	190	25	56	12	0	4	24	3	.295
2008 Richmond	Int.	2B-3B	3	12	1	3	0	0	0	1	0	.250
2008 Atlanta b-c-d	N.L.	3B-2B	88	102	10	24	5	0	2	8	1	.235
Major League Totals	4 Yrs.	316	726	84	185	38	5	12	77	6	.255

a Traded to New York Mets for infielder Jeff Keppinger, July 19, 2006.
b Claimed on waivers by Atlanta Braves, March 28, 2008.
c On disabled list from August 17 to September 1, 2008.
d Filed for free agency, October 6, 2008.

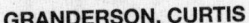

GRANDERSON, CURTIS

Born, Blue Island, Illinois, March 16, 1981.
Bats Left. Throws Right. Height, 6 feet, 1 inch. Weight, 185 pounds.

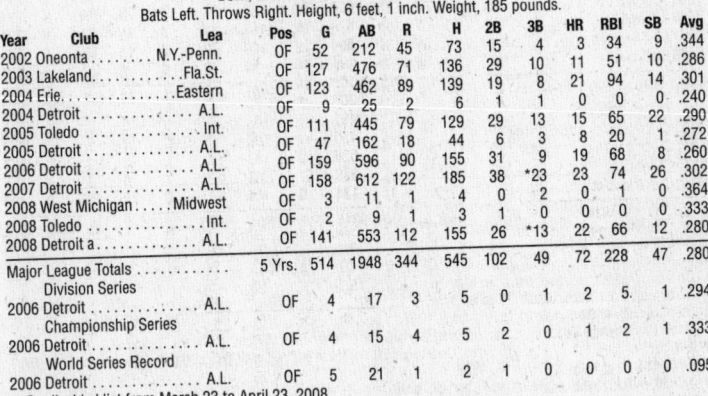

Year Club	Lea	Pos	G	AB	R	H	2B	3B	HR	RBI	SB	Avg
2002 Oneonta	N.Y.-Penn.	OF	52	212	45	73	15	4	3	34	9	.344
2003 Lakeland	Fla.St.	OF	127	476	71	136	29	10	11	51	10	.286
2004 Erie	Eastern	OF	123	462	89	139	19	8	21	94	14	.301
2004 Detroit	A.L.	OF	9	25	2	6	1	1	0	0	0	.240
2005 Toledo	Int.	OF	111	445	79	129	29	13	15	65	22	.290
2005 Detroit	A.L.	OF	47	162	18	44	6	3	8	20	1	.272
2006 Detroit	A.L.	OF	159	596	90	155	31	9	19	68	8	.260
2007 Detroit	A.L.	OF	158	612	122	185	38	*23	23	74	26	.302
2008 West Michigan	Midwest	OF	3	11	1	4	0	2	0	1	0	.364
2008 Toledo	Int.	OF	2	9	1	3	1	0	0	0	0	.333
2008 Detroit a	A.L.	OF	141	553	112	155	26	*13	22	66	12	.280
Major League Totals	5 Yrs.	514	1948	344	545	102	49	72	228	47	.280
Division Series												
2006 Detroit	A.L.	OF	4	17	3	5	0	1	2	5	1	.294
Championship Series												
2006 Detroit	A.L.	OF	4	15	4	5	2	0	1	2	1	.333
World Series Record												
2006 Detroit	A.L.	OF	5	21	1	2	1	0	0	0	0	.095

a On disabled list from March 23 to April 23, 2008.

GREENE, KHALIL TABIT

Born, Butler, Pennsylvania, October 21, 1979.
Bats Right. Throws Right. Height, 5 feet, 11 inches. Weight, 195 pounds.

Year Club	Lea	Pos	G	AB	R	H	2B	3B	HR	RBI	SB	Avg
2002 Eugene	Northwest	SS	10	37	5	10	1	0	0	6	0	.270
2002 Lake Elsinore	California	SS-2B-3B	46	183	33	58	9	1	9	32	0	.317
2003 Mobile	Southern	SS	59	229	20	63	17	2	3	20	2	.275
2003 Portland	P.C.	SS	76	319	42	92	19	0	10	47	5	.288
2003 San Diego	N.L.	SS	20	65	8	14	4	1	2	6	0	.215
2004 San Diego	N.L.	SS	139	484	67	132	31	4	15	65	4	.273
2005 Lake Elsinore	California	SS	4	12	4	6	1	0	0	3	0	.500
2005 San Diego a	N.L.	SS	121	436	51	109	30	2	15	70	5	.250
2006 San Diego b	N.L.	SS	121	412	56	101	26	2	15	55	5	.245
2007 San Diego	N.L.	SS	153	611	89	155	44	3	27	97	4	.254
2008 San Diego c-d	N.L.	SS	105	389	30	83	15	2	10	35	5	.213
Major League Totals	6 Yrs.	659	2397	301	594	150	14	84	328	23	.248
Division Series												
2005 San Diego	N.L.	SS	3	10	2	4	2	0	0	1	0	.400
2006 San Diego	N.L.	SS	3	4	0	0	0	0	0	0	0	.000
Division Series Totals			6	14	2	4	2	0	0	1	0	.286

a On disabled list from April 17 to May 9 and August 15 to August 30, 2005.
b On disabled list from August 18 to September 3, 2006.
c On disabled list from July 31 to October 2, 2008.
d Traded to St. Louis Cardinals for pitcher Mark Worrell and player to be named later, December 4, 2008.

GRIFFEY, GEORGE KENNETH, JR. (KEN)

Born, Donora, Pennsylvania, November 21, 1969.
Bats Left. Throws Left. Height, 6 feet, 3 inches. Weight, 220 pounds.

Year	Club	Lea	Pos	G	AB	R	H	2B	3B	HR	RBI	SB	Avg
1987 Bellingham	Northwest		OF	54	182	43	57	9	1	14	40	13	.313
1988 San Bernardino a	California		OF	58	219	50	74	13	3	11	42	32	.338
1988 Vermont	Eastern		OF	17	61	10	17	5	1	2	10	4	.279
1989 Seattle b	A.L.		OF	127	455	61	120	23	0	16	61	16	.264
1990 Seattle	A.L.		OF	155	597	91	179	28	7	22	80	16	.300
1991 Seattle	A.L.		OF	154	548	76	179	42	1	22	100	18	.327
1992 Seattle c	A.L.		OF	142	565	83	174	39	4	27	103	10	.308
1993 Seattle	A.L.		OF-1B	156	582	113	180	38	3	45	109	17	.309
1994 Seattle	A.L.		OF	111	433	94	140	24	4	*40	90	11	.323
1995 Tacoma	P.C.		DH	1	3	0	0	0	0	0	0	0	.000
1995 Seattle d	A.L.		OF	72	260	52	67	7	0	17	42	4	.258
1996 Seattle e	A.L.		OF	140	545	125	165	26	2	49	140	16	.303
1997 Seattle f	A.L.		OF	157	608	*125	185	34	3	*56	*147	15	.304
1998 Seattle	A.L.		OF-1B	161	633	120	180	33	3	*56	146	20	.284
1999 Seattle	A.L.		OF	160	606	123	173	26	3	*48	134	24	.285
2000 Cincinnati g	N.L.		OF	145	520	100	141	22	3	40	118	6	.271
2001 Cincinnati h	N.L.		OF	111	364	57	104	20	2	22	65	2	.286
2002 Cincinnati i	N.L.		OF	70	197	17	52	8	0	8	23	1	.264
2003 Cincinnati j	N.L.		OF	53	166	34	41	12	1	13	26	1	.247
2004 Cincinnati k	N.L.		OF	83	300	49	76	18	0	20	60	1	.253
2005 Cincinnati	N.L.		OF	128	491	85	148	30	0	35	92	0	.301
2006 Cincinnati l	N.L.		OF	109	428	62	108	19	0	27	72	0	.252
2007 Cincinnati	N.L.		OF	144	528	78	146	24	1	30	93	6	.277
2008 Cincinnati	N.L.		OF	102	359	51	88	20	1	15	53	0	.245
2008 Chicago m-n	A.L.		OF	41	131	16	34	10	0	3	18	0	.260
Major League Totals		20 Yrs.		2521	9316	1612	2680	503	38	611	1772	184	.288
Division Series													
1995 Seattle	A.L.		OF	5	23	9	9	0	0	5	7	1	.391
1997 Seattle	A.L.		OF	4	15	0	2	0	0	0	2	2	.133
2008 Chicago	A.L.		OF	3	10	1	2	0	0	0	0	0	.200
Division Series Totals				12	48	10	13	0	0	5	9	3	.271
Championship Series													
1995 Seattle	A.L.		OF	6	21	2	7	2	0	1	2	2	.333

a On disabled list from June 9 to August 15, 1988.
b On disabled list from July 24 to August 20, 1989.
c On disabled list from June 9 to June 25, 1992.
d On disabled list from May 27 to August 15, 1995.
e On disabled list from June 20 to July 13, 1996.
f Selected Most Valuable Player in American League for 1997.
g Traded to Cincinnati Reds for pitcher Brett Tomko, outfielder Mike Cameron, infielder Antonio Perez and pitcher Jake Meyer, February 10, 2000.
h On disabled list from April 29 to June 15, 2001.
i On disabled list from April 8 to May 24 and June 24 to July 22, 2002.
j On disabled list from April 6 to May 13 and July 18 to November 5, 2003.
k On disabled list from July 11 to August 3 and from August 12 to November 2, 2004.
l On disabled list from April 13 to May 11, 2006.
m Traded to Chicago White Sox for pitcher Nick Masset and infielder Danny Richar, July 31, 2008.
n Not offered contract, October 30, 2008.

GROSS, GABRIEL JORDAN (GABE)

Born, Baltimore, Maryland, October 21, 1979.
Bats Left. Throws Right. Height, 6 feet, 3 inches. Weight, 210 pounds.

Year	Club	Lea	Pos	G	AB	R	H	2B	3B	HR	RBI	SB	Avg
2001 Dunedin	Fla.St.		OF	35	126	23	38	9	2	4	15	4	.302
2001 Tennessee	Southern		OF	11	41	8	10	1	0	3	11	0	.244
2002 Tennessee	Southern		OF	112	403	57	96	17	5	10	54	8	.238
2003 New Haven	Eastern		OF	84	310	52	99	23	3	7	51	3	.319
2003 Syracuse	Int.		OF	53	182	22	48	16	2	5	23	1	.264
2004 Syracuse	Int.		OF	103	377	52	111	29	2	9	54	4	.294
2004 Toronto	A.L.		OF	44	129	18	27	4	0	3	16	2	.209
2005 Syracuse	Int.		OF	102	390	64	116	29	4	6	46	14	.297
2005 Toronto a	A.L.		OF	40	92	11	23	4	1	1	7	1	.250
2006 Milwaukee	N.L.		OF	117	208	42	57	15	0	9	38	1	.274
2007 Nashville	P.C.		OF	20	76	13	27	3	2	4	10	2	.355
2007 Milwaukee	N.L.		OF	93	183	28	43	12	2	7	24	3	.235

Year	Club	Lea	Pos	G	AB	R	H	2B	3B	HR	RBI	SB	Avg
2008 Milwaukee	....	N.L.	OF	16	43	6	9	3	0	0	2	2	.209
2008 Tampa Bay b	....	A.L.	OF	127	302	40	73	13	3	13	38	2	.242
Major League Totals	....		5 Yrs.	437	957	145	232	51	6	33	125	11	.242
Division Series													
2008 Tampa Bay	....	N.L.	OF	3	6	0	1	0	0	0	0	1	.167
Championship Series													
2008 Tampa Bay	....	N.L.	OF	6	10	0	0	0	0	0	0	1	.000
World Series Record													
2008 Tampa Bay	....	N.L.	OF	1	3	0	0	0	0	0	2	0	.000

a Traded to Milwaukee Brewers with pitcher Dave Bush and pitcher Zach Jackson for infielder Lyle Overbay and pitcher Ty Taubenheim, December 7, 2005.
b Traded to Tampa Bay Rays for pitcher Josh Butler, April 22, 2008.

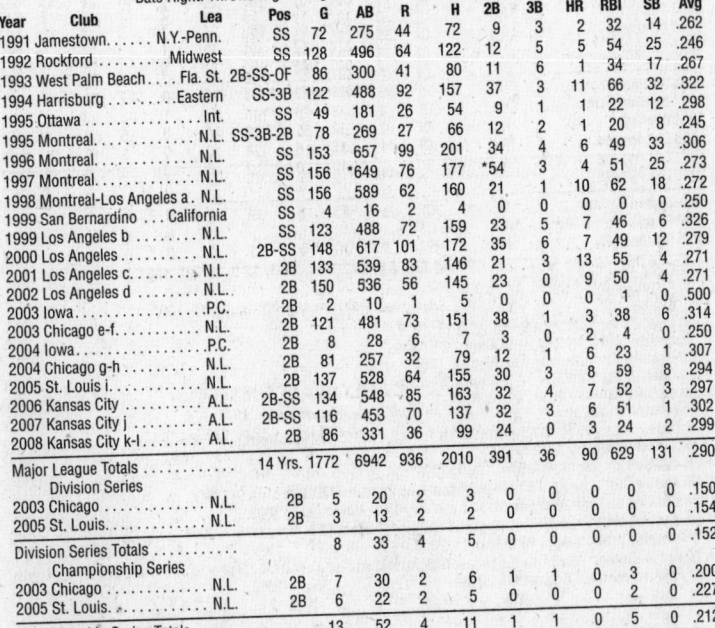

GRUDZIELANEK, MARK JAMES

Born, Milwaukee, Wisconsin, June 30, 1970.
Bats Right. Throws Right. Height, 6 feet, 1 inch. Weight, 190 pounds.

Year	Club	Lea	Pos	G	AB	R	H	2B	3B	HR	RBI	SB	Avg
1991 Jamestown	N.Y.-Penn.	SS	72	275	44	72	9	3	2	32	14	.262
1992 Rockford	Midwest	SS	128	496	64	122	12	5	5	54	25	.246
1993 West Palm Beach	Fla. St.	2B-SS-OF	86	300	41	80	11	6	1	34	17	.267
1994 Harrisburg	Eastern	SS-3B	122	488	92	157	37	3	11	66	32	.322
1995 Ottawa	Int.	SS	49	181	26	54	9	1	1	22	12	.298
1995 Montreal	N.L.	SS-3B-2B	78	269	27	66	12	2	1	20	8	.245
1996 Montreal	N.L.	SS	153	657	99	201	34	4	6	49	33	.306
1997 Montreal	N.L.	SS	156	*649	76	177	*54	3	4	51	25	.273
1998 Montreal-Los Angeles a	N.L.	SS	156	589	62	160	21	1	10	62	18	.272
1999 San Bernardino	California	SS	4	16	2	4	0	0	0	0	0	.250
1999 Los Angeles b	N.L.	SS	123	488	72	159	23	5	7	46	6	.326
2000 Los Angeles	N.L.	2B-SS	148	617	101	172	35	6	7	49	12	.279
2001 Los Angeles c	N.L.	2B	133	539	83	146	21	3	13	55	4	.271
2002 Los Angeles d	N.L.	2B	150	536	56	145	23	0	9	50	4	.271
2003 Iowa	P.C.	2B	2	10	1	5	0	0	0	1	0	.500
2003 Chicago e-f	N.L.	2B	121	481	73	151	38	1	3	38	6	.314
2004 Iowa	P.C.	2B	8	28	6	7	3	0	2	4	0	.250
2004 Chicago g-h	N.L.	2B	81	257	32	79	12	1	6	23	1	.307
2005 St. Louis i	N.L.	2B	137	528	64	155	30	3	8	59	8	.294
2006 Kansas City	A.L.	2B-SS	134	548	85	163	32	4	7	52	3	.297
2007 Kansas City j	A.L.	2B-SS	116	453	70	137	32	3	6	51	1	.302
2008 Kansas City k-l	A.L.	2B	86	331	36	99	24	0	3	24	2	.299
Major League Totals			14 Yrs.	1772	6942	936	2010	391	36	90	629	131	.290
Division Series													
2003 Chicago	N.L.	2B	5	20	2	3	0	0	0	0	0	.150
2005 St. Louis	N.L.	2B	3	13	2	2	0	0	0	0	0	.154
Division Series Totals				8	33	4	5	0	0	0	0	0	.152
Championship Series													
2003 Chicago	N.L.	2B	7	30	2	6	1	1	0	3	0	.200
2005 St. Louis	N.L.	2B	6	22	2	5	0	0	0	2	0	.227
Championship Series Totals				13	52	4	11	1	1	0	5	0	.212

a Traded to Los Angeles Dodgers with outfielder Hiram Bocachica and pitcher Carlos Perez for infielder Wilton Guerrero, outfielder Peter Bergeron, pitcher Ted Lilly and infielder Jonathan Tucker, July 31, 1998.
b On disabled list from June 3 to July 6, 1999.
c On disabled list from June 12 to June 28, 2001.
d Traded to Chicago Cubs with infielder Eric Karros for catcher Todd Hundley and outfielder Chad Hermansen, December 4, 2002.
e On disabled list from August 3 to September 2, 2003.
f Filed for free agency, October 29, 2003, re-signed with Chicago Cubs, December 7, 2003.
g On disabled list from April 10 to June 19, 2004.
h Filed for free agency, October 28, 2004. Signed with St. Louis Cardinals, January 5, 2005.
i Filed for free agency, October 27, 2005. Signed with Kansas City Royals, December 16, 2005.
j On disabled list from June 13 to July 5, 2007.
k On disabled list from August 2 to September 29, 2008.
l Filed for free agency, October 30, 2008.

GUERRERO, VLADIMIR NIZAO

Born, Nizao, Dominican Republic, February 9, 1976.
Bats Right. Throws Right. Height, 6 feet, 3 inches. Weight, 235 pounds.

Year Club	Lea	Pos	G	AB	R	H	2B	3B	HR	RBI	SB	Avg
1994 Montreal.......	Dominican	OF	25	92	34	39	11	0	12	35	5	.424
1994 Expos..........	Gulf Coast	OF	37	137	24	43	13	3	5	25	0	.314
1995 Albany	So.Atl.	OF	110	421	77	140	21	10	16	63	12	.333
1996 Wst Plm Bch	Fla.St.	OF	20	80	16	29	8	0	5	18	2	.363
1996 Harrisburg	Eastern	OF	118	417	84	150	32	8	19	78	17	.360
1996 Montreal...........	N.L.	OF	9	27	2	5	0	0	1	1	0	.185
1997 Wst. Plm. Bch	Fla. St.	OF	3	10	0	4	2	0	0	2	1	.400
1997 Montreal a	N.L.	OF	90	325	44	98	22	2	11	40	3	.302
1998 Montreal...........	N.L.	OF	159	623	108	202	37	7	38	109	11	.324
1999 Montreal...........	N.L.	OF	160	610	102	193	37	5	42	131	14	.316
2000 Montreal...........	N.L.	OF	154	571	101	197	28	11	44	123	9	.345
2001 Montreal...........	N.L.	OF	159	599	107	184	45	4	34	108	37	.307
2002 Montreal...........	N.L.	OF	161	614	106	*206	37	2	39	111	40	.336
2003 Brevard County	Fla.St.	OF	3	6	2	3	0	0	1	1	0	.500
2003 Montreal b-c	N.L.	OF	112	394	71	130	20	3	25	79	9	.330
2004 Anaheim d	A.L.	OF	156	612	*124	206	39	2	39	126	15	.337
2005 Los Angeles e........	A.L.	OF	141	520	95	165	29	2	32	108	13	.317
2006 Los Angeles	A.L.	OF	156	607	92	200	34	1	33	116	15	.329
2007 Los Angeles	A.L.	OF	150	574	89	186	45	1	27	125	2	.324
2008 Los Angeles	A.L.	OF	143	541	85	164	31	3	27	91	5	.303
Major League Totals	13 Yrs.		1750	6617	1126	2136	404	43	392	1268	173	.323
Division Series												
2004 Anaheim...........	A.L.	OF	3	12	1	2	0	0	1	6	0	.167
2005 Los Angeles........	A.L.	OF	5	18	5	6	0	0	0	0	1	.333
2007 Los Angeles........	A.L.	OF-DH	3	10	0	2	0	0	0	0	0	.200
2008 Los Angeles........	A.L.	DH	4	15	2	7	1	0	0	0	1	.467
Division Series Totals			15	55	8	17	1	0	1	6	2	.309
Championship Series												
2005 Los Angeles..........	A.L.	OF-DH	5	20	0	1	0	0	0	1	0	.050

a On disabled list from April 1 to May 2 and June 6 to June 21 and July 12 to July 27, 1997.
b On disabled list from June 5 to July 21, 2003.
c Filed for free agency, October 27, 2003. Signed with Anaheim Angels, January 12, 2004.
d Selected Most Valuable Player in American League for 2004.
e On disabled list from May 21 to June 10, 2005.

GUILLEN, CARLOS ALFONSO

Born, Maracay, Venezuela, September 30, 1975.
Bats Both. Throws Right. Height, 6 feet, 1 inch. Weight, 215 pounds.

Year Club	Lea	Pos	G	AB	R	H	2B	3B	HR	RBI	SB	Avg
1993 Houston	Dominican	SS	18	56	12	14	4	2	0	8	0	.250
1994 a.....................			INJURED—Did Not Play									
1995 Astros	Gulf Coast	DH	30	105	17	31	4	2	2	15	17	.295
1996 Quad City b	Midwest	SS	29	112	23	37	7	1	3	17	13	.330
1997 Jackson	Texas	SS	115	390	47	99	16	1	10	39	6	.254
1997 New Orleans..........	A.A.	SS	3	13	3	4	1	0	0	0	0	.308
1998 New Orleans.........	P.C.	SS	100	374	67	109	18	4	12	51	3	.291
1998 Tacoma.............	P.C.	2B	24	92	8	21	1	1	1	4	1	.228
1998 Seattle c-d	A.L.	2B	10	39	9	13	.1	1	0	5	2	.333
1999 Seattle e	A.L.	SS-2B	5	19	2	3	0	0	1	3	0	.158
2000 Tacoma	P.C.	3B	24	87	19	26	4	1	2	11	4	.299
2000 Seattle f	A.L.	3B-SS	90	288	45	74	15	2	7	42	1	.257
2001 Seattle	A.L.	SS	140	456	72	118	21	4	5	53	4	.259
2002 Seattle	A.L.	SS	134	475	73	124	24	6	9	56	4	.261
2003 Tacoma	P.C.	3B	4	14	2	5	1	0	2	4	0	.357
2003 Seattle g-h	A.L.	SS-3B	109	388	63	107	19	3	7	52	4	.276
2004 Detroit	A.L.	SS	136	522	97	166	37	10	20	97	12	.318
2005 Detroit i	A.L.	SS	87	334	48	107	15	4	5	23	2	.320
2006 Detroit	A.L.	SS-1B	153	543	100	174	41	5	19	85	20	.320
2007 Detroit	A.L.	SS-1B	151	564	86	167	35	9	21	102	13	.296
2008 Detroit	A.L.	3B-1B-OF	113	420	68	120	29	2	10	54	9	.286
Major League Totals	11 Yrs.		1128	4048	663	1173	237	46	104	572	71	.290
Division Series												
2000 Seattle	A.L.	PH	1	1	0	1	0	0	0	1	0	1.000
2006 Detroit	A.L.	SS	4	14	3	8	3	0	1	2	0	.571
Division Series Totals			5	15	3	9	3	0	1	3	0	.600

Year	Club	Lea	Pos	G	AB	R	H	2B	3B	HR	RBI	SB	Avg
	Championship Series												
2000 Seattle		A.L.	3B	2	5	1	1	0	0	0	1	2	0	.200
2001 Seattle		A.L.	SS	3	8	1	2	0	0	0	0	0	.250
2006 Detroit		A.L.	1B-SS	4	16	1	3	1	0	0	0	0	.188
Championship Series Totals				9	29	3	6	1	0	1	2	0	.207
	World Series Record												
2006 Detroit		A.L.	SS-1B	5	17	2	6	1	1	0	2	1	.353

a On disabled list from June 1 to September 12, 1994.
b On disabled list from May 21 to September 11, 1996.
c Traded by Houston Astros to Seattle Mariners with pitcher Freddy Garcia and player to be named later for pitcher Randy Johnson, July 31, 1998.
d Seattle Mariners received pitcher John Halama to complete trade, October 1, 1998.
e On disabled list from April 11 to November 12, 1999.
f On disabled list from April 13 to April 27, 2000.
g On disabled list from July 29 to August 23, 2003.
h Traded to Detroit Tigers for infielder Ramon Santiago and infielder Juan Gonzalez, January 8, 2004.
i On disabled list from June 8 to June 26 and August 11 to September 23, 2005.

GUILLEN, JOSE MANUEL

Born, San Cristobal, Dominican Republic, May 17, 1976.
Bats Right. Throws Right. Height, 5 feet, 11 inches. Weight, 195 pounds.

Year	Club	Lea	Pos	G	AB	R	H	2B	3B	HR	RBI	SB	Avg
1993 Pittsburgh	Dominican	OF	63	234	39	53	3	4	11	31	10	.226
1994 Pirates	Gulf Coast	OF	30	110	17	29	4	1	4	11	2	.264
1995 Erie	N.Y.-Penn.	OF	66	258	41	81	17	1	12	46	1	.314
1995 Augusta	So.Atl.	OF	10	34	6	8	1	1	2	6	0	.235
1996 Lynchburg	Carolina	OF	136	528	78	170	30	4	21	94	24	.322
1997 Pittsburgh	N.L.	OF	143	498	58	133	20	5	14	70	1	.267
1998 Pittsburgh	N.L.	OF	153	573	60	153	38	2	14	84	3	.267
1999 Pittsburgh	N.L.	OF	40	120	18	32	6	0	1	18	1	.267
1999 Nashville	P.C.	OF	35	132	28	44	10	1	5	22	0	.333
1999 Durham	Int.	OF	9	34	8	13	1	0	3	12	0	.382
1999 Tampa Bay a-b	A.L.	OF	47	168	24	41	10	0	2	13	0	.244
2000 Durham	Int.	OF	19	78	20	33	8	2	9	31	0	.423
2000 Tampa Bay c	A.L.	OF	105	316	40	80	16	5	10	41	3	.253
2001 Durham	Int.	OF	33	119	18	35	9	0	7	29	0	.294
2001 Tampa Bay d-e-f	A.L.	OF	41	135	14	37	5	0	3	11	2	.274
2002 Colorado Springs	P.C.	OF	5	17	2	7	3	0	0	5	0	.412
2002 Louisville	Int.	OF	8	29	4	9	4	0	2	8	0	.310
2002 Arizona-Cincinnati g	N.L.	OF	85	240	25	57	7	0	8	31	4	.237
2003 Louisville	Int.	OF	4	15	4	5	1	0	0	3	1	.333
2003 Cincinnati	N.L.	OF	91	315	52	106	21	1	23	63	1	.337
2003 Oakland h-i	A.L.	OF	45	170	25	45	7	1	8	23	0	.265
2004 Anaheim j	A.L.	OF	148	565	88	166	28	3	27	104	5	.294
2005 Washington	N.L.	OF	148	551	81	156	32	2	24	76	1	.283
2006 Potomac	Carolina	OF	3	6	2	3	0	0	2	3	0	.500
2006 Washington k-l	N.L.	OF	69	241	28	52	15	1	9	40	1	.216
2007 Seattle m	A.L.	OF	153	593	84	172	28	2	23	99	5	.290
2008 Kansas City	A.L.	OF	153	598	66	158	42	1	20	97	2	.264
Major League Totals			12 Yrs.	1421	5083	663	1388	275	23	186	770	29	.273
	Division Series												
2003 Oakland	A.L.	OF	4	11	1	5	1	0	0	1	0	.455

a Traded to Tampa Bay Devil Rays with pitcher Jeff Sparks for catcher Joe Oliver and catcher Humberto Cota, July 23, 1999.
b On disabled list from July 23 to 30, 1999.
c On disabled list from March 28 to April 11, 2000.
d On disabled list from May 18 to June 24 and June 25 to July 30, 2001.
e On disabled list from August 7 to 24, 2001.
f Released by Tampa Bay Devil Rays, November 27, 2001. Signed with Arizona Diamondbacks, December 12, 2001.
g Released by Arizona Diamondbacks, July 22, 2002. Signed with Cincinnati Reds organization, July 26, 2002.
h Traded to Oakland Athletics for pitcher Aaron Harang, pitcher Joe Valentine and pitcher Jeff Bruksch, July 30, 2003.
i Filed for free agency, October 30, 2003. Signed with Anaheim Angels, December 19, 2003.
j Traded to Washington Nationals for outfielder Juan Rivera and infielder Maicer Izturis, November 19, 2004.
k On disabled list from May 26 to June 10 and July 19 to October 9, 2006.
l Filed for free agency, October 29, 2006. Signed with Seattle Mariners, December 4, 2006.
m Filed for free agency, November 12, 2007. Signed with Kansas City Royals, December 6, 2007.

GUTIERREZ, FRANKLIN RAFAEL

Born, Caracas, Venezuela, February 21, 1983.
Bats Right. Throws Right. Height, 6 feet, 2 inches. Weight, 180 pounds.

Year Club	Lea	Pos	G	AB	R	H	2B	3B	HR	RBI	SB	Avg
2001 Dodgers.......	Gulf Coast	OF	56	234	38	63	16	0	4	30	9	.269
2002 Las Vegas.............	P.C.	OF	2	10	2	3	2	0	0	2	0	.300
2002 South Bend........	So.Atl.	OF	92	361	61	102	18	4	12	45	13	.283
2003 Vero Beach.........	Fla.St.	OF	110	425	65	120	28	5	20	68	17	.282
2003 Jacksonville......	Southern	OF	18	67	12	21	3	2	4	12	3	.313
2004 Akron.............	Eastern	OF	70	262	38	79	24	2	5	35	6	.302
2004 Buffalo a..........	Int.	DH	7	27	4	4	1	0	1	3	0	.148
2005 Akron.............	Eastern	OF	95	383	70	100	25	2	11	42	14	.261
2005 Buffalo...........	Int.	OF	19	67	10	17	6	2	0	7	2	.254
2005 Cleveland.........	A.L.	OF	7	1	2	0	0	0	0	0	0	.000
2006 Buffalo...........	Int.	OF	90	349	63	97	27	0	9	38	13	.278
2006 Cleveland.........	A.L.	OF	43	136	21	37	9	0	1	8	0	.272
2007 Buffalo...........	Int.	OF	30	129	29	44	7	0	4	16	7	.341
2007 Cleveland b.......	A.L.	OF	100	271	41	72	13	2	13	36	8	.266
2008 Cleveland c.......	A.L.	OF	134	399	54	99	26	2	8	41	9	.248
Major League Totals	4 Yrs.		284	807	118	208	48	4	22	85	17	.258
Division Series												
2007 Cleveland...........	A.L.	OF	4	10	2	2	0	0	0	0	0	.200
Championship Series												
2007 Cleveland............	A.L.	OF	6	19	3	4	0	0	1	4	0	.211

a Traded to Cleveland Indians with player to be named later for outfielder Milton Bradley, April 4, 2004. Cleveland Indians received pitcher Andrew Brown to complete trade, May 19, 2004.
b On disabled list from March 23 to April 13, 2007.
c Traded to Seattle Mariners for pitcher Luis Valbuena and pitcher Joe Smith, December 10, 2008.

GUZMAN, CRISTIAN

Born, Santo Domingo, Dominican Republic, March 21, 1978.
Bats Both. Throws Right. Height, 6 feet. Weight, 215 pounds.

Year Club	Lea	Pos	G	AB	R	H	2B	3B	HR	RBI	SB	Avg
1995 Yankees........	Dominican	SS	46	160	24	43	6	5	3	20	11	.269
1996 Yankees........	Gulf Coast	SS	42	170	37	50	8	2	1	21	7	.294
1997 Tampa.........	Fla.St.	SS	14	14	4	4	0	0	0	1	0	.286
1997 Greensboro........	So.Atl.	SS	124	495	68	135	21	4	4	52	23	.273
1998 New Britain a......	Eastern	SS	140	566	68	157	29	5	1	40	23	.277
1999 Minnesota..........	A.L.	SS	131	420	47	95	12	3	1	26	9	.226
2000 Minnesota..........	A.L.	SS	156	631	89	156	25	*20	8	54	28	.247
2001 Twins.........	Gulf Coast	SS	5	16	4	4	0	1	0	0	0	.250
2001 Minnesota c..........	A.L.	SS	118	493	80	149	28	*14	10	51	25	.302
2002 Minnesota..........	A.L.	SS	148	623	80	170	31	6	9	59	12	.273
2003 Minnesota..........	A.L.	SS	143	534	78	143	15	*14	3	53	18	.268
2004 Minnesota d..........	A.L.	SS	145	576	84	158	31	4	8	46	10	.274
2005 Washington.........	N.L.	SS	142	456	39	100	19	6	4	31	7	.219
2006 Washington e.........	N.L.				INJURED — Did Not Play							
2007 Washington f.........	N.L.	SS	46	174	31	57	6	6	2	14	2	.328
2008 Washington.........	N.L.	SS	138	579	77	183	35	5	9	55	6	.316
Major League Totals	9 Yrs.		1167	4486	605	1211	202	78	54	389	117	.270
Division Series												
2002 Minnesota	A.L.	SS	5	21	5	6	2	0	1	2	2	.286
2003 Minnesota	A.L.	SS	4	13	1	2	0	0	0	0	0	.154
2004 Minnesota	A.L.	SS	4	15	2	5	0	0	0	0	1	.333
Division Series Totals			13	49	8	13	2	0	1	2	3	.265
Championship Series												
2002 Minnesota	A.L.	SS	5	18	1	3	1	0	0	0	0	.167

a Traded by New York Yankees to Minnesota Twins with pitcher Eric Milton, pitcher Danny Mota, outfielder Brian Buchanan and cash for infielder Chuck Knoblauch, February 6, 1998.
b On disabled list from May 27 to June 11, 1999.
c On disabled list from July 13 to August 17, 2001.
d Filed for free agency, October 29, 2004. Signed with Washington Nationals, November 16, 2004.
e On disabled list from March 24 to October 9, 2006.
f On disabled list from April 3 to May 7 and June 25 to September 21, 2007.

HAFNER, TRAVIS LEE
Born, Jamestown, North Dakota, June 3, 1977.
Bats Left. Throws Right. Height, 6 feet, 3 inches. Weight, 240 pounds.

Year	Club	Lea	Pos	G	AB	R	H	2B	3B	HR	RBI	SB	Avg
1997 Rangers	Gulf Coast	1B-OF	55	189	38	54	14	0	5	24	7	.286
1998 Savannah	So.Atl.	1B-3B-OF	123	405	62	96	15	4	16	84	7	.237
1999 Savannah	So.Atl.	1B	134	480	94	140	30	4	28	111	5	.292
2000 Charlotte a	Fla.St.	1B-3B	122	436	90	151	34	1	22	109	0	.346
2001 Tulsa b	Texas	1B	88	323	59	91	25	0	20	74	3	.282
2002 Oklahoma	P.C.	1B	110	401	79	137	22	1	21	77	2	.342
2002 Texas c	A.L.	DH-1B	23	62	6	15	4	1	1	6	0	.242
2003 Buffalo	Int.	1B	29	100	15	27	4	0	2	10	2	.270
2003 Cleveland d	A.L.	DH-1B	91	291	35	74	19	3	14	40	2	.254
2004 Cleveland	A.L.	DH-1B	140	482	96	150	41	3	28	109	3	.311
2005 Akron	Eastern	DH	3	9	0	0	0	0	0	0	0	.000
2005 Cleveland e	A.L.	DH-1B	137	486	94	148	42	0	33	108	0	.305
2006 Cleveland	A.L.	DH-1B	129	454	100	140	31	1	42	117	0	.308
2007 Cleveland	A.L.	DH-1B	152	545	80	145	25	2	24	100	1	.266
2008 Buffalo	Int.	DH	7	22	4	7	3	0	0	4	0	.318
2008 Cleveland f	A.L.	DH	57	198	21	39	10	0	5	24	1	.197
Major League Totals			7 Yrs.	729	2518	432	711	172	10	147	504	7	.282
Division Series													
2007 Cleveland	A.L.	DH	4	16	4	4	0	0	1	2	0	.250
Championship Series													
2007 Cleveland	A.L.	DH	7	27	2	4	1	0	1	2	0	.148

a On disabled list from August 6 to 22, 2000.
b On disabled list from April 5 to May 11, 2001.
c Traded to Cleveland Indians with pitcher Aaron Myette for catcher Einar Diaz and pitcher Ryan Drese, December 6, 2002.
d On disabled list from May 10 to May 26, 2003.
e On disabled list from July 17 to August 4, 2005.
f On disabled list from May 26 to September 9, 2008.

HAIRSTON, JERRY WAYNE JR.
Born, Naperville, Illinois, May 29, 1976.
Bats Right. Throws Right. Height, 5 feet, 10 inches. Weight, 185 pounds.

Year	Club	Lea	Pos	G	AB	R	H	2B	3B	HR	RBI	SB	Avg
1997 Bluefield	Appal.	SS	59	221	44	73	13	4	2	36	13	.330
1998 Frederick	Carolina	SS-2B	80	293	56	83	22	3	5	33	13	.283
1998 Bowie	Eastern	2B-SS	55	221	42	72	12	3	5	37	6	.326
1998 Baltimore	A.L.	2B	6	7	2	0	0	0	0	0	0	.000
1999 Rochester	Int.	2B	107	413	65	120	24	5	7	48	19	.291
1999 Baltimore	A.L.	2B	50	175	26	47	12	1	4	17	9	.269
2000 Rochester	Int.	2B-SS	58	201	43	59	15	1	4	21	6	.294
2000 Orioles	Gulf Coast	2B	4	10	3	3	2	0	0	1	0	.300
2000 Frederick	Carolina	2B	2	8	1	3	2	0	0	1	0	.375
2000 Baltimore a	A.L.	2B	49	180	27	46	5	0	5	19	8	.256
2001 Baltimore	A.L.	2B	159	532	63	124	25	5	8	47	29	.233
2002 Baltimore	A.L.	2B	122	426	55	114	25	3	5	32	21	.268
2003 Aberdeen	N.Y.-Penn.	2B	2	3	2	1	0	0	0	0	1	.333
2003 Bowie	Eastern	2B	6	20	4	6	1	0	1	2	0	.300
2003 Baltimore b	A.L.	2B	58	218	25	59	12	2	2	21	14	.271
2004 Bowie	Eastern	2B	5	13	4	2	1	0	0	2	2	.154
2004 Baltimore c	A.L.	OF-2B-3B	86	287	43	87	19	1	2	24	13	.303
2005 Iowa	P.C.	2B-OF	5	22	3	7	0	1	0	2	3	.318
2005 Chicago d-e	N.L.	OF-2B-SS	114	380	51	99	25	2	4	30	8	.261
2006 Chicago	N.L.	2B-OF-1B	38	82	8	17	3	0	0	4	3	.207
2006 Texas f-g	A.L.	OF-SS-2B-3B	63	88	17	18	3	1	0	6	2	.205
2007 Frisco	Texas	DH	3	12	2	2	1	0	1	2	0	.167
2007 Oklahoma	P.C.	SS-OF	4	15	2	2	0	0	1	1	0	.133
2007 Texas h-i	A.L.	OF-2B-3B-SS	73	159	22	30	7	0	3	16	5	.189
2008 Louisville	Int.	OF-SS-3B-2B	20	79	11	30	8	2	4	19	1	.380
2008 Cincinnati j-k	N.L.	OF-SS-2B-3B	80	261	47	85	20	2	6	36	15	.326
Major League Totals			11 Yrs.	898	2795	386	726	156	17	39	252	127	.260

a On disabled list from May 16 to July 4, 2000.
b On disabled list from May 21 to September 4, 2003.
c On disabled list from March 31 to May 11 and from August 18 to November 3, 2004.
d Traded to Chicago Cubs with infielder Mike Fontenot and pitcher Dave Crouthers for outfielder Sammy Sosa, February 2, 2005.
e On disabled list from August 4 to August 19, 2005.

f Traded to Texas Rangers for infielder Phil Nevin, May 31, 2006.
g Filed for free agency, October 13, 2006. re-signed with Texas Rangers organization, January 5, 2007.
h On disabled list from May 17 to June 5 and August 8 to August 29, 2007.
i Filed for free agency, October 30, 2007. Signed with Cincinnati Reds organization, March 3, 2008.
j On disabled list from June 10 to June 26 and July 14 to August 1 and August 18 to September 8, 2008.
k Filed for free agency, October 31, 2008, re-signed with Cincinnati Reds, January 7, 2009.

HAIRSTON, SCOTT ALEXANDER

Born, Fort Worth, Texas, May 25, 1980.
Bats Right. Throws Right. Height, 6 feet. Weight, 190 pounds.

Year Club	Lea	Pos	G	AB	R	H	2B	3B	HR	RBI	SB	Avg
2001 Missoula ....Pioneer		2B	74	291	81	101	16	6	14	65	2	.347
2002 Lancaster ....Calif.		2B-3B	18	79	20	32	11	1	6	26	1	.405
2002 South Bend ....Midwest		2B-3B	109	394	79	131	35	4	16	72	9	.332
2003 Tucson .............P.C.		DH	1	0	0	0	0	0	0	1	0	.000
2003 El Paso .... Texas		2B	88	337	53	93	21	7	10	47	6	.276
2004 Tucson...............P.C.		2B-OF	28	115	29	36	8	3	5	20	0	.313
2004 Arizona..............N.L.		2B-OF	101	339	39	84	15	6	13	29	3	.248
2005 Arizona..............N.L.		OF	15	20	0	2	1	0	0	0	0	.100
2005 Tucson a..............P.C.		OF-2B	58	209	45	65	8	3	16	40	3	.311
2006 Tucson................P.C.		OF	98	381	83	123	22	1	26	81	3	.323
2006 Arizona b............N.L.		OF	9	15	2	6	2	0	0	2	0	.400
2007 Arizona-San Diego c-d .. N.L.		OF	107	263	37	64	18	2	11	36	0	.243
2008 San Diego e .........N.L.		OF-2B	112	326	42	81	18	3	17	31	3	.248
Major League Totals		5 Yrs.	344	963	120	237	54	11	41	98	8	.246

a On disabled list from September 2 to November 14, 2005.
b On disabled list from June 20 to July 29, 2006.
c Traded to San Diego Padres for pitcher Leo Rosales, July 27, 2007.
d On disabled list from August 10 to September 8, 2007.
e On disabled list from August 28 to October 2, 2008.

HALL, WILLIAM (BILL)

Born, Tupelo, Mississippi, December 28, 1979.
Bats Right. Throws Right. Height, 6 feet. Weight, 210 pounds.

Year Club	Lea	Pos	G	AB	R	H	2B	3B	HR	RBI	SB	Avg
1998 Helena ....Pioneer		SS	29	85	11	15	3	0	0	5	5	.176
1999 Ogden ....Pioneer		SS	69	280	41	81	15	2	6	31	19	.289
2000 Beloit .... Midwest		SS	130	470	57	123	30	6	3	41	10	.262
2001 High Desert .. California		SS	89	346	61	105	21	6	15	51	18	.303
2001 Huntsville.....Southern		SS	41	160	14	41	8	1	3	14	5	.256
2002 Indianapolis ....Int.		SS	134	465	35	106	20	1	4	31	17	.228
2002 Milwaukee .......N.L.		SS-3B	19	36	3	7	1	1	1	5	0	.194
2003 Indianapolis ....Int.		2B-SS-OF	89	354	57	100	25	2	5	32	10	.282
2003 Milwaukee .......N.L.		2B-SS-3B	52	142	23	37	9	2	5	20	1	.261
2004 Milwaukee .......N.L.		2B-SS-3B	126	390	43	93	20	3	9	53	12	.238
2005 Milwaukee ......N.L.		SS-3B-2B	146	501	69	146	39	6	17	62	18	.291
2006 Milwaukee .......N.L.		SS-3B-OF-2B	148	537	101	145	39	4	35	85	8	.270
2007 Azl Brewers ... Arizona		OF	2	6	0	1	0	0	0	0	0	.167
2007 Milwaukee a......N.L.		OF	136	452	59	115	35	0	14	63	4	.254
2008 Milwaukee .......N.L.		3B-2B	128	404	50	91	22	1	15	55	5	.225
Major League Totals		7 Yrs.	755	2462	348	634	165	17	96	343	48	.258
Division Series												
2008 Milwaukee ........N.L.		3B	3	8	1	2	0	0	0	0	0	.250

a On disabled list from July 6 to July 25, 2007.

HAMILTON, JOSHUA HOLT (JOSH)

Born, Raleigh, North Carolina, May 21, 1981.
Bats Left. Throws Left. Height, 6 feet, 4 inches. Weight, 235 pounds.

Year Club	Lea	Pos	G	AB	R	H	2B	3B	HR	RBI	SB	Avg
1999 Princeton ....Appal.		OF	56	236	49	82	20	4	10	48	17	.347
1999 Hudson Valley ... N.Y.-Penn.		OF	16	72	7	14	3	0	0	7	1	.194
2000 Charleston-SC ...... So.Atl.		OF	96	391	62	118	23	3	13	61	14	.302
2001 Charleston-SC ...... So.Atl.		OF	4	11	3	4	1	0	1	2	0	.364
2001 Orlando .... Southern		OF	23	89	5	16	5	0	0	4	2	.180
2002 Bakersfield ....Calif.		OF	56	211	32	64	14	1	9	44	10	.303
2003-05		Did Not Play										
2006 Hudson Valley a .. N.Y.-Penn.		OF	15	50	7	13	3	1	0	5	0	.260

Year Club	Lea	Pos	G	AB	R	H	2B	3B	HR	RBI	SB	Avg
2007 Louisville	Int.	OF	11	40	9	14	1	0	4	8	3	.350
2007 Cincinnati b-c	N.L.	OF	90	298	52	87	17	2	19	47	3	.292
2008 Texas	A.L.	OF	156	624	98	190	35	5	32	*130	9	.304
Major League Totals	2 Yrs.		246	922	150	277	52	7	51	177	12	.300

a Selected by Chicago Cubs from Tampa Bay Devil Rays in Rule V draft, December 7, 2006. Sold to Cincinnati Reds, December 7, 2006.
b On disabled list from May 19 to June 4 and July 8 to August 12, 2007.
c Traded to Texas Rangers for pitcher Edinson Volquez and pitcher Danny Herrera, December 21, 2007.

HANIGAN, RYAN M.

Born, Washington, District of Columbia, August 16, 1980.
Bats Right. Throws Right. Height, 6 feet. Weight, 195 pounds.

Year Club	Lea	Pos	G	AB	R	H	2B	3B	HR	RBI	SB	Avg
2002 Dayton	Midwest	C	6	11	1	3	1	0	0	0	0	.273
2003 Louisville	Int.	C	1	3	1	1	0	0	0	0	0	.333
2003 Dayton	Midwest	C	92	311	43	86	12	0	1	31	3	.277
2004 Potomac	Carolina	C	119	429	58	127	21	0	5	56	6	.296
2005 Chattanooga	Southern	1B-C	100	333	45	107	14	1	4	29	4	.321
2006 Louisville	Int.	C-1B	8	13	2	2	0	0	0	1	0	.154
2006 Chattanooga	Southern	C-1B-OF	56	126	17	31	2	0	0	14	0	.246
2007 Chattanooga	Southern	C-1B	60	197	30	59	14	1	3	27	0	.299
2007 Louisville	Int.	C-1B	41	127	16	32	5	0	1	9	0	.252
2007 Cincinnati	N.L.	C	5	10	3	3	1	0	0	2	0	.300
2008 Louisville	Int.	C-1B	75	272	37	88	14	0	4	35	1	.324
2008 Cincinnati	N.L.	C	31	85	9	23	2	0	2	9	0	.271
Major League Totals	2 Yrs.		36	95	12	26	3	0	2	11	0	.274

HANNAHAN, JOHN JOSEPH (JACK)

Born, St. Paul, Minnesota, March 4, 1980.
Bats Left. Throws Right. Height, 6 feet, 2 inches. Weight, 205 pounds.

Year Club	Lea	Pos	G	AB	R	H	2B	3B	HR	RBI	SB	Avg
2001 West Michigan .	Midwest	3B	46	170	24	54	11	0	1	27	4	.318
2001 Oneonta	N.Y.-Penn.	3B	14	55	11	16	4	1	0	8	2	.291
2002 Erie	Eastern	3B	65	226	17	54	12	1	3	20	2	.239
2002 Lakeland	Fla.St.	3B	66	246	28	67	11	1	6	42	9	.272
2003 Erie	Eastern	3B	135	471	64	121	18	0	9	45	2	.257
2004 Erie	Eastern	3B-SS	108	374	48	102	21	1	8	39	7	.273
2005 Erie	Eastern	3B	7	22	1	3	0	0	0	1	0	.136
2005 Toledo	Int.	1B	3	9	0	0	0	0	0	0	0	.000
2006 Detroit	A.L.	2B-3B-1B	68	238	31	64	15	0	4	28	6	.269
2006 Toledo	Int.	2B-3B-1B	119	415	59	117	27	0	9	62	9	.282
2007 Toledo	Int.	2B-3B-1B	101	336	56	99	20	1	13	63	5	.295
2007 Oakland a	A.L.	3B	41	144	16	40	12	0	3	24	1	.278
2008 Oakland	A.L.	3B-1B	143	436	48	95	27	0	9	47	2	.218
Major League Totals	3 Yrs.		187	589	64	135	39	0	12	71	3	.229

a Traded to Oakland Athletics for outfielder Jason Perry, August 13, 2007.

HARDY, JAMES JERRY (J.J.)

Born, Tucson, Arizona, August 19, 1982.
Bats Right. Throws Right. Height, 6 feet, 2 inches. Weight, 190 pounds.

Year Club	Lea	Pos	G	AB	R	H	2B	3B	HR	RBI	SB	Avg
2001 Brewers	Arizona	SS	5	20	6	5	2	1	0	1	0	.250
2001 Ogden	Pioneer	SS	35	125	20	31	5	0	2	15	1	.248
2002 High Desert	California	SS	84	335	53	98	19	1	6	48	9	.293
2002 Huntsville	Southern	SS	38	145	14	33	7	0	1	13	1	.228
2003 Huntsville	Southern	SS	114	416	67	116	26	0	12	62	6	.279
2004 Indianapolis	Int.	SS	26	101	17	28	10	0	4	20	0	.277
2005 Milwaukee	N.L.	SS	124	372	46	92	22	1	9	50	0	.247
2006 Milwaukee a	N.L.	SS	35	128	13	31	5	0	5	14	1	.242
2007 Milwaukee	N.L.	SS	151	592	89	164	30	1	26	80	2	.277
2008 Milwaukee	N.L.	SS	146	569	78	161	31	4	24	74	2	.283
Major League Totals	4 Yrs.		456	1661	226	448	88	6	64	218	5	.2703
Division Series												
2008 Milwaukee	N.L.	SS	4	14	2	6	1	0	0	2	0	.429

a On disabled list from May 17 to October 31, 2006.

HARRIS, BRENDAN MICHAEL

Born, Albany, New York, August 26, 1980.
Bats Right. Throws Right. Height, 6 feet, 1 inch. Weight, 200 pounds.

Year	Club	Lea	Pos	G	AB	R	H	2B	3B	HR	RBI	SB	Avg
2001 Lansing	Midwest		2B-3B-SS	32	113	25	31	5	1	4	22	5	.274
2002 Daytona	Fla.St.		3B-2B	110	425	82	140	35	6	13	54	16	.329
2002 West Tenn	Southern		3B-2B	13	53	8	17	4	1	2	11	1	.321
2003 West Tenn	Southern		3B-2B-SS	120	435	56	122	34	7	5	52	6	.280
2004 Iowa	P.C.		2B-SS-3B	69	254	48	79	21	1	11	35	0	.311
2004 Edmonton	P.C.		3B	33	123	20	35	6	0	6	24	0	.285
2004 Chicago-Montreal a	N.L.		2B-3B	23	59	4	10	3	0	1	3	0	.169
2005 Washington	N.L.		2B-3B	4	9	1	3	1	0	1	3	0	.333
2005 New Orleans	P.C.		2B-3B-OF	127	470	67	127	22	4	13	81	9	.270
2006 Louisville	Int.		3B-2B-SS	43	148	22	48	14	1	5	28	2	.324
2006 New Orleans	P.C.		3B-SS-2B-1B	59	219	37	62	14	0	5	32	3	.283
2006 Washington-Cincinnati b	N.L.		2B-SS-3B	25	42	5	10	2	0	1	3	0	.238
2007 Tampa Bay c-d	A.L.		SS-2B-3B	137	521	72	149	35	3	12	59	4	.286
2008 Minnesota	A.L.		SS-2B-3B-1B	130	434	57	115	29	3	7	49	1	.265
Major League Totals			5 Yrs.	319	1065	139	287	70	6	22	117	5	.269

a Traded to Montreal Expos with infielder Alex Gonzalez and pitcher Francis Beltran for infielder Orlando Cabrera, July 31, 2004.

b Traded to Cincinnati Reds with pitcher Gary Majewski, pitcher Bill Bray, infielder Royce Clayton and pitcher Daryl Thompson for outfielder Austin Kearns, infielder Felipe Lopez and pitcher Ryan Wagner, July 13, 2006.

c Traded to Tampa Bay Devil Rays for cash.

d Traded to Minnesota Twins with outfielder Jason Pridie and outfielder Delmon Young for infielder Jason Bartlett, pitcher Matt Garza and pitcher Eduardo Morlan, November 28, 2007.

HARRIS, WILLIAM CHARLES (WILLIE)

Born, Cairo, Georgia, June 22, 1978.
Bats Left. Throws Right. Height, 5 feet, 9 inches. Weight, 175 pounds.

Year	Club	Lea	Pos	G	AB	R	H	2B	3B	HR	RBI	SB	Avg
1999 Bluefield	Appal.		2B	5	22	3	6	1	0	0	3	1	.273
1999 Delmarva	So.Atl.		2B-OF	66	272	42	72	13	3	2	32	17	.265
2000 Delmarva	So.Atl.		2B-OF-SS	133	474	106	130	27	10	6	60	38	.274
2001 Bowie	Eastern		2B-OF	133	525	83	160	27	4	9	49	54	.305
2001 Baltimore	A.L.		OF	9	24	3	3	1	0	0	0	0	.125
2002 Charlotte	Int.		2B-OF	89	360	54	102	16	5	5	33	32	.283
2002 Chicago a	A.L.		2B-OF	49	163	14	38	4	0	2	12	8	.233
2003 Charlotte	Int.		2B-OF	28	100	22	38	6	1	6	13	9	.380
2003 Chicago b	A.L.		OF-2B	79	137	19	28	3	1	0	5	12	.204
2004 Chicago	A.L.		2B-OF	129	409	68	107	15	2	2	27	19	.262
2005 Charlotte	Int.		2B	28	109	21	29	11	1	1	10	10	.266
2005 Chicago	A.L.		2B-SS	56	121	17	31	2	1	1	8	10	.256
2006 Boston c-d	A.L.		OF-2B	47	45	17	7	2	0	0	1	6	.156
2006 Pawtucket	Int.		OF-2B	60	218	32	48	6	1	8	17	11	.220
2007 Richmond	Int.		3B-2B-OF	17	58	17	21	7	2	1	7	7	.362
2007 Atlanta e	N.L.		OF-3B	117	344	56	93	20	8	2	32	17	.270
2008 Washington	N.L.		OF-2B-3B-SS	140	367	58	92	14	4	13	43	13	.251
Major League Totals			8 Yrs.	626	1610	252	399	61	16	20	128	85	.248

Division Series

Year	Club	Lea	Pos	G	AB	R	H	2B	3B	HR	RBI	SB	Avg
2005 Chicago	A.L.		2B	1	1	0	1	0	0	0	1	0	1.000

World Series Record

Year	Club	Lea	Pos	G	AB	R	H	2B	3B	HR	RBI	SB	Avg
2005 Chicago	A.L.		2B	2	1	1	1	0	0	0	0	1	1.000

a Traded to Chicago White Sox for outfielder Chris Singleton, January 29, 2002.

b On disabled list from May 22 to June 16, 2003.

c Not offered contract, December 21, 2005. Signed with Boston Red Sox organization, January 19, 2006.

d Filed for free agency, October 2, 2006. Signed with Atlanta Braves organization, December 9, 2006.

e Released by Atlanta Braves, December 12, 2007. Signed with Washington Nationals, December 13, 2007.

HART, JON COREY (COREY)

Born, Bowling Green, Kentucky, March 24, 1982.
Bats Right. Throws Right. Height, 6 feet, 6 inches. Weight, 215 pounds.

Year	Club	Lea	Pos	G	AB	R	H	2B	3B	HR	RBI	SB	Avg
2000 Ogden	Pioneer		1B	57	216	32	62	9	1	2	30	6	.287
2001 Ogden	Pioneer		1B-OF	69	262	53	89	18	1	11	62	14	.340
2002 High Desert	Calif.		3B-1B	100	393	76	113	26	10	22	84	24	.288
2002 Huntsville	Southern		3B-1B	28	94	16	25	3	0	2	15	3	.266
2003 Huntsville	Southern		3B-OF	130	493	70	149	40	1	13	94	25	.302

81

Year Club	Lea	Pos	G	AB	R	H	2B	3B	HR	RBI	SB	Avg
2004 Indianapolis	Int.	OF-1B	121	440	68	124	29	8	15	67	17	.282
2004 Milwaukee	N.L.	DH	1	1	0	0	0	0	0	0	0	.000
2005 Milwaukee	N.L.	OF	21	57	9	11	2	1	2	7	2	.193
2005 Nashville	P.C.	OF-1B	113	429	85	132	29	9	17	69	31	.308
2006 Milwaukee	N.L.	OF-1B	87	237	32	67	13	2	9	33	5	.283
2007 Milwaukee	N.L.	OF	140	505	86	149	33	9	24	81	23	.295
2008 Milwaukee	N.L.	OF	157	612	76	164	45	6	20	91	23	.268
Major League Totals		5 Yrs.	406	1412	203	391	93	18	55	212	53	.277
Division Series												
2008 Milwaukee	N.L.	OF	4	13	0	3	0	0	0	0	0	.231

HAWPE, BRADLEY BONTE (BRAD)

Born, Fort Worth, Texas, June 22, 1979.
Bats Left. Throws Left. Height, 6 feet, 3 inches. Weight, 205 pounds.

Year Club	Lea	Pos	G	AB	R	H	2B	3B	HR	RBI	SB	Avg
2000 Portland	Northwest	OF-1B	62	205	38	59	19	2	7	29	2	.288
2001 Asheville	So.Atl.	OF-1B	111	393	78	105	22	3	22	72	7	.267
2002 Salem	Carolina	1B	122	450	87	156	38	2	22	97	1	.347
2003 Tulsa	Texas	OF-1B	93	346	52	96	27	0	17	68	1	.277
2004 Colorado Springs	P.C.	OF	92	345	62	111	19	1	31	86	3	.322
2004 Colorado	N.L.	OF	42	105	12	26	3	2	3	9	1	.248
2005 Colorado Springs	P.C.	OF	7	28	7	13	3	0	3	11	0	.464
2005 Colorado a	N.L.	OF	101	305	38	80	10	3	9	47	2	.262
2006 Colorado	N.L.	OF	150	499	67	146	33	6	22	84	5	.293
2007 Colorado	N.L.	OF	152	516	80	150	33	4	29	116	0	.291
2008 Colorado Springs	P.C.	OF	3	11	1	1	0	0	0	0	0	.091
2008 Colorado b	N.L.	OF	138	488	69	138	24	3	25	85	2	.283
Major League Totals		5 Yrs.	583	1913	266	540	103	18	88	341	10	.282
Division Series												
2007 Colorado	N.L.	OF	3	11	1	3	0	0	0	0	0	.273
Championship Series												
2007 Colorado	N.L.	OF	4	12	2	4	0	0	0	2	0	.333
World Series Record												
2007 Colorado	N.L.	OF	4	16	1	4	0	1	1	2	0	.250

a On disabled list from July 12 to September 2, 2005.
b On disabled list from May 21 to June 6, 2008.

HEADLEY, CHASE JORDAN

Born, Fountain, Colorado, May 9, 1984.
Bats Both. Throws Right. Height, 6 feet, 2 inches. Weight, 195 pounds.

Year Club	Lea	Pos	G	AB	R	H	2B	3B	HR	RBI	SB	Avg
2005 Fort Wayne	Midwest	3B	4	15	2	3	0	0	0	1	0	.200
2005 Eugene	Northwest	3B	57	220	29	59	14	3	6	33	1	.268
2006 Lake Elsinore	Calif.	3B	129	484	79	141	33	4	12	73	4	.291
2007 San Antonio	Texas	3B	121	433	82	143	38	5	20	78	1	.330
2007 San Diego	N.L.	3B	8	18	1	4	1	0	0	0	0	.222
2008 Portland	P.C.	OF-3B	65	259	49	79	24	1	13	40	0	.305
2008 San Diego	N.L.	OF-3B	91	331	34	89	19	2	9	38	4	.269
Major League Totals		2 Yrs.	99	349	35	93	20	2	9	38	4	.266

HELMS, WESLEY RAY (WES)

Born, Gastonia, North Carolina, May 12, 1976.
Bats Right. Throws Right. Height, 6 feet, 4 inches. Weight, 230 pounds.

Year Club	Lea	Pos	G	AB	R	H	2B	3B	HR	RBI	SB	Avg
1994 Braves	Gulf Coast	3B	56	184	22	49	15	1	4	29	6	.266
1995 Macon	So.Atl.	3B	136	539	89	149	32	1	11	85	2	.276
1996 Durham	Carolina	3B	67	258	40	83	19	2	13	54	1	.322
1996 Greenville	Southern	3B	64	231	24	59	13	2	4	22	2	.255
1997 Richmond	Int.	3B	32	110	11	21	4	0	3	15	1	.191
1997 Greenville	Southern	3B	86	314	50	93	14	1	11	44	3	.296
1998 Richmond	Int.	3B	125	451	56	124	27	1	13	75	6	.275
1998 Atlanta	N.L.	3B	7	13	2	4	1	0	1	2	0	.308
1999 Braves	Gulf Coast	DH	9	33	1	15	2	0	0	10	0	.455
1999 Greenville a-b	Southern	1B	30	113	15	34	6	0	8	26	1	.301
2000 Richmond	Int.	3B	136	539	74	155	27	7	20	88	0	.288

Year	Club	Lea	Pos	G	AB	R	H	2B	3B	HR	RBI	SB	Avg
2000 Atlanta	N.L.	3B	6	5	0	1	0	0	0	0	0	.200
2001 Atlanta	N.L.	1B-3B-OF	100	216	28	48	10	3	10	36	1	.222
2002 Atlanta c-d	N.L.	1B-3B-OF	85	210	20	51	16	0	6	22	1	.243
2003 Indianapolis	Int.	3B	2	5	0	2	0	0	0	0	0	.400
2003 Milwaukee e	N.L.	3B	134	476	56	124	21	0	23	67	0	.261
2004 Indianapolis	Int.	3B	6	19	4	6	1	0	0	1	0	.316
2004 Milwaukee f	N.L.	3B-1B	92	274	24	72	13	1	4	28	0	.263
2005 Milwaukee g	N.L.	3B-1B	95	168	18	50	13	1	4	24	0	.298
2006 Florida h	N.L.	1B-3B-OF	140	240	30	79	19	5	10	47	0	.329
2007 Philadelphia	N.L.	3B-1B	112	280	21	69	19	0	5	39	0	.246
2008 Florida i	N.L.	3B-1B-OF	132	251	28	61	11	0	5	31	0	.243
Major League Totals	10 Yrs.		903	2133	227	559	123	10	68	296	2	.262
Division Series													
2002 Atlanta	N.L.	1B	1	0	0	0	0	0	0	0	0	.000
2007 Philadelphia	N.L.	3B	2	2	1	0	0	0	0	0	0	.000
Division Series Totals			3	2	1	0	0	0	0	0	0	.000

a On Atlanta disabled list from April 3 to July 15 and September 4 to November 1, 1999.
b On Greenville disabled list from August 15 to September 4, 1999.
c On disabled list from August 10 to September 10, 2002.
d Traded to Milwaukee Brewers with pitcher John Foster for pitcher Ray King, December 16, 2002.
e On disabled list from August 6 to August 22, 2003.
f On disabled list from May 19 to June 28, 2004.
g Filed for free agency, October 27, 2005. Signed with Florida Marlins, December 30, 2005.
h Filed for free agency, October 28, 2006. Signed with Philadelphia Phillies, November 17, 2006.
i Traded to Florida Marlins for player to be named later, April 5, 2008.

HELTON, TODD LYNN
Born, Knoxville, Tennessee, August 20, 1973.
Bats Left. Throws Left. Height, 6 feet, 2 inches. Weight, 210 pounds.

Year	Club	Lea	Pos	G	AB	R	H	2B	3B	HR	RBI	SB	Avg
1995 Asheville	So. Atl.	1B	54	201	24	51	11	1	1	15	1	.254
1996 New Haven	Eastern	1B	93	319	46	106	24	2	7	51	2	.332
1996 Colo Sprngs	P.C.	1B-OF	21	71	13	25	4	1	2	13	0	.352
1997 Colo Sprngs	P.C.	1B-OF	99	392	87	138	31	2	16	88	3	.352
1997 Colorado	N.L.	OF-1B	35	93	13	26	2	1	5	11	0	.280
1998 Colorado	N.L.	1B	152	530	78	167	37	1	25	97	3	.315
1999 Colorado	N.L.	1B	159	578	114	185	39	5	35	113	7	.320
2000 Colorado	N.L.	1B	160	580	138	*216	*59	2	42	*147	5	*.372
2001 Colorado	N.L.	1B	159	587	132	197	54	2	49	146	7	.336
2002 Colorado	N.L.	1B	156	553	107	182	39	4	30	109	5	.329
2003 Colorado	N.L.	1B	160	583	135	209	49	5	33	117	0	.358
2004 Colorado	N.L.	1B	154	547	115	190	49	2	32	96	3	.347
2005 Colo Sprngs	P.C.	2B	2	5	1	3	2	0	0	1	0	.600
2005 Colorado a	N.L.	1B-3B-OF	144	509	92	163	45	2	20	79	3	.320
2006 Colorado Springs	P.C.	1B	2	6	0	2	0	0	0	0	0	.333
2006 Colorado b	N.L.	1B	145	546	94	165	40	5	15	81	3	.302
2007 Colorado	N.L.	1B	154	557	86	178	42	2	17	91	0	.320
2008 Colorado c	N.L.	1B	83	299	39	79	16	0	7	29	0	.264
Major League Totals	12 Yrs.		1661	5962	1143	1957	471	31	310	1116	36	.328
Division Series													
2007 Colorado	N.L.	1B	3	12	1	1	0	1	0	0	0	.083
Championship Series													
2007 Colorado	N.L.	1B	4	14	3	3	0	0	0	1	0	.214
World Series Record													
2007 Colorado	N.L.	1B	4	15	2	5	2	0	0	1	0	.333

a On disabled list from July 26 to August 10, 2005.
b On disabled list from April 20 to May 5, 2006.
c On disabled list from July 3 to September 12, 2008.

HERMIDA, JEREMY RYAN
Born, Atlanta, Georgia, January 30, 1984.
Bats Left. Throws Right. Height, 6 feet, 3 inches. Weight, 210 pounds.

Year	Club	Lea	Pos	G	AB	R	H	2B	3B	HR	RBI	SB	Avg
2002 Marlins	Gulf Coast	OF	38	134	15	30	7	3	0	14	5	.224
2002 Jamestown	N.Y.-Penn.	OF	13	47	8	15	2	1	0	7	1	.319
2003 Albuquerque	P.C.	OF	1	3	0	0	0	0	0	0	0	.000
2003 Greensboro	So.Atl.	OF	133	468	73	133	23	5	6	49	28	.284

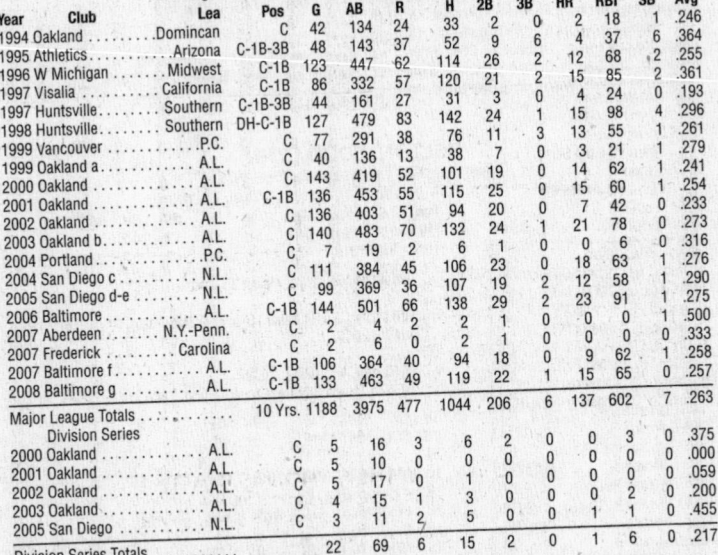

Year	Club	Lea	Pos	G	AB	R	H	2B	3B	HR	RBI	SB	Avg
2004	Jupiter	Fla.St.	OF	91	340	53	101	17	1	10	50	10	.297
2005	Carolina	Southern	OF	118	386	77	113	29	2	18	63	23	.293
2005	Florida	N.L.	OF	23	41	9	12	2	0	4	11	2	.293
2006	Jupiter	Fla.St.	OF	6	17	3	3	1	0	0	2	0	.176
2006	Florida a	N.L.	OF	99	307	37	77	19	1	5	28	4	.251
2007	Jupiter	Fla.St.	OF	3	12	4	4	0	1	2	5	0	.333
2007	Albuquerque	P.C.	OF	2	5	0	1	0	0	0	2	0	.200
2007	Florida b	N.L.	OF	123	429	54	127	32	1	18	63	3	.296
2008	Jupiter	Fla.St.	OF	5	15	6	5	1	0	1	1	0	.333
2008	Florida c	N.L.	OF	142	502	74	125	22	3	17	61	6	.249
Major League Totals			4 Yrs.	387	1279	174	341	75	5	44	163	15	.267

a On disabled list from April 12 to May 22, 2006.
b On disabled list from March 23 to May 14, 2007.
c On disabled list from March 21 to April 9, 2008.

HERNANDEZ (MARIN), RAMON JOSE
Born, Caracas, Venezuela, May 20, 1976.
Bats Right. Throws Right. Height, 6 feet. Weight, 225 pounds.

Year	Club	Lea	Pos	G	AB	R	H	2B	3B	HR	RBI	SB	Avg
1994 Oakland	Dominican		C	42	134	24	33	2	0	2	18	1	.246
1995 Athletics	Arizona		C-1B-3B	48	143	37	52	9	6	4	37	6	.364
1996 W Michigan	Midwest		C-1B	123	447	62	114	26	2	12	68	2	.255
1997 Visalia	California		C-1B	86	332	57	120	21	2	15	85	2	.361
1997 Huntsville	Southern		C-1B-3B	44	161	27	31	3	0	4	24	0	.193
1998 Huntsville	Southern		DH-C-1B	127	479	83	142	24	1	15	98	4	.296
1999 Vancouver	P.C.		C	77	291	38	76	11	3	13	55	1	.261
1999 Oakland a	A.L.		C	40	136	13	38	7	0	3	21	1	.279
2000 Oakland	A.L.		C	143	419	52	101	19	0	14	62	1	.241
2001 Oakland	A.L.		C-1B	136	453	55	115	25	0	15	60	1	.254
2002 Oakland	A.L.		C	136	403	51	94	20	0	7	42	0	.233
2003 Oakland b	A.L.		C	140	483	70	132	24	1	21	78	0	.273
2004 Portland c	P.C.		C	7	19	2	6	1	0	0	6	0	.316
2004 San Diego	N.L.		C	111	384	45	106	23	0	18	63	1	.276
2005 San Diego d-e	N.L.		C	99	369	36	107	19	2	12	58	1	.290
2006 Baltimore	A.L.		C-1B	144	501	66	138	29	2	23	91	1	.275
2007 Aberdeen	N.Y.-Penn.		C	2	4	2	2	1	0	0	0	1	.500
2007 Frederick	Carolina		C	2	6	0	2	1	0	0	0	0	.333
2007 Baltimore f	A.L.		C-1B	106	364	40	94	18	0	9	62	1	.258
2008 Baltimore g	A.L.		C-1B	133	463	49	119	22	1	15	65	0	.257
Major League Totals			10 Yrs.	1188	3975	477	1044	206	6	137	602	7	.263
Division Series													
2000 Oakland	A.L.		C	5	16	3	6	2	0	0	3	0	.375
2001 Oakland	A.L.		C	5	10	0	0	0	0	0	0	0	.000
2002 Oakland	A.L.		C	5	17	0	1	0	0	0	0	0	.059
2003 Oakland	A.L.		C	4	15	1	3	0	0	0	2	0	.200
2005 San Diego	N.L.		C	3	11	2	5	0	0	1	1	0	.455
Division Series Totals				22	69	6	15	2	0	1	6	0	.217

a On disabled list from July 26 to August 27, 1999.
b Traded to San Diego Padres with outfielder Terrence Long for outfielder Mark Kotsay, November 26, 2003.
c On disabled list from June 21 to July 26, 2004.
d On disabled list from June 18 to July and July 25 to September 2, 2005.
e Filed for free agency, October 27, 2005. Signed with Baltimore Orioles, December 13, 2005.
f On disabled list from March 31 to April 26 and June 7 to June 22, 2007.
g Traded to Cincinnati Reds with cash for outfielder Ryan Freel, infielder Brandon Waring and infielder Justin Turner, December 9, 2008.

HILL, AARON WALTER
Born, Visalia, California, March 21, 1982.
Bats Right. Throws Right. Height, 5 feet, 11 inches. Weight, 195 pounds.

Year	Club	Lea	Pos	G	AB	R	H	2B	3B	HR	RBI	SB	Avg
2003 Dunedin	Fla.St.		SS	32	119	26	34	7	0	0	11	1	.286
2003 Auburn	N.Y.-Penn.		SS	33	122	22	44	4	0	4	34	1	.361
2004 New Hampshire	Eastern		SS	135	479	78	134	26	2	11	80	3	.280
2005 Syracuse	Int.		SS	38	156	22	47	11	0	5	18	2	.301
2005 Toronto	A.L.		3B-2B-SS	105	361	49	99	25	3	3	40	2	.274
2006 Toronto	A.L.		2B-SS	155	546	70	159	28	3	6	50	5	.291

Year Club	Lea	Pos	G	AB	R	H	2B	3B	HR	RBI	SB	Avg
2007 Toronto	A.L.	2B	160	608	87	177	47	2	17	78	4	.291
2008 Toronto a	A.L.	2B	55	205	19	54	14	0	2	20	4	.263
Major League Totals		4 Yrs.	475	1720	225	489	114	8	28	188	15	.284

a On disabled list from June 5 to November 14, 2008.

HINSKE, ERIC SCOTT

Born, Menasha, Wisconsin, August 5, 1977.
Bats Left. Throws Right. Height, 6 feet, 2 inches. Weight, 235 pounds.

Year Club	Lea	Pos	G	AB	R	H	2B	3B	HR	RBI	SB	Avg
1998 Williamsprt.	N.Y.-Penn.	1B	68	248	46	74	20	0	9	57	19	.298
1998 Rockford	Midwest	1B-OF	6	20	8	9	4	0	1	4	1	.450
1999 Daytona	Fla.St.	3B	130	445	76	132	28	6	19	79	16	.297
1999 Iowa	P.C.	1B	4	15	3	4	0	1	1	2	0	.267
2000 West Tenn	Southern	3B-1B-OF	131	436	76	113	21	9	20	73	14	.259
2001 Sacramento a-b-c	P.C.	3B-2B	121	436	71	123	27	1	25	79	20	.282
2002 Toronto d	A.L.	3B	151	566	99	158	38	2	24	84	13	.279
2003 Syracuse	Int.	3B	2	8	2	4	1	0	1	2	0	.500
2003 Toronto e	A.L.	3B	124	449	74	109	45	3	12	63	12	.243
2004 Toronto	A.L.	3B	155	570	66	140	23	3	15	69	12	.246
2005 Toronto	A.L.	1B	147	477	79	125	31	2	15	68	8	.262
2006 Toronto-Boston f	A.L.	OF-1B-3B	109	277	43	75	17	2	13	34	2	.271
2007 Boston g	A.L.	1B-OF	84	186	25	38	12	3	6	21	3	.204
2008 Tampa Bay h	A.L.	OF-1B-3B	133	381	59	94	21	1	20	60	10	.247
Major League Totals		7 Yrs.	903	2906	445	739	187	16	105	399	60	.254
Division Series												
2007 Boston	A.L.	PH	1	1	0	0	0	0	0	0	0	.000
Championship Series												
2007 Boston	A.L.	PH	1	0	1	0	0	0	0	0	0	.000
World Series Record												
2007 Boston	A.L.	PH	1	1	0	0	0	0	0	0	0	.000
2008 Tampa Bay	N.L.	PH	2	2	1	1	0	0	1	1	0	.500
World Series Totals			3	3	1	1	0	0	1	1	0	.333

a Traded by Chicago Cubs to Oakland A's for infielder Miguel Cairo, March 28, 2001.
b On disabled list from May 1 to 12, 2001.
c Traded by Oakland A's to Toronto Blue Jays with pitcher Justin Miller for pitcher Billy Koch, December 7, 2001.
d Selected Rookie of the Year in American League for 2002.
e On disabled list from May 2 to June 26, 2003.
f Traded to Boston Red Sox for player to be named later, August 17, 2006.
g Filed for free agency, October 30, 2007. Signed with Tampa Bay Rays organization, February 7, 2008.
h Filed for free agency, November 1, 2008.

HOLLIDAY, MATTHEW THOMAS (MATT)

Born, Stillwater, Oklahoma, January 15, 1980.
Bats Right. Throws Right. Height, 6 feet, 4 inches. Weight, 235 pounds.

Year Club	Lea	Pos	G	AB	R	H	2B	3B	HR	RBI	SB	Avg
1998 Rockies	Arizona	3B	32	117	20	40	4	1	5	23	2	.342
1999 Asheville	So.Atl.	3B	121	444	76	117	28	0	16	64	10	.264
2000 Salem	Carolina	3B	123	460	64	126	28	2	7	72	11	.274
2001 Salem	Carolina	OF	72	255	36	70	16	1	11	52	11	.275
2002 Carolina	Southern	OF	130	463	79	128	19	2	10	64	16	.276
2003 Tulsa	Texas	OF	135	522	65	132	28	5	12	72	15	.253
2004 Colorado Springs	P.C.	OF	6	22	8	8	5	0	2	4	2	.364
2004 Colorado	N.L.	OF	121	400	65	116	31	3	14	57	3	.290
2005 Tulsa	Texas	OF	7	26	6	14	3	0	1	6	1	.538
2005 Colorado a	N.L.	OF	125	479	68	147	24	7	19	87	14	.307
2006 Colorado	N.L.	OF	155	602	119	196	45	5	34	114	10	.326
2007 Colorado	N.L.	OF	158	636	120	*216	*50	6	36	*137	11	*.340
2008 Colorado Springs	P.C.	OF	3	10	4	6	1	0	1	3	0	.600
2008 Colorado b-c	N.L.	OF	139	539	107	173	38	2	25	88	28	.321
Major League Totals		5 Yrs.	698	2656	479	848	188	23	128	483	66	.319
Division Series												
2007 Colorado	N.L.	OF	3	13	2	3	0	0	2	3	0	.231
Championship Series												
2007 Colorado	N.L.	OF	4	15	3	5	0	0	2	4	0	.333
World Series Record												
2007 Colorado	N.L.	OF	4	17	1	5	0	0	1	3	0	.294

b On disabled list from May 25 to June 10, 2008.
c Traded to Oakland Athletics for outfielder Carlos Gonzalez, pitcher Greg Smith and pitcher Huston Street, November 12, 2008.

HOPPER, NORRIS STEPHEN
Born, Shelby, North Carolina, March 24, 1979.
Bats Right. Throws Right. Height, 5 feet, 10 inches. Weight, 200 pounds.

Year Club	Lea	Pos	G	AB	R	H	2B	3B	HR	RBI	SB	Avg
1998 Royals	Gulf Coast	2B-SS	40	133	19	41	2	1	0	11	11	.308
1999 Royals	Gulf Coast	2B	46	179	33	46	3	2	0	13	22	.257
1999 Charleston-WV	So.Atl.	2B	5	22	3	11	0	2	0	2	1	.500
2000 Charleston-WV	So.Atl.	OF-2B	116	454	70	127	20	6	0	29	24	.280
2001 Wilmington	Carolina	OF-2B	110	389	38	96	6	2	1	38	16	.247
2002 Wilmington	Carolina	OF	125	514	78	140	12	3	1	46	22	.272
2003 Wichita	Texas	OF-2B	115	424	56	127	14	2	0	40	24	.300
2004 Wichita	Texas	OF-2B	98	363	48	101	5	3	0	40	17	.278
2005 Chattanooga a	Southern	OF-2B	116	451	70	140	15	4	1	37	25	.310
2006 Chattanooga	Southern	OF-2B	13	46	7	13	2	1	0	10	3	.283
2006 Louisville	Int.	OF-2B	98	383	47	133	11	3	0	26	25	.347
2006 Cincinnati	N.L.	OF	21	39	6	14	1	0	1	5	2	.359
2007 Sarasota	Fla.St.	OF	4	17	1	5	0	0	0	2	0	.294
2007 Louisville	Int.	OF	4	15	2	4	0	0	0	1	2	.267
2007 Cincinnati b	N.L.	OF	121	307	51	101	14	2	0	14	14	.329
2008 Sarasota	Fla.St.	OF	2	7	3	2	0	0	0	0	0	.286
2008 Louisville	Int.	OF	4	17	3	5	1	0	0	0	0	.294
2008 Cincinnati c-d	N.L.	OF	26	50	3	10	0	0	0	1	1	.200
Major League Totals		3 Yrs.	168	396	60	125	15	2	1	20	17	.316

a Filed for free agency, October 15, 2004. Signed with Cincinnati Reds organization, January 10, 2005.
b On disabled list from March 23 to April 18, 2007.
c On disabled list from April 20 to June 18 and July 2 to November 6, 2008.
d Not offered contract, December 12, 2008, re-signed with Cincinnati Reds, December 15, 2008.

HOWARD, RYAN JAMES
Born, St. Louis, Missouri, November 19, 1979.
Bats Left. Throws Left. Height, 6 feet, 4 inches. Weight, 250 pounds.

Year Club	Lea	Pos	G	AB	R	H	2B	3B	HR	RBI	SB	Avg
2001 Batavia	N.Y.-Penn.	1B	48	169	26	46	7	3	6	35	0	.272
2002 Lakewood	So.Atl.	1B	135	493	56	138	20	6	19	87	5	.280
2003 Clearwater	Fla.St.	1B	130	490	67	149	32	1	23	82	0	.304
2004 Reading	Eastern	1B	102	374	73	111	18	1	37	102	1	.297
2004 Scranton/W.B.	Int.	1B	29	111	21	30	10	0	9	29	0	.270
2004 Philadelphia	N.L.	1B	19	39	5	11	5	0	2	5	0	.282
2005 Scranton/WB	Int.	1B	61	210	38	78	19	0	16	54	0	.371
2005 Philadelphia a	N.L.	1B	88	312	52	90	17	2	22	63	0	.288
2006 Philadelphia b	N.L.	1B	159	581	104	182	25	1	*58	*149	0	.313
2007 Lakewood	So.Atl.	1B	2	6	1	2	1	0	1	4	0	.333
2007 Philadelphia c	N.L.	1B	144	529	94	142	26	0	47	136	1	.268
2008 Philadelphia	N.L.	1B	*162	610	105	153	26	4	*48	*146	1	.251
Major League Totals		5 Yrs.	572	2071	360	578	99	7	177	499	2	.279
Division Series												
2007 Philadelphia	N.L.	1B	3	12	1	3	0	0	1	1	0	.250
2008 Philadelphia	N.L.	1B	4	11	1	2	1	0	0	1	0	.182
Division Series Totals			7	23	2	5	1	0	1	2	0	.217
Championship Series												
2008 Philadelphia	N.L.	1B	5	20	4	6	1	0	0	2	0	.300
World Series Record												
2008 Philadelphia	N.L.	1B	5	21	3	6	1	0	3	6	0	.286

a Selected Rookie of the Year in National League for 2005.
b Selected Most Valuable Player in National League for 2006.
c On disabled list from May 10 to May 25, 2007.

HU, CHIN-LUNG (CHINH-LUNG)
Born, Tainan City, Taiwan, February 2, 1984.
Bats Right. Throws Right. Height, 5 feet, 11 inches. Weight, 190 pounds.

Year Club	Lea	Pos	G	AB	R	H	2B	3B	HR	RBI	SB	Avg
2003 Ogden	Pioneer	SS	53	220	34	67	9	5	3	23	5	.305
2004 Vero Beach	Fla.St.	SS	20	75	12	23	4	1	0	10	3	.307

Year	Club	Lea	Pos	G	AB	R	H	2B	3B	HR	RBI	SB	Avg
2004 Columbus	So.Atl.		SS	84	332	58	99	15	4	6	25	17	.298
2005 Vero Beach	Fla.St.		SS	116	470	80	147	29	1	8	56	23	.313
2006 Jacksonville	Southern		SS	125	488	71	124	20	2	5	34	11	.254
2007 Jacksonville	Southern		SS	82	325	56	107	30	5	6	34	12	.329
2007 Las Vegas	P.C.		SS-2B	45	192	33	61	10	1	8	28	3	.318
2007 Los Angeles	N.L.		SS	12	29	5	7	0	1	2	5	0	.241
2008 Las Vegas	P.C.		SS	41	156	21	46	5	3	1	15	2	.295
2008 Los Angeles	N.L.		SS-2B	65	116	16	21	2	2	0	9	2	.181
Major League Totals			2 Yrs.	77	145	21	28	2	3	2	14	2	.193

HUDSON, ORLANDO THILL

Born, Darlington, South Carolina, December 12, 1977.
Bats Both. Throws Right. Height, 6 feet. Weight, 185 pounds.

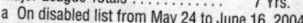

Year	Club	Lea	Pos	G	AB	R	H	2B	3B	HR	RBI	SB	Avg
1998 Medicine Hat	Pioneer		2B	65	242	50	71	18	1	8	42	6	.293
1999 Hagerstown	So.Atl.		3B	132	513	66	137	36	6	7	74	8	.267
2000 Dunedin	Fla.St.		3B-2B-SS	96	358	54	102	16	2	7	48	9	.285
2000 Tennessee	Southern		3B	39	134	17	32	4	3	2	15	3	.239
2001 Syracuse	Int.		2B-3B	55	194	31	59	14	3	4	27	11	.304
2001 Tennessee	Southern		2B-3B	84	306	51	94	22	8	4	52	8	.307
2002 Syracuse	Int.		2B	100	417	63	127	27	3	10	37	8	.305
2002 Toronto	A.L.		2B	54	192	20	53	10	5	4	23	0	.276
2003 Toronto	A.L.		2B	142	474	54	127	21	6	9	57	5	.268
2004 Toronto a	A.L.		2B	135	489	73	132	32	7	12	58	7	.270
2005 Toronto b	A.L.		2B	131	461	62	125	25	5	10	63	7	.271
2006 Arizona	N.L.		2B	157	579	87	166	34	9	15	67	9	.287
2007 Arizona	N.L.		2B	139	517	69	152	28	9	10	63	10	.294
2008 Arizona c-d	N.L.		2B	107	407	54	124	29	3	8	41	4	.305
Major League Totals			7 Yrs.	865	3119	419	879	179	44	68	372	42	.282

a On disabled list from May 24 to June 16, 2004.
b Traded to Arizona Diamondbacks with pitcher Miguel Batista for infielder Troy Glaus and infielder Sergio Santos, December 27, 2005.
c On disabled list from August 10 to November 1, 2008.
d Filed for free agency, November 1, 2008.

HUFF, AUBREY LEWIS

Born, Marion, Ohio, December 20, 1976.
Bats Left. Throws Right. Height, 6 feet, 4 inches. Weight, 230 pounds.

Year	Club	Lea	Pos	G	AB	R	H	2B	3B	HR	RBI	SB	Avg
1998 Chston-SC	So.Atl.		3B	69	265	38	85	19	1	13	54	3	.321
1999 Orlando	Southern		3B	133	491	85	148	40	4	22	78	2	.301
2000 Durham	Int.		3B	108	408	73	129	36	3	20	76	2	.316
2000 Tampa Bay	A.L.		3B	39	122	12	35	7	0	4	14	0	.287
2001 Durham	Int.		3B	17	66	14	19	6	0	3	10	0	.288
2001 Tampa Bay	A.L.		3B-1B	111	411	42	102	25	1	8	45	1	.248
2002 Durham	Int.		1B	32	126	18	41	9	0	3	20	0	.325
2002 Tampa Bay	A.L.		DH-1B-3B	113	454	67	142	25	0	23	59	4	.313
2003 Tampa Bay	A.L.		OF-1B-3B	162	636	91	198	47	3	34	107	4	.311
2004 Tampa Bay	A.L.		3B-1B-OF	157	600	92	178	27	2	29	104	5	.297
2005 Tampa Bay	A.L.		OF-1B-3B	154	575	70	150	26	2	22	92	8	.261
2006 Visalia	Calif.		3B	2	8	2	2	1	0	0	1	0	.250
2006 Tampa Bay	A.L.		3B	63	230	26	65	15	1	8	28	0	.283
2006 Houston a-b-c	N.L.		OF-3B-1B	68	224	31	56	10	1	13	38	0	.250
2007 Baltimore	A.L.		DH-1B-3B	151	550	68	154	34	5	15	72	1	.280
2008 Baltimore	A.L.		DH-1B-3B	154	598	96	182	48	2	32	108	4	.304
Major League Totals			9 Yrs.	1172	4400	595	1262	264	17	188	667	25	.287

a On disabled list from April 12 to May 5, 2006.
b Traded to Houston Astros with cash for pitcher Mitch Talbot and infielder Ben Zobrist, July 12, 2006.
c Filed for free agency, October 28, 2006. Signed with Baltimore Orioles, December 30, 2006.

HUNDLEY, NICHOLAS JOHN (NICK)

Born, Corvallis, Oregon, September 8, 1983.
Bats Right. Throws Right. Height, 6 feet, 1 inch. Weight, 210 pounds.

Year	Club	Lea	Pos	G	AB	R	H	2B	3B	HR	RBI	SB	Avg
2005 Fort Wayne	Midwest		C	10	36	2	8	2	0	0	5	0	.222
2005 Eugene	Northwest		C	43	148	30	37	7	1	7	22	1	.250

Year	Club	Lea	Pos	G	AB	R	H	2B	3B	HR	RBI	SB	Avg
2006 Lake Elsinore	Calif.	C	47	176	18	49	13	0	3	23	1	.278
2006 Fort Wayne	Midwest	C	57	215	29	59	19	0	8	44	1	.274
2007 San Antonio	Texas	C	101	373	55	92	23	1	20	72	0	.247
2008 Portland	P.C.	C	58	224	33	52	13	0	12	39	0	.232
2008 San Diego	N.L.	C	60	198	21	47	7	1	5	24	0	.237

HUNTER, TORII KEDAR

Born, Pine Bluff, Arkansas, July 18, 1975.
Bats Right. Throws Right. Height, 6 feet, 2 inches. Weight, 215 pounds.

Year	Club	Lea	Pos	G	AB	R	H	2B	3B	HR	RBI	SB	Avg
1993 Twins	Gulf Coast	OF	28	100	6	19	3	0	0	8	4	.190
1994 Fort Wayne	Midwest	OF	91	335	57	98	17	1	10	50	8	.293
1995 Fort Myers	Fla.St.	OF	113	391	64	96	15	2	7	36	7	.246
1996 Ft. Myers	Fla.St.	OF	4	16	1	3	0	0	0	1	1	.188
1996 New Britain	Eastern	OF	99	342	49	90	20	3	7	33	7	.263
1997 New Britain	Eastern	OF	127	471	57	109	22	2	8	56	8	.231
1997 Minnesota	A.L.	OF	1	0	0	0	0	0	0	0	0	.000
1998 New Britain	Eastern	OF	82	308	42	87	24	3	6	32	11	.282
1998 Salt Lake	P.C.	OF	26	92	15	31	7	0	4	20	2	.337
1998 Minnesota	A.L.	OF	6	17	0	4	1	0	0	2	0	.235
1999 Minnesota	A.L.	OF	135	384	52	98	17	2	9	35	10	.255
2000 Salt Lake	P.C.	OF	55	209	58	77	17	2	18	61	11	.368
2000 Minnesota	A.L.	OF	99	336	44	94	14	7	5	44	4	.280
2001 Minnesota a	A.L.	OF	148	564	82	147	32	5	27	92	9	.261
2002 Minnesota	A.L.	OF	148	561	89	162	37	4	29	94	23	.289
2003 Minnesota	A.L.	OF	154	581	83	145	31	4	26	102	6	.250
2004 Minnesota b	A.L.	OF	138	520	79	141	37	0	23	81	21	.271
2005 Minnesota c	A.L.	OF	98	372	63	100	24	1	14	56	23	.269
2006 Minnesota d	A.L.	OF	147	557	86	155	21	2	31	98	12	.278
2007 Minnesota e	A.L.	OF	160	600	94	172	45	1	28	107	18	.287
2008 Los Angeles	A.L.	OF	146	551	85	153	37	2	21	78	19	.278
Major League Totals		12 Yrs.	1380	5043	757	1371	296	28	213	789	145	.272
Division Series												
2002 Minnesota	A.L.	OF	5	20	4	6	4	0	0	2	0	.300
2003 Minnesota	A.L.	OF	4	14	3	6	0	1	1	2	0	.429
2004 Minnesota	A.L.	OF	4	17	5	6	1	0	1	2	2	.353
2006 Minnesota	A.L.	OF	3	11	1	3	1	0	1	2	0	.273
2008 Los Angeles	A.L.	OF	4	18	0	7	0	0	0	5	0	.389
Division Series Totals			20	80	13	28	6	1	3	13	2	.350
Championship Series												
2002 Minnesota	A.L.	OF	5	18	2	3	2	0	0	0	0	.167

a On disabled list from April 6 to April 21, 2001.
b On disabled list from April 7 to April 25, 2004.
c On disabled list from July 30 to October 6, 2005.
d On disabled list from July 16 to July 31, 2006.
e Filed for free agency, October 29, 2007. Signed with Los Angeles Angels, November 21, 2007.

IANNETTA, CHRISTOPHER DOMENIC (CHRIS)

Born, Providence, Rhode Island, April 8, 1983.
Bats Right. Throws Right. Height, 5 feet, 11 inches. Weight, 225 pounds.

Year	Club	Lea	Pos	G	AB	R	H	2B	3B	HR	RBI	SB	Avg
2004 Asheville	So.Atl.	C	36	121	23	38	5	1	5	17	0	.314
2005 Tulsa	Texas	C	19	60	7	14	3	1	2	11	0	.233
2006 Tulsa	Texas	C	44	156	38	50	10	2	11	26	1	.321
2006 Colorado Springs	P.C.	C	47	151	23	53	11	2	3	22	0	.351
2006 Colorado	N.L.	C	21	77	12	20	4	0	2	10	0	.260
2007 Colorado Springs	P.C.	C	16	54	8	16	3	0	1	7	0	.296
2007 Colorado	N.L.	C	67	197	22	43	8	3	4	27	0	.218
2008 Colorado	N.L.	C-3B	104	333	50	88	22	2	18	65	0	.264
Major League Totals		3 Yrs.	192	607	84	151	34	5	24	102	0	.249

88

IBANEZ, RAUL JAVIER

Born, New York, New York, June 2, 1972.
Bats Left. Throws Right. Height, 6 feet, 2 inches. Weight, 220 pounds.

Year	Club	Lea	Pos	G	AB	R	H	2B	3B	HR	RBI	SB	Avg
1992	Mariners	Arizona	DH-1B-C-OF	33	120	25	37	8	2	1	16	1	.308
1993	Appleton	Midwest	DH-1B-OF-C	52	157	26	43	9	0	5	21	0	.274
1993	Bellingham	Northwest	C	43	134	16	38	5	2	0	15	0	.284
1994	Appleton	Midwest	DH-C-1B-OF	91	327	55	102	30	3	7	59	10	.312
1995	Riverside	California	C-1B	95	361	59	120	23	9	20	108	4	.332
1996	Port City	Southern	OF-1B-C	19	76	12	28	8	1	1	13	3	.368
1996	Seattle	A.L.	DH	4	5	0	0	0	0	0	0	0	.000
1996	Tacoma	P.C.	OF-1B	111	405	59	115	20	3	11	47	7	.284
1997	Tacoma	P.C.	OF	111	438	84	133	30	5	15	84	7	.304
1997	Seattle	A.L.	OF	11	26	3	4	0	1	1	4	0	.154
1998	Tacoma	P.C.	OF	52	190	24	41	8	1	6	25	1	.216
1998	Seattle	A.L.	OF-1B	37	98	12	25	7	1	2	12	0	.255
1999	Tacoma	P.C.	OF	8	31	6	11	1	0	3	5	1	.355
1999	Seattle a	A.L.	OF-1B-C	87	209	23	54	7	0	9	27	5	.258
2000	Tacoma	P.C.	OF	10	40	3	10	4	0	0	6	0	.250
2000	Seattle b-c	A.L.	OF-1B	92	140	21	32	8	0	2	15	2	.229
2001	Omaha	P.C.	OF-SS	8	27	3	4	1	0	2	5	0	.148
2001	Kansas City d	A.L.	OF-1B-3B	104	279	44	78	11	5	13	54	0	.280
2002	Kansas City	A.L.	OF-1B	137	497	70	146	37	6	24	103	5	.294
2003	Kansas City d	A.L.	OF-1B	157	608	95	179	33	5	18	90	8	.294
2004	Tacoma	P.C.	OF	4	17	2	4	1	0	0	1	0	.235
2004	Seattle e	A.L.	OF-1B	123	481	67	146	31	1	16	62	1	.304
2005	Seattle	A.L.	DH-OF-1B	*162	614	92	172	32	2	20	89	9	.280
2006	Seattle	A.L.	OF	159	626	103	181	33	5	33	123	2	.289
2007	Seattle	A.L.	OF	149	573	80	167	35	5	21	105	0	.291
2008	Seattle f	A.L.	OF	162	635	85	186	43	3	23	110	2	.293
Major League Totals			**13 Yrs.**	**1384**	**4791**	**695**	**1370**	**277**	**34**	**182**	**794**	**34**	**.286**
Division Series													
2000	Seattle	A.L.	OF	3	8	2	3	0	0	0	0	0	.375
Championship Series													
2000	Seattle	A.L.	OF	6	9	0	0	0	0	0	0	0	.000

a On disabled list from May 18 to June 3, 1999.
b On disabled list from August 7 to August 21, 2000.
c Not offered contract, December 21, 2000. Signed with Kansas City Royals organization, January 13, 2001.
d Filed for free agency, October 27, 2003. Signed with Seattle Mariners, November 19, 2003.
e On disabled list from June 3 to July 10, 2004.
f Filed for free agency, October 30, 2008. Signed with Philadelphia Phillies, December 16, 2008.

IGUCHI, TADAHITO

Born, Tokyo, Japan, December 4, 1974.
Bats Right. Throws Right. Height, 5 feet, 10 inches. Weight, 200 pounds.

Year	Club	Lea	Pos	G	AB	R	H	2B	3B	HR	RBI	SB	Avg
1997	Fukuoka	Japan Pac.	SS	76	217	31	44	6	3	8	23	3	.203
1998	Fukuoka	Japan Pac.	SS	135	421	58	93	18	4	21	66	12	.221
1999	Fukuoka	Japan Pac.	SS	116	370	38	83	15	1	14	47	14	.224
2000	Fukuoka	Japan Pac.	SS	54	162	21	40	9	2	7	23	5	.247
2001	Fukuoka	Japan Pac.	2B	140	552	104	144	26	1	30	97	44	.261
2002	Fukuoka	Japan Pac.	2B	114	428	64	111	14	1	18	53	21	.259
2003	Fukuoka	Japan Pac.	2B	135	515	112	175	37	1	27	109	42	.340
2004	Fukuoka	Japan Pac.	2B	124	510	96	170	34	2	24	89	18	.333
2005	Chicago a	A.L.	2B	135	511	74	142	25	6	15	71	15	.278
2006	Chicago	A.L.	2B	138	555	97	156	24	5	18	67	11	.281
2007	Chicago	A.L.	2B	90	327	45	82	17	4	6	31	8	.251
2007	Philadelphia b-c	N.L.	2B	45	138	22	42	10	0	3	12	6	.304
2008	Lake Elsinore	Calif.	2B	3	10	4	4	0	0	2	3	0	.400
2008	San Diego-Philadelphia d-e-f	N.L.	2B	85	310	29	72	15	1	2	24	8	.232
Major League Totals			**4 Yrs.**	**493**	**1841**	**267**	**494**	**91**	**11**	**44**	**205**	**48**	**.268**
Division Series													
2005	Chicago	A.L.	2B	3	12	1	3	0	0	1	4	0	.250
2007	Philadelphia	N.L.	PH	3	1	0	0	0	0	0	0	0	.000
Division Series Totals				6	13	1	3	0	0	1	4	0	.231
Championship Series													
2005	Chicago	A.L.	2B	5	17	4	3	1	0	0	0	0	.176
World Series Record													
2005	Chicago	A.L.	2B	4	18	2	3	0	0	0	1	0	.167

a Signed with Chicago White Sox, January 27, 2005.
b Traded to Philadelphia Phillies for pitcher Michael Dubee, July 27, 2007.
c Released by Philadelphia Phillies, November 15, 2007. Signed with San Diego Padres, December 18, 2007.
d On disabled list from June 6 to August 1, 2008.
e Released by San Diego Padres, August 29, 2008. Signed with Philadelphia Phillies, September 5, 2008.
f Filed for free agency, November 13, 2008. Signed with Chiba Lotte Marines (Japan Pacific), January 20, 2009.

INFANTE, OMAR RAFAEL

Born, Puerto La Cruz, Venezuela, December 26, 1981.
Bats Right. Throws Right. Height, 6 feet. Weight, 180 pounds.

Year	Club	Lea	Pos	G	AB	R	H	2B	3B	HR	RBI	SB	Avg
1999 Tigers		Gulf Coast	SS	21	75	9	20	0	0	0	4	4	.267
2000 Lakeland		Fla.St.	SS	79	259	35	71	11	0	2	24	11	.274
2000 West Michigan		Midwest	SS-2B	12	48	7	11	0	0	0	5	1	.229
2001 Erie		Eastern	SS	132	540	86	163	21	4	2	62	27	.302
2002 Toledo		Int.	SS	120	436	49	117	16	8	4	51	19	.268
2002 Detroit		A.L.	SS-2B	18	72	4	24	3	0	1	6	0	.333
2003 Toledo		Int.	SS	64	224	28	50	10	0	2	18	22	.223
2003 Detroit		A.L.	SS-3B-2B	69	221	24	49	6	1	0	8	6	.222
2004 Detroit		A.L.	2B-SS-3B-OF	142	503	69	133	27	9	16	55	13	.264
2005 Detroit		A.L.	2B-SS	121	406	36	90	28	2	9	43	8	.222
2006 Detroit		A.L.	2B-SS-3B	78	224	35	62	11	4	4	25	3	.277
2007 Toledo		Int.	SS-2B	10	38	3	14	2	0	0	4	1	.368
2007 Detroit a-b		A.L.	2B-OF-SS-3B	66	166	24	45	6	1	2	17	4	.271
2008 Richmond		Int.	OF	3	11	3	4	1	0	0	3	0	.364
2008 Atlanta c		N.L.	OF-3B-SS-2B	96	317	45	93	24	3	3	40	0	.293
Major League Totals		7 Yrs.		590	1909	237	496	105	20	35	194	34	.260
Championship Series													
2006 Detroit		A.L.	DH	1	2	0	1	0	0	0	0	1	.500
World Series Record													
2006 Detroit		A.L.	PH	1	1	0	0	0	0	0	0	0	.000

a Traded to Chicago Cubs for outfielder Jacque Jones, November 12, 2007.
b Traded to Atlanta Braves with pitcher Will Ohman for pitcher Jose Ascanio, December 4, 2007.
c On disabled list from March 21 to May 8 and July 7 to July 22, 2008.

INGE, CHARLES BRANDON (BRANDON)

Born, Lynchburg, Virginia, May 19, 1977.
Bats Both. Throws Right. Height, 5 feet, 11 inches. Weight, 190 pounds.

Year	Club	Lea	Pos	G	AB	R	H	2B	3B	HR	RBI	SB	Avg
1998 Jamestown		N.Y.-Penn.	C	51	191	24	44	10	1	8	29	8	.230
1999 West Michigan		Midwest	C	100	352	54	86	25	2	9	46	15	.244
2000 Toledo		Int.	C	55	190	24	42	9	3	5	20	2	.221
2000 Jacksonville		Southern	C-OF	78	298	39	77	25	1	6	53	10	.258
2001 Toledo		Gulf Coast	C	3	10	1	1	0	0	1	2	0	.100
2001 West Michigan		Midwest	C	4	16	3	3	1	0	0	2	0	.188
2001 Toledo		Int.	C	27	90	11	26	11	1	2	15	1	.289
2001 Detroit a		A.L.	C	79	189	13	34	11	0	0	15	1	.180
2002 Toledo		Int.	C	21	65	10	17	2	4	3	13	1	.262
2002 Detroit b		A.L.	C	95	321	27	65	15	3	7	24	1	.202
2003 Toledo		Int.	C	39	142	15	39	9	0	5	15	3	.275
2003 Detroit		A.L.	C	104	330	32	67	15	3	8	30	4	.203
2004 Detroit c		A.L.	3B-C-OF	131	408	43	117	15	7	13	64	5	.287
2005 Detroit		A.L.	3B-OF	160	616	75	161	31	9	16	72	7	.261
2006 Detroit		A.L.	3B	159	542	83	137	29	2	27	83	7	.253
2007 Detroit		A.L.	3B	151	508	64	120	25	2	14	71	9	.236
2008 Toledo		Int.	C-3B	3	10	2	3	0	0	1	4	0	.300
2008 Detroit d		A.L.	C-3B-OF	113	347	41	71	16	4	11	51	4	.205
Major League Totals		8 Yrs.		992	3261	378	772	157	30	96	410	38	.237
Division Series													
2006 Detroit		A.L.	3B	4	15	1	2	0	0	0	0	0	.133
Championship Series													
2006 Detroit		A.L.	3B	4	12	3	4	1	0	1	3	0	.333
World Series Record													
2006 Detroit		A.L.	3B	5	17	0	6	2	0	0	1	0	.353

a On disabled list from June 25 to August 6, 2001.
b On disabled list from May 12 to May 27, 2002.
c On disabled list from June 26 to July 15, 2004.
d On disabled list from June 23 to July 10, 2008.

INGLETT, JOSEPH STEVEN (JOE)

Born, Sacramento, California, June 29, 1978.
Bats Left. Throws Right. Height, 5 feet, 10 inches. Weight, 180 pounds.

Year Club	Lea	Pos	G	AB	R	H	2B	3B	HR	RBI	SB	Avg
2000 Mahoning Valley	N.Y.-Penn.	2B-OF-1B	56	202	37	58	12	4	2	37	4	.287
2001 Columbus.......	So.Atl.	2B	62	237	34	71	9	2	2	33	5	.300
2002 Kinston......	Carolina	2B	66	238	24	67	12	0	0	29	5	.282
2002 Columbus......	So.Atl.	3B-2B	60	235	44	73	18	5	2	46	5	.311
2003 Kinston......	Carolina	2B	28	85	21	28	10	1	0	15	1	.329
2003 Akron........	Eastern	2B-OF	71	276	41	78	16	1	4	25	1	.283
2004 Akron......	Eastern	2B	66	266	49	85	19	7	1	20	3	.320
2005 Buffalo..........	Int.	2B-OF-SS	95	327	57	108	20	9	2	40	13	.330
2006 Akron......	Eastern	SS	18	64	20	33	9	0	3	9	7	.516
2006 Buffalo..........	Int.	2B-SS-OF	40	157	21	47	7	2	1	13	3	.299
2006 Cleveland........	A.L.	2B-OF-SS	64	201	26	57	8	3	2	21	5	.284
2007 Buffalo.........	Int.	2B-OF-SS	107	392	45	99	15	9	4	57	7	.253
2007 Toronto a-b	A.L.	3B	2	5	0	3	0	1	0	2	1	.600
2008 Syracuse.........	Int.	2B-OF	15	54	12	22	2	2	1	6	1	.407
2008 Toronto.......	A.L.	2B-OF-3B-SS	109	344	45	102	15	7	3	39	9	.297
Major League Totals		3 Yrs.	175	550	71	162	23	11	5	62	15	.295

a On disabled list from March 23 to April 17, 2007.
b Claimed on waivers by Toronto Blue Jays, September 14, 2007.

IWAMURA, AKINORI

Born, Ehime, Japan, February 9, 1979.
Bats Left. Throws Right. Height, 5 feet, 9 inches. Weight, 175 pounds.

Year Club	Lea	Pos	G	AB	R	H	2B	3B	HR	RBI	SB	Avg
1998 Yakult..........	Japan Pac.	3B	1	3	0	0	0	0	0	0	0	.000
1999 Yakult.........	Japan Pac.	3B	83	252	28	74	11	4	11	35	7	.341
2000 Yakult.........	Japan Pac.	3B	130	436	67	121	13	9	18	66	13	.342
2001 Yakult.........	Japan Pac.	3B	136	520	79	149	24	4	18	81	15	.329
2002 Yakult.........	Japan Pac.	3B	140	510	79	163	35	2	23	71	5	.390
2003 Yakult.........	Japan Pac.	3B	60	232	43	61	6	2	12	35	5	.328
2004 Yakult.........	Japan Pac.	3B	138	533	99	160	19	0	44	103	8	.383
2005 Yakult.........	Japan Pac.	3B	144	548	83	175	31	4	30	102	8	.388
2006 Yakult a ....,.,...	Japan Pac.	3B	145	546	84	170	27	2	32	77	6	.389
2007 Tampa Bay b..........	A.L.	3B-2B	123	491	82	140	21	10	7	34	12	.285
2008 Tampa Bay...........	A.L.	2B	152	627	91	172	30	9	6	48	8	.274
Major League Totals		2 Yrs.	275	1118	173	312	51	19	13	82	20	.279
Division Series												
2008 Tampa Bay..........	N.L.	2B	4	18	3	7	1	1	1	4	0	.389
Championship Series												
2008 Tampa Bay..........	N.L.	2B	7	29	4	6	2	0	0	0	2	.207
World Series Record												
2008 Tampa Bay..........	N.L.	2B	5	19	1	5	1	0	0	1	0	.263

a Signed with Tampa Bay Devil Rays, December 15, 2006.
b On disabled list from April 24 to May 28, 2007.

IZTURIS, CESAR DAVID

Born, Barquisimeto, Venezuela, February 10, 1980.
Bats Both. Throws Right. Height, 5 feet, 9 inches. Weight, 190 pounds.

Year Club	Lea	Pos	G	AB	R	H	2B	3B	HR	RBI	SB	Avg
1997 St.Cathrnes	N.Y.-Penn.	2B-SS	70	231	32	44	3	0	1	11	6	.190
1998 Hagerstown	So.Atl.	SS-2B-3B	130	413	56	108	13	1	1	38	20	.262
1999 Dunedin	Fla.St.	SS-2B-3B	131	536	77	165	28	12	3	77	32	.308
2000 Syracuse	Int.	SS	132	435	54	95	16	5	0	27	21	.218
2001 Syracuse	Int.	SS-2B	87	342	32	100	16	3	2	35	24	.292
2001 Toronto a	A.L.	2B-SS	46	134	19	36	6	2	2	9	8	.269
2002 Los Angeles	N.L.	SS-2B	135	439	43	102	24	2	1	31	7	.232
2003 Los Angeles	N.L.	SS	158	558	47	140	21	6	1	40	10	.251
2004 Los Angeles	N.L.	SS	159	670	90	193	32	9	4	62	25	.288
2005 Los Angeles b	N.L.	SS	106	444	48	114	19	2	2	31	8	.257
2006 Las Vegas..........	P.C.	SS-2B	15	59	9	16	3	0	0	3	0	.271
2006 Los Angeles-Chicago c-d-e.	N.L.	3B-SS-2B	54	192	14	47	9	1	1	18	1	.245
2007 Chicago-Pittsburgh f-g..	N.L.	SS-3B	110	314	31	81	14	2	0	16	3	.258
2008 St. Louis h-i	N.L.	SS-3B	135	414	50	109	10	3	1	24	24	.263
Major League Totals		8 Yrs.	903	3165	342	822	135	27	12	231	86	.260

Year	Club	Lea	Pos	G	AB	R	H	2B	3B	HR	RBI	SB	Avg
Division Series													
2004 Los Angeles		N.L.	SS	4	17	1	3	1	0	0	0	0	.176

a Traded to Los Angeles Dodgers with pitcher Paul Quantrill for pitcher Luke Prokopec and pitcher Chad Ricketts, December 13, 2001.
b On disabled list from June 30 to July 15 and August 23 to October 7, 2005.
c On disabled list from March 28 to June 20, 2006.
d Traded to Chicago Cubs for pitcher Greg Maddux, July 31, 2006.
e On disabled list from August 22 to September 6, 2006.
f Traded to Pittsburgh Pirates for cash for player to be named later, July 19, 2007.
g Filed for free agency, November 12, 2007. Signed with St. Louis Cardinals, November 30, 2007.
h On disabled list from June 21 to July 6, 2008.
i Filed for free agency, October 30, 2008. Signed with Baltimore Orioles, December 15, 2008.

IZTURIS, MAICER
Born, Barquisimeto, Venezuela, September 12, 1980.
Bats Both. Throws Right. Height, 5 feet, 8 inches. Weight, 160 pounds.

Year	Club	Lea	Pos	G	AB	R	H	2B	3B	HR	RBI	SB	Avg
1998 Burlington	Appal.	SS	55	217	33	63	8	2	2	33	16	.290
1999 Columbus	So.Atl.	SS	57	220	46	66	5	3	4	23	14	.300
2000 Columbus	So.Atl.	SS	10	29	4	8	1	0	0	1	0	.276
2001 Kinston	Carolina	2B	114	433	47	104	16	6	1	39	32	.240
2002 Kinston	Carolina	2B	58	233	28	61	13	1	1	30	24	.262
2002 Akron	Eastern	2B	67	253	34	70	12	7	0	32	8	.277
2003 Akron	Eastern	2B-SS-OF	54	218	31	61	11	5	1	20	14	.280
2003 Buffalo	Int.	SS-2B	85	301	43	79	16	4	2	29	14	.262
2004 Edmonton	P.C.	SS-2B	99	376	65	127	19	2	3	36	14	.338
2004 Montreal a-b	N.L.	SS-2B	32	107	10	22	5	2	1	4	4	.206
2005 Salt Lake	P.C.	SS-3B-2B	10	31	10	14	4	0	0	2	4	.452
2005 Los Angeles c	A.L.	3B-SS-2B-OF	77	191	18	47	8	4	1	15	9	.246
2006 Salt Lake	P.C.	SS-3B-2B	9	36	5	11	5	1	0	5	1	.306
2006 Los Angeles d	A.L.	3B-SS-2B	104	352	64	103	21	3	5	44	14	.293
2007 Rancho Cucamonga	Calif.	3B	7	22	5	7	1	0	0	3	0	.318
2007 Salt Lake	P.C.	2B-SS	5	17	3	6	1	0	0	0	0	.353
2007 Los Angeles e	A.L.	3B-2B-SS	102	336	47	97	17	2	6	51	7	.289
2008 Rancho Cucamonga	Calif.	2B	1	2	0	1	0	0	0	0	0	.500
2008 Los Angeles f	A.L.	SS-2B-3B	79	290	44	78	14	2	3	37	11	.269
Major League Totals		5 Yrs.	394	1276	183	347	65	13	16	151	45	.272
Division Series												
2007 Los Angeles	A.L.	3B	3	12	1	4	2	0	0	0	2	.333
Championship Series												
2005 Los Angeles	A.L.	SS	1	0	0	0	0	0	0	0	0	.000

a Traded by Cleveland Indians to Montreal Expos with outfielder Ryan Church for pitcher Scott Stewart, January 5, 2004.
b Traded to Anaheim Angels with outfielder Juan Rivera for outfielder Jose Guillen, November 19, 2004.
c On disabled list from April 26 to June 18, 2005.
d On disabled list from April 24 to June 9, 2006.
e On disabled list from April 30 to May 15 and May 21 to July 3, 2007.
f On disabled list from April 28 to May 13 and August 14 to October 9, 2008.

JACKSON, CONOR SIMS
Born, Austin, Texas, May 7, 1982.
Bats Right. Throws Right. Height, 6 feet, 2 inches. Weight, 225 pounds.

Year	Club	Lea	Pos	G	AB	R	H	2B	3B	HR	RBI	SB	Avg
2003 Yakima	Northwest	OF	68	257	44	82	35	1	6	60	3	.319
2004 Lancaster	Calif.	OF	67	258	64	89	19	2	11	54	4	.345
2004 El Paso	Texas	OF-3B	60	226	33	68	13	2	6	37	3	.301
2005 Tucson	P.C.	1B-OF	93	333	66	118	38	2	8	73	3	.354
2005 Arizona	N.L.	1B-OF	40	85	8	17	3	0	2	8	0	.200
2006 Arizona	N.L.	1B	140	485	75	141	26	1	15	79	1	.291
2007 Arizona	N.L.	1B-3B-OF	130	415	56	118	29	1	15	60	2	.284
2008 Arizona	N.L.	OF-1B	144	540	87	162	31	6	12	75	10	.300
Major League Totals		4 Yrs.	454	1525	226	438	89	8	44	222	13	.287
Division Series												
2007 Arizona	N.L.	1B	3	8	0	1	1	0	0	1	0	.125
Championship Series												
2007 Arizona	N.L.	1B	3	9	1	3	0	0	0	1	0	.333

JACOBS, MICHAEL JAMES (MIKE)

Born, Chula Vista, California, October 30, 1980.
Bats Left. Throws Right. Height, 6 feet, 2 inches. Weight, 215 pounds.

Year	Club	Lea	Pos	G	AB	R	H	2B	3B	HR	RBI	SB	Avg
1999 Mets	Gulf Coast		C-1B	44	147	18	49	12	0	4	30	2	.333
2000 Kingsport		Appal.	C	59	204	28	55	15	4	7	40	6	.270
2000 Columbia		So.Atl.	C	18	56	1	12	5	0	0	8	1	.214
2001 Brooklyn		N.Y.-Penn.	C	19	66	12	19	5	0	1	15	1	.288
2001 Columbia		So.Atl.	C	46	180	18	50	13	0	2	26	0	.278
2002 St. Lucie		Fla.St.	C-1B	118	467	62	117	26	1	11	64	2	.251
2003 Binghamton		Eastern	C-1B	119	407	56	134	36	1	17	81	0	.329
2004 Norfolk		Int.	C-1B-SS	27	96	8	17	3	0	2	6	0	.177
2005 Binghamton		Eastern	1B-C-OF	117	433	66	139	37	2	25	93	1	.321
2005 New York a		N.L.	1B	30	100	19	31	7	0	11	23	0	.310
2006 Florida		N.L.	1B	136	469	54	123	37	1	20	77	3	.262
2007 Jupiter		Fla.St.	1B	3	12	2	2	0	0	1	3	0	.167
2007 Carolina		Southern	1B	4	10	1	3	0	0	1	2	0	.300
2007 Florida b		N.L.	1B	114	426	57	113	27	2	17	54	1	.265
2008 Florida c		N.L.	1B	141	477	67	118	27	2	32	93	1	.247
Major League Totals			4 Yrs.	421	1472	197	385	98	5	80	247	5	.262

a Traded to Florida Marlins with pitcher Yusmeiro Petit and infielder Grant Psomas for infielder Carlos Delgado and cash, November 23, 2005.
b On disabled list from May 14 to June 23, 2007.
c Traded to Kansas City Royals for pitcher Leo Nunez, October 30, 2008.

JENKINS, GEOFFREY SCOTT (GEOFF)

Born, Olympia, Washington, July 21, 1974.
Bats Left. Throws Right. Height, 6 feet, 1 inch. Weight, 210 pounds.

Year	Club	Lea	Pos	G	AB	R	H	2B	3B	HR	RBI	SB	Avg
1995 Helena		Pioneer	OF	7	28	2	9	0	1	0	9	0	.321
1995 Stockton		California	OF	13	47	13	12	2	0	3	12	2	.255
1995 El Paso		Texas	OF	22	79	12	22	4	2	1	13	3	.278
1996 El Paso		Texas	DH	22	77	17	22	5	4	1	11	1	.286
1996 Stockton a		California	DH-OF	37	138	27	48	8	4	3	25	3	.348
1997 Tucson b		P.C.	OF-SS	93	347	44	82	24	3	10	56	0	.236
1998 Louisville		Int.	OF	55	215	38	71	10	4	7	52	1	.330
1998 Milwaukee		N.L.	OF	84	262	33	60	12	1	9	28	1	.229
1999 Milwaukee		N.L.	OF	135	447	70	140	43	3	21	82	5	.313
2000 Milwaukee c		N.L.	OF	135	512	100	155	36	4	34	94	11	.303
2001 Beloit		Midwest	OF	1	3	1	1	1	0	0	1	0	.333
2001 Milwaukee d		N.L.	OF	105	397	60	105	21	1	20	63	4	.264
2002 Milwaukee e		N.L.	OF	67	243	35	59	17	1	10	29	1	.243
2003 Huntsville		Southern	OF	6	20	6	5	0	0	2	3	1	.250
2003 Milwaukee f		N.L.	OF	124	487	81	144	30	2	28	95	0	.296
2004 Milwaukee		N.L.	OF	157	617	88	163	36	6	27	93	3	.264
2005 Milwaukee		N.L.	OF	148	538	87	157	42	1	25	86	0	.292
2006 Milwaukee		N.L.	OF	147	484	62	131	26	1	17	70	4	.271
2007 Milwaukee g		N.L.	OF	132	420	45	107	24	2	21	64	2	.255
2008 Philadelphia h		N.L.	OF	115	293	27	72	16	0	9	29	1	.246
Major League Totals			11 Yrs.	1349	4700	688	1293	303	22	221	733	32	.275
Division Series													
2008 Philadelphia		N.L.	OF	1	1	0	0	0	0	0	0	0	.000
Championship Series													
2008 Philadelphia		N.L.	PH	2	1	0	0	0	0	0	0	0	.000
World Series Record													
2008 Philadelphia		N.L.	PH	2	2	1	1	1	0	0	0	0	.500

a On disabled list from May 8 to July 13, 1996.
b On disabled list from July 4 to August 11, 1997.
c On disabled list from May 6 to May 28, 2000.
d On disabled list from May 2 to May 19 and July 29 to August 28, 2001.
e On disabled list from June 18 to September 30, 2002.
f On disabled list from March 21 to April 9 and August 29 to September 29, 2003.
g Filed for free agency, October 30, 2007. Signed with Philadelphia Phillies, December 20, 2007.
h On disabled list from August 23 to September 10, 2008.

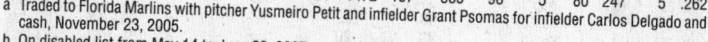

JETER, DEREK SANDERSON

Born, Pequannock, New Jersey, June 26, 1974.
Bats Right. Throws Right. Height, 6 feet, 3 inches. Weight, 195 pounds.

Year Club	Lea	Pos	G	AB	R	H	2B	3B	HR	RBI	SB	Avg
1992 Tampa Yankees	Gulf C.	SS	47	173	19	35	10	0	3	25	2	.202
1992 Greensboro	So. Atl.	SS	11	37	4	9	0	0	1	4	0	.243
1993 Greensboro	So. Atl.	SS	128	515	85	152	14	11	5	71	18	.295
1994 Tampa	Fla. St.	SS	69	292	61	96	13	8	0	39	28	.329
1994 Albany	Eastern	SS	34	122	17	46	7	2	2	13	12	.377
1994 Columbus	Int.	SS	35	126	25	44	7	1	3	16	10	.349
1995 Columbus	Int.	SS	123	486	96	154	27	9	2	45	20	.317
1995 New York	A.L.	SS	15	48	5	12	4	1	0	7	0	.250
1996 New York a	A.L.	SS	157	582	104	183	25	6	10	78	14	.314
1997 New York	A.L.	SS	159	654	116	190	31	7	10	70	23	.291
1998 Columbus	Int.	SS	1	5	2	2	2	0	0	0	0	.400
1998 New York b	A.L.	SS	149	626	*127	203	25	8	19	84	30	.324
1999 New York	A.L.	SS	158	627	134	219	37	9	24	102	19	.349
2000 Tampa	Fla.St.	SS	1	3	2	2	1	0	0	0	0	.667
2000 New York c	A.L.	SS	148	593	119	201	31	4	15	73	22	.339
2001 New York d	A.L.	SS	150	614	110	191	35	3	21	74	27	.311
2002 New York	A.L.	SS	157	644	124	191	26	0	18	75	32	.297
2003 Trenton	Eastern	SS	5	18	2	8	1	1	0	5	0	.444
2003 New York e	A.L.	SS	119	482	87	156	25	3	10	52	11	.324
2004 New York	A.L.	SS	154	643	111	188	44	1	23	78	23	.292
2005 New York	A.L.	SS	159	654	122	202	25	5	19	70	14	.309
2006 New York	A.L.	SS	154	623	118	214	39	3	14	97	34	.343
2007 New York	A.L.	SS	156	639	102	206	39	4	12	73	15	.322
2008 New York	A.L.	SS	150	596	88	179	25	3	11	69	11	.300
Major League Totals	14 Yrs.	1985	8025	1467	2535	411	57	206	1002	275	.316
Division Series												
1996 New York	A.L.	SS	4	17	2	7	1	0	0	1	0	.412
1997 New York	A.L.	SS	5	21	6	7	1	0	2	2	1	.333
1998 New York	A.L.	SS	3	9	0	1	0	0	0	0	0	.111
1999 New York	A.L.	SS	3	11	3	5	1	1	0	0	0	.455
2000 New York	A.L.	SS	5	19	1	4	0	0	0	2	0	.211
2001 New York	A.L.	SS	5	18	2	8	1	0	0	1	0	.444
2002 New York	A.L.	SS	4	16	6	8	0	0	2	3	0	.500
2003 New York	A.L.	SS	4	14	2	6	0	0	1	1	1	.429
2004 New York	A.L.	SS	4	19	3	6	1	0	1	4	1	.316
2005 New York	A.L.	SS	5	21	4	7	0	0	2	5	1	.333
2006 New York	A.L.	SS	4	16	4	8	4	0	1	1	0	.500
2007 New York	A.L.	SS	4	17	0	3	0	0	0	1	0	.176
Division Series Totals			50	198	33	70	9	1	9	21	4	.354
Championship Series												
1996 New York	A.L.	SS	5	24	5	10	2	0	1	1	2	.417
1998 New York	A.L.	SS	6	25	3	5	1	1	0	2	3	.200
1999 New York	A.L.	SS	5	20	3	7	1	0	1	3	0	.350
2000 New York	A.L.	SS	6	22	6	7	0	0	2	5	1	.318
2001 New York	A.L.	SS	5	17	0	2	0	0	0	0	0	.118
2003 New York	A.L.	SS	7	30	3	7	2	0	1	2	1	.233
2004 New York	A.L.	SS	7	30	5	6	1	0	0	5	1	.200
Championship Series Totals			41	168	25	44	7	1	5	20	8	.262
World Series												
1996 New York	A.L.	SS	6	20	5	5	0	0	0	1	1	.250
1998 New York	A.L.	SS	4	17	4	6	0	0	0	1	0	.353
1999 New York	A.L.	SS	4	17	4	6	1	0	0	1	3	.353
2000 New York	A.L.	SS	5	22	6	9	2	1	2	2	0	.409
2001 New York	A.L.	SS	7	27	3	4	0	0	1	1	0	.148
2003 New York	A.L.	SS	6	26	5	9	3	0	0	2	0	.346
World Series Totals			32	129	27	39	6	1	3	8	4	.302

a Selected Rookie of the Year in American League for 1996.
b On disabled list from June 4 to June 19, 1998.
c On disabled list from May 12 to May 26, 2000.
d On disabled list from March 23 to April 7, 2001.
e On disabled list from April 1 to May 13, 2003.

JOHJIMA, KENJI

Born, Nagasaki, Japan, June 8, 1976.
Bats Right. Throws Right. Height, 6 feet. Weight, 200 pounds.

Year	Club	Lea	Pos	G	AB	R	H	2B	3B	HR	RBI	SB	Avg
1995 Fukuoka	Japan Pac.		C	12	12	2	2	0	0	0	1	0	.167
1996 Fukuoka	Japan Pac.		C	17	58	5	14	2	0	4	9	1	.241
1997 Fukuoka	Japan Pac.		C	120	432	49	133	24	2	15	68	6	.308
1998 Fukuoka	Japan Pac.		C	122	395	53	99	19	0	16	58	5	.251
1999 Fukuoka	Japan Pac.		C	135	493	65	151	33	1	17	77	6	.306
2000 Fukuoka	Japan Pac.		C	84	303	38	94	22	2	9	50	10	.310
2001 Fukuoka	Japan Pac.		C	140	534	63	138	18	0	31	95	9	.258
2002 Fukuoka	Japan Pac.		C	115	416	60	122	18	0	25	74	8	.293
2003 Fukuoka	Japan Pac.		C	140	551	101	182	39	2	34	119	9	.330
2004 Fukuoka	Japan Pac.		C	116	426	91	144	25	1	36	91	6	.338
2005 Fukuoka a	Japan Pac.		C	116	411	70	127	22	4	24	57	3	.309
2006 Seattle	A.L.		C	144	506	61	147	25	1	18	76	3	.291
2007 Seattle	A.L.		C	135	485	52	139	29	0	14	61	0	.287
2008 Seattle	A.L.		C	112	379	29	86	19	0	7	39	2	.227
Major League Totals		3 Yrs.		391	1370	142	372	73	1	39	176	5	.272

a Signed with Seattle Mariners, November 21, 2005.

JOHNSON, KELLY ANDREW

Born, Austin, Texas, February 22, 1982.
Bats Left. Throws Right. Height, 6 feet, 1 inch. Weight, 205 pounds.

Year	Club	Lea	Pos	G	AB	R	H	2B	3B	HR	RBI	SB	Avg
2000 Braves	Gulf Coast	SS-3B	53	193	27	52	12	3	4	29	6	.269
2001 Macon	So.Atl.	SS	124	415	75	120	22	1	23	66	25	.289
2002 Myrtle Beach	Carolina	SS-3B	126	482	62	123	21	5	12	49	12	.255
2003 Braves	Gulf Coast	SS	6	26	10	10	1	1	1	3	1	.385
2003 Greenville	Southern	SS	98	334	46	92	22	5	6	45	10	.275
2004 Greenville	Southern	OF-3B-2B	135	479	70	135	35	3	16	50	9	.282
2005 Richmond	Int.	OF-3B-SS	44	155	35	48	12	3	8	22	7	.310
2005 Atlanta	N.L.	OF	87	290	46	70	12	3	9	40	2	.241
2006 Richmond	Int.	OF	10	39	3	13	4	0	1	7	1	.333
2006 Rome a	So.Atl.	OF	5	19	5	9	2	1	1	3	2	.474
2007 Atlanta	N.L.	2B	147	521	61	144	26	10	16	68	9	.276
2008 Atlanta	N.L.	2B	150	547	86	157	39	6	12	69	11	.287
Major League Totals		3 Yrs.	384	1358	223	371	77	19	37	177	22	.273
Division Series													
2005 Atlanta	N.L.	PH	4	2	0	0	0	0	0	0	0	.000

a On disabled list from March 24 to November 1, 2006.

JOHNSON, REED CAMERON

Born, Riverside, California, December 8, 1976.
Bats Right. Throws Right. Height, 5 feet, 10 inches. Weight, 180 pounds.

Year	Club	Lea	Pos	G	AB	R	H	2B	3B	HR	RBI	SB	Avg
1999 St. Catharines	N.Y.-Penn.	OF	60	189	24	44	8	2	2	23	5	.233
2000 Dunedin	Fla.St.	OF	36	133	26	42	9	2	4	28	3	.316
2000 Hagerstown	So.Atl.	OF	95	324	66	94	24	5	8	70	14	.290
2001 Tennessee	Southern	OF	136	554	104	174	29	4	13	74	42	.314
2002 Dunedin	Fla.St.	OF	8	33	7	9	3	0	0	6	0	.273
2002 Syracuse	Int.	OF	44	159	27	37	8	3	2	10	1	.233
2003 Syracuse	Int.	OF	26	101	14	33	4	1	2	16	3	.327
2003 Toronto	A.L.	OF	114	412	79	121	21	2	10	52	5	.294
2004 Toronto	A.L.	OF	141	537	68	145	25	2	10	61	6	.270
2005 Toronto	A.L.	OF	142	398	55	107	21	6	8	58	5	.269
2006 Toronto	A.L.	OF	134	461	86	147	34	2	12	49	8	.319
2007 Dunedin	Fla.St.	OF	4	12	1	4	1	0	1	1	0	.333
2007 Syracuse	Int.	OF	2	8	1	3	0	0	0	1	0	.375
2007 Toronto a	A.L.	OF	79	275	31	65	13	2	2	14	4	.236
2008 Chicago b-c	N.L.	OF	109	333	52	101	21	0	6	50	5	.303
Major League Totals		6 Yrs.	719	2416	371	686	135	14	48	284	33	.284

a On disabled list from April 12 to July 6, 2007.
b Released by Toronto Blue Jays, March 23, 2008. Signed with Chicago Cubs, March 25, 2008.
c On disabled list from June 18 to July 3, 2008.

JONES, ADAM LA MARQUE

Born, San Diego, California, August 1, 1985.
Bats Right. Throws Right. Height, 6 feet, 2 inches. Weight, 200 pounds.

Year	Club	Lea	Pos	G	AB	R	H	2B	3B	HR	RBI	SB	Avg
2003 Mariners	Arizona		SS	28	109	18	31	5	1	0	8	5	.284
2003 Everett	Northwest		SS	3	13	2	6	1	0	.0	4	0	.462
2004 Wisconsin	Midwest		SS-3B	130	510	76	136	23	7	11	72	8	.267
2005 Inland Empire	Calif.		SS	68	271	43	80	20	5	8	46	4	.295
2005 San Antonio	Texas		SS-OF	63	228	33	68	10	3	7	20	9	.298
2006 Tacoma	P.C.		OF	96	380	69	109	19	4	16	62	13	.287
2006 Seattle	A.L.		OF	32	74	6	16	4	0	1	8	3	.216
2007 Tacoma	P.C.		OF	101	420	75	132	27	6	25	84	8	.314
2007 Seattle	A.L.		OF	41	65	16	16	2	1	2	4	2	.246
2008 Baltimore a-b	A.L.		OF	132	477	61	129	21	7	9	57	10	.270
Major League Totals			3 Yrs.	205	616	83	161	27	8	12	69	15	.261

a Traded to Baltimore Orioles with pitcher Tony Butler, pitcher Kam Mickolio, pitcher George Sherrill and pitcher Chris Tillman for pitcher Erik Bedard, February 8, 2008.

b On disabled list from August 3 to September 1, 2008.

JONES, ANDRUW RUDOLF

Born, Willemstad, Curacao, Netherlands Antillies, April 23, 1977.
Bats Right. Throws Right. Height, 6 feet, 1 inch. Weight, 240 pounds.

Year	Club	Lea	Pos	G	AB	R	H	2B	3B	HR	RBI	SB	Avg
1994 Braves	Gulf Coast		OF	27	95	22	21	5	1	2	10	5	.221
1994 Danville	Appal.		OF	36	143	20	48	9	2	1	16	16	.336
1995 Macon	So.Atl.		OF	139	537	104	149	41	5	25	100	56	.277
1996 Durham	Carolina		OF	66	243	65	76	14	3	17	43	16	.313
1996 Greenville	Southern		OF	38	157	39	58	10	1	12	37	12	.369
1996 Richmond	Int.		OF	12	45	11	17	3	1	5	12	2	.378
1996 Atlanta	N.L.		OF	31	106	11	23	7	1	5	13	3	.217
1997 Atlanta	N.L.		OF	153	399	60	92	18	1	18	70	20	.231
1998 Atlanta	N.L.		OF	159	582	89	158	33	8	31	90	27	.271
1999 Atlanta	N.L.		OF	162	592	97	163	35	5	26	84	24	.275
2000 Atlanta	N.L.		OF	161	*656	122	199	36	6	36	104	21	.303
2001 Atlanta	N.L.		OF	161	625	104	157	25	2	34	104	11	.251
2002 Atlanta	N.L.		OF	154	560	91	148	34	0	35	94	8	.264
2003 Atlanta	N.L.		OF	156	595	101	165	28	2	36	116	4	.277
2004 Atlanta	N.L.		OF	154	570	85	149	34	4	29	91	6	.261
2005 Atlanta	N.L.		OF	160	586	95	154	24	3	*51	*128	5	.263
2006 Atlanta	N.L.		OF	156	565	107	148	29	0	41	129	4	.262
2007 Atlanta a	N.L.		OF	154	572	83	127	27	2	26	94	5	.222
2008 Las Vegas	P.C.		1B-OF	11	31	7	10	0	0	4	11	2	.323
2008 Los Angeles b	N.L.		OF	75	209	21	33	8	1	3	14	0	.158
Major League Totals			13 Yrs.	1836	6617	1066	1716	338	35	371	1131	138	.259
Division Series													
1996 Atlanta	N.L.		OF	3	0	0	0	0	0	0	0	0	.000
1997 Atlanta	N.L.		OF	3	5	1	0	0	0	0	1	0	.000
1998 Atlanta	N.L.		OF	3	9	2	0	0	0	0	1	2	.000
1999 Atlanta	N.L.		OF	4	18	1	4	1	0	0	2	0	.222
2000 Atlanta	N.L.		OF	3	9	3	1	0	0	1	1	0	.111
2001 Atlanta	N.L.		OF	3	12	2	6	0	0	1	1	0	.500
2002 Atlanta	N.L.		OF	5	19	4	6	1	0	0	2	0	.316
2003 Atlanta	N.L.		OF	5	17	1	1	0	0	0	1	0	.059
2004 Atlanta	N.L.		OF	5	19	4	10	2	0	2	5	1	.526
2005 Atlanta	N.L.		OF	4	17	5	8	3	0	1	5	0	.471
Division Series Totals				38	125	23	36	7	0	5	19	3	.288
Championship Series													
1996 Atlanta	N.L.		OF	5	9	3	2	0	0	1	3	0	.222
1997 Atlanta	N.L.		OF	5	9	0	4	0	0	0	1	0	.444
1998 Atlanta	N.L.		OF	6	22	3	6	0	0	1	2	1	.273
1999 Atlanta	N.L.		OF	6	23	5	5	0	0	0	1	0	.217
2001 Atlanta	N.L.		OF	5	17	4	3	0	0	1	1	0	.176
Championship Series Totals				27	80	15	20	0	0	3	8	1	.250
World Series													
1996 Atlanta	N.L.		OF	6	20	4	8	1	0	2	6	1	.400
1999 Atlanta	N.L.		OF	4	13	1	1	0	0	0	0	0	.077
World Series Totals				10	33	5	9	1	0	2	6	1	.273

a Filed for free agency, October 31, 2007. Signed with Los Angeles Dodgers, December 12, 2007.

b On disabled list from May 24 to July 4 and August 10 to September 1 and September 13 to November 4, 2008.

c Released, January 15, 2009.

JONES, BRANDON LAMON

Born, Panama City, Florida, December 10, 1983.
Bats Left. Throws Right. Height, 6 feet, 1 inch. Weight, 210 pounds.

Year	Club	Lea	Pos	G	AB	R	H	2B	3B	HR	RBI	SB	Avg
2004	Danville	Appal.	OF	57	209	35	62	6	5	3	33	4	.297
2005	Danville	Appal.	OF	2	7	0	2	0	0	0	1	0	.286
2005	Myrtle Beach	Carolina	OF	17	60	7	21	4	0	0	5	0	.350
2005	Braves	Gulf Coast	OF	2	8	0	1	0	0	0	2	0	.125
2005	Rome	So.Atl.	OF	43	156	37	48	12	3	8	27	4	.308
2006	Myrtle Beach	Carolina	OF	59	226	27	58	10	3	7	35	11	.257
2006	Mississippi	Southern	OF	48	176	18	48	9	3	7	25	4	.273
2007	Mississippi	Southern	OF	94	365	58	107	21	6	15	74	12	.293
2007	Richmond	Int.	OF	44	170	26	51	12	1	4	26	5	.300
2007	Atlanta	N.L.	OF	5	19	0	3	1	0	0	4	0	.158
2008	Richmond	Int.	OF	95	346	44	90	24	1	8	52	9	.260
2008	Atlanta	N.L.	OF	41	116	16	31	10	1	1	17	1	.267
Major League Totals			2 Yrs.	46	135	16	34	11	1	1	21	1	.252

JONES, LARRY WAYNE (CHIPPER)

Born, Deland, Florida, April 24, 1972.
Bats Both. Throws Right. Height, 6 feet, 4 inches. Weight, 210 pounds.

Year	Club	Lea	Pos	G	AB	R	H	2B	3B	HR	RBI	SB	Avg
1990	Bradenton Braves	Gulf C.	SS	44	140	20	32	1	1	1	18	5	.229
1991	Macon	So. Atl.	SS	136	473	*104	154	24	11	15	98	40	.326
1992	Durham	Carolina	SS	70	264	43	73	22	1	4	31	10	.277
1992	Greenville	Southern	SS	67	266	43	92	17	11	9	42	14	.346
1993	Richmond	Int.	SS	139	536	97	174	31	12	13	89	23	.325
1993	Atlanta	N.L.	SS	8	3	2	2	1	0	0	0	0	.667
1994	Atlanta a	N.L.				INJURED—Did Not Play								
1995	Atlanta	N.L.	3B-OF	140	524	87	139	22	3	23	86	8	.265
1996	Atlanta b	N.L.	3B-SS-OF	157	598	114	185	32	5	30	110	14	.309
1997	Atlanta	N.L.	3B-OF	157	597	100	176	41	3	21	111	20	.295
1998	Atlanta	N.L.	3B	160	601	123	188	29	5	34	107	16	.313
1999	Atlanta c	N.L.	3B-SS	157	567	116	181	41	1	45	110	25	.319
2000	Atlanta	N.L.	3B-SS	156	579	118	180	38	1	36	111	14	.311
2001	Atlanta	N.L.	3B-OF	159	572	113	189	33	5	38	102	8	.330
2002	Atlanta	N.L.	OF	.158	548	90	179	35	1	26	100	8	.327
2003	Atlanta	N.L.	OF	153	555	103	169	33	2	27	106	2	.305
2004	Rome	So.Atl.	OF	1	4	0	0	0	0	0	0	0	.000
2004	Atlanta d	N.L.	3B-OF	137	472	69	117	20	1	30	96	2	.248
2005	Rome	So.Atl.	3B	3	6	1	3	0	0	0	2	0	.500
2005	Atlanta e	N.L.	3B	109	358	66	106	30	0	21	72	5	.296
2006	Mississippi	Southern	3B	2	6	1	1	0	0	0	0	0	.167
2006	Atlanta f	N.L.	3B	110	411	87	133	28	3	26	86	6	.324
2007	Atlanta g	N.L.	3B-SS	134	513	108	173	42	4	29	102	5	.337
2008	Atlanta h	N.L.	3B	128	439	82	160	24	1	22	75	4	*.364
Major League Totals			15 Yrs.	2023	7337	1378	2277	449	35	408	1374	138	.310
Division Series													
1995	Atlanta	N.L.	3B	4	18	4	7	2	0	2	4	0	.389
1996	Atlanta	N.L.	3B	3	9	2	2	0	0	1	2	1	.222
1997	Atlanta	N.L.	3B	3	8	3	4	0	0	1	2	1	.500
1998	Atlanta	N.L.	3B	3	10	2	2	0	0	0	1	0	.200
1999	Atlanta	N.L.	3B	4	13	2	3	0	0	0	1	0	.231
2000	Atlanta	N.L.	3B	3	12	2	4	1	0	0	1	0	.333
2001	Atlanta	N.L.	3B	3	9	2	4	0	0	2	5	0	.444
2002	Atlanta	N.L.	OF	5	17	3	5	0	0	0	2	0	.294
2003	Atlanta	N.L.	OF	5	18	3	3	0	0	2	6	0	.167
2004	Atlanta	N.L.	3B	5	20	4	4	0	0	0	0	0	.200
2005	Atlanta	N.L.	3B	4	17	3	3	2	0	1	2	0	.176
Division Series Totals				42	151	30	41	5	0	9	26	2	.272
Championship Series													
1995	Atlanta	N.L.	3B	4	16	3	7	0	0	1	3	1	.438
1996	Atlanta	N.L.	3B	7	25	6	11	2	0	0	4	1	.440
1997	Atlanta	N.L.	3B	6	24	5	7	1	0	2	4	0	.292
1998	Atlanta	N.L.	3B	6	24	2	5	1	0	0	1	0	.208
1999	Atlanta	N.L.	3B	6	19	3	5	2	0	0	1	3	.263
2001	Atlanta	N.L.	3B	5	19	1	5	1	0	0	2	0	.263
Championship Series Totals				34	127	20	40	7	0	3	15	5	.315

Year	Club	Lea	Pos	G	AB	R	H	2B	3B	HR	RBI	SB	Avg
World Series Record													
1995 Atlanta	N.L.		3B	6	21	3	6	3	0	0	1	0	.286
1996 Atlanta	N.L.		3B-SS	6	21	3	6	3	0	0	3	1	.286
1999 Atlanta	N.L.		3B	4	13	2	3	0	0	1	2	0	.231
World Series Totals				16	55	8	15	6	0	1	6	1	.273

a On disabled list from March 20 to end of 1994 season.
b On disabled list from April 1 to April 6, 1996.
c Selected Most Valuable Player in National League for 1999.
d On disabled list from April 19 to May 8, 2004.
e On disabled list from June 6 to July 18, 2005.
f On disabled list from April 10 to April 25 and July 30 to August 13 and September 4 to September 19, 2006.
g On disabled list from May 24 to June 13, 2007.
h On disabled list from July 24 to August 8, 2008.

JOYCE, MATTHEW R. (MATT)
Born, Tampa, Florida, August 3, 1984.
Bats Left. Throws Right. Height, 6 feet, 2 inches. Weight, 185 pounds.

Year	Club	Lea	Pos	G	AB	R	H	2B	3B	HR	RBI	SB	Avg
2005 Oneonta	N.Y.-Penn.		OF	65	245	51	81	10	4	4	45	9	.331
2006 West Michigan	Midwest		OF	122	465	75	120	30	5	11	86	5	.258
2007 Erie	Eastern		OF	130	456	61	117	33	3	17	70	4	.257
2008 Toledo	Int.		OF	56	200	36	54	13	2	13	41	2	.270
2008 Detroit a	A.L.		OF	92	242	40	61	16	3	12	33	0	.252

a Traded to Tampa Bay Rays for pitcher Edwin Jackson, December 10, 2008.

KAPLER, GABRIEL STEFAN (GABE)
Born, Hollywood, California, July 31, 1975.
Bats Right. Throws Right. Height, 6 feet, 2 inches. Weight, 208 pounds.

Year	Club	Lea	Pos	G	AB	R	H	2B	3B	HR	RBI	SB	Avg
1995 Jamestown	N.Y.-Penn.		OF	63	236	38	68	19	4	4	34	1	.288
1996 Fayettevlle	So.Atl.		OF-3B	138	524	81	157	45	0	26	99	14	.300
1997 Lakeland	Fla.St.		OF	137	519	87	153	40	6	19	87	8	.295
1998 Jacksnville	Southern		OF-1B	139	547	113	176	47	6	28	146	6	.322
1998 Detroit	A.L.		OF	7	25	3	5	0	1	0	0	2	.200
1999 Detroit	A.L.		OF	130	416	60	102	22	4	18	49	11	.245
1999 Toledo a	Int.		OF	14	54	11	17	6	2	3	14	0	.315
2000 Texas	A.L.		OF	116	444	59	134	32	1	14	66	8	.302
2000 Oklahoma	P.C.		OF	3	9	3	3	0	0	0	0	0	.333
2000 Tulsa b	Texas		OF	3	12	3	7	0	0	1	4	0	.583
2001 Tulsa	Texas		OF	5	15	2	5	1	0	0	0	0	.333
2001 Texas c	A.L.		OF	134	483	77	129	29	1	17	72	23	.267
2002 Texas	A.L.		OF-1B	72	196	25	51	12	1	0	17	5	.260
2002 Oklahoma	P.C.		OF	5	17	6	8	2	0	1	5	1	.471
2002 Colorado d-e	N.L.		OF	40	119	12	37	4	3	2	17	6	.311
2003 Colorado	N.L.		OF	39	67	10	15	2	0	0	4	2	.224
2003 Colorado Springs	P.C.		OF	13	35	5	6	2	1	0	2	4	.171
2003 Lowell	N.Y.-Penn.		OF	1	3	2	2	0	0	0	0	1	.667
2003 Portland	Eastern		1B-OF	1	3	1	1	1	0	0	0	0	.333
2003 Boston f-g	A.L.		OF-1B	68	158	29	46	11	1	4	23	4	.291
2004 Boston	A.L.		OF	136	290	51	79	14	1	6	33	5	.272
2005 Lowell	N.Y.-Penn.		DH	2	8	1	1	0	0	0	0	0	.125
2005 Pawtucket	Int.		1B-C	6	22	7	14	3	1	2	6	0	.636
2005 Boston h-i	A.L.		OF	36	97	15	24	7	0	1	9	1	.247
2006 Pawtucket	Int.		OF	4	15	0	3	1	0	0	2	0	.200
2006 Portland	Eastern		OF	3	10	2	4	1	3	1	0	0	.400
2006 Boston j	A.L.		OF	72	130	21	33	7	0	2	12	1	.254
2007 k							RETIRED —Did Not Play						
2008 Milwaukee l	N.L.		OF	96	229	36	69	17	2	8	38	3	.301
Major League Totals		10 Yrs.		946	2654	398	724	157	15	72	340	71	.273
Division Series													
2003 Boston	A.L.		OF	4	9	0	0	0	0	0	0	0	.000
2004 Boston	A.L.		OF	2	5	2	1	0	0	0	0	0	.200
Division Series Totals				6	14	2	1	0	0	0	0	0	.071
Championship Series													
2003 Boston	A.L.		OF	3	8	0	1	0	0	0	0	0	.125
2004 Boston	A.L.		OF	2	3	0	1	0	0	0	0	0	.333
Championship Series Totals				5	11	0	2	0	0	0	0	0	.182

Year	Club	Lea	Pos	G	AB	R	H	2B	3B	HR	RBI	SB	Avg
	World Series Record												
2004 Boston		A.L.	OF	4	2	0	0	0	0	0	0	0	.000

a Traded to Texas Rangers with pitcher Justin Thompson, pitcher Francisco Cordero, pitcher Alan Webb, catcher Bill Haselman and infielder Frank Catalanotto for outfielder Juan Gonzalez, pitcher Danny Patterson and catcher Gregg Zaun, November 2, 1999.
b On disabled list from May 3 to June 8, 2000.
c On disabled list from March 23 to April 22, 2001.
d On disabled list from June 24 to July 16, 2002.
e Traded to Colorado Rockies with outfielder Jason Romano and cash for pitcher Dennys Reyes and outfielder Todd Hollandsworth, July 31, 2002.
f Released by Colorado Rockies, June 18, 2003. Signed with Boston Red Sox organization, June 24, 2003.
g Not offered contract, December 21, 2003, re-signed with Boston Red Sox, December 22, 2003.
h Filed for free agency, October 28, 2004. re-signed with Boston Red Sox, July 15, 2005.
i On disabled list from July 15 to July 30, 2005.
j Released by Boston Red Sox, November 18, 2005, re-signed with Boston Red Sox, January 23, 2006.
k Announced retirement to manage in minors, December 13, 2006. Signed with Milwaukee Brewers, December 20, 2007.
l Filed for free agency, October 30, 2008. Signed with Tampa Bay Rays, January 12, 2009.

KEARNS, AUSTIN RYAN
Born, Lexington, Kentucky, May 20, 1980.
Bats Right. Throws Right. Height, 6 feet, 3 inches. Weight, 235 pounds.

Year	Club	Lea	Pos	G	AB	R	H	2B	3B	HR	RBI	SB	Avg
1998 Billings	Pioneer		OF-3B	30	108	17	34	9	0	1	14	1	.315
1999 Rockford	Midwest		OF	124	426	72	110	36	5	13	48	21	.258
2000 Dayton	Midwest		OF	136	484	110	148	37	5	27	104	18	.306
2001 Reds	Gulf Coast		OF	6	17	2	3	2	0	0	4	0	.176
2001 Chattanooga a	Southern		OF	59	205	30	55	11	2	6	36	7	.268
2002 Chattanooga	Southern		OF	12	41	10	11	2	0	5	13	1	.268
2002 Louisville	Int.		OF	1	4	3	3	2	0	0	2	0	.750
2002 Cincinnati b	N.L.		OF	107	372	66	117	24	3	13	56	6	.315
2003 Chattanooga	Southern		OF	3	5	2	1	0	0	0	1	0	.200
2003 Cincinnati c	N.L.		OF	82	292	39	77	11	0	15	58	5	.264
2004 Louisville	Int.		OF	25	83	19	28	7	1	2	15	3	.337
2004 Cincinnati d	N.L.		OF	64	217	28	50	10	2	9	32	2	.230
2005 Louisville	Int.		OF	28	111	24	38	15	1	7	21	0	.342
2005 Cincinnati	N.L.		OF	112	387	62	93	26	1	18	67	0	.240
2006 Cincinnati-Washington e	N.L.		OF	150	537	86	142	33	2	24	86	9	.264
2007 Washington	N.L.		OF	161	587	84	156	35	1	16	74	2	.266
2008 Hagerstown	So.Atl.		DH	2	3	2	1	0	0	0	1	0	.333
2008 Columbus	Int.		OF	5	14	2	6	1	1	1	6	0	.429
2008 Washington f	N.L.		OF	86	313	40	68	10	0	7	32	2	.217
Major League Totals	7 Yrs.			762	2705	405	703	149	9	102	405	26	.260

a On disabled list from May 27 to August 13, 2001.
b On disabled list from August 27 to September 30, 2002.
c On disabled list from July 9 to November 5, 2003.
d On disabled list from April 27 to May 19 and from June 2 to August 24, 2004.
e Traded to Washington Nationals with infielder Felipe Lopez and pitcher Ryan Wagner for pitcher Gary Majewski, pitcher Bill Bray, infielder Royce Clayton, infielder Brendan Harris and pitcher Daryl Thompson, July 13, 2006.
f On disabled list from May 22 to July 3 and August 25 to October 3, 2008.

KEMP, MATTHEW RYAN (MATT)
Born, Midwest City, Oklahoma, September 23, 1984.
Bats Right. Throws Right. Height, 6 feet, 2 inches. Weight, 230 pounds.

Year	Club	Lea	Pos	G	AB	R	H	2B	3B	HR	RBI	SB	Avg
2003 Dodgers	Gulf Coast		OF	42	159	11	43	5	2	1	17	2	.270
2004 Vero Beach	Fla.St.		OF	11	37	5	13	5	0	1	9	2	.351
2004 Columbus	So.Atl.		OF	112	423	67	122	22	8	17	66	8	.288
2005 Vero Beach	Fla.St.		OF	109	418	76	128	21	4	27	90	23	.306
2006 Jacksonville	Southern		OF	48	199	38	65	15	2	7	34	11	.327
2006 Las Vegas	P.C.		OF	44	182	37	67	14	6	3	36	14	.368
2006 Los Angeles	N.L.		OF	52	154	30	39	7	1	7	23	6	.253
2007 Las Vegas	P.C.		OF	39	161	32	53	16	3	4	20	9	.329
2007 Los Angeles a	N.L.		OF	98	292	47	100	12	5	10	42	10	.342
2008 Los Angeles	N.L.		OF	155	606	93	176	38	5	18	76	35	.290
Major League Totals	3 Yrs.			305	1052	170	315	57	11	35	141	51	.299

Year Club	Lea	Pos	G	AB	R	H	2B	3B	HR	RBI	SB	Avg
Division Series												
2008 Los Angeles	N.L.	OF	3	13	0	2	2	0	0	1	0	.154
Championship Series												
2008 Los Angeles	N.L.	OF	5	15	1	5	1	0	0	0	0	.333

a On disabled list from April 10 to April 27, 2007.

KENDALL, JASON DANIEL

Born, San Diego, California, June 26, 1974.
Bats Right. Throws Right. Height, 6 feet. Weight, 205 pounds.

Year Club	Lea	Pos	G	AB	R	H	2B	3B	HR	RBI	SB	Avg
1992 Pirates	Gulf Coast	C	33	111	7	29	2	0	0	10	2	.261
1993 Augusta	So.Atl.	C	102	366	43	101	17	4	1	40	8	.276
1994 Salem..........	Carolina	C	101	371	68	118	19	2	7	66	14	.318
1994 Carolina	Southern	C	13	47	6	11	2	0	0	6	0	.234
1995 Carolina	Southern	C	117	429	87	140	26	1	8	71	10	.326
1996 Pittsburgh	N.L.	C	130	414	54	124	23	5	3	42	5	.300
1997 Pittsburgh	N.L.	C	144	486	71	143	36	4	8	49	18	.294
1998 Pittsburgh	N.L.	C	149	535	95	175	36	3	12	75	26	.327
1999 Pittsburgh a	N.L.	C	78	280	61	93	20	3	8	41	22	.332
2000 Pittsburgh	N.L.	C	152	579	112	185	33	6	14	58	22	.320
2001 Pittsburgh	N.L.	C-OF	157	606	84	161	22	2	10	53	13	.266
2002 Pittsburgh	N.L.	C	145	545	59	154	25	3	3	44	15	.283
2003 Pittsburgh	N.L.	C	150	587	84	191	29	3	6	58	8	.325
2004 Pittsburgh b	N.L.	C	147	574	86	183	32	0	3	51	11	.319
2005 Oakland	A.L.	C	150	601	70	163	28	1	0	53	8	.271
2006 Oakland	A.L.	C	143	552	76	163	23	0	1	50	11	.295
2007 Oakland	A.L.	C-OF	80	292	24	66	10	0	2	22	3	.226
2007 Chicago c-d	N.L.	C	57	174	21	47	10	1	1	19	0	.270
2008 Milwaukee	N.L.	C	151	516	46	127	30	2	2	49	8	.246
Major League Totals		13 Yrs.	1833	6741	943	1975	357	33	73	664	170	.293
Division Series												
2006 Oakland	A.L.	C	3	14	1	3	1	0	0	1	0	.214
2007 Chicago	N.L.	C	1	4	0	1	0	0	0	1	0	.250
2008 Milwaukee	N.L.	C	4	14	0	2	0	0	0	1	0	.143
Division Series Totals			8	32	1	6	1	0	0	3	0	.188
Championship Series												
2006 Oakland	A.L.	C	4	17	0	5	0	0	0	0	0	.294

a On disabled list from July 5 to November 17, 1999.
b Traded to Oakland Athletics with cash for pitcher Mark Redman and pitcher Arthur Rhodes, November 25, 2004.
c Traded to Chicago Cubs with cash for pitcher Jerry Blevins and catcher Rob Bowen, July 17, 2007.
d Filed for free agency, October 30, 2007. Signed with Milwaukee Brewers, November 28, 2007.

KENDRICK, HOWARD JOSEPH (HOWIE)

Born, Jacksonville, Florida, July 12, 1983.
Bats Right. Throws Right. Height, 5 feet, 10 inches. Weight, 195 pounds.

Year Club	Lea	Pos	G	AB	R	H	2B	3B	HR	RBI	SB	Avg
2002 Angels	Arizona	2B	42	157	24	50	6	4	0	13	12	.318
2003 Provo	Pioneer	2B	63	234	65	86	20	3	3	36	8	.368
2004 Angels	Arizona	2B	3	12	1	3	1	0	0	0	2	.250
2004 Cedar Rapids	Midwest	2B	75	313	66	115	24	6	10	49	15	.367
2005 Rancho Cucamonga....	Calif.	2B	63	279	69	107	23	6	12	47	13	.384
2005 Arkansas	Texas	2B	46	190	35	65	20	2	7	42	12	.342
2006 Salt Lake	P.C.	2B-3B	69	290	57	107	25	6	13	62	11	.369
2006 Los Angeles	A.L.	1B-2B-3B	72	267	25	76	21	1	4	30	6	.285
2007 Rancho Cucamonga....	Calif.	DH	1	4	0	1	0	0	0	0	0	.250
2007 Salt Lake	P.C.	2B	13	50	9	15	1	0	3	11	1	.300
2007 Los Angeles a	A.L.	2B	88	338	55	109	24	2	5	39	5	.322
2008 Rancho Cucamonga....	Calif.	2B	2	6	3	5	0	0	2	2	1	.833
2008 Salt Lake	P.C.	2B	2	5	0	1	0	0	0	1	0	.200
2008 Los Angeles b	A.L.	2B	92	340	43	104	26	2	3	37	11	.306
Major League Totals		3 Yrs.	252	945	123	289	71	5	12	106	22	.306
Division Series												
2007 Los Angeles	A.L.	2B	3	10	0	2	0	0	0	1	2	.200
2008 Los Angeles	A.L.	2B	4	17	0	2	0	0	0	0	0	.118
Division Series Totals			7	27	0	4	0	0	0	1	2	.148

a On disabled list from April 18 to May 23 and July 8 to August 20, 2007.
b On disabled list from April 14 to May 30 and August 28 to September 22, 2008.

KENNEDY, ADAM THOMAS

Born, Riverside, California, January 10, 1976.
Bats Left. Throws Right. Height, 6 feet. Weight, 185 pounds.

Year Club	Lea	Pos	G	AB	R	H	2B	3B	HR	RBI	SB	Avg
1997 New Jersey	N.Y.-Penn.	SS	29	114	20	39	6	3	0	19	9	.342
1997 Pr William	Carolina	SS	35	154	24	48	9	3	1	27	4	.312
1998 Pr William	Carolina	2B-SS	17	69	9	18	6	0	0	7	5	.261
1998 Arkansas	Texas	SS-2B	52	205	35	57	11	2	6	24	6	.278
1998 Memphis	P.C.	SS-2B	74	305	36	93	22	7	4	41	15	.305
1999 Memphis	P.C.	2B	91	367	69	120	22	4	10	63	20	.327
1999 St. Louis.	N.L.	2B	33	102	12	26	10	1	1	16	0	.255
2000 Anaheim a	A.L.	2B	156	598	82	159	33	11	9	72	22	.266
2001 Rancho Cucamonga....	Calif.	2B	3	8	3	3	2	0	0	1	3	.375
2001 Anaheim b...........	A.L.	2B	137	478	48	129	25	3	6	40	12	.270
2002 Anaheim.............	A.L.	2B-OF	144	474	65	148	32	6	7	52	17	.312
2003 Rancho Cucamonga....	Calif.	2B	3	11	3	3	1	0	1	1	0	.273
2003 Anaheim c...........	A.L.	2B	143	449	71	121	17	1	13	49	22	.269
2004 Anaheim.............	A.L.	2B	144	468	70	130	20	5	10	48	15	.278
2005 Rancho Cucamonga....	Calif.	2B	2	5	1	2	0	0	0	1	1	.400
2005 Salt Lake	P.C.	2B	4	17	4	7	1	0	0	4	2	.412
2005 Los Angeles d	A.L.	2B	129	416	49	125	23	0	0	37	19	.300
2006 Los Angeles e........	A.L.	2B	139	451	50	123	26	6	4	55	16	.273
2007 St. Louis f	N.L.	2B-SS-OF	87	279	27	61	9	1	3	18	6	.219
2008 St. Louis.	N.L.	2B-OF-1B	115	339	42	95	17	4	2	36	7	.280
Major League Totals	10 Yrs.		1227	4054	516	1117	212	38	57	423	136	.276
Division Series												
2002 Anaheim.............	A.L.	2B	4	8	4	4	1	0	1	3	1	.500
2005 Los Angeles	A.L.	2B	5	17	0	4	0	1	0	2	0	.235
Division Series Totals			9	25	4	8	1	1	1	5	1	.320
Championship Series												
2002 Anaheim.............	A.L.	2B	4	14	5	5	0	0	3	5	0	.357
2005 Los Angeles	A.L.	2B	5	14	3	4	0	0	0	1	0	.286
Championship Series Totals			9	28	8	9	0	0	3	6	0	.321
World Series Record												
2002 Anaheim.............	A.L.	2B	7	25	1	7	2	0	0	2	0	.280

a Traded to Anaheim Angels with pitcher Kent Bottenfield for outfielder Jim Edmonds, March 23, 2000.
b On disabled list from March 23 to April 13, 2001.
c On disabled list from April 7 to April 22, 2003.
d On disabled list from March 25 to May 2, 2005.
e Filed for free agency, October 29, 2006. Signed with St. Louis Cardinals, November 28, 2006.
f On disabled list from August 12 to November 2, 2007.

KENT, JEFFREY FRANKLIN (JEFF)

Born, Bellflower, California, March 7, 1968.
Bats Right. Throws Right. Height, 6 feet, 1 inch. Weight, 210 pounds.

Year Club	Lea	Pos	G	AB	R	H	2B	3B	HR	RBI	SB	Avg
1989 St. Catharines....	N.Y.-Penn.	3B-SS	73	268	34	60	14	1	*13	37	5	.224
1990 Dunedin...........	Fla. St.	2B	132	447	72	124	32	2	16	60	17	.277
1991 Knoxville	Southern	2B	139	445	68	114	34	1	12	61	25	.256
1992 Toronto a...........	A.L.	3B-2B-1B	65	192	36	46	13	1	12	35	2	.240
1992 New York........	N.L.	2B-3B-SS	37	113	16	27	8	1	3	15	0	.239
1993 New York........	N.L.	2B-3B-SS	140	496	65	134	24	0	21	80	4	.270
1994 New York........	N.L.	2B	107	415	53	121	24	5	14	68	1	.292
1995 New York b........	N.L.	2B	125	472	65	131	22	3	20	65	3	.278
1996 New York c........	N.L.	3B	89	335	45	97	20	1	9	39	4	.278
1996 Cleveland d	A.L.	1B-2B-3B	39	102	16	27	7	0	3	16	2	.265
1997 San Francisco	N.L.	2B-1B	155	580	90	145	38	2	29	121	11	.250
1998 San Francisco e.....	N.L.	2B-1B	137	526	94	156	37	3	31	128	9	.297
1999 San Francisco f	N.L.	2B-1B	138	511	86	148	40	2	23	101	13	.290
2000 San Francisco g.....	N.L.	2B-1B	159	587	114	196	41	7	33	125	12	.334
2001 San Francisco	N.L.	2B-1B	159	607	84	181	49	6	22	106	7	.298
2002 San Francisco h-i.....	N.L.	2B-1B	152	623	102	195	42	2	37	108	5	.313
2003 Round Rock j........	Texas	2B	3	10	1	3	0	0	1	6	0	.300
2003 Houston j...........	N.L.	2B	130	505	77	150	39	1	22	93	6	.297
2004 Houston k...........	N.L.	2B	145	540	96	156	34	8	27	107	7	.289
2005 Los Angeles	N.L.	2B-1B	149	553	100	160	36	0	29	105	6	.289
2006 Los Angeles l.........	N.L.	2B-1B	115	407	61	119	27	1	14	68	1	.292
2007 Los Angeles	N.L.	2B	136	494	78	149	36	3	20	79	1	.302
2008 Los Angeles m-n......	N.L.	2B-1B	121	440	42	123	23	1	12	59	0	.280
Major League Totals	17 Yrs.		2298	8498	1320	2461	560	47	377	1518	94	.290

Year	Club	Lea	Pos	G	AB	R	H	2B	3B	HR	RBI	SB	Avg
Division Series													
1996 Cleveland	A.L.	2B-1B-3B	4	8	2	1	1	0	0	0	0	.125
1997 San Francisco	N.L.	2B-1B	3	10	2	3	0	0	2	2	0	.300
2000 San Francisco	N.L.	2B-1B	4	16	3	6	1	0	0	1	1	.375
2002 San Francisco	N.L.	2B	5	19	1	5	2	0	0	1	0	.263
2004 Houston	N.L.	2B	5	22	3	5	3	0	0	3	0	.227
2006 Los Angeles	N.L.	2B-1B	3	13	2	8	1	0	1	2	0	.615
2008 Los Angeles	N.L.	PH	1	1	0	0	0	0	0	0	0	.000
Division Series Totals			25	89	13	28	8	0	3	9	1	.315
Championship Series													
2002 San Francisco	N.L.	2B	5	19	3	5	0	0	0	0	0	.263
2004 Houston.............	N.L.	2B	7	25	3	6	2	0	3	7	0	.240
2008 Los Angeles	N.L.	2B	5	8	0	0	0	0	0	0	0	.000
Championship Series Totals			17	52	6	11	2	0	3	7	0	.212
World Series Record													
2002 San Francisco	N.L.	2B	7	29	6	8	1	0	3	7	0	.276

a Traded to New York Mets with player to be named for pitcher David Cone, August 27, 1992. New York acquired outfielder Ryan Thompson to complete trade, September 1, 1992.

b On disabled list from July 6 to July 21, 1995.

c Traded to Cleveland Indians with infielder Jose Vizcaino for infielder Carlos Baerga and infielder Alvaro Espinoza, July 29, 1996.

d Traded to San Francisco Giants with pitcher Julian Taverez, infielder Jose Vizcaino and player to be named later for infielder Matt Williams and player to be named later, November 13, 1996. San Francisco Giants received pitcher Joe Roa and Cleveland Indians received outfielder Trenidad Hubbard to complete trade, December 16, 1996.

e On disabled list from June 10 to July 10, 1998.

f On disabled list from August 3 to August 21, 1999.

g Selected Most Valuable Player in National League for 2000.

h On disabled list from March 21 to April 6, 2002.

i Filed for free agency, October 29, 2002. Signed with Houston Astros, December 18, 2002.

j On disabled list from June 25 to July 16, 2003.

k Filed for free agency, November 1, 2004. Signed with Los Angeles Dodgers, December 9, 2004.

l On disabled list from May 28 to June 13 and July 18 to August 7, 2006.

m On disabled list from August 30 to September 20, 2008.

n Filed for free agency, November 5, 2008.

KEPPINGER, JEFFREY SCOTT (JEFF)

Born, Miami, Florida, April 21, 1980.
Bats Right. Throws Right. Height, 6 feet. Weight, 180 pounds.

Year	Club	Lea	Pos	G	AB	R	H	2B	3B	HR	RBI	SB	Avg
2002 Hickory.........	So.Atl.	2B	126	478	75	132	23	4	10	73	6	.276
2003 Lynchburg	Carolina	2B-3B-1B	92	342	55	111	21	2	3	51	3	.325
2004 Altoona.......	Eastern	2B	82	323	45	108	17	2	1	33	10	.334
2004 Binghamton ..	Eastern	2B-3B	14	47	14	17	3	1	0	5	2	.362
2004 Norfolk.........	Int.	2B	6	19	1	6	1	0	0	2	0	.316
2004 New York a.......	N.L.	2B	33	116	9	33	2	0	3	9	2	.284
2005 Norfolk b	Int.	2B-3B-SS	64	255	40	86	15	3	3	29	5	.337
2006 Norfolk.........	Int.	2B-OF-3B	87	323	36	97	13	0	2	26	0	.300
2006 Omaha..........	P.C.	2B-3B-1B-SS	32	127	21	45	6	1	2	17	0	.354
2006 Kansas City c......	A.L.	3B-1B-2B-OF	22	60	11	16	2	0	0	8	0	.267
2007 Sarasota........	Fla.St.	3B-2B	3	12	1	4	2	0	1	0	1	.333
2007 Louisville	Int.	3B-2B-OF-1B	57	228	31	84	15	1	2	18	1	.368
2007 Cincinnati d-e.......	N.L.	SS-3B-2B-OF	67	241	39	80	16	2	5	32	2	.332
2008 Sarasota........	Fla.St.	3B	2	7	1	2	0	0	0	1	0	.286
2008 Louisville :........	Int.	3B-SS	6	22	3	11	2	0	1	2	0	.500
2008 Cincinnati f.........	N.L.	SS-3B-1B-2B	121	459	45	122	24	2	3	43	3	.266
Major League Totals		4 Yrs.	243	876	104	251	44	4	13	92	7	.287

a Traded to New York Mets with pitcher Kris Benson for infielder Ty Wigginton, pitcher Matt Peterson and infielder Jose Bautista, July 30, 2004.

b On disabled list from September 9 to October 31, 2005.

c Traded to Kansas City Royals for infielder Ruben Gotay, July 19, 2006.

d Traded to Cincinnati Reds for pitcher Russ Haltiwanger, January 11, 2007.

e On disabled list from March 23 to April 22, 2007.

f On disabled list from May 14 to June 22, 2008.

KINSLER, IAN MICHAEL

Born, Tucson, Arizona, June 22, 1982.
Bats Right. Throws Right. Height, 6 feet. Weight, 200 pounds.

Year	Club	Lea	Pos	G	AB	R	H	2B	3B	HR	RBI	SB	Avg
2003 Spokane	Northwest		SS	51	188	32	52	10	6	1	15	11	.277
2004 Clinton	Midwest		SS	60	227	52	91	30	1	11	53	16	.401
2004 Frisco	Texas		SS	71	277	51	83	21	1	9	46	7	.300
2005 Oklahoma	P.C.		2B-SS-3B	131	530	102	145	28	2	23	94	19	.274
2006 Oklahoma	P.C.		2B	10	39	7	10	3	0	2	6	1	.256
2006 Texas a	A.L.		2B	120	423	65	121	27	1	14	55	11	.286
2007 Oklahoma	P.C.		2B	3	13	1	5	0	0	0	3	2	.385
2007 Texas b	A.L.		2B	130	483	96	127	22	2	20	61	23	.263
2008 Texas c	A.L.		2B	121	518	102	165	41	4	18	71	26	.319
Major League Totals		3 Yrs.		371	1424	263	413	90	7	52	187	60	.290

a On disabled list from April 12 to May 25, 2006.
b On disabled list from July 2 to July 31, 2007.
c On disabled list from August 18 to November 14, 2008.

KONERKO, PAUL HENRY

Born, Providence, Rhode Island, March 5, 1976.
Bats Right. Throws Right. Height, 6 feet, 2 inches. Weight, 220 pounds.

Year	Club	Lea	Pos	G	AB	R	H	2B	3B	HR	RBI	SB	Avg
1994 Yakima	Northwest		C	67	257	25	74	15	2	6	58	1	.288
1995 San Berndno	California		C	118	448	77	124	21	1	19	77	3	.277
1996 San Antonio	Texas		1B	133	470	78	141	23	2	29	86	1	.300
1996 Albuquerque	P.C.		1B	4	14	2	6	0	0	1	2	0	.429
1997 Albuquerque	P.C.		3B-1B-2B	130	483	97	156	31	1	37	127	2	.323
1997 Los Angeles	N.L.		1B-3B	6	7	0	1	0	0	0	0	0	.143
1998 Albuquerque	P.C.		OF-1B-3B	24	87	16	33	10	0	6	26	0	.379
1998 Indianapolis	Int.		3B	39	150	25	49	8	0	8	39	1	.327
1998 Los Angeles-Cinc. a-b	N.L.		1B-3B-OF	75	217	21	47	4	0	7	29	0	.217
1999 Chicago	A.L.		1B-3B	142	513	71	151	31	4	24	81	1	.294
2000 Chicago	A.L.		1B-3B	143	524	84	156	31	1	21	97	1	.298
2001 Chicago	A.L.		1B	156	582	92	164	35	0	32	99	1	.282
2002 Chicago	A.L.		1B	151	570	81	173	30	0	27	104	0	.304
2003 Chicago	A.L.		1B	137	444	49	104	19	0	18	65	0	.234
2004 Chicago c	A.L.		1B	155	563	84	156	22	0	41	117	1	.277
2005 Chicago	A.L.		1B	158	575	98	163	24	0	40	100	0	.283
2006 Chicago	A.L.		1B	152	566	97	177	30	0	35	113	1	.313
2007 Chicago	A.L.		1B	151	549	71	142	34	0	31	90	0	.259
2008 Charlotte	Int.		1B	4	11	3	5	2	0	0	3	0	.455
2008 Chicago d	A.L.		1B	122	438	59	105	19	1	22	62	2	.240
Major League Totals		12 Yrs.		1548	5548	807	1539	279	6	298	957	7	.277
Division Series													
2000 Chicago	A.L.		1B	3	9	1	0	0	0	0	0	0	.000
2005 Chicago	A.L.		1B	3	12	3	3	0	0	2	4	0	.250
2008 Chicago	A.L.		1B	4	16	3	5	0	0	2	2	0	.313
Division Series Totals				10	37	7	8	0	0	4	6	0	.216
Championship Series													
2005 Chicago	A.L.		1B	5	21	2	6	1	0	2	7	0	.286
World Series Record													
2005 Chicago	A.L.		1B	4	16	1	4	1	0	1	4	0	.250

a Traded to Cincinnati Reds with pitcher Dennis Reyes for pitcher Jeff Shaw, July 4, 1998.
b Traded to Chicago White Sox for outfielder Mike Cameron, November 11, 1998.
c Filed for free agency, October 27, 2005, re-signed with Chicago White Sox, November 30, 2005.
d On disabled list from June 15 to July 8, 2008.

KOTCHMAN, CASEY JOHN

Born, St. Petersburg, Florida, February 22, 1983.
Bats Left. Throws Left. Height, 6 feet, 3 inches. Weight, 215 pounds.

Year	Club	Lea	Pos	G	AB	R	H	2B	3B	HR	RBI	SB	Avg
2001 Angels	Arizona		1B	4	15	5	9	1	0	1	5	0	.600
2001 Provo	Pioneer		1B	7	22	6	11	3	0	0	7	0	.500
2002 Cedar Rapids	Midwest		1B	81	288	42	81	30	1	5	50	2	.281
2003 Angels	Arizona		1B	7	27	5	9	1	0	2	6	0	.333
2003 Rancho Cucamonga	Calif.		1B	57	206	42	72	12	0	8	28	2	.350
2004 Arkansas	Texas		1B	28	114	19	42	11	0	3	18	0	.368
2004 Anaheim	A.L.		1B	38	116	7	26	6	0	0	15	3	.224

103

Year	Club	Lea	Pos	G	AB	R	H	2B	3B	HR	RBI	SB	Avg
2004 Salt Lake	P.C.	1B	49	199	32	74	22	0	5	38	0	.372
2005 Salt Lake	P.C.	1B	94	363	62	105	23	1	10	58	0	.289
2005 Los Angeles	A.L.	1B	47	126	16	35	5	0	7	22	1	.278
2006 Salt Lake	P.C.	1B	3	7	0	0	0	0	0	1	0	.000
2006 Los Angeles a	A.L.	1B	29	79	6	12	2	0	1	6	0	.152
2007 Los Angeles	A.L.	1B	137	443	64	131	37	3	11	68	2	.296
2008 Los Angeles	A.L.	1B	100	373	47	107	24	0	12	54	2	.287
2008 Atlanta b	N.L.	1B	43	152	18	36	4	1	2	20	0	.237
Major League Totals		5 Yrs.	394	1289	158	347	78	4	33	185	8	.269
Division Series												
2004 Anaheim	A.L.	PH	2	1	0	0	0	0	0	0	0	.000
2005 Los Angeles	A.L.	PH	2	2	0	0	0	0	0	0	0	.000
2007 Los Angeles	A.L.	1B	2	5	1	0	0	0	0	0	0	.000
Division Series Totals			6	8	1	0	0	0	0	0	0	.000
Championship Series												
2005 Los Angeles	A.L.	DH	2	7	0	2	1	0	0	1	0	.286

a On disabled list from May 9 to October 2, 2006.
b Traded to Atlanta Braves with pitcher Steve Marek for infielder Mark Teixeira, July 29, 2008.

KOTSAY, MARK STEVEN
Born, Whittier, California, December 2, 1975.
Bats Left. Throws Left. Height, 6 feet. Weight, 205 pounds.

Year	Club	Lea	Pos	G	AB	R	H	2B	3B	HR	RBI	SB	Avg
1996 Kane County	Midwest	OF	17	60	16	17	5	0	2	8	3	.283
1997 Florida	N.L.	OF	14	52	5	10	1	1	0	4	3	.192
1997 Portland	Eastern	OF	114	438	103	134	27	2	20	77	17	.306
1998 Florida	N.L.	OF-1B	154	578	72	161	25	7	11	68	10	.279
1999 Florida	N.L.	OF-1B	148	495	57	134	23	9	8	50	7	.271
2000 Florida	N.L.	OF-1B	152	530	87	158	31	5	12	57	19	.298
2001 San Diego a-b	N.L.	OF	119	406	67	118	29	1	10	58	13	.291
2002 San Diego	N.L.	OF	153	578	82	169	27	7	17	61	11	.292
2003 San Diego c-d	N.L.	OF	128	482	64	128	28	4	7	38	6	.266
2004 Oakland	A.L.	OF	148	606	78	190	37	3	15	63	8	.314
2005 Oakland	A.L.	OF	139	582	75	163	35	1	15	82	5	.280
2006 Oakland	A.L.	OF-1B	129	502	57	138	29	3	7	59	6	.275
2007 Sacramento	P.C.	OF	10	37	2	10	1	0	0	2	2	.270
2007 Oakland e-f	A.L.	OF	56	206	20	44	14	0	1	20	1	.214
2008 Mississippi	Southern	OF	5	18	4	6	1	0	0	1	0	.333
2008 Atlanta	N.L.	OF	88	318	39	92	17	3	6	37	2	.289
2008 Boston g-h-i	A.L.	OF-1B	22	84	6	19	8	1	0	12	0	.226
Major League Totals		12 Yrs.	1450	5419	709	1524	304	45	109	609	91	.281
Division Series												
2006 Oakland	A.L.	OF	3	14	2	2	0	0	1	2	0	.143
2008 Boston	A.L.	1B	3	10	1	3	0	0	0	0	0	.300
Division Series Totals			6	24	3	5	0	0	1	2	0	.208
Championship Series												
2006 Oakland	A.L.	OF	4	16	3	4	2	0	0	0	0	.250
2008 Boston	A.L.	1B	7	30	1	7	3	0	0	0	0	.233
Championship Series Totals			11	46	4	11	5	0	0	0	0	.239

a Traded to San Diego Padres with outfielder Cesar Crespo for pitcher Matt Clement, pitcher Omar Ortiz and outfielder Eric Owens, March 28, 2001.
b On disabled list from April 16 to May 1, 2001.
c On disabled list from May 19 to June 5, 2003.
d Traded to Oakland Athletics for catcher Ramon Hernandez and outfielder Terrence Long, November 26, 2003.
e On disabled list from March 23 to June 1 and August 15 to October 8, 2007.
f Traded to Atlanta Braves for pitcher Joey Devine, pitcher Jamie Richmond and cash, January 14, 2008.
g On disabled list from May 26 to July 1, 2008.
h Traded to Boston Red Sox for outfielder Luis Sumoza, August 29, 2008.
i Filed for free agency, November 1, 2008, re-signed with Boston Red Sox, January 15, 2009.

KOUZMANOFF, KEVIN
Born, Newport Beach, California, July 25, 1981.
Bats Right. Throws Right. Height, 6 feet, 1 inch. Weight, 210 pounds.

Year	Club	Lea	Pos	G	AB	R	H	2B	3B	HR	RBI	SB	Avg
2003 Mahoning Valley	N.Y.-Penn.	3B	54	206	31	56	8	1	8	33	2	.272
2004 Akron	Eastern	3B	7	24	3	5	1	1	1	6	0	.208

Year	Club		Lea	Pos	G	AB	R	H	2B	3B	HR	RBI	SB	Avg
2004 Lake County		So.Atl.	3B	123	473	74	156	35	5	16	87	5	.330
2005 Kinston		Carolina	3B	68	254	47	86	20	4	12	58	3	.339
2005 Mahoning Valley		N.Y.-Penn.	3B	3	7	0	1	0	0	0	0	0	.143
2006 Akron		Eastern	3B	67	244	46	95	19	1	15	55	2	.389
2006 Buffalo		Int.	3B-1B	27	102	22	36	9	0	7	20	2	.353
2006 Cleveland a		A.L.	DH-3B	16	56	4	12	2	0	3	11	0	.214
2007 San Diego		N.L.	3B	145	484	57	133	30	2	18	74	1	.275
2008 San Diego		N.L.	3B	154	624	71	162	31	4	23	84	0	.260
Major League Totals				3 Yrs.	315	1164	132	307	63	6	44	169	1	.264

a Traded to San Diego Padres with pitcher Andrew Brown for infielder Josh Barfield, November 8, 2006.

KUBEL, JASON JAMES
Born, Belle Fourche, South Dakota, May 25, 1982.
Bats Left. Throws Right. Height, 5 feet, 11 inches. Weight, 200 pounds.

Year	Club		Lea	Pos	G	AB	R	H	2B	3B	HR	RBI	SB	Avg
2000 Twins		Gulf Coast	OF	23	78	17	22	3	2	0	13	0	.282
2001 Twins		Gulf Coast	OF	37	124	14	41	10	4	1	30	3	.331
2002 Quad Cities		Midwest	OF	115	424	60	136	26	4	17	69	3	.321
2003 Fort Myers		Fla.St.	OF	116	420	56	125	20	4	5	82	4	.298
2004 New Britain		Eastern	OF	37	138	25	52	14	4	6	29	0	.377
2004 Rochester		Int.	OF	90	350	71	120	28	5	16	71	16	.343
2004 Minnesota a		A.L.	OF	23	60	10	18	2	0	2	7	1	.300
2005 Minnesota		A.L.	INJURED—Did Not Play										
2006 Rochester		Int.	OF	30	120	18	34	7	2	4	22	2	.283
2006 Minnesota		A.L.	OF	73	220	23	53	8	0	8	26	2	.241
2007 Minnesota		A.L.	OF	128	418	49	114	31	2	13	65	5	.273
2008 Minnesota		A.L.	DH-OF	141	463	74	126	22	5	20	78	0	.272
Major League Totals				4 Yrs.	365	1161	156	311	63	7	43	176	8	.268
Division Series														
2004 Minnesota		A.L.	DH	2	7	0	1	1	0	0	0	0	.143

a On disabled list from March 15 to October 14, 2005.

LAIRD, GERALD LEE
Born, Westminster, California, November 13, 1979.
Bats Right. Throws Right. Height, 6 feet, 1 inch. Weight, 225 pounds.

Year	Club		Lea	Pos	G	AB	R	H	2B	3B	HR	RBI	SB	Avg
1999 Southern Oregon		Northwest	C	60	228	45	65	7	2	2	39	10	.285
2000 Athletics		Arizona	C	14	50	10	15	2	1	0	9	2	.300
2000 Visalia		Calif.	C	33	103	14	25	3	0	0	13	7	.243
2001 Modesto		Calif.	C-OF-1B-2B	119	443	71	113	13	5	5	46	10	.255
2002 Tulsa a		Texas	C-OF	123	442	70	122	21	4	11	67	8	.276
2003 Oklahoma		P.C.	C	99	338	50	88	20	5	9	42	9	.260
2003 Texas		A.L.	C	19	44	9	12	2	1	1	4	0	.273
2004 Texas		A.L.	C	49	147	20	33	6	0	1	16	0	.224
2004 Oklahoma b		P.C.	C	6	22	2	4	2	0	0	2	1	.182
2005 Rangers		Arizona	C	8	26	4	5	2	2	0	3	1	.192
2005 Oklahoma		P.C.	C	75	281	51	87	12	4	17	55	12	.310
2005 Texas		A.L.	C-OF	13	40	7	9	2	0	1	4	0	.225
2006 Texas		A.L.	C-OF	78	243	46	72	20	1	7	22	3	.296
2007 Texas		A.L.	C-OF	120	407	48	91	18	3	9	47	6	.224
2008 Oklahoma		P.C.	C	4	12	1	0	0	0	0	2	0	.000
2008 Texas c-d		A.L.	C-3B	95	344	54	95	24	0	6	41	2	.276
Major League Totals				6 Yrs.	374	1225	184	312	72	5	25	134	11	.255

a Traded to Texas Rangers with pitcher Mario Ramos, outfielder Ryan Ludwick and infielder Jason Hart for pitcher Mike Venafro and outfielder Carlos Pena, January 14, 2002.
b On disabled list from May 21 to July 23, 2004.
c On disabled list from June 21 to July 26, 2008.
d Traded to Detroit Tigers for pitcher Guillermo Moscoso and pitcher Carlos Melo, December 9, 2008.

LAMB, MICHAEL ROBERT (MIKE)
Born, West Covina, California, August 9, 1975.
Bats Left. Throws Right. Height, 6 feet, 1 inch. Weight, 190 pounds.

Year	Club		Lea	Pos	G	AB	R	H	2B	3B	HR	RBI	SB	Avg
1997 Pulaski		Appal.	3B	60	233	59	78	19	3	9	47	7	.335
1998 Charlotte		Fla.St.	3B-1B	135	536	83	162	35	3	9	93	18	.302

Year Club	Lea	Pos	G	AB	R	H	2B	3B	HR	RBI	SB	Avg
1999 Tulsa	Texas	3B-C	137	544	98	176	51	5	21	100	4	.324
1999 Oklahoma........	P.C.	3B	2	2	0	1	0	0	0	0	0	.500
2000 Oklahoma........	P.C.	3B	14	55	8	14	5	1	2	5	2	.255
2000 Texas	A.L.	3B	138	493	65	137	25	2	6	47	0	.278
2001 Oklahoma........	P.C.	3B	69	273	35	81	19	3	8	40	0	.297
2001 Texas	A.L.	3B	76	284	42	87	18	0	4	35	2	.306
2002 Oklahoma........	P.C.	C-3B	6	28	3	11	1	0	0	4	0	.393
2002 Texas	A.L.	1B-OF-3B	115	314	54	89	13	0	9	33	0	.283
2003 Texas	A.L.	1B-OF-3B	28	38	3	5	0	0	0	2	1	.132
2003 Oklahoma........	P.C.	3B-1B	73	274	45	79	19	4	9	46	1	.288
2004 Houston a	N.L.	3B-1B-2B	112	278	38	80	14	3	14	58	1	.288
2005 Houston	N.L.	1B-3B-OF	125	322	41	76	13	5	12	53	1	.236
2006 Houston	N.L.	1B-3B-2B	126	381	70	117	22	3	12	45	2	.307
2007 Houston b	N.L.	3B-1B-OF	124	311	45	90	14	2	11	40	0	.289
2008 Minnesota	A.L.	3B-1B	81	236	20	55	12	3	1	32	0	.233
2008 Milwaukee c-d	N.L.	3B	11	11	2	3	0	0	0	0	0	.273
Major League Totals		9 Yrs.	936	2668	380	739	131	18	69	345	7	.277
Division Series												
2004 Houston..........	N.L.	PH	4	3	0	0	0	0	0	1	0	.000
2005 Houston..........	N.L.	1B	2	6	1	3	0	0	1	1	0	.500
Division Series Totals			6	9	1	3	0	0	1	2	0	.333
Championship Series												
2004 Houston..........	N.L.	3B	2	5	2	2	0	0	2	2	0	.400
2005 Houston..........	N.L.	1B	4	16	3	3	1	0	1	2	0	.188
Championship Series Totals ..			6	21	5	5	1	0	3	4	0	.238
World Series Record												
2005 Houston..........	N.L.	1B	4	10	1	2	1	0	1	1	0	.200

a Traded to Houston Astros for pitcher Juan DeLeon, March 25, 2004.
b Filed for free agency, October 29, 2007. Signed with Minnesota Twins, December 14, 2007.
c Released by Minnesota Twins, September 3, 2008. Signed with Milwaukee Brewers, September 5, 2008.
d Filed for free agency, October 30, 2008, re-signed with Milwaukee Brewers, December 9, 2008.

LANGERHANS, RYAN DAVID

Born, San Antonio, Texas, February 20, 1980.
Bats Left. Throws Left. Height, 6 feet, 3 inches. Weight, 230 pounds.

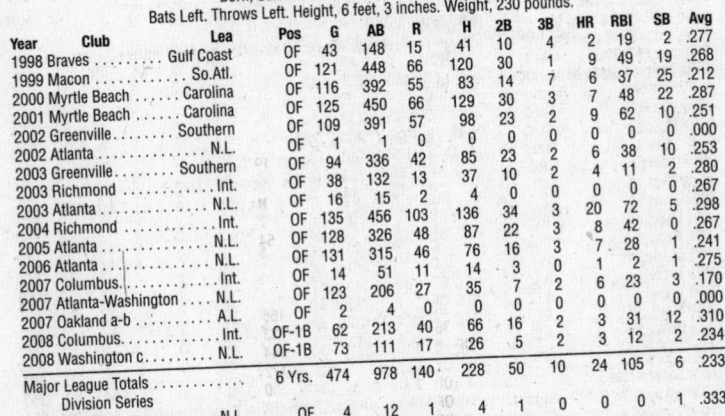

Year Club	Lea	Pos	G	AB	R	H	2B	3B	HR	RBI	SB	Avg
1998 Braves	Gulf Coast	OF	43	148	15	41	10	4	2	19	2	.277
1999 Macon	So.Atl.	OF	121	448	66	120	30	1	9	49	19	.268
2000 Myrtle Beach	Carolina	OF	116	392	55	83	14	7	6	37	25	.212
2001 Myrtle Beach	Carolina	OF	125	450	66	129	30	3	7	48	22	.287
2002 Greenville.......	Southern	OF	109	391	57	98	23	2	9	62	10	.251
2002 Atlanta............	N.L.	OF	1	1	0	0	0	0	0	0	0	.000
2003 Greenville........	Southern	OF	94	336	42	85	23	2	6	38	10	.253
2003 Richmond	Int.	OF	38	132	13	37	10	2	4	11	2	.280
2003 Atlanta............	N.L.	OF	16	15	2	4	0	0	0	0	0	.267
2004 Richmond	Int.	OF	135	456	103	136	34	3	20	72	5	.298
2005 Atlanta............	N.L.	OF	128	326	48	87	22	3	8	42	0	.267
2006 Atlanta ...	N.L.	OF	131	315	46	76	16	3	7	28	1	.241
2007 Columbus.	Int.	OF	14	51	11	14	3	0	1	2	1	.275
2007 Atlanta-Washington ...	N.L.	OF	123	206	27	35	7	2	6	23	3	.170
2007 Oakland a-b	A.L.	OF	2	4	0	0	0	0	0	0	0	.000
2008 Columbus	Int.	OF-1B	62	213	40	66	16	2	3	31	12	.310
2008 Washington c	N.L.	OF-1B	73	111	17	26	5	2	3	12	2	.234
Major League Totals		6 Yrs.	474	978	140	228	50	10	24	105	6	.233
Division Series												
2005 Atlanta	N.L.	OF	4	12	1	4	1	0	0	0	1	.333

a Traded to Oakland Athletics for player to be named later, April 29, 2007.
b Traded to Washington Nationals for outfielder Chis Snelling, May 2, 2007.
c Filed for free agency, October 23, 2008, re-signed with Washington Nationals organization, December 13, 2008.

LA ROCHE, ANDREW CHRISTIAN (ANDY)

Born, Fort Scott, Kansas, September 13, 1983.
Bats Right. Throws Right. Height, 6 feet, 1 inch. Weight, 215 pounds.

Year Club	Lea	Pos	G	AB	R	H	2B	3B	HR	RBI	SB	Avg
2003 Ogden	Pioneer	DH	6	19	1	4	1	0	0	5	0	.211
2004 Vero Beach........	Fla.St.	3B	62	219	26	52	13	0	10	34	2	.237
2004 Columbus..........	So.Atl.	3B	65	244	52	69	20	0	13	42	12	.283

Year	Club	Lea	Pos	G	AB	R	H	2B	3B	HR	RBI	SB	Avg
2005 Vero Beach	Fla.St.		3B	63	249	54	83	14	1	21	51	6	.333
2005 Jacksonville	Southern		3B-1B	64	227	41	62	12	0	9	43	2	.273
2006 Las Vegas	P.C.		3B	55	202	35	65	14	1	10	35	4	.322
2006 Jacksonville	Southern		3B	62	230	42	71	13	0	9	46	6	.309
2007 Las Vegas	P.C.		3B-OF	73	265	55	82	18	1	18	48	2	.309
2007 Los Angeles	N.L.		3B-OF	35	93	16	21	5	0	1	10	2	.226
2008 Jacksonville	Southern		3B	6	22	5	7	1	0	0	1	1	.318
2008 Las Vegas	P.C.		3B-2B-1B	39	123	35	36	3	0	5	28	2	.293
2008 Los Angeles-Pittsburgh a-b	N.L.		3B-2B-1B	76	223	17	37	5	0	5	18	2	.166
Major League Totals				2 Yrs.	111	316	33	58	10	0	6	28	4	.184

a On disabled list from March 21 to May 3, 2008.
b Traded to Pittsburgh Pirates with pitcher Bryan Morris for outfielder Manny Ramirez, July 31, 2008.

LA ROCHE, DAVID ADAM (ADAM)

Born, Orange Co., California, November 6, 1979.
Bats Left. Throws Left. Height, 6 feet, 3 inches. Weight, 200 pounds.

Year	Club	Lea	Pos	G	AB	R	H	2B	3B	HR	RBI	SB	Avg
2000 Danville	Appal.		1B	56	201	38	62	13	3	7	45	4	.308
2001 Myrtle Beach	Carolina		1B-OF	126	471	49	118	31	0	7	47	10	.251
2002 Myrtle Beach	Carolina		1B	69	250	30	84	17	0	9	53	0	.336
2002 Greenville	Southern		1B	45	173	17	50	9	0	4	19	1	.289
2003 Greenville	Southern		1B	61	219	42	62	12	1	12	37	1	.283
2003 Richmond	Int.		1B	72	264	33	78	21	0	8	35	1	.295
2004 Richmond	Int.		1B	4	11	1	2	0	0	1	2	0	.182
2004 Atlanta a	N.L.		1B	110	324	45	90	27	1	13	45	0	.278
2005 Atlanta	N.L.		1B	141	451	53	117	28	0	20	78	0	.259
2006 Atlanta b	N.L.		1B	149	492	89	140	38	1	32	90	0	.285
2007 Pittsburgh	N.L.		1B	152	563	71	153	42	0	21	88	1	.272
2008 Hickory	So.Atl.		1B	3	10	2	6	1	0	1	4	0	.600
2008 Pittsburgh c	N.L.		1B	136	492	66	133	32	3	25	85	1	.270
Major League Totals				5 Yrs.	688	2322	324	633	167	5	111	386	2	.273
Division Series													
2004 Atlanta	N.L.		1B	5	17	1	4	1	0	1	4	0	.235
2005 Atlanta	N.L.		1B	3	8	2	4	1	0	1	6	0	.500
Division Series Totals					8	25	3	8	2	0	2	10	0	.320

a On disabled list from May 29 to July 2, 2004.
b Traded to Pittsburgh Pirates with outfielder Jamie Romak for pitcher Mike Gonzalez and infielder Brent Lillibridge, January 17, 2007.
c On disabled list from July 28 to August 14, 2008.

LEE, CARLOS

Born, Aguadulce, Panama, June 20, 1976.
Bats Right. Throws Right. Height, 6 feet, 2 inches. Weight, 240 pounds.

Year	Club	Lea	Pos	G	AB	R	H	2B	3B	HR	RBI	SB	Avg
1994 White Sox	Gulf Coast		3B	29	56	6	7	1	0	0	1	0	.125
1995 Hickory	So.Atl.		3B-SS	63	218	18	54	9	1	4	30	1	.248
1995 Bristol	Appal.		3B-1B	67	269	43	93	17	1	7	45	17	.346
1996 Hickory	So.Atl.		3B-1B	119	480	65	150	23	6	8	70	18	.313
1997 Winston-Sal	Carolina		3B	139	546	81	173	50	4	17	84	11	.317
1998 Birmingham	Southern		3B	138	549	77	166	33	2	21	106	11	.302
1999 Charlotte	Int.		3B	25	94	16	33	5	0	4	20	2	.351
1999 Chicago	A.L.		OF-1B	127	492	66	144	32	2	16	84	4	.293
2000 Chicago	A.L.		OF	152	572	107	172	29	2	24	92	13	.301
2001 Chicago	A.L.		OF	150	558	75	150	33	3	24	84	17	.269
2002 Chicago	A.L.		OF	140	492	82	130	26	2	26	80	1	.264
2003 Chicago	A.L.		OF	158	623	100	181	35	1	31	113	18	.291
2004 Chicago a	A.L.		OF	153	591	103	180	37	0	31	99	11	.305
2005 Milwaukee	N.L.		OF	*162	618	85	164	41	0	32	114	13	.265
2006 Milwaukee	N.L.		OF	102	388	60	111	18	0	28	81	12	.286
2006 Texas b-c	A.L.		OF	59	236	42	76	19	1	9	35	7	.322
2007 Houston	N.L.		OF	*162	627	93	190	43	1	32	119	10	.303
2008 Houston d	N.L.		OF	115	436	61	137	27	2	28	100	4	.314
Major League Totals				10 Yrs.	1480	5633	874	1635	340	12	281	1001	110	.290
Division Series													
2000 Chicago	A.L.		OF	3	11	0	1	1	0	0	1	0	.091

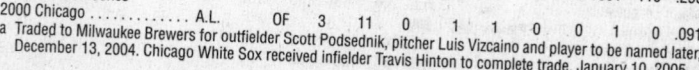

a Traded to Milwaukee Brewers for outfielder Scott Podsednik, pitcher Luis Vizcaino and player to be named later, December 13, 2004. Chicago White Sox received infielder Travis Hinton to complete trade, January 10, 2005.

b Traded to Texas Rangers with outfielder Nelson Cruz for pitcher Francisco Cordero, outfielder Kevin Mench, outfielder Laynce Nix and pitcher Julian Cordero, July 28, 2006.
c Filed for free agency, October 30, 2006. Signed with Houston Astros, November 24, 2006.
d On disabled list from August 10 to September 30, 2008.

LEE, DERREK LEON

Born, Sacramento, California, September 6, 1975.
Bats Right. Throws Right. Height, 6 feet, 5 inches. Weight, 245 pounds.

Year Club	Lea	Pos	G	AB	R	H	2B	3B	HR	RBI	SB	Avg
1993 Padres	Arizona	1B	15	52	11	17	1	1	2	5	4	.327
1993 Rancho Cucamonga	Calif.	1B	20	73	13	20	5	1	1	10	0	.274
1994 Rancho Cucamonga	Calif.	3B-1B	126	442	66	118	19	2	8	53	18	.267
1995 Rancho Cucamonga	Calif.	1B	128	502	82	151	25	2	23	95	14	.301
1995 Memphis	Southern	1B	2	9	0	1	0	0	0	1	0	.111
1996 Memphis	Southern	1B-3B	134	500	98	140	39	2	34	104	13	.280
1997 Las Vegas	P.C.	1B	124	468	85	152	29	2	13	64	17	.325
1997 San Diego a	N.L.	1B	22	54	9	14	3	0	1	4	0	.259
1998 Florida	N.L.	1B	141	454	62	106	29	1	17	74	5	.233
1999 Calgary	P.C.	1B	89	339	60	96	20	1	19	73	3	.283
1999 Florida	N.L.	1B	70	218	21	45	9	1	5	20	2	.206
2000 Florida	N.L.	1B	158	477	70	134	18	3	28	70	0	.281
2001 Florida	N.L.	1B	158	561	83	158	37	4	21	75	4	.282
2002 Florida	N.L.	1B	*162	581	95	157	35	7	27	86	19	.270
2003 Florida b	N.L.	1B	155	539	91	146	31	2	31	92	21	.271
2004 Chicago	N.L.	1B	161	605	90	168	39	1	32	98	12	.278
2005 Chicago	N.L.	1B	158	594	120	*199	*50	3	46	107	15	*.335
2006 Iowa	P.C.	1B	1	4	0	1	0	0	0	0	0	.250
2006 Chicago c	N.L.	1B	50	175	30	50	9	0	8	30	8	.286
2007 Chicago	N.L.	1B	150	567	91	180	43	1	22	82	6	.317
2008 Chicago	N.L.	1B	155	623	93	181	41	3	20	90	8	.291
Major League Totals		12 Yrs.	1540	5448	855	1538	344	26	258	828	100	.282
Division Series												
2003 Florida	N.L.	1B	4	16	2	4	1	0	0	2	1	.250
2007 Chicago	N.L.	1B	3	12	1	4	0	0	0	0	0	.333
2008 Chicago	N.L.	1B	3	11	2	6	3	0	0	1	0	.545
Division Series Totals			10	39	5	14	4	0	0	2	1	.359
Championship Series												
2003 Florida	N.L.	1B	7	32	2	6	2	0	1	4	1	.188
World Series Record												
2003 Florida	N.L.	1B	6	24	2	5	0	0	0	2	0	.208

a Traded to Florida Marlins with pitcher Rafael Medina and pitcher Steve Hoff for pitcher Kevin Brown, December 15, 1997.
b Traded to Chicago Cubs for infielder Hee Seop Choi and player to be named later, November 25, 2003. Florida Marlins received pitcher Mike Nannini to complete trade, December 15, 2003.
c On disabled list from April 20 to June 25 and July 24 to August 28, 2006.

LEWIS, FREDERICK DESHAUN (FRED)

Born, Hattiesburg, Mississippi, December 9, 1980.
Bats Left. Throws Right. Height, 6 feet, 2 inches. Weight, 190 pounds.

Year Club	Lea	Pos	G	AB	R	H	2B	3B	HR	RBI	SB	Avg
2002 Salem-Keizer	Northwest	OF	58	239	43	77	9	3	1	23	9	.322
2003 Hagerstown	So.Atl.	OF	114	420	61	105	17	8	1	27	30	.250
2004 San Jose	Calif.	OF	115	439	88	132	20	11	8	57	33	.301
2004 Fresno	P.C.	OF	6	23	3	7	1	0	1	2	1	.304
2005 Norwich	Eastern	OF	137	512	79	140	28	7	7	47	30	.273
2006 Fresno	P.C.	OF	120	439	85	121	20	11	12	56	18	.276
2006 San Francisco	N.L.	OF	13	11	5	5	1	0	0	2	0	.455
2007 Fresno	P.C.	OF	42	171	31	50	8	6	8	32	9	.292
2007 San Francisco a	N.L.	OF	58	157	34	45	6	2	3	19	5	.287
2008 San Francisco	N.L.	OF	133	468	81	132	25	11	9	40	21	.282
Major League Totals		3 Yrs.	204	636	120	182	32	13	12	61	26	.286

a On disabled list from June 9 to June 30, 2007.

LIND, ADAM ALAN

Born, Anderson, Indiana, July 17, 1983.
Bats Left. Throws Left. Height, 6 feet, 2 inches. Weight, 195 pounds.

Year	Club	Lea	Pos	G	AB	R	H	2B	3B	HR	RBI	SB	Avg
2004 Auburn	N.Y.-Penn.	OF	70	266	43	82	23	0	7	50	1	.308
2005 Dunedin	Fla.St.	OF	126	495	80	155	42	4	12	84	2	.313
2006 New Hampshire	Eastern	OF	91	348	43	108	24	0	19	71	2	.310
2006 Syracuse	Int.	OF	34	109	20	43	7	0	5	18	1	.394
2006 Toronto	A.L.	DH-OF	18	60	8	22	8	0	2	8	0	.367
2007 Syracuse	Int.	OF	46	174	20	52	8	2	6	28	0	.299
2007 Toronto	A.L.	OF	89	290	34	69	14	0	11	46	1	.238
2008 Syracuse	Int.	OF-1B	51	189	24	62	17	2	6	50	1	.328
2008 Toronto	A.L.	OF	88	326	48	92	16	4	9	40	2	.282
Major League Totals		3 Yrs.	195	676	90	183	38	4	22	94	3	.271

LO DUCA, PAUL ANTHONY

Born, Brooklyn, New York, April 12, 1972.
Bats Right. Throws Right. Height, 5 feet, 10 inches. Weight, 193 pounds.

Year	Club	Lea	Pos	G	AB	R	H	2B	3B	HR	RBI	SB	Avg
1993 Vero Beach	Fla.St.	C	39	134	17	42	6	0	0	13	0	.313
1994 Bakersfield	California	1B-C	123	455	65	141	32	1	6	68	16	.310
1995 San Antonio	Texas	C-1B-3B	61	199	27	49	8	0	1	8	5	.246
1996 Vero Beach	Fla.St.	C-1B-3B	124	439	54	134	22	0	3	66	8	.305
1997 San Antonio	Texas	C-1B	105	385	63	126	28	2	7	69	16	.327
1998 Albuquerque	P.C.	C-1B-3B	126	451	69	144	30	3	8	58	19	.319
1998 Los Angeles	N.L.	C	6	14	2	4	1	0	0	1	0	.286
1999 Los Angeles	N.L.	C	36	95	11	22	1	0	3	11	1	.232
1999 Albuquerque a	P.C.	C	26	76	17	28	9	0	1	8	1	.368
2000 Albuquerque	P.C.	C-OF-1B-3B	78	279	47	98	27	3	4	54	8	.351
2000 Los Angeles	N.L.	C-OF-3B	34	65	6	16	2	0	2	8	0	.246
2001 Las Vegas	P.C.	C-1B	3	9	3	3	2	0	0	3	0	.333
2001 Los Angeles b	N.L.	C-1B-OF	125	460	71	147	28	0	25	90	2	.320
2002 Los Angeles	N.L.	C-1B-OF	149	580	74	163	38	1	10	64	3	.281
2003 Los Angeles	N.L.	C-OF-1B	147	568	64	155	34	2	7	52	0	.273
2004 Los Angeles-Florida c	N.L.	C	143	535	68	153	29	2	13	80	4	.286
2005 Florida d-e	N.L.	C	132	445	45	126	23	1	6	57	4	.283
2006 New York	N.L.	C	124	512	80	163	39	1	5	49	3	.318
2007 Brooklyn	N.Y.-Penn.	C	2	5	1	2	0	0	1	2	0	.400
2007 Binghamton	Eastern	C	1	3	0	1	0	0	0	0	0	.333
2007 New York f-g	N.L.	C	119	445	46	121	18	1	9	54	2	.272
2008 Potomac	Carolina	C	5	14	0	2	1	0	0	1	0	.143
2008 Albuquerque	P.C.	C	7	26	5	11	1	0	0	7	0	.423
2008 Columbus	Int.	C-1B	4	13	0	2	0	0	0	2	0	.154
2008 Washington-Florida h-i-j	N.L.	C-1B-OF	67	173	16	42	9	0	0	15	1	.243
Major League Totals		11 Yrs.	1082	3892	483	1112	222	8	80	481	20	.286
Division Series												
2006 New York	N.L.	C	3	11	2	5	1	0	0	3	0	.455
Championship Series												
2006 New York	N.L.	C	7	29	3	6	1	0	0	3	0	.207

a On disabled list from June 4 to July 20, 1999.
b On disabled list from April 29 to May 21, 2001.
c Traded to Florida Marlins with outfielder Juan Encarnacion and pitcher Guillermo Mota for pitcher Brad Penny, pitcher Bill Murphy and infielder Hee Seop Choi, July 30, 2004.
d Traded to New York Mets two players to be named later, December 5, 2005.
e Florida Marlins received pitcher Gaby Hernandez and outfielder Dante Brinkley to complete trade, December 9, 2005.
f On disabled list from August 12 to August 27, 2007.
g Filed for free agency, October 29, 2007. Signed with Washington Nationals, December 11, 2007.
h On disabled list from April 14 to May 2 and May 9 to June 17, 2008.
i Released by Washington Nationals, July 31, 2008. Signed with Florida Marlins organization, August 8, 2008.
j Filed for free agency, October 30, 2008.

LONEY, JAMES ANTHONY

Born, Houston, Texas, May 7, 1984.
Bats Left. Throws Left. Height, 6 feet, 3 inches. Weight, 220 pounds.

Year	Club	Lea	Pos	G	AB	R	H	2B	3B	HR	RBI	SB	Avg
2002 Vero Beach	Fla.St.	1B	17	67	6	20	6	0	0	5	0	.299
2002 Great Falls	Pioneer	1B	47	170	33	63	22	3	5	30	5	.371

Year	Club	Lea	Pos	G	AB	R	H	2B	3B	HR	RBI	SB	Avg
2003 Vero Beach	Fla.St.	1B-OF	125	468	64	129	31	3	7	46	9	.276
2004 Jacksonville	Southern	1B	104	395	39	94	19	2	4	35	6	.238
2005 Jacksonville	Southern	1B-OF	138	504	74	143	31	2	11	65	1	.284
2006 Las Vegas	P.C.	1B-OF	98	366	64	139	33	2	8	67	9	.380
2006 Los Angeles	N.L.	1B-OF	48	102	20	29	6	5	4	18	1	.284
2007 Las Vegas	P.C.	1B-OF	58	233	28	65	19	1	1	32	2	.279
2007 Los Angeles	N.L.	1B-OF	96	344	41	114	18	4	15	67	0	.331
2008 Los Angeles	N.L.	1B	161	595	66	172	35	6	13	90	7	.289
Major League Totals		3 Yrs.	305	1041	127	315	59	15	32	175	8	.303
Division Series													
2006 Los Angeles	N.L.	1B	1	4	0	3	0	0	0	3	0	.750
2008 Los Angeles	N.L.	1B	3	14	2	3	1	0	1	6	0	.214
Division Series Totals			4	18	2	6	1	0	1	9	0	.333
Championship Series													
2008 Los Angeles	N.L.	1B	5	16	0	7	2	0	0	2	0	.438

LONGORIA, EVAN MICHAEL

Born, Downey, California, October 7, 1985.
Bats Right. Throws Right. Height, 6 feet, 2 inches. Weight, 210 pounds.

Year	Club	Lea	Pos	G	AB	R	H	2B	3B	HR	RBI	SB	Avg
2006 Visalia	Calif.	3B	28	110	22	36	8	0	8	28	1	.327
2006 Hudson Valley	N.Y.-Penn.	3B	8	33	5	14	1	1	4	11	1	.424
2006 Montgomery	Southern	3B	26	105	14	28	5	0	6	19	2	.267
2007 Durham	Int.	3B	31	104	19	28	8	0	5	19	0	.269
2007 Montgomery	Southern	3B	105	381	78	117	21	0	21	76	4	.307
2008 Durham	Int.	3B	7	25	2	5	0	0	1	0	0	.200
2008 Tampa Bay a-b	A.L.	3B-SS	122	448	67	122	31	2	27	85	7	.272
Division Series													
2008 Tampa Bay	N.L.	3B	4	15	2	4	0	0	2	3	1	.267
Championship Series													
2008 Tampa Bay	N.L.	3B	7	27	8	7	3	0	4	8	0	.259
World Series Record													
2008 Tampa Bay	N.L.	3B	5	20	0	1	0	0	0	2	0	.050

a On disabled list from August 8 to September 6, 2008.
b Selected Rookie of the Year in American League for 2008.

LOPEZ, FELIPE

Born, Bayamon, Puerto Rico, May 12, 1980.
Bats Both. Throws Right. Height, 6 feet, 1 inch. Weight, 205 pounds.

Year	Club	Lea	Pos	G	AB	R	H	2B	3B	HR	RBI	SB	Avg
1998 St.Cathrnes	N.Y.-Penn.	SS	19	83	14	31	5	2	1	11	4	.373
1998 Dunedin	Fla.St.	SS	4	13	3	5	0	1	1	1	0	.385
1999 Hagerstown	So.Atl.	SS	134	537	87	149	27	4	14	80	21	.277
2000 Tennessee	Southern	SS	127	463	52	119	18	4	9	41	12	.257
2001 Tennessee	Southern	SS-2B	19	72	12	16	2	1	2	4	4	.222
2001 Syracuse	Int.	SS-2B-3B	89	358	65	100	19	7	16	44	13	.279
2001 Toronto	A.L.	3B-SS	49	177	21	46	5	4	5	23	4	.260
2002 Toronto	A.L.	SS-3B	85	282	35	64	15	3	8	34	5	.227
2002 Syracuse a	Int.	SS	43	173	35	55	11	2	3	16	13	.318
2003 Cincinnati	N.L.	SS-3B-2B	59	197	28	42	7	2	2	13	8	.213
2003 Louisville	Int.	SS-2B	35	143	22	40	11	0	2	18	2	.280
2004 Louisville	Int.	SS-2B-3B	75	293	50	80	11	3	9	44	2	.273
2004 Cincinnati	N.L.	SS-3B-2B	79	264	35	64	18	2	7	31	1	.242
2005 Cincinnati	N.L.	SS-2B-3B	148	580	97	169	34	5	23	85	15	.291
2006 Cincinnati-Wash. b	N.L.	SS	156	617	98	169	27	3	11	52	44	.274
2007 Washington	N.L.	SS-2B	154	603	70	148	25	6	9	50	24	.245
2008 Wash.-St. Louis c-d	N.L.	2B-OF-3B-SS	143	481	64	136	28	2	6	46	8	.283
Major League Totals		8 Yrs.	873	3201	448	838	159	27	71	334	109	.262

a Traded by Toronto Blue Jays to Cincinnati Reds in four team deal. Cincinnati sent pitcher Elmer Dessens to Arizona Diamondbacks, who sent infield Eurbiel Durazo to Oakland A's, who sent pitcher Jamie Arnold to Toronto Blue Jays, December 15, 2002.
b Traded to Washington Nationals with outfielder Austin Kearns and pitcher Ryan Wagner for pitcher Gary Majewski, pitcher Bill Bray, infielder Royce Clayton, infielder Brendan Harris and pitcher Daryl Thompson, July 13, 2006.
c Released by Washington Nationals, July 31, 2008. Signed with St. Louis Cardinals, August 5, 2008.
d Filed for free agency, October 30, 2008. Signed with Arizona Diamondbacks, December 12, 2008.

LOPEZ, JOSE CELESTINO

Born, Barcelona, Venezuela, November 24, 1983.
Bats Right. Throws Right. Height, 6 feet. Weight, 200 pounds.

Year Club	Lea	Pos	G	AB	R	H	2B	3B	HR	RBI	SB	Avg
2001 Everett	Northwest	SS-2B	70	289	42	74	15	0	2	20	13	.256
2002 San Bernardino	Calif.	SS-2B	123	522	82	169	39	5	8	60	31	.324
2003 San Antonio	Texas	SS-2B-3B	132	538	82	139	35	2	13	69	18	.258
2004 Tacoma	P.C.	SS-2B-3B	74	275	40	81	19	0	13	39	5	.295
2004 Mariners	Arizona	3B-SS-2B	4	12	3	2	1	0	0	1	1	.167
2004 Seattle	A.L.	SS-3B	57	207	28	48	13	0	5	22	0	.232
2005 Tacoma	P.C.	2B	44	182	29	58	19	0	5	31	2	.319
2005 Seattle	A.L.	2B-3B	54	190	18	47	19	0	2	25	4	.247
2006 Seattle	A.L.	2B	151	603	78	170	28	8	10	79	5	.282
2007 Seattle	A.L.	2B-3B	149	524	58	132	17	2	11	62	2	.252
2008 Seattle	A.L.	2B-1B	159	644	80	191	41	1	17	89	6	.297
Major League Totals		5 Yrs.	570	2168	262	588	118	11	45	277	17	.271

LORETTA, MARK DAVID

Born, Santa Monica, California, August 14, 1971.
Bats Right. Throws Right. Height, 6 feet. Weight, 185 pounds.

Year Club	Lea	Pos	G	AB	R	H	2B	3B	HR	RBI	SB	Avg
1993 Helena	Pioneer	SS	6	28	5	9	1	0	1	8	0	.321
1993 Stockton	California	SS-3B	53	201	36	73	4	1	4	31	8	.363
1994 El Paso	Texas	SS-P	77	302	50	95	13	6	0	38	8	.315
1994 New Orleans	A.A.	SS-2B	43	138	16	29	7	0	1	14	2	.210
1995 New Orleans	A.A.	SS-3B-2B	127	479	48	137	22	5	7	79	8	.286
1995 Milwaukee	A.L.	SS-2B	19	50	13	13	3	0	1	3	1	.260
1996 New Orleans	A.A.	SS	19	71	10	18	5	1	0	11	1	.254
1996 Milwaukee	A.L.	2B-3B-SS	73	154	20	43	3	0	1	13	2	.279
1997 Milwaukee	A.L.	2B-SS-1B-3B	132	418	56	120	17	5	5	47	5	.287
1998 Milwaukee	N.L.	1B-SS-3B-2B	140	434	55	137	29	0	6	54	9	.316
1999 Milwaukee	N.L.	SS-1B-2B-3B	153	587	93	170	34	5	5	67	4	.290
2000 Indianapolis	Int.	SS	10	25	6	6	1	0	0	5	0	.240
2000 Milwaukee a	N.L.	SS-2B	91	352	49	99	21	1	7	40	0	.281
2001 Indianapolis	Int.	2B-3B	8	31	4	3	0	0	0	1	0	.097
2001 Milwaukee b	N.L.	2B-3B-SS-P	102	384	40	111	14	2	2	29	1	.289
2002 Milwaukee-Houston c-d-e	N.L.	3B-SS-2B-1B	107	283	33	86	18	0	4	27	1	.304
2003 San Diego	N.L.	2B-SS	154	589	74	185	28	4	13	72	5	.314
2004 San Diego	N.L.	2B	154	620	108	208	47	2	16	76	5	.335
2005 Portland	P.C.	2B	3	10	0	1	0	0	0	0	0	.100
2005 San Diego f-g	N.L.	2B-3B	105	404	54	113	16	1	3	38	6	.280
2006 Boston h	A.L.	2B-1B	155	635	75	181	33	0	5	59	4	.285
2007 Houston i	N.L.	SS-2B-1B-3B	133	460	52	132	23	2	4	41	1	.287
2008 Houston j	N.L.	2B-3B-SS-1B	101	261	27	73	15	0	4	38	0	.280
Major League Totals		14 Yrs.	1619	5631	749	1671	301	22	76	604	46	.297
Division Series												
2005 San Diego	N.L.	2B	3	15	0	4	0	0	0	2	0	.267

a On disabled list from June 3 to August 17, 2000.
b On disabled list from March 27 to May 19, 2001.
c Traded to Houston Astros with cash for two players to be named later, August 31, 2002.
d Milwaukee Brewers received pitcher Wayne Franklin to complete trade, September 3, 2002.
e Filed for free agency, October 28, 2002. Signed with San Diego Padres, December 16, 2002.
f On disabled list from May 19 to July 18, 2005.
g Traded to Boston Red Sox for catcher Doug Mirabelli, December 7, 2005.
h Filed for free agency, October 30, 2006. Signed with Houston Astros, January 4, 2007.
i Filed for free agency, October 29, 2007. Accepted arbitration to return to Houston, December 7, 2007.
j Filed for free agency, October 30, 2008. Signed with Los Angeles Dodgers, December 10, 2008.

LOWELL, MICHAEL AVERETT (MIKE)

Born, San Juan, Puerto Rico, February 24, 1974.
Bats Right. Throws Right. Height, 6 feet, 3 inches. Weight, 210 pounds.

Year Club	Lea	Pos	G	AB	R	H	2B	3B	HR	RBI	SB	Avg
1995 Oneonta	N.Y.-Penn.	3B	72	281	36	73	18	0	1	27	3	.260
1996 Greensboro	So.Atl.	3B-SS-P	113	433	58	122	33	0	8	64	10	.282
1996 Tampa	Fla.St.	3B	24	78	8	22	5	0	0	11	1	.282
1997 Norwich	Eastern	3B-SS	78	285	60	98	17	0	15	47	2	.344
1997 Columbus	Int.	3B-SS	57	210	36	58	13	1	15	45	2	.276
1998 Columbus	Int.	3B-1B-SS	126	510	79	155	34	3	26	99	4	.304

Year Club	Lea	Pos	G	AB	R	H	2B	3B	HR	RBI	SB	Avg
1998 New York	A.L.	3B	8	15	1	4	0	0	0	0	0	.267
1999 Calgary	P.C.	3B	24	83	11	26	3	0	2	9	0	.313
1999 Florida a-b	N.L.	3B	97	308	32	78	15	0	12	47	0	.253
2000 Florida c	N.L.	3B	140	508	73	137	38	0	22	91	4	.270
2001 Florida	N.L.	3B	146	551	65	156	37	0	18	100	1	.283
2002 Florida	N.L.	3B	160	597	88	165	44	0	24	92	4	.276
2003 Florida d	N.L.	3B	130	492	76	136	27	1	32	105	3	.276
2004 Florida	N.L.	3B	158	598	87	175	44	1	27	85	5	.293
2005 Florida e	N.L.	3B-2B	150	500	56	118	36	1	8	58	4	.236
2006 Boston	A.L.	3B	153	573	79	163	47	1	20	80	2	.284
2007 Boston f	A.L.	3B	154	589	79	191	37	2	21	120	3	.324
2008 Pawtucket	Int.	3B	3	13	0	3	0	0	0	3	0	.231
2008 Boston g	A.L.	3B	113	419	58	115	27	0	17	73	2	.274
Major League Totals	11 Yrs.		1409	5150	694	1438	352	6	201	851	28	.279
Division Series												
2003 Florida	N.L.	3B	2	3	0	0	0	0	0	0	0	.000
2007 Boston	A.L.	3B	3	9	1	3	2	0	0	3	0	.333
2008 Boston	A.L.	3B	2	8	0	0	0	0	0	0	0	.000
Division Series Totals			7	20	1	3	2	0	0	3	0	.150
Championship Series												
2003 Florida	N.L.	3B	7	20	5	4	0	0	2	3	0	.200
2007 Boston	A.L.	3B	7	27	3	9	2	0	1	8	0	.333
Championship Series Totals			14	47	8	13	2	0	3	11	0	.277
World Series Record												
2003 Florida	N.L.	3B	6	23	1	5	1	0	0	2	0	.217
2007 Boston	A.L.	3B	4	15	6	6	3	0	1	4	1	.400
World Series Totals			10	38	7	11	4	0	1	6	1	.289

a Traded to Florida Marlins for pitcher Ed Yarnall, pitcher Mark Johnson and pitcher Todd Noel, February 1, 1999.
b On disabled list from March 26 to May 29, 1999.
c On disabled list from May 13 to May 28, 2000.
d On disabled list from August 31 to September 28, 2003.
e Traded to Boston Red Sox with pitcher Josh Beckett and pitcher Guillermo Mota for infielder Hanley Ramirez, pitcher Anibal Sanchez and pitcher Jesus Delgado, November 24, 2005.
f Filed for free agency, November 6, 2007, re-signed with Boston Red Sox, November 20, 2007.
g On disabled list from April 10 to April 29 and August 13 to September 5, 2008.

LOWRIE, JED CARLSON
Born, Salem, Oregon, April 17, 1984.
Bats Both. Throws Right. Height, 6 feet. Weight, 180 pounds.

Year Club	Lea	Pos	G	AB	R	H	2B	3B	HR	RBI	SB	Avg
2005 Lowell	N.Y.-Penn.	SS-2B	53	201	36	66	12	0	4	32	7	.328
2006 Wilmington	Carolina	SS	97	374	43	98	21	6	3	50	2	.262
2007 Portland	Eastern	SS-2B	93	337	61	100	31	7	8	49	5	.297
2007 Pawtucket	Int.	SS-2B-3B	40	160	21	48	16	1	5	21	0	.300
2008 Pawtucket	Int.	SS-2B-3B	53	198	35	53	14	2	5	32	1	.268
2008 Boston	A.L.	SS-3B-2B	81	260	34	67	25	3	2	46	1	.258
Division Series												
2008 Boston	A.L.	SS-3B	3	11	2	4	0	0	0	1	0	.364
Championship Series												
2008 Boston	A.L.	SS	6	18	2	2	1	0	0	1	0	.111

LUDWICK, RYAN ANDREW
Born, Satellite Beach, Florida, July 13, 1978.
Bats Right. Throws Left. Height, 6 feet, 3 inches. Weight, 220 pounds.

Year Club	Lea	Pos	G	AB	R	H	2B	3B	HR	RBI	SB	Avg
1999 Modesto	Calif.	OF	43	171	28	47	11	3	4	34	2	.275
2000 Modesto	Calif.	OF	129	493	86	130	26	3	29	102	10	.264
2001 Sacramento	P.C.	OF	17	57	10	13	3	0	1	7	2	.228
2001 Midland	Texas	OF	119	443	82	119	23	3	25	96	9	.269
2002 Oklahoma	P.C.	OF	78	305	62	87	27	4	15	52	2	.285
2002 Texas a	A.L.	OF	23	81	10	19	6	0	1	9	2	.235
2003 Oklahoma	P.C.	OF	81	317	51	96	24	3	17	63	1	.303
2003 Texas-Cleveland b-c	A.L.	OF	47	162	17	40	8	1	7	26	2	.247
2004 Akron	Eastern	OF	8	26	4	7	2	0	1	5	0	.269
2004 Buffalo	Int.	OF	44	166	25	45	15	0	8	30	0	.271
2004 Cleveland d	A.L.	OF	15	50	3	11	2	0	2	4	0	.220

Year Club	Lea	Pos	G	AB	R	H	2B	3B	HR	RBI	SB	Avg
2005 Cleveland	A.L.	OF	19	41	8	9	0	0	4	5	0	.220
2005 Buffalo	Int.	OF	54	188	27	36	10	2	4	16	0	.191
2006 Toledo e-f	Int.	OF	134	508	81	135	34	2	28	80	2	.266
2007 Memphis	P.C.	OF	29	106	27	36	8	0	8	36	1	.340
2007 St. Louis	N.L.	OF	120	303	42	81	22	0	14	52	4	.267
2008 St. Louis	N.L.	OF	152	538	104	161	40	3	37	113	4	.299
Major League Totals		6 Yrs.	376	1175	184	321	78	4	65	209	12	.273

a Traded to Texas Rangers by Oakland Athletics with pitcher Mario Ramos, infielder Jason Hart and catcher Gerald Laird for pitcher Mike Venafro and outfielder Carlos Pena, January 14, 2002.
b On disabled list from September 9 to October 28, 2003.
c Traded to Cleveland Indians for outfielder Shane Spencer and pitcher Ricardo Rodriguez, July 18, 2003.
d On disabled list from April 2 to July 5, 2004.
e Filed for free agency, October 28, 2005. Signed with Detroit Tigers organization, January 4, 2006.
f Filed for free agency, October 15, 2006. Signed with St. Louis Cardinals organization, December 1, 2006.

LUGO, JULIO CESAR

Born, Barahona, Dominican Republic, November 16, 1975.
Bats Right. Throws Right. Height, 6 feet, 1 Inch. Weight, 175 pounds.

Year Club	Lea	Pos	G	AB	R	H	2B	3B	HR	RBI	SB	Avg
1995 Auburn	N.Y.-Penn.	2B-SS-OF	59	230	36	67	6	3	1	16	17	.291
1996 Quad City	Midwest	SS-2B-3B	101	393	60	116	18	2	10	50	24	.295
1997 Kissimmee	Fla.St.	SS-2B-3B	125	505	89	135	22	14	7	61	35	.267
1998 Kissimmee	Fla.St.	SS	128	509	81	154	20	14	7	62	51	.303
1999 Jackson a	Texas	SS	116	445	77	142	24	5	10	42	25	.319
2000 New Orleans	P.C.	2B	24	101	22	33	4	1	3	12	12	.327
2000 Houston	N.L.	SS-2B-OF	116	420	78	119	22	5	10	40	22	.283
2001 Houston	N.L.	SS-OF-2B	140	513	93	135	20	3	10	37	12	.263
2002 Houston b	N.L.	SS	88	322	45	84	15	1	8	35	9	.261
2003 Houston	N.L.	SS	22	65	6	16	3	0	0	2	2	.246
2003 Tampa Bay c	A.L.	SS	117	433	58	119	13	4	15	53	10	.275
2004 Tampa Bay	A.L.	SS-2B	157	581	83	160	41	4	7	75	21	.275
2005 Tampa Bay	A.L.	SS	158	616	89	182	36	6	6	57	39	.295
2006 Tampa Bay d	A.L.	SS	73	289	53	89	17	1	12	27	18	.308
2006 Los Angeles e-f	N.L.	2B-3B-SS-OF	49	146	16	32	5	1	1	10	6	.219
2007 Boston	A.L.	SS	147	570	71	135	36	2	8	73	33	.237
2008 Boston g	A.L.	SS-OF	82	261	27	70	13	0	1	22	12	.268
Major League Totals		9 Yrs.	1149	4216	619	1141	221	27	77	431	184	.271
Division Series												
2001 Houston	N.L.	SS	3	8	1	0	0	0	0	0	0	.000
2006 Los Angeles	N.L.	2B-3B	2	4	0	1	1	0	0	0	0	.250
2007 Boston	A.L.	SS	3	10	2	3	0	0	0	0	1	.300
Division Series Totals			8	22	3	4	1	0	0	0	1	.182
Championship Series												
2007 Boston	A.L.	SS	7	25	3	5	2	0	0	2	0	.200
World Series Record												
2007 Boston	A.L.	SS	4	13	2	5	1	0	0	1	0	.385

a On disabled list from July 21 to 29, 1999.
b On disabled list from August 13 to September 30, 2002.
c Released by Houston Astros, May 13, 2003. Signed with Tampa Bay Devil Rays, May 15, 2003.
d On disabled list from April 4 to May 5, 2006.
e Traded to Los Angeles Dodgers for infielder Joel Guzman and outfielder Sergio Pedroza, July 31, 2006.
f Filed for free agency, October 28, 2006. Signed with Boston Red Sox, December 13, 2006.
g On disabled list from July 12 to November 5, 2008.

MARKAKIS, NICHOLAS WILLIAM (NICK)

Born, Woodstock, Georgia, November 17, 1983.
Bats Left. Throws Left. Height, 6 feet, 2 inches. Weight, 195 pounds.

Year Club	Lea	Pos	G	AB	R	H	2B	3B	HR	RBI	SB	Avg
2003 Aberdeen	N.Y.-Penn.	OF	59	205	22	58	14	3	1	28	13	.283
2004 Delmarva	So.Atl.	OF	96	355	57	106	22	3	11	64	12	.299
2005 Frederick	Carolina	OF	91	350	59	105	25	1	12	62	2	.300
2005 Bowie	Eastern	OF	33	124	19	42	16	2	3	30	0	.339
2006 Baltimore	A.L.	OF	147	491	72	143	25	2	16	62	2	.291
2007 Baltimore	A.L.	OF	161	637	97	191	43	3	23	112	18	.300
2008 Baltimore	A.L.	OF	157	595	106	182	48	1	20	87	10	.306
Major League Totals		3 Yrs.	465	1723	275	516	116	6	59	261	30	.299

MARTE, ANDY MANUEL
Born, Villa Tapia, Dominican Republic, October 21, 1983.
Bats Right. Throws Right. Height, 6 feet, 1 inch. Weight, 185 pounds.

Year	Club	Lea	Pos	G	AB	R	H	2B	3B	HR	RBI	SB	Avg
2001 Danville	Appal.	3B-2B	37	125	12	25	6	0	1	12	3	.200
2002 Macon	So.Atl.	3B	126	488	69	137	32	4	21	105	2	.281
2003 Myrtle Beach	Carolina	3B	130	463	69	132	35	1	16	63	5	.285
2004 Braves	Gulf Coast	2B-3B	3	15	4	7	4	0	1	6	0	.467
2004 Greenville	Southern	3B	107	387	52	104	28	1	23	68	1	.269
2005 Richmond	Int.	3B	109	389	51	107	26	2	20	74	0	.275
2005 Atlanta a	N.L.	3B	24	57	3	8	2	1	0	4	0	.140
2006 Buffalo	Int.	3B	96	357	49	93	23	0	15	46	1	.261
2006 Cleveland b	A.L.	3B	50	164	20	37	15	1	5	23	0	.226
2007 Buffalo	Int.	3B	96	352	47	94	17	1	16	60	0	.267
2007 Cleveland c	A.L.	3B	20	57	3	11	4	0	1	8	0	.193
2008 Cleveland	A.L.	3B-1B	80	235	21	52	11	1	3	17	1	.221
Major League Totals		4 Yrs.	174	513	47	108	32	3	9	52	1	.211

a Traded to Boston Red Sox for infielder Edgar Renteria and cash, December 7, 2005.
b Traded to Cleveland Indians with catcher Kelly Shoppach and pitcher Guillermo Mota for outfielder Coco Crisp, pitcher David Riske and catcher Josh Bard, January 27, 2006.
c On disabled list from April 23 to May 19, 2007.

MARTIN, RUSSELL NATHAN
Born, East York, Ontario, Canada, February 15, 1983.
Bats Right. Throws Right. Height, 5 feet, 10 inches. Weight, 210 pounds.

Year	Club	Lea	Pos	G	AB	R	H	2B	3B	HR	RBI	SB	Avg
2002 Dodgers	Gulf Coast	3B-SS	41	126	22	36	3	3	0	10	7	.286
2003 Ogden	Pioneer	C	52	188	25	51	13	0	6	36	3	.271
2003 South Bend	So.Atl.	C-OF-3B	25	98	15	28	4	1	3	14	5	.286
2004 Vero Beach	Fla.St.	C	122	416	74	104	24	1	15	64	9	.250
2005 Jacksonville	Southern	C-OF	129	409	83	127	17	1	9	61	15	.311
2006 Las Vegas	P.C.	C	23	74	14	22	9	0	0	9	0	.297
2006 Los Angeles	N.L.	C	121	415	65	117	26	4	10	65	10	.282
2007 Los Angeles	N.L.	C	151	540	87	158	32	3	19	87	21	.293
2008 Los Angeles	N.L.	C-3B	155	553	87	155	25	0	13	69	18	.280
Major League Totals		3 Yrs.	427	1508	239	430	83	7	42	221	49	.285
Division Series													
2006 Los Angeles	N.L.	C	3	12	2	4	0	0	0	0	0	.333
2008 Los Angeles	N.L.	C	3	13	2	4	3	0	1	5	0	.308
Division Series Totals			6	25	4	8	3	0	1	5	0	.320
Championship Series													
2008 Los Angeles	N.L.	C	5	17	3	2	0	0	0	1	1	.118

MARTINEZ, VICTOR JESUS
Born, Ciudad Bolivar, Venezuela, December 23, 1978.
Bats Both. Throws Right. Height, 6 feet, 2 inches. Weight, 210 pounds.

Year	Club	Lea	Pos	G	AB	R	H	2B	3B	HR	RBI	SB	Avg
1997 Maracay-1	Venezuelan	C	53	122	21	42	12	0	0	26	6	.344
1998 Guacara-2	Venezuelan	C	55	160	28	43	13	0	1	27	8	.269
1999 Mahoning Valley	N.Y.-Penn.	C	64	235	37	65	9	0	4	36	0	.277
2000 Kinston	Carolina	C	26	83	9	18	7	0	0	8	1	.217
2000 Columbus a	So.Atl.	C	21	70	11	26	9	1	2	12	0	.371
2001 Kinston	Carolina	C	114	420	59	138	33	2	10	57	3	.329
2002 Akron	Eastern	C	121	443	84	149	40	0	22	85	3	.336
2002 Cleveland	A.L.	C	12	32	2	9	1	0	1	5	0	.281
2003 Buffalo	Int.	C-1B	73	274	42	90	19	0	7	45	3	.328
2003 Akron	Eastern	C	3	12	1	4	2	0	0	2	0	.333
2003 Cleveland b	A.L.	C	49	159	15	46	4	0	1	16	1	.289
2004 Cleveland	A.L.	C	141	520	77	147	38	1	23	108	0	.283
2005 Cleveland	A.L.	C	147	547	73	167	33	0	20	80	0	.305
2006 Cleveland	A.L.	C-1B	153	572	82	181	37	0	16	93	0	.316
2007 Cleveland	A.L.	C-1B	147	562	78	169	40	0	25	114	0	.301
2008 Akron	Eastern	DH	2	6	1	2	0	0	1	1	0	.333
2008 Buffalo	Int.	C	6	20	2	6	2	0	0	2	0	.300
2008 Cleveland c	A.L.	C-1B	73	266	30	74	17	0	2	35	0	.278
Major League Totals		7 Yrs.	722	2658	357	793	170	1	88	451	1	.298

Year	Club	Lea	Pos	G	AB	R	H	2B	3B	HR	RBI	SB	Avg
Division Series													
2007 Cleveland	A.L.	C-1B	4	17	2	6	1	0	1	4	0	.353
Championship Series													
2007 Cleveland	A.L.	C-1B	7	27	4	8	1	0	1	3	0	.296

a On minor league disabled list from May 25 to July 19, 2000.
b On disabled list from August 9 to September 2, 2003.
c On disabled list from June 12 to August 29, 2008.

MATHIS, JEFFERY STEPHEN (JEFF)

Born, Marianna, Florida, March 31, 1983.
Bats Right. Throws Right. Height, 6 feet. Weight, 180 pounds.

Year	Club	Lea	Pos	G	AB	R	H	2B	3B	HR	RBI	SB	Avg
2001 Angels	Arizona		C-OF	7	23	1	7	1	0	0	3	0	.304
2001 Provo	Pioneer		C	22	77	14	23	6	3	0	18	1	.299
2002 Cedar Rapids	Midwest		C	128	491	75	141	41	3	10	73	7	.287
2003 Rancho Cucamonga	Calif.		C	98	378	74	122	28	3	11	54	5	.323
2003 Arkansas	Texas		C	24	95	19	27	11	0	2	14	1	.284
2004 Arkansas	Texas		C	117	432	57	98	24	3	14	55	2	.227
2005 Salt Lake	P.C.		C	112	427	78	118	26	3	21	73	4	.276
2005 Los Angeles	A.L.		C	5	3	1	1	0	0	0	0	0	.333
2006 Salt Lake	P.C.		C	99	384	62	111	33	3	0	0	0	.289
2006 Los Angeles	A.L.		C	23	55	9	8	2	0	5	45	3	.145
2007 Salt Lake	P.C.		C	66	250	39	61	14	2	2	6	0	.244
2007 Los Angeles	A.L.		C	59	171	24	36	12	0	5	26	3	.211
2008 Los Angeles	A.L.		C	94	283	35	55	8	0	4	23	0	.194
Major League Totals		4 Yrs.		181	512	69	100	22	0	15	71	2	.195
Division Series													
2007 Los Angeles	A.L.		C	2	3	0	0	0	0	0	1	0	.000
2008 Los Angeles	A.L.		C	1	2	0	1	0	0	0	0	0	.500
Division Series Totals				3	5	0	1	0	0	0	1	0	.200

MATSUI, HIDEKI

Born: Ishikawa, Japan June 12, 1974
Bats Left, Throws Right, Height 6 feet two inches, Weight 230 pounds

Year	Club	Lea	Pos	G	AB	R	H	2B	3B	HR	RBI	SB	Avg
1993 Yomiuri Giants	Japan Cent.		OF	57	184	27	41	9	0	11	27	1	223
1994 Yomiuri Giants	Japan Cent.		OF	130	503	70	148	23	4	20	66	6	.294
1995 Yomiuri Giants	Japan Cent.		OF	131	501	76	142	31	1	22	80	9	283
1996 Yomiuri Giants	Japan Cent.		OF	130	487	97	153	34	1	38	99	7	.314
1997 Yomiuri Giants	Japan Cent.		OF	135	484	93	144	18	0	37	103	9	.298
1998 Yomiuri Giants	Japan Cent.		OF	135	487	103	142	24	3	34	100	3	.292
1999 Yomiuri Giants	Japan Cent.		OF	135	471	100	143	24	2	42	95	0	.304
2000 Yomiuri Giants	Japan Cent.		OF	135	474	116	150	32	1	42	108	5	.316
2001 Yomiuri Giants	Japan Cent.		OF	140	481	107	160	23	3	36	104	3	.333
2002 Yomiuri Giants a	Japan Cent.		OF	140	500	112	167	27	1	50	107	3	.334
Japan Central Totals		10 years		1268	4572	901	1390	245	16	332	889	46	.304
2003 New York	A.L.		OF	*163	623	82	179	42	1	16	106	2	.287
2004 New York	A.L.		OF	*162	584	109	174	34	2	31	108	3	.298
2005 New York b	A.L.		OF	*162	629	108	192	45	3	23	116	2	.305
2006 New York	A.L.		OF	51	172	32	52	9	0	8	29	1	.302
2007 Tampa	Fla.St.		OF	2	6	1	2	0	0	0	0	0	.333
2007 New York c	A.L.		OF	143	547	100	156	28	4	25	103	4	.285
2008 Tampa	Fla.St.		DH	3	8	1	2	0	0	1	1	0	.250
2008 New York d	A.L.		DH-OF	93	337	43	99	17	0	9	45	0	.294
Major League Totals		6 Yrs.		774	2892	474	852	175	10	112	507	12	.295
Division Series													
2003 New York	A.L.		OF	4	15	2	4	1	0	1	3	0	.267
2004 New York	A.L.		OF	4	17	3	7	1	0	1	3	0	.412
2005 New York	A.L.		OF	5	20	4	4	1	0	1	1	0	.200
2006 New York	A.L.		OF-DH	4	16	1	4	1	0	0	1	0	.250
2007 New York	A.L.		DH	4	11	4	2	0	0	0	0	0	.182
Division Series Totals				21	79	14	21	4	0	3	8	0	.266
Championship Series													
2003 New York	A.L.		OF	7	26	3	8	3	0	0	4	0	.308
2004 New York	A.L.		OF	7	34	9	14	6	1	2	10	0	.412

Year	Club	Lea	Pos	G	AB	R	H	2B	3B	HR	RBI	SB	Avg
Championship Series Totals				14	60	12	22	9	1	2	14	0	.367
World Series Record													
2003 New York	A.L.		OF	6	23	1	6	0	0	1	4	0	.261

a Reached agreement with New York Yankees on three year contract, December 19, 2002.
b On disabled list from May 12 to September 12, 2006.
c On disabled list from April 8 to April 23, 2007.
d On disabled list from June 23 to August 19 and September 22 to November 14, 2008.

MATSUI, KAZUO

Born, Osaka, Japan, October 23, 1975.
Bats Both. Throws Right. Height, 5 feet, 10 inches. Weight, 185 pounds.

Year	Club	Lea	Pos	G	AB	R	H	2B	3B	HR	RBI	SB	Avg
1995 Seibu	Japan Pac.		SS	69	204	25	45	9	1	2	15	21	.221
1996 Seibu	Japan Pac.		SS	130	473	51	134	22	5	1	29	50	.283
1997 Seibu	Japan Pac.		SS	135	645	91	178	23	13	7	63	62	.276
1998 Seibu	Japan Pac.		SS	135	641	92	179	38	5	9	58	43	.279
1999 Seibu	Japan Pac.		SS	135	609	87	178	29	4	15	67	32	.292
2000 Seibu	Japan Pac.		SS	135	611	99	177	40	11	23	90	26	.290
2001 Seibu	Japan Pac.		SS	140	613	94	170	28	2	24	76	26	.277
2002 Seibu	Japan Pac.		SS	140	651	119	193	46	6	36	87	33	.296
2003 Seibu a	Japan Pac.		SS	140	587	104	179	36	4	33	84	13	.305
2004 New York b	N.L.		SS-2B	114	460	65	125	32	2	7	44	14	.272
2005 Mets...........	Gulf Coast		2B	3	9	3	4	0	0	1	3	0	.444
2005 Binghamton	Eastern		2B	3	9	4	4	1	0	0	0	2	.444
2005 New York c	N.L.		2B	87	267	31	68	9	4	3	24	6	.255
2006 St. Lucie	Fla.St.		2B	2	7	1	2	0	0	0	0	0	.286
2006 Colorado Springs	P.C.		SS-2B	31	115	26	32	4	0	3	16	3	.278
2006 Norfolk........	Int.		2B	4	12	2	4	2	0	0	1	0	.333
2006 New York-Colorado d-e-f.	N.L.		2B-SS	70	243	32	65	12	3	3	26	10	.267
2007 Colorado Springs	P.C.		2B	2	6	1	3	0	0	0	0	1	.500
2007 Colorado g-h	N.L.		2B	104	410	84	118	24	6	4	37	32	.288
2008 Corpus Christi	Texas		2B	2	7	1	3	3	0	0	1	0	.429
2008 Round Rock.........	P.C.		2B	3	11	1	2	1	0	1	1	0	.182
2008 Houston i...........	N.L.		2B	96	375	58	110	26	3	6	33	20	.293
Major League Totals				5 Yrs.	471	1755	270	486	103	18	23	164	82	.277
Division Series													
2007 Colorado	N.L.		2B	3	12	2	5	1	2	1	6	0	.417
Championship Series													
2007 Colorado	N.L.		2B	4	17	2	4	0	0	0	2	1	.235
World Series Record													
2007 Colorado	N.L.		2B	4	17	1	5	1	0	0	0	1	.294

a Signed with New York Mets, December 9, 2003.
b On disabled list from August 9 to September 24, 2004.
c On disabled list from June 18 to August 9, 2005.
d On disabled list from March 18 to April 20, 2006.
e Traded to Colorado Rockies for outfielder Eli Marrero, June 9, 2006.
f Filed for free agency, October 31, 2006, re-signed with Colorado Rockies, November 13, 2006.
g On disabled list from April 15 to May 21, 2007.
h Filed for free agency, November 1, 2007. Signed with Houston Astros, December 2, 2007.
i On disabled list from March 21 to April 18 and June 23 to July 9 and August 16 to September 2, 2008.

MATTHEWS, GARY NATHANIEL, JR.

Born, San Francisco, California, August 25, 1974.
Bats Both. Throws Right. Height, 6 feet, 3 inches. Weight, 225 pounds.

Year	Club	Lea	Pos	G	AB	R	H	2B	3B	HR	RBI	SB	Avg
1994 Spokane........	Northwest		OF-2B	52	191	23	40	6	1	0	18	3	.209
1995 Clinton	Midwest		OF	128	421	57	100	18	4	2	40	28	.238
1996 Rancho Cuca	California		OF	123	435	65	118	21	11	7	54	7	.271
1997 Rancho Cuca	California		OF	69	268	66	81	15	4	8	40	10	.302
1997 Mobile	Southern		OF	28	90	14	22	4	1	2	12	3	.244
1998 Mobile	Southern		OF	72	254	62	78	15	4	7	51	11	.307
1999 Las Vegas	P.C.		OF	121	422	57	108	22	3	9	52	17	.256
1999 San Diego	N.L.		OF	23	36	4	8	0	0	0	7	2	.222
2000 Iowa..............	P.C.		OF	60	211	27	51	11	3	5	22	6	.242
2000 Chicago a	N.L.		OF	80	158	24	30	1	2	4	14	3	.190
2001 Chicago-Pittsburgh b-c .	N.L.		OF	152	405	63	92	15	2	14	44	8	.227
2002 New York	N.L.		PH	2	1	0	0	0	0	0	0	0	.000

Year Club	Lea	Pos	G	AB	R	H	2B	3B	HR	RBI	SB	Avg
2002 Baltimore d-e	A.L.	OF	109	344	54	95	25	3	7	38	15	.276
2003 Baltimore	A.L.	OF	41	162	21	33	12	1	2	20	0	.204
2003 San Diego f	N.L.	OF	103	306	50	83	19	1	4	22	12	.271
2004 Oklahoma	P.C.	OF	38	145	33	47	9	4	9	36	4	.324
2004 Texas g-h	A.L.	OF	87	280	37	77	17	1	11	36	5	.275
2005 Frisco	Texas	OF	1	5	0	2	0	0	0	1	0	.400
2005 Texas i	A.L.	OF	131	475	72	121	25	5	17	55	9	.255
2006 Oklahoma	P.C.	OF	6	21	10	9	2	0	0	1	2	.429
2006 Texas j-k	A.L.	OF	147	620	102	194	44	6	19	79	10	.313
2007 Los Angeles	A.L.	OF	140	516	79	130	26	3	18	72	18	.252
2008 Los Angeles	A.L.	OF	127	426	53	103	19	3	8	46	8	.242
Major League Totals		10 Yrs.	1142	3729	559	966	203	27	104	433	90	.259
Division Series												
2008 Los Angeles	A.L.	OF	3	5	0	0	0	0	0	0	0	.000

a Traded to Chicago Cubs for pitcher Rodney Myers, March 23, 2000.
b Claimed on waivers by Pittsburgh Pirates, August 10, 2001.
c Sold to New York Mets, December 28, 2001.
d Traded to Baltimore Orioles for pitcher John Bale, April 3, 2002.
e On disabled list from August 25 to September 11, 2002.
f Claimed on waivers by San Diego Padres, May 23, 2003.
g Claimed on waivers by Atlanta Braves, November 24, 2003.
h Released by Atlanta Braves, March 31, 2004. Signed with Texas Rangers organization, April 7, 2004.
i On disabled list from May 15 to June 8, 2005.
j On disabled list from March 24 to April 12, 2006.
k Filed for free agency, October 29, 2006. Signed with Los Angeles Angels, November 22, 2006.

MAUER, JOSEPH PATRICK (JOE)

Born, St. Paul, Minnesota, April 19, 1983.
Bats Left. Throws Right. Height, 6 feet, 4 inches. Weight, 220 pounds.

Year Club	Lea	Pos	G	AB	R	H	2B	3B	HR	RBI	SB	Avg
2001 Elizabethton	Appal.	C	32	110	14	44	6	2	0	14	4	.400
2002 Quad Cities	Midwest	C-1B	110	411	58	124	23	1	4	62	0	.302
2003 Fort Myers	Fla.St.	C-1B	62	233	25	78	13	1	1	44	3	.335
2003 New Britain	Eastern	C	73	276	48	94	17	1	4	41	0	.341
2004 Fort Myers	Fla.St.	C	2	6	0	4	0	0	0	2	0	.667
2004 Rochester	Int.	C	5	19	1	6	3	0	0	2	0	.316
2004 Minnesota a	A.L.	C	35	107	18	33	8	1	6	17	1	.308
2005 Minnesota	A.L.	C	131	489	61	144	26	2	9	55	13	.294
2006 Minnesota	A.L.	C	140	521	86	181	36	4	13	84	8	*.347
2007 Fort Myers	Fla.St.	C	1	3	0	0	0	0	0	0	0	.000
2007 Minnesota b	A.L.	C	109	406	62	119	27	3	7	60	7	.293
2008 Minnesota	A.L.	C	146	536	98	176	31	4	9	85	1	*.328
Major League Totals		5 Yrs.	561	2059	325	653	128	14	44	301	30	.317
Division Series												
2006 Minnesota	A.L.	C	3	11	0	2	0	0	0	0	0	.182

a On disabled list from April 7 to June 2 and from July 16 to October 11, 2004.
b On disabled list from May 5 to June 8, 2007.

MAYBIN, CAMERON KEITH

Born, Asheville, North Carolina, April 4, 1987.
Bats Right. Throws Right. Height, 6 feet, 4 inches. Weight, 205 pounds.

Year Club	Lea	Pos	G	AB	R	H	2B	3B	HR	RBI	SB	Avg
2006 West Michigan	Midwest	OF	101	385	59	117	20	6	9	69	27	.304
2007 Tigers	Gulf Coast	OF	2	7	1	4	0	0	0	1	0	.571
2007 Lakeland	Fla.St.	OF	83	296	58	90	14	5	10	44	25	.304
2007 Erie	Eastern	OF	6	20	9	8	1	0	4	8	0	.400
2007 Detroit a	A.L.	OF	24	49	8	7	3	0	1	2	5	.143
2008 Carolina	Southern	OF	108	390	73	108	15	8	13	49	21	.277
2008 Florida	N.L.	OF	8	32	9	16	2	0	0	2	4	.500
Major League Totals		2 Yrs.	32	81	17	23	5	0	1	4	9	.284

a Traded to Florida Marlins with pitcher Burke Badenhop, pitcher Eulogio De La Cruz, pitcher Andrew Miller and catcher Mike Rabelo for pitcher Dontrelle Willis and infielder Miguel Cabrera, December 5, 2007.

MC ANULTY, PAUL MICHAEL

Born, Oxnard, California, February 24, 1981.
Bats Left. Throws Right. Height, 5 feet, 10 inches. Weight, 220 pounds.

Year	Club	Lea	Pos	G	AB	R	H	2B	3B	HR	RBI	SB	Avg
2002 Idaho Falls	Pioneer		1B	67	235	56	89	29	0	8	51	7	.379
2003 Fort Wayne	Midwest		1B-OF	133	455	48	124	27	0	7	73	5	.273
2004 Lake Elsinore	Calif.		OF-1B	133	495	98	147	36	3	23	87	3	.297
2005 Mobile	Southern		OF-1B	79	298	39	84	17	2	10	42	5	.282
2005 Portland	P.C.		1B-OF	38	151	27	52	15	0	6	27	0	.344
2005 San Diego	N.L.		OF-1B	22	24	4	5	0	0	0	0	1	.208
2006 Portland	P.C.		1B-3B-OF	125	478	76	148	34	5	19	79	1	.310
2006 San Diego	N.L.		OF	16	13	3	3	1	0	1	3	0	.231
2007 San Diego	N.L.		OF	20	40	5	8	1	0	1	5	0	.200
2007 Padres	Arizona		OF	6	15	2	6	1	0	0	4	0	.400
2007 Portland	P.C.		OF-1B-3B	63	233	25	61	12	1	4	31	0	.262
2008 Portland	P.C.		OF-1B	53	181	34	62	14	1	13	50	0	.343
2008 San Diego a	N.L.		OF	66	135	9	28	7	1	3	13	0	.207
Major League Totals			4 Yrs.	124	212	21	44	9	1	5	21	1	.208

a Filed for free agency, October 29, 2008. Signed with Boston Red Sox organization, December 12, 2008.

MC CANN, BRIAN MICHAEL

Born, Athens, Georgia, February 20, 1984.
Bats Left. Throws Right. Height, 6 feet, 3 inches. Weight, 230 pounds.

Year	Club	Lea	Pos	G	AB	R	H	2B	3B	HR	RBI	SB	Avg
2002 Braves	Gulf Coast		C	29	100	9	22	5	0	2	11	0	.220
2003 Rome	So.Atl.		C	115	424	40	123	31	3	12	71	7	.290
2004 Myrtle Beach	Carolina		C	111	385	45	107	35	0	16	66	2	.278
2005 Mississippi	Southern		C	48	166	27	44	13	2	6	26	2	.265
2005 Atlanta	N.L.		C	59	180	20	50	7	0	5	23	1	.278
2006 Rome	So.Atl.		DH	2	7	0	2	0	0	0	0	0	.286
2006 Atlanta a	N.L.		C	130	442	61	147	34	0	24	93	2	.333
2007 Atlanta	N.L.		C	139	504	51	136	38	0	18	92	0	.270
2008 Atlanta	N.L.		C	145	509	68	153	42	1	23	87	5	.301
Major League Totals			4 Yrs.	473	1635	200	486	121	1	70	295	8	.297
Division Series													
2005 Atlanta	N.L.		C	3	16	2	3	0	0	2	5	0	.188

a On disabled list from May 24 to June 9, 2006.

MC DONALD, JOHN JOSEPH

Born, New London, Connecticut, September 24, 1974.
Bats Right. Throws Right. Height, 5 feet, 11 inches. Weight, 175 pounds.

Year	Club	Lea	Pos	G	AB	R	H	2B	3B	HR	RBI	SB	Avg
1996 Watertown	N.Y.-Penn.		SS	75	278	48	75	11	0	2	26	11	.270
1997 Kinston	Carolina		SS	130	541	77	140	27	3	5	53	6	.259
1998 Akron	Eastern		SS	132	514	68	118	18	2	2	43	17	.230
1999 Akron	Eastern		SS	55	226	31	67	12	0	1	26	7	.296
1999 Buffalo	Int.		SS	66	237	30	75	12	1	0	25	6	.316
1999 Cleveland	A.L.		2B-SS	18	21	2	7	0	0	0	0	0	.333
2000 Buffalo	Int.		SS-2B	75	286	37	77	17	2	1	36	4	.269
2000 Mahoning Valley	N.Y.-Penn.		SS	5	17	0	2	1	0	0	1	0	.118
2000 Cleveland	A.L.		SS-2B	9	9	3	4	0	0	0	0	0	.444
2000 Kinston a	Carolina		SS	1	3	0	1	0	0	0	0	0	.333
2001 Buffalo	Int.		SS-2B-3B	116	410	52	100	17	1	2	33	17	.244
2001 Cleveland b	A.L.		SS-2B-3B	17	22	1	2	1	0	0	0	0	.091
2002 Cleveland	A.L.		2B-SS-3B	93	264	35	66	11	3	1	12	3	.250
2003 Lake County	So.Atl.		SS	1	3	0	0	0	0	0	0	0	.000
2003 Mahoning Valley	N.Y.-Penn.		SS	1	2	1	0	0	0	0	0	0	.000
2003 Cleveland c	A.L.		2B-SS-3B	82	214	21	46	9	1	1	14	3	.215
2004 Cleveland d	A.L.		SS-2B-3B	66	93	17	19	5	1	2	7	0	.204
2005 Toronto-Detroit e-f	A.L.		SS-2B-3B	68	166	18	46	6	1	0	16	6	.277
2006 Toronto g	A.L.		SS-2B-3B	104	260	35	58	7	3	3	23	7	.223
2007 Toronto	A.L.		SS-3B	123	327	32	82	20	2	1	31	7	.251
2008 Dunedin	Fla.St.		SS	3	11	2	4	0	0	0	1	0	.364
2008 Toronto h	A.L.		SS-3B-2B	84	186	21	39	8	0	1	18	3	.210
Major League Totals			10 Yrs.	664	1562	182	369	67	11	9	121	29	.236

a On disabled list from April 27 to May 9 and May 10 to June 22, 2000.
b On disabled list from May 10 to 17, 2001.
c On disabled list from June 30 to July 17 and August 27 to October 3, 2003.

d Traded to Toronto Blue Jays for player to be named later, December 2, 2004. Cleveland received pitcher Tom Mastny to complete deal, December 13, 2004.
e Sold to Detroit Tigers, July 22, 2005.
f Sold to Toronto Blue Jays, November 10, 2005.
g On disabled list from May 28 to June 12, 2006.
h On disabled list from May 7 to June 7, 2008.

MC LOUTH, NATHAN RICHARD (NATE)

Born, Muskegon, Michigan, October 28, 1981.
Bats Left. Throws Right. Height, 5 feet, 11 inches. Weight, 185 pounds.

Year	Club	Lea	Pos	G	AB	R	H	2B	3B	HR	RBI	SB	Avg
2001	Hickory	So.Atl.	OF-2B	96	351	59	100	17	5	12	54	21	.285
2002	Lynchburg	Carolina	OF	114	393	58	96	23	4	9	46	20	.244
2003	Lynchburg	Carolina	OF	117	440	85	132	27	2	6	33	40	.300
2004	Altoona	Eastern	OF	133	515	93	166	40	4	8	73	31	.322
2005	Indianapolis	Int.	OF	110	397	64	118	20	3	5	39	34	.297
2005	Pittsburgh	N.L.	OF	41	109	20	28	6	0	5	12	2	.257
2006	Pittsburgh a	N.L.	OF	106	270	50	63	16	2	7	16	10	.233
2007	Pittsburgh	N.L.	OF	137	329	62	85	21	3	13	38	22	.258
2008	Pittsburgh	N.L.	OF	152	597	113	165	*46	4	26	94	23	.276
Major League Totals			4 Yrs.	436	1305	245	341	89	9	51	160	57	.261

a On disabled list from August 12 to October 3, 2006.

MICHAELS, JASON DREW

Born, Tampa, Florida, May 4, 1976.
Bats Right. Throws Right. Height, 6 feet. Weight, 205 pounds.

Year	Club	Lea	Pos	G	AB	R	H	2B	3B	HR	RBI	SB	Avg
1998	Batavia	N.Y.-Penn.	OF	67	235	45	63	14	3	11	49	4	.268
1999	Clearwater	Fla.St.	OF	122	452	91	138	31	6	14	65	10	.305
2000	Reading	Eastern	OF	113	437	71	129	30	4	10	74	7	.295
2001	Scranton-WB	Int.	OF	109	418	58	109	19	3	17	69	11	.261
2001	Philadelphia a	N.L.	OF	6	6	0	1	0	0	0	1	0	.167
2002	Scranton-WB	Int.	OF	9	32	3	9	2	0	0	7	1	.281
2002	Philadelphia	N.L.	OF-3B	81	105	16	28	10	3	2	11	1	.267
2003	Clearwater	Fla.St.	OF	4	14	1	0	0	0	0	0	0	.000
2003	Philadelphia b	N.L.	OF	76	109	20	36	11	0	5	17	0	.330
2004	Philadelphia	N.L.	OF	115	299	44	82	12	0	10	40	2	.274
2005	Philadelphia	N.L.	OF	105	289	54	88	16	2	4	31	3	.304
2006	Buffalo	Int.	OF	2	7	1	3	0	0	1	1	0	.429
2006	Cleveland c-d	A.L.	OF	123	494	77	132	32	1	9	55	9	.267
2007	Cleveland	A.L.	OF	105	267	43	72	11	1	7	39	3	.270
2008	Cleveland	A.L.	OF	21	58	3	12	4	0	0	9	1	.207
2008	Pittsburgh e-f	N.L.	OF	102	228	25	52	9	1	8	44	1	.228
Major League Totals			8 Yrs.	734	1855	282	503	105	8	45	247	20	.271
Division Series													
2007	Cleveland	A.L.	OF	1	1	0	1	1	0	0	0	0	1.000
Championship Series													
2007	Cleveland	A.L.	PH	1	0	1	0	0	0	0	0	0	.000

a On disabled list from May 1 to 10, 2001.
b On disabled list from March 21 to April 14, 2003.
c Traded to Cleveland Indians for pitcher Arthur Rhodes, January 27, 2006.
d On disabled list from June 16 to July 4, 2006.
e Traded to Pittsburgh Pirates for player to be named later, May 8, 2008.
f Not offered contract, October 31, 2008. Signed with Houston Astros, December 15, 2008.

MIENTKIEWICZ, DOUGLAS (DOUG)

Born, Toledo, Ohio, June 19, 1974.
Bats Left. Throws Right. Height, 6 feet, 2 inches. Weight, 205 pounds.

Year	Club	Lea	Pos	G	AB	R	H	2B	3B	HR	RBI	SB	Avg
1995	Fort Myers	Fla.St.	1B	38	110	9	27	6	1	1	15	2	.245
1996	Ft. Myers	Fla.St.	1B-C	133	492	69	143	36	4	5	79	12	.291
1997	New Britain	Eastern	1B-OF	132	467	87	119	28	2	15	61	21	.255
1998	New Britain	Eastern	1B-OF	139	502	96	162	45	0	16	88	11	.323
1998	Minnesota	A.L.	1B	8	25	1	5	1	0	0	2	1	.200
1999	Minnesota	A.L.	1B	118	327	34	75	21	3	2	32	1	.229
2000	Salt Lake	P.C.	1B-3B-2B-OF	130	485	96	162	32	3	18	96	9	.334

Year	Club	Lea	Pos	G	AB	R	H	2B	3B	HR	RBI	SB	Avg
2000 Minnesota		A.L.	1B	3	14	0	6	0	0	0	4	0	.429
2001 Minnesota		A.L.	1B	151	543	77	166	39	1	15	74	2	.306
2002 Minnesota		A.L.	1B	143	467	60	122	29	1	10	64	4	.261
2003 Minnesota		A.L.	1B-OF-2B-3B	142	487	67	146	38	1	11	65	4	.300
2004 Minn.-Boston a-b-c		A.L.	1B-2B	127	391	47	93	24	1	6	35	2	.238
2005 Mets		Gulf Coast	1B	4	10	2	5	1	0	1	5	0	.500
2005 St. Lucie		Fla.St.	1B	8	27	3	7	4	0	0	2	0	.259
2005 New York d-e-f		N.L.	1B	87	275	36	66	13	0	11	29	0	.240
2006 Kansas City g-h		A.L.	1B	91	314	37	89	24	2	4	43	3	.283
2007 Tampa		Fla.St.	1B	5	14	4	6	3	0	0	8	0	.429
2007 Scranton-WB		Int.	1B	5	21	5	8	3	0	1	7	0	.381
2007 New York i-j		A.L.	1B	72	166	26	46	12	0	5	24	0	.277
2008 Pittsburgh k		N.L.	1B-3B-OF	125	285	37	79	19	2	2	30	0	.277
Major League Totals			11 Yrs.	1067	3294	422	893	220	11	66	402	14	.271
Division Series													
2002 Minnesota		A.L.	1B	5	20	3	5	0	0	2	4	0	.250
2003 Minnesota		A.L.	1B	4	15	0	2	0	0	0	0	0	.133
2004 Boston		A.L.	1B	3	4	0	2	0	0	0	1	0	.500
2007 New York		A.L.	1B	4	6	0	0	0	0	0	0	0	.000
Division Series Totals				16	45	3	9	0	0	2	5	0	.200
Championship Series													
2002 Minnesota		A.L.	1B	5	18	1	5	1	0	0	2	0	.278
2004 Boston		A.L.	1B	4	4	0	2	1	0	0	0	0	.500
Championship Series Totals				9	22	1	7	2	0	0	2	0	.318
World Series Record													
2004 Boston		A.L.	1B	4	1	0	0	0	0	0	0	0	.000

a On disabled list from July 7 to July 23, 2004.
b Traded to Chicago Cubs for pitcher Justin Jones, July 31, 2004.
c Traded to Boston Red Sox with infielder Orlando Cabrera for infielder Nomar Garciaparra and outfielder Matt Murton, July 31, 2004.
d Traded to New York Mets for infielder Ian Bladergroen, January 26, 2005.
e On disabled list from June 26 to July 16 and August 4 to September 2, 2005.
f Filed for free agency, November 1, 2005. Signed with Kansas City Royals, December 16, 2005.
g On disabled list from July 31 to October 28, 2006.
h Filed for free agency, October 28, 2006. Signed with New York Yankees, January 5, 2007.
i On disabled list from June 3 to September 1, 2007.
j Filed for free agency, October 29, 2007. Signed with Pittsburgh Pirates organization, February 11, 2008.
k Filed for free agency, October 30, 2008.

MILES, AARON WADE

Born, Pittsburg, California, December 15, 1976.
Bats Both. Throws Right. Height, 5 feet, 8 inches. Weight, 175 pounds.

Year	Club	Lea	Pos	G	AB	R	H	2B	3B	HR	RBI	SB	Avg
1995 Astros		Gulf Coast	SS-2B	47	171	32	44	9	3	0	18	9	.257
1996 Astros		Gulf Coast	2B	55	214	48	63	3	2	0	15	14	.294
1997 Quad City		Midwest	2B	97	370	55	97	13	2	1	35	18	.262
1998 Quad City		Midwest	2B-3B-OF	108	369	42	90	22	6	2	37	28	.244
1999 Michigan		Midwest	2B	112	470	72	149	28	8	10	71	17	.317
2000 Kissimmee a		Fla.St.	2B	75	295	40	86	20	1	2	36	11	.292
2001 Birmingham b		Southern	3B-2B	84	343	53	89	16	3	8	42	3	.259
2002 Birmingham c		Southern	2B-3B	138	531	67	171	39	1	9	68	25	.322
2003 Charlotte		Int.	2B-3B	133	546	80	166	34	5	11	50	8	.304
2003 Chicago d		A.L.	2B	8	12	3	4	3	0	0	2	0	.333
2004 Colorado Springs		P.C.	2B	12	54	8	18	3	0	0	8	2	.333
2004 Colorado		N.L.	2B	134	522	75	153	15	3	6	47	12	.293
2005 Colorado Springs		P.C.	2B	8	32	6	7	0	1	0	1	1	.219
2005 Colorado e-f		N.L.	2B-SS	99	324	37	91	12	3	2	28	4	.281
2006 St. Louis		N.L.	2B-SS-3B	135	426	48	112	20	5	2	30	2	.263
2007 St. Louis g		N.L.	2B-SS-3B-P	133	414	55	120	16	1	2	32	2	.290
2008 St. Louis h		N.L.	2B-SS-3B-OF	134	379	49	120	15	2	4	31	3	.317
Major League Totals			6 Yrs.	643	2077	267	600	81	14	16	170	23	.289
Division Series													
2006 St. Louis		N.L.	2B	2	2	0	1	0	0	0	0	0	.500
Championship Series													
2006 St. Louis		N.L.	2B	3	3	0	2	0	1	0	0	0	.667
World Series Record													
2006 St. Louis		N.L.	2B	2	6	2	1	0	0	0	0	1	.167

a Selected by Chicago White Sox organization from Houston Astros organization in Rule V draft, December 11, 2000.
b Filed for free agency, October 15, 2001, re-signed with Chicago White Sox, November 16, 2001.
c Filed for free agency, October 15, 2002, re-signed with Chicago White Sox, October 25, 2002.
d Traded to Colorado Rockies for infielder Juan Uribe, December 2, 2003.
e On disabled list from May 26 to June 28, 2005.
f Traded to St. Louis Cardinals with outfielder Larry Bigbie for pitcher Ray King, December 7, 2005.
g Not offered contract, December 12, 2007, re-signed with St. Louis Cardinals organization, January 4, 2008.
h Not offered contract, December 12, 2008. Signed with Chicago Cubs, December 31, 2008.

MILLAR, KEVIN CHARLES

Born, Los Angeles, California, September 24, 1971.
Bats Right. Throws Right. Height, 6 feet. Weight, 215 pounds.

Year	Club	Lea	Pos	G	AB	R	H	2B	3B	HR	RBI	SB	Avg
1993	St. Paul	Northern	3B-2B	63	227	33	59	11	1	5	30	2	.260
1994	Kane County	Midwest	1B	135	477	75	144	35	2	19	93	3	.302
1995	Brevard Cty	Fla.St.	1B	129	459	53	132	32	2	13	68	4	.288
1996	Portland	Eastern	1B-3B	130	472	69	150	32	0	18	86	6	.318
1997	Portland	Eastern	1B-3B	135	511	94	175	34	2	32	131	2	.342
1998	Charlotte	Int.	3B-1B	14	46	14	15	3	0	4	15	1	.326
1998	Florida	N.L.	3B	2	2	1	1	0	0	0	0	0	.500
1999	Calgary	P.C.	OF	36	143	24	43	11	1	7	26	2	.301
1999	Florida	N.L.	1B-3B-OF	105	351	48	100	17	4	9	67	1	.285
2000	Florida	N.L.	1B-OF-3B	123	259	36	67	14	3	14	42	0	.259
2001	Florida	N.L.	OF-1B-3B	144	449	62	141	39	5	20	85	0	.314
2002	Portland	Eastern	OF	3	12	1	1	0	0	1	3	0	.083
2002	Florida b-c	N.L.	OF-1B-3B	126	438	58	134	41	0	16	57	0	.306
2003	Boston d	A.L.	1B-OF	148	544	83	150	30	1	25	96	3	.276
2004	Boston	A.L.	OF-1B	150	508	74	151	36	0	18	74	1	.297
2005	Boston e	A.L.	1B-OF	134	449	57	122	28	1	9	50	0	.272
2006	Baltimore f	A.L.	1B	132	430	64	117	26	0	15	64	1	.272
2007	Baltimore	A.L.	1B-OF	140	476	63	121	26	1	17	63	1	.254
2008	Baltimore g	A.L.	1B	145	531	73	124	25	0	20	72	0	.234
Major League Totals			11 Yrs.	1349	4437	619	1228	282	15	163	670	7	.277
Division Series													
2003	Boston	A.L.	1B	5	21	0	5	0	0	0	0	0	.238
2004	Boston	A.L.	1B	3	10	2	3	0	0	1	4	0	.300
2005	Boston	A.L.	1B	2	3	0	1	1	0	0	1	0	.333
Division Series Totals				10	34	2	9	1	0	1	5	0	.265
Championship Series													
2003	Boston	A.L.	1B	7	29	3	7	0	0	1	3	0	.241
2004	Boston	A.L.	1B	7	24	4	6	3	0	0	2	0	.250
Championship Series Totals				14	53	7	13	3	0	1	5	0	.245
World Series Record													
2004	Boston	A.L.	1B	4	8	2	1	1	0	0	0	0	.125

a Filed for free agency, December 19, 1997, re-signed with Florida Marlins, December 21, 1997.
b On disabled list from April 29 to May 28, 2002.
c Sold to Chunichi Dragons, January 8, 2003.
d Sale to Japan voided and sold to Boston Red Sox, February 15, 2003.
e Filed for free agency, October 27, 2005. Signed with Baltimore Orioles, January 13, 2006.
f Filed for free agency, October 31, 2006, re-signed with Baltimore Orioles, December 2, 2006.
g Filed for free agency, October 30, 2008.

MILLEDGE, LASTINGS DARNELL

Born, Bradenton, Florida, April 5, 1985.
Bats Right. Throws Right. Height, 6 feet, 1 inch. Weight, 205 pounds.

Year	Club	Lea	Pos	G	AB	R	H	2B	3B	HR	RBI	SB	Avg
2003	Kingsport	Appal.	DH	7	26	4	6	2	0	0	2	5	.231
2004	St. Lucie	Fla.St.	OF	22	81	6	19	6	2	2	8	3	.235
2004	Capital City	So.Atl.	OF	65	262	66	89	22	1	13	58	23	.340
2005	Binghamton	Eastern	OF	48	193	33	65	17	0	4	24	11	.337
2005	St. Lucie	Fla.St.	OF	62	232	48	70	15	0	4	22	18	.302
2006	Norfolk	Int.	OF	84	307	52	85	21	4	7	36	13	.277
2006	New York	N.L.	OF	56	166	14	40	7	2	4	22	1	.241
2007	Mets	Gulf Coast	OF	2	7	1	1	1	0	0	0	0	.143
2007	St. Lucie	Fla.St.	OF	1	4	2	1	0	0	0	0	0	.250
2007	Binghamton	Eastern	OF	5	23	7	10	1	1	3	8	1	.435
2007	New Orleans	P.C.	OF	11	39	9	13	1	0	1	5	5	.333

Year	Club	Lea	Pos	G	AB	R	H	2B	3B	HR	RBI	SB	Avg
2007 New York a	N.L.		OF	59	184	27	50	9	1	7	29	3	.272
2008 Nationals	Gulf Coast		OF	2	4	1	1	0	0	1	1	0	.250
2008 Columbus	Int.		OF	3	13	0	1	0	0	0	2	0	.077
2008 Washington b	N.L.		OF	138	523	65	140	24	2	14	61	24	.268
Major League Totals		3 Yrs.		253	873	106	230	40	5	25	112	28	.263

a Traded to Washington Nationals for outfielder Ryan Church and catcher Brian Schneider, November 30, 2007.
b On disabled list from June 28 to July 24, 2008.

MOLINA, BENJAMIN JOSE (BENGIE)
Born, Rio Piedras, Puerto Rico, July 20, 1974.
Bats Right. Throws Right. Height, 5 feet, 11 inches. Weight, 225 pounds.

Year	Club	Lea	Pos	G	AB	R	H	2B	3B	HR	RBI	SB	Avg
1993 Angels	Arizona		DH-C	27	80	9	21	6	2	0	10	0	.262
1994 Cedar Rapds	Midwest		C	48	171	14	48	8	0	3	16	1	.281
1995 Vancouver	P.C.		C	1	2	0	0	0	0	0	0	0	.000
1995 Cedar Rapds	Midwest		C	39	133	15	39	9	0	4	17	1	.293
1995 Lk Elsinore	California		C	27	96	21	37	7	2	2	12	0	.385
1996 Midland	Texas		C	108	365	45	100	21	2	8	54	0	.274
1997 Lk Elsinore	California		C	36	149	18	42	10	2	4	33	0	.282
1997 Midland	Texas		DH-C	29	106	18	35	8	0	6	30	0	.330
1998 Midland	Texas		C	41	154	28	55	8	0	9	39	0	.357
1998 Vancouver	P.C.		C	49	184	13	54	9	1	1	22	1	.293
1998 Anaheim a	A.L.		C	2	1	0	0	0	0	0	0	0	.000
1999 Edmonton	P.C.		C	65	241	28	69	16	0	7	41	1	.286
1999 Anaheim b	A.L.		C	31	101	8	26	5	0	1	10	0	.257
2000 Anaheim	A.L.		C	130	473	59	133	20	2	14	71	1	.281
2001 Salt Lake	P.C.		C	5	18	2	5	1	0	0	3	0	.278
2001 Rancho Cucamonga	Calif.		C	3	11	1	6	1	0	0	2	0	.545
2001 Anaheim c	A.L.		C	96	325	31	85	11	0	6	40	0	.262
2002 Rancho Cucamonga	Calif.		C	1	2	0	1	0	0	0	0	0	.500
2002 Anaheim d	A.L.		C	122	428	34	105	18	0	5	47	0	.245
2003 Anaheim e	A.L.		C	119	409	37	115	24	0	14	71	1	.281
2004 Anaheim f	A.L.		C	97	337	36	93	13	0	10	54	0	.276
2005 Los Angeles g-h	A.L.		C	119	410	45	121	17	0	15	69	0	.295
2006 Toronto i	A.L.		C	117	433	44	123	20	1	19	57	1	.284
2007 San Francisco	N.L.		C	134	497	38	137	19	1	19	81	0	.276
2008 San Francisco	N.L.		C	145	530	46	155	33	0	16	95	0	.292
Major League Totals		11 Yrs.		1112	3944	378	1093	180	4	119	595	3	.277
Division Series													
2002 Anaheim	A.L.		C	4	15	0	4	2	0	0	2	0	.267
2004 Anaheim	A.L.		C	3	6	0	1	0	0	0	0	0	.167
2005 Los Angeles	A.L.		C	5	18	5	8	0	0	3	5	0	.444
Division Series Totals				12	39	5	13	2	0	3	7	0	.333
Championship Series													
2002 Anaheim	A.L.		C	5	14	0	3	0	1	0	2	0	.214
2005 Los Angeles	A.L.		C-DH	5	17	0	2	0	0	0	1	0	.118
Championship Series Totals				10	31	0	5	0	1	0	3	0	.161
World Series Record													
2002 Anaheim	A.L.		C	7	21	2	6	2	0	0	2	0	.286

a On disabled list from May 13 to 22, 1998.
b On disabled list from June 4 to 14, 1999.
c On disabled list from May 5 to June 27, 2001.
d On disabled list from July 17 to August 1, 2002.
e On disabled list from September 4 to October 6, 2003.
f On disabled list from June 4 to June 19 and from August 1 to August 17, 2004.
g On disabled list from April 18 to May 13, 2005.
h Filed for free agency, October 27, 2005. Signed with Toronto Blue Jays, February 28, 2006.
i Filed for free agency, November 31, 2006, re-signed with San Francisco Giants, December 6, 2006.

MOLINA (MATTA), JOSE BENJAMIN
Born, Bayamon, Puerto Rico, June 3, 1975.
Bats Right. Throws Right. Height, 6 feet, 2 inch. Weight, 245 pounds.

Year	Club	Lea	Pos	G	AB	R	H	2B	3B	HR	RBI	SB	Avg
1993 Cubs	Gulf Coast		C-1B	33	78	5	17	2	0	0	4	3	.218
1993 Daytona	Fla.St.		C	3	7	0	1	0	0	0	1	0	.143
1994 Peoria	Midwest		C	78	253	31	58	13	1	1	33	4	.229

Year Club	Lea	Pos	G	AB	R	H	2B	3B	HR	RBI	SB	Avg
1995 Daytona	Fla.St.	C	82	233	27	55	9	1	1	19	1	.236
1996 Rockford	Midwest	C	96	305	35	69	10	1	2	27	2	.226
1997 Iowa	A.A.	C	1	3	0	1	0	0	0	0	0	.333
1997 Daytona	Fla.St.	C	55	179	17	45	9	1	0	23	4	.251
1997 Orlando	Southern	C	37	99	10	17	3	0	1	15	0	.172
1998 West Tenn	Southern	C-1B	109	320	33	71	10	1	2	28	1	.222
1999 West Tenn	Southern	C	14	35	2	6	3	0	0	5	0	.171
1999 Iowa	P.C.	C	74	240	24	63	11	1	4	26	0	.262
1999 Chicago	N.L.	C	10	19	3	5	1	0	0	1	0	.263
2000 Iowa	P.C.	C-1B	76	248	22	58	9	0	0	17	1	.234
2001 Salt Lake	P.C.	C	61	213	29	64	11	1	5	31	1	.300
2001 Anaheim a-b	A.L.	C	15	37	8	10	3	0	2	4	0	.270
2002 Salt Lake	P.C.	C	79	290	30	89	14	2	4	43	0	.307
2002 Anaheim	A.L.	C	29	70	5	19	3	0	0	5	0	.271
2003 Anaheim	A.L.	C	53	114	12	21	4	0	0	6	0	.184
2004 Anaheim	A.L.	C-1B	73	203	26	53	10	2	3	25	4	.261
2005 Los Angeles	A.L.	C-1B	75	184	14	42	4	0	6	25	2	.228
2006 Los Angeles	A.L.	C-1B	78	225	18	54	17	0	4	22	1	.240
2007 Los Angeles-New York c-d	A.L.	C	69	191	18	49	13	0	1	19	2	.257
2008 New York	A.L.	C-1B	100	268	32	58	17	0	3	18	0	.216
Major League Totals	9 Yrs.		502	1311	136	311	72	2	19	125	9	.237
Division Series												
2004 Anaheim	A.L.	C	2	3	2	1	0	0	0	0	0	.333
2005 Los Angeles	A.L.	C	1	1	1	1	0	0	0	0	1	1.000
Division Series Totals			3	4	3	2	0	0	0	1	0	.500
Championship Series												
2002 Anaheim	A.L.	C	3	1	0	0	0	0	0	0	0	.000
2005 Los Angeles	A.L.	C	1	3	0	1	0	0	0	0	0	.333
Championship Series Totals			4	4	0	1	0	0	0	0	0	.250
World Series Record												
2002 Anaheim	A.L.	C	3	0	0	0	0	0	0	0	0	.000

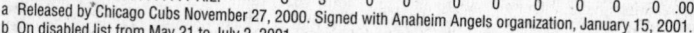

a Released by Chicago Cubs November 27, 2000. Signed with Anaheim Angels organization, January 15, 2001.
b On disabled list from May 21 to July 2, 2001.
c Traded to New York Yankees for pitcher Jeff Kennard, July 21, 2007.
d Filed for free agency, October 30, 2007, re-signed with New York Yankees, December 3, 2007.

MOLINA, YADIER B.

Born, Bayamon, Puerto Rico, July 13, 1982.
Bats Right. Throws Right. Height, 5 feet, 11 inches. Weight, 225 pounds.

Year Club	Lea	Pos	G	AB	R	H	2B	3B	HR	RBI	SB	Avg
2001 Johnson City	Appal.	C	44	158	18	41	11	0	4	18	1	.259
2002 Peoria	Midwest	C	112	393	39	110	20	0	7	50	2	.280
2003 Tennessee	Southern	C	104	364	32	100	13	1	2	51	0	.275
2004 Memphis	P.C.	C	37	129	19	39	6	0	1	14	0	.302
2004 St. Louis	N.L.	C	51	135	12	36	6	0	2	15	0	.267
2005 St. Louis a	N.L.	C-1B	114	385	36	97	15	1	8	49	2	.252
2006 St. Louis	N.L.	C-1B	129	417	29	90	26	0	6	49	1	.216
2007 St. Louis b	N.L.	C-1B	111	353	30	97	15	0	6	40	1	.275
2008 St. Louis	N.L.	C-1B	124	444	37	135	18	0	7	56	0	.304
Major League Totals	5 Yrs.		529	1734	144	455	80	1	29	209	4	.262
Division Series												
2005 St. Louis	N.L.	C	3	13	1	3	0	0	0	3	0	.231
2006 St. Louis	N.L.	C	4	13	0	4	1	0	0	1	0	.308
Division Series Totals			7	26	1	7	1	0	0	4	0	.269
Championship Series												
2004 St. Louis	N.L.	C	1	4	0	1	0	0	0	0	0	.250
2005 St. Louis	N.L.	C	6	22	1	7	3	0	0	0	0	.318
2006 St. Louis	N.L.	C	7	23	2	8	1	0	2	6	0	.348
Championship Series Totals			14	49	3	16	4	0	2	6	0	.327
World Series Record												
2004 St. Louis	N.L.	C	3	3	0	0	0	0	0	0	0	.000
2006 St. Louis	N.L.	C	5	17	3	7	2	0	0	1	0	.412
World Series Totals			8	20	3	7	2	0	0	1	0	.350

a On disabled list from July 9 to August 18, 2005.
b On disabled list from May 30 to June 28, 2007.

MONTERO, MIGUEL ANGEL

Born, Caracas, Venezuela, July 9, 1983.
Bats Left. Throws Right. Height, 5 feet, 11 inches. Weight, 195 pounds.

Year	Club	Lea	Pos	G	AB	R	H	2B	3B	HR	RBI	SB	Avg
2002	Missoula	Pioneer	C-3B-1B	50	152	21	40	10	1	3	14	2	.263
2003	Missoula	Pioneer	C	59	196	24	59	10	2	4	32	2	.301
2004	South Bend	Midwest	C-1B-SS	115	403	47	106	22	2	11	59	8	.263
2005	Lancaster	Calif.	C-1B	85	355	73	124	24	1	24	82	1	.349
2005	Tennessee	Southern	C-1B	30	108	13	27	1	2	2	13	1	.250
2006	Tennessee	Southern	C	81	289	24	78	18	0	10	46	0	.270
2006	Tucson	P.C.	C	36	134	21	43	5	0	7	29	1	.321
2006	Arizona	N.L.	C	6	16	0	4	1	0	0	3	0	.250
2007	Arizona	N.L.	C	84	214	30	48	7	0	10	37	0	.224
2008	Tucson	P.C.	C	11	32	3	9	2	0	1	5	0	.281
2008	Arizona a	N.L.	C	70	184	24	47	16	1	5	18	0	.255
Major League Totals			3 Yrs.	160	414	54	99	24	1	15	58	0	.239
Division Series													
2007	Arizona	N.L.	C	1	2	1	0	0	0	0	0	0	.000
Championship Series													
2007	Arizona	N.L.	C	3	5	0	2	0	0	0	0	0	.400

a On disabled list from March 23 to April 23, 2008.

MORA, MELVIN

Born, Agua Negra, Venezuela, February 2, 1972.
Bats Right. Throws Right. Height, 5 feet, 11 inches. Weight, 200 pounds.

Year	Club	Lea	Pos	G	AB	R	H	2B	3B	HR	RBI	SB	Avg
1992	Astros	Gulf Coast	OF-2B-3B	49	144	28	32	3	0	0	8	16	.222
1993	Asheville	So.Atl.	2B-OF-3B	108	365	66	104	22	2	2	31	20	.285
1994	Osceola	Fla.St.	OF-3B-2B	118	425	57	120	29	4	8	46	24	.282
1995	Jackson	Texas	OF-2B-3B	123	467	63	139	32	0	3	45	22	.298
1995	Tucson	P.C.	OF	2	5	3	3	0	1	0	1	1	.600
1996	Tucson	P.C.	3B-OF-2B	62	228	35	64	11	2	3	26	3	.281
1996	Jackson	Texas	OF-2B-SS-3B	70	255	36	73	6	1	5	23	4	.286
1997	New Orleans	A.A.	OF-3B-2B-SS	119	370	55	95	15	3	2	38	7	.257
1998	St. Lucie	Fla.St.	2B-SS-OF	17	55	5	15	0	0	0	8	1	.273
1998	Norfolk a	Int.	3B-OF-2B	11	28	5	5	1	0	0	2	0	.179
1999	Norfolk	Int.	SS	82	304	55	92	17	2	8	36	18	.303
1999	New York b	N.L.	OF-2B-3B-SS	66	31	6	5	0	0	0	1	2	.161
2000	Norfolk	Int.	OF	8	27	7	9	2	0	0	7	2	.333
2000	New York	N.L.	SS-OF-2B-3B	79	215	35	56	13	2	6	30	7	.260
2000	Baltimore c	A.L.	SS-2B	53	199	25	58	9	3	2	17	5	.291
2001	Baltimore	A.L.	OF-SS-2B	128	436	49	109	28	0	7	48	11	.250
2002	Baltimore	A.L.	OF-SS-2B	149	557	86	130	30	4	19	64	16	.233
2003	Bowie	Eastern	OF	6	21	3	6	0	0	2	5	0	.286
2003	Baltimore d	A.L.	OF-SS-2B-1B	96	344	68	109	17	1	15	48	6	.317
2004	Baltimore e	A.L.	3B-SS	140	550	111	187	41	0	27	104	11	.340
2005	Baltimore	A.L.	3B	149	593	86	168	30	1	27	88	7	.283
2006	Baltimore	A.L.	3B-2B	155	624	96	171	25	0	16	83	11	.274
2007	Orioles	Gulf Coast	DH	2	7	1	2	1	0	0	1	0	.286
2007	Baltimore f	A.L.	3B	126	467	67	128	23	1	14	58	9	.274
2008	Baltimore	A.L.	3B-SS	135	513	77	146	29	2	23	104	3	.285
Major League Totals			10 Yrs.	1276	4529	706	1267	245	14	156	645	88	.280
Division Series													
1999	New York	N.L.	OF	3	1	1	0	0	0	0	0	0	.000
Championship Series													
1999	New York	N.L.	OF	6	14	3	6	0	0	0	1	2	.429

a Filed for free agency from Houston Astros, October 17, 1997. Signed with New York Mets, July 24, 1998.
b Filed for free agency, October 16, 1998, re-signed with New York Mets, February 2, 1999.
c Traded to Baltimore Orioles with infielder Mike Kinkade, pitcher Pat Gorman and pitcher Leslie Brea for infielder Mike Bordick, July 28, 2000.
d On disabled list from August 1 to September 2, 2003.
e On disabled list from July 3 to July 18, 2004.
f On disabled list from July 13 to August 5, 2007.

MORGAN, NYJER JAMID

Born, San Francisco, California, July 2, 1980.
Bats Left. Throws Left. Height, 6 feet. Weight, 170 pounds.

Year Club	Lea	Pos	G	AB	R	H	2B	3B	HR	RBI	SB	Avg
2003 Williamsport	N.Y.-Penn.	OF	72	268	49	92	7	4	0	23	26	.343
2004 Hickory	So.Atl.	OF	134	514	83	131	16	7	4	41	55	.255
2005 Lynchburg	Carolina	OF	60	252	36	72	12	3	0	24	24	.286
2006 Lynchburg	Carolina	OF	61	228	43	69	7	3	0	22	38	.303
2006 Altoona	Eastern	OF	56	219	39	67	6	5	1	10	21	.306
2007 Pirates	Gulf Coast	OF	4	13	3	4	0	0	1	1	0	.308
2007 Indianapolis	Int.	OF	44	164	30	50	4	2	0	10	26	.305
2007 Pittsburgh a	N.L.	OF	28	107	15	32	3	4	1	7	7	.299
2008 Indianapolis	Int.	OF	82	322	54	96	13	4	1	33	44	.298
2008 Pittsburgh	N.L.	OF	58	160	26	47	13	0	0	7	9	.294
Major League Totals		2 Yrs.	86	267	41	79	16	4	1	14	16	.296

a On minor league disabled list from May 14 through August 23, 2007.

MORNEAU, JUSTIN ERNEST GEORGE

Born, New Westminster, British Columbia, Canada, May 15, 1981.
Bats Left. Throws Right. Height, 6 feet, 4 inches. Weight, 225 pounds.

Year Club	Lea	Pos	G	AB	R	H	2B	3B	HR	RBI	SB	Avg
1999 Twins	Gulf Coast	DH	17	53	3	16	5	0	0	9	0	.302
2000 Twins	Gulf Coast	1B-C-OF	52	194	47	78	21	0	10	58	3	.402
2000 Elizabethton	Appal.	C	6	23	4	5	0	0	1	3	0	.217
2001 Quad Cities	Midwest	1B	64	236	50	84	17	2	12	53	0	.356
2001 Fort Myers	Fla.St.	1B	53	197	25	58	10	3	4	40	0	.294
2001 New Britain	Eastern	1B	10	38	3	6	1	0	0	4	0	.158
2002 New Britain	Eastern	1B	126	494	72	147	31	4	16	80	7	.298
2003 New Britain	Eastern	1B	20	79	14	26	3	1	6	13	0	.329
2003 Rochester	Int.	1B	71	265	39	71	11	1	16	42	0	.268
2003 Minnesota	A.L.	DH-1B	40	106	14	24	4	0	4	16	0	.226
2004 Rochester	Int.	1B	72	288	51	88	23	0	22	63	1	.306
2004 Minnesota	A.L.	1B	74	280	39	76	17	0	19	58	0	.271
2005 Minnesota a	A.L.	1B	141	490	62	117	23	4	22	79	0	.239
2006 Minnesota b	A.L.	1B	157	592	97	190	37	1	34	130	3	.321
2007 Minnesota	A.L.	1B	157	590	84	160	31	3	31	111	1	.271
2008 Minnesota	A.L.	1B	*163	623	97	187	47	4	23	129	0	.300
Major League Totals		6 Yrs.	732	2681	393	754	159	12	133	523	4	.281
Division Series												
2004 Minnesota	A.L.	1B	4	17	1	4	2	0	0	2	0	.235
2006 Minnesota	A.L.	1B	3	12	3	5	1	0	2	2	0	.417
Division Series Totals			7	29	4	9	3	0	2	4	0	.310

a On disabled list from April 7 to April 22, 2005.
b Selected Most Valuable Player in American League for 2006.

MORSE, MICHAEL JOHN (MIKE)

Born, Fort Lauderdale, Florida, March 22, 1982.
Bats Right. Throws Right. Height, 6 feet, 4 inches. Weight, 220 pounds.

Year Club	Lea	Pos	G	AB	R	H	2B	3B	HR	RBI	SB	Avg
2000 White Sox	Arizona	SS	45	180	32	46	6	1	2	24	5	.256
2001 Bristol	Appal.	SS	57	181	23	41	7	3	4	27	6	.227
2002 Kannapolis	So.Atl.	SS-3B	113	417	43	107	30	4	2	56	7	.257
2003 Winston-Salem	Carolina	SS	122	432	45	106	30	2	10	55	4	.245
2004 Birmingham	Southern	SS	54	209	30	60	9	5	11	38	0	.287
2004 San Antonio a	Texas	SS	41	157	18	43	10	1	6	33	0	.274
2005 Tacoma	P.C.	SS	49	182	20	46	12	2	4	23	1	.253
2005 Seattle	A.L.	SS-OF	72	230	27	64	10	1	3	23	3	.278
2006 Tacoma	P.C.	1B-3B-SS-OF	57	206	23	51	15	1	5	34	0	.248
2006 Seattle	A.L.	OF-3B-1B-SS	21	43	5	16	5	0	0	11	1	.372
2007 Mariners	Arizona	3B-SS	5	15	2	3	1	0	0	2	0	.200
2007 Tacoma	P.C.	3B-SS-OF	76	291	48	90	26	0	6	39	5	.309
2007 Seattle	A.L.	1B-3B-SS-OF	9	18	1	8	2	0	0	3	0	.444
2008 Seattle b	A.L.	OF	5	9	0	2	1	0	0	0	0	.222
Major League Totals		4 Yrs.	107	300	33	90	18	1	3	37	4	.300

a Traded by Chicago White Sox to Seattle Mariners with catcher Miguel Olivo and outfielder Jeremy Reed for pitcher Freddy Garcia, catcher Ben Davis and cash, June 27, 2004.
b On disabled list from April 14 to September 29, 2008.

MOSS, BRANDON DOUGLAS

Born, Monroe, Georgia, September 16, 1983.
Bats Left. Throws Right. Height, 6 feet. Weight, 205 pounds.

Year	Club	Lea	Pos	G	AB	R	H	2B	3B	HR	RBI	SB	Avg
2002 Red Sox	Gulf Coast	2B-3B	42	113	10	23	6	2	0	6	1	.204
2003 Lowell	N.Y.-Penn.	OF	65	228	29	54	15	4	7	34	7	.237
2004 Sarasota	Fla.St.	OF	23	83	16	35	2	1	2	10	2	.422
2004 Augusta	So.Atl.	OF	109	433	66	147	25	6	13	101	19	.339
2005 Portland	Eastern	OF	135	503	87	135	31	4	16	61	6	.268
2006 Portland	Eastern	OF	133	508	76	145	36	3	12	83	8	.285
2007 Pawtucket	Int.	OF-1B	133	493	66	139	41	2	16	78	3	.282
2007 Boston	A.L.	OF	15	25	6	7	2	1	0	1	0	.280
2008 Pawtucket	Int.	1B-OF	43	163	29	46	8	4	8	30	2	.282
2008 Boston	A.L.	OF-1B	34	78	7	23	5	1	2	11	1	.295
2008 Pittsburgh a-b	N.L.	OF	45	158	12	35	10	2	6	23	0	.222
Major League Totals			2 Yrs.	94	261	25	65	17	4	8	35	1	.249

a On disabled list from May 3 to May 23, 2008.
b Traded to Pittsburgh Pirates with outfielder Manny Ramirez and pitcher Craig Hansen for outfielder Jason Bay, July 31, 2008.

MURPHY, DAVID MATTHEW

Born, Houston, Texas, October 18, 1981.
Bats Left. Throws Left. Height, 6 feet, 4 inches. Weight, 205 pounds.

Year	Club	Lea	Pos	G	AB	R	H	2B	3B	HR	RBI	SB	Avg
2003 Sarasota	Fla.St.	OF	45	153	18	37	5	1	1	18	6	.242
2003 Lowell	N.Y.-Penn.	OF	21	78	13	27	4	0	0	13	4	.346
2004 Sarasota	Fla.St.	OF	73	272	35	71	11	0	4	38	3	.261
2004 Red Sox	Gulf Coast	OF	5	18	3	5	1	0	0	1	1	.278
2005 Portland	Eastern	OF	135	484	71	133	25	4	14	75	13	.275
2006 Portland	Eastern	OF	42	172	22	47	17	1	3	25	4	.273
2006 Pawtucket	Int.	OF	84	318	45	85	23	5	8	44	3	.267
2006 Boston	A.L.	OF	20	22	4	5	1	0	1	2	0	.227
2007 Oklahoma	P.C.	OF	2	7	0	2	0	0	0	0	0	.286
2007 Pawtucket	Int.	OF	100	400	50	112	20	5	9	47	8	.280
2007 Boston-Texas a	A.L.	OF	46	105	17	36	12	2	2	14	0	.343
2008 Texas b	A.L.	OF	108	415	64	114	28	3	15	74	7	.275
Major League Totals			3 Yrs.	174	542	85	155	41	5	18	90	7	.286

a Traded to Texas Rangers with pitcher Kason Gabbard and outfielder Engle Beltre for pitcher Eric Gagne, July 31, 2007.
b On disabled list from August 7 to October 2, 2008.

NADY, XAVIER CLIFFORD

Born, Salinas, California, November 14, 1978.
Bats Right. Throws Right. Height, 6 feet, 2 inches. Weight, 205 pounds.

Year	Club	Lea	Pos	G	AB	R	H	2B	3B	HR	RBI	SB	Avg
2000 San Diego	N.L.	PH	1	1	1	1	0	0	0	0	0	1.000
2001 Lake Elsinore	California	1B	137	524	96	158	38	1	26	100	6	.302
2002 Lake Elsinore	California	OF	45	169	41	47	6	3	13	37	2	.278
2002 Portland	P.C.	OF	85	315	46	89	12	1	10	43	0	.283
2003 Portland	P.C.	OF	37	136	19	36	7	0	7	23	0	.265
2003 San Diego	N.L.	OF	110	371	50	99	17	1	9	39	6	.267
2004 Portland	P.C.	OF-1B	74	291	52	96	19	1	22	70	3	.330
2004 San Diego	N.L.	OF	34	77	7	19	4	0	3	9	0	.247
2005 San Diego a	N.L.	OF-1B-3B	124	326	40	85	15	2	13	43	2	.261
2006 Norfolk	Int.	OF	3	11	2	4	1	0	0	3	0	.364
2006 New York-Pittsburgh b-c	N.L.	OF-1B	130	468	57	131	28	1	17	63	3	.280
2007 Pittsburgh	N.L.	OF	125	431	55	120	23	1	20	72	5	.278
2008 Pittsburgh	N.L.	OF	89	327	50	108	26	1	13	57	1	.330
2008 New York d	A.L.	OF-1B	59	228	26	61	11	0	12	40	1	.268
Major League Totals			7 Yrs.	672	2229	286	624	124	6	87	323	16	.280
Division Series													
2005 San Diego	N.L.	1B	2	3	0	1	0	0	0	2	0	.333

a Traded to New York Mets for outfielder Mike Cameron, November 18, 2005.
b On disabled list from May 30 to June 18, 2006.
c Traded to Pittsburgh Pirates for pitcher Oliver Perez and pitcher Roberto Hernandez, July 31, 2006.
d Traded to New York Yankees with pitcher Damaso Marte for outfielder Jose Tabata, pitcher Ross Ohlendorf, pitcher Jeff Karstens and pitcher Dan McCutchen, July 26, 2008.

NAPOLI, MICHAEL ANTHONY (MIKE)

Born, Hollywood, Florida, October 31, 1981.
Bats Right. Throws Right. Height, 6 feet. Weight, 205 pounds.

Year	Club	Lea	Pos	G	AB	R	H	2B	3B	HR	RBI	SB	Avg
2000 Butte	....	Pioneer	1B-C	10	26	3	6	2	0	0	3	1	.231
2001 Rancho Cucamonga	....	Calif.	C	7	20	3	4	0	0	1	4	0	.200
2001 Cedar Rapids	......	Midwest	C-1B	43	155	23	36	10	1	5	18	3	.232
2002 Cedar Rapids	......	Midwest	C-1B-3B	106	362	57	91	19	1	10	50	6	.251
2003 Rancho Cucamonga	....	Calif.	C-1B	47	165	28	44	10	1	4	26	5	.267
2004 Rancho Cucamonga	....	Calif.	C-1B-3B	132	482	94	136	29	4	29	118	9	.282
2005 Arkansas	....	Texas	C-1B	131	439	96	104	22	2	31	99	12	.237
2006 Salt Lake	....	P.C.	C-1B	21	78	12	19	6	0	3	10	1	.244
2006 Los Angeles	....	A.L.	C	99	268	47	61	13	0	16	42	2	.228
2007 Los Angeles a	....	A.L.	C	75	219	40	54	11	1	10	34	5	.247
2008 Rancho Cucamonga	....	Calif.	C	5	14	3	8	3	0	1	4	0	.571
2008 Los Angeles b	....	A.L.	C	78	227	39	62	9	1	20	49	7	.273
Major League Totals	....		3 Yrs.	252	714	126	177	33	2	46	125	14	.248
Division Series													
2007 Los Angeles	....	A.L.	C	3	6	0	1	0	0	0	0	0	.167
2008 Los Angeles	....	A.L.	C	4	12	3	3	0	0	2	4	0	.250
Division Series Totals	....			7	18	3	4	0	0	2	4	0	.222

a On disabled list from July 2 to July 18 and July 28 to September 1, 2007.
b On disabled list from July 6 to August 8, 2008.

NAVARRO, DIONER FAVIAU

Born, Caracas, Venezuela, February 9, 1984.
Bats Both. Throws Right. Height, 5 feet, 10 inches. Weight, 215 pounds.

Year	Club	Lea	Pos	G	AB	R	H	2B	3B	HR	RBI	SB	Avg
2001 Yankees	....	Gulf Coast	C	43	143	27	40	10	1	2	22	6	.280
2002 Tampa	....	Fla.St.	C	1	2	1	1	0	0	0	0	0	.500
2002 Greensboro	....	So.Atl.	C	92	328	41	78	12	2	8	36	1	.238
2003 Trenton	....	Eastern	C	58	208	28	71	15	0	4	37	2	.341
2003 Tampa	....	Fla.St.	C	52	197	28	59	16	4	3	28	1	.299
2004 Trenton	....	Eastern	C	70	255	32	69	14	1	3	29	1	.271
2004 Columbus	....	Int.	C	40	136	18	34	8	2	1	16	1	.250
2004 New York	....	A.L.	C	5	7	2	3	0	0	0	1	0	.429
2005 Las Vegas	....	P.C.	C	75	241	31	64	12	0	6	29	2	.266
2005 Los Angeles a-b	....	N.L.	C	50	176	21	48	9	0	3	14	0	.273
2006 Las Vegas	....	P.C.	C	11	40	3	7	2	0	0	2	1	.175
2006 Los Angeles c	....	N.L.	C	25	75	5	21	2	0	2	8	1	.280
2006 Tampa Bay d	....	A.L.	C	56	193	23	47	7	0	2	20	1	.244
2007 Tampa Bay	....	A.L.	C	119	388	46	88	19	2	9	44	3	.227
2008 Vero Beach	....	Fla.St.	C	4	10	4	4	1	0	1	4	1	.400
2008 Tampa Bay e	....	A.L.	C	120	427	43	126	27	0	7	54	0	.295
Major League Totals	....		5 Yrs.	375	1266	140	333	64	2	25	141	5	.263
Division Series													
2008 Tampa Bay	....	N.L.	C	4	15	1	6	3	0	0	3	0	.400
Championship Series													
2008 Tampa Bay	....	N.L.	C	7	26	1	5	0	0	0	2	0	.192
World Series Record													
2008 Tampa Bay	....	N.L.	C	5	17	2	6	1	0	0	0	0	.353

a Traded to Arizona Diamondbacks with pitcher Javier Vazquez, pitcher Brad Halsey and cash for pitcher Randy Johnson, January 11, 2005.
b Traded to Los Angeles Dodgers with pitcher Danny Muegge, pitcher Beltran Perez and pitcher William Juarez for outfielder Shawn Green, January 11, 2005.
c On disabled list from May 5 to June 15, 2006.
d Traded to Tampa Bay Devil Rays with pitcher Jae Seo and player to be named later for pitcher Mark Hendrickson, catcher Toby Hall and cash, June 27, 2006.
e On disabled list from April 5 to April 22, 2008.

NEWHAN, DAVID MATTHEW

Born, Fullerton, California, September 7, 1973.
Bats Left. Throws Right. Height, 5 feet, 10 inches. Weight, 180 pounds.

Year	Club	Lea	Pos	G	AB	R	H	2B	3B	HR	RBI	SB	Avg
1995 Sou Oregon	..	Northwest	OF	42	145	25	39	8	1	6	21	10	.269
1995 W Michigan	...	Midwest	OF	25	96	9	21	5	0	3	8	3	.219
1996 Modesto	....	Calif.	OF-2B	117	455	96	137	27	3	25	75	17	.301
1997 Visalia	....	Calif.	2B	67	241	52	67	15	2	7	48	9	.278

Year	Club	Lea	Pos	G	AB	R	H	2B	3B	HR	RBI	SB	Avg
1997 Huntsville a	...Southern		2B	57	212	40	67	13	2	5	35	5	.316
1998 Mobile	...Southern		2B-3B-SS	121	491	89	128	26	3	12	45	27	.261
1999 Las Vegas	...P.C.		2B-SS	98	374	49	107	25	1	14	49	22	.286
1999 San Diego	...N.L.		2B-1B-3B	32	43	7	6	1	0	2	6	2	.140
2000 Las Vegas	...P.C.		2B-OF	66	244	41	62	5	2	5	35	9	.254
2000 Scranton-WB	...Int.		2B	25	83	10	21	3	0	3	8	3	.253
2000 San Diego-Philadelphia b N.L.			2B-OF-3B	24	37	8	6	1	0	1	2	0	.162
2001 Philadelphia	...N.L.		2B	7	6	2	2	1	0	0	1	0	.333
2001 Scranton-WB c	...Int.		2B	13	55	4	6	1	0	0	2	0	.109
2002 d-e	...		INJURED—Did Not Play										
2003 Colorado Springs f-g P.C.			2B-1B-OF	72	244	43	85	17	2	3	28	6	.348
2004 Oklahoma	...P.C.		2B-3B-1B	61	262	57	86	21	6	9	38	10	.328
2004 Baltimore h	...A.L.		OF-3B-1B	95	373	66	116	15	7	8	54	11	.311
2005 Ottawa	...Int.		OF	11	41	11	15	4	0	1	8	2	.366
2005 Baltimore	...A.L.		OF-3B	96	218	31	44	9	0	5	21	9	.202
2006 Bowie	...Eastern		OF-2B	6	17	4	4	0	1	0	3	1	.235
2006 Baltimore i	...A.L.		OF-1B	39	131	14	33	4	0	4	18	4	.252
2007 New Orleans	...P.C.		2B-OF-1B-3B	44	173	27	60	12	3	7	30	7	.347
2007 New York j-k	...N.L.		OF-2B-3B	56	74	9	15	1	1	1	6	2	.203
2008 Round Rock	...P.C.		OF-2B-3B	60	198	39	61	14	2	9	36	8	.308
2008 Houston l	...N.L.		2B-OF	64	104	11	27	5	2	2	12	1	.260
Major League Totals			8 Yrs.	413	986	148	249	37	10	23	120	29	.253

a Traded by Oakland Athletics to San Diego Padres with pitcher Don Wengert for pitcher Doug Bochtler and infielder Jorge Velandia, November 26, 1997.
b Sent to Philadelphia Phillies as player to be named later for infielder Desi Relaford, August 7, 2000.
c On disabled list from April 14 to October 9, 2001.
d Filed for free agency, October 15, 2001. Signed with Los Angeles Dodgers organization, February 5, 2002.
e On minor league disabled list from April 4 to September 16, 2002.
f Filed for free agency, October 15, 2002. Signed with Colorado Rockies organization, May 8, 2003.
g Filed for free agency, October 15, 2003. Signed with Texas Rangers organization, November 10, 2003.
h Released by Texas Rangers June 15, 2004. Signed with Baltimore Orioles, June 18, 2004.
i On disabled list from April 18 to August 29, 2006.
j Not offered contract, December 13, 2006. Signed with New York Mets organization, January 9, 2007.
k Filed for free agency, November 5, 2007. Signed with Houston Astros organization, January 29, 2008.
l Filed for free agency, November 23, 2008.

NIEVES, WILBERT (WIL)

Born, San Juan, Puerto Rico, September 25, 1977.
Bats Right. Throws Right. Height, 5 feet, 11 inches. Weight, 190 pounds.

Year	Club	Lea	Pos	G	AB	R	H	2B	3B	HR	RBI	SB	Avg
1996 Padres	...Arizona		C-3B-OF	43	113	23	39	5	0	2	22	3	.345
1997 Clinton	...Midwest		C	18	55	6	12	1	1	1	7	2	.218
1997 Padres	...Arizona		DH-OF	8	27	2	8	2	0	0	2	1	.296
1998 Clinton	...Midwest		C	115	380	47	97	22	0	3	55	7	.255
1999 Rancho Cucamonga	...Calif.		C	120	427	58	140	26	2	7	61	2	.328
2000 Rancho Cucamonga	...Calif.		C	31	101	16	26	5	0	0	9	2	.257
2000 Las Vegas	...P.C.		PH	1	1	0	0	0	0	0	0	0	.000
2000 Mobile	...Southern		C-1B-2B	68	214	18	57	4	0	4	30	1	.266
2001 Mobile	...Southern		C	95	330	28	99	24	0	3	41	1	.300
2002 Portland	...P.C.		C-1B	70	237	24	73	20	2	7	29	0	.308
2002 San Diego a	...N.L.		C	28	72	2	13	3	1	0	3	1	.181
2003 Salt Lake	...P.C.		C-1B	102	361	48	102	16	2	4	38	1	.283
2004 Salt Lake	...P.C.		C-1B-3B	108	421	60	125	22	8	10	53	3	.297
2005 Columbus	...Int.		C	102	380	45	110	22	3	4	37	1	.289
2005 New York b	...A.L.		C	3	4	0	0	0	0	0	0	0	.000
2006 Columbus	...Int.		C	88	321	29	83	13	0	5	34	2	.259
2006 New York	...A.L.		C	6	6	0	0	0	0	0	0	0	.000
2007 New York	...A.L.		C-1B	26	61	6	10	4	0	0	8	0	.164
2007 Scranton-WB c	...Int.		C	27	90	5	23	1	2	1	8	1	.256
2008 Columbus	...Int.		C	9	25	3	6	1	0	0	2	1	.240
2008 Washington	...N.L.		C	68	176	15	46	9	1	1	20	0	.261
Major League Totals			5 Yrs.	131	319	23	69	16	2	1	31	1	.216

a Claimed on waivers by Anaheim Angels, December 18, 2002.
b Traded to New York Yankees for pitcher Bret Prinz, March 29, 2005.
c Filed for free agency, October 9, 2007. Signed with Washington Nationals organization, February 6, 2008.

NORTON, GREGORY BLAKEMOOR (GREG)

Born, San Leandro, California, July 6, 1972.
Bats Both. Throws Right. Height, 6 feet, 1 inch. Weight, 205 pounds.

Year	Club	Lea	Pos	G	AB	R	H	2B	3B	HR	RBI	SB	Avg
1993	White Sox	Gulf Coast	3B	3	9	1	2	0	0	0	2	0	.222
1993	Hickory	So.Atl.	3B-SS	71	254	36	62	12	2	4	36	0	.244
1994	South Bend	Midwest	3B	127	477	73	137	22	2	6	64	5	.287
1995	Birmingham	Southern	3B	133	469	65	117	23	2	6	60	19	.249
1996	Birmingham	Southern	SS	76	287	40	81	14	3	8	44	5	.282
1996	Nashville	A.A.	SS-3B	43	164	28	47	14	2	7	26	2	.287
1996	Chicago	A.L.	SS-3B	11	23	4	5	0	0	2	3	0	.217
1997	Nashville	A.A.	3B-SS-2B	114	414	82	114	27	1	26	76	3	.275
1997	Chicago	A.L.	3B	18	34	5	9	2	2	0	1	0	.265
1998	Chicago	A.L.	1B-3B-2B	105	299	38	71	17	2	9	36	3	.237
1999	Chicago	A.L.	3B-1B	132	436	62	111	26	0	16	50	4	.255
2000	Chicago	A.L.	3B-1B	71	201	25	49	6	1	6	28	1	.244
2000	Charlotte	Int.	3B-1B-SS	29	97	18	28	4	0	5	17	1	.289
2001	Colorado a	N.L.	OF-3B-1B	117	225	30	60	13	2	13	40	1	.267
2002	Colorado Springs	P.C.	1B-3B	3	12	2	1	0	0	0	0	0	.083
2002	Colorado b	N.L.	3B-1B-OF	113	168	19	37	8	1	7	37	2	.220
2003	Colorado	N.L.	3B-1B-OF	114	179	19	47	15	0	6	31	2	.263
2004	Detroit	A.L.	3B-1B-OF	41	86	9	15	1	0	2	2	0	.174
2004	Toledo c-d-e	Int.	3B-1B	53	184	26	38	6	1	4	16	1	.207
2005	Charlotte f	Int.	3B-1B	90	330	57	94	19	1	17	56	0	.285
2006	Durham	Int.	1B	3	9	0	1	0	0	0	1	0	.111
2006	Tampa Bay g	A.L.	OF-1B	98	294	47	87	15	0	17	45	1	.296
2007	Montgomery	Southern	1B	7	25	2	7	2	0	0	4	0	.280
2007	Tampa Bay h-i	A.L.	DH-OF-1B	75	202	25	49	9	0	4	23	1	.243
2008	Tacoma	P.C.	1B-OF	8	22	3	9	2	0	0	3	1	.409
2008	Seattle	A.L.	1B-OF	6	16	2	7	2	0	0	4	0	.438
2008	Atlanta j-k	N.L.	OF-1B	111	171	27	42	10	0	7	31	0	.246
Major League Totals			12 Yrs.	1012	2334	312	589	124	8	89	331	15	.252

a Not offered contract, December 21, 2000. Signed with Colorado Rockies, January 5, 2001.
b On disabled list from June 30 to July 18, 2002.
c Filed for free agency, October 28, 2003. Signed with Detroit Tigers organization, January 14, 2004.
d On disabled list from June 18 to July 25, 2004.
e Filed for free agency, October 4, 2004. Signed with Colorado Rockies organization, December 21, 2004.
f Released by Colorado Rockies, March 29, 2005. Signed with Chicago White Sox organization, April 24, 2005.
g Filed for free agency, October 15, 2005. Signed with Tampa Bay Devil Rays organization, January 11, 2006.
h On disabled list from March 31 to May 17, 2007.
i Filed for free agency, November 9, 2007. Signed with Seattle Mariners organization, February 13, 2008.
j Sold to Atlanta Braves, May 5, 2008.
k Filed for free agency, October 30, 2008, re-signed with Atlanta Braves, December 19, 2008.

OJEDA, OCTAVIO AUGIE (AUGIE)

Born, Los Angeles, California, December 20, 1974.
Bats Both. Throws Right. Height, 5 feet, 9 inches. Weight, 165 pounds.

Year	Club	Lea	Pos	G	AB	R	H	2B	3B	HR	RBI	SB	Avg
1997	Frederick	Carolina	SS	34	128	25	44	11	1	1	20	2	.344
1997	Bowie	Eastern	SS	58	204	33	60	9	1	2	23	7	.294
1997	Rochester	Int.	SS	15	47	5	11	3	1	0	6	1	.234
1998	Orioles	Gulf Coast	SS	4	15	6	6	2	0	0	2	3	.400
1998	Bowie	Eastern	SS-3B	73	254	36	65	10	2	1	19	0	.256
1999	Bowie	Eastern	SS-3B	134	460	73	123	18	4	10	60	6	.267
1999	Rochester a	Int.	SS	1	1	1	0	0	0	0	0	0	.000
2000	Iowa	P.C.	SS-2B	113	396	56	111	23	2	8	43	16	.280
2000	Chicago	N.L.	SS-2B	28	77	10	17	3	1	2	8	0	.221
2001	Chicago	N.L.	3B-SS-2B	78	144	16	29	5	1	1	12	1	.201
2002	Chicago	N.L.	SS-2B-3B	30	70	4	13	4	0	0	4	1	.186
2002	Iowa	P.C.	SS-3B	73	291	54	67	20	4	1	27	5	.230
2003	Iowa	P.C.	SS-2B-3B	106	283	42	71	10	3	2	23	4	.251
2003	Chicago b-c	N.L.	SS-2B-3B	12	25	2	3	0	0	0	0	0	.120
2004	Rochester	Int.	SS-3B-2B	89	327	49	80	19	0	2	21	7	.245
2004	Minnesota	A.L.	2B-SS-3B	30	59	16	20	1	0	2	7	1	.339
2005	Rochester	Int.	SS-2B-3B	105	313	42	70	16	0	3	33	3	.224
2006	Iowa d-e	P.C.	SS	115	306	40	76	11	1	3	25	4	.248
2007	Tucson	P.C.	SS-2B	32	99	20	32	8	0	1	7	1	.323
2007	Arizona	N.L.	2B-SS-3B-P	57	113	16	31	2	1	1	12	1	.274
2008	Arizona	N.L.	2B-3B-SS	105	231	27	56	9	2	0	17	0	.242
Major League Totals			7 Yrs.	340	719	91	169	24	6	6	60	4	.235

Year	Club	Lea	Pos	G	AB	R	H	2B	3B	HR	RBI	SB	Avg
Division Series													
2007 Arizona...........N.L.			2B	3	9	1	4	1	0	0	1	0	.444
Championship Series													
2007 Arizona...........N.L.			2B	4	12	0	2	0	0	0	0	0	.167

a Traded by Baltimore Orioles to Chicago Cubs for pitcher Richard Negrette, December 13, 1999.
b Claimed on waivers by Minnesota Twins, November 25, 2003.
c Not offered contract, December 21, 2003, re-signed with Minnesota Twins, December 22, 2003.
d Filed for free agency, October 3, 2005. Signed with Chicago Cubs organization, January 3, 2006.
e Filed for free agency, October 14, 2006. Signed with Arizona Diamondbacks organization, November 20, 2006.

OLIVO (PENA), MIGUEL EDUARDO

Born, Villa Vasquez, Dominican Republic, July 15, 1978.
Bats Right. Throws Right. Height, 6 feet. Weight, 220 pounds.

Year	Club	Lea	Pos	G	AB	R	H	2B	3B	HR	RBI	SB	Avg
1997 Oakland-East	Dominican		C	63	221	37	60	11	4	6	57	6	.271
1998 Athletics..........	Arizona		C-OF	46	164	30	51	11	3	2	23	2	.311
1999 Modesto........	California		C	73	243	46	74	13	6	9	42	4	.305
2000 Modesto........	California		C	58	227	40	64	11	5	5	35	5	.282
2000 Midland a-b-c.......	Texas		C	19	59	8	14	2	0	1	9	0	.237
2001 Birmingham d	Southern		C	93	316	45	82	23	1	14	55	6	.259
2002 Birmingham	Southern		C	106	359	51	110	24	10	6	49	29	.306
2002 Chicago e	A.L.		C	6	19	2	4	1	0	1	5	0	.211
2003 Chicago	A.L.		C	114	317	37	75	19	1	6	27	6	.237
2004 Everett	Northwest		C	2	6	0	0	0	0	0	0	0	.000
2004 Chicago-Seattle f-g	A.L.		C	96	301	46	70	15	4	13	40	7	.233
2005 Tacoma	P.C.		C	24	90	13	21	4	1	3	21	8	.233
2005 Seattle	A.L.		C	54	152	14	23	4	0	5	18	1	.151
2005 San Diego h	N.L.		C	37	115	16	35	7	1	4	16	6	.304
2006 Florida i	N.L.		C-1B	127	430	52	113	22	3	16	58	2	.263
2007 Florida j	N.L.		C	122	452	43	107	20	4	16	60	3	.237
2008 Kansas City	A.L.		C	84	306	29	78	22	0	12	41	7	.255
Major League Totals			7 Yrs.	640	2092	239	505	110	13	73	265	32	.241
Division Series													
2005 San Diego	N.L.		PH	1	1	0	0	0	0	0	0	0	.000

a On disabled list from August 8 to September 29, 2000.
b Chicago White Sox traded pitcher Chad Bradford to Oakland Athletics for player to be named later, December 7, 2000.
c Sent by Oakland Athletics to Chicago White Sox to complete trade, December 12, 2000.
d On disabled list from April 22 to May 2, 2001.
e On disabled list from June 4 to 11, 2002.
f Traded to Seattle Mariners with outfielder Jeremy Reed and infielder Michael Morse for pitcher Freddy Garcia, catcher Ben Davis and cash, June 27, 2004.
g On disabled list from June 30 to July 15, 2004.
h Traded to San Diego Padres for catcher Miguel Ojeda and pitcher Nathaniel Mateo, July 31, 2005.
i Filed for free agency, December 21, 2005. Signed with Florida Marlins, January 3, 2006.
j Not offered contract, December 12, 2007. Signed with Kansas City Royals, December 27, 2007.

ORDONEZ, MAGGLIO

Born, Caracas, Venezuela, January 28, 1974.
Bats Right. Throws Right. Height, 6 feet. Weight, 215 pounds.

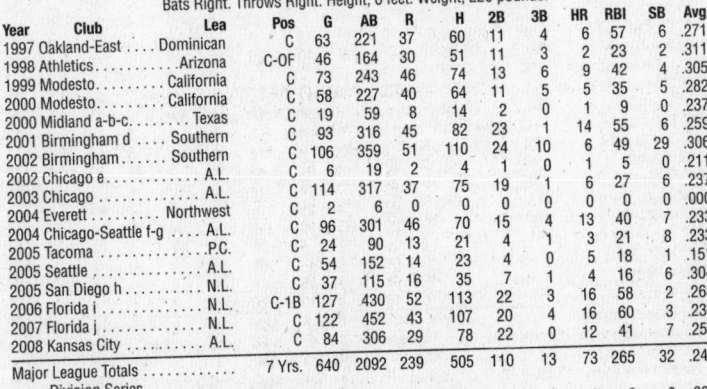

Year	Club	Lea	Pos	G	AB	R	H	2B	3B	HR	RBI	SB	Avg
1993 Hickory...........	So. Atl.		OF	84	273	32	59	14	4	3	20	5	.216
1994 Hickory...........	So. Atl.		OF	132	490	86	144	24	5	11	69	16	.294
1995 Pr William	Carolina		OF	131	487	61	116	24	2	12	65	11	.238
1996 Birmingham	Southern		OF	130	479	66	126	41	0	18	67	9	.263
1997 Nashville	A.A.		OF	135	523	65	172	29	3	14	90	14	.329
1997 Chicago	A.L.		OF	21	69	12	22	6	0	4	11	1	.319
1998 Chicago	A.L.		OF	145	535	70	151	25	2	14	65	9	.282
1999 Chicago	A.L.		OF	157	624	100	188	34	3	30	117	13	.301
2000 Chicago	A.L.		OF	153	588	102	185	34	3	32	126	18	.315
2001 Chicago	A.L.		OF	160	593	97	181	40	1	31	113	25	.305
2002 Chicago	A.L.		OF	153	590	116	189	47	1	38	135	7	.320
2003 Chicago	A.L.		OF	160	606	95	192	46	3	29	99	9	.317
2004 Chicago a-b.........	A.L.		OF	52	202	32	59	8	2	9	37	0	.292
2005 Toledo	Int.		OF	4	14	3	3	1	0	1	2	0	.214
2005 Detroit c...........	A.L.		OF	82	305	38	92	17	0	8	46	0	.302
2006 Detroit	A.L.		OF	155	593	82	177	32	1	24	104	1	.298
2007 Detroit	A.L.		OF	157	595	117	216	*54	0	28	139	4	*.363

Year Club	Lea	Pos	G	AB	R	H	2B	3B	HR	RBI	SB	Avg
2008 West Michigan.....	Midwest	DH	1	4	1	1	0	0	0	0	0	.250
2008 Detroit d...........	A.L.	OF	146	561	72	178	32	2	21	103	1	.317
Major League Totals	12 Yrs.		1541	5861	933	1830	375	18	268	1095	88	.312
Division Series												
2000 Chicago	A.L.	OF	3	11	0	2	0	1	0	1	1	.182
2006 Detroit	A.L.	OF	4	15	3	4	1	0	1	2	0	.267
Division Series Totals			7	26	3	6	1	1	1	3	1	.231
Championship Series												
2006 Detroit	A.L.	OF	4	17	3	4	0	0	2	6	0	.235
World Series Record												
2006 Detroit	A.L.	OF	5	19	2	2	0	0	0	0	0	.105

a On disabled list from May 26 to July 8 and from July 22 to October 12, 2004.
b Filed for free agency, October 28, 2004. Signed with Detroit Tigers organization, February 7, 2005.
c On disabled list from April 13 to July 1, 2005.
d On disabled list from June 29 to July 17, 2008.

ORTIZ (ARIAS), DAVID AMERICO

Born, Santo Domingo, Dominican Republic, November 18, 1975.
Bats Left. Throws Left. Height, 6 feet, 4 inches. Weight, 230 pounds.

Year Club	Lea	Pos	G	AB	R	H	2B	3B	HR	RBI	SB	Avg
1993 Seattle	Dominican	1B	61	201	37	53	17	1	7	31	1	.264
1994 Mariners..........	Arizona	1B	53	167	14	41	10	1	2	20	1	.246
1995 Mariners..........	Arizona	1B	48	184	30	61	18	4	4	37	2	.332
1996 Wisconsin a......	Midwest	1B	129	485	89	156	34	2	18	93	3	.322
1997 Salt Lake	P.C.	1B	10	42	5	9	1	0	4	10	0	.214
1997 New Britain	Eastern	DH-1B	69	258	40	83	22	2	18	56	2	.322
1997 Ft. Myers	Fla.St.	1B	61	239	45	79	15	0	13	58	2	.331
1997 Minnesota	A.L.	1B	15	49	10	16	3	0	1	6	0	.327
1998 Salt Lake	P.C.	1B	11	37	5	9	3	0	2	6	0	.243
1998 Minnesota b.........	A.L.	1B	86	278	47	77	20	0	9	46	1	.277
1999 Salt Lake	P.C.	1B	130	476	85	150	35	3	30	110	2	.315
1999 Minnesota	A.L.	1B	10	20	1	0	0	0	0	0	0	.000
2000 Minnesota	A.L.	DH-1B	130	415	59	117	36	1	10	63	1	.282
2001 Twins	Gulf Coast	DH	4	10	3	4	0	0	1	1	1	.400
2001 Fort Myers	Fla.St.	1B	1	3	0	0	0	0	0	0	0	.000
2001 New Britain	Eastern	1B	9	37	3	9	4	0	0	1	0	.243
2001 Minnesota c..........	A.L.	DH-1B	89	303	46	71	17	1	18	48	1	.234
2002 Minnesota d-e.......	A.L.	DH-1B	125	412	52	112	32	1	20	75	1	.272
2003 Boston	A.L.	DH-1B	128	448	79	129	39	2	31	101	0	.288
2004 Boston	A.L.	DH-1B	150	582	94	175	47	3	41	139	0	.301
2005 Boston	A.L.	DH-1B	159	601	119	180	40	1	47	*148	1	.300
2006 Boston	A.L.	DH-1B	151	558	115	160	29	2	*54	*137	1	.287
2007 Boston	A.L.	DH-1B	149	549	116	182	52	1	35	117	3	.332
2008 Portland	Eastern	DH	3	8	2	2	0	0	0	1	0	.250
2008 Pawtucket	Int.	DH	3	9	4	3	0	0	3	5	0	.333
2008 Boston f.............	A.L.	DH	109	416	74	110	30	1	23	89	1	.264
Major League Totals	12 Yrs.		1301	4631	812	1329	345	13	289	969	10	.287
Division Series												
2002 Minnesota	A.L.	DH	4	13	0	3	2	0	0	2	0	.231
2003 Boston	A.L.	DH	5	21	0	2	1	0	0	2	0	.095
2004 Boston	A.L.	DH	3	11	4	6	2	0	1	4	0	.545
2005 Boston	A.L.	DH	3	12	2	4	2	0	1	1	0	.333
2007 Boston	A.L.	DH	3	7	5	5	0	0	2	3	0	.714
2008 Boston	A.L.	DH	4	17	1	4	1	0	0	1	0	.235
Division Series Totals			22	81	12	24	8	0	4	13	0	.296
Championship Series												
2002 Minnesota	A.L.	DH	5	16	0	5	1	0	0	2	0	.313
2003 Boston	A.L.	DH	7	26	4	7	1	0	2	6	0	.269
2004 Boston	A.L.	DH	7	31	6	12	0	1	3	11	0	.387
2007 Boston	A.L.	DH	7	24	7	7	3	0	1	3	0	.292
2008 Boston	A.L.	DH	7	26	3	4	1	1	1	4	0	.154
Championship Series Totals			33	123	20	35	6	2	7	26	0	.285
World Series Record												
2004 Boston	A.L.	1B-DH	4	13	3	4	1	0	1	4	0	.308
2007 Boston	A.L.	1B-DH	4	15	4	5	3	0	0	4	0	.333
World Series Totals.............			8	28	7	9	4	0	1	8	0	.321

a Sent to Minnesota Twins by Seattle Mariners to complete trade for infielder Dave Hollins, September 13, 1996.

b On disabled list from May 10 to July 9, 1998.
c On disabled list from May 5 to July 21, 2001.
d On disabled list from April 20 to May 13, 2002.
e Released by Minnesota Twins, December 16, 2002. Signed with Boston Red Sox, January 22, 2003.
f On disabled list from June 1 to July 25, 2008.

OVERBAY, LYLE STEFAN

Born, Centralia, Washington, January 28, 1977.
Bats Left. Throws Left. Height, 6 feet, 2 inches. Weight, 235 pounds.

Year Club	Lea	Pos	G	AB	R	H	2B	3B	HR	RBI	SB	Avg
1999 Missoula	Pioneer	1B	75	306	66	105	25	7	12	101	10	.343
2000 South Bend	Midwest	1B	71	259	47	86	19	3	6	47	9	.332
2000 El Paso	Texas	1B	62	244	43	86	16	2	8	49	3	.352
2001 El Paso	Texas	1B-OF	138	532	82	187	49	3	13	100	5	.352
2001 Arizona	N.L.	PH	2	2	0	1	0	0	0	0	0	.500
2002 Tucson	P.C.	1B	134	525	83	180	40	0	19	109	0	.343
2002 Arizona	N.L.	PH	10	10	0	1	0	0	0	1	0	.100
2003 Tucson	P.C.	1B	35	119	24	34	11	0	4	16	0	.286
2003 Arizona a	N.L.	1B	86	254	23	70	20	0	4	28	1	.276
2004 Milwaukee	N.L.	1B	159	579	83	174	*53	1	16	87	2	.301
2005 Milwaukee b	N.L.	1B	158	537	80	148	34	1	19	72	1	.276
2006 Toronto	A.L.	1B	157	581	82	181	46	1	22	92	5	.312
2007 New Hampshire	Eastern	1B	4	15	2	4	1	0	1	5	0	.267
2007 Toronto c	A.L.	1B	122	425	49	102	30	2	10	44	2	.240
2008 Toronto	A.L.	1B	158	544	74	147	32	2	15	69	1	.270
Major League Totals	8 Yrs.		852	2932	391	824	215	7	86	393	12	.281

a Traded to Milwaukee Brewers with infielder Junior Spivey, infielder Craig Counsell, catcher Chad Moeller, pitcher Chris Capuano and pitcher Jorge De La Rosa for infielder Richie Sexson, pitcher Shane Nance and player to be named later, December 1, 2003. Arizona Diamondbacks received outfielder Gary Varner to complete trade, December 15, 2003.
b Traded to Toronto Blue Jays with pitcher Ty Taubenheim for pitcher Dave Bush, outfielder Gabe Gross and pitcher Zach Jackson, December 7, 2005.
c On disabled list from June 4 to July 12, 2007.

OZUNA, PABLO JOSE

Born, Santo Domingo, Dominican Republic, August 25, 1974.
Bats Right. Throws Right. Height, 6 feet. Weight, 160 pounds.

Year Club	Lea	Pos	G	AB	R	H	2B	3B	HR	RBI	SB	Avg
1996 St. Louis	Dominican	SS	74	295	57	107	12	4	6	60	18	.363
1997 Johnson Cty	Appal.	SS	56	232	40	75	13	1	5	24	23	.323
1998 Peoria a	Midwest	SS	133	538	122	192	27	10	9	62	62	.357
1999 Portland	Eastern	SS	117	502	62	141	25	7	7	46	31	.281
2000 Portland	Eastern	2B	118	464	74	143	25	6	7	59	35	.308
2000 Florida	N.L.	2B	14	24	2	8	1	0	0	0	1	.333
2001				INJURED—Did Not Play								
2002 Florida	N.L.	2B-OF	34	47	4	13	2	2	0	3	1	.277
2002 Calgary b-c	P.C.	2B-OF	77	261	37	85	16	1	7	33	16	.326
2003 Visalia	Calif.	2B-SS	2	8	1	5	0	0	0	1	1	.625
2003 Tulsa	Texas	2B-SS-3B	12	59	4	15	3	0	0	4	4	.254
2003 Colorado Springs	P.C.	2B-OF-SS-3B	56	219	30	59	13	7	1	17	12	.269
2003 Colorado d	N.L.	2B-OF-SS	17	40	5	8	1	0	0	2	3	.200
2004 Scranton-WB e-f	Int.	2B-SS-OF	126	472	77	145	27	3	6	76	31	.307
2005 Chicago g	A.L.	3B-SS-OF-2B	70	203	27	56	7	2	0	11	14	.276
2006 Chicago	A.L.	OF-3B-2B	79	189	25	62	12	2	2	17	6	.328
2007 Chicago h	A.L.	3B-OF-2B-SS	27	78	9	19	3	0	0	3	3	.244
2008 Chicago	A.L.	3B-2B	32	64	5	18	3	0	0	6	0	.281
2008 Los Angeles i-j	N.L.	2B-SS-OF-3B	36	32	6	7	0	1	1	3	1	.219
Major League Totals	7 Yrs.		309	677	83	191	29	7	3	45	29	.282
Championship Series												
2005 Chicago	A.L.	PH	2	0	1	0	0	0	0	0	1	.000
2008 Los Angeles	N.L.	PH	1	1	0	0	0	0	0	0	0	.000
Championship Series Totals			3	1	1	0	0	0	0	0	1	.000

a Traded by St. Louis Cardinals to Florida Marlins with pitcher Braden Looper and pitcher Armando Almanza for infielder Edgar Renteria, December 14, 1998.
b On disabled list from March 23 to November 13, 2001.
c Traded to Colorado Rockies with outfielder Preston Wilson, catcher Charles Johnson and pitcher Vic Darensbourg for pitcher Mike Hampton and outfielder Juan Pierre, November 16, 2002.
d On disabled list from March 26 to June 6, 2003.
e Released by Colorado Rockies, December 15, 2003. Signed with Detroit Tigers organization, January 9, 2004.

f Sold to Philadelphia Phillies, March 27, 2004.
g Filed for free agency, October 15, 2004. Signed with Chicago White Sox organization, January 19, 2005.
h On disabled list from May 28 to October 26, 2007.
i Released by Chicago White Sox, July 18, 2008. Signed with Los Angeles Dodgers, July 20, 2008.
j Filed for free agency, November 12, 2008. Signed with Philadelphia Phillies organization, January 15, 2009.

PAGAN, ANGEL ANTHONY

Born, Rio Piedras, Puerto Rico, July 2, 1981.
Bats Both. Throws Right. Height, 6 feet, 1 inch. Weight, 195 pounds.

Year	Club	Lea	Pos	G	AB	R	H	2B	3B	HR	RBI	SB	Avg
2000 Kingsport	Appal.	OF	19	72	13	26	5	1	0	8	6	.361
2001 Brooklyn	N.Y.-Penn.	OF	62	238	46	75	10	2	0	15	30	.315
2001 Columbia	So.Atl.	OF	15	57	4	17	1	1	0	5	3	.298
2002 St. Lucie	Fla.St.	OF	16	67	12	23	2	1	1	7	10	.343
2002 Columbia	So.Atl.	OF	108	458	79	128	14	5	1	36	52	.279
2003 St. Lucie	Fla.St.	OF	113	441	64	110	15	5	1	33	35	.249
2004 Binghamton	Eastern	OF	112	448	71	129	25	8	4	63	29	.288
2004 Norfolk	Int.	OF	12	45	13	13	3	3	0	1	4	.289
2005 Norfolk	Int.	OF	129	516	69	140	20	10	8	40	27	.271
2006 Cubs	Arizona	OF	3	9	1	1	0	0	0	0	1	.111
2006 Iowa	P.C.	OF	4	15	2	4	1	0	0	0	1	.267
2006 Chicago a-b	N.L.	OF	77	170	28	42	6	2	5	18	4	.247
2007 Iowa	P.C.	OF	33	116	18	29	4	3	3	9	6	.250
2007 Chicago c-d	N.L.	OF	71	148	21	39	10	2	4	21	4	.264
2008 Mets	Gulf Coast	OF	2	5	1	3	1	0	0	0	4	.600
2008 Brooklyn	N.Y.-Penn.	OF	4	13	0	4	0	0	0	1	3	.308
2008 St. Lucie	Fla.St.	OF	1	4	1	0	0	0	0	0	0	.000
2008 New York e	N.L.	OF	31	91	12	25	7	1	0	13	4	.275
Major League Totals			3 Yrs.	179	409	61	106	23	5	9	52	12	.259

a Sold to Chicago by New York Mets, January 25, 2006.
b On disabled list from April 16 to June 30, 2006.
c On disabled list from August 8 to November 1, 2007.
d Traded to New York Mets for pitcher Ryan Meyers and outfielder Corey Coles, January 5, 2008.
e On disabled list from May 13 to November 3, 2008.

PATTERSON, DONALD COREY (COREY)

Born, Atlanta, Georgia, August 13, 1979.
Bats Left. Throws Right. Height, 5 feet, 9 inches. Weight, 175 pounds.

Year	Club	Lea	Pos	G	AB	R	H	2B	3B	HR	RBI	SB	Avg
1999 Lansing	Midwest	OF	112	475	94	152	35	17	20	79	33	.320
2000 West Tenn	Southern	OF	118	444	73	116	26	5	22	82	27	.261
2000 Chicago	N.L.	OF	11	42	9	7	1	0	2	2	1	.167
2001 Iowa	P.C.	OF	89	367	63	93	22	3	7	32	19	.253
2001 Chicago	N.L.	OF	59	131	26	29	3	0	4	14	4	.221
2002 Chicago	N.L.	OF	153	592	71	150	30	5	14	54	18	.253
2003 Chicago a	N.L.	OF	83	329	49	98	17	7	13	55	16	.298
2004 Chicago	N.L.	OF	157	631	91	168	33	6	24	72	32	.266
2005 Iowa	P.C.	OF	24	91	16	27	4	0	5	12	6	.297
2005 Chicago b	N.L.	OF	126	451	47	97	15	3	13	34	15	.215
2006 Baltimore	A.L.	OF	135	463	75	128	19	5	16	53	45	.276
2007 Baltimore c	A.L.	OF	132	461	65	124	26	2	8	45	37	.269
2008 Louisville	Int.	OF	5	22	3	9	2	0	0	1	4	.409
2008 Cincinnati d	N.L.	OF	135	366	46	75	17	2	10	34	14	.205
Major League Totals			9 Yrs.	991	3466	479	876	161	30	104	363	182	.253

a On disabled list from July 7 to October 31, 2003.
b Traded to Baltimore Orioles for infielder Nate Spears and pitcher Carlos Perez, January 9, 2006.
c Filed for free agency, October 31, 2007. Signed with Cincinnati Reds organization, March 3, 2008.
d Filed for free agency, November 3, 2008. Signed with Washington Nationals organization, December 18, 2008.

PAYTON, JASON LEE (JAY)

Born, Zanesville, Ohio, November 22, 1972.
Bats Right. Throws Right. Height, 5 feet, 10 inches. Weight, 205 pounds.

Year	Club	Lea	Pos	G	AB	R	H	2B	3B	HR	RBI	SB	Avg
1994 Pittsfield	N.Y.-Penn.	OF	58	219	47	80	16	2	3	37	10	.365
1994 Binghamton	Eastern	OF	8	25	3	7	1	0	0	1	1	.280
1995 Binghamton	Eastern	OF	85	357	59	123	20	3	14	54	16	.345
1995 Norfolk	Int.	OF	50	196	33	47	11	4	4	30	11	.240

Year Club Lea	Pos	G	AB	R	H	2B	3B	HR	RBI	SB	Avg
1996 Mets..........Gulf Coast	DH	3	13	3	5	1	0	1	2	1	.385
1996 Binghamton.......Eastern	DH	4	10	0	2	0	0	0	2	0	.200
1996 St. Lucie.......Fla.St.	DH	9	26	4	8	2	0	0	1	2	.308
1996 Norfolk a-b..........Int.	DH-OF	55	153	30	47	6	3	6	26	10	.307
1997......................			INJURED—Did Not Play								
1998 St. Lucie.......Fla.St.	OF	3	7	0	1	0	0	0	0	0	.143
1998 Norfolk.......Int.	OF-1B	82	322	45	84	14	4	8	30	12	.261
1998 New York c.......N.L.	OF	15	22	2	7	1	0	0	0	0	.318
1999 Norfolk.......Int.	OF	38	144	27	56	13	2	8	35	2	.389
1999 St. Lucie.......Fla.St.	OF	7	26	3	9	1	1	0	3	0	.346
1999 New York d-e.......N.L.	OF	13	8	1	2	1	0	0	1	1	.250
2000 New York.......N.L.	OF	149	488	63	142	23	1	17	62	5	.291
2001 St. Lucie.......Fla.St.	OF	4	16	7	6	3	0	0	0	0	.375
2001 New York f.......N.L.	OF	104	361	44	92	16	1	8	34	4	.255
2002 New York-Colorado g...N.L.	OF	134	445	69	135	20	7	16	59	7	.303
2003 Colorado h.......N.L.	OF	157	600	93	181	32	5	28	89	6	.302
2004 San Diego i.......N.L.	OF	143	458	57	119	17	4	8	55	2	.260
2005 Boston-Oakland j.......A.L.	OF	124	408	62	109	16	1	18	63	0	.267
2006 Oakland k.......A.L.	OF	142	557	78	165	32	3	10	59	8	.296
2007 Norfolk.......Int.	OF	2	8	3	2	1	0	0	0	0	.250
2007 Baltimore l.......A.L.	OF	131	434	48	111	21	5	7	58	5	.256
2008 Baltimore m.......A.L.	OF	127	338	41	82	10	2	7	41	8	.243
Major League Totals	11 Yrs.	1239	4119	558	1145	189	29	119	521	46	.278
Division Series											
2000 New York.......N.L.	OF	4	17	1	3	0	0	0	2	1	.176
2006 Oakland.......A.L.	OF	3	12	3	4	0	0	0	0	0	.333
Division Series Totals		7	29	4	7	0	0	0	2	1	.241
Championship Series											
2000 New York.......N.L.	OF	5	19	1	3	0	0	1	3	0	.158
2006 Oakland.......A.L.	OF	4	14	1	4	2	0	1	2	0	.286
Championship Series Totals		9	33	2	7	2	0	2	5	0	.212
World Series Record											
2000 New York.......N.L.	OF	5	21	3	7	0	0	1	3	0	.333

a On disabled list from April 29 to July 3, 1996.
b On disabled list from April 3 to September 1, 1997.
c On disabled list from May 27 to June 15 and June 24 to July 20, 1998.
d On disabled list from March 21 to June 8, 1999.
e On disabled list from July 10 to August 19, 1999.
f On disabled list from May 8 to June 26, 2001.
g Traded to Colorado Rockies with outfielder Robert Stratton and pitcher Mark Corey for pitcher John Thomson and outfielder Mark Little, July 31, 2002.
h Not offered contract, December 21, 2003. Signed with San Diego Padres, January 13, 2004.
i Traded to Boston Red Sox with infielder Ramon Vazquez, pitcher David Pauley and cash for outfielder Dave Roberts, December 20, 2004.
j Traded to Oakland Athletics for pitcher Chad Bradford, July 13, 2005.
k Filed for free agency, October 29, 2006. Signed with Baltimore Orioles, December 11, 2006.
l On disabled list from March 27 to April 20, 2007.
m Filed for free agency, October 30, 2008.

PEDROIA, DUSTIN LUIS

Born, Woodland, California, August 17, 1983.
Bats Right. Throws Right. Height, 5 feet, 9 inches. Weight, 180 pounds.

Year Club Lea	Pos	G	AB	R	H	2B	3B	HR	RBI	SB	Avg
2004 Sarasota........Fla.St.	SS	30	107	23	36	8	3	2	14	0	.336
2004 Augusta.......So.Atl.	SS	12	50	11	20	5	0	1	5	2	.400
2005 Portland.......Eastern	2B-SS	66	256	39	83	19	2	8	40	7	.324
2005 Pawtucket.......Int.	2B-SS	51	204	39	52	9	1	5	24	1	.255
2006 Pawtucket.......Int.	SS-2B-3B	111	423	55	129	30	3	5	50	1	.305
2006 Boston.......A.L.	2B-SS	31	89	5	17	4	0	2	7	0	.191
2007 Boston a.......A.L.	2B	139	520	86	165	39	1	8	50	7	.317
2008 Boston b.......A.L.	2B	157	653	*118	*213	*54	2	17	83	20	.326
Major League Totals	3 Yrs.	327	1262	209	395	97	3	27	140	27	.313
Division Series											
2007 Boston..........A.L.	2B	3	13	2	2	2	0	0	1	0	.154
2008 Boston..........A.L.	2B	4	17	0	1	1	0	0	1	0	.059
Division Series Totals		7	30	2	3	3	0	0	2	0	.100
Championship Series											
2007 Boston..........A.L.	2B	7	29	8	10	3	0	1	5	0	.345

Year Club	Lea	Pos	G	AB	R	H	2B	3B	HR	RBI	SB	Avg
2008 Boston .... A.L.		2B	7	26	9	9	1	0	3	5	2	.346
Championship Series Totals			14	55	17	19	4	0	4	10	2	.345
World Series Record												
2007 Boston .... A.L.		2B	4	18	2	5	1	0	1	4	0	.278

a Selected Rookie of the Year in American League for 2007.
b Selected Most Valuable Player in American League for 2008.

PENA, CARLOS FELIPE

Born, Santo Domingo, Dominican Republic, May 17, 1978.
Bats Left. Throws Left. Height, 6 feet, 2 inches. Weight, 210 pounds.

Year Club	Lea	Pos	G	AB	R	H	2B	3B	HR	RBI	SB	Avg
1998 Rangers	Gulf Coast	1B	2	5	1	2	0	0	0	0	1	.400
1998 Savannah	So.Atl.	1B-OF	30	117	22	38	14	0	6	20	3	.325
1998 Charlotte	Fla.St.	1B	7	22	1	6	1	0	0	3	0	.273
1999 Charlotte	Fla.St.	1B	136	501	85	128	31	8	18	103	2	.255
2000 Tulsa	Texas	1B	138	529	117	158	36	2	28	105	12	.299
2001 Oklahoma.............	P.C.	1B	119	431	71	124	38	3	23	74	11	.288
2001 Texas	A.L.	1B	22	62	6	16	4	1	3	12	0	.258
2002 Sacramento	P.C.	1B	44	175	30	42	10	1	10	33	3	.240
2002 Oakland-Detroit a-b ...	A.L.	1B	115	397	46	96	17	4	19	52	2	.242
2003 Toledo	Int.	1B	8	30	4	10	4	1	0	5	0	.333
2003 Detroit c.............	A.L.	1B	131	452	51	112	21	6	18	50	4	.248
2004 Detroit	A.L.	1B	142	481	89	116	22	4	27	82	7	.241
2005 Toledo	Int.	1B	71	257	43	80	17	1	12	45	3	.311
2005 Detroit	A.L.	1B	79	260	37	61	9	0	18	44	0	.235
2006 Columbus.............	Int.	1B	105	381	65	99	17	0	19	66	4	.260
2006 Pawtucket	Int.	1B	11	37	7	17	3	0	4	8	0	.459
2006 Boston d-e-f.........	A.L.	1B-OF	18	33	3	9	2	0	1	3	0	.273
2007 Tampa Bay	A.L.	1B	148	490	99	138	29	1	46	121	1	.282
2008 Vero Beach.........	Fla.St.	DH	1	4	0	0	0	0	0	1	0	.000
2008 Tampa Bay g	A.L.	1B	139	490	76	121	24	2	31	102	1	.247
Major League Totals	8 Yrs.		794	2665	404	669	128	18	163	466	15	.251
Division Series												
2008 Tampa Bay	N.L.	1B	3	10	0	5	0	0	0	2	2	.500
Championship Series												
2008 Tampa Bay	N.L.	1B	7	26	8	7	1	0	3	6	1	.269
World Series Record												
2008 Tampa Bay	N.L.	1B	5	17	1	2	1	0	0	2	0	.118

a Traded to Oakland Athletics with pitcher Mike Venafro for pitcher Mario Ramos, outfielder Ryan Ludwick, infielder Jason Hart and catcher Gerald Laird, January 14, 2002.
b Traded to Detroit Tigers with pitcher Franklyn German and player to be named later for pitcher Jeff Weaver, July 5, 2002. Detroit Tigers received pitcher Jeremy Bonderman to complete trade, August 22, 2002.
c On disabled list from June 2 to June 27, 2003.
d Released by Detroit Tigers, March 26, 2006. Signed with New York Yankees organization, April 15, 2006.
e Filed for free agency, August 16, 2006. Signed with Boston Red Sox organization, August 17, 2006.
f Filed for free agency, October 13, 2006. Signed with Tampa Bay Devil Rays organization, February 1, 2007.
g On disabled list from June 4 to June 27, 2008.

PENA, TONY FRANCISCO

Born, Santiago, Dominican Republic, March 23, 1981.
Bats Right. Throws Right. Height, 6 feet, 1 inch. Weight, 180 pounds.

Year Club	Lea	Pos	G	AB	R	H	2B	3B	HR	RBI	SB	Avg
2000 Danville	Appal.	SS-2B	55	215	22	46	5	0	2	20	6	.214
2001 Jamestown......	N.Y.-Penn.	SS	72	264	26	65	12	2	0	18	8	.246
2002 Macon	So.Atl.	SS	118	405	42	101	9	5	2	36	11	.249
2003 Myrtle Beach	Carolina	SS	120	405	43	105	14	1	4	30	17	.259
2004 Greenville........	Southern	SS	130	495	65	126	22	0	11	34	25	.255
2005 Richmond	Int.	SS	138	490	49	122	25	4	5	40	17	.249
2006 Richmond	Int.	SS	81	298	38	84	12	4	1	23	12	.282
2006 Atlanta	N.L.	SS-3B	40	44	12	10	2	0	1	3	0	.227
2007 Kansas City a	A.L.	SS-2B	152	509	58	136	25	7	2	47	5	.267
2008 Kansas City	A.L.	SS-P	95	225	22	38	4	1	1	14	3	.169
Major League Totals	3 Yrs.		287	778	92	184	31	8	4	64	8	.237

a Traded to Kansas City Royals for pitcher Erik Cordier, March 23, 2007.

PENCE, HUNTER ANDREW
Born, Arlington, Texas, April 13, 1983.
Bats Right. Throws Right. Height, 6 feet, 4 inches. Weight, 210 pounds.

Year	Club	Lea	Pos	G	AB	R	H	2B	3B	HR	RBI	SB	Avg
2004 Tri-City	N.Y.-Penn.	OF	51	199	36	59	18	1	8	37	3	.296
2005 Lexington	So.Atl.	OF	80	302	59	102	14	3	25	60	8	.338
2005 Salem	Carolina	OF	41	151	24	46	8	1	6	30	1	.305
2006 Corpus Christi	Texas	OF	136	523	97	148	31	8	28	95	17	.283
2007 Round Rock	P.C.	OF	25	95	17	31	11	1	3	21	2	.326
2007 Houston a	N.L.	OF	108	456	57	147	30	9	17	69	11	.322
2008 Houston	N.L.	OF	157	595	78	160	34	4	25	83	11	.269
Major League Totals			2 Yrs.	265	1051	135	307	64	13	42	152	22	.292

a On disabled list from July 23 to August 21, 2007.

PERALTA, JHONNY ANTONIO
Born, Santiago, Dominican Republic, May 28, 1982.
Bats Right. Throws Right. Height, 6 feet, 1 inch. Weight, 210 pounds.

Year	Club	Lea	Pos	G	AB	R	H	2B	3B	HR	RBI	SB	Avg
2001 Kinston	Carolina	SS	125	441	57	106	24	2	7	47	4	.240
2002 Akron	Eastern	SS	130	470	62	132	28	5	15	62	4	.281
2003 Buffalo	Int.	SS-3B	63	237	25	61	12	1	1	21	1	.257
2003 Cleveland	A.L.	SS-3B	77	242	24	55	10	1	4	21	1	.227
2004 Buffalo	Int.	SS-3B	138	556	109	181	44	2	15	86	8	.326
2004 Cleveland	A.L.	SS-3B	8	25	2	6	1	0	0	2	0	.240
2005 Cleveland	A.L.	SS	141	504	82	147	35	4	24	78	0	.292
2006 Cleveland	A.L.	SS	149	569	84	146	28	3	13	68	4	.257
2007 Cleveland	A.L.	SS	152	574	87	155	27	1	21	72	4	.270
2008 Cleveland	A.L.	SS-3B	154	605	104	167	42	4	23	89	3	.276
Major League Totals			6 Yrs.	681	2519	383	676	143	13	85	330	8	.268
Division Series													
2007 Cleveland	A.L.	SS	4	15	2	7	3	0	0	2	1	.467
Championship Series													
2007 Cleveland	A.L.	SS	7	27	4	7	2	0	2	8	0	.259

PHILLIPS, BRANDON EMIL
Born, Raleigh, North Carolina, June 28, 1981.
Bats Right. Throws Right. Height, 6 feet. Weight, 195 pounds.

Year	Club	Lea	Pos	G	AB	R	H	2B	3B	HR	RBI	SB	Avg
1999 Expos	Gulf Coast	SS	47	169	23	49	11	3	1	21	12	.290
2000 Cape Fear	So.Atl.	SS-2B	126	484	74	117	17	8	11	72	23	.242
2001 Harrisburg	Eastern	SS-2B-3B	67	265	35	79	19	0	7	36	13	.298
2001 Jupiter	Fla.St.	SS	55	194	36	55	12	2	4	23	17	.284
2002 Harrisburg	Eastern	SS	60	245	40	80	13	2	9	35	6	.327
2002 Ottawa	Int.	SS	10	35	1	9	4	0	1	5	0	.257
2002 Buffalo	Int.	SS-2B	55	223	30	63	14	0	8	27	8	.283
2002 Cleveland a-b	A.L.	2B	11	31	5	8	3	1	0	4	0	.258
2003 Cleveland	A.L.	2B	112	370	36	77	18	1	6	33	4	.208
2003 Buffalo	Int.	2B	43	154	14	27	7	0	3	13	7	.175
2004 Buffalo	Int.	2B-SS	135	521	83	158	34	4	8	50	14	.303
2004 Cleveland	A.L.	2B	6	22	1	4	2	0	0	1	0	.182
2005 Cleveland	A.L.	2B-SS	6	9	1	0	0	0	0	0	0	.000
2005 Buffalo	Int.	SS	112	465	79	119	24	1	15	46	7	.256
2006 Cincinnati c-d	N.L.	2B-SS	149	536	65	148	28	1	17	75	25	.276
2007 Cincinnati	N.L.	2B-SS	158	650	107	187	26	6	30	94	32	.288
2008 Cincinnati e	N.L.	2B	141	559	80	146	24	7	21	78	23	.261
Major League Totals			7 Yrs.	583	2177	295	570	101	16	74	285	84	.262

a Traded to Cleveland Indians with infielder Lee Stevens, outfielder Grady Sizemore and pitcher Cliff Lee for pitcher Bartolo Colon and player to be named later, June 27, 2002.
b Montreal Expos received pitcher Tim Drew to complete trade, June 28, 2002.
c Traded to Cincinnati Reds for player to be named later, April 7, 2006.
d Cleveland Indians received pitcher Jeff Stevens to complete trade, June 13, 2006.
e On disabled list from September 12 to November 6, 2008.

PIERRE, JUAN D'VAUGHN

Born, Mobile, Alabama, August 14, 1977.
Bats Left. Throws Left. Height, 6 feet. Weight, 180 pounds.

Year	Club	Lea	Pos	G	AB	R	H	2B	3B	HR	RBI	SB	Avg
1998 Portland	Northwest		OF	64	264	55	93	9	2	0	30	38	.352
1999 Asheville	So.Atl.		OF	140	585	93	187	28	5	1	55	66	.320
2000 Carolina	Southern		OF	107	439	63	143	16	4	0	32	46	.326
2000 Colorado Spgs	P.C.		OF	4	17	3	8	0	1	0	1	1	.471
2000 Colorado	N.L.		OF	51	200	26	62	2	0	0	20	7	.310
2001 Colorado	N.L.		OF	156	617	108	202	26	11	2	55	*46	.327
2002 Colorado a	N.L.		OF	152	592	90	170	20	5	1	35	47	.287
2003 Florida	N.L.		OF	*162	*668	100	204	28	7	1	41	*65	.305
2004 Florida	N.L.		OF	*162	*678	100	*221	22	*12	3	49	45	.326
2005 Florida b	N.L.		OF	*162	656	96	181	19	13	2	47	57	.276
2006 Chicago c	N.L.		OF	*162	*699	87	*204	32	13	3	40	58	.292
2007 Los Angeles	N.L.		OF	*162	668	96	196	24	8	0	41	64	.293
2008 Las Vegas	P.C.		OF	2	6	2	3	1	0	0	0	0	.500
2008 Los Angeles d	N.L.		OF	119	375	44	106	10	2	1	28	40	.283
Major League Totals		9 Yrs.		1288	5153	747	1546	183	71	13	356	429	.300
Division Series													
2003 Florida	N.L.		OF	4	19	5	5	1	0	0	3	1	.263
2008 Los Angeles	N.L.		OF	1	1	1	0	0	0	0	0	0	.000
Division Series Totals				5	20	6	5	1	0	0	3	1	.250
Championship Series													
2003 Florida	N.L.		OF	7	33	5	10	1	2	0	1	1	.303
2008 Los Angeles	N.L.		OF	1	3	1	2	1	0	0	0	0	.667
Championship Series Totals				8	36	6	12	2	2	0	1	1	.333
World Series Record													
2003 Florida	N.L.		OF	6	21	2	7	2	0	0	3	1	.333

a Traded to Florida Marlins with pitcher Mike Hampton for outfielder Preston Wilson, catcher Charles Johnson, pitcher Vic Darensbourg and infielder Pablo Ozuna, November 16, 2002.
b Traded to Chicago Cubs for pitcher Sergio Mitre, pitcher Ricky Nolasco and pitcher Renyel Pinto, December 7, 2005.
c Filed for free agency, October 29, 2006. Signed with Los Angeles Dodgers, November 22, 2006.
d On disabled list from June 30 to July 25, 2008.

PIERZYNSKI, ANTHONY JOHN (A.J.)

Born, Bridgehampton, New York, December 30, 1976.
Bats Left. Throws Right. Height, 6 feet, 3 inches. Weight, 235 pounds.

Year	Club	Lea	Pos	G	AB	R	H	2B	3B	HR	RBI	SB	Avg
1994 Twins	Gulf Coast		C	43	152	21	44	8	1	1	19	0	.289
1995 Ft. Wayne	Midwest		C	22	84	10	26	5	1	2	14	0	.310
1995 Elizabethtn	Appal.		C-1B	56	205	29	68	13	1	7	45	0	.332
1996 Ft. Wayne	Midwest		C-OF	114	431	48	118	30	3	7	70	0	.274
1997 Ft. Myers	Fla.St.		C-1B	118	412	49	115	23	1	9	64	2	.279
1998 New Britain	Eastern		C	59	212	30	63	11	0	3	17	0	.297
1998 Salt Lake	P.C.		C	59	208	29	53	7	2	7	30	3	.255
1998 Minnesota	A.L.		C	7	10	1	3	0	0	0	1	0	.300
1999 Salt Lake	P.C.		C	67	228	29	59	10	0	1	25	0	.259
1999 Minnesota a	A.L.		C	9	22	3	6	2	0	0	3	0	.273
2000 New Britain	Eastern		C	62	228	36	68	17	2	4	34	0	.298
2000 Salt Lake	P.C.		C	41	155	22	52	14	1	4	25	1	.335
2000 Minnesota	A.L.		C	33	88	12	27	5	1	2	11	1	.307
2001 Minnesota	A.L.		C	114	381	51	110	33	2	7	55	1	.289
2002 Minnesota	A.L.		C	130	440	54	132	31	6	6	49	1	.300
2003 Minnesota b	A.L.		C	137	487	63	152	35	3	11	74	3	.312
2004 San Francisco c	N.L.		C	131	471	45	128	28	2	11	77	0	.272
2005 Chicago	A.L.		C	128	460	61	118	21	0	18	56	0	.257
2006 Chicago	A.L.		C	140	509	65	150	24	0	16	64	1	.295
2007 Chicago	A.L.		C	136	472	54	124	24	0	14	50	1	.263
2008 Chicago	A.L.		C	134	534	66	150	31	1	13	60	1	.281
Major League Totals		11 Yrs.		1099	3874	475	1100	234	15	98	500	9	.284
Division Series													
2002 Minnesota	A.L.		C	5	16	4	7	0	1	1	4	0	.438
2003 Minnesota	A.L.		C	4	13	1	3	0	0	1	1	0	.231
2005 Chicago	A.L.		C	3	9	5	4	2	0	2	4	1	.444
2008 Chicago	A.L.		C	4	13	1	5	1	0	0	1	0	.385
Division Series Totals				16	51	11	19	3	1	4	10	1	.373

Year	Club	Lea	Pos	G	AB	R	H	2B	3B	HR	RBI	SB	Avg
Championship Series													
2002 Minnesota	....	A.L.	C	5	16	1	4	0	0	0	2	0	.250
2005 Chicago	....	A.L.	C	5	18	1	3	0	0	1	2	0	.167
Championship Series Totals				10	34	2	7	0	0	1	4	0	.206
World Series Record													
2005 Chicago	....	A.L.	C	4	15	3	4	2	0	0	3	1	.267

a On disabled list from August 24 to September 30, 1999.
b Traded to San Francisco Giants with player to be named later for pitcher Joe Nathan, pitcher Boof Bonser and pitcher Francisco Liriano, November 14, 2003.
c Released by San Francisco Giants, December 16, 2004. Signed with Chicago White Sox, January 5, 2005.

PODSEDNIK, SCOTT ERIC

Born, West, Texas, March 18, 1976.
Bats Left. Throws Left. Height, 6 feet, 1 inch. Weight, 190 pounds.

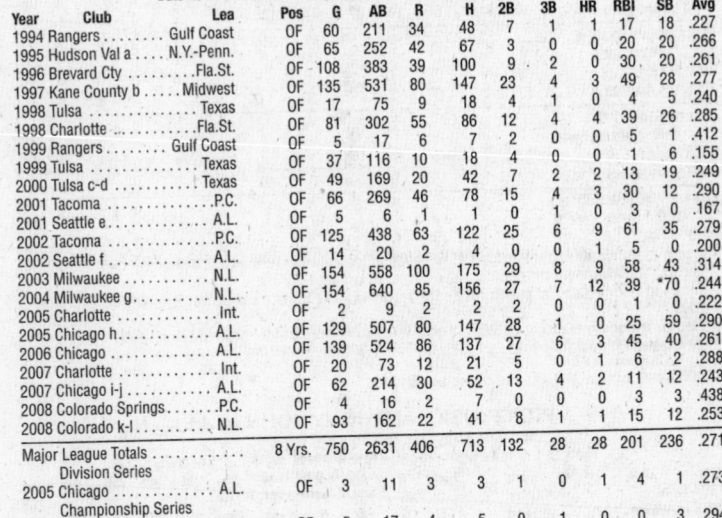

Year	Club	Lea	Pos	G	AB	R	H	2B	3B	HR	RBI	SB	Avg
1994 Rangers	....	Gulf Coast	OF	60	211	34	48	7	1	1	17	18	.227
1995 Hudson Val a	....	N.Y.-Penn.	OF	65	252	42	67	3	0	0	20	20	.266
1996 Brevard Cty	....	Fla.St.	OF	108	383	39	100	9	2	0	30	20	.261
1997 Kane County b	.....	Midwest	OF	135	531	80	147	23	4	3	49	28	.277
1998 Tulsa	....	Texas	OF	17	75	9	18	4	1	0	4	5	.240
1998 Charlotte	....	Fla.St.	OF	81	302	55	86	12	4	4	39	26	.285
1999 Rangers	....	Gulf Coast	OF	5	17	6	7	2	0	0	5	1	.412
1999 Tulsa	....	Texas	OF	37	116	10	18	4	0	0	1	6	.155
2000 Tulsa c-d	....	Texas	OF	49	169	20	42	7	2	2	13	19	.249
2001 Tacoma	....	P.C.	OF	66	269	46	78	15	4	3	30	12	.290
2001 Seattle e	....	A.L.	OF	5	6	.1	1	0	1	0	3	0	.167
2002 Tacoma	....	P.C.	OF	125	438	63	122	25	6	9	61	35	.279
2002 Seattle f	....	A.L.	OF	14	20	2	4	0	0	1	5	0	.200
2003 Milwaukee	....	N.L.	OF	154	558	100	175	29	8	9	58	43	.314
2004 Milwaukee g	....	N.L.	OF	154	640	85	156	27	7	12	39	*70	.244
2005 Charlotte	....	Int.	OF	2	9	2	2	2	0	0	1	0	.222
2005 Chicago h	....	A.L.	OF	129	507	80	147	28	1	0	25	59	.290
2006 Chicago	....	A.L.	OF	139	524	86	137	27	6	3	45	40	.261
2007 Charlotte	....	Int.	OF	20	73	12	21	5	0	1	6	2	.288
2007 Chicago i-j	....	A.L.	OF	62	214	30	52	13	4	2	11	12	.243
2008 Colorado Springs	....	P.C.	OF	4	16	2	7	0	0	0	3	3	.438
2008 Colorado k-l	....	N.L.	OF	93	162	22	41	8	1	1	15	12	.253
Major League Totals		8 Yrs.		750	2631	406	713	132	28	28	201	236	.271
Division Series													
2005 Chicago	....	A.L.	OF	3	11	3	3	1	0	1	4	1	.273
Championship Series													
2005 Chicago	....	A.L.	OF	5	17	4	5	0	1	0	0	3	.294
World Series Record													
2005 Chicago	....	A.L.	OF	4	21	2	6	0	2	1	2	2	.286

a Sent to Florida Marlins by Texas Rangers to complete trade for pitcher Bobby Witt, August 8, 1995.
b Selected by Texas Rangers organization in Rule V draft, December 15, 1997.
c On disabled list from April 6 to May 22, 2000.
d Filed for free agency, October 15, 2000. Signed with Seattle Mariners organization, November 7, 2000.
e On disabled list from May 4 to June 12 and August 14 to 26, 2001.
f Claimed on waivers by Milwaukee Brewers, October 11, 2002.
g Traded to Chicago White Sox with pitcher Luis Vizcaino and player to be named later for outfielder Carlos Lee, December 13, 2004. Chicago White Sox received infielder Travis Hinton to complete trade, January 10, 2005.
h On disabled list from August 13 to August 29, 2005.
i On disabled list from April 16 to June 23 and July 2 to July 24, 2007.
j Released by Chicago White Sox, November 28, 2007. Signed with Colorado Rockies organization, February 5, 2008.
k On disabled list from July 28 to August 22, 2008.
l Filed for free agency, November 1, 2008, re-signed with Colorado Rockies organization, January 14, 2009.

POLANCO, PLACIDO ENRIQUE

Born, Santo Domingo, Dominican Republic, October 10, 1975.
Bats Right. Throws Right. Height, 5 feet, 10 inches. Weight, 195 pounds.

Year	Club	Lea	Pos	G	AB	R	H	2B	3B	HR	RBI	SB	Avg
1994 Cardinals	......	Arizona	SS-2B	32	127	17	27	4	0	1	10	4	.213
1995 Peoria	....	Midwest	SS-2B	103	361	43	96	7	4	2	41	7	.266
1996 St. Pete	....	Fla.St.	2B	137	540	65	157	29	5	0	51	4	.291
1997 Arkansas	....	Texas	2B	129	508	71	148	16	3	2	51	19	.291
1998 Memphis	....	P.C.	2B-SS	70	246	36	69	19	1	1	21	6	.280

Year Club	Lea	Pos	G	AB	R	H	2B	3B	HR	RBI	SB	Avg
1998 St. Louis.........N.L.		SS-2B	45	114	10	29	3	2	1	11	2	.254
1999 Memphis.........P.C.		2B	29	120	18	33	4	1	0	10	2	.275
1999 St. Louis.........N.L.		2B-3B-SS	88	220	24	61	9	3	1	19	1	.277
2000 St. Louis a.........N.L.		2B-3B-SS-1B	118	323	50	102	12	3	5	39	4	.316
2001 St. Louis.........N.L.		3B-SS-2B	144	564	87	173	26	4	3	38	12	.307
2002 St. Louis-Phil. b....N.L.		3B-SS-2B	147	548	75	158	32	2	9	49	5	.288
2003 Philadelphia c.....N.L.		2B-3B	122	492	87	142	30	3	14	63	14	.289
2004 Reading.......Eastern		2B	1	3	0	2	0	0	0	0	0	.667
2004 Scranton/W.B......Int.		2B	1	3	1	0	0	0	0	0	0	.000
2004 Philadelphia d-e....N.L.		2B-3B	126	503	74	150	21	0	17	55	7	.298
2005 Philadelphia.......N.L.		2B-3B-OF-SS	43	158	26	50	7	0	3	20	7	.316
2005 Detroit f-g.........A.L.		2B-3B	86	343	58	116	20	2	6	36	4	.338
2006 Detroit h.........A.L.		2B	110	461	58	136	18	1	4	52	1	.295
2007 Detroit .........A.L.		2B	142	587	105	200	36	3	9	67	7	.341
2008 Detroit .........A.L.		2B	141	580	90	178	34	3	8	58	7	.307
Major League Totals	11 Yrs.		1312	4893	744	1495	248	26	80	507	64	.306
Division Series												
2000 St. Louis.........N.L.		3B	3	10	1	3	0	0	0	3	1	.300
2001 St. Louis.........N.L.		3B	5	15	1	4	0	0	0	1	1	.267
2006 Detroit ..........A.L.		2B	4	17	3	7	1	0	0	2	0	.412
Division Series Totals			12	42	5	14	1	0	0	6	2	.333
Championship Series												
2000 St. Louis.........N.L.		3B	4	5	0	1	0	0	0	0	0	.200
2006 Detroit .........A.L.		2B	4	17	2	9	1	0	0	2	0	.529
Championship Series Totals ..			8	22	2	10	1	0	0	2	0	.455
World Series Record												
2006 Detroit ...........A.L.		2B	5	17	0	0	0	0	0	0	0	.000

a On disabled list from July 1 to July 15, 2000.
b Traded to Philadelphia Phillies with pitcher Bud Smith and pitcher Mike Timlin for infielder Scott Rolen and pitcher Doug Nickle, July 29, 2002.
c On disabled list from April 16 to May 1, 2003.
d On disabled list from May 8 to June 7, 2004.
e Filed for free agency, October 29, 2004, re-signed with Philadelphia Phillies, December 19, 2004.
f Traded to Detroit Tigers for pitcher Ugueth Urbina and infielder Ramon Martinez, June 8, 2005.
g On disabled list from July 12 to July 27, 2005.
h On disabled list from August 16 to September 22, 2006.

POSADA, JORGE RAFAEL

Born, Santurce, Puerto Rico, August 17, 1971.
Bats Both. Throws Right. Height, 6 feet, 2 inches. Weight, 205 pounds

Year Club	Lea	Pos	G	AB	R	H	2B	3B	HR	RBI	SB	Avg
1991 Oneonta.........N.Y.-Penn		2B-C	71	217	34	51	5	5	4	33	6	.235
1992 Greensboro.........So. Atl.		DH-C-3B	101	339	60	94	22	4	12	58	11	.277
1993 Pr William........Carolina		C-3B	118	410	71	106	27	2	17	61	17	.259
1993 Albany............Eastern		C	7	25	3	7	0	0	0	0	0	.280
1994 Columbus.............Int.		C-OF	92	313	46	75	13	3	11	48	5	.240
1995 Columbus.............Int.		C	108	368	60	94	32	5	8	51	4	.255
1995 New York ...........A.L.		C	1	0	0	0	0	0	0	0	0	.000
1996 Columbus.............Int.		C-OF	106	354	76	96	22	6	11	62	3	.271
1996 New York ...........A.L.		C	8	14	1	1	0	0	0	0	0	.071
1997 New York ...........A.L.		C	60	188	29	47	12	0	6	25	1	.250
1998 New York ...........A.L.		C-1B	111	358	56	96	23	0	17	63	0	.268
1999 New York ...........A.L.		C-1B	112	379	50	93	19	2	12	57	1	.245
2000 New York ...........A.L.		C-1B	151	505	92	145	35	1	28	86	2	.287
2001 New York ...........A.L.		C-1B	138	484	59	134	28	1	22	95	2	.277
2002 New York ...........A.L.		C	143	511	79	137	40	1	20	99	1	.268
2003 New York ...........A.L.		C	142	481	83	135	24	0	30	101	2	.281
2004 New York ...........A.L.		C	137	449	72	122	31	0	21	81	1	.272
2005 New York ...........A.L.		C	142	474	67	124	23	0	19	71	1	.262
2006 New York ...........A.L.		C-1B	143	465	65	129	27	2	23	93	3	.277
2007 New York a.........A.L.		C-1B	144	506	91	171	42	1	20	90	2	.338
2008 New York b.........A.L.		C-1B	51	168	18	45	13	1	3	22	0	.268
Major League Totals	14 Yrs.		1483	4982	762	1379	317	9	221	883	16	.277
Division Series												
1995 New York ...........A.L.		C	1	0	1	0	0	0	0	0	0	.000
1997 New York ...........A.L.		C	2	2	0	0	0	0	0	0	0	.000
1998 New York ...........A.L.		C	1	2	1	0	0	0	0	0	0	.000
1999 New York ...........A.L.		C	1	4	0	1	1	0	0	0	0	.250

Year Club	Lea	Pos	G	AB	R	H	2B	3B	HR	RBI	SB	Avg
2000 New York	A.L.	C	5	17	2	4	2	0	0	1	0	.235
2001 New York	A.L.	C	5	18	3	8	1	0	1	2	1	.444
2002 New York	A.L.	C	4	17	2	4	0	0	1	3	0	.235
2003 New York	A.L.	C	4	17	1	3	1	0	0	0	0	.176
2004 New York	A.L.	C	4	18	2	4	0	0	0	0	0	.222
2005 New York	A.L.	C	5	13	3	3	1	0	1	2	0	.231
2006 New York	A.L.	C	4	14	2	7	1	0	1	2	0	.500
2007 New York	A.L.	C	4	15	1	2	1	0	0	0	0	.133
Division Series Totals			40	137	18	36	8	0	4	10	1	.263
Championship Series												
1998 New York	A.L.	C	5	11	1	2	0	0	1	2	0	.182
1999 New York	A.L.	C	3	10	1	1	0	0	1	2	0	.100
2000 New York	A.L.	C	6	19	2	3	1	0	0	3	0	.158
2001 New York	A.L.	C	5	14	4	3	1	0	0	0	0	.214
2003 New York	A.L.	C	7	27	5	8	4	0	1	6	0	.296
2004 New York	A.L.	C	7	27	4	7	1	0	0	2	0	.259
Championship Series Totals			33	108	17	24	7	0	3	15	0	.222
World Series Record												
1998 New York	A.L.	C	3	9	2	3	0	0	1	2	0	.333
1999 New York	A.L.	C	2	8	0	2	1	0	0	1	0	.250
2000 New York	A.L.	C	5	18	2	4	1	0	0	1	0	.222
2001 New York	A.L.	C	7	23	2	4	1	0	1	1	0	.174
2003 New York	A.L.	C	6	19	0	3	1	0	0	1	1	.158
World Series Totals			23	77	6	16	4	0	2	6	1	.208

a Filed for free agency, October 29, 2007, re-signed with New York Yankees, November 29, 2007.
b On disabled list from April 27 to June 4 and July 21 to November 14, 2008.

PRADO, MARTIN MANUEL
Born, Maracay, Venezuela, October 27, 1983.
Bats Right. Throws Right. Height, 6 feet, 1 inch. Weight, 170 pounds.

Year Club	Lea	Pos	G	AB	R	H	2B	3B	HR	RBI	SB	Avg
2003 Braves	Gulf Coast	2B-3B	59	220	28	63	2	6	0	23	9	.286
2004 Rome	So.Atl.	2B	107	429	68	135	25	6	3	38	14	.315
2005 Myrtle Beach	Carolina	2B	75	297	44	91	13	3	4	34	9	.306
2005 Mississippi	Southern	2B	39	143	17	40	7	1	1	11	3	.280
2006 Richmond	Int.	2B-3B	60	241	30	68	12	1	2	23	2	.282
2006 Mississippi	Southern	2B-3B	43	176	17	49	6	2	1	15	2	.278
2006 Atlanta	N.L.	2B-3B	24	42	3	11	1	1	1	9	0	.262
2007 Richmond	Int.	2B-3B-SS	103	395	61	125	23	3	4	41	5	.316
2007 Atlanta	N.L.	2B-3B	28	59	5	17	3	0	0	2	0	.288
2008 Mississippi	Southern	2B-3B-SS-OF	5	19	2	5	2	0	0	3	0	.320
2008 Atlanta a	N.L.	3B-1B-2B-OF	78	228	36	73	18	4	2	33	3	.320
Major League Totals	3 Yrs.		130	329	44	101	22	5	3	44	3	.307

a On disabled list from May 5 to July 3, 2008.

PUJOLS, JOSE ALBERTO (ALBERT)
Born, Santo Domingo, Dominican Republic, January 16, 1980.
Bats Right. Throws Right. Height, 6 feet, 3 inches. Weight, 225 pounds.

Year Club	Lea	Pos	G	AB	R	H	2B	3B	HR	RBI	SB	Avg
2000 Potomac	Carolina	3B	21	81	11	23	8	1	2	10	1	.284
2000 Peoria	Midwest	3B	109	395	62	128	32	6	17	84	2	.324
2000 Memphis	P.C.	3B-OF	3	14	1	3	1	0	0	2	1	.214
2001 St. Louis a	N.L.	OF-3B-1B	161	590	112	194	47	4	37	130	1	.329
2002 St. Louis	N.L.	OF-3B-1B-SS	157	590	118	185	40	2	34	127	2	.314
2003 St. Louis	N.L.	OF-1B	157	591	*137	*212	*51	1	43	124	5	*.359
2004 St. Louis	N.L.	1B	154	592	*133	196	51	2	46	123	5	.331
2005 St. Louis b	N.L.	1B	161	591	*129	195	38	2	41	117	16	.330
2006 St. Louis c	N.L.	1B	143	535	119	177	33	1	49	137	7	.331
2007 St. Louis	N.L.	1B	158	565	99	185	38	1	32	103	2	.327
2008 St. Louis d-e	N.L.	1B-2B	148	524	100	187	44	0	37	116	7	.357
Major League Totals	8 Yrs.		1239	4578	947	1531	342	13	319	977	45	.334
Division Series												
2001 St. Louis	N.L.	1B-OF	5	18	1	2	0	0	1	2	0	.111
2002 St. Louis	N.L.	OF-1B-3B	3	10	3	3	0	1	0	3	0	.300
2004 St. Louis	N.L.	1B	4	15	4	5	0	0	2	5	0	.333
2005 St. Louis	N.L.	1B	3	9	4	5	2	0	0	2	0	.556

Year	Club		Lea	Pos	G	AB	R	H	2B	3B	HR	RBI	SB	Avg
2006 St. Louis		N.L.		1B	4	15	3	5	1	0	1	3	0	.333
Division Series Totals					19	67	15	20	3	1	4	15	0	.299
Championship Series														
2002 St. Louis		N.L.		OF-3B-1B	5	19	2	5	1	0	1	2	0	.263
2004 St. Louis		N.L.		1B	7	28	10	14	2	0	4	9	0	.500
2005 St. Louis		N.L.		1B	6	23	3	7	0	0	2	6	0	.304
2006 St. Louis		N.L.		1B	7	22	5	7	1	0	1	1	0	.318
Championship Series Totals					25	92	20	33	4	0	8	18	0	.359
World Series Record														
2004 St. Louis		N.L.		1B	4	15	1	5	2	0	0	0	0	.333
2006 St. Louis		N.L.		1B	5	15	3	3	1	0	1	2	0	.200
World Series Totals					9	30	4	8	3	0	1	2	0	.267

a Selected Rookie of the Year in National League for 2001.
b Selected Most Valuable Player in National League for 2005.
c On disabled list from June 4 to June 22, 2006.
d On disabled list from June 11 to June 26, 2008.
e Selected Most Valuable Player in National League for 2008.

PUNTO, NICHOLAS PAUL (NICK)

Born, San Diego, California, November 8, 1977.
Bats Both. Throws Right. Height, 5 feet, 9 inches. Weight, 185 pounds.

Year	Club		Lea	Pos	G	AB	R	H	2B	3B	HR	RBI	SB	Avg
1998 Batavia		N.Y.-Penn.		SS-2B	72	279	51	69	9	4	1	20	19	.247
1999 Clearwater		Fla.St.		SS	106	400	65	122	18	6	1	48	16	.305
2000 Reading		Eastern		SS	121	456	77	116	15	4	5	47	33	.254
2001 Scranton-WB		Int.		SS	123	463	57	106	19	5	1	39	33	.229
2001 Philadelphia		N.L.		SS	4	5	0	2	0	0	0	0	0	.400
2002 Philadelphia		N.L.		2B-SS	9	6	1	1	0	0	0	0	0	.167
2002 Scranton-WB		Int.		SS	115	443	74	120	12	5	1	29	42	.271
2003 Philadelphia		N.L.		2B-3B-SS	64	92	14	20	2	0	1	4	2	.217
2003 Scranton/WB a		Int.		SS	25	111	19	35	7	1	0	9	7	.315
2004 Minnesota		A.L.		2B-SS-3B-OF	38	91	17	23	0	0	2	12	6	.253
2004 Quad Cities b		Midwest		SS-2B-3B	4	16	4	7	1	0	1	6	1	.438
2005 Rochester		Int.		2B	4	15	2	3	1	0	0	1	0	.200
2005 Minnesota c		A.L.		2B-SS-3B-OF	112	394	45	94	18	4	4	26	13	.239
2006 Minnesota		A.L.		3B-SS-2B-OF	135	459	73	133	21	7	1	45	17	.290
2007 Minnesota		A.L.		3B-SS-2B	150	472	53	99	18	4	1	25	16	.210
2008 Fort Myers		Fla.St.		SS	3	12	0	3	0	0	0	1	1	.250
2008 Minnesota d-e		A.L.		SS-2B-3B-OF	99	338	43	96	19	4	2	28	15	.284
Major League Totals				8 Yrs.	611	1857	245	468	78	19	11	140	69	.252
Division Series														
2006 Minnesota		A.L.		3B	3	12	0	2	0	0	0	0	0	.167

a Traded to Minnesota Twins with pitcher Carlos Silva and player to be named later for pitcher Eric Milton, December 3, 2003.
b On disabled list from May 9 to June 30 and July 27 to October 28, 2004.
c On disabled list from June 3 to July 3, 2005.
d On disabled list from May 8 to May 31 and June 6 to June 24, 2008.
e Filed for free agency, October 30, 2008, re-signed with Minnesota Twins, December 11, 2008.

QUENTIN, CARLOS JOSE

Born, Bellflower, California, August 28, 1982.
Bats Right. Throws Right. Height, 6 feet, 1 inch. Weight, 225 pounds.

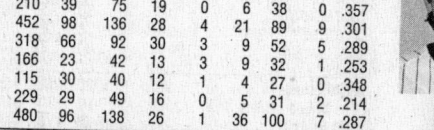

Year	Club		Lea	Pos	G	AB	R	H	2B	3B	HR	RBI	SB	Avg
2004 Lancaster		Calif.		OF	65	242	64	75	14	1	15	51	5	.310
2004 El Paso		Texas		OF	60	210	39	75	19	0	6	38	0	.357
2005 Tucson		P.C.		OF	136	452	98	136	28	4	21	89	9	.301
2006 Tucson		P.C.		OF	85	318	66	92	30	3	9	52	5	.289
2006 Arizona		N.L.		OF	57	166	23	42	13	3	9	32	1	.253
2007 Tucson		P.C.		OF	33	115	30	40	12	1	4	27	0	.348
2007 Arizona a-b		N.L.		OF	81	229	29	49	16	0	5	31	2	.214
2008 Chicago		A.L.		OF	130	480	96	138	26	1	36	100	7	.287
Major League Totals				3 Yrs.	268	875	148	229	55	4	50	163	10	.262

a On disabled list from March 23 to April 16 and August 2 to September 1, 2007.
b Traded to Chicago White Sox for infielder Chris Carter, December 3, 2008.

QUINLAN, ROBB WILLIAM
Born, St. Paul, Minnesota, March 17, 1977.
Bats Right. Throws Right. Height, 6 feet, 1 inch. Weight, 215 pounds.

Year Club	Lea	Pos	G	AB	R	H	2B	3B	HR	RBI	SB	Avg
1999 Boise	Northwest	3B-2B-1B	73	295	51	95	20	1	9	77	5	.322
2000 Lake Elsinore	Calif.	1B-OF	127	482	79	153	35	5	5	85	6	.317
2001 Arkansas	Texas	1B-OF	129	492	82	145	33	7	14	79	0	.295
2002 Salt Lake	P.C.	OF-1B	136	528	95	176	31	13	20	112	8	.333
2003 Salt Lake	P.C.	1B-OF	95	393	55	122	18	4	9	68	10	.310
2003 Anaheim	A.L.	1B-OF	38	94	13	27	4	2	0	4	1	.287
2004 Salt Lake	P.C.	1B-3B-OF	27	108	15	32	9	1	2	17	1	.296
2004 Anaheim a	A.L.	3B-1B-OF	56	160	23	55	14	0	5	23	3	.344
2005 Angels	Arizona	1B-3B	4	12	3	3	2	0	1	4	0	.250
2005 Salt Lake	P.C.	1B-3B	15	60	13	23	6	0	1	4	0	.383
2005 Los Angeles b	A.L.	3B-1B-OF	54	134	17	31	8	0	5	14	0	.231
2006 Los Angeles	A.L.	1B-3B-OF	86	234	28	75	11	1	9	32	2	.321
2007 Los Angeles	A.L.	1B-OF-3B	79	178	21	44	9	0	3	21	3	.247
2008 Los Angeles	A.L.	3B-1B-OF	68	164	15	43	1	2	1	11	4	.262
Major League Totals		6 Yrs.	381	964	117	275	47	5	23	105	13	.285
Division Series												
2005 Los Angeles	A.L.	3B	2	2	0	1	0	0	0	0	0	.500
2007 Los Angeles	A.L.	PH	1	1	0	0	0	0	0	0	0	.000
Division Series Totals			3	3	0	1	0	0	0	0	0	.333
Championship Series												
2005 Los Angeles	A.L.	3B	1	3	1	1	0	0	1	1	0	.333

a On disabled list from August 16 to October 14, 2004.
b On disabled list from July 1 to August 23, 2005.

QUINTANILLA, OMAR
Born, El Paso, Texas, October 24, 1981.
Bats Left. Throws Right. Height, 5 feet, 9 inches. Weight, 190 pounds.

Year Club	Lea	Pos	G	AB	R	H	2B	3B	HR	RBI	SB	Avg
2003 Modesto	Calif.	SS	8	36	9	15	3	0	2	6	0	.417
2003 Vancouver	Northwest	SS	32	129	22	44	5	4	0	14	7	.341
2004 Modesto	Calif.	SS	108	451	75	142	32	5	11	72	1	.315
2004 Midland	Texas	SS	23	94	20	33	10	0	2	20	2	.351
2005 Midland	Texas	SS-2B	78	294	46	86	14	2	4	25	2	.293
2005 Colorado Springs	P.C.	SS	13	52	16	18	3	2	1	7	0	.346
2005 Colorado a	N.L.	SS-2B	39	128	16	28	1	1	0	7	2	.219
2006 Colorado	N.L.	SS-2B	11	34	3	6	1	1	0	3	1	.176
2006 Colorado Springs b	P.C.	SS-2B	82	308	48	85	23	2	4	29	4	.319
2007 Colorado Springs	P.C.	SS-2B	98	348	54	111	30	4	3	43	3	.319
2007 Colorado	N.L.	2B-SS	27	70	6	16	4	0	0	5	0	.229
2008 Colorado Springs	P.C.	SS-2B	20	73	18	24	4	0	1	8	3	.329
2008 Colorado	N.L.	2B-SS	81	210	28	50	17	0	2	15	0	.238
Major League Totals		4 Yrs.	158	442	53	100	23	2	2	30	3	.226

a Traded to Colorado Rockies with outfielder Eric Byrnes for pitcher Jay Witasick and pitcher Joe Kennedy, July 13, 2005.
b On disabled list from July 16 to August 4, 2006.

RABURN, RYAN NEIL
Born, Tampa, Florida, April 17, 1981.
Bats Right. Throws Right. Height, 6 feet. Weight, 185 pounds.

Year	Club	Lea	Pos	G	AB	R	H	2B	3B	HR	RBI	SB	Avg
2001 Tigers	Gulf Coast		3B	19	58	4	9	2	0	1	5	2	.155
2001 Oneonta	N.Y.-Penn.		3B-2B	44	171	25	62	17	8	8	42	1	.363
2002 Tigers	Gulf Coast		3B	8	30	4	9	3	1	1	5	0	.300
2002 West Michigan	Midwest		3B	40	150	27	33	10	1	6	28	0	.220
2003 Lakeland	Fla.St.		3B	95	325	52	72	14	3	12	56	2	.222
2003 West Michigan	Midwest		3B	16	57	14	20	7	0	3	12	1	.351
2004 Lakeland	Fla.St.		2B	3	11	1	3	1	0	1	3	0	.273
2004 Erie	Eastern		2B	98	366	66	110	29	4	16	63	3	.301
2004 Detroit	A.L.		2B	12	29	4	4	1	0	0	1	1	.138
2005 Toledo	Int.		2B-OF	130	471	62	119	22	4	19	64	8	.253
2006 Toledo	Int.		OF-2B	118	451	68	124	29	4	20	79	16	.275
2007 Toledo	Int.		OF-2B	85	315	60	92	21	3	17	64	12	.292
2007 Detroit	A.L.		OF-2B-3B	49	138	28	42	12	2	4	27	3	.304
2008 Toledo	Int.		OF	5	19	6	6	2	0	0	2	6	.316

Year Club	Lea	Pos	G	AB	R	H	2B	3B	HR	RBI	SB	Avg
2008 Detroit	A.L.	OF-3B-2B	92	182	26	43	10	1	4	20	3	.236
Major League Totals		3 Yrs.	153	349	58	89	23	3	8	48	7	.255

RAMIREZ, ALEXEI FERNANDO
Born, Pinar Del Rio, Cuba, September 22, 1981.
Bats Right. Throws Right. Height, 6 feet, 3 inches. Weight, 185 pounds.

Year Club	Lea	Pos	G	AB	R	H	2B	3B	HR	RBI	SB	Avg
2008 Chicago a-b	A.L.	2B-SS-OF-3B	136	480	65	139	22	2	21	77	13	.290
Division Series												
2008 Chicago	A.L.	2B	4	12	1	3	0	0	0	2	0	.250

a Played in Cuba 2001-2007.
b Signed with Chicago White Sox, January 1, 2008.

RAMIREZ (NIN), ARAMIS
Born, Santo Domingo, Dominican Republic, June 25, 1978.
Bats Right. Throws Right. Height, 6 feet, 1 inch. Weight, 215 pounds.

Year Club	Lea	Pos	G	AB	R	H	2B	3B	HR	RBI	SB	Avg
1995 Pittsburgh	Dominican	3B	64	214	41	63	13	0	11	54	2	.294
1996 Erie.	N.Y.-Penn.	3B	61	223	37	68	14	4	9	42	0	.305
1996 Augusta	So.Atl.	3B	6	20	3	4	1	0	1	2	0	.200
1997 Lynchburg	Carolina	3B	137	482	85	134	24	2	29	114	5	.278
1998 Nashville	P.C.	3B-SS	47	168	19	46	10	0	5	18	0	.274
1998 Pittsburgh a	N.L.	3B	72	251	23	59	9	1	6	24	0	.235
1999 Nashville	P.C.	3B	131	460	92	151	35	1	21	74	5	.328
1999 Pittsburgh	N.L.	3B	18	56	2	10	2	1	0	7	0	.179
2000 Nashville	P.C.	3B	44	167	28	59	12	2	4	26	0	.353
2000 Pittsburgh b	N.L.	3B	73	254	19	65	15	2	6	35	0	.256
2001 Pittsburgh	N.L.	3B	158	603	83	181	40	0	34	112	5	.300
2002 Pittsburgh	N.L.	3B	142	522	51	122	26	0	18	71	2	.234
2003 Pittsburgh-Chicago c-d .	N.L.	3B	159	607	75	165	32	2	27	106	2	.272
2004 Chicago	N.L.	3B	145	547	99	174	32	1	36	103	0	.318
2005 Chicago e	N.L.	3B	123	463	72	140	30	0	31	92	0	.302
2006 Chicago f	N.L.	3B	157	594	93	173	38	4	38	119	2	.291
2007 Chicago g	N.L.	3B	132	506	72	157	35	4	26	101	0	.310
2008 Chicago	N.L.	3B	149	554	97	160	44	1	27	111	0	.289
Major League Totals		11 Yrs.	1328	4957	686	1406	303	16	249	881	13	.284
Division Series												
2003 Chicago	N.L.	3B	5	18	2	5	1	0	1	3	0	.278
2007 Chicago	N.L.	3B	3	12	0	0	0	0	0	0	0	.000
2008 Chicago	N.L.	3B	3	11	1	2	1	0	0	0	0	.182
Division Series Totals			11	41	3	7	2	0	1	3	0	.171
Championship Series												
2003 Chicago	N.L.	3B	7	26	4	6	0	1	3	7	0	.231

a On disabled list from August 10 to September 4, 1998.
b On disabled list from August 29 to October 1, 2000.
c Traded to Chicago Cubs with outfielder Kenny Lofton for infielder Jose Hernandez, pitcher Matt Bruback and player to be named later, July 22, 2003.
d Pittsburgh Pirates received infielder Bobby Hill to complete trade, August 15, 2003.
e On disabled list from August 25 to October 3, 2005.
f Filed for free agency, October 30, 2006, re-signed with Chicago Cubs, November 12, 2006.
g On disabled list from June 7 to June 22, 2007.

RAMIREZ, HANLEY
Born, Samana, Dominican Republic, December 23, 1983.
Bats Right. Throws Right. Height, 6 feet, 3 inches. Weight, 195 pounds.

Year Club	Lea	Pos	G	AB	R	H	2B	3B	HR	RBI	SB	Avg
2002 Red Sox	Gulf Coast	SS-2B-3B	45	164	29	56	11	3	6	26	8	.341
2002 Lowell	N.Y.-Penn.	SS	22	97	17	36	9	2	1	19	4	.371
2003 Augusta	So.Atl.	SS	111	422	69	116	24	3	6	50	36	.275
2004 Portland	Eastern	SS	32	129	26	40	7	2	5	15	12	.310
2004 Sarasota	Fla.St.	SS	62	239	33	74	8	4	1	24	12	.310
2004 Red Sox	Gulf Coast	SS-2B	6	20	5	8	0	1	0	7	1	.400
2005 Portland	Eastern	SS-2B-3B	122	465	66	126	21	7	6	52	26	.271
2005 Boston a	A.L.	SS	2	2	0	0	0	0	0	0	0	.000
2006 Florida b	N.L.	SS	158	633	119	185	46	11	17	59	51	.292
2007 Florida	N.L.	SS	154	639	125	212	48	6	29	81	51	.332
2008 Florida	N.L.	SS	153	589	*125	177	34	4	33	67	35	.301
Major League Totals		4 Yrs.	467	1863	369	574	128	21	79	207	137	.308

a Traded to Florida Marlins with pitcher Anibal Sanchez and pitcher Jesus Delgado for pitcher Josh Beckett, infielder Mike Lowell and pitcher Guillermo Mota, November 24, 2005.
b Selected Rookie of the Year in National League for 2006.

RAMIREZ, MANUEL ARISTIDES (MANNY)

Born, Santo Domingo, Domininican Republic, May 30, 1972.
Bats Right. Throws Right. Height, 6 feet. Weight, 200 pounds.

Year Club	Lea	Pos	G	AB	R	H	2B	3B	HR	RBI	SB	Avg
1991 Burlington	Appal.	OF	59	215	44	70	11	4	19	63	7	.326
1992 Kinston a	Carolina	OF	81	291	52	81	18	4	13	63	1	.278
1993 Canton	Eastern	OF	89	344	67	117	32	0	17	79	2	.340
1993 Charlotte	Int.	OF	40	145	38	46	12	0	14	36	1	.317
1993 Cleveland	A.L.	DH-OF	22	53	5	9	1	0	2	5	0	.170
1994 Cleveland	A.L.	OF	91	290	51	78	22	0	17	60	4	.269
1995 Cleveland	A.L.	OF	137	484	85	149	26	1	31	107	6	.308
1996 Cleveland	A.L.	OF	152	550	94	170	45	3	33	112	8	.309
1997 Cleveland	A.L.	OF	150	561	99	184	40	0	26	88	2	.328
1998 Cleveland	A.L.	OF	150	571	108	168	35	2	45	145	5	.294
1999 Cleveland	A.L.	OF	147	522	131	174	34	3	44	*165	2	.333
2000 Akron	Eastern	PH	1	2	1	1	0	0	1	2	0	.500
2000 Buffalo	Int.	PH	5	11	5	5	1	0	3	7	0	.455
2000 Cleveland b-c	A.L.	OF	118	439	92	154	34	2	38	122	1	.351
2001 Boston	A.L.	DH-OF	142	529	93	162	33	2	41	125	0	.306
2002 Pawtucket	Int.	OF	11	30	2	3	1	0	1	2	0	*.349
2002 Boston d	A.L.	OF	120	436	84	152	31	0	33	107	0	.349
2003 Boston	A.L.	OF	154	569	117	185	36	1	37	104	3	.325
2004 Boston	A.L.	OF	152	568	108	175	44	0	*43	130	2	.308
2005 Boston	A.L.	OF	152	554	112	162	30	1	45	144	1	.292
2006 Boston	A.L.	OF	130	449	79	144	27	1	35	102	0	.321
2007 Boston	A.L.	OF	133	483	84	143	33	1	20	88	0	.296
2008 Boston	A.L.	OF	100	365	66	109	22	1	20	68	1	.299
2008 Los Angeles e-f-g	N.L.	OF	53	187	36	74	14	0	17	53	2	.396
Major League Totals		16 Yrs.	2103	7610	1444	2392	507	18	527	1725	37	.314

Division Series

Year Club	Lea	Pos	G	AB	R	H	2B	3B	HR	RBI	SB	Avg
1995 Cleveland	A.L.	OF	3	12	1	0	0	0	0	0	0	.000
1996 Cleveland	A.L.	OF	4	16	4	6	2	0	2	2	0	.375
1997 Cleveland	A.L.	OF	5	21	2	3	1	0	0	3	0	.143
1998 Cleveland	A.L.	OF	4	14	2	5	2	0	2	3	0	.357
1999 Cleveland	A.L.	OF	5	18	5	1	1	0	0	1	0	.056
2003 Boston	A.L.	OF	5	20	2	4	0	0	1	3	0	.200
2004 Boston	A.L.	OF	3	13	3	5	2	0	1	7	0	.385
2005 Boston	A.L.	OF	3	10	2	3	0	0	2	4	0	.300
2007 Boston	A.L.	OF	3	8	3	3	0	0	2	4	0	.375
2008 Los Angeles	N.L.	OF	3	10	5	5	0	0	2	3	0	.500
Division Series Totals			38	142	29	35	8	0	12	30	0	.246

Championship Series

Year Club	Lea	Pos	G	AB	R	H	2B	3B	HR	RBI	SB	Avg
1995 Cleveland	A.L.	OF	6	21	2	6	0	0	2	2	0	.286
1997 Cleveland	A.L.	OF	6	21	3	6	1	0	2	3	0	.286
1998 Cleveland	A.L.	OF	6	21	2	7	1	0	2	4	0	.333
2003 Boston	A.L.	OF	7	29	6	9	1	0	2	4	0	.310
2004 Boston	A.L.	OF	7	30	3	9	1	0	0	0	0	.300
2007 Boston	A.L.	OF	7	22	5	9	1	0	2	10	0	.409
2008 Los Angeles	N.L.	OF	5	15	4	8	2	0	2	7	0	.533
Championship Series Totals			44	159	25	54	7	0	12	30	0	.340

World Series Record

Year Club	Lea	Pos	G	AB	R	H	2B	3B	HR	RBI	SB	Avg
1995 Cleveland	A.L.	OF	6	18	2	4	0	0	1	2	1	.222
1997 Cleveland	A.L.	OF	7	26	3	4	0	0	2	6	0	.154
2004 Boston	A.L.	OF	4	17	2	7	0	0	1	4	0	.412
2007 Boston	A.L.	OF	4	16	3	4	1	0	0	2	0	.250
World Series Totals			21	77	10	19	1	0	4	14	1	.247

a On disabled list from July 10 to end of 1992 season.
b On disabled list from May 30 to July 12, 2000.
c Filed for free agency, October 27, 2000. Signed with Boston Red Sox, December 13, 2000.
d On disabled list from May 14 to June 25, 2002.
e Traded to Pittsburgh Pirates with outfielder Brandon Moss and pitcher Craig Hansen for outfielder Jason Bay, July 31, 2008.
f Traded to Los Angeles Dodgers for infielder Andy LaRoche and pitcher Bryan Morris, July 31, 2008.
g Filed for free agency, October 30, 2008.

REED, JEREMY THOMAS

Born, San Dimas, California, June 15, 1981.
Bats Left. Throws Left. Height, 6 feet. Weight, 180 pounds.

Year Club	Lea	Pos	G	AB	R	H	2B	3B	HR	RBI	SB	Avg
2002 Kannapolis	So.Atl.	OF	57	210	37	67	15	0	4	32	17	.319
2003 Winston-Salem	Carolina	OF	65	222	37	74	18	1	4	52	27	.333
2003 Birmingham	Southern	OF	66	242	51	99	17	3	7	43	18	.409
2004 Charlotte	Int.	OF	73	276	44	76	14	1	8	37	12	.275
2004 Tacoma	P.C.	OF	61	233	40	71	10	5	5	36	13	.305
2004 Seattle a	A.L.	OF	18	58	11	23	4	0	0	5	3	.397
2005 Seattle	A.L.	OF	141	488	61	124	33	3	3	45	12	.254
2006 Seattle b	A.L.	OF	67	212	27	46	6	5	6	17	2	.217
2007 Tacoma	P.C.	OF	135	564	92	169	37	5	13	64	14	.300
2007 Seattle	A.L.	OF	13	17	2	3	0	1	0	0	0	.176
2008 Tacoma	P.C.	OF	38	149	26	52	11	1	6	21	6	.349
2008 Seattle c	A.L.	OF-1B	97	286	30	77	18	1	2	31	2	.269
Major League Totals	5 Yrs.		336	1061	131	273	61	10	11	98	19	.257

a Traded by Chicago White Sox to Seattle Mariners with catcher Miguel Olivo and infielder Michael Morse for pitcher Freddy Garcia, catcher Ben Davis and cash, June 27, 2004.
b On disabled list from July 3 to November 2, 2006.
c Traded to New York Mets with pitcher J.J. Putz and pitcher Sean Green for pitcher Aaron Heilman, outfielder Endy Chavez, pitcher Jason Vargas, infielder Mike Carp, outfielder Ezequiel Carrera, pitcher Maikel Cleto and pitcher Joe Smith, December 10, 2008.

RENTERIA, EDGAR ENRIQUE

Born, Barranquilla, Colombia, August 7, 1976.
Bats Right. Throws Right. Height, 6 feet, 1 inch. Weight, 200 pounds.

Year Club	Lea	Pos	G	AB	R	H	2B	3B	HR	RBI	SB	Avg
1992 Marlins	Gulf Coast	SS	43	163	25	47	8	1	0	9	10	.288
1993 Kane County	Midwest	SS	116	384	40	78	8	0	1	35	7	.203
1994 Brevard Cty	Fla. St.	SS	128	439	46	111	15	1	0	36	6	.253
1995 Portland	Eastern	SS	135	508	70	147	15	7	7	68	30	.289
1996 Charlotte	Int.	SS	35	132	17	37	8	0	2	16	10	.280
1996 Florida a	N.L.	SS	106	431	68	133	18	3	5	31	16	.309
1997 Florida	N.L.	SS	154	617	90	171	21	3	4	52	32	.277
1998 Florida b-c	N.L.	SS	133	517	79	146	18	2	3	31	41	.282
1999 St. Louis	N.L.	SS	154	585	92	161	36	2	11	63	37	.275
2000 St. Louis	N.L.	SS	150	562	94	156	32	1	16	76	21	.278
2001 St. Louis	N.L.	SS-1B	141	493	54	128	19	3	10	57	17	.260
2002 St. Louis	N.L.	SS	152	544	77	166	36	2	11	83	22	.305
2003 St. Louis	N.L.	SS	157	587	96	194	47	1	13	100	34	.330
2004 St. Louis d	N.L.	SS	149	586	84	168	37	0	10	72	17	.287
2005 Boston e	A.L.	SS	153	623	100	172	36	4	8	70	9	.276
2006 Atlanta	N.L.	SS	149	598	100	175	40	2	14	70	17	.293
2007 Atlanta f-g	N.L.	SS	124	494	87	164	30	1	12	57	11	.332
2008 Detroit h	A.L.	SS	138	503	69	136	22	2	10	55	6	.270
Major League Totals	13 Yrs.		1860	7140	1090	2070	392	26	127	817	280	.290
Division Series												
1997 Florida	N.L.	SS	3	13	1	2	0	0	0	1	0	.154
2000 St. Louis	N.L.	SS	3	10	5	2	0	0	0	0	2	.200
2001 St. Louis	N.L.	SS	5	17	2	4	1	0	1	1	0	.235
2002 St. Louis	N.L.	SS	3	12	3	3	0	0	0	0	2	.250
2004 St. Louis	N.L.	SS	4	11	4	5	2	0	0	4	1	.455
2005 Boston	A.L.	SS	3	13	1	3	2	0	0	0	0	.231
Division Series Totals			21	76	16	19	5	0	1	6	5	.250
Championship Series												
1997 Florida	N.L.	SS	6	22	4	5	1	0	0	0	1	.227
2000 St. Louis	N.L.	SS	5	20	4	6	1	0	0	4	3	.300
2002 St. Louis	N.L.	SS	5	19	0	3	0	0	0	1	0	.158
2004 St. Louis	N.L.	SS	7	24	1	4	0	0	0	2	0	.167
Championship Series Totals			23	85	9	18	2	0	0	7	4	.212
World Series Record												
1997 Florida	N.L.	SS	7	31	3	9	2	0	0	3	0	.290
2004 St. Louis	N.L.	SS	4	15	2	5	3	0	0	1	0	.333
World Series Totals			11	46	5	14	5	0	0	4	0	.304

a On disabled list from June 24 to July 11, 1996.
b On disabled list from August 25 to September 9, 1998.
c Traded to St. Louis Cardinals for infielder Pablo Ozuna, pitcher Armando Almanza and pitcher Braden Looper, December 14, 1998.

d Filed for free agency, October 29, 2004. Signed with Boston Red Sox, December 17, 2004.
e Traded to Atlanta Braves with cash for infielder Andy Marte, December 7, 2005.
f On disabled list from August 3 to August 22 and from August 23 to September 7, 2007.
g Traded to Detroit Tigers for pitcher Jair Jurrjens and outfielder Gorkys Hernandez, October 29, 2007.
h Not offered contract, October 30, 2008. Signed with San Francisco Giants, December 4, 2008.

REYES, JOSE BERNABE
Born, Villa Gonzalez, Dominican Republic, June 11, 1983.
Bats Both. Throws Right. Height, 6 feet. Weight, 200 pounds.

Year Club	Lea	Pos	G	AB	R	H	2B	3B	HR	RBI	SB	Avg
2000 Kingsport......	Appal.	SS-3B-2B-OF	49	132	22	33	3	3	0	8	10	.250
2001 Columbia......	So.Atl.	SS	108	407	71	125	22	15	5	48	30	.307
2002 Binghamton....	Eastern	SS	65	275	46	79	16	8	2	24	27	.287
2002 St. Lucie......	Fla.St.	SS	69	288	58	83	10	11	6	38	31	.288
2003 Norfolk.........	Int.	SS	42	160	28	43	6	4	0	13	26	.269
2003 New York a.......	N.L.	SS	69	274	47	84	12	4	5	32	13	.307
2004 St. Lucie......	Fla.St.	2B	6	23	3	6	2	0	0	1	2	.261
2004 Binghamton....	Eastern	2B	4	18	2	2	0	0	0	3	3	.111
2004 New York b.....	N.L.	2B-SS	53	220	33	56	16	2	2	14	19	.255
2005 New York.......	N.L.	SS	161	*696	99	190	24	*17	7	58	*60	.273
2006 New York.......	N.L.	SS	153	647	*122	194	30	17	19	81	*64	.300
2007 New York.......	N.L.	SS	160	681	119	191	36	12	12	57	*78	.280
2008 New York......	N.L.	SS	159	*688	113	*204	37	*19	16	68	56	.297
Major League Totals		6 Yrs.	755	3206	533	919	155	71	61	310	290	.287
Division Series												
2006 New York.......	N.L.	SS	3	12	2	2	0	0	0	3	1	.167
Championship Series												
2006 New York........	N.L.	SS	7	32	5	9	1	1	1	2	2	.281

a On disabled list from September 1 to November 6, 2003.
b On disabled list from March 26 to June 19 and August 12 to September 24, 2004.

REYNOLDS, MARK ANDREW
Born, Pikeville, Kentucky, August 3, 1983.
Bats Right. Throws Right. Height, 6 feet, 1 inch. Weight, 220 pounds.

Year Club	Lea	Pos	G	AB	R	H	2B	3B	HR	RBI	SB	Avg
2004 Lancaster.........	Calif.	3B-SS	4	12	1	1	0	0	0	1	0	.083
2004 South Bend ...	Midwest	3B	4	15	0	1	1	0	0	0	0	.067
2004 Yakima......	Northwest	SS-3B-2B	64	234	58	64	19	1	12	41	5	.274
2005 South Bend ...	Midwest	SS-3B	118	434	65	110	26	2	19	76	4	.253
2006 Lancaster........	Calif.	SS-3B-2B-1B	76	273	64	92	18	2	23	77	1	.337
2006 Tennessee	Southern	OF-3B-2B	30	114	23	31	7	0	8	21	0	.272
2007 Mobile	Southern	3B-2B	37	134	28	41	9	2	6	22	2	.306
2007 Arizona..........	N.L.	3B-2B-OF	111	366	62	102	20	4	17	62	0	.279
2008 Arizona..........	N.L.	3B-1B	152	539	87	129	28	3	28	97	11	.239
Major League Totals		2 Yrs.	263	905	149	231	48	7	45	159	11	.255
Division Series												
2007 Arizona..........	N.L.	3B	3	10	2	2	0	0	1	1	0	.200
Championship Series												
2007 Arizona..........	N.L.	3B	4	16	1	2	0	0	1	1	0	.125

RIOS, ALEXIS ISRAEL
Born, Coffee County, Alabama, February 18, 1981.
Bats Right. Throws Right. Height, 6 feet, 5 inches. Weight, 195 pounds.

Year Club	Lea	Pos	G	AB	R	H	2B	3B	HR	RBI	SB	Avg
1999 Medicine Hat	Pioneer	OF	67	234	35	63	7	3	0	13	8	.269
2000 Hagerstown	So.Atl.	DH	22	74	5	17	3	1	0	5	2	.230
2000 Queens	N.Y.-Penn.	OF	50	206	22	55	9	2	1	25	5	.267
2001 Charleston-W.V......	So.Atl.	OF	130	480	40	126	20	9	2	58	22	.262
2002 Dunedin	Fla.St.	OF	111	456	60	139	22	8	3	61	14	.305
2003 New Haven	Eastern	OF	127	514	86	181	32	11	11	82	11	.352
2004 Syracuse	Int.	OF	46	185	14	48	10	1	3	23	2	.259
2004 Toronto	A.L.	OF	111	426	55	122	24	7	1	28	15	.286
2005 Toronto	A.L.	OF	146	481	71	126	23	6	10	59	14	.262
2006 Syracuse	Int.	OF	3	10	0	3	1	0	0	1	0	.300
2006 Toronto a	A.L.	OF	128	450	68	136	33	6	17	82	15	.302
2007 Toronto	A.L.	OF	161	643	114	191	43	7	24	85	17	.297
2008 Toronto	A.L.	OF	155	635	91	185	47	8	15	79	32	.291
Major League Totals		5 Yrs.	701	2635	399	760	170	34	67	333	93	.288

a On disabled list from June 28 to July 28, 2006.

RIVAS, LUIS WILFREDO

Born, LaGuaira, Venezuela, August 30, 1979.
Bats Right. Throws Right. Height, 5 feet, 10 inches. Weight, 175 pounds.

Year	Club	Lea	Pos	G	AB	R	H	2B	3B	HR	RBI	SB	Avg
1996	Twins	Gulf Coast	SS	53	201	29	52	12	1	1	13	35	.259
1997	Ft. Wayne	Midwest	SS	121	419	61	100	20	6	1	30	28	.239
1998	Fort Myers	Fla.St.	SS	126	463	58	130	21	5	4	51	34	.281
1999	New Britain	Eastern	SS-2B	132	527	78	134	30	7	7	49	31	.254
2000	New Britain	Eastern	2B-SS	82	328	56	82	23	6	3	40	11	.250
2000	Salt Lake	P.C.	2B-SS	41	157	33	50	14	1	3	25	7	.318
2000	Minnesota a	A.L.	2B-SS	16	58	8	18	4	1	0	6	2	.310
2001	Minnesota	A.L.	2B	153	563	70	150	21	6	7	47	31	.266
2002	Minnesota b	A.L.	2B	93	316	46	81	23	4	4	35	9	.256
2002	Fort Myers	Fla.St.	2B	6	22	1	2	0	1	0	3	1	.091
2003	Minnesota	A.L.	2B	135	475	69	123	16	9	8	43	17	.259
2004	Rochester	Int.	2B	3	14	2	3	0	0	0	1	1	.214
2004	Minnesota c	A.L.	2B	109	336	44	86	19	5	10	34	15	.256
2005	Rochester	Int.	2B-SS	43	145	17	36	14	0	2	22	3	.248
2005	Minnesota d	A.L.	2B-SS	59	136	21	35	3	1	1	12	4	.257
2006	Durham	Int.	2B	69	229	21	50	8	1	2	24	2	.218
2007	Buffalo	Int.	SS-2B	105	410	58	108	17	3	11	43	13	.263
2007	Cleveland e-f	A.L.	2B-SS	4	11	3	3	0	1	1	4	0	.273
2008	Pittsburgh g	N.L.	SS-2B-3B	79	206	25	45	6	2	3	20	3	.218
Major League Totals		8 Yrs.		648	2101	286	541	92	29	34	201	81	.257
Division Series													
2002	Minnesota	A.L.	2B	4	12	2	3	1	0	0	0	0	.250
2003	Minnesota	A.L.	2B	4	13	0	0	0	0	0	0	0	.000
2004	Minnesota	A.L.	2B	3	1	0	0	0	0	0	1	0	.000
Division Series Totals				11	26	2	3	1	0	0	1	0	.115
Championship Series													
2002	Minnesota	A.L.	2B	5	12	1	3	0	0	0	0	0	.250

a On disabled list July 7 to 21, 2000.
b On disabled list from April 4 to June 4, 2002.
c On disabled list from May 19 to June 8, 2004.
d On disabled list from June 1 to June 17, 2005.
e Filed for free agency, October 12, 2005. Signed with Cleveland Indians organization, January 2, 2007.
f Filed for free agency, October 29, 2007. Signed with Pittsburgh Pirates organization, December 11, 2007.
g Filed for free agency, October 31, 2008.

RIVERA, JUAN LUIS

Born, Guarenas, Venezuela, July 3, 1978.
Bats Right. Throws Right. Height, 6 feet, 2 inches. Weight, 225 pounds.

Year	Club	Lea	Pos	G	AB	R	H	2B	3B	HR	RBI	SB	Avg
1996	NY Yankees	Dominican	OF	10	18	0	3	0	0	0	2	0	.167
1997	Maracay-2	Venezuelan	OF	52	142	25	40	9	0	0	14	12	.282
1998	Yankees	Gulf Coast	OF	57	210	43	70	9	1	12	45	8	.333
1998	Oneonta	N.Y.-Penn.	OF	6	18	2	5	0	0	1	3	1	.278
1999	Tampa	Fla.St.	OF	109	427	50	112	20	2	14	77	5	.262
1999	Yankees	Gulf Coast	OF	5	18	7	6	0	0	1	4	0	.333
2000	Norwich	Eastern	OF	17	62	9	14	5	0	2	12	0	.226
2000	Tampa	Fla.St.	OF-1B	115	409	62	113	26	1	14	69	11	.276
2001	Norwich	Eastern	OF	77	316	50	101	18	3	14	58	5	.320
2001	Columbus	Int.	OF	55	199	39	65	11	1	14	40	4	.327
2001	New York	A.L.	OF	3	4	0	0	0	0	0	0	0	.000
2002	Columbus	Int.	OF	65	265	40	86	21	1	8	47	5	.325
2002	New York a	A.L.	OF	28	83	9	22	5	0	1	6	1	.265
2003	Columbus	Int.	OF	79	308	47	100	21	0	7	37	1	.325
2003	New York b	A.L.	OF	57	173	22	46	14	0	7	26	0	.266
2004	Montreal c	N.L.	OF	134	391	48	120	24	1	12	49	6	.307
2005	Los Angeles	A.L.	OF	106	350	46	95	17	1	15	59	1	.271
2006	Salt Lake	P.C.	OF	2	9	3	5	3	0	1	6	0	.556
2006	Los Angeles d	A.L.	OF	124	448	65	139	27	0	23	85	0	.310
2007	Rancho Cucamonga	Calif.	OF	3	10	3	4	1	0	0	2	0	.400
2007	Salt Lake	P.C.	OF	15	61	4	16	8	0	0	17	0	.262
2007	Los Angeles e	A.L.	OF	14	43	3	12	1	0	2	8	0	.279
2008	Los Angeles f-g	A.L.	OF-1B-2B	89	256	31	63	13	0	12	45	1	.246
Major League Totals		8 Yrs.		555	1748	224	497	101	2	72	278	9	.284
Division Series													
2002	New York	A.L.	OF	4	12	2	3	0	0	0	3	0	.250

147

Year	Club	Lea	Pos	G	AB	R	H	2B	3B	HR	RBI	SB	Avg
2003 New York	A.L.	OF	4	12	2	4	0	0	0	0	0	.333
2005 Los Angeles	A.L.	DH	5	17	3	6	1	0	1	1	0	.353
2007 Los Angeles	A.L.	DH	2	3	0	1	0	0	0	0	0	.333
2008 Los Angeles	A.L.	OF	3	8	1	1	0	0	0	1	0	.125
Division Series Totals				18	52	8	15	1	0	1	5	0	.288
Championship Series													
2003 New York	A.L.	OF	2	2	0	0	0	0	0	0	0	.000
2005 Los Angeles	A.L.	OF-DH	3	9	1	1	1	0	0	0	0	.111
Championship Series Totals				5	11	1	1	1	0	0	0	0	.091
World Series Record													
2003 New York	A.L.	OF	4	6	0	1	1	0	0	1	0	.167

a On disabled list from June 8 to August 19, 2002.
b Traded to Montreal Expos with infielder Nick Johnson and pitcher Randy Choate for pitcher Javier Vazquez, December 4, 2003.
c Traded to Anaheim Angels with infielder Maicer Izturis for outfielder Jose Guillen, November 19, 2004.
d On disabled list from April 17 to May 8, 2006.
e On disabled list from March 23 to September 2, 2007.
f Traded to Kansas City Royals for infielder Angel Berroa, June 6, 2008.
g Filed for free agency, October 31, 2008, re-signed with Los Angeles Angels, December 19, 2008.

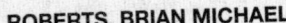

ROBERTS, BRIAN MICHAEL

Born, Durham, North Carolina, October 9, 1977.
Bats Both. Throws Right. Height, 5 feet, 9 inches. Weight, 175 pounds.

Year	Club	Lea	Pos	G	AB	R	H	2B	3B	HR	RBI	SB	Avg
1999 Delmarva a	So.Atl.	SS	47	167	22	40	12	1	0	21	17	.240
2000 Frederick	Carolina	SS	48	163	27	49	6	3	0	16	13	.301
2000 Orioles b	Gulf Coast	SS	9	29	8	9	1	2	1	3	7	.310
2001 Bowie	Eastern	2B-SS	22	81	12	24	7	0	1	7	10	.296
2001 Rochester	Int.	SS	44	161	16	43	4	1	1	12	23	.267
2001 Baltimore	A.L.	SS-2B	75	273	42	69	12	3	2	17	12	.253
2002 Rochester	Int.	2B	78	313	49	86	9	7	3	30	22	.275
2002 Baltimore	A.L.	2B	38	128	18	29	6	0	1	11	9	.227
2003 Ottawa	Int.	2B-SS	44	178	36	56	13	1	0	15	19	.315
2003 Baltimore	A.L.	2B-SS	112	460	65	124	22	4	5	41	23	.270
2004 Baltimore	A.L.	2B	159	641	107	175	*50	2	4	53	29	.273
2005 Baltimore	A.L.	2B	143	561	92	176	45	7	18	73	27	.314
2006 Bowie	Eastern	2B	2	5	0	1	0	0	0	0	0	.200
2006 Baltimore c	A.L.	2B	138	563	85	161	34	3	10	55	36	.286
2007 Baltimore	A.L.	2B	156	621	103	180	42	5	12	57	*50	.290
2008 Baltimore	A.L.	2B	155	611	107	181	51	8	9	57	40	.296
Major League Totals	8 Yrs.		976	3858	619	1095	262	32	61	364	226	.284

a Drafted by Baltimore Orioles with choice received for Texas Rangers signing infielder Rafael Palmeiro, June 2, 1999.
b On disabled list from April 19 to July 13, 2000.
c On disabled list from April 30 to May 24, 2006.

ROBERTS, DAVID RAY (DAVE)

Born, Okinawa, Japan, May 31, 1972.
Bats Left. Throws Left. Height, 5 feet, 10 inches. Weight, 180 pounds.

Year	Club	Lea	Pos	G	AB	R	H	2B	3B	HR	RBI	SB	Avg
1994 Jamestown	N.Y.-Penn.	DH-OF	54	178	33	52	7	2	0	12	12	.292
1995 Lakeland	Fla.St.	DH-OF	92	357	67	108	10	5	3	30	30	.303
1996 Visalia	California	OF	126	482	112	131	24	7	0	37	65	.272
1996 Jacksnville a	Southern	OF	3	9	0	2	0	0	0	0	0	.222
1997 Jacksonville	Southern	DH-OF	105	415	76	123	24	2	4	41	23	.296
1998 Jacksonville	Southern	OF	69	279	71	91	14	5	5	42	21	.326
1998 Buffalo	Int.	OF	5	15	2	2	0	0	0	2	2	.133
1998 Akron b-c	Eastern	OF	56	227	49	82	10	5	7	33	28	.361
1999 Buffalo	Int.	OF	89	350	65	95	17	10	0	38	39	.271
1999 Cleveland	A.L.	OF	41	143	26	34	4	0	2	12	11	.238
2000 Buffalo	Int.	OF	120	462	93	135	16	3	13	55	39	.292
2000 Cleveland	A.L.	OF	19	10	1	2	0	0	0	0	1	.203
2001 Akron	Eastern	OF	17	64	9	13	5	0	0	2	4	.203
2001 Buffalo	Int.	OF	62	241	34	73	12	4	0	22	17	.303
2001 Cleveland d-e	A.L.	OF	15	12	3	4	1	0	0	2	0	.333
2002 Los Angeles	N.L.	OF	127	422	63	117	14	7	3	34	45	.277
2003 Ogden	Pioneer	OF	3	10	4	4	0	0	0	0	1	.400
2003 Las Vegas	P.C.	OF	2	5	2	0	0	0	0	0	0	.000

Year Club	Lea	Pos	G	AB	R	H	2B	3B	HR	RBI	SB	Avg
2003 Los Angeles f	N.L.	OF	107	388	56	97	6	5	2	16	40	.250
2004 Vero Beach	Fla.St.	OF	2	8	0	0	0	0	0	0	0	.000
2004 Los Angeles	N.L.	OF	68	233	45	59	4	7	2	21	33	.253
2004 Boston g-h-i	A.L.	OF	45	86	19	22	10	0	2	14	5	.256
2005 Lake Elsinore	California	OF	3	10	2	2	1	0	0	0	0	.200
2005 San Diego j	N.L.	OF	115	411	65	113	19	10	8	38	23	.275
2006 Lake Elsinore	Calif.	OF	1	3	0	1	0	0	0	0	0	.333
2006 San Diego k-l	N.L.	OF	129	499	80	146	18	13	2	44	49	.293
2007 Fresno	P.C.	OF	2	7	1	1	0	0	0	0	0	.143
2007 San Francisco m	N.L.	OF	114	396	61	103	17	9	2	23	31	.260
2008 Fresno	P.C.	OF	11	31	4	12	4	1	2	5	0	.387
2008 San Francisco n	N.L.	OF	52	107	18	24	2	2	0	9	5	.224
Major League Totals		10 Yrs.	832	2707	437	721	95	53	23	213	243	.266
Division Series												
1999 Cleveland	A.L.	OF	2	3	0	0	0	0	0	0	0	.000
2004 Boston	A.L.	PH	1	0	0	0	0	0	0	0	0	.000
2005 San Diego	N.L.	OF	3	9	1	2	0	0	1	1	0	.222
2006 San Diego	N.L.	OF	4	16	1	7	0	1	0	0	1	.438
Division Series Totals			10	28	2	9	0	1	1	1	1	.321
Championship Series												
2004 Boston	A.L.	PH	2	0	2	0	0	0	0	0	1	.000

a Loaned by Detroit Tigers to Oakland A's organization from March 30 to August 30, 1996.
b Traded by Detroit Tigers to Cleveland Indians with pitcher Tim Worrell for outfielder Geronimo Berroa, June 22, 1998.
c On disabled list from August 10 to 18, 1998.
d On disabled list from March 21 to June 24, 2001.
e Traded to Los Angeles Dodgers for pitcher Christian Bridenbaugh and pitcher Nial Hughes, December 21, 2001.
f On disabled list from May 17 to June 1 and July 2 to July 26, 2003.
g On disabled list from May 5 to May 28, 2004.
h Traded to Boston Red Sox for outfielder Henri Stanley, July 31, 2004.
i Traded to San Diego Padres for outfielder Jay Payton, infielder Ramon Vazquez, pitcher David Pauley and cash, December 20, 2004.
j On disabled list from March 30 to April 18, 2005.
k On disabled list from June 18 to July 5, 2006.
l Filed for free agency, October 28, 2006. Signed with San Francisco Giants, December 1, 2006.
m On disabled list from May 10 to June 9, 2007.
n On disabled list from April 8 to July 22, 2008.

RODRIGUEZ, ALEXANDER EMMANUEL (ALEX)

Born, New York, New York, July 27, 1975.
Bats Right. Throws Right. Height, 6 feet, 3 inches. Weight, 225 pounds.

Year Club	Lea	Pos	G	AB	R	H	2B	3B	HR	RBI	SB	Avg
1994 Appleton	Midwest	SS	65	248	49	79	17	6	14	55	16	.319
1994 Jacksonville	Southern	SS	17	59	7	17	4	1	1	8	2	.288
1994 Seattle	A.L.	SS	17	54	4	11	0	0	0	2	3	.204
1994 Calgary	P.C.	SS	32	119	22	37	7	4	6	21	2	.311
1995 Tacoma	P.C.	SS	54	214	37	77	12	3	15	45	2	.360
1995 Seattle	A.L.	SS	48	142	15	33	6	2	5	19	4	.232
1996 Tacoma a	P.C.	SS	2	5	0	1	0	0	0	0	0	.200
1996 Seattle	A.L.	SS	146	601	*141	215	*54	1	36	123	15	*.358
1997 Seattle b	A.L.	SS	141	587	100	176	40	3	23	84	29	.300
1998 Seattle	A.L.	SS	161	*686	123	*213	35	5	42	124	46	.310
1999 Seattle c	A.L.	SS	129	502	110	143	25	0	42	111	21	.285
2000 Seattle d-e	A.L.	SS	148	554	134	175	34	2	41	132	15	.316
2001 Texas	A.L.	SS	*162	632	*133	201	34	1	*52	135	18	.318
2002 Texas	A.L.	SS	*162	624	125	187	27	2	*57	*142	9	.300
2003 Texas	A.L.	SS	161	607	*124	181	30	6	*47	118	17	.298
2004 New York f-g	A.L.	3B-SS	155	601	112	172	24	2	36	106	28	.286
2005 New York h	A.L.	3B-SS	*162	605	*124	194	29	1	*48	130	21	.321
2006 New York	A.L.	3B	154	572	113	166	26	1	35	121	15	.290
2007 New York i-j	A.L.	3B	158	583	*143	183	31	0	*54	*156	24	.314
2008 New York k	A.L.	3B	138	510	104	154	33	0	35	103	18	.302
Major League Totals		15 Yrs.	2042	7860	1605	2404	428	26	553	1606	283	.306
Division Series												
1995 Seattle	A.L.	SS	1	1	1	0	0	0	0	0	0	.000
1997 Seattle	A.L.	SS	4	16	1	5	1	0	1	1	0	.313
2000 Seattle	A.L.	SS	3	13	0	4	0	0	0	2	0	.308
2004 New York	A.L.	3B	4	19	3	8	3	0	1	3	2	.421

Year	Club	Lea	Pos	G	AB	R	H	2B	3B	HR	RBI	SB	Avg
2005 New York		A.L.	3B	5	15	2	2	1	0	0	0	1	.133
2006 New York		A.L.	3B	4	14	0	1	0	0	0	0	0	.071
2007 New York		A.L.	3B	4	15	2	4	0	0	1	1	0	.267
Division Series Totals				25	93	9	24	5	0	3	7	3	.258
Championship Series													
1995 Seattle		A.L.	PH	1	1	0	0	0	0	0	0	0	.000
2000 Seattle		A.L.	SS	6	22	4	9	2	0	2	5	1	.409
2004 New York		A.L.	3B	7	31	8	8	2	0	2	5	0	.258
Championship Series Totals				14	54	12	17	4	0	4	10	1	.315

a On disabled list from April 22 to May 7, 1996.
b On disabled list from June 12 to June 27, 1997.
c On disabled list from April 7 to May 14, 1999.
d On disabled list from July 8 to July 23, 2000.
e Filed for free agency, October 30, 2000. Signed with Texas Rangers, December 11, 2000.
f Traded to New York Yankees for infielder Alfonso Soriano and player to be named later, February 16, 2004.
g Texas Rangers received infielder Joaquin Arias to complete trade, March 23, 2004.
h Selected Most Valuable Player in American League for 2005.
i Filed for free agency, October 29, 2007, re-signed with New York Yankees, December 13, 2007.
j Selected Most Valuable Player in American League for 2007.
k On disabled list from April 30 to May 20, 2008.

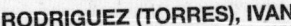

RODRIGUEZ (TORRES), IVAN

Born, Manati, Puerto Rico, November 27, 1971.
Bats Right. Throws Right. Height, 5 feet, 9 inches. Weight, 195 pounds.

Year	Club	Lea	Pos	G	AB	R	H	2B	3B	HR	RBI	SB	Avg
1989 Gastonia		So. Atl.	C	112	386	38	92	22	1	7	42	2	.238
1990 Charlotte		Fla. St.	C	109	408	48	117	17	7	2	55	1	.287
1991 Tulsa		Texas	C	50	175	16	48	7	2	3	28	1	.274
1991 Texas		A.L.	C	88	280	24	74	16	0	3	27	0	.264
1992 Texas a		A.L.	C	123	420	39	109	16	1	8	37	0	.260
1993 Texas		A.L.	C	137	473	56	129	28	4	10	66	8	.273
1994 Texas		A.L.	C	99	363	56	108	19	1	16	57	6	.298
1995 Texas		A.L.	C	130	492	56	149	32	2	12	67	0	.303
1996 Texas		A.L.	C	153	639	116	192	47	3	19	86	5	.300
1997 Texas		A.L.	C	150	597	98	187	34	4	20	77	7	.313
1998 Texas		A.L.	C	145	579	88	186	40	4	21	91	9	.321
1999 Texas b		A.L.	C	144	600	116	199	29	1	35	113	25	.332
2000 Texas c		A.L.	C	91	363	66	126	27	4	27	83	5	.347
2001 Texas d		A.L.	C	111	442	70	136	24	2	25	65	10	.308
2002 Charlotte		Fla.St.	C	3	9	1	3	0	0	0	0	0	.333
2002 Texas e-f		A.L.	C	108	408	67	128	32	2	19	60	5	.314
2003 Florida g		N.L.	C	144	511	90	152	36	3	16	85	10	.297
2004 Detroit		A.L.	C	135	527	72	176	32	2	19	86	7	.334
2005 Detroit		A.L.	C	129	504	71	139	33	5	14	50	7	.276
2006 Detroit		A.L.	C-1B-2B	136	547	74	164	28	4	13	69	8	.300
2007 Detroit		A.L.	C	129	502	50	141	31	3	11	63	2	.281
2008 Detroit-New York h-i		A.L.	C	115	398	44	110	20	3	7	35	10	.276
Major League Totals			18 Yrs.	2267	8645	1253	2605	524	48	295	1217	124	.301
Division Series													
1996 Texas		A.L.	C	4	16	1	6	1	0	0	2	0	.375
1998 Texas		A.L.	C	3	10	0	1	0	0	0	1	0	.100
1999 Texas		A.L.	C	3	12	0	3	1	0	0	0	1	.250
2003 Florida		N.L.	C	4	17	3	6	1	0	1	6	0	.353
2006 Detroit		A.L.	C	4	13	3	3	1	0	0	3	0	.231
Division Series Totals				18	68	7	19	4	0	1	12	1	.279
Championship Series													
2003 Florida		N.L.	C	7	28	5	9	2	0	2	10	0	.321
2006 Detroit		A.L.	C	4	16	2	2	0	0	1	1	0	.125
Championship Series Totals				11	44	7	11	2	0	3	11	0	.250
World Series Record													
2003 Florida		N.L.	C	6	22	2	6	2	0	0	1	0	.273
2006 Detroit		A.L.	C	5	19	1	3	1	0	0	1	0	.158
World Series Totals				11	41	3	9	3	0	0	2	0	.220

a On disabled list from June 6 to June 27, 1992.
b Selected Most Valuable Player in American League for 1999.
c On disabled list from July 25 to October 1, 2000.
d On disabled list from May 2 to May 17 and August 31 to November 19, 2001.

e On disabled list from April 17 to June 7, 2002.
f Filed for free agency, October 28, 2002. Signed with Florida Marlins, January 24, 2003
g Filed for free agency, November 2, 2003. Signed with Detroit Tigers, February 2, 2004.
h Traded to New York Yankees for pitcher Kyle Farnsworth, July 30, 2008.
i Filed for free agency, October 30, 2008.

RODRIGUEZ, LUIS ORLANDO

Born, San Carlos, Venezuela, June 27, 1980.
Bats Both. Throws Right. Height, 5 feet, 9 inches. Weight, 180 pounds.

Year	Club	Lea	Pos	G	AB	R	H	2B	3B	HR	RBI	SB	Avg
1997	Maracay-1 ...	Venzuelan	2B	51	107	21	33	6	1	0	12	5	.308
1998	Twins	Gulf Coast	2B-SS-3B	52	180	33	50	11	1	0	15	14	.278
1999	Quad Cities....	Midwest	2B-3B	119	434	63	117	20	0	3	50	8	.270
2000	Quad Cities....	Midwest	2B-SS-3B	106	342	35	77	11	2	0	28	4	.225
2001	Fort Myers	Fla.St.	SS-2B-3B	125	463	71	127	21	3	4	64	11	.274
2002	New Britain	Eastern	SS-2B	129	455	60	117	18	2	8	40	3	.257
2003	Rochester.......	Int.	2B-SS	131	518	65	153	35	2	1	44	6	.295
2004	Rochester........	Int.	2B-3B-SS	127	486	73	139	33	1	5	52	3	.286
2005	Rochester........	Int.	2B-SS-3B	40	138	19	42	10	0	1	17	0	.304
2005	Minnesota	A.L.	2B-3B-SS	79	175	21	47	10	2	2	20	2	.269
2006	Minnesota a	A.L.	3B-2B-SS-1B	59	115	11	27	4	0	2	6	0	.235
2007	Rochester.........	Int.	SS	6	19	3	8	1	0	0	1	0	.421
2007	Minnesota b	A.L.	3B-2B-1B	68	155	18	34	5	1	2	12	1	.219
2008	Portland	P.C.	SS	31	96	10	29	5	1	1	8	0	.302
2008	San Diego	N.L.	SS-2B-1B-3B	64	202	22	58	11	1	0	12	1	.287
Major League Totals		4 Yrs.		270	647	72	166	30	4	6	50	4	.257

a Not offered contract, December 12, 2006, re-signed with Minnesota Twins organization, December 13, 2006.
b Claimed on waivers by San Diego Padres, October 4, 2007.

ROLEN, SCOTT BRUCE

Born, Evansville, Indiana, April 4, 1975.
Bats Right. Throws Right. Height, 6 feet, 4 inches. Weight, 240 pounds.

Year	Club	Lea	Pos	G	AB	R	H	2B	3B	HR	RBI	SB	Avg
1993	Martinsville	Appal.	3B	25	80	8	25	5	0	0	12	3	.313
1994	Spartanburg........	So.Atl.	3B	138	513	83	151	34	5	14	72	6	.294
1995	Clearwater	Fla.St.	3B	66	238	45	69	13	2	10	39	4	.290
1995	Reading	Eastern	3B	20	76	16	22	3	0	3	15	1	.289
1996	Reading	Eastern	3B	61	230	44	83	22	2	9	42	6	.361
1996	Scranton-WB	Int.	3B	45	168	23	46	17	0	2	19	4	.274
1996	Philadelphia	N.L.	3B	37	130	10	33	7	0	4	18	0	.254
1997	Philadelphia a	N.L.	3B	156	561	93	159	35	3	21	92	16	.283
1998	Philadelphia	N.L.	3B	160	601	120	174	45	4	31	110	14	.290
1999	Philadelphia b	N.L.	3B	112	421	74	113	28	1	26	77	12	.268
2000	Philadelphia	N.L.	3B	128	483	88	144	32	6	26	89	8	.298
2001	Philadelphia	N.L.	3B	151	554	96	160	39	1	25	107	16	.289
2002	Philadelphia-St. Louis c	N.L.	3B	155	580	89	154	29	8	31	110	8	.266
2003	St. Louis	N.L.	3B	154	559	98	160	49	1	28	104	13	.286
2004	St. Louis	N.L.	3B	142	500	109	157	32	4	34	124	4	.314
2005	St. Louis d	N.L.	3B	56	196	28	46	12	1	5	28	1	.235
2006	St. Louis	N.L.	3B	142	521	94	154	48	1	22	95	7	.296
2007	St. Louis e-f	N.L.	3B	112	392	55	104	24	2	8	58	5	.265
2008	Dunedin	Fla.St.	3B	3	9	0	0	0	0	0	0	0	.000
2008	Toronto g	A.L.	3B	115	408	58	107	30	3	11	50	5	.262
Major League Totals		13 Yrs.		1620	5906	1012	1665	410	35	272	1062	109	.282
Division Series													
2002	St. Louis............	N.L.	3B	2	7	1	3	0	0	1	2	0	.429
2004	St. Louis............	N.L.	3B	4	12	1	0	0	0	0	0	0	.000
2006	St. Louis............	N.L.	3B	3	11	0	1	1	0	0	0	0	.091
Division Series Totals				9	30	2	4	1	0	1	2	0	.133
Championship Series													
2004	St. Louis............	N.L.	3B	7	29	6	9	2	0	3	6	0	.310
2006	St. Louis............	N.L.	3B	7	21	4	5	1	0	0	0	0	.238
Championship Series Totals				14	50	10	14	3	0	3	6	0	.280
World Series Record													
2004	St. Louis............	N.L.	3B	4	15	0	0	0	0	0	1	0	.000
2006	St. Louis............	N.L.	3B	5	19	5	8	3	0	1	2	0	.421
World Series Totals				9	34	5	8	3	0	1	3	0	.235

a Selected Rookie of the Year in National League for 1997.
b On disabled list from May 24 to June 8, 2000.
c Traded to St. Louis Cardinals with pitcher Doug Nickle for infielder Placido Polanco, pitcher Bud Smith and pitcher Mike Timlin, July 29, 2002.
d On disabled list from May 11 to June 18 and July 22 to October 31, 2005.
e On disabled list from August 29 to November 2, 2007.
f Traded to Toronto Blue Jays for infielder Troy Glaus, January 14, 2008.
g On disabled list from March 21 to April 25 and from August 11 to August 26, 2008.

ROLLINS, JAMES CALVIN (JIMMY)

Born, Oakland, California, November 27, 1978.
Bats Both. Throws Right. Height, 5 feet, 8 inches. Weight, 170 pounds.

Year	Club	Lea	Pos	G	AB	R	H	2B	3B	HR	RBI	SB	Avg
1996 Martinsvlle	Appal.	SS	49	172	22	41	3	1	1	16	11	.238
1997 Piedmont	So.Atl.	SS	139	560	94	151	22	8	6	59	46	.270
1998 Clearwater	Fla.St.	SS	119	495	72	121	18	9	6	35	23	.244
1999 Reading	Eastern	SS	133	532	81	145	21	8	11	56	24	.273
1999 Scranton-WB	Int.	SS	4	13	0	1	1	0	0	0	1	.077
2000 Scranton-WB	Int.	SS	133	470	67	129	28	11	12	69	24	.274
2000 Philadelphia	N.L.	SS	14	53	5	17	1	1	1	0	5	.321
2001 Philadelphia	N.L.	SS	158	*656	97	180	29	*12	14	54	*46	.274
2002 Philadelphia	N.L.	SS-2B	154	*637	82	156	33	*10	11	60	31	.245
2003 Philadelphia	N.L.	SS	156	628	85	165	42	6	8	62	20	.263
2004 Philadelphia	N.L.	SS	154	657	119	190	43	*12	14	73	30	.289
2005 Philadelphia	N.L.	SS	158	677	115	196	38	11	12	54	41	.290
2006 Philadelphia	N.L.	SS	158	689	127	191	45	9	25	83	36	.277
2007 Philadelphia a	N.L.	SS	*162	*716	*139	212	38	*20	30	94	41	.296
2008 Clearwater	Fla.St.	SS	1	3	2	0	0	0	0	0	0	.000
2008 Philadelphia b	N.L.	SS	137	556	76	154	38	9	11	59	47	.277
Major League Totals			9 Yrs.	1251	5269	845	1461	307	90	125	544	295	.277
Division Series													
2007 Philadelphia	N.L.	SS	3	11	1	2	0	1	1	4	.1	.182
2008 Philadelphia	N.L.	SS	4	16	2	6	2	0	1	1	1	.375
Division Series Totals				7	27	3	8	2	1	2	5	2	.296
Championship Series													
2008 Philadelphia	N.L.	SS	5	21	4	3	0	0	1	1	2	.143
World Series Record													
2008 Philadelphia	N.L.	SS	5	22	4	5	2	0	0	0	0	.227

a Selected Most Valuable Player in National League for 2007.
b On disabled list from April 20 to May 9, 2008.

ROMERO, ALEXANDER RAFAEL (ALEX)

Born, Maracaibo, Venezuela, September 9, 1983.
Bats Left. Throws Right. Height, 6 feet. Weight, 200 pounds.

Year	Club	Lea	Pos	G	AB	R	H	2B	3B	HR	RBI	SB	Avg
2002 Twins	Gulf Coast	OF-1B	56	186	31	62	13	2	2	42	16	.333
2003 Quad Cities	Midwest	OF	120	423	50	125	16	3	4	40	11	.296
2004 Fort Myers	Fla.St.	OF	104	380	59	111	21	2	6	42	6	.292
2005 New Britain	Eastern	OF	139	509	65	153	31	2	15	77	12	.301
2006 New Britain	Eastern	OF	48	167	29	47	11	2	5	16	15	.281
2006 Rochester	Int.	OF	71	236	20	59	8	2	0	26	6	.250
2007 Tucson a	P.C.	OF	131	535	82	166	32	6	5	66	12	.310
2008 Tucson	P.C.	OF	41	173	28	56	9	2	3	19	4	.324
2008 Arizona	N.L.	OF	78	135	13	31	8	2	1	12	4	.230

a Claimed on waivers by Arizona Diamondbacks from Minnesota Twins, January 19, 2007.

ROSS, CODY JOSEPH

Born, Portales, New Mexico, December 23, 1980.
Bats Right. Throws Left. Height, 5 feet, 9 inches. Weight, 205 pounds.

Year	Club	Lea	Pos	G	AB	R	H	2B	3B	HR	RBI	SB	Avg
1999 Tigers	Gulf Coast	OF	42	142	19	31	8	3	4	18	3	.218
2000 West Michigan	Midwest	OF	122	434	71	116	17	9	7	68	11	.267
2001 Lakeland	Fla.St.	OF	127	482	84	133	34	5	15	80	28	.276
2002 Erie	Eastern	OF	105	400	73	112	28	3	19	72	16	.280
2003 Toledo	Int.	OF	124	470	74	135	35	6	20	61	15	.287
2003 Detroit	A.L.	OF	6	19	1	4	1	0	1	5	0	.211
2004 Las Vegas a	P.C.	OF	60	238	44	65	17	2	14	49	2	.273

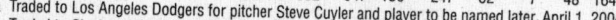

Year	Club	Lea	Pos	G	AB	R	H	2B	3B	HR	RBI	SB	Avg
2005 Los Angeles	N.L.		OF	14	25	1	4	1	0	0	1	0	.160
2005 Las Vegas	P.C.		OF	115	393	79	105	21	4	22	63	4	.267
2006 L.A.-Cin.-Florida b-c-d-e	N.L.		OF	101	269	34	61	12	2	13	46	1	.227
2007 Jupiter	Fla.St.		OF	7	23	2	6	1	0	2	3	0	.261
2007 Florida f	N.L.		OF	66	173	35	58	19	0	12	39	2	.335
2008 Florida	N.L.		OF	145	461	59	120	29	5	22	73	6	.260
Major League Totals		5 Yrs.		332	947	130	247	62	7	48	164	9	.261

a Traded to Los Angeles Dodgers for pitcher Steve Cuyler and player to be named later, April 1, 2004.
b Traded to Cincinnati Reds for player to be named later, April 24, 2006.
c Los Angeles Dodgers received pitcher Ben Kozlowski to complete trade, June 1, 2006.
d On disabled list from April 29 to May 23, 2006.
e Sold to Florida Marlins, May 27, 2006.
f On disabled list from May 6 to July 19, 2007.

ROWAND, AARON RYAN
Born, Portland, Oregon, August 29, 1977.
Bats Right. Throws Right. Height, 6 feet. Weight, 220 pounds.

Year	Club	Lea	Pos	G	AB	R	H	2B	3B	HR	RBI	SB	Avg
1998 Hickory a	So.Atl.		OF	60	218	42	75	13	3	5	32	7	.344
1999 Winston-Salem	Carolina		OF	133	512	96	143	37	3	24	88	15	.279
2000 Birmingham	Southern		OF	139	532	80	137	26	5	20	98	22	.258
2001 Charlotte	Int.		OF	82	329	54	97	28	0	16	48	8	.295
2001 Chicago	A.L.		OF	63	123	21	36	5	0	4	20	5	.293
2002 Chicago	A.L.		OF	126	302	41	78	16	2	7	29	0	.258
2003 Charlotte	Int.		OF	32	120	15	29	9	0	3	13	0	.242
2003 Chicago	A.L.		OF	93	157	22	45	8	0	6	24	0	.287
2004 Chicago	A.L.		OF	140	487	94	151	38	2	24	69	17	.310
2005 Chicago b	A.L.		OF	157	578	77	156	30	5	13	69	16	.270
2006 Philadelphia c	N.L.		OF	109	405	59	106	24	3	12	47	10	.262
2007 Philadelphia d	N.L.		OF	161	612	105	189	45	0	27	89	6	.309
2008 San Francisco	N.L.		OF	152	549	57	149	37	0	13	70	2	.271
Major League Totals		8 Yrs.		1001	3213	476	910	203	12	106	417	56	.283
Division Series													
2005 Chicago	A.L.		OF	3	10	3	4	2	0	0	2	1	.400
2007 Philadelphia	N.L.		OF	3	12	1	1	0	0	1	1	0	.083
Division Series Totals				6	22	4	5	2	0	1	3	1	.227
Championship Series													
2005 Chicago	A.L.		OF	5	18	3	3	3	0	0	1	0	.167
World Series Record													
2005 Chicago	A.L.		OF	4	17	2	5	1	0	0	0	0	.294

a Drafted by Chicago White Sox with choice received for Tampa Bay Devil Rays signing of outfielder Dave Martinez, June 2, 1998.
b Traded to Philadelphia Phillies with pitcher Dan Haigwood and player to be named later for infielder Jim Thome, November 25, 2005. Philadelphia Phillies received pitcher Giovany Gonzalez to complete trade, December 8, 2005.
c On disabled list from May 12 to May 27 and August 22 to October 4, 2006.
d Filed for free agency, October 29, 2007. Signed with San Francisco Giants, December 12, 2007.

RUIZ, CARLOS JOAQUIN
Born, David, Panama, January 22, 1979.
Bats Right. Throws Right. Height, 5 feet, 10 inches. Weight, 200 pounds.

Year	Club	Lea	Pos	G	AB	R	H	2B	3B	HR	RBI	SB	Avg
2000 Phillies	Gulf Coast		C	38	130	11	36	7	1	1	22	3	.277
2001 Lakewood	So.Atl.		C-OF	73	249	21	65	14	3	4	32	5	.261
2002 Clearwater	Fla.St.		C	92	342	35	73	18	3	5	32	3	.213
2003 Reading	Eastern		C-OF	52	169	22	45	6	0	2	16	1	.266
2003 Clearwater	Fla.St.		C	15	54	5	17	0	0	2	9	2	.315
2004 Reading	Eastern		C	101	349	45	99	15	2	17	50	8	.284
2005 Scranton-WB	Int.		C-1B	100	347	50	104	25	9	4	40	4	.300
2006 Scranton-WB	Int.		C	100	368	56	113	25	0	16	69	4	.307
2006 Philadelphia	N.L.		C	27	69	5	18	1	1	3	10	0	.261
2007 Philadelphia	N.L.		C	115	374	42	97	29	2	6	54	6	.259
2008 Philadelphia	N.L.		C-3B	117	320	47	70	14	0	4	31	1	.219
Major League Totals		3 Yrs.		259	763	94	185	44	3	13	95	7	.242
Division Series													
2007 Philadelphia	N.L.		C	3	9	1	3	1	0	0	0	1	.333

Year	Club	Lea	Pos	G	AB	R	H	2B	3B	HR	RBI	SB	Avg
2008 Philadelphia	N.L.	C	4	14	1	1	0	0	0	0	0	.071
Division Series Totals			7	23	2	4	1	0	0	0	1	.174
Championship Series													
2008 Philadelphia	N.L.	C	5	16	3	5	1	0	0	1	0	.313
World Series Record													
2008 Philadelphia	N.L.	C	5	16	2	6	2	0	1	3	1	.375

RYAN, BRENDAN WOOD

Born, Los Angeles, California, March 26, 1982.
Bats Right. Throws Right. Height, 6 feet, 2 inches. Weight, 195 pounds.

Year	Club	Lea	Pos	G	AB	R	H	2B	3B	HR	RBI	SB	Avg
2003 New Jersey	..N.Y.-Penn.	SS-3B	53	193	20	60	14	4	0	13	11	.311
2004 Peoria.......	Midwest	SS	105	426	72	137	21	4	2	59	30	.322
2005 Palm Beach	Fla.St.	SS	49	188	29	57	17	0	1	16	8	.303
2005 Springfield	Texas	SS	43	154	28	42	8	1	2	9	6	.273
2006 Palm Beach	Fla.St.	SS	3	14	2	6	1	0	0	1	1	.429
2006 State College	..N.Y.-Penn.	SS	8	34	5	8	0	0	0	3	1	.235
2006 Memphis	P.C.	SS	7	26	4	4	0	0	0	1	1	.154
2006 Springfield	Texas	SS	10	43	6	13	1	0	0	3	1	.302
2007 Memphis	P.C.	SS	81	323	55	88	9	5	1	15	17	.272
2007 St. Louis	N.L.	SS-3B-2B	67	180	30	52	9	0	4	12	7	.289
2008 Palm Beach	Fla.St.	SS	3	12	1	3	1	0	0	0	1	.250
2008 Springfield	Texas	3B-2B-SS	4	19	5	7	3	0	1	3	1	.368
2008 Memphis	P.C.	OF-2B-SS	21	80	13	19	5	0	3	10	1	.237
2008 St. Louis a	N.L.	SS-2B-3B-OF	80	197	30	48	9	0	0	10	7	.244
Major League Totals	2 Yrs.	147	377	60	100	18	0	4	22	14	.265		

a On disabled list from March 21 to April 23, 2008.

RYAN, DUSTY MITCHELL

Born, Merced, California, September 2, 1984.
Bats Right. Throws Right. Height, 6 feet, 4 inches. Weight, 220 pounds.

Year	Club	Lea	Pos	G	AB	R	H	2B	3B	HR	RBI	SB	Avg
2004 Oneonta	N.Y.-Penn.	C	54	157	20	43	11	1	4	26	6	.274
2005 West Michigan.....	Midwest	C	75	241	21	44	11	0	4	21	3	.183
2006 West Michigan.....	Midwest	C	98	322	49	79	13	2	6	35	3	.245
2007 Lakeland..........	Fla.St.	C	46	145	17	31	0	0	7	22	0	.214
2007 Tigers.........	Gulf Coast	C	6	16	1	1	0	0	0	1	0	.063
2008 Erie............	Eastern	C-1B	82	296	46	75	17	2	15	50	2	.253
2008 Toledo	Int.	C	20	73	12	23	7	2	2	13	0	.315
2008 Detroit	A.L.	C	15	44	6	14	2	0	2	7	0	.318

SALAZAR, JEFFREY DEWAN (JEFF)

Born, Oklahoma City, Oklahoma, November 24, 1980.
Bats Left. Throws Left. Height, 6 feet. Weight, 190 pounds.

Year	Club	Lea	Pos	G	AB	R	H	2B	3B	HR	RBI	SB	Avg
2002 Tri-City	Northwest	OF	72	268	38	63	5	4	4	21	10	.235
2003 Visalia	Calif.	OF	1	5	1	0	0	0	0	0	0	.000
2003 Asheville...........	So.Atl.	OF	129	486	109	138	23	4	29	98	28	.284
2004 Visalia	Calif.	OF	75	314	79	109	18	9	13	44	17	.347
2004 Tulsa	Texas	OF	58	224	39	50	13	2	1	17	10	.223
2005 Colorado Springs.......	P.C.	OF	59	236	42	62	17	3	6	26	5	.263
2005 Tulsa	Texas	OF	69	266	47	74	13	2	6	35	12	.278
2006 Colorado Springs.......	P.C.	OF	85	328	62	87	14	7	9	39	12	.265
2006 Colorado	N.L.	OF	19	53	13	15	4	0	1	8	2	.283
2007 Tucson	P.C.	OF	108	402	76	120	31	9	10	68	18	.299
2007 Arizona a	N.L.	OF	38	94	13	26	6	1	1	10	2	.277
2008 Tucson	P.C.	OF	24	99	29	36	6	3	4	18	3	.364
2008 Arizona b	N.L.	OF	90	128	17	27	5	3	2	12	0	.211
Major League Totals	3 Yrs.	147	275	43	68	15	4	4	30	4	.247		
Division Series													
2007 Arizona.............	N.L.	OF	2	3	0	0	0	0	0	0	0	.000
Championship Series													
2007 Arizona.............	N.L.	OF	4	7	0	1	0	0	0	0	0	.143

a Claimed on waivers by Arizona Diamondbacks, March 28, 2007.
b Not offered contract, December 12, 2008. Signed with Pittsburgh Pirates organization, December 22, 2008.

SALTALAMACCHIA, JARROD SCOTT

Born, West Palm Beach, Florida, May 2, 1985.
Bats Both. Throws Right. Height, 6 feet, 4 inches. Weight, 235 pounds.

Year Club	Lea	Pos	G	AB	R	H	2B	3B	HR	RBI	SB	Avg
2003 Braves	Gulf Coast	C-3B	46	134	23	32	11	2	2	14	0	.239
2004 Rome	So.Atl.	C	91	323	42	88	19	2	10	51	1	.272
2005 Myrtle Beach	Carolina	C	129	459	70	144	35	1	19	81	4	.314
2006 Mississippi.......	Southern	C	92	313	30	72	18	1	9	39	0	.230
2007 Mississippi.......	Southern	C	22	81	18	25	7	0	6	13	2	.309
2007 Atlanta	N.L.	C-1B	47	141	11	40	6	0	4	12	0	.284
2007 Texas a.............	A.L.	1B-C	46	167	28	42	7	1	7	21	0	.251
2008 Oklahoma............	P.C.	C	15	55	10	16	3	1	2	13	0	.291
2008 Texas	A.L.	C	61	198	27	50	13	0	3	26	0	.253
Major League Totals		2 Yrs.	154	506	66	132	26	1	14	59	0	.261

a Traded to Texas Rangers with infielder Elvis Andrus, pitcher Neftali Feliz, pitcher Matt Harrison and pitcher Beau James for infielder Mark Teixeira and pitcher Ron Mahay, July 31, 2007.

SANCHEZ, FREDERICK PHILLIP (FREDDY)

Born, Hollywood, California, December 21, 1977.
Bats Right. Throws Right. Height, 5 feet, 10 inches. Weight, 185 pounds.

Year Club	Lea	Pos	G	AB	R	H	2B	3B	HR	RBI	SB	Avg
2000 Lowell	N.Y.-Penn.	SS	34	132	24	38	13	2	1	14	2	.288
2000 Augusta	So.Atl.	SS	30	109	17	33	7	0	0	15	4	.303
2001 Trenton	Eastern	SS	44	178	25	58	20	0	2	19	3	.326
2001 Sarasota........	Fla.St.	SS	69	280	40	95	19	4	1	24	5	.339
2002 Trenton.......	Eastern	SS-2B	80	311	60	102	23	1	3	38	19	.328
2002 Pawtucket	Int.	SS-2B	45	183	25	55	10	1	4	28	5	.301
2002 Boston	A.L.	2B-SS	12	16	3	3	0	0	0	2	0	.188
2003 Pawtucket	Int.	SS-2B-3B	58	211	46	72	17	0	5	25	8	.341
2003 Boston	A.L.	3B-SS-2B	20	34	6	8	2	0	0	2	0	.235
2003 Nashville a	P.C.	2B	1	5	1	2	1	0	0	0	0	.400
2004 Nashville	P.C.	2B-SS	44	125	10	33	7	1	1	11	4	.264
2004 Pittsburgh b	N.L.	SS-2B-3B	9	19	2	3	0	0	0	2	0	.158
2005 Pittsburgh	N.L.	3B-2B-SS	132	453	54	132	26	4	5	35	2	.291
2006 Pittsburgh	N.L.	3B-SS-2B	157	582	85	200	*53	2	6	85	3	*.344
2007 Indianapolis	Int.	2B	1	2	1	1	1	0	0	0	0	.500
2007 Pittsburgh c	N.L.	2B-SS	147	602	77	183	42	4	11	81	0	.304
2008 Pittsburgh	N.L.	2B	145	569	75	154	26	2	9	52	0	.271
Major League Totals		7 Yrs.	622	2275	302	683	149	12	31	259	5	.300

a Traded to Pittsburgh Pirates with pitcher Mike Gonzalez and cash for pitcher Jeff Suppan, pitcher Brandon Lyon and pitcher Anastacio Martinez, July 31, 2003.
b On disabled list from March 26 to July 9, 2004.
c On disabled list from March 23 to April 8, 2007.

SANCHEZ, GABRIEL (GABY)

Born, Miami, Florida, September 2, 1983.
Bats Right. Throws Right. Height, 6 feet, 2 inches. Weight, 225 pounds.

Year Club	Lea	Pos	G	AB	R	H	2B	3B	HR	RBI	SB	Avg
2005 Jamestown......	N.Y.-Penn.	3B-1B-C	62	234	34	83	16	0	5	42	11	.355
2006 Jupiter	Fla.St.	1B-3B-C	16	55	13	10	3	1	1	7	1	.182
2006 Marlins.......	Gulf Coast	1B	3	6	1	2	1	0	0	3	0	.333
2006 Greensboro	So.Atl.	1B-C	55	189	43	60	12	0	14	40	6	.317
2007 Jupiter	Fla.St.	1B-3B-C	133	473	89	132	40	3	9	70	6	.279
2008 Carolina	Southern	1B-3B	133	478	70	150	42	1	17	92	17	.314
2008 Florida	N.L.	1B	5	8	0	3	2	0	0	1	0	.375

SANDOVAL, PABLO E.

Born, Puerto Cabello, Venezuela, August 11, 1986.
Bats Both. Throws Right. Height, 5 feet, 11 inches. Weight, 245 pounds.

Year Club	Lea	Pos	G	AB	R	H	2B	3B	HR	RBI	SB	Avg
2004 Giants............	Arizona	C	46	177	21	47	9	5	0	26	4	.266
2005 Salem-Keizer	Northwest	3B-1B-C	75	294	46	97	15	2	3	50	2	.330
2006 Augusta	So.Atl.	1B-3B	117	438	43	116	20	1	1	49	3	.265
2007 San Jose	Calif.	C-1B	102	401	56	115	33	5	11	52	3	.287
2008 San Jose	Calif.	C-1B	68	273	61	98	25	2	12	59	2	.359
2008 Connecticut	Eastern	C-1B	44	175	29	59	13	0	8	37	0	.337
2008 San Francisco	N.L.	1B-3B-C	41	145	24	50	10	1	3	24	0	.345

SANTIAGO, RAMON D.
Born, Las Matas de Farfan, Dominican Republic, August 31, 1979.
Bats Both. Throws Right. Height, 5 feet, 11 inches. Weight, 150 pounds.

Year	Club	Lea	Pos	G	AB	R	H	2B	3B	HR	RBI	SB	Avg
1999 Tigers	Gulf Coast		SS	35	134	25	43	9	2	0	11	20	.321
1999 Oneonta	N.Y.-Penn.		SS	12	50	9	17	1	2	1	8	5	.340
2000 West Michigan	Midwest		SS	98	379	69	103	15	1	1	42	39	.272
2001 Lakeland	Fla.St.		DH	120	429	64	115	15	3	2	46	34	.268
2002 Erie	Eastern		SS	22	75	9	21	0	2	1	7	6	.280
2002 Toledo	Int.		SS	9	28	8	12	1	0	2	6	0	.429
2002 Detroit	A.L.		SS	65	222	33	54	5	5	4	20	8	.243
2003 Detroit	A.L.		SS-2B	141	444	41	100	18	1	2	29	10	.225
2004 Tacoma	P.C.		SS-2B	71	243	35	47	7	2	1	24	9	.193
2004 Seattle a	A.L.		SS	19	39	8	7	1	0	0	2	0	.179
2005 Tacoma	P.C.		2B-SS-3B-C	129	441	68	111	22	3	10	50	18	.252
2005 Seattle	A.L.		2B-SS	8	8	2	1	0	0	0	0	0	.125
2006 Toledo	Int.		2B-SS	25	83	13	21	6	0	2	12	2	.253
2006 Detroit b	A.L.		SS-2B-3B	43	80	9	18	1	1	0	3	2	.225
2007 Toledo ,	Int.		SS-2B	91	365	40	96	19	4	3	30	8	.263
2007 Detroit	A.L.		SS	32	67	10	19	5	1	0	7	3	.284
2008 Toledo	Int.		SS	8	28	3	6	2	0	0	3	0	.214
2008 Detroit c	A.L.		SS-2B-3B	58	124	30	35	6	2	4	18	1	.282
Major League Totals			7 Yrs.	366	984	133	234	36	10	10	79	24	.238
Championship Series													
2006 Detroit	A.L.		SS	3	7	0	0	0	0	0	0	0	.000
World Series Record													
2006 Detroit	A.L.		SS	3	5	0	1	0	0	0	0	0	.200

a Traded to Seattle Mariners with infielder Juan Gonzalez for infielder Carlos Guillen, January 8, 2004.
b Released by Seattle Mariners, November 18, 2005. Signed with Detroit Tigers organization, January 4, 2006.
c On disabled list from June 5 to July 8, 2008.

SCHNEIDER, BRIAN DUNCAN
Born, Jacksonville, Florida, November 26, 1976.
Bats Left. Throws Right. Height, 6 feet, 1 inch. Weight, 195 pounds.

Year	Club	Lea	Pos	G	AB	R	H	2B	3B	HR	RBI	SB	Avg
1995 Expos	Gulf Coast		C	30	97	7	22	3	0	0	4	2	.227
1996 Expos	Gulf Coast		C	52	164	26	44	5	2	0	23	2	.268
1996 Delmarva	So.Atl.		C	5	9	0	3	0	0	0	1	0	.333
1997 Cape Fear	So.Atl.		C	113	381	46	96	20	1	4	49	3	.252
1998 Cape Fear	So.Atl.		C	38	134	33	40	7	2	7	30	6	.299
1998 Jupiter	Fla.St.		C	82	302	32	82	12	1	3	30	4	.272
1999 Harrisburg	Eastern		C	121	421	48	111	19	1	17	66	2	.264
2000 Ottawa	Int.		C-1B	67	238	22	59	22	3	4	31	1	.248
2000 Montreal	N.L.		C	45	115	6	27	6	0	0	11	0	.235
2001 Ottawa	Int.		C	97	338	33	93	27	1	6	43	2	.275
2001 Montreal	N.L.		C	27	41	4	13	3	0	1	6	0	.317
2002 Montreal	N.L.		C-OF	73	207	21	57	19	2	5	29	1	.275
2003 Montreal	N.L.		C	108	335	34	77	26	1	9	46	0	.230
2004 Montreal	N.L.		C	135	436	40	112	20	3	12	49	0	.257
2005 Washington	N.L.		C	116	369	38	99	20	1	10	44	1	.268
2006 Potomac	Carolina		DH	2	9	1	2	1	0	0	1	0	.222
2006 Washington a	N.L.		C-1B	124	410	30	105	18	0	4	55	2	.256
2007 Washington b	N.L.		C-1B	129	408	33	96	21	1	6	54	0	.235
2008 New York	N.L.		C	110	335	30	86	10	0	9	38	0	.257
Major League Totals			9 Yrs.	867	2656	236	672	143	8	56	332	4	.253

a On disabled list from May 11 to May 26, 2006.
b Traded to New York Mets with outfielder Ryan Church for outfielder Lastings Milledge, November 30, 2007.

SCHUMAKER, JARED MICHAEL (SKIP)
Born, Torrance, California, February 3, 1980.
Bats Left. Throws Right. Height, 5 feet, 10 inches. Weight, 195 pounds.

Year	Club	Lea	Pos	G	AB	R	H	2B	3B	HR	RBI	SB	Avg
2001 New Jersey	N.Y.-Penn.		OF	49	162	22	41	10	1	0	14	11	.253
2002 Potomac	Carolina		OF	136	551	71	158	22	4	2	44	26	.287
2003 Tennessee	Southern		OF	91	342	43	86	20	3	2	22	6	.251
2004 Tennessee	Southern		OF-3B	138	516	78	163	29	6	4	43	19	.316
2005 Memphis	P.C.		OF	115	443	66	127	24	3	7	34	14	.287
2005 St. Louis	N.L.		OF	27	24	9	6	1	0	0	1	1	.250

Year Club	Lea	Pos	G	AB	R	H	2B	3B	HR	RBI	SB	Avg
2006 Memphis	P.C.	OF	95	369	47	113	13	3	3	27	11	.306
2006 St. Louis	N.L.	OF	28	54	3	10	1	0	1	2	2	.185
2007 Memphis	P.C.	OF	59	232	34	71	16	0	7	31	2	.306
2007 St. Louis	N.L.	OF	88	177	19	59	12	2	2	19	1	.333
2008 St. Louis	N.L.	OF	153	540	87	163	22	5	8	46	8	.302
Major League Totals	4 Yrs.		296	795	118	238	36	7	11	68	12	.299

SCOTT, LUKE BRANDON

Born, DeLeon Springs, Florida, June 25, 1978.
Bats Left. Throws Right. Height, 6 feet. Weight, 210 pounds.

Year Club	Lea	Pos	G	AB	R	H	2B	3B	HR	RBI	SB	Avg
2001 Kinston a	Carolina				INJURED — Did Not Play							
2002 Kinston	Carolina	OF-1B	48	163	22	39	7	1	8	30	2	.239
2002 Columbus	So.Atl.	OF	49	171	28	44	15	4	7	32	9	.257
2003 Kinston	Carolina	OF	67	241	37	67	12	1	13	44	6	.278
2003 Akron	Eastern	OF	50	183	21	50	13	1	7	37	0	.273
2004 Salem	Carolina	OF	66	241	45	67	20	1	8	35	6	.278
2004 Round Rock b	Texas	OF	63	208	45	62	17	0	19	62	0	.298
2005 Round Rock	P.C.	OF	103	398	69	114	25	4	31	87	2	.286
2005 Houston	N.L.	OF	34	80	6	15	4	2	0	4	1	.188
2006 Round Rock	P.C.	OF	87	318	63	95	15	1	20	63	6	.299
2006 Houston	N.L.	OF	65	214	31	72	19	6	10	37	2	.336
2007 Houston c	N.L.	OF	132	369	49	94	28	5	18	64	3	.255
2008 Baltimore	A.L.	OF	148	475	67	122	29	2	23	65	2	.257
Major League Totals			4 Yrs. 379	1138	153	303	80	15	51	170	8	.266
Division Series												
2005 Houston	N.L.	OF	2	2	1	0	0	0	0	0	0	.000
World Series Record												
2005 Houston	N.L.	PH	0	0	0	0	0	0	0	0	0	.000

a On disabled list from June 21 to September 14, 2001.
b Traded by Cleveland Indians to Houston Astros with outfielder Willy Taveras for pitcher Jeriome Robertston, March 31, 2004.
c Traded to Baltimore Orioles with pitcher Troy Patton, pitcher Matt Albers, pitcher Dennis Sarfate and infielder Michael Costanzo for infielder Miguel Tejada, December 12, 2007.

SCUTARO, MARCOS (MARCO)

Born, San Felipe, Venezuela, October 30, 1975.
Bats Right. Throws Right. Height, 5 feet, 10 inches. Weight, 190 pounds.

Year Club	Lea	Pos	G	AB	R	H	2B	3B	HR	RBI	SB	Avg
1995 Cleveland	Dominican	3B	66	262	71	103	18	6	0	38	32	.393
1996 Columbus	So.Atl.	2B-SS-3B	85	315	66	79	12	3	10	45	6	.251
1997 Buffalo	A.A.	2B-3B-SS	21	57	8	15	3	0	1	6	0	.263
1997 Kinston	Carolina	2B-3B	97	378	58	103	17	6	10	59	23	.272
1998 Buffalo	Int.	2B-3B	8	26	3	6	3	0	0	4	0	.231
1998 Akron	Eastern	2B-SS	124	462	68	146	27	6	11	62	33	.316
1999 Buffalo	Int.	2B-SS	129	462	76	126	24	2	8	51	21	.273
2000 Buffalo	Int.	2B-SS	124	425	67	117	20	5	5	54	9	.275
2000 Indianapolis a	Int.	2B-SS	4	13	5	7	1	1	1	3	1	.538
2001 Indianapolis	Int.	2B-3B-SS	132	495	87	146	29	3	11	50	11	.295
2002 Norfolk	Int.	2B-SS-OF-3B	97	354	48	113	22	6	7	28	7	.319
2002 New York b	N.L.	2B-SS-3B-OF	27	36	2	8	0	1	1	6	0	.222
2003 Norfolk	Int.	3B-2B-SS-OF	70	244	42	76	18	3	9	32	11	.311
2003 New York c	N.L.	2B-SS	48	75	10	16	4	0	2	6	2	.213
2004 Oakland	A.L.	2B-SS-3B	137	455	50	124	32	1	7	43	0	.273
2005 Oakland	A.L.	SS-2B-3B-OF	118	381	48	94	22	3	9	37	5	.247
2006 Oakland	A.L.	SS-3B-2B-OF	117	365	52	97	21	6	5	41	5	.266
2007 Oakland d	A.L.	SS-2B-3B-OF	104	338	49	88	13	0	7	41	2	.260
2008 Toronto	A.L.	SS-2B-3B-1B	145	517	76	138	23	1	7	60	7	.267
Major League Totals			7 Yrs. 696	2167	287	565	115	12	38	234	21	.261
Division Series												
2006 Oakland	A.L.	SS	3	12	1	4	4	0	0	6	0	.333
Championship Series												
2006 Oakland	A.L.	SS	4	15	0	1	0	0	0	0	0	.067

a Sent by Cleveland Indians to Milwaukee Brewers as player to be named later in Richie Sexson trade, August 30, 2000.
b Claimed on waivers by New York Mets, April 3, 2002.
c Claimed on waivers by Oakland Athletics, October 9, 2003.
d Traded to Toronto Blue Jays for pitcher Kristian Bell and pitcher Graham Godfrey, November 18, 2007.

SEXSON, RICHMOND LOCKWOOD (RICHIE)

Born, Portland, Oregon, December 29, 1974.
Bats Right. Throws Right. Height, 6 feet, 8 inches. Weight, 235 pounds.

Year	Club	Lea	Pos	G	AB	R	H	2B	3B	HR	RBI	SB	Avg
1993 Burlington	Appal.		1B	40	97	11	18	3	0	1	5	1	.186
1994 Columbus	So.Atl.		1B	130	488	88	133	25	2	14	77	7	.273
1995 Kinston	Carolina		1B	131	494	80	151	34	0	22	85	4	.306
1996 Canton-Akron	Eastern		1B	133	518	85	143	33	3	16	76	2	.276
1997 Buffalo	A.A.		1B	115	434	57	113	20	2	31	88	5	.260
1997 Cleveland	A.L.		1B	5	11	1	3	0	0	0	0	0	.273
1998 Buffalo	Int.		OF-1B	89	344	58	102	20	1	21	74	1	.297
1998 Cleveland	A.L.		1B-OF	49	174	28	54	14	1	11	35	1	.310
1999 Cleveland	A.L.		1B-OF	134	479	72	122	17	7	31	116	3	.255
2000 Cleveland	A.L.		OF-1B	91	324	45	83	16	1	16	44	1	.256
2000 Milwaukee a-b	N.L.		1B	57	213	44	63	14	0	14	47	1	.296
2001 Milwaukee	N.L.		1B	158	598	94	162	24	3	45	125	2	.271
2002 Milwaukee	N.L.		1B	157	570	86	159	37	2	29	102	0	.279
2003 Milwaukee c	N.L.		1B	*162	606	97	165	28	2	45	124	2	.272
2004 Arizona d-e	N.L.		1B	23	90	20	21	4	0	9	23	0	.233
2005 Seattle	A.L.		1B	156	558	99	147	36	1	39	121	1	.263
2006 Seattle	A.L.		1B	158	591	75	156	40	0	34	107	1	.264
2007 Seattle	A.L.		1B	121	434	58	89	21	0	21	63	1	.205
2008 Seattle-New York f-g	A.L.		1B	96	280	29	62	9	0	12	36	1	.221
Major League Totals	12 Yrs.			1367	4928	748	1286	260	17	306	943	14	.261
Division Series													
1998 Cleveland	A.L.		1B	3	2	0	0	0	0	0	0	0	.000
1999 Cleveland	A.L.		1B-OF	3	6	1	1	0	0	0	1	0	.167
Division Series Totals				6	8	1	1	0	0	0	1	0	.125
Championship Series													
1998 Cleveland	A.L.		1B	3	6	0	0	0	0	0	0	0	.000

a Traded to Milwaukee Brewers with pitcher Paul Rigdon, pitcher Kane Davis and player to be named later for pitcher Bob Wickman, pitcher Steve Woodard and pitcher Jason Bere, July 28, 2000.
b Milwaukee Brewers received infielder Marcus Scutaro to complete trade, August 30, 2000.
c Traded to Arizona Diamondbacks with pitcher Shane Nance and player to be named later for infielder Junior Spivey, infielder Craig Counsell, infielder Lyle Overbay, catcher Chad Moeller, pitcher Chris Capuano and pitcher Jorge DeRosa, December 1, 2003. Arizona Diamondbacks received outfielder Gary Varner to complete trade, December 15, 2003.
d On disabled list from April 29 to May 21 and from May 23 to November 1, 2004.
e Filed for free agency, November 1, 2004. Signed with Seattle Mariners, December 15, 2004.
f Released by Seattle Mariners, July 10, 2008. Signed with New York Yankees, July 18, 2008.
g Released by New York Yankees, August 21, 2008.

SHEALY, RYAN NELSON

Born, Fort Lauderdale, Florida, August 29, 1979.
Bats Right. Throws Right. Height, 6 feet, 5 inches. Weight, 250 pounds.

Year	Club	Lea	Pos	G	AB	R	H	2B	3B	HR	RBI	SB	Avg
2002 Casper	Pioneer		1B	69	231	55	85	21	1	19	70	0	.368
2003 Visalia	Calif.		1B	93	341	70	102	31	1	14	73	0	.299
2004 Tulsa	Texas		1B	132	469	88	149	32	3	29	99	1	.318
2005 Colorado Springs	P.C.		1B-OF	108	411	85	135	30	2	26	88	4	.328
2005 Colorado	N.L.		1B	36	91	14	30	7	0	2	16	1	.330
2006 Colorado Springs	P.C.		1B	58	222	37	63	16	1	15	55	0	.284
2006 Colorado	N.L.		1B	5	9	2	2	2	0	0	1	0	.222
2006 Kansas City a-b	A.L.		1B	51	193	29	54	10	1	7	36	1	.280
2007 Omaha	P.C.		1B	34	122	14	32	7	0	7	24	0	.262
2007 Kansas City c	A.L.		1B	52	172	18	38	6	0	3	21	0	.221
2008 Omaha	P.C.		1B	111	400	53	113	22	0	22	65	0	.283
2008 Kansas City	A.L.		1B	20	73	12	22	1	0	7	20	0	.301
Major League Totals	4 Yrs.			164	538	75	146	26	1	19	94	2	.271

a On disabled list from March 24 to May 12, 2006.
b Traded to Kansas City Royals with pitcher Scott Dohmann for pitcher Jeremy Affeldt and pitcher Denny Bautista, July 31, 2006.
c On disabled list from May 1 to May 16 and June 26 to August 11 and August 30 to November 13, 2007.

SHEFFIELD, GARY ANTONIAN

Born, Tampa, Florida, November 18, 1968.
Bats Right. Throws Right. Height, 6 feet. Weight, 215 pounds.

Year	Club	Lea	Pos	G	AB	R	H	2B	3B	HR	RBI	SB	Avg
1986 Helena	Pioneer		SS	57	222	53	81	12	2	15	71	14	.365
1987 Stockton	California		SS	129	469	84	130	23	3	17	*103	25	.277
1988 El Paso	Texas		SS	77	296	70	93	19	3	19	65	5	.314
1988 Denver	A.A.		3B-SS	57	212	42	73	9	5	9	54	8	.344
1988 Milwaukee	A.L.		SS	24	80	12	19	1	0	4	12	3	.238
1989 Denver a	A.A.		SS	7	29	3	4	1	1	0	0	0	.138
1989 Milwaukee	A.L.		SS-3B	95	368	34	91	18	0	5	32	10	.247
1990 Milwaukee b	A.L.		3B	125	487	67	143	30	1	10	67	25	.294
1991 Milwaukee c-d	A.L.		3B	50	175	25	34	12	2	2	22	5	.194
1992 San Diego	N.L.		3B	146	557	87	184	34	3	33	100	5	*.330
1993 San Diego-Florida e-f	N.L.		3B	140	494	67	145	20	5	20	73	17	.294
1994 Portland	Eastern		OF	2	7	1	2	1	0	0	0	0	.286
1994 Florida g	N.L.		OF	87	322	61	89	16	1	27	78	12	.276
1995 Florida h	N.L.		OF	63	213	46	69	8	0	16	46	19	.324
1996 Florida	N.L.		OF	161	519	118	163	33	1	42	120	16	.314
1997 Florida i	N.L.		OF	135	444	86	111	22	1	21	71	11	.250
1998 Florida-Los Angeles j	N.L.		OF	130	437	73	132	27	2	22	85	22	.302
1999 Los Angeles	N.L.		OF	152	549	103	165	20	0	34	101	11	.301
2000 Los Angeles	N.L.		OF	141	501	105	163	24	3	43	109	4	.325
2001 Los Angeles k-l	N.L.		OF	143	515	98	160	28	2	36	100	10	.311
2002 Atlanta	N.L.		OF	135	492	82	151	26	0	25	84	12	.307
2003 Atlanta m	N.L.		OF	155	576	126	190	37	2	39	132	18	.330
2004 New York	A.L.		OF-3B	154	573	117	166	30	1	36	121	5	.290
2005 New York	A.L.		OF	154	584	104	170	27	0	34	123	10	.291
2006 Trenton	Eastern		DH	1	3	0	1	0	0	0	1	0	.333
2006 New York n-o	A.L.		OF-1B	39	151	22	45	5	0	6	25	5	.298
2007 Detroit p	A.L.		DH-OF	133	494	107	131	20	1	25	75	22	.265
2008 Lakeland	Fla.St.		DH	5	13	7	2	0	0	2	2	0	.154
2008 Detroit q	A.L.		DH-OF	114	418	52	94	16	0	19	57	9	.225
Major League Totals			21 Yrs.	2476	8949	1592	2615	454	25	499	1633	251	.292

Division Series

Year	Club	Lea	Pos	G	AB	R	H	2B	3B	HR	RBI	SB	Avg
1997 Florida	N.L.		OF	3	9	2	5	1	0	1	1	1	.556
2002 Atlanta	N.L.		OF	5	16	3	1	0	0	1	1	0	.063
2003 Atlanta	N.L.		OF	4	14	0	2	0	0	0	1	0	.143
2004 New York	A.L.		OF	4	18	2	4	1	0	1	2	0	.222
2005 New York	A.L.		OF	5	21	1	6	0	0	0	2	0	.286
2006 New York	A.L.		1B	3	12	1	1	0	0	0	1	0	.083
Division Series Totals				24	90	10	19	2	0	3	8	1	.211

Championship Series

Year	Club	Lea	Pos	G	AB	R	H	2B	3B	HR	RBI	SB	Avg
1997 Florida	N.L.		OF	6	17	6	4	0	0	1	1	0	.235
2004 New York	A.L.		OF	7	30	7	10	3	0	1	5	0	.333
Championship Series Totals				13	47	13	14	3	0	2	6	0	.298

World Series Record

Year	Club	Lea	Pos	G	AB	R	H	2B	3B	HR	RBI	SB	Avg
1997 Florida	N.L.		OF	7	24	4	7	1	0	1	5	0	.292

a On disabled list from July 14 to September 9, 1989.
b Suspended three games by American League for June 30 fight, August 31 to September 2, 1990.
c On disabled list from June 2 to July 3 and July 25 to end of 1991 season.
d Traded to San Diego Padres with pitcher Geoff Kellogg for pitcher Ricky Bones, infielder Jose Valentin and outfielder Matt Mieske, March 27, 1992.
e Suspended three games by National League for June 10 fight from July 9 to July 11, 1993.
f Traded to Florida Marlins with pitcher Rich Rodriguez for pitchers Trevor Hoffman, Andres Berumen and Jose Martinez, June 25, 1993.
g On disabled list from May 10 to May 25 and May 28 to June 11, 1994.
h On disabled list from June 11 to September 1, 1995.
i On disabled list from May 14 to May 29, 1997.
j Traded to Los Angeles Dodgers with outfielder Jim Eisenreich, catcher Charles Johnson, infielder Bobby Bonilla and pitcher Manuel Barrios for catcher Mike Piazza and infielder Todd Zeile, May 15, 1998.
k On disabled list from May 24 to June 8, 2001.
l Traded to Atlanta Braves for outfielder Brian Jordan, pitcher Odalis Perez and pitcher Andy Brown, January 15, 2002.
m Filed for free agency, October 27, 2003. Signed with New York Yankees, December 17, 2003.
n On disabled list from May 6 to May 23 and May 30 to September 19, 2006.
o Traded to Detroit Tigers for pitcher Humberto Sanchez, pitcher Kevin Whelan and pitcher Anthony Claggett, November 10, 2006.
p On disabled list from August 22 to September 6, 2007.
q On disabled list from May 27 to June 24, 2008.

SHOPPACH, KELLY BRIAN
Born, Fort Worth, Texas, April 29, 1980.
Bats Right. Throws Right. Height, 6 feet, 1 inch. Weight, 210 pounds.

Year	Club	Lea	Pos	G	AB	R	H	2B	3B	HR	RBI	SB	Avg
2002 Sarasota	Fla.St.	C	116	414	54	112	35	1	10	66	2	.271
2003 Portland	Eastern	C	92	340	45	96	30	2	12	60	0	.282
2004 Pawtucket	Int.	C	113	399	62	93	25	0	22	64	0	.233
2005 Pawtucket	Int.	C	102	371	60	94	16	0	26	75	0	.253
2005 Boston	A.L.	C	9	15	1	0	0	0	0	0	0	.000
2006 Buffalo	Int.	C	21	78	11	22	8	0	4	9	0	.282
2006 Cleveland a.	A.L.	C	41	110	7	27	6	0	3	16	0	.245
2007 Cleveland	A.L.	C	59	161	26	42	13	0	7	30	0	.261
2008 Cleveland	A.L.	C	112	352	67	92	27	0	21	55	0	.261
Major League Totals		4 Yrs.	221	638	101	161	46	0	31	101	0	.252
Division Series													
2007 Cleveland	A.L.	C	1	3	1	2	2	0	0	0	0	.667
Championship Series													
2007 Cleveland	A.L.	C	1	3	0	1	0	0	0	0	0	.333

a Traded to Cleveland Indians with infielder Andy Marte and pitcher Guillermo Mota for outfielder Coco Crisp, pitcher David Riske and catcher Josh Bard, January 27, 2006.

SIZEMORE, GRADY
Born, Seattle, Washington, August 2, 1982.
Bats Left. Throws Left. Height, 6 feet, 2 inches. Weight, 200 pounds.

Year	Club	Lea	Pos	G	AB	R	H	2B	3B	HR	RBI	SB	Avg
2000 Expos	Gulf Coast	OF	55	205	31	60	8	3	1	14	16	.293
2001 Clinton	Midwest	OF	123	451	64	121	16	4	2	61	14	.268
2002 Kinston	Carolina	OF	47	172	31	59	9	3	3	20	14	.343
2002 Brevard County a	Fla.St.	OF	75	256	37	66	15	4	0	26	9	.258
2003 Akron	Eastern	OF-2B	128	496	96	151	26	11	13	78	10	.304
2004 Buffalo	Int.	OF	101	418	73	120	23	8	8	51	15	.287
2004 Cleveland	A.L.	OF	43	138	15	34	6	2	4	24	2	.246
2005 Cleveland	A.L.	OF	158	640	111	185	37	11	22	81	22	.289
2006 Cleveland	A.L.	OF	*162	655	*134	190	*53	11	28	76	22	.290
2007 Cleveland	A.L.	OF	*162	628	118	174	34	5	24	78	33	.277
2008 Cleveland	A.L.	OF	157	634	101	170	39	5	33	90	38	.268
Major League Totals		5 Yrs.	682	2695	479	753	169	34	111	349	117	.279
Division Series													
2007 Cleveland	A.L.	OF	4	16	3	6	0	1	1	1	1	.375
Championship Series													
2007 Cleveland	A.L.	OF	7	27	6	6	2	0	1	2	1	.222

a Traded by Montreal Expos to Cleveland Indians with infielder Lee Stevens, infielder Brandon Phillips and pitcher Cliff Lee for pitcher Bartolo Colon and player to be named later, June 27, 2002. Montreal Expos received pitcher Tim Drew to complete trade, June 28, 2002.

SMITH, GARRY SETH (SETH)
Born, Jackson, Mississippi, September 30, 1982.
Bats Left. Throws Left. Height, 6 feet, 3 inches. Weight, 215 pounds.

Year	Club	Lea	Pos	G	AB	R	H	2B	3B	HR	RBI	SB	Avg
2004 Tri-Cities	Northwest	OF	9	27	6	7	1	1	2	5	0	.259
2004 Casper	Pioneer	OF	56	233	46	86	21	3	9	61	9	.369
2005 Modesto	Calif.	OF	129	533	87	160	45	6	9	72	5	.300
2006 Tulsa	Texas	OF	130	524	79	154	46	4	15	71	4	.294
2007 Colorado Springs	P.C.	OF	129	451	68	143	32	6	17	82	7	.317
2007 Colorado	N.L.	OF	7	8	4	5	0	1	0	0	0	.625
2008 Colorado Springs	P.C.	OF	68	248	55	80	16	2	10	53	11	.323
2008 Colorado	N.L.	OF	67	108	13	28	7	0	4	15	1	.259
Major League Totals		2 Yrs.	74	116	17	33	7	1	4	15	1	.284
Division Series													
2007 Colorado	N.L.	PH	2	2	1	1	0	0	0	0	0	.500
Championship Series													
2007 Colorado	N.L.	PH	2	2	1	1	1	0	0	2	0	.500
World Series Record													
2007 Colorado	N.L.	PH	2	2	0	1	0	0	0	0	0	.500

SNIDER, TRAVIS JAMES

Born, Kirkland, Washington, February 2, 1988.
Bats Left. Throws Left. Height, 5 feet, 11 inches. Weight, 245 pounds.

Year Club	Lea	Pos	G	AB	R	H	2B	3B	HR	RBI	SB	Avg
2006 Pulaski............Appal.		OF	54	194	36	63	12	1	11	41	6	.325
2007 Lansing..........Midwest		OF	118	457	72	143	35	7	16	93	3	.313
2008 Dunedin............Fla.St.		DH	17	61	15	17	5	0	4	7	1	.279
2008 New Hampshire.....Eastern		OF	98	362	65	95	21	0	17	67	1	.262
2008 Syracuse............Int.		OF	18	64	9	22	5	0	2	17	1	.344
2008 Toronto............A.L.		OF	24	73	9	22	6	0	2	13	0	.301

SNYDER, CHRISTOPHER RYAN (CHRIS)

Born, Houston, Texas, February 12, 1981.
Bats Right. Throws Right. Height, 6 feet, 3 inches. Weight, 245 pounds.

Year Club	Lea	Pos	G	AB	R	H	2B	3B	HR	RBI	SB	Avg
2002 Lancaster........California		C	60	217	32	56	16	0	9	44	0	.258
2003 Lancaster........California		C	69	245	53	77	16	2	10	53	0	.314
2003 El Paso............Texas		C	53	188	21	38	14	0	4	26	0	.202
2004 El Paso............Texas		C-1B	99	346	66	104	31	0	15	57	3	.301
2004 Arizona............N.L.		C	29	96	10	23	6	0	5	15	0	.240
2005 Arizona............N.L.		C	115	326	24	66	14	0	6	28	0	.202
2006 Arizona............N.L.		C	61	184	19	51	9	0	6	32	0	.277
2007 Arizona............N.L.		C-1B-OF	110	326	37	82	20	0	13	47	0	.252
2008 Visalia............Calif.		C	1	5	1	2	0	0	1	4	0	.400
2008 Arizona a............N.L.		C	115	334	47	79	22	1	16	64	0	.237
Major League Totals............5 Yrs.			430	1266	137	301	71	1	46	186	0	.238
Division Series												
2007 Arizona............N.L.		C	3	7	2	1	0	0	0	0	0	.143
Championship Series												
2007 Arizona............N.L.		C	3	12	1	4	2	0	1	3	0	.333

a On disabled list from July 1 to July 20, 2008.

SORIANO, ALFONSO GUILLEARD

Born, San Pedro de Macoris, Dominican Republic, January 7, 1976.
Bats Right. Throws Right. Height, 6 feet, 1 inch. Weight, 180 pounds.

Year Club	Lea	Pos	G	AB	R	H	2B	3B	HR	RBI	SB	Avg
1995 Hiroshima......Dominican		SS	63	227	52	83	12	3	4	55	8	.366
1996 Hiroshima......Japan East		SS	57	131	11	28	0	0	0	13	0	.214
1997 Hiroshima......Japan Cent.		SS	9	17	2	2	0	0	0	2	0	.118
1998 a..................				Did Not Play								
1999 Norwich..........Eastern		SS	89	361	57	110	20	3	15	68	24	.305
1999 Yankees........Gulf Coast		SS	5	19	7	5	2	0	1	5	0	.263
1999 Columbus..........Int.		SS	20	82	8	15	5	1	2	11	1	.183
1999 New York b..........A.L.		SS	9	8	2	1	0	0	1	1	0	.125
2000 Columbus..........Int.		SS-2B	111	459	90	133	32	6	12	66	14	.290
2000 New York..........A.L.		3B-SS-2B	22	50	5	9	3	0	2	3	2	.180
2001 New York..........A.L.		2B	158	574	77	154	34	3	18	73	43	.268
2002 New York..........A.L.		2B	156	*696	*128	*209	51	2	39	102	41	.300
2003 New York..........A.L.		2B	156	*682	114	198	36	5	38	91	35	.290
2004 Texas c-d..........A.L.		2B	145	608	77	170	32	4	28	91	18	.280
2005 Texas e..........A.L.		2B	156	637	102	171	43	2	36	104	30	.268
2006 Washington f..........N.L.		OF	159	647	119	179	41	2	46	95	41	.277
2007 Chicago g..........N.L.		OF-2B	135	579	97	173	42	5	33	70	19	.299
2008 Azl Cubs..........Arizona		DH	1	2	1	0	0	0	0	0	0	.000
2008 Iowa..............P.C.		OF	1	3	0	1	0	0	0	0	0	.333
2008 Chicago h..........N.L.		OF-2B	109	453	76	127	27	0	29	75	19	.280
Major League Totals............10 Yrs.			1205	4934	797	1391	309	23	270	705	248	.282
Division Series												
2001 New York..........A.L.		2B	5	18	2	4	0	0	0	3	2	.222
2002 New York..........A.L.		2B	4	17	2	2	1	0	1	2	1	.118
2003 New York..........A.L.		2B	4	19	2	7	1	0	0	4	2	.368
2007 Chicago..........N.L.		OF	3	14	0	2	0	0	0	0	0	.143
2008 Chicago..........N.L.		OF	3	14	0	1	0	0	0	0	0	.071
Division Series Totals............			19	82	6	16	2	0	1	9	5	.195
Championship Series												
2001 New York..........A.L.		2B	5	15	5	6	0	0	1	2	2	.500
2003 New York..........A.L.		2B	7	30	0	4	1	0	0	3	2	.133
Championship Series Totals......			12	45	5	10	1	0	1	5	4	.222

Year	Club	Lea	Pos	G	AB	R	H	2B	3B	HR	RBI	SB	Avg
	World Series Record												
2001 New York		A.L.	2B	7	25	1	6	0	0	1	2	0	.240
2003 New York		A.L.	2B-OF	6	22	2	5	0	0	1	2	1	.227
World Series Totals				13	47	3	11	0	0	2	4	1	.234

a Signed by New York Yankees as free agent, September 29, 1998.
b On disabled list from July 15 to August 15, 1999.
c Traded to Texas Rangers with player to be named later for infielder Alex Rodriguez, February 16, 2004.
d Texas Rangers received infielder Joaquin Arias to complete trade, March 23, 2004.
e Traded to Washington Nationals for outfielder Brad Wilkerson, outfielder Terrmel Sledge and pitcher Armando Galarraga, December 13, 2005.
f Filed for free agency, October 29, 2006. Signed with Chicago Cubs, November 20, 2006.
g On disabled list from August 6 to August 28, 2007.
h On disabled list from April 16 to May 1 and June 12 to July 23, 2008.

SOTO, GEOVANY

Born, San Juan, Puerto Rico, January 20, 1983.
Bats Right. Throws Right. Height, 6 feet, 1 inch. Weight, 230 pounds.

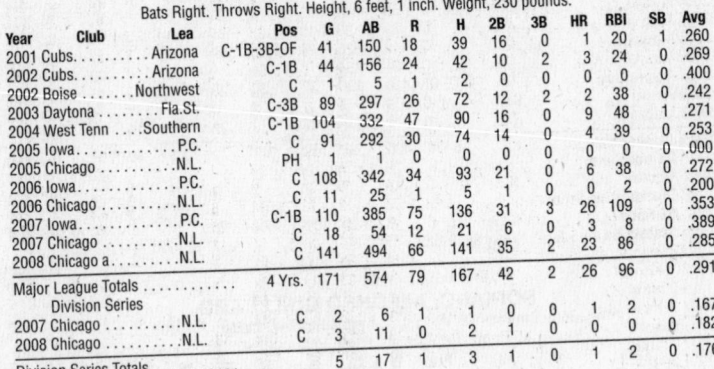

Year	Club	Lea	Pos	G	AB	R	H	2B	3B	HR	RBI	SB	Avg
2001 Cubs	Arizona	C-1B-3B-OF	41	150	18	39	16	0	1	20	1	.260
2002 Cubs	Arizona	C-1B	44	156	24	42	10	2	3	24	0	.269
2002 Boise	Northwest	C	1	5	1	2	0	0	0	0	0	.400
2003 Daytona	Fla.St.	C-3B	89	297	26	72	12	2	2	38	0	.242
2004 West Tenn	Southern	C-1B	104	332	47	90	16	0	9	48	1	.271
2005 Iowa	P.C.	C	91	292	30	74	14	0	4	39	0	.253
2005 Chicago	N.L.	PH	1	1	0	0	0	0	0	0	0	.000
2006 Iowa	P.C.	C	108	342	34	93	21	0	6	38	0	.272
2006 Chicago	N.L.	C	11	25	1	5	1	0	0	2	0	.200
2007 Iowa	P.C.	C-1B	110	385	75	136	31	3	26	109	0	.353
2007 Chicago	N.L.	C	18	54	12	21	6	0	3	8	0	.389
2008 Chicago a	N.L.	C	141	494	66	141	35	2	23	86	0	.285
Major League Totals			4 Yrs.	171	574	79	167	42	2	26	96	0	.291
	Division Series												
2007 Chicago	N.L.	C	2	6	1	1	0	0	1	2	0	.167
2008 Chicago	N.L.	C	3	11	0	2	1	0	0	0	0	.182
Division Series Totals				5	17	1	3	1	0	1	2	0	.176

a Selected Rookie of the Year in National League for 2008.

SPAN, KEIUNTA DENARD (DENARD)

Born, Tampa, Florida, February 17, 1984.
Bats Left. Throws Left. Height, 6 feet. Weight, 205 pounds.

Year	Club	Lea	Pos	G	AB	R	H	2B	3B	HR	RBI	SB	Avg
2003 Elizabethton	Appal.	OF	50	207	34	56	5	1	1	18	14	.271
2004 Twins	Gulf Coast	OF	5	16	1	6	2	0	0	1	0	.375
2004 Quad Cities	Midwest	OF	64	240	29	64	4	3	0	14	15	.267
2005 New Britain	Eastern	OF	68	267	47	76	6	5	0	26	10	.285
2005 Fort Myers	Fla.St.	OF	49	186	38	63	3	3	1	19	13	.339
2006 New Britain	Eastern	OF	134	536	80	153	16	6	2	45	24	.285
2007 Rochester	Int.	OF	139	487	59	130	20	7	3	55	25	.267
2008 Rochester	Int.	OF	40	156	32	53	11	1	3	14	15	.340
2008 Minnesota	A.L.	OF	93	347	70	102	16	7	6	47	18	.294

SPILBORGHS, RYAN ADAM

Born, Santa Barbara, California, September 5, 1979.
Bats Right. Throws Right. Height, 6 feet, 1 inch. Weight, 190 pounds.

Year	Club	Lea	Pos	G	AB	R	H	2B	3B	HR	RBI	SB	Avg
2002 Tri-City	Northwest	OF	71	261	34	60	11	1	4	34	11	.230
2003 Asheville	So.Atl.	OF	119	434	78	122	22	2	15	61	10	.281
2004 Visalia	Calif.	OF-SS	125	444	59	115	26	3	8	57	8	.259
2005 Tulsa	Texas	OF	71	255	52	87	23	3	6	54	10	.341
2005 Colorado	N.L.	OF	1	4	0	2	0	0	0	1	0	.500
2005 Colorado Springs a	P.C.	OF	60	227	49	77	23	5	5	30	7	.339
2006 Colorado Springs	P.C.	OF	68	269	50	91	20	1	5	34	8	.338
2006 Colorado	N.L.	OF	67	167	26	48	6	3	4	21	5	.287
2007 Colorado Springs	P.C.	OF-1B	34	124	25	40	7	1	5	17	4	.323
2007 Colorado	N.L.	OF	97	264	40	79	14	1	11	51	4	.299

Year Club	Lea	Pos	G	AB	R	H	2B	3B	HR	RBI	SB	Avg
2008 Colorado Springs.......P.C.		OF	11	30	9	9	1	0	1	4	0	.300
2008 Colorado b..........	N.L.	OF	89	233	38	73	14	2	6	36	7	.313
Major League Totals		4 Yrs.	254	668	104	202	34	6	21	109	16	.302
Division Series												
2007 Colorado	N.L.	OF	3	8	2	2	0	0	0	0	0	.250
Championship Series												
2007 Colorado	N.L.	OF	2	2	1	1	0	0	0	0	0	.500
World Series Record												
2007 Colorado	N.L.	OF-DH	4	10	0	0	0	0	0	0	0	.000

a Not offered contract, December 21, 2005, re-signed with Colorado Rockies organization, December 22, 2005.
b On disabled list from July 9 to September 1, 2008.

STAIRS, MATTHEW WADE (MATT)

Born, St. John, New Brunswick, Canada, February 27, 1969.
Bats Left. Throws Right. Height, 5 feet, 9 inches. Weight, 215 pounds.

Year Club	Lea	Pos	G	AB	R	H	2B	3B	HR	RBI	SB	Avg
1989 Jamestown......N.Y.Penn.		2B-3B	14	43	8	11	1	0	1	5	1	.256
1989 West Palm Bch.....	Fla. St.	3B-SS-2B	36	111	12	21	3	1	1	9	0	.189
1989 Rockford	Midwest	3B	44	141	20	40	9	2	2	14	5	.284
1990 West Palm Bch.....	Fla. St.	3B-SS	55	183	30	62	9	3	3	30	15	.339
1990 Jacksonville.....	Southern	3B-OF-2B	79	280	26	71	17	0	3	34	5	.254
1991 Harrisburg.......	Eastern	2B-3B-OF	129	505	87	168	30	10	13	78	23	.333
1992 Montreal...........	N.L.	OF	13	30	2	5	2	0	0	5	0	.167
1992 Indianapolis........	A.A.	OF	110	401	57	107	23	4	11	56	11	.267
1993 Ottawa a - b..........	Int.	OF	34	125	18	35	4	2	3	20	4	.280
1993 Montreal...........	N.L.	OF	6	8	1	3	1	0	0	2	0	.375
1993 Chunichi.......	Japan Cent.	OF	60	132	10	33	6	0	6	23	1	.250
1994 New Britain	Eastern	OF-1B	93	317	44	98	25	2	9	61	10	.309
1995 Pawtucket	Int.	OF	75	271	40	77	17	0	13	56	3	.284
1995 Boston c.............	A.L.	OF	39	88	8	23	7	1	1	17	0	.261
1996 Edmonton	P.C.	DH-OF-1B	51	180	35	62	16	1	8	41	0	.344
1996 Oakland	A.L.	OF-1B	61	137	21	38	5	1	10	23	1	.277
1997 Oakland	A.L.	OF-1B	133	352	62	105	19	0	27	73	3	.298
1998 Oakland	A.L.	DH-OF-1B	149	523	88	154	33	1	26	106	8	.294
1999 Oakland	A.L.	OF-1B	146	531	94	137	26	3	38	102	2	.258
2000 Oakland d.............	A.L.	OF-1B	143	476	74	108	26	0	21	81	5	.227
2001 Chicago e...........	N.L.	1B-OF-2B	128	340	48	85	21	0	17	61	2	.250
2002 Milwaukee f-g....	N.L.	OF	107	270	41	66	15	0	16	41	2	.244
2003 Nashville	P.C.	OF-1B	7	18	4	3	0	0	2	3	0	.167
2003 Pittsburgh h-i........	N.L.	OF-1B	121	305	49	89	20	1	20	57	0	.292
2004 Kansas City j.......	A.L.	OF-1B	126	439	48	117	21	3	18	66	1	.267
2005 Kansas City	A.L.	1B-OF	127	396	55	109	26	1	13	66	1	.275
2006 K.C.-Texas-Detroit k-l-m..	A.L.	DH-1B-OF	117	348	42	86	21	0	13	51	0	.247
2007 Toronto n.............	A.L.	OF-1B	125	357	58	103	28	1	21	64	2	.289
2008 Toronto	A.L.	DH-OF	105	320	42	80	11	1	11	44	1	.250
2008 Philadelphia o	N.L.	OF	16	17	4	5	1	0	2	5	0	.294
Major League Totals		16 Yrs.	1662	4937	737	1313	283	13	254	864	28	.266
Division Series												
1995 Boston	A.L.	PH	1	1	F0	0	0	0	0	0	0	.000
2000 Oakland	A.L.	OF	3	9	0	1	0	0	0	0	0	.111
2008 Philadelphia	N.L.	PH	2	2	0	0	0	0	0	0	0	.000
Division Series Totals			6	12	0	1	0	0	0	0	0	.083
Championship Series												
2008 Philadelphia	N.L.	PH	1	1	1	1	0	0	1	2	0	1.000
World Series Record												
2008 Philadelphia	N.L.	PH	1	1	0	0	0	0	0	0	0	.000

a Released, June 8, 1993, played in Japan, re-signed by Montreal Expos organization, December 15, 1993.
b Traded to Boston Red Sox with pitcher Pete Young for player to be named later and cash, February 18, 1994.
c Filed for free agency, October 14, 1995. Signed by Oakland Athletics organization, December 1, 1995.
d Traded to Chicago Cubs for pitcher Eric Ireland, November 20, 2000.
e Filed for free agency, November 5, 2001. Signed with Milwaukee Brewers, January 25, 2002.
f On disabled list from May 16 to June 3, 2002.
g Filed for free agency, October 28, 2002. Signed with Pittsburgh Pirates, December 15, 2002.
h On disabled list from May 19 to June 10, 2003.
i Filed for free agency, October 31, 2003. Signed with Kansas City Royals, December 9, 2003.
j On disabled list from August 7 to August 22, 2004.
k Traded to Texas Rangers for pitcher Joselo Diaz, July 31, 2006.
l Claimed on waivers by Detroit Tigers, September 15, 2006.

m Filed for free agency, October 30, 2006. Signed with Toronto Blue Jays organization, December 12, 2006.
n Filed for free agency, October 29, 2007, re-signed with Toronto Blue Jays, November 2, 2007.
o Traded to Philadelphia Phillies August 30, 2008. Toronto Blue Jay received pitcher Fabio Castro to complete trade, September 29, 2008.

STEWART, IAN KENNETH

Born, Long Beach, California, April 5, 1985.
Bats Left. Throws Right. Height, 6 feet, 3 inches. Weight, 205 pounds.

Year Club	Lea	Pos	G	AB	R	H	2B	3B	HR	RBI	SB	Avg
2003 Casper	Pioneer	3B	57	224	40	71	14	5	10	43	4	.317
2004 Asheville	So.Atl.	3B	131	505	92	161	31	9	30	101	19	.319
2005 Modesto	Calif.	3B	112	435	83	119	32	7	17	86	2	.274
2006 Tulsa	Texas	3B	120	462	75	124	41	7	10	71	3	.268
2007 Colorado Springs	P.C.	3B	112	414	72	126	23	2	15	65	11	.304
2007 Colorado	N.L.	3B	35	43	3	9	4	0	1	9	0	.209
2008 Colorado Springs	P.C.	3B-2B	69	257	65	72	15	6	19	57	7	.280
2008 Colorado	N.L.	3B-2B	81	266	33	69	18	2	10	41	1	.259
Major League Totals		2 Yrs.	116	309	36	78	22	2	11	50	1	.252

SUZUKI, ICHIRO

Born, Kasugai, Japan, October 22, 1973.
Bats Left. Throws Right. Height, 5 feet, 9 inches. Weight, 170 pounds.

Year Club	Lea	Pos	G	AB	R	H	2B	3B	HR	RBI	SB	Avg
1992 Orix	Japan Pac.	OF	40	95	9	24	5	0	0	5	3	.253
1993 Orix	Japan Pac.	OF	43	64	4	12	2	0	1	2	0	.188
1994 Orix	Japan Pac.	OF	130	546	111	210	41	5	13	54	29	.385
1995 Orix	Japan Pac.	OF	130	524	104	179	23	4	25	80	49	.342
1996 Orix	Japan Pac.	OF	130	542	104	193	24	4	16	84	35	.356
1997 Orix	Japan Pac.	OF	135	536	94	185	31	4	17	91	39	.345
1998 Orix	Japan Pac.	OF	135	506	79	181	36	3	13	71	11	.358
1999 Orix	Japan Pac.	OF	103	411	80	141	27	2	21	68	12	.343
2000 Orix a	Japan Pac.	OF	105	395	73	153	22	1	12	73	21	.387
2001 Seattle b-c	A.L.	OF	157	*692	127	*242	34	8	8	69	*56	*.350
2002 Seattle	A.L.	OF	157	647	111	208	27	8	8	51	31	.321
2003 Seattle	A.L.	OF	159	679	111	212	29	8	13	62	34	.312
2004 Seattle	A.L.	OF	161	*704	101	*262	24	5	8	60	36	*.372
2005 Seattle	A.L.	OF	*162	679	111	206	21	12	15	68	33	.303
2006 Seattle	A.L.	OF	161	*695	110	*224	20	9	9	49	45	.322
2007 Seattle	A.L.	OF	161	*678	111	*238	22	7	6	68	37	.351
2008 Seattle	A.L.	OF	162	*686	103	*213	20	7	6	42	43	.310
Major League Totals		8 Yrs.	1280	5460	885	1805	197	64	73	469	315	.331
Division Series												
2001 Seattle	A.L.	OF	5	20	4	12	1	0	0	2	1	.600
Championship Series												
2001 Seattle	A.L.	OF	5	18	3	4	1	0	0	1	2	.222

a Signed by Seattle Mariners as free agent, November 18, 2000.
b Selected Rookie of the Year in American League for 2001.
c Selected Most Valuable Player in American League for 2001.

SUZUKI, KURT KIYOSHI

Born, Wailuku, Hawaii, October 4, 1983.
Bats Right. Throws Right. Height, 6 feet. Weight, 205 pounds.

Year Club	Lea	Pos	G	AB	R	H	2B	3B	HR	RBI	SB	Avg
2004 Vancouver	Northwest	C	46	175	27	52	10	3	3	31	0	.297
2005 Stockton	Calif.	C	114	441	85	122	26	5	12	65	5	.277
2006 Midland	Texas	C-1B	99	376	64	107	26	1	7	55	5	.285
2007 Sacramento	P.C.	C	55	211	32	59	9	0	3	27	0	.280
2007 Oakland	A.L.	C	68	213	27	53	13	0	7	39	0	.249
2008 Oakland	A.L.	C	148	530	54	148	25	1	7	42	2	.279
Major League Totals		2 Yrs.	216	743	81	201	38	1	14	81	2	.271

SWEENEY, MARK PATRICK

Born, Framingham, Massachusetts, October 26, 1969.
Bats Left. Throws Left. Height, 6 feet, 1 inch. Weight, 195 pounds.

Year Club	Lea	Pos	G	AB	R	H	2B	3B	HR	RBI	SB	Avg
1991 Boise	Northwest	OF	70	234	45	66	10	3	4	34	9	.282
1992 Quad City	Midwest	OF	120	424	65	115	20	5	14	76	15	.271
1993 Palm Springs	California	OF-1B	66	245	41	87	18	3	3	47	9	.355
1993 Midland	Texas	OF	51	188	41	67	13	2	9	32	1	.356
1994 Midland	Texas	OF-1B	14	50	13	15	3	0	3	18	1	.300
1994 Vancouver	P.C.	DH-1B-OF	103	344	59	98	12	3	8	49	3	.285
1995 Vancouver	P.C.	OF-1B	69	226	48	78	14	2	7	59	3	.345
1995 Louisville	A.A.	1B	22	76	15	28	8	0	2	22	2	.368
1995 St. Louis............	N.L.	1B-OF	37	77	5	21	2	0	2	13	1	.273
1996 St. Louis a	N.L.	OF-1B	98	170	32	45	9	0	3	22	3	.265
1997 St. Louis-San Diego b ..	N.L.	OF-1B	115	164	16	46	7	0	2	23	2	.280
1998 San Diego	N.L.	OF-1B	122	192	17	45	8	3	2	15	1	.234
1999 Cincinnati	N.L.	1B-OF	37	31	6	11	3	0	2	7	0	.355
1999 Indianapolis c.........	Int.	OF	86	311	66	100	17	1	12	51	3	.322
2000 Milwaukee..........	N.L.	OF-1B	71	73	9	16	6	0	1	6	0	.219
2000 Indianapolis d-e.......	Int.	1B-OF	18	55	13	28	8	0	2	14	0	.509
2001 Indianapolis	Int.	OF-1B	109	404	65	116	34	1	6	69	3	.287
2001 Milwaukee f	N.L.	OF-1B	48	89	9	23	3	1	3	11	2	.258
2002 San Diego	N.L.	1B-OF	48	65	3	11	3	0	1	4	0	.169
2002 Portland g-h-i-j	P.C.	1B	1	1	0	1	0	0	0	0	0	1.000
2003 Colorado Springs	P.C.	OF-1B	51	165	24	49	10	1	5	35	1	.297
2003 Colorado k-l..........	N.L.	OF-1B	67	97	13	25	9	0	2	14	0	.258
2004 Colorado m	N.L.	OF-1B	122	177	25	47	12	2	9	40	1	.266
2005 San Diego n-o	N.L.	1B-OF	135	221	31	65	12	1	8	40	1	.294
2006 San Francisco	N.L.	1B-OF	114	259	32	65	15	2	5	37	0	.251
2007 San Fran.-L.A. p-q	N.L.	1B-OF	106	123	20	32	9	0	2	13	2	.260
2008 Las Vegas............	P.C.	1B	4	16	2	4	0	0	0	0	0	.250
2008 Los Angeles r-s	N.L.	1B-OF	98	92	2	12	3	0	0	5	0	.130
Major League Totals		14 Yrs.	1218	1830	220	464	101	9	42	250	16	.254
Division Series												
1996 St. Louis..............	N.L.	PH	1	1	0	1	0	0	0	0	0	1.000
1998 San Diego	N.L.	PH	2	1	0	0	0	0	0	0	0	.000
2005 San Diego	N.L.	1B	3	3	1	2	1	0	0	0	0	.667
Division Series Totals			6	5	1	3	1	0	0	0	0	.600
Championship Series												
1996 St. Louis..............	N.L.	OF	5	4	1	0	0	0	0	0	0	.000
1998 San Diego	N.L.	PH	3	2	1	0	0	0	0	0	0	.000
Championship Series Totals			8	6	2	0	0	0	0	0	0	.000
World Series Record												
1998 San Diego	N.L.	PH	3	3	0	2	0	0	0	0	1	.000

a Traded by California Angels to St. Louis Cardinals with player to be named later for pitcher John Habyan, July 8, 1995. St. Louis Cardinals received infielder Rod Correia to complete trade, January 31, 1996.

b Traded to San Diego Padres with pitcher Danny Jackson and pitcher Rich Batchelor for outfielder Phil Plantier, infielder Scott Livingstone and pitcher Fernando Valenzuela, June 14, 1997.

c Traded to Cincinnati Reds with pitcher Greg Vaughn for outfielder Reggie Sanders, infielder Damian Jackson and pitcher Josh Harris, February 2, 1999.

d Traded to Milwaukee Brewers with player to be named later for outfielder Alex Ochoa, January 14, 2000. Milwaukee Brewers received infielder Gene Altman to complete trade, May 15, 2000.

e On disabled list from March 31 to May 6 and July 18 to August 14, 2000.

f Filed for free agency, October 5, 2000, re-signed with Milwaukee Brewers, January 3, 2001.

g Traded to New York Mets with outfielder Jeromy Burnitz, pitcher Jeff D'Amico, infielder Lou Collier and cash for outfielder Alex Ochoa, pitcher Glendon Rusch and infielder Lenny Harris, January 21, 2002.

h Released by New York Mets, March 13, 2002. Signed with San Diego Padres organization, March 16, 2002.

i On disabled list from June 6 to June 26, 2002.

j Released by San Diego Padres, July 13, 2002, re-signed with San Diego Padres, August 13, 2002.

k Released by San Diego Padres, August 16, 2002. Signed with Colorado Rockies, January 21, 2003.

l Filed for free agency, October 27, 2003. Signed with Colorado Rockies organization, January 5, 2004.

m Filed for free agency, October 28, 2004. Signed with San Diego Padres, December 22, 2004.

n Filed for free agency, October 28, 2005. Signed with San Francisco Giants, December 8, 2005.

o On disabled list from March 29 to April 13, 2007.

p Traded to Los Angeles Dodgers for player to be named later, August 9, 2007. San Francisco Giants received infielder Travis Denker to complete trade, August 26, 2007.

q Filed for free agency, October 30, 2007, re-signed with Los Angeles Dodgers organization, February 12, 2008.

r On disabled list from July 3 to July 27, 2008.

s Filed for free agency, October 31, 2008.

SWEENEY, RYAN JOSEPH

Born, Cedar Rapids, Iowa, February 20, 1985.
Bats Left. Throws Left. Height, 6 feet, 4 inches. Weight, 200 pounds.

Year	Club	Lea	Pos	G	AB	R	H	2B	3B	HR	RBI	SB	Avg
2003 Bristol		Appal.	OF	19	67	11	21	3	0	2	5	3	.313
2003 Great Falls		Pioneer	OF	10	34	0	12	2	0	0	4	0	.353
2004 Winston-Salem		Carolina	OF	134	515	71	146	22	3	7	66	8	.283
2005 Birmingham		Southern	OF	113	429	64	128	22	3	1	47	6	.298
2006 Charlotte		Int.	OF	118	449	64	133	25	3	3	70	7	.296
2006 Chicago		A.L.	OF	18	35	1	8	0	0	0	5	0	.229
2007 Chicago		A.L.	OF	15	45	5	9	3	0	1	5	0	.200
2007 Charlotte		Int.	OF	105	397	50	107	17	2	10	47	8	.270
2008 Azl Athletics		Arizona	DH	1	3	0	0	0	0	0	0	0	.000
2008 Sacramento		P.C.	OF	8	34	5	14	4	0	1	5	0	.412
2008 Oakland a-b		A.L.	OF	115	384	53	110	18	2	5	45	9	.286
Major League Totals		3 Yrs.		148	464	59	127	21	2	6	55	9	.274

a Traded to Oakland Athletics with pitcher Gio Gonzalez and pitcher Fautino de los Santos for outfielder Nick Swisher, January 3, 2008.
b On disabled list from May 29 to June 13 and August 13 to August 28, 2008.

SWISHER, NICHOLAS THOMPSON (NICK)

Born, Columbus, Ohio, January 25, 1980.
Bats Both. Throws Left. Height, 6 feet. Weight, 215 pounds.

Year	Club	Lea	Pos	G	AB	R	H	2B	3B	HR	RBI	SB	Avg
2002 Visalia		California	OF	49	183	22	44	13	2	4	23	3	.240
2002 Vancouver		Northwest	OF	13	44	10	11	3	0	2	12	3	.250
2003 Modesto		California	OF-1B	51	189	38	56	14	2	10	43	0	.296
2003 Midland		Texas	OF-1B	76	287	36	66	24	2	5	43	0	.230
2004 Sacramento		P.C.	OF-1B	125	443	109	119	28	2	29	92	3	.269
2004 Oakland		A.L.	OF-1B	20	60	11	15	4	0	2	8	0	.250
2005 Sacramento		P.C.	OF-1B	6	23	4	9	3	0	0	1	0	.391
2005 Oakland a		A.L.	OF-1B	131	462	66	109	32	1	21	74	0	.236
2006 Oakland		A.L.	1B-OF	157	556	106	141	24	2	35	95	1	.254
2007 Oakland b		A.L.	OF-1B	150	539	84	141	36	1	22	78	3	.262
2008 Chicago c		A.L.	OF-1B	153	497	86	109	21	1	24	69	3	.219
Major League Totals		5 Yrs.		611	2114	353	515	117	5	104	324	7	.244
Division Series													
2006 Oakland		A.L.	1B	3	10	3	3	2	0	0	1	0	.300
2008 Chicago		A.L.	OF-1B	3	4	1	1	0	0	0	0	0	.250
Division Series Totals				6	14	4	4	2	0	0	1	0	.286
Championship Series													
2006 Oakland		A.L.	1B	4	10	0	1	0	0	0	0	0	.100

a On disabled list from May 2 to May 25, 2005.
b Traded to Chicago White Sox for pitcher Gio Gonzalez, pitcher Fautino de los Santos and outfielder Ryan Sweeney, January 3, 2008.
c Traded to New York Yankees with pitcher Kaneoka Texeira for infielder Wilson Betemit, pitcher Jeff Marquez and pitcher Jhonny Nunez, November 13, 2008.

TAGUCHI, SO

Born, Hyogo, Japan, July 22, 1969.
Bats Right. Throws Right. Height, 5 feet, 10 inches. Weight, 165 pounds.

Year	Club	Lea	Pos	G	AB	R	H	2B	3B	HR	RBI	SB	Avg
1992 Orix		Japan Pac.	OF	47	123	12	33	10	0	1	7	5	.268
1993 Orix		Japan Pac.	OF	31	83	12	23	7	1	0	5	3	.277
1994 Orix		Japan Pac.	OF	108	329	55	101	17	1	6	43	10	.307
1995 Orix		Japan Pac.	OF	130	495	76	122	24	2	9	61	14	.246
1996 Orix		Japan Pac.	OF	128	509	74	142	24	1	7	44	10	.279
1997 Orix		Japan Pac.	OF	135	572	92	168	32	4	10	56	7	.294
1998 Orix		Japan Pac.	OF	132	497	85	135	26	2	9	41	8	.272
1999 Orix		Japan Pac.	OF	133	524	77	141	21	3	9	56	11	.269
2000 Orix		Japan Pac.	OF	129	509	77	142	26	6	8	49	9	.279
2001 Orix		Japan Pac.	OF	134	453	70	127	21	0	8	42	6	.280
2002 Memphis		P.C.	OF	91	304	37	75	17	0	5	36	6	.247
2002 St. Louis		N.L.	OF	19	15	4	6	0	0	0	2	1	.400
2002 New Haven a		Eastern	OF	26	107	21	33	10	0	1	15	3	.308
2003 Memphis		P.C.	OF	90	258	31	66	8	2	2	24	14	.256
2003 St. Louis		N.L.	OF-2B	43	54	9	14	3	1	3	13	0	.259

Year	Club	Lea	Pos	G	AB	R	H	2B	3B	HR	RBI	SB	Avg
2004 Memphis	...P.C.		OF	17	55	5	18	4	0	1	7	6	.327
2004 St. Louis b	...N.L.		OF	109	179	26	52	10	2	3	25	6	.291
2005 St. Louis	...N.L.		OF	143	396	45	114	21	2	8	53	11	.288
2006 St. Louis	...N.L.		OF-2B	134	316	46	84	19	1	2	31	11	.266
2007 St. Louis c	...N.L.		OF-2B	130	307	48	89	15	0	3	30	7	.290
2008 Philadelphia d	...N.L.		OF	88	91	18	20	5	1	0	9	3	.220
Major League Totals			7 Yrs.	666	1358	196	379	73	7	19	163	39	.279
Division Series													
2004 St. Louis	...N.L.		OF	1	0	0	0	0	0	0	0	0	.000
2005 St. Louis	...N.L.		OF	3	1	0	0	0	0	0	0	0	.000
2006 St. Louis	...N.L.		OF	2	1	1	1	0	0	0	1	1	1.000
Division Series Totals				6	2	1	1	0	0	0	1	1	.500
Championship Series													
2004 St. Louis	...N.L.		OF	3	2	0	0	0	0	0	0	0	.000
2005 St. Louis	...N.L.		OF	6	6	0	0	0	0	0	0	0	.000
2006 St. Louis	...N.L.		OF	5	3	1	3	1	0	1	3	0	1.000
2008 Philadelphia	...N.L.		PH	4	4	0	0	0	0	0	0	0	.000
Championship Series Totals				18	15	1	3	1	0	1	3	0	.200
World Series Record													
2004 St. Louis	...N.L.		OF	2	4	1	1	0	0	0	1	0	.250
2006 St. Louis	...N.L.		OF	4	11	3	2	0	0	0	0	0	.182
World Series Totals				6	15	4	3	0	0	0	1	0	.200

a Signed by St. Louis Cardinals, January 9, 2002.
b Not offered contract, December 21, 2004, re-signed with St. Louis Cardinals, December 22, 2004.
c Released by St. Louis Cardinals, December 5, 2007. Signed with Philadelphia Phillies, December 23, 2007.
d Released by Philadelphia Phillies, November 6, 2008. Signed with Chicago Cubs organization, January 15, 2009.

TATIS, FERNANDO

Born, San Pedro de Macoris, Dominican Republic, January 1, 1975.
Bats Right. Throws Right. Height, 5 feet, 10 inches. Weight, 170 pounds.

Year	Club	Lea	Pos	G	AB	R	H	2B	3B	HR	RBI	SB	Avg
1993 Tex/Chi Cub	. Dominican		3B	59	198	22	54	5	1	4	34	7	.273
1994 Rangers	...Gulf Coast		3B-2B	60	212	34	70	10	2	6	32	21	.330
1995 Chston-SC	...So.Atl.		3B	131	499	74	151	43	4	15	84	22	.303
1996 Charlotte	...Fla.St.		3B	85	325	46	93	25	0	12	53	9	.286
1996 Okla City	...A.A.		3B	2	4	0	2	1	0	0	0	0	.500
1997 Tulsa	...Texas		3B	102	382	73	120	26	1	24	61	17	.314
1997 Texas	...A.L.		3B	60	223	29	57	9	0	8	29	3	.256
1998 Texas	...A.L.		3B	95	330	41	89	17	2	3	32	6	.270
1998 St. Louis a	...N.L.		3B-SS	55	202	28	58	16	2	8	26	7	.287
1999 St. Louis	...N.L.		3B	149	537	104	160	31	2	34	107	21	.298
2000 St. Louis	...N.L.		3B-1B	96	324	59	82	21	1	18	64	2	.253
2000 Memphis b-c	...P.C.		3B	3	9	0	0	0	0	0	0	0	.000
2001 Montreal d-e	...N.L.		3B	41	145	20	37	9	0	2	11	0	.255
2002 Brevard County	. Fla.St.		3B	6	17	2	4	1	0	0	2	0	.235
2002 Montreal f	...N.L.		3B	114	381	43	87	18	1	15	55	2	.228
2003 Montreal g	...N.L.		3B	53	175	15	34	6	0	2	15	2	.194
2004-05 h				Did Not Play									
2006 Ottawa	...Int.		3B	90	326	44	97	15	2	7	37	8	.298
2006 Baltimore i	...A.L.		3B-1B-OF-2B	28	56	7	14	6	1	2	8	0	.250
2007 New Orleans j-k	...P.C.		3B	131	497	90	137	31	5	21	67	8	.276
2008 New Orleans	...P.C.		3B-OF-2B-SS	37	120	18	29	6	0	1	12	0	.242
2008 New York	...N.L.		OF-1B-3B	92	273	33	81	16	1	11	47	3	.297
Major League Totals			9 Yrs.	783	2646	379	699	149	10	103	394	46	.264
Championship Series													
2000 St. Louis	...N.L.		3B	5	13	1	3	2	0	0	2	0	.231

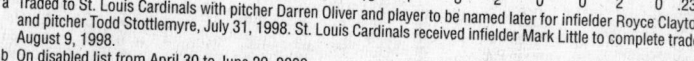

a Traded to St. Louis Cardinals with pitcher Darren Oliver and player to be named later for infielder Royce Clayton and pitcher Todd Stottlemyre, July 31, 1998. St. Louis Cardinals received infielder Mark Little to complete trade, August 9, 1998.
b On disabled list from April 30 to June 29, 2000.
c Traded to Montreal Expos with pitcher Britt Reames for pitcher Dustin Hermanson and pitcher Steve Kline, December 14, 2000.
d On disabled list from May 11 to May 26, 2001.
e On disabled list from June 3 to November 14, 2001.
f On disabled list from March 22 to April 29, 2002.
g On disabled list from June 16 to October 27, 2003.
h Filed for free agency, October 27, 2003. Signed with Tampa Bay Devil Rays organization, January 12, 2004.

i Released by Tampa Bay Devil Rays, March 24, 2004. Signed with Baltimore Orioles organization, January 11, 2006.
j Filed for free agency, November 2, 2006. Signed with Los Angeles Dodgers organization, January 23, 2007.
k Released by Los Angeles Dodgers, March 13, 2007. Signed with New York Mets organization, March 23, 2007.

TAVERAS, WILLY

Born, Tenares, Dominican Republic, December 25, 1981.
Bats Right. Throws Right. Height, 6 feet. Weight, 160 pounds.

Year	Club	Lea	Pos	G	AB	R	H	2B	3B	HR	RBI	SB	Avg
2000 Burlington	Appal.		OF	50	190	46	50	4	3	1	16	36	.263
2001 Columbus	So.Atl.		OF	97	395	55	107	15	7	3	32	29	.271
2002 Columbus	So.Atl.		OF	85	313	68	83	14	1	4	27	54	.265
2003 Kinston	Carolina		OF	113	397	64	112	9	6	2	35	57	.282
2004 Round Rock	Texas		OF	103	409	76	137	13	1	2	27	55	.335
2004 Houston a	N.L.		OF	10	1	2	0	0	0	0	0	1	.000
2005 Houston	N.L.		OF	152	592	82	172	13	4	3	29	34	.291
2006 Houston b	N.L.		OF	149	529	83	147	19	5	1	30	33	.278
2007 Colorado Springs	P.C.		OF	4	14	0	5	0	0	0	0	1	.357
2007 Colorado c	N.L.		OF	97	372	64	119	13	2	2	24	33	.320
2008 Colorado d	N.L.		OF	133	479	64	120	15	2	1	26	*68	.251
Major League Totals			5 Yrs.	541	1973	295	558	60	13	7	109	169	.283
Division Series													
2005 Houston	N.L.		OF	4	14	2	5	1	0	0	0	0	.357
Championship Series													
2005 Houston	N.L.		OF	6	14	1	5	0	0	0	0	0	.357
2007 Colorado	N.L.		OF	4	18	3	3	1	0	0	1	1	.167
Championship Series Totals				10	32	4	8	1	0	0	1	1	.250
World Series Record													
2005 Houston	N.L.		OF	4	15	2	5	2	1	0	0	1	.333
2007 Colorado	N.L.		OF	3	8	1	0	0	0	0	0	0	.000
World Series Totals				7	23	3	5	2	1	0	0	1	.217

a Traded by Cleveland Indians to Houston Astros with outfielder Luke Scott for pitcher Jeriome Robertson, March 31, 2004.
b Traded to Colorado Rockies with pitcher Taylor Buchholz and pitcher Jason Hirsh for pitcher Jason Jennings and pitcher Miguel Asencio, December 12, 2006.
c On disabled list from August 15 to September 1, 2007.
d Not offered contract, December 12, 2008. Signed with Cincinnati Reds, December 27, 2008.

TEAGARDEN, TAYLOR HILL

Born, Dallas, Texas, December 21, 1983.
Bats Right. Throws Right. Height, 6 feet, 1 inch. Weight, 200 pounds.

Year	Club	Lea	Pos	G	AB	R	H	2B	3B	HR	RBI	SB	Avg
2005 Spokane	Northwest		C	31	96	23	27	5	4	7	16	1	.281
2006 Rangers	Arizona		DH	7	20	4	1	0	0	0	1	1	.050
2007 Bakersfield	Calif.		C	81	292	75	92	25	0	20	67	2	.315
2007 Frisco	Texas		C	29	102	19	30	3	0	7	16	0	.294
2008 Frisco	Texas		C	16	59	6	10	2	0	2	6	1	.169
2008 Oklahoma	P.C.		C	57	187	26	42	5	3	7	16	0	.225
2008 Texas	A.L.		C	16	47	10	15	5	0	6	17	0	.319

TEAHEN, MARK THOMAS

Born, Redlands, California, September 6, 1981.
Bats Left. Throws Right. Height, 6 feet, 3 inches. Weight, 220 pounds.

Year	Club	Lea	Pos	G	AB	R	H	2B	3B	HR	RBI	SB	Avg
2002 Modesto	California		3B	59	234	25	56	9	1	1	26	1	.239
2002 Vancouver	Northwest		3B	13	57	10	23	5	1	0	6	4	.404
2003 Modesto	California		3B	121	453	68	128	27	4	3	71	4	.283
2004 Omaha	P.C.		3B	66	246	33	69	15	1	8	31	0	.280
2004 Sacramento	P.C.		3B	20	69	9	19	8	0	0	10	0	.275
2004 Midland a	Texas		3B	53	197	31	66	15	4	6	36	0	.335
2005 Omaha	P.C.		3B	8	27	4	7	2	0	0	4	0	.259
2005 Kansas City b	A.L.		3B	130	447	60	110	29	4	7	55	7	.246
2006 Omaha	P.C.		3B	24	79	14	30	4	2	2	14	0	.380
2006 Kansas City	A.L.		3B	109	393	70	114	21	7	18	69	10	.290
2007 Kansas City c	A.L.		OF-1B	144	544	78	155	31	8	7	60	13	.285

Year Club	Lea	Pos	G	AB	R	H	2B	3B	HR	RBI	SB	Avg
2008 Kansas City	A.L.	OF-3B-1B	149	572	66	146	31	4	15	59	4	.255
Major League Totals		4 Yrs.	532	1956	274	525	112	23	47	243	34	.268

a Traded to Kansas City Royals with pitcher Mike Wood for outfielder Octavio Dotel and cash, June 24, 2004.
b On disabled list from April 12 to May 3, 2005.
c On disabled list from August 19 to September 3, 2007.

TEIXEIRA, MARK CHARLES

Born, Annapolis, Maryland, April 11, 1980.
Bats Both. Throws Right. Height, 6 feet, 3 inches. Weight, 220 pounds.

Year Club	Lea	Pos	G	AB	R	H	2B	3B	HR	RBI	SB	Avg
2002 Charlotte	Fla.St.	3B	38	150	32	48	10	2	9	41	2	.320
2002 Tulsa	Texas	3B	48	171	31	54	11	3	10	28	2	.316
2003 Texas	A.L.	1B-OF-3B	146	529	66	137	29	5	26	84	1	.259
2004 Frisco	Texas	1B	1	3	0	0	0	0	0	0	0	.000
2004 Texas a	A.L.	1B-OF	145	545	101	153	34	2	38	112	4	.281
2005 Texas	A.L.	1B	*162	644	112	194	41	3	43	144	4	.301
2006 Texas	A.L.	1B	*162	628	99	177	45	1	33	110	2	.282
2007 Frisco	Texas	1B	1	2	0	0	0	0	0	0	0	.000
2007 Texas	A.L.	1B	78	286	48	85	24	1	13	49	0	.297
2007 Atlanta b-c	N.L.	1B	54	208	38	66	9	1	17	56	0	.317
2008 Atlanta	N.L.	1B	103	381	63	108	27	0	20	78	0	.283
2008 Los Angeles d-e	A.L.	1B	54	193	39	69	14	0	13	43	2	.358
Major League Totals		6 Yrs.	904	3414	566	989	223	13	203	676	13	.290
Division Series												
2008 Los Angeles	A.L.	1B	4	15	4	7	0	0	0	1	0	.467

a On disabled list from April 13 to April 29, 2004.
b On disabled list from June 9 to July 13, 2007.
c Traded to Atlanta Braves with pitcher Ron Mahay for catcher Jarrod Saltalamacchia, infielder Elvis Andrus, pitcher Neftali Feliz, pitcher Matt Harrison and pitcher Beau James, July 31, 2007.
d Traded to Los Angeles Angels for infielder Casey Kotchman and pitcher Steve Marek, July 29, 2008.
e Filed for free agency, October 30, 2008. Signed with New York Yankees, January 6, 2009.

TEJADA, MIGUEL ODALIS

Born, Bani, Dominican Republic, May 25, 1976.
Bats Right. Throws Right. Height, 5 feet, 9 inches. Weight, 215 pounds.

Year Club	Lea	Pos	G	AB	R	H	2B	3B	HR	RBI	SB	Avg
1994 Oakland	Dominican	2B	74	218	51	64	9	1	18	62	13	.294
1995 Sou. Oregon	Northwest	SS	74	269	45	66	15	5	8	44	19	.245
1996 Modesto	California	SS-3B	114	458	97	128	12	5	20	72	27	.279
1997 Huntsville	Southern	SS	128	502	85	138	20	3	22	97	15	.275
1997 Oakland	A.L.	SS	26	99	10	20	3	2	2	10	2	.202
1998 Edmonton	P.C.	SS	1	3	0	0	0	0	0	0	0	.000
1998 Huntsville	Southern	SS	15	52	9	17	6	0	2	7	1	.327
1998 Oakland a	A.L.	SS	105	365	53	85	20	1	11	45	5	.233
1999 Oakland	A.L.	SS	159	593	93	149	33	4	21	84	8	.251
2000 Oakland	A.L.	SS	160	607	105	167	32	1	30	115	6	.275
2001 Oakland	A.L.	SS	*162	622	107	166	31	3	31	113	11	.267
2002 Oakland b	A.L.	SS	*162	662	108	204	30	0	34	131	7	.308
2003 Oakland c	A.L.	SS	162	636	98	177	42	0	27	106	10	.278
2004 Baltimore	A.L.	SS	*162	653	107	203	40	2	34	106	10	.278
2005 Baltimore	A.L.	SS	*162	654	89	199	*50	5	26	98	5	.304
2006 Baltimore	A.L.	SS	*162	648	99	214	37	0	24	100	6	.330
2007 Frederick	Carolina	3B	1	2	1	2	0	0	1	1	0	1.000
2007 Bowie	Eastern	SS	1	3	0	0	0	0	0	1	0	.000
2007 Baltimore d-e	A.L.	SS	133	514	72	152	19	1	18	81	2	.296
2008 Houston	N.L.	SS	158	632	92	179	38	3	13	66	7	.283
Major League Totals		12 Yrs.	1713	6685	1033	1915	375	22	271	1099	73	.286
Division Series												
2000 Oakland	A.L.	SS	5	20	5	7	2	0	0	1	1	.350
2001 Oakland	A.L.	SS	5	21	1	6	3	0	0	1	0	.286
2002 Oakland	A.L.	SS	5	21	3	3	1	0	1	4	0	.143
2003 Oakland	A.L.	SS	5	23	0	2	1	0	0	2	0	.087
Division Series Totals			20	85	9	18	7	0	1	8	1	.212

a On disabled list from March 31 to May 20, 1998.
b Selected Most Valuable Player in American League for 2002.
c Filed for free agency, October 27, 2003. Signed with Baltimore Orioles, December 14, 2003.

THAMES, MARCUS MARKLEY

Born, Louisville, Mississippi, March 6, 1977.
Bats Right. Throws Right. Height, 6 feet, 2 inches. Weight, 220 pounds.

Year	Club	Lea	Pos	G	AB	R	H	2B	3B	HR	RBI	SB	Avg
1997 Yankees	Gulf Coast	OF	57	195	51	67	17	4	7	36	6	.344
1997 Greensboro	So.Atl.	OF	4	16	2	5	1	0	0	2	1	.313
1998 Tampa	Fla.St.	OF	122	457	62	130	18	3	11	59	13	.284
1999 Norwich	Eastern	OF	51	182	25	41	6	2	4	26	0	.225
1999 Tampa	Fla.St.	OF	69	266	47	65	12	4	11	38	3	.244
2000 Norwich	Eastern	OF	131	474	72	114	30	2	15	79	1	.241
2001 Norwich	Eastern	OF	139	520	114	167	43	4	31	97	10	.321
2002 Columbus	Int.	OF	107	386	51	80	21	3	13	45	5	.207
2002 New York	A.L.	OF	7	13	2	3	1	0	1	2	0	.231
2003 Columbus	Int.	OF	52	194	26	54	15	2	2	28	3	.278
2003 Oklahoma	P.C.	OF	18	66	9	17	4	0	2	7	1	.258
2003 Texas a-b	A.L.	OF	30	73	12	15	2	0	1	4	0	.205
2004 Toledo	Int.	OF	64	234	57	77	21	1	24	59	4	.329
2004 Detroit	A.L.	OF	61	165	24	42	12	0	10	33	0	.255
2005 Toledo	Int.	OF	73	265	53	90	18	3	22	56	4	.340
2005 Detroit	A.L.	OF	38	107	11	21	2	0	7	16	0	.196
2006 Detroit	A.L.	OF	110	348	61	89	20	2	26	60	1	.256
2007 Toledo	Int.	1B	2	8	2	3	0	0	1	2	0	.375
2007 Detroit c	A.L.	OF-1B	86	269	37	65	15	0	18	54	2	.242
2008 Detroit	A.L.	OF-1B	103	316	50	76	12	0	25	56	0	.241
Major League Totals		7 Yrs.	435	1291	197	311	64	2	88	225	3	.241	
Division Series													
2006 Detroit	A.L.	DH	4	15	2	5	2	0	0	1	0	.333
Championship Series													
2006 Detroit	A.L.	DH	2	5	1	0	0	0	0	0	0	.000
World Series Record													
2006 Detroit	A.L.	OF	2	1	0	0	0	0	0	0	0	.000

a Traded to Texas Rangers for outfielder Ruben Sierra, June 6, 2003.
b Filed for free agency, October 14, 2003. Signed with Detroit Tigers organization, December 7, 2003.
c On disabled list from July 19 to August 9, 2007.

THERIOT, RYAN STEWART

Born, Baton Rouge, Louisiana, December 7, 1979.
Bats Right. Throws Right. Height, 5 feet, 11 inches. Weight, 175 pounds.

Year	Club	Lea	Pos	G	AB	R	H	2B	3B	HR	RBI	SB	Avg
2001 Daytona	Fla.St.	SS	30	103	20	21	5	0	0	9	2	.204
2002 Lansing	Midwest	2B-SS	130	489	75	123	19	4	1	37	32	.252
2003 Lansing	Midwest	2B-SS	58	220	29	57	8	1	1	17	21	.259
2003 West Tenn	Southern	SS	53	178	20	42	3	0	1	9	9	.236
2004 Daytona	Fla.St.	2B-SS-3B	103	330	47	90	14	3	1	34	13	.273
2005 West Tenn	Southern	2B-SS-3B	120	448	52	136	28	4	1	53	24	.304
2005 Chicago	N.L.	2B	9	13	3	2	1	0	0	0	0	.154
2006 Iowa	P.C.	SS-2B-OF-3B	73	280	41	85	11	5	0	22	14	.304
2006 Chicago	N.L.	2B-SS-3B	53	134	34	44	11	3	3	16	13	.328
2007 Chicago	N.L.	SS-2B-3B-OF	148	537	80	143	30	2	3	45	28	.266
2008 Chicago	N.L.	SS	149	580	85	178	19	4	1	38	22	.307
Major League Totals		4 Yrs.	359	1264	202	367	61	9	7	99	63	.290	
Division Series													
2007 Chicago	N.L.	SS	3	12	0	3	0	0	0	1	1	.250
2008 Chicago	N.L.	SS	3	11	0	3	0	0	0	0	0	.273
Division Series Totals			6	23	0	6	0	0	0	1	1	.261	

THOMAS, FRANK EDWARD

Born, Columbus, Georgia, May 27, 1968.
Bats Right. Throws Right. Height, 6 feet, 5 inches. Weight, 275 pounds.

Year	Club	Lea	Pos	G	AB	R	H	2B	3B	HR	RBI	SB	Avg
1989 Sarasota White Sox	Gulf C.	1B	16	48	7	16	5	0	1	11	4	.333
1989 Sarasota	Fla. St.	1B	55	188	27	52	9	1	4	30	0	.277
1990 Birmingham	Southern	1B	109	353	84	114	27	5	18	71	7	.323

Year Club	Lea	Pos	G	AB	R	H	2B	3B	HR	RBI	SB	Avg
1990 Chicago	A.L.	1B	60	191	39	63	11	3	7	31	0	.330
1991 Chicago	A.L.	1B	158	559	104	178	31	2	32	109	1	.318
1992 Chicago	A.L.	1B	160	573	108	185	*46	2	24	115	6	.323
1993 Chicago a	A.L.	1B	153	549	106	174	36	0	41	128	4	.317
1994 Chicago b	A.L.	1B	113	399	*106	141	34	1	38	101	2	.353
1995 Chicago	A.L.	1B	*145	493	102	152	27	0	40	111	3	.308
1996 Chicago c	A.L.	1B	141	527	110	184	26	0	40	134	1	.349
1997 Chicago d	A.L.	1B	146	530	110	184	35	0	35	125	1	*.347
1998 Chicago	A.L.	DH-1B	160	585	109	155	35	2	29	109	7	.265
1999 Chicago	A.L.	DH-1B	135	486	74	148	36	0	15	77	3	.305
2000 Chicago	A.L.	DH-1B	159	582	115	191	44	0	43	143	1	.328
2001 Chicago e	A.L.	DH-1B	20	68	8	15	3	0	4	10	0	.221
2002 Chicago f	A.L.	DH-1B	148	523	77	132	29	1	28	92	3	.252
2003 Chicago	A.L.	DH-1B	153	546	87	146	35	0	42	105	0	.267
2004 Chicago g	A.L.	DH-1B	74	240	53	65	16	0	18	49	0	.271
2005 Charlotte	Int.	DH	11	42	3	8	1	0	1	4	0	.190
2005 Chicago h-i	A.L.	DH	34	105	19	23	3	0	12	26	0	.219
2006 Oakland j-k..........	A.L.	DH	137	466	77	126	11	0	39	114	0	.270
2007 Toronto l.............	A.L.	DH	155	531	63	147	30	0	26	95	0	.277
2008 Toronto-Oakland m-n-o.	A.L.	DH	71	246	27	59	7	1	8	30	0	.240
Major League Totals		19 Yrs.	2322	8199	1494	2468	495	12	521	1704	32	.301
Division Series												
2000 Chicago	A.L.	DH-1B	3	9	0	0	0	0	0	0	0	.000
2006 Oakland	A.L.	DH	3	10	3	5	1	0	2	2	0	.500
Division Series Totals			6	19	3	5	1	0	2	2	0	.263
Championship Series												
1993 Chicago	A.L.	1B	6	17	2	6	0	0	1	3	0	.353
2006 Oakland	A.L.	DH	4	13	0	0	0	0	0	0	0	.000
Championship Series Totals			10	30	2	6	0	0	1	3	0	.200

a Selected Most Valuable Player in American League for 1993.
b Selected Most Valuable Player in American League for 1994.
c On disabled list from July 8 to July 30, 1996.
d On disabled list from June 7 to June 22, 1997.
e On disabled list from April 30 to October 12, 2001.
f Filed for free agency, October 31, 2002, re-signed with Chicago White Sox, December 6, 2002.
g On disabled list from July 7 to October 12, 2004.
h On disabled list from March 25 to May 30 and July 21 to October 31, 2005.
i Filed for free agency, November 8, 2005. Signed with Oakland Athletics, January 24, 2006.
j On disabled list from June 15 to June 30, 2006.
k Filed for free agency, October 28, 2006. Signed with Toronto Blue Jays, November 17, 2006.
l On disabled list from March 31 to June 16, 2007.
m Released by Toronto Blue Jays, April 20, 2008. Signed with Oakland Athletics, April 24, 2008.
n On disabled list from May 28 to July 31 and August 30 to September 29, 2008.
o Filed for free agency, October 31, 2008.

THOME, JAMES HOWARD (JIM)

Born, Peoria, Illinois, August 27, 1970.
Bats Left. Throws Right. Height, 6 feet, 4 inches. Weight, 245 pounds.

Year Club	Lea	Pos	G	AB	R	H	2B	3B	HR	RBI	SB	Avg
1989 Indians..........	Gulf Coast	SS-3B	55	186	22	44	5	3	0	22	6	.237
1990 Burlington	Appal.	3B	34	118	31	44	7	1	12	34	6	.373
1990 Kinston	Carolina	3B	33	117	19	36	4	1	4	16	4	.308
1991 Canton	Eastern	3B	84	294	47	99	20	2	5	45	8	.337
1991 Colorado Springs.......	P.C.	3B	41	151	20	43	7	3	2	28	0	.285
1991 Cleveland	A.L.	3B	27	98	7	25	4	2	1	9	1	.255
1992 Colorado Springs.......	P.C.	3B	12	48	11	15	4	1	2	14	0	.313
1992 Cleveland a..........	A.L.	3B	40	117	8	24	3	1	2	12	2	.205
1993 Charlotte	Int.	3B	115	410	85	136	21	4	25	*102	1	*.332
1993 Cleveland	A.L.	3B	47	154	28	41	11	0	7	22	2	.266
1994 Cleveland	A.L.	3B	98	321	58	86	20	1	20	52	3	.268
1995 Cleveland	A.L.	3B	137	452	92	142	29	3	25	73	4	.314
1996 Cleveland	A.L.	3B	151	505	122	157	28	5	38	116	2	.311
1997 Cleveland	A.L.	1B	147	496	104	142	25	0	40	102	1	.286
1998 Cleveland b..........	A.L.	1B	123	440	89	129	34	2	30	85	1	.293
1999 Cleveland	A.L.	1B	146	494	101	137	27	2	33	108	0	.277
2000 Cleveland	A.L.	1B	158	557	106	150	33	1	37	106	1	.269
2001 Cleveland	A.L.	1B	156	526	101	153	26	1	49	124	0	.291
2002 Cleveland c..........	A.L.	1B	147	480	101	146	19	2	52	118	1	.304

Year	Club	Lea	Pos	G	AB	R	H	2B	3B	HR	RBI	SB	Avg
2003 Philadelphia	N.L.		1B	159	578	111	154	30	3	*47	131	0	.266
2004 Philadelphia	N.L.		1B	143	508	97	139	28	1	42	105	0	.274
2005 Clearwater	Fla.St.		DH	5	12	2	4	0	0	1	3	0	.333
2005 Philadelphia d-e	N.L.		1B	59	193	26	40	7	0	7	30	0	.207
2006 Chicago	A.L.		DH-1B	143	490	108	141	26	0	42	109	0	.288
2007 Charlotte	Int.		DH	5	14	2	3	1	0	0	5	0	.214
2007 Chicago f	A.L.		DH-1B	130	432	79	119	19	0	35	96	0	.275
2008 Chicago	A.L.		DH	149	503	93	123	28	0	34	90	1	.245
Major League Totals			18 Yrs.	2160	7344	1431	2048	397	24	541	1488	19	.279
Division Series													
1995 Cleveland	A.L.		3B	3	13	1	2	0	0	1	3	0	.154
1996 Cleveland	A.L.		3B	4	10	1	3	0	0	0	0	0	.300
1997 Cleveland	A.L.		1B	5	15	1	3	0	0	0	1	0	.200
1998 Cleveland	A.L.		1B-DH	4	15	2	2	0	0	2	2	0	.133
1999 Cleveland	A.L.		1B	5	17	7	6	0	0	4	10	0	.353
2001 Cleveland	A.L.		1B	5	19	2	3	0	0	1	1	0	.158
2008 Chicago	A.L.		DH	4	16	1	2	1	0	0	1	0	.125
Division Series Totals				29	105	15	21	1	0	8	18	0	.200
Championship Series													
1995 Cleveland	A.L.		3B	5	15	2	4	0	0	2	5	0	.267
1997 Cleveland	A.L.		1B	6	14	3	1	0	0	0	0	0	.071
1998 Cleveland	A.L.		1B-DH	6	23	4	7	0	0	4	8	0	.304
Championship Series Totals				17	52	9	12	0	0	6	13	0	.231
World Series Record													
1995 Cleveland	A.L.		3B	6	19	1	4	1	0	1	2	0	.211
1997 Cleveland	A.L.		1B	7	28	8	8	0	1	2	4	0	.286
World Series Totals				13	47	9	12	1	1	3	6	0	.255

a On disabled list from March 28 to May 18 and May 29 to June 15, 1992.
b On disabled list from August 8 to September 16, 1998.
c Filed for free agency, October 28, 2002. Signed with Philadelphia Phillies, December 3, 2002.
d On disabled list from May 1 to May 21 and July 1 to November 1, 2005.
e Traded to Chicago White Sox for outfielder Aaron Rowand, pitcher Dan Haigwood and player to be named later, November 25, 2005. Philadelphia Phillies received pitcher Giovany Gonzalez to complete trade, December 8, 2005.
f On disabled list from April 28 to May 20, 2007.

TORREALBA, YORVIT ADOLFO

Born, Caracas, Venezuela, July 19, 1978.
Bats Right. Throws Right. Height, 5 feet, 11 inches. Weight, 200 pounds.

Year	Club	Lea	Pos	G	AB	R	H	2B	3B	HR	RBI	SB	Avg
1995 Bellingham	Northwest		C	26	71	2	11	3	0	0	8	0	.155
1996 San Jose	California		C	2	5	0	0	0	0	0	0	0	.000
1996 Burlington	Midwest		C	1	4	0	0	0	0	0	0	0	.000
1996 Bellingham	Northwest		C	48	150	23	40	4	0	1	10	4	.267
1997 Bakersfield	California		C	119	446	52	122	15	3	4	40	4	.274
1998 San Jose	California		C	21	70	10	20	2	0	0	10	2	.286
1998 Shreveport	Texas		C	59	196	18	46	7	0	0	13	0	.235
1998 Fresno	P.C.		C	4	11	1	2	1	0	0	1	0	.182
1999 San Jose	California		C	19	73	10	23	3	0	2	14	0	.315
1999 Fresno	P.C.		C	17	63	9	16	2	0	2	10	0	.254
1999 Shreveport	Texas		C	65	217	25	53	10	1	4	19	0	.244
2000 Shreveport	Texas		C	108	398	50	114	21	1	4	32	2	.286
2001 Fresno	P.C.		C	115	394	56	108	23	3	8	36	2	.274
2001 San Francisco	N.L.		C	3	4	0	2	0	1	0	2	0	.500
2002 San Francisco	N.L.		C	53	136	17	38	10	0	2	14	0	.279
2003 San Francisco	N.L.		C-OF	66	200	22	52	10	2	4	29	1	.260
2004 San Francisco	N.L.		C	64	172	19	39	7	3	6	23	2	.227
2005 San Francisco	N.L.		C	34	93	18	21	8	0	1	7	1	.226
2005 Seattle a-b	A.L.		C	42	108	14	26	4	0	2	8	0	.241
2006 Colorado Springs	P.C.		C	10	36	0	6	2	0	0	2	0	.167
2006 Colorado c	N.L.		C	65	223	23	55	16	3	7	43	4	.247
2007 Colorado d	N.L.		C	113	396	47	101	22	1	8	47	2	.255
2008 Colorado e	N.L.		C	70	236	19	58	17	0	6	31	0	.246
Major League Totals			8 Yrs.	510	1568	179	392	94	10	36	204	10	.250
Division Series													
2003 San Francisco	N.L.		C	2	3	0	0	0	0	0	1	0	.000
2007 Colorado	N.L.		C	3	10	3	5	1	0	0	3	0	.500
Division Series Totals				5	13	3	5	1	0	0	4	0	.385

Year	Club	Lea	Pos	G	AB	R	H	2B	3B	HR	RBI	SB	Avg
	Championship Series												
2007	Colorado	N.L.	C	4	15	2	3	1	0	1	4	0	.200
	World Series Record												
2007	Colorado	N.L.	C	4	14	0	2	0	0	0	1	0	.143

a Traded to Seattle Mariners with pitcher Jesse Foppert for outfielder Randy Winn, July 31, 2005.
b Traded to Colorado Rockies for player to be named later, December 7, 2005. Seattle Mariners received pitcher Marcos Carvajal to complete trade, December 8, 2005.
c On disabled list from March 24 to June 2 and September 10 to November 1, 2006.
d Filed for free agency, October 31, 2007, re-signed with Colorado Rockies, November 29, 2007.
e On disabled list from August 26 to October 1, 2008.

TRACY, CHAD AUSTIN

Born, Charlotte, North Carolina, May 22, 1980.
Bats Left. Throws Right. Height, 6 feet, 2 inches. Weight, 215 pounds.

Year	Club	Lea	Pos	G	AB	R	H	2B	3B	HR	RBI	SB	Avg
2001	South Bend ...	Midwest	3B-1B	54	215	43	73	11	0	4	36	3	.340
2001	Yakima	Northwest	3B	10	36	2	10	1	0	0	5	1	.278
2002	El Paso	Texas	3B-1B	129	514	80	177	39	5	8	74	2	.344
2003	Tucson	P.C.	3B	133	522	91	169	31	4	10	80	0	.324
2004	Tucson	P.C.	3B-OF	11	40	7	16	4	0	2	11	2	.400
2004	Arizona	N.L.	3B-1B-OF	143	481	45	137	29	3	8	53	2	.285
2005	Arizona	N.L.	1B-OF	145	503	73	155	34	4	27	72	3	.308
2006	Arizona	N.L.	3B-1B	154	597	91	168	41	0	20	80	5	.281
2007	Tucson	P.C.	3B	3	15	3	7	2	0	1	4	0	.467
2007	Arizona a	N.L.	3B-1B	76	227	30	60	18	2	7	35	0	.264
2008	Tucson	P.C.	3B-1B	12	49	5	15	2	0	0	6	0	.306
2008	Arizona b	N.L.	1B-3B	88	273	25	73	16	0	8	39	0	.267
Major League Totals			5 Yrs.	606	2081	264	593	138	9	70	279	10	.285

a On disabled list from May 16 to June 10 and August 13 to September 16, 2007.
b On disabled list from March 23 to May 26, 2008.

TREANOR, MATTHEW AARON (MATT)

Born, Garden Grove, California, March 3, 1976.
Bats Right. Throws Right. Height, 6 feet, 2 inches. Weight, 220 pounds.

Year	Club	Lea	Pos	G	AB	R	H	2B	3B	HR	RBI	SB	Avg
1994	Royals	Gulf Coast	C-2B-OF	46	99	17	18	5	0	1	12	1	.182
1995	Springfield	Midwest	C	75	211	17	39	6	2	3	19	1	.185
1996	Lansing	Midwest	C-OF	119	384	56	100	18	2	6	33	5	.260
1997	Wilmington	Carolina	C	80	257	22	51	6	1	5	25	1	.198
1997	Brevard Cty a	Fla.St.	C	23	70	11	15	4	1	0	3	1	.214
1998	Brevard Cty	Fla.St.	C-1B-3B	80	243	24	57	8	0	3	28	3	.235
1999	Kane County	Midwest	C	86	308	56	88	21	1	10	53	4	.286
2000	Brevard County b	Fla.St.	C-1B	109	350	51	86	17	0	3	37	3	.246
2001	Portland	Eastern	C-1B	35	89	7	14	2	0	2	8	1	.157
2001	Marlins	N.L.	C	11	34	10	14	4	0	1	4	3	.412
2001	Kane County	Midwest	C	1	1	2	1	0	0	0	0	1	1.000
2002	Portland	Eastern	C	50	156	24	39	5	1	9	28	3	.250
2002	Calgary c	P.C.	C-1B	36	95	10	27	8	0	1	18	1	.284
2003	Albuquerque d	P.C.	C	98	315	45	86	18	1	11	40	9	.273
2004	Albuquerque.	P.C.	C	62	198	32	51	8	0	8	38	2	.258
2004	Florida	N.L.	C	29	55	7	13	2	0	0	1	0	.236
2005	Florida	N.L.	C	58	134	10	27	8	0	0	13	0	.201
2006	Florida e	N.L.	C	67	157	12	36	6	1	2	14	0	.229
2007	Florida	N.L.	C	55	171	16	46	7	1	4	19	0	.269
2008	Jupiter	Fla.St.	C	5	16	7	5	1	0	1	5	0	.313
2008	Florida f-g	N.L.	C	65	206	18	49	7	0	2	23	1	.238
Major League Totals			5 Yrs.	274	723	63	171	30	2	8	70	1	.237

a Traded by Kansas City Royals to Florida Marlins for pitcher Matt Whisenant, July 29, 1997.
b Filed for free agency, October 15, 2000, re-signed with Florida Marlins, November 13, 2000.
c Filed for free agency, October 15, 2002, re-signed with Florida Marlins, November 25, 2002.
d Filed for free agency, October 15, 2003, re-signed with Florida Marlins, December 4, 2003.
e On disabled list from August 2 to August 16, 2006.
f On disabled list from July 8 to August 6, 2008.
g Released by Florida Marlins, December 10, 2008. Signed with Detroit Tigers, December 18, 2008.

TULOWITZKI, TROY TREVER

Born, Santa Clara, California, October 10, 1984.
Bats Right. Throws Right. Height, 6 feet, 3 inches. Weight, 205 pounds.

Year	Club	Lea	Pos	G	AB	R	H	2B	3B	HR	RBI	SB	Avg
2005	Modesto	Calif.	SS	22	94	17	25	6	0	4	14	1	.266
2006	Tulsa	Texas	SS	104	423	75	123	34	2	13	61	6	.291
2006	Colorado	N.L.	SS	25	96	15	23	2	0	1	6	3	.240
2007	Colorado	N.L.	SS	155	609	104	177	33	5	24	99	7	.291
2008	Modesto	Calif.	SS	5	12	3	4	3	0	0	1	0	.333
2008	Tulsa	Texas	SS	5	21	5	7	0	0	2	3	0	.333
2008	Colorado Springs	P.C.	SS	2	7	2	3	1	0	0	1	1	.429
2008	Colorado a	N.L.	SS	101	377	48	99	24	2	8	46	1	.263
Major League Totals			3 Yrs.	281	1082	167	299	59	7	33	151	11	.276
Division Series													
2007	Colorado	N.L.	SS	3	12	1	2	1	0	1	2	0	.167
Championship Series													
2007	Colorado	N.L.	SS	4	16	1	3	0	0	0	0	0	.188
World Series Record													
2007	Colorado	N.L.	SS	4	13	1	3	2	0	0	1	0	.231

a On disabled list from April 30 to June 20 and July 5 to July 21, 2008.

UGGLA, DANIEL COOLEY (DAN)

Born, Louisville, Kentucky, March 11, 1980.
Bats Right. Throws Right. Height, 5 feet, 11 inches. Weight, 200 pounds.

Year	Club	Lea	Pos	G	AB	R	H	2B	3B	HR	RBI	SB	Avg
2001	Yakima	Northwest	2B	72	278	39	77	21	0	5	40	8	.277
2002	Lancaster	Calif.	2B-3B	54	184	21	42	7	2	3	16	3	.228
2002	South Bend	Midwest	3B-2B	53	171	16	34	5	1	2	10	0	.199
2003	Lancaster	Calif.	3B-2B	134	534	104	155	31	7	23	90	24	.290
2004	Lancaster	Calif.	2B-3B-SS-1B	37	140	29	47	13	3	6	38	2	.336
2004	El Paso	Texas	3B-OF-2B	83	295	29	76	12	2	4	30	10	.258
2005	Tennessee a	Southern	2B-3B-1B-SS	135	498	88	148	33	3	21	87	15	.297
2006	Florida	N.L.	2B	154	611	105	172	26	7	27	90	6	.282
2007	Florida	N.L.	2B	159	632	113	155	49	3	31	88	2	.245
2008	Florida	N.L.	2B	146	531	97	138	37	1	32	92	5	.260
Major League Totals			3 Yrs.	459	1774	315	465	112	11	90	270	13	.262

a Selected by Florida Marlins from Arizona Diamondbacks in Rule V draft, December 8, 2005.

UPTON, JUSTIN IRVIN

Born, Norfolk, Virginia, August 25, 1987.
Bats Right. Throws Right. Height, 6 feet, 3 inches. Weight, 205 pounds.

Year	Club	Lea	Pos	G	AB	R	H	2B	3B	HR	RBI	SB	Avg
2006	South Bend	Midwest	OF	113	438	71	115	28	1	12	66	15	.263
2007	Visalia	Calif.	OF	32	126	27	43	6	2	5	17	9	.341
2007	Mobile	Southern	OF	71	259	48	80	17	4	13	53	10	.309
2007	Arizona	N.L.	OF	43	140	17	31	8	3	2	11	2	.221
2008	Tucson	P.C.	OF	15	61	13	17	3	1	3	10	2	.279
2008	Arizona a	N.L.	OF	108	356	52	89	19	6	15	42	1	.250
Major League Totals			2 Yrs.	151	496	69	120	27	9	17	53	3	.242
Division Series													
2007	Arizona	N.L.	OF	2	5	2	3	0	0	0	1	1	.600
Championship Series													
2007	Arizona	N.L.	OF	4	9	0	2	1	1	0	0	0	.222

a On disabled list from July 9 to August 29, 2008.

UPTON, MELVIN EMANUEL (B.J.)

Born, Norfolk, Virginia, August 21, 1984.
Bats Right. Throws Right. Height, 6 feet, 3 inches. Weight, 180 pounds.

Year	Club	Lea	Pos	G	AB	R	H	2B	3B	HR	RBI	SB	Avg
2003	Charleston	So.Atl.	SS	101	384	70	116	22	6	7	46	38	.302
2003	Orlando	Southern	SS	29	105	14	29	8	0	1	16	2	.276
2004	Montgomery	Southern	SS	29	104	21	34	7	1	2	15	3	.327
2004	Durham	Int.	SS	69	264	65	82	17	1	12	36	17	.311
2004	Tampa Bay	A.L.	SS-3B-OF	45	159	19	41	8	2	4	12	4	.258
2005	Durham	Int.	SS	139	545	98	165	36	6	18	74	44	.303
2006	Durham	Int.	SS-3B	106	398	72	107	18	4	8	41	6	.269

Year Club	Lea	Pos	G	AB	R	H	2B	3B	HR	RBI	SB	Avg
2006 Tampa Bay	A.L.	3B	50	175	20	43	5	0	1	10	11	.246
2007 Vero Beach.........	Fla.St.	2B-OF	7	17	4	4	0	0	1	3	0	.235
2007 Durham	Int.	2B	2	7	1	3	0	0	1	1	0	.429
2007 Tampa Bay a.........	A.L.	OF-2B	129	474	86	142	25	1	24	82	22	.300
2008 Tampa Bay	A.L.	OF	145	531	85	145	37	2	9	67	44	.273
Major League Totals		4 Yrs.	369	1339	210	371	75	5	38	171	81	.277
Division Series												
2008 Tampa Bay	N.L.	OF	4	18	5	5	0	1	3	4	0	.278
Championship Series												
2008 Tampa Bay	N.L.	OF	7	28	8	9	1	0	4	11	2	.321
World Series Record												
2008 Tampa Bay	N.L.	OF	5	20	3	5	0	0	0	1	4	.250

a On disabled list from June 9 to July 13, 2007.

URIBE (TENA), JUAN C.
Born, Bani, Dominican Republic, July 22, 1979.
Bats Right. Throws Right. Height, 6 feet. Weight, 220 pounds.

Year Club	Lea	Pos	G	AB	R	H	2B	3B	HR	RBI	SB	Avg
1997 Colorado	Domincan	SS	65	234	32	63	12	0	0	29	7	.269
1998 Rockies	Arizona	SS	40	148	25	41	5	3	0	17	8	.277
1999 Asheville.......	So.Atl.	SS	125	430	57	115	28	3	9	46	11	.267
2000 Salem.......	Carolina	SS	134	485	64	124	22	7	13	65	22	.256
2001 Carolina	Southern	SS	3	13	1	3	1	0	0	1	1	.231
2001 Colo Spmgs.......	P.C.	SS	74	281	40	87	27	7	7	48	11	.310
2001 Colorado	N.L.	SS	72	273	32	82	15	11	8	53	3	.300
2002 Colorado	N.L.	SS	155	566	69	136	25	7	6	49	9	.240
2003 Visalia	California	2B-SS	2	9	4	5	1	0	1	5	1	.556
2003 Tulsa	Texas	2B-3B-SS-OF	5	20	3	5	2	0	1	4	0	.250
2003 Colorado a-b	N.L.	SS-2B-OF	87	316	45	80	19	3	10	33	7	.253
2004 Chicago	A.L.	2B-SS-3B	134	502	82	142	31	6	23	74	9	.283
2005 Chicago	A.L.	SS	146	481	58	121	23	3	16	71	4	.252
2006 Chicago	A.L.	SS	132	463	53	109	28	2	21	71	1	.235
2007 Chicago	A.L.	SS	150	513	55	120	18	2	20	68	1	.234
2008 Charlotte	Int.	2B-SS	3	11	0	2	0	0	0	2	0	.182
2008 Chicago c-d	A.L.	3B-2B-SS	110	324	38	80	22	1	7	40	1	.247
Major League Totals		8 Yrs.	986	3438	432	870	181	35	111	459	35	.253
Division Series												
2005 Chicago	A.L.	SS	3	10	4	4	1	0	1	4	0	.400
2008 Chicago	A.L.	3B	4	12	0	2	0	0	0	1	1	.167
Division Series Totals			7	22	4	6	1	0	1	5	1	.273
Championship Series												
2005 Chicago	A.L.	SS	5	16	1	4	1	0	0	0	0	.250
World Series Record												
2005 Chicago	A.L.	SS	4	16	2	4	3	0	0	2	1	.250

a On disabled list from March 18 to June 3, 2003.
b Traded to Chicago White Sox for infielder Aaron Miles, December 2, 2003.
c On disabled list from May 16 to May 31, 2008.
d Filed for free agency, October 30, 2008.

UTLEY, CHASE CAMERON
Born, Pasadena, California, December 17, 1978.
Bats Left. Throws Right. Height, 6 feet, 1 inch. Weight, 200 pounds.

Year Club	Lea	Pos	G	AB	R	H	2B	3B	HR	RBI	SB	Avg
2000 Batavia.........	N.Y.-Penn.	2B	40	153	21	47	13	1	2	22	5	.307
2001 Clearwater	Fla.St.	2B	122	467	65	120	25	2	16	59	19	.257
2002 Scranton/W.B.	Int.	3B	125	464	73	122	39	1	17	70	8	.263
2003 Scranton/W.B.	Int.	2B	113	431	80	139	26	2	18	77	10	.323
2003 Philadelphia	N.L.	2B	43	134	13	32	10	1	2	21	2	.239
2004 Scranton/W.B.	Int.	2B	33	123	23	35	8	1	6	25	4	.285
2004 Philadelphia	N.L.	2B-1B	94	267	36	71	11	2	13	57	4	.266
2005 Philadelphia	N.L.	2B-1B	147	543	93	158	39	6	28	105	16	.291
2006 Philadelphia	N.L.	2B-1B	160	658	*131	203	40	4	32	102	15	.309
2007 Reading	Eastern	2B	3	10	0	1	0	0	0	0	0	.100
2007 Philadelphia a.........	N.L.	2B-1B	132	530	104	176	48	5	22	103	9	.332
2008 Philadelphia	N.L.	2B-1B	159	607	113	177	41	4	33	104	14	.292
Major League Totals		6 Yrs.	735	2739	490	817	189	22	130	492	60	.298

Year	Club	Lea	Pos	G	AB	R	H	2B	3B	HR	RBI	SB	Avg
Division Series													
2007 Philadelphia	N.L.		2B	3	11	0	2	0	0	0	0	0	.182
2008 Philadelphia	N.L.		2B	4	15	1	2	1	0	0	2	0	.133
Division Series Totals				7	26	1	4	1	0	0	2	0	.154
Championship Series													
2008 Philadelphia	N.L.		2B	5	17	4	6	2	0	1	3	0	.353
World Series Record													
2008 Philadelphia	N.L.		2B	5	18	5	3	0	0	2	4	3	.167

a On disabled list from July 27 to August 27, 2007.

VALENTIN, JOSE JAVIER (JAVIER)

Born, Manati, Puerto Rico, September 19, 1975.
Bats Both. Throws Right. Height, 5 feet, 10 inches. Weight, 210 pounds.

Year	Club	Lea	Pos	G	AB	R	H	2B	3B	HR	RBI	SB	Avg
1993 Twins	Gulf Coast	C-3B-OF	32	103	18	27	6	1	1	19	0	.262	
1993 Elizabethtn	Appal.	C	9	24	3	5	1	0	0	3	0	.208	
1994 Elizabethtn	Appal.	C-OF-3B	54	210	23	44	5	0	9	27	0	.210	
1995 Ft. Wayne	Midwest	C-3B	112	383	59	123	26	5	19	65	0	.321	
1996 Ft. Myers	Fla.St.	C-3B	87	338	34	89	26	1	7	54	1	.263	
1996 New Britain	Eastern	C-3B	48	165	22	39	8	0	3	14	0	.236	
1997 New Britain	Eastern	C-3B	102	370	41	90	17	0	8	50	2	.243	
1997 Minnesota	A.L.	C	4	7	1	2	0	0	0	0	0	.286	
1998 Minnesota	A.L.	C	55	162	11	32	7	1	3	18	0	.198	
1999 Minnesota	A.L.	C	78	218	22	54	12	1	5	28	0	.248	
2000 Salt Lake	P.C.	C	39	140	25	50	16	2	7	35	1	.357	
2001 Edmonton	P.C.	C-3B-1B	121	431	53	121	29	2	17	71	0	.281	
2002 Edmonton	P.C.	C-3B-1B	127	455	69	130	33	1	21	80	0	.286	
2002 Minnesota a	A.L.	C	4	4	0	2	0	0	0	0	0	.500	
2003 Tampa Bay b	A.L.	C	49	135	13	30	7	1	3	15	0	.222	
2004 Cincinnati c	N.L.	C-1B	82	202	18	47	10	1	6	20	0	.233	
2005 Cincinnati	N.L.	C-1B	76	221	36	62	11	0	14	50	0	.281	
2006 Cincinnati	N.L.	C-1B	92	186	24	50	6	1	8	27	0	.269	
2007 Cincinnati	N.L.	C-1B	97	243	19	67	21	0	2	34	0	.276	
2008 Cincinnati d	N.L.	C-1B-3B	94	129	10	33	8	0	4	18	0	.256	
Major League Totals		10 Yrs.	631	1507	154	379	82	5	45	210	0	.251	

a Traded to Milwaukee Brewers with pitcher Matt Kinney for pitcher Matt Yeatman and pitcher Gerry Oakes, November 14, 2002.
b Traded to Tampa Bay Devil Rays for outfielder Jason Conti, March 24, 2003.
c Filed for free agency, October 15, 2003. Signed with Cincinnati Reds organization, January 9, 2004.
d Filed for free agency, October 31, 2008.

VARITEK, JASON ANDREW

Born, Rochester, Minnesota, April 11, 1972.
Bats Both. Throws Right. Height, 6 feet, 2 inches. Weight, 230 pounds.

Year	Club	Lea	Pos	G	AB	R	H	2B	3B	HR	RBI	SB	Avg
1995 Port City	Southern	C	104	352	42	79	14	2	10	44	0	.224	
1996 Port City	Southern	C-3B-OF	134	503	63	132	34	1	12	67	7	.262	
1997 Tacoma	P.C.	C	87	307	54	78	13	0	15	48	0	.254	
1997 Pawtucket	Int.	C	20	66	6	13	5	0	1	5	0	.197	
1997 Boston a	A.L.	C	1	1	0	1	0	0	0	0	0	1.000	
1998 Boston	A.L.	C	86	221	31	56	13	0	7	33	2	.253	
1999 Boston	A.L.	C	144	483	70	130	39	2	20	76	1	.269	
2000 Boston	A.L.	C	139	448	55	111	31	1	10	65	1	.248	
2001 Boston b	A.L.	C	51	174	19	51	11	1	7	25	0	.293	
2002 Boston	A.L.	C	132	467	58	124	27	1	10	61	4	.266	
2003 Boston	A.L.	C	142	451	63	123	31	1	25	85	3	.273	
2004 Boston c	A.L.	C	137	463	67	137	30	1	18	73	10	.296	
2005 Boston	A.L.	C	133	470	70	132	30	1	22	70	2	.281	
2006 Pawtucket	Int.	C	2	7	2	3	0	0	1	1	0	.429	
2006 Boston d	A.L.	C	103	365	46	87	19	2	12	55	1	.238	
2007 Boston	A.L.	C	131	435	57	111	15	3	17	68	1	.255	
2008 Boston e	A.L.	C	131	423	37	93	20	2	13	43	0	.220	
Major League Totals		12 Yrs.	1330	4401	573	1156	266	13	161	654	25	.263	
Division Series													
1998 Boston	A.L.	C	1	4	0	1	0	0	0	0	1	.250	
1999 Boston	A.L.	C	5	21	7	5	3	0	1	3	0	.238	

Year Club	Lea	Pos	G	AB	R	H	2B	3B	HR	RBI	SB	Avg
2003 Boston	A.L.	C	5	14	4	4	0	0	2	2	0	.286
2004 Boston	A.L.	C	3	12	3	2	0	0	1	2	0	.167
2005 Boston	A.L.	C	3	10	1	3	0	0	0	1	0	.300
2007 Boston	A.L.	C	3	11	1	2	1	0	0	1	0	.182
2008 Boston	A.L.	C	4	14	2	3	0	0	0	0	0	.214
Division Series Totals			24	86	18	20	4	0	4	10	0	.233
Championship Series												
1999 Boston	A.L.	C	5	20	1	4	1	1	1	1	0	.200
2003 Boston	A.L.	C	6	20	4	6	2	0	2	3	0	.300
2004 Boston	A.L.	C	7	28	5	9	1	0	2	7	0	.321
2007 Boston	A.L.	C	7	26	3	7	3	0	1	4	0	.269
2008 Boston	A.L.	C	6	20	2	1	0	0	1	1	0	.050
Championship Series Totals			31	114	15	27	7	1	7	16	0	.237
World Series Record												
2004 Boston	A.L.	C	4	13	2	2	0	1	0	2	0	.154
2007 Boston	A.L.	C	4	15	2	5	1	0	0	5	0	.333
World Series Totals			8	28	4	7	1	1	0	7	0	.250

a Traded to Boston Red Sox by Seattle Mariners with pitcher Derek Lowe for pitcher Heathcliff Slocumb, July 31, 1997.

b On disabled list from June 8 to November 7, 2001.

c Filed for free agency, November 1, 2004, re-signed with Boston Red Sox, December 24, 2004.

d On disabled list from August 1 to September 3, 2006.

e Filed for free agency, October 30, 2008.

VAZQUEZ, RAMON LUIS

Born, Aibonito, Puerto Rico, August 21, 1976.
Bats Left. Throws Right. Height, 5 feet, 11 inches. Weight, 195 pounds.

Year Club	Lea	Pos	G	AB	R	H	2B	3B	HR	RBI	SB	Avg
1995 Mariners	Arizona	SS-3B-2B	39	141	20	29	3	1	0	11	4	.206
1996 Everett	Northwest	SS	33	126	25	35	5	2	1	18	7	.278
1996 Tacoma	P.C.	2B-SS	18	49	7	11	2	1	0	4	0	.224
1996 Wisconsin	Midwest	3B	3	10	1	3	1	0	0	1	0	.300
1997 Wisconsin	Midwest	SS	131	479	79	129	25	5	5	49	16	.269
1998 Lancaster	Calif.	SS	121	468	77	129	26	4	2	72	15	.276
1999 New Haven.....	Eastern	SS-3B	127	438	58	113	27	3	5	45	8	.258
2000 New Haven.....	Eastern	SS	124	405	58	116	25	4	8	59	1	.286
2001 Tacoma	P.C.	SS	127	466	85	140	28	1	10	79	9	.300
2001 Seattle a	A.L.	SS-2B-3B	17	35	5	8	0	0	0	4	0	.229
2002 San Diego	N.L.	2B-SS-3B	128	423	50	116	21	5	2	32	7	.274
2003 Lake Elsinore	Calif.	SS	5	16	3	3	0	0	1	4	0	.188
2003 San Diego b	N.L.	SS-3B-2B	116	422	56	110	17	4	3	30	0	.261
2004 San Diego	N.L.	SS-2B-3B-1B	52	115	12	27	3	2	1	13	1	.235
2004 Portland c-d	P.C.	2B-3B-SS	53	184	36	55	21	1	8	34	2	.299
2005 Buffalo	Int.	SS-2B-3B	21	84	13	18	3	1	0	4	1	.214
2005 Boston-Cleveland e	A.L.	SS-2B-3B	34	85	7	18	5	0	0	5	0	.212
2006 Cleveland	A.L.	3B-2B-SS	34	67	11	14	2	0	1	8	0	.209
2006 Buffalo f	Int.	SS-2B-1B-3B	28	99	19	24	2	1	2	11	2	.242
2007 Oklahoma........	P.C.		35	132	27	34	10	2	2	13	3	.258
2007 Texas	A.L.	3B-SS-2B-1B	104	300	42	69	13	3	8	28	1	.230
2008 Texas g..........	A.L.	3B-SS-2B-1B	105	300	44	87	18	3	6	40	0	.290
Major League Totals		8 Yrs.	595	1747	227	449	79	17	21	160	19	.257
Division Series												
2001 Seattle ...........A.L.		SS	1	0	0	0	0	0	0	0	0	.000

a Traded to San Diego Padres with pitcher Brett Tomko and catcher Tom Lampkin for catcher Ben Davis, pitcher Wascar Serrano and infielder Alex Arias, December 11, 2001.

b On disabled list from June 1 to July 7, 2003.

c On disabled list from May 20 to June 20, 2004.

d Traded to Boston Red Sox with outfielder Jay Payton, pitcher David Pauley and cash for outfielder Dave Roberts, December 20, 2004.

e Traded to Cleveland Indians for infielder Alex Cora, July 7, 2005.

f Filed for free agency, October 2, 2006. Signed with Texas Rangers organization, November 17, 2006.

g Filed for free agency, October 30, 2008. Signed with Pittsburgh Pirates, December 12, 2008.

VELEZ (VANCOMPER), EUGENIO
Born, San Pedro de Macoris, Dominican Republic, May 16, 1982.
Bats Both. Throws Right. Height, 6 feet, 1 inch. Weight, 160 pounds.

Year	Club	Lea	Pos	G	AB	R	H	2B	3B	HR	RBI	SB	Avg
2003	Pulaski	Appal.	SS-2B	50	186	20	48	7	2	2	24	3	.258
2003	Auburn	N.Y.-Penn.	2B-SS	7	26	2	5	2	0	1	7	0	.192
2004	Pulaski	Appal.	SS-3B	44	168	27	49	14	4	1	26	1	.292
2004	Auburn	N.Y.-Penn.	3B-2B-SS	10	19	5	5	0	0	0	2	0	.263
2005	Lansing a	Midwest	2B-3B	67	239	25	68	11	3	4	34	7	.285
2006	Augusta	So.Atl.	2B-SS-3B	126	460	90	145	29	20	14	90	64	.315
2007	Connecticut	Eastern	OF-2B	96	376	55	112	17	9	1	25	49	.298
2007	Fresno	P.C.	OF	4	18	5	5	0	0	0	0	5	.278
2007	San Francisco	N.L.	2B-OF	14	11	5	3	0	2	0	2	4	.273
2008	Fresno	P.C.	OF-2B	42	171	25	53	11	4	5	15	13	.310
2008	San Francisco	N.L.	2B-OF	98	275	32	72	16	7	1	30	15	.262
Major League Totals			2 Yrs.	112	286	37	75	16	9	1	32	19	.262

a Selected by San Francisco Giants from Toronto Blue Jays in Rule V draft, December 8, 2005.

VENABLE, WILLIAM DION (WILL)
Born, Greenbrae, California, October 29, 1982.
Bats Left. Throws Left. Height, 6 feet, 2 inches. Weight, 205 pounds.

Year	Club	Lea	Pos	G	AB	R	H	2B	3B	HR	RBI	SB	Avg
2005	Padres	Arizona	OF	15	59	13	19	4	2	1	12	4	.322
2005	Eugene	Northwest	OF	42	139	17	30	5	2	2	14	2	.216
2006	Fort Wayne	Midwest	OF	124	472	86	148	34	5	11	91	18	.314
2007	San Antonio	Texas	OF	134	515	66	143	19	3	8	68	21	.278
2008	Portland	P.C.	OF	120	442	70	129	26	4	14	58	7	.292
2008	San Diego	N.L.	OF	28	110	16	29	4	2	2	10	1	.264

VICTORINO, SHANE PATRICK
Born, Wailuku, Hawaii, November 30, 1980.
Bats Both. Throws Right. Height, 5 feet, 9 inches. Weight, 180 pounds.

Year	Club	Lea	Pos	G	AB	R	H	2B	3B	HR	RBI	SB	Avg
1999	Great Falls	Pioneer	OF	55	225	53	63	7	6	2	25	20	.280
2000	Yakima	Northwest	2B-SS	61	236	32	58	7	2	2	20	21	.246
2001	Vero Beach	Fla.St.	OF	2	6	2	1	0	0	0	0	0	.167
2001	Wilmington	So.Atl.	OF	112	435	71	123	21	9	4	32	47	.283
2002	Jacksonville	Southern	OF	122	481	61	124	15	4	1	34	45	.258
2003	Jacksonville	Southern	OF	66	266	37	75	9	4	2	15	16	.282
2003	Las Vegas	P.C.	OF	11	41	6	16	1	2	1	9	0	.390
2003	San Diego a	N.L.	OF	36	73	8	11	2	0	0	4	7	.151
2004	Las Vegas	P.C.	OF-2B	55	200	28	47	9	1	3	20	7	.235
2004	Jacksonville b	Southern	OF	75	293	70	96	13	7	16	43	9	.328
2005	Scranton/WB	Int.	OF	126	494	93	153	25	16	18	70	17	.310
2005	Philadelphia	N.L.	OF	21	17	5	5	0	0	2	8	0	.294
2006	Philadelphia	N.L.	OF	153	415	70	119	19	8	6	46	4	.287
2007	Lakewood	So.Atl.	DH	1	5	1	1	0	0	0	0	0	.200
2007	Reading	Eastern	OF	2	6	0	2	0	0	0	1	1	.333
2007	Philadelphia c	N.L.	OF	131	456	78	128	23	3	12	46	37	.281
2008	Clearwater	Fla.St.	OF	2	5	1	2	0	0	0	0	0	.400
2008	Reading	Eastern	OF	1	3	0	1	0	0	0	0	0	.333
2008	Lehigh	Int.	OF	2	8	0	3	0	0	0	0	0	.375
2008	Philadelphia d	N.L.	OF	146	570	102	167	30	8	14	58	36	.293
Major League Totals			5 Yrs.	487	1531	263	430	74	19	34	162	84	.281
Division Series													
2007	Philadelphia	N.L.	OF	3	9	2	2	0	0	1	1	1	.222
2008	Philadelphia	N.L.	OF	4	14	2	5	3	0	1	5	3	.357
Division Series Totals				7	23	4	7	3	0	2	6	4	.304
Championship Series													
2008	Philadelphia	N.L.	OF	5	18	2	4	0	1	1	6	0	.222
World Series Record													
2008	Philadelphia	N.L.	OF	5	20	1	5	0	0	0	2	0	.250

a Selected by San Diego Padres from Los Angeles Dodgers in Rule V draft, December 16, 2002. Returned to Los Angeles Dodgers, May 28, 2003.
b Selected by Philadelphia Phillies in Rule V draft, December 13, 2004.
c On disabled list from July 31 to August 22, 2007.
d On disabled list from April 13 to April 29, 2008.

VIDRO, JOSE ANGEL

Born, Mayaguez, Puerto Rico, August 27, 1974.
Bats Both. Throws Right. Height, 5 feet, 11 inches. Weight, 195 pounds.

Year Club	Lea	Pos	G	AB	R	H	2B	3B	HR	RBI	SB	Avg
1992 Expos	Gulf Coast	2B	54	200	29	66	6	2	4	31	10	.330
1993 Burlington	Midwest	2B	76	287	39	69	19	0	2	34	3	.240
1994 Wst Plm Bch	Fla. St.	2B	125	465	57	124	30	2	4	49	8	.267
1995 Harrisburg	Eastern	2B-SS-3B	64	246	33	64	16	2	4	38	3	.260
1995 Wst Plm Bch	Fla. St.	2B-SS-3B	44	163	20	53	15	2	3	24	0	.325
1996 Harrisburg	Eastern	3B-2B-SS	126	452	57	117	25	3	18	82	3	.259
1997 Ottawa	Int.	3B-2B	73	279	40	90	17	0	13	47	2	.323
1997 Montreal	N.L.	3B-2B	67	169	19	42	12	1	2	17	1	.249
1998 Ottawa	Int.	2B-3B	63	235	35	68	14	2	2	32	5	.289
1998 Montreal	N.L.	2B-3B	83	205	24	45	12	0	0	18	2	.220
1999 Montreal	N.L.	2B-1B-OF-3B	140	494	67	150	45	2	12	59	0	.304
2000 Montreal	N.L.	2B	153	606	101	200	51	2	24	97	5	.330
2001 Montreal a	N.L.	2B	124	486	82	155	34	1	15	59	4	.319
2002 Montreal	N.L.	2B	152	604	103	190	43	3	19	96	2	.315
2003 Montreal	N.L.	2B	144	509	77	158	36	0	15	65	3	.310
2004 Montreal b	N.L.	2B	110	412	51	121	24	0	14	60	3	.294
2005 Potomac	Carolina	2B	5	13	3	2	1	0	0	3	0	.154
2005 Washington c	N.L.	2B	87	309	38	85	21	2	7	32	0	.275
2006 Potomac	Carolina	DH	1	3	0	1	1	0	0	0	0	.333
2006 Harrisburg	Eastern	2B	3	8	0	2	0	0	0	1	0	.250
2006 Washington d-e	N.L.	2B-1B	126	463	52	134	26	1	7	47	1	.289
2007 Seattle	A.L.	DH-1B-2B	147	548	78	172	26	0	6	59	0	.314
2008 Seattle f	A.L.	DH-1B	85	308	28	72	11	0	7	45	2	.234
Major League Totals		12 Yrs.	1418	5113	720	1524	341	12	128	654	23	.298

a On disabled list from May 20 to June 12, 2001.
b On disabled list from August 26 to November 1, 2004.
c On disabled list from May 5 to July 5, 2005.
d On disabled list from July 18 to August 18, 2006.
e Traded to Seattle Mariners for pitcher Emiliano Fruto and outfielder Chris Snelling, December 18, 2006.
f Released by Seattle Mariners, August 13, 2008.

VIZQUEL, OMAR ENRIQUE

Born, Caracas, Venezuela, April 24, 1967.
Bats Both. Throws Right. Height, 5 feet, 9 inches. Weight, 175 pounds.

Year Club	Lea	Pos	G	AB	R	H	2B	3B	HR	RBI	SB	Avg
1984 Butte a	Pioneer	SS-2B	15	45	7	14	2	0	0	4	2	.311
1985 Bellingham	Northwest	SS-2B	50	187	24	42	9	0	5	17	4	.225
1986 Wausau	Midwest	SS-2B	105	352	60	75	13	2	4	28	19	.213
1987 Salinas	California	SS-2B	114	407	61	107	12	8	0	38	25	.263
1988 Vermont	Eastern	SS	103	375	54	95	18	2	2	35	30	.253
1988 Calgary	P.C.	SS	33	107	10	24	2	3	1	12	2	.224
1989 Seattle	A.L.	SS	143	387	45	85	7	3	1	20	1	.220
1989 Calgary	P.C.	SS	7	28	3	6	2	0	0	3	0	.214
1990 San Bernardino	California	SS	6	28	5	7	0	0	0	3	1	.250
1990 Calgary	P.C.	SS	48	150	18	35	6	2	0	8	4	.233
1990 Seattle b	A.L.	SS	81	255	19	63	3	2	2	18	4	.247
1991 Seattle	A.L.	SS-2B	142	426	42	98	16	4	1	41	7	.230
1992 Seattle c	A.L.	SS	136	483	49	142	20	4	0	21	15	.294
1992 Calgary	P.C.	SS	6	22	0	6	1	0	0	2	0	.273
1993 Seattle d	A.L.	SS	158	560	68	143	14	2	2	31	12	.255
1994 Charlotte e	Int.	SS	7	26	3	7	1	0	0	1	1	.269
1994 Cleveland e	A.L.	SS	69	286	39	78	10	1	1	33	13	.273
1995 Cleveland	A.L.	SS	136	542	87	144	28	0	6	56	29	.266
1996 Cleveland	A.L.	SS	151	542	98	161	36	1	9	64	35	.297
1997 Cleveland	A.L.	SS	153	565	89	158	23	6	5	49	43	.280
1998 Cleveland	A.L.	SS	151	576	86	166	30	6	2	50	37	.288
1999 Cleveland	A.L.	SS-OF	144	574	112	191	36	4	5	66	42	.333
2000 Cleveland	A.L.	SS	156	613	101	176	27	3	7	66	22	.287
2001 Cleveland	A.L.	SS	155	611	84	156	26	8	2	50	13	.255
2002 Cleveland	A.L.	SS	151	582	85	160	31	5	14	72	18	.275
2003 Lake County	So.Atl.	SS	4	14	0	1	0	0	0	0	1	.071
2003 Cleveland f	A.L.	SS	64	250	43	61	13	2	2	19	8	.244
2004 Cleveland g	A.L.	SS	148	567	82	165	28	3	7	59	19	.291
2005 San Francisco	N.L.	SS	152	568	66	154	28	4	3	45	24	.271
2006 San Francisco	N.L.	SS	153	579	88	171	22	10	4	58	24	.295
2007 San Francisco	N.L.	SS	145	513	54	126	18	3	4	51	14	.246

Year Club	Lea	Pos	G	AB	R	H	2B	3B	HR	RBI	SB	Avg
2008 San Jose	Calif.	SS	3	8	3	3	0	0	0	1	0	.375
2008 Fresno	P.C.	SS	2	5	0	1	0	0	0	0	0	.200
2008 San Francisco h-i ..	N.L.	SS	92	266	24	59	10	1	0	23	5	.222
Major League Totals	20 Yrs.		2680	9745	1361	2657	426	72	77	892	385	.273
Division Series												
1995 Cleveland	A.L.	SS	3	12	2	2	1	0	0	4	1	.167
1996 Cleveland	A.L.	SS	4	14	4	6	1	0	0	2	4	.429
1997 Cleveland	A.L.	SS	5	18	3	9	0	0	0	1	4	.500
1998 Cleveland	A.L.	SS	4	15	1	1	0	0	0	0	0	.067
1999 Cleveland	A.L.	SS	5	21	3	5	1	1	0	3	0	.238
2001 Cleveland	A.L.	SS	5	22	2	9	1	1	0	6	1	.409
Division Series Totals			26	102	15	32	4	2	0	16	10	.314
Championship Series												
1995 Cleveland	A.L.	SS	6	23	2	2	1	0	0	2	3	.087
1997 Cleveland	A.L.	SS	6	25	1	1	0	0	0	0	0	.040
1998 Cleveland	A.L.	SS	6	25	2	11	0	1	0	0	4	.440
Championship Series Totals			18	73	5	14	1	1	0	2	7	.192
World Series Record												
1995 Cleveland	A.L.	SS	6	23	3	4	0	1	0	1	-1	.174
1997 Cleveland	A.L.	SS	7	30	5	7	2	0	0	1	5	.233
World Series Totals			13	53	8	11	2	1	0	2	6	.208

a Batted righthanded only from 1984 through 1988 season.
b On disabled list from April 7 to May 14, 1990.
c On disabled list from April 13 to May 11, 1992.
d Traded to Cleveland Indians for shortstop Felix Fermin and first baseman Reggie Jefferson, December 20, 1993.
e On disabled list from April 23 to June 13, 1994.
f On disabled list from June 12 to August 26 and September 6 to October 28, 2003.
g Filed for free agency, October 29, 2004. Signed with San Francisco Giants, November 14, 2004.
h On disabled list from March 21 to May 10, 2008.
i Not offered contract, November 3, 2008.

VOTTO, JOSEPH DANIEL (JOEY)

Born, Toronto, Ontario, Canada, September 10, 1983.
Bats Left. Throws Right. Height, 6 feet, 3 inches. Weight, 220 pounds.

Year Club	Lea	Pos	G	AB	R	H	2B	3B	HR	RBI	SB	Avg
2002 Reds	Gulf Coast	3B-C-OF	50	175	29	47	13	3	9	33	7	.269
2003 Dayton	Midwest	1B	60	195	19	45	8	0	1	20	2	.231
2003 Billings..........	Pioneer	1B	70	240	47	76	17	3	6	37	4	.317
2004 Potomac.........	Carolina	1B	24	84	11	25	7	0	5	20	1	.298
2004 Dayton..........	Midwest	1B	111	391	60	118	26	2	14	73	9	.302
2005 Sarasota.........	Fla.St.	1B	124	464	64	119	23	2	17	83	4	.256
2006 Chattanooga.....	Southern	1B	136	508	85	162	46	2	22	77	24	.319
2007 Louisville	Int.	1B-OF	133	496	74	146	21	2	22	92	17	.294
2007 Cincinnati........	N.L.	1B-OF	24	84	11	27	7	0	4	17	1	.321
2008 Cincinnati........	N.L.	1B	151	526	69	156	32	3	24	84	7	.297
Major League Totals		2 Yrs.	175	610	80	183	39	3	28	101	8	.300

WARD, DARYLE LAMAR

Born, Lynwood, California, June 27, 1975.
Bats Left. Throws Left. Height, 6 feet, 2 inches. Weight, 240 pounds.

Year Club	Lea	Pos	G	AB	R	H	2B	3B	HR	RBI	SB	Avg
1994 Bristol	Appal.	1B	48	161	17	43	6	0	5	30	4	.267
1995 Fayetteville	So.Atl.	1B	137	524	75	149	32	0	14	106	1	.284
1996 Toledo	Int.	1B	6	23	1	4	0	0	0	1	0	.174
1996 Lakeland a	Fla.St.	1B	128	464	65	135	29	4	10	68	1	.291
1997 Jackson	Texas	1B	114	422	72	139	25	0	19	90	4	.329
1997 New Orleans........	A.A.	1B	14	48	4	18	1	0	2	8	0	.375
1998 Houston	N.L.	PH	4	3	1	1	0	0	0	0	0	.333
1998 New Orleans........	P.C.	OF-1B	116	463	78	141	31	1	23	96	2	.305
1999 New Orleans........	P.C.	1B-OF	61	241	56	85	15	1	28	65	1	.353
1999 Houston	N.L.	OF-1B	64	150	11	41	6	0	8	30	0	.273
2000 Houston	N.L.	OF-1B	119	264	36	68	10	2	20	47	0	.258
2001 Houston	N.L.	OF-1B	95	213	21	56	15	0	9	39	0	.263
2002 Houston	N.L.	OF	136	453	41	125	31	0	12	72	1	.276
2003 Jacksonville	Southern	1B-OF	4	16	0	2	0	0	1	0	0	.125
2003 Los Angeles	N.L.	1B-OF	52	109	6	20	1	0	1	9	0	.183

Year Club	Lea	Pos	G	AB	R	H	2B	3B	HR	RBI	SB	Avg
2003 Las Vegas b-c-d.......P.C.		1B	34	128	16	38	9	0	4	24	0	.297
2004 Nashville............P.C.		1B-OF	28	96	14	27	7	0	7	17	0	.281
2004 Pittsburgh e.........N.L.		1B-OF	79	293	39	73	17	2	15	57	0	.249
2005 Pittsburgh f.........N.L.		1B	133	407	46	106	21	1	12	63	0	.260
2006 Washington-Atlanta g-h. N.L.		OF-1B	98	130	17	40	10	0	7	26	0	.308
2007 Iowa................P.C.		1B	4	13	0	1	1	0	0	1	0	.077
2007 Chicago i...........N.L.		1B-OF	79	110	16	36	13	0	3	19	0	.327
2008 Iowa................P.C.		1B	3	10	3	5	0	0	0	0	0	.500
2008 Chicago j-k.........N.L.		1B-OF	89	102	8	22	7	0	4	17	0	.216
Major League Totals............	11 Yrs.		948	2234	242	588	131	5	90	379	1	.263
Division Series												
1999 Houston.............N.L.		OF	3	7	1	1	0	0	1	1	0	.143
2001 Houston.............N.L.		PH	2	2	1	1	0	0	1	2	0	.500
2007 Chicago.............N.L.		PH	3	2	0	1	1	0	0	2	0	.500
2008 Chicago.............N.L.		PH	3	3	0	1	0	0	0	1	0	.333
Division Series Totals...........			11	14	2	4	1	0	2	6	0	.286

a Traded by Detroit Tigers to Houston Astros with catcher Brad Ausmus, pitcher C.J. Nitkowski, pitcher Jose Lima and pitcher Trever Miller for outfielder Brian Hunter, infielder Orlando Miller, pitcher Todd Jones and pitcher Doug Brocail, December 10, 1996.
b Traded to Los Angeles Dodgers for infielder Ruddy Lugo, January 28, 2003.
c On disabled list from May 29 to June 17, 2003.
d Filed for free agency, September 30, 2003. Signed with Pittsburgh Pirates organization, December 10, 2003.
e On disabled list from June 26 to August 15, 2004.
f Filed for free agency, October 27, 2005. Signed with Washington Nationals organization, January 27, 2006.
g Traded to Atlanta Braves for pitcher Luis Atilano, August 31, 2006.
h Filed for free agency, October 28, 2006. Signed with Chicago Cubs, December 15, 2006.
i On disabled list from June 3 to June 18 and July 20 to August 12, 2007.
j On disabled list from May 14 to June 24, 2008.
k Filed for free agency, November 1, 2008.

WEEKS, RICKIE DARNELL

Born, Altamonte Springs, Florida, September 13, 1982.
Bats Right. Throws Right. Height, 6 feet. Weight, 205 pounds.

Year Club	Lea	Pos	G	AB	R	H	2B	3B	HR	RBI	SB	Avg
2003 Brewers..........Arizona		DH	1	4	0	2	0	0	0	4	1	.500
2003 Beloit...........Midwest		2B	20	63	13	22	8	1	1	16	2	.349
2003 Milwaukee..........N.L.		2B	7	12	1	2	1	0	0	0	0	.167
2004 Huntsville.......Southern		2B	133	479	67	124	35	6	8	42	11	.259
2005 Nashville.........P.C.		2B	55	203	43	65	14	9	12	48	10	.320
2005 Milwaukee a........N.L.		2B	96	360	56	86	13	2	13	42	15	.239
2006 Milwaukee a........N.L.		2B	95	359	73	100	15	3	8	34	19	.279
2007 Nashville.........P.C.		2B	6	22	5	10	3	1	0	3	1	.455
2007 Milwaukee b........N.L.		2B	118	409	87	96	21	6	16	36	25	.235
2008 Milwaukee c........N.L.		2B	129	475	89	111	22	7	14	46	19	.234
Major League Totals............	5 Yrs.		445	1615	306	395	72	18	51	158	78	.245
Division Series												
2008 Milwaukee..........N.L.		2B	3	4	0	0	0	0	0	0	0	.000

a On disabled list from July 29 to October 31, 2006.
b On disabled list from May 30 to June 18, 2007.
c On disabled list from June 7 to June 22, 2008.

WELLS, VERNON M.

Born, Shreveport, Louisiana, December 8, 1978.
Bats Right. Throws Right. Height, 6 feet, 1 inch. Weight, 225 pounds.

Year Club	Lea	Pos	G	AB	R	H	2B	3B	HR	RBI	SB	Avg
1997 St.Catherines...N.Y.-Penn.		OF	66	264	52	81	20	1	10	31	8	.307
1998 Hagerstown........So.Atl.		OF	134	509	86	145	35	2	11	65	13	.285
1999 Dunedin...........Fla.St.		OF	70	265	43	91	16	2	11	43	13	.343
1999 Knoxville.......Southern		OF	26	106	18	36	6	2	3	17	6	.340
1999 Syracuse...........Int.		OF	33	129	20	40	8	1	4	21	5	.310
1999 Toronto............A.L.		OF	24	88	8	23	5	0	1	8	1	.261
2000 Syracuse...........Int.		OF	127	493	76	120	31	7	16	66	23	.243
2000 Toronto............A.L.		OF	3	2	0	0	0	0	0	0	0	.000
2001 Syracuse...........Int.		OF	107	413	57	116	27	4	12	52	15	.281
2001 Toronto a.........A.L.		OF	30	96	14	30	8	0	1	6	5	.313
2002 Toronto............A.L.		OF	159	608	87	167	34	4	23	100	9	.275
2003 Toronto............A.L.		OF	161	678	118	*215	*49	5	33	117	4	.317

Year Club	Lea	Pos	G	AB	R	H	2B	3B	HR	RBI	SB	Avg
2004 Toronto b	A.L.	OF	134	536	82	146	34	2	23	67	9	.272
2005 Toronto	A.L.	OF	156	620	78	167	30	3	28	97	8	.269
2006 Toronto	A.L.	OF	154	611	91	185	40	5	32	106	17	.303
2007 Toronto c	A.L.	OF	149	584	85	143	36	4	16	80	10	.245
2008 Dunedin	Fla.St.	OF	2	8	3	4	0	0	0	4	0	.500
2008 Syracuse	Int.	OF	2	6	0	0	0	0	0	0	0	.000
2008 Toronto d	A.L.	OF	108	427	63	128	22	1	20	78	4	.300
Major League Totals	10 Yrs.		1078	4250	626	1204	258	24	177	659	67	.283

a On disabled list from April 14 to 24, 2001.
b On disabled list from June 16 to July 16, 2004.
c On disabled list from September 22 to November 13, 2007.
d On disabled list from May 10 to June 7 and July 10 to August 10, 2008.

WERTH, JAYSON RICHARD GOWAN
Born, Springfield, Illinois, May 20, 1979.
Bats Right. Throws Right. Height, 6 feet, 5 inches. Weight, 220 pounds.

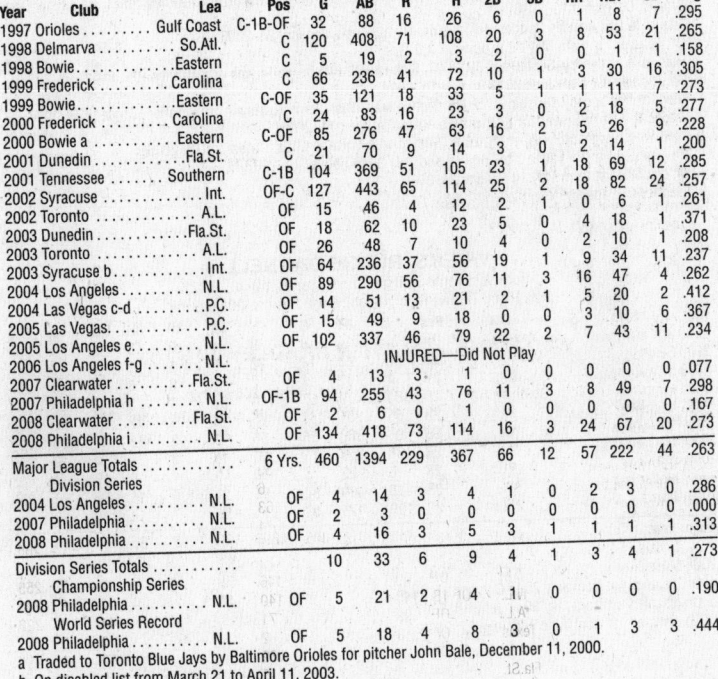

Year Club	Lea	Pos	G	AB	R	H	2B	3B	HR	RBI	SB	Avg
1997 Orioles	Gulf Coast	C-1B-OF	32	88	16	26	6	0	1	8	7	.295
1998 Delmarva	So.Atl.	C	120	408	71	108	20	3	8	53	21	.265
1998 Bowie	Eastern	C	5	19	2	3	2	0	0	1	1	.158
1999 Frederick	Carolina	C	66	236	41	72	10	1	3	30	16	.305
1999 Bowie	Eastern	C-OF	35	121	18	33	5	1	1	11	7	.273
2000 Frederick	Carolina	C	24	83	16	23	3	0	2	18	5	.277
2000 Bowie a	Eastern	C-OF	85	276	47	63	16	2	5	26	9	.228
2001 Dunedin	Fla.St.	C	21	70	9	14	3	0	2	14	1	.200
2001 Tennessee	Southern	C-1B	104	369	51	105	23	1	18	69	12	.285
2002 Syracuse	Int.	OF-C	127	443	65	114	25	2	18	82	24	.257
2002 Toronto	A.L.	OF	15	46	4	12	2	1	0	6	1	.261
2003 Dunedin	Fla.St.	OF	18	62	10	23	5	0	4	18	1	.371
2003 Toronto	A.L.	OF	26	48	7	10	4	0	2	10	1	.208
2003 Syracuse b	Int.	OF	64	236	37	56	19	1	9	34	11	.237
2004 Los Angeles	N.L.	OF	89	290	56	76	11	3	16	47	4	.262
2004 Las Vegas c-d	P.C.	OF	14	51	13	21	2	1	5	20	2	.412
2005 Las Vegas.	P.C.	OF	15	49	9	18	0	0	3	10	6	.367
2005 Los Angeles e	N.L.	OF	102	337	46	79	22	2	7	43	11	.234
2006 Los Angeles f-g	N.L.		INJURED—Did Not Play									
2007 Clearwater	Fla.St.	OF	4	13	3	1	0	0	0	0	0	.077
2007 Philadelphia h	N.L.	OF-1B	94	255	43	76	11	3	8	49	7	.298
2008 Clearwater	Fla.St.	OF	2	6	0	1	0	0	0	0	0	.167
2008 Philadelphia i	N.L.	OF	134	418	73	114	16	3	24	67	20	.273
Major League Totals	6 Yrs.		460	1394	229	367	66	12	57	222	44	.263
Division Series												
2004 Los Angeles	N.L.	OF	4	14	3	4	1	0	2	3	0	.286
2007 Philadelphia	N.L.	OF	2	3	0	0	0	0	0	0	0	.000
2008 Philadelphia	N.L.	OF	4	16	3	5	3	1	1	1	1	.313
Division Series Totals			10	33	6	9	4	1	3	4	1	.273
Championship Series												
2008 Philadelphia	N.L.	OF	5	21	2	4	1	0	0	0	0	.190
World Series Record												
2008 Philadelphia	N.L.	OF	5	18	4	8	3	0	1	3	3	.444

a Traded to Toronto Blue Jays by Baltimore Orioles for pitcher John Bale, December 11, 2000.
b On disabled list from March 21 to April 11, 2003.
c On disabled list from April 6 to June 4, 2004.
d Traded to Los Angeles Dodgers for pitcher Jason Frasor, March 30, 2004.
e On disabled list from March 25 to May 25 and from July 27 to August 11, 2005.
f On disabled list from April 1 to November 2, 2006.
g Not offered contract, December 12, 2006. Signed with Philadelphia Phillies, December 19, 2006.
h On disabled list from June 29 to August 1, 2007.
i On disabled list from May 23 to June 7, 2008.

WIETERS, MATTHEW RICHARD (MATT)
Born, Goose Creek, South Carolina, May 21, 1986.
Bats Both. Throws Right. Height, 6 feet, 5 inches. Weight, 230 pounds.

Year Club	Lea	Pos	G	AB	R	H	2B	3B	HR	RBI	SB	Avg
2008 Frederick a	Carolina	C	69	229	48	79	8	0	15	40	1	.345
2008 Bowie	Eastern	C	61	208	41	76	14	2	12	51	1	.365

a Drafted by Baltimore Orioles in first round, 2007.

WIGGINTON, TY ALLEN (TY)

Born, San Diego, California, October 11, 1977.
Bats Right. Throws Right. Height, 6 feet. Weight, 225 pounds.

Year Club	Lea	Pos	G	AB	R	H	2B	3B	HR	RBI	SB	Avg
1998 Pittsfield.....N.Y.-Penn.		2B-3B-OF	70	272	39	65	14	4	8	29	11	.239
1999 St. Lucie........	Fla.St.	2B	123	456	69	133	23	5	8	73	9	.292
2000 Binghamton....	Eastern	2B-3B	122	453	64	129	27	3	20	77	5	.285
2001 Binghamton....	Eastern	2B-3B	8	28	5	8	3	0	0	0	1	.286
2001 St. Lucie........	Fla.St.	2B	3	9	1	3	1	0	0	1	0	.333
2001 Norfolk..........	Int.	3B-2B-1B-OF	78	260	29	65	12	0	7	24	3	.250
2002 Norfolk..........	Int.	3B-2B-OF-1B	104	383	49	115	26	3	6	48	5	.300
2002 New York.........	N.L.	3B-1B-2B-OF	46	116	18	35	8	0	6	18	2	.302
2003 New York.........	N.L.	3B	156	573	73	146	36	6	11	71	12	.255
2004 St. Lucie........	Fla.St.	3B	2	8	1	3	0	0	0	0	0	.375
2004 N.Y.-Pittsburgh a-b .N.L.		3B-2B-1B	144	494	63	129	30	2	17	66	7	.261
2005 Indianapolis.......	Int.	3B-1B-2B	72	280	53	82	18	0	14	52	8	.293
2005 Pittsburgh c.......	N.L.	3B-1B-2B	57	155	20	40	9	1	7	25	0	.258
2006 Durham..........	Int.	1B	2	8	2	3	2	0	1	2	0	.375
2006 Tampa Bay d	A.L.	1B-2B-3B-OF	122	444	55	122	25	1	24	79	4	.275
2007 Tampa Bay........	A.L.	2B-3B-1B	98	378	47	104	21	0	16	49	1	.275
2007 Houston e	N.L.	3B-OF-1B	50	169	24	48	12	0	6	18	2	.284
2008 Round Rock........	P.C.	3B	3	9	1	1	0	1	0	1	0	.111
2008 Houston f-g	N.L.	3B-OF	111	386	50	110	22	1	23	58	4	.285
Major League Totals	7 Yrs.		784	2715	350	734	163	11	110	384	32	.270

a On disabled list from April 21 to May 7, 2004.
b Traded to Pittsburgh Pirates with pitcher Matt Peterson and infielder Jose Bautista for pitcher Kris Benson and infielder Jeff Keppinger, July 30, 2004.
c Released by Pittsburgh Pirates, December 8, 2005. Signed with Tampa Bay Devil Rays, January 10, 2006.
d On disabled list from July 31 to September 1, 2006.
e Traded to Houston Astros for pitcher Dan Wheeler, July 28, 2007.
f On disabled list from April 6 to May 2, 2008.
g Not offered contract, December 12, 2008.

WILKERSON, STEPHEN BRADLEY (BRAD)

Born, Owensboro, Kentucky, June 1, 1977.
Bats Left. Throws Left. Height, 6 feet. Weight, 205 pounds.

Year Club	Lea	Pos	G	AB	R	H	2B	3B	HR	RBI	SB	Avg
1999 Harrisburg a.......	Eastern	OF	138	422	66	99	21	3	8	49	3	.235
2000 Harrisburg.........	Eastern	OF-1B	66	229	53	77	36	2	6	44	8	.336
2000 Ottawa.............	Int.	OF	63	212	40	53	11	1	12	35	5	.250
2001 Jupiter.............	Fla.St.	DH	6	26	3	6	3	0	0	1	0	.231
2001 Ottawa.............	Int.	OF	69	233	43	63	10	0	12	48	12	.270
2001 Montreal b.........	N.L.	OF	47	117	11	24	7	2	1	5	2	.205
2002 Montreal...........	N.L.	OF-1B	153	507	92	135	27	8	20	59	7	.266
2003 Montreal...........	N.L.	OF-1B	146	504	78	135	34	4	19	77	13	.268
2004 Montreal c.........	N.L.	1B-OF	160	572	112	146	39	2	32	67	13	.255
2005 Washington.........	N.L.	OF-1B	148	565	76	140	42	7	11	57	8	.248
2006 Texas d...........	A.L.	OF	95	320	56	71	15	2	15	44	8	.222
2007 Frisco.............	Texas	OF	3	10	3	2	1	0	0	0	0	.200
2007 Texas e-f..........	A.L.	1B-OF	119	338	54	79	17	1	20	62	4	.234
2008 Dunedin...........	Fla.St.	DH	3	11	4	5	3	0	1	1	0	.455
2008 Seattle-Toronto g-h-i ...	A.L.	OF-1B	104	264	21	58	12	2	4	28	3	.220
Major League Totals	8 Yrs.		972	3187	500	788	193	28	122	399	53	.247

a Drafted by Montreal Expos with choice received for Toronto Blue Jays signing of catcher Darrin Fletcher, June 2, 1998.
b On disabled list from April 5 to May 5, 2001.
c Traded to Texas Rangers with outfielder Terrmel Sledge and pitcher Armando Galarraga for infielder Alfonso Soriano, December 13, 2005.
d On disabled list from August 10 to November 8, 2006.
e On disabled list from May 16 to June 9, 2007.
f Filed for free agency, October 31, 2007. Signed with Seattle Mariners, January 31, 2008.
g Released by Seattle Mariners, May 7, 2008. Signed with Toronto Blue Jays, May 9, 2008.
h On disabled list from August 18 to September 2, 2008.
i Filed for free agency, October 30, 2008.

WILLINGHAM, JOSHUA DAVID (JOSH)
Born, Florence, Alabama, February 17, 1979.
Bats Right. Throws Right. Height, 6 feet, 1 inch. Weight, 215 pounds.

Year Club	Lea	Pos	G	AB	R	H	2B	3B	HR	RBI	SB	Avg
2000 Utica........N.Y.-Penn.		OF-2B-3B-SS	65	205	37	54	16	0	6	29	9	.263
2001 Kane County...	Midwest	3B-OF-2B	97	320	57	83	20	2	7	36	24	.259
2002 Jupiter.........Fla.St.		1B-3B-OF	107	376	72	103	21	4	17	69	18	.274
2003 Jupiter.........Fla.St.		C-1B-OF-3B	59	193	46	51	17	1	12	34	9	.264
2003 Marlins.....Gulf Coast		DH	2	7	3	3	1	0	1	3	0	.429
2003 Carolina......Southern		1B-C-3B-OF	22	67	15	20	2	1	5	14	0	.299
2004 Carolina......Southern		C-1B-OF-3B	112	338	81	95	24	0	24	76	6	.281
2004 Florida..........N.L.		C-OF	12	25	2	5	0	0	1	1	0	.200
2005 Jupiter.........Fla.St.		C	2	9	1	2	1	0	0	1	0	.222
2005 Albuquerque.......P.C.		C-3B	66	219	56	71	14	3	19	54	5	.324
2005 Florida a.........N.L.		C-OF	16	23	3	7	1	0	0	4	0	.304
2006 Carolina......Southern		OF	2	8	0	2	0	0	0	0	0	.250
2006 Florida b.........N.L.		OF-C-1B	142	502	62	139	28	2	26	74	2	.277
2007 Florida..........N.L.		OF	144	521	75	138	32	4	21	89	8	.265
2008 Carolina......Southern		OF	8	26	6	6	2	0	0	5	0	.231
2008 Florida c-d........N.L.		OF	102	351	54	89	21	5	15	51	3	.254
Major League Totals............			5 Yrs.	416	1422	196	378	82	11	63	219	13	.266

a On disabled list from June 30 to September 2, 2005.
b On disabled list from June 7 to June 22, 2006.
c On disabled list from April 28 to June 23, 2008.
d Traded to Washington Nationals with pitcher Scott Olsen for infielder Emilio Bonifacio, pitcher P.J. Dean and
infielder Jake Smolinkski, November 11, 2008.

WILLITS, REGGIE GENE
Born, Chickasha, Oklahoma, May 30, 1981.
Bats Both. Throws Right. Height, 5 feet, 11 inches. Weight, 185 pounds.

Year Club	Lea	Pos	G	AB	R	H	2B	3B	HR	RBI	SB	Avg
2003 Provo.............Pioneer		OF	59	230	53	69	14	4	4	27	14	.300
2004 Rancho Cucamonga....Calif.		OF	135	526	99	150	17	5	5	52	45	.285
2005 Arkansas ....Texas		OF	123	487	75	148	23	6	2	46	40	.304
2006 Salt Lake ...........P.C.		OF	97	352	85	115	18	4	3	39	31	.327
2006 Los Angeles .........A.L.		OF	28	45	12	12	1	0	0	2	4	.267
2007 Los Angeles .........A.L.		OF	136	430	74	126	20	1	0	34	27	.293
2008 Rancho Cucamonga....Calif.		OF	4	14	4	5	0	0	0	0	2	.357
2008 Salt Lake ...........P.C.		OF	10	37	7	14	2	1	0	4	1	.378
2008 Los Angeles a.......A.L.		OF	82	108	21	21	4	0	0	7	2	.194
Major League Totals.............			3 Yrs.	246	583	107	159	25	1	0	43	33	.273
Division Series												
2007 Los Angeles .........A.L.		OF	3	4	0	0	0	0	0	0	1	.000
2008 Los Angeles..........A.L.		OF	3	0	0	0	0	0	0	0	0	.000
Division Series Totals...........				6	4	0	0	0	0	0	0	1	.000

a On disabled list from August 9 to August 27, 2008.

WILSON, JACK EUGENE
Born, Westlake Village, California, December 29, 1977.
Bats Right. Throws Right. Height, 6 feet. Weight, 185 pounds.

Year Club	Lea	Pos	G	AB	R	H	2B	3B	HR	RBI	SB	Avg
1998 Johnson Cty........Appal.		SS	61	241	50	90	18	4	4	29	22	.373
1999 Potomac..........Carolina		SS	64	257	44	76	10	1	2	18	7	.296
1999 Peoria...........Midwest		SS	64	251	47	86	22	4	3	28	11	.343
2000 Potomac..........Carolina		SS	13	47	7	13	0	1	2	7	2	.277
2000 Altoona...........Eastern		SS	33	139	17	35	7	2	1	16	1	.252
2000 Arkansas a ....Texas		SS	88	343	65	101	20	8	6	34	2	.294
2001 Nashville ............P.C.		SS	27	103	20	38	6	1	1	6	2	.369
2001 Pittsburgh .........N.L.		SS	108	390	44	87	17	1	3	25	1	.223
2002 Pittsburgh .........N.L.		SS	147	527	77	133	22	4	4	47	5	.252
2003 Pittsburgh .........N.L.		SS	150	558	58	143	21	3	9	62	5	.256
2004 Pittsburgh .........N.L.		SS	157	652	82	201	41	*12	11	59	8	.308
2005 Pittsburgh .........N.L.		SS	158	587	60	151	24	7	8	52	7	.257
2006 Pittsburgh .........N.L.		SS	142	543	70	148	27	1	8	35	4	.273
2007 Pittsburgh .........N.L.		SS	135	477	67	141	29	2	12	56	2	.296
2008 Altoona............Eastern		SS	7	19	1	6	0	0	0	0	1	.316
2008 Indianapolis ....Int.		SS	4	12	2	4	1	0	0	0	0	.333

Year	Club	Lea	Pos	G	AB	R	H	2B	3B	HR	RBI	SB	Avg
2008 Pittsburgh b		N.L.	SS	87	305	24	83	18	1	1	22	2	.272
Major League Totals		8 Yrs.		1084	4039	482	1087	199	31	56	358	34	.269

a Traded by St. Louis Cardinals to Pittsburgh Pirates for pitcher Jason Christiansen, July 30, 2000.
b On disabled list from April 4 to May 27, 2008.

WINN, DWIGHT RANDOLPH (RANDY)

Born, Los Angeles, California, June 9, 1974.
Bats Both. Throws Right. Height, 6 feet, 2 inches. Weight, 195 pounds.

Year	Club	Lea	Pos	G	AB	R	H	2B	3B	HR	RBI	SB	Avg
1995 Elmira a	N.Y.-Penn.		OF	51	213	38	67	7	4	0	22	19	.315
1996 Kane County	Midwest		OF	130	514	90	139	16	3	0	35	30	.270
1997 Brevard Cty	Fla.St.		OF	36	143	26	45	8	2	0	15	16	.315
1997 Portland b	Eastern		OF	96	384	66	112	15	6	8	36	35	.292
1998 Durham	Int.		OF	29	123	25	35	5	2	1	16	10	.285
1998 Tampa Bay	A.L.		OF	109	338	51	94	9	9	1	17	26	.278
1999 Tampa Bay	A.L.		OF	79	303	44	81	16	4	2	24	9	.267
1999 Durham	Int.		OF	46	207	38	73	20	3	3	30	9	.353
2000 Durham	Int.		OF	79	303	67	100	24	5	7	40	18	.330
2000 Tampa Bay	A.L.		OF	51	159	28	40	5	0	1	16	6	.252
2001 Tampa Bay	A.L.		OF	128	429	54	117	25	6	6	50	12	.273
2002 Tampa Bay c	A.L.		OF	152	607	87	181	39	9	14	75	27	.298
2003 Seattle	A.L.		OF	157	600	103	177	37	4	11	75	23	.295
2004 Seattle	A.L.		OF	157	626	84	179	34	6	14	81	21	.286
2005 Seattle	A.L.		OF	102	386	46	106	25	1	6	37	12	.275
2005 San Francisco d	N.L.		OF	58	231	39	83	22	5	14	26	7	.359
2006 San Francisco	N.L.		OF	149	573	82	150	34	5	11	56	10	.262
2007 San Francisco	N.L.		OF-3B	155	593	73	178	42	1	14	65	15	.300
2008 San Francisco	N.L.		OF	155	598	84	183	38	2	10	64	25	.306
Major League Totals		11 Yrs.		1452	5443	775	1569	326	52	104	586	193	.288

a On disabled list from August 22 to September 11, 1995.
b Selected in expansion draft by Tampa Bay Devil Rays, November 18, 1997.
c Traded to Seattle Mariners for infielder Antonio Perez and manager Lou Piniella, October 28, 2002.
d Traded to San Francisco Giants for pitcher Jesse Foppert and catcher Yorvit Torrealba, July 31, 2005.

WRIGHT, DAVID ALLEN

Born, Norfolk, Virginia, December 20, 1982.
Bats Right. Throws Right. Height, 6 feet. Weight, 215 pounds.

Year	Club	Lea	Pos	G	AB	R	H	2B	3B	HR	RBI	SB	Avg
2001 Kingsport	Appal.		3B	35	116	27	35	7	0	4	16	9	.302
2002 Columbia	So.Atl.		3B	135	496	85	132	30	2	11	93	21	.266
2003 St. Lucie	Fla.St.		3B	133	466	69	126	39	2	15	75	19	.270
2004 Binghamton	Eastern		3B	60	223	44	81	27	0	10	40	20	.363
2004 Norfolk	Int.		3B	31	114	18	34	8	0	8	17	2	.298
2004 New York	N.L.		3B	69	263	41	77	17	1	14	40	6	.293
2005 New York	N.L.		3B	160	575	99	176	42	1	27	102	17	.306
2006 New York	N.L.		3B	154	582	96	181	40	5	26	116	20	.311
2007 New York	N.L.		3B	160	604	113	196	42	1	30	107	34	.325
2008 New York	N.L.		3B	160	626	115	189	42	2	33	124	15	.302
Major League Totals		5 Yrs.		703	2650	464	819	183	10	130	489	92	.309
Division Series													
2006 New York	N.L.		3B	3	12	1	4	2	0	0	4	0	.333
Championship Series													
2006 New York	N.L.		3B	7	25	2	4	1	0	1	2	0	.160

YOUKILIS, KEVIN EDMUND

Born, Cincinnati, Ohio, March 15, 1979.
Bats Right. Throws Right. Height, 6 feet, 1 inch. Weight, 220 pounds.

Year	Club	Lea	Pos	G	AB	R	H	2B	3B	HR	RBI	SB	Avg
2001 Lowell	N.Y.-Penn.		3B	59	183	52	58	14	2	3	28	4	.317
2001 Augusta	So.Atl.		3B	5	12	0	2	0	0	0	0	0	.167
2002 Augusta	So.Atl.		3B	15	53	5	15	5	0	0	6	0	.283
2002 Sarasota	Fla.St.		1B-3B	76	268	45	79	16	0	3	48	0	.295
2002 Trenton	Eastern		3B	44	160	34	55	14	0	5	26	5	.344
2003 Portland	Eastern		3B	94	312	74	102	23	1	6	37	7	.327
2003 Pawtucket	Int.		3B	32	109	9	18	3	0	2	15	0	.165

185

Year Club	Lea	Pos	G	AB	R	H	2B	3B	HR	RBI	SB	Avg
2004 Lowell .... N.Y.-Penn.		3B	2	4	1	3	1	1	0	0	0	.750
2004 Pawtucket .... Int.		3B-1B	38	154	25	41	12	0	3	18	2	.266
2004 Boston a. .... A.L.		3B	72	208	38	54	11	0	7	35	0	.260
2005 Pawtucket .... Int.		3B-1B-2B	43	152	30	49	15	1	8	27	1	.322
2005 Boston .... A.L.		3B-1B-2B	44	79	11	22	7	0	1	9	0	.278
2006 Boston .... A.L.		1B-OF-3B	147	569	100	159	42	2	13	72	5	.279
2007 Boston .... A.L.		1B-3B	145	528	85	152	35	2	16	83	4	.288
2008 Boston .... A.L.		1B-3B-OF	145	538	91	168	43	4	29	115	3	.312
Major League Totals		5 Yrs.	553	1922	325	555	138	8	66	314	12	.289
Division Series												
2004 Boston .... A.L.		3B	1	2	0	0	0	0	0	0	0	.000
2007 Boston .... A.L.		1B	3	12	3	3	1	0	1	2	0	.250
2008 Boston .... A.L.		1B-3B	4	18	2	4	1	0	0	1	0	.222
Division Series Totals			8	32	5	7	2	0	1	3	0	.219
Championship Series												
2007 Boston .... A.L.		1B	7	28	10	14	1	1	3	7	0	.500
2008 Boston .... A.L.		3B	7	30	4	10	3	0	2	6	0	.333
Championship Series Totals			14	58	14	24	4	1	5	13	0	.414
World Series Record												
2007 Boston .... A.L.		1B	4	9	3	2	2	0	0	1	0	.222

a On disabled list from August 16 to September 1, 2004.

YOUNG, CHRISTOPHER BRANDON (CHRIS)

Born, Houston, Texas, September 5, 1983.
Bats Right. Throws Right. Height, 6 feet, 2 inches. Weight, 200 pounds.

Year Club	Lea	Pos	G	AB	R	H	2B	3B	HR	RBI	SB	Avg
2002 White Sox ....Arizona		OF	55	184	26	40	13	1	5	17	7	.217
2003 Bristol ....Appal.		OF	64	238	47	69	18	3	7	28	21	.290
2003 Great Falls ....Pioneer		OF	10	34	5	6	3	0	0	0	0	.176
2004 Kannapolis ....So.Atl.		OF	136	467	83	122	31	5	24	56	31	.261
2005 Birmingham a .... Southern		OF	126	466	100	129	41	3	26	77	32	.277
2006 Tucson ..............P.C.		OF	100	402	78	111	32	4	21	77	17	.276
2006 Arizona..............N.L.		OF	30	70	10	17	4	0	2	10	2	.243
2007 Arizona..............N.L.		OF	148	569	85	135	29	3	32	68	27	.237
2008 Arizona..............N.L.		OF	160	625	85	155	42	7	22	85	14	.248
Major League Totals		3 Yrs.	338	1264	180	307	75	10	56	163	43	.243
Division Series												
2007 Arizona..............N.L.		OF	3	11	3	3	0	0	2	4	1	.273
Championship Series												
2007 Arizona..............N.L.		OF	4	14	1	4	1	0	0	1	0	.286

a Traded to Arizona Diamondbacks by Chicago White Sox with pitcher Orlando Hernandez and pitcher Luis Vizcaino for pitcher Javier Vazquez, December 20, 2005.

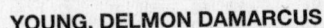

YOUNG, DELMON DAMARCUS

Born, Birmingham, Alabama, September 14, 1985.
Bats Right. Throws Right. Height, 6 feet, 3 inches. Weight, 205 pounds.

Year Club	Lea	Pos	G	AB	R	H	2B	3B	HR	RBI	SB	Avg
2004 Charleston .... So.Atl.		OF	131	513	95	165	26	5	25	116	21	.322
2005 Durham .... Int.		OF	52	228	33	65	13	3	6	28	7	.285
2005 Montgomery ..... Southern		OF	84	330	59	111	13	4	20	71	25	.336
2006 Durham .... Int.		OF	86	342	50	108	22	4	8	59	22	.316
2006 Tampa Bay .... A.L.		OF	30	126	16	40	9	1	3	10	2	.317
2007 Tampa Bay a .... A.L.		OF	*162	645	65	186	38	0	13	93	10	.288
2008 Minnesota .... A.L.		OF	152	575	80	167	28	4	10	69	14	.290
Major League Totals		3 Yrs.	344	1346	161	393	75	5	26	172	26	.292

a Traded to Minnesota Twins with infielder Brendan Harris and outfielder Jason Pridie for infielder Jason Bartlett, pitcher Matt Garza and pitcher Eduardo Morlan, November 28, 2007.

YOUNG, DELWYN RUDY

Born, Los Angeles, California, June 30, 1982.
Bats Both. Throws Right. Height, 5 feet, 8 inches. Weight, 210 pounds.

Year Club	Lea	Pos	G	AB	R	H	2B	3B	HR	RBI	SB	Avg
2002 Great Falls ....Pioneer		2B-1B	59	240	42	72	18	1	10	41	4	.300
2003 South Bend .... So.Atl.		2B	119	443	67	143	38	7	15	73	5	.323

Year	Club	Lea	Pos	G	AB	R	H	2B	3B	HR	RBI	SB	Avg
2004 Vero Beach.........Fla.St.			2B	129	470	76	132	36	3	22	85	11	.281
2005 Las Vegas...........P.C.			2B	36	160	23	52	12	0	4	14	0	.325
2005 Jacksonville...... Southern			2B-3B-OF	95	371	52	110	25	1	16	62	0	.296
2006 Las Vegas..........P.C.			OF-2B	140	532	76	145	42	1	18	98	3	.273
2006 Los Angeles..........N.L.			OF	8	5	0	0	0	0	0	0	0	.000
2007 Las Vegas..........P.C.			OF	121	490	107	165	54	5	17	97	4	.337
2007 Los Angeles..........N.L.			OF-2B	19	34	4	13	1	1	2	3	1	.382
2008 Las Vegas............P.C.			OF	13	49	14	17	5	1	3	10	0	.347
2008 Los Angeles a.........N.L.			OF-2B	83	126	10	31	9	0	1	7	0	.246
Major League Totals .... 3 Yrs.				110	165	14	44	10	1	3	10	1	.267

a On disabled list from July 24 to September 1, 2008.

YOUNG, DMITRI DELL

Born, Vicksburg, Mississippi, October 11, 1973.
Bats Both. Throws Right. Height, 6 feet, 2 inches. Weight, 235 pounds.

Year	Club	Lea	Pos	G	AB	R	H	2B	3B	HR	RBI	SB	Avg
1991 Johnson Cty..... Appal.			3B	37	129	22	33	10	0	2	22	2	.256
1992 Springfield .... Midwest			3B	135	493	74	153	36	6	14	72	14	.310
1993 St.Pete ....Fla.St.			3B-1B	69	270	31	85	13	3	5	43	3	.315
1993 Arkansas .... Texas			1B-3B	45	166	13	41	11	2	3	21	4	.247
1994 Arkansas .... Texas			OF-1B	125	453	53	123	33	2	8	54	0	.272
1995 Arkansas .... Texas			OF	97	367	54	107	18	6	10	62	2	.292
1995 Louisville .........A.A.			OF	2	7	3	2	0	0	0	0	0	.286
1996 Louisville .........A.A.			1B	122	459	90	153	31	8	15	64	16	.333
1996 St. Louis..........N.L.			1B	16	29	3	7	0	0	0	2	0	.241
1997 Louisville .........A.A.			OF-1B	24	84	10	23	7	0	4	14	1	.274
1997 St. Louis a-b-c.....N.L.			1B-OF	110	333	38	86	14	3	5	34	6	.258
1998 Cincinnati .........N.L.			OF-1B	144	536	81	166	48	1	14	83	2	.310
1999 Cincinnati .........N.L.			OF-1B	127	373	63	112	30	2	14	56	3	.300
2000 Cincinnati .........N.L.			OF-1B	152	548	68	166	37	6	18	88	0	.303
2001 Cincinnati d .......N.L.			OF-1B-3B	142	540	68	163	28	3	21	69	8	.302
2002 Detroit e .........A.L.			DH-1B-3B-OF	54	201	25	57	14	0	7	27	2	.284
2003 Detroit .........A.L.			DH-OF-3B-1B	155	562	78	167	34	7	29	85	2	.297
2004 Toledo ....Int.			DH	2	10	1	5	1	1	1	5	0	.500
2004 Detroit f .........A.L.			DH-1B-OF-3B	104	389	72	106	23	2	18	60	0	.272
2005 Detroit .........A.L.			DH-1B-OF	126	469	61	127	25	3	21	72	1	.271
2006 Lakeland. ......Fla.St.			DH	2	5	1	2	1	0	0	0	0	.400
2006 Erie. ....Eastern			1B-OF	6	20	2	3	1	0	0	1	0	.150
2006 Toledo ....Int.			1B	8	31	4	14	3	0	1	6	0	.452
2006 Detroit g .........A.L.			DH-1B	48	172	19	43	4	1	7	23	1	.250
2007 Washington h .....N.L.			1B	136	460	57	147	38	1	13	74	0	.320
2008 Vermont.... N.Y.-Penn.			1B	5	12	0	4	2	0	0	2	0	.333
2008 Harrisburg .....Eastern			1B	3	8	0	3	1	0	0	0	0	.375
2008 Washington i .....N.L.			1B	50	150	15	42	6	0	4	10	0	.280
Major League Totals .... 13 Yrs.				1364	4762	648	1389	301	29	171	683	25	.292
Championship Series													
1996 St. Louis...........N.L.			1B	4	7	1	2	0	1	0	2	0	.286

a Traded to Cincinnati Reds for pitcher Jeff Brantley, November 10, 1997.
b Selected in expansion draft by Tampa Bay Devil Rays, November 18, 1997.
c Sent to Cincinnati Reds as player to be named later for outfielder Mike Kelly, November 18, 1997.
d Traded to Detroit Tigers for outfielder Juan Encarnacion and pitcher Luis Pineda, December 11, 2001.
e On disabled list from April 23 to May 14 and July 6 to November 18, 2002.
f On disabled list from April 7 to May 31, 2004.
g On disabled list from April 15 to May 5 and May 22 to July 21, 2006.
h Released by Detroit Tigers, September 6, 2006. Signed with Washington Nationals organization, February 14, 2007.
i On disabled list from April 3 to May 15 and July 12 to July 29 and September 15 to November 4, 2008.

YOUNG, MICHAEL BRIAN

Born, Covina, California, October 19, 1976.
Bats Right. Throws Right. Height, 6 feet, 1 inch. Weight, 200 pounds.

Year	Club	Lea	Pos	G	AB	R	H	2B	3B	HR	RBI	SB	Avg
1997 St.Catherines .... N.Y.-Penn.			SS-2B	74	276	49	85	18	3	9	48	9	.308
1998 Hagerstown .... So.Atl.			2B-SS-OF	140	522	86	147	33	5	16	87	16	.282
1999 Dunedin ....Fla.St.			2B	129	495	86	155	36	3	5	83	30	.313
2000 Tennessee .... Southern			2B-SS	91	345	51	95	24	5	6	47	16	.275
2000 Tulsa .... Texas			SS	43	188	30	60	13	5	1	32	9	.319
2000 Texas a.............. A.L.			2B	2	2	0	0	0	0	0	0	0	.000

Year	Club	Lea	Pos	G	AB	R	H	2B	3B	HR	RBI	SB	Avg
2001 Oklahoma	P.C.	2B-SS	47	189	28	55	8	0	8	28	3	.291
2001 Texas	A.L.	2B	106	386	57	96	18	4	11	49	3	.249
2002 Texas	A.L.	2B-SS-3B	156	573	77	150	26	8	9	62	6	.262
2003 Texas	A.L.	2B-SS	160	666	106	204	33	9	14	72	13	.306
2004 Texas	A.L.	SS	160	690	114	216	33	9	22	99	12	.313
2005 Texas	A.L.	SS	159	668	*114	*221	40	5	24	91	5	*.331
2006 Texas	A.L.	SS	*162	691	93	217	52	3	14	103	7	.314
2007 Texas	A.L.	SS	156	639	80	201	37	1	9	94	13	.315
2008 Texas	A.L.	SS	155	645	102	183	36	2	12	82	10	.284
Major League Totals		9 Yrs.	1216	4960	743	1488	275	41	115	652	69	.300

a Traded by Toronto Blue Jays to Texas Rangers with pitcher Darwin Cubillan for pitcher Esteban Loaiza, July 19, 2000.

ZAUN, GREGORY OWEN (GREGG)

Born, Glendale, California, April 14, 1971.
Bats Both. Throws Right. Height, 5 feet, 10 inches. Weight, 205 pounds.

Year	Club	Lea	Pos	G	AB	R	H	2B	3B	HR	RBI	SB	Avg
1990 Wausau	Midwest	C	37	100	3	13	0	1	1	7	0	.130
1990 Bluefield	Appal.	C-3B-SS-P	61	184	29	55	5	2	2	21	5	.299
1991 Kane County	Midwest	C	113	409	67	112	17	5	4	51	4	.274
1992 Frederick	Carolina	C-2B	108	383	54	96	18	6	6	52	3	.251
1993 Bowie	Eastern	C-2B-3B	79	258	25	79	10	0	3	38	4	.306
1993 Rochester a	Int.	C	21	78	10	20	4	2	1	11	0	.256
1994 Rochester	Int.	C	123	388	61	92	16	4	7	43	4	.237
1995 Rochester	Int.	C	42	140	26	41	13	1	6	18	0	.293
1995 Baltimore	A.L.	C	40	104	18	27	5	0	3	14	1	.260
1996 Baltimore	A.L.	C	50	108	16	25	8	1	1	13	0	.231
1996 Rochester	Int.	C	14	47	11	15	2	1	0	4	0	.319
1996 Florida b	N.L.	C	10	31	4	9	1	0	1	2	1	.290
1997 Florida	N.L.	C-1B	58	143	21	43	10	2	2	20	1	.301
1998 Florida c	N.L.	C-2B	106	298	19	56	12	2	5	29	5	.188
1999 Texas d-e	A.L.	C	43	93	12	23	2	1	1	12	1	.247
2000 Omaha	P.C.	DH	9	25	7	7	3	0	0	3	1	.280
2000 Kansas City f-g	A.L.	C-1B-2B	83	234	36	64	11	0	7	33	7	.274
2001 Royals	Gulf Coast	C	6	18	3	1	0	0	0	1	0	.056
2001 Omaha	P.C.	C	11	43	5	12	4	0	1	8	0	.279
2001 Kansas City h-i	A.L.	C	39	125	15	40	9	0	6	18	1	.320
2002 Houston	N.L.	C	76	185	18	41	7	1	3	24	1	.222
2003 Houston-Colorado k-l	N.L.	C	74	166	15	38	8	0	4	21	1	.229
2004 Syracuse	Int.	C	7	23	4	7	1	0	0	2	1	.304
2004 Toronto m-n	A.L.	C	107	338	46	91	24	0	6	36	0	.269
2005 New Hampshire	Eastern	C	2	6	1	2	1	0	0	0	0	.333
2005 Toronto o	A.L.	C	133	434	61	109	18	1	11	61	2	.251
2006 Dunedin	Fla.St.	C	1	4	0	0	0	0	0	0	0	.000
2006 Toronto p-q	A.L.	C	99	290	39	79	19	0	12	40	0	.272
2007 Syracuse	Int.	C	3	11	1	1	0	0	0	0	0	.091
2007 Toronto r	A.L.	C	110	331	43	80	24	1	10	52	0	.242
2008 Syracuse	Int.	C	2	8	1	2	0	0	1	1	0	.250
2008 Toronto s-t	A.L.	C	86	245	29	58	12	0	6	30	2	.237
Major League Totals		14 Yrs.	1114	3125	392	783	170	9	78	405	23	.251
Championship Series												
1997 Florida	N.L.	C	1	0	0	0	0	0	0	0	0	.000
World Series Record												
1997 Florida	N.L.	C	2	2	0	0	0	0	0	0	0	.000

a On disabled list from June 17 to July 15, 1993.
b Sent to Florida Marlins to complete trade for pitcher Terry Mathews, August 23, 1996.
c Traded to Texas Rangers for player to be named later, November 23, 1998.
d Florida Marlins received cash to complete trade, April 15, 1999.
e Traded to Detroit Tigers with outfielder Juan Gonzalez and pitcher Danny Patterson for pitcher Justin Thompson, pitcher Francisco Cordero, pitcher Alan Webb, outfielder Gabe Kapler, catcher Bill Haselman and infielder Frank Catalanotto, November 2, 1999.
f Traded to Kansas City Royals for player to be named later, March 7, 2000.
g On disabled list from April 15 to May 28, 2000.
h On disabled list from March 31 to July 23, 2001.
i Filed for free agency, November 5, 2001. Signed with Houston Astros, December 8, 2001.
k Released by Houston Astros, August 20, 2003. Signed with Colorado Rockies, August 26, 2003.
l Filed for free agency, October 27, 2003. Signed with Montreal Expos organization January 13, 2004.
m Released by Montreal Expos, April 4, 2004. Signed with Toronto Blue Jays organization, April 9, 2004.
n Filed for free agency, November 1, 2004, re-signed with Toronto Blue Jays, January 5, 2005.

o On disabled list from May 9 to May 24, 2005.
p On disabled list from March 24 to April 8, 2006.
q Filed for free agency, October 30, 2006, re-signed with Toronto Blue Jays, November 28, 2006.
r On disabled list from April 25 to June 8, 2007.
s On disabled list from May 27 to June 15, 2008.
t Filed for free agency, November 3, 2008. Signed with Baltimore Orioles, January 16, 2009.

ZIMMERMAN, RYAN WALLACE
Born, Washington, North Carolina, September 28, 1984.
Bats Right. Throws Right. Height, 6 feet, 3 inches. Weight, 230 pounds.

Year	Club	Lea	Pos	G	AB	R	H	2B	3B	HR	RBI	SB	Avg
2005	Savannah	So.Atl.	1B-SS	4	17	5	8	2	1	2	6	0	.471
2005	Harrisburg	Eastern	3B-SS	63	233	40	76	20	0	9	32	1	.326
2005	Washington	N.L.	3B-SS	20	58	6	23	10	0	0	6	0	.397
2006	Washington	N.L.	3B	157	614	84	176	47	3	20	110	11	.287
2007	Washington	N.L.	3B	*162	653	99	174	43	5	24	91	4	.266
2008	Potomac	Carolina	DH	2	10	1	3	2	0	0	0	0	.300
2008	Columbus	Int.	3B	4	15	4	4	1	0	1	3	0	.267
2008	Washington a	N.L.	3B	106	428	51	121	24	1	14	51	1	.283
Major League Totals			4 Yrs.	445	1753	240	494	124	9	58	258	16	.282

a On disabled list from May 26 to July 22, 2008.

ZOBRIST, BENJAMIN THOMAS (BEN)
Born, Eureka, Illinois, May 26, 1981.
Bats Both. Throws Right. Height, 6 feet, 3 inches. Weight, 200 pounds.

Year	Club	Lea	Pos	G	AB	R	H	2B	3B	HR	RBI	SB	Avg
2004	Tri-City	N.Y.-Penn.	SS	68	257	50	87	14	3	4	45	15	.339
2005	Salem	Carolina	SS	42	141	25	47	12	1	3	13	2	.333
2005	Lexington	So.Atl.	SS	68	247	45	75	17	2	2	32	16	.304
2006	Corpus Christi	Texas	SS-3B	83	315	57	103	25	6	3	30	9	.327
2006	Durham	Int.	SS	18	69	12	21	3	1	0	6	4	.304
2006	Tampa Bay a	A.L.	SS	52	183	10	41	6	2	2	18	2	.224
2007	Durham	Int.	SS	61	222	42	62	14	2	7	22	8	.279
2007	Tampa Bay b	A.L.	SS	31	97	8	15	2	0	1	9	2	.155
2008	Vero Beach	Fla.St.	2B-SS	4	14	1	4	1	0	0	2	0	.286
2008	Durham	Int.	SS-3B-2B	20	71	15	26	3	0	4	13	4	.366
2008	Tampa Bay c	A.L.	SS-OF-2B-3B	62	198	32	50	10	2	12	30	3	.253
Major League Totals			3 Yrs.	145	478	50	106	18	4	15	57	7	.222
Championship Series													
2008	Tampa Bay	N.L.	OF-SS	3	4	0	0	0	0	0	0	0	.000
World Series Record													
2008	Tampa Bay	N.L.	OF	4	7	0	1	0	0	0	0	0	.143

a Traded by Houston Astros to Tampa Bay Devil Rays with pitcher Mitch Talbot for infielder Aubrey Huff and cash, July 12, 2006.
b On disabled list from August 19 to November 12, 2007.
c On disabled list from March 25 to May 13, 2008.

PITCHERS

AARDSMA, DAVID ALLAN
Born, Denver, Colorado, December 27, 1981.
Bats Right. Throws Right. Height, 6 feet, 5 inches. Weight, 205 pounds.

Year Club	Lea	G	IP	W	L	Pct	SO	BB	H	ERA	SAVES
2003 San Jose	Calif.	18	18⅓	1	1	.500	28	7	14	1.96	8
2004 San Francisco	N.L.	11	10⅔	1	0	1.000	5	10	20	6.75	0
2004 Fresno	P.C.	44	55⅓	6	4	.600	53	29	46	3.09	11
2005 Norwich	Eastern	9	46	6	2	.750	30	13	44	2.93	0
2005 West Tenn a	Southern	33	50⅔	4	1	.800	43	32	48	3.91	2
2006 Iowa	P.C.	29	36⅓	2	3	.400	36	15	31	3.22	8
2006 Chicago b	N.L.	45	53	3	0	1.000	49	28	41	4.08	0
2007 Chicago	A.L.	25	32⅓	2	1	.667	36	17	39	6.40	0
2007 Charlotte	Int.	28	35⅓	3	2	.600	45	11	26	4.33	15
2008 Pawtucket	Int.	2	2	0	0	.000	2	2	0	0.00	0
2008 Boston c-d	A.L.	47	48⅔	4	2	.667	49	35	49	5.55	0
Major League Totals	4 Yrs.	128	144⅔	10	3	.769	139	90	149	5.29	0

a Traded to Chicago Cubs with pitcher Jerome Williams for pitcher La Troy Hawkins, May 28, 2005.
b Traded to Chicago White Sox with pitcher Carlos Vazquez for pitcher Neal Cotts, November 16, 2006.
c Traded to Boston Red Sox for pitcher Willy Mota and pitcher Miguel Socolovich, January 29, 2008.
d On disabled list from July 19 to August 8 and August 21 to September 10, 2008.

ACEVES, ALFREDO
Born, San Luis Rio Colorado, Mexico, December 8, 1982.
Bats Right. Throws Right. Height, 6 feet, 3 inches. Weight, 220 pounds.

Year Club	Lea	G	IP	W	L	Pct	SO	BB	H	ERA	SAVES
2002 Yucatan	Mexican	23	4	1	2	.333	25	20	42	3.00	0
2003 Yucatan	Mexican	27	4	1	1	.500	29	18	49	3.35	1
2004 Yucatan	Mexican	17	6⅓	4	2	.667	37	37	64	4.55	0
2005 Yucatan	Mexican	22	14⅔	9	8	.529	101	44	155	4.32	0
2006 Monterrey	Mexican	19	12	8	5	.615	95	26	126	4.50	0
2007 Monterrey	Mexican	18	10⅓	11	5	.688	70	33	96	3.64	0
2008 Tampa	Fla.St.	8	47	4	1	.800	37	8	32	2.11	0
2008 Trenton	Eastern	7	50	2	2	.500	35	6	37	1.80	0
2008 Scranton-WB	Int.	10	43⅔	2	3	.400	42	13	42	4.12	0
2008 New York a	A.L.	6	30	1	0	1.000	16	10	25	2.40	0

a Signed by New York Yankees organization, March 10, 2008.

ACOSTA, MANUEL ALCIDES (MANNY)
Born, Colon, Panama, May 1, 1981.
Bats Both. Throws Right. Height, 6 feet, 4 inches. Weight, 170 pounds.

Year Club	Lea	G	IP	W	L	Pct	SO	BB	H	ERA	SAVES
2000 Yankees	Gulf Coast	12	62⅓	4	2	.667	46	21	64	3.47	0
2001 Tampa	Fla.St.	2	7	0	1	.000	8	6	7	7.71	0
2001 Greensboro	So.Atl.	10	65⅔	5	2	.714	67	37	37	1.51	0
2002 Staten Island	N.Y.-Penn.	3	15⅓	2	1	.667	12	8	20	4.11	0
2002 Greensboro	So.Atl.	13	52	2	5	.286	35	44	65	6.40	0
2003 Myrtle Beach	Carolina	8	12⅔	2	0	1.000	10	11	19	6.39	1
2003 Battle Creek a	Midwest	15	61	0	8	.000	45	29	80	6.64	0
2004 Myrtle Beach	Carolina	11	23⅓	4	0	1.000	21	11	20	4.24	0
2004 Braves	Gulf Coast	2	2⅔	0	0	.000	2	2	5	3.38	0
2005 Danville	Appal.	3	6	0	0	.000	8	1	3	3.00	0
2005 Myrtle Beach	Carolina	18	22⅓	2	2	.500	18	9	22	4.43	7
2006 Richmond	Int.	38	44⅔	1	6	.143	44	32	38	3.63	17
2006 Mississippi	Southern	13	15⅓	0	0	.000	13	15	7	2.35	4
2007 Richmond	Int.	40	59⅔	9	3	.750	56	35	46	2.26	12
2007 Atlanta	N.L.	21	23⅔	1	1	.500	22	14	13	2.28	0
2008 Richmond	Int.	4	3⅔	0	0	.000	4	2	4	0.00	0
2008 Atlanta b	N.L.	46	53	3	5	.375	31	26	48	3.57	3
Major League Totals	2 Yrs.	67	76⅔	4	6	.400	53	40	61	3.17	3

a Released by New York Yankees, July 24, 2003. Signed with Atlanta Braves organization, July 29, 2003.
b On disabled list from July 7 to August 23, 2008.

ADAMS, JON MICHAEL (MIKE)

Born, Corpus Christi, Texas, July 29, 1978.
Bats Right. Throws Right. Height, 6 feet, 5 inches. Weight, 190 pounds.

Year	Club	Lea	G	IP	W	L	Pct	SO	BB	H	ERA	SAVES
2001	Ogden	Pioneer	23	32	2	2	.500	44	6	26	2.81	12
2002	High Desert	Calif.	10	14	2	1	.667	23	7	9	2.57	5
2002	Beloit	Midwest	11	15¹/₃	0	0	.000	21	2	13	2.93	5
2002	Huntsville	Southern	13	18²/₃	1	0	1.000	17	12	14	3.38	1
2003	Huntsville	Southern	45	74¹/₃	3	7	.300	83	33	58	3.15	14
2004	Indianapolis	Int.	10	31	2	0	1.000	37	4	23	2.61	0
2004	Milwaukee	N.L.	46	53	2	3	.400	39	14	50	3.40	0
2005	Milwaukee	N.L.	13	13¹/₃	0	1	.000	14	10	12	2.70	1
2005	Nashville	P.C.	26	36	3	4	.429	45	12	35	5.75	2
2006	Milwaukee	N.L.	2	2¹/₃	0	0	.000	1	2	4	11.57	0
2006	Nashville	P.C.	15	16¹/₃	1	1	.500	18	8	17	3.31	2
2006	Norfolk	Int.	13	14²/₃	0	0	.000	12	7	13	4.91	0
2006	Buffalo	Int.	3	4²/₃	0	0	.000	3	0	4	1.93	0
2006	Portland a-b-c	P.C.	17	23²/₃	0	2	.000	15	7	29	4.18	0
2007						INJURED—Did Not Play						
2008	Portland	P.C.	12	14²/₃	3	1	.750	16	9	21	5.52	0
2008	San Diego d	N.L.	54	65¹/₃	2	3	.400	74	19	49	2.48	0
Major League Totals		4 Yrs.	115	134	4	7	.364	128	45	115	3.02	1

a Traded to New York Mets for pitcher Jeremi Gonzalez, May 26, 2006.
b Claimed on waivers by Cleveland Indians, July 6, 2006.
c Traded to San Diego Padres for pitcher Brian Sikorski, July 18, 2006.
d Released by San Diego Padres, March 14, 2007, re-signed with San Diego Padres organization, April 12, 2007.

AFFELDT, JEREMY DAVID

Born, Phoenix, Arizona, June 6, 1979.
Bats Left. Throws Left. Height, 6 feet, 4 inches. Weight, 225 pounds.

Year	Club	Lea	G	IP	W	L	Pct	SO	BB	H	ERA	SAVES
1997	Royals	Gulf Coast	10	40	2	0	1.000	36	21	34	4.50	0
1998	Royals	Gulf Coast	12	56	4	3	.571	67	24	50	2.89	0
1998	Lansing	Midwest	6	17	0	3	.000	8	12	27	9.53	0
1999	Charleston-WV	So.Atl.	27	143¹/₃	7	7	.500	111	80	140	3.83	0
2000	Wilmington	Carolina	27	147¹/₃	5	15	.250	92	59	158	4.09	0
2001	Wichita	Texas	25	145¹/₃	10	6	.625	128	46	153	3.90	0
2002	Wichita	Texas	3	6	0	0	.000	3	3	1	1.50	0
2002	Kansas City a	A.L.	34	77²/₃	3	4	.429	67	37	85	4.64	0
2003	Kansas City b	A.L.	36	126	7	6	.538	98	38	126	3.93	4
2004	Omaha	P.C.	4	4	0	0	.000	5	0	2	0.00	3
2004	Kansas City c	A.L.	38	76¹/₃	3	4	.429	49	32	91	4.95	13
2005	Omaha	P.C.	9	8¹/₃	0	1	.000	9	6	9	6.48	0
2005	Kansas City d	A.L.	49	49²/₃	0	2	.000	39	29	56	5.26	0
2006	Kansas City	A.L.	27	70	4	6	.400	28	42	71	5.91	0
2006	Colorado e	N.L.	27	27¹/₃	4	2	.667	20	13	30	6.91	1
2007	Colorado f	N.L.	75	59	4	3	.571	46	33	47	3.51	0
2008	Cincinnati g	N.L.	74	78¹/₃	1	1	.500	80	25	78	3.33	0
Major League Totals		7 Yrs.	360	564¹/₃	26	28	.481	427	249	585	4.55	18
Division Series												
2007	Colorado	N.L.	1	1	0	0	.000	2	1	1	9.00	0
Championship Series												
2007	Colorado	N.L.	2	1¹/₃	0	0	.000	0	0	0	0.00	0
World Series Record												
2007	Colorado	N.L.	4	3	0	0	.000	2	1	2	0.00	0

a On disabled list from June 9 to August 1, 2002.
b On disabled list from April 20 to May 6, 2003.
c On disabled list from June 27 to August 21, 2004.
d On disabled list from April 16 to June 4 and June 19 to July 7, 2005.
e Traded to Colorado Rockies with pitcher Denny Bautista for infielder Ryan Shealy and pitcher Scott Dohmann, July 31, 2006.
f Filed for free agency, October 29, 2007. Signed with Cincinnati Reds, January 23, 2008.
g Filed for free agency, October 30, 2008. Signed with San Francisco Giants, November 17, 2008.

ALBERS, MATTHEW JAMES (MATT)

Born, Houston, Texas, January 20, 1983.
Bats Left. Throws Right. Height, 6 feet. Weight, 205 pounds.

Year	Club	Lea	G	IP	W	L	Pct	SO	BB	H	ERA	SAVES
2002	Martinsville	Appal.	13	59²/₃	2	3	.400	72	38	61	5.13	0
2003	Tri-City	N.Y.-Penn.	15	86¹/₃	5	4	.556	94	25	69	2.92	0

Year	Club	Lea	G	IP	W	L	Pct	SO	BB	H	ERA	SAVES
2004 Lexington	So.Atl.	22	111⅓	8	3	.727	140	57	95	3.31	0
2005 Salem	Carolina	28	148⅔	8	12	.400	146	62	161	4.66	0
2006 Corpus Christi	Texas	19	116	10	2	.833	95	47	96	2.17	0
2006 Round Rock	P.C.	4	25	2	1	.667	26	10	24	3.96	0
2006 Houston	N.L.	4	15	0	2	.000	11	7	17	6.00	0
2007 Round Rock	P.C.	9	53	2	3	.400	43	22	50	3.74	0
2007 Houston a	N.L.	31	110⅔	4	11	.267	71	50	127	5.86	0
2008 Aberdeen	N.Y.-Penn.	2	2	0	0	.000	4	1	1	0.00	0
2008 Baltimore b	A.L.	28	49	3	3	.500	26	22	43	3.49	0
Major League Totals ....3 Yrs.		63	174⅔	7	16	.304	108	79	187	5.20	0

a Traded to Baltimore Orioles with pitcher Troy Patton, outfielder Luke Scott, pitcher Dennis Sarfate and infielder Michael Costanzo for infielder Miguel Tejada, December 12, 2007.

b On disabled list from June 26 to October 21, 2008.

ARREDONDO, JOSE JUAN

Born, San Pedro de Macoris, Dominican Republic, March 30, 1984.
Bats Right. Throws Right. Height, 6 feet. Weight, 175 pounds.

Year	Club	Lea	G	IP	W	L	Pct	SO	BB	H	ERA	SAVES
2004 Angels	Arizona	8	12⅓	0	0	.000	14	4	14	2.92	1
2005 Orem	Pioneer	15	68⅔	5	0	1.000	60	20	76	4.19	0
2005 Arkansas	Texas	5	5⅓	0	0	.000	4	4	5	3.38	0
2006 Rancho Cucamonga	Calif.	15	90	5	6	.455	115	35	62	2.30	0
2006 Arkansas	Texas	11	60⅔	2	3	.400	48	22	80	6.53	4
2007 Rancho Cucamonga	Calif.	28	35	2	4	.333	34	11	46	6.43	4
2007 Salt Lake	P.C.	2	3	0	0	.000	1	2	2	3.00	0
2007 Arkansas	Texas	23	25	0	1	.000	28	12	16	2.52	10
2008 Salt Lake	P.C.	15	17	1	1	.500	15	4	12	2.12	10
2008 Los Angeles	A.L.	52	61	10	2	.833	55	22	42	1.62	0
Division Series											
2008 Los Angeles	A.L.	3	3⅔	0	0	.000	4	2	2	0.00	0

ARROYO, BRONSON ANTHONY

Born, Key West, Florida, February 24, 1977.
Bats Right. Throws Right. Height, 6 feet, 5 inches. Weight, 190 pounds.

Year	Club	Lea	G	IP	W	L	Pct	SO	BB	H	ERA	SAVES
1995 Pirates	Gulf Coast	13	61⅓	5	4	.556	48	9	72	4.26	1
1996 Augusta	So.Atl.	26	135⅔	8	6	.571	107	36	123	3.52	0
1997 Lynchburg	Carolina	24	160⅓	12	4	.750	121	33	154	3.31	0
1998 Carolina a	Southern	23	127	9	8	.529	90	51	158	5.46	0
1999 Altoona	Eastern	25	153	15	4	.789	100	58	167	3.65	0
1999 Nashville	P.C.	3	13	0	2	.000	11	10	22	10.38	0
2000 Nashville	P.C.	13	88⅔	8	2	.800	52	25	82	3.65	0
2000 Pittsburgh	N.L.	20	71⅔	2	6	.250	50	36	88	6.40	0
2000 Lynchburg	Carolina	1	7	0	0	.000	3	2	8	3.86	0
2001 Pittsburgh	N.L.	24	88⅓	5	7	.417	39	34	99	5.09	0
2001 Nashville	P.C.	9	66⅓	6	2	.750	49	15	63	3.93	0
2002 Nashville	P.C.	22	143	8	6	.571	116	28	126	2.96	0
2002 Pittsburgh	N.L.	9	27	2	1	.667	22	15	30	4.00	0
2003 Pawtucket	Int.	24	149⅔	12	6	.667	155	23	148	3.43	0
2003 Boston b	A.L.	6	17⅓	0	0	.000	14	4	10	2.08	0
2004 Boston	A.L.	32	178⅔	10	9	.526	142	47	171	4.03	0
2005 Boston	A.L.	35	205⅓	14	10	.583	100	54	213	4.51	0
2006 Cincinnati c	N.L.	35	*240⅔	14	11	.560	184	64	222	3.29	0
2007 Cincinnati	N.L.	34	210⅔	9	15	.375	156	63	232	4.23	0
2008 Cincinnati	N.L.	34	200	15	11	.577	163	68	219	4.77	0
Major League Totals ....9 Yrs.		229	1239⅔	71	70	.504	870	385	1284	4.31	1
Division Series											
2004 Boston	A.L.	1	6	0	0	.000	7	2	3	3.00	0
2005 Boston	A.L.	1	1	0	0	.000	1	2	2	18.00	0
Division Series Totals		2	7	0	0	.000	8	4	5	5.14	0
Championship Series											
2003 Boston	A.L.	3	3⅓	0	0	.000	5	2	2	2.70	0
2004 Boston	A.L.	3	4	0	0	.000	3	2	8	15.75	0
Championship Series Totals		6	7⅓	0	0	.000	8	4	10	9.82	0
World Series Record											
2004 Boston	A.L.	2	2⅔	0	0	.000	4	1	4	6.75	0

a On minor league disabled list from May 18 to June 7 and June 18 to July 4, 1998.
b Claimed on waivers by Boston Red Sox, February 4, 2003.
c Traded to Cincinnati Reds for outfielder Wily Mo Pena, March 20, 2006.

AYALA, LUIS IGNACIO

Born, Los Mochis, Mexico, January 12, 1978.
Bats Right. Throws Right. Height, 6 feet, 2 inches. Weight, 200 pounds.

Year Club	Lea	G	IP	W	L	Pct	SO	BB	H	ERA	SAVES
1997 Saltillo . . . . .Mexican		37	62	7	5	.583	30	21	76	4.62	0
1998 Saltillo . . . . .Mexican		47	83	7	8	.467	29	45	105	5.62	7
1999 Saltillo a . . . . .Mexican		61	79	7	3	.700	28	22	54	1.71	41
2000 Saltillo . . . . .Mexican		55	65	5	3	.625	38	13	54	2.76	25
2001 Salem. . . . . .Carolina		13	13¹/₃	0	1	.000	10	5	19	4.05	7
2001 Saltillo b . . . . .Mexican		33	40	1	2	.333	34	11	34	2.03	21
2002 Saltillo . . . . .Mexican		49	54	3	5	.375	43	15	43	1.68	23
2002 Ottawa c-d-e . . . . .Int.		6	7²/₃	0	0	.000	6	4	7	3.52	0
2003 Expos . . . . Gulf Coast		3	3²/₃	0	0	.000	2	2	2	0.00	0
2003 Montreal f . . . . .N.L.		65	71	10	3	.769	66	13	65	2.92	5
2004 Montreal. . . . . .N.L.		81	90¹/₃	6	12	.333	63	15	92	2.69	2
2005 Washington . . . . .N.L.		68	71	8	7	.533	40	14	75	2.66	1
2006 Washington g. . . . . .N.L.					INJURED—Did Not Play						
2007 Potomac. . . . . .Carolina		3	2²/₃	0	0	.000	1	1	1	0.00	0
2007 Columbus. . . . . .Int.		5	7	0	0	.000	5	2	4	1.29	0
2007 Washington h. . . . . .N.L.		44	42¹/₃	2	2	.500	28	12	43	3.19	1
2008 Washington-New York i-j N.L.		81	75²/₃	2	10	.167	50	24	86	5.71	9
Major League Totals . . . . . . .5 Yrs.		339	350¹/₃	28	34	.452	227	78	361	3.44	18

a Sold to Colorado Rockies by Saltillo (Mexican), October 14, 1999.
b Sold to Saltillo (Mexican), May 15, 2001.
c Sold to Montreal Expos, August 18, 2002.
d Filed for free agency, October 15, 2002. Signed with Arizona Diamondbacks organization, October 23, 2002.
e Selected by Montreal Expos organization in Rule V draft, December 16, 2002.
f On disabled list from June 22 to July 21, 2003.
g On disabled list from March 24 to October 9, 2006.
h On disabled list from March 28 to June 20, 2007.
i Traded to New York Mets for player to be named later, August 17, 2008. Washington Nationals received infielder Anderson Hernandez to complete trade, August 20, 2008.
j Filed for free agency, October 31, 2008.

BACKE, BRANDON ALLEN

Born, Galveston, Texas, April 5, 1978.
Bats Right. Throws Right. Height, 6 feet. Weight, 195 pounds.

Year Club	Lea	G	IP	W	L	Pct	SO	BB	H	ERA	SAVES
1998 Princeton . . . . .Appal.		1	2	0	0	.000	3	2	0	0.00	0
2001 Bakersfield . . . . .Calif.		17	24²/₃	1	0	1.000	33	8	13	1.09	3
2001 Charleston-SC . . . . . . .So.Atl.		16	24²/₃	2	1	.667	20	7	17	2.92	7
2001 Orlando a-b . . . . .Southern		14	22	1	0	1.000	20	11	20	5.73	0
2002 Orlando . . . . .Southern		20	92¹/₃	4	6	.400	45	37	91	4.68	2
2002 Tampa Bay . . . . .A.L.		9	13	0	0	.000	6	7	15	6.92	0
2003 Durham . . . . .Int.		16	33	2	1	.667	27	13	33	4.64	0
2003 Tampa Bay c. . . . . .A.L.		28	44²/₃	1	1	.500	36	25	40	5.44	0
2004 New Orleans. . . . . .P.C.		19	64¹/₃	6	5	.545	74	26	57	2.80	0
2004 Houston . . . . .N.L.		33	67	5	3	.625	54	27	75	4.30	0
2005 Corpus Christi . . . . . . .Texas		2	8	0	1	.000	11	1	4	2.25	0
2005 Houston d . . . . .N.L.		26	149¹/₃	10	8	.556	97	67	151	4.76	0
2006 Round Rock. . . . . .P.C.		4	20¹/₃	1	2	.333	13	13	23	5.31	0
2006 Houston e . . . . .N.L.		8	43	3	2	.600	19	18	43	3.77	0
2007 Corpus Christi . . . . . . .Texas		1	5	1	0	1.000	4	2	5	5.40	0
2007 Round Rock. . . . . .P.C.		5	25	3	2	.600	25	11	27	4.32	0
2007 Houston f. . . . . .N.L.		5	28²/₃	3	1	.750	11	11	27	3.77	0
2008 Houston . . . . .N.L.		31	166²/₃	9	14	.391	127	77	202	6.05	0
Major League Totals . . . . . . .7 Yrs.		140	512¹/₃	31	29	.517	350	232	553	5.09	0
Division Series											
2004 Houston . . . . .N.L.		1	6	1	0	1.000	5	2	5	3.00	0
2005 Houston . . . . .N.L.		2	5¹/₃	0	0	.000	3	3	6	8.44	0
Division Series Totals		3	11¹/₃	1	0	1.000	8	5	11	5.56	0
Championship Series											
2004 Houston . . . . .N.L.		2	12²/₃	0	0	.000	10	4	6	2.84	0
2005 Houston . . . . .N.L.		1	5²/₃	0	0	.000	7	3	2	1.59	0
Championship Series Totals		3	18¹/₃	0	0	.000	17	7	8	2.45	0

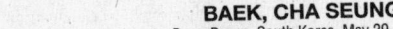

Year Club	Lea	G	IP	W	L	Pct	SO	BB	H	ERA	SAVES
World Series Record											
2005 Houston..............	N.L.	1	7	0	0	.000	7	0	5	0.00	0

a Played outfield in minors 1998 through 2000.
b On minor league disabled list from April 5 to 19, 2001.
c Traded to Houston Astros for infielder Geoff Blum, December 14, 2003.
d On disabled list from July 25 to September 3, 2005.
e On disabled list from April 14 to July 22 and August 19 to October 25, 2006.
f On disabled list from March 28 to September 1, 2007.

BAEK, CHA SEUNG

Born, Pusan, South Korea, May 29, 1980.
Bats Right. Throws Right. Height, 6 feet, 4 inches. Weight, 220 pounds.

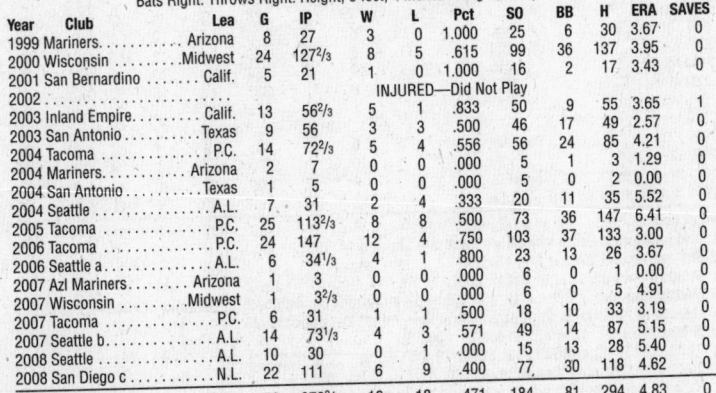

Year Club	Lea	G	IP	W	L	Pct	SO	BB	H	ERA	SAVES
1999 Mariners...........	Arizona	8	27	3	0	1.000	25	6	30	3.67	0
2000 Wisconsin	Midwest	24	127²/₃	8	5	.615	99	36	137	3.95	0
2001 San Bernardino	Calif.	5	21	1	0	1.000	16	2	17	3.43	0
2002				INJURED—Did Not Play							
2003 Inland Empire........	Calif.	13	56²/₃	5	1	.833	50	9	55	3.65	1
2003 San Antonio	Texas	9	56	3	3	.500	46	17	49	2.57	0
2004 Tacoma	P.C.	14	72²/₃	5	4	.556	56	24	85	4.21	0
2004 Mariners...........	Arizona	2	7	0	0	.000	5	1	3	1.29	0
2004 San Antonio	Texas	1	5	0	0	.000	5	0	2	0.00	0
2004 Seattle	A.L.	7	31	2	4	.333	20	11	35	5.52	0
2005 Tacoma	P.C.	25	113²/₃	8	8	.500	73	36	147	6.41	0
2006 Tacoma	P.C.	24	147	12	4	.750	103	37	133	3.00	0
2006 Seattle a............	A.L.	6	34¹/₃	4	1	.800	23	13	26	3.67	0
2007 Azl Mariners........	Arizona	1	3	0	0	.000	6	0	1	0.00	0
2007 Wisconsin	Midwest	1	3²/₃	0	0	.000	6	0	5	4.91	0
2007 Tacoma	P.C.	6	31	1	1	.500	18	10	33	3.19	0
2007 Seattle b............	A.L.	14	73¹/₃	4	3	.571	49	14	87	5.15	0
2008 Seattle	A.L.	10	30	0	1	.000	15	13	28	5.40	0
2008 San Diego c........	N.L.	22	111	6	9	.400	77	30	118	4.62	0
Major League Totals .... 4 Yrs.		59	279²/₃	16	18	.471	184	81	294	4.83	0

a On disabled list from September 25 to November 2, 2006.
b On disabled list from June 17 to September 17, 2007.
c Traded to San Diego Padres for pitcher Jared Wells, May 28, 2008.

BAKER, TIMOTHY SCOTT (SCOTT)

Born, Shreveport, Louisiana, September 19, 1981.
Bats Right. Throws Right. Height, 6 feet, 4 inches. Weight, 210 pounds.

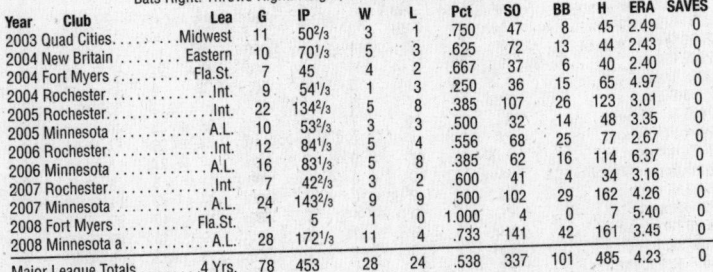

Year Club	Lea	G	IP	W	L	Pct	SO	BB	H	ERA	SAVES
2003 Quad Cities........	Midwest	11	50²/₃	3	1	.750	47	8	45	2.49	0
2004 New Britain	Eastern	10	70¹/₃	5	3	.625	72	13	44	2.43	0
2004 Fort Myers	Fla.St.	7	45	4	2	.667	37	6	40	2.40	0
2004 Rochester.............	Int.	9	54¹/₃	1	3	.250	36	15	65	4.97	0
2005 Rochester.............	Int.	22	134²/₃	5	8	.385	107	26	123	3.01	0
2005 Minnesota	A.L.	10	53²/₃	3	3	.500	32	14	48	3.35	0
2006 Rochester.............	Int.	12	84¹/₃	5	4	.556	68	25	77	2.67	0
2006 Minnesota	A.L.	16	83¹/₃	5	8	.385	62	16	114	6.37	0
2007 Rochester.............	Int.	7	42²/₃	3	2	.600	41	4	34	3.16	1
2007 Minnesota	A.L.	24	143²/₃	9	9	.500	102	29	162	4.26	0
2008 Fort Myers	Fla.St.	1	5	1	0	1.000	4	0	7	5.40	0
2008 Minnesota a............	A.L.	28	172¹/₃	11	4	.733	141	42	161	3.45	0
Major League Totals .... 4 Yrs.		78	453	28	24	.538	337	101	485	4.23	0

a On disabled list from May 4 to June 5, 2008.

BALESTER, COLLIN THOMAS

Born, Huntington Beach, California, June 6, 1986.
Bats Right. Throws Right. Height, 6 feet, 5 inches. Weight, 195 pounds.

Year Club	Lea	G	IP	W	L	Pct	SO	BB	H	ERA	SAVES
2004 Expos............	Gulf Coast	5	24²/₃	1	2	.333	21	5	20	2.19	0
2005 Savannah	So.Atl.	24	125	8	6	.571	95	42	105	3.67	0
2006 Potomac..........	Carolina	23	118	4	5	.444	87	53	126	5.19	0
2006 Harrisburg	Eastern	3	19²/₃	1	0	1.000	10	6	15	1.83	0
2007 Harrisburg	Eastern	17	98²/₃	2	7	.222	77	25	103	3.74	0

Year Club	Lea	G	IP	W	L	Pct	SO	BB	H	ERA	SAVES
2007 Columbus............Int.		10	51²/₃	2	3	.400	40	23	49	4.18	0
2008 Columbus............Int.		15	78²/₃	9	3	.750	64	23	79	4.00	0
2008 Washington...........N.L.		15	80	3	7	.300	50	28	92	5.51	0

BALFOUR, GRANT ROBERT
Born, Sydney, New South Wales, Australia, December 30, 1977.
Bats Right. Throws Right. Height, 6 feet, 2 inches. Weight, 190 pounds.

Year Club	Lea	G	IP	W	L	Pct	SO	BB	H	ERA	SAVES
1997 Twins...........Gulf Coast		13	67	2	4	.333	43	20	73	3.76	0
1998 Elizabethtn..........Appal.		13	77²/₃	7	2	.778	75	27	70	3.36	0
1999 Quad Cities........Midwest		19	91²/₃	8	5	.615	95	37	66	3.53	1
2000 Fort Myers..........Fla.St.		35	89	8	5	.615	90	34	91	4.25	6
2001 New Britain........Eastern		35	50	2	1	.667	72	22	26	1.08	13
2001 Minnesota..........A.L.		2	2²/₃	0	0	.000	2	3	3	13.50	0
2001 Edmonton............P.C.		11	16¹/₃	2	2	.500	17	10	18	5.51	0
2002 Edmonton............P.C.		58	71¹/₃	2	4	.333	88	30	60	4.16	8
2003 Rochester...........Int.		21	71	5	2	.714	87	16	48	2.41	5
2003 Minnesota..........A.L.		17	26	1	0	1.000	30	14	23	4.15	0
2004 Minnesota a.........A.L.		36	39¹/₃	4	1	.800	42	21	35	4.35	0
2005 Minnesota b.........A.L.					INJURED—Did Not Play						
2006 Sarasota............Fla.St.		5	5²/₃	0	0	.000	7	3	8	7.94	0
2006 Reds...........Gulf Coast		2	1¹/₃	0	0	.000	2	3	1	13.50	0
2006 Dayton c-d........Midwest		2	2	0	0	.000	3	0	0	0.00	0
2007 Huntsville........Southern		8	11¹/₃	0	0	.000	21	4	8	2.38	2
2007 Nashville...........P.C.		24	32	1	1	.500	47	11	17	1.69	5
2007 Tampa Bay..........A.L.		22	22	1	0	1.000	27	16	26	6.14	0
2007 Milwaukee e..........N.L.		3	2²/₃	0	2	.000	3	4	4	20.25	0
2008 Durham.............Int.		15	23²/₃	1	0	1.000	39	10	5	0.38	8
2008 Tampa Bay..........A.L.		51	58¹/₃	6	2	.750	82	24	28	1.54	4
Major League Totals.......5 Yrs.		131	151	12	5	.706	186	82	119	3.93	4
Division Series											
2004 Minnesota...........A.L.		2	2²/₃	0	0	.000	2	0	0	0.00	0
2008 Tampa Bay..........N.L.		3	3¹/₃	0	0	.000	4	1	2	0.00	0
Division Series Totals..........		5	6	0	0	.000	6	1	2	0.00	0
Championship Series											
2008 Tampa Bay..........N.L.		4	2¹/₃	0	0	.000	1	4	5	19.29	0
World Series Record											
2008 Tampa Bay..........N.L.		3	3	0	0	.000	2	3	4	3.00	0

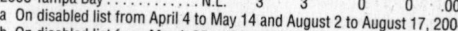

a On disabled list from April 4 to May 14 and August 2 to August 17, 2004.
b On disabled list from March 25 to October 14, 2005. Signed with Cincinnati Reds organization, January 12, 2006.
c Filed for free agency, October 15, 2005.
d On disabled list from March 31 to October 3, 2006.
e Traded to Tampa Bay Devil Rays for pitcher Seth McClung, July 27, 2007.

BANKS, JOSHUA CHARLES (JOSH)
Born, Baltimore, Maryland, July 18, 1982.
Bats Right. Throws Right. Height, 6 feet, 3 inches. Weight, 210 pounds.

Year Club	Lea	G	IP	W	L	Pct	SO	BB	H	ERA	SAVES
2003 Auburn...........N.Y.-Penn.		15	66²/₃	7	2	.778	81	10	58	2.43	0
2004 New Hampshire.....Eastern		18	91¹/₃	6	6	.500	76	28	89	5.03	0
2004 Dunedin............Fla.St.		11	60	7	1	.875	60	8	49	1.80	0
2005 New Hampshire.....Eastern		27	162¹/₃	8	12	.400	145	11	159	3.83	0
2006 Syracuse.............Int.		29	170²/₃	10	11	.476	126	28	184	5.17	0
2007 Syracuse.............Int.		27	169	12	10	.545	101	24	192	4.63	0
2007 Toronto.............A.L.		3	7¹/₃	0	0	.000	2	2	11	7.36	0
2008 Portland............P.C.		9	30¹/₃	1	1	.500	22	8	39	5.93	0
2008 Syracuse.............Int.		3	16²/₃	0	2	.000	12	5	21	7.02	0
2008 San Diego a..........N.L.		17	85¹/₃	3	6	.333	43	32	94	4.75	0
Major League Totals.......2 Yrs.		20	92²/₃	3	6	.333	45	34	105	4.95	0

a Claimed on waivers by San Diego Padres, April 23, 2008.

BANNISTER, BRIAN P.

Born, Scottsdale, Arizona, February 28, 1981.
Bats Right. Throws Right. Height, 6 feet, 2 inches. Weight, 210 pounds.

Year	Club	Lea	G	IP	W	L	Pct	SO	BB	H	ERA	SAVES
2003	Brooklyn	N.Y.-Penn.	12	46	4	1	.800	42	18	27	2.15	1
2004	Binghamton	Eastern	8	44$^{1}/_{3}$	3	3	.500	28	17	45	4.06	0
2004	St. Lucie	Fla.St.	20	110$^{1}/_{3}$	5	7	.417	106	27	111	4.32	0
2005	Binghamton	Eastern	18	109	9	4	.692	94	27	91	2.56	0
2005	Norfolk	Int.	8	45$^{1}/_{3}$	4	1	.800	48	13	48	3.18	0
2006	St. Lucie	Fla.St.	2	12	1	0	1.000	9	4	10	1.50	0
2006	Norfolk	Int.	6	30$^{1}/_{3}$	3	3	.500	24	5	34	3.86	0
2006	New York a-b	N.L.	8	38	2	1	.667	19	22	34	4.26	0
2007	Omaha	P.C.	4	20$^{2}/_{3}$	1	1	.500	14	4	16	2.61	0
2007	Kansas City	A.L.	27	165	12	9	.571	77	44	156	3.87	0
2008	Kansas City	A.L.	32	182$^{2}/_{3}$	9	16	.360	113	58	215	5.76	0
Major League Totals		3 Yrs.	67	385$^{2}/_{3}$	23	26	.469	209	124	405	4.81	0

a On disabled list from April 27 to August 25, 2006.
b Traded to Kansas City Royals for pitcher Ambiorix Burgos, December 6, 2006.

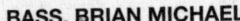

BASS, BRIAN MICHAEL

Born, Pinehurst, North Carolina, January 6, 1982.
Bats Right. Throws Right. Height, 6 feet, 2 inches. Weight, 215 pounds.

Year	Club	Lea	G	IP	W	L	Pct	SO	BB	H	ERA	SAVES
2000	Royals	Gulf Coast	12	44	3	5	.375	44	18	36	3.89	0
2000	Charleston-WV	So.Atl.	1	4	0	0	.000	1	0	6	6.75	0
2001	Burlington	Midwest	26	139$^{1}/_{3}$	3	10	.231	75	53	138	4.65	0
2002	Burlington	Midwest	20	110$^{1}/_{3}$	5	7	.417	60	31	103	3.83	0
2003	Wilmington	Carolina	26	152$^{1}/_{3}$	9	8	.529	119	43	129	2.84	0
2004	Royals	Arizona	5	17$^{2}/_{3}$	0	1	.000	23	3	17	2.55	0
2004	Wichita	Texas	9	31$^{2}/_{3}$	0	4	.000	20	22	53	8.53	0
2005	Wichita	Texas	27	165	12	8	.600	102	53	185	5.24	0
2006	Royals	Arizona	3	12	1	1	.500	9	0	15	4.50	0
2006	Omaha	P.C.	7	32	1	5	.167	11	14	49	7.59	0
2006	Wichita	Texas	6	27	4	1	.800	18	6	29	4.00	0
2007	Rochester a-b	Int.	37	103$^{1}/_{3}$	7	3	.700	80	24	96	3.48	1
2008	Rochester	Int.	2	9	1	0	1.000	6	4	8	4.00	0
2008	Minnesota-Baltimore c	A.L.	49	89$^{1}/_{3}$	4	4	.500	45	31	98	4.84	1
Major League Totals		1 Yrs.	49	89$^{1}/_{3}$	4	4	.500	45	31	98	4.84	1

a Filed for free agency from Baltimore Orioles, October 15, 2006. Signed with Minnesota Twins organization, February 14, 2007.
b Filed for free agency, October 29, 2007, re-signed with Minnesota Twins organization, November 29, 2007.
c Traded to Baltimore Orioles for player to be named later, September 5, 2008.

BATISTA, MIGUEL JEREZ

Born, Santo Domingo, Dominican Republic, February 19, 1971.
Bats Right. Throws Right. Height, 6 feet, 1 inch. Weight, 195 pounds.

Year	Club	Lea	G	IP	W	L	Pct	SO	BB	H	ERA	SAVES
1990	Expos	Gulf Coast	9	39$^{1}/_{3}$	4	3	.571	21	17	33	2.06	0
1990	Rockford	Midwest	3	12$^{1}/_{3}$	0	1	.000	7	5	16	8.76	0
1991	Rockford a	Midwest	23	133$^{2}/_{3}$	11	5	.688	90	57	126	4.04	0
1992	Pittsburgh b	N.L.	1	2	0	0	.000	1	3	4	9.00	0
1992	Wst Plm Bch	Fla. St.	24	135$^{1}/_{3}$	7	7	.500	92	54	130	3.79	0
1993	Harrisburg	Eastern	26	141	13	5	.722	91	86	139	4.34	0
1994	Harrisburg c-d-e	Eastern	3	11$^{1}/_{3}$	0	1	.000	5	9	8	2.38	0
1995	Charlotte	Int.	34	116$^{1}/_{3}$	6	12	.333	58	60	118	4.80	0
1996	Charlotte	Int.	47	77	4	3	.571	56	39	93	5.38	4
1996	Florida f	N.L.	9	11$^{1}/_{3}$	0	0	.000	6	7	9	5.56	0
1997	Iowa	A.A.	31	122	9	4	.692	95	38	117	4.20	0
1997	Chicago g	N.L.	11	36$^{1}/_{3}$	0	5	.000	27	24	36	5.70	0
1998	Montreal	N.L.	56	135	3	5	.375	92	65	141	3.80	0
1999	Ottawa h	Int.	3	8	0	1	.000	7	4	3	2.25	0
2000	Montreal i	N.L.	4	8$^{1}/_{3}$	0	1	.000	7	3	19	14.04	0
2000	Omaha	P.C.	18	28$^{1}/_{3}$	2	2	.500	27	7	35	6.04	3
2000	Kansas City j	A.L.	14	57	2	6	.250	30	34	66	7.74	0
2001	Arizona	N.L.	48	139$^{1}/_{3}$	11	8	.579	90	60	113	3.36	0
2002	Arizona	N.L.	36	184$^{2}/_{3}$	8	9	.471	112	70	172	4.29	0
2003	Arizona k	N.L.	36	193$^{1}/_{3}$	10	9	.526	142	60	197	3.54	0
2004	Toronto	A.L.	38	198$^{2}/_{3}$	10	13	.435	104	*96	206	4.80	5

Year	Club	Lea	G	IP	W	L	Pct	SO	BB	H	ERA	SAVES
2005	Toronto l.	A.L.	71	74²/₃	5	8	.385	54	27	80	4.10	31
2006	Arizona m.	N.L.	34	206¹/₃	11	8	.579	110	84	231	4.58	0
2007	Seattle	A.L.	33	193	16	11	.593	133	85	209	4.29	0
2008	Seattle	A.L.	44	115	4	14	.222	73	79	135	6.26	1
Major League Totals	14 Yrs.		474	1689²/₃	88	104	.458	1076	755	1764	4.56	38
Division Series												
2001	Arizona.	N.L.	2	6²/₃	1	0	1.000	4	1	3	2.70	0
2002	Arizona.	N.L.	1	3²/₃	0	1	.000	1	3	5	9.82	0
Division Series Totals			3	10¹/₃	1	1	.500	5	4	8	5.23	0
Championship Series												
2001	Arizona.	N.L.	2	7	0	1	.000	3	2	5	5.14	0
World Series Record												
2001	Arizona.	N.L.	2	8	0	0	.000	6	5	5	0.00	0

a Selected by Pittsburgh Pirates from Montreal Expos in Rule V draft, December 9, 1991.
b Returned to Montreal Expos by Pittsburgh Pirates, April 23, 1992.
c On disabled list April 14 to 30 and May 7 to September 26, 1994.
d Released by Montreal Expos, November 18, 1994.
e Signed as free agent by Florida Marlins organization, December 9, 1994.
f Claimed on waivers by Chicago Cubs, December 10, 1996.
g Traded to Montreal Expos for outfielder Henry Rodriguez, December 12, 1997.
h On disabled list from July 16 to August 10, 1999.
i Traded to Kansas City Royals for pitcher Brad Rigby, April 25, 2000.
j Filed for free agency, October 2, 2000. Signed with Arizona Diamondbacks, November 15, 2000.
k Filed for free agency, November 7, 2003. Signed with Toronto Blue Jays, December 12, 2003.
l Traded to Arizona Diamondbacks with infielder Orlando Hudson for infielder Troy Glaus and infielder Sergio Santos, December 27, 2005.
m Filed for free agency, October 30, 2006. Signed with Seattle Mariners, December 14, 2006.

BAUTISTA (GERMAN), DENNY M.

Born, Sanchez, Samana, Dominican Republic, August 23, 1980.
Bats Right. Throws Right. Height, 6 feet, 5 inches. Weight, 190 pounds.

Year	Club	Lea	G	IP	W	L	Pct	SO	BB	H	ERA	SAVES
2000	Marlins.	Gulf Coast	11	63	6	2	.750	58	17	49	2.43	0
2000	Utica.	N.Y.-Penn.	1	5	0	0	.000	5	2	4	3.60	0
2001	Kane County.	Midwest	8	39¹/₃	3	1	.750	20	14	43	4.35	0
2001	Utica.	N.Y.-Penn.	7	39	3	1	.750	31	6	25	2.08	0
2002	Jupiter	Fla.St.	19	88¹/₃	4	6	.400	79	40	80	4.99	0
2003	Jupiter	Fla.St.	14	84	8	4	.667	77	35	68	3.21	0
2003	Carolina a.	Southern	11	53¹/₃	4	5	.444	61	35	45	3.71	0
2004	Bowie.	Eastern	14	62²/₃	3	5	.375	72	33	58	4.74	0
2004	Wichita.	Texas	12	81²/₃	4	3	.571	73	32	68	2.53	0
2004	Baltimore-Kansas City b. .	A.L.	7	29²/₃	0	4	.000	19	13	44	8.49	0
2005	Kansas City	A.L.	7	35²/₃	2	2	.500	23	17	36	5.80	0
2005	Omaha c.	P.C.	6	13	0	1	.000	12	6	8	2.77	0
2006	Kansas City	A.L.	8	35	0	2	.000	22	17	38	7.36	0
2006	Omaha	P.C.	10	44	2	5	.286	28	32	52	7.36	0
2006	Colorado Springs	P.C.	6	36	1	4	.200	35	16	46	4.50	0
2006	Colorado d-e	N.L.	4	6²/₃	0	1	.000	5	4	9	5.40	0
2007	Colorado Springs	P.C.	51	64²/₃	3	2	.600	63	31	54	2.92	0
2007	Colorado f	N.L.	9	8²/₃	2	1	.667	8	4	18	12.46	0
2008	Toledo	Int.	5	6¹/₃	0	1	.000	7	3	2	0.00	0
2008	Detroit	A.L.	16	19	0	1	.000	10	14	15	3.32	0
2008	Pittsburgh g-h-i	N.L.	35	41¹/₃	4	3	.571	34	28	46	6.10	0
Major League Totals	5 Yrs.		86	176	8	14	.364	121	97	206	6.34	0

a Traded by Florida Marlins to Baltimore Orioles with pitcher Don Levinski for infielder Jeff Conine, August 31, 2003.
b Traded to Kansas City Royals for pitcher Jason Grimsley, June 22, 2004.
c On disabled list from May 12 to November 14, 2005.
d On disabled list from April 14 to May 8, 2006.
e Traded to Colorado Rockies with pitcher Jeremy Affeldt for infielder Ryan Shealy and pitcher Scott Dohmann, July 31, 2006.
f Traded to Detroit Tigers for pitcher Jose Capellan, December 4, 2007.
g On disabled list from May 3 to June 5, 2008.
h Traded to Pittsburgh Pirates for pitcher Kyle Pearson, June 25, 2008.
i Not offered contract, December 12, 2008, re-signed with Pittsburgh Pirates organization, December 19, 2008.

BECKETT, JOSHUA PATRICK (JOSH)
Born, Spring, Texas, May 15, 1980.
Bats Right. Throws Right. Height, 6 feet, 5 inches. Weight, 220 pounds.

Year	Club	Lea	G	IP	W	L	Pct	SO	BB	H	ERA	SAVES
2000 Kane County	Midwest		13	59 1/3	2	3	.400	61	15	45	2.12	0
2001 Brevard County	Fla.St.		13	65 2/3	6	0	1.000	101	15	32	1.23	0
2001 Portland	Eastern		13	74 1/3	8	1	.889	102	19	50	1.82	0
2001 Florida	N.L.		4	24	2	2	.500	24	11	14	1.50	0
2002 Marlins	Gulf Coast		1	4	0	0	.000	7	1	5	4.50	0
2002 Jupiter	Fla.St.		1	6	1	0	1.000	12	1	4	0.00	0
2002 Florida a	N.L.		23	107 2/3	6	7	.462	113	44	93	4.10	0
2003 Carolina	Southern		1	4	0	0	.000	7	0	4	4.50	0
2003 Jupiter	Fla.St.		1	3	0	0	.000	5	0	2	0.00	0
2003 Florida b	N.L.		24	142	9	8	.529	152	56	132	3.04	0
2004 Florida c	N.L.		26	156 2/3	9	9	.500	152	54	137	3.79	0
2005 Florida d-e	N.L.		29	178 2/3	15	8	.652	166	58	153	3.38	0
2006 Boston	A.L.		33	204 2/3	16	11	.593	158	74	191	5.01	0
2007 Boston f	A.L.		30	200 2/3	*20	7	.741	194	40	189	3.27	0
2008 Boston g	A.L.		27	174 1/3	12	10	.545	172	34	173	4.03	0
Major League Totals	8 Yrs.		196	1188 2/3	89	62	.589	1131	371	1082	3.78	0
Division Series												
2003 Florida	N.L.		1	7	0	1	.000	9	5	2	1.29	0
2007 Boston	A.L.		1	9	1	0	1.000	8	0	4	0.00	0
2008 Boston	A.L.		1	5	0	0	.000	6	4	9	7.20	0
Division Series Totals			3	21	1	1	.500	23	9	15	2.14	0
Championship Series												
2003 Florida	N.L.		3	19 1/3	1	0	1.000	19	2	11	3.26	0
2007 Boston	A.L.		2	14	2	0	1.000	18	1	9	1.93	0
2008 Boston	A.L.		2	9 1/3	1	0	1.000	8	2	13	9.64	0
Championship Series Totals			7	42 2/3	4	0	1.000	45	5	33	4.22	0
World Series Record												
2003 Florida	N.L.		2	16 1/3	1	1	.500	19	5	8	1.10	0
2007 Boston	A.L.		1	7	1	0	1.000	9	1	6	1.29	0
World Series Totals			3	23 1/3	2	1	.667	28	6	14	1.16	0

a On disabled list from April 29 to May 14 and June 5 to July 16 and August 23 to September 11, 2002.
b On disabled list from May 8 to July 1, 2003.
c On disabled list from May 31 to June 17 and from June 18 to July 5 and July 6 to July 30, 2004.
d On disabled list from June 15 to June 30 and July 6 to July 23, 2005.
e Traded to Boston Red Sox with infielder Mike Lowell and pitcher Guillermo Mota for infielder Hanley Ramirez, pitcher Anibal Sanchez and pitcher Jesus Delgado, November 24, 2005.
f On disabled list from May 14 to May 29, 2007.
g On disabled list from March 19 to April 6 and August 18 to September 5, 2008.

BEDARD, ERIK JOSEPH
Born, Navan, Ontario, Canada, March 5, 1979.
Bats Left. Throws Left. Height, 6 feet, 1 inch. Weight, 190 pounds.

Year	Club	Lea	G	IP	W	L	Pct	SO	BB	H	ERA	SAVES
1999 Orioles	Gulf Coast		8	29	2	1	.667	41	13	20	1.86	0
2000 Delmarva	So.Atl.		29	111	9	4	.692	131	35	98	3.57	2
2001 Frederick	Carolina		17	96 1/3	9	2	.818	130	26	68	2.15	0
2001 Orioles	Gulf Coast		2	6	0	1	.000	7	3	4	3.00	0
2002 Bowie	Eastern		13	68 2/3	6	3	.667	66	30	43	1.97	0
2002 Baltimore	A.L.		2	0 2/3	0	0	.000	1	0	2	13.50	0
2003 Orioles	Gulf Coast		3	8	0	0	.000	11	2	4	1.13	0
2003 Aberdeen	N.Y.-Penn.		2	7 2/3	0	0	.000	13	1	7	2.35	0
2003 Frederick a	Carolina		1	3 2/3	0	1	.000	2	1	5	7.36	0
2004 Ottawa	Int.		2	5	0	1	.000	3	3	8	7.20	0
2004 Baltimore	A.L.		27	137 1/3	6	10	.375	121	71	149	4.59	0
2005 Delmarva	So.Atl.		1	5	1	0	1.000	9	1	3	0.00	0
2005 Bowie	Eastern		1	2	0	1	.000	4	1	2	9.00	0
2005 Baltimore b	A.L.		24	141 2/3	6	8	.429	125	57	139	4.00	0
2006 Baltimore	A.L.		33	196 1/3	15	11	.577	171	69	196	3.76	0
2007 Baltimore c	A.L.		28	182	13	5	.722	221	57	141	3.16	0
2008 Seattle d-e	A.L.		15	81	6	4	.600	72	37	70	3.67	0
Major League Totals	6 Yrs.		129	739	46	38	.548	711	291	697	3.81	0

a On disabled list from March 28 to September 29, 2003.
b On disabled list from May 22 to July 18, 2005.
c On disabled list from September 9 to October 23, 2007.

d Traded to Seattle Mariners for pitcher Tony Butler, outfielder Adam Jones, pitcher Kam Mickolio, pitcher George Sherrill and pitcher Chris Tillman, February 8, 2008.
e On disabled list from April 9 to April 26 and July 5 to October 1, 2008.

BEIMEL, JOSEPH RONALD (JOE)
Born, St. Marys, Pennsylvania, April 19, 1977.
Bats Left. Throws Left. Height, 6 feet, 2 inches. Weight, 215 pounds.

Year Club	Lea	G	IP	W	L	Pct	SO	BB	H	ERA	SAVES
1998 Erie.............	N.Y.-Penn.	17	47	1	4	.200	37	22	56	6.32	0
1999 Hickory.............	So.Atl.	29	130	5	11	.313	102	43	146	4.43	0
2000 Lynchburg.........	Carolina	18	120²/₃	10	6	.625	82	44	111	3.36	0
2000 Altoona..........	Eastern	10	62²/₃	1	6	.143	28	21	72	4.16	0
2001 Pittsburgh.............	N.L.	42	115¹/₃	7	11	.389	58	49	131	5.23	0
2002 Pittsburgh.............	N.L.	53	85¹/₃	2	5	.286	53	45	88	4.64	0
2003 Pittsburgh.............	N.L.	69	62¹/₃	1	3	.250	42	33	69	5.05	0
2004 Rochester..........	Int.	49	62	2	4	.333	44	24	83	6.97	2
2004 Minnesota a.........	A.L.	3	1²/₃	0	0	.000	2	2	8	43.20	0
2005 Durham..........	Int.	48	52²/₃	1	2	.333	36	21	58	3.93	0
2005 Tampa Bay b-c	A.L.	7	11	0	0	.000	3	4	15	3.27	0
2006 Las Vegas........	P.C.	10	13	3	0	1.000	9	4	9	1.38	0
2006 Los Angeles.........	N.L.	62	70	2	1	.667	30	21	70	2.96	2
2007 Los Angeles.........	N.L.	83	67¹/₃	4	2	.667	39	24	63	3.88	1
2008 Los Angeles d.........	N.L.	71	49	5	1	.833	32	21	50	2.02	0
Major League Totals.......8 Yrs.		390	462	21	23	.477	259	199	494	4.31	3
Championship Series											
2008 Los Angeles.........	N.L.	3	0²/₃	0	0	.000	0	2	0	0.00	0

a Released by Pittsburgh Pirates, March 31, 2004. Signed with Minnesota Twins organization, April 11, 2004.
b Filed for free agency, October 9, 2004. Signed with Tampa Bay Devil Rays organization, November 21, 2005.
c Released by Tampa Bay Devil Rays, November 22, 2005. Signed with Los Angeles Dodgers organization, January 23, 2006.
d Filed for free agency, October 30, 2008.

BELL, HEATH JUSTIN
Born, Oceanside, California, September 29, 1977.
Bats Right. Throws Right. Height, 6 feet, 3 inches. Weight, 240 pounds.

Year Club	Lea	G	IP	W	L	Pct	SO	BB	H	ERA	SAVES
1998 Kingsport..........	Appal.	22	46	1	0	1.000	61	11	40	2.54	8
1999 Columbia..........	So.Atl.	55	62¹/₃	1	7	.125	68	17	47	2.60	25
2000 St. Lucie.........	Fla.St.	48	60	5	1	.833	75	21	43	2.55	23
2001 Binghamton.......	Eastern	43	61¹/₃	3	1	.750	55	19	82	6.02	4
2002 Binghamton.......	Eastern	24	38	1	0	1.000	49	6	22	1.18	6
2002 Norfolk..........	Int.	22	31²/₃	3	4	.429	28	9	38	4.26	5
2003 Norfolk...........	Int.	40	49²/₃	2	3	.400	54	8	54	4.71	3
2004 Binghamton.......	Eastern	2	2	0	0	.000	0	0	2	0.00	0
2004 Norfolk...........	Int.	45	55²/₃	3	1	.750	68	24	42	3.23	16
2004 New York.........	N.L.	17	24¹/₃	0	2	.000	27	6	42	3.33	0
2005 Norfolk...........	Int.	13	26²/₃	1	0	1.000	29	5	15	1.69	6
2005 New York.........	N.L.	42	46²/₃	1	3	.250	43	13	56	5.59	0
2006 Norfolk...........	Int.	30	35	3	3	.500	56	8	21	1.29	12
2006 New York a.......	N.L.	22	37	0	0	.000	35	11	51	5.11	0
2007 San Diego.........	N.L.	81	93²/₃	6	4	.600	102	30	60	2.02	2
2008 San Diego..........	N.L.	74	78	6	6	.500	71	28	66	3.58	0
Major League Totals.......5 Yrs.		236	279²/₃	13	15	.464	278	88	255	3.57	2

a Traded to San Diego Padres with pitcher Royce Ring for pitcher Jon Adkins and outfielder Ben Johnson, November 15, 2006.

BENNETT, DAVID JEFFREY (JEFF)
Born, Donelson, Tennessee, June 10, 1980.
Bats Right. Throws Right. Height, 6 feet, 3 inches. Weight, 200 pounds.

Year Club	Lea	G	IP	W	L	Pct	SO	BB	H	ERA	SAVES
1998 Pirates..........	Gulf Coast	13	46²/₃	2	4	.333	18	13	50	4.63	0
1999 Pirates..........	Gulf Coast	8	44²/₃	3	4	.429	28	9	53	4.23	0
1999 Hickory...........	So.Atl.	8	35	2	2	.500	16	9	48	5.91	0
2000 Hickory...........	So.Atl.	27	171²/₃	10	13	.435	126	47	189	4.40	0
2001 Lynchburg........	Carolina	25	166	11	10	.524	98	30	171	3.42	0
2001 Altoona...........	Eastern	1	7	0	1	.000	6	2	9	3.86	0
2002 Lynchburg........	Carolina	24	124¹/₃	10	6	.625	90	30	137	3.62	0

Year	Club	Lea	G	IP	W	L	Pct	SO	BB	H	ERA	SAVES
2003 Altoona	Eastern	33	59⅔	4	4	.500	62	23	45	2.72	1	
2003 Nashville a	P.C.	9	23⅓	1	3	.250	16	12	26	6.56	0	
2004 Milwaukee	N.L.	60	71⅓	1	5	.167	45	26	78	4.79	0	
2005 Nashville	P.C.	49	62⅓	2	3	.400	56	25	44	3.03	13	
2006 b				INJURED—Did Not Play								
2007 Mississippi	Southern	6	8⅔	0	0	.000	7	6	7	4.15	0	
2007 Richmond	Int.	36	86	3	5	.375	45	34	84	3.35	1	
2007 Atlanta	N.L.	3	13	2	1	.667	14	3	14	3.46	0	
2008 Myrtle Beach	Carolina	4	4	0	0	.000	3	0	3	0.00	0	
2008 Atlanta c	N.L.	72	97⅓	3	7	.300	68	47	86	3.70	3	
Major League Totals ....3 Yrs.		135	181⅔	6	13	.316	127	76	178	4.11	3	

a Selected by Milwaukee Brewers from Pittsburgh Pirates in Rule V draft, December 15, 2003.
b Filed for free agency, December 21, 2005. Signed with Atlanta Braves organization, November 13, 2006.
c On disabled list from July 6 to July 28, 2008.

BERGMANN, JASON CHRIS
Born, Neptune, New Jersey, September 25, 1981.
Bats Right. Throws Right. Height, 6 feet, 4 inches. Weight, 215 pounds.

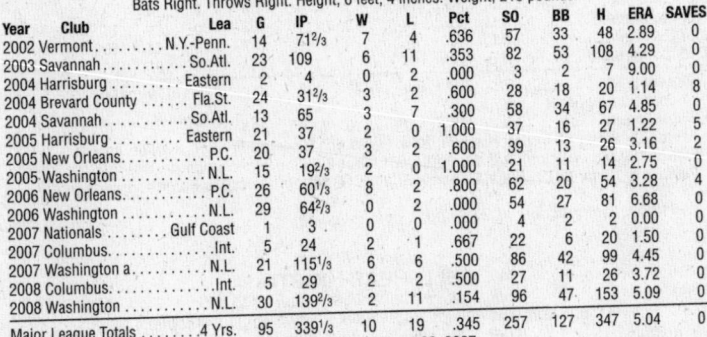

Year	Club	Lea	G	IP	W	L	Pct	SO	BB	H	ERA	SAVES
2002 Vermont	N.Y.-Penn.	14	71⅔	7	4	.636	57	33	48	2.89	0	
2003 Savannah	So.Atl.	23	109	6	11	.353	82	53	108	4.29	0	
2004 Harrisburg	Eastern	2	4	0	2	.000	3	2	7	9.00	0	
2004 Brevard County	Fla.St.	24	31⅔	3	2	.600	28	18	20	1.14	8	
2004 Savannah	So.Atl.	13	65	3	7	.300	58	34	67	4.85	0	
2005 Harrisburg	Eastern	21	37	2	0	1.000	37	16	27	1.22	5	
2005 New Orleans	P.C.	20	37	3	2	.600	39	13	26	3.16	2	
2005 Washington	N.L.	15	19⅔	2	0	1.000	21	11	14	2.75	0	
2006 New Orleans	P.C.	26	60⅓	8	2	.800	62	20	54	3.28	4	
2006 Washington	N.L.	29	64⅔	0	2	.000	54	27	81	6.68	0	
2007 Nationals	Gulf Coast	1	3	0	0	.000	4	2	2	0.00	0	
2007 Columbus	Int.	5	24	2	1	.667	22	6	20	1.50	0	
2007 Washington a	N.L.	21	115⅓	6	6	.500	86	42	99	4.45	0	
2008 Columbus	Int.	5	29	2	2	.500	27	11	26	3.72	0	
2008 Washington	N.L.	30	139⅔	2	11	.154	96	47	153	5.09	0	
Major League Totals ....4 Yrs.		95	339⅓	10	19	.345	257	127	347	5.04	0	

a On disabled list from May 15 to June 25 and July 25 to August 26, 2007.

BETANCOURT, RAFAEL JOSE
Born, Cumana, Venezuela, April 29, 1975.
Bats Right. Throws Right. Height, 6 feet, 2 inches. Weight, 200 pounds.

Year	Club	Lea	G	IP	W	L	Pct	SO	BB	H	ERA	SAVES
1997 Michigan	Midwest	27	32⅓	0	3	.000	52	2	26	1.95	11	
1998 Red Sox	Gulf Coast	4	5	0	2	.000	4	1	6	7.20	0	
1998 Sarasota	Fla.St.	20	28	3	1	.750	33	6	22	3.54	2	
1998 Trenton	Eastern	7	9⅓	0	0	.000	9	3	9	6.75	0	
1999 Sarasota	Fla.St.	6	7	0	0	.000	6	1	5	0.00	4	
1999 Trenton a	Eastern	39	54⅔	6	2	.750	57	10	50	3.62	13	
2000 Yokohama	Japan Cen.	11	29	1	2	.333	16	11	30	4.08	0	
2000 Searex b	Japan East	20	23	1	0	1.000	29	6	17	1.17	6	
2001 Trenton	Eastern	16	24	0	1	.000	27	3	28	5.63	4	
2002 Trenton	Eastern			INJURED—Did Not Play								
2003 Akron	Eastern	31	45⅓	0	0	.000	75	13	33	1.39	16	
2003 Buffalo	Int.	4	6⅔	0	0	.000	6	2	6	4.05	1	
2003 Cleveland c	A.L.	33	38	2	2	.500	36	13	27	2.13	1	
2004 Akron	Eastern	1	1	0	0	.000	2	1	0	0.00	0	
2004 Cleveland d	A.L.	68	66⅔	5	6	.455	76	18	71	3.92	4	
2005 Cleveland e	A.L.	54	67⅔	4	3	.571	73	17	57	2.79	1	
2006 Akron f	Eastern	1	1	0	0	.000	2	1	0	0.00	0	
2007 Cleveland	A.L.	68	79⅓	5	1	.833	80	9	51	1.47	3	
2008 Cleveland	A.L.	69	71	3	4	.429	64	25	76	5.07	4	
Major League Totals ....6 Yrs.		342	379⅓	22	20	.524	377	93	334	3.23	16	
Division Series												
2007 Cleveland	A.L.	2	2	0	0	.000	3	0	1	0.00	0	
Championship Series												
2007 Cleveland	A.L.	5	8	0	0	.000	6	1	6	6.75	0	
Major League Totals ....4 Yrs.		205	229	14	15	.483	233	59	207	3.26	9	

a Sold by Boston Red Sox to Yokohama, November 18,1999.
b Sold to Boston Red Sox, December 13, 2000.
c Filed for free agency, October 15, 2001. Signed with Cleveland Indians organization, January 20, 2003.
d On disabled list from June 26 to July 11, 2004.
e On disabled list from June 30 to July 18, 2005.
f On disabled list from April 20 to May 16, 2006.

BILLINGSLEY, CHAD RYAN

Born, Defiance, Ohio, July 29, 1984.
Bats Right. Throws Right. Height, 6 feet. Weight, 245 pounds.

Year	Club	Lea	G	IP	W	L	Pct	SO	BB	H	ERA	SAVES
2003 Ogden	Pioneer	11	54	5	4	.556	62	15	49	2.83	0
2004 Vero Beach	Fla.St.	18	92	7	4	.636	111	49	68	2.35	0
2004 Jacksonville	Southern	8	42⅓	4	0	1.000	47	22	32	2.98	0
2005 Jacksonville	Southern	28	146	13	6	.684	162	50	116	3.51	0
2006 Las Vegas	P.C.	13	70⅔	6	3	.667	78	32	57	3.95	0
2006 Los Angeles	N.L.	18	90	7	4	.636	59	58	92	3.80	0
2007 Los Angeles	N.L.	43	147	12	5	.706	141	64	131	3.31	0
2008 Los Angeles	N.L.	35	200⅔	16	10	.615	201	80	188	3.14	0
Major League Totals	3 Yrs.	96	437⅔	35	19	.648	401	202	411	3.33	0
Division Series											
2006 Los Angeles	N.L.	2	2	0	0	.000	3	0	1	0.00	0
2008 Los Angeles	N.L.	1	6⅔	1	0	1.000	7	1	5	1.35	0
Division Series Totals		3	8⅔	1	0	1.000	10	1	6	1.04	0
Championship Series											
2008 Los Angeles	N.L.	2	5	0	2	.000	9	7	12	18.00	0

BLACKBURN, ROBERT NICHOLAS (NICK)

Born, Ada, Oklahoma, February 24, 1982.
Bats Right. Throws Right. Height, 6 feet, 4 inches. Weight, 225 pounds.

Year	Club	Lea	G	IP	W	L	Pct	SO	BB	H	ERA	SAVES
2002 Elizabethton	Appal.	13	66⅔	3	3	.500	62	21	70	4.99	0
2003 Quad Cities	Midwest	16	76	2	9	.182	40	18	78	4.86	1
2004 Fort Myers	Fla.St.	9	37⅓	3	3	.500	21	7	51	6.27	0
2004 Quad Cities	Midwest	20	84⅓	6	4	.600	66	23	69	2.77	1
2005 New Britain	Eastern	7	49	2	4	.333	27	10	35	1.84	0
2005 Fort Myers	Fla.St.	15	93⅔	7	5	.583	55	16	95	3.36	0
2005 Rochester	Int.	3	14	0	0	.000	7	3	20	5.14	0
2006 New Britain	Eastern	30	132⅓	7	8	.467	81	37	141	4.42	0
2007 New Britain	Eastern	8	38	3	1	.750	18	7	36	3.08	0
2007 Rochester	Int.	17	110⅔	7	3	.700	57	12	96	2.11	0
2007 Minnesota	A.L.	6	11⅔	0	2	.000	8	2	19	7.71	0
2008 Minnesota	A.L.	33	193⅓	11	11	.500	96	39	224	4.05	0
Major League Totals	2 Yrs.	39	205	11	13	.458	104	41	243	4.26	0

BLANTON, JOSEPH MATTHEW (JOE)

Born, Bowling Green, Kentucky, December 11, 1980.
Bats Right. Throws Right. Height, 6 feet, 3 inches. Weight, 255 pounds.

Year	Club	Lea	G	IP	W	L	Pct	SO	BB	H	ERA	SAVES
2002 Modesto	California	2	6	0	1	.000	6	6	8	7.50	0
2002 Vancouver	Northwest	4	14⅓	1	1	.500	15	2	11	3.14	0
2003 Kane County	Midwest	21	133	8	7	.533	144	19	110	2.57	0
2003 Midland	Texas	7	35⅔	3	1	.750	30	7	21	1.26	1
2004 Sacramento	P.C.	28	176⅓	11	8	.579	143	34	199	4.19	0
2004 Oakland	A.L.	3	8	0	0	.000	6	2	6	5.63	0
2005 Oakland	A.L.	33	201⅓	12	12	.500	116	67	178	3.53	0
2006 Oakland	A.L.	32	194⅓	16	12	.571	107	58	241	4.82	0
2007 Oakland	A.L.	34	230	14	10	.583	140	40	*240	3.95	0
2008 Oakland	A.L.	20	127	5	12	.294	62	35	145	4.96	0
2008 Philadelphia a	N.L.	13	70⅔	4	0	1.000	49	31	66	4.20	0
Major League Totals	5 Yrs.	135	831⅓	51	46	.526	480	233	876	4.24	0
Division Series											
2008 Philadelphia	N.L.	1	6	1	0	1.000	7	0	5	1.50	0
Championship Series											
2006 Oakland	A.L.	1	2	0	0	.000	2	2	0	0.00	0
2008 Philadelphia	N.L.	1	5	0	0	.000	4	4	7	5.40	0
Championship Series Totals		2	7	0	0	.000	6	6	7	3.86	0

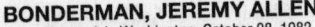

Year	Club	Lea	G	IP	W	L	Pct	SO	BB	H	ERA	SAVES
World Series Record												
2008 Philadelphia		N.L.	1	6	1	0	1.000	7	2	4	3.00	0

a Traded to Philadelphia Phillies for pitcher Josh Outman, infielder Adrian Cardenas and outfielder Matt Spencer, July 17, 2008.

BONDERMAN, JEREMY ALLEN

Born, Kennewick, Washington, October 28, 1982.
Bats Right. Throws Right. Height, 6 feet, 2 inches. Weight, 220 pounds.

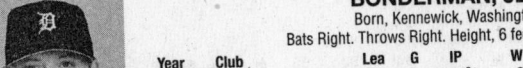

Year	Club	Lea	G	IP	W	L	Pct	SO	BB	H	ERA	SAVES
2002 Modesto.........	California	25	144²/₃	9	8	.529	160	55	129	3.61	0	
2002 Lakeland a	Fla.St.	2	12	0	1	.000	10	4	11	6.00	0	
2003 Detroit	A.L.	33	162	6	19	.240	108	58	193	5.56	0	
2004 Detroit	A.L.	33	184	11	13	.458	168	73	168	4.89	0	
2005 Detroit	A.L.	29	189	14	13	.519	145	57	199	4.57	0	
2006 Detroit	A.L.	34	214	14	8	.636	202	64	214	4.08	0	
2007 Detroit b...............	A.L.	28	174¹/₃	11	9	.550	145	48	193	5.01	0	
2008 Detroit c...............	A.L.	12	71¹/₃	3	4	.429	44	36	75	4.29	0	
Major League Totals	6 Yrs.	169	994²/₃	59	66	.472	812	336	1042	4.74	0	
Division Series												
2006 Detroit	A.L.	1	8¹/₃	1	0	1.000	4	1	5	2.16	0	
Championship Series												
2006 Detroit	A.L.	1	6²/₃	0	0	.000	3	2	6	4.05	0	
World Series Record												
2006 Detroit	A.L.	1	5¹/₃	0	0	.000	4	4	6	3.38	0	

a Sent by Oakland Athletics to Detroit Tigers to complete trade involving Jeff Weaver, Carlos Pena and Ted Lilly, August 22, 2002.

b On disabled list from May 9 to May 24, 2007.

c On disabled list from June 7 to September 30, 2008.

BONSER, BOOF

Born, St. Petersburg, Florida, October 14, 1981.
Bats Right. Throws Right. Height, 6 feet, 4 inches. Weight, 245 pounds.

Year	Club	Lea	G	IP	W	L	Pct	SO	BB	H	ERA	SAVES
2000 Salem-Keizer	Northwest	10	33	1	4	.200	41	29	21	6.00	0	
2001 Hagerstown	So.Atl.	27	134	16	4	.800	178	61	91	2.49	0	
2002 San Jose	Calif.	23	128¹/₃	8	6	.571	139	70	89	2.88	0	
2002 Shreveport	Texas	5	24¹/₃	1	2	.333	23	14	30	5.55	0	
2003 Norwich	Eastern	24	135	7	10	.412	103	67	122	4.00	0	
2003 Fresno a..............	P.C.	4	23	1	2	.333	28	8	17	3.13	0	
2004 New Britain	Eastern	27	154¹/₃	12	9	.571	146	56	160	4.37	0	
2004 Rochester..............	Int.	1	7	1	0	1.000	7	1	5	1.29	0	
2005 Rochester..............	Int.	28	160¹/₃	11	9	.550	168	57	153	3.99	0	
2006 Rochester..............	Int.	14	86¹/₃	6	4	.600	83	35	68	2.81	0	
2006 Minnesota	A.L.	18	100¹/₃	7	6	.538	84	24	104	4.22	0	
2007 Minnesota	A.L.	31	173	8	12	.400	136	65	199	5.10	0	
2008 Minnesota	A.L.	47	118¹/₃	3	7	.300	97	36	139	5.93	0	
Major League Totals	3 Yrs.	96	391²/₃	18	25	.419	317	125	442	5.12	0	
Division Series												
2006 Minnesota	A.L.	1	6	0	0	.000	3	1	7	3.00	0	

a Traded by San Francisco Giants to Minnesota Twins with pitcher Joe Nathan and pitcher Francisco Liriano for catcher A.J. Pierzynski and cash, November 14, 2003.

BOYER, BLAINE THOMAS

Born, Atlanta, Georgia, July 11, 1981.
Bats Right. Throws Right. Height, 6 feet, 3 inches. Weight, 215 pounds.

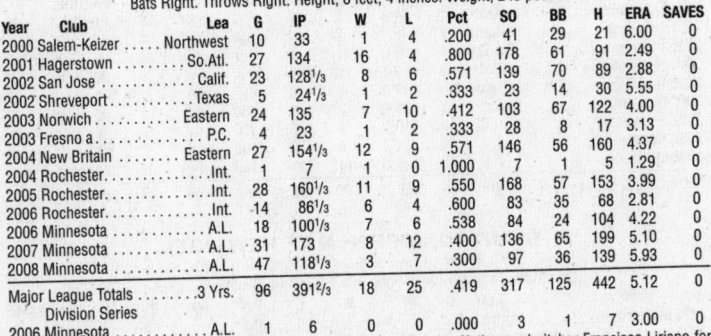

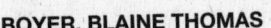

Year	Club	Lea	G	IP	W	L	Pct	SO	BB	H	ERA	SAVES
2000 Braves	Gulf Coast	11	32¹/₃	1	3	.250	27	19	24	2.51	1
2001 Danville	Appal.	13	50	4	5	.444	57	19	48	4.32	1
2002 Macon	So.Atl.	43	70¹/₃	5	9	.357	73	39	52	3.07	1
2003 Rome	So.Atl.	30	136²/₃	12	8	.600	115	58	146	3.69	0
2004 Myrtle Beach	Carolina	28	154	10	10	.500	95	49	138	2.98	0
2005 Mississippi........	Southern	14	48¹/₃	2	4	.333	40	18	62	5.03	0
2005 Atlanta	N.L.	43	37²/₃	4	2	.667	33	17	32	3.11	0
2006 Atlanta a...............	N.L.	2	0²/₃	0	0	.000	0	1	4	40.50	0
2007 Atlanta	N.L.	5	5¹/₃	0	0	.000	3	1	10	3.38	0

Year Club	Lea	G	IP	W	L	Pct	SO	BB	H	ERA	SAVES
2007 Richmond	Int.	21	73⅓	4	3	.571	62	50	76	4.30	2
2008 Atlanta	N.L.	76	72	2	6	.250	67	25	73	5.88	1
Major League Totals	4 Yrs.	126	115⅔	6	8	.429	103	44	119	5.06	1

a On disabled list from June 24 to November 1, 2006.

BRADEN, DALLAS LEE
Born, Phoenix, Arizona, August 13, 1983.
Bats Left. Throws Left. Height, 6 feet, 1 inch. Weight, 195 pounds.

Year Club	Lea	G	IP	W	L	Pct	SO	BB	H	ERA	SAVES
2004 Kane County	Midwest	5	23	2	1	.667	33	6	22	4.70	0
2004 Vancouver	Northwest	8	19⅓	2	0	1.000	26	3	15	2.33	2
2005 Stockton	Calif.	7	43⅔	6	0	1.000	64	11	31	2.68	0
2005 Midland	Texas	16	97	9	5	.643	71	32	104	3.90	0
2006 Athletics	Arizona	6	21	2	0	1.000	36	3	12	0.86	0
2006 Stockton	Calif.	3	13	2	0	1.000	17	5	12	6.23	0
2006 Midland	Texas	1	3⅓	0	0	.000	2	0	9	16.20	0
2007 Midland	Texas	2	12	1	0	1.000	13	3	5	2.25	0
2007 Sacramento	P.C.	11	64	2	3	.400	74	18	51	2.95	0
2007 Oakland	A.L.	20	72⅓	1	8	.111	55	26	91	6.72	0
2008 Sacramento	P.C.	11	53⅓	3	1	.750	54	11	49	2.36	0
2008 Oakland	A.L.	19	71⅔	5	4	.556	41	25	77	4.14	0
Major League Totals	2 Yrs.	39	144	6	12	.333	96	51	168	5.44	0

BRADFORD, CHADWICK LEE (CHAD)
Born, Jackson, Mississippi, September 14, 1974.
Bats Right. Throws Right. Height, 6 feet, 5 inches. Weight, 205 pounds.

Year Club	Lea	G	IP	W	L	Pct	SO	BB	H	ERA	SAVES
1996 Hickory	So.Atl.	28	30	0	2	.000	27	7	21	0.90	18
1997 Winston-Sal	Carolina	46	54⅔	3	7	.300	43	25	51	3.95	15
1998 Birmingham	Southern	10	17⅓	1	1	.500	14	8	13	2.60	1
1998 Calgary	P.C.	29	51	4	1	.800	27	11	50	1.94	0
1998 Chicago	A.L.	29	30⅔	2	1	.667	11	7	27	3.23	1
1999 Charlotte	Int.	47	74⅓	9	3	.750	56	15	63	1.94	5
1999 Chicago	A.L.	3	3⅔	0	0	.000	0	5	9	19.64	0
2000 Charlotte	Int.	55	53⅔	2	4	.333	42	12	38	1.51	10
2000 Chicago a-b-c	A.L.	12	13⅔	1	0	1.000	9	1	13	1.98	0
2001 Sacramento	P.C.	12	23⅔	0	0	.000	24	2	15	0.38	2
2001 Oakland	A.L.	35	36⅔	2	1	.667	34	6	41	2.70	1
2002 Oakland	A.L.	75	75⅓	4	2	.667	56	14	73	3.11	2
2003 Oakland	A.L.	72	77	7	4	.636	62	30	67	3.04	2
2004 Sacramento	P.C.	2	2	0	0	.000	3	0	1	0.00	0
2004 Oakland d	A.L.	68	59	5	7	.417	34	24	51	4.42	1
2005 Athletics	Arizona	3	3	0	0	.000	2	0	3	0.00	0
2005 Sacramento	P.C.	3	3	0	0	.000	1	0	4	6.00	0
2005 Stockton	Calif.	3	2⅓	0	0	.000	1	1	3	3.86	0
2005 Boston e-f-g	A.L.	31	23⅓	2	1	.667	10	4	29	3.86	0
2006 New York h	N.L.	70	62	4	2	.667	45	13	59	2.90	2
2007 Baltimore	A.L.	78	64⅔	4	7	.364	29	16	77	3.34	2
2008 Baltimore-Tampa Bay i	A.L.	68	59⅓	4	3	.571	17	15	59	2.12	0
Major League Totals	11 Yrs.	541	505⅓	35	28	.556	307	135	505	3.24	11
Division Series											
2000 Chicago	A.L.	1	0⅔	0	0	.000	0	0	2	0.00	0
2001 Oakland	A.L.	1	1	0	0	.000	1	0	0	0.00	0
2002 Oakland	A.L.	2	3	0	0	.000	1	0	0	0.00	0
2003 Oakland	A.L.	4	3⅔	0	0	.000	1	0	1	0.00	0
2005 Boston	A.L.	2	1⅓	0	0	.000	5	2	4	0.00	0
2006 New York	N.L.	2	0⅓	0	0	.000	0	1	1	0.00	0
2008 Tampa Bay	N.L.	2	3	0	0	.000	2	0	1	0.00	0
Division Series Totals		14	13	0	0	.000	10	3	10	0.00	0
Championship Series											
2006 New York	N.L.	5	5⅓	0	0	.000	2	0	3	0.00	0
2008 Tampa Bay	N.L.	3	3	0	0	.000	1	2	4	3.00	0
Championship Series Totals		8	8⅓	0	0	.000	3	2	7	1.08	0
World Series Record											
2008 Tampa Bay	N.L.	2	2	0	0	.000	0	1	1	0.00	0

a On disabled list from June 18 to July 5, 2000.

b Traded to Oakland Athletics for player to be named later, December 7, 2000.
c Chicago White Sox received catcher Miguel Olivo to complete trade, December 13, 2000.
d On disabled list from August 8 to August 23, 2004.
e On disabled list from March 30 to July 13, 2005.
f Traded to Boston Red Sox for outfielder Jay Payton, July 13, 2005.
g Not offered contract, December 21, 2005. Signed with New York Mets, December 28, 2005.
h Filed for free agency, October 30, 2006. Signed with Baltimore Orioles, November 30, 2006.
i Sold to Tampa Bay Rays, August 2, 2008.

BRAY, WILLIAM PAUL (BILL)
Born, Virginia Beach, Virginia, June 5, 1983.
Bats Left. Throws Left. Height, 6 feet, 3 inches. Weight, 220 pounds.

Year	Club	Lea	G	IP	W	L	Pct	SO	BB	H	ERA	SAVES
2004	Brevard County	Fla.St.	6	7⅓	0	2	.000	6	1	9	4.91	1
2005	Potomac	Carolina	8	12⅔	1	0	1.000	18	3	8	2.13	3
2005	Harrisburg	Eastern	3	5⅔	1	0	1.000	6	1	10	6.35	1
2005	New Orleans	P.C.	23	21⅓	1	4	.200	25	9	23	5.06	2
2006	New Orleans	P.C.	21	31⅔	4	1	.800	45	9	26	3.98	5
2006	Washington-Cincinnati a	N.L.	48	50⅔	3	2	.600	39	18	57	4.09	2
2007	Sarasota	Fla.St.	2	2	0	0	.000	2	1	0	0.00	0
2007	Louisville	Int.	18	19	1	2	.333	29	6	19	4.26	0
2007	Cincinnati b	N.L.	19	14⅓	3	3	.500	14	5	16	6.28	1
2008	Louisville	Int.	9	9	0	0	.000	15	5	6	3.00	1
2008	Cincinnati	N.L.	63	47	2	2	.500	54	24	50	2.87	0
Major League Totals		3 Yrs.	130	112	8	7	.533	107	47	123	3.86	3

a Traded to Cincinnati Reds with pitcher Gary Majewski, infielder Royce Clayton, infielder Brendan Harris and pitcher Daryl Thompson for outfielder Austin Kearns, infielder Felipe Lopez and pitcher Ryan Wagner, July 13, 2006.
b On disabled list from March 23 to July 20, 2007.

BRESLOW, CRAIG ANDREW
Born, New Haven, Connecticut, August 8, 1980.
Bats Left. Throws Left. Height, 6 feet, 1 inch. Weight, 185 pounds.

Year	Club	Lea	G	IP	W	L	Pct	SO	BB	H	ERA	SAVES
2002	Ogden	Pioneer	23	54⅓	6	2	.750	56	24	42	1.82	2
2003	Beloit	Midwest	33	65	3	4	.429	80	27	64	5.12	2
2004	High Desert	Calif.	23	41⅓	1	3	.250	41	24	54	7.19	0
2004	New Jersey a	Northeast	19	26⅓	3	1	.750	37	13	19	4.10	0
2005	Mobile	Southern	40	52⅓	2	1	.667	47	17	38	2.75	0
2005	Portland	P.C.	7	9	0	1	.000	9	1	11	4.00	0
2005	San Diego b	N.L.	14	16⅓	0	0	.000	14	13	15	2.20	0
2006	Pawtucket	Int.	39	67	7	1	.875	77	24	49	2.69	7
2006	Boston c	A.L.	13	12	0	2	.000	12	6	12	3.75	0
2007	Pawtucket	Int.	49	68⅔	2	3	.400	73	25	70	4.06	1
2008	Cleveland-Minnesota d-e	A.L.	49	47	0	2	.000	39	19	34	1.91	1
Major League Totals		3 Yrs.	76	75⅓	0	4	.000	65	38	61	2.27	1

a Released by Milwaukee Brewers, July 6, 2004. Signed with independent New Jersey (Northeast), July 2004.
b Signed with San Diego Padres organization, March 6, 2005.
c Not offered contract, December 21, 2005. Signed with Boston Red Sox organization, February 1, 2006.
d Claimed on waivers by Cleveland Indians, March 23, 2008.
e Claimed on waivers by Minnesota Twins, May 29, 2008.

BROCAIL, DOUGLAS KEITH (DOUG)
Born, Clearfield, Pennsylvania, May 16, 1967.
Bats Left. Throws Right. Height, 6 feet, 5 inches. Weight, 250 pounds.

Year	Club	Lea	G	IP	W	L	Pct	SO	BB	H	ERA	SAVES
1986	Spokane	Northwest	16	85	5	4	.556	77	53	85	3.81	0
1987	Chston-SC	So.Atl.	19	92⅓	2	6	.250	68	28	94	4.09	0
1988	Chston-SC	So.Atl.	22	107	8	6	.571	107	25	107	2.69	2
1989	Wichita	Texas	23	134⅔	5	9	.357	95	50	158	5.21	0
1990	Wichita	Texas	12	52	2	2	.500	27	24	53	4.33	0
1991	Wichita	Texas	34	146⅓	10	7	.588	108	43	147	3.87	6
1992	Las Vegas	P.C.	29	172⅓	10	10	.500	103	63	187	3.97	0
1992	San Diego	N.L.	3	14	0	0	.000	15	5	17	6.43	0
1993	Las Vegas	P.C.	10	51⅓	4	2	.667	32	14	51	3.68	1
1993	San Diego	N.L.	24	128⅓	4	13	.235	70	42	143	4.56	0
1994	Wichita	Texas	2	4	0	0	.000	2	1	3	0.00	0

Year Club	Lea	G	IP	W	L	Pct	SO	BB	H	ERA	SAVES
1994 Las Vegas............	P.C.	7	12 2/3	0	0	.000	8	2	21	7.11	0
1994 San Diego a..........	N.L.	12	17	0	0	.000	11	5	21	5.82	0
1995 Tucson...............	P.C.	3	16 1/3	1	0	1.000	16	4	18	3.86	0
1995 Houston b...........	N.L.	36	77 1/3	6	4	.600	39	22	87	4.19	1
1996 Jackson.............	Texas	2	4	0	0	.000	5	1	1	0.00	0
1996 Tucson.............	P.C.	5	7 1/3	0	0	.000	4	1	12	7.36	0
1996 Houston c-d.........	N.L.	23	53	1	5	.167	34	23	58	4.58	0
1997 Detroit e............	A.L.	61	78	3	4	.429	60	36	74	3.23	2
1998 Detroit.............	A.L.	60	62 2/3	5	2	.714	55	18	47	2.73	0
1999 Detroit.............	A.L.	70	82	4	4	.500	78	25	60	2.52	2
2000 Detroit f-g..........	A.L.	49	50 2/3	5	4	.556	41	14	57	4.09	0
2001 New Orleans.........	P.C.	2	2 1/3	0	0	.000	2	1	2	0.00	0
2001 Round Rock h-i......	Texas	1	1	0	0	.000	1	0	0	0.00	0
2002 Houston j...........	N.L.	1	1	0	0	.000	0	0	0	0.00	0
2003			INJURED—Did Not Play								
2004 Oklahoma...........	P.C.	12	19 1/3	2	0	1.000	19	2	20	4.19	0
2004 Texas..............	A.L.	43	52 1/3	4	1	.800	43	20	54	4.13	1
2004 Frisco k-l-m........	Texas	1	4 1/3	0	0	.000	6	0	2	2.08	0
2005 Texas n............	A.L.	61	73 1/3	5	3	.625	61	34	90	5.52	1
2006 Lake Elsinore.......	Calif.	6	6 1/3	0	0	.000	12	2	3	0.00	0
2006 San Diego o-p.......	N.L.	25	28 1/3	2	2	.500	19	8	27	4.76	0
2007 Lake Elsinore.......	Calif.	1	2	0	0	.000	3	0	2	0.00	0
2007 San Diego q-r.......	N.L.	67	76 2/3	5	1	.833	43	24	66	3.05	0
2008 Houston s..........	N.L.	72	68 2/3	7	5	.583	64	21	63	3.93	2
Major League Totals......14 Yrs.		606	862 1/3	51	48	.515	633	297	864	3.99	9

a Traded to Houston Astros with outfielder Derek Bell, outfielder Phil Plantier, pitcher Pedro A. Martinez, infielder Craig Shipley and infielder Ricky Gutierrez for infielder Ken Caminiti, infielder Andujar Cedeno, pitcher Brian Williams, infielder Roberto Petagine and player to be named later, December 28, 1994.

b San Diego received pitcher Sean Fesh to complete trade, May 1, 1995.

c On disabled list from May 11 to August 15, 1996.

d Traded to Detroit Tigers with outfielder Brian Hunter, infielder Orlando Miller and pitcher Todd Jones for catcher Brad Ausmus, pitcher C.J. Nitkowski, pitcher Jose Lima, pitcher Trever Miller and infielder Daryle Ward, December 10, 1996.

e On disabled list from August 9 to August 24, 1998.

f On disabled list from August 14 to August 31 and September 29 to November 6, 2000.

g Traded to Houston Astros with catcher Brad Ausmus and pitcher Nelson Cruz for pitcher Chris Holt, outfielder Roger Cedeno and catcher Mitch Meluskey, December 11, 2000.

h On disabled list from March 22 to October 30, 2001.

i Filed for free agency, November 8, 2001, re-signed with Houston Astros, December 4, 2001.

j On disabled list from March 22 to November 11, 2002.

k Filed for free agency, October 15, 2003. Signed with Texas Rangers organization, February 17, 2004.

l On disabled list from May 9 to June 7 and July 25 to August 9, 2004.

m Filed for free agency, October 29, 2004, re-signed with Texas Rangers, November 12, 2004.

n Filed for free agency, October 31, 2005. Signed with San Diego Padres, December 16, 2005.

o On disabled list from March 24 to July 13 and September 20 to October 30, 2006.

p Filed for free agency, October 30, 2006, re-signed with San Diego Padres, December 20, 2006.

q On disabled list from June 21 to July 7, 2007.

r Filed for free agency, October 30, 2007. Signed with Houston Astros, November 27, 2007.

s Filed for free agency, November 3, 2008, re-signed with Houston Astros, December 2, 2008.

BROWN, ANDREW AARON

Born, Chardon, Ohio, February 17, 1981.
Bats Right. Throws Right. Height, 6 feet, 6 inches. Weight, 230 pounds.

Year Club	Lea	G	IP	W	L	Pct	SO	BB	H	ERA	SAVES
1999 Braves..........	Gulf Coast	11	42 1/3	1	1	.500	57	16	40	2.34	0
2000 a....................			INJURED—Did Not Play								
2001 Jamestown.......	N.Y.-Penn.	14	64 1/3	3	4	.429	59	31	50	3.92	0
2002 Vero Beach b.......	Fla.St.	25	127	10	10	.500	129	62	97	4.11	0
2003 Jacksonville......	Southern	1	1	0	0	.000	1	0	0	0.00	0
2004 Akron............	Eastern	17	77 1/3	3	6	.333	67	36	66	4.66	0
2004 Buffalo................	Int.	1	5	1	0	1.000	4	3	4	0.00	0
2004 Jacksonville c......	Southern	8	40 1/3	1	3	.250	58	14	36	4.02	0
2005 Buffalo............	Int.	49	69 2/3	4	2	.667	81	19	52	3.36	4
2006 Buffalo............	Int.	39	62 1/3	5	4	.556	53	36	52	2.60	5
2006 Cleveland d.........	A.L.	9	10	0	0	.000	7	6	8	3.60	0
2007 Portland............	P.C.	32	35 2/3	2	3	.400	43	15	26	2.78	0
2007 Sacramento.........	P.C.	5	5	0	0	.000	6	0	6	3.60	4
2007 Oakland e.........	A.L.	33	41 2/3	3	3	.500	43	17	38	4.54	0
2008 Stockton...........	Calif.	1	2	0	0	.000	0	0	0	0.00	0

Year Club	Lea	G	IP	W	L	Pct	SO	BB	H	ERA	SAVES
2008 Sacramento	P.C.	1	1⅓	0	0	.000	1	1	1	6.75	0
2008 Oakland f	A.L.	31	35	1	0	1.000	28	21	23	3.09	0
Major League Totals 3 Yrs.		73	86⅔	4	3	.571	78	46	67	3.84	0

a On minor league disabled list from June 19 to September 6, 2000.
b Traded by Atlanta Braves to Los Angeles Dodgers with outfielder Brian Jordan and pitcher Odalis Perez for outfielder Gary Sheffield, January 15, 2002.
c Sent to Cleveland Indians as player to be named later for outfielder Milton Bradley, May 19, 2004.
d Traded to San Diego Padres with infielder Kevin Kouzmanoff for infielder Josh Barfield, November 8, 2006.
e Traded to Oakland Athletics for outfielder Milton Bradley, June 29, 2007.
f On disabled list from May 14 to June 8 and July 26 to November 14, 2008.

BROXTON, JONATHAN ROY
Born, Augusta, Georgia, June 16, 1984.
Bats Right. Throws Right. Height, 6 feet, 4 inches. Weight, 290 pounds.

Year Club	Lea	G	IP	W	L	Pct	SO	BB	H	ERA	SAVES
2002 Great Falls	Pioneer	11	29⅓	2	0	1.000	33	16	22	2.76	2
2003 South Bend	So.Atl.	9	37⅓	4	2	.667	30	22	27	3.13	0
2004 Vero Beach	Fla.St.	23	128⅓	11	6	.647	144	43	110	3.23	0
2005 Jacksonville	Southern	33	96⅔	5	3	.625	107	31	79	3.17	5
2005 Los Angeles	N.L.	14	13⅔	1	0	1.000	22	12	13	5.93	0
2006 Las Vegas	P.C.	11	11⅓	1	0	1.000	18	3	6	0.00	5
2006 Los Angeles	N.L.	68	76⅓	4	1	.800	97	33	61	2.59	3
2007 Los Angeles	N.L.	83	82	4	4	.500	99	25	69	2.85	2
2008 Los Angeles	N.L.	70	69	3	5	.375	88	27	54	3.13	14
Major League Totals 4 Yrs.		235	241	12	10	.545	306	97	197	3.02	19
Division Series											
2006 Los Angeles	N.L.	2	2	0	1	.000	3	2	5	13.50	0
2008 Los Angeles	N.L.	3	3⅓	0	0	.000	5	2	0	0.00	1
Division Series Totals		5	5⅓	0	1	.000	8	4	5	5.06	1
Championship Series											
2008 Los Angeles	N.L.	2	2⅓	0	0	.000	2	1	3	3.86	0

BRUNEY, BRIAN ANTHONY
Born, Astoria, Oregon, February 17, 1982.
Bats Right. Throws Right. Height, 6 feet, 3 inches. Weight, 245 pounds.

Year Club	Lea	G	IP	W	L	Pct	SO	BB	H	ERA	SAVES
2000 Diamondbacks	Arizona	20	25	4	1	.800	24	29	21	6.48	2
2001 South Bend	Midwest	26	32⅔	1	4	.200	40	19	24	4.13	8
2001 Yakima	Northwest	15	21	1	2	.333	28	11	19	5.14	2
2002 South Bend	Midwest	37	48⅓	4	3	.571	54	17	37	1.68	10
2002 El Paso	Texas	10	12⅓	0	2	.000	14	4	11	2.92	0
2003 Tucson	P.C.	32	32	3	1	.750	32	18	24	2.81	12
2003 El Paso	Texas	28	31⅓	0	2	.000	28	13	29	2.59	14
2004 Tucson	P.C.	31	38	2	0	1.000	42	20	18	1.42	5
2004 Arizona a	N.L.	30	31⅓	3	4	.429	34	27	20	4.31	0
2005 Tucson	P.C.	4	4⅔	1	0	1.000	3	5	3	1.93	0
2005 Arizona	N.L.	47	46	1	3	.250	51	35	56	7.43	12
2006 Tucson	P.C.	4	2⅔	0	1	.000	4	4	10	33.75	0
2006 Yankees	Gulf Coast	3	3⅔	0	0	.000	5	3	1	4.91	0
2006 Columbus	Int.	11	14⅓	1	1	.500	22	8	10	3.14	3
2006 New York b	A.L.	19	20⅔	1	1	.500	25	15	14	0.87	0
2007 Scranton-WB	Int.	4	6	2	0	1.000	5	2	5	6.00	1
2007 New York	A.L.	58	50	3	2	.600	39	37	44	4.68	0
2008 Yankees	Gulf Coast	3	4	0	1	.000	6	2	3	2.25	0
2008 Trenton	Eastern	2	2⅓	0	1	.000	2	2	2	3.86	0
2008 Scranton-WB	Int.	7	7⅓	0	0	.000	7	7	7	3.68	0
2008 New York c	A.L.	32	34⅓	3	0	1.000	33	16	18	1.83	1
Major League Totals 5 Yrs.		186	182⅓	11	10	.524	182	130	152	4.34	13
Division Series											
2006 New York	A.L.	3	2⅔	0	0	.000	4	0	1	3.38	0

a On disabled list from May 27 to July 6, 2004.
b Released by Arizona Diamondbacks, May 22, 2006. Signed with New York Yankees organization, July 19, 2006.
c On disabled list from April 23 to August 1, 2008.

BUCHHOLZ, CLAY DANIEL
Born, Nederland, Texas, August 14, 1984.
Bats Left. Throws Right. Height, 6 feet, 3 inches. Weight, 190 pounds.

Year Club	Lea	G	IP	W	L	Pct	SO	BB	H	ERA	SAVES
2005 Lowell ...... N.Y.-Penn.	15	$41^{1/3}$	0	1	.000	45	9	34	2.61	0
2006 Wilmington .... Carolina	3	16	2	0	1.000	23	4	10	1.13	0
2006 Greenville .... So.Atl.	21	103	9	4	.692	117	29	78	2.62	0
2007 Portland .... Eastern	16	$86^{2/3}$	7	2	.778	116	22	55	1.77	0
2007 Pawtucket .... Int.	8	$38^{2/3}$	1	3	.250	55	13	32	3.96	0
2007 Boston a .... A.L.	4	$22^{2/3}$	3	1	.750	22	10	14	1.59	0
2008 Portland .... Eastern	2	15	1	0	1.000	18	1	7	1.80	0
2008 Pawtucket .... Int.	9	$43^{2/3}$	4	2	.667	43	17	36	2.47	0
2008 Boston b .... A.L.	16	76	2	9	.182	72	41	93	6.75	0
Major League Totals .... 2 Yrs.	20	$98^{2/3}$	5	10	.333	94	51	107	5.56	0

a Pitched no-hit, no-run game against Baltimore Orioles, September 1, 2007.
b On disabled list from May 13 to May 31, 2008.

BUCHHOLZ, TAYLOR
Born, Lower Merion Twsp., Pennsylvania, October 13, 1981.
Bats Right. Throws Right. Height, 6 feet, 4 inches. Weight, 220 pounds.

Year Club	Lea	G	IP	W	L	Pct	SO	BB	H	ERA	SAVES
2000 Phillies .... Gulf Coast	12	44	2	3	.400	41	14	46	2.25	0
2001 Lakewood .... So.Atl.	28	$176^{2/3}$	9	14	.391	136	57	165	3.36	0
2002 Reading .... Eastern	4	23	0	2	.000	17	6	29	7.43	0
2002 Clearwater .... Fla.St.	23	$158^{2/3}$	10	6	.625	129	51	140	3.29	0
2003 Reading a .... Eastern	25	$144^{2/3}$	9	11	.450	114	33	136	3.55	0
2004 New Orleans .... P.C.	20	98	6	7	.462	74	29	107	5.23	0
2005 Round Rock .... P.C.	20	$76^{2/3}$	6	6	1.000	45	27	79	4.81	0
2006 Round Rock .... P.C.	7	44	1	3	.250	37	17	47	4.91	0
2006 Houston b .... N.L.	22	113	6	10	.375	77	34	107	5.89	0
2007 Colorado .... N.L.	41	$93^{2/3}$	6	5	.545	61	20	105	4.23	0
2008 Colorado .... N.L.	63	$66^{1/3}$	6	6	.500	56	18	45	2.17	1
Major League Totals .... 3 Yrs.	126	273	18	21	.462	194	72	257	4.42	1

a Traded by Philadelphia Phillies to Houston Astros with pitcher Brandon Duckworth and pitcher Ezequiel Astacio for pitcher Billy Wagner, November 3, 2003.
b Traded to Colorado Rockies with outfielder Willy Taveras and pitcher Jason Hirsh for pitcher Jason Jennings and pitcher Miguel Asencio, December 12, 2006.

BUEHRLE, MARK ANTHONY
Born, St. Charles, Missouri, March 23, 1979.
Bats Left. Throws Left. Height, 6 feet, 2 inches. Weight, 225 pounds.

Year Club	Lea	G	IP	W	L	PCT	SO	BB	H	ERA	SAVES
1999 Burlington ....Midwest	20	$98^{2/3}$	7	4	.636	91	16	105	4.10	3
2000 Birmingham .... Southern	16	$118^{2/3}$	8	4	.667	68	17	95	2.28	0
2000 Chicago .... A.L.	28	$51^{1/3}$	4	1	.800	37	19	55	4.21	0
2001 Chicago .... A.L.	32	$221^{1/3}$	16	8	.667	126	48	188	3.29	0
2002 Chicago .... A.L.	34	239	19	12	.613	134	61	236	3.58	0
2003 Chicago .... A.L.	35	$230^{1/3}$	14	14	.500	119	61	250	4.14	0
2004 Chicago .... A.L.	35	$*245^{1/3}$	16	10	.615	165	51	257	3.89	0
2005 Chicago .... A.L.	33	$*236^{2/3}$	16	8	.667	149	40	*240	3.12	0
2006 Chicago .... A.L.	32	204	12	13	.480	98	48	*247	4.99	0
2007 Chicago a .... A.L.	30	201	10	9	.526	115	45	208	3.63	0
2008 Chicago .... A.L.	34	$218^{2/3}$	15	12	.556	140	52	*240	3.79	0
Major League Totals .... 9 Yrs.	293	$1847^{2/3}$	122	87	.584	1083	425	1921	3.80	0
Division Series										
2000 Chicago .... A.L.	1	$0^{1/3}$	0	0	.000	1	0	2	0.00	0
2005 Chicago .... A.L.	1	7	1	0	1.000	2	1	8	5.14	0
2008 Chicago .... A.L.	1	7	0	1	.000	3	0	10	6.43	0
Division Series Totals	3	$14^{1/3}$	1	1	.500	6	1	20	5.65	0
Championship Series										
2005 Chicago .... A.L.	1	9	1	0	1.000	4	0	5	1.00	0
World Series Record										
2005 Chicago .... A.L.	2	$7^{1/3}$	0	0	.000	6	0	7	4.91	1

a Pitched no-hit, no-run game against Texas Rangers, April 18, 2007.

BURNETT, ALLAN JAMES (A.J.)

Born, North Little Rock, Arkansas, January 3, 1977.
Bats Right. Throws Right. Height, 6 feet, 4 inches. Weight, 230 pounds.

Year	Club	Lea	G	IP	W	L	Pct	SO	BB	H	ERA	SAVES
1995 Mets	Gulf Coast	9	33²/₃	2	3	.400	26	23	27	4.28	0
1996 Kingsport	Appal.	12	58	4	0	1.000	68	54	31	3.88	0
1997 Mets	Gulf Coast	3	11¹/₃	0	1	.000	15	8	8	3.18	0
1997 Pittsfield	N.Y.-Penn.	9	44	3	1	.750	48	35	28	4.70	0
1998 Kane County a	Midwest	20	119	10	4	.714	186	45	74	1.97	0
1999 Portland	Eastern	26	120²/₃	6	12	.333	121	71	132	5.52	0
1999 Florida	N.L.	7	41¹/₃	4	2	.667	33	25	37	3.48	0
2000 Brevard County	Fla.St.	2	7¹/₃	0	0	.000	6	6	4	3.68	0
2000 Calgary	P.C.	1	5	0	0	.000	6	3	0	0.00	0
2000 Florida b	N.L.	13	82²/₃	3	7	.300	57	44	80	4.79	0
2001 Brevard County	Fla.St.	2	9¹/₃	0	0	.000	10	4	4	1.93	0
2001 Florida c-d	N.L.	27	173¹/₃	11	12	.478	128	83	145	4.05	0
2002 Florida e	N.L.	31	204¹/₃	12	9	.571	203	90	153	3.30	0
2003 Florida f	N.L.	4	23	0	2	.000	21	18	18	4.70	0
2004 Jupiter	Fla.St.	1	4	0	0	.000	4	2	2	0.00	0
2004 Albuquerque	P.C.	1	3¹/₃	0	0	.000	6	2	7	10.80	0
2004 Florida g	N.L.	20	120	7	6	.538	113	38	102	3.68	0
2005 Florida h	N.L.	32	209	12	12	.500	198	79	184	3.44	0
2006 Dunedin	Fla.St.	2	8	0	0	.000	6	2	9	3.38	0
2006 New Hampshire	Eastern	1	6	1	0	1.000	9	3	2	1.50	0
2006 Syracuse	Int.	1	5	1	0	1.000	7	1	0	0.00	0
2006 Toronto i	A.L.	21	135²/₃	10	8	.556	118	39	138	3.98	0
2007 Syracuse	Int.	1	5	0	0	.000	7	1	3	1.80	0
2007 Toronto j	A.L.	25	165²/₃	10	8	.556	176	66	131	3.75	0
2008 Toronto k	A.L.	35	221¹/₃	18	10	.643	*231	86	211	4.07	0
Major League Totals	10 Yrs.	215	1376¹/₃	87	76	.534	1278	568	1199	3.81	0

a Traded to Florida Marlins with pitcher Jesus Sanchez and outfielder Robert Stratton for pitcher Al Leiter and infielder Ralph Milliard, February 6, 1998.
b On disabled list from March 17 to July 19, 2000.
c On disabled list from March 23 to May 7, 2001.
d Pitched no-hit, no-run game against San Diego Padres, May 12, 2001.
e On disabled list from August 19 to September 14, 2002.
f On disabled list from March 21 to April 9 and April 26 to September 29, 2003.
g On disabled list from March 26 to June 3, 2004.
h Filed for free agency, October 27, 2005. Signed with Toronto Blue Jays, December 6, 2005.
i On disabled list from March 24 to April 15 and April 22 to June 22, 2006.
j On disabled list from June 13 to June 28 and June 29 to August 12, 2007.
k Filed for free agency, November 13, 2008. Signed with New York Yankees, December 18, 2008.

BURNETT, SEAN RICHARD

Born, Dunedin, Florida, September 17, 1982.
Bats Left. Throws Left. Height, 5 feet, 11 inches. Weight, 190 pounds.

Year	Club	Lea	G	IP	W	L	Pct	SO	BB	H	ERA	SAVES
2000 Pirates	Gulf Coast	8	31	2	1	.667	24	3	31	4.06	0
2001 Hickory	So.Atl.	26	161¹/₃	11	8	.579	134	33	164	2.62	0
2002 Lynchburg	Carolina	26	155¹/₃	13	4	.765	96	33	118	1.80	0
2003 Altoona	Eastern	27	159²/₃	14	6	.700	86	29	158	3.21	0
2004 Nashville	P.C.	10	47	1	5	.167	25	17	58	5.36	0
2004 Pittsburgh a	N.L.	13	71²/₃	5	5	.500	30	28	86	5.02	0
2005 Pittsburgh b	N.L.					INJURED—Did Not Play					
2006 Indianapolis	Int.	25	120¹/₃	8	11	.421	46	46	136	5.16	0
2007 Indianapolis	Int.	15	70¹/₃	4	5	.444	31	39	83	4.48	0
2008 Indianapolis	Int.	12	17¹/₃	1	1	.500	15	8	9	1.04	3
2008 Pittsburgh	N.L.	58	56²/₃	1	1	.500	42	34	57	4.76	0
Major League Totals	2 Yrs.	71	128¹/₃	6	6	.500	72	62	143	4.91	0

a On disabled list from August 22 to October 4, 2004.
b On disabled list from April 2 to October 3, 2005.

BURRES, BRIAN JAMES

Born, Oregon City, Oregon, April 8, 1981.
Bats Left. Throws Left. Height, 6 feet, 1 inch. Weight, 180 pounds.

Year	Club	Lea	G	IP	W	L	Pct	SO	BB	H	ERA	SAVES
2001 Salem-Keizer	Northwest	14	40²/₃	3	1	.750	38	11	43	3.10	1
2002 Hagerstown	So.Atl.	32	119¹/₃	5	10	.333	119	53	114	4.75	0

Year	Club	Lea	G	IP	W	L	Pct	SO	BB	H	ERA	SAVES
2003 San Jose	Calif.	39	60²/₃	3	3	.500	64	36	55	3.86	1
2004 San Jose	Calif.	36	123²/₃	12	1	.923	114	30	115	2.84	0
2005 Norwich	Eastern	26	128²/₃	9	6	.600	105	57	130	4.20	0
2006 Ottawa	Int.	26	139	10	6	.625	110	57	133	3.76	0
2006 Baltimore a.	A.L.	11	8	0	0	.000	6	1	6	2.25	0
2007 Norfolk.	Int.	2	4	1	0	1.000	5	1	2	2.25	0
2007 Baltimore	A.L.	37	121	6	8	.429	96	66	140	5.95	0
2008 Norfolk.	Int.	4	11	1	0	1.000	11	1	9	0.82	0
2008 Baltimore	A.L.	31	129²/₃	7	10	.412	63	50	165	6.04	0
Major League Totals ...... .3 Yrs.	79	258²/₃	13	18	.419	165	117	311	5.88	0

a Claimed on waivers by Baltimore Orioles from San Francisco Giants, January 6, 2006.

BURTON, LEVI JARED (JARED)
Born, Westminster, South Carolina, June 2, 1981.
Bats Right. Throws Right. Height, 6 feet, 5 inches. Weight, 225 pounds.

Year	Club	Lea	G	IP	W	L	Pct	SO	BB	H	ERA	SAVES
2002 Vancouver	Northwest	13	37²/₃	0	4	.000	38	14	32	3.58	1
2003 Kane County........	Midwest	15	31²/₃	2	1	.667	33	7	19	2.27	1
2004 Athletics	Arizona	5	21²/₃	1	0	1.000	15	4	21	4.15	0
2004 Modesto	Calif.	10	32	3	2	.600	25	20	34	4.78	0
2005 Stockton.	Calif.	52	55¹/₃	4	4	.500	67	20	44	2.60	24
2006 Midland a	Texas	53	74	6	5	.545	66	27	71	4.14	1
2007 Chattanooga	Southern	4	5¹/₃	0	1	.000	3	5	10	11.81	0
2007 Louisville	Int.	10	14	1	0	1.000	13	4	11	0.64	1
2007 Cincinnati b	N.L.	47	43	4	2	.667	36	22	28	2.51	0
2008 Louisville	Int.	2	2	0	0	.000	1	2	1	4.50	0
2008 Cincinnati c	N.L.	54	58²/₃	5	1	.833	58	25	56	3.22	0
Major League Totals .... .2 Yrs.	101	101²/₃	9	3	.750	94	47	84	2.92	0

a Selected by Cincinnati Reds from Oakland Athletics in Rule V draft, December 7, 2006.
b On disabled list from April 8 to May 9 and June 11 to July 7, 2007.
c On disabled list from July 11 to September 2, 2008.

BUSH, DAVID THOMAS (DAVE)
Born, Pittsburgh, Pennsylvania, November 9, 1979.
Bats Right. Throws Right. Height, 6 feet, 2 inches. Weight, 210 pounds.

Year	Club	Lea	G	IP	W	L	Pct	SO	BB	H	ERA	SAVES
2002 Auburn	N.Y.-Penn.	18	22¹/₃	1	1	.500	39	7	13	2.82	10
2002 Dunedin	Fla.St.	7	13¹/₃	0	1	.000	9	2	10	2.03	0
2003 Dunedin	Fla.St.	14	77	7	3	.700	75	9	64	2.81	0
2003 New Haven	Eastern	14	81	7	3	.700	73	19	73	2.78	0
2004 Syracuse	Int.	16	99²/₃	6	6	.500	88	20	108	4.06	0
2004 Toronto	A.L.	16	97¹/₃	5	4	.556	64	25	95	3.69	0
2005 Syracuse	Int.	9	55	2	2	.500	40	9	65	4.42	0
2005 Toronto a	A.L.	25	136¹/₃	5	11	.313	75	29	142	4.49	0
2006 Milwaukee	N.L.	34	210	12	11	.522	166	38	201	4.41	0
2007 Milwaukee	N.L.	33	186¹/₃	12	10	.545	134	44	217	5.12	0
2008 Nashville	P.C.	1	6	0	0	.000	7	2	3	1.50	0
2008 Milwaukee	N.L.	31	185	9	10	.474	109	48	163	4.18	0
Major League Totals .... .5 Yrs.	139	815¹/₃	43	46	.483	548	184	818	4.45	0
Division Series											
2008 Milwaukee	N.L.	1	5¹/₃	1	0	1.000	3	0	5	1.69	0

a Traded to Milwaukee Brewers with outfielder Gabe Gross and pitcher Zach Jackson for infielder Lyle Overbay and pitcher Ty Taubenheim, December 7, 2005.

BYRD, PAUL GREGORY
Born, Louisville, Kentucky, December 3, 1970.
Bats Right. Throws Right. Height, 6 feet, 1 inches. Weight, 190 pounds.

Year	Club	Lea	G	IP	W	L	Pct	SO	BB	H	ERA	SAVES
1991 Kinston............	Carolina	14	62²/₃	4	3	.571	62	36	40	3.16	0
1992 Canton-Akron......	Eastern	24	152¹/₃	14	6	.700	118	75	122	3.01	0
1993 Canton-Akron......	Eastern	2	10	0	0	.000	8	3	7	3.60	0
1993 Charlotte	Int.	14	81	7	4	.636	54	30	80	3.89	0
1994 Canton-Akron a	Eastern	21	139¹/₃	5	9	.357	106	52	135	3.81	0
1994 Charlotte	Int.	9	36²/₃	2	2	.500	15	11	33	3.93	1
1995 Norfolk.	Int.	22	87	3	5	.375	61	21	71	2.79	6

Year Club	Lea	G	IP	W	L	Pct	SO	BB	H	ERA	SAVES
1995 New York	N.L.	17	22	2	0	1.000	26	7	18	2.05	0
1996 Norfolk...............	Int.	5	7 2/3	2	0	1.000	8	4	4	3.52	1
1996 New York b-c	N.L.	38	46 2/3	1	2	.333	31	21	48	4.24	0
1997 Richmond	Int.	3	17	2	1	.667	14	1	14	3.18	0
1997 Atlanta	N.L.	31	53	4	4	.500	37	28	47	5.26	0
1998 Richmond	Int.	17	102 1/3	5	5	.500	84	36	92	3.69	0
1998 Atlanta-Philadelphia d ...	N.L.	9	57	5	2	.714	39	18	45	2.68	0
1999 Philadelphia	N.L.	32	199 2/3	15	11	.577	106	70	205	4.60	0
2000 Scranton-WB	Int.	3	26	2	0	1.000	10	6	20	1.73	0
2000 Philadelphia e-f	N.L.	17	83	2	9	.182	53	35	89	6.51	0
2001 Clearwater	Fla.St.	4	23 2/3	0	3	.000	17	5	24	3.42	0
2001 Scranton-WB	Int.	5	37	1	3	.250	35	7	34	3.65	0
2001 Philadelphia	N.L.	3	10	0	1	.000	3	4	10	8.10	0
2001 Kansas City g-h	A.L.	16	93 1/3	6	6	.500	49	22	110	4.05	0
2002 Kansas City i-j	A.L.	33	228 1/3	17	11	.607	129	38	224	3.90	0
2003 Atlanta	N.L.	INJURED—Did Not Play									
2004 Greenville..........	Southern	3	12 2/3	1	1	.500	8	5	13	7.11	0
2004 Richmond	Int.	1	4 2/3	0	1	.000	5	2	3	7.71	0
2004 Atlanta k-l	N.L.	19	114 1/3	8	7	.533	79	19	123	3.94	0
2005 Los Angeles m	A.L.	31	204 1/3	12	11	.522	102	28	216	3.74	0
2006 Cleveland	A.L.	31	179	10	9	.526	88	38	232	4.88	0
2007 Cleveland	A.L.	31	192 1/3	15	8	.652	88	28	239	4.59	0
2008 Cleveland-Boston n-o ..	A.L.	30	180	11	12	.478	82	34	204	4.60	0
Major League Totals ...13 Yrs.		338	1663	108	93	.537	912	390	1810	4.38	0
Division Series											
2004 Atlanta	N.L.	2	5 2/3	0	1	.000	3	3	8	6.35	0
2005 Los Angeles	A.L.	1	3 2/3	0	0	.000	2	2	7	9.82	0
2007 Cleveland	A.L.	1	5	1	0	1.000	2	2	8	3.60	0
Division Series Totals		4	14 1/3	1	1	.500	7	7	23	6.28	0
Championship Series											
2005 Los Angeles	A.L.	2	10 2/3	1	0	1.000	2	2	10	3.38	0
2007 Cleveland	A.L.	1	5	1	0	1.000	4	0	6	3.60	0
2008 Boston	A.L.	1	3 1/3	0	0	.000	2	0	5	10.80	0
Championship Series Totals		4	19	2	0	1.000	8	2	21	4.74	0

a Traded to New York Mets by Cleveland Indians with pitcher Dave Mlicki and pitcher Jerry DiPoto and player to be named later for outfielder Jeromy Burnitz and pitcher Joe Roa, November 18, 1994. New York Mets received infielder Jesus Azuaje to complete trade, December 6, 1994.

b On disabled list from April 1 to June 9, 1996.

c Traded to Atlanta Braves with player to be named later for pitcher Greg McMichael, November 25, 1996. Atlanta Braves received pitcher Andy Zwirchitz to complete trade, June 1, 1997.

d Claimed on waivers by Philadelphia Phillies, August 10, 1998.

e On disabled list from July 27 to October 5, 2000.

f Filed for free agency, October 12, 2000, re-signed with Philadelphia Phillies organization, January 29, 2001.

g Traded to Kansas City Royals for pitcher Jose Santiago, June 5, 2001.

h On disabled list from September 22 to November 8, 2001.

i Not offered 2002 contract, December 21, 2001, re-signed with Kansas City Royals, January 10, 2002.

j Filed for free agency, October 28, 2002. Signed with Atlanta Braves, December 17, 2002.
   On disabled list from March 21 to November 7, 2003. On disabled list from March 21 to November 7, 2003.

k On disabled list from March 26 to June 19, 2004. Signed with Anaheim Angels, December 14, 2004.

l Filed for free agency, October 28, 2004. Signed with Anaheim Angels, December 14, 2004.

m Filed for free agency, October 27, 2005. Signed with Cleveland Indians, December 5, 2005.

n Traded to Boston Red Sox for player to be named later, August 12, 2008.

o Filed for free agency, November 3, 2008.

BYRDAK, TIMOTHY CHRISTOPHER (TIM)

Born, Oak Lawn, Illinois, October 31, 1973.

Bats Left. Throws Left. Height, 5 feet, 11 inches. Weight, 195 pounds.

Year Club	Lea	G	IP	W	L	Pct	SO	BB	H	ERA	SAVES
1994 Eugene..........	Northwest	15	73 1/3	4	5	.444	77	20	60	3.07	0
1995 Wilmington	Carolina	27	166 1/3	11	5	.688	127	45	118	2.16	0
1996 Wichita..............	Texas	15	84 2/3	5	7	.417	47	44	112	6.91	3
1997 Wilmington	Carolina	22	41	4	3	.571	47	12	34	3.51	3
1998 Wichita..........	Texas	34	52	3	5	.375	37	28	58	4.15	2
1998 Kansas City	A.L.	3	1 2/3	0	0	.000	1	0	5	5.40	0
1998 Omaha...............	P.C.	26	36 2/3	2	1	.667	32	20	31	2.45	1
1999 Omaha...............	P.C.	33	49 2/3	3	1	.750	51	28	39	1.81	4
1999 Kansas City	A.L.	33	24 2/3	0	3	.000	17	20	32	7.66	1
2000 Omaha...............	P.C.	34	52 2/3	6	2	.750	47	29	59	4.44	4

Year Club	Lea	G	IP	W	L	Pct	SO	BB	H	ERA	SAVES
2000 Kansas City	A.L.	12	6⅓	0	1	.000	8	4	11	11.37	0
2000 Wichita a	Texas	4	6⅔	0	0	.000	1	3	9	5.40	0
2001 Buffalo	Int.	4	17⅓	2	0	1.000	17	5	18	4.67	0
2002 Kinston...........	Carolina	2	4	1	0	1.000	3	4	3	4.50	0
2002 Akron........	Eastern	9	13	0	0	.000	8	11	16	6.23	1
2003 Joliet	Northern	5	34	2	1	.667	18	10	31	2.67	0
2003 Gary...........	Northern	10	66	2	4	.333	58	25	60	4.34	0
2004 Ottawa	Int.	33	34⅓	2	1	.667	43	12	46	4.19	2
2004 Portland b-c-d.......	P.C.	20	38	3	0	1.000	25	17	47	5.45	0
2005 Ottawa	Int.	37	38⅔	3	2	.600	44	15	23	2.09	11
2005 Baltimore	A.L.	41	26⅔	0	1	.000	31	21	27	4.05	1
2006 Aberdeen	N.Y.-Penn.	1	1	0	0	.000	3	0	2	9.00	0
2006 Frederick	Carolina	1	1⅓	0	0	.000	0	1	4	13.50	0
2006 Bowie.............	Eastern	3	4	0	0	.000	7	2	4	2.25	0
2006 Baltimore e-f.......	A.L.	16	7	1	0	1.000	2	8	14	12.86	0
2007 Toledo	Int.	17	24⅓	1	0	1.000	30	8	22	2.59	0
2007 Detroit g.............	A.L.	39	45	3	0	1.000	49	26	38	3.20	1
2008 Round Rock..........	P.C.	7	7⅓	0	0	.000	10	0	8	3.68	0
2008 Houston h	N.L.	59	55⅓	2	1	.667	47	29	45	3.90	0
Major League Totals ....7 Yrs.		203	166⅔	6	6	.500	155	108	172	4.97	3

a Not offered contract, December 1, 2000. Signed with Cleveland Indians organization, December 24, 2000.
b Released by Cleveland Indians, June 28, 2001. Signed with San Diego Padres organization, January 30, 2004.
c Traded to Baltimore Orioles for player to be named later, June 22, 2004.
d Filed for free agency, October 15, 2004, re-signed with Baltimore Orioles organization, November 16, 2004.
e On disabled list from April 19 to July 30, 2006.
f Filed for free agency, October 15, 2006. Signed with Detroit Tigers organization, November 18, 2006.
g On disabled list from June 27 to July 25, 2007.
h Released by Detroit Tigers, March 26, 2008. Signed with Houston Astros organization, April 3, 2008.

CABRERA, DANIEL ALBERTO

Born, San Pedro de Macoris, Dominican Republic, May 28, 1981.
Bats Right. Throws Right. Height, 6 feet, 7 inches. Weight, 260 pounds.

Year Club	Lea	G	IP	W	L	Pct	SO	BB	H	ERA	SAVES
2001 Orioles	Gulf Coast	12	40⅔	2	3	.400	36	39	31	5.53	0
2002 Bluefield	Appal.	12	60⅓	5	2	.714	69	25	52	3.28	0
2003 Delmarva	So.Atl.	26	125⅓	5	9	.357	120	78	105	4.24	0
2004 Bowie.............	Eastern	5	27⅓	0	1	.000	35	12	11	2.63	0
2004 Baltimore	A.L.	28	147⅔	12	8	.600	76	89	145	5.00	1
2005 Bowie.............	Eastern	1	6	1	0	1.000	7	2	8	3.00	0
2005 Baltimore a...........	A.L.	29	161⅓	10	13	.435	157	87	144	4.52	0
2006 Bowie.............	Eastern	1	4	0	0	.000	7	1	0	0.00	0
2006 Ottawa	Int.	4	24⅓	3	1	.750	27	9	20	4.07	0
2006 Baltimore b	A.L.	26	148	9	10	.474	157	*104	130	4.74	0
2007 Baltimore	A.L.	34	204⅓	9	*18	.333	166	*108	207	5.55	0
2008 Baltimore c-d........	A.L.	30	180	8	10	.444	95	90	199	5.25	0
Major League Totals ....5 Yrs.		147	841⅓	48	59	.449	651	478	825	5.05	1

a On disabled list from August 17 to September 6, 2005.
b On disabled list from May 15 to June 5, 2006.
c On disabled list from September 14 to October 2, 2008.
d Not offered contract, December 13, 2008. Signed with Washington Nationals, December 29, 2008.

CAIN, MATTHEW THOMAS (MATT)

Born, Dothan, Alabama, October 1, 1984.
Bats Right. Throws Right. Height, 6 feet, 3 inches. Weight, 235 pounds.

Year Club	Lea	G	IP	W	L	Pct	SO	BB	H	ERA	SAVES
2002 Giants.............	Arizona	8	19⅓	0	1	.000	20	11	13	3.72	0
2003 Hagerstown	So.Atl.	14	74	4	4	.500	90	24	57	2.55	0
2004 San Jose	Calif.	13	72⅔	7	1	.875	89	17	58	1.86	0
2004 Norwich	Eastern	15	86	6	4	.600	72	40	73	3.35	0
2005 Fresno	P.C.	26	145⅔	10	5	.667	176	73	118	4.39	0
2005 San Francisco	N.L.	7	46⅓	2	1	.667	30	19	24	2.33	0
2006 San Francisco	N.L.	32	190⅔	13	12	.520	179	87	157	4.15	0
2007 San Francisco	N.L.	32	200	7	16	.304	163	79	173	3.65	0
2008 San Francisco	N.L.	34	217⅔	8	14	.364	186	91	206	3.76	0
Major League Totals ....4 Yrs.		105	654⅔	30	43	.411	558	276	560	3.74	0

CAMPILLO, JORGE HIDALGO
Born, Tijuana, Mexico, August 10, 1978.
Bats Right. Throws Right. Height, 6 feet, 1 inch. Weight, 225 pounds.

Year	Club	Lea	G	IP	W	L	Pct	SO	BB	H	ERA	SAVES
1997	Tigres a-b	Mexican	2	4	1	0	1.000	4	5	2	4.50	0
1998	Tigres	Mexican	24	68²/₃	6	2	.750	42	55	76	5.11	0
1999	Tigres	Mexican	32	71	1	2	.333	41	46	50	2.90	0
2000	Tigres	Mexican	25	99	9	7	.563	58	42	128	6.84	0
2001	Tigres	Mexican	30	87	6	3	.667	64	37	95	3.53	1
2002	Tigres	Mexican	25	94	5	5	.500	64	37	111	5.53	0
2003	Tigres	Mexican	21	119	12	5	.706	63	30	116	2.79	2
2004	Tigres	Mexican	17	99	5	5	.500	66	28	120	5.38	0
2005	Mariners	Arizona	4	11	0	2	.000	10	2	18	5.73	0
2005	Tacoma	P.C.	12	66¹/₃	4	1	.800	43	18	63	2.71	0
2005	Seattle c-d	A.L.	2	2	0	0	.000	1	1	1	0.00	0
2006	Mariners	Arizona	6	13	0	0	.000	15	0	13	4.15	0
2006	Inland Empire	Calif.	2	9	1	1	.500	6	2	8	4.00	0
2006	San Antonio	Texas	2	10²/₃	2	0	1.000	3	2	12	2.53	0
2006	Seattle	A.L.	1	2¹/₃	0	0	.000	1	0	4	15.43	0
2007	Tacoma	P.C.	24	149¹/₃	9	6	.600	99	39	151	3.07	0
2007	Seattle f	A.L.	5	13¹/₃	0	0	.000	9	6	18	6.75	0
2008	Richmond	Int.	1	4¹/₃	0	0	.000	4	0	5	0.00	0
2008	Atlanta	N.L.	39	158²/₃	8	7	.533	107	38	158	3.91	0
Major League Totals		4 Yrs.	47	176¹/₃	8	7	.533	118	45	181	4.24	0

a Loaned by Atlanta Braves to Mexico City Tigers June 23, 1996.
b Released by Atlanta Braves, January 27, 1997. Signed by Mexico City Tigers, 1997.
c Signed by Seattle Mariners organization, March 26, 2005.
d On disabled list from August 3 to October 7, 2005.
f Filed for free agency, October 25, 2007. Signed with Atlanta Braves organization, December 26, 2007.

CAPPS, MATTHEW DICUS (MATT)
Born, Douglasville, Georgia, September 3, 1983.
Bats Right. Throws Right. Height, 6 feet, 2 inches. Weight, 240 pounds.

Year	Club	Lea	G	IP	W	L	Pct	SO	BB	H	ERA	SAVES
2002	Pirates	Gulf Coast	7	13	1	0	1.000	8	6	13	0.69	1
2003	Lynchburg	Carolina	1	5	0	0	.000	5	4	5	5.40	0
2003	Pirates	Gulf Coast	10	62²/₃	5	1	.833	54	9	40	1.87	0
2004	Williamsport	N.Y.-Penn.	11	65	3	5	.375	27	16	82	10.07	0
2004	Hickory	So.Atl.	12	42	2	3	.400	33	4	84	4.85	0
2005	Hickory	So.Atl.	35	53²/₃	3	4	.429	39	5	47	2.52	14
2005	Altoona	Eastern	17	20	0	2	.000	26	1	21	2.70	7
2005	Pittsburgh	N.L.	4	4	0	0	.000	3	0	5	4.50	0
2006	Pittsburgh	N.L.	85	80²/₃	9	1	.900	56	12	81	3.79	1
2007	Pittsburgh	N.L.	76	79	4	7	.364	64	16	64	2.28	18
2008	Pirates	Gulf Coast	2	2	0	0	.000	2	0	2	0.00	0
2008	Altoona	Eastern	3	3	0	0	.000	5	1	0	0.00	0
2008	Indianapolis	Int.	1	1²/₃	0	0	.000	1	3	0	0.00	0
2008	Pittsburgh a	N.L.	49	53²/₃	2	3	.400	39	5	47	3.02	21
Major League Totals		4 Yrs.	214	217¹/₃	15	11	.577	162	33	197	3.06	40

a On disabled list from July 2 to August 23, 2008.

CARLSON, JESSE CRAIG
Born, New Britain, Connecticut, December 31, 1980.
Bats Left. Throws Left. Height, 6 feet, 1 inch. Weight, 160 pounds.

Year	Club	Lea	G	IP	W	L	Pct	SO	BB	H	ERA	SAVES
2002	Oneonta	N.Y.-Penn.	19	38	2	2	.500	47	10	19	1.66	0
2003	Lexington a	So.Atl.	53	63¹/₃	3	0	1.000	84	16	37	1.56	13
2004	Round Rock b	Texas	41	55¹/₃	5	0	1.000	51	21	57	5.04	1
2005	New Hampshire	Eastern	39	39¹/₃	3	2	.600	42	5	28	1.83	5
2005	Syracuse c	Int.	22	18²/₃	1	1	.500	17	7	26	4.82	0
2006	Oklahoma	P.C.	10	11	0	0	.000	5	4	6	0.00	0
2006	Frisco	Texas	43	58	6	5	.545	45	18	65	4.66	3
2007	New Hampshire d	Eastern	58	70¹/₃	8	2	.800	81	18	77	4.86	6
2008	Syracuse	Int.	2	3²/₃	0	0	.000	2	0	1	0.00	0
2008	Toronto	A.L.	69	60	7	2	.778	55	21	41	2.25	2

a Released by Detroit Tigers, March 28, 2003. Signed with Houston Astros organization, March 31, 2003.
b Filed for free agency, October 15, 2004. Signed with Toronto Blue Jays organization, November 11, 2004.
c Filed for free agency, October 15, 2005. Signed with Texas Rangers organization, November 10, 2005.
d Filed for free agency, October 15, 2006. Signed with Toronto Blue Jays organization, January 23, 2007.

CARLYLE, EARL L. (BUDDY)

Born, Omaha, Nebraska, December 21, 1977.
Bats Left. Throws Right. Height, 6 feet, 3 inches. Weight, 210 pounds.

Year	Club	Lea	G	IP	W	L	Pct	SO	BB	H	ERA	SAVES
1996	Princeton	Appal.	10	46 1/3	2	4	.333	42	16	47	4.66	0
1997	Chston-WV.	So.Atl.	23	143	14	5	.737	111	27	130	2.77	0
1998	Chattanooga	Southern	1	5	0	1	.000	3	0	6	5.40	0
1998	Mobile a	Southern	27	183 2/3	14	6	.700	97	46	179	3.38	0
1999	Las Vegas	P.C.	25	160	11	8	.579	138	42	180	4.89	0
1999	San Diego	N.L.	7	37 2/3	1	3	.250	29	17	36	5.97	0
2000	San Diego	N.L.	4	3	0	0	.000	2	3	6	21.00	0
2000	Las Vegas b	P.C.	27	151	8	6	.571	127	44	165	4.29	0
2001	Hanshin	Japan Pac.	28	153 1/3	7	10	.412	111	65	151	3.87	0
2002	Hanshin c	Japan Pac.	3	14 1/3	0	2	.000	13	5	17	7.53	0
2003	Omaha	P.C.	2	5	0	1	.000	4	1	5	5.40	0
2003	Wichita d	Texas	15	27 1/3	3	2	.600	41	7	19	1.98	3
2004	Trenton	Eastern	8	37 1/3	4	0	1.000	48	4	23	0.72	0
2004	Columbus e	Int.	19	104	8	5	.615	92	21	113	4.15	0
2005	Los Angeles	N.L.	10	14	0	0	.000	13	4	16	8.36	0
2005	Dodgers	Gulf Coast	1	3	0	0	.000	1	0	3	3.00	0
2005	Las Vegas f	P.C.	20	48	1	2	.333	53	21	51	4.88	2
2006	Albuquerque g	P.C.	13	28	3	1	.750	22	7	17	1.93	0
2007	Richmond	Int.	9	48 2/3	5	2	.714	56	9	40	2.59	0
2007	Atlanta	N.L.	22	107	8	7	.533	74	32	117	5.21	0
2008	Richmond	Int.	2	7 2/3	0	0	.000	7	3	11	7.04	0
2008	Atlanta h	N.L.	45	62 2/3	2	0	1.000	59	26	52	3.59	0
Major League Totals	5 Yrs.		88	224 1/3	11	10	.524	177	82	227	5.30	0

a Traded to San Diego Padres by Cincinnati Reds for pitcher Marc Kroon, April 8, 1998.
b Sold to Hanshin Tigers, November 3, 2000.
c Signed with Kansas City Royals organization, December 18, 2002.
d Filed for free agency, October 15, 2003. Signed with New York Yankees organization, December 23, 2003.
e Filed for free agency, October 15, 2004. Signed with Los Angeles Dodgers organization, November 18, 2004.
f Filed for free agency, October 3, 2005. Signed with Florida Marlins organization, December 15, 2005.
g Released by Florida Marlins, May 18, 2006. Signed with Atlanta Braves organization, December 4, 2006.
h On disabled list from May 9 to May 26, 2008.

CARMONA, FAUSTO C.

Born, Santo Domingo, Dominican Republic, December 7, 1983.
Bats Right. Throws Right. Height, 6 feet, 4 inches. Weight, 220 pounds.

Year	Club	Lea	G	IP	W	L	Pct	SO	BB	H	ERA	SAVES
2002	Burlington	Appal.	13	76 1/3	2	4	.333	42	10	89	3.30	1
2002	Mahoning Valley.	N.Y.-Penn.	3	4	0	0	.000	0	1	2	0.00	0
2003	Akron	Eastern	1	6	0	0	.000	3	0	8	4.50	0
2003	Lake County	So.Atl.	24	148 1/3	17	4	.810	83	14	117	2.06	0
2004	Kinston	Carolina	13	70	5	2	.714	57	20	68	2.83	0
2004	Akron	Eastern	15	87	4	8	.333	63	21	114	4.97	0
2004	Buffalo	Int.	1	6	1	0	1.000	2	3	6	6.00	0
2005	Akron	Eastern	14	90 2/3	6	5	.545	57	20	100	4.07	0
2005	Buffalo	Int.	13	83	7	4	.636	49	15	76	3.25	0
2006	Buffalo	Int.	6	27 2/3	1	3	.250	28	8	28	5.53	0
2006	Cleveland	A.L.	38	74 2/3	1	10	.091	58	31	88	5.42	0
2007	Cleveland	A.L.	32	215	19	8	.704	137	61	199	3.06	0
2008	Lake County	So.Atl.	1	4	0	0	.000	3	0	1	0.00	0
2008	Akron	Eastern	1	5	1	0	1.000	2	0	9	1.80	0
2008	Cleveland a	A.L.	22	120 2/3	8	7	.533	58	70	126	5.44	0
Major League Totals	3 Yrs.		92	410 1/3	28	25	.528	253	162	413	4.19	0
Division Series												
2007 Cleveland	A.L.		1	9	0	0	.000	5	2	3	1.00	0
Championship Series												
2007 Cleveland	A.L.		2	6	0	1	.000	7	9	10	16.50	0

a On disabled list from May 24 to July 26, 2008.

CARPENTER, CHRISTOPHER JOHN (CHRIS)

Born, Exeter, New Hampshire, April 27, 1975.
Bats Right. Throws Right. Height, 6 feet, 6 inches. Weight, 230 pounds.

Year	Club	Lea	G	IP	W	L	Pct	SO	BB	H	ERA	SAVES
1994	Medicne Hat	Pioneer	15	84 2/3	6	3	.667	80	39	76	2.76	0
1995	Dunedin	Fla.St.	15	99 1/3	3	5	.375	56	50	83	2.17	0
1995	Knoxville	Southern	12	64 1/3	3	7	.300	53	31	71	5.18	0

Year	Club	Lea	G	IP	W	L	Pct	SO	BB	H	ERA	SAVES
1996 Knoxville	Southern		28	171⅓	7	9	.438	150	91	161	3.94	0
1997 Syracuse	Int.		19	120	4	9	.308	97	53	113	4.50	0
1997 Toronto	A.L.		14	81⅓	3	7	.300	55	37	108	5.09	0
1998 Toronto	A.L.		33	175	12	7	.632	136	61	177	4.37	0
1999 Toronto	A.L.		24	150	9	8	.529	106	48	177	4.38	0
1999 St. Catharines a	N.Y.-Penn.		1	4	0	0	.000	6	1	5	4.50	0
2000 Toronto	A.L.		34	175⅓	10	12	.455	113	83	204	6.26	0
2001 Toronto	A.L.		34	215⅔	11	11	.500	157	75	229	4.09	0
2002 Toronto	A.L.		13	73⅓	4	5	.444	45	27	89	5.28	0
2002 Tennessee	Southern		5	18⅔	0	1	.000	9	8	26	8.20	0
2002 Syracuse b-c	Int.		1	6	0	1	.000	6	2	8	4.50	0
2003 Palm Beach	Fla.St.		4	7	0	1	.000	6	1	6	1.29	0
2003 Memphis	P.C.		3	8⅓	0	0	.000	4	2	11	5.40	0
2003 Tennessee d-e	Southern		1	3⅓	0	1	.000	2	2	7	13.50	0
2004 St. Louis	N.L.		28	182	15	5	.750	152	38	169	3.46	0
2005 St. Louis f	N.L.		33	241⅔	21	5	*.808	213	51	204	2.83	0
2006 St. Louis g	N.L.		32	221⅔	15	8	.652	184	43	194	3.09	0
2007 Palm Beach	Fla.St.		2	4⅓	0	1	.000	4	1	7	6.23	0
2007 St. Louis h	N.L.		1	6	0	1	.000	3	1	9	7.50	0
2008 Springfield	Texas		1	4	0	0	.000	4	4	1	0.00	0
2008 Memphis	P.C.		1	5⅔	0	1	.000	5	1	4	3.18	0
2008 St. Louis i	N.L.		4	15⅓	0	1	.000	7	4	16	1.76	0
Major League Totals	11 Yrs.		250	1537⅓	100	70	.588	1171	468	1576	4.08	0
Division Series												
2005 St. Louis	N.L.		1	6	1	0	1.000	3	3	3	0.00	0
2006 St. Louis	N.L.		2	13⅓	2	0	1.000	12	4	12	2.03	0
Division Series Totals			3	19⅓	3	0	1.000	15	7	15	1.40	0
Championship Series												
2005 St. Louis	N.L.		2	15	1	0	1.000	9	4	14	3.00	0
2006 St. Louis	N.L.		2	11	0	1	.000	5	4	13	5.73	0
Championship Series Totals			4	26	1	1	.500	14	8	27	4.15	0
World Series Record												
2006 St. Louis	N.L.		1	8	1	0	1.000	6	0	3	0.00	0

a On disabled list from June 3 to June 28, 1999.
b On disabled list from April 2 to April 20 and April 22 to June 21 and August 14 to October 7, 2002.
c Filed for free agency, October 9, 2002. Signed with St. Louis Cardinals, December 15, 2002.
d On disabled list from March 27 to September 30, 2003.
e Filed for free agency, November 3, 2003, re-signed with St. Louis Cardinals, December 1, 2003.
f Selected Cy Young Award Winner in National League for 2005.
g On disabled list from May 22 to June 6, 2006.
h On disabled list from April 2 to November 2, 2007.
i On disabled list from March 21 to July 30 and August 11 to September 1, 2008.

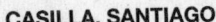

CASILLA, SANTIAGO

Born, Don Gregorio, Dominican Republic, June 25, 1980.
Bats Right. Throws Right. Height, 6 feet. Weight, 200 pounds.

Year	Club	Lea	G	IP	W	L	Pct	SO	BB	H	ERA	SAVES
2001 Athletics	Arizona		12	47⅓	4	2	.667	50	6	37	2.85	1
2002 Athletics	Arizona		13	59	2	1	.667	66	17	56	2.44	1
2002 Vancouver	Northwest		3	12⅓	0	3	.000	16	7	15	7.30	0
2003 Kane County	Midwest		14	42⅓	0	1	.000	28	19	40	2.55	0
2004 Kane County	Midwest		25	30	1	0	1.000	49	6	16	0.30	16
2004 Midland	Texas		13	18	2	0	1.000	32	15	10	1.50	2
2004 Sacramento	P.C.		11	13⅔	1	2	.333	21	9	5	12.71	0
2004 Oakland	A.L.		4	5⅔	0	0	.000	5	9	9	1.08	6
2005 Midland	Texas		10	16⅔	0	0	.000	30	9	9	4.47	20
2005 Sacramento	P.C.		44	48⅓	3	6	.333	73	20	45	4.44	20
2005 Oakland a	A.L.		3	3	0	0	.000	1	1	2	3.00	0
2006 Oakland	A.L.		2	2⅓	0	0	.000	2	2	2	11.57	0
2006 Sacramento	P.C.		25	33	2	0	1.000	32	10	25	3.27	4
2007 Sacramento	P.C.		22	24	2	1	.667	29	14	18	4.13	3
2007 Oakland	A.L.		46	50⅔	3	1	.750	52	23	43	4.44	2
2008 Stockton	Calif.		1	1	0	0	.000	2	0	0	0.00	0
2008 Sacramento	P.C.		2	2⅔	0	0	.000	5	1	3	3.38	0
2008 Oakland b	A.L.		51	50⅓	2	1	.667	43	20	60	3.93	2
Major League Totals	5 Yrs.		106	112	5	2	.714	103	55	112	4.74	4

a Played under name of Jairo Garcia 2001-2005
b On disabled list from May 16 to June 19, 2008.

214

CHACON, SHAWN ANTHONY

Born, Anchorage, Alaska, December 23, 1977.
Bats Right. Throws Right. Height, 6 feet, 3 inches. Weight, 220 pounds.

Year Club	Lea	G	IP	W	L	Pct	SO	BB	H	ERA	SAVES
1996 Rockies .... Arizona		11	56⅓	1	2	.333	64	15	46	1.60	0
1996 Portland .... Northwest		4	19⅔	0	2	.000	17	9	24	6.86	0
1997 Asheville............ So.Atl.		28	162	11	7	.611	149	63	155	3.89	0
1998 Salem............ Carolina		12	56	0	4	.000	54	31	53	5.30	0
1999 Salem............ Carolina		12	72	5	5	.500	66	34	69	4.13	0
2000 Carolina .... Southern		27	173⅔	10	10	.500	172	85	151	3.16	0
2001 Colo Sprngs.......... P.C.		4	24	2	0	1.000	28	7	18	2.25	0
2001 Colorado .... N.L.		27	160	6	10	.375	134	87	157	5.06	0
2002 Colorado a .... N.L.		21	119⅓	5	11	.313	67	60	122	5.73	0
2002 Colorado Springs....... P.C.		4	20⅔	2	0	1.000	15	10	23	4.79	0
2003 Colorado Springs....... P.C.		1	3	0	0	.000	2	0	5	6.00	0
2003 Colorado b .... N.L.		23	137	11	8	.579	93	58	124	4.60	0
2004 Colorado .... N.L.		66	63⅓	1	9	.100	52	52	71	7.11	35
2005 Colorado Springs....... P.C.		3	12⅔	0	2	.000	11	4	19	9.95	0
2005 Colorado .... N.L.		13	72⅔	1	7	.125	39	36	69	4.09	0
2005 New York c-d .... A.L.		14	79	7	3	.700	40	30	66	2.85	0
2006 Trenton........... Eastern		1	5	0	0	.000	3	2	4	5.40	0
2006 New York e............ A.L.		17	63	5	3	.625	35	36	77	7.00	0
2006 Pittsburgh f .... N.L.		9	46	2	3	.400	27	27	47	5.48	0
2007 Pittsburgh g .... N.L.		64	96	5	4	.556	79	48	95	3.94	1
2008 Houston h .... N.L.		15	85⅔	2	3	.400	53	41	88	5.04	0
Major League Totals ....8 Yrs.		269	922	45	61	.425	619	475	916	4.99	36
Division Series											
2005 New York............. A.L.		1	6⅓	0	0	.000	5	1	4	2.84	0

a On disabled list from May 9 to June 6, 2002.
b On disabled list from June 30 to July 19 and August 17 to October 8, 2003.
c On disabled list from June 3 to July 6, 2005.
d Traded to New York Yankees for outfielder Ramon Ramirez and pitcher Eduardo Sierra, July 28, 2005.
e On disabled list from May 17 to June 11, 2006.
f Traded to Pittsburgh Pirates for outfielder Craig Wilson, July 31, 2006.
g Filed for free agency, October 30, 2007. Signed with Houston Astros, February 20, 2008.
h Released by Houston Astros, June 26, 2008.

CHAMBERLAIN, JUSTIN LOUIS (JOBA)

Born, Lincoln, Nebraska, September 23, 1985.
Bats Right. Throws Right. Height, 6 feet, 2 inches. Weight, 230 pounds.

Year Club	Lea	G	IP	W	L	Pct	SO	BB	H	ERA	SAVES
2007 Tampa .... Fla.St.		7	40	4	0	1.000	51	11	25	2.03	0
2007 Trenton.......... Eastern		8	40⅓	4	2	.667	66	15	32	3.35	0
2007 Scranton-WB ....Int.		3	8	1	0	1.000	18	1	5	0.00	0
2007 New York .... A.L.		19	24	2	0	1.000	34	6	12	0.38	1
2008 New York a............. A.L.		42	100⅓	4	3	.571	118	39	87	2.60	1
Major League Totals ....2 Yrs.		61	124⅓	6	3	.667	152	45	99	2.17	1
Division Series											
2007 New York .... A.L.		2	3⅔	0	0	.000	4	3	3	4.91	0

a On disabled list from August 5 to September 2, 2008.

CHICO, MATTHEW BRYAN (MATT)

Born, Fullerton, California, June 10, 1983.
Bats Left. Throws Left. Height, 6 feet. Weight, 220 pounds.

Year Club	Lea	G	IP	W	L	Pct	SO	BB	H	ERA	SAVES
2003 Yakima.......... Northwest		17	71⅓	7	4	.636	71	25	75	3.53	0
2004 South Bend .... Midwest		14	87⅔	8	5	.615	89	27	59	2.57	0
2004 El Paso .... Texas		14	62⅓	3	7	.300	59	36	82	5.78	0
2005 Lancaster .... Calif.		18	110	7	2	.778	102	39	101	3.76	0
2005 Tennessee .... Southern		10	52⅔	1	7	.125	35	15	75	5.98	0
2006 Lancaster .... Calif.		10	50⅓	3	4	.429	49	11	48	3.75	0
2006 Harrisburg .... Eastern		4	22	2	0	1.000	13	8	28	3.27	0
2006 Tennessee a .... Southern		13	81	7	2	.778	63	21	62	2.22	0
2007 Columbus ....Int.		2	11	1	1	.500	7	5	9	3.27	0
2007 Washington .... N.L.		31	167	7	9	.438	94	74	183	4.63	0
2008 Columbus ....Int.		1	4	0	0	.000	1	2	7	9.00	0
2008 Washington b.......... N.L.		11	48	0	6	.000	31	17	63	6.19	0
Major League Totals ....2 Yrs.		42	215	7	15	.318	125	91	246	4.98	0

a Traded to Washington Nationals by Arizona Diamondbacks with pitcher Garrett Mock for pitcher Livan Hernandez and cash, August 7, 2006.
b On disabled list from May 23 to October 3, 2008.

COKE, PHILLIP DOUGLAS (PHIL)

Born, Sonora, California, July 19, 1982.
Bats Left. Throws Left. Height, 6 feet, 1 inch. Weight, 210 pounds.

Year Club	Lea	G	IP	W	L	Pct	SO	BB	H	ERA	SAVES
2003 Yankees	Gulf Coast	10	12	0	0	.000	5	3	13	3.75	0
2004 Yankees	Gulf Coast	7	11⅓	0	1	.000	13	3	18	3.97	0
2004 Staten Island	N.Y.-Penn.	3	8	0	0	.000	7	3	9	6.75	0
2005 Charleston	So.Atl.	24	103	8	11	.421	68	34	122	5.42	0
2006 Tampa	Fla.St.	22	110	5	7	.417	88	35	101	3.60	0
2006 Charleston	So.Atl.	5	17	0	1	.000	19	4	10	0.53	1
2007 Tampa	Fla.St.	17	99	7	3	.700	76	37	93	3.09	0
2008 Trenton	Eastern	23	118⅓	9	4	.692	115	39	105	2.51	0
2008 Scranton-WB	Int.	14	17⅓	2	2	.500	22	5	19	4.67	0
2008 New York	A.L.	12	14⅔	1	0	1.000	14	2	8	0.61	0

COLOME (DE LA CRUZ), JESUS

Born, San Pedro de Macoris, Dominican Republic, December 23, 1977.
Bats Right. Throws Right. Height, 6 feet, 2 inches. Weight, 240 pounds.

Year Club	Lea	G	IP	W	L	Pct	SO	BB	H	ERA	SAVES
1997 Oaklnd-West	Dominican	18	89⅔	9	3	.750	55	22	73	2.71	0
1998 Athletics	Arizona	12	56⅔	2	5	.286	62	16	47	3.18	0
1999 Modesto	Calif.	31	128⅔	8	4	.667	127	60	125	3.36	1
2000 Orlando	Southern	3	14⅔	1	2	.333	9	7	18	6.75	0
2000 Midland a	Texas	20	110⅓	9	4	.692	95	50	99	3.59	0
2001 Durham	Int.	13	17⅓	0	0	.000	18	6	22	6.23	0
2001 Tampa Bay	A.L.	30	48⅔	2	3	.400	31	25	37	3.33	0
2002 Tampa Bay	A.L.	32	41⅓	2	7	.222	33	33	56	8.27	0
2002 Durham	Int.	18	29	2	2	.500	30	13	18	2.17	1
2003 Tampa Bay	A.L.	54	74	3	7	.300	69	46	69	4.50	2
2004 Durham	Int.	18	30⅔	2	1	.667	17	16	27	3.52	2
2004 Tampa Bay b	A.L.	33	41⅓	2	2	.500	40	18	28	3.27	3
2005 Montgomery	Southern	3	4	0	0	.000	3	0	2	0.00	0
2005 Tampa Bay c	A.L.	36	45⅓	2	3	.400	28	18	54	4.57	0
2006 Tampa Bay	A.L.	1	0⅓	0	0	.000	0	1	0	27.00	0
2006 Trenton	Eastern	3	4⅔	2	0	1.000	2	3	2	1.93	0
2006 Columbus d-e	Int.	25	33⅓	1	1	.500	25	15	35	3.78	0
2007 Nationals	Gulf Coast	2	3	1	0	1.000	2	0	2	0.00	0
2007 Columbus	Int.	1	1	0	0	.000	2	0	0	0.00	0
2007 Washington f	N.L.	61	66	5	1	.833	43	27	64	3.82	1
2008 Washington g	N.L.	61	71	2	2	.500	55	39	61	4.31	0
Major League Totals	8 Yrs.	308	388	18	25	.419	299	207	369	4.50	6

a Traded to Tampa Bay Devil Rays by Oakland Athletics with player to be named later for pitcher Jim Mecir and pitcher Todd Belitz, July 27, 2000.
b On disabled list from September 14 to October 29, 2004.
c On disabled list from April 14 to May 10 and June 10 to July 22, 2005.
d Released by Tampa Bay Devil Rays, April 6, 2006. Signed with New York Yankees organization, April 15, 2006.
e Filed for free agency, October 15, 2006. Signed with Washington Nationals organization, November 8, 2006.
f On disabled list from June 25 to August 18, 2007.
g Released by Washington Nationals, December 10, 2008. Signed with Washington Nationals organization, January 15, 2009.

CONDREY, CLAYTON LEE (CLAY)

Born, Beaumont, Texas, November 19, 1975.
Bats Right. Throws Right. Height, 6 feet, 3 inches. Weight, 215 pounds.

Year Club	Lea	G	IP	W	L	Pct	SO	BB	H	ERA	SAVES
1998 Padres	Arizona	5	5⅓	0	1	.000	4	5	6	3.38	0
1998 Idaho Falls	Pioneer	18	24⅔	2	1	.667	19	4	31	2.55	5
1999 Rancho Cucamonga	Calif.	6	7⅓	0	0	.000	9	3	4	3.68	0
1999 Fort Wayne	Midwest	42	47⅔	2	3	.400	47	19	40	3.78	20
2000 Rancho Cucamonga	Calif.	18	20⅔	1	1	.500	21	7	18	3.48	4
2000 Mobile	Southern	35	43⅔	2	2	.500	25	20	41	5.36	6
2001 Portland	P.C.	39	53	1	3	.250	45	13	63	4.75	2
2001 Mobile	Southern	27	33⅔	2	2	.500	21	15	33	4.54	12
2002 Portland	P.C.	25	133⅔	10	4	.714	73	40	128	3.50	0
2002 San Diego	N.L.	9	26⅔	1	2	.333	16	8	20	1.69	0

Year Club	Lea	G	IP	W	L	Pct	SO	BB	H	ERA	SAVES
2003 San Diego	N.L.	9	34	1	2	.333	25	21	43	8.47	0
2003 Portland a	P.C.	11	63	3	3	.500	46	12	64	4.14	0
2004 Scranton/WB b-c	Int.	27	155	9	9	.500	70	34	206	5.46	0
2005 Scranton-WB	Int.	25	132 1/3	7	8	.467	74	29	159	4.15	0
2006 Scranton-WB	Int.	39	51 1/3	4	2	.667	28	15	41	1.93	6
2006 Philadelphia d	N.L.	21	28 2/3	2	2	.500	16	9	35	3.14	0
2007 Ottawa	Int.	10	22	1	0	1.000	10	5	19	2.45	1
2007 Philadelphia	N.L.	39	50	5	0	1.000	27	16	61	5.04	2
2008 Philadelphia	N.L.	56	69	3	4	.429	34	19	85	3.26	1
Major League Totals	5 Yrs.	134	208 1/3	12	10	.545	118	73	244	4.32	3
Division Series											
2007 Philadelphia	N.L.	1	1 2/3	0	0	.000	2	0	4	5.40	0
2008 Philadelphia	N.L.	1	1	0	0	.000	1	2	1	9.00	0
Division Series Totals		2	2 2/3	0	0	.000	3	2	5	6.75	0
Championship Series											
2008 Philadelphia	N.L.	1	0 2/3	0	0	.000	0	1	0	0.00	0

a On disabled list from May 13 to July 7, 2003.
b Traded to Philadelphia Phillies for infielder Trinio Aguilar, March 28, 2004.
c Filed for free agency, October 15, 2004, re-signed with Philadelphia Phillies organization, November 15, 2004.
d Filed for free agency, October 3, 2005, re-signed with Philadelphia Phillies organization, January 11, 2006.

CONTRERAS, JOSE ARIEL

Born, Las Martinas, Cuba, December 6, 1971.
Bats Right. Throws Right. Height, 6 feet, 4 inches. Weight, 245 pounds.

Year Club	Lea	G	IP	W	L	Pct	SO	BB	H	ERA	SAVES
2003 Staten Island	N.Y.-Penn.	1	7	0	0	.000	15	0	2	0.00	0
2003 Tampa	Fla.St.	1	4	0	0	.000	5	3	4	4.50	0
2003 Trenton	Eastern	1	1 2/3	0	0	.000	3	2	1	0.00	0
2003 Columbus	Int.	3	15	2	0	1.000	18	2	10	1.20	0
2003 New York a-b-c	A.L.	18	71	7	2	.778	72	30	52	3.30	0
2004 New York-Chicago d	A.L.	31	170 1/3	13	9	.591	150	84	166	5.50	0
2005 Chicago	A.L.	32	204 2/3	15	7	.682	154	75	177	3.61	0
2006 Chicago e	A.L.	30	196	13	9	.591	134	55	194	4.27	0
2007 Chicago	A.L.	32	189	10	17	.370	113	62	232	5.57	0
2008 Charlotte	Int.	1	5	0	0	.000	4	3	4	5.40	0
2008 Chicago f	A.L.	20	121	7	6	.538	70	35	130	4.54	0
Major League Totals	6 Yrs.	163	952	65	50	.565	693	341	951	4.57	0
Division Series											
2005 Chicago	A.L.	1	7 2/3	1	0	1.000	6	0	8	2.35	0
Championship Series											
2003 New York	A.L.	4	4 2/3	0	1	.000	7	2	6	5.79	0
2005 Chicago	A.L.	2	17 1/3	1	1	.500	6	2	12	3.12	0
Championship Series Totals		6	22	1	2	.333	13	4	18	3.68	0
World Series Record											
2003 New York	A.L.	4	6 1/3	0	1	.000	10	5	5	5.68	0
2005 Chicago	A.L.	1	7	1	0	1.000	2	0	6	3.86	0
World Series Totals		5	13 1/3	1	1	.500	12	5	11	4.72	0

a Played in Cuba 1996 through 2002.
b Signed as free agent by New York Yankees, February 6, 2003.
c On disabled list from June 7 to August 24, 2003.
d Traded to Chicago White Sox for pitcher Esteban Loaiza, July 31, 2004.
e On disabled list from May 5 to May 21, 2006.
f On disabled list from July 18 to August 9 and August 10 to October 17, 2008.

COOK, AARON LANE

Born, Fort Campbell, Kentucky, February 8, 1979.
Bats Right. Throws Right. Height, 6 feet, 3 inches. Weight, 215 pounds.

Year Club	Lea	G	IP	W	L	Pct	SO	BB	H	ERA	SAVES
1997 Rockies	Arizona	9	46	1	3	.250	35	17	48	3.13	0
1998 Portland	Northwest	15	79 1/3	5	8	.385	38	39	87	4.88	0
1999 Asheville	So.Atl.	25	121 2/3	4	12	.250	73	42	157	6.44	0
2000 Salem	Carolina	7	43	1	6	.143	37	12	52	5.44	0
2000 Asheville	So.Atl.	21	142 2/3	10	7	.588	118	23	130	2.96	0
2001 Salem	Carolina	27	155	11	11	.500	122	38	157	3.08	0
2002 Carolina	Southern	14	95	7	2	.778	58	19	73	1.42	0
2002 Colorado Springs	P.C.	10	64 1/3	4	4	.500	32	18	67	3.78	0

Year	Club	Lea	G	IP	W	L	Pct	SO	BB	H	ERA	SAVES
2002 Colorado	N.L.	9	35²/₃	2	1	.667	14	13	41	4.54	0
2003 Colorado Springs	P.C.	2	16	1	1	.500	12	4	10	2.25	0
2003 Colorado	N.L.	43	124	4	6	.400	43	57	160	6.02	0
2004 Colorado Springs	P.C.	7	46	3	1	.750	25	8	34	2.74	0
2004 Colorado a	N.L.	16	96²/₃	6	4	.600	40	39	112	4.28	0
2005 Tri-City	Northwest	2	7	0	0	.000	0	0	1	0.00	0
2005 Modesto	California	1	5	1	0	1.000	5	0	5	1.80	0
2005 Tulsa	Texas	1	3²/₃	0	1	.000	1	1	10	17.18	0
2005 Colorado Springs	P.C.	3	16¹/₃	1	0	1.000	11	7	18	5.51	0
2005 Colorado b	N.L.	13	83¹/₃	7	2	.778	24	16	101	3.67	0
2006 Colorado	N.L.	32	212²/₃	9	15	.375	92	55	242	4.23	0
2007 Colorado Springs	P.C.	1	1	0	1	.000	0	1	4	27.00	0
2007 Colorado c	N.L.	25	166	8	7	.533	61	44	178	4.12	0
2008 Colorado	N.L.	32	211¹/₃	16	9	.640	96	48	*236	3.96	0
Major League Totals	7 Yrs.	170	929²/₃	52	44	.542	370	272	1070	4.36	0
World Series Record											
2007 Colorado	N.L.	1	6	0	1	.000	2	0	6	4.50	0

a On disabled list from August 8 to November 3, 2004.
b On disabled list from March 25 to July 30, 2005.
c On disabled list from August 16 to October 10, 2007.

CORCORAN, ROY ELLIOT
Born, Baton Rouge, Louisiana, May 11, 1980.
Bats Right. Throws Right. Height, 5 feet, 10 inches. Weight, 170 pounds.

Year	Club	Lea	G	IP	W	L	Pct	SO	BB	H	ERA	SAVES
2001 Jupiter	Fla.St.	1	2	0	0	.000	0	2	0	0.00	0
2001 Expos	Gulf Coast	13	17¹/₃	2	0	1.000	21	2	12	1.56	2
2002 Clinton	Midwest	48	80	3	4	.429	106	24	82	4.16	11
2003 Brevard County	Fla.St.	28	33	5	3	.625	35	11	19	1.91	12
2003 Harrisburg	Eastern	14	23²/₃	1	1	.500	26	7	14	0.38	3
2003 Montreal	N.L.	5	7¹/₃	0	0	.000	2	3	7	1.23	0
2003 Edmonton	P.C.	2	2	0	0	.000	1	0	0	0.00	0
2004 Edmonton	P.C.	30	44¹/₃	5	1	.833	35	24	39	3.05	5
2004 Montreal	N.L.	5	5¹/₃	0	0	.000	4	5	7	6.75	0
2005 New Orleans	P.C.	52	68²/₃	4	4	.500	55	36	67	4.85	3
2006 Harrisburg	Eastern	21	26	0	2	.000	40	10	12	0.35	16
2006 Washington	N.L.	6	5²/₃	0	1	.000	6	4	12	11.12	0
2006 New Orleans a	P.C.	28	33²/₃	2	4	.333	37	25	24	2.41	11
2007 Albuquerque b	P.C.	53	61	4	4	.500	52	33	63	3.54	15
2007 Tacoma	P.C.	15	14¹/₃	0	0	.000	11	13	14	5.02	4
2008 Seattle	A.L.	50	72²/₃	6	2	.750	39	36	65	3.22	3
Major League Totals	4 Yrs.	66	91	6	3	.667	51	48	91	3.76	3

a Filed for free agency, October 6, 2006. Signed with Florida Marlins organization, December 1, 2006.
b Filed for free agency, October 29, 2007. Signed with Seattle Mariners organization, November 21, 2007.

CORDERO, CHAD PATRICK
Born, Upland, California, April 18, 1982.
Bats Right. Throws Right. Height, 6 feet. Weight, 225 pounds.

Year	Club	Lea	G	IP	W	L	Pct	SO	BB	H	ERA	SAVES
2003 Brevard County	Fla.St.	19	26¹/₃	1	1	.500	17	10	17	2.05	6
2003 Montreal	N.L.	12	11	1	0	1.000	12	3	4	1.64	1
2004 Montreal	N.L.	69	82²/₃	7	3	.700	83	43	68	2.94	14
2005 Washington	N.L.	74	74¹/₃	2	4	.333	61	17	55	1.82	*47
2006 Washington	N.L.	68	73¹/₃	7	4	.636	69	22	59	3.19	29
2007 Washington	N.L.	76	75	3	3	.500	62	29	75	3.36	37
2008 Potomac	Carolina	2	2	1	0	1.000	2	0	1	0.00	0
2008 Washington a-b	N.L.	6	4¹/₃	0	0	.000	5	3	6	2.08	0
Major League Totals	6 Yrs.	305	320²/₃	20	14	.588	292	117	267	2.78	128

a On disabled list from March 27 to April 13 and April 30 to September 29, 2008.
b Filed for free agency, October 30, 2008.

CORDERO, FRANCISCO JAVIER
Born, Santo Domingo, Dominican Republic, May 11, 1975.
Bats Right. Throws Right. Height, 6 feet, 2 inches. Weight, 235 pounds.

Year	Club	Lea	G	IP	W	L	Pct	SO	BB	H	ERA	SAVES
1994 Detroit	Dominican	12	60	4	3	.571	36	27	65	3.90	0
1995 Fayetteville	So.Atl.	4	20	0	3	.000	19	12	26	6.30	0

Year	Club	Lea	G	IP	W	L	Pct	SO	BB	H	ERA	SAVES
1995 Jamestown	N.Y.-Penn.	15	88	4	7	.364	54	37	96	5.22	0
1996 Fayettevlle	So.Atl.	2	7	0	0	.000	7	6	2	2.57	0
1996 Jamestown a	N.Y.-Penn.	2	11	0	0	.000	10	2	5	0.82	0
1997 W Michigan	Midwest	50	54¹/₃	6	1	.857	67	15	36	0.99	35
1998 Jacksnville	Southern	17	16²/₃	1	1	.500	18	9	19	4.86	8
1998 Lakeland b	Fla.St.	1	0	0	0	.000	0	0	1	0.00	0
1999 Jacksonville	Southern	47	52¹/₃	4	1	.800	58	22	35	1.38	27
1999 Detroit c	A.L.	20	19	2	2	.500	19	18	19	3.32	0
2000 Texas	A.L.	56	77¹/₃	1	2	.333	49	48	87	5.35	0
2000 Oklahoma	P.C.	3	4¹/₃	0	0	.000	5	3	7	4.15	1
2001 Oklahoma	P.C.	12	15¹/₃	0	1	.000	20	3	8	0.59	6
2001 Texas d	A.L.	3	2¹/₃	0	1	.000	1	2	3	3.86	0
2002 Oklahoma	P.C.	11	12¹/₃	0	2	.000	21	7	15	5.84	2
2002 Texas e	A.L.	39	45¹/₃	2	0	1.000	41	13	33	1.79	10
2003 Texas	A.L.	73	82²/₃	5	8	.385	90	38	70	2.94	15
2004 Texas	A.L.	67	71²/₃	3	4	.429	79	32	60	2.13	49
2005 Texas	A.L.	69	69	3	1	.750	79	30	61	3.39	37
2006 Texas	A.L.	49	48²/₃	7	4	.636	54	16	49	4.81	6
2006 Milwaukee f	N.L.	28	26²/₃	3	1	.750	30	16	20	1.69	16
2007 Milwaukee g	N.L.	66	63¹/₃	0	4	.000	86	18	52	2.98	44
2008 Cincinnati	N.L.	72	70¹/₃	5	4	.556	78	38	61	3.33	34
Major League Totals	10 Yrs.	542	576¹/₃	31	31	.500	606	269	515	3.29	211

a On disabled list from June 28 to September 30, 1996.
b On disabled list from May 22 to June 18 and June 26 to September 30, 1998.
c Traded to Texas Rangers with pitcher Justin Thompson, pitcher Alan Webb, outfielder Gabe Kapler, catcher Bill Haselman and infielder Frank Catalanotto for outfielder Juan Gonzalez, pitcher Danny Patterson and catcher Greg Zaun, November 2, 1999.
d On disabled list from March 23 to June 22 and June 26 to October 11, 2001.
e On disabled list from June 25 to July 27, 2002.
f Traded to Milwaukee Brewers with outfielder Kevin Mench, outfielder Laynce Nix and pitcher Julian Cordero for outfielder Carlos Lee and outfielder Nelson Cruz, July 28, 2006.
g Filed for free agency, October 29, 2007. Signed with Cincinnati Reds, November 28, 2007.

COREY, BRYAN SCOTT
Born, Thousand Oaks, California, October 21, 1973.
Bats Right. Throws Right. Height, 6 feet, 1 inch. Weight, 175 pounds.

Year	Club	Lea	G	IP	W	L	Pct	SO	BB	H	ERA	SAVES
1995 Jamestown	N.Y.-Penn.	29	28	2	2	.500	41	12	21	3.86	10
1996 Fayetteville	So.Atl.	60	82	6	4	.600	101	17	50	1.21	34
1997 Jacksnville a	Southern	52	68	3	8	.273	37	21	74	4.76	9
1998 Arizona	N.L.	3	4	0	0	.000	1	2	6	9.00	0
1998 Tucson b	P.C.	39	87²/₃	4	6	.400	50	24	116	5.44	2
1999 Toledo c	Int.	48	69¹/₃	5	2	.714	36	34	63	2.86	2
2000 Sacramento d	P.C.	47	85	8	3	.727	55	29	88	4.24	4
2001 Portland e	P.C.	47	106	8	7	.533	66	31	124	4.67	6
2002 Las Vegas	P.C.	37	53²/₃	5	4	.556	33	18	79	4.36	1
2002 Los Angeles f-g	N.L.	1	1	0	0	.000	0	0	0	0.00	0
2003 Las Vegas h	P.C.	60	91	4	5	.444	46	29	94	2.97	3
2004 Iowa i	P.C.	10	13¹/₃	2	0	1.000	13	5	10	3.38	5
2005 Albuquerque	P.C.	44	60	3	6	.333	44	20	78	7.65	0
2006 Frisco	Texas	13	17¹/₃	1	0	1.000	19	6	16	2.08	7
2006 Oklahoma	P.C.	12	15	0	0	.000	16	2	9	0.60	8
2006 Pawtucket	Int.	3	5	0	0	.000	4	2	7	7.20	0
2006 Texas-Boston j-k-l-m	A.L.	32	39	2	1	.667	28	15	35	3.69	0
2007 Pawtucket	Int.	58	68¹/₃	6	8	.429	67	20	57	3.69	3
2007 Boston	A.L.	9	9¹/₃	1	0	1.000	6	4	6	1.93	0
2008 Portland	P.C.	5	6²/₃	0	0	.000	4	1	9	1.35	0
2008 Pawtucket	Int.	5	5	0	0	.000	5	1	4	0.00	1
2008 Boston	A.L.	7	6	0	0	.000	4	3	11	10.50	0
2008 San Diego n-o-p-q	N.L.	39	39	1	3	.250	18	9	42	6.23	0
Major League Totals	5 Yrs.	91	98¹/₃	4	4	.500	57	33	100	5.13	0

a Selected in expansion draft by Arizona Diamondbacks from Detroit Tigers, November 18, 1997.
b Claimed on waivers by Detroit Tigers, December 4, 1998.
c Filed for free agency, October 15, 1999. Signed with Oakland Athletics organization, December 3, 1999.
d Filed for free agency, October 15, 2000. Signed with San Diego Padres organization, November 20, 2000.
e Filed for free agency, October 15, 2001. Signed with Los Angeles Dodgers organization, December 27, 2001.
f On disabled list from May 29 to June 13, 2002.
g Filed for free agency, October 8, 2002, re-signed with Los Angeles Dodgers organization, November 26, 2002.
h Filed for free agency, October 15, 2003. Signed with Chicago Cubs organization, November 12, 2003.

i Released by Chicago Cubs, May 5, 2004. Signed with Florida Marlins organization, November 17, 2004.
j Filed for free agency, October 15, 2005. Signed with Chicago Cubs organization, February 22, 2006.
k Released by Chicago Cubs, March 13, 2006. Signed with Texas Rangers organization, March 15, 2006.
l Traded to Boston Red Sox for pitcher Luis Mendoza, July 30, 2006.
m Filed for free agency, August 9, 2006, re-signed with Boston Red Sox organization, October 13, 2006.
n Filed for free agency, April 17, 2008, re-signed with Boston Red Sox organization, April 22, 2008.
o Traded to San Diego Padres for player to be named later, May 11, 2008.
p On disabled list from August 10 to August 27, 2008.
q Filed for free agency, October 1, 2008.

CORMIER, LANCE ROBERT
Born, Lafayette, Louisiana, August 19, 1980.
Bats Right. Throws Right. Height, 6 feet, 1 inch. Weight, 200 pounds.

Year Club	Lea	G	IP	W	L	Pct	SO	BB	H	ERA	SAVES
2002 South Bend	Midwest	11	27²/₃	3	0	1.000	17	2	29	2.93	1
2002 Yakima	Northwest	1	1	0	0	.000	3	0	4	27.00	0
2003 Lancaster	Calif.	15	94¹/₃	6	5	.545	59	16	102	3.82	0
2003 Tucson	P.C.	5	27²/₃	1	1	.500	11	5	26	2.60	0
2003 El Paso	Texas	9	41¹/₃	2	3	.400	26	22	59	6.10	0
2004 El Paso	Texas	10	63	2	3	.400	58	17	66	2.29	0
2004 Tucson	P.C.	8	50¹/₃	3	3	.500	37	17	50	2.68	0
2004 Arizona	N.L.	17	45¹/₃	1	4	.200	24	25	62	8.14	0
2005 Tucson	P.C.	1	3²/₃	0	1	.000	5	5	6	14.73	0
2005 Arizona a	N.L.	67	79¹/₃	7	3	.700	63	43	86	5.11	0
2006 Rome	So.Atl.	1	1	0	0	.000	2	0	0	0.00	0
2006 Richmond	Int.	9	54²/₃	4	3	.571	27	14	65	3.95	0
2006 Atlanta b	N.L.	29	73²/₃	4	5	.444	43	39	90	4.89	0
2007 Rome	So.Atl.	1	2	0	0	.000	4	0	5	4.50	0
2007 Mississippi	Southern	2	8	1	1	.500	6	0	8	4.50	0
2007 Richmond	Int.	10	52	4	2	.667	31	15	56	3.46	0
2007 Atlanta c	N.L.	10	45²/₃	2	6	.250	27	22	56	7.09	0
2008 Norfolk	Int.	9	18²/₃	1	1	.500	12	5	12	0.96	0
2008 Baltimore d-e	A.L.	45	71²/₃	3	3	.500	46	34	78	4.02	1
Major League Totals ...... 5 Yrs.		168	315²/₃	17	21	.447	203	163	372	5.53	1

a Traded to Atlanta Braves with pitcher Oscar Villarreal for catcher Johnny Estrada, December 7, 2005.
b On disabled list from May 3 to May 18, 2006.
c On disabled list from March 31 to June 3 and June 9 to June 30, 2007.
d Released by Atlanta Braves, December 7, 2007. Signed with Baltimore Orioles organization, January 22, 2008.
e Not offered contract, December 13, 2008. Signed with Tampa Bay Rays, January 16, 2009.

CORPAS, MANUEL (MANNY)
Born, Panama City, Panama, December 3, 1982.
Bats Right. Throws Right. Height, 6 feet, 3 inches. Weight, 170 pounds.

Year Club	Lea	G	IP	W	L	Pct	SO	BB	H	ERA	SAVES
2002 Casper	Pioneer	29	33	2	4	.333	42	18	37	5.73	2
2003 Tri-Cities	Northwest	15	84	5	6	.455	47	22	98	5.79	0
2004 Asheville	So.Atl.	43	44¹/₃	2	2	.500	52	13	48	3.05	3
2005 Modesto	Calif.	47	69	3	2	.600	52	14	83	3.78	2
2006 Tulsa	Texas	34	36²/₃	2	1	.667	35	4	22	0.98	19
2006 Colorado Springs	P.C.	8	8²/₃	0	0	.000	7	2	5	1.04	0
2006 Colorado	N.L.	35	32¹/₃	1	2	.333	27	8	36	3.62	0
2007 Colorado	N.L.	78	78	4	2	.667	58	20	63	2.08	19
2008 Colorado	N.L.	76	79²/₃	3	4	.429	50	23	93	4.52	4
Major League Totals .... 3 Yrs.		189	190	8	8	.500	135	51	192	3.36	23
Division Series											
2007 Colorado	N.L.	3	3¹/₃	0	0	.000	3	0	2	0.00	3
Championship Series											
2007 Colorado	N.L.	4	5¹/₃	1	0	1.000	3	0	3	1.69	2
World Series Record											
2007 Colorado	N.L.	2	1²/₃	0	0	.000	1	0	1	0.00	0

CORREIA, KEVIN JOHN
Born, San Diego, California, August 24, 1980.
Bats Right. Throws Right. Height, 6 feet, 3 inches. Weight, 200 pounds.

Year Club	Lea	G	IP	W	L	Pct	SO	BB	H	ERA	SAVES
2002 Salem-Keizer	Northwest	10	37²/₃	2	2	.500	31	14	37	4.54	0
2003 Norwich	Eastern	16	86¹/₃	6	6	.500	73	30	80	3.65	0

Year Club	Lea	G	IP	W	L	Pct	SO	BB	H	ERA	SAVES
2003 San Francisco	N.L.	10	39⅓	3	1	.750	28	18	41	3.66	0
2003 Fresno	P.C.	3	19	1	0	1.000	23	2	16	2.84	0
2004 Fresno	P.C.	29	105⅓	3	7	.300	70	35	118	4.53	0
2004 San Francisco	N.L.	12	19	0	1	.000	14	10	25	8.05	0
2005 San Jose	California	1	7	0	1	.000	7	5	5	2.57	0
2005 Fresno	P.C.	31	46	3	2	.600	35	23	50	6.07	7
2005 San Francisco	N.L.	16	58⅓	2	5	.286	44	31	61	4.63	0
2006 San Francisco	N.L.	48	69⅔	2	0	1.000	57	22	64	3.49	0
2007 San Francisco	N.L.	59	101⅔	4	7	.364	80	40	94	3.45	0
2008 San Jose	Calif.	1	3⅓	0	0	.000	1	1	1	0.00	0
2008 Fresno	P.C.	2	12	1	0	1.000	15	0	8	1.50	0
2008 San Francisco a-b	N.L.	25	110	3	8	.273	66	47	141	6.05	0
Major League Totals ....6 Yrs.		170	398	14	22	.389	289	168	426	4.59	0

a On disabled list from April 27 to June 15, 2008.

b Filed for free agency, October 14, 2008. Signed with San Diego Padres organization, December 24, 2008.

COTTS, NEAL JAMES

Born, Belleville, Illinois, March 25, 1980.
Bats Left. Throws Left. Height, 6 feet, 2 inches. Weight, 200 pounds.

Year Club	Lea	G	IP	W	L	Pct	SO	BB	H	ERA	SAVES
2001 Visalia	Calif.	7	31	3	2	.600	34	15	27	2.32	0
2001 Vancouver a	Northwest	9	35	1	0	1.000	44	13	28	3.09	0
2002 Modesto	Calif.	28	137⅔	12	6	.667	178	87	123	4.12	0
2003 Birmingham	Southern	21	108⅓	9	7	.563	133	56	67	2.16	0
2003 Chicago	A.L.	4	13⅓	1	1	.500	10	17	15	8.10	0
2004 Chicago	A.L.	56	65⅓	4	4	.500	58	30	61	5.65	0
2005 Chicago	A.L.	69	60⅓	4	0	1.000	58	29	38	1.94	0
2006 Chicago b	A.L.	70	54	1	2	.333	43	24	64	5.17	1
2007 Chicago	N.L.	16	16⅔	0	1	.000	14	9	15	4.86	0
2007 Iowa	P.C.	24	50⅓	2	2	.500	48	30	43	4.83	0
2008 Iowa	P.C.	19	27	2	0	1.000	33	10	23	2.00	3
2008 Chicago	N.L.	50	35⅔	0	2	.000	43	13	38	4.29	0
Major League Totals ....6 Yrs.		265	245⅓	10	10	.500	226	122	231	4.51	1
Division Series											
2005 Chicago	A.L.	1	0⅓	0	0	.000	0	0	0	0.00	0
2008 Chicago	N.L.	2	1⅔	0	0	.000	3	1	1	0.00	0
Division Series Totals		3	2	0	0	.000	3	1	1	0.00	0
Championship Series											
2005 Chicago	A.L.	1	0⅔	0	0	.000	0	0	0	0.00	0
World Series Record											
2005 Chicago	A.L.	4	1⅓	1	0	1.000	2	1	1	0.00	0

a Sent by Oakland Athletics to Chicago White Sox with outfielder Daylan Holt as two players to be named later in Keith Foulke trade of December 3, 2002.

b Traded to Chicago Cubs for pitcher David Aardsma and pitcher Carlos Vazquez, November 16, 2006.

CRAIN, JESSE ALAN

Born, Toronto, Ontario, Canada, July 5, 1981.
Bats Right. Throws Right. Height, 6 feet, 1 inch. Weight, 205 pounds.

Year Club	Lea	G	IP	W	L	Pct	SO	BB	H	ERA	SAVES
2002 Elizabethton	Appal.	9	15⅔	2	1	.667	18	7	4	0.57	2
2002 Quad Cities	Midwest	9	12	1	1	.500	11	4	6	1.50	1
2003 New Britain	Eastern	22	39	1	1	.500	56	10	13	0.69	9
2003 Fort Myers	Fla.St.	10	19	2	1	.667	25	5	10	2.84	0
2003 Rochester	Int.	23	26	3	1	.750	33	10	24	3.12	10
2004 Rochester	Int.	41	50⅔	3	2	.600	64	17	38	2.49	19
2004 Minnesota	A.L.	22	27	3	0	1.000	14	12	17	2.00	0
2005 Minnesota	A.L.	75	79⅔	12	5	.706	25	29	61	2.71	0
2006 Minnesota	A.L.	68	76⅔	4	5	.444	60	18	79	3.52	1
2007 Minnesota a	A.L.	18	16⅓	1	2	.333	10	4	19	5.51	0
2008 Minnesota	A.L.	66	62⅔	5	4	.556	50	24	62	3.59	0
Major League Totals ....5 Yrs.		249	262⅓	25	16	.610	159	87	238	3.26	2
Division Series											
2004 Minnesota	A.L.	1	0⅓	0	0	.000	0	0	1	0.00	0
2006 Minnesota	A.L.	2	1	0	0	.000	1	1	3	9.00	0
Division Series Totals		3	1⅓	0	0	.000	1	1	4	6.75	0

a On disabled list from May 16 to October 10, 2007.

CRUZ, JUAN CARLOS
Born, Bonao, Dominican Republic, October 15, 1978.
Bats Right. Throws Right. Height, 6 feet, 2 inches. Weight, 155 pounds.

Year	Club	Lea	G	IP	W	L	Pct	SO	BB	H	ERA	SAVES
1998	Cubs	Arizona	12	41⅓	2	4	.333	36	14	61	6.10	0
1999	Eugene	Northwest	15	80⅓	5	6	.455	65	33	97	5.94	0
2000	Daytona	Fla.St.	8	44⅓	3	0	1.000	54	18	30	3.25	0
2000	Lansing	Midwest	17	96	5	5	.500	106	60	75	3.28	0
2001	West Tenn	Southern	23	121⅓	9	6	.600	137	60	107	4.01	0
2001	Chicago	N.L.	8	44⅔	3	1	.750	39	17	40	3.22	1
2002	Chicago a	N.L.	45	97⅓	3	11	.214	81	59	84	3.98	0
2003	Chicago	N.L.	25	61	2	7	.222	65	28	66	6.05	0
2003	Iowa	P.C.	9	50⅔	4	0	1.000	47	11	37	1.95	0
2004	Atlanta b-c	N.L.	50	72	6	2	.750	70	30	59	2.75	0
2005	Sacramento	P.C.	13	75	5	1	.833	90	28	51	2.40	0
2005	Oakland	A.L.	28	32⅔	0	3	.000	34	22	38	7.44	0
2006	Tucson	P.C.	1	3⅓	0	0	.000	4	1	4	2.70	0
2006	Arizona d-e	N.L.	31	94⅔	5	6	.455	88	47	80	4.18	0
2007	Tucson	P.C.	1	2	0	0	.000	5	0	0	0.00	0
2007	Arizona f	N.L.	53	61	6	1	.857	87	32	45	3.10	0
2008	Tucson	P.C.	2	3	0	0	.000	4	0	3	3.00	0
2008	Arizona g-h	N.L.	57	51⅔	4	0	1.000	71	31	34	2.61	0
Major League Totals		8 Yrs.	297	515	29	31	.483	535	266	446	4.00	1
Division Series												
2003	Chicago	N.L.	1	1	0	0	.000	2	1	0	0.00	0
2004	Atlanta	N.L.	3	3⅔	0	0	.000	4	4	6	9.82	0
2007	Arizona	N.L.	1	0⅓	0	0	.000	1	0	1	0.00	0
Division Series Totals			5	5	0	0	.000	7	5	7	7.20	0
Championship Series												
2007	Arizona	N.L.	3	4	0	0	.000	8	3	0	0.00	0

a On disabled list from August 10 to August 25, 2002.
b Traded to Atlanta Braves with pitcher Steve Smyth for pitcher Andy Pratt and pitcher Richard Lewis, March 25, 2004.
c Traded to Oakland Athletics with pitcher Dan Meyer and outfielder Charles Thomas for pitcher Tim Hudson, December 16, 2004.
d Traded to Arizona Diamondbacks for pitcher Brad Halsey, March 26, 2006.
e On disabled list from June 4 to July 3, 2006.
f On disabled list from April 21 to May 11, 2007.
g On disabled list from July 6 to August 1, 2008.
h Filed for free agency, October 30, 2008.

CUETO (ORTIZ), JOHNNY
Born, San Pedro de Macoris, Dominican Republic, February 15, 1985.
Bats Right. Throws Right. Height, 5 feet, 10 inches. Weight, 185 pounds.

Year	Club	Lea	G	IP	W	L	Pct	SO	BB	H	ERA	SAVES
2005	Sarasota	Fla.St.	2	6	0	1	.000	6	2	5	3.00	0
2005	Reds	Gulf Coast	13	43	2	2	.500	38	8	49	5.02	1
2006	Sarasota	Fla.St.	12	61⅔	7	2	.778	61	23	48	3.50	0
2006	Dayton	Midwest	14	76⅓	8	1	.889	82	15	52	2.59	0
2007	Sarasota	Fla.St.	14	78⅓	4	5	.444	72	21	72	3.33	0
2007	Louisville	Int.	4	22	2	1	.667	21	2	22	2.05	0
2007	Chattanooga	Southern	10	61	6	3	.667	77	11	52	3.10	0
2008	Cincinnati	N.L.	31	174	9	14	.391	158	68	178	4.81	0

DANKS, JOHN WILLIAM
Born, Austin, Texas, April 15, 1985.
Bats Left. Throws Left. Height, 6 feet, 1 inch. Weight, 200 pounds.

Year	Club	Lea	G	IP	W	L	Pct	SO	BB	H	ERA	SAVES
2003	Rangers	Arizona	5	13	1	0	1.000	22	4	6	0.69	0
2003	Spokane	Northwest	5	12⅔	0	2	.000	13	7	12	8.53	0
2004	Stockton	Calif.	13	55	1	4	.200	48	26	62	5.24	0
2004	Clinton	Midwest	14	49⅔	3	2	.600	64	14	38	2.17	0
2005	Bakersfield	Calif.	10	57⅔	3	3	.500	53	16	50	2.50	0
2005	Frisco	Texas	18	98⅓	4	10	.286	85	34	117	5.49	0
2006	Oklahoma	P.C.	14	70⅔	4	5	.444	72	34	67	4.15	0
2006	Frisco a	Texas	13	69⅓	5	4	.556	82	22	74	4.15	0
2007	Chicago	A.L.	26	139	6	13	.316	109	54	160	5.50	0

Year Club	Lea	G	IP	W	L	Pct	SO	BB	H	ERA	SAVES
2008 Chicago .... A.L.	33	195	12	9	.571	159	57	182	3.32	0
Major League Totals .... 2 Yrs.	59	334	18	22	.450	268	111	342	4.23	0
Division Series										
2008 Chicago .... A.L.	1	6²/₃	1	0	1.000	7	3	7	4.05	0

a Traded to Chicago White Sox by Texas Rangers with pitcher Nick Masset and pitcher Jacob Rasner for pitcher Brandon McCarthy and outfielder David Paisano, December 23, 2006.

DAVIES, HIRAM KYLE (KYLE)
Born, Decatur, Georgia, September 9, 1983.
Bats Right. Throws Right. Height, 6 feet, 2 inches. Weight, 205 pounds.

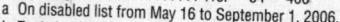

Year Club	Lea	G	IP	W	L	Pct	SO	BB	H	ERA	SAVES
2001 Braves .... Gulf Coast	12	56	4	2	.667	53	8	47	2.25	0
2001 Macon .... So.Atl.	1	5²/₃	1	0	1.000	7	1	2	0.00	0
2002 Danville .... Appal.	14	69¹/₃	5	3	.625	62	23	73	3.50	0
2002 Macon .... So.Atl.	2	6	0	1	.000	4	4	6	6.00	0
2003 Rome.............. So.Atl.	27	146¹/₃	8	8	.500	148	53	128	2.89	0
2004 Myrtle Beach .... Carolina	14	75¹/₃	9	2	.818	95	32	55	2.63	0
2004 Richmond .... Int.	1	5	0	1	.000	5	3	5	9.00	0
2004 Greenville........ Southern	11	62	4	0	1.000	73	22	40	2.32	0
2005 Richmond .... Int.	13	73¹/₃	5	2	.714	62	34	66	3.44	0
2005 Atlanta .... N.L.	21	87²/₃	7	6	.538	62	49	98	4.93	0
2006 Mississippi........ Southern	4	14	1	1	.500	9	5	11	4.50	0
2006 Richmond .... Int.	2	15	2	0	1.000	8	3	7	0.60	0
2006 Atlanta a.............. N.L.	14	63¹/₃	3	7	.300	51	33	90	8.38	0
2007 Richmond .... Int.	2	10	0	1	.000	12	6	11	4.50	0
2007 Atlanta .... N.L.	17	86	4	8	.333	59	44	92	5.76	0
2007 Kansas City b .... A.L.	11	50	3	7	.300	40	26	63	6.66	0
2008 Omaha................ P.C.	11	57²/₃	6	2	.750	38	21	47	2.03	0
2008 Kansas City .... A.L.	21	113	9	7	.563	71	43	121	4.06	0
Major League Totals .... 4 Yrs.	84	400	26	35	.426	283	195	464	5.63	0

a On disabled list from May 16 to September 1, 2006.
b Traded to Kansas City Royals for pitcher Octavio Dotel, July 31, 2007.

DAVIS, DOUGLAS (DOUG)
Born, Sacramento, California, September 21, 1975.
Bats Right. Throws Left. Height, 6 feet, 4 inches. Weight, 210 pounds.

Year Club	Lea	G	IP	W	L	Pct	SO	BB	H	ERA	SAVES
1996 Rangers .... Gulf Coast	8	42²/₃	3	1	.750	49	26	28	1.90	0
1997 Rangers .... Gulf Coast	4	21	3	1	.750	27	15	14	1.71	0
1997 Charlotte .... Fla.St.	9	49¹/₃	5	3	.625	52	33	29	3.10	0
1998 Charlotte .... Fla.St.	27	155¹/₃	11	7	.611	173	74	129	3.24	0
1999 Oklahoma............. P.C.	13	78	7	0	1.000	74	31	77	3.00	0
1999 Tulsa .... Texas	12	74¹/₃	4	4	.500	79	25	65	2.42	0
1999 Texas .... A.L.	2	2²/₃	0	0	.000	3	0	12	33.75	0
2000 Oklahoma............. P.C.	12	69²/₃	8	3	.727	53	34	62	2.84	0
2000 Texas .... A.L.	30	98²/₃	7	6	.538	66	58	109	5.38	0
2001 Oklahoma............. P.C.	2	15²/₃	2	0	1.000	14	4	10	2.87	0
2001 Texas .... A.L.	30	186	11	10	.524	115	69	220	4.45	0
2002 Texas .... A.L.	10	59²/₃	3	5	.375	28	22	67	4.98	0
2002 Oklahoma............. P.C.	9	61¹/₃	4	3	.571	48	11	70	4.99	0
2003 Oklahoma............. P.C.	4	27²/₃	3	0	1.000	18	1	29	3.25	0
2003 Texas-Toronto a ...... A.L.	13	57	4	6	.400	27	30	74	5.37	0
2003 Indianapolis .... Int.	5	34²/₃	1	2	.333	19	10	33	4.15	0
2003 Huntsville .... Southern	1	6	1	0	1.000	6	3	5	3.00	0
2003 Milwaukee b........... N.L.	8	52¹/₃	3	2	.600	35	21	49	2.58	0
2004 Milwaukee .... N.L.	34	207¹/₃	12	12	.500	166	79	192	3.39	0
2005 Milwaukee .... N.L.	35	222²/₃	11	11	.500	208	93	190	3.84	0
2006 Milwaukee c........... N.L.	34	203¹/₃	11	11	.500	159	102	206	4.91	0
2007 Arizona............... N.L.	33	192²/₃	13	12	.520	144	95	211	4.25	0
2008 Tucson .... P.C.	2	9²/₃	1	1	.500	6	3	10	3.72	0
2008 Arizona d............. N.L.	26	146	6	8	.429	112	64	160	4.32	0
Major League Totals .... 10 Yrs.	255	1428¹/₃	81	83	.494	1063	633	1496	4.34	0
Division Series										
2007 Arizona............... N.L.	1	5²/₃	1	0	1.000	8	4	5	6.35	0
Championship Series										
2007 Arizona............... N.L.	1	5	0	0	.000	5	4	5	1.80	0

a Claimed on waivers by Toronto Blue Jays, April 30, 2003.
b Filed for free agency, July 12, 2003. Signed with Milwaukee Brewers organization, July 13, 2003.

c Traded to Arizona Diamondbacks with pitcher Dana Eveland and outfielder David Krynzel for pitcher Greg Aquino, catcher Johnny Estrada and pitcher Claudio Vargas, November 25, 2006.
d On disabled list from April 9 to May 22, 2008.

DE LA ROSA, JORGE ALBERTO

Born, Monterrey, Nuevo Leon, Mexico, April 5, 1981.
Bats Left. Throws Left. Height, 6 feet, 1 inch. Weight, 210 pounds.

Year	Club	Lea	G	IP	W	L	Pct	SO	BB	H	ERA	SAVES
1998 Arizona	Dominican	13	14	1	0	1.000	21	8	8	4.50	1
1999 Diamondbacks	Arizona	8	14	0	0	.000	17	3	12	3.21	2
1999 High Desert	California	2	3	0	0	.000	3	2	1	0.00	0
1999 Missoula	Pioneer	13	14²/₃	0	1	.000	14	9	22	7.98	2
2000 Monterrey a	Mexican	37	39	3	2	.600	50	32	38	6.28	1
2001 Trenton	Eastern	29	37	1	3	.250	27	20	56	5.84	0
2001 Sarasota b	Fla.St.	12	29²/₃	0	1	.000	27	12	13	1.21	2
2002 Trenton	Eastern	4	18	1	2	.333	15	9	17	5.50	0
2002 Sarasota	Fla.St.	23	120²/₃	7	7	.500	95	52	105	3.65	0
2003 Portland	Eastern	22	99²/₃	6	3	.667	102	36	87	2.80	1
2003 Pawtucket c-d	Int.	5	24	1	2	.333	17	12	27	3.75	0
2004 Indianapolis	Int.	20	85²/₃	5	6	.455	86	36	80	4.52	0
2004 Milwaukee	N.L.	5	22²/₃	0	3	.000	5	14	29	6.35	0
2005 Milwaukee	N.L.	38	42¹/₃	2	2	.500	42	38	48	4.46	0
2006 Huntsville	Southern	6	30	3	1	.750	23	3	31	2.40	0
2006 Milwaukee	N.L.	18	30¹/₃	2	2	.500	31	22	32	8.60	0
2006 Kansas City e-f	A.L.	10	48²/₃	3	4	.429	36	32	49	5.18	0
2007 Wichita	Texas	3	5²/₃	0	1	.000	7	4	10	11.12	0
2007 Kansas City g	A.L.	26	130	8	12	.400	82	53	160	5.82	0
2008 Omaha	P.C.	4	22	3	0	1.000	23	7	18	1.64	0
2008 Colorado h	N.L.	28	130	10	8	.556	128	62	128	4.92	0
Major League Totals	5 Yrs.	125	404	25	31	.446	324	221	446	5.55	0

a Sold by Arizona Diamondbacks to Monterrey, April 2, 2000.
b Sold to Boston Red Sox, February 22, 2001.
c Traded by Boston Red Sox to Arizona Diamondbacks with pitcher Casey Fossum, pitcher Brandon Lyon and outfielder Michael Goss for pitcher Curt Schilling, November 28, 2003.
d Traded to Milwaukee Brewers with infielder Junior Spivey, infielder Craig Counsell, infielder Lyle Overbay, catcher Chad Moeller and pitcher Chris Capuano for infielder Richie Sexson, pitcher Shane Nance and player to be named later, December 1, 2003. Arizona Diamondbacks received outfielder Noochie Varner to complete trade, December 15, 2003.
e Traded to Kansas City Royals for infielder Tony Graffanino, July 25, 2006.
f On disabled list from June 10 to July 25, 2006.
g On disabled list from August 1 to September 11, 2007.
h Sent to Colorado Rockies as player to be named later for pitcher Ramon Ramirez, April 30, 2008.

DELCARMEN, MANUEL (MANNY)

Born, Boston, Massachusetts, February 16, 1982.
Bats Right. Throws Right. Height, 6 feet, 2 inches. Weight, 205 pounds.

Year	Club	Lea	G	IP	W	L	Pct	SO	BB	H	ERA	SAVES
2001 Red Sox	Gulf Coast	11	46	4	2	.667	62	19	35	2.54	1
2002 Augusta	So.Atl.	26	136	7	8	.467	136	56	124	4.10	0
2003 Sarasota	Fla.St.	4	23	1	1	.500	16	7	16	3.13	0
2004 Sarasota	Fla.St.	19	73	3	6	.333	76	20	84	4.68	0
2005 Portland	Eastern	31	39	4	4	.500	49	20	31	3.23	3
2005 Pawtucket	Int.	15	21	3	1	.750	23	13	17	1.29	2
2005 Boston	A.L.	10	9	0	0	.000	9	7	8	3.00	0
2006 Pawtucket	Int.	10	17	0	1	.000	19	6	9	2.12	0
2006 Boston	A.L.	50	53¹/₃	2	0	1.000	45	17	68	5.06	0
2007 Boston	A.L.	44	44	0	0	.000	41	17	28	2.05	1
2008 Boston	A.L.	73	74¹/₃	1	2	.333	72	28	55	3.27	2
Major League Totals	4 Yrs.	177	180²/₃	3	2	.600	167	69	159	3.49	3
Division Series												
2007 Boston	A.L.	1	1¹/₃	0	0	.000	1	0	0	0.00	0
2008 Boston	A.L.	2	2¹/₃	1	0	1.000	1	0	1	0.00	0
Division Series Totals		3	3²/₃	1	0	1.000	2	0	1	0.00	0
Championship Series												
2007 Boston	A.L.	3	1²/₃	0	0	.000	3	2	4	16.20	0
2008 Boston	A.L.	3	2	0	0	.000	2	5	3	31.50	0
Championship Series Totals		6	3²/₃	0	0	.000	5	7	7	24.55	0
World Series Record												
2007 Boston	A.L.	2	1¹/₃	0	0	.000	1	1	3	6.75	0

DEMPSTER, RYAN SCOTT

Born, Sechelt, British Columbia, Canada, May 3, 1977.
Bats Right. Throws Right. Height, 6 feet, 2 inches. Weight, 215 pounds.

Year Club	Lea	G	IP	W	L	Pct	SO	BB	H	ERA	SAVES
1995 Rangers	Gulf Coast	8	34⅓	3	1	.750	37	17	34	2.36	0
1995 Hudson Val.	N.Y.-Penn.	1	5⅔	1	0	1.000	6	1	7	3.18	0
1996 Chston-SC	So.Atl.	23	144⅓	7	11	.389	141	58	120	3.30	0
1996 Kane County a	Midwest	4	26⅓	2	1	.667	16	18	18	2.73	0
1997 Brevard Cty	Fla.St.	28	165⅓	10	9	.526	131	46	190	4.90	0
1998 Portland	Eastern	7	44⅔	4	3	.571	33	15	34	3.22	0
1998 Florida	N.L.	14	54⅔	1	5	.167	35	38	72	7.08	0
1998 Charlotte	Int.	5	33	3	1	.750	24	12	33	3.27	0
1999 Calgary	P.C.	5	30⅔	1	1	.500	29	10	30	4.99	0
1999 Florida	N.L.	25	147	7	8	.467	126	93	146	4.71	0
2000 Florida	N.L.	33	226⅓	14	10	.583	209	97	210	3.66	0
2001 Florida	N.L.	34	211⅓	15	12	.556	171	112	218	4.94	0
2002 Florida-Cincinnati b	N.L.	33	209	10	13	.435	153	93	228	5.38	0
2003 Cincinnati	N.L.	22	115⅔	3	7	.300	84	70	134	6.54	0
2003 Louisville c	Int.	2	13⅔	1	1	.500	9	3	13	3.29	0
2004 Lansing	Midwest	5	18⅓	0	0	.000	21	2	20	1.96	0
2004 Iowa	P.C.	6	21	1	1	.500	20	10	19	3.86	0
2004 Chicago d-e	N.L.	23	20⅔	1	1	.500	18	13	16	3.92	2
2005 Chicago	N.L.	63	92	5	3	.625	89	49	83	3.13	33
2006 Chicago	N.L.	74	75	1	9	.100	67	36	77	4.80	24
2007 Iowa	P.C.	2	2	0	0	.000	4	1	1	0.00	0
2007 Chicago f	N.L.	66	66⅔	2	7	.222	55	30	59	4.72	28
2008 Chicago g	N.L.	33	206⅔	17	6	.739	187	76	174	2.96	0
Major League Totals	11 Yrs.	420	1425	76	81	.484	1194	707	1417	4.55	87
Division Series											
2007 Chicago	N.L.	1	1	0	0	.000	2	0	0	0.00	0
2008 Chicago	N.L.	1	4⅔	0	1	.000	2	7	4	7.71	0
Division Series Totals		2	5⅔	0	1	.000	4	7	4	6.35	0

a Traded by Texas Rangers to Florida Marlins with player to be named later for pitcher John Burkett, August 8, 1996. Florida Marlins received pitcher Rick Helling to complete trade, September 3, 1996.
b Traded to Cincinnati Reds for outfielder Juan Encarnacion, infielder Wilton Guerrero and pitcher Ryan Snare, July 11, 2002.
c On disabled list from May 23 to June 7 and July 29 to November 3, 2003.
d Waived by Cincinnati Reds, November 4, 2003. Signed with Chicago Cubs, January 21, 2004.
e On disabled list from March 26 to August 1, 2004.
f On disabled list from June 23 to July 20, 2007.
g Filed for free agency, October 30, 2008, re-signed with Chicago Cubs, November 18, 2008.

DEVINE, JOSEPH NEAL (JOEY)

Born, Junction City, Kansas, September 19, 1983.
Bats Right. Throws Right. Height, 6 feet. Weight, 205 pounds.

Year Club	Lea	G	IP	W	L	Pct	SO	BB	H	ERA	SAVES
2005 Myrtle Beach	Carolina	4	5	0	0	.000	7	3	0	0.00	1
2005 Mississippi	Southern	18	20	1	1	.500	28	12	19	2.70	5
2005 Richmond	Int.	1	1	0	0	.000	1	1	3	18.00	0
2005 Atlanta	N.L.	5	5	0	1	.000	3	5	6	12.60	0
2006 Richmond	Int.	1	0	0	0	.000	0	1	1	0.00	0
2006 Myrtle Beach	Carolina	13	18⅓	1	3	.250	28	11	13	5.89	0
2006 Mississippi	Southern	6	11	2	0	1.000	20	4	2	0.82	0
2006 Atlanta	N.L.	10	6⅓	0	0	.000	10	9	8	9.95	0
2007 Mississippi	Southern	33	35	2	4	.333	51	13	26	2.06	16
2007 Richmond	Int.	17	22	3	0	1.000	27	6	15	1.64	4
2007 Atlanta	N.L.	10	8⅓	1	0	1.000	7	8	7	1.08	0
2008 Sacramento	P.C.	4	4	0	1	.000	8	1	4	6.75	0
2008 Oakland a-b	A.L.	42	45⅔	6	1	.857	49	15	23	0.59	1
Major League Totals	4 Yrs.	67	65⅓	7	2	.778	69	37	44	2.48	1
Division Series											
2005 Atlanta	N.L.	3	1⅔	0	1	.000	3	1	3	10.80	0

a Traded to Oakland Athletics with pitcher Jamie Richmond for outfielder Mark Kotsay, January 14, 2008.
b On disabled list from May 26 to August 2, 2008.

DICKEY, ROBERT ALAN (R.A.)

Born, Nashville, Tennessee, October 29, 1974.
Bats Right. Throws Right. Height, 6 feet, 3 inches. Weight, 220 pounds.

Year Club	Lea	G	IP	W	L	Pct	SO	BB	H	ERA	SAVES
1997 Charlotte	Fla.St.	8	35	1	4	.200	32	12	51	6.94	0
1998 Charlotte	Fla.St.	57	60	1	5	.167	53	22	58	3.30	38
1999 Oklahoma	P.C.	6	22 2/3	2	2	.500	17	7	23	4.37	0
1999 Tulsa	Texas	35	95	6	7	.462	59	40	105	4.55	10
2000 Oklahoma	P.C.	30	158 1/3	8	9	.471	85	65	167	4.49	1
2001 Oklahoma	P.C.	24	163	11	7	.611	120	45	164	3.75	0
2001 Texas	A.L.	4	12	0	1	.000	4	7	13	6.75	0
2002 Oklahoma	P.C.	37	154	8	7	.533	109	47	176	4.09	0
2003 Oklahoma	P.C.	3	15	1	1	.500	4	3	14	1.20	0
2003 Texas	A.L.	38	116 2/3	9	8	.529	94	38	135	5.09	1
2004 Frisco	Texas	4	13 2/3	1	1	.500	9	1	16	1.98	0
2004 Texas a	A.L.	25	104 1/3	6	7	.462	57	33	136	5.61	1
2005 Oklahoma	P.C.	19	121 2/3	10	6	.625	81	39	152	5.99	0
2005 Texas b	A.L.	9	29 2/3	1	2	.333	15	17	29	6.67	0
2006 Texas	A.L.	1	3 1/3	0	1	.000	1	1	8	18.90	0
2006 Oklahoma	P.C.	22	131 2/3	9	8	.529	61	46	134	4.92	1
2007 Nashville c-d-e	P.C.	31	169 1/3	13	6	.684	119	60	159	3.72	0
2008 Tacoma	P.C.	7	49 2/3	2	5	.286	30	8	58	3.44	0
2008 Seattle f	A.L.	32	112 1/3	5	8	.385	58	51	124	5.21	0
Major League Totals .... 6 Yrs.		109	378 1/3	21	27	.438	229	147	445	5.57	2

a On disabled list from June 25 to July 19 and July 30 to August 23, 2004.
b On disabled list from April 13 to May 25, 2005.
c Filed for free agency, October 11, 2006. Signed with Milwaukee Brewers organization, January 10, 2007.
d Filed for free agency, October 29, 2007. Signed with Minnesota Twins organization, November 29, 2007.
e Selected by Seattle Mariners in Rule V draft, December 6, 2007.
f Traded to Seattle Mariners for catcher Jair Fernandez, March 29, 2008.

DOLSI, FREDDY

Born, San Pedro de Macoris, Dominican Republic, January 9, 1983.
Bats Right. Throws Right. Height, 6 feet. Weight, 160 pounds.

Year Club	Lea	G	IP	W	L	Pct	SO	BB	H	ERA	SAVES
2003 Tigers	Gulf Coast	8	23	1	1	.500	19	12	27	4.70	0
2005 West Michigan	Midwest	23	37	1	0	1.000	27	14	36	2.43	0
2006 Lakeland	Fla.St.	30	42 2/3	4	4	.500	29	17	47	4.01	1
2007 Erie	Eastern	1	1	0	0	.000	0	1	1	0.00	0
2007 Lakeland	Fla.St.	48	51 2/3	5	3	.625	44	17	52	3.48	23
2008 Lakeland	Fla.St.	9	7 1/3	0	1	.000	11	3	7	6.14	5
2008 Erie	Eastern	3	3	0	0	.000	1	1	1	0.00	2
2008 Toledo	Int.	4	9	0	0	.000	7	3	5	1.00	1
2008 Detroit	A.L.	42	47 2/3	1	5	.167	29	28	50	3.97	2

DOTEL (DIAZ), OCTAVIO EDUARDO

Born, Santo Domingo, Dominican Republic, November 25, 1973.
Bats Right. Throws Right. Height, 6 feet. Weight, 215 pounds.

Year Club	Lea	G	IP	W	L	Pct	SO	BB	H	ERA	SAVES
1993 Mets	Dominican	15	59 1/3	6	2	.750	48	38	46	4.10	0
1994 Mets	Dominican	15	81 1/3	5	0	1.000	95	31	84	4.32	0
1995 Mets	Gulf Coast	13	74 1/3	7	4	.636	86	17	48	2.18	0
1995 St. Lucie	Fla.St.	3	8	1	0	1.000	9	4	10	5.63	0
1996 Columbia	So.Atl.	22	115 1/3	11	3	.786	142	49	89	3.59	0
1997 Mets	Gulf Coast	3	9 1/3	0	0	.000	7	2	9	0.96	1
1997 St. Lucie	Fla.St.	9	50	5	2	.714	39	23	44	2.52	0
1997 Binghamton	Eastern	12	55 2/3	3	4	.429	40	38	66	5.98	0
1998 Binghamton	Eastern	10	68 2/3	4	2	.667	82	24	41	1.97	0
1998 Norfolk	Int.	17	99	8	6	.571	118	43	82	3.45	0
1999 Norfolk	Int.	13	70 1/3	5	2	.714	90	34	52	3.84	0
1999 New York	N.L.	19	85 1/3	8	3	.727	85	49	69	5.38	0
2000 Houston	N.L.	50	125	3	7	.300	142	61	127	5.40	16
2001 Houston	N.L.	61	105	7	5	.583	145	47	79	2.66	2
2002 Houston	N.L.	83	97 1/3	6	4	.600	118	27	58	1.85	6
2003 Houston	N.L.	76	87	6	4	.600	97	31	53	2.48	4
2004 Houston	N.L.	32	34 2/3	0	4	.000	50	15	27	3.12	14
2004 Oakland a-b	A.L.	45	50 2/3	6	2	.750	72	18	41	4.09	22
2005 Oakland c-d	A.L.	15	15 1/3	1	2	.333	16	11	10	3.52	7
2006 Staten Island	N.Y.-Penn.	1	1	0	0	.000	1	0	2	0.00	0

Year Club	Lea	G	IP	W	L	Pct	SO	BB	H	ERA	SAVES
2006 Yankees .... Gulf Coast		3	3	0	0	.000	6	1	0	0.00	0
2006 Tampa .... Fla.St.		2	2	0	0	.000	2	0	1	0.00	0
2006 Trenton........... Eastern		2	2	0	0	.000	3	0	1	0.00	0
2006 Columbus..............Int.		5	5 1/3	0	0	.000	8	0	6	3.38	0
2006 New York e-f .... A.L.		14	10	0	0	.000	7	11	18	10.80	0
2007 Wichita.............. Texas		3	3	0	1	.000	4	0	2	3.00	1
2007 Kansas City .... A.L.		24	23	2	1	.667	29	11	24	3.91	11
2007 Atlanta g-h-i.......... N.L.		9	7 2/3	0	0	.000	12	1	5	4.70	0
2008 Chicago .... A.L.		72	67	4	4	.500	92	29	52	3.76	1
Major League Totals ....10 Yrs.		500	708	43	36	.544	865	311	563	3.76	83
Division Series											
1999 New York .... N.L.		1	0 1/3	0	0	.000	0	2	1	54.00	0
2001 Houston............... N.L.		2	3 1/3	0	0	.000	5	0	5	5.40	0
2008 Chicago .... A.L.		4	1 1/3	0	0	.000	3	0	2	13.50	0
Division Series Totals		7	5	0	0	.000	8	2	8	10.80	0
Championship Series											
1999 New York .... N.L.		1	3	1	0	1.000	5	2	4	3.00	0

a Traded to Kansas City Royals with catcher John Buck for outfielder Carlos Beltran, June 24, 2004.
b Traded to Oakland Athletics with cash for pitcher Mike Wood and infielder Mark Teahen, June 24, 2004.
c On disabled list from May 19 to October 28, 2005.
d Filed for free agency, October 28, 2005. Signed with New York Yankees, December 29, 2005.
e On disabled list from March 24 to August 16, 2006.
f Filed for free agency, October 28, 2006. Signed with Kansas City Royals, December 8, 2006.
g On disabled list from August 8 to September 20 and March 30 to May 22, 2007.
h Traded to Atlanta Braves for pitcher Kyle Davies, July 31, 2007.
i Filed for free agency, November 6, 2007. Signed with Chicago White Sox, January 22, 2008.

DOWNS, SCOTT JEREMY
Born, Louisville, Kentucky, March 17, 1976.
Bats Left. Throws Left. Height, 6 feet, 2 inches. Weight, 210 pounds.

Year Club	Lea	G	IP	W	L	Pct	SO	BB	H	ERA	SAVES
1997 Williamsprt........ N.Y.-Penn.		5	23	0	2	.000	28	7	15	2.74	0
1997 Rockford .... Midwest		5	36	3	0	1.000	43	8	17	1.25	0
1998 Daytona a........... Fla.St.		27	161 2/3	8	9	.471	117	55	179	3.90	0
1999 New Britain .... Eastern		6	19 2/3	0	0	.000	22	10	33	8.69	0
1999 Daytona .... Fla.St.		7	48	5	0	1.000	41	11	41	1.88	0
1999 Fort Myers .... Fla.St.		2	9 2/3	0	1	.000	9	6	7	0.00	0
1999 West Tenn b......... Southern		13	80	8	1	.889	101	28	56	1.35	0
2000 Chicago-Montreal c-d .. N.L.		19	97	4	3	.571	63	40	122	5.29	0
2001 Montreal.............. N.L.			INJURED—Did Not Play								
2002 Brevard County ...... Fla.St.		7	9	0	0	.000	7	2	7	3.00	1
2002 Ottawa e-f .... Int.		17	23 1/3	2	1	.667	15	3	31	5.79	0
2003 Edmonton .... P.C.		21	121 2/3	8	9	.471	54	39	119	4.29	0
2003 Montreal.............. N.L.		1	3	0	1	.000	4	3	5	15.00	0
2004 Edmonton .... P.C.		22	135 1/3	10	6	.625	67	26	143	3.52	0
2004 Montreal g .... N.L.		12	63	3	6	.333	38	23	79	5.14	0
2005 Syracuse .... Int.		7	39 1/3	2	3	.400	35	3	45	4.81	0
2005 Toronto .... A.L.		26	94	4	3	.571	75	34	93	4.31	0
2006 Toronto .... A.L.		59	77	6	2	.750	61	30	73	4.09	1
2007 Toronto .... A.L.		*81	58	4	2	.667	57	24	47	2.17	1
2008 Toronto h .... A.L.		66	70 2/3	0	3	.000	57	27	54	1.78	5
Major League Totals ....7 Yrs.		264	462 2/3	21	20	.512	355	181	473	4.01	7

a Sent by Chicago Cubs to Minnesota Twins as player to be named later for pitcher Mike Morgan, November 3, 1998.
b Traded to Chicago Cubs with pitcher Rick Aguilera for pitcher Jason Ryan and pitcher Kyle Lohse, May 21, 1999.
c On disabled list from August 9 to October 1, 2000.
d Traded to Montreal Expos for outfielder Rondell White, July 31, 2000.
e On disabled list from March 23 to November 14, 2001.
f On disabled list from March 27 to June 10, 2002.
g Released by Montreal Expos, November 29, 2004. Signed with Toronto Blue Jays organization, December 16, 2004.
h On disabled list from September 20 to October 2, 2008.

DUCHSCHERER, JUSTIN CRAIG
Born, Aberdeen, South Dakota, November 19, 1977.
Bats Right. Throws Right. Height, 6 feet, 3 inches. Weight, 200 pounds.

Year Club	Lea	G	IP	W	L	Pct	SO	BB	H	ERA	SAVES
1996 Red Sox .... Gulf Coast		13	54 2/3	0	2	.000	45	14	52	3.13	1
1997 Red Sox .... Gulf Coast		10	44 2/3	2	3	.400	59	17	34	1.81	0

Year	Club	Lea	G	IP	W	L	Pct	SO	BB	H	ERA	SAVES
1997 Michigan	Midwest	4	24	1	1	.500	19	10	26	5.63	0
1998 Michigan	Midwest	30	142²/₃	7	12	.368	106	47	166	4.79	0
1999 Augusta	So.Atl.	6	41	4	0	1.000	39	8	21	0.22	0
1999 Sarasota	Fla.St.	21	112¹/₃	7	7	.500	105	30	101	4.49	0
2000 Trenton	Eastern	24	143¹/₃	7	9	.438	126	35	134	3.39	0
2001 Trenton	Eastern	12	73²/₃	6	3	.667	69	14	49	2.44	0
2001 Tulsa	Texas	6	43¹/₃	4	0	1.000	55	10	39	2.08	0
2001 Texas	A.L.	5	14²/₃	1	1	.500	11	4	24	12.27	0
2001 Oklahoma a	P.C.	7	50²/₃	3	3	.500	52	10	48	2.84	0
2002 Sacramento b	P.C.	14	63	2	4	.333	52	17	73	5.57	0
2003 Sacramento	P.C.	24	155	14	2	.875	117	18	151	3.25	0
2003 Oakland	A.L.	4	16¹/₃	1	1	.500	15	3	17	3.31	0
2004 Oakland	A.L.	53	96¹/₃	7	6	.538	59	32	85	3.27	0
2005 Oakland	A.L.	65	85²/₃	7	4	.636	85	19	67	2.21	5
2006 Sacramento	P.C.	2	2	0	0	.000	1	0	2	0.00	0
2006 Oakland c	A.L.	53	55²/₃	2	1	.667	51	9	52	2.91	9
2007 Stockton	Calif.	1	1	0	0	.000	1	0	0	0.00	0
2007 Oakland d	A.L.	17	16¹/₃	3	3	.500	13	8	18	4.96	0
2008 Sacramento	P.C.	1	2²/₃	0	1	.000	1	0	5	6.75	0
2008 Oakland e	A.L.	22	141²/₃	10	8	.556	95	34	107	2.54	0
Major League Totals	7 Yrs.	219	426²/₃	31	24	.564	329	109	370	3.14	14
Division Series											
2006 Oakland	A.L.	2	4	0	0	.000	4	0	1	2.25	0

a Traded by Boston Red Sox to Texas Rangers for catcher Doug Mirabelli, June 12, 2001.
b Traded to Oakland Athletics for pitcher Luis Vizcaino, March 18, 2002.
c On disabled list from May 7 to June 23, 2006.
d On disabled list from May 15 to October 8, 2007.
e On disabled list from April 5 to April 26 and August 19 to October 3, 2008.

DUKE, ZACHARY THOMAS (ZACH)

Born, Clifton, Texas, April 19, 1983.
Bats Left. Throws Left. Height, 6 feet, 2 inches. Weight, 220 pounds.

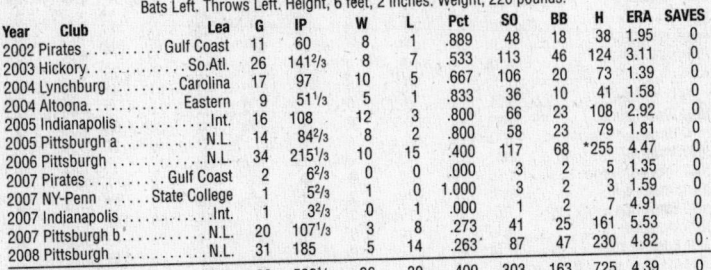

Year	Club	Lea	G	IP	W	L	Pct	SO	BB	H	ERA	SAVES
2002 Pirates	Gulf Coast	11	60	8	1	.889	48	18	38	1.95	0
2003 Hickory	So.Atl.	26	141²/₃	8	7	.533	113	46	124	3.11	0
2004 Lynchburg	Carolina	17	97	10	5	.667	106	20	73	1.39	0
2004 Altoona	Eastern	9	51¹/₃	5	1	.833	36	10	41	1.58	0
2005 Indianapolis	Int.	16	108	12	3	.800	66	23	108	2.92	0
2005 Pittsburgh a	N.L.	14	84²/₃	8	2	.800	58	23	79	1.81	0
2006 Pittsburgh	N.L.	34	215¹/₃	10	15	.400	117	68	*255	4.47	0
2007 Pirates	Gulf Coast	2	6²/₃	0	0	.000	3	2	5	1.35	0
2007 NY-Penn	State College	1	5²/₃	1	0	1.000	3	2	3	1.59	0
2007 Indianapolis	Int.	1	3²/₃	0	1	.000	1	2	7	4.91	0
2007 Pittsburgh b	N.L.	20	107¹/₃	3	8	.273	41	25	161	5.53	0
2008 Pittsburgh	N.L.	31	185	5	14	.263	87	47	230	4.82	0
Major League Totals	4 Yrs.	99	592¹/₃	26	39	.400	303	163	725	4.39	0

a On disabled list from August 24 to September 16, 2005.
b On disabled list from June 29 to September 11, 2007.

DUMATRAIT, PHILLIP ANTHONY (PHIL)

Born, Bakersfield, California, July 12, 1981.
Bats Right. Throws Left. Height, 6 feet, 2 inches. Weight, 195 pounds.

Year	Club	Lea	G	IP	W	L	Pct	SO	BB	H	ERA	SAVES
2000 Red Sox	Gulf Coast	6	16¹/₃	0	1	.000	12	12	10	1.65	0
2001 Red Sox	Gulf Coast	8	32²/₃	3	0	1.000	33	9	27	2.76	0
2001 Lowell	N.Y.-Penn.	2	10¹/₃	1	1	.500	15	4	9	3.48	0
2002 Sarasota	Fla.St.	4	14	0	2	.000	16	15	10	3.86	0
2002 Augusta	So.Atl.	22	120¹/₃	8	5	.615	108	47	109	2.77	0
2003 Potomac	Carolina	7	37²/₃	4	1	.800	32	14	36	3.35	0
2003 Sarasota a	Fla.St.	21	104¹/₃	7	5	.583	74	59	74	3.02	1
2004 b	INJURED—Did Not Play										
2005 Sarasota	Fla.St.	3	10	0	0	.000	13	3	8	2.70	0
2005 Chattanooga	Southern	24	127²/₃	4	12	.250	101	70	115	3.17	0
2006 Louisville	Int.	16	87²/₃	5	7	.417	58	36	104	4.72	0
2006 Chattanooga	Southern	10	49²/₃	3	4	.429	45	22	39	3.62	0
2007 Louisville	Int.	22	125	10	6	.625	76	49	114	3.53	0
2007 Cincinnati c	N.L.	6	18	0	4	.000	9	12	39	15.00	0

Year Club	Lea	G	IP	W	L	Pct	SO	BB	H	ERA	SAVES
2008 Pittsburgh d	N.L.	21	78²/₃	3	4	.429	52	42	82	5.26	0
Major League Totals .... 2 Yrs.		27	96²/₃	3	8	.273	61	54	121	7.08	0

a Traded by Boston Red Sox to Cincinnati Reds with player to be named later and cash for pitcher Scott Williamson, July 29, 2003. Cincinnati Reds received pitcher Tyler Pelland to complete trade, August 18, 2003.
b On minor league disabled list from April 10 to September 17, 2004.
c Claimed on waivers by Pittsburgh Pirates, October 26, 2007.
d On disabled list from June 20 to July 7 and July 8 to November 13, 2008.

DURBIN, CHAD GRIFFIN

Born, Spring Valley, Illinois, December 3, 1977.
Bats Both. Throws Right. Height, 6 feet, 2 inches. Weight, 200 pounds.

Year Club	Lea	G	IP	W	L	Pct	SO	BB	H	ERA	SAVES
1996 Royals	Gulf Coast	11	44¹/₃	3	2	.600	43	25	34	4.26	0
1997 Lansing	Midwest	26	144²/₃	5	8	.385	116	53	157	4.79	0
1998 Wilmington	Carolina	26	147²/₃	10	7	.588	162	59	126	2.93	0
1999 Wichita	Texas	28	157	8	10	.444	122	49	154	4.64	0
1999 Kansas City	A.L.	1	2¹/₃	0	0	.000	3	1	1	0.00	0
2000 Kansas City	A.L.	16	72¹/₃	2	5	.286	37	43	91	8.21	0
2000 Omaha	P.C.	12	72²/₃	4	4	.500	53	22	75	4.46	0
2001 Omaha	P.C.	5	27	2	2	.500	35	6	22	3.33	0
2001 Kansas City	A.L.	29	179	9	16	.360	95	58	201	4.93	0
2002 Omaha	P.C.	1	1²/₃	0	1	.000	2	0	4	10.80	0
2002 Royals	Gulf Coast	3	6	0	0	.000	5	1	4	0.00	0
2002 Wichita	Texas	3	5¹/₃	0	0	.000	6	4	5	5.06	0
2002 Kansas City	A.L.	2	8¹/₃	0	1	.000	5	4	13	11.88	0
2003 Mahoning Valley...	N.Y.-Penn.	2	12	1	1	.500	8	3	9	2.25	0
2003 Akron	Eastern	3	12	2	0	1.000	11	1	7	1.50	0
2003 Buffalo	Int.	10	58²/₃	3	6	.333	64	16	51	4.60	0
2003 Cleveland a	A.L.	3	8²/₃	0	1	.000	8	3	18	7.27	0
2004 Cleveland	A.L.	17	51¹/₃	5	6	.455	38	24	63	6.66	0
2004 Buffalo	Int.	9	52	3	3	.500	40	16	55	3.46	0
2004 Arizona b-c	N.L.	7	9¹/₃	1	1	.500	10	11	9	8.68	0
2005 New Orleans	P.C.	26	115¹/₃	4	5	.444	99	48	121	5.77	0
2006 Toledo	Int.	28	185	11	8	.579	149	46	169	3.11	0
2006 Detroit	A.L.	3	6	0	0	.000	3	0	6	1.50	0
2007 Detroit e	A.L.	36	127²/₃	8	7	.533	76	49	133	4.72	1
2008 Philadelphia	N.L.	71	87¹/₃	5	4	.556	63	35	81	2.87	1
Major League Totals ...... 9 Yrs.		185	552²/₃	30	41	.423	328	228	616	5.29	2
Division Series											
2008 Philadelphia	N.L.	1	0²/₃	0	0	.000	1	0	3	0.00	0
Championship Series											
2008 Philadelphia	N.L.	3	2	0	0	.000	2	2	3	4.50	0
World Series Record											
2008 Philadelphia	N.L.	2	0²/₃	0	0	.000	0	1	1	0.00	0

a Not offered contract, December 20, 2002. Signed with Cleveland Indians organization, February 17, 2003.
b Claimed on waivers by Arizona Diamondbacks, August 13, 2004.
c Filed for free agency, October 11, 2004. Signed with Washington Nationals organization, December 23, 2004.
d Filed for free agency, October 28, 2005. Signed with Detroit Tigers organization, January 10, 2006.
e Not offered contract, December 12, 2007. Signed with Philadelphia Phillies, December 20, 2007.

EATON, ADAM THOMAS

Born; Seattle, Washington, November 23, 1977.
Bats Right. Throws Right. Height, 6 feet, 2 inches. Weight, 200 pounds.

Year Club	Lea	G	IP	W	L	Pct	SO	BB	H	ERA	SAVES
1997 Piedmont	So.Atl.	14	71¹/₃	5	6	.455	57	30	81	4.16	0
1998 Clearwater	Fla.St.	24	131²/₃	9	8	.529	89	47	152	4.44	0
1999 Reading	Eastern	12	77	5	4	.556	67	28	60	2.92	0
1999 Clearwater	Fla.St.	13	69	5	5	.500	50	24	81	3.91	0
1999 Scranton-WB a	Int.	3	21	1	1	.500	10	6	17	3.00	0
2000 Mobile	Southern	10	57	4	1	.800	58	18	47	2.68	0
2000 San Diego	N.L.	22	135	7	4	.636	90	61	134	4.13	0
2001 San Diego b	N.L.	17	116²/₃	8	5	.615	109	40	108	4.32	0
2002 Lake Elsinore	California	3	13¹/₃	0	0	.000	19	3	10	2.70	0
2002 Portland	P.C.	2	12¹/₃	1	1	.500	6	3	9	2.92	0
2002 San Diego c	N.L.	6	33¹/₃	1	1	.500	25	17	28	5.40	0
2003 San Diego d	N.L.	31	183	9	12	.429	146	68	173	4.08	0
2004 San Diego	N.L.	33	199¹/₃	11	14	.440	153	52	204	4.61	0

Year	Club	Lea	G	IP	W	L	Pct	SO	BB	H	ERA	SAVES
2005 Lake Elsinore	California		1	3	0	0	.000	2	2	1	0.00	0
2005 Portland	P.C.		2	8	0	0	.000	4	1	11	5.63	0
2005 San Diego e-f	N.L.		24	128²/₃	11	5	.688	100	44	140	4.27	0
2006 Frisco	Texas		2	6¹/₃	0	0	.000	5	1	7	1.42	0
2006 Oklahoma	P.C.		2	6	0	0	.000	8	2	3	1.50	0
2006 Texas g-h	A.L.		13	65	7	4	.636	43	24	78	5.12	0
2007 Reading	Eastern		1	2	0	0	.000	1	0	3	9.00	0
2007 Philadelphia i	N.L.		30	161²/₃	10	10	.500	97	71	192	6.29	0
2008 Lakewood	So.Atl.		1	3²/₃	0	1	.000	2	1	5	9.82	0
2008 Reading	Eastern		5	26²/₃	0	3	.000	23	4	34	7.09	0
2008 Lehigh	Int.		1	3	0	1	.000	2	1	5	3.00	0
2008 Philadelphia	N.L.		21	107	4	8	.333	57	44	131	5.80	0
Major League Totals	9 Yrs.		197	1129²/₃	68	63	.519	820	421	1188	4.80	0

a Traded to San Diego Padres by Philadelphia Phillies with pitcher Carlton Loewer and pitcher Steve Montgomery for pitcher Andy Ashby, November 10, 1999.
b On disabled list from July 6 to October 10, 2001.
c On disabled list from March 27 to September 1, 2002.
d On disabled list from May 5 to May 20, 2003.
e On disabled list from June 16 to August 1 and August 5 to August 26, 2005.
f Traded to Texas Rangers with pitcher Akinori Otsuka and catcher Billy Killian for pitcher Chris Young, infielder Adrian Gonzalez and outfielder Terrmel Sledge, January 4, 2006.
g On disabled list from March 30 to July 25, 2006.
h Filed for free agency, October 28, 2006. Signed with Philadelphia Phillies, November 30, 2006.
i On disabled list from August 12 to August 28, 2007.

EMBREE, ALAN DUANE

Born, The Dalles, Oregon, January 23, 1970.
Bats Left. Throws Left. Height, 6 feet, 2 inches. Weight, 190 pounds.

Year	Club	Lea	G	IP	W	L	Pct	SO	BB	H	ERA	SAVES
1990 Burlington	Appal.		15	81²/₃	4	4	.500	58	30	87	2.64	0
1991 Columbus	So. Atl.		27	155¹/₃	10	8	.556	137	77	126	3.59	0
1992 Kinston	Carolina		15	101	10	5	.667	115	32	89	3.30	0
1992 Canton-Akron	Eastern		12	79	7	2	.778	56	28	61	2.28	0
1992 Cleveland	A.L.		4	18	0	2	.000	12	8	19	7.00	0
1993 Canton-Akron	Eastern		1	5¹/₃	0	0	.000	4	3	3	3.38	0
1994 Canton-Akron	Eastern		30	157	9	16	.360	81	64	183	5.50	0
1995 Buffalo	A.A.		30	40²/₃	3	4	.429	56	19	31	0.89	.5
1995 Cleveland	A.L.		23	24²/₃	3	2	.600	23	16	23	5.11	.5
1996 Buffalo	A.A.		20	34¹/₃	4	1	.800	46	14	26	3.93	.5
1996 Cleveland a	A.L.		24	31	1	1	.500	33	21	36	6.39	0
1997 Atlanta b	N.L.		66	46	3	1	.750	45	20	36	2.54	0
1998 Atlanta-Arizona c-d	N.L.		55	53²/₃	4	2	.667	43	23	56	4.19	1
1999 San Francisco	N.L.		68	58²/₃	3	2	.600	53	26	42	3.38	0
2000 San Francisco	N.L.		63	60	3	5	.375	49	25	62	4.95	2
2001 Fresno	P.C.		7	8	1	0	1.000	6	1	5	1.13	1
2001 San Francisco e	N.L.		22	20	0	2	.000	25	10	34	11.25	0
2001 Chicago f-g	A.L.		39	34	1	2	.333	34	7	31	5.03	0
2002 San Diego	N.L.		36	28²/₃	3	4	.429	38	9	23	2.97	2
2002 Boston h-i	A.L.		32	33¹/₃	1	2	.333	43	11	24	2.97	0
2003 Sarasota	Fla.St.		1	0²/₃	0	0	.000	2	0	2	13.50	0
2003 Boston j	A.L.		65	55	4	1	.800	45	16	49	4.25	1
2004 Boston	A.L.		71	52¹/₃	2	2	.500	37	11	49	4.13	0
2005 Boston-New York k-l	A.L.		67	52	2	5	.286	38	14	62	7.62	1
2006 San Diego m-n	N.L.		73	52¹/₃	4	3	.571	53	15	50	3.27	17
2007 Oakland	A.L.		68	68	1	2	.333	51	19	67	3.97	0
2008 Oakland o	A.L.		70	61²/₃	2	5	.286	57	30	59	4.96	0
Major League Totals	15 Yrs.		846	749¹/₃	37	43	.463	679	281	716	4.55	25
Division Series												
1996 Cleveland	A.L.		3	1	0	0	.000	1	0	0	9.00	0
2000 San Francisco	N.L.		2	1²/₃	0	0	.000	0	0	0	0.00	0
2003 Boston	A.L.		3	2	0	0	.000	0	0	1	0.00	0
2004 Boston	A.L.		2	1	0	0	.000	0	1	0	0.00	0
2006 San Diego	N.L.		1	0¹/₃	0	0	.000	1	0	0	0.00	0
Division Series Totals			11	6	0	0	.000	2	1	1	1.50	0
Championship Series												
1995 Cleveland	A.L.		1	0¹/₃	0	0	.000	1	0	0	0.00	0
1997 Atlanta	N.L.		1	1	0	0	.000	1	1	0	0.00	0

Year Club	Lea	G	IP	W	L	Pct	SO	BB	H	ERA	SAVES
2003 Boston	A.L.	5	4 2/3	1	0	1.000	1	0	3	0.00	0
2004 Boston	A.L.	6	4 2/3	0	0	.000	2	1	9	3.86	0
Championship Series Totals		13	10 2/3	1	0	1.000	5	2	12	1.69	0
World Series Record											
1995 Cleveland	A.L.	4	3 1/3	0	0	.000	2	2	2	2.70	0
2004 Boston	A.L.	3	1 2/3	0	0	.000	4	0	1	0.00	0
World Series Totals.............		7	5	0	0	.000	6	2	3	1.80	0

a On disabled list from August 1 to September 7, 1996.
b Traded to Atlanta Braves with outfielder Kenny Lofton for outfielder Marquis Grissom and outfielder David Justice, March 25, 1997.
c Traded to Arizona Diamondbacks for pitcher Russ Springer, June 22, 1998.
d Traded to San Francisco Giants for outfielder Dante Powell, November 10, 1998.
e On disabled list from May 23 to June 12, 2001.
f Traded to Chicago White Sox with cash for pitcher Derek Hasselhoff, June 29, 2001.
g Filed for free agency, November 6, 2001. Signed with San Diego Padres, December 27, 2001.
h Traded to Boston Red Sox with pitcher Andy Shibilo for pitcher Brad Baker and pitcher Dan Giese, June 23, 2002.
i On disabled list from July 14 to July 29, 2002.
j On disabled list from April 9 to April 29, 2003.
k Released by Boston Red Sox, July 27, 2005. Signed with New York Yankees, July 30, 2005.
l Filed for free agency, November 3, 2005. Signed with San Diego Padres organization, January 12, 2006.
m On disabled list from July 2 to July 17, 2006.
n Filed for free agency, October 29, 2006. Signed with Oakland Athletics, December 6, 2006.
o Not offered contract, October 31, 2008. Signed with Colorado Rockies, December 13, 2008.

ESCOBAR, KELVIM JOSE

Born, La Guaira, Venezuela, April 11, 1976.
Bats Right. Throws Right. Height, 6 feet, 1 inch. Weight, 230 pounds.

Year Club	Lea	G	IP	W	L	Pct	SO	BB	H	ERA	SAVES
1994 Blue Jays	Gulf Coast	11	65	4	4	.500	64	18	56	2.35	0
1995 Medcine Hat........	Pioneer	14	69 1/3	3	3	.500	75	33	66	5.71	0
1996 Dunedin	Fla. St.	18	110 1/3	9	5	.643	113	33	101	2.69	0
1996 Knoxville	Southern	10	54	3	4	.429	44	24	61	5.33	0
1997 Dunedin	Fla. St.	3	12	0	1	.000	16	3	16	3.75	0
1997 Knoxville	Southern	5	24 1/3	2	1	.667	31	16	20	3.70	0
1997 Toronto	A.L.	27	31	3	2	.600	36	19	28	2.90	14
1998 Syracuse	Int.	13	59 2/3	2	2	.500	64	24	51	3.77	1
1998 Toronto a	A.L.	22	79 2/3	7	3	.700	72	35	72	3.73	0
1999 Toronto	A.L.	33	174	14	11	.560	129	81	203	5.69	0
2000 Toronto	A.L.	43	180	10	15	.400	142	85	186	5.35	2
2001 Toronto	A.L.	59	126	6	8	.429	121	52	93	3.50	0
2002 Toronto	A.L.	76	78	5	7	.417	85	44	75	4.27	38
2003 Toronto b	A.L.	41	180 1/3	13	9	.591	159	78	189	4.29	4
2004 Anaheim	A.L.	33	208 1/3	11	12	.478	191	76	192	3.93	0
2005 Rancho Cucamonga....	Calif.	1	3	0	0	.000	7	2	1	0.00	0
2005 Salt Lake	P.C.	4	14 1/3	1	0	1.000	22	8	14	2.51	0
2005 Los Angeles c	A.L.	16	59 2/3	3	2	.600	63	21	45	3.02	1
2006 Los Angeles d	A.L.	30	189 1/3	11	14	.440	147	50	192	3.61	0
2007 Los Angeles e.........	A.L.	30	195 2/3	18	7	.720	160	66	182	3.40	0
2008 Los Angeles f.........	A.L.		INJURED—Did Not Play								
Major League Totals	11 Yrs.	410	1502	101	90	.529	1305	607	1457	4.15	59
Division Series											
2004 Anaheim.................	A.L.	1	3 1/3	0	0	.000	4	5	5	8.10	0
2005 Los Angeles	A.L.	4	7	1	0	1.000	5	5	2	1.29	0
2007 Los Angeles	A.L.	1	5	0	0	.000	5	5	4	5.40	0
Division Series Totals...........		6	15 1/3	1	0	1.000	14	15	11	4.11	0
Championship Series											
2005 Los Angeles	A.L.	2	4 1/3	0	2	.000	10	2	4	2.08	0

a On disabled list from April 16 to May 6, 1998.
b Filed for free agency, October 26, 2003. Signed with Anaheim Angels, November 24, 2003.
c On disabled list from March 31 to April 24 and May 12 to May 28 and June 9 to September 6, 2005.
d On disabled list from July 7 to July 22, 2006.
e On disabled list from April 9 to April 24, 2007.
f On disabled list from March 21 to November 7, 2008.

EVELAND, DANA JAMES
Born, Olympia, Washington, October 29, 1983.
Bats Left. Throws Left. Height, 6 feet, 1 inch. Weight, 240 pounds.

Year	Club	Lea	G	IP	W	L	Pct	SO	BB	H	ERA	SAVES
2003 Helena	....	Pioneer	19	26	2	1	.667	41	8	30	2.08	14
2004 Beloit	....	Midwest	22	117⅓	9	6	.600	119	24	108	2.84	2
2004 Huntsville	....	Southern	4	23⅔	0	2	.000	14	4	23	2.28	0
2005 Huntsville	....	Southern	18	109	10	4	.714	98	38	96	2.72	0
2005 Milwaukee	....	N.L.	27	31⅔	1	1	.500	23	18	40	5.97	1
2006 Milwaukee	....	N.L.	9	27⅔	0	3	.000	32	16	39	8.13	0
2006 Nashville a	....	P.C.	20	105	6	5	.545	110	41	71	2.74	0
2007 Visalia	....	Calif.	2	5	0	0	.000	9	2	1	0.00	0
2007 Tucson	....	P.C.	7	27⅔	1	0	1.000	15	10	29	1.95	0
2007 Arizona b	....	N.L.	5	5	1	0	1.000	3	5	8	14.40	0
2008 Sacramento	....	P.C.	3	21	3	0	1.000	21	4	23	2.57	0
2008 Oakland	....	A.L.	29	168	9	9	.500	118	77	172	4.34	0
Major League Totals	4 Yrs.		70	232⅓	11	13	.458	176	116	259	5.23	1

a Traded to Arizona Diamondbacks with pitcher Doug Davis and outfielder David Krynzel for pitcher Greg Aquino, catcher Johnny Estrada and pitcher Claudio Vargas, November 25, 2006.
b Traded to Oakland Athletics with pitcher Brett Anderson, pitcher Greg Smith, infielder Chris Carter, outfielder Aaron Cunningham and outfielder Carlos Gonzalez for pitcher Danny Haren and pitcher Connor Robertson, December 14, 2007.

FARNSWORTH, KYLE LYNN
Born, Wichita, Kansas, April 14, 1976.
Bats Right. Throws Right. Height, 6 feet, 4 inches. Weight, 240 pounds.

Year	Club	Lea	G	IP	W	L	Pct	SO	BB	H	ERA	SAVES
1995 Cubs	....	Gulf Coast	16	31	3	2	.600	18	11	22	0.87	1
1996 Rockford	....	Midwest	20	112	9	6	.600	82	35	122	3.70	0
1997 Daytona	....	Fla.St.	27	156⅓	10	10	.500	105	47	178	4.09	0
1998 West Tenn	....	Southern	13	81⅓	8	2	.800	73	21	70	2.77	0
1998 Iowa	....	P.C.	18	102⅔	5	9	.357	79	36	129	6.93	0
1999 Iowa	....	P.C.	6	39⅓	2	2	.500	29	9	38	3.20	0
1999 Chicago	....	N.L.	27	130	5	9	.357	70	52	140	5.05	0
2000 Chicago	....	N.L.	46	77	2	9	.182	74	50	90	6.43	1
2000 Iowa	....	P.C.	22	25⅓	0	2	.000	22	18	24	3.20	2
2001 Chicago	....	N.L.	76	82	4	6	.400	107	29	65	2.74	1
2002 Chicago a	....	N.L.	45	46⅔	4	6	.400	46	24	53	7.33	0
2002 Iowa	....	P.C.	2	3	0	1	.000	2	0	3	6.00	0
2003 Chicago	....	N.L.	77	76⅓	3	2	.600	92	36	53	3.30	0
2004 Chicago b	....	N.L.	72	66⅔	4	5	.444	78	33	67	4.72	6
2005 Detroit	....	A.L.	46	42⅔	1	1	.500	55	20	29	2.32	6
2005 Atlanta c-d-e	....	N.L.	26	27⅓	0	0	.000	32	7	15	1.98	10
2006 New York	....	A.L.	72	66	3	6	.333	75	28	62	4.36	6
2007 New York	....	A.L.	64	60	2	1	.667	48	27	60	4.80	0
2008 New York-Detroit f-g	....	A.L.	61	60⅓	2	3	.400	61	22	70	4.48	1
Major League Totals	10 Yrs.		612	735	30	48	.385	738	328	704	4.47	27
Division Series												
2003 Chicago	....	N.L.	3	2⅔	0	0	.000	2	1	1	0.00	0
2005 Atlanta	....	N.L.	2	3	0	0	.000	4	1	2	9.00	0
2006 New York	....	A.L.	2	2	0	0	.000	1	1	1	0.00	0
2007 New York	....	A.L.	1	1	0	0	.000	2	0	1	0.00	0
Division Series Totals			8	8⅔	0	0	.000	9	3	5	3.12	0
Championship Series												
2003 Chicago	....	N.L.	5	5⅓	0	0	.000	7	2	6	10.13	0

a On disabled list from April 10 to June 4, 2002.
b On disabled list from August 28 to September 12, 2004.
c Traded to Detroit Tigers with player to be named later for pitcher Roberto Novoa, infielder Scott Moore and outfielder Clarence Flowers, February 9, 2005.
d Traded to Atlanta Braves for pitcher Roman Colon and pitcher Zach Miner, July 26, 2005.
e Filed for free agency, October 31, 2005. Signed with New York Yankees, December 5, 2005.
f Traded to Detroit Tigers for catcher Ivan Rodriguez, July 30, 2008.
g Filed for free agency, November 3, 2008. Signed with Kansas City Royals, December 13, 2008.

FELDMAN, SCOTT WAYNE

Born, Kailua, Hawaii, February 7, 1983.
Bats Left. Throws Right. Height, 6 feet, 5 inches. Weight, 210 pounds.

Year Club	Lea	G	IP	W	L	Pct	SO	BB	H	ERA	SAVES
2003 Rangers	Arizona	3	6⅓	1	1	.500	7	1	4	4.26	0
2004 Rangers	Arizona	4	7	0	0	.000	5	1	2	0.00	0
2005 Bakersfield	Calif.	6	9	0	0	.000	11	2	5	0.00	3
2005 Frisco	Texas	46	61	1	2	.333	41	23	43	2.36	14
2005 Texas	A.L.	8	9⅓	0	1	.000	4	2	9	0.96	0
2006 Oklahoma	P.C.	23	27⅓	2	2	.500	24	9	20	1.98	4
2006 Texas	A.L.	36	41⅓	0	2	.000	30	10	42	3.92	4
2007 Oklahoma	P.C.	21	30	1	1	.500	24	12	28	4.50	2
2007 Texas	A.L.	29	39	1	2	.333	19	32	44	5.77	0
2008 Frisco	Texas	2	12⅔	2	0	1.000	4	2	11	4.26	0
2008 Texas	A.L.	28	151⅓	6	8	.429	74	56	161	5.29	0
Major League Totals ....4 Yrs.		101	241	7	13	.350	127	100	256	4.97	0

FELICIANO (MOLINA), PEDRO JUAN

Born, Rio Piedras, Puerto Rico, August 25, 1976.
Bats Left. Throws Left. Height, 5 feet, 10 inches. Weight, 185 pounds.

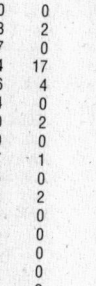

Year Club	Lea	G	IP	W	L	Pct	SO	BB	H	ERA	SAVES
1995 Great Falls	Pioneer	6	6⅔	0	0	.000	9	7	12	13.50	0
1996 Great Falls	Pioneer	22	41	2	3	.400	39	26	50	5.71	3
1997 Savannah	So.Atl.	36	105⅔	3	7	.300	94	39	90	2.64	4
1997 Vero Beach	Fla.St.	1	2	0	0	.000	1	0	3	4.50	0
1998 Vero Beach	Fla.St.	22	68⅓	2	5	.286	51	30	68	4.61	2
1999					INJURED—Did Not Play						
2000 Vero Beach	Fla.St.	25	61⅓	4	5	.444	48	24	76	3.82	0
2000 Albuquerque	P.C.	1	1	0	0	.000	2	1	3	18.00	0
2000 San Antonio a	Texas	9	9⅓	0	0	.000	11	4	7	1.93	2
2001 Las Vegas	P.C.	6	8⅔	0	1	.000	5	5	16	7.27	0
2001 Jacksonville b	Southern	54	60⅓	5	4	.556	55	11	41	1.94	17
2002 Chattanooga	Southern	28	38⅔	2	1	.667	26	11	33	2.56	4
2002 Louisville	Int.	20	26⅔	1	1	.500	19	4	35	3.04	0
2002 Norfolk	Int.	5	9	0	0	.000	11	1	14	7.00	2
2002 New York c-d-e	N.L.	6	6	0	0	.000	4	1	9	7.50	0
2003 Norfolk	Int.	15	22⅔	3	2	.600	18	6	20	3.97	1
2003 New York f-g	N.L.	23	48⅓	0	0	.000	43	21	52	3.35	0
2004 Norfolk	Int.	32	35⅔	4	3	.571	25	15	35	5.30	2
2004 New York	N.L.	22	18⅓	1	1	.500	14	12	14	5.40	0
2005 Fukuoka h-i	Japan Pac.	37	37	3	2	.600	36	13	30	3.89	0
2006 Norfolk	Int.	3	4⅓	0	0	.000	5	1	4	6.23	0
2006 New York	N.L.	64	60⅓	7	2	.778	54	20	56	2.09	0
2007 New York	N.L.	78	64	2	2	.500	61	31	47	3.09	2
2008 New York	N.L.	*86	53⅓	3	4	.429	50	26	57	4.05	2
Major League Totals ....6 Yrs.		279	250⅓	13	9	.591	226	111	235	3.38	4
Division Series											
2006 New York	N.L.	3	1⅔	1	0	1.000	2	2	0	0.00	0
Championship Series											
2006 New York	N.L.	3	3	0	0	.000	1	0	2	3.00	0

a On minor league disabled list from April 8 to September 22, 1999.
b Filed for free agency from Los Angeles Dodgers, October 15, 2001. Signed with Cincinnati Reds organization, December 21, 2001.
c Traded to New York Mets with outfielder Elvin Andujar, player to be named later and two players to be named later for pitcher Shawn Estes and cash, August 16, 2002.
d New York Mets received outfielder Raul Gonzalez (August 20, 2002) and Brady Clark to complete trade, September 9, 2002.
e Claimed on waivers by Detroit Tigers, October 11, 2002.
f Released by Detroit Tigers, December 17, 2002. Signed with New York Mets organization, April 3, 2003.
g Not offered contract, December 21, 2003, re-signed with New York Mets organization, December 22, 2003.
h Sold to Fukuoka Daiei Hawks (Japan), January 21, 2005.
i Signed with New York Mets organization, December 19, 2005.

FLOYD, GAVIN CHRISTOPHER

Born, Annapolis, Maryland, January 27, 1983.
Bats Right. Throws Right. Height, 6 feet, 4 inches. Weight, 230 pounds.

Year Club	Lea	G	IP	W	L	Pct	SO	BB	H	ERA	SAVES
2002 Lakewood	So.Atl.	27	166	11	10	.524	140	64	119	2.77	0
2003 Clearwater	Fla.St.	24	138	7	8	.467	115	45	128	3.00	0

Year Club	Lea	G	IP	W	L	Pct	SO	BB	H	ERA	SAVES
2004 Reading	Eastern	20	119	6	6	.500	94	46	93	2.57	0
2004 Scranton-WB	Int.	5	30²/₃	1	3	.250	18	9	39	4.99	0
2004 Philadelphia	N.L.	6	28¹/₃	2	0	1.000	24	16	25	3.49	0
2005 Scranton-WB	Int.	24	137¹/₃	6	9	.400	97	66	155	6.16	0
2005 Philadelphia	N.L.	7	26	1	2	.333	17	16	30	10.04	0
2006 Philadelphia	N.L.	11	54¹/₃	4	3	.571	34	32	70	7.29	0
2006 Scranton-WB a	Int.	17	115	7	4	.636	85	38	117	4.23	0
2007 Charlotte	Int.	17	106²/₃	7	3	.700	96	35	93	3.12	0
2007 Chicago	A.L.	16	70	1	5	.167	49	19	85	5.27	0
2008 Chicago	A.L.	33	206¹/₃	17	8	.680	145	70	190	3.84	0
Major League Totals .....5 Yrs.		73	385	25	18	.581	269	153	400	4.98	0
Division Series											
2008 Chicago	A.L.	1	3	0	1	.000	4	2	5	12.00	0

a Traded to Chicago White Sox with player to be named later for pitcher Freddy Garcia, December 6, 2006. Chicago White Sox received pitcher Gio Gonzalez to complete trade, December 7, 2006.

FOGG, JOSHUA SMITH (JOSH)

Born, Lynn, Massachusetts, December 13, 1976.
Bats Right. Throws Right. Height, 6 feet. Weight, 205 pounds.

Year Club	Lea	G	IP	W	L	Pct	SO	BB	H	ERA	SAVES
1998 White Sox	Arizona	2	4	1	0	1.000	5	1	0	0.00	0
1998 Hickory	So.Atl.	8	41¹/₃	1	3	.250	29	13	36	2.18	0
1998 Winston-Sal	Carolina	1	1	0	1	.000	2	0	2	0.00	0
1999 Winston-Salem	Carolina	17	103¹/₃	10	5	.667	109	33	93	2.96	0
1999 Birmingham	Southern	10	55	3	2	.600	40	18	66	5.89	0
2000 Birmingham	Southern	27	192¹/₃	11	7	.611	136	44	190	2.57	4
2001 Charlotte	Int.	40	114²/₃	4	7	.364	89	30	129	4.79	4
2001 Chicago a	A.L.	11	13¹/₃	0	0	.000	17	3	10	2.03	0
2002 Pittsburgh	N.L.	33	194¹/₃	12	12	.500	113	69	199	4.35	0
2003 Nashville	P.C.	2	10	0	1	.000	7	1	12	5.40	0
2003 Pittsburgh b	N.L.	26	142	10	9	.526	71	40	166	5.26	0
2004 Pittsburgh	N.L.	33	178¹/₃	11	10	.524	82	66	193	4.64	0
2005 Pittsburgh c	N.L.	34	169¹/₃	6	11	.353	85	53	196	5.05	0
2006 Colorado	N.L.	31	172	11	9	.550	93	60	206	5.49	0
2007 Colorado Springs	P.C.	1	5	0	1	.000	3	0	6	3.60	0
2007 Colorado d-e	N.L.	30	165²/₃	10	9	.526	94	59	194	4.94	0
2008 Sarasota	Fla.St.	3	19	1	0	1.000	14	3	24	3.32	0
2008 Louisville	Int.	2	17	1	1	.500	12	3	14	1.59	0
2008 Cincinnati f-g	N.L.	22	78¹/₃	2	7	.222	45	27	97	7.58	0
Major League Totals ......8 Yrs.		219	1113¹/₃	62	67	.481	600	377	1261	5.08	0
Division Series											
2007 Colorado	N.L.	1	2	1	0	1.000	1	0	1	0.00	0
Championship Series											
2007 Colorado	N.L.	1	6	1	0	1.000	3	1	7	1.50	0
World Series Record											
2007 Colorado	N.L.	1	2²/₃	0	1	.000	2	2	10	20.25	0

a Traded to Pittsburgh Pirates with pitcher Kip Wells and pitcher Sean Lowe for pitcher Todd Ritchie and catcher Lee Evans, December 13, 2001.
b On disabled list from April 21 to May 26, 2003.
c Not offered contract, December 21, 2005. Signed with Colorado Rockies, February 11, 2006.
d On disabled list from May 23 to June 7, 2007.
e Filed for free agency, November 2, 2007. Signed with Cincinnati Reds, February 21, 2008.
f On disabled list from June 1 to July 5 and September 9 to November 1, 2008.
g Filed for free agency, November 1, 2008.

FRANCIS, JEFFREY WILLIAM (JEFF)

Born, Vancouver, British Columbia, Canada, January 8, 1981.
Bats Left. Throws Left. Height, 6 feet, 5 inches. Weight, 205 pounds.

Year Club	Lea	G	IP	W	L	Pct	SO	BB	H	ERA	SAVES
2002 Tri-City	Northwest	4	10²/₃	0	0	.000	16	4	5	0.00	0
2002 Asheville	So.Atl.	4	20	0	0	.000	23	4	16	1.80	0
2003 Visalia	California	27	160²/₃	12	9	.571	153	45	135	3.47	0
2004 Tulsa	Texas	17	113²/₃	13	1	.929	147	22	73	1.98	0
2004 Colorado Springs	P.C.	7	41	3	2	.600	49	7	35	2.85	0
2004 Colorado	N.L.	7	36²/₃	3	2	.600	32	13	42	5.15	0
2005 Colorado	N.L.	33	183²/₃	14	12	.538	128	70	228	5.68	0
2006 Colorado	N.L.	32	199	13	11	.542	117	69	187	4.16	0
2007 Colorado	N.L.	34	215¹/₃	17	9	.654	165	63	234	4.22	0

Year Club	Lea	G	IP	W	L	Pct	SO	BB	H	ERA	SAVES
2008 Tulsa .... Texas		3	14⅓	1	0	1.000	19	2	12	0.63	0
2008 Colorado a .... N.L.		24	143⅔	4	10	.286	94	49	164	5.01	0
Major League Totals .... 5 Yrs.		130	778⅓	51	44	.537	536	264	855	4.74	0
Division Series											
2007 Colorado .... N.L.		1	6	1	0	1.000	8	2	4	3.00	0
Championship Series											
2007 Colorado .... N.L.		1	6⅔	1	0	1.000	4	1	7	1.35	0
World Series Record											
2007 Colorado .... N.L.		1	4	0	1	.000	3	3	10	13.50	0

a On disabled list from June 29 to August 6, 2008.

FRANCISCO, FRANKLIN (FRANK)
Born, Santo Domingo, Dominican Republic, September 11, 1979.
Bats Right. Throws Right. Height, 6 feet, 2 inches. Weight, 235 pounds.

Year Club	Lea	G	IP	W	L	Pct	SO	BB	H	ERA	SAVES
1997						INJURED—Did Not Play					
1998 Co-op .... Dominican		16	48	0	5	.000	53	76	44	10.31	0
1999 Red Sox .... Gulf Coast		12	53⅓	2	4	.333	48	35	58	4.56	0
2000 Red Sox .... Gulf Coast		1	1	0	0	.000	1	2	2	18.00	0
2001 Augusta .... So.Atl.		37	68	4	3	.571	90	30	40	2.91	2
2002 Winston-Salem ..... Carolina		6	25⅔	0	4	.000	25	18	31	8.06	0
2002 Trenton .... Eastern		9	16	2	2	.500	18	16	10	5.63	0
2002 Sarasota a .... Fla.St.		16	53	1	5	.167	58	27	33	2.55	0
2003 Winston-Salem ... Carolina		16	78⅓	7	3	.700	67	36	59	3.56	0
2003 Frisco b .... Texas		7	35⅓	2	3	.400	22	18	43	8.41	0
2004 Frisco............... Texas		15	17⅔	1	3	.250	30	10	7	2.55	6
2004 Texas .... A.L.		45	51⅓	5	1	.833	60	28	36	3.33	0
2005 Oklahoma............. P.C.		2	3	0	0	.000	4	2	2	3.00	1
2005 Frisco c .... Texas		4	3⅓	0	1	.000	3	2	4	8.10	0
2006 Frisco............... Texas		13	14⅔	0	0	.000	22	4	10	1.84	0
2006 Spokane......... Northwest		4	4	0	0	.000	6	0	3	0.00	0
2006 Texas d.............. A.L.		8	7⅓	0	1	.000	6	2	8	4.91	0
2007 Oklahoma........... P.C.		5	6	1	0	1.000	14	3	0	0.00	2
2007 Texas .... A.L.		59	59⅓	1	1	.500	49	38	57	4.55	0
2008 Oklahoma........... P.C.		8	9	0	0	.000	16	3	3	0.00	5
2008 Texas .... A.L.		58	63⅓	3	5	.375	83	26	47	3.13	5
Major League Totals ...... 4 Yrs.		170	181⅓	9	8	.529	198	94	148	3.72	5

a Traded to Chicago White Sox by Boston Red Sox with pitcher Byeong An for pitcher Bob Howry, July 31, 2002.
b Sent to Texas Rangers as one of the players to be named later for outfielder Carl Everett, July 23, 2003.
c On disabled list from March 25 to October 12, 2005.
d On disabled list from March 24 to June 19, 2006.

FRANKLIN, RYAN RAY
Born, Fort Smith, Arkansas, March 5, 1973.
Bats Right. Throws Right. Height, 6 feet, 3 inches. Weight, 190 pounds.

Year Club	Lea	G	IP	W	L	Pct	SO	BB	H	ERA	SAVES
1993 Bellingham....... Northwest		15	74	5	3	.625	55	27	72	2.92	0
1994 Appleton...........Midwest		18	118	9	6	.600	102	23	105	3.13	0
1994 Calgary.............. P.C.		1	5⅔	0	0	.000	2	1	9	7.94	0
1994 Riverside .... California		8	61⅔	4	2	.667	35	2	61	3.06	0
1995 Port City.......... Southern		31	146	6	10	.375	102	43	153	4.32	0
1996 Port City.......... Southern		28	182	6	12	.333	127	37	186	4.01	0
1997 Memphis .... Southern		11	59⅓	4	2	.667	49	14	45	3.03	0
1997 Tacoma .... P.C.		14	90⅓	5	5	.500	59	24	97	4.18	0
1998 Tacoma .... P.C.		34	127⅔	5	6	.455	90	32	148	4.51	1
1999 Tacoma .... P.C.		29	135⅔	6	9	.400	94	33	142	4.71	2
1999 Seattle .... A.L.		6	11⅓	0	0	.000	6	8	10	4.76	0
2000 Tacoma .... P.C.		31	164	11	5	.688	142	35	147	3.90	0
2001 Tacoma .... P.C.		1	3⅔	0	0	.000	3	0	2	0.00	0
2001 Seattle .... A.L.		38	78⅓	5	1	.833	60	24	76	3.56	0
2002 Everett .... Northwest		1	2⅔	0	0	.000	1	0	2	0.00	0
2002 Seattle a .... A.L.		41	118⅔	7	5	.583	65	22	117	4.02	0
2003 Seattle .... A.L.		32	212	11	13	.458	99	61	199	3.57	0
2004 Seattle .... A.L.		32	200⅓	4	16	.200	104	61	224	4.90	0
2005 Seattle b............. A.L.		32	190⅔	8	15	.348	93	62	212	5.10	0
2006 Philadelphia-Cincinnati c-d . N.L.		66	77⅓	6	7	.462	43	33	86	4.54	0
2007 St. Louis.............. N.L.		69	80	4	4	.500	44	11	70	3.04	1

Year Club	Lea	G	IP	W	L	Pct	SO	BB	H	ERA	SAVES
2008 St. Louis.............	N.L.	74	78²/₃	6	6	.500	51	30	86	3.55	17
Major League Totals........9 Yrs.		390	1047¹/₃	51	67	.432	565	312	1080	4.19	18

a On disabled list from June 28 to July 15, 2002.
b Not offered contract, December 21, 2005. Signed with Philadelphia Phillies, January 5, 2006.
c Traded to Cincinnati Reds for pitcher Zac Scott, August 7, 2006.
d Filed for free agency, October 30, 2006. Signed with St. Louis Cardinals, January 11, 2007.

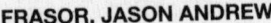

FRASOR, JASON ANDREW

Born, Chicago, Illinois, August 9, 1977.
Bats Right. Throws Right. Height, 5 feet, 10 inches. Weight, 170 pounds.

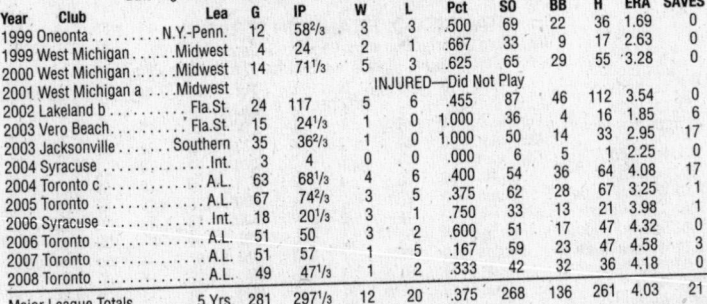

Year Club	Lea	G	IP	W	L	Pct	SO	BB	H	ERA	SAVES
1999 Oneonta.........N.Y.-Penn.	12	58²/₃	3	3	.500	69	22	36	1.69	0	
1999 West Michigan......Midwest	4	24	2	1	.667	33	9	17	2.63	0	
2000 West Michigan......Midwest	14	71¹/₃	5	3	.625	65	29	55	3.28	0	
2001 West Michigan a ...Midwest					INJURED—Did Not Play						
2002 Lakeland b ....Fla.St.	24	117	5	6	.455	87	46	112	3.54	0	
2003 Vero Beach........Fla.St.	15	24¹/₃	1	0	1.000	36	4	16	1.85	6	
2003 Jacksonville.......Southern	35	36²/₃	1	0	1.000	50	14	33	2.95	17	
2004 Syracuse..............Int.	3	4	0	0	.000	6	5	1	2.25	0	
2004 Toronto c..............A.L.	63	68¹/₃	4	6	.400	54	36	64	4.08	17	
2005 Toronto..............A.L.	67	74²/₃	3	5	.375	62	28	67	3.25	1	
2006 Syracuse..............Int.	18	20¹/₃	3	1	.750	33	13	21	3.98	1	
2006 Toronto..............A.L.	51	50	3	2	.600	51	17	47	4.32	0	
2007 Toronto..............A.L.	51	57	1	5	.167	59	23	47	4.58	3	
2008 Toronto..............A.L.	49	47¹/₃	1	2	.333	42	32	36	4.18	0	
Major League Totals........5 Yrs.	281	297¹/₃	12	20	.375	268	136	261	4.03	21	

a On minor league disabled list, April 5 to September 14, 2001.
b Sent by Detroit Tigers to Los Angeles Dodgers as player to be named later for infielder Hiram Bocachica, September 18, 2002.
c Traded to Toronto Blue Jays for outfielder Jayson Werth, March 30, 2004.

FUENTES, BRIAN CHRISTOPHER

Born, Merced, California, August 9, 1975.
Bats Left. Throws Left. Height, 6 feet, 4 inches. Weight, 230 pounds.

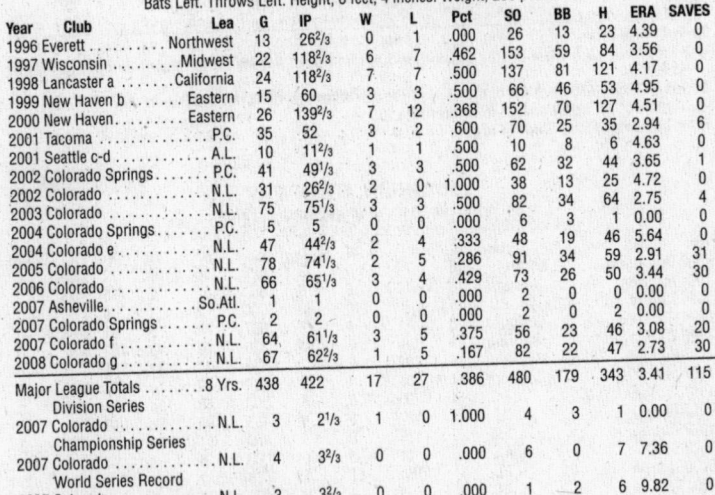

Year Club	Lea	G	IP	W	L	Pct	SO	BB	H	ERA	SAVES
1996 Everett.........Northwest	13	26²/₃	0	1	.000	26	13	23	4.39	0	
1997 Wisconsin........Midwest	22	118²/₃	6	7	.462	153	59	84	3.56	0	
1998 Lancaster a ......California	24	118²/₃	7	7	.500	137	81	121	4.17	0	
1999 New Haven b ....Eastern	15	60	3	3	.500	66	46	53	4.95	0	
2000 New Haven.........Eastern	26	139²/₃	7	12	.368	152	70	127	4.51	0	
2001 Tacoma..............P.C.	35	52	3	2	.600	70	25	35	2.94	6	
2001 Seattle c-d............A.L.	10	11²/₃	1	1	.500	10	8	6	4.63	0	
2002 Colorado Springs......P.C.	41	49¹/₃	3	3	.500	62	32	44	3.65	1	
2002 Colorado............N.L.	31	26²/₃	2	0	1.000	38	13	25	4.72	0	
2003 Colorado............N.L.	75	75¹/₃	3	3	.500	82	34	64	2.75	4	
2004 Colorado Springs......P.C.	5	5	0	0	.000	6	3	1	0.00	0	
2004 Colorado e............N.L.	47	44²/₃	2	4	.333	48	19	46	5.64	0	
2005 Colorado............N.L.	78	74¹/₃	2	5	.286	91	34	59	2.91	31	
2006 Colorado............N.L.	66	65¹/₃	3	4	.429	73	26	50	3.44	30	
2007 Asheville.........So.Atl.	1	1	0	0	.000	2	0	0	0.00	0	
2007 Colorado Springs.......P.C.	2	2	0	0	.000	2	0	2	0.00	0	
2007 Colorado f............N.L.	64	61¹/₃	3	5	.375	56	23	46	3.08	20	
2008 Colorado g............N.L.	67	62²/₃	1	5	.167	82	22	47	2.73	30	
Major League Totals........8 Yrs.	438	422	17	27	.386	480	179	343	3.41	115	
Division Series											
2007 Colorado............N.L.	3	2¹/₃	1	0	1.000	4	3	1	0.00	0	
Championship Series											
2007 Colorado............N.L.	4	3²/₃	0	0	.000	6	0	7	7.36	0	
World Series Record											
2007 Colorado............N.L.	3	3²/₃	0	0	.000	1	2	6	9.82	0	

a On disabled list from April 2 to 20, 1998.
b On disabled list from June 9 to August 22, 1999.
c On disabled list from August 26 to September 29, 2001.
d Traded to Colorado Rockies with pitcher Dennis Stark and pitcher Jose Paniagua for infielder Jeff Cirillo, December 15, 2001.
e On disabled list from June 7 to August 15, 2004.
f On disabled list from July 4 to August 14, 2007.
g Filed for free agency, November 1, 2008. Signed with Los Angeles Angels, December 31, 2008.

GAGNE, ERIC SERGE

Born, Montreal, Quebec, Canada, January 7, 1976.
Bats Right. Throws Right. Height, 6 feet, 2 inches. Weight, 245 pounds.

Year	Club	Lea	G	IP	W	L	Pct	SO	BB	H	ERA	SAVES
1996	Savannah	So.Atl.	23	115⅓	7	6	.538	131	43	94	3.28	0
1997							INJURED—Did Not Play					
1998	Vero Beach	Fla.St.	25	139⅔	9	7	.563	144	48	118	3.74	0
1999	San Antonio	Texas	26	167⅔	12	4	.750	185	64	122	2.63	0
1999	Los Angeles	N.L.	5	30	1	1	.500	30	15	18	2.10	0
2000	Albuquerque	P.C.	9	55⅔	5	1	.833	59	15	56	3.88	0
2000	Los Angeles	N.L.	20	101⅓	4	6	.400	79	60	106	5.15	0
2001	Las Vegas	P.C.	4	23⅔	3	0	1.000	31	8	15	1.52	0
2001	Los Angeles	N.L.	33	151⅔	6	7	.462	130	46	144	4.75	0
2002	Los Angeles	N.L.	77	82⅓	4	1	.800	114	16	55	1.97	52
2003	Los Angeles a	N.L.	77	82⅓	2	3	.400	137	20	37	1.20	*55
2004	Los Angeles	N.L.	70	82⅓	7	3	.700	114	22	53	2.19	45
2005	Las Vegas	P.C.	3	4	0	0	.000	7	0	0	0.00	0
2005	Los Angeles b	N.L.	14	13⅓	1	0	1.000	22	3	10	2.70	8
2006	Las Vegas	P.C.	2	2	0	0	.000	3	1	0	0.00	2
2006	Los Angeles c-d	N.L.	2	2	0	0	.000	3	1	0	0.00	2
2007	Frisco	Texas	3	2⅔	0	1	.000	3	1	2	3.38	0
2007	Texas-Boston e-f-g	A.L.	54	52	4	2	.667	51	21	49	3.81	16
2008	Nashville	P.C.	2	1⅔	0	0	.000	3	1	2	10.80	0
2008	Milwaukee h-i	N.L.	50	46⅓	4	3	.571	38	22	46	5.44	10
Major League Totals	10 Yrs.		402	643⅔	33	26	.559	718	226	518	3.47	187
Division Series												
2004	Los Angeles	N.L.	2	3	0	0	.000	3	1	1	0.00	0
2007	Boston	A.L.	1	1	0	0	.000	1	0	9	9.00	0
2008	Milwaukee	N.L.	2	2	0	0	.000	1	0	1	0.00	0
Division Series Totals			5	6	0	0	.000	5	1	3	1.50	0
Championship Series												
2007	Boston	A.L.	3	2⅓	0	0	.000	4	2	3	7.71	0
World Series Record												
2007	Boston	A.L.	1	1	0	0	.000	1	0	0	0.00	0

a Selected Cy Young Award Winner in National League for 2003.
b On disabled list from April 1 to May 14 and June 13 to November 16, 2005.
c On disabled list from April 1 to May 30 and June 7 to October 26, 2006.
d Filed for free agency, October 31, 2006. Signed with Texas Rangers, December 12, 2006.
e On disabled list from March 28 to April 13 and April 23 to May 8, 2007.
f Traded to Boston Red Sox for pitcher Kason Gabbard, outfielder David Murphy and outfielder Engle Beltre, July 31, 2007.
g Filed for free agency, October 31, 2007. Signed with Milwaukee Brewers, December 10, 2007.
h On disabled list from May 21 to June 30, 2008.
i Filed for free agency, October 30, 2008.

GALARRAGA, ARMANDO ANTONIO

Born, Cumana, Venezuela, January 15, 1982.
Bats Right. Throws Right. Height, 6 feet, 4 inches. Weight, 180 pounds.

Year	Club	Lea	G	IP	W	L	Pct	SO	BB	H	ERA	SAVES
2001	Expos	Gulf Coast	14	34⅔	1	3	.250	24	15	37	3.12	2
2002	Expos	Gulf Coast	2	3⅔	0	0	.000	1	0	1	2.45	0
2003	Expos	Gulf Coast	5	15	1	1	.500	7	5	13	1.80	0
2004	Savannah	So.Atl.	23	110⅓	5	5	.500	94	31	104	4.65	0
2005	Potomac	Carolina	14	80	3	4	.429	79	23	69	2.48	0
2005	Harrisburg a	Eastern	13	76⅓	3	4	.429	58	21	80	5.19	0
2006	Rangers	Arizona	6	16⅓	0	2	.000	16	6	18	3.31	0
2006	Bakersfield	Calif.	2	8⅔	0	1	.000	7	7	6	6.23	0
2006	Spokane	Northwest	1	4	0	1	.000	3	0	6	4.50	0
2006	Frisco	Texas	9	41	1	6	.143	38	13	56	5.49	0
2007	Frisco	Texas	23	127⅔	9	6	.600	114	47	122	4.02	0
2007	Oklahoma	P.C.	4	24⅔	2	2	.500	21	11	23	4.74	0
2007	Texas	A.L.	3	8⅔	0	0	.000	6	7	8	6.23	0
2008	Toledo	Int.	2	12	2	0	1.000	11	1	7	2.25	0
2008	Detroit b	A.L.	30	178⅔	13	7	.650	126	61	152	3.73	0
Major League Totals	2 Yrs.		33	187⅓	13	7	.650	132	68	160	3.84	0

a Traded by Washington Nationals to Texas Rangers with outfielder Brad Wilkerson and outfielder Terrmel Sledge for infielder Alfonso Soriano, December 13, 2005.
b Traded to Detroit Tigers for outfielder Michael Hernandez, February 5, 2008.

GALLAGHER, SEAN PATRICK

Born, Boston, Massachusetts, December 30, 1985.
Bats Right. Throws Right. Height, 6 feet, 2 inches. Weight, 235 pounds.

Year	Club	Lea	G	IP	W	L	Pct	SO	BB	H	ERA	SAVES
2004 Cubs	Arizona	10	34²/₃	1	2	.333	44	11	38	3.12	0
2005 Daytona	Fla.St.	1	5	0	0	.000	7	0	6	1.80	0
2005 Peoria	Midwest	26	146	14	5	.737	139	55	107	2.71	0
2006 Daytona	Fla.St.	13	78¹/₃	4	0	1.000	80	21	75	2.30	0
2006 West Tenn	Southern	15	86¹/₃	7	5	.583	91	55	74	2.71	0
2007 Tennessee	Southern	11	61	7	2	.778	54	24	54	3.39	0
2007 Iowa	P.C.	8	40²/₃	3	1	.750	37	13	33	2.66	0
2007 Chicago	N.L.	8	14²/₃	0	0	.000	5	12	19	8.59	1
2008 Iowa	P.C.	5	29	2	2	.500	30	9	21	3.10	0
2008 Chicago	N.L.	12	58²/₃	3	4	.429	49	22	58	4.45	0
2008 Oakland a-b	A.L.	11	56²/₃	2	3	.400	54	36	60	5.88	0
Major League Totals ....2 Yrs.		31	130	5	7	.417	108	70	137	5.54	1

a Traded to Oakland Athletics with outfielder Matt Murton, outfielder Eric Patterson and catcher Josh Donaldson for pitcher Rich Harden and pitcher Chad Gaudin, July 8, 2008.
b On disabled list from August 20 to September 10, 2008.

GALLARDO, YOVANI

Born, La Piedad, Mexico, February 27, 1986.
Bats Right. Throws Right. Height, 6 feet, 1 inch. Weight, 210 pounds.

Year	Club	Lea	G	IP	W	L	Pct	SO	BB	H	ERA	SAVES
2004 Brewers	Arizona	6	19¹/₃	0	0	.000	23	4	14	0.47	0
2004 Beloit	Midwest	2	7¹/₃	0	1	.000	8	4	12	12.27	0
2005 West Tenn	So.Atl.	26	121¹/₃	8	3	.727	110	51	100	2.74	1
2006 Brevard County	Fla.St.	13	77²/₃	6	3	.667	103	23	54	2.09	0
2006 Huntsville	Southern	13	77¹/₃	5	2	.714	85	28	50	1.63	0
2007 Nashville	P.C.	13	77²/₃	8	3	.727	110	28	53	2.90	0
2007 Milwaukee	N.L.	20	110¹/₃	9	5	.643	101	37	103	3.67	0
2008 Nashville	P.C.	3	15²/₃	0	1	.000	18	5	20	5.17	0
2008 Milwaukee a	N.L.	4	24	0	0	.000	20	8	22	1.88	0
Major League Totals ....2 Yrs.		24	134¹/₃	9	5	.643	121	45	125	3.35	0
Division Series											
2008 Milwaukee	N.L.	2	7	0	1	.000	4	5	4	0.00	0

a On disabled list from March 21 to April 20 and May 2 to September 23, 2008.

GARLAND, JON STEVEN

Born, Valencia, California, September 27, 1979.
Bats Right. Throws Right. Height, 6 feet, 6 inches. Weight, 215 pounds.

Year	Club	Lea	G	IP	W	L	Pct	SO	BB	H	ERA	SAVES
1997 Cubs	Arizona	10	40	3	2	.600	39	10	37	2.70	0
1998 Rockford	Midwest	19	107¹/₃	4	7	.364	70	45	124	5.03	0
1998 Hickory a	So.Atl.	5	26²/₃	1	4	.200	19	13	36	5.40	0
1999 Winston-Salem	Carolina	19	119	5	7	.417	84	39	109	3.33	0
1999 Birmingham	Southern	7	39	3	1	.750	27	18	39	4.38	0
2000 Charlotte	Int.	16	103²/₃	9	2	.818	63	32	99	2.26	0
2000 Birmingham	Southern	1	6	0	0	.000	10	1	4	0.00	0
2000 Chicago b	A.L.	15	69²/₃	4	8	.333	42	40	82	6.46	0
2001 Charlotte	Int.	5	33	0	3	.000	26	11	31	2.73	0
2001 Chicago	A.L.	35	117	6	7	.462	61	55	123	3.69	1
2002 Chicago	A.L.	33	192²/₃	12	12	.500	112	83	188	4.58	0
2003 Chicago	A.L.	32	191²/₃	12	13	.480	108	74	188	4.51	0
2004 Chicago	A.L.	34	217	12	11	.522	113	76	223	4.89	0
2005 Chicago	A.L.	32	221	18	10	.643	115	47	212	3.50	0
2006 Chicago	A.L.	33	211¹/₃	18	7	.720	112	41	*247	4.51	0
2007 Chicago c	A.L.	32	208¹/₃	10	13	.435	98	57	219	4.23	0
2008 Los Angeles d	A.L.	32	196²/₃	14	8	.636	90	59	237	4.90	0
Major League Totals ....9 Yrs.		278	1625¹/₃	106	89	.544	851	532	1719	4.47	1
Championship Series											
2005 Chicago	A.L.	1	9	1	0	1.000	7	1	4	2.00	0
World Series Record											
2005 Chicago	A.L.	1	7	0	0	.000	4	2	7	2.57	0

a Traded by Chicago Cubs to Chicago White Sox for pitcher Matt Karcher, July 29, 1998.
b On disabled list from August 19 to September 2, 2000.
c Traded to Los Angeles Angels for infielder Orlando Cabrera, November 19, 2007.
d Filed for free agency, October 30, 2008.

GARZA, MATTHEW SCOTT (MATT)
Born, Selma, California, November 11, 1983.
Bats Right. Throws Right. Height, 6 feet, 4 inches. Weight, 205 pounds.

Year Club	Lea	G	IP	W	L	Pct	SO	BB	H	ERA	SAVES
2005 Elizabethton	Appal.	4	19²/₃	1	1	.500	25	6	14	3.66	0
2006 Fort Myers	Fla.St.	8	44¹/₃	5	1	.833	53	11	27	1.42	0
2006 New Britain	Eastern	10	57¹/₃	6	2	.750	68	14	40	2.51	0
2006 Rochester	Int.	5	34	3	1	.750	33	7	20	1.85	0
2006 Minnesota	A.L.	10	50	3	6	.333	38	23	62	5.76	0
2007 Rochester	Int.	16	92	4	6	.400	95	31	93	3.62	0
2007 Minnesota a	A.L.	16	83	5	7	.417	67	32	96	3.69	0
2008 Vero Beach	Fla.St.	1	3²/₃	0	0	.000	4	3	8	9.82	0
2008 Tampa Bay b	A.L.	30	184²/₃	11	9	.550	128	59	170	3.70	0
Major League Totals	3 Yrs.	56	317²/₃	19	22	.463	233	114	328	4.02	0
Division Series											
2008 Tampa Bay	N.L.	1	6	0	1	.000	4	4	7	7.50	0
Championship Series											
2008 Tampa Bay	N.L.	2	13	2	0	1.000	14	6	8	1.38	0
World Series Record											
2008 Tampa Bay	N.L.	1	6	0	0	.000	7	2	6	6.00	0

a Traded to Tampa Bay Devil Rays with infielder Jason Bartlett and pitcher Eduardo Morlan for infielder Brendan Harris, outfielder Jason Pridie and outfielder Delmon Young, November 28, 2007.
b On disabled list from April 9 to April 25, 2008.

GAUDIN, CHAD EDWARD
Born, Metairie, Louisiana, March 24, 1983.
Bats Right. Throws Right. Height, 5 feet, 11 inches. Weight, 190 pounds.

Year Club	Lea	G	IP	W	L	Pct	SO	BB	H	ERA	SAVES
2002 Charleston-SC	So.Atl.	26	119¹/₃	4	6	.400	106	37	106	2.26	1
2003 Bakersfield	Calif.	14	80¹/₃	5	3	.625	70	23	63	2.13	0
2003 Orlando	Southern	3	19	2	0	1.000	23	3	8	0.47	0
2003 Tampa Bay	A.L.	15	40	2	0	1.000	23	16	37	3.60	0
2004 Tampa Bay	A.L.	26	42²/₃	1	2	.333	30	16	59	4.85	0
2004 Durham a	Int.	17	47²/₃	1	3	.250	52	17	48	4.72	2
2005 Toronto	A.L.	5	13	1	3	.250	12	6	31	13.15	0
2005 Syracuse b-c	Int.	23	150¹/₃	9	8	.529	113	35	140	3.35	0
2006 Sacramento	P.C.	4	24¹/₃	3	0	1.000	26	8	14	0.37	0
2006 Oakland	A.L.	55	64	4	2	.667	36	42	51	3.09	2
2007 Oakland	A.L.	34	199¹/₃	11	13	.458	154	100	205	4.42	0
2008 Oakland	A.L.	26	62²/₃	5	3	.625	44	17	63	3.59	0
2008 Chicago d-e	N.L.	24	27¹/₃	4	2	.667	27	10	29	6.26	0
Major League Totals	6 Yrs.	185	449	28	25	.528	326	207	475	4.45	2
Championship Series											
2006 Oakland	A.L.	3	3¹/₃	0	0	.000	1	3	2	0.00	0

a Traded to Toronto Blue Jays for catcher Kevin Cash, December 13, 2004.
b Traded to Oakland Athletics for player to be named later, December 5, 2005.
c Toronto Blue Jays received outfielder Dustin Majewski to complete trade, December 8, 2005.
d On disabled list from March 19 to April 8, 2008.
e Traded to Chicago Cubs with pitcher Rich Harden for pitcher Sean Gallagher, outfielder Matt Murton, outfielder Eric Patterson and catcher Josh Donaldson, July 8, 2008.

GEARY, GEOFFREY MICHAEL (GEOFF)
Born, Buffalo, New York, August 26, 1976.
Bats Right. Throws Right. Height, 6 feet. Weight, 175 pounds.

Year Club	Lea	G	IP	W	L	Pct	SO	BB	H	ERA	SAVES
1998 Batavia	N.Y.-Penn.	16	95¹/₃	9	1	.900	101	14	78	1.60	0
1999 Clearwater	Fla.St.	24	139	10	5	.667	77	31	175	3.95	0
2000 Reading	Eastern	22	129¹/₃	7	6	.538	112	22	141	4.11	0
2001 Reading	Eastern	29	112¹/₃	9	7	.563	88	21	101	3.61	2
2001 Scranton-W.B.	Int.	7	22	0	3	.000	21	6	35	6.95	0
2002 Scranton-W.B.	Int.	38	101	4	2	.667	82	32	108	3.03	1
2003 Scranton/W.B.	Int.	46	87²/₃	9	4	.692	80	13	73	2.16	5
2003 Philadelphia	N.L.	5	6	0	0	.000	3	3	8	4.50	0
2004 Scranton/W.B.	Int.	21	23¹/₃	1	2	.333	23	13	20	2.31	10
2004 Philadelphia a	N.L.	33	44²/₃	1	0	1.000	30	16	52	5.44	0
2005 Reading	Eastern	1	2	0	0	.000	2	0	0	0.00	0
2005 Scranton/W.B.	Int.	10	16²/₃	1	2	.333	14	2	15	2.70	1
2005 Philadelphia b	N.L.	40	58	2	1	.667	42	21	54	3.72	0

Year Club	Lea	G	IP	W	L	Pct	SO	BB	H	ERA	SAVES
2006 Philadelphia............	N.L.	81	91⅓	7	1	.875	60	20	103	2.96	1
2007 Ottawa................	Int.	14	25	2	1	.667	21	1	28	2.52	0
2007 Philadelphia c..........	N.L.	57	67⅓	3	2	.600	38	25	72	4.41	0
2008 Houston d.............	N.L.	55	64	2	3	.400	45	28	45	2.53	0
Major League Totals........	6 Yrs.	271	331⅓	15	7	.682	218	113	334	3.67	1

a Filed for free agency, December 21, 2004, re-signed with Philadelphia Phillies organization, December 21, 2004.

b On disabled list from July 9 to July 24, 2005.

c Traded to Houston Astros with outfielder Michael Bourn and infielder Mike Costanzo for infielder Eric Bruntlett and pitcher Brad Lidge, November 12, 2007.

d On disabled list from May 16 to June 3, 2008.

GEER, JOSHUA BRENT (JOSH)

Born, Dallas, Texas, June 2, 1983.
Bats Right, Throws Right. Height, 6 feet, 3 inches. Weight, 190 pounds.

Year Club	Lea	G	IP	W	L	Pct	SO	BB	H	ERA	SAVES
2005 Fort Wayne........	Midwest	5	29⅔	1	1	.500	23	9	29	4.25	0
2005 Eugene............	Northwest	7	31⅔	3	1	.750	13	4	35	3.69	0
2006 Lake Elsinore........	Calif.	15	89	7	4	.636	56	16	116	4.96	0
2006 Fort Wayne........	Midwest	12	72⅔	6	2	.750	46	13	72	3.10	0
2007 Portland...........	P.C.	1	6	1	0	1.000	6	1	6	3.00	0
2007 San Antonio........	Texas	26	171⅓	16	6	.727	102	27	163	3.20	0
2008 Portland...........	P.C.	28	166⅔	8	9	.471	107	45	187	4.54	0
2008 San Diego	N.L.	5	27	2	1	.667	16	9	29	2.67	0

GLAVINE, THOMAS MICHAEL (TOM)

Born, Concord, Massachusetts, March 25, 1966.
Bats Left, Throws Left. Height, 6 feet. Weight, 185 pounds.

Year Club	Lea	G	IP	W	L	Pct	SO	BB	H	ERA	SAVES
1984 Bradenton Braves.....	Gulf C.	8	32⅓	2	3	.400	34	13	29	3.34	0
1985 Sumter............	So. Atl.	26	168⅔	9	6	.600	174	73	114	*2.35	0
1986 Greenville........	Southern	22	145⅓	11	6	.647	114	70	129	3.41	0
1986 Richmond	Int.	7	40	1	5	.167	12	27	40	5.63	0
1987 Richmond	Int.	22	150⅓	6	12	.333	91	56	142	3.35	0
1987 Atlanta............	N.L.	9	50⅓	2	4	.333	20	33	55	5.54	0
1988 Atlanta............	N.L.	34	195⅓	7	*17	.292	84	63	201	4.56	0
1989 Atlanta............	N.L.	29	186	14	8	.636	90	40	172	3.68	0
1990 Atlanta a..........	N.L.	33	214⅓	10	12	.455	129	78	232	4.28	0
1991 Atlanta b-c........	N.L.	34	246⅔	*20	11	.645	192	69	201	2.55	0
1992 Atlanta d..........	N.L.	33	225	*20	8	.714	129	70	197	2.76	0
1993 Atlanta............	N.L.	36	239⅓	*22	6	.786	120	90	236	3.20	0
1994 Atlanta e..........	N.L.	25	165⅓	13	9	.591	140	70	173	3.97	0
1995 Atlanta............	N.L.	29	198⅔	16	7	.696	127	66	182	3.08	0
1996 Atlanta............	N.L.	36	235⅓	15	10	.600	181	85	222	2.98	0
1997 Atlanta............	N.L.	33	240	14	7	.667	152	79	197	2.96	0
1998 Atlanta f..........	N.L.	33	229⅓	*20	6	.769	157	74	202	2.47	0
1999 Atlanta............	N.L.	35	234	14	11	.560	138	83	*259	4.12	0
2000 Atlanta............	N.L.	35	241	*21	9	.700	152	65	222	3.40	0
2001 Atlanta............	N.L.	35	219⅓	16	7	.696	116	97	213	3.57	0
2002 Atlanta g..........	N.L.	36	224⅔	18	11	.621	127	78	210	2.96	0
2003 New York..........	N.L.	32	183⅓	9	14	.391	82	66	205	4.52	0
2004 New York..........	N.L.	33	212⅓	11	14	.440	109	70	204	3.60	0
2005 New York..........	N.L.	33	211⅓	13	13	.500	105	61	227	3.53	0
2006 New York h........	N.L.	32	198	15	7	.682	131	62	202	3.82	0
2007 New York i........	N.L.	34	200⅓	13	8	.619	89	64	219	4.45	0
2008 Myrtle Beach	Carolina	1	4	0	0	.000	4	1	3	2.25	0
2008 Mississippi........	Southern	1	5	0	1	.000	1	1	4	3.60	0
2008 Atlanta j-k........	N.L.	13	63⅓	2	4	.333	37	37	67	5.54	0
Major League Totals.......	22 Yrs.	682	4413⅓	305	203	.600	2607	1500	4298	3.54	0
Division Series											
1995 Atlanta.............	N.L.	1	7	0	0	.000	3	1	5	2.57	0
1996 Atlanta.............	N.L.	1	6⅔	1	0	1.000	7	3	5	1.35	0
1997 Atlanta.............	N.L.	1	6	1	0	1.000	4	5	5	4.50	0
1998 Atlanta.............	N.L.	1	7	0	0	.000	8	1	3	1.29	0
1999 Atlanta.............	N.L.	1	6	0	0	.000	6	3	5	3.00	0
2000 Atlanta.............	N.L.	1	2⅓	0	1	.000	2	1	6	27.00	0
2001 Atlanta.............	N.L.	1	8	1	0	1.000	3	2	6	0.00	0

Year Club	Lea	G	IP	W	L	Pct	SO	BB	H	ERA	SAVES
2002 Atlanta	N.L.	2	7⅔	0	2	.000	4	7	17	15.26	0
2006 New York	N.L.	1	6	1	0	1.000	2	2	4	0.00	0
Division Series Totals		10	56⅔	4	3	.571	39	25	56	4.61	0
Championship Series											
1991 Atlanta	N.L.	2	14	0	2	.000	11	6	12	3.21	0
1992 Atlanta	N.L.	2	7⅓	0	2	.000	2	3	13	12.27	0
1993 Atlanta	N.L.	1	7	1	0	1.000	5	0	6	2.57	0
1995 Atlanta	N.L.	1	7	0	0	.000	5	2	7	1.29	0
1996 Atlanta	N.L.	2	13	1	1	.500	9	0	10	2.08	0
1997 Atlanta	N.L.	2	13⅓	1	1	.500	9	11	13	5.40	0
1998 Atlanta	N.L.	2	11⅓	0	2	.000	8	9	13	2.31	0
1999 Atlanta	N.L.	1	7	1	0	1.000	8	1	7	0.00	0
2001 Atlanta	N.L.	2	12	1	1	.500	5	5	10	1.50	0
2006 New York	N.L.	2	11	1	1	.500	4	5	11	2.45	0
Championship Series Totals		17	103⅓	6	10	.375	66	42	102	3.22	0
World Series Record											
1991 Atlanta	N.L.	2	13⅓	1	1	.500	8	7	8	2.70	0
1992 Atlanta	N.L.	2	17	1	1	.500	8	4	10	1.59	0
1995 Atlanta	N.L.	2	14	2	0	1.000	11	6	4	1.29	0
1996 Atlanta	N.L.	1	7	0	1	.000	8	3	4	1.29	0
1999 Atlanta	N.L.	1	7	0	0	.000	3	0	7	5.14	0
World Series Totals		8	58⅓	4	3	.571	38	20	33	2.16	0

a Appeared in one additional game as pinch runner.
b Appeared in one additional game as pinch hitter and one additional game as pinch runner.
c Selected Cy Young Award winner in National League for 1991.
d Appeared in two additional games as pinch hitter.
e Appeared in one additional game as pinch hitter.
f Selected Cy Young Award Winner in National League for 1998.
g Filed for free agency, October 28, 2002. Signed with New York Mets, December 5, 2002.
h Filed for free agency, November 9, 2006, re-signed with New York Mets, December 1, 2006.
i Filed for free agency, October 31, 2007. Signed with Atlanta Braves, November 19, 2007.
j On disabled list from April 14 to April 29 and June 11 to August 14 and August 15 to November 3, 2008.
k Filed for free agency, November 5, 2008.

GLOVER, JOHN GARY (GARY)

Born, Cleveland, Ohio, December 3, 1976.
Bats Right. Throws Right. Height, 6 feet, 5 inches. Weight, 220 pounds.

Year Club	Lea	G	IP	W	L	Pct	SO	BB	H	ERA	SAVES
1994 Blue Jays	Gulf Coast	2	1⅓	0	0	.000	2	4	4	47.25	0
1995 Blue Jays	Gulf Coast	12	62⅓	3	7	.300	46	26	62	4.91	0
1996 Medicine Hat	Pioneer	15	83⅔	3	12	.200	54	29	119	7.75	0
1997 Hagerstown	So.Atl.	28	173⅔	6	17	.261	155	58	165	3.73	0
1998 Knoxville	Southern	8	37⅓	0	5	.000	14	28	41	6.75	0
1998 Dunedin	Fla.St.	19	109⅓	7	6	.538	88	36	117	4.28	0
1999 Knoxville	Southern	13	86	8	2	.800	77	27	70	3.56	0
1999 Syracuse	Int.	14	76⅓	4	6	.400	57	35	93	5.19	0
1999 Toronto	A.L.	1	1	0	0	.000	0	1	0	0.00	0
2000 Syracuse a	Int.	27	166⅔	9	9	.500	119	62	181	5.02	0
2001 Charlotte	Int.	6	38⅓	2	1	.667	29	5	21	1.88	0
2001 Chicago	A.L.	46	100⅓	5	5	.500	63	32	98	4.93	0
2002 Chicago	A.L.	41	138⅓	7	8	.467	70	52	136	5.20	1
2003 Chicago-Anaheim b-c	A.L.	42	62⅔	2	0	1.000	37	22	77	4.74	0
2004 Iowa	P.C.	20	30⅔	3	2	.600	18	14	43	7.92	0
2004 Rochester	Int.	5	16	0	1	.000	8	5	27	8.44	0
2004 Indianapolis	Int.	8	40⅔	3	3	.500	18	11	47	3.98	0
2004 Milwaukee d-e	N.L.	4	18	2	1	.667	8	8	18	3.50	0
2005 Nashville	P.C.	17	92	6	4	.600	75	29	91	3.03	1
2005 Milwaukee f	N.L.	15	64⅔	5	4	.556	58	20	74	5.57	0
2006 Yomiuri g	Japan Cent.	20	96	5	7	.417	63	23	125	4.97	0
2007 Tampa Bay	A.L.	67	77⅓	6	5	.545	51	27	87	4.89	2
2008 Toledo	Int.	3	4	0	0	.000	4	0	3	0.00	1
2008 Tampa Bay-Detroit h-i-j	A.L.	47	54⅓	2	3	.400	37	22	64	5.30	0
Major League Totals	8 Yrs.	263	516⅔	29	26	.527	324	184	554	5.03	3

a Traded to Chicago White Sox for pitcher Scott Eyre, November 7, 2000.
b Traded to Anaheim Angels with pitcher Scott Dunn and pitcher Tim Bittner for pitcher Scott Schoeneweis and pitcher Doug Nickle, July 29, 2003.
c Filed for free agency October 15, 2003. Signed with Chicago Cubs organization, December 18, 2003.
d Released by Chicago Cubs, June 5, 2004. Signed with Minnesota Twins organization, June 7, 2004.

e Released by Minnesota Twins, July 1, 2004. Signed with Milwaukee Brewers organization, July 15, 2004.
f Released by Milwaukee Brewers, November 22, 2005. Signed with Yomuri Giants, November 29, 2005.
g Signed with Tampa Bay Devil Rays organization, December 21, 2006.
h On disabled list from April 26 to May 12 and July 11 to July 28, 2008.
i Filed for free agency, August 2, 2008. Signed with Detroit Tigers organization, August 9, 2008.
j Filed for free agency, October 30, 2008.

GONZALEZ, MICHAEL VELA (MIKE)

Born, Corpus Christi, Texas, May 23, 1978.
Bats Right. Throws Left. Height, 6 feet, 2 inches. Weight, 220 pounds.

Year	Club	Lea	G	IP	W	L	Pct	SO	BB	H	ERA	SAVES
1997	Pirates	Gulf Coast	7	29	2	0	1.000	33	8	21	2.48	0
1997	Augusta	So.Atl.	4	19⅓	1	1	.500	22	8	11	1.86	0
1998	Lynchburg	Carolina	7	28⅓	0	3	.000	22	13	40	6.67	0
1998	Augusta	So.Atl.	11	50⅔	4	2	.667	72	26	43	2.84	0
1999	Lynchburg	Carolina	20	112	10	4	.714	119	63	98	4.02	0
1999	Altoona	Eastern	7	26⅔	2	3	.400	31	19	34	8.10	0
2000	Pirates	Gulf Coast	2	6	1	0	1.000	7	4	8	4.50	0
2000	Lynchburg	Carolina	12	56	4	3	.571	53	34	57	4.66	0
2001	Lynchburg	Carolina	14	30⅔	2	2	.500	32	7	28	2.93	0
2001	Altoona	Eastern	14	87⅓	5	4	.556	66	36	81	3.71	0
2002	Altoona	Eastern	16	85⅓	8	4	.667	82	47	77	3.80	0
2002	Pirates	Gulf Coast	2	13⅓	2	0	1.000	14	3	5	0.00	0
2003	Lynchburg	Carolina	5	7	0	1	.000	9	5	7	5.14	0
2003	Altoona	Eastern	5	7⅓	0	0	.000	10	2	4	1.23	1
2003	Nashville	P.C.	7	10	0	0	.000	10	4	9	4.50	2
2003	Pawtucket	Int.	2	1⅔	0	0	.000	2	1	2	0.00	1
2003	Pittsburgh a-b	N.L.	16	8⅓	0	1	.000	6	6	7	7.56	2
2004	Nashville	P.C.	14	20	2	0	1.000	35	7	12	0.90	2
2004	Pittsburgh	N.L.	47	43⅓	3	1	.750	55	6	32	1.25	1
2005	Indianapolis	Int.	2	3⅓	0	0	.000	5	0	0	0.00	0
2005	Pittsburgh c	N.L.	51	50	1	3	.250	58	31	35	2.70	3
2006	Pittsburgh d-e	N.L.	54	54	3	4	.429	64	31	42	2.17	24
2007	Atlanta f	N.L.	18	17	2	0	1.000	13	8	15	1.59	2
2008	Mississippi	Southern	4	5	0	0	.000	4	0	7	0.00	0
2008	Richmond	Int.	5	6	1	0	1.000	8	1	5	1.50	1
2008	Atlanta g	N.L.	36	33⅔	0	3	.000	44	14	26	4.28	14
Major League Totals		6 Yrs.	222	206⅓	9	12	.429	240	96	157	2.62	44

a Traded to Boston Red Sox with pitcher Scott Sauerbeck for pitcher Brandon Lyon and pitcher Anastacio Martinez, July 22, 2003.
b Traded to Pittsburgh Pirates with infielder Freddy Sanchez and cash for pitcher Jeff Suppan, pitcher Brandon Lyon and pitcher Anastacio Martinez, July 31, 2003.
c On disabled list from June 23 to August 16, 2005.
d On disabled list from August 25 to October 3, 2006.
e Traded to Atlanta Braves with infielder Brent Lillibridge for infielder Adam LaRoche and outfielder Jamie Romak, January 17, 2007.
f On disabled list from May 16 to November 13, 2007.
g On disabled list from March 21 to June 18, 2008.

GORZELANNY, THOMAS STEPHEN (TOM)

Born, Evergreen Park, Illinois, July 12, 1982.
Bats Left. Throws Left. Height, 6 feet, 2 inches. Weight, 210 pounds.

Year	Club	Lea	G	IP	W	L	Pct	SO	BB	H	ERA	SAVES
2003	Williamsport	N.Y.-Penn.	8	30⅓	1	2	.333	22	10	23	1.78	0
2004	Lynchburg	Carolina	10	55⅔	3	5	.375	61	19	54	4.85	0
2004	Hickory	So.Atl.	16	93	7	2	.778	106	34	63	2.23	0
2005	Altoona	Eastern	23	129⅔	8	5	.615	124	46	114	3.26	0
2005	Pittsburgh	N.L.	3	6	0	1	.000	3	3	10	12.00	0
2006	Indianapolis	Int.	16	99⅔	6	5	.545	94	27	67	2.35	0
2006	Pittsburgh a	N.L.	11	61⅔	2	5	.286	40	31	50	3.79	0
2007	Pittsburgh	N.L.	32	201⅔	14	10	.583	135	68	214	3.88	0
2008	Indianapolis	Int.	7	35	3	1	.750	33	4	28	2.06	0
2008	Pittsburgh b	N.L.	21	105⅓	6	9	.400	67	70	120	6.66	0
Major League Totals		4 Yrs.	67	374⅔	22	25	.468	245	172	394	4.78	0

a On disabled list from August 18 to September 16, 2006.
b On disabled list from September 24 to November 13, 2008.

GRABOW, JOHN WILLIAM

Born, Arcadia, California, November 4, 1978.
Bats Left. Throws Left. Height, 6 feet, 2 inches. Weight, 210 pounds.

Year	Club	Lea	G	IP	W	L	Pct	SO	BB	H	ERA	SAVES
1997 Pirates	Gulf Coast		11	45⅓	2	7	.222	28	14	57	4.57	0
1998 Augusta	So.Atl.		17	71⅔	6	3	.667	67	34	84	5.78	0
1999 Hickory	So.Atl.		26	156⅓	9	10	.474	164	32	152	3.80	0
2000 Altoona	Eastern		24	145⅓	8	7	.533	109	65	145	4.33	0
2001 Altoona	Eastern		10	50⅔	2	5	.286	42	39	30	3.38	0
2001 Pirates	Gulf Coast		6	12	0	1	.000	9	4	11	3.75	0
2001 Lynchburg	Carolina		7	36⅔	1	3	.250	35	26	42	6.38	0
2002 Altoona	Eastern		28	146⅓	8	13	.381	97	47	181	5.47	0
2003 Altoona	Eastern		24	83	6	1	.857	73	19	87	3.36	1
2003 Nashville	P.C.		17	24⅔	0	2	.000	26	7	31	4.74	0
2003 Pittsburgh	N.L.		5	5	0	0	.000	9	0	6	3.60	0
2004 Pittsburgh	N.L.		68	61⅔	2	5	.286	64	28	81	5.11	1
2005 Pittsburgh	N.L.		63	52	2	3	.400	42	25	46	4.85	0
2006 Pittsburgh	N.L.		72	69⅔	4	2	.667	66	30	68	4.13	0
2007 Indianapolis	Int.		4	4	0	0	.000	4	2	4	2.25	0
2007 Pittsburgh a	N.L.		63	51⅔	3	2	.600	42	19	56	4.53	1
2008 Pittsburgh	N.L.		74	76	6	3	.667	62	37	60	2.84	4

Major League Totals .... 6 Yrs. 345 316 17 15 .531 285 139 317 4.19 6
a On disabled list from March 23 to April 23, 2007.

GREEN, SEAN WILLIAM

Born, Louisville, Kentucky, April 20, 1979.
Bats Right. Throws Right. Height, 6 feet, 6 inches. Weight, 235 pounds.

Year	Club	Lea	G	IP	W	L	Pct	SO	BB	H	ERA	SAVES
2000 Portland	Northwest		22	28⅔	1	4	.200	17	19	45	8.48	0
2001 Asheville	So.Atl.		43	58	3	4	.429	37	28	66	5.90	0
2002 Salem	Carolina		52	67	2	5	.286	26	31	92	3.90	2
2003 Visalia	Calif.		46	80	3	4	.429	56	38	90	4.84	0
2004 Tulsa a	Texas		52	77⅓	4	3	.571	50	29	63	3.03	2
2005 Tacoma	P.C.		33	49⅓	4	2	.667	44	29	40	3.65	1
2005 San Antonio	Texas		21	24⅓	0	1	.000	18	8	17	2.96	14
2006 Tacoma	P.C.		15	24	4	1	.800	12	11	18	2.25	5
2006 Seattle b	A.L.		24	32	0	0	.000	15	10	34	4.50	1
2007 Tacoma	P.C.		10	17⅔	2	1	.667	10	8	13	2.04	1
2007 Seattle	A.L.		64	68	5	2	.714	53	34	77	3.84	0
2008 Seattle c	A.L.		72	79	4	5	.444	62	36	80	4.67	1

Major League Totals .... 3 Yrs. 160 179 9 7 .563 130 83 191 4.32 1
a Traded to Seattle Mariners by Colorado Rockies for pitcher Aaron Taylor, December 20, 2004.
b On disabled list from July 3 to July 29 and September 8 to November 2, 2006.
c Traded to New York Mets with pitcher J.J. Putz and infielder Jeremy Reed for pitcher Aaron Heilman, outfielder Endy Chavez, pitcher Jason Vargas, infielder Mike Carp, outfielder Ezequiel Carrera, pitcher Maikel Cleto and pitcher Joe Smith, December 10, 2008.

GREGG, KEVIN MARSCHALL

Born, Corvallis, Oregon, June 20, 1978.
Bats Right. Throws Right. Height, 6 feet, 6 inches. Weight, 235 pounds.

Year	Club	Lea	G	IP	W	L	Pct	SO	BB	H	ERA	SAVES
1996 Athletics	Arizona		11	40⅔	3	3	.500	48	21	30	3.10	0
1997 Visalia	California		25	115⅓	6	8	.429	136	74	116	5.70	0
1998 Modesto	California		30	144	8	7	.533	141	76	139	3.81	0
1999 Visalia	California		13	64	4	4	.500	48	24	60	3.74	1
1999 Midland	Texas		16	91⅓	4	7	.364	66	31	75	3.74	0
1999 Vancouver	P.C.		1	5	1	0	1.000	4	2	6	3.60	0
2000 Midland	Texas		28	140⅔	5	14	.263	97	73	171	6.40	0
2001 Midland	Texas		44	81⅓	5	5	.500	72	40	88	4.54	1
2002 Midland	Texas		11	37⅔	3	3	.500	45	18	31	4.30	0
2002 Sacramento	P.C.		16	58⅔	2	5	.286	45	23	82	7.52	0
2002 Visalia a	California		3	17⅓	2	1	.667	11	9	8	2.08	0
2003 Arkansas	Texas		15	66⅓	4	3	.571	60	19	60	3.53	0
2003 Salt Lake	P.C.		15	91⅔	7	4	.636	75	18	90	4.03	0
2003 Anaheim	A.L.		5	24⅔	2	0	1.000	15	14	18	3.28	0
2004 Anaheim	A.L.		55	87⅔	5	2	.714	84	28	86	4.21	1
2005 Salt Lake	P.C.		7	34⅔	3	1	.750	36	10	36	3.89	0
2005 Los Angeles	A.L.		33	64⅓	1	2	.333	52	29	70	5.04	0
2006 Salt Lake	P.C.		3	10	1	0	1.000	8	4	5	0.00	0
2006 Los Angeles b	A.L.		32	78⅓	3	4	.429	71	21	88	4.14	0

Year	Club	Lea	G	IP	W	L	Pct	SO	BB	H	ERA	SAVES
2007 Florida		N.L.	74	84	0	5	.000	87	40	63	3.54	32
2008 Florida c		N.L.	72	68²/₃	7	8	.467	58	37	51	3.41	29
Major League Totals	6 Yrs.		271	407²/₃	18	21	.462	366	163	376	4.00	62
Division Series												
2004 Anaheim		A.L.	1	2	0	0	.000	0	1	3	0.00	0
Championship Series												
2005 Los Angeles		A.L.	1	2	0	0	.000	3	1	1	0.00	0

a Filed for free agency from Oakland Athletics, October 15, 2002. Signed with Anaheim Angels organization, November 20, 2002.

b Traded to Florida Marlins for pitcher Chris Resop, November 20, 2006.

c Traded to Chicago Cubs for pitcher Jose Ceda, November 13, 2008.

GREINKE, DONALD ZACKARY (ZACK)

Born, Orlando, Florida, October 21, 1983.
Bats Right. Throws Right. Height, 6 feet, 2 inches. Weight, 185 pounds.

Year	Club	Lea	G	IP	W	L	Pct	SO	BB	H	ERA	SAVES
2002 Wilmington	Carolina		1	2	0	0	.000	0	0	1	0.00	0
2002 Royals	Gulf Coast		3	4²/₃	0	0	.000	4	3	3	1.93	0
2002 Spokane	Northwest		2	4²/₃	0	0	.000	5	0	9	7.71	0
2003 Wilmington	Carolina		14	87	11	1	.917	78	13	56	1.14	0
2003 Wichita	Texas		9	53	4	3	.571	34	5	58	3.23	0
2004 Omaha	P.C.		6	28²/₃	1	1	.500	23	6	25	2.51	0
2004 Kansas City	A.L.		24	145	8	11	.421	100	26	143	3.97	0
2005 Kansas City	A.L.		33	183	5	17	.227	114	53	233	5.80	0
2006 Wichita	Texas		18	105²/₃	8	3	.727	94	27	96	4.34	0
2006 Kansas City a	A.L.		3	6¹/₃	1	0	1.000	5	3	7	4.26	0
2007 Kansas City	A.L.		52	122	7	7	.500	106	36	122	3.69	1
2008 Kansas City	A.L.		32	202¹/₃	13	10	.565	183	56	202	3.47	0
Major League Totals	5 Yrs.		144	658²/₃	34	45	.430	508	174	707	4.28	1

a On disabled list from April 1 to June 21, 2006.

GRILLI, JASON MICHAEL

Born, Royal Oak, Michigan, November 11, 1976.
Bats Right. Throws Right. Height, 6 feet, 5 inches. Weight, 225 pounds.

Year	Club	Lea	G	IP	W	L	Pct	SO	BB	H	ERA	SAVES
1998 Shreveport	Texas		21	123¹/₃	7	10	.412	100	37	113	3.79	0
1998 Fresno	P.C.		8	42	2	3	.400	37	18	49	5.14	0
1999 Calgary	P.C.		8	41	1	5	.167	27	23	56	7.68	0
1999 Fresno a	P.C.		19	100²/₃	7	5	.583	76	39	124	5.54	0
2000 Calgary	P.C.		8	41¹/₃	1	4	.200	21	23	58	7.19	0
2000 Florida	N.L.		1	6²/₃	1	0	1.000	3	2	11	5.40	0
2001 Florida	N.L.		6	26²/₃	2	2	.500	17	11	30	6.07	0
2001 Calgary	P.C.		8	47	1	2	.333	35	20	46	4.02	0
2001 Marlins	Gulf Coast		2	4	0	0	.000	6	0	2	0.00	0
2001 Brevard County	Fla.St.		3	13²/₃	2	0	1.000	14	5	12	1.98	0
2001 Portland	Eastern		1	4	0	1	.000	3	0	3	2.25	0
2002 Calgary	P.C.		1	5²/₃	0	1	.000	8	3	3	1.59	0
2003 Jupiter	Fla.St.		7	42²/₃	4	2	.667	30	6	38	2.53	0
2003 Albuquerque b	P.C.		12	66²/₃	6	2	.750	38	30	64	3.38	0
2004 Charlotte	Int.		25	152²/₃	9	9	.500	101	58	163	4.83	0
2004 Chicago	A.L.		8	45	2	3	.400	26	20	52	7.40	0
2005 Toledo	Int.		28	167¹/₃	12	9	.571	120	58	170	4.09	0
2005 Detroit c	A.L.		3	16	1	1	.500	5	6	14	3.38	0
2006 Detroit	A.L.		51	62	2	3	.400	31	25	61	4.21	0
2007 Detroit	A.L.		57	79²/₃	5	3	.625	62	32	81	4.74	0
2008 Detroit	A.L.		9	13²/₃	0	1	.000	10	7	12	3.29	0
2008 Colorado d	N.L.		51	61¹/₃	3	2	.600	59	31	55	2.93	1
Major League Totals	7 Yrs.		186	311	16	15	.516	213	134	316	4.66	1
Division Series												
2006 Detroit		A.L.	1	0¹/₃	0	0	.000	0	0	0	0.00	0
Championship Series												
2006 Detroit		A.L.	2	1	0	0	.000	1	3	1	0.00	0
World Series Record												
2006 Detroit		A.L.	2	1²/₃	0	0	.000	0	1	0	0.00	0

a Traded by San Francisco Giants to Florida Marlins with pitcher Nathan Bump for pitcher Livan Hernandez, July 24, 1999.

b Selected by Chicago White Sox in Rule V draft, December 15, 2003.

c Released by Chicago White Sox, January 28, 2005. Signed with Detroit Tigers organization, February 10, 2005.

d Traded to Colorado Rockies for pitcher Zachary Simons, April 30, 2008.

GUARDADO, EDWARD ADRIAN (EDDIE)

Born, Stockton, California, October 2, 1970.
Bats Right. Throws Left. Height, 6 feet. Weight, 225 pounds.

Year	Club	Lea	G	IP	W	L	Pct	SO	BB	H	ERA	SAVES
1991	Elizabethtn	Appal.	14	92	8	4	.667	106	31	67	1.86	0
1992	Kenosha	Midwest	18	101	5	10	.333	103	30	106	4.37	0
1992	Visalia	Calif.	7	49⅓	7	0	1.000	39	10	47	1.64	0
1993	Nashville	Southern	10	65⅓	4	0	1.000	57	10	53	1.24	0
1993	Minnesota	A.L.	19	94⅔	3	8	.273	46	36	123	6.18	0
1994	Minnesota	A.L.	4	17	0	2	.000	8	4	26	8.47	0
1994	Salt Lake	P.C.	24	151	12	7	.632	87	51	171	4.83	0
1995	Minnesota	A.L.	51	91⅓	4	9	.308	71	45	99	5.12	2
1996	Minnesota	A.L.	*83	73⅔	6	5	.545	74	33	61	5.25	4
1997	Minnesota	A.L.	69	46	0	0	.000	54	17	45	3.91	1
1998	Minnesota	A.L.	79	65⅔	3	1	.750	53	28	66	4.52	0
1999	Minnesota	A.L.	63	48	2	5	.286	50	25	37	4.50	2
1999	New Britain a	Eastern	3	4⅔	0	0	.000	5	0	3	1.93	0
2000	Minnesota	A.L.	70	61⅔	7	4	.636	52	25	55	3.94	9
2001	Minnesota b	A.L.	67	66⅔	7	1	.875	67	23	47	3.51	12
2002	Minnesota	A.L.	68	67⅔	1	3	.250	70	18	53	2.93	*45
2003	Minnesota c	A.L.	66	65⅓	3	5	.375	60	14	50	2.89	41
2004	Seattle d	A.L.	41	45⅓	2	2	.500	45	14	31	2.78	18
2005	Seattle	A.L.	58	56⅓	2	3	.400	48	15	52	2.72	36
2006	Seattle	A.L.	28	23	1	3	.250	22	11	29	5.48	5
2006	Cincinnati e-f	N.L.	15	14	0	0	.000	17	2	15	1.29	8
2007	Dayton	Midwest	3	3	0	0	.000	3	0	2	0.00	1
2007	Louisville	Int.	9	8	0	0	.000	3	4	11	4.50	0
2007	Cincinnati g-h	N.L.	15	13⅔	0	0	.000	8	4	16	7.24	0
2008	Texas-Minnesota i-j-k-l	A.L.	64	56⅓	4	4	.500	33	19	50	4.15	4
Major League Totals	16 Yrs.		860	906⅓	45	59	.433	778	333	855	4.30	187
Division Series												
2002	Minnesota	A.L.	2	2	0	0	.000	1	1	5	13.50	1
2003	Minnesota	A.L.	2	2	0	0	.000	2	0	5	9.00	1
Division Series Totals			4	4	0	0	.000	3	1	10	11.25	2
Championship Series												
2002	Minnesota	A.L.	1	1	0	0	.000	2	1	0	0.00	1

a On disabled list from May 22 to June 29, 1999.
b On disabled list from June 5 to June 20, 2001.
c Filed for free agency, October 26, 2003. Signed with Seattle Mariners, December 9, 2003.
d On disabled list from August 1 to November 1, 2004.
e On disabled list from August 20 to October 31, 2006.
f Traded to Cincinnati Reds with cash for outfielder Travis Chick, July 6, 2006.
g Filed for free agency, October 31, 2006, re-signed with Cincinnati Reds organization, February 5, 2007.
h On disabled list from April 1 to August 7, 2007.
i Filed for free agency, November 1, 2007. Signed with Texas Rangers, January 11, 2008.
j On disabled list from April 5 to April 25, 2008.
k Traded to Minnesota Twins for pitcher Mike Hamburger, August 25, 2008.
l Filed for free agency, October 30, 2008.

GUERRIER, MATTHEW OLSON (MATT)

Born, Cleveland, Ohio, August 2, 1978.
Bats Right. Throws Right. Height, 6 feet, 3 inches. Weight, 195 pounds.

Year	Club	Lea	G	IP	W	L	Pct	SO	BB	H	ERA	SAVES
1999	Bristol	Appal.	21	25⅔	5	0	1.000	37	14	18	1.05	10
1999	Winston-Salem	Carolina	4	3⅓	0	0	.000	5	0	3	5.40	2
2000	Winston-Salem	Carolina	30	34⅔	0	3	.000	35	12	25	1.30	19
2000	Birmingham	Southern	23	23⅓	3	1	.750	19	12	17	2.70	7
2001	Charlotte	Int.	12	81⅓	7	1	.875	43	18	75	3.54	0
2001	Birmingham	Southern	15	98⅔	11	3	.786	75	32	85	3.10	0
2002	Nashville a	P.C.	27	157	7	12	.368	130	47	154	4.59	0
2003	Nashville b	P.C.	20	105⅓	4	6	.400	78	18	108	4.53	0
2004	Rochester	Int.	24	144	5	10	.333	97	25	135	3.19	0
2004	Minnesota	A.L.	9	19	0	1	.000	11	6	22	5.68	0
2005	Minnesota	A.L.	43	71⅔	0	3	.000	46	24	71	3.39	0
2006	New Britain	Eastern	4	8⅔	2	0	1.000	10	3	3	1.04	0
2006	Minnesota c	A.L.	39	69⅔	1	0	1.000	37	21	78	3.36	1
2007	Minnesota	A.L.	73	88	2	4	.333	68	21	71	2.35	1
2008	Minnesota	A.L.	*76	76⅓	6	9	.400	59	37	84	5.19	1
Major League Totals	5 Yrs.		240	324⅔	9	17	.346	221	109	326	3.66	3

Year	Club	Lea	G	IP	W	L	Pct	SO	BB	H	ERA	SAVES
Division Series												
2006 Minnesota		A.L.	1	1	0	0	.000	0	0	0	0.00	0

a Traded by Chicago White Sox to Pittsburgh Pirates for pitcher Damaso Marte and infielder Edwin Yan, March 27, 2002.
b Claimed on waivers by Minnesota Twins, November 20, 2003.
c On disabled list from June 9 to August 1, 2006.

GUTHRIE, JEREMY SHANE
Born, Roseburg, Oregon, April 8, 1979.
Bats Right. Throws Right. Height, 6 feet, 1 inch. Weight, 200 pounds.

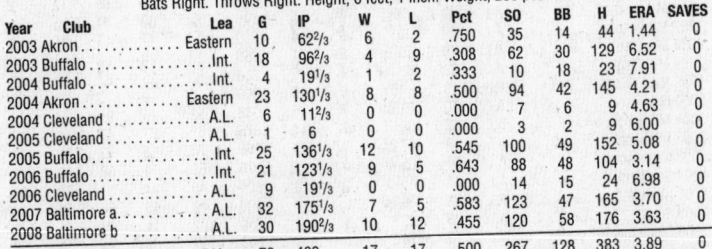

Year	Club	Lea	G	IP	W	L	Pct	SO	BB	H	ERA	SAVES
2003 Akron	Eastern	10	62²/₃	6	2	.750	35	14	44	1.44	0	
2003 Buffalo	Int.	18	96²/₃	4	9	.308	62	30	129	6.52	0	
2004 Buffalo	Int.	4	19¹/₃	1	2	.333	10	18	23	7.91	0	
2004 Akron	Eastern	23	130¹/₃	8	8	.500	94	42	145	4.21	0	
2004 Cleveland	A.L.	6	11²/₃	0	0	.000	7	6	9	4.63	0	
2005 Cleveland	A.L.	1	6	0	0	.000	3	2	9	6.00	0	
2005 Buffalo	Int.	25	136¹/₃	12	10	.545	100	49	152	5.08	0	
2006 Buffalo	Int.	21	123¹/₃	9	5	.643	88	48	104	3.14	0	
2006 Cleveland	A.L.	9	19¹/₃	0	0	.000	14	15	24	6.98	0	
2007 Baltimore a	A.L.	32	175¹/₃	7	5	.583	123	47	165	3.70	0	
2008 Baltimore b	A.L.	30	190²/₃	10	12	.455	120	58	176	3.63	0	
Major League Totals	5 Yrs.	78	403	17	17	.500	267	128	383	3.89	0	

a Claimed on waivers by Baltimore Orioles, January 29, 2007.
b On disabled list from September 6 to September 27, 2008.

HALLADAY, HARRY LEROY (ROY)
Born, Denver, Colorado, May 14, 1977.
Bats Right. Throws Right. Height, 6 feet, 6 inches. Weight, 225 pounds.

Year	Club	Lea	G	IP	W	L	Pct	SO	BB	H	ERA	SAVES
1995 Blue Jays	Gulf Coast	10	50¹/₃	3	5	.375	48	16	35	3.40	0
1996 Dunedin	Fla.St.	27	164²/₃	15	7	.682	109	46	158	2.73	0
1997 Knoxville	Southern	7	36²/₃	2	3	.400	30	11	46	5.40	0
1997 Syracuse	Int.	22	125²/₃	7	10	.412	64	53	132	4.58	0
1998 Syracuse	Int.	21	116¹/₃	9	5	.643	71	53	107	3.79	0
1998 Toronto	A.L.	2	14	1	0	1.000	13	2	9	1.93	0
1999 Toronto	A.L.	36	149¹/₃	8	7	.533	82	79	156	3.92	1
2000 Syracuse	Int.	11	73²/₃	2	3	.400	38	21	85	5.50	0
2000 Toronto	A.L.	19	67²/₃	4	7	.364	44	42	107	10.64	0
2001 Dunedin	Fla.St.	13	22²/₃	0	1	.000	15	3	28	3.97	2
2001 Tennessee	Southern	5	34	2	1	.667	29	6	25	2.12	1
2001 Syracuse	Int.	2	14	1	0	1.000	13	0	12	3.21	0
2001 Toronto	A.L.	17	105¹/₃	5	3	.625	96	25	97	3.16	0
2002 Toronto	A.L.	34	*239¹/₃	19	7	.731	168	62	223	2.93	0
2003 Toronto a	A.L.	36	*266	*22	7	*.759	204	32	*253	3.25	0
2004 Toronto b	A.L.	21	133	8	8	.500	95	39	140	4.20	0
2005 Toronto c	A.L.	19	141²/₃	12	4	.750	108	18	118	2.41	0
2006 Toronto	A.L.	32	220	16	5	*.762	132	34	208	3.19	0
2007 Toronto d	A.L.	31	225¹/₃	16	7	.696	139	48	232	3.71	0
2008 Toronto	A.L.	34	*246	20	11	.645	206	39	220	2.78	0
Major League Totals	11 Yrs.	281	1807²/₃	131	66	.665	1287	420	1763	3.52	1

a Selected Cy Young Award Winner in American League for 2003.
b On disabled list from May 28 to June 12 and from July 17 to September 21, 2004.
c On disabled list from July 9 to October 3, 2005.
d On disabled list from May 11 to May 31, 2007.

HAMELS, COLBERT RICHARD (COLE)
Born, San Diego, California, December 27, 1983.
Bats Left. Throws Left. Height, 6 feet, 4 inches. Weight, 195 pounds.

Year	Club	Lea	G	IP	W	L	Pct	SO	BB	H	ERA	SAVES
2003 Clearwater	Fla.St.	5	26¹/₃	0	2	.000	32	14	29	2.73	0
2003 Lakewood	So.Atl.	13	74²/₃	6	1	.857	115	25	32	0.84	0
2004 Clearwater	Fla.St.	4	16	1	0	1.000	24	4	10	1.13	0
2005 Reading	Eastern	3	19	2	0	1.000	19	12	10	2.37	0
2005 Clearwater	Fla.St.	3	16	2	0	1.000	18	7	7	2.25	0
2006 Lakewood	So.Atl.	1	5²/₃	0	0	.000	3	2	3	1.59	0

Year Club	Lea	G	IP	W	L	Pct	SO	BB	H	ERA	SAVES
2006 Clearwater .... Fla.St.		4	20⅓	1	1	.500	29	9	16	1.77	0
2006 Scranton/WB .... Int.		3	23	2	0	1.000	36	1	10	0.39	0
2006 Philadelphia a .... N.L.		23	132⅓	9	8	.529	145	48	117	4.08	0
2007 Philadelphia b .... N.L.		28	183⅓	15	5	.750	177	43	163	3.39	0
2008 Philadelphia .... N.L.		33	227⅓	14	10	.583	196	53	193	3.09	0
Major League Totals .... 3 Yrs.		84	543	38	23	.623	518	144	473	3.43	0
Division Series											
2007 Philadelphia .... N.L.		1	6⅔	0	1	.000	7	4	3	4.05	0
2008 Philadelphia .... N.L.		1	8	1	0	1.000	9	1	2	0.00	0
Division Series Totals		2	14⅔	1	1	.500	16	5	5	1.84	0
Championship Series											
2008 Philadelphia .... N.L.		2	14	2	0	1.000	13	5	11	1.93	0
World Series Record											
2008 Philadelphia .... N.L.		2	13	1	0	1.000	8	3	10	2.77	0

a On disabled list from May 19 to June 6, 2006.
b On disabled list from August 17 to September 18, 2007.

HAMMEL, JASON AARON
Born, Greenville, South Carolina, September 2, 1982.
Bats Right. Throws Right. Height, 6 feet, 6 inches. Weight, 220 pounds.

Year Club	Lea	G	IP	W	L	Pct	SO	BB	H	ERA	SAVES
2002 Princeton .... Appal.		2	5⅓	0	0	.000	5	0	7	0.00	1
2002 Hudson Valley .... N.Y.-Penn.		13	51⅔	1	5	.167	38	14	71	5.23	1
2003 Charleston .... So.Atl.		14	76⅔	6	2	.750	50	27	70	3.40	0
2004 Bakersfield .... Calif.		11	71⅓	6	2	.750	65	20	52	1.89	0
2004 Charleston .... So.Atl.		18	94⅔	4	7	.364	88	27	94	3.23	0
2005 Durham .... Int.		10	54⅔	3	2	.600	48	27	57	4.12	0
2005 Montgomery ...... Southern		12	81⅓	8	2	.800	76	19	70	2.66	0
2006 Durham .... Int.		24	127⅔	5	9	.357	117	36	133	4.23	0
2006 Tampa Bay .... A.L.		9	44	0	6	.000	32	21	61	7.77	0
2007 Durham .... Int.		13	76⅓	4	5	.444	75	28	61	3.42	0
2007 Tampa Bay .... A.L.		24	85	3	5	.375	64	40	100	6.14	0
2008 Tampa Bay .... A.L.		40	78⅓	4	4	.500	44	35	83	4.60	2
Major League Totals .... 3 Yrs.		73	207⅓	7	15	.318	140	96	244	5.90	2

HAMPTON, MICHAEL WILLIAM (MIKE)
Born, Brooksville, Florida, September 9, 1972.
Bats Right. Throws Left. Height, 5 feet, 10 inches. Weight, 195 pounds.

Year Club	Lea	G	IP	W	L	Pct	SO	BB	H	ERA	SAVES
1990 Mariners .... Arizona		14	64⅓	7	2	.778	59	40	52	2.66	0
1991 San Berndno ...... Calif.		18	73⅔	1	7	.125	57	47	71	5.25	0
1991 Bellingham .... Northwest		9	57	5	2	.714	65	26	32	1.58	0
1992 San Berndno ...... Calif.		25	170	13	8	.619	132	66	163	3.12	0
1992 Jacksnville .... Southern		2	10⅓	0	1	.000	6	1	13	4.35	0
1993 Seattle .... A.L.		13	17	1	3	.250	8	17	28	9.53	1
1993 Jacksnville a ...... Southern		15	87⅓	6	4	.600	84	33	71	3.71	0
1994 Houston .... N.L.		44	41⅓	2	1	.667	24	16	46	3.70	0
1995 Houston b .... N.L.		24	150⅔	9	8	.529	115	49	141	3.35	0
1996 Houston .... N.L.		27	160⅓	10	10	.500	101	49	175	3.59	0
1997 Houston .... N.L.		34	223	15	10	.600	139	77	217	3.83	0
1998 Houston c .... N.L.		32	211⅔	11	7	.611	137	81	227	3.36	0
1999 Houston d .... N.L.		34	239	*22	4	*.846	177	101	206	2.90	0
2000 New York e .... N.L.		33	217⅔	15	10	.600	151	99	194	3.14	0
2001 Colorado .... N.L.		32	203	14	13	.519	122	85	236	5.41	0
2002 Colorado f-g .... N.L.		30	178⅔	7	15	.318	74	91	228	6.15	0
2003 Atlanta h .... N.L.		31	190	14	8	.636	110	78	186	3.84	0
2004 Atlanta .... N.L.		29	172⅓	13	9	.591	87	65	198	4.28	0
2005 Richmond .... Int.		1	4	0	0	.000	3	0	4	2.25	0
2005 Braves .... Gulf Coast		1	5	0	0	.000	4	0	6	0.00	0
2005 Atlanta i-j .... N.L.		12	69⅓	5	3	.625	27	18	74	3.50	0
2006 Atlanta k .... N.L.		INJURED—Did Not Play									
2007 Atlanta l .... N.L.		INJURED—Did Not Play									
2008 Braves .... Gulf Coast		2	5⅔	0	0	.000	4	0	4	0.00	0
2008 Rome .... So.Atl.		1	3	0	0	.000	4	0	8	9.00	0
2008 Myrtle Beach .... Carolina		1	5	0	0	.000	6	0	5	0.00	0
2008 Mississippi........ Southern		2	7	0	0	.000	6	1	7	3.86	0

Year Club	Lea	G	IP	W	L	Pct	SO	BB	H	ERA	SAVES
2008 Richmond ....Int.		2	6 1/3	0	1	.000	6	3	6	1.42	0
2008 Atlanta m-n ..........N.L.		13	78	3	4	.429	38	28	83	4.85	0
Major League Totals ....14 Yrs.		388	2152	141	105	.573	1310	854	2239	4.01	1
Division Series											
1997 Houston ..............N.L.		1	4 2/3	0	1	.000	2	8	2	11.57	0
1998 Houston ..............N.L.		1	6	0	0	.000	2	1	2	1.50	0
1999 Houston ..............N.L.		1	7	0	0	.000	9	1	6	3.86	0
2000 New York ............N.L.		1	5 1/3	0	1	.000	2	3	6	8.44	0
2003 Atlanta ...............N.L.		2	12 2/3	0	1	.000	16	6	11	4.26	0
2004 Atlanta ...............N.L.		2	7 1/3	0	0	.000	6	4	4	2.45	0
Division Series Totals		8	43	0	3	.000	37	23	31	4.81	0
Championship Series											
2000 New York ............N.L.		2	16	2	0	1.000	12	4	9	0.00	0
World Series Record											
2000 New York ............N.L.		1	6	0	1	.000	4	5	8	6.00	0

a Traded to Houston Astros with outfielder Mike Felder for outfielder Eric Anthony, December 10, 1993.
b On disabled list from May 15 to June 13, 1995.
c On disabled list from June 16 to July 4, 1998.
d Traded to New York Mets with outfielder Derek Bell for pitcher Octavio Dotel, outfielder Roger Cedeno and pitcher Kyle Kessel, December 23, 1999.
e Filed for free agency, November 4, 2000. Signed with Colorado Rockies, December 9, 2000.
f Traded to Florida Marlins with outfielder Juan Pierre for outfielder Preston Wilson, catcher Charles Johnson, pitcher Vic Darensbourg and infielder Pablo Ozuna, November 16, 2002.
g Traded to Atlanta Braves for pitcher Tim Spooneybarger and pitcher Ryan Baker, November 18, 2002.
h On disabled list from March 28 to April 19, 2003.
i On disabled list from May 15 to May 31 and June 1 to July 17 and July 18 to August 14, 2005.
j On disabled list from August 24 to September 11 and September 12 to November 1, 2005.
k On disabled list from March 24 to November 1, 2006.
l On disabled list from March 24 to November 13, 2007.
m On disabled list from March 30 to July 26, 2008.
n Filed for free agency, November 5, 2008. Signed with Houston Astros, December 3, 2008.

HANRAHAN, JOEL RYAN
Born, Des Moines, Iowa, October 6, 1981.
Bats Right. Throws Right. Height, 6 feet, 3 inches. Weight, 250 pounds.

Year Club	Lea	G	IP	W	L	Pct	SO	BB	H	ERA	SAVES
2000 Great Falls ....Pioneer		12	55	3	1	.750	40	23	49	4.75	0
2001 Wilmington ....So.Atl.		27	144	9	11	.450	116	55	136	3.38	0
2002 Vero Beach..........Fla.St.		25	143 2/3	10	6	.625	139	51	129	4.20	0
2002 Jacksonville ......Southern		3	11	1	1	.500	10	7	15	10.64	0
2003 Las Vegas............P.C.		5	25	1	2	.333	13	20	36	10.08	0
2003 Jacksonville ....Southern		23	133 1/3	10	4	.714	130	53	117	2.43	0
2004 Las Vegas............P.C.		25	119 1/3	7	7	.500	97	75	128	5.05	0
2005 Vero Beach..........Fla.St.		5	21 1/3	1	0	1.000	25	11	25	5.91	0
2005 Jacksonville ......Southern		23	111 2/3	9	8	.529	102	55	118	4.92	0
2006 Las Vegas............P.C.		14	74 1/3	4	3	.571	46	39	70	4.48	0
2006 Jacksonville a......Southern		12	66 1/3	7	2	.778	67	38	49	2.58	0
2007 Columbus...............Int.		15	75 1/3	5	4	.556	71	36	65	3.70	0
2007 Washington ...........N.L.		12	51	5	3	.625	43	38	59	6.00	0
2008 Washington ...........N.L.		69	84 1/3	6	3	.667	93	42	73	3.95	9
Major League Totals ....2 Yrs.		81	135 1/3	11	6	.647	136	80	132	4.72	9

a Filed for free agency from Los Angeles Dodgers, October 15, 2006. Signed with Washington Nationals organization, November 6, 2006.

HANSEN, CRAIG ROBERT
Born, Glen Cove, New York, November 15, 1983.
Bats Right. Throws Right. Height, 6 feet, 6 inches. Weight, 230 pounds.

Year Club	Lea	G	IP	W	L	Pct	SO	BB	H	ERA	SAVES
2005 Red Sox ....Gulf Coast		2	3	1	0	1.000	4	0	2	0.00	0
2005 Portland...........Eastern		8	9 2/3	0	0	.000	10	1	9	0.00	1
2005 Boston ...............A.L.		4	3	0	0	.000	3	1	6	6.00	0
2006 Portland...........Eastern		5	11	1	0	1.000	12	4	4	0.82	0
2006 Pawtucket.............Int.		14	36	1	2	.333	26	19	31	2.75	0
2006 Boston ...............A.L.		38	38	2	2	.500	30	15	46	6.63	3
2007 Pawtucket.............Int.		40	51 1/3	3	1	.750	48	32	58	3.86	3
2008 Indianapolis ....Int.		2	2	0	0	.000	2	1	4	9.00	0
2008 Pawtucket.............Int.		11	16 2/3	1	0	1.000	17	5	6	1.62	0

Year Club	Lea	G	IP	W	L	Pct	SO	BB	H	ERA	SAVES
2008 Boston	A.L.	32	30⅔	1	3	.250	25	23	29	5.58	2
2008 Pittsburgh a	N.L.	16	15⅔	1	4	.200	7	20	11	7.47	1
Major League Totals .... 3 Yrs.		90	87⅓	4	9	.308	65	59	92	6.39	3

a Traded to Pittsburgh Pirates with outfielder Manny Ramirez and outfielder Brandon Moss for outfielder Jason Bay, July 31, 2008.

HARANG, AARON MICHAEL
Born, San Diego, California, May 9, 1978.
Bats Right. Throws Right. Height, 6 feet, 7 inches. Weight, 270 pounds.

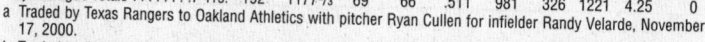

Year Club	Lea	G	IP	W	L	Pct	SO	BB	H	ERA	SAVES
1999 Pulaski.............	Appal.	16	78⅓	9	2	.818	87	17	64	2.30	1
2000 Charlotte a	Fla.St.	28	157	13	5	.722	136	50	128	3.32	0
2001 Midland	Texas	27	150	10	8	.556	112	37	173	4.14	0
2002 Midland	Texas	3	16⅔	2	0	1.000	21	7	12	1.08	0
2002 Sacramento	P.C.	8	38⅔	3	3	.500	39	9	41	3.26	0
2002 Oakland	A.L.	16	78⅓	5	4	.556	64	45	78	4.83	0
2003 Louisville	Int.	1	3	0	1	.000	4	2	5	15.00	0
2003 Sacramento	P.C.	12	69⅔	8	2	.800	60	17	62	2.71	0
2003 Oakland	A.L.	7	30⅓	1	3	.250	16	9	41	5.34	0
2003 Cincinnati b	N.L.	9	46	4	3	.571	26	10	48	5.28	0
2004 Louisville	Int.	1	3	0	1	.000	3	3	9	12.00	0
2004 Cincinnati c	N.L.	28	161	10	9	.526	125	53	177	4.86	0
2005 Cincinnati..........	N.L.	32	211⅔	11	13	.458	163	51	217	3.83	0
2006 Cincinnati..........	N.L.	36	234⅓	*16	11	.593	*216	56	242	3.76	0
2007 Cincinnati..........	N.L.	34	231⅔	16	6	.727	218	52	213	3.73	0
2008 Louisville	Int.	1	6	1	0	1.000	6	0	5	0.00	0
2008 Cincinnati d	N.L.	30	184⅓	6	*17	.261	153	50	205	4.78	0
Major League Totals .... 7 Yrs.		192	1177⅔	69	66	.511	981	326	1221	4.25	0

a Traded by Texas Rangers to Oakland Athletics with pitcher Ryan Cullen for infielder Randy Velarde, November 17, 2000.

b Traded to Cincinnati Reds with pitcher Joe Valentine and pitcher Jeff Bruksch for outfielder Jose Guillen, July 30, 2003.

c On disabled list from June 2 to June 26, 2004.

d On disabled list from July 9 to August 10, 2008.

HARDEN, JAMES RICHARD (RICH)
Born, Victoria, British Columbia, Canada, November 30, 1981.
Bats Left. Throws Right. Height, 6 feet, 1 inch. Weight, 195 pounds.

Year Club	Lea	G	IP	W	L	Pct	SO	BB	H	ERA	SAVES
2001 Vancouver	Northwest	18	74⅓	2	4	.333	100	38	47	3.39	0
2002 Visalia...........	California	12	68	4	3	.571	85	24	49	2.91	0
2002 Midland	Texas	16	85⅓	8	3	.727	102	52	67	2.95	0
2003 Midland	Texas	2	13	2	0	1.000	17	0	0	0.00	0
2003 Sacramento	P.C.	16	88⅔	9	4	.692	91	35	72	3.15	0
2003 Oakland	A.L.	15	74⅔	5	4	.556	67	40	72	4.46	0
2004 Sacramento	P.C.	1	5	0	0	.000	6	3	6	5.40	0
2004 Oakland	A.L.	31	189⅔	11	7	.611	167	81	171	3.99	0
2005 Sacramento	P.C.	1	3	0	0	.000	7	0	1	0.00	0
2005 Oakland a	A.L.	22	128	10	5	.667	121	43	93	2.53	0
2006 Sacramento	P.C.	1	2	0	0	.000	3	0	1	0.00	0
2006 Oakland b	A.L.	9	46⅔	4	0	1.000	49	26	31	4.24	0
2007 Sacramento	P.C.	1	1	0	0	.000	1	0	1	0.00	0
2007 Oakland c	A.L.	7	25⅔	1	2	.333	27	11	18	2.45	0
2008 Stockton..........	Calif.	1	6	1	0	1.000	9	0	3	0.00	0
2008 Sacramento	P.C.	1	3⅔	0	0	.000	4	0	3	2.45	0
2008 Oakland	A.L.	13	77	5	1	.833	92	31	57	2.34	0
2008 Chicago d-e	N.L.	12	71	5	1	.833	89	30	39	1.77	0
Major League Totals .... 6 Yrs.		109	612⅔	41	20	.672	612	262	481	3.23	0
Division Series											
2003 Oakland	A.L.	2	1⅓	1	1	.500	1	2	2	13.50	0
2008 Chicago	N.L.	1	4⅓	0	1	.000	4	3	5	6.23	0
Division Series Totals...........		3	5⅔	1	2	.333	5	5	7	7.94	0
Championship Series											
2006 Oakland	A.L.	1	5⅔	0	1	.000	4	5	5	4.76	0

a On disabled list from May 14 to June 21, 2005.

b On disabled list from April 27 to June 4 and June 5 to September 21, 2006.

c On disabled list from April 16 to June 22 and July 8 to October 8, 2007.
d On disabled list from April 3 to May 11, 2008.
e Traded to Chicago Cubs with pitcher Chad Gaudin for pitcher Sean Gallagher, outfielder Matt Murton, outfielder Eric Patterson and catcher Josh Donaldson, July 8, 2008.

HAREN, DANIEL JOHN (DANNY)
Born, Monterey Park, California, September 17, 1980.
Bats Right. Throws Right. Height, 6 feet, 5 inches. Weight, 220 pounds.

Year	Club	Lea	G	IP	W	L	Pct	SO	BB	H	ERA	SAVES
2001 New Jersey	N.Y.-Penn.	12	52⅓	3	3	.500	57	8	47	3.10	1
2002 Potomac	Carolina	14	92	3	6	.333	82	19	90	3.62	0
2002 Peoria	Midwest	14	101⅔	7	3	.700	89	12	89	1.95	0
2003 Memphis	P.C.	8	45⅔	2	1	.667	35	8	50	4.93	0
2003 Tennessee	Southern	8	55	6	0	1.000	49	6	36	0.82	0
2003 St. Louis	N.L.	14	72⅔	3	7	.300	43	22	84	5.08	0
2004 Memphis	P.C.	21	128	11	4	.733	150	33	136	4.15	0
2004 St. Louis a	N.L.	14	46	3	3	.500	32	17	45	4.50	0
2005 Oakland	A.L.	34	217	14	12	.538	163	53	212	3.73	0
2006 Oakland	A.L.	34	223	14	13	.519	176	45	224	4.12	0
2007 Oakland b	A.L.	34	222⅔	15	9	.625	192	55	214	3.07	0
2008 Arizona	N.L.	33	216	16	8	.667	206	40	204	3.33	0
Major League Totals	6 Yrs.	163	997⅓	65	52	.556	812	232	983	3.72	0
Division Series											
2004 St. Louis	N.L.	1	2	1	0	1.000	3	1	1	0.00	0
2006 Oakland	A.L.	1	6	1	0	1.000	2	1	9	3.00	0
Division Series Totals		2	8	2	0	1.000	5	2	10	2.25	0
Championship Series											
2004 St. Louis	N.L.	2	1⅔	0	0	.000	2	0	3	10.80	0
2006 Oakland	A.L.	1	5	0	0	.000	7	2	7	5.40	0
Championship Series Totals		3	6⅔	0	0	.000	9	2	10	6.75	0
World Series Record											
2004 St. Louis	N.L.	2	4⅔	0	0	.000	2	3	4	0.00	0

a Traded to Oakland Athletics with pitcher Kiko Calero and catcher Daric Barton for pitcher Mark Mulder, December 18, 2004.
b Traded to Arizona Diamondbacks with pitcher Connor Robertson for pitcher Brett Anderson, pitcher Dana Eveland, pitcher Greg Smith, infielder Chris Carter, outfielder Aaron Cunningham and outfielder Carlos Gonzalez, December 14, 2007.

HARRISON, MATTHEW REID (MATT)
Born, Durham, North Carolina, August 16, 1985.
Bats Left. Throws Left. Height, 6 feet, 4 inches. Weight, 225 pounds.

Year	Club	Lea	G	IP	W	L	Pct	SO	BB	H	ERA	SAVES
2003 Braves	Gulf Coast	11	39	3	1	.750	33	9	40	3.69	1
2004 Danville	Appal.	13	66	4	4	.500	49	10	72	4.09	0
2005 Rome	So.Atl.	27	167	12	7	.632	118	30	151	3.23	0
2006 Myrtle Beach	Carolina	13	81⅓	8	4	.667	60	16	77	3.10	0
2006 Mississippi	Southern	13	77⅓	3	4	.429	54	17	83	3.61	0
2007 Mississippi a	Southern	20	116⅔	5	7	.417	78	34	118	3.39	0
2008 Frisco	Texas	9	46	3	2	.600	35	14	49	3.33	0
2008 Oklahoma	P.C.	6	38	3	1	.750	20	14	40	3.55	0
2008 Texas	A.L.	15	83⅔	9	3	.750	42	31	100	5.49	0

a Traded to Texas Rangers with catcher Jarrod Saltalamacchia, infielder Elvis Andrus, pitcher Neftali Feliz and pitcher Beau James for infielder Mark Teixeira and pitcher Ron Mahay, July 31, 2007.

HAWKINS, LA TROY
Born, Gary, Indiana, December 21, 1972.
Bats Right. Throws Right. Height, 6 feet, 5 inches. Weight, 215 pounds.

Year	Club	Lea	G	IP	W	L	Pct	SO	BB	H	ERA	SAVES
1991 Twins	Gulf Coast	11	55	4	3	.571	47	26	62	4.75	0
1992 Twins	Gulf Coast	6	36⅓	3	2	.600	35	10	36	3.22	0
1992 Elizabethton	Appal.	5	26⅔	0	1	.000	36	11	21	3.38	0
1993 Ft. Wayne	Midwest	26	157⅓	15	5	.750	179	41	110	2.06	0
1994 Ft. Myers	Fla. St.	6	38⅔	4	0	1.000	36	6	32	2.33	0
1994 Nashville	Southern	11	73⅓	9	2	.818	53	28	50	2.33	0
1994 Salt Lake	P.C.	12	81⅔	5	4	.556	37	33	92	4.08	0
1995 Salt Lake	P.C.	22	144⅓	9	7	.563	74	40	150	3.55	0
1995 Minnesota	A.L.	6	27	2	3	.400	9	12	39	8.67	0

Year	Club	Lea	G	IP	W	L	Pct	SO	BB	H	ERA	SAVES
1996	Minnesota	A.L.	7	26⅓	1	1	.500	24	9	42	8.20	0
1996	Salt Lake	P.C.	20	137⅔	9	8	.529	99	31	138	3.92	0
1997	Salt Lake	P.C.	14	76	9	4	.692	53	16	100	5.45	0
1997	Minnesota	A.L.	20	103⅓	6	12	.333	58	47	134	5.84	0
1998	Minnesota	A.L.	33	190⅓	7	14	.333	105	61	227	5.25	0
1999	Minnesota	A.L.	33	174⅓	10	14	.417	103	60	238	6.66	0
2000	Minnesota	A.L.	66	87⅔	2	5	.286	59	32	85	3.39	14
2001	Minnesota	A.L.	62	51⅓	1	5	.167	36	39	59	5.96	28
2002	Minnesota a	A.L.	65	80⅓	6	0	1.000	63	15	63	2.13	0
2003	Minnesota a	A.L.	74	77⅓	9	3	.750	75	15	69	1.86	2
2004	Chicago	N.L.	77	82	5	4	.556	69	14	72	2.63	25
2005	Fresno	P.C.	2	2	0	0	.000	1	0	2	0.00	0
2005	Chicago-San Francisco b-c-d	N.L.	66	56⅓	2	8	.200	43	24	58	3.83	6
2006	Baltimore e	A.L.	60	60⅓	3	2	.600	27	15	73	4.48	0
2007	Colorado Springs	P.C.	4	4	1	0	1.000	5	2	2	2.25	0
2007	Colorado f-g	N.L.	62	55⅓	2	5	.286	29	16	52	3.42	0
2008	New York	A.L.	33	41	1	1	.500	23	17	46	5.71	0
2008	Houston h-i	N.L.	24	21	2	0	1.000	25	5	11	0.43	1
Major League Totals	14 Yrs.		688	1134	59	77	.434	748	381	1264	4.64	76
Division Series												
2002	Minnesota	A.L.	3	2⅓	0	0	.000	5	0	0	0.00	0
2003	Minnesota	A.L.	3	3	1	0	1.000	5	0	5	6.00	0
2007	Colorado	N.L.	1	1	0	0	.000	0	1	0	0.00	0
Division Series Totals			7	6⅓	1	0	1.000	10	1	5	2.84	0
Championship Series												
2002	Minnesota	A.L.	4	1⅓	0	0	.000	1	1	4	20.25	0
2007	Colorado	N.L.	2	2	0	0	.000	1	0	1	0.00	0
Championship Series Totals			6	3⅓	0	0	.000	2	1	5	8.10	0
World Series Record												
2007	Colorado	N.L.	2	2	0	0	.000	3	2	1	4.50	0

a Filed for free agency, October 27, 2003. Signed with Chicago Cubs, December 3, 2003.
b Traded to San Francisco Giants for pitcher Jerome Williams and pitcher David Aardsma, May 28, 2005.
c On disabled list from June 10 to July 4, 2005.
d Traded to Baltimore Orioles for pitcher Steve Kline, December 6, 2005.
e Filed for free agency, October 31, 2006. Signed with Colorado Rockies, December 5, 2006.
f On disabled list from April 21 to May 22, 2007.
g Filed for free agency, November 1, 2007. Signed with New York Yankees, December 27, 2007.
h Traded to Houston Astros for infielder Matt Cusick and cash, July 30, 2008.
i Filed for free agency, October 31, 2008, re-signed with Houston Astros, November 11, 2008.

HEILMAN, AARON MICHAEL

Born, Logansport, Indiana, November 12, 1978.
Bats Right. Throws Right. Height, 6 feet, 5 inches. Weight, 220 pounds.

Year	Club	Lea	G	IP	W	L	Pct	SO	BB	H	ERA	SAVES
2001	St. Lucie	Fla.St.	7	38⅓	0	1	.000	39	13	26	2.35	0
2002	Binghamton	Eastern	17	96⅔	4	4	.500	97	28	85	3.82	0
2002	Norfolk	Int.	10	49⅓	2	3	.400	35	16	42	3.28	0
2003	Norfolk	Int.	16	94⅓	6	4	.600	71	32	99	3.24	0
2003	New York	N.L.	14	65⅓	2	7	.222	51	41	79	6.75	0
2004	Norfolk	Int.	26	151⅔	7	10	.412	123	66	156	4.33	0
2004	New York	N.L.	5	28	1	3	.250	22	13	27	5.46	0
2005	New York	N.L.	53	108	5	3	.625	106	37	87	3.17	5
2006	New York	N.L.	74	87	4	5	.444	73	28	73	3.62	0
2007	New York	N.L.	81	86	7	7	.500	63	20	72	3.03	1
2008	New York a	N.L.	78	76	3	8	.273	80	46	75	5.21	3
Major League Totals	6 Yrs.		305	450⅓	22	33	.400	395	185	413	4.24	9
Division Series												
2006	New York	N.L.	3	3	0	0	.000	1	0	3	3.00	0
Championship Series												
2006	New York	N.L.	3	4⅓	0	1	.000	5	1	4	4.15	0

a Traded to Seattle Mariners with outfielder Endy Chavez, pitcher Jason Vargas, infielder Mike Carp, outfielder Ezequiel Carrera and pitcher Maikel Cleto for pitcher J.J. Putz, pitcher Sean Green and infielder Jeremy Reed, December 10, 2008.

HENDRICKSON, MARK ALLAN

Born, Mount Vernon, Washington, June 23, 1974.
Bats Left. Throws Left. Height, 6 feet, 9 inches. Weight, 230 pounds.

Year	Club	Lea	G	IP	W	L	Pct	SO	BB	H	ERA	SAVES
1998 Dunedin	Fla.St.	16	$49\frac{1}{3}$	4	3	.571	38	26	44	2.37	1
1999 Knoxville	Southern	12	$55\frac{2}{3}$	2	7	.222	39	21	73	6.63	0
2000 Dunedin	Fla.St.	12	$51\frac{1}{3}$	2	2	.500	38	29	63	5.61	0
2000 Tennessee	Southern	6	$39\frac{2}{3}$	3	1	.750	29	12	32	3.63	0
2001 Syracuse	Int.	38	$73\frac{1}{3}$	2	9	.182	33	18	80	4.66	0
2002 Syracuse	Int.	19	92	7	5	.583	68	22	90	3.52	0
2002 Toronto a	A.L.	16	$36\frac{2}{3}$	3	0	1.000	21	12	25	2.45	0
2003 Syracuse	Int.	1	6	0	0	.000	5	1	8	4.50	0
2003 Dunedin	Fla.St.	1	$5\frac{2}{3}$	1	0	1.000	3	4	5	1.59	0
2003 Toronto b-c	A.L.	30	$158\frac{1}{3}$	9	9	.500	76	40	207	5.51	0
2004 Tampa Bay	A.L.	32	$183\frac{1}{3}$	10	15	.400	87	46	211	4.81	0
2005 Tampa Bay d	A.L.	31	$178\frac{1}{3}$	11	8	.579	89	49	227	5.90	0
2006 Tampa Bay	A.L.	13	$89\frac{2}{3}$	4	8	.333	51	34	81	3.81	0
2006 Los Angeles e-f	N.L.	18	75	2	7	.222	48	28	92	4.68	0
2007 Los Angeles g	N.L.	39	$122\frac{2}{3}$	4	8	.333	92	29	142	5.21	0
2008 Florida h	N.L.	36	$132\frac{2}{3}$	7	8	.467	81	48	148	5.45	0
Major League Totals	7 Yrs.	215	$977\frac{2}{3}$	50	63	.442	545	286	1133	5.07	0
Division Series											
2006 Los Angeles	N.L.	3	$2\frac{2}{3}$	0	0	.000	1	1	1	0.00	0

a On disabled list from June 18 to July 12, 2002.
b Traded to Colorado Rockies with player named later for pitcher Justin Speier, December 14, 2003.
c Traded to Tampa Bay Devil Rays for pitcher Joe Kennedy, December 14, 2003.
d On disabled list from April 14 to April 30, 2005.
e On disabled list from April 7 to April 25, 2006.
f Traded to Los Angeles Dodgers with catcher Toby Hall and cash for catcher Dioner Navarro, pitcher Jae Seo and player named later, June 27, 2006.
g Not offered contract, December 12, 2007. Signed with Florida Marlins, January 16, 2008.
h Filed for free agency, October 31, 2008. Signed with Baltimore Orioles, December 31, 2008.

HERGES, MATTHEW TYLER (MATT)

Born, Champaign, Illinois, April 1, 1970.
Bats Left. Throws Right. Height, 6 feet. Weight, 210 pounds.

Year	Club	Lea	G	IP	W	L	Pct	SO	BB	H	ERA	SAVES
1992 Yakima	Northwest	27	$44\frac{2}{3}$	2	3	.400	57	24	33	3.22	9
1993 Bakersfield	Calif.	51	$90\frac{1}{3}$	2	6	.250	84	56	70	3.69	2
1994 Vero Beach	Fla.St.	48	111	8	9	.471	61	33	115	3.32	3
1995 San Antonio	Texas	19	$27\frac{2}{3}$	0	3	.000	18	16	34	4.88	8
1995 San Bernardino	Calif.	22	$51\frac{1}{3}$	5	2	.714	35	15	58	3.66	1
1996 San Antonio	Texas	30	83	3	2	.600	45	28	83	2.71	3
1996 Albuquerque	P.C.	10	$34\frac{2}{3}$	4	1	.800	15	14	33	2.60	0
1997 Albuquerque	P.C.	31	85	0	8	.000	61	46	120	8.89	0
1997 San Antonio	Texas	4	$15\frac{1}{3}$	0	1	.000	12	10	22	8.80	0
1998 San Antonio	Texas	3	6	0	0	.000	3	2	3	0.00	0
1998 Albuquerque	P.C.	34	$88\frac{1}{3}$	3	5	.375	75	37	115	5.71	0
1999 Albuquerque	P.C.	21	$131\frac{1}{3}$	8	3	.727	88	47	135	4.73	0
1999 Los Angeles a	N.L.	17	$24\frac{1}{3}$	0	2	.000	18	8	24	4.07	0
2000 Los Angeles	N.L.	59	$110\frac{2}{3}$	11	3	.786	75	40	100	3.17	1
2001 Los Angeles	N.L.	75	$99\frac{1}{3}$	9	8	.529	76	46	97	4.04	1
2002 Montreal b-c	N.L.	62	$64\frac{2}{3}$	2	5	.286	50	26	80	1.80	6
2003 Portland	P.C.	4	5	0	0	.000	5	2	1	1.80	0
2003 San Diego-San Fran. d-e-f	N.L.	67	79	3	2	.600	68	29	68	2.62	3
2004 San Francisco	N.L.	70	$65\frac{1}{3}$	4	5	.444	39	21	89	3.14	23
2005 Tucson	P.C.	26	$28\frac{2}{3}$	1	2	.333	29	8	39	3.14	0
2005 San Fran.-Arizona g-h	N.L.	28	29	1	1	.500	9	12	35	7.14	0
2006 Florida i	N.L.	66	71	2	3	.400	36	28	94	4.31	0
2007 Colorado Springs	P.C.	32	$35\frac{1}{3}$	2	1	.667	33	10	24	1.27	1
2007 Colorado j	N.L.	35	$48\frac{2}{3}$	5	1	.833	30	15	34	2.96	0
2008 Colorado Springs	P.C.	2	2	0	0	.000	1	0	2	4.50	0
2008 Colorado k-l	N.L.	58	$64\frac{1}{3}$	3	4	.429	46	24	79	5.04	0
Major League Totals	10 Yrs.	537	$656\frac{1}{3}$	40	34	.541	447	249	701	3.94	34
Division Series											
2003 San Francisco	N.L.	3	$4\frac{1}{3}$	0	0	.000	5	2	1	0.00	0
2007 Colorado	N.L.	1	$0\frac{2}{3}$	0	0	.000	0	0	0	0.00	0
Division Series Totals		4	5	0	0	.000	5	2	1	0.00	0
Championship Series											
2007 Colorado	N.L.	3	3	1	0	1.000	2	1	1	0.00	0

Year Club	Lea	G	IP	W	L	Pct	SO	BB	H	ERA	SAVES
World Series Record											
2007 Colorado .............N.L.		3	3⅓	0	0	.000	4	2	1	0.00	0

a Filed for free agency, October 15, 1998, re-signed by Los Angeles Dodgers organization, January 6, 1999.
b Traded to Montreal Expos with infielder Jorge Nunez for pitcher Guillermo Mota and outfielder Wilkin Ruan, March 23, 2002.
c Traded to Pittsburgh Pirates for pitcher Chris Young and pitcher Jon Searles, December 20, 2002.
d Released by Pittsburgh Pirates, March 26, 2003. Signed with San Diego Padres organization, March 30, 2003.
e Traded to San Francisco Giants for pitcher Clay Hensley and player to be named later, July 13, 2003.
f San Diego Padres received pitcher R.D. Spiehs to complete trade, July 27, 2003.
g Traded to Arizona Diamondbacks for outfielder Doug DeVore, June 3, 2005.
h Filed for free agency, October 3, 2005. Signed with Florida Marlins organization, February 1, 2006.
i Filed for free agency, October 28, 2006. Signed with Colorado Rockies organization, February 12, 2007.
j Filed for free agency, November 6, 2007, re-signed with Colorado Rockies organization, November 30, 2007.
k On disabled list from August 18 to September 2, 2008.
l Filed for free agency, November 1, 2008. Signed with Cleveland Indians organization, January 16, 2009.

HERNANDEZ, EISLER LIVAN

Born, Villa Clara, Cuba, February 20, 1975.
Bats Right. Throws Right. Height, 6 feet, 2 inches. Weight, 245 pounds.

Year Club	Lea	G	IP	W	L	Pct	SO	BB	H	ERA	SAVES
1996 Charlotte ....Int.		10	49	2	4	.333	45	34	61	5.14	0
1996 Portland ....Eastern		15	93⅓	9	2	.818	95	34	81	4.34	0
1996 Florida ...............N.L.		1	3	0	0	.000	2	2	3	0.00	0
1997 Portland ....Eastern		1	4	0	0	.000	2	7	2	2.25	0
1997 Charlotte ....Int.		14	81⅓	5	3	.625	58	38	76	3.98	0
1997 Florida ...............N.L.		17	96⅓	9	3	.750	72	38	81	3.18	0
1998 Florida ...............N.L.		33	234⅓	10	12	.455	162	104	*265	4.72	0
1999 Florida-San Francisco a ..	N.L.	30	199⅔	8	12	.400	144	76	227	4.64	0
2000 San Francisco .........N.L.		33	240	17	11	.607	165	73	*254	3.75	0
2001 San Francisco .........N.L.		34	226⅔	13	15	.464	138	85	*266	5.24	0
2002 San Francisco .........N.L.		33	216	12	*16	.429	134	71	233	4.38	0
2003 Montreal b-c ..........N.L.		33	*233⅓	15	10	.600	178	57	225	3.20	0
2004 Montreal...............N.L.		35	*255	11	15	.423	186	83	234	3.60	0
2005 Washington ...........N.L.		35	*246⅓	15	10	.600	147	84	*268	3.98	0
2006 Washington-Arizona d ...N.L.		34	216	13	13	.500	128	78	246	4.83	0
2007 Arizona e .............N.L.		33	204⅓	11	11	.500	90	79	*247	4.93	0
2008 Minnesota .............A.L.		23	139⅔	10	8	.556	54	29	199	5.48	0
2008 Colorado f-g...........N.L.		8	40⅓	3	3	.500	13	14	58	8.03	0
Major League Totals .... 13 Yrs.		382	2551	147	139	.514	1613	873	2806	4.37	0
Division Series											
1997 Florida ...............N.L.		1	4	0	0	.000	3	0	3	2.25	0
2000 San Francisco .........N.L.		1	7⅔	1	0	1.000	5	5	5	1.17	0
2002 San Francisco .........N.L.		1	8⅓	1	0	1.000	6	2	8	3.24	0
2007 Arizona................N.L.		1	6	1	0	1.000	2	5	5	1.50	0
Division Series Totals		4	26	3	0	1.000	16	12	21	2.08	0
Championship Series											
1997 Florida ................N.L.		2	10⅔	2	0	1.000	16	2	5	0.84	0
2002 San Francisco .........N.L.		1	6⅓	0	0	.000	0	1	9	2.84	0
2007 Arizona................N.L.		1	5⅔	0	1	.000	4	2	8	6.35	0
Championship Series Totals		4	22⅔	2	1	.667	20	5	22	2.78	0
World Series Record											
1997 Florida ................N.L.		2	13⅔	2	0	1.000	7	10	15	5.27	0
2002 San Francisco .........N.L.		2	5⅔	0	2	.000	4	9	9	14.29	0
World Series Totals..............		4	19⅓	2	2	.500	11	19	24	7.91	0

a Traded to San Francisco Giants for pitcher Jason Grilli and pitcher Nathan Bump, July 24, 1999.
b Traded to Montreal Expos with catcher Edwards Guzman for pitcher Jim Brower and player to be named later, March 24, 2003.
c San Francisco Giants received pitcher Matt Blank to complete trade, April 30, 2003.
d Traded to Arizona Diamondbacks with cash for pitcher Garrett Mock and pitcher Matt Chico, August 7, 2006.
e Filed for free agency, October 29, 2007. Signed with Minnesota Twins, February 12, 2008.
f Claimed on waivers by Colorado Rockies, August 6, 2008.
g Filed for free agency, November 1, 2008.

HERNANDEZ, FELIX ABRAHAM
Born, Valencia, Venezuela, April 8, 1986.
Bats Right. Throws Right. Height, 6 feet, 3 inches. Weight, 230 pounds.

Year Club	Lea	G	IP	W	L	Pct	SO	BB	H	ERA	SAVES
2003 Wisconsin	Midwest	2	14	0	0	.000	18	3	9	1.93	0
2003 Everett	Northwest	11	55	7	2	.778	73	24	43	2.29	0
2004 Inland Empire	California	16	92	9	3	.750	114	26	85	2.74	0
2004 San Antonio	Texas	10	57¹/₃	5	1	.833	58	21	47	3.30	0
2005 Tacoma	P.C.	19	88	9	4	.692	100	48	62	2.25	0
2005 Seattle	A.L.	12	84¹/₃	4	4	.500	77	23	61	2.67	0
2006 Seattle	A.L.	31	191	12	14	.462	176	60	195	4.52	0
2007 Seattle a	A.L.	30	190¹/₃	14	7	.667	165	53	209	3.92	0
2008 Seattle b	A.L.	31	200²/₃	9	11	.450	175	80	198	3.45	0
Major League Totals ....4 Yrs.		104	666¹/₃	39	36	.520	593	216	663	3.80	0

a On disabled list from April 19 to May 15, 2007.
b On disabled list from June 24 to July 11, 2008.

HILL, RICHARD JOSEPH (RICH)
Born, Boston, Massachusetts, March 11, 1980.
Bats Left. Throws Left. Height, 6 feet, 5 inches. Weight, 205 pounds.

Year Club	Lea	G	IP	W	L	Pct	SO	BB	H	ERA	SAVES
2002 Boise	Northwest	6	14	0	2	.000	12	14	15	8.36	0
2003 Lansing	Midwest	15	29¹/₃	0	1	.000	50	36	14	2.76	0
2003 Boise	Northwest	14	68¹/₃	1	6	.143	99	32	57	4.35	0
2004 Daytona	Fla.St.	28	109¹/₃	7	6	.538	136	72	88	4.03	0
2005 West Tenn	Southern	10	57²/₃	4	3	.571	90	21	42	3.28	0
2005 Peoria	Midwest	1	8	1	0	1.000	12	0	5	1.13	0
2005 Iowa	P.C.	11	65	6	1	.857	92	14	53	3.60	0
2005 Chicago	N.L.	10	23²/₃	0	2	.000	21	17	25	9.13	0
2006 Iowa	P.C.	15	100	7	1	.875	135	21	62	1.80	0
2006 Chicago	N.L.	17	99¹/₃	6	7	.462	90	39	83	4.17	0
2007 Chicago	N.L.	32	195	11	8	.579	183	63	170	3.92	0
2008 Azl Cubs	Arizona	3	9¹/₃	1	1	.500	11	5	5	2.89	0
2008 Daytona	Fla.St.	3	12¹/₃	1	2	.333	14	11	12	8.03	0
2008 Iowa	P.C.	7	26	2	4	.333	32	28	22	5.88	0
2008 Chicago a	N.L.	5	19²/₃	1	0	1.000	15	18	13	4.12	0
Major League Totals ....4 Yrs.		64	337²/₃	18	17	.514	309	137	291	4.37	0

Division Series

| 2007 Chicago | N.L. | 1 | 3 | 0 | 1 | .000 | 3 | 2 | 6 | 9.00 | 0 |

a On disabled list from August 31 to October 8, 2008.

HINSHAW, ALEXANDER OMAR (ALEX)
Born, Pomona, California, October 31, 1982.
Bats Left. Throws Left. Height, 6 feet, 4 inches. Weight, 190 pounds.

Year Club	Lea	G	IP	W	L	Pct	SO	BB	H	ERA	SAVES
2005 Salem-Keizer	Northwest	25	22	0	1	.000	33	18	17	3.68	0
2006 San Jose	Calif.	30	69²/₃	6	3	.667	78	60	58	4.26	0
2007 Connecticut	Eastern	17	41¹/₃	3	1	.750	50	19	22	1.96	0
2008 Fresno	P.C.	13	15²/₃	0	0	.000	21	4	5	0.57	7
2008 San Francisco	N.L.	48	39²/₃	2	1	.667	47	29	31	3.40	0

HOCHEVAR, LUKE ANTHONY
Born, Denver, Colorado, September 15, 1983.
Bats Right. Throws Right. Height, 6 feet, 5 inches. Weight, 205 pounds.

Year Club	Lea	G	IP	W	L	Pct	SO	BB	H	ERA	SAVES
2006 Burlington	Midwest	4	15¹/₃	0	1	.000	16	2	8	1.17	0
2007 Wichita	Texas	17	94	3	6	.333	94	26	110	4.69	0
2007 Omaha	P.C.	10	58	1	3	.250	44	21	53	5.12	0
2007 Kansas City	A.L.	4	12²/₃	0	1	.000	5	4	11	2.13	0
2008 Omaha	P.C.	3	17¹/₃	1	1	.500	12	6	11	2.60	0
2008 Kansas City a	A.L.	22	129	6	12	.333	72	47	143	5.51	0
Major League Totals ....2 Yrs.		26	141²/₃	6	13	.316	77	51	154	5.21	0

a On disabled list from August 20 to November 14, 2008.

HOFFMAN, TREVOR WILLIAM
Born, Bellflower, California, October 13, 1967.
Bats Right. Throws Right. Height, 6 feet, 1 inch. Weight, 215 pounds.

Year Club	Lea	G	IP	W	L	Pct	SO	BB	H	ERA	SAVES
1991 Cedar Rapids ....Midwest		27	33⅔	1	1	.500	52	13	22	1.87	12
1991 Chattanooga.......	Southern	14	14	1	0	1.000	23	7	10	1.93	8
1992 Chattanooga......	Southern	6	29⅔	3	0	1.000	31	11	22	1.52	0
1992 Nashville a	A.A.	42	65⅓	4	6	.400	63	32	57	4.27	6
1993 Florida-San Diego b	N.L.	67	90	4	6	.400	79	39	80	3.90	5
1994 San Diego	N.L.	47	56	4	4	.500	68	20	39	2.57	20
1995 San Diego	N.L.	55	53⅓	7	4	.636	52	14	48	3.88	31
1996 San Diego	N.L.	70	88	9	5	.643	111	31	50	2.25	42
1997 San Diego	N.L.	70	81⅓	6	4	.600	111	24	59	2.66	37
1998 San Diego	N.L.	66	73	4	2	.667	86	21	41	1.48	*53
1999 San Diego	N.L.	64	67⅓	2	3	.400	73	15	48	2.14	40
2000 San Diego	N.L.	70	72⅓	4	7	.364	85	11	61	2.99	43
2001 San Diego	N.L.	62	60⅓	3	4	.429	63	21	48	3.43	43
2002 San Diego	N.L.	61	59⅓	2	5	.286	69	18	52	2.73	38
2003 Lake Elsinore	California	3	3	0	0	.000	4	0	2	0.00	0
2003 San Diego c	N.L.	9	9	0	0	.000	11	3	7	2.00	0
2004 San Diego	N.L.	55	54⅔	3	3	.500	53	8	42	2.30	41
2005 San Diego d	N.L.	60	57⅔	1	6	.143	54	12	52	2.97	43
2006 San Diego	N.L.	65	63	0	2	.000	50	13	48	2.14	*46
2007 San Diego	N.L.	61	57⅓	4	5	.444	44	15	49	2.98	42
2008 San Diego e	N.L.	48	45⅓	3	3	.333	46	9	38	3.77	30
Major League Totals ....16 Yrs.		930	988	56	66	.459	1055	274	762	2.78	554
Division Series											
1996 San Diego	N.L.	2	1⅔	0	1	.000	2	1	3	10.80	0
1998 San Diego	N.L.	4	3	0	0	.000	4	1	3	0.00	2
2005 San Diego	N.L.	1	1	0	0	.000	0	0	1	0.00	0
2006 San Diego	N.L.	1	1	0	0	.000	1	0	0	0.00	1
Division Series Totals		8	6⅔	0	1	.000	7	2	7	2.70	3
Championship Series											
1998 San Diego	N.L.	3	4⅓	1	0	1.000	7	2	2	2.08	1
World Series Record											
1998 San Diego	N.L.	1	2	0	1	.000	0	1	2	9.00	0

Record as Position Player

Year Club	Lea	Pos	G	AB	R	H	2B	3B	HR	RBI	SB	Avg
1989 Bellingham.........	Pioneer	SS	61	201	22	50	5	0	1	20	1	.249
1990 Charleston.........	So. Atl.	SS-3B	103	278	41	59	10	1	2	23	3	.212

a Selected by Florida Marlins from Cincinnati Reds organization in expansion draft, November 17, 1992.
b Traded to San Diego Padres with pitchers Andres Berumen and Jose Martinez for infielder Greg Sheffield and pitcher Rich Rodriguez, June 25, 1993.
c On disabled list from March 25 to September 2, 2003.
d Filed for free agency, October 28, 2005, re-signed with San Diego Padres, December 7, 2005.
e Filed for free agency, November 1, 2008. Signed with Milwaukee Brewers, January 13, 2009.

HOWELL, JAMES PHILLIP (J.P.)
Born, Modesto, California, April 25, 1983.
Bats Left. Throws Left. Height, 6 feet. Weight, 175 pounds.

Year Club	Lea	G	IP	W	L	Pct	SO	BB	H	ERA	SAVES
2004 Idaho Falls	Pioneer	6	26	3	1	.750	38	12	16	2.77	0
2005 High Desert	Calif.	8	46	3	1	.750	48	24	33	1.96	0
2005 Wichita.............	Texas	3	18	2	0	1.000	23	5	12	2.50	0
2005 Omaha.............	P.C.	7	37⅔	3	1	.750	29	19	40	4.06	0
2005 Kansas City	A.L.	15	72⅔	3	5	.375	54	39	73	6.19	0
2006 Omaha..............	P.C.	8	36	3	2	.600	33	14	39	4.75	0
2006 Durham.............	Int.	10	55	5	3	.625	49	15	53	2.62	0
2006 Tampa Bay a...........	A.L.	8	42⅓	1	3	.250	33	14	52	5.10	0
2007 Durham.............	Int.	21	128	7	8	.467	145	34	110	3.38	0
2007 Tampa Bay	A.L.	10	51	1	6	.143	49	21	69	7.59	0
2008 Tampa Bay	A.L.	64	89⅓	6	1	.857	92	39	62	2.22	3
Major League Totals ....4 Yrs.		97	255⅓	11	15	.423	228	113	256	4.90	3
Division Series											
2008 Tampa Bay	N.L.	3	4⅓	0	0	.000	6	0	2	0.00	0
Championship Series											
2008 Tampa Bay	N.L.	6	5⅓	0	1	.000	6	3	5	3.38	0
World Series Record											
2008 Tampa Bay	N.L.	3	2⅓	0	2	.000	5	1	2	7.71	0

a Traded to Tampa Bay Devil Rays for outfielder Joey Gathright and infielder Fernando Cortez, June 20, 2006.

HOWRY, BOBBY DEAN (BOB)

Born, Phoenix, Arizona, August 4, 1973.
Bats Left. Throws Right. Height, 6 feet, 5 inches. Weight, 220 pounds.

Year	Club	Lea	G	IP	W	L	Pct	SO	BB	H	ERA	SAVES
1994 Everett	Northwest		5	19	0	4	.000	16	10	29	7.11	0
1994 Clinton	Midwest		9	49 1/3	1	3	.250	22	16	61	4.20	0
1995 San Jose	California		27	165 1/3	12	10	.545	107	54	171	3.54	0
1996 Shreveport	Texas		27	156 2/3	10	8	.556	57	56	163	4.65	0
1997 Shreveport	Texas		48	55	6	3	.667	43	21	58	4.91	22
1997 Birmingham a	Southern		12	12 2/3	0	0	.000	3	3	16	2.84	2
1998 Calgary	P.C.		23	31 2/3	1	2	.333	22	10	25	3.41	5
1998 Chicago	A.L.		44	54 1/3	0	3	.000	51	19	37	3.15	9
1999 Chicago	A.L.		69	67 2/3	5	3	.625	80	38	58	3.59	28
2000 Chicago	A.L.		65	71	2	4	.333	60	29	54	3.17	7
2001 Chicago	A.L.		69	78 2/3	4	5	.444	64	30	85	4.69	5
2002 Chicago-Boston b	A.L.		67	68 2/3	3	5	.375	45	21	67	4.19	0
2003 Boston	A.L.		4	4 1/3	0	0	.000	4	3	11	12.46	0
2003 Pawtucket c-d	Int.		13	17	2	0	1.000	10	1	14	1.06	0
2004 Buffalo	Int.		18	26	1	1	.500	24	6	22	5.19	0
2004 Cleveland	A.L.		37	42 2/3	4	2	.667	39	12	37	2.74	0
2005 Cleveland e	A.L.		79	73	7	4	.636	48	16	49	2.47	3
2006 Chicago	N.L.		84	76 2/3	4	5	.444	71	17	70	3.17	5
2007 Chicago	N.L.		78	81 1/3	6	7	.462	72	19	76	3.32	8
2008 Chicago f	N.L.		72	70 2/3	7	5	.583	59	13	90	5.35	1
Major League Totals	11 Yrs.		668	689	42	43	.494	593	217	634	3.68	66
Division Series												
2000 Chicago	A.L.		2	2 2/3	0	0	.000	4	2	2	3.38	0
2007 Chicago	N.L.		2	3	0	0	.000	6	0	1	0.00	0
Division Series Totals			4	5 2/3	0	0	.000	10	2	3	1.59	0

a Traded by San Francisco Giants to Chicago White Sox with infielder Mike Caruso, outfielder Brian Manning, pitcher Lorenzo Barcelo and pitcher Ken Vining for pitcher Wilson Alvarez, pitcher Danny Darwin and pitcher Roberto Hernandez, July 31, 1997.
b Traded to Boston Red Sox for pitcher Franklin Francisco and pitcher Byeong An, July 31, 2002.
c On disabled list from August 22 to September 29, 2003.
d Released by Boston Red Sox October 24, 2003. Signed with Cleveland Indians organization, December 17, 2003.
e Filed for free agency, October 27, 2005. Signed with Chicago Cubs, November 29, 2005.
f Filed for free agency, October 30, 2008. Signed with San Francisco Giants, December 3, 2008.

HUDSON, TIMOTHY ADAM (TIM)

Born, Columbus, Georgia, July 14, 1975.
Bats Right. Throws Right. Height, 6 feet, 1 inch. Weight, 170 pounds.

Year	Club	Lea	G	IP	W	L	Pct	SO	BB	H	ERA	SAVES
1997 Sou Oregon	Northwest		8	28 2/3	3	1	.750	37	15	12	2.51	0
1998 Modesto	California		8	37 2/3	4	0	1.000	48	18	19	1.67	0
1998 Huntsville	Southern		22	134 2/3	10	9	.526	104	71	136	4.54	0
1999 Midland	Texas		3	18	3	0	1.000	18	3	9	0.50	0
1999 Vancouver	P.C.		8	49	4	0	1.000	61	21	38	2.20	0
1999 Oakland	A.L.		21	136 1/3	11	2	.846	132	62	121	3.23	0
2000 Oakland	A.L.		32	202 1/3	*20	6	*.769	169	82	169	4.14	0
2001 Oakland	A.L.		35	235	18	9	.667	181	71	216	3.37	0
2002 Oakland	A.L.		34	238 1/3	15	9	.625	152	62	237	2.98	0
2003 Oakland	A.L.		34	240	16	7	.696	162	61	197	2.70	0
2004 Sacramento	P.C.		1	3	0	0	.000	3	2	2	6.00	0
2004 Oakland a-b	A.L.		27	188 2/3	12	6	.667	103	44	194	3.53	0
2005 Atlanta c	N.L.		29	192	14	9	.609	115	65	194	3.52	0
2006 Atlanta	N.L.		35	218 1/3	13	12	.520	141	79	235	4.86	0
2007 Atlanta	N.L.		34	224 1/3	16	10	.615	132	53	221	3.33	0
2008 Atlanta d	N.L.		23	142	11	7	.611	85	40	125	3.17	0
Major League Totals	10 Yrs.		304	2017 1/3	146	77	.655	1372	619	1909	3.48	0
Division Series												
2000 Oakland	A.L.		1	8	0	1	.000	5	4	6	3.38	0
2001 Oakland	A.L.		2	9 2/3	1	0	1.000	5	1	8	0.93	0
2002 Oakland	A.L.		2	8 2/3	0	1	.000	8	4	13	6.23	0
2003 Oakland	A.L.		2	7 2/3	0	0	.000	6	1	10	3.52	0
2005 Atlanta	N.L.		2	13 2/3	0	1	.000	8	6	13	5.27	0
Division Series Totals			9	47 2/3	1	3	.250	32	16	50	3.97	0

a On disabled list from June 23 to August 7, 2004.
b Traded to Atlanta Braves for pitcher Juan Cruz, pitcher Dan Meyer and outfielder Charles Thomas, December 16, 2004.
c On disabled list from June 14 to July 16, 2005.
d On disabled list from July 27 to November 3, 2008.

HUGHES, PHILIP JOSEPH

Born, Mission Viejo, California, June 24, 1986.
Bats Right. Throws Right. Height, 6 feet, 5 inches. Weight, 220 pounds.

Year Club	Lea	G	IP	W	L	Pct	SO	BB	H	ERA	SAVES
2004 Yankees .... Gulf Coast		3	5	0	0	.000	8	0	4	0.00	0
2005 Tampa .... Fla.St.		5	17²/₃	2	0	1.000	21	4	8	3.06	0
2005 Charleston .... So.Atl.		12	68²/₃	7	1	.875	72	16	46	1.97	0
2006 Trenton........... Eastern		21	116	10	3	.769	138	32	73	2.25	0
2006 Tampa .... Fla.St.		5	30	2	3	.400	30	2	19	1.80	0
2007 Tampa .... Fla.St.		1	2	0	0	.000	3	2	0	0.00	0
2007 Trenton............ Eastern		2	7	0	0	.000	11	2	5	1.29	0
2007 Scranton-WB ....Int.		5	28²/₃	4	1	.800	28	8	16	2.20	0
2007 New York a..........A.L.		13	72²/₃	5	3	.625	58	29	64	4.46	0
2008 Charleston .... So.Atl.		2	6²/₃	2	0	1.000	6	2	3	0.00	0
2008 Scranton-WB ....Int.		6	29	1	0	1.000	31	9	34	5.90	0
2008 New York b..........A.L.		8	34	0	4	.000	23	15	43	6.62	0
Major League Totals ....2 Yrs.		21	106²/₃	5	7	.417	81	44	107	5.15	0
Division Series											
2007 New York .... A.L.		2	5²/₃	1	0	1.000	6	0	3	1.59	0

a On disabled list from May 2 to August 4, 2007.
b On disabled list from April 30 to July 30, 2008.

ISRINGHAUSEN, JASON DERIK

Born, Brighton, Illinois, September 7, 1972.
Bats Right. Throws Right. Height, 6 feet, 3 inches. Weight, 230 pounds.

Year Club	Lea	G	IP	W	L	Pct	SO	BB	H	ERA	SAVES
1992 Mets .... Gulf Coast		6	29	2	4	.333	25	17	26	4.34	0
1992 Kingsport.......... Appal.		7	36	4	1	.800	24	12	32	3.25	0
1993 Pittsfield .... N.Y.-Penn.		15	90¹/₃	7	4	.636	104	28	68	3.29	0
1994 St. Lucie............ Fla.St.		14	101	6	4	.600	59	27	76	2.23	0
1994 Binghamton .... Eastern		14	92¹/₃	5	4	.556	69	23	78	3.02	0
1995 Binghamton .... Eastern		6	41	2	1	.667	59	12	26	2.85	0
1995 Norfolk...............Int.		12	87	9	1	.900	75	24	64	1.55	0
1995 New York........... N.L.		14	93	9	2	.818	55	31	88	2.81	0
1996 New York a.......... N.L.		27	171²/₃	6	14	.300	114	73	190	4.77	0
1997 Mets .... Gulf Coast		1	4²/₃	1	0	1.000	7	1	2	1.93	0
1997 St. Lucie............ Fla.St.		2	12	1	0	1.000	15	5	8	0.00	0
1997 Norfolk...............Int.		3	20	0	2	.000	17	8	20	4.05	0
1997 New York b.......... N.L.		6	29²/₃	2	2	.500	25	22	40	7.58	0
1998 New York c.......... N.L.					INJURED—Did Not Play						
1999 New York .... N.L.		13	39¹/₃	1	3	.250	31	22	43	6.41	1
1999 Oakland d............. A.L.		20	25¹/₃	0	1	.000	20	12	21	2.13	8
2000 Oakland .... A.L.		66	69	6	4	.600	57	32	67	3.78	33
2001 Oakland e............. A.L.		65	71¹/₃	4	3	.571	74	23	54	2.65	34
2002 St. Louis............. N.L.		60	65¹/₃	3	2	.600	68	18	46	2.48	32
2003 Tennessee .... Southern		2	2	0	0	.000	3	0	1	0.00	0
2003 St. Louis f .... N.L.		40	42	0	1	.000	41	18	31	2.36	22
2004 St. Louis............. N.L.		74	75¹/₃	4	2	.667	71	23	55	2.87	*47
2005 St. Louis g........... N.L.		63	59	1	2	.333	51	27	43	2.14	39
2006 St. Louis............. N.L.		59	58¹/₃	4	8	.333	52	38	47	3.55	33
2007 St. Louis............. N.L.		63	65¹/₃	4	0	1.000	54	28	42	2.48	32
2008 Palm Beach .... Fla.St.		1	2	0	0	.000	1	0	1	0.00	0
2008 Springfield ....Texas		1	1²/₃	0	0	.000	2	0	1	0.00	0
2008 St. Louis h-i........ N.L.		42	42²/₃	1	5	.167	36	22	48	5.70	12
Major League Totals ....13 Yrs.		612	907¹/₃	45	49	.479	749	389	815	3.61	293
Division Series											
2000 Oakland .... A.L.		2	2	0	0	.000	3	0	1	0.00	1
2001 Oakland .... A.L.		2	2	0	0	.000	3	1	1	0.00	2
2002 St. Louis............. N.L.		2	2	0	0	.000	1	0	0	0.00	2
2004 St. Louis............. N.L.		2	2	0	0	.000	2	2	1	4.50	0
2005 St. Louis............. N.L.		3	3	0	0	.000	4	1	5	3.00	1
Division Series Totals		11	11	0	0	.000	13	4	8	1.64	6
Championship Series											
2002 St. Louis............. N.L.		2	2	0	0	.000	3	3	1	4.50	1
2004 St. Louis............. N.L.		6	7²/₃	0	1	.000	3	4	4	4.70	3
2005 St. Louis............. N.L.		3	4	1	0	1.000	2	0	3	0.00	1
Championship Series Totals		11	13²/₃	1	1	.500	8	7	8	3.29	5
World Series Record											
2004 St. Louis............. N.L.		1	2	0	0	.000	2	1	1	0.00	0

a On disabled list from August 13 to September 1, 1996.
b On disabled list from March 24 to August 27, 1997.
c On disabled list from March 21 to September 28, 1998.
d Traded to Oakland Athletics with pitcher Greg McMichael for pitcher Billy Taylor, July 31, 1999.
e Filed for free agency, November 5, 2001. Signed with St. Louis Cardinals, December 10, 2001.
f On disabled list from March 21 to June 10, 2003.
g On disabled list from April 27 to May 13, 2005.
h On disabled list from May 16 to June 14 and August 17 to November 1, 2008.
i Filed for free agency, November 1, 2008.

JACKSON, EDWIN
Born, Neu-Ulm, West Germany, September 9, 1983.
Bats Right. Throws Right. Height, 6 feet, 3 inches. Weight, 210 pounds.

Year	Club	Lea	G	IP	W	L	Pct	SO	BB	H	ERA	SAVES
2001 Dodgers		Gulf Coast	12	22	2	1	.667	23	19	14	2.45	0
2002 South Bend		So.Atl.	19	104²/₃	5	2	.714	85	33	79	1.98	0
2003 Jacksonville		Southern	27	148¹/₃	7	7	.500	157	53	121	3.70	0
2003 Los Angeles		N.L.	4	22	2	1	.667	19	11	17	2.45	0
2004 Las Vegas		P.C.	19	90²/₃	6	4	.600	70	55	90	5.86	0
2004 Los Angeles a		N.L.	8	24²/₃	2	1	.667	16	11	31	7.30	0
2005 Jacksonville		Southern	11	62	6	4	.600	44	18	52	3.48	0
2005 Las Vegas		P.C.	12	55¹/₃	3	7	.300	33	37	76	8.62	0
2005 Los Angeles		N.L.	7	28²/₃	2	2	.500	13	17	31	6.28	0
2006 Durham		Int.	22	73	3	7	.300	66	35	84	5.55	5
2006 Tampa Bay b		A.L.	23	36¹/₃	0	0	.000	27	25	42	5.45	0
2007 Tampa Bay		A.L.	32	161	5	15	.250	128	88	195	5.76	0
2008 Tampa Bay c		A.L.	32	183¹/₃	14	11	.560	108	77	199	4.42	0
Major League Totals	6 Yrs.		106	456	25	30	.455	311	229	515	5.15	0
Championship Series												
2008 Tampa Bay		N.L.	2	2¹/₃	0	0	.000	4	2	0	0.00	0
World Series Record												
2008 Tampa Bay c		N.L.	1	2	0	0	.000	1	1	2	4.50	0

a On disabled list from July 9 to September 7, 2004.
b Traded to Tampa Bay Devil Rays with pitcher Chuck Tiffany for pitcher Danys Baez and pitcher Lance Carter, January 14, 2006.
c Traded to Detroit Tigers for outfielder Matt Joyce, December 10, 2008.

JANSSEN, ROBERT CASEY (CASEY)
Born, Orange, California, September 17, 1981.
Bats Right. Throws Right. Height, 6 feet, 4 inches. Weight, 205 pounds.

Year	Club	Lea	G	IP	W	L	Pct	SO	BB	H	ERA	SAVES
2004 Auburn		N.Y.-Penn.	10	50	3	1	.750	45	10	47	3.60	0
2005 New Hampshire		Eastern	9	43	3	3	.500	47	4	49	2.93	0
2005 Dunedin		Fla.St.	10	59²/₃	6	1	.857	51	12	46	2.26	0
2005 Lansing		Midwest	7	46	4	0	1.000	38	4	27	1.37	0
2006 Syracuse		Int.	9	42²/₃	1	5	.167	32	8	47	4.85	0
2006 Toronto		A.L.	19	94	6	10	.375	44	21	103	5.07	0
2007 Toronto		A.L.	70	72²/₃	2	3	.400	39	20	67	2.35	6
2008 Toronto a		A.L.					INJURED—Did Not Play					
Major League Totals	2 Yrs.		89	166²/₃	8	13	.381	83	41	170	3.89	6

a On disabled list from March 17 to November 14, 2008.

JENKS, ROBERT SCOTT (BOBBY)
Born, Mission Hills, California, March 14, 1981.
Bats Right. Throws Right. Height, 6 feet, 3 inches. Weight, 280 pounds.

Year	Club	Lea	G	IP	W	L	Pct	SO	BB	H	ERA	SAVES
2000 Butte		Pioneer	14	52²/₃	1	7	.125	42	44	61	7.86	0
2001 Cedar Rapids		Midwest	21	99	3	7	.300	98	64	90	5.27	0
2001 Arkansas		Texas	2	10	1	0	1.000	10	5	8	3.60	0
2002 Rancho Cucamonga		California	11	65¹/₃	3	5	.375	64	46	50	4.82	0
2002 Arkansas		Texas	10	58	3	6	.333	58	44	49	4.66	0
2003 Angels		Arizona	1	4	0	0	.000	5	0	2	0.00	0
2003 Arkansas		Texas	16	83	7	2	.778	103	51	56	2.17	0
2004 Angels		Arizona	1	3¹/₃	0	0	.000	5	3	2	8.10	0
2004 Rancho Cucamonga		California	1	3²/₃	0	1	.000	3	7	5	19.64	0
2004 Salt Lake a		P.C.	3	12¹/₃	0	1	.000	13	6	19	8.76	0
2005 Birmingham		Southern	35	41	1	2	.333	48	20	34	2.85	19

Year Club	Lea	G	IP	W	L	Pct	SO	BB	H	ERA	SAVES
2005 Chicago	A.L.	32	39 1/3	1	1	.500	50	15	34	2.75	6
2006 Chicago	A.L.	67	69 2/3	3	4	.429	80	31	66	4.00	41
2007 Chicago	A.L.	66	65	3	5	.375	56	13	45	2.77	40
2008 Winston-Salem	Carolina	1	1	0	0	.000	0	0	3	9.00	0
2008 Birmingham	Southern	1	1	0	0	.000	3	0	0	0.00	0
2008 Chicago b	A.L.	57	61 2/3	3	1	.750	38	17	51	2.63	30
Major League Totals ... 4 Yrs.		222	235 2/3	10	11	.476	224	76	196	3.09	117
Division Series											
2005 Chicago	A.L.	2	3	0	0	.000	1	1	1	0.00	2
2008 Chicago	A.L.	1	1	0	0	.000	1	0	1	0.00	1
Division Series Totals		3	4	0	0	.000	2	1	2	0.00	3
World Series Record											
2005 Chicago	A.L.	4	5	0	0	.000	7	2	3	3.60	2

a Claimed on waivers by Chicago White Sox from Anaheim Angels, December 17, 2004.
b On disabled list from June 30 to July 18, 2008.

JIMENEZ, UBALDO

Born, Nagua, Dominican Republic, January 22, 1984.
Bats Right. Throws Right. Height, 6 feet, 4 inches. Weight, 200 pounds.

Year Club	Lea	G	IP	W	L	Pct	SO	BB	H	ERA	SAVES
2002 Casper	Pioneer	14	62	3	5	.375	65	29	72	6.53	0
2003 Visalia	Calif.	1	5	1	0	1.000	7	1	3	0.00	0
2003 Asheville	So.Atl.	27	153 2/3	10	6	.625	138	67	129	3.46	0
2004 Visalia	Calif.	9	44 1/3	4	1	.800	61	12	29	2.23	0
2005 Modesto	Calif.	14	72 1/3	5	3	.625	78	40	61	3.98	0
2005 Tulsa	Texas	12	63	2	5	.286	53	31	58	5.43	0
2006 Tulsa	Texas	13	73 1/3	9	2	.818	86	40	49	2.45	0
2006 Colorado Springs	P.C.	13	78 1/3	5	2	.714	64	43	74	5.06	0
2006 Colorado	N.L.	2	7 2/3	0	0	.000	3	3	5	3.52	0
2007 Colorado Springs	P.C.	19	103	8	5	.615	89	62	110	5.85	0
2007 Colorado	N.L.	15	82	4	4	.500	68	37	70	4.28	0
2008 Colorado	N.L.	34	198 2/3	12	12	.500	172	103	182	3.99	0
Major League Totals ... 3 Yrs.		51	288 1/3	16	16	.500	243	143	257	4.06	0
Division Series											
2007 Colorado	N.L.	1	6 1/3	0	0	.000	5	4	3	1.42	0
Championship Series											
2007 Colorado	N.L.	1	5	0	0	.000	6	4	5	1.80	0
World Series Record											
2007 Colorado	N.L.	1	4 2/3	0	0	.000	2	5	3	3.86	0

JOHNSON, JAMES ROBERT (JIM)

Born, Johnson City, New York, June 27, 1983.
Bats Right. Throws Right. Height, 6 feet, 5 inches. Weight, 230 pounds.

Year Club	Lea	G	IP	W	L	Pct	SO	BB	H	ERA	SAVES
2001 Orioles	Gulf Coast	7	18 2/3	0	1	.000	19	7	17	3.86	0
2002 Bluefield	Appal.	11	55 2/3	4	2	.667	36	16	52	4.37	0
2003 Bluefield	Appal.	11	51 1/3	3	2	.600	46	18	62	3.68	0
2004 Frederick	Carolina	1	3	0	0	.000	6	1	6	9.00	0
2004 Delmarva	So.Atl.	20	106 2/3	8	7	.533	93	30	97	3.29	0
2005 Frederick	Carolina	28	159 2/3	12	9	.571	168	64	139	3.49	1
2005 Bowie	Eastern	1	7	0	0	.000	6	2	3	0.00	0
2006 Baltimore	A.L.	1	3	0	1	.000	0	3	9	24.00	0
2006 Bowie	Eastern	27	156	13	6	.684	124	57	165	4.44	0
2007 Baltimore	A.L.	1	2	0	0	.000	1	2	3	9.00	0
2007 Norfolk	Int.	26	148	6	12	.333	109	48	164	4.07	0
2008 Norfolk	Int.	1	4	0	1	.000	2	1	2	2.25	0
2008 Baltimore a	A.L.	54	68 2/3	2	4	.333	38	28	54	2.23	1
Major League Totals ... 3 Yrs.		56	73 2/3	2	5	.286	39	33	66	3.30	1

a On disabled list from September 1 to October 2, 2008.

JOHNSON, JOSHUA MICHAEL (JOSH)

Born, Minneapolis, Minnesota, January 31, 1984.
Bats Left. Throws Right. Height, 6 feet, 7 inches. Weight, 230 pounds.

Year Club	Lea	G	IP	W	L	Pct	SO	BB	H	ERA	SAVES
2002 Marlins	Gulf Coast	4	15	2	0	1.000	11	3	8	0.60	0
2003 Greensboro	So.Atl.	17	82 1/3	4	7	.364	59	29	69	3.61	0

Year	Club	Lea	G	IP	W	L	Pct	SO	BB	H	ERA	SAVES
2004 Jupiter	Fla.St.	23	114$\frac{1}{3}$	5	12	.294	103	47	124	3.38	0
2005 Carolina	Southern	26	139$\frac{2}{3}$	12	4	.750	113	50	139	3.87	0
2005 Florida	N.L.	4	12$\frac{1}{3}$	0	0	.000	10	10	11	3.65	0
2006 Florida	N.L.	31	157	12	7	.632	133	68	136	3.10	0
2007 Carolina	Southern	2	10$\frac{1}{3}$	0	0	.000	9	5	8	1.74	0
2007 Florida	N.L.	4	15$\frac{2}{3}$	0	3	.000	14	12	26	7.47	0
2007 Jupiter a	Fla.St.	3	11$\frac{1}{3}$	0	0	.000	13	0	9	0.79	0
2008 Greensboro	So.Atl.	1	5	0	1	.000	7	0	8	3.60	0
2008 Jupiter	Fla.St.	1	5$\frac{1}{3}$	0	0	.000	2	2	6	5.06	0
2008 Carolina	Southern	3	19	1	1	.500	14	3	22	3.32	0
2008 Florida b	N.L.	14	87$\frac{1}{3}$	7	1	.875	77	27	91	3.61	0
Major League Totals	4 Yrs.	53	272$\frac{1}{3}$	19	11	.633	234	117	264	3.54	0

a On disabled list from March 23 to June 18 and July 5 to November 12, 2007.
b On disabled list from March 21 to July 10, 2008.

JOHNSON, RANDALL DAVID (RANDY)

Born, Walnut Creek, California, September 10, 1963.
Bats Right. Throws Left. Height, 6 feet, 10 inches. Weight, 230 pounds.

Year	Club	Lea	G	IP	W	L	Pct	SO	BB	H	ERA	SAVES
1985 Jamestown	N.Y.-Penn.	8	27$\frac{1}{3}$	0	3	.000	21	24	29	5.93	0
1986 West Palm Beach	Fla. St.	26	119$\frac{2}{3}$	8	7	.533	133	94	89	3.16	0
1987 Jacksonville	Southern	25	140	11	8	.579	*163	128	100	3.73	0
1988 Indianapolis	A.A.	20	113$\frac{1}{3}$	8	7	.533	111	72	85	3.26	0
1988 Montreal	N.L.	4	26	3	0	1.000	25	7	23	2.42	0
1989 Montreal	N.L.	7	29$\frac{2}{3}$	0	4	.000	26	26	29	6.67	0
1989 Indianapolis a	A.A.	3	18	1	1	.500	17	9	13	2.00	0
1989 Seattle	A.L.	22	131	7	9	.438	104	70	118	4.40	0
1990 Seattle b-c	A.L.	33	219$\frac{2}{3}$	14	11	.560	194	*120	174	3.65	0
1991 Seattle	A.L.	33	201$\frac{1}{3}$	13	10	.565	228	*152	151	3.98	0
1992 Seattle d	A.L.	31	210$\frac{1}{3}$	12	14	.462	*241	*144	154	3.77	0
1993 Seattle	A.L.	35	255$\frac{1}{3}$	19	8	.704	*308	99	185	3.24	1
1994 Seattle	A.L.	23	172	13	6	.684	*204	72	132	3.19	0
1995 Seattle e	A.L.	30	214$\frac{1}{3}$	18	2	*.900	*294	65	159	*2.48	0
1996 Everett	Northwest	1	2	0	0	.000	5	0	0	0.00	0
1996 Seattle f	A.L.	14	61$\frac{1}{3}$	5	0	1.000	85	25	48	3.67	1
1997 Seattle	A.L.	30	213	20	4	*.833	291	77	147	2.28	0
1998 Seattle	A.L.	23	160	9	10	.474	213	60	146	4.33	0
1998 Houston g-h-i	N.L.	11	84$\frac{1}{3}$	10	1	.909	116	26	57	1.28	0
1999 Arizona j	N.L.	35	*271$\frac{2}{3}$	17	9	.654	364	70	*207	*2.48	0
2000 Arizona k	N.L.	35	248$\frac{2}{3}$	19	7	*.731	*347	76	202	2.64	0
2001 Arizona l	N.L.	35	249$\frac{2}{3}$	21	6	.778	*372	71	181	*2.49	0
2002 Arizona m	N.L.	35	*260	*24	5	*.828	*334	71	197	*2.32	0
2003 Lancaster	California	1	6	0	1	.000	6	0	11	6.00	0
2003 Tucson	P.C.	1	4	0	0	.000	4	0	0	0.00	0
2003 El Paso	Texas	1	4	0	0	.000	5	1	3	0.00	0
2003 Arizona n	N.L.	18	114	6	8	.429	125	27	125	4.26	0
2004 Arizona o-p	N.L.	35	245$\frac{2}{3}$	16	14	.533	*290	44	177	2.60	0
2005 New York	A.L.	34	225$\frac{2}{3}$	17	8	.680	211	47	207	3.79	0
2006 New York q	A.L.	33	205	17	11	.607	172	60	194	5.00	0
2007 Visalia	Calif.	1	6	0	0	.000	4	0	4	3.00	0
2007 Tucson	P.C.	2	12	1	0	1.000	10	2	15	3.00	0
2007 Arizona r	N.L.	10	56$\frac{2}{3}$	4	3	.571	72	13	52	3.81	0
2008 Tucson	P.C.	2	10	0	0	.000	8	3	11	7.20	0
2008 Arizona s-t	N.L.	30	184	11	10	.524	173	44	184	3.91	0
Major League Totals	21 Yrs.	596	4039$\frac{1}{3}$	295	160	.648	4789	1466	3249	3.26	2
Division Series											
1995 Seattle	A.L.	2	10	2	0	1.000	16	6	5	2.70	0
1997 Seattle	A.L.	2	13	0	2	.000	16	6	14	5.54	0
1998 Houston	N.L.	2	14	0	2	.000	17	2	12	1.93	0
1999 Arizona	N.L.	1	8$\frac{1}{3}$	0	1	.000	11	3	8	7.56	0
2001 Arizona	N.L.	1	8	0	1	.000	9	2	6	3.38	0
2002 Arizona	N.L.	1	6	0	1	.000	4	2	10	7.50	0
2005 New York	A.L.	2	7$\frac{1}{3}$	0	0	.000	4	1	12	6.14	0
2006 New York	A.L.	1	5$\frac{2}{3}$	0	1	.000	4	2	8	7.94	0
Division Series Totals		12	72$\frac{1}{3}$	2	8	.200	81	24	75	4.85	0
Championship Series											
1995 Seattle	A.L.	2	15$\frac{1}{3}$	0	1	.000	13	2	12	2.35	0
2001 Arizona	N.L.	2	16	2	0	1.000	19	3	10	1.13	0
Championship Series Totals		4	31$\frac{1}{3}$	2	1	.667	32	5	22	1.72	0

Year	Club	Lea	G	IP	W	L	Pct	SO	BB	H	ERA	SAVES
	World Series Record											
2001 Arizona	N.L.	3	17$\frac{1}{3}$	3	0	1.000	19	3	9	1.04	0	

a Traded by Montreal Expos to Seattle Mariners with pitchers Brian Holman and Gene Harris for pitcher Mark Langston and player to be named, May 25; Montreal acquired pitcher Mike Campbell to complete trade, July 31, 1989.
b Pitched no-hit, no-run game against Detroit Tigers, winning 2-0, June 2, 1990.
c Suspended three games by American League for June 30 fight from July 11 to July 13, 1990.
d On disabled list from June 11 to June 27, 1992.
e Selected Cy Young Award Winner in American League for 1995.
f On disabled list from May 13 to August 6 and August 27 to September 30, 1996.
g Traded to Houston Astros for infielder Carlos Guillen, pitcher Freddy Garcia and player to be named later, July 31, 1998.
h Seattle Mariners received pitcher John Halama to complete trade, October 1, 1998.
i Filed for free agency, October 28, 1998. Signed with Arizona Diamondbacks, November 30, 1998.
j Selected Cy Young Award Winner in National League for 1999.
k Selected Cy Young Award Winner in National League for 2000.
l Selected Cy Young Award Winner in National League for 2001.
m Selected Cy Young Award Winner in National League for 2002.
n On disabled list from April 12 to April 27 and April 28 to July 20, 2003.
o Pitched no-hit, no-run perfect game against Atlanta Braves, May 18, 2004.
p Traded to New York Yankees for pitcher Javier Vazquez, pitcher Brad Halsey, catcher Dioner Navarro and cash, January 11, 2005.
q Traded to Arizona Diamondbacks with cash for pitcher Luis Vizcaino, pitcher Steven Jackson, pitcher Ross Ohlendorf and infielder Alberto Gonzalez, January 9, 2007.
r On disabled list from March 30 to April 24 and June 11 to June 28 and June 29 to November 9, 2007.
s On disabled list from March 22 to April 14, 2008.
t Filed for free agency, November 13, 2008. Signed with San Francisco Giants, December 26, 2008.

JONES, TODD BARTON

Born, Marietta, Georgia, April 24, 1968.
Bats Left. Throws Right. Height, 6 feet, 3 inches. Weight, 230 pounds.

Year	Club	Lea	G	IP	W	L	Pct	SO	BB	H	ERA	SAVES
1989 Auburn	N.Y.-Penn.	11	49$\frac{2}{3}$	2	3	.400	71	42	47	5.44	0
1990 Osceola	Fla. St.	27	151$\frac{1}{3}$	12	10	.545	106	109	124	3.51	0
1991 Osceola	Fla. St.	14	72$\frac{1}{3}$	4	4	.500	51	35	69	4.35	0
1991 Jackson	Texas	10	55$\frac{1}{3}$	4	3	.571	37	39	51	4.88	0
1992 Jackson	Texas	61	66	3	7	.300	60	44	52	3.14	25
1992 Tucson	P.C.	3	4	0	1	.000	4	10	1	4.50	0
1993 Tucson	P.C.	41	48$\frac{2}{3}$	4	2	.667	45	31	49	4.44	12
1993 Houston	N.L.	27	37$\frac{1}{3}$	1	2	.333	25	15	28	3.13	2
1994 Houston	N.L.	48	72$\frac{2}{3}$	5	2	.714	63	26	52	2.72	5
1995 Houston	N.L.	68	99$\frac{2}{3}$	6	5	.545	96	52	89	3.07	15
1996 Tucson	P.C.	1	2	0	0	.000	0	2	1	0.00	0
1996 Houston a-b	N.L.	51	57$\frac{1}{3}$	6	3	.667	44	32	61	4.40	17
1997 Detroit	A.L.	68	70	5	4	.556	70	35	60	3.09	31
1998 Detroit	A.L.	65	63$\frac{1}{3}$	1	4	.200	57	36	58	4.97	28
1999 Detroit	A.L.	65	66$\frac{1}{3}$	4	4	.500	64	35	64	3.80	30
2000 Detroit	A.L.	67	64	2	4	.333	67	25	67	3.52	*42
2001 Detroit-Minnesota c-d	A.L.	69	68	5	5	.500	54	29	87	4.24	13
2002 Colorado	N.L.	79	82$\frac{1}{3}$	1	4	.200	73	28	84	4.70	1
2003 Colorado	N.L.	33	39$\frac{1}{3}$	1	4	.200	28	18	61	8.24	0
2003 Boston e-f	A.L.	26	29$\frac{1}{3}$	2	1	.667	31	13	32	5.52	0
2004 Cincinnati-Philadelphia g-h-i	N.L.	78	82$\frac{1}{3}$	11	5	.688	59	33	84	4.15	2
2005 Florida j	N.L.	68	73	1	5	.167	62	14	61	2.10	40
2006 Detroit k	A.L.	62	64	2	6	.250	28	11	70	3.94	37
2007 Detroit l	A.L.	63	61$\frac{1}{3}$	1	4	.200	33	23	64	4.26	38
2008 Detroit m-n	A.L.	45	41$\frac{2}{3}$	4	1	.800	14	18	50	4.97	18
Major League Totals	16 Yrs.	982	1072	58	63	.479	868	443	1072	3.97	319
	Division Series											
2006 Detroit	A.L.	2	2	0	0	.000	2	0	1	0.00	1
	Championship Series											
2003 Boston	A.L.	1	0$\frac{1}{3}$	0	0	.000	1	1	1	0.00	0
2006 Detroit	A.L.	3	3	0	0	.000	2	1	3	0.00	2
Championship Series Totals		4	3$\frac{1}{3}$	0	0	.000	3	2	4	0.00	2
	World Series Record											
2006 Detroit	A.L.	2	1$\frac{2}{3}$	0	0	.000	0	0	3	0.00	1

a On disabled list from July 19 to August 12 and August 18 to September 12, 1996.
b Traded to Detroit Tigers with outfielder Brian Hunter, infielder Orlando Miller and pitcher Doug Brocail for catcher Brad Ausmus, pitcher C.J. Nitkowski, pitcher Jose Lima, pitcher Trever Miller and infielder Daryle Ward, December 10, 1996.

c Traded to Minnesota Twins for pitcher Mark Redman, July 28, 2001.
d Filed for free agency, November 5, 2001. Signed with Colorado Rockies, January 11, 2002.
e Released by Colorado Rockies, June 30, 2003. Signed with Boston Red Sox, July 2, 2003.
f Filed for free agency, October 30, 2003. Signed with Tampa Bay Devil Rays organization, January 12, 2004.
g Released by Tampa Bay Devil Rays, March 24, 2004. Signed with Cincinnati Reds organization, March 25, 2004.
h Traded to Philadelphia Phillies with outfielder Brad Correll for pitcher Josh Hancock and infielder Anderson Machado, July 30, 2004.
i Filed for free agency, October 29, 2004. Signed with Florida Marlins, December 13, 2004.
j Filed for free agency, October 28, 2005. Signed with Detroit Tigers, December 8, 2005.
k On disabled list from April 5 to April 21, 2006.
l Filed for free agency, October 29, 2007, re-signed with Detroit Tigers, November 12, 2007.
m On disabled list from July 31 to August 15 and August 16 to October 1, 2008.
n Announced retirement at end of season, September 24, 2008.

JURRJENS, JAIR FRANCOISE

Born, Santa Maria, Curacao, Netherlands Antilles, January 29, 1986.
Bats Right. Throws Right. Height, 6 feet, 1 inch. Weight, 200 pounds.

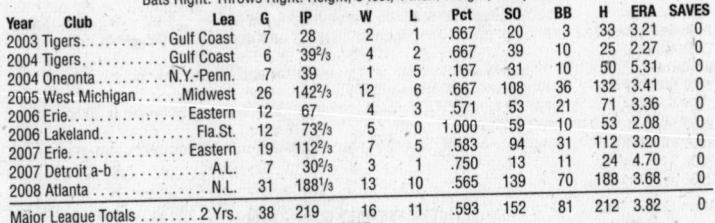

Year Club	Lea	G	IP	W	L	Pct	SO	BB	H	ERA	SAVES
2003 Tigers	Gulf Coast	7	28	2	1	.667	20	3	33	3.21	0
2004 Tigers	Gulf Coast	6	39²/₃	4	2	.667	39	10	25	2.27	0
2004 Oneonta	N.Y.-Penn.	7	39	1	5	.167	31	10	50	5.31	0
2005 West Michigan	Midwest	26	142²/₃	12	6	.667	108	36	132	3.41	0
2006 Erie	Eastern	12	67	4	3	.571	53	21	71	3.36	0
2006 Lakeland	Fla.St.	12	73²/₃	5	0	1.000	59	10	53	2.08	0
2007 Erie	Eastern	19	112²/₃	7	5	.583	94	31	112	3.20	0
2007 Detroit a-b	A.L.	7	30²/₃	3	1	.750	13	11	24	4.70	0
2008 Atlanta	N.L.	31	188¹/₃	13	10	.565	139	70	188	3.68	0
Major League Totals 2 Yrs.		38	219	16	11	.593	152	81	212	3.82	0

a On disabled list from August 27 to September 11, 2007.
b Traded to Atlanta Braves with outfielder Gorkys Hernandez for infielder Edgar Renteria, October 29, 2007.

KAZMIR, SCOTT EDWARD

Born, Houston, Texas, January 24, 1984.
Bats Left. Throws Left. Height, 6 feet. Weight, 190 pounds.

Year Club	Lea	G	IP	W	L	Pct	SO	BB	H	ERA	SAVES
2002 Brooklyn	N.Y.-Penn.	5	18	0	1	.000	34	7	5	0.50	0
2003 St. Lucie	Fla.St.	7	33	1	2	.333	40	16	29	3.27	0
2003 Capital City	So.Atl.	18	76¹/₃	4	4	.500	105	28	50	2.36	0
2004 St. Lucie	Fla.St.	11	50	1	2	.333	51	22	49	3.42	0
2004 Binghamton	Eastern	4	26	2	1	.667	29	9	16	1.73	0
2004 Montgomery	Southern	4	25	1	2	.333	24	11	14	1.44	0
2004 Tampa Bay a	A.L.	8	33¹/₃	2	3	.400	41	21	33	5.67	0
2005 Tampa Bay	A.L.	32	186	10	9	.526	174	*100	172	3.77	0
2006 Tampa Bay b	A.L.	24	144²/₃	10	8	.556	163	52	132	3.24	0
2007 Tampa Bay	A.L.	34	206²/₃	13	9	.591	*239	89	196	3.48	0
2008 Vero Beach	Fla.St.	2	7²/₃	0	1	.000	7	0	8	4.70	0
2008 Durham	Int.	1	5	0	0	.000	3	1	3	1.80	0
2008 Tampa Bay c	A.L.	27	152¹/₃	12	8	.600	166	70	123	3.49	0
Major League Totals 5 Yrs.		125	723	47	37	.560	783	332	656	3.61	0
Division Series											
2008 Tampa Bay	N.L.	1	5¹/₃	1	0	1.000	4	2	8	3.38	0
Championship Series											
2008 Tampa Bay	N.L.	2	10¹/₃	0	0	.000	9	6	8	4.35	0
World Series Record											
2008 Tampa Bay	N.L.	2	10	0	1	.000	9	10	10	4.50	0

a Traded by New York Mets to Tampa Bay Devil Rays with pitcher Jose Diaz for pitcher Victor Zambrano and pitcher Bartolome Fortunado, July 30, 2004.
b On disabled list from July 31 to August 8 and August 23 to October 2, 2006.
c On disabled list from March 25 to May 4, 2008.

KENDRICK, KYLE RODNEY

Born, Houston, Texas, August 26, 1984.
Bats Right. Throws Right. Height, 6 feet, 3 inches. Weight, 190 pounds.

Year Club	Lea	G	IP	W	L	Pct	SO	BB	H	ERA	SAVES
2003 Phillies	Gulf Coast	9	31¹/₃	0	4	.000	26	12	40	5.46	0
2004 Batavia	N.Y.-Penn.	13	70²/₃	2	8	.200	53	18	94	5.48	0

Year Club	Lea	G	IP	W	L	Pct	SO	BB	H	ERA	SAVES
2004 Lakewood	So.Atl.	15	66 2/3	3	8	.273	36	33	85	6.07	0
2005 Clearwater	Fla.St.	1	4	0	1	.000	1	2	5	0.00	0
2005 Batavia	N.Y.-Penn.	14	91 1/3	5	4	.556	70	22	94	3.74	0
2005 Lakewood	So.Atl.	5	22 2/3	0	3	.000	11	10	38	9.13	0
2006 Clearwater	Fla.St.	21	130	9	7	.563	79	37	117	3.53	0
2006 Lakewood	So.Atl.	7	46	3	2	.600	54	15	34	2.15	0
2007 Reading	Eastern	12	81 1/3	4	7	.364	50	18	82	3.21	0
2007 Philadelphia	N.L.	20	121	10	4	.714	49	25	129	3.87	0
2008 Philadelphia	N.L.	31	155 2/3	11	9	.550	68	57	194	5.49	0
Major League Totals	2 Yrs.	51	276 2/3	21	13	.618	117	82	323	4.78	0
Division Series											
2007 Philadelphia	N.L.	1	3 2/3	0	1	.000	2		5	12.27	0

KENNEDY, IAN PATRICK

Born, Huntington Beach, California, December 19, 1984.
Bats Right. Throws Right. Height, 6 feet. Weight, 195 pounds.

Year Club	Lea	G	IP	W	L	Pct	SO	BB	H	ERA	SAVES
2006 Staten Island	N.Y.-Penn.	1	2 2/3	0	0	.000	2	2	2	0.00	0
2007 Tampa	Fla.St.	11	63	6	1	.857	72	22	39	1.29	0
2007 Trenton	Eastern	9	48 2/3	5	1	.833	57	17	27	2.59	0
2007 Scranton-WB	Int.	6	34 2/3	1	1	.500	34	11	25	2.08	0
2007 New York	A.L.	3	19	1	0	1.000	15	9	13	1.89	0
2008 Yankees	Gulf Coast	1	3	1	0	1.000	7	0	3	3.00	0
2008 Tampa	Fla.St.	1	5	0	0	.000	4	1	2	0.00	0
2008 Scranton-WB	Int.	13	69	5	3	.625	72	17	52	2.35	0
2008 New York a	A.L.	10	39 2/3	0	4	.000	27	26	50	8.17	0
Major League Totals	2 Yrs.	13	58 2/3	1	4	.200	42	35	63	6.14	0

a On disabled list from May 28 to June 24, 2008.

KENSING, LOGAN FRENCH

Born, San Antonio, Texas, July 3, 1982.
Bats Right. Throws Right. Height, 6 feet, 1 inch. Weight, 185 pounds.

Year Club	Lea	G	IP	W	L	Pct	SO	BB	H	ERA	SAVES
2003 Jamestown	N.Y.-Penn.	8	33	2	4	.333	20	6	48	5.73	0
2003 Greensboro	So.Atl.	4	20	0	2	.000	11	5	18	4.50	0
2004 Jupiter	Fla.St.	23	127 2/3	6	7	.462	100	35	120	2.96	0
2004 Florida	N.L.	5	13 2/3	0	3	.000	7	9	19	9.88	0
2005 Carolina	Southern	7	39 2/3	4	1	.800	33	14	35	3.18	0
2005 Florida a	N.L.	3	5 2/3	0	0	.000	4	3	11	11.12	0
2006 Albuquerque	P.C.	13	18	1	1	.500	18	5	11	3.00	2
2006 Florida b	N.L.	37	37 2/3	1	3	.250	45	19	30	4.54	1
2007 Marlins	Gulf Coast	3	3	0	0	.000	5	0	0	0.00	0
2007 Jupiter	Fla.St.	1	0 2/3	0	0	.000	2	0	4	27.00	0
2007 Carolina	Southern	3	3	0	0	.000	6	1	2	3.00	0
2007 Albuquerque	P.C.	8	9	0	1	.000	8	7	4	4.00	0
2007 Florida c	N.L.	9	13 1/3	3	0	1.000	13	7	11	1.35	0
2008 Albuquerque	P.C.	13	12 2/3	1	0	1.000	17	12	8	6.39	3
2008 Florida	N.L.	48	55 1/3	3	1	.750	55	33	50	4.23	0
Major League Totals	5 Yrs.	102	125 2/3	7	7	.500	124	71	121	4.94	1

a On disabled list from May 26 to November 3, 2005.
b On disabled list from August 7 to November 10, 2006.
c On disabled list from March 23 to August 7, 2007.

KERSHAW, CLAYTON EDWARD

Born, Dallas, Texas, March 19, 1988.
Bats Left. Throws Left. Height, 6 feet, 3 inches. Weight, 220 pounds.

Year Club	Lea	G	IP	W	L	Pct	SO	BB	H	ERA	SAVES
2006 Dodgers	Gulf Coast	10	37	2	0	1.000	54	5	28	1.95	1
2007 Great Lakes	Midwest	20	97 1/3	7	5	.583	134	50	72	2.77	0
2007 Jacksonville	Southern	5	24 2/3	1	2	.333	29	17	17	3.65	0
2008 Jacksonville	Southern	13	61 1/3	2	3	.400	59	19	39	1.91	0
2008 Los Angeles	N.L.	22	107 2/3	5	5	.500	100	52	109	4.26	0
Championship Series											
2008 Los Angeles	N.L.	2	2	0	0	.000	1	2	1	4.50	0

KOBAYASHI, MASAHIDE

Born, Yamanashi, Japan, May 24, 1974.
Bats Right. Throws Right. Height, 6 feet. Weight, 195 pounds.

Year	Club	Lea	G	IP	W	L	Pct	SO	BB	H	ERA	SAVES
1999 Chiba Lotte	Japan Pac.		46	124$^{1}/_3$	5	5	.500	107	55	93	2.68	0
2000 Chiba Lotte	Japan Pac.		65	109$^{2}/_3$	11	6	.647	72	37	87	2.13	14
2001 Chiba Lotte	Japan Pac.		48	52	0	4	.000	47	13	54	4.33	33
2002 Chiba Lotte	Japan Pac.		43	43$^{1}/_3$	2	1	.667	41	6	26	0.83	37
2003 Chiba Lotte	Japan Pac.		44	47	0	2	.000	30	11	45	2.87	33
2004 Chiba Lotte	Japan Pac.		51	57$^{2}/_3$	8	5	.615	50	19	51	3.90	20
2005 Chiba Lotte	Japan Pac.		46	45$^{1}/_3$	2	2	.500	33	9	49	2.58	29
2006 Chiba Lotte	Japan Pac.		53	53$^{2}/_3$	6	2	.750	48	8	49	2.68	34
2007 Chiba Lotte a	Japan Pac.		49	47$^{1}/_3$	2	7	.222	35	12	53	3.61	27
2008 Cleveland	A.L.		57	55$^{2}/_3$	4	5	.444	35	14	65	4.53	6

a Signed with Cleveland Indians, November 20, 2007.

KUO, HONG-CHIH

Born, Tainan City, Taiwan, July 23, 1981.
Bats Left. Throws Left. Height, 6 feet. Weight, 235 pounds.

Year	Club	Lea	G	IP	W	L	Pct	SO	BB	H	ERA	SAVES
2000 San Bernardino	Calif.		1	3	0	0	.000	7	0	0	0.00	0
2001 Dodgers	Gulf Coast		7	19$^{1}/_3$	0	0	.000	21	4	13	2.33	0
2002 Vero Beach	Fla.St.		4	8	0	1	.000	8	2	11	6.75	0
2002 Dodgers	Gulf Coast		3	6	0	0	.000	9	1	4	4.50	0
2003 Columbus a	So.Atl					INJURED—Did Not Play						
2004 Columbus	So.Atl		3	6	1	0	1.000	10	4	8	4.50	0
2005 Vero Beach	Fla.St.		11	26	1	1	.500	42	10	19	2.08	0
2005 Jacksonville	Southern		17	28$^{1}/_3$	1	1	.500	44	11	22	1.91	3
2005 Los Angeles	N.L.		9	5$^{1}/_3$	0	1	.000	10	5	5	6.75	0
2006 Las Vegas	P.C.		23	53	4	3	.571	63	22	52	3.06	1
2006 Los Angeles	N.L.		28	59$^{2}/_3$	1	5	.167	71	33	54	4.22	0
2007 Las Vegas	P.C.		7	20	0	1	.000	28	8	18	3.60	0
2007 Los Angeles b	N.L.		8	30$^{1}/_3$	1	4	.200	27	14	35	7.42	0
2008 Los Angeles	N.L.		42	80	5	3	.625	96	21	60	2.14	1
Major League Totals	4 Yrs.		87	175$^{1}/_3$	7	13	.350	204	73	154	3.90	1
Division Series												
2006 Los Angeles	N.L.		1	4$^{1}/_3$	0	1	.000	4	2	4	4.15	0
Championship Series												
2008 Los Angeles	N.L.		3	3	0	0	.000	3	0	2	3.00	0

a On minor league disabled list from April 3 to September 8, 2003.
b On disabled list from March 23 to May 3 and June 30 to October 31, 2007.

KURODA, HIROKI

Born, Osaka, Japan, February 10, 1975.
Bats Right. Throws Right. Height, 6 feet, 1 inch. Weight, 210 pounds.

Year	Club	Lea	G	IP	W	L	Pct	SO	BB	H	ERA	SAVES
1997 Hiroshima	Japan Cent.		23	135	6	9	.400	64	63	147	4.40	0
1998 Hiroshima	Japan Cent.		18	45	1	4	.200	25	24	53	6.60	0
1999 Hiroshima	Japan Cent.		21	87$^{2}/_3$	5	8	.385	55	39	106	6.78	0
2000 Hiroshima	Japan Cent.		29	144	9	6	.600	116	61	147	4.31	0
2001 Hiroshima	Japan Cent.		27	190	12	8	.600	146	45	175	3.03	0
2002 Hiroshima	Japan Cent.		23	164$^{1}/_3$	10	10	.500	144	34	166	3.67	0
2003 Hiroshima	Japan Cent.		28	205$^{2}/_3$	13	9	.591	137	45	197	3.11	0
2004 Hiroshima	Japan Cent.		21	147	7	9	.438	138	29	187	4.65	0
2005 Hiroshima	Japan Cent.		29	212$^{2}/_3$	15	12	.556	165	42	183	3.17	0
2006 Hiroshima	Japan Cent.		26	189$^{1}/_3$	13	6	.684	144	21	169	1.85	1
2007 Hiroshima a	Japan Cent.		26	179$^{2}/_3$	12	8	.600	123	42	176	3.56	0
2008 Los Angeles b	N.L.		31	183$^{1}/_3$	9	10	.474	116	42	181	3.73	0
Division Series												
2008 Los Angeles	N.L.		1	6$^{1}/_3$	1	0	1.000	4	2	6	0.00	0
Championship Series												
2008 Los Angeles	N.L.		1	6	1	0	1.000	3	1	5	3.00	0

a Signed with Los Angeles Dodgers, December 16, 2007.
b On disabled list from June 13 to July 2, 2008.

LACKEY, JOHN DERRAN

Born, Abilene, Texas, October 23, 1978.
Bats Right. Throws Right. Height, 6 feet, 6 inches. Weight, 235 pounds.

Year	Club	Lea	G	IP	W	L	Pct	SO	BB	H	ERA	SAVES
1999 Boise	Northwest		15	81⅓	6	2	.750	77	50	81	4.98	0
2000 Lake Elsinore	California		15	100⅔	6	6	.500	74	42	94	3.40	0
2000 Erie	Eastern		8	57⅓	6	1	.857	43	9	58	3.30	0
2000 Cedar Rapids	Midwest		5	30⅓	3	2	.600	21	5	20	2.08	0
2001 Salt Lake	P.C.		10	57⅔	3	4	.429	42	16	75	6.71	0
2001 Arkansas	Texas		18	127⅓	9	7	.563	94	29	106	3.46	0
2002 Salt Lake	P.C.		16	101⅔	8	2	.800	82	28	89	2.57	0
2002 Anaheim	A.L.		18	108⅓	9	4	.692	69	33	113	3.66	0
2003 Anaheim	A.L.		33	204	10	16	.385	151	66	223	4.63	0
2004 Anaheim	A.L.		33	198⅓	14	13	.519	144	60	215	4.67	0
2005 Los Angeles	A.L.		33	209	14	5	.737	199	71	208	3.44	0
2006 Los Angeles	A.L.		33	217⅔	13	11	.542	190	72	203	3.56	0
2007 Los Angeles	A.L.		33	224	19	9	.679	179	52	219	*3.01	0
2008 Rancho Cucamonga	Calif.		3	9	0	0	.000	11	2	8	4.00	0
2008 Los Angeles a	A.L.		24	163⅓	12	5	.706	130	40	161	3.75	0
Major League Totals	7 Yrs.		207	1324⅔	91	63	.591	1062	394	1342	3.81	0
Division Series												
2002 Anaheim	A.L.		1	3	0	0	.000	3	1	3	0.00	0
2005 Los Angeles	A.L.		2	11⅓	0	0	.000	9	9	7	2.38	0
2007 Los Angeles	A.L.		1	6	0	1	.000	4	2	9	6.00	0
2008 Los Angeles	A.L.		2	13⅔	0	1	.000	6	4	11	2.63	0
Division Series Totals			6	34	0	2	.000	22	16	30	2.91	0
Championship Series												
2002 Anaheim	A.L.		1	7	1	0	1.000	7	0	3	0.00	0
2005 Los Angeles	A.L.		1	5	0	1	.000	3	1	8	9.00	0
Championship Series Totals			2	12	1	1	.500	10	1	11	3.75	0
World Series Record												
2002 Anaheim	A.L.		3	12⅓	1	0	1.000	7	5	15	4.38	0

a On disabled list from March 21 to May 14, 2008.

LAFFEY, AARON STEVEN

Born, Cumberland, Maryland, April 15, 1985.
Bats Left. Throws Left. Height, 6 feet. Weight, 185 pounds.

Year	Club	Lea	G	IP	W	L	Pct	SO	BB	H	ERA	SAVES
2003 Burlington	Appal.		9	34	3	1	.750	46	15	22	2.91	0
2004 Mahoning Valley	N.Y.-Penn.		8	43⅔	3	1	.750	30	10	38	1.24	0
2004 Lake County	So.Atl.		19	74	3	7	.300	69	44	79	6.45	1
2005 Akron	Eastern		1	5	1	0	1.000	6	2	8	3.60	0
2005 Lake County	So.Atl.		25	142⅓	7	7	.500	69	52	123	3.22	1
2006 Kinston	Carolina		10	41⅓	4	1	.800	24	6	38	2.18	1
2006 Akron	Eastern		19	112⅓	8	3	.727	61	33	121	3.53	0
2007 Akron	Eastern		6	35	4	1	.800	24	7	29	2.31	0
2007 Buffalo	Int.		16	96⅓	9	3	.750	75	23	89	3.08	0
2007 Cleveland	A.L.		9	49⅓	4	2	.667	25	12	54	4.56	0
2008 Buffalo	Int.		11	61⅔	6	2	.750	47	18	72	4.38	0
2008 Cleveland	A.L.		16	93⅔	5	7	.417	43	31	103	4.23	0
Major League Totals	2 Yrs.		25	143	9	9	.500	68	43	157	4.34	0
Championship Series												
2007 Cleveland	A.L.		1	4⅔	0	0	.000	3	1	1	0.00	0

LANNAN, JOHN E.

Born, Long Beach, New York, September 27, 1984.
Bats Left. Throws Left. Height, 6 feet, 5 inches. Weight, 225 pounds.

Year	Club	Lea	G	IP	W	L	Pct	SO	BB	H	ERA	SAVES
2005 Vermont	N.Y.-Penn.		14	63⅓	3	5	.375	41	31	74	5.26	0
2006 Savannah	So.Atl.		27	138	6	8	.429	114	54	149	4.76	0
2007 Potomac	Carolina		8	50⅔	6	0	1.000	35	15	31	2.13	0
2007 Harrisburg	Eastern		6	36	3	2	.600	20	15	31	3.25	0
2007 Columbus	Int.		7	38	3	1	.750	19	12	30	1.66	0
2007 Washington	N.L.		6	34⅔	2	2	.500	10	17	36	4.15	0
2008 Washington	N.L.		31	182	9	15	.375	117	72	172	3.91	0
Major League Totals	2 Yrs.		37	216⅔	11	17	.393	127	89	208	3.95	0

LEDEZMA, WILFREDO JOSE
Born, Guarico, Venezuela, January 21, 1981.
Bats Left. Throws Left. Height, 6 feet, 4 inches. Weight, 210 pounds.

Year Club	Lea	G	IP	W	L	Pct	SO	BB	H	ERA	SAVES
1998 Sp Red Sox	Dominican	11	47	2	4	.333	34	38	38	4.40	0
1999 Red Sox	Gulf Coast	13	57¹/₃	5	1	.833	52	20	51	3.30	1
2000 Augusta	So.Atl.	14	52²/₃	2	4	.333	60	36	51	5.13	0
2001 Augusta a	So.Atl.	INJURED—Did Not Play									
2002 Red Sox	Gulf Coast	1	3	0	0	.000	3	0	4	6.00	0
2002 Augusta b	So.Atl.	5	23²/₃	2	2	.500	38	8	23	3.80	0
2003 Detroit	A.L.	34	84	3	7	.300	49	35	99	5.79	0
2004 Erie	Eastern	17	111²/₃	10	3	.769	98	24	95	2.42	0
2004 Detroit	A.L.	15	53¹/₃	4	3	.571	29	18	55	4.39	0
2005 Detroit	A.L.	10	49²/₃	2	4	.333	30	24	61	7.07	0
2005 Toledo	Int.	11	51	5	3	.625	44	27	52	5.29	0
2006 Toledo	Int.	12	71¹/₃	4	3	.571	66	23	60	2.52	0
2006 Detroit	A.L.	24	60¹/₃	3	3	.500	39	23	60	3.58	0
2007 Detroit	A.L.	23	35²/₃	3	1	.750	24	26	38	4.79	0
2007 Atlanta-San Diego c-d	N.L.	21	23²/₃	0	2	.000	23	12	32	6.85	0
2008 Portland	P.C.	11	16¹/₃	1	0	1.000	20	4	14	4.41	1
2008 San Diego-Arizona e-f	N.L.	28	58¹/₃	0	2	.000	53	41	51	4.17	0
Major League Totals . . . . . . .6 Yrs.		155	365	15	22	.405	247	179	396	5.10	0
Championship Series											
2006 Detroit	A.L.	2	2²/₃	1	0	1.000	1	1	2	3.38	0
World Series Record											
2006 Detroit	A.L.	2	1¹/₃	0	0	.000	1	0	2	0.00	0

a On minor league disabled list from June 19 to September 6, 2001.
b Selected by Detroit Tigers from Boston Red Sox in Rule V draft, December 16, 2002.
c Traded to Atlanta Braves for pitcher Macay McBride, June 20, 2007.
d Traded to San Diego Padres with pitcher Will Startup for pitcher Royce Ring, July 31, 2007.
e Claimed on waivers by Arizona Diamondbacks, August 29, 2008.
f Not offered contract, December 12, 2008. Signed with Washington Nationals organization, January 15, 2009.

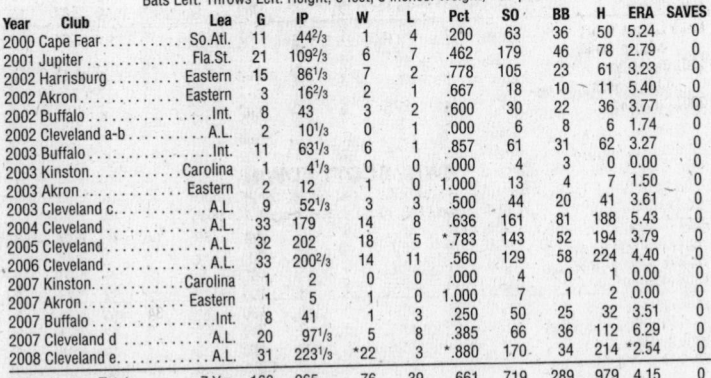

LEE, CLIFTON PHIFER (CLIFF)
Born, Benton, Arkansas, August 30, 1978.
Bats Left. Throws Left. Height, 6 feet, 3 inches. Weight, 190 pounds.

Year Club	Lea	G	IP	W	L	Pct	SO	BB	H	ERA	SAVES
2000 Cape Fear	So.Atl.	11	44²/₃	1	4	.200	63	36	50	5.24	0
2001 Jupiter	Fla.St.	21	109²/₃	6	7	.462	179	46	78	2.79	0
2002 Harrisburg	Eastern	15	86¹/₃	7	2	.778	105	23	61	3.23	0
2002 Akron	Eastern	3	16²/₃	2	1	.667	18	10	11	5.40	0
2002 Buffalo	Int.	8	43	3	2	.600	30	22	36	3.77	0
2002 Cleveland a-b	A.L.	2	10¹/₃	0	1	.000	6	8	6	1.74	0
2003 Buffalo	Int.	11	63¹/₃	6	1	.857	61	31	62	3.27	0
2003 Kinston	Carolina	1	4¹/₃	0	0	.000	4	3	0	0.00	0
2003 Akron	Eastern	2	12	1	0	1.000	13	4	7	1.50	0
2003 Cleveland c	A.L.	9	52¹/₃	3	3	.500	44	20	41	3.61	0
2004 Cleveland	A.L.	33	179	14	8	.636	161	81	188	5.43	0
2005 Cleveland	A.L.	32	202	18	5	*.783	143	52	194	3.79	0
2006 Cleveland	A.L.	33	200²/₃	14	11	.560	129	58	224	4.40	0
2007 Kinston	Carolina	1	2	0	0	.000	4	0	1	0.00	0
2007 Akron	Eastern	1	5	1	0	1.000	7	1	2	0.00	0
2007 Buffalo	Int.	8	41	1	3	.250	50	25	32	3.51	0
2007 Cleveland d	A.L.	20	97¹/₃	5	8	.385	66	36	112	6.29	0
2008 Cleveland e	A.L.	31	223¹/₃	*22	3	*.880	170	34	214	*2.54	0
Major League Totals . . . . . . .7 Yrs.		160	965	76	39	.661	719	289	979	4.15	0

a Traded to Cleveland Indians with infielder Lee Stevens, infielder Brandon Phillips and outfielder Grady Sizemore for pitcher Bartolo Colon and player to be named later, June 27, 2002.
b Montreal Expos received pitcher Tim Drew to complete trade, June 28, 2002.
c On disabled list from March 29 to May 30, 2003.
d On disabled list from March 23 to May 3, 2007.
e Selected Cy Young Award Winner in American League for 2008.

LESTER, JONATHAN TYLER (JON)
Born, Tacoma, Washington, January 7, 1984.
Bats Left. Throws Left. Height, 6 feet, 2 inches. Weight, 190 pounds.

Year Club	Lea	G	IP	W	L	Pct	SO	BB	H	ERA	SAVES
2002 Red Sox	Gulf Coast	1	0²/₃	0	1	.000	1	1	5	13.50	0
2003 Augusta	So.Atl.	24	106	6	9	.400	71	44	102	3.65	0

Year Club	Lea	G	IP	W	L	Pct	SO	BB	H	ERA	SAVES
2004 Sarasota...........Fla.St.	21	90⅓	7	6	.538	97	37	82	4.28	0	
2004 Red Sox.........Gulf Coast	1	1	0	0	.000	1	2	0	0.00	0	
2005 Portland.........Eastern	26	148⅓	11	6	.647	163	57	114	2.61	0	
2006 Pawtucket.............Int.	11	46⅔	3	4	.429	43	25	43	2.70	0	
2006 Boston a.............A.L.	15	81⅓	7	2	.778	60	43	91	4.76	0	
2007 Greenville.........So.Atl.	3	13	0	0	.000	15	2	11	2.08	0	
2007 Portland..........Eastern	1	6	1	0	1.000	4	4	5	1.50	0	
2007 Pawtucket.............Int.	14	71⅔	4	5	.444	51	31	67	3.89	0	
2007 Boston b.............A.L.	12	63	4	0	1.000	50	31	61	4.57	0	
2008 Boston c.............A.L.	33	210⅓	16	6	.727	152	66	202	3.21	0	
Major League Totals........3 Yrs.	60	354⅔	27	8	.771	262	140	354	3.81	0	
Division Series											
2008 Boston...............A.L.	2	14	1	0	1.000	11	3	10	0.00	0	
Championship Series											
2007 Boston...............A.L.	2	3⅔	0	0	.000	5	1	3	4.91	0	
2008 Boston...............A.L.	2	12⅔	0	2	.000	15	2	14	4.97	0	
Championship Series Totals......	4	16⅓	0	2	.000	20	3	17	4.96	0	
World Series Record											
2007 Boston...............A.L.	1	5⅔	1	0	1.000	3	3	3	0.00	0	

a On disabled list from August 24 to November 6, 2006.
b On disabled list from March 23 to June 11, 2007.
c Pitched no-hit, no-run game against Kansas City Royals, May 19, 2008.

LEWIS, JENSEN DANIEL
Born, Cincinnati, Ohio, May 16, 1984.
Bats Right. Throws Right. Height, 6 feet, 3 inches. Weight, 210 pounds.

Year Club	Lea	G	IP	W	L	Pct	SO	BB	H	ERA	SAVES
2005 Mahoning Valley...N.Y.-Penn.	13	59	4	2	.667	59	11	58	3.20	0	
2006 Kinston............Carolina	21	108⅓	7	6	.538	94	29	110	3.99	0	
2006 Akron.............Eastern	7	39⅓	1	2	.333	44	12	41	3.89	0	
2007 Buffalo..............Int.	24	39	2	0	1.000	49	13	27	1.85	1	
2007 Buffalo..............Int.	10	13	1	0	1.000	12	4	5	1.38	1	
2007 Cleveland.............A.L.	26	29⅓	1	1	.500	34	10	26	2.15	0	
2008 Buffalo..............Int.	11	20	1	2	.333	18	8	16	3.60	1	
2008 Cleveland.............A.L.	51	66	0	4	.000	52	27	68	3.82	13	
Major League Totals........2 Yrs.	77	95⅓	1	5	.167	86	37	94	3.30	13	
Division Series											
2007 Cleveland.............A.L.	2	2	0	0	.000	4	0	0	0.00	0	
Championship Series											
2007 Cleveland.............A.L.	5	5⅔	0	0	.000	3	0	6	6.35	0	

LEWIS, SCOTT EDWIN
Born, West Covina, California, September 26, 1983.
Bats Both. Throws Left. Height, 6 feet. Weight, 195 pounds.

Year Club	Lea	G	IP	W	L	Pct	SO	BB	H	ERA	SAVES
2004 Mahoning Valley...N.Y.-Penn.	2	3⅓	0	2	.000	13	1	5	8.10	0	
2005 Mahoning Valley...N.Y.-Penn.	7	15⅔	0	1	.000	24	6	13	4.60	0	
2006 Kinston............Carolina	27	115⅔	3	3	.500	123	28	84	1.48	0	
2007 Akron.............Eastern	27	134⅔	7	9	.438	121	34	135	3.68	0	
2008 Akron.............Eastern	13	73⅓	6	2	.750	61	9	62	2.33	0	
2008 Buffalo..............Int.	4	24	2	2	.500	21	4	19	2.63	0	
2008 Cleveland.............A.L.	4	24	4	0	1.000	15	6	20	2.63	0	

LIDGE, BRADLEY THOMAS (BRAD)
Born, Sacramento, California, December 23, 1976.
Bats Right. Throws Right. Height, 6 feet, 5 inches. Weight, 210 pounds.

Year Club	Lea	G	IP	W	L	Pct	SO	BB	H	ERA	SAVES
1998 Quad City a-b....Midwest	4	11	0	1	.000	6	5	10	3.27	0	
1999 Kissimmee c........Fla.St.	6	21⅓	0	2	.000	19	11	13	3.38	0	
2000 Kissimmee d........Fla.St.	8	41⅔	2	1	.667	46	15	28	2.81	0	
2001 Round Rock e.......Texas	5	26	2	0	1.000	42	7	21	1.73	0	
2002 Round Rock.........Texas	5	11	1	1	.500	18	3	9	2.45	0	
2002 Houston..............N.L.	6	8⅔	1	0	1.000	12	9	12	6.23	0	
2002 New Orleans..........P.C.	24	111⅔	5	5	.500	110	47	83	3.39	0	
2003 Houston..............N.L.	78	85	6	3	.667	97	42	60	3.60	1	

Year	Club	Lea	G	IP	W	L	Pct	SO	BB	H	ERA	SAVES
2004 Houston	N.L.	80	94⅔	6	5	.545	157	30	57	1.90	29	
2005 Houston	N.L.	70	70⅔	4	4	.500	103	23	58	2.29	42	
2006 Houston	N.L.	78	75	1	5	.167	104	36	69	5.28	32	
2007 Corpus Christi	Texas	1	1	0	0	.000	0	0	0	0.00	0	
2007 Houston f-g	N.L.	66	67	5	3	.625	88	30	54	3.36	19	
2008 Clearwater	Fla.St.	1	1	0	0	.000	2	1	2	9.00	0	
2008 Philadelphia h	N.L.	72	69⅓	2	0	1.000	92	35	50	1.95	41	
Major League Totals	7 Yrs.	450	470⅓	25	20	.556	653	205	360	3.10	164	
Division Series												
2004 Houston	N.L.	3	4⅓	0	0	.000	6	1	4	2.08	1	
2005 Houston	N.L.	3	4	0	0	.000	5	4	2	0.00	0	
2008 Philadelphia	N.L.	3	3	0	0	.000	4	1	3	3.00	2	
Division Series Totals		9	11⅓	0	0	.000	15	6	9	1.59	3	
Championship Series												
2004 Houston	N.L.	4	8	1	0	1.000	14	2	1	0.00	2	
2005 Houston	N.L.	4	5	0	1	.000	7	2	6	7.20	3	
2008 Philadelphia	N.L.	4	4⅓	0	0	.000	6	2	2	0.00	3	
Championship Series Totals		12	17⅓	1	1	.500	27	6	9	2.08	8	
World Series Record												
2005 Houston	N.L.	3	3⅔	0	2	.000	6	0	4	4.91	0	
2008 Philadelphia	N.L.	2	2	0	0	.000	3	0	1	0.00	2	
World Series Totals		5	5⅔	0	2	.000	9	0	5	3.18	2	

a Drafted by Texas Rangers with choice received for Colorado Rockies signing pitcher Darryl Kile, June 2, 1998.
b On disabled list from August 18 to September 29, 1998.
c On disabled list from April 1 to June 1 and July 10 to September 29, 1999.
d On disabled list from April 24 to June 13 and July 1 to September 29, 2000.
e On disabled list from May 5 to September 29, 2001.
f On disabled list from June 16 to July 13, 2007.
g Traded to Philadelphia Phillies with infielder Eric Bruntlett for pitcher Geoff Geary, outfielder Michael Bourn and infielder Mike Costanzo, November 12, 2007.
h On disabled list from March 21 to April 5, 2008.

LIEBER, JONATHAN RAY (JON)
Born, Council Bluffs, Iowa, April 2, 1970.
Bats Left. Throws Right. Height, 6 feet, 2 inches. Weight, 235 pounds.

Year	Club	Lea	G	IP	W	L	Pct	SO	BB	H	ERA	SAVES
1992 Eugene	Northwest	5	31	3	0	1.000	23	2	26	1.16	0	
1992 Baseball City	Fla. St.	7	31	3	3	.500	19	8	45	4.65	0	
1993 Wilmington	Carolina	17	114⅔	9	3	.750	89	9	125	2.67	0	
1993 Memphis-Carol. a	Southern	10	55	6	3	.667	45	16	71	5.07	0	
1994 Carolina	Southern	3	21	2	0	1.000	21	2	13	1.29	0	
1994 Buffalo	A.A.	3	21⅓	1	1	.500	21	1	16	1.69	0	
1994 Pittsburgh	N.L.	17	108⅔	6	7	.462	71	25	116	3.73	0	
1995 Calgary	P.C.	14	77	1	5	.167	34	19	122	7.01	0	
1995 Pittsburgh	N.L.	21	72⅔	4	7	.364	45	14	103	6.32	0	
1996 Pittsburgh	N.L.	51	142	9	5	.643	94	28	156	3.99	1	
1997 Pittsburgh	N.L.	33	188⅓	11	14	.440	160	51	193	4.49	0	
1998 Pittsburgh b	N.L.	29	171	8	14	.364	138	40	182	4.11	1	
1999 Chicago c	N.L.	31	203⅓	10	11	.476	186	46	226	4.07	0	
2000 Chicago	N.L.	35	*251	12	11	.522	192	54	248	4.41	0	
2001 Chicago	N.L.	34	232⅓	20	6	.769	148	41	226	3.80	0	
2002 Chicago d	N.L.	21	141	6	8	.429	87	12	153	3.70	0	
2003 New York e	A.L.				INJURED—Did Not Play						0	
2004 Tampa	Fla.St.	1	7	1	0	1.000	4	0	2	0.00	0	
2004 New York f-g	A.L.	27	176⅔	14	8	.636	102	18	216	4.33	0	
2005 Philadelphia	N.L.	35	218⅓	17	13	.567	149	41	223	4.20	0	
2006 Phillies	Gulf Coast	1	3	0	0	.000	1	0	4	3.00	0	
2006 Clearwater	Fla.St.	2	11⅓	0	2	.000	6	0	19	7.15	0	
2006 Philadelphia h	N.L.	27	168	9	11	.450	100	24	196	4.93	0	
2007 Clearwater	Fla.St.	1	3⅔	0	0	.000	4	0	4	2.45	0	
2007 Philadelphia i-j	N.L.	14	78	3	6	.333	54	22	91	4.73	0	
2008 Azl Cubs	Arizona	1	3	0	0	.000	1	0	4	0.00	0	
2008 Peoria	Midwest	3	7	0	1	.000	6	0	8	3.86	0	
2008 Chicago k-l	N.L.	26	46⅔	2	3	.400	27	6	59	4.05	0	
Major League Totals	14 Yrs.	401	2198	131	124	.514	1553	422	2388	4.27	2	

Year	Club	Lea	G	IP	W	L	Pct	SO	BB	H	ERA	SAVES
	Division Series											
2004 New York	A.L.	1	6 2/3	0	0	.000	4	1	7	4.05	0
	Championship Series											
2004 New York	A.L.	2	14 1/3	1	1	.500	5	1	12	3.14	0

a Traded by Kansas City Royals to Pittsburgh Pirates with pitcher Dan Miceli for pitcher Stan Belinda, July 31, 1993.
b On disabled list from August 21 to September 14, 1998.
c On disabled list from April 21 to May 8, 1999.
d On disabled list from August 2 to October 9, 2002.
e Filed for free agency, November 1, 2002. Signed with New York Yankees, January 24, 2003. On disabled list from March 21 to November 13, 2003.
f On disabled list from March 19 to May 1, 2004.
g Filed for free agency, November 5, 2004. Signed with Philadelphia Phillies, December 8, 2004.
h On disabled list from May 30 to July 7, 2006.
i On disabled list from March 23 to April 9 and June 21 to October 29, 2007.
j Filed for free agency, October 29, 2007. Signed with Chicago Cubs, January 16, 2008.
k On disabled list from July 11 to September 1 and September 9 to September 29, 2008.
l Filed for free agency, October 31, 2008.

LILLY, THEODORE ROOSEVELT (TED)

Born, Lamita, California, January 4, 1976.
Bats Left. Throws Left. Height, 6 feet, 1 inch. Weight, 190 pounds.

Year	Club	Lea	G	IP	W	L	Pct	SO	BB	H	ERA	SAVES
1996 Yakima	Northwest	13	53 2/3	4	0	1.000	75	14	25	0.84	0
1997 San Bernardino	California	23	134 2/3	7	8	.467	158	32	116	2.81	0
1998 San Antonio	Texas	17	111 2/3	8	4	.667	96	37	114	3.30	0
1998 Albuquerque.........	P.C.	5	31	1	3	.250	25	9	39	4.94	0
1998 Ottawa a.............	Int.	7	39	2	2	.500	49	19	45	4.85	0
1999 Ottawa	Int.	16	89	8	5	.615	78	23	81	3.84	0
1999 Montreal b-c	N.L.	9	23 2/3	0	1	.000	28	9	30	7.61	0
2000 Tampa	Fla.St.	1	6 2/3	0	0	.000	6	1	5	1.35	0
2000 Columbus.............	Int.	22	137 1/3	8	11	.421	127	48	157	4.19	0
2000 New York d-e	A.L.	7	8	0	0	.000	11	5	5	5.63	0
2001 Columbus.............	Int.	5	25 1/3	0	0	.000	30	8	16	2.84	0
2001 New York	A.L.	26	120 2/3	5	6	.455	112	51	126	5.37	0
2002 New York-Oakland f-g	A.L.	22	100	5	7	.417	77	31	80	3.69	0
2003 Oakland h.............	A.L.	32	178 1/3	12	10	.545	147	58	179	4.34	0
2004 Toronto	A.L.	32	197 1/3	12	10	.545	168	89	171	4.06	0
2005 Syracuse	Int.	2	8 2/3	0	1	.000	9	5	5	3.12	0
2005 Toronto i.	A.L.	25	126 1/3	10	11	.476	96	58	135	5.56	0
2006 Toronto j.............	A.L.	32	181 2/3	15	13	.536	160	81	179	4.31	0
2007 Chicago	N.L.	34	207	15	8	.652	174	55	181	3.83	0
2008 Chicago	N.L.	34	204 2/3	17	9	.654	184	64	187	4.09	0
Major League Totals ....10 Yrs.		253	1347 2/3	91	75	.548	1157	501	1276	4.40	0
	Division Series											
2002 Oakland	A.L.	2	4	0	1	.000	3	1	10	13.50	0
2003 Oakland	A.L.	2	9	0	0	.000	7	2	2	0.00	0
2007 Chicago	N.L.	1	3 1/3	0	1	.000	4	4	7	16.20	0
Division Series Totals		5	16 1/3	0	2	.000	14	7	19	6.61	0

a Traded by Los Angeles Dodgers to Montreal Expos with infielder Wilton Guerrero, outfielder Peter Bergeron and infielder Jonathan Tucker for infielder Mark Grudzielanek, outfielder Hiram Bocachica and pitcher Carlos Perez, July 31, 1998.
b Montreal Expos traded pitcher Jake Westbrook and two players to be named later to New York Yankees for pitcher Hideki Irabu, December 22, 1999.
c On disabled list from June 21 to September 30, 1999.
d Sent to New York Yankees with pitcher Christian Parker as players to be named later for Jake Westbrook, March 17 and March 22, 2000.
e On disabled list from March 25 to May 22, 2000.
f Traded to Oakland Athletics with pitcher Jason Arnold and outfielder John-Ford Griffin for pitcher Jeff Weaver, July 5, 2002.
g On disabled list from July 23 to September 10, 2002.
h Traded to Toronto Blue Jays for outfielder Bobby Kielty and cash, November 18, 2003.
i On disabled list from March 25 to April 10 and July 25 to September 6, 2005.
j Filed for free agency, October 28, 2006. Signed with Chicago Cubs, December 15, 2006.

LINCECUM, TIMOTHY LEROY (TIM)

Born, Bellevue, Washington, June 15, 1984.
Bats Left. Throws Right. Height, 5 feet, 11 inches. Weight, 160 pounds.

Year Club	Lea	G	IP	W	L	Pct	SO	BB	H	ERA	SAVES
2006 San Jose	Calif.	6	27²/₃	2	0	1.000	48	12	13	1.95	0
2006 Salem-Keizer	Northwest	2	4	0	0	.000	10	0	1	0.00	0
2007 Fresno	P.C.	5	31	4	0	1.000	46	11	12	0.29	0
2007 San Francisco	N.L.	24	146¹/₃	7	5	.583	150	65	122	4.00	0
2008 San Francisco a	N.L.	34	227	18	5	*.783	*265	84	182	2.62	0
Major League Totals .... 2 Yrs.		58	373¹/₃	25	10	.714	415	149	304	3.16	0

a Selected Cy Young Award Winner in National League for 2008.

LINCOLN, MICHAEL GEORGE (MIKE)

Born, Carmichael, California, April 10, 1975.
Bats Right. Throws Right. Height, 6 feet, 2 inches. Weight, 215 pounds.

Year Club	Lea	G	IP	W	L	Pct	SO	BB	H	ERA	SAVES
1996 Ft. Myers	Fla.St.	12	59²/₃	5	2	.714	24	25	64	4.07	0
1997 Ft. Myers	Fla.St.	20	134	13	4	.765	75	25	130	2.28	0
1998 New Britain	Eastern	26	173¹/₃	15	7	.682	109	35	180	3.22	0
1999 Minnesota	A.L.	18	76¹/₃	3	10	.231	27	26	102	6.84	0
1999 Salt Lake	P.C.	9	59	5	2	.714	39	21	82	7.78	0
2000 Salt Lake	P.C.	12	74¹/₃	4	1	.800	37	16	72	3.87	0
2000 Minnesota a............	A.L.	8	20²/₃	0	3	.000	15	13	36	10.89	0
2001 Nashville	P.C.	18	91²/₃	5	4	.556	71	25	90	3.44	0
2001 Pittsburgh b-c	N.L.	31	40¹/₃	2	1	.667	24	11	34	2.68	2
2002 Nashville	P.C.	10	14²/₃	0	0	.000	15	2	14	1.23	2
2002 Pittsburgh	N.L.	55	72¹/₃	2	4	.333	50	27	80	3.11	0
2003 Nashville	P.C.	8	12²/₃	1	1	.500	9	4	8	0.71	0
2003 Pittsburgh d...........	N.L.	36	36¹/₃	3	4	.429	28	13	38	5.20	5
2004 St. Louis e-f...........	N.L.	13	17¹/₃	3	2	.600	14	6	10	5.19	0
2005 St. Louis g-h...........	N.L.		INJURED—Did Not Play								
2006			INJURED—Did Not Play								
2007			INJURED—Did Not Play								
2008 Cincinnati i............	N.L.	64	70¹/₃	2	5	.286	57	24	66	4.48	0
Major League Totals .... 7 Yrs.		225	333²/₃	15	29	.341	215	120	366	5.02	5

a On disabled list from July 23 to October 1, 2000.
b Released by Minnesota Twins, January 15, 2001. Signed with Pittsburgh Pirates organization, February 17, 2001.
c On disabled list from August 13 to August 28, 2001.
d On disabled list from March 24 to July 1, 2003.
e Not offered contract, December 21, 2003. Signed with St. Louis Cardinals, January 6, 2004.
f On disabled list from May 4 to November 2, 2004.
g On disabled list from April 1 to October 31, 2005.
h Not offered contract, December 21, 2005. Signed with Cincinnati Reds organization, February 5, 2008.
i Filed for free agency, October 30, 2008, re-signed with Cincinnati Reds, December 4, 2008.

LINDSTROM, MATTHEW JAMES (MATT)

Born, Rexburg, Idaho, February 11, 1980.
Bats Right. Throws Right. Height, 6 feet, 4 inches. Weight, 210 pounds.

Year Club	Lea	G	IP	W	L	Pct	SO	BB	H	ERA	SAVES
2002 Kingsport	Appal.	12	48¹/₃	0	6	.000	39	21	56	4.84	0
2003 Brooklyn..........	N.Y.-Penn.	14	65¹/₃	7	3	.700	52	27	61	3.44	0
2003 Capital City	So.Atl.	12	56²/₃	2	3	.400	50	33	46	2.86	0
2004 St. Lucie............	Fla.St.	14	79²/₃	5	5	.500	50	20	83	3.73	0
2004 Capital City..........	So.Atl.	12	56	3	2	.600	64	10	47	3.21	0
2005 Binghamton	Eastern	35	73¹/₃	2	5	.286	58	55	90	5.40	11
2006 Binghamton	Eastern	35	40²/₃	2	4	.333	54	14	42	3.76	11
2006 St. Lucie a	Fla.St.	11	18	1	0	1.000	16	7	14	2.50	2
2007 Florida	N.L.	71	67	3	4	.429	62	21	66	3.09	0
2008 Albuquerque..........	P.C.	3	4	0	0	.000	4	1	5	9.00	0
2008 Florida	N.L.	66	57¹/₃	3	3	.500	43	26	57	3.14	5
Major League Totals .... 2 Yrs.		137	124¹/₃	6	7	.462	105	47	123	3.11	5

a Traded to Florida Marlins by New York Mets with pitcher Henry Owens for pitcher Adam Bostick and pitcher Jason Vargas, November 20, 2006.

LINEBRINK, SCOTT CAMERON
Born, Austin, Texas, August 4, 1976.
Bats Right. Throws Right. Height, 6 feet, 2 inches. Weight, 215 pounds.

Year Club	Lea	G	IP	W	L	Pct	SO	BB	H	ERA	SAVES
1997 Salem-Keizr	Northwest	3	10	0	0	.000	6	6	7	4.50	0
1997 San Jose	California	6	28⅓	2	1	.667	40	10	29	3.18	0
1998 Shreveport	Texas	21	113	10	8	.556	128	58	101	5.02	0
1999 Shreveport	Texas	10	43⅓	1	8	.111	33	14	48	6.44	0
2000 Fresno	P.C.	28	62	1	4	.200	49	12	54	5.23	4
2000 San Francisco-Houston	N.L.	11	12	0	0	.000	6	8	18	6.00	0
2000 New Orleans a	P.C.	11	15	2	0	1.000	22	7	15	1.80	1
2001 New Orleans	P.C.	50	72	7	6	.538	72	24	52	3.50	8
2001 Houston	N.L.	9	10⅓	0	0	.000	9	6	6	2.61	0
2002 Houston	N.L.	22	24⅓	0	0	.000	24	13	31	7.03	0
2002 New Orleans	P.C.	13	15	1	1	.500	16	11	17	6.00	0
2002 Round Rock b	Texas	2	2	0	0	.000	1	2	2	0.00	0
2003 New Orleans	P.C.	2	10	0	2	.000	6	5	8	2.70	0
2003 Houston-San Diego c-d	N.L.	52	92⅓	3	2	.600	68	36	93	3.31	0
2004 San Diego	N.L.	73	84	7	3	.700	83	26	61	2.14	0
2005 San Diego	N.L.	73	73⅔	8	1	.889	70	23	55	1.83	1
2006 San Diego	N.L.	73	75⅔	7	4	.636	68	22	70	3.57	2
2007 San Diego-Milwaukee e-f	N.L.	71	70⅓	5	6	.455	50	25	68	3.71	1
2008 Chicago g	A.L.	50	46⅓	2	2	.500	40	9	41	3.69	1
Major League Totals ... 9 Yrs.		434	489	32	18	.640	418	168	443	3.26	5
Division Series											
2005 San Diego	N.L.	1	1	0	0	.000	1	0	2	0.00	0
2006 San Diego	N.L.	2	1⅓	0	0	.000	0	1	1	6.75	0
2008 Chicago	A.L.	1	1	0	0	.000	1	1	1	0.00	0
Division Series Totals		4	3⅓	0	0	.000	2	2	4	2.70	0

a Traded to Houston Astros for pitcher Doug Henry, July 30, 2000.
b On disabled list from May 20 to June 17, 2002.
c Signed with Houston Astros organization, January 31, 2003.
d Claimed on waivers by San Diego Padres, May 29, 2003.
e Traded to Milwaukee Brewers for pitcher Will Inman, pitcher Joe Thatcher and pitcher Steve Garrison, July 25, 2007.
f Filed for free agency, October 29, 2007. Signed with Chicago White Sox, November 28, 2007.
g On disabled list from July 23 to September 1, 2008.

LIRIANO, FRANCISCO CASILLAS
Born, San Cristobal, Dominican Republic, October 26, 1983.
Bats Left. Throws Left. Height, 6 feet, 2 inches. Weight, 225 pounds.

Year Club	Lea	G	IP	W	L	Pct	SO	BB	H	ERA	SAVES
2001 Giants	Arizona	13	62	5	4	.556	67	24	51	3.63	0
2001 Salem-Keizer	Northwest	2	9	0	0	.000	12	1	7	5.00	0
2002 Hagerstown	So.Atl.	16	80	3	6	.333	85	31	61	3.49	0
2003 Giants	Arizona	4	8⅓	0	1	.000	9	6	5	4.32	0
2003 San Jose a	Calif.	1	0⅔	0	1	.000	0	2	5	54.00	0
2004 New Britain	Eastern	7	39⅔	3	2	.600	49	17	45	3.18	0
2004 Fort Myers	Fla.St.	21	117	6	7	.462	125	43	118	4.00	0
2005 New Britain	Eastern	13	76⅔	3	5	.375	92	26	70	3.64	0
2005 Rochester	Int.	14	91	9	2	.818	112	24	56	1.78	0
2005 Minnesota	A.L.	6	23⅔	1	2	.333	33	7	19	5.70	0
2006 Minnesota b	A.L.	28	121	12	3	.800	144	32	89	2.16	1
2007 Minnesota c	A.L.	INJURED—Did Not Play									
2008 Fort Myers	Fla.St.	1	5⅓	0	1	.000	8	2	6	6.75	0
2008 Rochester	Int.	19	118	10	2	.833	113	31	102	3.28	0
2008 Minnesota	A.L.	14	76	6	4	.600	67	32	74	3.91	0
Major League Totals ... 3 Yrs.		48	220⅔	19	9	.679	244	71	182	3.14	1

a Traded by San Francisco Giants to Minnesota Twins with pitcher Joe Nathan and pitcher Boof Bonser for catcher A.J. Pierzynski and player to be named later, November 14, 2003.
b On disabled list from August 8 to September 11, 2006.
c On disabled list from March 24 to October 10, 2007.

LITSCH, JESSE ALLEN
Born, Pinellas Park, Florida, March 9, 1985.
Bats Right. Throws Right. Height, 6 feet, 1 inch. Weight, 205 pounds.

Year Club	Lea	G	IP	W	L	Pct	SO	BB	H	ERA	SAVES
2005 Pulaski	Appal.	11	65⅔	5	1	.833	67	10	51	2.74	0
2005 Auburn	N.Y.-Penn.	4	10	0	1	.000	7	6	11	3.60	0

Year	Club	Lea	G	IP	W	L	Pct	SO	BB	H	ERA	SAVES
2006 New Hampshire	Eastern	12	69 1/3	3	4	.429	54	13	85	5.06	0	
2006 Dunedin	Fla.St.	16	89 1/3	6	6	.500	81	8	94	3.53	0	
2007 New Hampshire	Eastern	10	61 1/3	7	2	.778	46	14	51	2.35	0	
2007 Syracuse	Int.	2	15	1	0	1.000	10	3	12	1.80	0	
2007 Toronto	A.L.	20	111	7	9	.438	50	36	116	3.81	0	
2008 Syracuse	Int.	3	20	1	1	.500	18	4	18	3.60	0	
2008 Toronto	A.L.	29	176	13	9	.591	99	39	178	3.58	0	
Major League Totals	2 Yrs.	49	287	20	18	.526	149	75	294	3.67	0	

LIZ, RADHAMES COREY

Born, ElSeibo, Dominican Republic, June 10, 1983.
Bats Right. Throws Right. Height, 6 feet, 2 inches. Weight, 185 pounds.

Year	Club	Lea	G	IP	W	L	Pct	SO	BB	H	ERA	SAVES
2005 Aberdeen	N.Y.-Penn.	11	56	5	4	.556	82	19	36	1.77	0	
2005 Delmarva	So.Atl.	10	38 1/3	2	3	.400	55	23	33	4.46	0	
2006 Frederick	Carolina	16	83	6	5	.545	95	44	57	2.82	0	
2006 Bowie	Eastern	10	50 1/3	3	1	.750	54	31	55	5.36	0	
2007 Bowie	Eastern	25	137	11	4	.733	161	70	101	3.22	0	
2007 Baltimore	A.L.	9	24 2/3	0	2	.000	24	23	25	6.93	0	
2008 Norfolk	Int.	15	87	3	7	.300	85	32	77	3.62	0	
2008 Baltimore	A.L.	17	84 1/3	6	6	.500	57	51	99	6.72	0	
Major League Totals	2 Yrs.	26	109	6	8	.429	81	74	124	6.77	0	

LOGAN, BOONE

Born, San Antonio, Texas, August 13, 1984.
Bats Right. Throws Left. Height, 6 feet, 5 inches. Weight, 200 pounds.

Year	Club	Lea	G	IP	W	L	Pct	SO	BB	H	ERA	SAVES
2003 Great Falls	Pioneer	16	67	3	3	.500	48	31	76	6.58	0	
2004 Great Falls	Pioneer	18	64 1/3	3	7	.300	48	31	74	5.60	1	
2005 Winston-Salem	Carolina	4	5 1/3	0	0	.000	5	4	7	5.06	0	
2005 Great Falls	Pioneer	21	35 1/3	1	1	.500	29	4	34	3.31	2	
2006 Charlotte	Int.	38	42 2/3	3	1	.750	57	12	35	3.38	11	
2006 Chicago	A.L.	21	17 1/3	0	0	.000	15	15	21	8.31	1	
2007 Charlotte	Int.	4	8 1/3	0	1	.000	11	4	8	2.16	1	
2007 Chicago	A.L.	68	50 2/3	2	1	.667	35	20	59	4.97	0	
2008 Charlotte	Int.	5	9	0	1	.000	7	6	10	6.00	0	
2008 Chicago a	A.L.	55	42 1/3	2	3	.400	42	14	57	5.95	0	
Major League Totals	3 Yrs.	144	110 1/3	4	4	.500	92	49	137	5.87	1	

a Traded to Atlanta Braves with pitcher Javier Vazquez for catcher Tyler Flowers, infielder Jonathan Gilmore, infielder Brent Lillibridge and pitcher Santos Rodriguez, December 4, 2008.

LOHSE, KYLE MATTHEW

Born, Chico, California, October 4, 1978.
Bats Right. Throws Right. Height, 6 feet, 2 inches. Weight, 210 pounds.

Year	Club	Lea	G	IP	W	L	Pxt	SO	BB	H	ERA	SAVES
1997 Cubs	Arizona	12	47 2/3	2	2	.500	49	22	46	3.02	0	
1998 Rockford	Midwest	28	170 2/3	13	8	.619	121	45	158	3.22	0	
1999 New Britain	Eastern	11	70 1/3	3	4	.429	41	23	87	5.89	0	
1999 Daytona	Fla.St.	9	53	5	3	.625	41	16	48	2.89	0	
1999 Fort Myers a	Fla.St.	7	41 2/3	2	3	.400	33	9	47	5.18	0	
2000 New Britain	Eastern	28	167	3	18	.143	124	55	196	6.04	0	
2001 New Britain	Eastern	6	38	3	1	.750	32	4	32	2.37	0	
2001 Edmonton	P.C.	8	49	4	2	.667	48	13	50	3.12	0	
2001 Minnesota	A.L.	19	90 1/3	4	7	.364	64	29	102	5.68	0	
2002 Minnesota	A.L.	32	180 2/3	13	8	.619	124	70	181	4.23	0	
2003 Minnesota	A.L.	33	201	14	11	.560	130	45	211	4.61	0	
2004 Minnesota	A.L.	35	194	9	13	.409	111	76	240	5.34	0	
2005 Minnesota	A.L.	31	178 2/3	9	13	.409	86	44	211	4.18	0	
2006 Rochester	Int.	4	24	2	1	.667	12	6	15	1.50	0	
2006 Minnesota	A.L.	22	63 2/3	2	5	.286	46	25	80	7.07	0	
2006 Cincinnati b	N.L.	12	63	3	5	.375	51	19	70	4.57	0	
2007 Cincinnati-Philadelphia c-d	N.L.	34	192 2/3	9	12	.429	122	57	207	4.62	0	
2008 St. Louis e	N.L.	33	200	15	6	.714	119	49	211	3.78	0	
Major League Totals	8 Yrs.	251	1364	78	80	.494	853	414	1513	4.67	0	

Year	Club	Lea	G	IP	W	L	Pct	SO	BB	H	ERA	SAVES
	Division Series											
2002	Minnesota	A.L.	2	4	0	0	.000	5	0	2	0.00	0
2003	Minnesota	A.L.	1	5	0	1	.000	5	2	6	5.40	0
2004	Minnesota	A.L.	1	2	0	1	.000	3	0	1	4.50	0
2007	Philadelphia	N.L.	1	1²/₃	0	0	.000	1	0	1	6.75	0
	Division Series Totals		5	12²/₃	0	2	.000	14	2	10	3.65	0
	Championship Series											
2002	Minnesota	A.L.	1	1	0	0	.000	1	0	0	0.00	0

a Traded by Chicago Cubs to Minnesota Twins with pitcher Jason Ryan for pitcher Rick Aguilera and pitcher Scott Downs, May 21, 1999.

b Traded to Cincinnati Reds for pitcher Zach Ward, July 31, 2006.

c Traded to Philadelphia Phillies for pitcher Matt Maloney, July 30, 2007.

d Filed for free agency, October 31, 2007. Signed with St. Louis Cardinals, March 14, 2008.

LOOPER, BRADEN LA VERN

Born, Weatherford, Oklahoma, October 28, 1974.
Bats Right. Throws Right. Height, 6 feet, 3 inches. Weight, 235 pounds.

Year	Club	Lea	G	IP	W	L	Pct	SO	BB	H	ERA	SAVES
1997	Pr William	Carolina	12	64¹/₃	3	6	.333	58	25	71	4.48	0
1997	Arkansas	Texas	19	21¹/₃	1	4	.200	20	7	24	5.91	5
1998	Memphis	P.C.	40	40²/₃	2	3	.400	43	13	43	3.10	20
1998	St. Louis a	N.L.	4	3¹/₃	0	1	.000	4	1	5	5.40	0
1999	Florida	N.L.	72	83	3	3	.500	50	31	96	3.80	0
2000	Florida	N.L.	73	67¹/₃	5	1	.833	29	36	71	4.41	2
2001	Florida	N.L.	71	71	3	3	.500	52	30	63	3.55	3
2002	Florida b	N.L.	78	86	2	5	.286	55	28	73	3.14	13
2003	Florida b	N.L.	74	80²/₃	6	4	.600	56	29	82	3.68	28
2004	New York	N.L.	71	83¹/₃	2	5	.286	60	16	86	2.70	29
2005	New York c	N.L.	60	59¹/₃	4	7	.364	27	22	65	3.94	28
2006	St. Louis	N.L.	69	73¹/₃	9	3	.750	41	20	76	3.56	0
2007	St. Louis d	N.L.	31	175	12	12	.500	87	51	183	4.94	0
2008	St. Louis e	N.L.	33	199	12	14	.462	108	45	216	4.16	0
	Major League Totals	11 Yrs.	636	981¹/₃	58	58	.500	569	309	1016	3.93	103
	Division Series											
2003	Florida	N.L.	2	1²/₃	1	0	1.000	0	2	1	0.00	0
2006	St. Louis	N.L.	1	1²/₃	0	0	.000	0	0	1	0.00	0
	Division Series Totals		3	3¹/₃	1	0	1.000	0	2	2	0.00	0
	Championship Series											
2003	Florida	N.L.	2	1²/₃	0	0	.000	1	1	1	0.00	1
2006	St. Louis	N.L.	3	4²/₃	0	0	.000	1	0	7	5.79	0
	Championship Series Totals		5	6¹/₃	0	0	.000	2	1	8	4.26	1
	World Series Record											
2003	Florida	N.L.	4	3²/₃	1	0	1.000	4	0	6	9.82	0
2006	St. Louis	N.L.	3	2¹/₃	0	0	.000	1	0	1	3.86	0
	World Series Totals		7	6	1	0	1.000	5	0	7	7.50	0

a Traded to Florida Marlins with pitcher Armando Almanza and infielder Pablo Ozuna for infielder Edgar Renteria, December 14, 1998.

b Not offered contract, December 21, 2003. Signed with New York Mets, January 6, 2004.

c Filed for free agency, November 4, 2005. Signed with St. Louis Cardinals, December 15, 2005.

d On disabled list from June 16 to July 2, 2007.

e Filed for free agency, October 30, 2008.

LOPEZ (ROA), AQUILINO

Born, Villa Altagracia, Dominican Republic, April 21, 1975.
Bats Right. Throws Right. Height, 6 feet, 3 inches. Weight, 185 pounds.

Year	Club	Lea	G	IP	W	L	Pct	SO	BB	H	ERA	SAVES
1997	Seattle	Dominican	15	20¹/₃	2	1	.667	19	7	19	3.10	2
1998	Seattle	Dominican	28	70	5	1	.833	100	19	53	2.19	3
1999	Everett	Northwest	15	87²/₃	7	6	.538	93	30	76	3.80	0
2000	Wisconsin	Midwest	39	68	6	1	.857	67	20	47	1.85	17
2001	San Antonio	Texas	42	62²/₃	4	3	.571	79	25	48	3.02	2
2002	Tacoma a	P.C.	34	109¹/₃	4	4	.500	103	27	89	2.39	5
2003	Toronto	A.L.	72	73²/₃	1	3	.250	64	34	58	3.42	14
2004	Toronto	A.L.	18	21	1	1	.500	13	13	21	6.00	0
2004	Syracuse b	Int.	32	42²/₃	1	6	.143	32	10	58	7.17	5
2005	Las Vegas	P.C.	27	36²/₃	3	4	.429	32	6	40	5.89	5

<table>
Year	Club	Lea	G	IP	W	L	Pct	SO	BB	H	ERA	SAVES
2005	Colorado Springs.......	P.C.	14	19²/₃	2	0	1.000	25	4	14	2.75	0
2005	Scranton-WB	Int.	4	9	0	0	.000	11	1	5	1.00	0
2005	Colorado-Philadelphia c-d ..	N.L.	11	16²/₃	0	1	.000	22	7	16	2.16	0
2006	Portland e	P.C.	41	62	3	4	.429	72	24	66	5.52	2
2007	Detroit	A.L.	10	17¹/₃	0	0	.000	7	6	18	5.19	1
2007	Toledo f	Int.	48	53²/₃	3	5	.375	58	11	46	2.35	26
2008	Toledo	Int.	3	11	0	0	.000	14	0	5	2.45	0
2008	Detroit g	A.L.	48	78²/₃	4	1	.800	61	22	86	3.55	0
Major League Totals	5 Yrs.		159	207¹/₃	6	6	.500	167	82	199	3.78	15
</table>

a Selected by Toronto Blue Jays from Seattle Mariners in Rule V draft, December 16, 2002.
b Filed for free agency, October 15, 2004. Signed with Los Angeles Dodgers organization, December 2, 2004.
c Released by Los Angeles Dodgers, June 15, 2005. Signed with Colorado Rockies organization, June 21, 2005.
d Claimed on waivers by Philadelphia Phillies, August 2, 2005.
e Traded to San Diego Padres for outfielder Matt Thayer and infielder Trey Johnson, March 28, 2006.
f Released by San Diego Padres, July 19, 2006. Signed with Detroit Tigers organization, March 26, 2007.
g Not offered contract, December 12, 2008.

LOPEZ, JAVIER ALFONSO

Born, San Juan, Puerto Rico, June 11, 1977.
Bats Left. Throws Left. Height, 6 feet, 4 inches. Weight, 220 pounds.

<table>
Year	Club	Lea	G	IP	W	L	Pct	SO	BB	H	ERA	SAVES
1998	South Bend	Midwest	16	44	2	4	.333	31	30	60	6.55	0
1999	South Bend	Midwest	20	99	4	6	.400	70	43	122	6.00	0
2000	High Desert	Calif.	30	136¹/₃	4	8	.333	98	57	152	5.22	2
2001	Lancaster	Calif.	17	24	1	3	.250	18	5	30	2.63	1
2001	El Paso	Texas	22	40	1	0	1.000	21	14	64	7.43	0
2002	El Paso a	Texas	61	46¹/₃	2	2	.500	47	16	34	2.72	6
2003	Colorado b	N.L.	75	58¹/₃	4	1	.800	40	12	58	3.70	1
2004	Colorado Springs.......	P.C.	8	9	0	1	.000	9	2	10	4.00	0
2004	Colorado	N.L.	64	40²/₃	1	2	.333	20	26	45	7.52	0
2005	Tucson	P.C.	27	24¹/₃	0	1	.000	16	12	17	2.22	2
2005	Arizona-Colorado c	N.L.	32	16¹/₃	1	1	.500	12	11	26	11.02	2
2006	Charlotte	Int.	26	33	2	1	.667	26	6	28	0.55	12
2006	Pawtucket	Int.	13	16²/₃	0	0	.000	12	8	20	4.86	4
2006	Boston d-e	A.L.	27	16²/₃	1	0	1.000	11	10	13	2.70	1
2007	Pawtucket	Int.	17	16²/₃	2	1	.667	15	8	19	3.78	0
2007	Boston	A.L.	61	40²/₃	2	1	.667	26	18	36	3.10	0
2008	Boston	A.L.	70	59¹/₃	2	0	1.000	38	27	53	2.43	0
Major League Totals	6 Yrs.		329	232	11	5	.688	147	104	231	4.38	4
</table>

Division Series

<table>
Year	Club	Lea	G	IP	W	L	Pct	SO	BB	H	ERA	SAVES
2007	Boston	A.L.	1	0¹/₃	0	0	.000	0	0	0	0.00	0
2008	Boston	A.L.	1	1	0	1	.000	1	0	3	9.00	0
Division Series Totals			2	1¹/₃	0	1	.000	1	0	3	6.75	0
</table>

Championship Series

<table>
Year	Club	Lea	G	IP	W	L	Pct	SO	BB	H	ERA	SAVES
2007	Boston	A.L.	3	2	0	0	.000	0	2	3	18.00	0
2008	Boston	A.L.	2	1²/₃	0	0	.000	0	0	3	0.00	0
Championship Series Totals			5	3²/₃	0	0	.000	0	2	6	9.82	0
</table>

World Series Record

<table>
Year	Club	Lea	G	IP	W	L	Pct	SO	BB	H	ERA	SAVES
2007	Boston	A.L.	1	0	0	0	.000	0	0	2	INF	0
</table>

a Selected by Boston Red Sox from Arizona Diamondbacks in Rule V draft, December 16, 2002.
b Traded to Colorado Rockies for player to be named later, March 28, 2003. Boston Red Sox received pitcher Ryan Cameron to complete trade, March 29, 2003.
c Claimed on waivers by Arizona Diamondbacks, April 14, 2005.
d Filed for free agency, October 14, 2005. Signed with Chicago White Sox organization, January 19, 2006.
e Traded to Boston Red Sox for pitcher David Riske, June 15, 2006.

LOWE, DEREK CHRISTOPHER

Born, Dearborn, Michigan, June 1, 1973.
Bats Right. Throws Right. Height, 6 feet, 6 inches. Weight, 230 pounds.

<table>
Year	Club	Lea	G	IP	W	L	Pct	SO	BB	H	ERA	SAVES
1991	Mariners...........	Arizona	12	71	5	3	.625	60	21	58	2.41	0
1992	Bellingham.......	Northwest	14	85²/₃	7	3	.700	66	22	69	2.42	0
1993	Riverside	California	27	154	12	9	.571	80	60	189	5.26	0
1994	Jacksnville	Southern	26	151¹/₃	7	10	.412	75	50	177	4.94	0
1995	Mariners...........	Arizona	2	9²/₃	1	0	1.000	11	2	5	0.93	0
1995	Port City.........	Southern	10	53¹/₃	1	6	.143	30	22	70	6.07	0
1996	Port City.........	Southern	10	65	5	3	.625	33	17	56	3.05	0
</table>

Year	Club	Lea	G	IP	W	L	Pct	SO	BB	H	ERA	SAVES
1996 Tacoma		P.C.	17	105	6	9	.400	54	37	118	4.54	0
1997 Tacoma		P.C.	10	57⅓	3	4	.429	49	20	53	3.45	0
1997 Pawtucket		Int.	6	30⅓	4	0	1.000	21	11	23	2.37	0
1997 Seattle-Boston a		A.L.	20	69	2	6	.250	52	23	74	6.13	0
1998 Boston		A.L.	63	123	3	9	.250	77	42	126	4.02	4
1999 Boston		A.L.	74	109⅓	6	3	.667	80	25	84	2.63	15
2000 Boston		A.L.	74	91⅓	4	4	.500	79	22	90	2.56	*42
2001 Boston		A.L.	67	91⅔	5	10	.333	82	29	103	3.53	24
2002 Boston b		A.L.	32	219⅔	21	8	.724	127	48	166	2.58	0
2003 Boston		A.L.	33	203⅓	17	7	.708	110	72	216	4.47	0
2004 Boston c		A.L.	33	182⅔	14	12	.538	105	71	224	5.42	0
2005 Los Angeles		N.L.	35	222	12	15	.444	146	55	223	3.61	0
2006 Los Angeles		N.L.	35	218	*16	8	.667	123	55	221	3.63	0
2007 Los Angeles		N.L.	33	199⅓	12	14	.462	147	59	194	3.88	0
2008 Los Angeles d		N.L.	34	211	14	11	.560	147	45	194	3.24	0
Major League Totals	12 Yrs.		533	1940⅓	126	107	.541	1275	546	1915	3.75	85
Division Series												
1998 Boston		A.L.	2	4⅓	0	0	.000	2	1	3	2.08	0
1999 Boston		A.L.	3	8⅓	1	1	.500	7	1	6	4.32	0
2003 Boston		A.L.	3	9⅔	0	1	.000	6	7	7	0.93	1
2004 Boston		A.L.	1	1	1	0	1.000	0	1	1	0.00	0
2006 Los Angeles		N.L.	1	5⅓	0	0	.000	6	2	6	6.75	0
2008 Los Angeles		N.L.	1	6	1	0	1.000	6	1	7	3.00	0
Division Series Totals			11	34⅔	3	2	.600	27	13	30	3.12	1
Championship Series												
1999 Boston		A.L.	3	6⅓	0	0	.000	7	2	6	1.42	0
2003 Boston		A.L.	2	14	0	2	.000	5		14	6.43	0
2004 Boston		A.L.	2	11⅓	1	0	1.000	6	1	7	3.18	0
2008 Los Angeles		N.L.	2	10⅓	0	1	.000	6	2	12	3.48	0
Championship Series Totals			9	42	1	3	.250	24	12	39	4.07	0
World Series Record												
2004 Boston		A.L.	1	7	1	0	1.000	4	1	3	0.00	0

a Traded to Boston Red Sox with catcher Jason Varitek for pitcher Heathcliff Slocumb, July 31, 1997.
b Pitched no-hit, no-run game against Tampa Bay Devil Rays, April 27, 2002.
c Filed for free agency, November 1, 2004. Signed with Los Angeles Dodgers, January 11, 2005.
d Filed for free agency, October 30, 2008. Signed with Atlanta Braves, January 13, 2009.

LOWE, MARK CHRISTOPHER

Born, Houston, Texas, June 7, 1983.
Bats Left. Throws Right. Height, 6 feet, 3 inches. Weight, 200 pounds.

Year	Club	Lea	G	IP	W	L	Pct	SO	BB	H	ERA	SAVES
2004 Everett		Northwest	18	38⅓	1	2	.333	38	14	42	4.93	7
2005 Wisconsin		Midwest	22	102⅔	6	6	.500	72	49	107	5.47	0
2006 Inland Empire		Calif.	13	29⅓	1	0	1.000	46	11	14	1.84	2
2006 San Antonio		Texas	11	16⅔	0	2	.000	14	3	14	2.16	4
2006 Seattle a		A.L.	15	18⅔	1	0	1.000	20	9	12	1.93	0
2007 Everett		Northwest	1	1	0	0	.000	0	0	0	0.00	0
2007 West Tenn		Southern	3	2⅔	0	0	.000	1	2	2	3.38	0
2007 Seattle		A.L.	4	2⅔	0	0	.000	3	3	2	6.75	0
2007 Tacoma b		P.C.	7	6⅓	0	0	.000	5	3	12	5.68	0
2008 Seattle		A.L.	57	63⅔	1	5	.167	55	34	78	5.37	1
Major League Totals	3 Yrs.		76	85	2	5	.286	78	46	92	4.66	1

a On disabled list from August 20 to November 2, 2006.
b On disabled list from March 23 to July 24 and August 28 to October 25, 2007.

LOWRY, NOAH RYAN

Born, Ventura, California, October 10, 1980.
Bats Right. Throws Left. Height, 6 feet, 2 inches. Weight, 200 pounds.

Year	Club	Lea	G	IP	W	L	Pct	SO	BB	H	ERA	SAVES
2001 Salem-Keizer		Northwest	8	25	1	1	.500	28	8	26	3.60	0
2002 San Jose		California	15	58⅔	6	5	.545	62	20	38	2.15	0
2003 Norwich		Eastern	23	118⅓	9	6	.600	97	47	127	4.72	0
2003 Fresno		P.C.	4	19	1	0	1.000	13	6	15	2.37	0
2003 San Francisco		N.L.	4	6⅓	0	0	.000	5	2	1	0.00	0
2004 Fresno		P.C.	17	89⅓	7	5	.583	73	28	98	4.13	0
2004 San Francisco		N.L.	16	92	6	0	1.000	72	28	91	3.82	0

Year	Club	Lea	G	IP	W	L	Pct	SO	BB	H	ERA	SAVES
2005 San Francisco	N.L.	33	204²/₃	13	13	.500	172	76	193	3.78	0
2006 San Jose	Calif.	1	4²/₃	0	0	.000	9	1	5	0.00	0
2006 Fresno	P.C.	1	6	0	0	.000	6	1	5	4.50	0
2006 San Francisco a	N.L.	27	159¹/₃	7	10	.412	84	56	166	4.74	0
2007 San Francisco	N.L.	26	156	14	8	.636	87	87	155	3.92	0
2008 San Francisco b	N.L.		INJURED—Did Not Play								

Major League Totals .... 5 Yrs.	106	618¹/₃	40	31	.563	420	249	606	4.03	0

a On disabled list from April 7 to May 8, 2006.
b On disabled list from March 21 to October 9, 2008.

LYON, BRANDON JAMES

Born, Salt Lake City, Utah, August 10, 1979.
Bats Right. Throws Right. Height, 6 feet, 1 inch. Weight, 195 pounds.

Year	Club	Lea	G	IP	W	L	Pct	SO	BB	H	ERA	SAVES
2000 Queens	N.Y.-Penn.	15	60¹/₃	5	3	.625	55	6	43	2.39	0
2001 Tennessee	Southern	9	58²/₃	5	0	1.000	45	9	57	3.68	0
2001 Syracuse	Int.	11	68¹/₃	5	3	.625	53	10	68	3.69	0
2001 Toronto	A.L.	11	63	5	4	.556	35	15	63	4.29	0
2002 Toronto	A.L.	15	62	1	4	.200	30	19	78	6.53	0
2002 Syracuse a	Int.	14	75²/₃	4	9	.308	35	19	99	5.11	0
2003 Boston	A.L.	49	59	4	6	.400	50	19	73	4.12	9
2003 Pawtucket b-c-d-e	Int.	5	8¹/₃	0	0	.000	7	2	7	3.24	0
2004 Tucson f	P.C.	6	8¹/₃	2	3	.400	4	4	15	15.12	0
2005 Tucson	P.C.	5	5	0	1	.000	4	0	5	5.40	0
2005 Arizona g	N.L.	32	29¹/₃	0	2	.000	17	10	44	6.44	14
2006 Arizona	N.L.	68	69¹/₃	2	4	.333	46	22	68	3.89	0
2007 Arizona	N.L.	73	74	6	4	.600	40	22	70	2.68	2
2008 Arizona h	N.L.	61	59¹/₃	3	5	.375	44	13	75	4.70	26

Major League Totals .... 7 Yrs.	309	416	21	29	.420	262	120	471	4.46	51
Division Series										
2007 Arizona	N.L.	3	3	0	0	.000	1	1	1	0.00	0
Championship Series										
2007 Arizona	N.L.	2	3	0	0	.000	4	0	0	0.00	0

a Claimed on waivers by Boston Red Sox, October 9, 2002.
b Traded to Pittsburgh Pirates with pitcher Anastacio Martinez for pitcher Scott Sauerbeck and pitcher Mike Gonzalez, July 22, 2003.
c On disabled list from July 24 to September 1, 2003.
d Traded to Boston Red Sox with pitcher Jeff Suppan and pitcher Anastacio Martinez for infielder Freddy Sanchez, pitcher Mike Gonzalez and cash, July 31, 2003.
e Traded to Arizona Diamondbacks with pitcher Casey Fossum, pitcher Jorge DeRosa and outfielder Michael Goss for pitcher Curt Schilling, November 28, 2003.
f On disabled list from April 3 to October 4, 2004.
g On disabled list from May 13 to August 13, 2005.
h Filed for free agency, November 3, 2008.

MADDUX, GREGORY ALAN

Born, San Angelo, Texas, April 14, 1966.
Bats Right. Throws Right. Height, 6 feet. Weight, 195 pounds.

Year	Club	Lea	G	IP	W	L	Pct	SO	BB	H	ERA	SAVES
1984 Pikeville	Appalachian	14	85²/₃	6	2	.750	62	41	63	2.63	0
1985 Peoria	Midland	27	186	13	9	.591	125	52	176	3.19	0
1986 Pittsfield	Eastern	8	62²/₃	4	3	.571	35	15	49	2.69	0
1986 Iowa	A.A.	18	128¹/₃	10	1	*.909	65	30	127	3.02	0
1986 Chicago	N.L.	6	31	2	4	.333	20	11	44	5.52	0
1987 Iowa	A.A.	4	27²/₃	3	0	1.000	22	12	17	0.98	0
1987 Chicago a	N.L.	30	155²/₃	6	14	.300	101	74	181	5.61	0
1988 Chicago	N.L.	34	249	18	8	.692	140	81	230	3.18	0
1989 Chicago	N.L.	35	238¹/₃	19	12	.613	135	82	222	2.95	0
1990 Chicago	N.L.	35	237	15	15	.500	144	71	*242	3.46	0
1991 Chicago	N.L.	39	*263	15	11	.577	198	66	232	3.35	0
1992 Chicago b-c	N.L.	35	*268	*20	11	.645	199	70	201	2.18	0
1993 Atlanta d	N.L.	36	*267	20	10	.667	197	52	228	*2.36	0
1994 Atlanta e	N.L.	25	*202	*16	6	.727	156	31	150	*1.56	0
1995 Atlanta f	N.L.	28	*209²/₃	*19	2	*.905	181	23	147	*1.63	0
1996 Atlanta	N.L.	35	245	15	11	.577	172	28	225	2.72	0
1997 Atlanta	N.L.	33	232²/₃	19	4	*.826	177	20	200	2.20	0
1998 Atlanta	N.L.	34	251	18	9	.667	204	45	201	*2.22	0
1999 Atlanta	N.L.	33	219¹/₃	19	9	.679	136	37	258	3.57	0

Year Club	Lea	G	IP	W	L	Pct	SO	BB	H	ERA	SAVES
2000 Atlanta	N.L.	35	249⅓	19	9	.679	190	42	225	3.00	0
2001 Atlanta	N.L.	34	233	17	11	.607	173	27	220	3.05	0
2002 Atlanta g-h	N.L.	34	199⅓	16	6	.727	118	45	194	2.62	0
2003 Atlanta i	N.L.	36	218⅓	16	11	.593	124	33	225	3.96	0
2004 Chicago	N.L.	33	212⅔	16	11	.593	151	33	218	4.02	0
2005 Chicago	N.L.	35	225	13	15	.464	136	36	239	4.24	0
2006 Chicago-Los Angeles j-k	N.L.	34	210	15	14	.517	117	37	219	4.20	0
2007 San Diego	N.L.	34	198	14	11	.560	104	25	221	4.14	0
2008 San Diego-Los Angeles l-m	N.L.	33	194	8	13	.381	98	30	204	4.22	0
Major League Totals 23 Yrs.		744	5008⅓	355	227	.610	3371	999	4726	3.16	0
Division Series											
1995 Atlanta	N.L.	2	14	1	0	1.000	7	2	19	4.50	0
1996 Atlanta	N.L.	1	7	1	0	1.000	7	0	3	0.00	0
1997 Atlanta	N.L.	1	9	1	0	1.000	6	1	7	1.00	0
1998 Atlanta	N.L.	1	7	1	0	1.000	4	0	7	2.57	0
1999 Atlanta	N.L.	2	7	0	1	.000	5	5	10	2.57	0
2000 Atlanta	N.L.	1	4	0	1	.000	2	3	9	11.25	0
2001 Atlanta	N.L.	1	6	0	0	.000	5	3	4	3.00	0
2002 Atlanta	N.L.	1	6	1	0	1.000	3	1	5	3.00	0
2003 Atlanta	N.L.	1	6	0	1	.000	1	1	6	3.00	0
2006 Los Angeles	N.L.	1	4	0	0	.000	1	2	7	9.00	0
2008 Los Angeles	N.L.	1	1	0	0	.000	0	0	1	0.00	0
Division Series Totals		13	71	5	3	.625	40	18	78	3.42	0
Championship Series											
1989 Chicago	N.L.	2	7⅓	0	1	.000	5	4	13	13.50	0
1993 Atlanta	N.L.	2	12⅔	1	1	.500	11	7	11	4.97	0
1995 Atlanta	N.L.	1	8	1	0	1.000	4	2	7	1.13	0
1996 Atlanta	N.L.	2	14⅓	1	1	.500	10	2	15	2.51	0
1997 Atlanta	N.L.	2	13	0	2	.000	16	4	9	1.38	0
1998 Atlanta	N.L.	2	6	0	1	.000	4	3	5	3.00	0
1999 Atlanta	N.L.	2	14	1	0	1.000	7	1	12	1.93	0
2001 Atlanta	N.L.	2	10	0	2	.000	7	2	14	5.40	0
2008 Los Angeles	N.L.	2	3	0	0	.000	3	1	3	0.00	0
Championship Series Totals		17	88⅓	4	8	.333	67	26	89	3.67	1
World Series Record											
1995 Atlanta	N.L.	2	16	1	1	.500	8	3	9	2.25	0
1996 Atlanta	N.L.	2	15⅔	1	1	.500	5	1	14	1.72	0
1999 Atlanta	N.L.	1	7	0	1	.000	5	3	5	2.57	0
World Series Totals		5	38⅔	2	3	.400	18	7	28	2.09	0

a Appeared in two games as pinch hitter.
b Selected Cy Young Award winner in National League for 1992.
c Filed for free agency, October 26; signed with Atlanta Braves, December 9, 1992.
d Selected Cy Young Award winner in National League for 1993.
e Selected Cy Young Award winner in National League for 1994.
f Selected Cy Young Award Winner in National League for 1995.
g On disabled list from March 26 to April 12, 2002.
h Filed for free agency, October 29, 2002, re-signed with Atlanta Braves, December 19, 2002.
i Filed for free agency, October 29, 2002. Signed with Chicago Cubs, February 18, 2004.
j Traded to Los Angeles Dodgers for infielder Cesar Izturis, July 31, 2006.
k Filed for free agency, October 31, 2006. Signed with San Diego Padres, December 13, 2006.
l Traded to Los Angeles Dodgers for two players to be named later, August 19, 2008. San Diego Padres received pitcher Eduardo Perez and pitcher Michael Watt to complete trade, September 30, 2008.
m Announced retirement, December 8, 2008.

MADSON, RYAN MICHAEL

Born, Long Beach, California, August 28, 1980.
Bats Left. Throws Right. Height, 6 feet, 6 inches. Weight, 195 pounds.

Year Club	Lea	G	IP	W	L	Pct	SO	BB	H	ERA	SAVES
1998 Martinsvlle	Appal.	12	54	3	3	.500	52	20	57	4.83	0
1999 Batavia	N.Y.-Penn.	15	87⅔	5	5	.500	75	43	80	4.72	0
2000 Piedmont	So.Atl.	21	135⅔	14	5	.737	123	45	113	2.59	0
2001 Clearwater	Fla.St.	22	117⅔	9	9	.500	101	49	137	3.90	0
2002 Reading	Eastern	26	171⅓	16	4	.800	132	53	150	3.20	0
2003 Clearwater	Fla.St.	2	8	0	0	.000	9	7	11	5.63	0
2003 Scranton/WB	Int.	26	157	12	8	.600	138	42	157	3.50	0
2003 Philadelphia	N.L.	1	2	0	0	.000	0	0	2	0.00	0
2004 Reading	Eastern	2	2	0	0	.000	1	2	3	4.50	0
2004 Philadelphia a	N.L.	52	77	9	3	.750	55	19	68	2.34	1
2005 Philadelphia	N.L.	78	87	6	5	.545	79	25	84	4.14	0

Year	Club	Lea	G	IP	W	L	Pct	SO	BB	H	ERA	SAVES
2006 Philadelphia		N.L.	50	134⅓	11	9	.550	99	50	176	5.69	2
2007 Reading		Eastern	2	3	0	0	.000	4	0	3	0.00	0
2007 Philadelphia a		N.L.	38	56	2	2	.500	43	23	48	3.05	1
2008 Philadelphia		N.L.	76	82⅔	4	2	.667	67	23	79	3.05	1
Major League Totals	6 Yrs.		295	439	32	21	.604	343	140	455	3.94	5
Division Series												
2008 Philadelphia		N.L.	3	4	0	0	.000	2	0	3	2.25	0
Championship Series												
2008 Philadelphia		N.L.	4	5	1	0	1.000	4	1	4	0.00	0
World Series Record												
2008 Philadelphia		N.L.	4	3⅔	0	0	.000	6	0	3	4.91	0

a On disabled list from May 4 to May 22 and July 30 to November 2, 2007.

MAHAY, RONALD MATTHEW (RON)

Born, Crestwood, Illinois, June 28, 1971.
Bats Left. Throws Left. Height, 6 feet, 2 inches. Weight, 190 pounds.

Year	Club	Lea	G	IP	W	L	Pct	SO	BB	H	ERA	SAVES
1996 Sarasota		Fla.St.	31	70⅔	2	2	.500	68	35	61	3.82	2
1996 Trenton		Eastern	1	3⅔	0	1	.000	0	6	12	29.45	0
1997 Trenton		Eastern	17	40⅓	3	3	.500	47	13	29	3.10	5
1997 Pawtucket		Int.	2	4⅔	1	0	1.000	6	1	3	0.00	0
1997 Boston		A.L.	28	25	3	0	1.000	22	11	19	2.52	0
1998 Pawtucket		Int.	23	41	3	1	.750	41	19	37	4.17	3
1998 Boston		A.L.	29	26	1	1	.500	14	15	26	3.46	1
1999 Vancouver		P.C.	32	107	7	2	.778	73	45	116	4.29	0
1999 Oakland a		A.L.	6	19⅓	2	0	1.000	15	3	8	1.86	1
2000 Oakland		A.L.	5	16	0	0	.000	5	9	26	9.00	0
2000 Florida		N.L.	18	25⅓	1	0	1.000	27	16	31	6.04	0
2000 Calgary b-c		P.C.	8	13	0	1	.000	15	7	7	4.85	0
2001 Portland		P.C.	14	16⅔	1	2	.333	18	5	13	3.78	0
2001 Iowa		P.C.	36	46⅔	3	1	.750	52	10	29	2.31	14
2001 Chicago d		N.L.	17	20⅔	0	0	.000	24	15	14	2.61	0
2002 Iowa		P.C.	39	46⅔	0	1	.000	50	15	32	1.93	2
2002 Chicago e-f		N.L.	11	14⅔	2	0	1.000	14	8	13	8.59	0
2003 Oklahoma		P.C.	26	42⅔	4	2	.667	51	10	36	4.22	3
2003 Texas		A.L.	35	45⅓	3	3	.500	38	20	33	3.18	0
2004 Texas		A.L.	60	67	3	0	1.000	54	29	60	2.55	0
2005 Oklahoma		P.C.	3	3⅔	0	0	.000	5	1	2	0.00	0
2005 Texas		A.L.	30	35⅔	0	2	.000	30	16	47	6.81	1
2005 Frisco g		Texas	5	19⅔	1	0	1.000	20	9	24	1.42	2
2006 Oklahoma		P.C.	5	6⅓	0	1	.000	11	0	5	1.42	2
2006 Texas		A.L.	62	57	1	3	.250	56	28	54	3.95	0
2007 Frisco		Texas	3	4⅔	0	0	.000	4	1	5	0.00	0
2007 Oklahoma		P.C.	4	5⅔	0	1	.000	5	4	10	11.12	0
2007 Texas h		A.L.	28	39	2	0	1.000	32	21	33	2.77	1
2007 Atlanta i-j		N.L.	30	28	1	0	1.000	23	16	19	2.25	0
2008 Kansas City k		A.L.	57	64⅔	5	0	1.000	49	29	61	3.48	0
Major League Totals	12 Yrs.		416	483⅔	24	10	.706	403	236	444	3.81	4

a Claimed on waivers by Oakland Athletics, March 30, 1999.
b Sold to Florida Marlins, May 11, 2000.
c Filed for free agency, October 2, 2000. Signed with San Diego Padres organization, November 20, 2000.
d Released by San Diego Padres, May 15, 2001. Signed with Chicago Cubs organization, May 19, 2001.
e On disabled list from May 24 to June 13, 2002.
f Filed for free agency, September 30, 2002. Signed with Texas Rangers organization, November 13, 2002.
g On disabled list from June 8 to June 24, 2005.
h On disabled list from May 12 to June 15, 2007.
i Traded to Atlanta Braves with infielder Mark Teixeira for catcher Jarrod Saltalamacchia, infielder Elvis Andrus, pitcher Neftali Feliz, pitcher Matt Harrison and pitcher Beau James, July 31, 2007.
j Filed for free agency, October 29, 2007. Signed with Kansas City Royals, December 20, 2007.
k On disabled list from August 16 to September 2, 2008.

MAHOLM, PAUL GURNER

Born, Greenwood, Mississippi, June 25, 1982.
Bats Left. Throws Left. Height, 6 feet, 2 inches. Weight, 230 pounds.

Year	Club	Lea	G	IP	W	L	Pct	SO	BB	H	ERA	SAVES
2003 Williamsport		N.Y.-Penn.	8	34⅓	2	1	.667	32	10	25	1.83	0
2004 Lynchburg		Carolina	8	44	1	3	.250	28	15	39	1.84	0

Year Club	Lea	G	IP	W	L	Pct	SO	BB	H	ERA	SAVES
2004 Pirates . . . . Gulf Coast	1	4	0	0	.000	2	1	5	2.25	0
2004 Hickory . . . . So.Atl.	3	12⅓	0	2	.000	12	10	17	9.49	0
2005 Altoona . . . . Eastern	16	81⅔	6	2	.750	75	26	73	3.20	0
2005 Indianapolis . . . . Int.	6	35⅔	1	1	.500	21	12	40	3.53	0
2005 Pittsburgh . . . . N.L.	6	41⅓	3	1	.750	26	17	31	2.18	0
2006 Pittsburgh . . . . N.L.	30	176	8	10	.444	117	81	202	4.76	0
2007 Pittsburgh . . . . N.L.	29	177⅔	10	15	.400	105	49	204	5.02	0
2008 Pittsburgh . . . . N.L.	31	206⅓	9	9	.500	139	63	201	3.71	0
Major League Totals . . . . 4 Yrs.	96	601⅓	30	35	.462	387	210	638	4.30	0

MAINE, JOHN KEVIN

Born, Fredericksburg, Virginia, May 8, 1981.
Bats Right. Throws Right. Height, 6 feet, 4 inches. Weight, 205 pounds.

Year Club	Lea	G	IP	W	L	Pct	SO	BB	H	ERA	SAVES
2002 Aberdeen . . . . N.Y.-Penn.	4	10⅓	1	1	.500	21	3	6	1.74	0
2002 Delmarva . . . . So.Atl.	6	33	1	1	.500	39	4	21	1.36	0
2003 Frederick . . . . Carolina	12	70⅓	6	1	.857	77	20	48	3.07	0
2003 Delmarva . . . . So.Atl.	14	76⅓	7	3	.700	108	18	43	1.53	0
2004 Bowie . . . . Eastern	5	28	4	0	1.000	34	7	16	2.25	0
2004 Ottawa . . . . Int.	22	119⅔	5	7	.417	105	52	123	3.91	0
2004 Baltimore . . . . A.L.	1	3⅔	1	0	.000	1	3	7	9.82	0
2005 Ottawa . . . . Int.	23	128⅓	6	11	.353	111	42	128	4.56	0
2005 Baltimore . . . . A.L.	10	40	2	3	.400	24	24	39	6.30	0
2006 St. Lucie . . . . Fla.St.	1	5	1	0	1.000	7	2	3	0.00	0
2006 Norfolk . . . . Int.	10	56⅔	3	5	.375	48	20	55	3.49	0
2006 New York a-b . . . . N.L.	16	90	6	5	.545	71	33	69	3.60	0
2007 New York . . . . N.L.	32	191	15	10	.600	180	75	168	3.91	0
2008 New York c . . . . N.L.	25	140	10	8	.556	122	67	122	4.18	0
Major League Totals . . . . 5 Yrs.	84	464⅔	33	27	.550	398	202	405	4.18	0
Division Series										
2006 New York . . . . N.L.	1	4⅓	0	0	.000	5	2	6	2.08	0
Championship Series										
2006 New York . . . . N.L.	2	9⅓	1	0	1.000	8	9	4	2.89	0

a Traded to New York Mets with pitcher Jorge Julio for pitcher Kris Benson, January 21, 2006.
b On disabled list from May 3 to June 12, 2006.
c On disabled list from July 29 to August 13 and August 24 to September 24, 2008.

MANNING, CHARLES NELSON (CHARLIE)

Born, Winter Haven, Florida, March 31, 1979.
Bats Left. Throws Left. Height, 6 feet, 2 inches. Weight, 185 pounds.

Year Club	Lea	G	IP	W	L	Pct	SO	BB	H	ERA	SAVES
2001 Staten Island . . . . . N.Y.-Penn.	14	80	8	4	.667	87	21	73	3.49	0
2002 Norwich . . . . Eastern	11	63	4	2	.667	61	26	55	3.57	0
2002 Tampa . . . . Fla.St.	17	100	6	4	.600	85	31	82	3.24	0
2003 Potomac . . . . Carolina	6	37⅔	5	0	1.000	31	11	24	1.19	0
2003 Trenton . . . . Eastern	23	46	0	2	.000	34	35	53	6.26	0
2003 Tampa a . . . . Fla.St.	6	31⅓	2	4	.333	25	15	27	3.45	0
2004 Trenton . . . . Eastern	15	24⅓	2	1	.667	19	6	31	4.07	0
2004 Columbus . . . . Int.	11	12⅓	1	1	.500	11	6	10	3.65	0
2004 Chattanooga b . . . . Southern	13	70⅓	4	4	.500	71	21	79	5.12	0
2005 Trenton . . . . Eastern	45	73	4	3	.571	67	37	64	3.33	2
2005 Columbus . . . . Int.	7	9⅔	1	1	.500	6	9	8	5.59	0
2006 Trenton . . . . Eastern	48	83	8	3	.727	81	28	60	2.71	1
2006 Columbus . . . . Int.	1	1	0	0	.000	1	0	3	0.00	0
2007 Trenton . . . . Eastern	7	9⅔	1	0	1.000	9	2	4	0.00	1
2007 Scranton-WB c . . . . Int.	34	51⅓	3	2	.600	59	24	41	4.38	2
2008 Columbus . . . . Int.	19	27⅔	0	0	.000	34	13	20	1.95	6
2008 Washington . . . . N.L.	57	42	1	3	.250	37	31	35	5.14	0

a Traded by New York Yankees to Cincinnati Reds with pitcher Brandon Claussen and cash for infielder Aaron Boone, July 31, 2003.
b Traded to New York Yankees for pitcher Gabe White, player to be named later and cash, June 18, 2004.
c Filed for free agency, October 29, 2007. Signed with Washington Nationals organization, November 18, 2007.

MARCUM, SHAUN MICHAL
Born, Kansas City, Missouri, December 14, 1981.
Bats Right. Throws Right. Height, 6 feet. Weight, 190 pounds.

Year	Club	Lea	G	IP	W	L	Pct	SO	BB	H	ERA	SAVES
2003 Auburn	N.Y.-Penn.	21	34	1	0	1.000	47	7	15	1.32	8
2004 Dunedin	Fla.St.	12	69⅓	3	2	.600	72	4	74	3.12	0
2004 Charleston	So.Atl.	13	79	7	4	.636	83	16	64	3.19	0
2005 New Hampshire	Eastern	9	53⅓	7	1	.875	40	10	44	2.53	0
2005 Syracuse	Int.	18	103⅔	6	4	.600	90	18	112	4.95	0
2005 Toronto	A.L.	5	8	0	0	.000	4	4	6	0.00	0
2006 Syracuse	Int.	18	52⅔	4	0	1.000	60	9	48	3.42	0
2006 Toronto	A.L.	21	78⅓	3	4	.429	65	38	87	5.06	0
2007 Toronto	A.L.	38	159	12	6	.667	122	49	149	4.13	1
2008 Dunedin	Fla.St.	1	4	0	0	.000	6	0	0	0.00	0
2008 Syracuse	Int.	2	13	0	1	.000	15	3	10	2.77	0
2008 Toronto a	A.L.	25	151⅓	9	7	.563	123	50	126	3.39	0
Major League Totals	4 Yrs.	89	396⅔	24	17	.585	314	141	368	3.95	1

a On disabled list from June 19 to July 22, 2008.

MARMOL, CARLOS AGUSTIN
Born, Bonao, Dominican Republic, October 14, 1982.
Bats Right. Throws Right. Height, 6 feet, 2 inches. Weight, 180 pounds.

Year	Club	Lea	G	IP	W	L	Pct	SO	BB	H	ERA	SAVES
2002 Cubs	Arizona	1	1	0	0	.000	1	1	1	0.00	0
2003 Cubs	Arizona	15	64⅓	3	5	.375	74	37	59	4.76	0
2004 Lansing	Midwest	26	154⅔	14	8	.636	154	53	131	3.20	0
2005 Daytona	Fla.St.	13	72⅓	6	2	.750	71	37	60	2.99	0
2005 West Tenn	Southern	14	81⅓	3	4	.429	70	40	70	3.65	0
2006 West Tenn	Southern	11	58	3	2	.600	67	25	42	2.33	0
2006 Iowa	P.C.	2	3	0	0	.000	1	1	4	9.00	0
2006 Chicago a	N.L.	19	77	5	7	.417	59	59	71	6.08	0
2007 Iowa	P.C.	8	41	4	1	.800	48	12	30	3.95	0
2007 Chicago	N.L.	59	69⅓	5	1	.833	96	35	41	1.43	1
2008 Chicago	N.L.	82	87⅓	2	4	.333	114	41	40	2.68	7
Major League Totals	3 Yrs.	160	233⅔	12	12	.500	269	135	152	3.43	8
Division Series											
2007 Chicago	N.L.	2	3	0	1	.000	6	3	3	9.00	0
2008 Chicago	N.L.	2	2⅔	0	0	.000	3	0	3	6.75	0
Division Series Totals		4	5⅔	0	1	.000	9	3	6	7.94	0

a On disabled list from August 19 to September 4, 2006.

MARQUIS, JASON SCOTT
Born, Manhasset, New York, August 21, 1978.
Bats Left. Throws Right. Height, 6 feet, 1 inch. Weight, 210 pounds.

Year	Club	Lea	G	IP	W	L	Pct	SO	BB	H	ERA	SAVES
1996 Danville	Appal.	7	23⅓	1	1	.500	24	7	30	4.63	0
1997 Macon	So.Atl.	28	141⅔	14	10	.583	121	55	156	4.38	0
1998 Danville	Carolina	22	114⅔	2	12	.143	135	41	120	4.87	0
1999 Myrtle Beach	Carolina	6	32	3	0	1.000	41	17	22	0.28	0
1999 Greenville a	Southern	12	55	3	4	.429	35	29	52	4.58	0
2000 Greenville	Southern	11	68	4	2	.667	49	23	68	3.57	0
2000 Atlanta	N.L.	15	23⅓	1	0	1.000	17	12	23	5.01	0
2000 Richmond	Int.	6	20	0	3	.000	18	13	26	9.00	0
2001 Atlanta	N.L.	38	129⅓	5	6	.455	98	59	113	3.48	0
2002 Richmond	Int.	1	5	0	1	.000	6	1	5	3.60	0
2002 Atlanta b	N.L.	22	114⅓	8	9	.471	84	49	127	5.04	0
2003 Richmond	Int.	15	94	8	4	.667	75	34	93	3.35	0
2003 Atlanta c	N.L.	21	40⅔	0	0	.000	19	18	43	5.53	1
2004 St. Louis	N.L.	32	201⅓	15	7	.682	138	70	215	3.71	0
2005 St. Louis	N.L.	33	207	13	14	.481	100	69	206	4.13	0
2006 St. Louis d	N.L.	33	194⅓	14	*16	.467	96	75	221	6.02	0
2007 Chicago	N.L.	34	191⅔	12	9	.571	109	76	190	4.60	0
2008 Chicago e	N.L.	29	167	11	9	.550	91	70	172	4.53	0
Major League Totals	9 Yrs.	257	1269	79	70	.530	752	498	1310	4.55	1
Division Series											
2004 St. Louis	N.L.	1	3⅓	0	0	.000	0	4	4	8.10	0
2008 Chicago	N.L.	1	1	0	0	.000	1	0	1	9.00	0
Division Series Totals		2	4⅓	0	0	.000	1	4	5	8.31	0

Year	Club	Lea	G	IP	W	L	Pct	SO	BB	H	ERA	SAVES
	Championship Series											
2001	Atlanta	N.L.	2	2	0	0	.000	3	2	2	0.00	0
2004	St. Louis.............	N.L.	1	4	0	0	.000	2	2	5	6.75	0
2005	St. Louis.............	N.L.	3	5⅓	0	1	.000	4	3	6	3.38	0
	Championship Series Totals		6	11⅓	0	1	.000	9	7	13	3.97	0
	World Series Record											
2004	St. Louis.............	N.L.	2	7	0	1	.000	4	7	6	3.86	0

a On disabled list from July 5 to 31, 1999.
b On disabled list from April 15 to May 11, 2002.
c Traded to St. Louis Cardinals with pitcher Ray King and pitcher Adam Wainwright for catcher Eli Marrero and outfielder J.D. Drew, December 13, 2003.
d Filed for free agency, October 30, 2006. Signed with Chicago Cubs, December 19, 2006.
e Traded to Colorado Rockies for pitcher Luis Vizcaino, January 6, 2009.

MARSHALL, SEAN CHRISTOPHER

Born, Richmond, Virginia, August 30, 1982.
Bats Left. Throws Left. Height, 6 feet, 7 inches. Weight, 220 pounds.

Year	Club	Lea	G	IP	W	L	Pct	SO	BB	H	ERA	SAVES
2003	Lansing	Midwest	1	7	1	0	1.000	11	0	5	0.00	0
2003	Boise	Northwest	14	73⅔	5	6	.455	88	23	66	2.57	0
2004	Lansing	Midwest	7	48⅔	2	0	1.000	51	4	29	1.11	0
2004	West Tenn	Southern	6	29	2	2	.500	23	12	36	5.90	0
2005	Daytona	Fla.St.	12	69	4	4	.500	61	26	63	2.74	0
2005	West Tenn	Southern	4	25	0	1	.000	24	5	16	2.52	0
2006	Iowa..............	P.C.	4	21⅔	0	2	.000	21	14	17	3.32	0
2006	Chicago a	N.L.	24	125⅔	6	9	.400	77	59	132	5.59	0
2007	Daytona	Fla.St.	1	6	1	0	1.000	4	1	7	3.00	0
2007	Iowa..............	P.C.	4	24⅔	2	0	1.000	15	8	17	1.82	0
2007	Chicago	N.L.	21	103⅓	7	8	.467	67	35	107	3.92	0
2008	Iowa..............	P.C.	7	31⅔	1	1	.500	25	6	26	3.41	0
2008	Chicago	N.L.	34	65⅓	3	5	.375	58	23	60	3.86	1
	Major League Totals	3 Yrs.	79	294⅓	16	22	.421	202	117	299	4.62	1
	Division Series											
2008	Chicago	N.L.	2	3⅓	0	0	.000	5	1	2	2.70	0

a On disabled list from July 23 to September 1, 2006.

MARTE, DAMASO

Born, Santo Domingo, Dominican Republic, February 14, 1975.
Bats Left. Throws Left. Height, 6 feet, 2 inches. Weight, 210 pounds.

Year	Club	Lea	G	IP	W	L	Pct	SO	BB	H	ERA	SAVES
1993	Seattle	Dominican	17	56⅓	2	5	.286	29	50	62	6.55	0
1994	Seattle	Dominican	17	65⅓	7	0	1.000	80	48	53	3.86	0
1995	Everett	Northwest	11	36⅔	2	2	.500	39	10	25	2.21	0
1996	Wisconsin	Midwest	26	142⅓	8	6	.571	115	75	134	4.49	0
1997	Lancaster.........	California	25	139⅓	8	8	.500	127	62	144	4.13	0
1998	Orlando	Southern	22	121⅓	7	6	.538	99	47	136	5.27	0
1999	Tacoma	P.C.	31	73⅔	3	3	.500	59	40	79	5.13	0
1999	Seattle	A.L.	5	8⅔	0	1	.000	3	6	16	9.35	0
2000	Mariners...........	Arizona	2	5	0	0	.000	6	0	1	0.00	0
2000	New Haven a	Eastern	4	5⅔	0	0	.000	4	2	6	1.59	0
2001	Norwich...........	Eastern	23	36	3	1	.750	36	7	29	3.50	1
2001	Nashville	P.C.	4	5⅓	0	0	.000	4	0	3	3.38	0
2001	Pittsburgh b...........	N.L.	23	36⅓	0	1	.000	39	12	34	4.71	0
2002	Chicago c..........	A.L.	68	60⅓	1	1	.500	72	18	44	2.83	10
2003	Chicago	A.L.	71	79⅔	4	2	.667	87	34	50	1.58	11
2004	Chicago	A.L.	74	73⅔	6	5	.545	68	34	56	3.42	6
2005	Charlotte	Int.	1	1⅔	0	0	.000	2	1	4	5.40	0
2005	Chicago d-e	A.L.	66	45⅓	3	4	.429	54	33	45	3.77	4
2006	Pittsburgh	N.L.	75	58⅓	1	7	.125	63	31	51	3.70	0
2007	Pittsburgh	N.L.	65	45⅓	2	0	1.000	51	18	32	2.38	0
2008	Pittsburgh	N.L.	47	46⅔	4	1	1.000	47	16	38	3.47	5
2008	New York f-g	A.L.	25	18⅓	1	3	.250	24	10	14	5.40	0
	Major League Totals	9 Yrs.	519	472⅔	22	24	.478	508	212	380	3.29	36
	Division Series											
2005	Chicago	A.L.	1	0	0	0	.000	0	2	1	INF	0
	World Series Record											
2005	Chicago	A.L.	1	1⅔	1	0	1.000	3	2	0	0.00	0

a Filed for free agency, October 15, 2000. Signed with New York Yankees organization, November 21, 2000.
b Traded to Pittsburgh Pirates for infielder Enrique Wilson, June 13, 2001.
c Traded to Chicago White Sox with infielder Edwin Yan for pitcher Matt Guerrier, March 27, 2002.
d On disabled list from June 27 to July 14, 2005.
e Traded to Pittsburgh Pirates for outfielder Rob Mackowiak, December 13, 2005.
f Traded to New York Yankees with outfielder Xavier Nady for outfielder Jose Tabata, pitcher Ross Ohlendorf, pitcher Jeff Karstens and pitcher Dan McCutchen, July 26, 2008.
g Filed for free agency, November 5, 2008, re-signed with New York Yankees, November 12, 2008.

MARTINEZ, PEDRO JAMIE

Born, Manoguyabo, Dominican Republic, October 25, 1971.
Bats Right. Throws Right. Height, 5 feet, 11 inches. Weight, 195 pounds.

Year	Club	Lea	G	IP	W	L	Pct	SO	BB	H	ERA	SAVES
1988 Santo Domingo	Domin. Sum.		8	49⅓	5	1	.833	28	16	45	3.12	0
1989 Santo Domingo	Domin. Sum.		13	85⅔	7	2	.778	63	25	59	2.75	0
1990 Great Falls	Pioneer		14	77	8	3	.727	82	40	74	3.62	0
1991 Bakersfield	California		10	61⅓	8	0	1.000	83	19	41	2.05	0
1991 San Antonio	Texas		12	76⅔	7	5	.583	74	31	57	1.76	0
1991 Albuquerque	P.C.		6	39⅓	3	3	.500	35	16	28	3.66	0
1992 Albuquerque	P.C.		20	125⅓	7	6	.538	124	57	104	3.81	0
1992 Los Angeles	N.L.		2	8	0	1	.000	8	1	6	2.25	0
1993 Albuquerque	P.C.		1	3	0	0	.000	4	1	1	3.00	0
1993 Los Angeles a	N.L.		65	107	10	5	.667	119	57	76	2.61	2
1994 Montreal	N.L.		24	144⅔	11	5	.688	142	45	115	3.42	1
1995 Montreal	N.L.		30	194⅔	14	10	.583	174	66	158	3.51	0
1996 Montreal	N.L.		33	216⅔	13	10	.565	222	70	189	3.70	0
1997 Montreal b-c	N.L.		31	241⅓	17	8	.680	305	67	158	*1.90	0
1998 Boston	A.L.		33	233⅔	19	7	.731	251	67	188	2.89	0
1999 Boston d-e	A.L.		31	213⅓	*23	4	*.852	*313	37	160	*2.07	0
2000 Boston f-g	A.L.		29	217	18	6	.750	*284	32	128	*1.74	0
2001 Boston h	A.L.		18	116⅔	7	3	.700	163	25	84	2.39	0
2002 Boston	A.L.		30	199¼	20	4	*.833	*239	40	144	*2.26	0
2003 Boston i	A.L.		29	186⅔	14	4	.778	206	47	147	*2.22	0
2004 Boston j	A.L.		33	217	16	9	.640	227	61	193	3.90	0
2005 New York	N.L.		31	217	15	8	.652	208	47	159	2.82	0
2006 New York k	N.L.		23	132⅔	9	8	.529	137	39	108	4.48	0
2007 Mets	Gulf Coast		1	4	0	0	.000	4	1	3	6.75	0
2007 St. Lucie	Fla.St.		3	14	1	1	.500	13	3	13	3.21	0
2007 New York l	N.L.		5	28	3	1	.750	32	7	33	2.57	0
2008 St. Lucie	Fla.St.		1	6	0	1	.000	6	0	4	3.00	0
2008 New York m-n	N.L.		20	109	5	6	.455	87	44	127	5.61	0
Major League Totals	17 Yrs.		467	2782⅔	214	99	.684	3117	752	2173	2.91	3
Division Series												
1998 Boston	A.L.		1	7	1	0	1.000	8	0	6	3.86	0
1999 Boston	A.L.		2	10	1	0	1.000	11	4	3	0.00	0
2003 Boston	A.L.		2	14	1	0	1.000	9	5	13	3.86	0
2004 Boston	A.L.		1	7	1	0	1.000	6	2	6	3.86	0
Division Series Totals			6	38	4	0	1.000	34	11	28	2.84	0
Championship Series												
1999 Boston	A.L.		1	7	1	0	1.000	12	2	2	0.00	0
2003 Boston	A.L.		2	14⅓	0	1	.000	14	2	16	5.65	0
2004 Boston	A.L.		3	13	0	1	.000	14	9	14	6.23	0
Championship Series Totals			6	34⅓	1	2	.333	40	13	32	4.72	0
World Series Record												
2004 Boston	A.L.		1	7	1	0	1.000	6	2	3	0.00	0

a Traded to Montreal Expos for second baseman Delino DeShields, November 19, 1993.
b Traded to Boston Red Sox for pitcher Carl Pavano and player to be named later, November 18, 1997. Montreal Expos received pitcher Tony Armas to complete trade, December 18, 1997.
c Selected Cy Young Award Winner for National League for 1997.
d On disabled list from July 19 to August 3, 1999.
e Selected Cy Young Award Winner in American League for 1999.
f On disabled list from June 26 to July 12, 2000.
g Selected Cy Young Award Winner in American League for 2000.
h On disabled list from June 27 to August 26 and September 8 to November 7, 2001.
i On disabled list from May 16 to June 11, 2003.
j Filed for free agency, November 2, 2004. Signed with New York Mets, December 16, 2004.
k On disabled list from June 29 to July 28 and August 15 to September 15, 2006.
l On disabled list from March 23 to September 3, 2007.
m On disabled list from April 2 to June 3, 2008.
n Filed for free agency, October 31, 2008.

MARTIS, SHAIRON B.

Born, Willemstad, Curacao, Netherlands Antilles, March 30, 1987.
Bats Right. Throws Right. Height, 6 feet, 1 inch. Weight, 175 pounds.

Year Club	Lea	G	IP	W	L	Pct	SO	BB	H	ERA	SAVES
2005 Giants..........	Arizona	11	34	2	1	.667	50	9	28	1.85	1
2006 Potomac........	Carolina	2	12	0	2	.000	7	3	9	3.00	0
2006 Harrisburg......	Eastern	1	5	0	1	.000	1	3	8	12.60	0
2006 Augusta........	So.Atl.	15	76⅔	6	4	.600	66	21	76	3.64	0
2006 Savannah a.....	So.Atl.	4	21⅓	1	1	.500	14	4	23	3.80	0
2007 Potomac.......	Carolina	27	151	14	8	.636	108	52	150	4.23	0
2008 Harrisburg......	Eastern	14	74⅔	4	4	.500	57	28	73	3.98	0
2008 Columbus.......	Int.	7	41⅔	1	2	.333	42	17	42	3.02	0
2008 Washington.....	N.L.	5	20⅔	1	3	.250	23	12	18	5.66	0

a Traded by San Francisco Giants to Washington Nationals for pitcher Mike Stanton, July 28, 2006.

MASSET, NICHOLAS ALLEN (NICK)

Born, St. Petersburg, Florida, May 17, 1982.
Bats Right. Throws Right. Height, 6 feet, 4 inches. Weight, 235 pounds.

Year Club	Lea	G	IP	W	L	Pct	SO	BB	H	ERA	SAVES
2001 Rangers........	Gulf Coast	15	31	0	6	.000	32	7	34	4.35	0
2002 Savannah.......	So.Atl.	33	120⅓	5	8	.385	93	47	129	4.56	0
2003 Clinton.........	Midwest	30	123⅔	7	7	.500	63	43	144	4.08	2
2004 Stockton.......	Calif.	16	77	6	5	.545	43	19	71	3.51	0
2004 Frisco.........	Texas	2	10	1	0	1.000	8	4	8	1.80	0
2005 Frisco.........	Texas	29	157⅓	7	12	.368	105	61	197	6.18	0
2006 Frisco.........	Texas	8	48	2	2	.500	40	20	38	2.06	0
2006 Oklahoma......	P.C.	24	67⅓	4	5	.444	65	28	79	4.81	3
2006 Texas a.......	A.L.	8	8⅔	0	0	.000	4	2	9	4.15	0
2007 Chicago.......	A.L.	27	39⅓	2	3	.400	21	26	52	7.09	0
2007 Charlotte......	Int.	11	45⅓	4	0	.000	33	9	51	4.57	0
2008 Chicago.......	A.L.	32	44⅔	1	0	1.000	32	21	55	4.63	1
2008 Cincinnati b....	N.L.	10	17⅓	1	0	1.000	11	5	16	2.08	0
Major League Totals ....3 Yrs.		77	110	4	3	.571	68	54	132	5.07	1

a Traded to Chicago White Sox by Texas Rangers with pitcher John Danks and pitcher Jacob Rasner for pitcher Brandon McCarthy and outfielder David Paisano, December 23, 2006.
b Traded to Cincinnati Reds with infielder Danny Richar for outfielder Ken Griffey, July 31, 2008.

MASTERSON, JUSTIN DANIEL

Born, Kingston, Jamaica, March 22, 1985.
Bats Right. Throws Right. Height, 6 feet, 6 inches. Weight, 250 pounds.

Year Club	Lea	G	IP	W	L	Pct	SO	BB	H	ERA	SAVES
2006 Lowell..........	N.Y.-Penn.	14	31⅔	3	1	.750	33	2	20	0.85	0
2007 Lancaster......	Calif.	17	95⅔	8	5	.615	56	22	103	4.33	0
2007 Portland.......	Eastern	10	58	4	3	.571	59	18	49	4.34	0
2008 Portland.......	Eastern	8	38⅓	1	3	.250	37	16	37	4.23	0
2008 Pawtucket......	Int.	4	9⅓	1	0	1.000	8	1	6	2.89	0
2008 Boston........	A.L.	36	88⅓	6	5	.545	68	40	68	3.16	0
Division Series											
2008 Boston........	A.L.	4	4	0	0	.000	3	3	6	2.25	0
Championship Series											
2008 Boston........	A.L.	5	5⅔	1	0	1.000	6	2	4	1.59	0

MATSUZAKA, DAISUKE

Born, Tokoyo, Japan, September 13, 1980.
Bats Right. Throws Right. Height, 6 feet. Weight, 185 pounds.

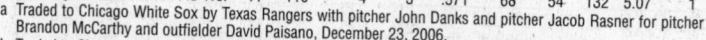

Year Club	Lea	G	IP	W	L	Pct	SO	BB	H	ERA	SAVES
1999 Seibu........	Japan Pac.	25	180	16	5	.762	151	87	124	2.60	0
2000 Seibu........	Japan Pac.	27	167⅔	14	7	.667	144	95	132	3.97	1
2001 Seibu........	Japan Pac.	33	240⅓	15	15	.500	214	117	184	3.60	0
2002 Seibu........	Japan Pac.	14	73⅔	6	2	.750	78	15	60	3.68	0
2003 Seibu........	Japan Pac.	29	194	16	7	.696	215	63	165	2.83	0
2004 Seibu........	Japan Pac.	23	146	10	6	.625	127	42	127	2.90	0
2005 Seibu........	Japan Pac.	28	215	14	13	.519	226	49	172	2.30	0
2006 Seibu a-b....	Japan Pac.	25	186⅓	17	5	.773	200	34	138	2.13	0
2007 Boston......	A.L.	32	204⅔	15	12	.556	201	80	191	4.40	0
2008 Pawtucket....	Int.	1	5	1	0	1.000	5	1	4	3.60	0
2008 Boston c.....	A.L.	29	167⅔	18	3	.857	154	*94	128	2.90	0
Major League Totals ....2 Yrs.		61	372⅓	33	15	.688	355	174	319	3.72	0

Year	Club	Lea	G	IP	W	L	Pct	SO	BB	H	ERA	SAVES
	Division Series											
2007 Boston	A.L.		1	4²/₃	0	0	.000	3	3	7	5.79	0
2008 Boston	A.L.		1	5	0	0	.000	5	3	8	5.40	0
Division Series Totals			2	9²/₃	0	0	.000	8	6	15	5.59	0
	Championship Series											
2007 Boston	A.L.		2	9²/₃	1	1	.500	9	2	12	5.59	0
2008 Boston	A.L.		2	11	1	0	1.000	11	6	9	4.09	0
Championship Series Totals			4	20²/₃	2	1	.667	20	8	21	4.79	0
	World Series Record											
2007 Boston	A.L.		1	5¹/₃	1	0	1.000	5	3	3	3.38	0

a Signed with Boston Red Sox, December 14, 2006.
b World Baseball Classic most valuable player.
c On disabled list from May 28 to June 21, 2008.

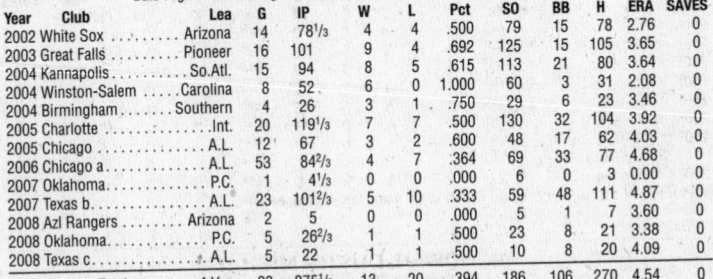

MC CARTHY, BRANDON PATRICK
Born, Glendale, California, July 7, 1983.
Bats Right. Throws Right. Height, 6 feet, 7 inches. Weight, 190 pounds.

Year	Club	Lea	G	IP	W	L	Pct	SO	BB	H	ERA	SAVES
2002 White Sox	Arizona	14	78¹/₃	4	4	.500	79	15	78	2.76	0
2003 Great Falls	Pioneer	16	101	9	4	.692	125	15	105	3.65	0
2004 Kannapolis..........	So.Atl.	15	94	8	5	.615	113	21	80	3.64	0
2004 Winston-Salem	Carolina	8	52	6	0	1.000	60	3	31	2.08	0
2004 Birmingham	Southern	4	26	3	1	.750	29	6	23	3.46	0
2005 Charlotte	Int.	20	119¹/₃	7	7	.500	130	32	104	3.92	0
2005 Chicago	A.L.	12	67	3	2	.600	48	17	62	4.03	0
2006 Chicago a	A.L.	53	84²/₃	4	7	.364	69	33	77	4.68	0
2007 Oklahoma...........	P.C.	1	4¹/₃	0	0	.000	6	0	3	0.00	0
2007 Texas b.............	A.L.	23	101²/₃	5	10	.333	59	48	111	4.87	0
2008 Azl Rangers	Arizona	2	5	0	0	.000	5	1	7	3.60	0
2008 Oklahoma..........	P.C.	5	26²/₃	1	1	.500	23	8	21	3.38	0
2008 Texas c............	A.L.	5	22	1	1	.500	10	8	20	4.09	0
Major League Totals ....4 Yrs.		93	275¹/₃	13	20	.394	186	106	270	4.54	0

a Traded to Texas Rangers with outfielder David Paisano for pitcher John Danks, pitcher Nick Masset and pitcher Jacob Rasner, December 23, 2006.
b On disabled list from June 10 to July 2 and August 11 to September 11, 2007.
c On disabled list from March 30 to August 7, 2008.

MC CLELLAN, KYLE WILLIAM
Born, Florissant, Missouri, June 12, 1984.
Bats Right. Throws Right. Height, 6 feet, 4 inches. Weight, 205 pounds.

Year	Club	Lea	G	IP	W	L	Pct	SO	BB	H	ERA	SAVES
2002 Johnson City	Appal.	7	12	0	2	.000	8	7	17	11.25	0
2003 Johnson City	Appal.	12	67²/₃	3	6	.333	44	16	74	3.99	0
2004 Peoria.............	Midwest	24	128	4	12	.250	84	34	143	5.34	0
2005 Quad Cities........	Midwest	17	54	1	4	.200	36	26	59	4.83	1
2006 Johnson City	Appal.	3	6²/₃	0	1	.000	4	3	7	9.45	0
2007 Palm Beach	Fla.St.	16	29	4	1	.800	24	4	22	1.24	0
2007 Springfield	Texas	24	30²/₃	2	0	1.000	30	6	24	2.35	0
2008 St. Louis.............	N.L.	68	75²/₃	2	7	.222	59	26	79	4.04	1

MC CLUNG, MICHAEL SETH (SETH)
Born, Lewisburg, West Virginia, February 7, 1981.
Bats Left. Throws Right. Height, 6 feet, 6 inches. Weight, 250 pounds.

Year	Club	Lea	G	IP	W	L	Pct	SO	BB	H	ERA	SAVES
1999 Princeton	Appal.	13	45²/₃	2	4	.333	46	48	53	7.69	0
2000 Hudson Valley	N.Y.-Penn.	8	43²/₃	2	2	.500	38	17	37	1.85	0
2000 Charleston-SC	So.Atl.	6	31	2	1	.667	26	19	30	3.19	0
2001 Charleston-SC	So.Atl.	28	164¹/₃	10	11	.476	165	53	142	2.79	0
2002 Bakersfield	Calif.	7	37	3	2	.600	48	11	35	2.92	0
2002 Orlando	Southern	20	114	5	7	.417	64	53	138	5.37	0
2003 Tampa Bay a........	A.L.	12	38²/₃	4	1	.800	25	25	33	5.35	0
2004 Durham	Int.	11	13²/₃	2	1	.667	12	7	10	3.29	0
2004 Charleston	So.Atl.	3	9¹/₃	0	0	.000	10	4	5	0.00	0
2004 Montgomery b	Southern	3	13¹/₃	1	1	.500	16	4	10	4.72	0
2005 Durham	Int.	6	18¹/₃	2	0	1.000	19	6	23	3.93	0

Year Club	Lea	G	IP	W	L	Pct	SO	BB	H	ERA	SAVES
2005 Tampa Bay	A.L.	34	109⅓	7	11	.389	92	62	106	6.59	0
2006 Durham	Int.	14	16⅓	1	0	1.000	26	2	16	2.20	5
2006 Tampa Bay	A.L.	39	103	6	12	.333	59	68	120	6.29	6
2007 Durham	Int.	40	58⅔	1	5	.167	68	43	38	1.99	5
2007 Nashville	P.C.	5	19	2	0	1.000	25	5	14	1.42	0
2007 Milwaukee c	N.L.	14	12	0	1	.000	11	5	11	3.75	0
2008 Milwaukee	N.L.	37	105⅓	6	6	.500	87	55	93	4.02	0
Major League Totals . . . . 5 Yrs.		136	368⅓	23	31	.426	274	215	363	5.55	6
Division Series											
2008 Milwaukee	N.L.	1	2	0	0	.000	1	3	2	0.00	0

a On disabled list from May 23 to October 31, 2003.
b On disabled list from February 23 to August 3, 2004.
c Traded to Milwaukee Brewers for pitcher Grant Balfour, July 27, 2007.

MC DONALD, JAMES ZELL

Born, Long Beach, California, October 19, 1984.
Bats Left. Throws Right. Height, 6 feet, 5 inches. Weight, 195 pounds.

Year Club	Lea	G	IP	W	L	Pct	SO	BB	H	ERA	SAVES
2003 Dodgers	Gulf Coast	12	48⅔	2	4	.333	47	15	39	3.33	0
2005 Ogden a	Pioneer	4	6	0	0	.000	9	2	4	1.50	0
2006 Columbus.	So.Atl.	30	142⅓	5	10	.333	146	65	119	3.98	0
2007 Inland Empire.	Calif.	16	82	6	7	.462	104	21	79	3.95	0
2007 Jacksonville	Southern	10	52⅔	7	2	.778	64	16	42	1.71	0
2008 Jacksonville	Southern	22	118⅔	5	3	.625	113	46	98	3.19	0
2008 Las Vegas.	P.C.	5	22⅓	2	1	.667	28	7	17	3.63	0
2008 Los Angeles . . . . N.L.		4	6	0	0	.000	2	1	5	0.00	0
Championship Series											
2008 Los Angeles	N.L.	2	5⅓	0	0	.000	7	2	3	0.00	0

a Played outfield for Dodgers (Gulf Coast) in 2004 and Ogden (Pioneer) in 2005.

MC GOWAN, DUSTIN MICHAEL

Born, Savannah, Georgia, March 24, 1982.
Bats Right. Throws Right. Height, 6 feet, 3 inches. Weight, 220 pounds.

Year Club	Lea	G	IP	W	L	Pct	SO	BB	H	ERA	SAVES
2000 Medicine Hat	Pioneer	8	25	0	3	.000	19	25	26	6.48	0
2001 Auburn.	N.Y.-Penn.	15	67	3	6	.333	80	49	57	3.76	0
2002 Charleston-WV.	So.Atl.	28	148⅓	11	10	.524	163	59	143	4.19	0
2003 New Haven.	Eastern	14	76⅔	7	0	1.000	72	19	78	3.17	0
2003 Dunedin	Fla.St.	14	75⅔	5	6	.455	66	25	62	2.85	0
2004 New Hampshire	Eastern	6	31	2	0	1.000	29	15	24	4.06	0
2005 Dunedin	Fla.St.	5	21	0	1	.000	20	5	21	4.29	0
2005 New Hampshire	Eastern	6	35	0	2	.000	33	10	35	3.34	0
2005 Toronto	A.L.	13	45⅓	1	3	.250	34	17	49	6.35	0
2006 Syracuse	Int.	23	84	4	5	.444	86	39	77	4.39	1
2006 Toronto	A.L.	16	27⅓	1	2	.333	22	25	35	7.24	0
2007 Syracuse	Int.	5	22	0	2	.000	29	9	16	1.64	0
2007 Toronto	A.L.	27	169⅔	12	10	.545	144	61	146	4.08	0
2008 Toronto a	A.L.	19	111⅓	6	7	.462	85	38	115	4.37	0
Major League Totals . . . . 4 Yrs.		75	353⅔	20	22	.476	285	141	345	4.71	0

a On disabled list from July 9 to October 2, 2008.

MECHE, GILBERT ALLEN (GIL)

Born, Lafayette, Louisiana, September 8, 1978.
Bats Right. Throws Right. Height, 6 feet, 3 inches. Weight, 220 pounds.

Year Club	Lea	G	IP	W	L	Pct	SO	BB	H	ERA	SAVES
1996 Mariners.	Arizona	2	9	0	1	.000	4	1	4	6.00	0
1997 Everett	Northwest	12	74⅔	3	4	.429	62	24	75	3.98	0
1997 Wisconsin	Midwest	2	12	0	2	.000	14	4	12	3.00	0
1998 Wisconsin	Midwest	26	149	8	7	.533	168	63	136	3.44	0
1999 New Haven	Eastern	10	59	3	4	.429	56	26	51	3.05	0
1999 Tacoma	P.C.	6	31	2	2	.500	24	13	31	3.19	0
1999 Seattle	A.L.	16	85⅔	8	4	.667	47	57	73	4.73	0
2000 Seattle	A.L.	15	85⅔	4	4	.500	60	40	75	3.78	0
2000 Tacoma	P.C.	3	14	1	1	.500	15	10	10	3.86	0
2000 Wisconsin	Midwest	1	5	0	0	.000	6	2	1	0.00	0
2000 Everett a	Northwest	1	1	0	1	.000	0	0	3	9.00	0

Year	Club	Lea	G	IP	W	L	Pct	SO	BB	H	ERA	SAVES
2001 Seattle b		A.L.			INJURED—Did Not Play							0
2002 San Antonio	Texas		25	65	4	6	.400	56	32	68	6.51	0
2003 Seattle		A.L.	32	186¹/₃	15	13	.536	130	63	187	4.59	0
2004 Tacoma		P.C.	10	57	1	3	.250	45	27	55	5.05	0
2004 Seattle		A.L.	23	127²/₃	7	7	.500	99	47	139	5.01	0
2005 Seattle c		A.L.	29	143¹/₃	10	8	.556	83	72	153	5.09	0
2006 Seattle d		A.L.	32	186²/₃	11	8	.579	156	84	183	4.48	0
2007 Kansas City		A.L.	34	216	9	13	.409	156	62	218	3.67	0
2008 Kansas City		A.L.	34	210¹/₃	14	11	.560	183	73	204	3.98	0
Major League Totals	8 Yrs.		215	1241²/₃	78	68	.534	914	498	1232	4.36	0

a On disabled list from May 29 to June 12 and July 31 to October 1, 2000.
b On disabled list from March 31 to November 6, 2001.
c On disabled list from August 20 to September 16, 2005.
d Filed for free agency, October 28, 2006. Signed with Kansas City Royals, December 7, 2006.

MEREDITH, OLISE CLA (CLA)

Born, Richmond, Virginia, June 4, 1983.
Bats Right. Throws Right. Height, 6 feet. Weight, 180 pounds.

Year	Club	Lea	G	IP	W	L	Pct	SO	BB	H	ERA	SAVES
2004 Sarasota		Fla.St.	16	16¹/₃	0	2	.000	16	3	15	2.20	12
2004 Augusta		So.Atl.	13	15¹/₃	1	0	1.000	18	3	8	0.00	6
2005 Portland		Eastern	12	15	1	0	1.000	12	3	5	0.00	9
2005 Boston		A.L.	3	2¹/₃	0	0	.000	0	4	1	27.00	0
2005 Wilmington		Carolina	1	1	0	0	.000	2	0	1	0.00	0
2005 Pawtucket		Int.	40	48¹/₃	2	5	.286	42	12	63	5.59	10
2006 Portland		P.C.	24	32¹/₃	3	0	1.000	24	4	26	1.39	2
2006 Pawtucket		Int.	8	13²/₃	0	0	.000	14	5	16	5.27	0
2006 San Diego a		N.L.	45	50²/₃	5	1	.833	37	6	30	1.07	0
2007 San Diego		N.L.	80	79²/₃	5	6	.455	59	17	94	3.50	0
2008 Portland		P.C.	6	6²/₃	0	0	.000	4	3	6	2.70	0
2008 San Diego		N.L.	73	70¹/₃	0	3	.000	49	24	79	4.09	0
Major League Totals	4 Yrs.		201	203	10	10	.500	145	51	209	3.37	0
Division Series												
2006 San Diego		N.L.	2	3²/₃	0	0	.000	3	0	3	0.00	0

a Traded to San Diego Padres with catcher Josh Bard for catcher Doug Mirabelli, May 1, 2006.

MIJARES, JOSE MANUEL

Born, Caracas, Venezuela, October 29, 1984.
Bats Left. Throws Left. Height, 6 feet. Weight, 230 pounds.

Year	Club	Lea	G	IP	W	L	Pct	SO	BB	H	ERA	SAVES
2004 Twins		Gulf Coast	19	29²/₃	4	0	1.000	25	15	22	2.43	5
2005 Fort Myers		Fla.St.	5	12	0	0	.000	17	5	5	1.50	0
2005 Beloit		Midwest	20	54¹/₃	6	3	.667	78	40	43	4.31	2
2006 Fort Myers		Fla.St.	27	63	3	5	.375	77	27	52	3.57	9
2007 New Britain		Eastern	46	61	5	3	.625	75	48	40	3.54	5
2007 Rochester		Int.	5	8²/₃	0	1	.000	6	5	9	6.23	0
2008 Twins		Gulf Coast	7	11	2	1	.667	16	1	10	2.45	0
2008 Fort Myers		Fla.St.	5	10¹/₃	0	0	.000	8	3	7	2.61	0
2008 New Britain		Eastern	11	15¹/₃	1	1	.500	17	7	16	2.93	2
2008 Minnesota		A.L.	10	10¹/₃	0	0	.000	5	0	3	0.87	0

MILLER, ANDREW MARK

Born, Gainesville, Florida, May 21, 1985.
Bats Left. Throws Left. Height, 6 feet, 6 inches. Weight, 210 pounds.

Year	Club	Lea	G	IP	W	L	Pct	SO	BB	H	ERA	SAVES
2006 Lakeland		Fla.St.	3	5	0	0	.000	9	1	2	0.00	0
2006 Detroit		A.L.	8	10¹/₃	0	1	.000	6	10	8	6.10	0
2007 Aberdeen		N.Y.-Penn.	16	55	3	5	.375	40	17	66	4.91	0
2007 Lakeland		Fla.St.	7	41¹/₃	1	4	.200	28	15	43	3.48	0
2007 Erie		Eastern	4	30²/₃	2	0	1.000	24	5	22	0.59	0
2007 Toledo		Int.	2	6	0	0	.000	9	5	6	9.00	0
2007 Detroit a-b		A.L.	13	64	5	5	.500	56	39	73	5.63	0
2008 Marlins		Gulf Coast	1	1	0	1	.000	0	1	2	18.00	0
2008 Jupiter		Fla.St.	4	12²/₃	1	0	1.000	11	1	10	0.71	0
2008 Carolina		Southern	1	5²/₃	0	0	.000	6	4	2	3.18	0

Year Club	Lea	G	IP	W	L	Pct	SO	BB	H	ERA	SAVES
2008 Florida c	N.L.	29	107¹/₃	6	10	.375	89	56	120	5.87	0
Major League Totals . . . . 3 Yrs.		50	181²/₃	11	16	.407	151	105	201	5.80	0

a On disabled list from August 4 to August 24, 2007.
b Traded to Florida Marlins with pitcher Burke Badenhop, pitcher Eulogio De La Cruz, catcher Mike Rabelo and outfielder Cameron Maybin for pitcher Dontrelle Willis and infielder Miguel Cabrera, December 5, 2007.
c On disabled list from July 14 to September 1, 2008.

MILLER, JUSTIN MARK

Born, Torrance, California, August 27, 1977.
Bats Right. Throws Right. Height, 6 feet, 2 inches. Weight, 200 pounds.

Year Club	Lea	G	IP	W	L	Pct	SO	BB	H	ERA	SAVES
1997 Portland	Northwest	14	67¹/₃	4	2	.667	54	20	68	2.14	0
1998 Asheville	So.Atl.	27	163¹/₃	13	8	.619	142	40	177	3.69	0
1999 Salem a-b	Carolina	8	37	1	2	.333	35	11	35	4.14	0
2000 Sacramento	P.C.	9	54²/₃	4	1	.800	34	13	42	2.47	0
2000 Midland	Texas	18	87	5	4	.556	82	41	74	4.55	0
2001 Sacramento c	P.C.	29	165	7	10	.412	134	64	174	4.75	0
2002 Syracuse	Int.	8	44²/₃	3	2	.600	29	16	34	1.61	0
2002 Toronto	A.L.	25	102¹/₃	9	5	.643	68	66	103	5.54	0
2003 Dunedin	Fla.St.	1	6	0	1	.000	5	2	3	4.50	0
2004 Syracuse	Int.	3	16²/₃	1	1	.500	21	4	16	2.16	0
2004 Toronto d	A.L.	19	81²/₃	3	4	.429	47	42	101	6.06	0
2005 Toronto	A.L.	1	2¹/₃	0	0	.000	2	0	5	15.43	0
2005 Syracuse	Int.	28	50¹/₃	3	1	.750	56	14	39	2.32	2
2006 Durham e	Int.	5	7	2	0	1.000	11	2	5	3.86	1
2007 Albuquerque	P.C.	11	12	0	0	.000	20	4	9	1.50	6
2007 Ottawa	Int.	3	2¹/₃	0	0	.000	2	3	4	3.86	0
2007 Florida f-g	N.L.	62	61²/₃	5	0	1.000	74	24	53	3.65	0
2008 Marlins	Gulf Coast	1	1	0	0	.000	2	0	2	9.00	0
2008 Jupiter	Fla.St.	3	3	1	0	1.000	3	1	2	0.00	0
2008 Albuquerque	P.C.	1	0²/₃	0	0	.000	1	0	4	40.50	0
2008 Florida h-i	N.L.	46	46²/₃	4	2	.667	43	20	46	4.24	0
Major League Totals . . . . 5 Yrs.		153	294²/₃	21	11	.656	234	152	308	5.16	0

a Traded to Milwaukee Brewers by Colorado Rockies with catcher Henry Blanco and pitcher Jamey Wright for infielder Jeff Cirillo and pitcher Scott Karl, December 13, 1999.
b Traded to Oakland A's for pitcher Jimmy Haynes, December 13, 1999.
c Traded to Toronto Blue Jays with infielder Eric Hinske for pitcher Billy Koch, December 7, 2001.
d On disabled list from May 31 to August 4, 2004.
e Filed for free agency, October 3, 2005. Signed with Tampa Bay Devil Rays, January 11, 2006.
f Released by Tampa Bay Devil Rays, March 31, 2007. Signed with Philadelphia Phillies organization, April 1, 2007.
g Released by Philadelphia Phillies, April 19, 2007. Signed with Florida Marlins organization, April 24, 2007.
h On disabled list from July 5 to July 24, 2008.
i Elected free agency, August 15, 2008. Signed with San Francisco Giants organization, November 2, 2008.

MILLER, TREVER DOUGLAS

Born, Louisville, Kentucky, May 29, 1973.
Bats Right. Throws Left. Height, 6 feet, 3 inches. Weight, 200 pounds.

Year Club	Lea	G	IP	W	L	Pct	SO	BB	H	ERA	SAVES
1991 Bristol	Appal.	13	54	2	7	.222	46	29	60	5.67	0
1992 Bristol	Appal.	12	69¹/₃	3	8	.273	64	27	75	4.93	0
1993 Fayetteville	So.Atl.	28	161	8	13	.381	116	67	151	4.19	0
1994 Trenton	Eastern	26	174¹/₃	7	16	.304	73	51	198	4.39	0
1995 Jacksonville	Southern	31	122¹/₃	8	2	.800	77	34	122	2.72	0
1996 Toledo	Int.	27	165¹/₃	13	6	.684	115	65	167	4.90	0
1996 Detroit a	A.L.	5	16²/₃	0	4	.000	8	9	28	9.18	0
1997 New Orleans	A.A.	29	163²/₃	6	7	.462	99	54	177	3.30	0
1998 Houston	N.L.	37	53¹/₃	2	0	1.000	30	20	57	3.04	1
1999 Houston	N.L.	47	49²/₃	3	2	.600	37	29	58	5.07	1
2000 Phil.-Los Angeles b-c . .	N.L.	16	16¹/₃	0	0	.000	11	12	27	10.47	0
2000 Albuquerque	P.C.	12	58	4	2	.667	39	20	60	3.41	0
2001 Sarasota	Fla.St.	3	8	0	0	.000	6	1	3	2.25	0
2001 Pawtucket d-e	Int.	33	116	3	11	.214	93	34	142	5.20	0
2002 Louisville f	Int.	65	82	9	5	.643	80	23	76	3.18	0
2003 Toronto g	A.L.	*79	52²/₃	2	2	.500	44	28	46	4.61	4
2004 Tampa Bay	A.L.	60	49	1	1	.500	43	15	48	3.12	1
2005 Tampa Bay h-i	A.L.	61	44¹/₃	2	2	.500	35	29	45	4.06	0
2006 Round Rock	P.C.	2	2	0	0	.000	3	0	0	0.00	0

Year	Club	Lea	G	IP	W	L	Pct	SO	BB	H	ERA	SAVES
2006 Houston j	N.L.	70	50²/₃	2	3	.400	56	13	42	3.02	1
2007 Houston k	N.L.	76	46¹/₃	0	0	.000	46	23	45	4.86	1
2008 Tampa Bay l	A.L.	68	43¹/₃	2	0	1.000	44	20	39	4.15	2
Major League Totals .... 10 Yrs.		519	422¹/₃	14	14	.500	354	198	435	4.43	10
Division Series											
1998 Houston	N.L.	1	0	0	0	.000	0	1	0	INF	0
1999 Houston	N.L.	2	1¹/₃	0	0	.000	2	0	1	0.00	0
2008 Tampa Bay	N.L.	1	0	0	0	.000	0	1	0	INF	0
Division Series Totals		4	1¹/₃	0	0	.000	2	2	1	0.00	0
Championship Series											
2008 Tampa Bay	N.L.	3	0²/₃	0	0	.000	1	1	1	0.00	0
World Series Record											
2008 Tampa Bay	N.L.	2	1	0	0	.000	1	1	1	18.00	0

a Traded to Houston Astros with catcher Brad Ausmus, pitcher C.J. Nitkowski, pitcher Jose Lima and infielder Daryle Ward for outfielder Brian Hunter, infielder Orlando Miller, pitcher Todd Jones and pitcher Doug Brocail, December 10, 1996.
b Traded to Philadelphia Phillies for pitcher Yorkis Perez, March 29, 2000.
c Claimed on waivers by Los Angeles Dodgers, May 19, 2000.
d Filed for free agency, October 15, 2000. Signed with Boston Red Sox organization, January 22, 2001.
e Filed for free agency, October 15, 2001. Signed with Cincinnati Reds organization, November 8, 2001.
f Released by Cincinnati Reds, September 4, 2002. Signed with Toronto Blue Jays, November 13, 2002.
g Not offered contract, December 21, 2003. Signed with Tampa Bay Devil Rays, January 6, 2004.
h On disabled list from June 13 to June 28, 2005.
i Not offered contract, December 21, 2005. Signed with Houston Astros, January 9, 2006.
j On disabled list from April 19 to May 12, 2006.
k Filed for free agency, October 29, 2007. Signed with Tampa Bay Rays, February 6, 2008.
l Not offered contract, November 3, 2008. Signed with St. Louis Cardinals, December 3, 2008.

MILLWOOD, KEVIN AUSTIN

Born, Gastonia, North Carolina, December 24, 1974.
Bats Right. Throws Right. Height, 6 feet, 4 inches. Weight, 230 pounds.

Year	Club	Lea	G	IP	W	L	Pct	SO	BB	H	ERA	SAVES
1993 Braves	Gulf Coast	12	50	3	3	.500	49	28	36	3.06	0
1994 Macon	So. Atl.	12	32²/₃	0	5	.000	24	32	31	5.79	1
1994 Danville	Appal.	13	46	3	3	.500	56	34	42	3.72	1
1995 Macon	So. Atl.	29	103	5	6	.455	89	57	86	4.63	1
1996 Durham	Carolina	33	149¹/₃	6	9	.400	139	58	138	4.28	1
1997 Greenville	Southern	11	61¹/₃	3	5	.375	61	24	59	4.11	0
1997 Richmond	Int.	9	60²/₃	7	0	1.000	46	16	38	1.93	0
1997 Atlanta	N.L.	12	51¹/₃	5	3	.625	42	21	55	4.03	0
1998 Atlanta	N.L.	31	174¹/₃	17	8	.680	163	56	175	4.08	0
1999 Atlanta	N.L.	33	228	18	7	.720	205	59	168	2.68	0
2000 Atlanta	N.L.	36	212²/₃	10	13	.435	168	62	213	4.66	0
2001 Macon	So.Atl.	1	3	0	0	.000	5	0	0	0.00	0
2001 Greenville	Southern	2	10	0	1	.000	10	3	9	4.50	0
2001 Atlanta a	N.L.	21	121	7	7	.500	84	40	121	4.31	0
2002 Atlanta b	N.L.	35	217	18	8	.692	178	65	186	3.24	0
2003 Philadelphia c-d	N.L.	35	222	14	12	.538	169	68	210	4.01	0
2004 Philadelphia e-f	N.L.	25	141	9	6	.600	125	51	155	4.85	0
2005 Cleveland g-h	A.L.	30	192	9	11	.450	146	52	182	*2.86	0
2006 Texas	A.L.	34	215	16	12	.571	157	53	228	4.52	0
2007 Frisco	Texas	1	5	0	0	.000	3	1	1	0.00	0
2007 Texas i	A.L.	31	172²/₃	10	14	.417	123	67	213	5.16	0
2008 Frisco	Texas	1	4	0	1	.000	6	2	5	2.25	0
2008 Texas j	A.L.	29	168²/₃	9	10	.474	125	49	220	5.07	0
Major League Totals .... 12 Yrs.		352	2115²/₃	142	111	.561	1685	643	2126	4.06	0
Division Series											
1999 Atlanta	N.L.	2	10	1	0	1.000	9	0	1	0.90	1
2000 Atlanta	N.L.	1	4²/₃	0	1	.000	3	3	4	7.71	0
2002 Atlanta	N.L.	2	11	1	1	.500	14	0	7	3.27	0
Division Series Totals		5	25²/₃	2	2	.500	26	3	12	3.16	1
Championship Series											
1999 Atlanta	N.L.	2	12²/₃	1	0	1.000	9	1	13	3.55	0
2001 Atlanta	N.L.	1	1	0	0	.000	1	0	0	0.00	0
Championship Series Totals		3	13²/₃	1	0	1.000	10	1	13	3.29	0
World Series											
1999 Atlanta	N.L.	1	2	0	1	.000	2	2	8	18.00	0

a On disabled list from May 7 to July 20, 2001.

b Traded to Philadelphia Phillies for catcher Johnny Estrada, December 20, 2002.
c Pitched no-hit, no-run game against San Francisco Giants, April 27, 2003.
d Filed for free agency, October 29, 2003, re-signed with Philadelphia Phillies, December 19, 2003.
e On disabled list from August 6 to September 12, 2004.
f Filed for free agency, October 28, 2004. Signed with Cleveland Indians, January 7, 2005.
g On disabled list from May 26 to June 16, 2005.
h Filed for free agency, October 28, 2005. Signed with Texas Rangers, December 29, 2005.
i On disabled list from April 29 to May 14 and May 15 to June 1, 2007.
j On disabled list from May 11 to May 28 and July 24 to August 15, 2008.

MINER, ZACHARY CHARLES (ZACH)
Born, St. Louis, Missouri, March 12, 1982.
Bats Right. Throws Right. Height, 6 feet, 3 inches. Weight, 200 pounds.

Year	Club	Lea	G	IP	W	L	Pct	SO	BB	H	ERA	SAVES
2001 Jamestown	N.Y.-Penn.	15	90²/₃	3	4	.429	68	16	76	1.89	0
2002 Macon	So.Atl.	29	159	8	9	.471	131	51	143	3.28	0
2003 Myrtle Beach	Carolina	27	153²/₃	6	10	.375	88	61	150	3.69	0
2004 Greenville	Southern	27	129¹/₃	6	10	.375	111	55	132	5.22	0
2005 Richmond	Int.	17	89¹/₃	2	7	.222	63	45	97	4.23	0
2005 Toledo	Int.	6	34¹/₃	3	1	.750	20	20	28	2.36	0
2005 Mississippi a	Southern	4	16²/₃	0	1	.000	18	5	21	4.32	1
2006 Toledo	Int.	9	51	6	0	1.000	40	21	43	2.82	0
2006 Detroit	A.L.	27	93	7	6	.538	59	32	100	4.84	0
2007 Erie	Eastern	2	2	0	0	.000	2	1	4	4.50	0
2007 Toledo	Int.	11	51²/₃	1	4	.200	33	22	43	4.88	0
2007 Detroit b	A.L.	34	53²/₃	3	4	.429	34	22	56	3.02	0
2008 Toledo	Int.	4	10²/₃	0	1	.000	15	3	11	3.38	0
2008 Detroit	A.L.	45	118	8	5	.615	62	46	118	4.27	0
Major League Totals	3 Yrs.	106	264²/₃	18	15	.545	155	100	274	4.22	0
World Series Record											
2006 Detroit	A.L.	1	0²/₃	0	0	.000	0	0	0	0.00	0

a Traded by Atlanta Braves to Detroit Tigers with pitcher Roman Colon for pitcher Kyle Farnsworth, July 26, 2005.
b On disabled list from June 6 to June 29, 2007.

MOEHLER, BRIAN MERRITT
Born, Rockingham, North Carolina, December 31, 1971.
Bats Right. Throws Right. Height, 6 feet, 3 inches. Weight, 235 pounds.

Year	Club	Lea	G	IP	W	L	Pct	SO	BB	H	ERA	SAVES
1993 Niagara Fls	N.Y.-Penn.	12	58²/₃	6	5	.545	38	27	51	3.22	0
1994 Lakeland	Fla.St.	26	164²/₃	12	12	.500	92	65	153	3.01	0
1995 Jacksnville	Southern	28	162¹/₃	8	10	.444	89	52	176	4.82	0
1996 Jacksnville	Southern	28	173¹/₃	15	6	.714	120	50	186	3.48	0
1996 Detroit	A.L.	2	10¹/₃	0	1	.000	2	8	11	4.35	0
1997 Detroit a	A.L.	31	175¹/₃	11	12	.478	97	61	198	4.67	0
1998 Detroit	A.L.	33	221¹/₃	14	13	.519	123	56	220	3.90	0
1999 Detroit	A.L.	32	196¹/₃	10	*16	.385	106	59	229	5.04	0
2000 Detroit	A.L.	29	178	12	9	.571	103	40	222	4.50	0
2000 West Michigan b	Midwest	1	6¹/₃	0	1	.000	4	1	5	4.26	0
2001 Detroit	A.L.	1	8	0	0	.000	2	1	6	3.38	0
2001 Toledo c	Int.	2	10¹/₃	0	2	.000	6	2	12	4.35	0
2002 Lakeland	Fla.St.	2	12¹/₃	1	1	.500	7	1	10	2.92	0
2002 Toledo	Int.	4	24	2	1	.667	7	3	28	4.88	0
2002 Detroit	A.L.	3	19²/₃	1	1	.500	13	2	17	2.29	0
2002 Cincinnati d-e-f	N.L.	10	43¹/₃	2	4	.333	18	11	61	6.02	0
2003 Houston	N.L.	3	13²/₃	0	0	.000	5	6	22	7.90	0
2003 New Orleans g-h	P.C.	1	2	0	0	.000	3	0	3	4.50	0
2004 Greenville i-j	Southern	20	108	3	9	.250	57	27	113	4.17	0
2005 Florida k	N.L.	37	158¹/₃	6	12	.333	95	42	198	4.55	0
2006 Marlins	Gulf Coast	1	5	0	1	.000	4	0	8	3.60	0
2006 Florida l-m	N.L.	29	122	7	11	.389	58	38	164	6.57	0
2007 Houston n-o	N.L.	42	59²/₃	1	4	.200	36	17	67	4.07	1
2008 Houston	N.L.	31	150	11	8	.579	82	36	166	4.56	0
Major League Totals	12 Yrs.	283	1356	75	91	.452	740	377	1581	4.73	1

a On disabled list from August 7 to August 22, 1997.
b On disabled list from April 17 to May 18, 2000.
c On disabled list from April 6 to November 14, 2001.
d On disabled list from August 28 to September 13, 2002.
e On disabled list from March 22 to July 3, 2002.

f Traded to Cincinnati Reds with infielder Matt Boone for infielder David Espinosa, two players to be named later, July 23, 2002. Detroit Tigers received outfielder Gary Varner to complete trade, August 30, 2002.
g Filed for free agency, October 28, 2002. Signed with Houston Astros, January 17, 2003.
h On disabled list from April 17 to September 29, 2003.
i Filed for free agency, October 27, 2003. Signed with Atlanta Braves organization, February 17, 2004.
j Filed for free agency, October 15, 2004. Signed with Florida Marlins organization, December 14, 2004.
k Filed for free agency, October 27, 2005, re-signed with Florida Marlins, December 7, 2005.
l On disabled list from July 2 to July 30, 2006.
m Filed for free agency, October 28, 2006. Signed with Houston Astros organization, January 19, 2007.
n Filed for free agency, October 29, 2007.
o Signed with Houston Astros organization, January 29, 2008.

MORROW, BRANDON JOHN

Born, Santa Rosa, California, July 26, 1984.
Bats Right. Throws Right. Height, 6 feet, 3 inches. Weight, 190 pounds.

Year	Club	Lea	G	IP	W	L	Pct	SO	BB	H	ERA	SAVES
2006 Mariners	Arizona		7	13	0	2	.000	13	9	10	2.77	0
2006 Inland Empire	Calif.		1	3	0	0	.000	4	0	0	0.00	0
2007 Seattle	A.L.		60	63⅓	3	4	.429	66	50	56	4.12	0
2008 West Tenn	Southern		6	7⅓	0	0	.000	8	6	3	0.00	0
2008 Tacoma	P.C.		6	23⅓	1	2	.333	26	11	17	5.01	0
2008 Seattle	A.L.		45	64⅔	3	4	.429	75	34	40	3.34	10
Major League Totals	2 Yrs.		105	128	6	8	.429	141	84	96	3.73	10

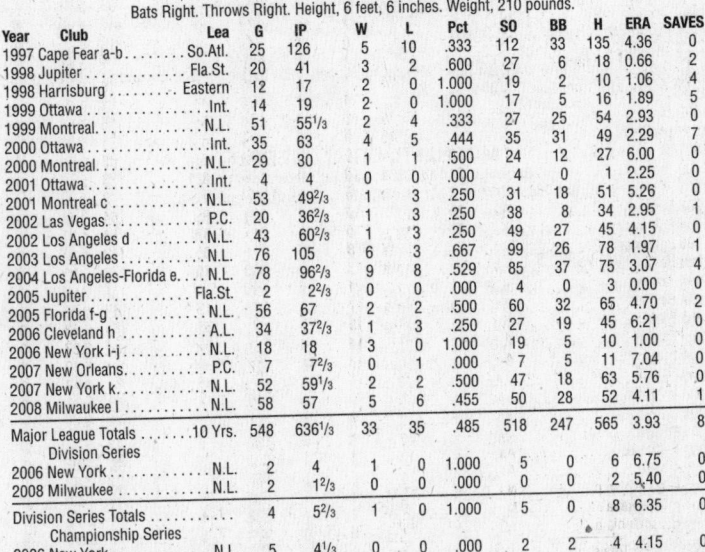

MOTA, GUILLERMO

Born, San Pedro de Macoris, Dominican Republic, July 25, 1973.
Bats Right. Throws Right. Height, 6 feet, 6 inches. Weight, 210 pounds.

Year	Club	Lea	G	IP	W	L	Pct	SO	BB	H	ERA	SAVES
1997 Cape Fear a-b	So.Atl.		25	126	5	10	.333	112	33	135	4.36	0
1998 Jupiter	Fla.St.		20	41	3	2	.600	27	6	18	0.66	2
1998 Harrisburg	Eastern		12	17	2	0	1.000	19	2	10	1.06	4
1999 Ottawa	Int.		14	19	2	0	1.000	17	5	16	1.89	5
1999 Montreal	N.L.		51	55⅓	2	4	.333	35	25	54	2.93	0
2000 Ottawa	Int.		35	63	4	5	.444	35	31	49	2.29	7
2000 Montreal	N.L.		29	30	1	1	.500	24	12	27	6.00	0
2001 Ottawa	Int.		4	4	0	0	.000	4	0	1	2.25	0
2001 Montreal c	N.L.		53	49⅔	1	3	.250	31	18	51	5.26	0
2002 Las Vegas	P.C.		20	36⅔	1	3	.250	38	8	34	2.95	1
2002 Los Angeles d	N.L.		43	60⅔	1	3	.250	49	27	45	4.15	0
2003 Los Angeles	N.L.		76	105	6	3	.667	99	26	78	1.97	1
2004 Los Angeles-Florida e	N.L.		78	96⅔	9	8	.529	85	37	75	3.07	4
2005 Jupiter	Fla.St.		2	2⅔	0	0	.000	4	0	3	0.00	2
2005 Florida f-g	N.L.		56	67	2	2	.500	60	32	65	4.70	2
2006 Cleveland h	A.L.		34	37⅔	1	3	.250	27	19	45	6.21	0
2006 New York i-j	N.L.		18	18	3	0	1.000	19	5	10	1.00	0
2007 New Orleans	P.C.		7	7⅔	0	1	.000	7	5	11	7.04	0
2007 New York k	N.L.		52	59⅓	2	2	.500	47	18	63	5.76	0
2008 Milwaukee l	N.L.		58	57	5	6	.455	50	28	52	4.11	1
Major League Totals	10 Yrs.		548	636⅓	33	35	.485	518	247	565	3.93	8
Division Series												
2006 New York	N.L.		2	4	1	0	1.000	5	0	6	6.75	0
2008 Milwaukee	N.L.		2	1⅔	0	0	.000	0	0	2	5.40	0
Division Series Totals			4	5⅔	1	0	1.000	5	0	8	6.35	0
Championship Series												
2006 New York	N.L.		5	4⅓	0	0	.000	2	2	4	4.15	0

a Played infield, starting in the Dominican Summer League and finishing in the Florida State League, from 1991 to 1996.
b Selected by Montreal Expos from New York Mets in Rule V draft, December 9, 1996.
c On disabled list from July 13 to September 1, 2001.
d Traded to Los Angeles Dodgers with outfielder Wilkin Ruan for pitcher Matt Herges and infielder Jorge Nunez, March 23, 2002.
e Traded to Florida Marlins with catcher Paul LoDuca and outfielder Juan Encarnacion for pitcher Brad Penny, pitcher Bill Murphy and infielder Hee Seop Choi, July 30, 2004.
f On disabled list from May 1 to May 27, 2005.
g Traded to Boston Red Sox with pitcher Josh Beckett and infielder Mike Lowell for infielder Hanley Ramirez, pitcher Anibal Sanchez and pitcher Jesus Delgado, November 24, 2005.
h Traded to Cleveland Indians with infielder Andy Marte and catcher Kelly Shoppach for outfielder Coco Crisp, pitcher David Riske and catcher Josh Bard, January 27, 2006.

i Traded to New York Mets for player to be named later, August 20, 2006.
j Filed for free agency, October 30, 2006, re-signed with New York Mets, December 7, 2006.
k Traded to Milwaukee Brewers for catcher Johnny Estrada, November 20, 2007.
l Filed for free agency, November 3, 2008. Signed with Los Angeles Dodgers, January 14, 2009.

MOTTE, JASON LOUIS
Born, Port Huron, Michigan, June 22, 1982.
Bats Right. Throws Right. Height, 6 feet. Weight, 195 pounds.

Year	Club	Lea	G	IP	W	L	Pct	SO	BB	H	ERA	SAVES
2006 Quad Cities	....	Midwest	8	12²/₃	1	1	.500	13	3	16	4.97	0
2006 State College a	....	N.Y.-Penn.	21	26¹/₃	1	2	.333	25	4	30	3.08	8
2007 Palm Beach	....	Fla.St.	9	10	1	0	1.000	6	1	7	0.90	3
2007 Springfield	....	Texas	44	49	3	3	.500	63	22	36	2.20	8
2008 Memphis	....	P.C.	63	66²/₃	4	3	.571	110	26	64	3.24	9
2008 St. Louis	....	N.L.	12	11	0	0	.000	16	3	5	0.82	1

a Played catcher 2003-2006.

MOYER, JAMIE
Born, Sellersville, Pennsylvania, November 18, 1962.
Bats Left. Throws Left. Height, 6 feet. Weight, 180 pounds.

Year	Club	Lea	G	IP	W	L	Pct	SO	BB	H	ERA	SAVES
1984 Geneva	....	N.Y.-Penn.	14	*104²/₃	*9	3	.750	*120	31	59	1.89	0
1985 Winston-Salem	....	Carolina	12	94	8	2	.800	94	22	82	2.30	0
1985 Pittsfield	....	Eastern	15	96²/₃	7	6	.538	51	32	99	3.72	0
1986 Pittsfield	....	Eastern	6	41	3	1	.750	42	16	27	0.88	0
1986 Iowa	....	A.A.	6	42¹/₃	3	2	.600	25	11	25	2.55	0
1986 Chicago	....	N.L.	16	87¹/₃	7	4	.636	45	42	107	5.05	0
1987 Chicago	....	N.L.	35	201	12	15	.444	147	97	210	5.10	0
1988 Chicago a	....	N.L.	34	202	9	15	.375	121	55	212	3.48	0
1989 Charlotte Rangers	....	Gulf C.	3	11	1	0	1.000	18	1	8	1.64	0
1989 Tulsa	....	Texas	2	12¹/₃	1	1	.500	9	3	16	5.11	0
1989 Texas b	....	A.L.	15	76	4	9	.308	44	33	84	4.86	0
1990 Texas c	....	A.L.	33	102¹/₃	2	6	.250	58	39	115	4.66	0
1991 Louisville	....	A.A.	20	125²/₃	5	10	.333	69	43	125	3.80	0
1991 St. Louis d-e	....	N.L.	8	31¹/₃	0	5	.000	20	16	38	5.74	0
1992 Toledo f	....	Int.	21	138²/₃	10	8	.556	80	37	128	2.86	0
1993 Rochester	....	Int.	8	54	6	0	1.000	41	13	42	1.67	0
1993 Baltimore	....	A.L.	25	152	12	9	.571	90	38	154	3.43	0
1994 Baltimore	....	A.L.	23	149	5	7	.417	87	38	158	4.77	0
1995 Baltimore g-h	....	A.L.	27	115²/₃	8	6	.571	65	30	117	5.21	0
1996 Boston-Seattle i-j-k	....	A.L.	34	160²/₃	13	3	*.813	79	46	177	3.98	0
1997 Tacoma	....	P.C.	1	5	1	0	1.000	6	0	1	0.00	0
1997 Seattle l	....	A.L.	30	188²/₃	17	5	.773	113	43	187	3.86	0
1998 Seattle	....	A.L.	34	234¹/₃	15	9	.625	158	42	234	3.53	0
1999 Seattle	....	A.L.	32	228	14	8	.636	137	48	235	3.87	0
2000 Seattle m	....	A.L.	26	154	13	10	.565	98	53	173	5.49	0
2001 Seattle	....	A.L.	33	209²/₃	20	6	.769	119	44	187	3.43	0
2002 Seattle n	....	A.L.	34	230²/₃	13	8	.619	147	50	198	3.32	0
2003 Seattle	....	A.L.	33	215	21	7	.750	129	66	199	3.27	0
2004 Seattle	....	A.L.	34	202	7	13	.350	125	63	217	5.21	0
2005 Seattle o	....	A.L.	32	200	13	7	.650	102	52	225	4.28	0
2006 Seattle	....	A.L.	25	160	6	12	.333	82	44	179	4.39	0
2006 Philadelphia p	....	N.L.	8	51¹/₃	5	2	.714	26	7	49	4.03	0
2007 Philadelphia	....	N.L.	33	199¹/₃	14	12	.538	133	66	222	5.01	0
2008 Philadelphia q	....	N.L.	33	196¹/₃	16	7	.696	123	62	199	3.71	0
Major League Totals	....	22 Yrs.	637	3746²/₃	246	185	.571	2248	1074	3876	4.19	0
Divisional Series												
1997 Seattle	....	A.L.	1	4²/₃	0	1	.000	2	1	5	5.79	0
2001 Seattle	....	A.L.	2	12	2	0	1.000	10	2	8	1.50	0
2007 Philadelphia	....	N.L.	1	6	0	0	.000	2	2	5	1.50	0
2008 Philadelphia	....	N.L.	1	4	0	1	.000	3	3	4	4.50	0
Division Series Totals	....		5	26²/₃	2	2	.500	17	8	22	2.70	0
Championship Series												
2001 Seattle	....	A.L.	1	7	1	0	1.000	5	1	4	2.57	0
2008 Philadelphia	....	N.L.	1	1¹/₃	0	1	.000	2	0	6	40.50	0
Championship Series Totals	......		2	8¹/₃	1	1	.500	7	1	10	8.64	0
World Series Record												
2008 Philadelphia	....	N.L.	1	6¹/₃	0	0	.000	5	1	5	4.26	0

a Traded to Texas Rangers with outfielder Rafael Palmeiro and pitcher Drew Hall for infielders Curtis Wilkerson and Luis Benitez, pitchers Mitch Williams, Paul Kilgus and Steve Wilson, and outfielder Pablo Delgado, December 5, 1988.
b On disabled list from May 31 to September 1, 1989.
c Released, November 13, 1990. Signed with St. Louis Cardinals organization, January 10, 1991.
d Became free agent, October 15, 1991. Signed with Chicago Cubs organization, January 8, 1992.
e Released by Chicago Cubs, March 30. Signed with Detroit Tigers organization, March 30, 1992.
f Became free agent, October 15. Signed with Baltimore Orioles organization, December 19, 1992.
g Filed for free agency, November 12, 1995.
h Signed with Signed with Boston Red Sox, January 2, 1996.
i Traded to Seattle Mariners for outfielder Darren Bragg, July 30, 1996.
j Filed for free agency, October 29, 1996.
k Re-signed with Seattle Mariners, November 20, 1996.
l On disabled list from April 1 to April 29, 1997.
m On disabled list from April 15 to June 1, 2000.
n Filed for free agency, October 28, 2002, re-signed with Seattle Mariners, December 7, 2002.
o Filed for free agency, November 7, 2005, re-signed with Seattle Mariners, December 7, 2005.
p Traded to Philadelphia Phillies for pitcher Andrew Baldwin and pitcher Andrew Barb, August 19, 2006.
q Filed for free agency, November 6, 2008, re-signed with Philadelphia Phillies, December 15, 2008.

MOYLAN, PETER MICHAEL

Born, Attadale, Western Australia,Australia, December 2, 1978.
Bats Right. Throws Right. Height, 6 feet, 2 inches. Weight, 200 pounds.

Year	Club	Lea	G	IP	W	L	Pct	SO	BB	H	ERA	SAVES
1996 Twins	Gulf Coast		13	28²/₃	1	1	.500	16	9	34	4.08	1
1997 Twins	Gulf Coast		12	40	4	2	.667	40	10	46	4.05	0
2006 Richmond		Int.	35	56²/₃	1	7	.125	54	38	61	6.35	1
2006 Atlanta		N.L.	15	15	0	0	.000	14	5	18	4.80	0
2007 Richmond a		Int.	2	2	0	0	.000	3	1	0	0.00	1
2007 Atlanta		N.L.	80	90	5	3	.625	63	31	65	1.80	1
2008 Atlanta b		N.L.	7	5²/₃	0	1	.000	5	1	5	1.59	1
Major League Totals	3 Yrs.		102	110²/₃	5	4	.556	82	37	88	2.20	2

a Released by Minnesota Twins, April 1, 1998. Joined the Australian World Baseball team in 2006. Signed with Atlanta Braves organization, March 10, 2006.
b On disabled list from April 12 to November 3, 2008.

MULDER, MARK ALAN

Born, South Holland, Illinois, August 5, 1977.
Bats Left. Throws Left. Height, 6 feet, 6 inches. Weight, 215 pounds.

Year	Club	Lea	G	IP	W	L	Pct	SO	BB	H	ERA	SAVES
1999 Vancouver	P.C.		22	128²/₃	6	7	.462	81	31	152	4.06	0
2000 Sacramento	P.C.		2	8¹/₃	1	1	.500	6	4	15	5.40	0
2000 Oakland	A.L.		27	154	9	10	.474	88	69	191	5.44	0
2001 Oakland	A.L.		34	229¹/₃	*21	8	.724	153	51	214	3.45	0
2002 Oakland a	A.L.		30	207¹/₃	19	7	.731	159	55	182	3.47	0
2003 Oakland b	A.L.		26	186²/₃	15	9	.625	128	40	180	3.13	0
2004 Oakland c	A.L.		33	225²/₃	17	8	.680	140	83	223	4.43	0
2005 St. Louis	N.L.		32	205	16	8	.667	111	70	212	3.64	0
2006 Quad Cities	Midwest		1	5	0	0	.000	1	2	2	1.80	0
2006 Memphis	P.C.		2	8	0	1	.000	5	9	11	9.00	0
2006 St. Louis d-e	N.L.		17	93¹/₃	6	7	.462	50	35	124	7.14	0
2007 Palm Beach	Fla.St.		3	9¹/₃	0	2	.000	5	3	7	1.93	0
2007 Memphis	P.C.		1	5	0	0	.000	4	2	5	3.60	0
2007 St. Louis f	N.L.		3	11	0	0	.000	3	7	22	12.27	0
2008 Palm Beach	Fla.St.		1	5	0	0	.000	1	0	6	1.80	0
2008 Springfield	Texas		3	16	3	0	1.000	9	7	14	2.25	0
2008 Memphis	P.C.		3	13¹/₃	0	3	.000	8	5	28	13.50	0
2008 St. Louis g-h	N.L.		3	1²/₃	0	0	.000	2	4	4	10.80	0
Major League Totals	9 Yrs.		205	1314	103	60	.632	834	412	1352	4.18	0
Division Series												
2001 Oakland	A.L.		2	11	1	1	.500	7	2	14	2.45	0
2002 Oakland	A.L.		2	13	1	1	.500	12	3	14	2.08	0
2005 St. Louis	N.L.		1	6²/₃	1	0	1.000	2	1	8	1.35	0
Division Series Totals			5	30²/₃	3	2	.600	21	6	36	2.05	0
Championship Series												
2005 St. Louis	N.L.		2	11²/₃	0	2	.000	8	3	14	3.09	0

a On disabled list from April 12 to May 10, 2002.
b On disabled list from August 20 to October 7, 2003.

c Traded to St. Louis Cardinals for pitcher Danny Haren, pitcher Kiko Calero and catcher Daric Barton, December 18, 2004.
d On disabled list from June 21 to August 23 and August 30 to November 2, 2006.
e Filed for free agency, November 2, 2006, re-signed with St. Louis Cardinals, January 11, 2007.
f On disabled list from March 23 to September 5, 2007.
g On disabled list from March 21 to June 27 and July 10 to November 4, 2008.
h Not offered contract, October 21, 2008.

MUSSINA, MICHAEL COLE (MIKE)

Born, Williamsport, Pennsylvania, December 8, 1968.
Bats Right. Throws Right. Height, 6 feet, 2 inches. Weight, 190 pounds.

Year	Club	Lea	G	IP	W	L	Pct	SO	BB	H	ERA	SAVES
1990 Hagerstown	Eastern	7	42 1/3	3	0	1.000	40	7	34	1.49	0
1990 Rochester	Int.	2	13 1/3	0	0	.000	15	4	8	1.35	0
1991 Rochester a	Int.	19	122 1/3	10	4	.714	107	31	108	2.87	0
1991 Baltimore	A.L.	12	87 2/3	4	5	.444	52	21	77	2.87	0
1992 Baltimore	A.L.	32	241	18	5	*.783	130	48	212	2.54	0
1993 Bowie	Eastern	2	8	1	0	1.000	10	1	5	2.25	0
1993 Baltimore b	A.L.	25	167 2/3	14	6	.700	117	44	163	4.46	0
1994 Baltimore	A.L.	24	176 1/3	16	5	.762	99	42	163	3.06	0
1995 Baltimore	A.L.	32	221 2/3	*19	9	.679	158	50	187	3.29	0
1996 Baltimore	A.L.	36	243 1/3	19	11	.633	204	69	264	4.81	0
1997 Baltimore	A.L.	33	224 2/3	15	8	.652	218	54	197	3.20	0
1998 Baltimore c	A.L.	29	206 1/3	13	10	.565	175	41	189	3.49	0
1999 Baltimore	A.L.	31	203 1/3	18	7	.720	172	52	207	3.50	0
2000 Baltimore d	A.L.	34	*237 2/3	11	15	.423	210	46	236	3.79	0
2001 New York	A.L.	34	228 2/3	17	11	.607	214	42	202	3.15	0
2002 New York	A.L.	33	215 2/3	18	10	.643	182	48	208	4.05	0
2003 New York	A.L.	31	214 2/3	17	8	.680	195	40	192	3.40	0
2004 Columbus	Int.	1	3	0	0	.000	5	0	2	0.00	0
2004 New York e	A.L.	27	164 2/3	12	9	.571	132	40	178	4.59	0
2005 New York	A.L.	30	179 2/3	13	8	.619	142	47	199	4.41	0
2006 New York f-g	A.L.	32	197 1/3	15	7	.682	172	35	184	3.51	0
2007 New York h	A.L.	28	152	11	10	.524	91	35	188	5.15	0
2008 New York i	A.L.	34	200 1/3	20	9	.690	150	31	214	3.37	0
Major League Totals	18 Yrs.	537	3562 2/3	270	153	.638	2813	785	3460	3.68	0
Division Series											
1996 Baltimore	A.L.	1	6	0	0	.000	6	2	7	4.50	0
1997 Baltimore	A.L.	2	14	2	0	1.000	16	3	7	1.93	0
2001 New York	A.L.	1	7	1	0	1.000	4	1	4	0.00	0
2002 New York	A.L.	1	4	0	0	.000	2	0	6	9.00	0
2003 New York	A.L.	1	7	0	1	.000	6	3	7	3.86	0
2004 New York	A.L.	1	7	0	0	.000	7	1	2	2.57	0
2005 New York	A.L.	2	8 1/3	1	1	.500	7	1	11	5.40	0
2006 New York	A.L.	1	7	0	1	.000	5	0	8	5.14	0
2007 New York	A.L.	1	4 2/3	0	0	.000	3	4	4	3.86	0
Division Series Totals		11	65	4	4	.500	56	15	61	3.60	0
Championship Series											
1996 Baltimore	A.L.	1	7 2/3	0	1	.000	6	2	8	5.87	0
1997 Baltimore	A.L.	2	15	0	0	.000	25	4	4	0.60	0
2001 New York	A.L.	1	6	1	0	1.000	3	1	4	3.00	0
2003 New York	A.L.	3	15 1/3	0	2	.000	17	4	16	4.11	0
2004 New York	A.L.	2	12 2/3	1	0	1.000	15	2	10	4.26	0
Championship Series Totals		9	56 2/3	2	3	.400	66	13	42	3.34	0
World Series Record											
2001 New York	A.L.	2	11	0	1	.000	14	4	11	4.09	0
2003 New York	A.L.	1	7	1	0	1.000	9	1	7	1.29	0
World Series Totals		3	18	1	1	.500	23	5	18	3.00	0

a On disabled list from May 5 to May 12, 1991.
b On disabled list from July 22 to August 20, 1993.
c On disabled list from April 17 to May 3 and May 15 to June 6, 1998.
d Filed for free agency, October 27, 2000. Signed with New York Yankees, November 30, 2000.
e On disabled list from July 7 to August 18, 2004.
f On disabled list from August 23 to September 5, 2006.
g Filed for free agency, November 11, 2006, re-signed with New York Yankees, November 27, 2006.
h On disabled list from April 12 to May 3, 2007.
i Announced retirement, November 20, 2008.

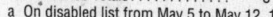

MYERS, BRETT ALLEN
Born, Jacksonville, Florida, August 17, 1980.
Bats Right. Throws Right. Height, 6 feet, 4 inches. Weight, 240 pounds.

Year	Club	Lea	G	IP	W	L	Pct	SO	BB	H	ERA	SAVES
1999	Phillies	Gulf Coast	7	27	2	1	.667	30	7	17	2.33	0
2000	Piedmont	So.Atl.	27	175 1/3	13	7	.650	140	69	165	3.18	0
2001	Reading	Eastern	26	156	13	4	.765	130	43	156	3.87	0
2002	Scranton-WB	Int.	19	128	9	6	.600	97	20	121	3.59	0
2002	Philadelphia	N.L.	12	72	4	5	.444	34	29	73	4.25	0
2003	Philadelphia	N.L.	32	193	14	9	.609	143	76	205	4.43	0
2004	Philadelphia	N.L.	32	176	11	11	.500	116	62	196	5.52	0
2005	Philadelphia	N.L.	34	215 1/3	13	8	.619	208	68	193	3.72	0
2006	Philadelphia	N.L.	31	198	12	7	.632	189	63	194	3.91	0
2007	Clearwater	Fla.St.	3	3 1/3	0	0	.000	4	1	2	0.00	0
2007	Philadelphia a	N.L.	51	68 2/3	5	7	.417	83	27	61	4.33	21
2008	Clearwater	Fla.St.	1	6 2/3	0	1	.000	6	1	7	2.70	0
2008	Reading	Eastern	1	8	0	1	.000	10	2	5	2.25	0
2008	Lehigh	Int.	2	12 1/3	1	1	.500	12	4	12	3.65	0
2008	Philadelphia	N.L.	30	190	10	13	.435	163	65	197	4.55	0
Major League Totals	7 Yrs.		222	1113	69	60	.535	936	390	1119	4.37	21
Division Series												
2007	Philadelphia	N.L.	2	1 1/3	0	0	.000	3	0	2	0.00	0
2008	Philadelphia	N.L.	1	7	1	0	1.000	4	3	2	2.57	0
Division Series Totals			3	8 1/3	1	0	1.000	7	3	4	2.16	0
Championship Series												
2008	Philadelphia	N.L.	1	5	1	0	1.000	6	4	6	9.00	0
World Series Record												
2008	Philadelphia	N.L.	1	7	0	1	.000	2	3	7	3.86	0

a On disabled list from May 24 to July 27, 2007.

NATHAN, JOSEPH MICHAEL (JOE)
Born, Houston, Texas, November 22, 1974.
Bats Right. Throws Right. Height, 6 feet, 4 inches. Weight, 220 pounds.

Year	Club	Lea	G	IP	W	L	Pct	SO	BB	H	ERA	SAVES
1995	San Francisco a	N.L.				Did Not Play						
1996						Did Not Play						
1997	Salem-Keizer	Northwest	18	62	2	1	.667	44	26	53	2.47	2
1998	Shreveport	Texas	4	15 1/3	1	3	.250	10	9	20	8.80	0
1998	San Jose	California	22	122	8	6	.571	118	48	100	3.32	0
1999	Shreveport	Texas	2	8 2/3	0	1	.000	7	7	5	3.12	0
1999	San Francisco	N.L.	19	90 1/3	7	4	.636	54	46	84	4.18	1
1999	Fresno	P.C.	13	74 2/3	6	4	.600	82	36	68	4.46	0
2000	San Francisco	N.L.	20	93 1/3	5	2	.714	61	63	89	5.21	0
2000	San Jose	California	1	5	0	1	.000	2	1	4	3.60	0
2000	Bakersfield	California	1	5 1/3	1	0	1.000	6	7	2	5.06	0
2000	Fresno b	P.C.	3	14 1/3	0	2	.000	9	7	15	4.40	0
2001	Fresno	P.C.	10	46 1/3	0	5	.000	21	33	63	7.77	0
2001	Shreveport	Texas	21	62 1/3	3	6	.333	33	37	73	6.93	0
2002	Fresno	P.C.	31	146 1/3	6	12	.333	117	74	167	5.60	0
2002	San Francisco	N.L.	4	3 2/3	0	0	.000	2	0	1	0.00	0
2003	San Francisco c	N.L.	78	79	12	4	.750	83	33	51	2.96	0
2004	Minnesota	A.L.	73	72 1/3	1	2	.333	89	23	48	1.62	44
2005	Minnesota	A.L.	69	70	7	4	.636	94	22	46	2.70	43
2006	Minnesota	A.L.	64	68 1/3	7	0	1.000	95	16	38	1.58	36
2007	Minnesota	A.L.	68	71 2/3	4	2	.667	77	19	54	1.88	37
2008	Minnesota	A.L.	68	67 2/3	1	2	.333	74	18	43	1.33	39
Major League Totals	9 Yrs.		463	616 1/3	44	20	.688	629	240	454	2.82	200
Division Series												
2003	San Francisco	N.L.	2	0 1/3	0	1	.000	1	1	4	81.00	0
2004	Minnesota	A.L.	3	5	0	1	.000	6	5	2	3.60	1
2006	Minnesota	A.L.	1	0 2/3	0	0	.000	1	0	1	0.00	0
Division Series Totals			6	6	0	2	.000	8	6	7	7.50	1

a Drafted by San Francisco Giants, June 1, 1995.
b On disabled list from May 13 to June 5 and July 14 to August 18, 2000.
c Traded to Minnesota Twins with pitcher Boof Bonser and pitcher Francisco Liriano for catcher A.J. Pierzynski and player to be named later, November 14, 2003.

NELSON, JOSEPH GEORGE (JOE)

Born, Alameda, California, October 25, 1974.
Bats Right. Throws Right. Height, 6 feet, 2 inches. Weight, 200 pounds.

Year Club	Lea	G	IP	W	L	Pct	SO	BB	H	ERA	SAVES
1996 Eugene.........	Northwest	14	70	5	3	.625	67	29	69	4.37	0
1997 Durham..........	Carolina	15	124²/₃	10	6	.625	99	61	114	4.76	0
1998 Greenville.......	Southern	45	108¹/₃	6	9	.400	74	69	124	4.98	2
1999 Richmond	Int.	12	33²/₃	2	3	.400	31	15	33	4.54	1
1999 Greenville........	Southern	25	30¹/₃	1	1	.500	37	14	19	2.37	8
2000 Braves.............	Gulf Coast	5	9	2	0	1.000	14	4	6	1.00	1
2000 Jamestown.......	N.Y.-Penn.	3	4	0	0	.000	7	1	3	2.25	0
2001 Richmond	Int.	29	39²/₃	1	2	.333	40	14	23	1.13	8
2001 Atlanta a..........	N.L.	2	2	0	0	.000	0	2	7	36.00	0
2002 Trenton b-c........	Eastern	4	4¹/₃	0	0	.000	3	2	9	14.54	0
2003 d.....................				INJURED—Did Not Play							
2004 Portland...........	Eastern	25	30¹/₃	3	2	.600	49	15	16	1.78	13
2004 Pawtucket	Int.	16	21¹/₃	0	0	.000	31	9	27	4.64	0
2004 Boston e-f.........	A.L.	3	2²/₃	0	0	.000	5	3	4	16.88	0
2005 Durham.............	Int.	35	46	0	3	.000	62	21	41	4.11	6
2005 Springfield g-h-i.......	Texas	9	13¹/₃	0	0	.000	22	7	4	2.03	1
2006 Omaha...............	P.C.	24	32	2	2	.500	39	12	19	1.97	7
2006 Kansas City.........	A.L.	43	44²/₃	1	1	.500	44	24	37	4.43	9
2007 Kansas City j-k.........	A.L.			INJURED—Did Not Play							
2008 Albuquerque...........	P.C.	19	25²/₃	1	1	.500	36	6	17	2.10	11
2008 Florida l...............	N.L.	59	54	3	1	.750	60	22	42	2.00	1
Major League Totals ....4 Yrs.		107	103¹/₃	4	2	.667	109	51	90	4.09	10

a On disabled list from June 20 to November 6, 2001.
b Released by Atlanta Braves, August 2, 2002. Signed with Boston Red Sox organization, August 9, 2002.
c Released by Boston Red Sox, August 27, 2002.
d On minor league disabled list from April 1 to September 21, 2003.
e Signed with Boston Red Sox organization, March 30, 2004.
f Filed for free agency, October 15, 2004. Signed with New York Mets organization, December 28, 2004.
g Released by New York Mets, April 1, 2005. Signed with Tampa Bay Devil Rays organization, April 19, 2005.
h Released by Tampa Bay Devil Rays, July 25, 2005. Signed with St. Louis Cardinals organization, July 31, 2005.
i Filed for free agency, October 15, 2005. Signed with Kansas City Royals organization, November 15, 2005.
j On disabled list from March 23 to November 13, 2007.
k Filed for free agency, November 16, 2007. Signed with Florida Marlins organization, December 12, 2007.
l Not offered contract, December 13, 2008. Signed with Tampa Bay Rays, December 30, 2008.

NIESE, JONATHON JOSEPH

Born, Lima, Ohio, October 27, 1986.
Bats Left. Throws Left. Height, 6 feet, 4 inches. Weight, 215 pounds.

Year Club	Lea	G	IP	W	L	Pct	SO	BB	H	ERA	SAVES
2005 Mets...........	Gulf Coast	7	24²/₃	1	0	1.000	24	10	23	3.65	0
2006 St. Lucie.............	Fla.St.	2	10	0	2	.000	10	5	8	4.50	0
2006 Hagerstown.........	So.Atl.	25	123²/₃	11	9	.550	132	62	121	3.93	0
2007 St. Lucie.............	Fla.St.	27	134¹/₃	11	11	.611	110	31	151	4.29	0
2008 Binghamton.......	Eastern	22	124¹/₃	6	7	.462	112	44	118	3.04	0
2008 New Orleans...........	P.C.	7	39²/₃	5	1	.833	32	14	34	3.40	0
2008 New York	N.L.	3	14	1	1	.500	11	8	20	7.07	0

NOLASCO, CARLOS ENRIQUE (RICKY)

Born, Corona, California, December 13, 1982.
Bats Right. Throws Right. Height, 6 feet, 2 inches. Weight, 220 pounds.

Year Club	Lea	G	IP	W	L	Pct	SO	BB	H	ERA	SAVES
2001 Cubs.............	Arizona	5	18	1	0	1.000	23	5	11	1.50	0
2002 Boise	Northwest	15	90²/₃	7	2	.778	92	25	72	2.48	0
2003 Daytona............	Fla.St.	26	149	11	5	.688	136	48	129	2.96	0
2004 Iowa................	P.C.	9	40²/₃	2	3	.400	28	16	68	9.30	0
2004 West Tenn........	Southern	19	107	6	4	.600	115	37	104	3.70	0
2005 West Tenn a.......	Southern	27	161²/₃	14	3	.824	173	46	151	2.89	0
2006 Florida...............	N.L.	35	140	11	11	.500	99	41	157	4.82	0
2007 Florida...............	N.L.	5	21¹/₃	1	2	.333	11	9	26	5.48	0
2007 Marlins.........	Gulf Coast	2	3¹/₃	0	0	.000	8	0	4	2.70	0
2007 Jupiter	Fla.St.	5	12	1	1	.500	9	1	10	0.75	0
2007 Carolina	Southern	1	3	1	0	1.000	2	1	2	6.00	0
2007 Albuquerque b.......	P.C.	4	15¹/₃	0	2	.000	15	4	29	14.09	0
2008 Florida	N.L.	34	212¹/₃	15	8	.652	186	42	192	3.52	0
Major League Totals ....3 Yrs.		74	373²/₃	27	21	.563	296	92	375	4.12	0

a Traded by Chicago Cubs to Florida Marlins with pitcher Sergio Mitre and pitcher Renyel Pinto for outfielder Juan Pierre, December 7, 2005.
b On disabled list from April 7 to May 1 AND May 18 to August 20, 2007.

NUNEZ (MORALES), LEONEL (LEO)

Born, Jamao Norte, Dominican Republic, August 14, 1983.
Bats Right. Throws Right. Height, 6 feet, 1 inch. Weight, 165 pounds.

Year Club	Lea	G	IP	W	L	Pct	SO	BB	H	ERA	SAVES
2001 Pirates . . . . Gulf Coast	10	53⅓	2	2	.500	34	9	62	4.39	0
2002 Pirates . . . . Gulf Coast	11	60⅓	4	2	.667	52	5	54	3.43	0
2002 Hickory. . . . . So.Atl.	1	4	0	0	.000	1	3	5	0.00	0
2003 Williamsport. . . . . . N.Y.-Penn.	8	38⅓	4	3	.571	41	12	31	3.05	0
2003 Hickory. . . . . So.Atl.	13	48⅓	2	1	.667	37	14	59	5.59	0
2004 Hickory a . . . . So.Atl.	27	144	10	4	.714	140	46	121	3.13	1
2005 High Desert . . . . Calif.	8	13	0	0	.000	15	3	23	9.00	0
2005 Wichita. . . . . Texas	12	13	1	0	1.000	14	2	8	0.69	4
2005 Kansas City . . . . A.L.	41	53⅔	3	2	.600	32	18	73	7.55	0
2006 Wichita. . . . . Texas	15	21	1	2	.333	22	12	18	4.29	3
2006 Kansas City . . . . A.L.	7	13⅓	0	0	.000	7	5	15	4.72	0
2006 Omaha . . . . P.C.	23	38	2	2	.500	33	13	37	2.13	5
2007 Wichita. . . . . Texas	6	20⅔	1	0	1.000	13	6	10	0.87	0
2007 Omaha . . . . P.C.	5	23	1	2	.333	19	4	16	2.74	0
2007 Kansas City b . . . . A.L.	13	43⅔	2	4	.333	37	10	44	3.92	0
2008 Nw Arkansas . . . . Texas	1	2	0	0	.000	2	0	0	0.00	0
2008 Omaha . . . . P.C.	4	4	0	0	.000	3	1	7	6.75	0
2008 Kansas City c-d . . . . A.L.	45	48⅓	4	1	.800	26	15	45	2.98	0
Major League Totals . . . . . . .4 Yrs.	106	159	9	7	.563	102	48	177	4.92	0

a Traded to Kansas City Royals by Pittsburgh Pirates for catcher Benito Santiago, December 16, 2004.
b On disabled list from April 1 to June 10, 2007.
c On disabled list from May 28 to July 21, 2008.
d Traded to Florida Marlins for infielder Mike Jacobs, October 30, 2008.

OHLENDORF, CURTIS ROSS (ROSS)

Born, Austin, Texas, August 8, 1982.
Bats Right. Throws Right. Height, 6 feet, 4 inches. Weight, 235 pounds.

Year Club	Lea	G	IP	W	L	Pct	SO	BB	H	ERA	SAVES
2004 Yakima . . . . Northwest	7	29	2	3	.400	28	19	22	2.79	0
2005 South Bend . . . , . . . Midwest	27	157	11	10	.524	144	48	181	4.53	0
2006 Tucson . . . . P.C.	1	5	0	0	.000	4	0	6	1.80	0
2006 Tennessee . . . . Southern	27	177⅔	10	8	.556	125	29	180	3.29	0
2007 Yankees . . . . Gulf Coast	4	16	1	1	.500	17	1	13	3.94	0
2007 Scranton-WB . . . - . . . . . Int.	21	66⅓	3	3	.500	48	24	86	5.02	0
2007 New York a . . . . A.L.	6	6⅓	0	0	.000	9	2	5	2.84	0
2008 Indianapolis . . . . Int.	7	46⅔	4	3	.571	40	8	46	3.47	0
2008 Scranton-WB . . . . Int.	5	22⅓	1	1	.500	25	5	28	4.03	0
2008 New York . . . . A.L.	25	40	1	1	.500	36	19	50	6.52	0
2008 Pittsburgh b . . . . N.L.	5	22⅔	0	3	.000	13	12	36	6.35	0
Major League Totals . . . . . . .2 Yrs.	36	69	1	4	.200	58	33	91	6.13	0
Division Series										
2007 New York . . . . A.L.	1	1	0	0	.000	0	1	4	27.00	

a Traded by Arizona Diamondbacks to New York Yankees with pitcher Steven Jackson, pitcher Luis Vizcaino and infielder Alberto González for pitcher Randy Johnson and cash, January 9, 2007.
b Traded to Pittsburgh Pirates with outfielder Jose Tabata, pitcher Jeff Karstens and pitcher Dan McCutchen for outfielder Xavier Nady and pitcher Damaso Marte, July 26, 2008.

OHMAN, WILLIAM MC DANIEL (WILL)

Born, Frankfurt, West Germany, August 13, 1977.
Bats Left. Throws Left. Height, 6 feet, 2 inches. Weight, 210 pounds.

Year Club	Lea	G	IP	W	L	Pct	SO	BB	H	ERA	SAVES
1998 Williamsprt. . . . . . N.Y.-Penn.	10	39	4	4	.500	35	13	39	6.46	0
1998 Rockford . . . . Midwest	4	24⅓	1	1	.500	21	7	25	4.44	0
1999 Daytona . . . . Fla.St.	31	106⅔	4	7	.364	97	41	102	3.46	5
2000 West Tenn . . . . Southern	59	71⅓	6	4	.600	85	36	53	1.89	8
2000 Chicago . . . . N.L.	6	3⅓	1	0	1.000	2	4	4	8.10	0
2001 Iowa. . . . . P.C.	40	51	5	2	.714	66	18	51	4.06	4
2001 Chicago . . . . N.L.	11	11⅔	0	1	.000	12	6	14	7.71	0
2002 Chicago a . . . . N.L.					INJURED—Did Not Play					

Year Club	Lea	G	IP	W	L	Pct	SO	BB	H	ERA	SAVES
2003 Chicago b............N.L.			INJURED—Did Not Play								
2004 Iowa c ...............P.C.	45	52⅓	3	3	.500	75	29	53	4.30	0
2005 Iowa.................P.C.	8	8⅔	1	0	1.000	12	2	4	4.15	1
2005 Chicago..............N.L.	69	43⅓	2	2	.500	45	24	32	2.91	0
2006 Chicago..............N.L.	78	65⅓	1	1	.500	74	34	51	4.13	0
2007 Iowa.................P.C.	9	6⅔	0	0	.000	9	5	7	2.70	0
2007 Chicago d............N.L.	56	36⅓	2	4	.333	33	16	42	4.95	1
2008 Atlanta e............N.L.	83	58⅔	4	1	.800	53	22	51	3.68	1
Major League Totals ....6 Yrs.	303	218⅔	10	9	.526	219	106	194	4.16	2

a On disabled list from March 15 to October 9, 2002.
b On disabled list from March 28 to September 29, 2003.
c Released by Chicago Cubs, October 20, 2003, re-signed with Chicago Cubs organization, February 11, 2004.
d Traded to Atlanta Braves with infielder Omar Infante for pitcher Jose Ascanio, December 4, 2007.
e Filed for free agency, October 30, 2008.

OKAJIMA, HIDEKI (HIDEKI)

Born, Kyoto, Japan, December 25, 1975.
Bats Left. Throws Left. Height, 6 feet, 1 inch. Weight, 195 pounds.

Year Club	Lea	G	IP	W	L	Pct	SO	BB	H	ERA	SAVES
1995 Yomiuri ....Japan Cent.	1	5	0	0	.000	9	2	5	1.80	0
1996 Yomiuri ....Japan Cent.	5	12⅔	1	0	1.000	8	9	13	0.71	0
1997 Yomiuri ....Japan Cent.	25	109⅓	4	9	.308	102	59	92	3.46	0
1998 Yomiuri ....Japan Cent.	14	62⅓	3	6	.333	54	32	61	4.33	0
1999 Yomiuri ....Japan Cent.	37	69⅔	4	1	.800	77	28	42	2.97	0
2000 Yomiuri ....Japan Cent.	56	72⅓	5	4	.556	102	31	53	3.11	7
2001 Yomiuri ....Japan Cent.	58	62	2	1	.667	70	39	62	2.76	25
2002 Yomiuri ....Japan Cent.	52	55⅔	6	3	.667	58	33	42	3.40	1
2003 Yomiuri ....Japan Cent.	41	38⅔	2	3	.400	29	20	45	4.89	0
2004 Yomiuri ....Japan Cent.	53	46⅔	4	3	.571	53	20	33	3.09	5
2005 Yomiuri ....Japan Cent.	42	53	1	0	1.000	56	19	55	4.75	0
2006 Hokkaido a......Japan Pac.	55	54⅔	2	2	.500	63	14	46	2.14	4
2007 Boston ..............A.L.	66	69	3	2	.600	63	17	50	2.22	5
2008 Boston ..............A.L.	64	62	3	2	.600	60	23	49	2.61	1
Major League Totals ....2 Yrs.	130	131	6	4	.600	123	40	99	2.40	6
Division Series											
2007 Boston ..............A.L.	2	2⅓	0	0	.000	2	1	1	0.00	0
2008 Boston ..............A.L.	3	2⅔	0	0	.000	0	1	3	6.75	0
Division Series Totals	5	5	0	0	.000	2	2	4	3.60	0
Championship Series											
2007 Boston ..............A.L.	3	5	0	0	.000	3	2	4	0.00	0
2008 Boston ..............A.L.	5	7⅓	0	0	.000	5	1	1	0.00	0
Championship Series Totals	8	12⅓	0	0	.000	8	3	5	0.00	0
World Series Record											
2007 Boston ..............A.L.	3	3⅔	0	0	.000	6	0	4	7.36	0

a Signed with Boston Red Sox, November 30, 2006.

OLIVER, DARREN CHRISTOPHER

Born, Rio Linda, California, October 6, 1970.
Bats Right. Throws Left. Height, 6 feet, 2 inches. Weight, 200 pounds.

Year Club	Lea	G	IP	W	L	Pct	SO	BB	H	ERA	SAVES
1988 Rangers ....Gulf Coast	12	54⅓	5	1	.833	59	18	39	2.15	0
1989 Gastonia............So.Atl.	24	122⅓	8	7	.533	108	82	86	3.16	0
1990 Rangers ....Gulf Coast	3	6	0	0	.000	7	1	1	0.00	0
1990 Gastonia............So.Atl.	1	2	0	0	.000	2	4	1	13.50	0
1991 Charlotte ....Fla.St.	2	8	0	1	.000	12	3	6	4.50	0
1992 Charlotte ....Fla.St.	8	25	1	0	1.000	33	10	11	0.72	0
1992 Tulsa ....Texas	14	14⅓	0	1	.000	14	4	15	3.14	2
1993 Tulsa ....Texas	46	73⅓	7	5	.583	77	41	51	1.96	6
1993 Texas ...............A.L.	2	3⅓	0	0	.000	4	1	2	2.70	0
1994 Okla City. .........A.A.	6	7⅓	0	0	.000	6	3	1	0.00	1
1994 Texas ...............A.L.	43	50	4	0	1.000	50	35	40	3.42	2
1995 Texas ...............A.L.	17	49	4	2	.667	39	32	47	4.22	0
1996 Charlotte ....Fla.St.	2	12	0	1	.000	9	3	8	3.00	0
1996 Texas ..............A.L.	30	173⅔	14	6	.700	112	76	190	4.66	0
1997 Texas ...............A.L.	32	201⅓	13	12	.520	104	82	213	4.20	0
1998 Oklahoma...........P.C.	1	5	0	0	.000	1	1	2	0.00	0
1998 Texas a.............A.L.	19	103⅓	6	7	.462	58	43	140	6.53	0

Year	Club	Lea	G	IP	W	L	Pct	SO	BB	H	ERA	SAVES
1998 St. Louis b-c	N.L.	10	57	4	4	.500	29	23	64	4.26	0
1999 St. Louis	N.L.	30	196$^{1}/_3$	9	9	.500	119	74	197	4.26	0
2000 Texas	A.L.	21	108	2	9	.182	49	42	151	7.42	0
2000 Oklahoma	P.C.	7	32	2	1	.667	28	14	22	1.97	0
2000 Tulsa d-e	Texas	1	4$^{2}/_3$	0	1	.000	5	2	10	11.57	0
2001 Texas	A.L.	28	154	11	11	.500	104	65	189	6.02	0
2001 Oklahoma	P.C.	1	3	0	0	.000	3	0	3	0.00	0
2001 Tulsa f-g	Texas	1	5	0	1	.000	5	2	4	5.40	0
2002 Memphis	P.C.	5	16	0	2	.000	9	17	17	7.87	0
2002 Boston h	A.L.	14	58	4	5	.444	32	27	70	4.66	0
2003 Colorado i	N.L.	33	180$^{1}/_3$	13	11	.542	88	61	201	5.04	0
2004 Florida-Houston j-k-l	N.L.	27	72$^{2}/_3$	3	3	.500	46	21	87	5.94	0
2005 Iowa	P.C.	3	13$^{1}/_3$	0	3	.000	10	5	28	13.50	0
2005 Tucson m-n-o-p	P.C.	4	18$^{1}/_3$	1	0	1.000	8	3	33	6.38	0
2006 New York q	N.L.	45	81	4	1	.800	60	21	70	3.44	0
2007 Los Angeles	A.L.	61	64$^{1}/_3$	3	1	.750	51	23	58	3.78	0
2008 Los Angeles r	A.L.	54	72	7	1	.875	48	16	67	2.88	0
Major League Totals	15 Yrs.	466	1624$^{1}/_3$	101	82	.552	993	642	1786	4.84	2
Division Series											
1996 Texas	A.L.	1	8	0	1	.000	3	2	6	3.38	0
2006 New York	N.L.	1	1$^{1}/_3$	0	0	.000	0	0	3	20.25	0
2007 Los Angeles	A.L.	1	0$^{2}/_3$	0	0	.000	0	0	2	27.00	0
2008 Los Angeles	A.L.	2	1$^{1}/_3$	0	0	.000	1	1	0	0.00	0
Division Series Totals		5	11$^{1}/_3$	0	1	.000	4	3	11	6.35	0
Championship Series											
2006 New York	N.L.	1	6	0	0	.000	3	1	3	0.00	0

a On disabled list from June 11 to June 26, 1998.
b Traded to St. Louis Cardinals with infielder Fernando Tatis and player to be named later for infielder Royce Clayton and pitcher Todd Stottlemyre, July 31, 1998.
c St. Louis Cardinals received infielder Mark Little to complete trade, August 9, 1998.
d Filed for free agency, October 29, 1999. Signed with Texas Rangers, January 27, 2000.
e On disabled list from June 17 to July 19 and July 31 to August 31, 2000.
f On disabled list from May 8 to June 6, 2001.
g Traded to Boston Red Sox for outfielder Carl Everett, December 12, 2001.
h Released by Boston Red Sox, July 2, 2002. Signed with St. Louis Cardinals organization, July 20, 2002.
i Released by St. Louis Cardinals, August 13, 2002. Signed with Colorado Rockies organization, January 29, 2003.
j Filed for free agency, October 26, 2003. Signed with Florida Marlins, January 28, 2004.
k Sold to Houston Astros, July 22, 2004.
l On disabled list from August 6 to September 6, 2004.
m Filed for free agency, November 8, 2004. Signed with Colorado Rockies organization, January 22, 2005.
n Released by Colorado Rockies, March 31, 2005. Signed with Arizona Diamondbacks organization, April 12, 2005.
o Released by Arizona Diamondbacks, May 3, 2005. Signed with Chicago Cubs organization, May 7, 2005.
p Released by Chicago Cubs, May 20, 2005. Signed with New York Mets organization, December 16, 2005.
q Filed for free agency, October 31, 2006. Signed with Los Angeles Angels, December 11, 2006.
r Filed for free agency, October 31, 2008. Accepted arbitration, December 8, 2008.

OLSEN, SCOTT MATTHEW

Born, Kalamazoo, Michigan, January 12, 1984.
Bats Left. Throws Left. Height, 6 feet, 4 inches. Weight, 215 pounds.

Year	Club	Lea	G	IP	W	L	Pct	SO	BB	H	ERA	SAVES
2002 Marlins	Gulf Coast	13	51$^{2}/_3$	2	3	.400	50	17	39	2.96	0
2003 Greensboro	So.Atl.	25	128$^{1}/_3$	7	9	.438	129	59	101	2.81	0
2004 Jupiter	Fla.St.	25	136$^{1}/_3$	7	6	.538	158	53	127	2.97	0
2005 Carolina	Southern	14	80$^{1}/_3$	6	4	.600	94	27	75	3.92	0
2005 Florida	N.L.	5	20$^{1}/_3$	1	1	.500	21	10	21	3.98	0
2006 Albuquerque	P.C.	1	6$^{1}/_3$	0	0	.000	5	3	5	0.00	0
2006 Florida	N.L.	31	180$^{2}/_3$	12	10	.545	166	75	160	4.04	0
2007 Florida	N.L.	33	176$^{2}/_3$	10	15	.400	133	85	226	5.81	0
2008 Florida a	N.L.	33	201$^{2}/_3$	8	11	.421	113	69	195	4.20	0
Major League Totals	4 Yrs.	102	579$^{1}/_3$	31	37	.456	433	239	602	4.63	0

a Traded to Washington Nationals with outfielder Josh Willingham for infielder Emilio Bonifacio, pitcher P.J. Dean and infielder Jake Smolinkski, November 11, 2008.

OLSON, GARRETT ANDREW

Born, Fresno, California, October 18, 1983.
Bats Right. Throws Left. Height, 6 feet, 1 inch. Weight, 195 pounds.

Year	Club	Lea	G	IP	W	L	Pct	SO	BB	H	ERA	SAVES
2005 Aberdeen	N.Y.-Penn.	11	40	2	1	.667	40	13	22	1.58	1
2005 Frederick	Carolina	3	14$^{1}/_3$	0	0	.000	7	5	10	3.14	0

Year	Club	Lea	G	IP	W	L	Pct	SO	BB	H	ERA	SAVES
2006 Frederick	Carolina	14	81⅓	4	4	.500	77	19	81	2.77	0
2006 Bowie	Eastern	14	84⅓	6	5	.545	85	31	78	3.42	0
2007 Norfolk	Int.	22	128	9	7	.563	120	39	95	3.16	0
2007 Baltimore	A.L.	7	32⅓	1	3	.250	28	28	42	7.79	0
2008 Norfolk	Int.	7	36⅓	1	2	.333	39	16	35	2.97	0
2008 Baltimore a	A.L.	26	132⅔	9	10	.474	83	62	168	6.65	0
Major League Totals .... 2 Yrs.		33	165	10	13	.435	111	90	210	6.87	0

a Traded to Chicago Cubs with pitcher Henry Williamson for outfielder Felix Pie, January 18, 2009.

OSORIA, FRANQUELIS ANTONIO
Born, Santiago, Dominican Republic, September 12, 1981.
Bats Right. Throws Right. Height, 6 feet. Weight, 200 pounds.

Year	Club	Lea	G	IP	W	L	Pct	SO	BB	H	ERA	SAVES
2002 Vero Beach	Fla.St.	3	7⅓	0	1	.000	10	2	4	2.45	0
2002 South Bend	So.Atl.	21	43⅓	2	2	.500	30	13	40	3.32	1
2003 Vero Beach	Fla.St.	33	75	3	6	.333	53	19	69	3.00	6
2004 Las Vegas	P.C.	4	8⅓	0	0	.000	3	1	13	6.48	0
2004 Jacksonville	Southern	51	81	8	5	.615	73	18	71	3.67	5
2005 Las Vegas	P.C.	40	55	6	4	.600	35	13	63	2.62	9
2005 Los Angeles	N.L.	24	29⅔	0	2	.000	15	8	28	3.94	0
2006 Los Angeles	N.L.	12	17⅔	0	2	.000	13	9	27	7.13	0
2006 Las Vegas a	P.C.	44	51⅔	2	2	.500	28	21	81	4.35	2
2007 Indianapolis	Int.	39	54⅔	2	5	.286	33	19	51	2.63	11
2007 Pittsburgh	N.L.	25	28⅓	0	2	.000	13	8	33	4.76	0
2008 Indianapolis	Int.	10	12⅔	2	1	.667	14	3	13	3.55	1
2008 Pittsburgh b-c	N.L.	43	60⅔	4	3	.571	31	12	87	6.08	0
Major League Totals .... 4 Yrs.		104	136⅓	4	9	.308	72	37	175	5.48	0

a Claimed on waivers by Pittsburgh Pirates, December 12, 2006.
b On disabled list from June 27 to July 12, 2008.
c Filed for free agency, October 15, 2008. Signed with Kansas City Royals organization, December 2, 2008.

OSWALT, ROY EDWARD
Born, Kosciusko, Mississippi, August 29, 1977.
Bats Right. Throws Right. Height, 6 feet. Weight, 185 pounds.

Year	Club	Lea	G	IP	W	L	Pct	SO	BB	H	ERA	SAVES
1997 Astros	Gulf Coast	5	28⅓	1	1	.500	28	7	25	0.64	0
1997 Auburn	N.Y.-Penn.	9	51⅔	2	4	.333	44	15	50	4.53	0
1998 Astros	Gulf Coast	4	16	1	1	.500	27	1	10	2.25	0
1998 Auburn	N.Y.-Penn.	11	70⅓	4	5	.444	67	31	49	2.18	0
1999 Michigan	Midwest	22	151⅓	13	4	.765	143	54	144	4.46	0
2000 Kissimmee	Fla.St.	8	45⅓	4	3	.571	47	11	52	2.98	0
2000 Round Rock	Texas	19	129⅔	11	4	.733	141	22	106	1.94	2
2001 New Orleans	P.C.	5	31	2	3	.400	34	6	32	4.35	0
2001 Houston	N.L.	28	141⅔	14	3	.824	144	24	126	2.73	0
2002 Houston	N.L.	35	233	19	9	.679	208	62	215	3.01	0
2003 New Orleans	P.C.	1	3	0	0	.000	2	0	3	3.00	0
2003 Houston a	N.L.	21	127⅓	10	5	.667	108	29	116	2.97	0
2004 Houston	N.L.	36	237	*20	10	.667	206	62	233	3.49	0
2005 Houston	N.L.	35	241⅔	20	12	.625	184	48	243	2.94	0
2006 Houston b	N.L.	33	220⅔	15	8	.652	166.	38	220	*2.98	0
2007 Houston	N.L.	33	212	14	7	.667	154	60	221	3.18	0
2008 Houston c	N.L.	32	208⅔	17	10	.630	165	47	199	3.54	0
Major League Totals .... 8 Yrs.		253	1622	129	64	.668	1335	370	1573	3.13	0
Division Series											
2004 Houston	N.L.	2	11⅓	1	0	1.000	8	4	15	2.38	0
2005 Houston	N.L.	1	7⅓	1	0	1.000	7	2	6	3.68	0
Division Series Totals		3	18⅔	2	0	1.000	15	6	21	2.89	0
Championship Series											
2004 Houston	N.L.	2	8	0	0	.000	2	4	11	6.75	0
2005 Houston	N.L.	2	14	2	0	1.000	12	4	8	1.29	0
Championship Series Totals		4	22	2	0	1.000	14	8	19	3.27	0
World Series Record											
2005 Houston	N.L.	1	6	0	0	.000	3	5	8	7.50	0

a On disabled list from May 16 to May 31 and June 19 to July 7 and July 30 to September 8, 2003.
b On disabled list from May 30 to June 14, 2006.
c On disabled list from July 12 to July 28, 2008.

OUTMAN, JOSHUA S. (JOSH)

Born, St. Louis, Missouri, September 14, 1984.
Bats Left. Throws Left. Height, 6 feet, 1 inch. Weight, 185 pounds.

Year	Club	Lea	G	IP	W	L	Pct	SO	BB	H	ERA	SAVES
2005 Batavia	N.Y.-Penn.		11	29⅓	2	1	.667	31	14	23	2.76	0
2006 Lakewood	So.Atl.		27	155⅓	14	6	.700	161	75	119	2.95	0
2007 Reading	Eastern		7	42	2	3	.400	34	23	38	4.50	0
2007 Clearwater	Fla.St.		20	117⅓	10	4	.714	117	54	104	2.45	0
2008 Midland	Texas		4	12⅔	1	0	1.000	5	3	13	4.26	1
2008 Reading	Eastern		33	70⅓	5	4	.556	66	37	68	3.20	1
2008 Sacramento	P.C.		5	15⅓	1	0	1.000	15	5	9	1.76	0
2008 Oakland a	A.L.		6	25⅔	1	2	.333	19	8	34	4.56	0

a Traded to Oakland Athletics with infielder Adrian Cardenas and outfielder Matt Spencer for pitcher Joe Blanton, July 17, 2008.

PADILLA, VICENTE DE LA CRUZ

Born, Chinandega, Nicaraqua, September 27, 1977.
Bats Right. Throws Right. Height, 6 feet, 2 inches. Weight, 220 pounds.

Year	Club	Lea	G	IP	W	L	Pct	SO	BB	H	ERA	SAVES
1999 High Desert	California		9	50⅔	4	1	.800	55	17	50	3.73	0
1999 Tucson	P.C.		18	93⅔	7	4	.636	58	24	107	3.75	0
1999 Arizona	N.L.		5	2⅔	0	1	.000	0	3	7	16.88	0
2000 Tucson	P.C.		12	18⅓	0	1	.000	22	8	22	4.42	1
2000 Arizona-Philadelphia a	N.L.		55	65⅓	4	7	.364	51	28	72	3.72	2
2001 Scranton-WB	Int.		16	81⅔	7	0	1.000	75	11	64	2.42	0
2001 Philadelphia b	N.L.		23	34	3	1	.750	29	12	36	4.24	0
2002 Philadelphia	N.L.		32	206	14	11	.560	128	53	198	3.28	0
2003 Philadelphia	N.L.		32	208⅔	14	12	.538	133	62	196	3.62	0
2004 Clearwater	Fla.St.		1	2	0	1	.000	1	1	3	9.00	0
2004 Scranton/WB	Int.		2	4⅔	0	0		6	5	6	13.50	0
2004 Philadelphia c	N.L.		20	115⅓	7	7	.500	82	36	119	4.53	0
2005 Clearwater	Fla.St.		1	5	0	1	.000	3	1	4	1.80	0
2005 Scranton/WB	Int.		1	5	1	0	1.000	4	2	6	3.60	0
2005 Philadelphia d-e	N.L.		27	147	9	12	.429	103	74	146	4.71	0
2006 Texas f	A.L.		33	200	15	10	.600	156	70	206	4.50	0
2007 Frisco	Int.		6	12	0	1	.000	12	9	14	8.25	0
2007 Texas g	A.L.		23	120⅓	6	10	.375	71	50	146	5.76	0
2008 Texas h	A.L.		29	171	14	8	.636	127	65	185	4.74	0
Major League Totals	10 Yrs.		279	1270⅓	86	79	.521	880	453	1311	4.31	2

a Traded to Philadelphia Phillies with infielder Travis Lee, pitcher Omar Daal and pitcher Nelson Figueroa for pitcher Curt Schilling, July 26, 2000.
b On disabled list from May 4 to May 30, 2001.
c On disabled list from May 30 to August 10, 2004.
d On disabled list from March 25 to April 19, 2005.
e Traded to Texas Rangers for player to be named later, December 12, 2005. Philadelphia Phillies received pitcher Ricardo Rodriguez to complete trade, December 19, 2005.
f Filed for free agency, October 30, 2006, re-signed with Texas Rangers, December 9, 2006.
g On disabled list from June 22 to August 15, 2007.
h On disabled list from July 5 to July 20 and August 25 to September 9, 2008.

PAPELBON, JONATHAN ROBERT

Born, Baton Rouge, Louisiana, November 23, 1980.
Bats Right. Throws Right. Height, 6 feet, 4 inches. Weight, 230 pounds.

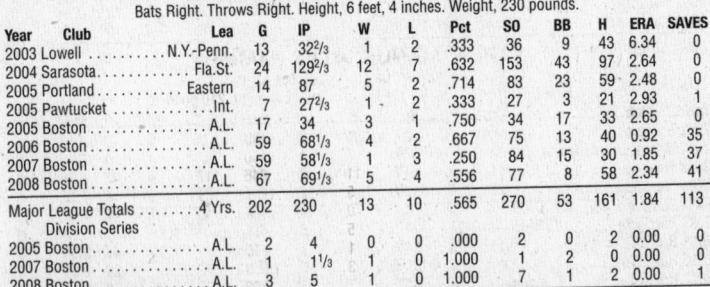

Year	Club	Lea	G	IP	W	L	Pct	SO	BB	H	ERA	SAVES
2003 Lowell	N.Y.-Penn.		13	32⅔	1	2	.333	36	9	43	6.34	0
2004 Sarasota	Fla.St.		24	129⅔	12	7	.632	153	43	97	2.64	0
2005 Portland	Eastern		14	87	5	2	.714	83	23	59	2.48	0
2005 Pawtucket	Int.		7	27⅔	1	2	.333	27	3	21	2.93	1
2005 Boston	A.L.		17	34	3	1	.750	34	17	33	2.65	0
2006 Boston	A.L.		59	68⅓	4	2	.667	75	13	40	0.92	35
2007 Boston	A.L.		59	58⅓	1	3	.250	84	15	30	1.85	37
2008 Boston	A.L.		67	69⅓	5	4	.556	77	8	58	2.34	41
Major League Totals	4 Yrs.		202	230	13	10	.565	270	53	161	1.84	113
Division Series												
2005 Boston	A.L.		2	4	0	0	.000	2	0	2	0.00	0
2007 Boston	A.L.		1	1⅓	1	0	1.000	1	2	0	0.00	0
2008 Boston	A.L.		3	5	1	0	1.000	7	1	2	0.00	1
Division Series Totals			6	10⅓	2	0	1.000	10	3	4	0.00	1

Year Club	Lea	G	IP	W	L	Pct	SO	BB	H	ERA	SAVES
Championship Series											
2007 Boston	A.L.	3	5	0	0	.000	3	2	3	0.00	1
2008 Boston	A.L.	4	5 1/3	0	0	.000	6	1	1	0.00	2
Championship Series Totals		7	10 1/3	0	0	.000	9	3	4	0.00	3
World Series Record											
2007 Boston	A.L.	3	4 1/3	0	0	.000	3	0	2	0.00	3

PARK, CHAN HO

Born, Kongju, South Korea, June 30, 1973.
Bats Right. Throws Right. Height, 6 feet, 2 inches. Weight, 210 pounds.

Year Club	Lea	G	IP	W	L	Pct	SO	BB	H	ERA	SAVES
1994 Los Angeles	N.L.	2	4	0	0	.000	6	5	5	11.25	0
1994 San Antonio	Texas	20	101 1/3	5	7	.417	100	57	91	3.55	0
1995 Albuquerque	P.C.	23	110	6	7	.462	101	76	93	4.91	0
1995 Los Angeles	N.L.	2	4	0	0	.000	7	2	2	4.50	0
1996 Los Angeles	N.L.	48	108 2/3	5	5	.500	119	71	82	3.64	0
1997 Los Angeles	N.L.	32	192	14	8	.636	166	70	149	3.38	0
1998 Los Angeles	N.L.	34	220 2/3	15	9	.625	191	97	199	3.71	0
1999 Los Angeles	N.L.	33	194 1/3	13	11	.542	174	100	208	5.23	0
2000 Los Angeles	N.L.	34	226	18	10	.643	217	124	173	3.27	0
2001 Los Angeles	N.L.	36	234	15	11	.577	218	91	183	3.50	0
2002 Oklahoma	P.C.	1	3	0	1	.000	3	3	9	27.00	0
2002 Texas a-b	A.L.	25	145 2/3	9	8	.529	121	78	154	5.75	0
2003 Texas	A.L.	7	29 2/3	1	3	.250	16	25	34	7.58	0
2003 Frisco	Texas	2	11	1	0	1.000	6	4	10	2.45	0
2003 Oklahoma c	P.C.	3	18 1/3	1	0	1.000	12	8	27	5.89	0
2004 Rangers	Arizona	4	21	1	1	.500	20	6	15	1.71	0
2004 Frisco	Texas	2	11 1/3	0	2	.000	5	5	16	8.74	0
2004 Oklahoma	P.C.	4	19 1/3	0	2	.000	19	3	21	3.72	0
2004 Texas d	A.L.	16	95 2/3	4	7	.364	63	33	105	5.46	0
2005 Texas	A.L.	20	109 2/3	8	5	.615	80	54	130	5.66	0
2005 San Diego e	N.L.	10	45 2/3	4	3	.571	33	26	50	5.91	0
2006 San Diego f	N.L.	24	136 2/3	7	7	.500	96	44	146	4.81	0
2007 New York	N.L.	1	4	0	1	.000	4	2	6	15.75	0
2007 New Orleans	P.C.	9	51 2/3	4	4	.500	49	16	64	5.57	0
2007 Round Rock g-h-i	P.C.	15	84	2	10	.167	70	24	100	6.21	0
2008 Los Angeles j	N.L.	54	95 1/3	4	4	.500	79	36	97	3.40	2
Major League Totals	15 Yrs.	378	1846	117	92	.560	1590	858	1723	4.34	2
Division Series											
2006 San Diego	N.L.	1	2	0	0	.000	0	0	1	0.00	0
Championship Series											
2008 Los Angeles	N.L.	4	1 2/3	0	0	.000	1	1	1	0.00	0

a Filed for free agency, November 5, 2001. Signed with Texas Rangers, January 16, 2002.
b On disabled list from April 2 to May 12 and August 7 to August 23, 2002.
c On disabled list from April 28 to June 7 and June 8 to November 14, 2003.
d On disabled list from May 20 to August 26, 2004.
e Traded to San Diego Padres for infielder Phil Nevin and cash, July 30, 2005.
f On disabled list from July 26 to August 11 and August 21 to September 22, 2006.
g Filed for free agency, October 31, 2006. Signed with New York Mets, February 9, 2007.
h Released by New York Mets, June 3, 2007. Signed with Houston Astros organization, June 12, 2007.
i Filed for free agency, October 29, 2007. Signed with Los Angeles Dodgers organization, November 8, 2007.
j Filed for free agency, November 1, 2008. Signed with Philadelphia Phillies, January 6, 2009.

PARRA, MANUEL ALEX (MANNY)

Born, Carmichael, California, October 30, 1982.
Bats Left. Throws Left. Height, 6 feet, 3 inches. Weight, 210 pounds.

Year Club	Lea	G	IP	W	L	Pct	SO	BB	H	ERA	SAVES
2002 Brewers	Arizona	1	2	0	0	.000	4	0	1	4.50	0
2002 Ogden	Pioneer	11	47 2/3	3	1	.750	51	10	59	3.21	0
2003 Beloit	Midwest	23	138 2/3	11	2	.846	117	24	127	2.73	0
2004 High Desert	Calif.	13	67 1/3	5	2	.714	64	19	76	3.48	0
2004 Huntsville	Southern	3	6	0	1	.000	10	1	5	3.00	0
2005 Huntsville	Southern	16	91	5	6	.455	86	21	111	3.96	0
2006 Brevard County	Fla.St.	15	54 2/3	1	3	.250	61	37	47	2.96	0
2006 Huntsville	Southern	6	31 1/3	3	0	1.000	29	8	26	2.87	0
2007 Huntsville	Southern	13	80 2/3	7	3	.700	81	26	70	2.68	0
2007 Nashville	P.C.	4	26	3	1	.750	25	7	15	1.73	0

Year	Club	Lea	G	IP	W	L	Pct	SO	BB	H	ERA	SAVES
2007 Milwaukee a	N.L.	9	26⅓	0	1	.000	26	12	25	3.76	0
2008 Milwaukee	N.L.	32	166	10	8	.556	147	75	181	4.39	0
Major League Totals	2 Yrs.	41	192⅓	10	9	.526	173	87	206	4.31	0
Division Series											
2008 Milwaukee	N.L.	2	21/3	0	0	.000	3	1	2	0.00	0

a On disabled list from August 31 to September 21, 2007.

PEAVY, JACOB EDWARD (JAKE)

Born, Mobile, Alabama, May 3, 1981.
Bats Right. Throws Right. Height, 6 feet, 1 inch. Weight, 195 pounds.

Year	Club	Lea	G	IP	W	L	Pct	SO	BB	H	ERA	SAVES
1999 Padres	Arizona	13	73⅔	7	1	.875	90	23	52	1.34	0
1999 Idaho Falls	Pioneer	2	11	2	0	1.000	13	1	5	0.00	0
2000 Fort Wayne	Midwest	26	133⅔	13	8	.619	164	53	107	2.90	0
2001 Mobile	Southern	5	28	2	1	.667	44	12	19	2.57	0
2002 Mobile	Southern	14	80⅓	4	5	.444	89	30	65	2.80	0
2002 San Diego	N.L.	17	97⅔	6	7	.462	90	33	106	4.52	0
2003 San Diego	N.L.	32	194⅔	12	11	.522	156	82	173	4.11	0
2004 Mobile	Southern	1	4⅔	0	1	.000	4	2	7	5.79	0
2004 San Diego a	N.L.	27	166⅓	15	6	.714	173	53	146	*2.27	0
2005 San Diego	N.L.	30	203	13	7	.650	*216	50	162	2.88	0
2006 San Diego	N.L.	32	202⅓	11	14	.440	215	62	187	4.09	0
2007 San Diego b	N.L.	34	223⅓	*19	6	.760	*240	68	169	*2.54	0
2008 San Diego c	N.L.	27	173⅔	10	11	.476	166	59	146	2.85	0
Major League Totals	7 Yrs.	199	1261	86	62	.581	1256	407	1089	3.25	0
Division Series											
2005 San Diego	N.L.	1	4⅓	0	1	.000	3	3	8	16.62	0
2006 San Diego	N.L.	1	5⅓	0	1	.000	2	1	11	8.44	0
Division Series Totals		2	9⅔	0	2	.000	5	4	19	12.10	0

a On disabled list from May 20 to July 2, 2004.
b Selected Cy Young Award Winner in National League for 2007.
c On disabled list from May 15 to June 12, 2008.

PELFREY, MICHAEL ALAN (MIKE)

Born, Wright-Patterson AFB, Ohio, January 14, 1984.
Bats Right. Throws Right. Height, 6 feet, 7 inches. Weight, 230 pounds.

Year	Club	Lea	G	IP	W	L	Pct	SO	BB	H	ERA	SAVES
2006 St. Lucie	Fla.St.	4	22	2	1	.667	26	2	17	1.64	0
2006 Binghamton	Eastern	12	66⅓	4	2	.667	77	26	60	2.71	0
2006 New York	N.L.	4	21⅓	2	1	.667	13	12	25	5.48	0
2006 Norfolk	Int.	2	8	1	0	1.000	6	5	4	2.25	0
2007 St. Lucie	Fla.St.	1	6	0	0	.000	2	3	5	3.00	0
2007 New Orleans	P.C.	14	74	3	6	.333	56	26	74	4.01	0
2007 New York	N.L.	15	72⅔	3	8	.273	45	39	85	5.57	0
2008 New York	N.L.	32	200⅔	13	11	.542	110	64	209	3.72	0
Major League Totals	3 Yrs.	51	294⅔	18	20	.474	168	115	319	4.31	0

PENA, RAMON ANTONIO (TONY)

Born, Santo Domingo, Dominican Republic, January 9, 1982.
Bats Right. Throws Right. Height, 6 feet, 1 inch. Weight, 220 pounds.

Year	Club	Lea	G	IP	W	L	Pct	SO	BB	H	ERA	SAVES
2005 Tennessee	Southern	25	148⅓	7	13	.350	95	40	165	4.43	0
2006 Tennessee	Southern	17	20⅓	2	0	1.000	17	5	18	0.89	6
2006 Tucson	P.C.	24	26⅓	3	1	.750	21	2	17	1.71	7
2006 Arizona	N.L.	25	30⅔	3	4	.429	21	8	36	5.58	1
2007 Arizona	N.L.	75	85⅓	5	4	.556	63	31	63	3.27	2
2008 Arizona	N.L.	72	72⅔	3	2	.600	52	17	80	4.33	3
Major League Totals	3 Yrs.	172	188⅔	11	10	.524	136	56	179	4.05	6
Division Series											
2007 Arizona	N.L.	2	2	0	0	.000	0	0	2	0.00	0
Championship Series											
2007 Arizona	N.L.	3	3⅓	0	0	.000	7	0	1	0.00	0

PENNY, BRADLEY WAYNE (BRAD)

Born, Broken Arrow, Oklahoma, May 24, 1978.
Bats Right. Throws Right. Height, 6 feet, 4 inches. Weight, 260 pounds.

Year Club	Lea	G	IP	W	L	Pct.	SO	BB	H	ERA	SAVES
1996 Diamondbcks	Arizona	11	49²/₃	2	2	.500	52	14	36	2.36	0
1997 South Bend	Midwest	25	118²/₃	10	5	.667	116	43	91	2.73	0
1998 High Desert	California	28	164	14	5	.737	207	35	138	2.96	0
1999 El Paso a-b-c	Texas	17	90	2	7	.222	100	25	109	4.80	0
1999 Portland	Eastern	6	32¹/₃	1	0	1.000	35	14	28	3.90	0
2000 Brevard County	Fla.St.	2	8	0	1	.000	11	4	5	1.13	0
2000 Calgary	P.C.	3	15	2	0	1.000	16	10	8	1.80	0
2000 Florida d	N.L.	23	119²/₃	8	7	.533	80	60	120	4.81	0
2001 Florida	N.L.	31	205	10	10	.500	154	54	183	3.69	0
2002 Jupiter	Fla.St.	2	7²/₃	0	0	.000	9	0	5	0.00	0
2002 Florida e	N.L.	24	129¹/₃	8	7	.533	93	50	148	4.66	0
2003 Florida	N.L.	32	196¹/₃	14	10	.583	138	56	195	4.13	0
2004 Florida-Los Angeles f-g	N.L.	24	143	9	10	.474	111	45	130	3.15	0
2005 Vero Beach	Fla.St.	1	5	1	0	1.000	3	1	2	1.80	0
2005 Las Vegas	P.C.	1	6	1	0	1.000	9	2	5	3.00	0
2005 Los Angeles h	N.L.	29	175¹/₃	7	9	.438	122	41	185	3.90	0
2006 Los Angeles	N.L.	34	189	*16	9	.640	148	54	206	4.33	0
2007 Los Angeles	N.L.	33	208	16	4	*.800	135	73	199	3.03	0
2008 Las Vegas	P.C.	1	4	0	0	.000	4	1	6	4.50	0
2008 Los Angeles i-j	N.L.	19	94²/₃	6	9	.400	51	42	112	6.27	0
Major League Totals ....9 Yrs.		249	1460¹/₃	94	75	.556	1032	475	1478	4.06	0
Division Series											
2003 Florida	N.L.	2	5²/₃	0	0	.000	6	1	5	6.35	0
2006 Los Angeles	N.L.	1	1	0	1	.000	1	2	2	18.00	0
Division Series Totals		3	6²/₃	0	1	.000	7	3	7	8.10	0
Championship Series											
2003 Florida	N.L.	3	4	1	1	.500	0	3	9	15.75	0
World Series Record											
2003 Florida	N.L.	2	12¹/₃	2	0	1.000	7	5	15	2.19	0

a On disabled list from April 20 to 30, 1999.
b Traded by Arizona Diamondbacks to Florida Marlins with pitcher Vladimir Nunez and player to be named later for pitcher Matt Mantei, July 9, 1999.
c Florida Marlins received outfielder Abraham Nunez to complete trade, December 13, 1999.
d On disabled list from July 20 to September 1, 2000.
e On disabled list from May 19 to July 2, 2002.
f Traded to Los Angeles Dodgers with pitcher Bill Murphy and infielder Hee Seop Choi for catcher Paul LoDuca, outfielder Juan Encarnacion and pitcher Guillermo Mota, July 30, 2004.
g On disabled list from August 9 to September 22, 2004.
h On disabled list from March 25 to April 24, 2005.
i On disabled list from June 15 to August 8 and August 14 to September 10 and September 24 to November 4, 2008.
j Not offered contract, November 5, 2008. Signed with Boston Red Sox, January 9, 2009.

PERALTA (GUTIERREZ), JOEL

Born, Bonao, Dominican Republic, March 23, 1976.
Bats Right. Throws Right. Height, 5 feet, 11 inches. Weight, 180 pounds.

Year Club	Lea	G	IP	W	L	Pct.	SO	BB	H	ERA	SAVES
2000 Boise	Northwest	4	8¹/₃	0	0	.000	9	5	12	6.48	0
2000 Butte	Pioneer	10	19	2	1	.667	17	10	24	6.63	1
2001 Cedar Rapids	Midwest	41	42¹/₃	0	0	.000	53	5	27	2.13	23
2001 Arkansas	Texas	9	10	0	1	.000	14	5	15	6.30	2
2002 Cedar Rapids	Midwest	41	47¹/₃	5	0	1.000	53	11	28	0.95	21
2002 Arkansas	Texas	12	17²/₃	0	0	.000	11	10	25	6.62	0
2003 Salt Lake	P.C.	1	0	0	0	.000	0	1	0	0.00	0
2003 Arkansas	Texas	47	52¹/₃	5	4	.556	48	12	39	2.24	20
2004 Angels	Arizona	2	4¹/₃	0	0	.000	9	0	1	2.08	0
2004 Rancho Cucamonga	Calif.	1	2	0	0	.000	1	1	5	9.00	0
2004 Salt Lake	P.C.	39	56	4	2	.667	68	18	64	4.98	1
2005 Los Angeles	A.L.	28	34²/₃	1	0	1.000	30	14	28	3.89	0
2005 Salt Lake a	P.C.	19	20	4	1	.800	18	6	11	2.70	10
2006 Omaha	P.C.	6	7²/₃	1	0	1.000	8	3	8	2.35	2
2006 Kansas City	A.L.	64	73²/₃	1	3	.250	57	17	74	4.40	1
2007 Kansas City	A.L.	62	87²/₃	1	3	.250	66	19	93	3.80	1
2008 Omaha	P.C.	10	18²/₃	1	0	1.000	19	6	9	0.00	2
2008 Kansas City	A.L.	40	52²/₃	1	2	.333	38	14	56	5.98	0
Major League Totals ....4 Yrs.		194	248²/₃	4	8	.333	191	64	251	4.45	2

a Claimed on waivers by Kansas City Royals, October 7, 2005.

PERCIVAL, TROY EUGENE

Born, Fontana, California, August 9, 1969.
Bats Right. Throws Right. Height, 6 feet, 3 inches. Weight, 240 pounds.

Year Club	Lea	G	IP	W	L	Pct	SO	BB	H	ERA	SAVES
1991 Boise	Northwest	28	38⅓	2	0	1.000	63	18	23	1.41	12
1992 Palm Sprngs	Calif.	11	10⅔	1	1	.500	16	8	6	5.06	2
1992 Midland	Texas	20	19	3	0	1.000	21	11	18	2.37	5
1993 Vancouver	P.C.	18	18⅔	0	1	.000	19	13	24	6.27	4
1994 Vancouver	P.C.	49	61	2	6	.250	73	29	63	4.13	15
1995 California	A.L.	62	74	3	2	.600	94	26	37	1.95	3
1996 California	A.L.	62	74	0	2	.000	100	31	38	2.31	36
1997 Lake Elsinore	Calif.	2	2	0	0	.000	3	0	1	0.00	0
1997 Anaheim a	A.L.	55	52	5	5	.500	72	22	40	3.46	27
1998 Anaheim	A.L.	67	66⅔	2	7	.222	87	37	45	3.65	42
1999 Anaheim	A.L.	60	57	4	6	.400	58	22	38	3.79	31
2000 Anaheim	A.L.	54	50	5	5	.500	49	30	42	4.50	32
2000 Lake Elsinore b	Calif.	2	2	0	0	.000	1	1	1	4.50	0
2001 Anaheim	A.L.	57	57⅔	4	2	.667	71	18	39	2.65	39
2002 Anaheim c	A.L.	58	56⅓	4	1	.800	68	25	38	1.92	40
2003 Anaheim d	A.L.	52	49⅓	0	5	.000	48	23	33	3.47	33
2004 Anaheim e-f	A.L.	52	49⅔	2	3	.400	33	19	43	2.90	33
2005 Detroit g	A.L.	26	25	1	3	.250	20	11	19	5.76	8
2006 Detroit h	A.L.				INJURED—Did Not Play						
2007 Memphis	P.C.	6	6⅔	0	0	.000	9	5	4	1.35	0
2007 St. Louis i-j-k-l	N.L.	34	40	3	0	1.000	36	10	24	1.80	0
2008 Tampa Bay m	A.L.	50	45⅔	2	1	.667	38	27	29	4.53	28
Major League Totals	13 Yrs.	689	697⅓	35	42	.455	774	301	465	3.12	352
Division Series											
2002 Anaheim	A.L.	3	3⅓	0	0	.000	4	0	6	5.40	2
Championship Series											
2002 Anaheim	A.L.	3	3⅓	0	0	.000	3	0	0	0.00	2
World Series Record											
2002 Anaheim	A.L.	3	3	0	0	.000	3	1	2	3.00	3

a On disabled list from April 7 to May 16, 1997.
b On disabled list from August 5 to August 25, 2000.
c On disabled list from April 3 to April 18 and July 12 to July 27, 2002.
d On disabled list from May 23 to June 7, 2003.
e On disabled list from June 2 to June 27, 2004.
f Filed for free agency, October 28, 2004. Signed with Detroit Tigers, November 17, 2004.
g On disabled list from May 8 to June 5 and July 10 to October 31, 2005.
h On disabled list from April 1 to November 1, 2006.
i Filed for free agency, November 2, 2006.
j Signed with Los Angeles Angels organization, April 2, 2007.
k Announced retirement, April 2, 2007. Signed with St. Louis Cardinals organization, June 8, 2007.
l Filed for free agency, October 29, 2007. Signed with Tampa Bay Devil Rays, November 30, 2007.
m On disabled list from May 29 to June 13 and July 1 to July 20 and August 15 to September 2, 2008.

PEREZ, CHRISTOPHER RALPH (CHRIS)

Born, Bradenton, Florida, July 1, 1985.
Bats Right. Throws Right. Height, 6 feet, 4 inches. Weight, 225 pounds.

Year Club	Lea	G	IP	W	L	Pct	SO	BB	H	ERA	SAVES
2006 Quad Cities	Midwest	25	29⅓	2	0	1.000	32	19	20	1.84	12
2007 Memphis	P.C.	15	14	0	1	.000	15	13	6	4.50	8
2007 Springfield	Texas	39	40⅔	2	0	1.000	62	28	17	2.43	27
2008 Memphis	P.C.	26	25⅓	1	1	.500	38	12	18	3.20	11
2008 St. Louis	N.L.	41	41⅔	3	3	.500	42	22	34	3.46	7

PEREZ, ODALIS AMADOL

Born, Las Matas de Farfan, Dominican Republic, June 11, 1977.
Bats Left. Throws Left. Height, 6 feet. Weight, 220 pounds.

Year Club	Lea	G	IP	W	L	Pct	SO	BB	H	ERA	SAVES
1995 Braves	Gulf Coast	12	65	3	5	.375	62	18	48	2.22	0
1996 Eugene	Northwest	10	23⅔	2	1	.667	38	11	26	3.80	0
1997 Macon	So.Atl.	36	87⅓	4	5	.444	100	27	67	1.65	5
1998 Greenville	Southern	23	132	6	5	.545	143	53	127	4.02	0
1998 Richmond	Int.	13	24⅓	1	2	.333	22	7	26	2.96	3
1998 Atlanta	N.L.	10	10⅔	0	1	.000	5	4	10	4.22	0
1999 Atlanta a	N.L.	18	93	4	6	.400	82	53	100	6.00	0
2000 Atlanta b	N.L.				INJURED—Did Not Play						

Year Club	Lea	G	IP	W	L	Pct	SO	BB	H	ERA	SAVES
2001 Richmond ....Int.	Int.	5	23	1	0	1.000	22	2	23	2.74	0
2001 Atlanta c-d ...........N.L.	N.L.	24	95$\frac{1}{3}$	7	8	.467	71	39	108	4.91	0
2002 Los Angeles ..........N.L.	N.L.	32	222$\frac{1}{3}$	15	10	.600	155	38	182	3.00	0
2003 Los Angeles ..........N.L.	N.L.	30	185$\frac{1}{3}$	12	12	.500	141	46	191	4.52	0
2004 Los Angeles e-f ......N.L.	N.L.	31	196$\frac{1}{3}$	7	6	.538	128	44	180	3.25	0
2005 Las Vegas. ...........P.C.	P.C.	4	14$\frac{2}{3}$	1	0	1.000	11	4	14	4.30	0
2005 Los Angeles g ........N.L.	N.L.	19	108$\frac{2}{3}$	7	8	.467	74	28	109	4.56	0
2006 Los Angeles ..........N.L.	N.L.	20	59$\frac{1}{3}$	4	4	.500	33	13	89	6.83	0
2006 Kansas City h ........A.L.	A.L.	12	67	2	4	.333	48	18	80	5.64	0
2007 Kansas City i-j .......A.L.	A.L.	26	137$\frac{1}{3}$	8	11	.421	64	50	178	5.57	0
2008 Potomac. ....Carolina	Carolina	1	4	0	0	.000	5	0	3	2.25	0
2008 Washington k-l ........N.L.	N.L.	30	159$\frac{2}{3}$	7	12	.368	119	55	182	4.34	0
Major League Totals ....10 Yrs.		252	1335	73	82	.471	920	388	1409	4.46	0
Division Series											
1998 Atlanta ..............N.L.	N.L.	1	0$\frac{2}{3}$	1	0	1.000	1	0	0	0.00	0
2004 Los Angeles ..........N.L.	N.L.	2	5	0	1	.000	3	7	8	14.40	0
Division Series Totals		3	5$\frac{2}{3}$	1	1	.500	4	7	8	12.71	0
Championship Series											
1998 Atlanta ..............N.L.	N.L.	2	0$\frac{1}{3}$	0	0	.000	0	2	5	54.00	0

a On disabled list from July 23 to November 1, 1999.
b On disabled list from April 2 to October 30, 2000.
c On disabled list from July 22 to September 1, 2001.
d Traded to Los Angeles Dodgers with outfielder Brian Jordan and pitcher Andy Brown for outfielder Gary Sheffield, January 15, 2002.
e On disabled list from June 27 to July 17, 2004.
f Filed for free agency, November 1, 2004, re-signed with Los Angeles Dodgers, January 7, 2005.
g On disabled list from May 15 to July 5 and August 18 to September 24, 2005.
h Traded to Kansas City Royals with pitcher Blake Johnson, pitcher Julio Pimental and cash for pitcher Elmer Dessens, July 25, 2006.
i On disabled list from August 19 to October 31, 2007.
j Filed for free agency, October 31, 2007. Signed with Washington Nationals organization, February 19, 2008.
k On disabled list from June 11 to June 26, 2008.
l Filed for free agency, October 31, 2008.

PEREZ, OLIVER

Born, Culiacan, Mexico, August 15, 1981.
Bats Left. Throws Left. Height, 6 feet, 3 inches. Weight, 210 pounds.

Year Club	Lea	G	IP	W	L	Pct	SO	BB	H	ERA	SAVES
1999 Padres ....Arizona	Arizona	15	28$\frac{1}{3}$	1	2	.333	37	16	28	5.08	3
2000 Yucatan ....Mexican	Mexican	11	43	3	2	.600	37	17	39	4.36	1
2000 Idaho Falls a ......Pioneer	Pioneer	5	24$\frac{1}{3}$	3	1	.750	27	9	24	4.07	0
2001 Lake Elsinore .....California	California	9	53	2	4	.333	62	25	45	2.72	0
2001 Fort Wayne........Midwest	Midwest	19	101$\frac{1}{3}$	8	5	.615	98	43	84	3.46	0
2002 Lake Elsinore .....California	California	9	48$\frac{2}{3}$	3	3	.500	66	24	36	1.85	0
2002 Mobile ....Southern	Southern	4	23	1	0	1.000	34	16	11	1.17	0
2002 San Diego b .........N.L.	N.L.	16	90	4	5	.444	94	48	71	3.50	0
2003 Portland ............P.C.	P.C.	8	47$\frac{2}{3}$	3	3	.500	48	12	44	3.02	0
2003 San Diego-Pittsburgh c-d N.L.	N.L.	24	126$\frac{2}{3}$	4	10	.286	141	77	129	5.47	0
2004 Pittsburgh ...........N.L.	N.L.	30	196	12	10	.545	239	81	145	2.98	0
2005 Indianapolis ....Int.	Int.	3	10	0	1	.000	4	12	14	9.90	0
2005 Pittsburgh e .........N.L.	N.L.	20	103	7	5	.583	97	70	102	5.85	0
2006 Indianapolis ....Int.	Int.	6	32	1	3	.250	34	11	28	5.63	0
2006 Norfolk...............Int.	Int.	4	19$\frac{1}{3}$	1	2	.333	26	12	18	6.05	0
2006 Pittsburgh-New York f ...N.L.	N.L.	22	112$\frac{2}{3}$	3	13	.188	102	68	129	6.55	0
2007 Mets...........Gulf Coast	Gulf Coast	1	4	0	0	.000	7	0	2	0.00	0
2007 New York g............N.L.	N.L.	29	177	15	10	.600	174	79	153	3.56	0
2008 New York h............N.L.	N.L.	34	194	10	7	.588	180	*105	167	4.22	0
Major League Totals ....7 Yrs.		175	999$\frac{1}{3}$	55	60	.478	1027	528	896	4.39	0
Championship Series											
2006 New York .............N.L.	N.L.	2	11$\frac{2}{3}$	1	0	1.000	7	3	13	4.63	0

a Loaned to Yucatan by San Diego Padres, June 2 to 22 and July 18 to September 6, 2000.
b On disabled list from August 7 to September 2, 2002.
c Traded to Pittsburgh Pirates with outfielder Jason Bay and player to be named later for outfielder Brian Giles, August 26, 2003.
d Pittsburgh Pirates received pitcher Cory Stewart to complete trade, October 2, 2003.
e On disabled list from June 27 to September 3, 2005.
f Traded to New York Mets with pitcher Roberto Hernandez for outfielder Xavier Nady, July 31, 2006.
g On disabled list from June 27 to July.15, 2007.
h Filed for free agency, October 30, 2008.

PEREZ, RAFAEL JEROME
Born, Santo Domingo, Dominican Republic, May 15, 1982.
Bats Left. Throws Left. Height, 6 feet, 3 inches. Weight, 185 pounds.

Year Club	Lea	G	IP	W	L	Pct	SO	BB	H	ERA	SAVES
2003 Burlington	Appal.	13	69	9	3	.750	63	16	56	1.70	0
2004 Kinston...........	Carolina	1	4²/₃	0	0	.000	3	2	10	11.57	0
2004 Lake County........	So.Atl.	23	115	7	6	.538	99	47	121	4.85	0
2005 Kinston...........	Carolina	14	77²/₃	8	5	.615	48	32	54	3.36	0
2005 Akron	Eastern	15	66²/₃	4	3	.571	46	12	53	1.75	1
2006 Akron	Eastern	12	67¹/₃	4	5	.444	53	22	53	2.81	0
2006 Buffalo	Int.	13	27¹/₃	0	3	.000	33	8	20	2.63	0
2006 Cleveland	A.L.	18	12¹/₃	0	0	.000	15	6	10	4.38	0
2007 Buffalo	Int.	8	46²/₃	3	3	.500	31	11	53	3.66	0
2007 Cleveland	A.L.	44	60²/₃	1	2	.333	62	15	41	1.78	1
2008 Cleveland	A.L.	73	76¹/₃	4	4	.500	86	23	67	3.54	2
Major League Totals ....3 Yrs.		135	149¹/₃	5	6	.455	163	44	118	2.89	3
Division Series											
2007 Cleveland	A.L.	3	6	1	0	1.000	6	1	3	1.50	0
Championship Series											
2007 Cleveland	A.L.	3	1	0	0	.000	0	2	7	45.00	0

PERKINS, GLEN WESTON
Born, St.Paul, Minnesota, March 2, 1983.
Bats Left. Throws Left. Height, 5 feet, 11 inches. Weight, 200 pounds.

Year Club	Lea	G	IP	W	L	Pct	SO	BB	H	ERA	SAVES
2004 Elizabethton	Appal.	3	12	1	0	1.000	22	4	8	2.25	0
2004 Quad Cities........	Midwest	9	48¹/₃	2	1	.667	49	12	33	1.30	0
2005 New Britain	Eastern	14	79	4	4	.500	67	35	80	4.90	0
2005 Fort Myers	Fla.St.	10	55	3	2	.600	66	13	41	2.13	0
2006 New Britain	Eastern	23	117¹/₃	4	11	.267	131	45	109	3.91	0
2006 Rochester...........	Int.	1	4¹/₃	0	1	.000	3	5	6	2.08	0
2006 Minnesota	A.L.	4	5²/₃	0	0	.000	6	0	3	1.59	0
2007 Rochester...........	Int.	1	6	0	0	.000	2	1	2	1.50	0
2007 Fort Myers	Fla.St.	1	1	0	0	.000	0	0	3	27.00	0
2007 Twins	Gulf Coast	3	5	0	0	.000	6	2	3	1.80	0
2007 New Britain	Eastern	3	7¹/₃	0	2	.000	7	7	11	11.05	0
2007 Minnesota a.........	A.L.	19	28²/₃	0	0	.000	20	12	23	3.14	0
2008 Rochester..........	Int.	7	33¹/₃	2	1	.667	27	19	28	2.97	0
2008 Minnesota	A.L.	26	151	12	4	.750	74	39	183	4.41	0
Major League Totals ......3 Yrs.		49	185¹/₃	12	4	.750	100	51	209	4.13	0
Division Series											
2006 Minnesota	A.L.	1	0¹/₃	0	0	.000	0	0	2	0.00	0

a On disabled list from May 22 to September 11, 2007.

PETTITTE, ANDREW EUGENE (ANDY)
Born, Baton Rouge, Louisiana, June 15, 1972.
Bats Left. Throws Left. Height, 6 feet, 5 inches. Weight, 225 pounds.

Year Club	Lea	G	IP	W	L	Pct	SO	BB	H	ERA	SAVES
1991 Yankees	Gulf Coast	6	36²/₃	4	1	.800	51	8	16	0.98	0
1991 Oneonta	N.Y.-Penn.	6	33	2	2	.500	32	16	33	2.18	0
1992 Greensboro	So. Atl.	27	168	10	4	.714	130	55	141	2.20	0
1993 Prince William	Carolina	26	159²/₃	11	9	.550	129	47	146	3.04	0
1993 Albany	Eastern	1	5	1	0	1.000	6	2	5	3.60	0
1994 Albany	Eastern	11	73	7	2	.778	50	18	60	2.71	0
1994 Columbus..........	Int.	16	96²/₃	7	2	.778	61	21	101	2.98	0
1995 Columbus..........	Int.	2	11²/₃	0	0	.000	8	0	7	0.00	0
1995 New York	A.L.	31	175	12	9	.571	114	63	183	4.17	0
1996 New York	A.L.	35	221	*21	8	.724	162	72	229	3.87	0
1997 New York	A.L.	35	240¹/₃	18	7	.720	166	65	233	2.88	0
1998 New York	A.L.	33	216¹/₃	16	11	.593	146	87	226	4.24	0
1999 Tampa	Fla.St.	1	5	1	0	1.000	8	2	4	0.00	0
1999 New York a.........	A.L.	31	191²/₃	14	11	.560	121	89	216	4.70	0
2000 New York b.........	A.L.	32	204²/₃	19	9	.679	125	80	219	4.35	0
2001 New York c.........	A.L.	31	200²/₃	15	10	.600	164	41	224	3.99	0
2002 Tampa	Fla.St.	2	5	0	0	.000	4	0	3	0.00	0
2002 Norwich	Eastern	1	6¹/₃	0	0	.000	5	0	2	1.42	0
2002 New York d.........	A.L.	22	134²/₃	13	5	.722	97	32	144	3.27	0

Year Club	Lea	G	IP	W	L	Pct	SO	BB	H	ERA	SAVES
2003 New York e	A.L.	33	208 1/3	21	8	.724	180	50	227	4.02	0
2004 Round Rock	Texas	2	8	0	0	.000	9	2	4	2.25	0
2004 Houston f	N.L.	15	83	6	4	.600	79	31	71	3.90	0
2005 Houston	N.L.	33	221 1/3	17	9	.654	171	41	188	2.39	0
2006 Houston g	N.L.	36	214 1/3	14	13	.519	178	70	238	4.20	0
2007 New York h	A.L.	36	215 1/3	15	9	.625	141	69	238	4.05	0
2008 New York i-j	A.L.	33	204	14	14	.500	158	55	233	4.54	0
Major League Totals ....14 Yrs.		436	2731 2/3	215	127	.629	2002	845	2869	3.89	0

Division Series

Year Club	Lea	G	IP	W	L	Pct	SO	BB	H	ERA	SAVES
1995 New York	A.L.	1	7	0	0	.000	0	3	9	5.14	0
1996 New York	A.L.	1	6 1/3	0	0	.000	3	6	4	5.68	0
1997 New York	A.L.	2	11 2/3	0	2	.000	5	1	15	8.49	0
1998 New York	A.L.	1	7	1	0	1.000	8	0	3	1.29	0
1999 New York	A.L.	1	7 1/3	1	0	1.000	5	0	7	1.23	0
2000 New York	A.L.	2	11 1/3	1	0	1.000	7	3	15	3.97	0
2001 New York	A.L.	1	6 1/3	0	1	.000	4	2	7	1.42	0
2002 New York	A.L.	1	3	0	0	.000	1	0	8	12.00	0
2003 New York	A.L.	1	7	1	0	1.000	10	3	4	1.29	0
2005 Houston	N.L.	1	7	1	0	1.000	6	2	4	3.86	0
2007 New York	A.L.	1	6 1/3	0	0	.000	5	2	7	0.00	0
Division Series Totals		13	80 1/3	5	3	.625	54	22	83	3.92	0

Championship Series

Year Club	Lea	G	IP	W	L	Pct	SO	BB	H	ERA	SAVES
1996 New York	A.L.	2	15	1	0	1.000	7	5	10	3.60	0
1998 New York	A.L.	1	4 2/3	0	1	.000	1	3	8	11.57	0
1999 New York	A.L.	1	7 1/3	1	0	1.000	5	1	8	2.45	0
2000 New York	A.L.	1	6 2/3	1	0	1.000	2	1	9	2.70	0
2001 New York	A.L.	2	14 1/3	2	0	1.000	8	2	11	2.51	0
2003 New York	A.L.	2	11 2/3	1	0	1.000	10	4	17	4.63	0
2005 Houston	N.L.	2	12 1/3	0	1	.000	6	4	15	5.11	0
Championship Series Totals		11	72	6	2	.750	39	20	78	4.13	0

World Series Record

Year Club	Lea	G	IP	W	L	Pct	SO	BB	H	ERA	SAVES
1996 New York	A.L.	2	10 2/3	1	1	.500	5	4	11	5.91	0
1998 New York	A.L.	1	7 1/3	1	0	1.000	4	3	5	0.00	0
1999 New York	A.L.	1	3 2/3	0	0	.000	1	1	10	12.27	0
2000 New York	A.L.	2	13 2/3	0	0	.000	9	4	16	1.98	0
2001 New York	A.L.	2	9	0	2	.000	9	2	12	10.00	0
2003 New York	A.L.	2	15 2/3	1	1	.500	14	4	12	0.57	0
2005 Houston	N.L.	1	6	0	0	.000	4	0	8	3.00	0
World Series Totals		11	66	3	4	.429	46	18	74	3.82	0

a On disabled list from March 26 to April 17, 1999.
b On disabled list from April 8 to April 25, 2000.
c On disabled list from June 16 to July 1, 2001.
d On disabled list from April 16 to June 14, 2002.
e Filed for free agency, November 6, 2003. Signed with Houston Astros, December 11, 2003.
f On disabled list from April 7 to April 29 and from May 27 to June 29 and from August 18 to October 28, 2004.
g Filed for free agency, November 6, 2006. Signed with New York Yankees, December 8, 2006.
h Filed for free agency, November 12, 2007, re-signed with New York Yankees, December 12, 2007.
i On disabled list from March 21 to April 5, 2008.
j Filed for free agency, November 9, 2008.

PINEIRO, JOEL ALBERTO

Born, Rio Piedras, Puerto Rico, September 25, 1978.
Bats Right. Throws Right. Height, 6 feet, 1 inch. Weight, 200 pounds.

Year Club	Lea	G	IP	W	L	Pct	SO	BB	H	ERA	SAVES
1997 Mariners	Arizona	1	3	1	0	1.000	4	0	1	0.00	0
1997 Everett	Northwest	18	49	4	2	.667	59	18	54	5.33	2
1998 Wisconsin	Midwest	16	96	8	4	.667	84	28	92	3.19	0
1998 Lancaster	California	9	45	2	0	1.000	48	22	58	7.80	0
1998 Orlando	Southern	1	5	1	0	1.000	2	2	7	5.40	0
1999 New Haven	Eastern	28	166	10	15	.400	116	52	190	4.72	0
2000 New Haven	Eastern	9	52 1/3	2	1	.667	43	12	42	4.13	0
2000 Tacoma	P.C.	10	61	7	1	.875	41	22	53	2.80	0
2000 Seattle	A.L.	8	19 1/3	1	0	1.000	10	13	25	5.59	0
2001 Tacoma	P.C.	18	77	6	3	.667	64	33	68	3.62	0
2001 Seattle	A.L.	17	75 1/3	6	2	.750	56	21	50	2.03	0
2002 Seattle	A.L.	37	194 1/3	14	7	.667	136	54	189	3.24	0
2003 Seattle	A.L.	32	211 2/3	16	11	.593	151	76	192	3.78	0
2004 Seattle a	A.L.	21	140 2/3	6	11	.353	111	43	144	4.67	0

Year	Club	Lea	G	IP	W	L	Pct	SO	BB	H	ERA	SAVES
2005 Tacoma	P.C.	1	7	0	0	.000	6	0	5	1.29	0
2005 Seattle b	A.L.	30	189	7	11	.389	107	56	224	5.62	0
2006 Seattle c	A.L.	40	165²/₃	8	13	.381	87	64	209	6.36	1
2007 Lowell	N.Y.-Penn.	1	1	0	0	.000	2	0	0	0.00	0
2007 Pawtucket	Int.	2	8	0	0	.000	3	4	3	2.25	0
2007 Boston	A.L.	31	34	1	1	.500	20	14	41	5.03	0
2007 St. Louis d-e-f	N.L.	11	63²/₃	6	4	.600	40	12	69	3.96	0
2008 Memphis	P.C.	1	6	0	0	.000	5	1	6	3.00	0
2008 St. Louis g	N.L.	26	148²/₃	7	7	.500	81	35	180	5.15	1
Major League Totals	9 Yrs.	253	1242¹/₃	72	67	.518	799	388	1323	4.55	2
Championship Series											
2001 Seattle	A.L.	1	2	0	0	.000	5	2	4	4.50	0

a On disabled list from July 26 to November 1, 2004.
b On disabled list from March 27 to April 15, 2005.
c Not offered contract, December 12, 2006. Signed with Boston Red Sox, January 4, 2007.
d On disabled list from June 28 to July 13, 2007.
e Traded to St. Louis Cardinals for player to be named later, July 31, 2007.
f Boston Red Sox received outfielder Sean Danielson to complete trade, November 2, 2007.
g On disabled list from March 21 to April 13 and May 21 to June 12, 2008.

PINTO, RENYEL ELIGIO
Born, Cupira, Venezuela, July 8, 1982.
Bats Left. Throws Left. Height, 6 feet, 4 inches. Weight, 215 pounds.

Year	Club	Lea	G	IP	W	L	Pct	SO	BB	H	ERA	SAVES
2000 Cubs	Arizona	9	30	0	2	.000	23	16	42	6.30	0
2001 Lansing	Midwest	20	88	4	8	.333	69	44	94	5.22	0
2002 Daytona	Fla.St.	7	32²/₃	3	3	.500	24	11	45	5.51	0
2002 Lansing	Midwest	17	98	7	5	.583	92	28	80	3.31	0
2003 Daytona	Fla.St.	20	114²/₃	3	8	.273	104	45	91	3.22	0
2004 Iowa	P.C.	2	9¹/₃	1	1	.500	9	8	9	7.71	0
2004 West Tenn	Southern	25	141²/₃	11	8	.579	179	72	107	2.92	0
2005 Iowa	P.C.	6	22²/₃	1	2	.333	24	24	31	9.53	0
2005 West Tenn a	Southern	22	129²/₃	10	3	.769	123	58	101	2.71	0
2006 Albuquerque	P.C.	18	95¹/₃	8	2	.800	96	47	82	3.40	0
2006 Florida	N.L.	27	29²/₃	0	0	.000	36	27	20	3.03	1
2007 Florida b	N.L.	57	58²/₃	2	4	.333	56	32	45	3.68	1
2008 Florida c	N.L.	67	64²/₃	2	5	.286	56	39	52	4.45	0
Major League Totals	3 Yrs.	151	153	4	9	.308	148	98	117	3.88	2

a Traded to Florida Marlins by Chicago Cubs with pitcher Sergio Mitre and pitcher Ricky Nolasco for outfielder Juan Pierre, December 7, 2005.
b On disabled list from August 3 to September 14, 2007.
c On disabled list from August 26 to September 8, 2008.

PONSON, SIDNEY ALTON
Born, Noord, Aruba, November 2, 1976.
Bats Right. Throws Right. Height, 6 feet, 2 inches. Weight, 260 pounds.

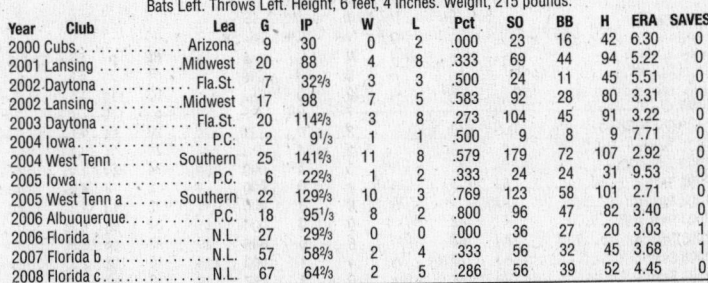

Year	Club	Lea	G	IP	W	L	Pct	SO	BB	H	ERA	SAVES
1994 Orioles	Gulf Coast	12	73	4	3	.571	53	17	68	2.96	0
1995 Bluefield	Appal.	13	77²/₃	6	3	.667	56	16	79	4.17	0
1996 Frederick	Carolina	18	107	7	6	.538	110	28	98	3.45	0
1997 Bowie	Eastern	13	74²/₃	2	7	.222	56	32	77	5.42	0
1997 Orioles a	Gulf Coast	1	2	1	0	1.000	1	0	0	0.00	0
1998 Rochester	Int.	1	5	1	0	1.000	3	1	4	0.00	0
1998 Baltimore	A.L.	31	135	8	9	.471	85	42	157	5.27	1
1999 Baltimore	A.L.	32	210	12	12	.500	112	80	227	4.71	0
2000 Baltimore	A.L.	32	222	9	13	.409	152	83	223	4.82	0
2001 Bowie	Eastern	1	4	0	0	.000	2	1	3	0.00	0
2001 Baltimore b	A.L.	23	138¹/₃	5	10	.333	84	37	161	4.94	0
2002 Baltimore c	A.L.	28	176	7	9	.438	120	63	172	4.09	0
2003 Baltimore	A.L.	21	148	14	6	.700	100	43	147	3.77	0
2003 San Francisco d	N.L.	10	68	3	6	.333	34	18	64	3.71	0
2004 Baltimore e	A.L.	33	215²/₃	11	15	.423	115	69	265	5.30	0
2005 Baltimore f-g	A.L.	23	130¹/₃	7	11	.389	68	48	177	6.21	0
2006 St. Louis	N.L.	14	68²/₃	4	4	.500	33	29	82	5.24	0
2006 New York h-i-j	A.L.	5	16¹/₃	0	1	.000	15	7	26	10.47	0
2007 Minnesota k-l	A.L.	7	37²/₃	2	5	.286	23	17	54	6.93	0
2008 Oklahoma	P.C.	5	23¹/₃	1	2	.333	12	9	25	3.47	0

Year Club	Lea	G	IP	W	L	Pct	SO	BB	H	ERA	SAVES
2008 Scranton-WB	Int.	1	4	0	0	.000	2	3	3	2.25	0
2008 Texas-New York m-n	A.L.	25	135²/₃	8	5	.615	58	48	170	5.04	0
Major League Totals ....11 Yrs.		284	1701²/₃	90	106	.459	999	584	1925	4.95	1
Division Series											
2003 San Francisco	N.L.	1	5	0	0	.000	3	0	7	7.20	0

a On disabled list from June 13 to July 15, 1997.
b On disabled list from April 16 to May 9, 2001.
c On disabled list from August 7 to September 1, 2002.
d Traded to San Francisco Giants for pitcher Damian Moss, pitcher Kurt Ainsworth and pitcher Ryan Hannaman, July 31, 2003.
e Filed for free agency, October 26, 2003. Signed with Baltimore Orioles, January 14, 2004.
f On disabled list from August 8 to September 1, 2005.
g Released by Baltimore Orioles, September 1, 2005. Signed with St. Louis Cardinals, December 21, 2005.
h On disabled list from May 8 to May 27, 2006.
i Designated for assignment by St. Louis Cardinals, July 8, 2006.
j Released by St. Louis Cardinals, July 11, 2006. Signed with New York Yankees, July 14, 2006.
k Released by New York Yankees, August 23, 2006. Signed with Minnesota Twins organization , January 3, 2007.
l Released by Minnesota Twins, May 18, 2007. Signed with Texas Rangers organization, March 9, 2008.
m Released by Texas Rangers, June 16, 2008. Signed with New York Yankees, June 18, 2008.
n Filed for free agency, October 30, 2008.

PUTZ, JOSEPH JASON (J.J.)

Born, Trenton, Michigan, February 2, 1977.
Bats Right. Throws Right. Height, 6 feet, 5 inches. Weight, 250 pounds.

Year Club	Lea	G	IP	W	L	Pct	SO	BB	H	ERA	SAVES
1999 Everett	Northwest	10	22¹/₃	0	0	.000	17	11	23	4.84	2
2000 Wisconsin	Midwest	26	142²/₃	12	6	.667	105	63	130	3.15	0
2001 San Antonio	Texas	27	148	7	9	.438	135	59	145	3.83	0
2002 San Antonio	Texas	15	84	3	10	.231	60	28	84	3.64	0
2002 Tacoma	P.C.	9	54	2	4	.333	39	21	51	3.83	0
2003 Tacoma	P.C.	41	86	0	3	.000	60	34	69	2.51	11
2003 Seattle	A.L.	3	3²/₃	0	0	.000	3	3	4	4.91	0
2004 Tacoma	P.C.	7	8¹/₃	0	0	.000	13	3	10	4.32	3
2004 Seattle	A.L.	54	63	0	3	.000	47	24	66	4.71	9
2005 Seattle	A.L.	64	60	6	5	.545	45	23	58	3.60	1
2006 Seattle	A.L.	72	78¹/₃	4	1	.800	104	13	59	2.30	36
2007 Seattle	A.L.	68	71²/₃	6	1	.857	82	13	37	1.38	40
2008 Azl Mariners........	Arizona	2	3	0	0	.000	4	0	2	0.00	0
2008 Tacoma	P.C.	1	1²/₃	0	0	.000	1	0	0	0.00	0
2008 Seattle a-b	A.L.	47	46¹/₃	6	5	.545	56	28	46	3.88	15
Major League Totals ....6 Yrs.		308	323	22	15	.595	337	104	270	3.07	101

a On disabled list from April 2 to April 22 and June 12 to July 20, 2008.
b Traded to New York Mets with pitcher Sean Green and outfielder Jeremy Reed for pitcher Aaron Heilman, outfielder Endy Chavez, pitcher Jason Vargas, infielder Mike Carp, outfielder Ezequiel Carrera and pitcher Maikel Cleto, December 10, 2008.

QUALLS, CHAD MICHAEL

Born, Lomita, California, August 17, 1978.
Bats Right. Throws Right. Height, 6 feet, 5 inches. Weight, 220 pounds.

Year Club	Lea	G	IP	W	L	Pct	SO	BB	H	ERA	SAVES
2001 Michigan	Midwest	26	162	15	6	.714	125	31	149	3.72	0
2002 Round Rock.......	Texas	29	163	6	13	.316	142	67	174	4.36	0
2003 Round Rock.........	Texas	28	175¹/₃	8	11	.421	132	61	174	3.85	0
2004 New Orleans........	P.C.	32	106²/₃	3	6	.333	72	30	134	5.57	1
2004 Houston.............	N.L.	25	33	4	0	1.000	24	8	34	3.55	1
2005 Houston.............	N.L.	77	79²/₃	6	4	.600	60	23	73	3.28	0
2006 Houston.............	N.L.	81	88²/₃	7	3	.700	56	28	76	3.76	0
2007 Houston a...........	N.L.	79	82²/₃	6	5	.545	78	25	84	3.05	5
2008 Arizona.............	N.L.	77	73²/₃	4	8	.333	71	18	61	2.81	9
Major League Totals ....5 Yrs.		339	357²/₃	27	20	.574	289	102	328	3.27	15
Division Series											
2004 Houston.............	N.L.	4	4	0	0	.000	3	1	4	6.75	0
2005 Houston.............	N.L.	2	3	0	0	.000	1	2	5	6.00	0
Division Series Totals		6	7	0	0	.000	4	3	9	6.43	0
Championship Series											
2004 Houston.............	N.L.	2	4	0	1	.000	4	2	8	11.25	0

Year	Club	Lea	G	IP	W	L	Pct	SO	BB	H	ERA	SAVES
2005 Houston		N.L.	4	4²/₃	1	0	1.000	4	0	0	0.00	0
Championship Series Totals			6	8²/₃	1	1	.500	8	2	8	5.19	0
World Series Record												
2005 Houston		N.L.	3	5¹/₃	0	0	.000	5	2	3	1.69	0

a Traded to Arizona Diamondbacks with pitcher Juan Gutierrez and outfielder Chris Burke for pitcher Jose Valverde, December 14, 2007.

RAMIREZ, EDWAR EMILIO
Born, El Cerdado, Dominican Republic, March 28, 1981.
Bats Right. Throws Right. Height, 6 feet, 3 inches. Weight, 165 pounds.

Year	Club	Lea	G	IP	W	L	Pct	SO	BB	H	ERA	SAVES
2002 Angels		Arizona	13	46¹/₃	2	5	.286	45	13	47	3.69	0
2002 Provo		Pioneer	2	9²/₃	1	0	1.000	4	4	14	9.31	0
2003 Rancho Cucamonga		Calif.	4	16²/₃	0	2	.000	9	7	29	8.10	0
2003 Cedar Rapids		Midwest	6	19	1	1	.500	15	8	17	3.32	0
2004							INJURED—Did Not Play					
2005 Pensacola		Central	43	62	2	2	.500	93	15	37	1.45	11
2005 Salt Lake a-b		P.C.	1	2	0	0	.000	2	0	0	0.00	0
2006 Edinburg		United	25	25	1	1	.500	46	10	14	1.07	16
2006 Tampa c		Fla.St.	19	30²/₃	4	1	.800	47	6	14	1.17	3
2007 Trenton		Eastern	9	16²/₃	3	0	1.000	33	8	6	0.54	1
2007 Scranton-WB		Int.	25	40	1	0	1.000	69	14	20	0.90	6
2007 New York		A.L.	21	21	1	1	.500	31	14	24	8.14	1
2008 Scranton-WB		Int.	8	9	1	0	1.000	13	1	2	0.00	0
2008 New York		A.L.	55	55¹/₃	5	1	.833	63	24	44	3.90	1
Major League Totals	2 Yrs.		76	76¹/₃	6	2	.750	94	38	68	5.07	2

a Released by Anaheim Angels, March 31, 2004. Signed by independent Pensacola (Central), 2005.
b Signed with Anaheim Angels, September 1, 2005. Filed for free agency, December 19, 2005.
c Signed with independent Edinburg (United), 2006. Sold to New York Yankees, July 9, 2006.

RAMIREZ, RAMON SANTO
Born, Puerto Plata, Dominican Republic, August 31, 1981.
Bats Right. Throws Right. Height, 5 feet, 11 inches. Weight, 190 pounds.

Year	Club	Lea	G	IP	W	L	Pct	SO	BB	H	ERA	SAVES
2002 Hiroshima a-b		Japan Cent.	2	3	0	0	.000	3	2	3	3.00	0
2003 Tampa		Fla.St.	14	74¹/₃	2	8	.200	70	20	88	5.21	0
2003 Trenton		Eastern	4	21¹/₃	1	1	.500	21	8	18	1.69	0
2003 Columbus c		Int.	2	6	0	1	.000	5	1	5	4.50	0
2004 Trenton		Eastern	18	114	4	6	.400	128	32	116	4.66	0
2004 Columbus		Int.	4	18	0	3	.000	17	8	25	8.50	0
2005 Columbus		Int.	6	27	1	3	.250	26	9	32	5.33	0
2005 Trenton		Eastern	15	89	6	5	.545	82	35	79	3.84	0
2005 Tulsa d		Texas	9	25¹/₃	2	1	.667	23	8	27	5.33	0
2006 Colorado Springs		P.C.	1	1	0	0	.000	1	0	0	0.00	0
2006 Colorado		N.L.	61	67²/₃	4	3	.571	61	27	58	3.46	0
2007 Colorado Springs		P.C.	25	27²/₃	4	0	1.000	35	16	18	2.28	0
2007 Colorado e		N.L.	22	17¹/₃	2	2	.500	15	6	21	8.31	0
2008 Kansas City f-g		A.L.	71	71²/₃	3	2	.600	70	31	57	2.64	1
Major League Totals	3 Yrs.		154	156²/₃	9	7	.563	146	64	136	3.62	1

a Played for Texas Rangers in the Dominican Summer League as an infielder 1997. Did not play 1998 through 2001.
b Released by Texas Rangers, June 4, 1998. Signed with Hiroshima (Japan) 2002.
c Signed with New York Yankees organization, March 5, 2003.
d Traded to Colorado Rockies with pitcher Eduardo Sierra for pitcher Shawn Chacon, July 28, 2005.
e On disabled list from April 18 to May 15 and September 8 to October 31, 2007.
f Traded to Kansas City Royals for player to be named later, March 26, 2008. Colorado Rockies received pitcher Jorge De La Rosa to complete trade, April 30, 2008.
g Traded to Boston Red Sox for outfielder Coco Crisp, November 19, 2008.

RASNER, DARRELL WAYNE
Born, Carson City, Nevada, January 13, 1981.
Bats Right. Throws Right. Height, 6 feet, 3 inches. Weight, 210 pounds.

Year	Club	Lea	G	IP	W	L	Pct	SO	BB	H	ERA	SAVES
2002 Vermont		N.Y.-Penn.	10	43²/₃	2	5	.286	49	18	44	4.33	0
2003 Savannah		So.Atl.	22	105¹/₃	7	7	.500	90	36	106	4.19	0
2004 Harrisburg		Eastern	5	29²/₃	1	1	.500	15	9	21	1.21	0

Year	Club	Lea	G	IP	W	L	Pct	SO	BB	H	ERA	SAVES
2004 Brevard County	Fla.St.	22	119⅓	6	5	.545	88	31	133	3.17	0
2005 Harrisburg	Eastern	27	150⅓	6	7	.462	96	29	150	3.59	0
2005 Washington	N.L.	5	7⅓	0	1	.000	4	2	5	3.68	0
2006 Yankees	Gulf Coast	2	6	0	0	.000	6	1	5	4.50	0
2006 Tampa	Fla.St.	2	7	0	0	.000	6	3	12	2.57	0
2006 Columbus	Int.	10	58⅔	4	0	1.000	47	11	60	2.76	0
2006 New York a-b	A.L.	6	20⅓	3	1	.750	11	5	18	4.43	0
2007 Scranton-WB	Int.	2	8	1	0	1.000	3	2	5	0.00	0
2007 Staten Island	N.Y.-Penn.	2	7	0	0	.000	3	3	8	5.14	0
2007 New York c-d	A.L.	6	24⅔	1	3	.250	11	8	29	4.01	0
2008 Scranton-WB	Int.	5	31	4	0	1.000	27	6	18	0.87	0
2008 New York e	A.L.	24	113⅓	5	10	.333	67	39	135	5.40	0
Major League Totals	4 Yrs.	41	165⅔	9	15	.375	93	54	187	5.00	0

a On disabled list from June 2 to August 24, 2006.
b Claimed on waivers by New York Yankees, February 11, 2006.
c On disabled list from May 20 to October 31, 2007.
d Not offered contract, December 12, 2007, re-signed by New York Yankees organization, December 15, 2007.
e Released by New York Yankees, November 21, 2008. Signed with Tohoku Rakuten (Japanese Pacific), December 7, 2008.

RAUCH, JON ERICH

Born, Louisville, Kentucky, September 27, 1978.
Bats Right. Throws Right. Height, 6 feet, 11 inches. Weight, 290 pounds.

Year	Club	Lea	G	IP	W	L	Pct	SO	BB	H	ERA	SAVES
1999 Bristol	Appal.	14	56⅔	4	4	.500	66	16	65	4.45	2
1999 Winston-Salem	Carolina	1	6	0	0	.000	7	3	4	3.00	0
2000 Winston-Salem	Carolina	18	110	11	3	.786	124	33	102	2.86	0
2000 Birmingham	Southern	8	56	5	1	.833	63	16	36	2.25	0
2001 Charlotte	Int.	6	28	1	3	.250	27	7	28	5.79	0
2002 Chicago	A.L.	8	28⅔	2	1	.667	19	14	28	6.59	0
2002 Charlotte	Int.	19	109⅓	7	8	.467	97	42	91	4.28	0
2003 Charlotte	Int.	24	124⅔	7	1	.875	94	35	121	4.11	0
2004 Charlotte	Int.	14	72⅓	6	3	.667	61	25	57	3.11	0
2004 Chicago	A.L.	2	8⅔	1	1	.500	4	4	16	6.23	0
2004 Edmonton	P.C.	3	18	1	1	.500	13	2	17	4.50	0
2004 Montreal a-b	N.L.	9	23⅓	3	0	1.000	18	7	14	1.54	0
2005 New Orleans	P.C.	7	21⅓	1	1	.500	25	2	19	2.53	0
2005 Washington c	N.L.	15	30	2	4	.333	23	11	24	3.60	0
2006 Washington	N.L.	85	91⅓	4	5	.444	86	36	78	3.35	2
2007 Washington	N.L.	*88	87⅓	8	4	.667	71	21	75	3.61	4
2008 Washington-Arizona d	N.L.	74	71⅔	4	8	.333	66	16	69	4.14	18
Major League Totals	6 Yrs.	281	341	24	23	.511	287	109	304	3.83	24

a Traded to Montreal Expos with pitcher Gary Majewski for outfielder Carl Everett, July 18, 2004.
b On disabled list from August 14 to September 14, 2004.
c On disabled list from May 26 to September 6, 2005.
d Traded to Arizona Diamondbacks for infielder Emilio Bonifacio, July 22, 2008.

REDDING, TIMOTHY JAMES (TIM)

Born, Rochester, New York, February 12, 1978.
Bats Right. Throws Right. Height, 6 feet. Weight, 225 pounds.

Year	Club	Lea	G	IP	W	L	Pct	SO	BB	H	ERA	SAVES
1998 Auburn	N.Y.-Penn.	16	73⅔	7	3	.700	98	50	49	4.52	1
1999 Michigan	Midwest	43	105	8	6	.571	141	76	84	4.97	14
2000 Kissimmee	Fla.St.	24	154⅔	12	5	.706	170	57	125	2.68	0
2000 Round Rock	Texas	5	26	2	0	1.000	22	22	14	3.46	0
2001 Round Rock	Texas	14	90⅔	10	2	.833	113	25	64	2.18	0
2001 New Orleans	P.C.	6	37⅔	4	1	.800	42	19	22	4.54	0
2001 Houston	N.L.	13	55⅔	3	1	.750	55	24	62	5.50	0
2002 New Orleans	P.C.	11	38	3	3	.500	50	13	32	5.21	0
2002 Houston	N.L.	18	73⅓	3	6	.333	63	35	78	5.40	0
2003 Houston	N.L.	33	176	10	14	.417	116	65	179	3.68	0
2004 Houston	N.L.	27	100⅔	5	7	.417	56	43	125	5.72	0
2004 New Orleans	P.C.	5	28⅓	1	3	.250	26	12	30	6.04	0
2005 Portland	P.C.	2	10	0	0	.000	5	2	7	0.90	0
2005 San Diego	N.L.	9	29⅔	0	5	.000	17	13	40	9.10	0
2005 New York	A.L.	1	1	0	1	.000	2	4	4	54.00	0
2005 Columbus a-b-c	Int.	10	51⅓	3	4	.429	47	13	62	5.08	0
2006 Charlotte d-e	Int.	29	187⅔	12	10	.545	148	56	168	3.40	0

311

Year	Club	Lea	G	IP	W	L	Pct	SO	BB	H	ERA	SAVES
2007 Columbus............Int.		Int.	17	89²/₃	9	5	.643	63	24	110	5.32	0
2007 Washington...........N.L.		N.L.	15	84	3	6	.333	47	38	84	3.64	0
2008 Washington f.........N.L.		N.L.	33	182	10	11	.476	120	65	195	4.95	0
Major League Totals........7 Yrs.			149	702¹/₃	34	51	.400	476	287	767	4.92	0

a Traded to San Diego Padres with cash for catcher Humberto Quintero, March 28, 2005.
b On disabled list from May 9 to June 22, 2005.
c Traded to New York Yankees with pitcher Darrell May and cash for pitcher Paul Quantrill, July 2, 2005.
d Filed for free agency, October 6, 2005. Signed with Chicago White Sox, January 19, 2006.
e Filed for free agency, October 15, 2006. Signed with Washington Nationals, November 6, 2006.
f Not offered contract, December 12, 2008. Signed with New York Mets, January 9, 2009.

REYES, ANTHONY LOZA
Born, Downey, California, October 16, 1981.
Bats Right. Throws Right. Height, 6 feet, 2 inches. Weight, 230 pounds.

Year	Club	Lea	G	IP	W	L	Pct	SO	BB	H	ERA	SAVES
2004 Palm Beach.........Fla.St.		Fla.St.	6	30²/₃	3	0	1.000	38	7	41	5.58	0
2004 Tennessee........Southern		Southern	12	74¹/₃	6	2	.750	102	13	62	2.91	0
2005 Memphis...........P.C.		P.C.	23	128²/₃	7	6	.538	136	34	105	3.64	0
2005 St. Louis...........N.L.		N.L.	4	13¹/₃	1	1	.500	12	4	6	2.70	0
2006 Memphis...........P.C.		P.C.	13	84	6	1	.857	82	11	70	2.57	0
2006 St. Louis...........N.L.		N.L.	17	85¹/₃	5	8	.385	72	34	84	5.06	0
2007 Memphis...........P.C.		P.C.	6	38²/₃	1	1	.500	33	11	27	2.79	0
2007 St. Louis...........N.L.		N.L.	22	107¹/₃	2	14	.125	74	43	108	6.04	0
2008 Memphis...........P.C.		P.C.	11	52²/₃	2	3	.400	47	21	51	3.25	0
2008 Buffalo..............Int.		Int.	2	13	2	0	1.000	8	4	10	2.77	0
2008 St. Louis...........N.L.		N.L.	10	14²/₃	2	1	.667	10	3	16	4.91	1
2008 Cleveland a-b.........A.L.		A.L.	6	34¹/₃	2	1	.667	15	12	31	1.83	0
Major League Totals........4 Yrs.			59	255	12	25	.324	183	96	245	4.91	1
Championship Series												
2006 St. Louis............N.L.		N.L.	1	4	0	0	.000	4	4	3	4.50	0
World Series Record												
2006 St. Louis............N.L.		N.L.	1	8	1	0	1.000	4	1	4	2.25	0

a On disabled list from June 16 to July 5, 2008.
b Traded to Cleveland Indians for pitcher Luis Perdomo, July 26, 2008.

REYES (VALARDE), DENNYS
Born, Higuera de Zaragoza, Mexico, April 19, 1977.
Bats Left. Throws Left. Height, 6 feet, 3 inches. Weight, 246 pounds.

Year	Club	Lea	G	IP	W	L	Pct	SO	BB	H	ERA	SAVES
1993 Mexico City Reds a..Mexican		Mexican	7	5¹/₃	0	1	.000	5	9	4	5.06	0
1994 Vero Beach.........Fla.St.		Fla.St.	9	41²/₃	2	4	.333	25	18	58	6.70	0
1994 Great Falls.........Pioneer		Pioneer	14	66²/₃	7	1	.875	70	25	71	3.78	0
1995 Mexico...........Mexican		Mexican	17	58²/₃	5	5	.500	44	41	76	6.60	0
1995 Vero Beach.........Fla.St.		Fla.St.	3	10	1	0	1.000	9	6	8	1.80	0
1996 San Bernardino.......Calif.		Calif.	29	166	11	12	.478	176	77	166	4.17	0
1997 San Antonio........Texas		Texas	12	80¹/₃	8	1	.889	66	28	79	3.02	0
1997 Albuquerque.........P.C.		P.C.	10	57¹/₃	6	3	.667	45	33	70	5.65	0
1997 Los Angeles..........N.L.		N.L.	14	47	2	3	.400	36	18	51	3.83	0
1998 Albuquerque.........P.C.		P.C.	7	43²/₃	1	4	.200	58	18	31	1.44	0
1998 Indianapolis...........Int.		Int.	4	24	2	0	1.000	27	14	20	3.00	0
1998 Los Angeles-Cincinnati b N.L.		N.L.	19	67¹/₃	3	5	.375	77	47	62	4.54	0
1999 Cincinnati............N.L.		N.L.	65	61²/₃	2	2	.500	72	39	53	3.79	2
2000 Cincinnati............N.L.		N.L.	62	43²/₃	2	1	.667	36	29	43	4.53	0
2001 Cincinnati............N.L.		N.L.	35	53	2	6	.250	52	35	51	4.92	0
2001 Louisville c-d...........Int.		Int.	7	34¹/₃	4	2	.667	34	16	34	3.67	0
2002 Colorado............N.L.		N.L.	43	40¹/₃	0	1	.000	30	24	43	4.24	0
2002 Texas e..............A.L.		A.L.	15	42¹/₃	4	3	.571	29	21	55	6.38	0
2003 Tucson.............P.C.		P.C.	33	31²/₃	2	1	.667	30	22	24	2.84	2
2003 Pittsburgh-Arizona f-g-h N.L.		N.L.	15	12²/₃	0	0	.000	16	10	15	10.66	0
2004 Kansas City i.........A.L.		A.L.	40	108	4	8	.333	91	50	114	4.75	0
2005 San Diego j...........N.L.		N.L.	36	43²/₃	3	2	.600	35	32	57	5.15	0
2006 Rochester.............Int.		Int.	4	18	1	0	1.000	13	3	11	0.50	0
2006 Minnesota...........A.L.		A.L.	66	50²/₃	5	0	1.000	49	15	35	0.89	0
2007 Minnesota k..........A.L.		A.L.	50	29¹/₃	2	1	.667	21	21	34	3.99	0
2008 Minnesota l...........A.L.		A.L.	75	46¹/₃	3	0	1.000	39	15	40	2.33	0
Major League Totals.......12 Yrs.			535	646	32	32	.500	583	356	653	4.28	2
Division Series												
2006 Minnesota............A.L.		A.L.	2	1	0	0	.000	0	2	1	9.00	0

a Sold to Los Angeles Dodgers, July 5, 1993.
b Traded to Cincinnati Reds with infielder Paul Konerko for pitcher Jeff Shaw, July 4, 1998.
c On disabled list from May 30 to July 2, 2001.
d Traded to Colorado Rockies with infielder Pokey Reese for pitcher Gabe White and pitcher Luke Hudson, December 18, 2001.
e Traded to Texas Rangers with outfielder Todd Hollandsworth for outfielder Gabe Kapler, outfielder Jason Romano and cash, July 31, 2002.
f Not offered contract, December 20, 2002. Signed with Pittsburgh Pirates organization, February 7, 2003.
g Filed for free agency, May 19, 2003. Signed with Arizona Diamondbacks organization, June 11, 2003.
h Filed for free agency, October 3, 2003. Signed with Kansas City Royals organization, November 6, 2003.
i Filed for free agency, October 29, 2004. Signed with San Diego Padres, November 29, 2004.
j Released by San Diego Padres, July 18, 2005. Signed with Minnesota Twins organization, December 23, 2005.
k On disabled list from May 21 to June 14 and August 22 to October 10, 2007.
l Filed for free agency, October 30, 2008.

REYES, JOSEPH ALBERT (JO-JO)

Born, West Covina, California, November 20, 1984.
Bats Left. Throws Left. Height, 6 feet, 2 inches. Weight, 230 pounds.

Year	Club	Lea	G	IP	W	L	Pct	SO	BB	H	ERA	SAVES
2003 Braves	Gulf Coast	11	45²/₃	5	3	.625	55	14	34	2.56	0
2004 Rome	So.Atl.	15	74	2	4	.333	71	25	84	5.35	0
2005 Danville	Appal.	9	43¹/₃	3	0	1.000	27	6	37	3.53	0
2005 Braves	Gulf Coast	3	5¹/₃	0	1	.000	6	1	6	1.69	0
2006 Myrtle Beach	Carolina	14	65²/₃	4	4	.500	58	36	52	4.11	0
2006 Rome	So.Atl.	13	75¹/₃	8	1	.889	54	25	62	2.99	0
2007 Mississippi	Southern	13	73¹/₃	8	1	.889	71	35	63	3.56	0
2007 Richmond	Int.	6	36	4	0	1.000	39	12	25	1.00	0
2007 Atlanta	N.L.	11	50²/₃	2	2	.500	27	30	55	6.22	0
2008 Richmond	Int.	8	39	1	1	.500	38	16	31	2.31	0
2008 Atlanta	N.L.	23	113	3	11	.214	78	52	134	5.81	0
Major League Totals	2 Yrs.	34	163²/₃	5	13	.278	105	82	189	5.94	0

RHODES, ARTHUR LEE

Born, Waco, Texas, October 24, 1969.
Bats Left. Throws Left. Height, 6 feet, 2 inches. Weight, 210 pounds.

Year	Club	Lea	G	IP	W	L	Pct	SO	BB	H	ERA	SAVES
1988 Bluefield	Appal.	11	35¹/₃	3	4	.429	44	15	29	3.31	0
1989 Erie	N.Y.-Penn.	5	31	2	0	1.000	45	10	13	1.16	0
1989 Frederick	Carolina	7	24¹/₃	2	2	.500	28	19	19	5.18	0
1990 Frederick	Carolina	13	80²/₃	4	6	.400	103	21	62	2.12	0
1990 Hagerstown	Eastern	12	72¹/₃	3	4	.429	60	39	62	3.73	0
1991 Hagerstown	Eastern	19	106²/₃	7	4	.636	115	47	73	2.70	0
1991 Baltimore	A.L.	8	36	0	3	.000	23	23	47	8.00	0
1992 Rochester	Int.	17	101¹/₃	6	6	.500	115	46	84	3.72	0
1992 Baltimore	A.L.	15	94¹/₃	7	5	.583	77	38	87	3.63	0
1993 Rochester	Int.	6	26²/₃	1	1	.500	33	15	26	4.05	0
1993 Baltimore	A.L.	17	85²/₃	5	5	.455	49	49	91	6.51	0
1994 Frederick	Carolina	1	5	0	0	.000	7	0	3	0.00	0
1994 Baltimore	A.L.	10	52²/₃	3	5	.375	47	30	51	5.81	0
1994 Rochester	Int.	15	90¹/₃	7	5	.583	86	34	70	2.79	0
1995 Rochester	Int.	4	30	2	1	.667	33	8	27	2.70	0
1995 Baltimore	A.L.	19	75¹/₃	2	5	.286	77	48	68	6.21	0
1996 Baltimore	A.L.	28	53	9	1	.900	62	23	48	4.08	1
1997 Baltimore	A.L.	53	95¹/₃	10	3	.769	102	26	75	3.02	1
1998 Rochester	Int.	1	2	0	0	.000	1	1	3	4.50	0
1998 Baltimore a	A.L.	45	77	4	4	.500	83	34	65	3.51	4
1999 Baltimore b	A.L.	43	53	3	4	.429	59	45	43	5.43	3
2000 Seattle	A.L.	72	69¹/₃	5	8	.385	77	29	51	4.28	0
2001 Seattle	A.L.	71	68	8	0	1.000	83	12	46	1.72	3
2002 Seattle	A.L.	66	69²/₃	10	4	.714	81	13	45	2.33	2
2003 Seattle c	A.L.	67	54	3	3	.500	48	18	53	4.17	3
2004 Sacramento	P.C.	2	2	0	0	.000	3	1	0	0.00	0
2004 Oakland d-e-f	A.L.	37	38²/₃	3	3	.500	34	21	46	5.12	9
2005 Akron	Eastern	1	1	0	0	.000	0	0	0	0.00	0
2005 Cleveland g	A.L.	47	43¹/₃	3	1	.750	43	12	33	2.08	0
2006 Philadelphia h	N.L.	55	45²/₃	0	5	.000	48	30	47	5.32	4
2007 Seattle i-j	A.L.		INJURED—Did Not Play								
2008 West Tenn	Southern	1	0¹/₃	0	1	.000	1	1	2	27.00	0

Year Club	Lea	G	IP	W	L	Pct	SO	BB	H	ERA	SAVES
2008 Seattle	A.L.	36	22	2	1	.667	26	13	17	2.86	1
2008 Florida k-l	N.L.	25	13⅓	2	0	1.000	14	3	11	0.68	1
Major League Totals .... 17 Yrs.		714	1046⅓	79	61	.564	1033	467	924	4.23	32
Division Series											
1996 Baltimore	A.L.	2	1	0	0	.000	1	1	1	9.00	0
1997 Baltimore	A.L.	1	2⅓	0	0	.000	4	0	0	0.00	0
2000 Seattle	A.L.	3	2⅔	0	0	.000	2	2	0	0.00	0
2001 Seattle	A.L.	3	2⅔	0	0	.000	1	0	1	0.00	0
Division Series Totals		9	8⅔	0	0	.000	8	3	2	1.04	0
Championship Series											
1996 Baltimore	A.L.	3	2	0	0	.000	2	0	2	0.00	0
1997 Baltimore	A.L.	2	2⅓	0	0	.000	2	3	2	0.00	0
2000 Seattle	A.L.	4	2	0	1	.000	5	4	8	31.50	0
2001 Seattle	A.L.	2	2	0	0	.000	2	0	2	4.50	0
Championship Series Totals		11	8⅓	0	1	.000	11	7	14	8.64	0

a On disabled list from July 5 to August 17, 1998.
b Filed for free agency, November 1, 1999. Signed with Seattle Mariners, December 21, 1999.
c Filed for free agency, October 27, 2003. Signed with Oakland Athletics, December 22, 2003.
d On disabled list from June 28 to August 18, 2004.
e Traded to Pittsburgh Pirates with pitcher Mark Redman for catcher Jason Kendall and cash, November 25, 2004.
f Traded to Cleveland Indians for outfielder Matt Lawton, December 11, 2004.
g On disabled list from August 12 to September 2, 2005.
h Traded to Philadelphia Phillies for outfielder Jason Michaels, January 27, 2006.
i Filed for free agency, October 28, 2006. Signed with Seattle Mariners, January 25, 2007.
j On disabled list from April 2 to October 24, 2007.
k Traded to Florida Marlins for pitcher Gaby Hernandez, July 31, 2008.
l Filed for free agency, November 1, 2008. Signed with Cincinnati Reds, December 12, 2008.

RICHARD, CLAYTON C.
Born, Lafayette, Indiana, September 12, 1983.
Bats Left. Throws Left. Height, 6 feet, 5 inches. Weight, 240 pounds.

Year Club	Lea	G	IP	W	L	Pct	SO	BB	H	ERA	SAVES
2005 Great Falls	Pioneer	10	41	2	1	.667	39	12	37	2.85	0
2005 Kannapolis	So.Atl.	3	10⅓	0	1	.000	8	1	14	5.23	0
2006 Winston-Salem	Carolina	4	23⅔	1	3	.250	12	6	29	4.56	0
2006 Kannapolis	So.Atl.	18	95⅔	6	6	.500	54	28	117	3.67	0
2007 Winston-Salem	Carolina	28	161⅓	8	12	.400	99	59	159	3.63	0
2008 Birmingham	Southern	13	83⅔	6	6	.500	53	16	66	2.47	0
2008 Charlotte	Int.	7	44	6	0	1.000	33	4	33	2.45	0
2008 Chicago a.............	A.L.	13	47⅔	2	5	.286	29	13	61	6.04	0
Division Series											
2008 Chicago	A.L.	2	6⅓	0	0	.000	6	3	5	1.42	0

a On disabled list from March 22 to May 29, 2008.

RINCON, JUAN MANUEL
Born, Maracaibo, Venezuela, January 23, 1979.
Bats Right. Throws Right. Height, 5 feet, 11 inches. Weight, 205 pounds.

Year Club	Lea	G	IP	W	L	Pct	SO	BB	H	ERA	SAVES
1997 Twins	Gulf Coast	11	58	3	3	.500	46	24	55	2.95	0
1997 Elizabethtown........	Appal.	2	9⅓	0	1	.000	7	3	11	3.86	0
1998 Fort Wayne........	Midwest	37	96⅓	6	4	.600	74	54	84	3.83	6
1999 Quad City	Midwest	28	163⅓	14	8	.636	153	66	146	2.92	0
2000 New Britain	Eastern	15	89	3	9	.250	79	39	96	4.65	0
2000 Fort Myers	Fla.St.	13	76⅓	5	3	.625	55	23	67	2.12	0
2001 New Britain	Eastern	29	153⅓	14	6	.700	133	57	130	2.88	0
2001 Minnesota	A.L.	4	5⅔	0	0	.000	4	5	7	6.35	0
2002 Edmonton	P.C.	19	101⅔	7	4	.636	75	35	111	4.78	0
2002 Minnesota	A.L.	10	28⅔	0	2	.000	21	9	44	6.28	0
2003 Rochester............	Int.	2	8⅓	0	2	.000	8	5	12	7.56	0
2003 Minnesota	A.L.	58	85⅔	5	6	.455	63	38	74	3.68	0
2004 Minnesota	A.L.	77	82	11	6	.647	106	32	52	2.63	2
2005 Minnesota	A.L.	75	77	6	6	.500	84	30	63	2.45	0
2006 Minnesota	A.L.	75	74⅓	3	1	.750	65	24	76	2.91	1
2007 Minnesota	A.L.	63	59⅔	3	3	.500	49	28	65	5.13	0
2008 Buffalo	Int.	4	5⅓	0	1	.000	4	3	11	6.75	0
2008 Minnesota-Cleveland a-b	A.L.	47	55⅓	3	3	.500	39	24	67	5.86	0
Major League Totals .... 8 Yrs.		409	468⅓	31	27	.534	431	190	448	3.80	3

Year Club	Lea	G	IP	W	L	Pct	SO	BB	H	ERA	SAVES
Division Series											
2003 Minnesota .... A.L.		3	2⅓	0	0	.000	1	4	1	0.00	0
2004 Minnesota .... A.L.		3	3⅓	0	0	.000	5	2	4	10.80	0
2006 Minnesota .... A.L.		2	3	0	0	.000	3	0	1	3.00	0
Division Series Totals		8	8⅔	0	0	.000	9	6	6	5.19	0

a Released by Minnesota Twins, June 18, 2008. Signed with Cleveland Indians organization, June 24, 2008.
b Filed for free agency, November 1, 2008.

RIVERA, MARIANO

Born, Panama City, Panama, November 29, 1969.
Bats Right. Throws Right. Height, 6 feet, 2 inches. Weight, 195 pounds.

Year Club	Lea	G	IP	W	L	Pct	SO	BB	H	ERA	SAVES
1990 Yankees	Gulf Coast	22	52	5	1	.833	58	7	17	0.17	1
1991 Greensboro	So. Atl.	29	114⅔	4	9	.308	123	36	103	2.75	0
1992 Ft. Lauderdale	Fla. St.	10	59⅓	5	3	.625	42	5	40	2.28	0
1993 Yankees	Gulf Coast	2	4	0	1	.000	6	1	2	2.25	0
1993 Greensboro	So. Atl.	10	39⅓	1	0	1.000	32	15	31	2.06	0
1994 Tampa	Fla. St.	7	36⅔	3	0	1.000	27	12	34	2.21	0
1994 Albany	Eastern	9	63⅓	3	0	1.000	39	8	58	2.27	0
1994 Columbus..............	Int.	6	31	4	2	.667	23	10	34	5.81	0
1995 Columbus..............	Int.	7	30	2	2	.500	30	3	25	2.10	0
1995 New York	A.L.	19	67	5	3	.625	51	30	71	5.51	0
1996 New York	A.L.	61	107⅔	8	3	.727	130	34	73	2.09	5
1997 New York	A.L.	66	71⅔	6	4	.600	68	20	65	1.88	43
1998 New York a.............	A.L.	54	61⅓	3	0	1.000	36	17	48	1.91	36
1999 New York	A.L.	66	69	4	3	.571	52	18	43	1.83	*45
2000 New York	A.L.	66	75⅔	7	4	.636	58	25	58	2.85	36
2001 New York	A.L.	71	80⅔	4	6	.400	83	12	61	2.34	*50
2002 Yankees	Gulf Coast	1	2	0	0	.000	2	1	2	0.00	0
2002 New York b.............	A.L.	45	46	1	4	.200	41	11	35	2.74	28
2003 New York c.............	A.L.	64	70⅔	5	2	.714	63	10	61	1.66	40
2004 New York	A.L.	74	78⅔	4	2	.667	66	20	65	1.94	*53
2005 New York	A.L.	71	78⅓	7	4	.636	80	18	50	1.38	43
2006 New York	A.L.	63	75	5	5	.500	55	11	61	1.80	34
2007 New York d.............	A.L.	67	71⅓	3	4	.429	74	12	68	3.15	30
2008 New York	A.L.	64	70⅔	6	5	.545	77	6	41	1.40	39
Major League Totals .... 14 Yrs.		851	1023⅔	68	49	.581	934	244	800	2.29	482
Division Series											
1995 New York	A.L.	3	5⅓	1	0	1.000	8	1	3	0.00	0
1996 New York	A.L.	2	4⅔	0	0	.000	1	1	0	0.00	0
1997 New York	A.L.	2	2	0	0	.000	1	0	2	4.50	1
1998 New York	A.L.	3	3⅓	0	0	.000	2	1	1	0.00	2
1999 New York	A.L.	2	3	0	0	.000	3	0	1	0.00	2
2000 New York	A.L.	3	5	0	0	.000	2	0	2	0.00	3
2001 New York	A.L.	3	5	0	0	.000	4	0	4	0.00	2
2002 New York	A.L.	1	1	0	0	.000	0	0	1	0.00	1
2003 New York	A.L.	2	4	0	0	.000	4	0	0	0.00	2
2004 New York	A.L.	4	5⅔	1	0	1.000	2	0	2	0.00	2
2005 New York	A.L.	2	3	0	0	.000	2	1	1	3.00	2
2006 New York	A.L.	1	1	0	0	.000	0	0	1	0.00	0
2007 New York	A.L.	3	4⅔	0	0	.000	6	1	2	0.00	0
Division Series Totals		31	47⅔	2	0	1.000	35	5	20	0.38	15
Championship Series											
1996 New York	A.L.	2	4	1	0	1.000	5	1	6	0.00	0
1998 New York	A.L.	4	5⅔	0	0	.000	5	1	0	0.00	1
1999 New York	A.L.	3	4⅔	1	0	1.000	3	0	5	0.00	2
2000 New York	A.L.	3	4⅔	0	0	.000	1	0	4	1.93	1
2001 New York	A.L.	4	4⅔	1	0	1.000	3	1	2	1.93	2
2003 New York	A.L.	4	8	1	0	1.000	6	0	5	1.13	2
2004 New York	A.L.	5	7	0	0	.000	6	2	6	1.29	2
Championship Series Totals		25	38⅔	4	0	1.000	29	5	28	0.93	10
World Series Record											
1996 New York	A.L.	4	5⅔	0	0	.000	4	3	4	1.59	0
1998 New York	A.L.	3	4⅓	0	0	.000	4	0	5	0.00	3
1999 New York	A.L.	3	4⅔	1	0	1.000	3	1	3	0.00	2
2000 New York	A.L.	4	6	0	0	.000	7	1	4	3.00	2
2001 New York	A.L.	4	6⅓	1	1	.500	7	1	6	1.42	0

Year	Club	Lea	G	IP	W	L	Pct	SO	BB	H	ERA	SAVES
2003 New York	A.L.	2	4	0	0	.000	4	0	2	0.00	1
World Series Totals		20	31	2	1	.667	29	6	24	1.16	9

a On disabled list from April 6 to April 24, 1998.
b On disabled list from June 9 to June 25 and July 21 to August 8 and August 18 to September 20, 2002.
c On disabled list from March 25 to April 29, 2003.
d Filed for free agency, October 30, 2007, re-signed with New York Yankees, December 17, 2007.

RIVERA, RABELL SAUL (SAUL)

Born, San Juan, Puerto Rico, December 7, 1977.
Bats Both. Throws Right. Height, 5 feet, 11 inches. Weight, 185 pounds.

Year	Club	Lea	G	IP	W	L	Pct	SO	BB	H	ERA	SAVES
1998 Elizabethtown	Appal.	23	36	3	3	.500	65	19	19	2.25	7
1999 Quad Cities	Midwest	60	69²/₃	4	1	.800	102	36	42	1.42	23
2000 New Britain	Eastern	22	37	1	0	1.000	47	22	28	3.89	0
2000 Fort Myers	Fla.St.	29	37²/₃	8	1	.889	45	19	34	3.58	5
2001 New Britain	Eastern	33	42²/₃	5	2	.714	55	18	35	3.16	13
2001 Twins a	Gulf Coast	3	3	0	0	.000	4	1	2	0.00	0
2002 Binghamton	Eastern	30	38²/₃	2	3	.400	32	23	25	3.03	13
2002 Harrisburg b	Eastern	15	19	0	2	.000	15	9	21	3.32	3
2003		INJURED—Did Not Play									
2004 Harrisburg	Eastern	18	20²/₃	0	2	.000	15	12	27	7.84	3
2004 Huntsville c-d	Southern	26	33¹/₃	2	1	.667	25	16	30	1.62	1
2005 Harrisburg e	Eastern	40	76²/₃	3	3	.500	70	20	72	2.47	9
2006 New Orleans	P.C.	12	28¹/₃	1	1	.500	25	12	25	1.59	1
2006 Washington	N.L.	54	60¹/₃	3	0	1.000	41	32	59	3.43	1
2007 Columbus	Int.	1	0²/₃	0	1	.000	0	0	2	13.50	0
2007 Washington	N.L.	85	93	4	6	.400	64	42	88	3.68	3
2008 Washington	N.L.	76	84	5	6	.455	65	35	90	3.96	0
Major League Totals	3 Yrs.	215	237¹/₃	12	12	.500	170	109	237	3.72	4

a Claimed on waivers by New York Mets from Minnesota Twins, November 20, 2001.
b Sent to Montreal Expos by New York Mets to complete trade for pitcher Scott Strickland, July 14, 2002.
c Traded to Milwaukee Brewers with outfielder Peter Bergeron for outfielder Jason Belcher and pitcher Jason Childers, June 6, 2004.
d Filed for free agency, October 15, 2004. Signed with Montreal Expos, November 16, 2004.
e Filed for free agency, October 15, 2005, re-signed with Washington Nationals, November 21, 2005.

ROBERTSON, NATHAN DANIEL (NATE)

Born, Wichita, Kansas, September 3, 1977.
Bats Right. Throws Left. Height, 6 feet, 2 inches. Weight, 225 pounds.

Year	Club	Lea	G	IP	W	L	Pct	SO	BB	H	ERA	SAVES
1999 Utica	N.Y.-Penn.	5	26	2	0	1.000	26	8	22	2.77	0
1999 Kane County	Midwest	8	51	6	1	.857	33	12	42	2.29	0
2000 Kane County	Midwest	6	17²/₃	0	2	.000	15	6	24	5.09	0
2001 Brevard County	Fla.St.	19	106¹/₃	11	4	.733	67	43	95	2.88	0
2002 Portland	Eastern	27	163	10	9	.526	109	50	156	3.42	0
2002 Florida	N.L.	6	8¹/₃	0	1	.000	8	4	15	11.88	0
2003 Toledo	Int.	24	155	9	7	.563	102	47	145	3.14	0
2003 Detroit a	A.L.	8	44²/₃	1	2	.333	23	23	55	5.44	0
2004 Detroit	A.L.	34	196²/₃	12	10	.545	155	66	210	4.90	1
2005 Detroit	A.L.	32	196²/₃	7	16	.304	122	65	202	4.48	0
2006 Detroit	A.L.	32	208²/₃	13	13	.500	137	67	206	3.84	0
2007 Erie	Eastern	1	6	1	0	1.000	6	1	0	0.00	0
2007 Detroit b	A.L.	30	177²/₃	9	13	.409	119	63	199	4.76	0
2008 Detroit	A.L.	32	168²/₃	7	11	.389	108	62	218	6.35	0
Major League Totals	7 Yrs.	174	1001¹/₃	49	66	.426	677	350	1105	4.90	1
Division Series											
2006 Detroit	A.L.	1	5²/₃	0	1	.000	1	0	12	11.12	0
Championship Series											
2006 Detroit	A.L.	1	5	1	0	1.000	4	3	6	0.00	0
World Series Record											
2006 Detroit	A.L.	1	5	0	1	.000	3	3	5	3.60	0

a Traded to Detroit Tigers with pitcher Gary Knotts and pitcher Rob Henkel for pitcher Mark Redman and pitcher Jerrod Fuell, January 11, 2003.
b On disabled list from June 6 to June 26, 2007.

RODNEY, FERNANDO

Born, Samana, Dominican Republic, March 17, 1977.
Bats Right. Throws Right. Height, 5 feet, 11 inches. Weight, 220 pounds.

Year	Club	Lea	G	IP	W	L	Pct	SO	BB	H	ERA	SAVES
1998 Detroit	....	Dominican	11	32	1	3	.250	37	19	25	3.38	1
1999 Lakeland	....	Fla.St.	4	6⅓	1	0	1.000	5	1	7	1.42	2
1999 Tigers	....	Gulf Coast	22	30	3	3	.500	39	21	20	2.40	9
2000 West Michigan	......	Midwest	22	82⅔	6	4	.600	56	35	74	2.94	0
2001 Erie	....	Eastern	4	6⅓	0	0	.000	8	3	7	4.26	1
2001 Lakeland	....	Fla.St.	16	55⅓	4	2	.667	44	19	53	3.42	0
2001 Tigers	....	Gulf Coast	1	1	0	0	.000	1	1	0	0.00	0
2002 Erie	....	Eastern	21	20⅓	1	0	1.000	18	5	14	1.33	11
2002 Detroit	....	A.L.	20	18	1	3	.250	10	10	25	6.00	0
2002 Toledo	....	Int.	20	22⅓	1	1	.500	25	9	13	0.81	4
2003 Toledo	....	Int.	38	40⅔	1	1	.500	58	13	22	1.33	23
2003 Detroit	....	A.L.	27	29⅔	1	3	.250	33	17	35	6.07	3
2004 Detroit a	....	A.L.			INJURED—Did Not Play							
2005 Toledo	....	Int.	3	3	0	0	.000	4	1	2	3.00	0
2005 Detroit b	....	A.L.	39	44	2	3	.400	42	17	39	2.86	9
2006 Detroit	....	A.L.	63	71⅔	7	4	.636	65	34	51	3.52	7
2007 Toledo	....	Int.	4	3	0	0	.000	4	2	4	0.00	0
2007 Detroit c	....	A.L.	48	50⅔	2	6	.250	54	21	46	4.26	1
2008 Toledo	....	Int.	4	5⅓	1	0	1.000	8	5	3	6.75	0
2008 Detroit d	....	A.L.	38	40⅓	0	6	.000	49	30	34	4.91	13
Major League Totals	........6 Yrs.		235	254⅓	13	25	.342	253	129	230	4.25	33
Championship Series												
2006 Detroit	....	A.L.	3	3⅔	0	0	.000	4	1	1	0.00	0
World Series Record												
2006 Detroit	....	A.L.	4	4	0	0	.000	5	4	5	4.50	0

a On disabled list from March 26 to October 4, 2004.
b On disabled list from March 29 to June 9, 2005.
c On disabled list from May 21 to June 5 and June 24 to August 4, 2007.
d On disabled list from March 30 to June 16, 2008.

RODRIGUEZ, FRANCISCO JOSE

Born, Caracas, Venezuela, January 7, 1982.
Bats Right. Throws Right. Height, 6 feet. Weight, 195 pounds.

Year	Club	Lea	G	IP	W	L	Pct	SO	BB	H	ERA	SAVES
1999 Boise	....	Northwest	1	5	1	0	1.000	6	1	3	5.40	0
1999 Butte	....	Pioneer	12	51⅔	1	1	.500	69	21	33	3.31	0
2000 Lake Elsinore	......	California	13	64	4	4	.500	79	32	43	2.81	0
2001 Rancho Cucamonga		California	20	113⅔	5	7	.417	147	55	127	5.38	0
2002 Arkansas	....	Texas	23	41⅓	3	3	.500	61	15	32	1.96	9
2002 Salt Lake	....	P.C.	27	42	2	3	.400	59	13	30	2.57	6
2002 Anaheim	....	A.L.	5	5⅔	0	0	.000	13	2	3	0.00	0
2003 Anaheim	....	A.L.	59	86	8	3	.727	95	35	50	3.03	2
2004 Anaheim	....	A.L.	69	84	4	1	.800	123	33	51	1.82	12
2005 Los Angeles a	....	A.L.	66	67⅓	2	5	.286	91	32	45	2.67	*45
2006 Los Angeles	....	A.L.	69	73	2	3	.400	98	28	52	1.73	*47
2007 Los Angeles	....	A.L.	64	67⅓	5	2	.714	90	34	50	2.81	40
2008 Los Angeles b	......	A.L.	*76	68⅓	2	3	.400	77	34	54	2.24	*62
Major League Totals	........7 Yrs.		408	451⅔	23	17	.575	587	198	305	2.35	208
Division Series												
2002 Anaheim	....	A.L.	3	5⅔	2	0	1.000	8	2	2	3.18	0
2004 Anaheim	....	A.L.	2	4⅔	0	2	.000	5	3	4	3.86	0
2005 Los Angeles	....	A.L.	3	3⅓	0	0	.000	2	0	5	2.70	2
2007 Los Angeles	....	A.L.	1	0⅓	0	0	.000	1	1	1	54.00	0
2008 Los Angeles	....	A.L.	2	2⅓	0	1	.000	2	2	5	7.71	0
Division Series Totals	....		11	16⅓	2	3	.400	18	8	17	4.96	2
Championship Series												
2002 Anaheim	....	A.L.	4	4⅓	2	0	1.000	7	2	2	0.00	0
2005 Los Angeles	....	A.L.	2	2⅓	0	0	.000	3	3	2	0.00	1
Championship Series Totals	......		6	6⅔	2	0	1.000	10	5	4	0.00	1
World Series Record												
2002 Anaheim	....	A.L.	4	8⅔	1	1	.500	13	1	6	2.08	0

a On disabled list from May 15 to June 1, 2005.
b Filed for free agency, November 3, 2008. Signed with New York Mets, December 10, 2008.

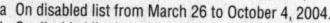

RODRIGUEZ, WANDY FULTON

Born, Santiago Rodriguez, Dominican Republic, January 18, 1979.
Bats Both. Throws Left. Height, 5 feet, 11 inches. Weight, 160 pounds.

Year Club	Lea	G	IP	W	L	Pct	SO	BB	H	ERA	SAVES
2001 Martinsville	Appal.	12	74	4	3	.571	67	20	54	1.58	0
2002 Lexington...........	So.Atl.	28	159⅓	11	4	.733	137	44	167	3.78	0
2003 Salem...............	Carolina	20	111	8	7	.533	72	41	102	3.49	0
2004 Round Rock..........	Texas	26	142⅔	11	6	.647	115	57	159	4.48	0
2005 Corpus Christi	Texas	1	3⅓	0	0	.000	3	2	3	2.70	0
2005 Round Rock..........	P.C.	8	46⅓	4	2	.667	48	16	43	3.69	0
2005 Houston.............	N.L.	25	128⅔	10	10	.500	80	53	135	5.53	0
2006 Round Rock...........	P.C.	5	26	2	2	.500	13	13	32	6.92	0
2006 Houston.............	N.L.	30	135⅔	9	10	.474	98	63	154	5.64	0
2007 Houston.............	N.L.	31	182⅔	9	13	.409	158	62	179	4.58	0
2008 Corpus Christi	Texas	1	6	0	0	.000	0	1	4	1.50	0
2008 Houston a...........	N.L.	25	137⅓	9	7	.563	131	44	136	3.54	0
Major League Totals........	4 Yrs.	111	584⅓	37	40	.481	467	222	604	4.79	0
Division Series											
2005 Houston.............	N.L.	1	1	0	0	.000	2	0	1	9.00	0
World Series Record											
2005 Houston.............	N.L.	2	3⅔	0	1	.000	2	5	4	2.45	0

a On disabled list from April 20 to May 28, 2008.

ROGERS, KENNETH SCOTT (KENNY)

Born, Savannah, Georgia, November 10, 1964.
Bats Left. Throws Left. Height, 6 feet, 1 inch. Weight, 190 pounds.

Year Club	Lea	G	IP	W	L	Pct	SO	BB	H	ERA	SAVES
1982 Sarasota Rangers.....	Gulf C.	2	3	0	0	.000	4	0	0	0.00	0
1983 Sarasota Rangers.....	Gulf C.	15	53⅓	4	1	.800	36	20	40	2.36	1
1984 Burlington	Midwest	39	92⅔	4	7	.364	93	33	87	3.98	3
1985 Daytona Beach.......	Fla. St.	6	10	0	1	.000	9	11	12	7.20	0
1985 Burlington	Midwest	33	95	2	5	.286	96	61	67	2.84	4
1986 Tulsa a.............	Texas	10	26⅓	0	3	.000	23	18	39	9.91	0
1986 Salem.............	Carolina	12	66	2	7	.222	46	26	75	6.27	0
1987 Charlotte b..........	Fla. St.	5	17	0	3	.000	14	8	17	4.76	0
1987 Tulsa.............	Texas	28	69	1	5	.167	59	35	80	5.35	2
1988 Charlotte c..........	Fla. St.	8	35⅓	2	0	1.000	26	11	22	1.27	1
1988 Tulsa	Texas	13	83⅓	4	6	.400	76	34	73	4.00	0
1989 Texas	A.L.	73	73⅔	3	4	.429	63	42	60	2.93	2
1990 Texas	A.L.	69	97⅔	10	6	.625	74	42	93	3.13	15
1991 Texas	A.L.	63	109⅔	10	10	.500	73	61	121	5.42	5
1992 Texas	A.L.	*81	78⅔	3	6	.333	70	26	80	3.09	6
1993 Texas	A.L.	35	208⅓	16	10	.615	140	71	210	4.10	0
1994 Texas d-e-f............	A.L.	24	167⅓	11	8	.579	120	52	169	4.46	0
1995 Texas g-h.............	A.L.	31	208	17	7	.708	140	76	192	3.38	0
1996 New York.............	A.L.	30	179	12	8	.600	92	83	179	4.68	0
1997 New York i............	A.L.	31	145	6	7	.462	78	62	161	5.65	0
1998 Oakland	A.L.	34	238⅔	16	8	.667	138	67	215	3.17	0
1999 Oakland j.............	A.L.	19	119⅓	5	3	.625	68	41	135	4.30	0
1999 New York k...........	N.L.	12	76	5	1	.833	58	28	71	4.03	0
2000 Texas	A.L.	34	227⅓	13	13	.500	127	78	257	4.55	0
2001 Texas	A.L.	20	120⅔	5	7	.417	74	49	150	6.19	0
2002 Texas l..............	A.L.	33	210⅔	13	8	.619	107	70	212	3.84	0
2003 Minnesota m	A.L.	33	195	13	8	.619	116	50	227	4.57	0
2004 Texas	A.L.	35	211⅔	18	9	.667	126	66	248	4.76	0
2005 Texas n..............	A.L.	30	195⅓	14	8	.636	87	53	205	3.46	0
2006 Detroit	A.L.	34	204	17	8	.680	99	62	195	3.84	0
2007 West Michigan......	Midwest	1	5	0	1	.000	4	2	7	1.80	0
2007 Toledo	Int.	1	3⅔	0	0	.000	2	0	3	0.00	0
2007 Detroit o-p	A.L.	11	63	3	4	.429	36	25	65	4.43	0
2008 Detroit q............	A.L.	30	173⅔	9	13	.409	82	71	212	5.70	0
Major League Totals	20 Yrs.	762	3302⅔	219	156	.584	1968	1175	3457	4.27	28
Division Series											
1996 New York.............	A.L.	2	2	0	0	.000	1	2	5	9.00	0
1999 New York	N.L.	1	4⅓	0	1	.000	6	2	5	8.31	0
2003 Minnesota	A.L.	1	1⅓	0	0	.000	3	1	1	0.00	0
2006 Detroit	A.L.	1	7⅔	1	0	1.000	8	2	5	0.00	0
Division Series Totals		5	15⅓	1	1	.500	18	7	16	3.52	0

Year	Club	Lea	G	IP	W	L	Pct	SO	BB	H	ERA	SAVES
	Championship Series											
1996 New York		A.L.	1	3	0	0	.000	3	2	5	12.00	0
1999 New York		N.L.	3	$7^2/3$	0	2	.000	2	7	11	5.87	0
2006 Detroit		A.L.	1	$7^1/3$	1	0	1.000	6	2	2	0.00	0
Championship Series Totals			5	18	1	2	.333	11	11	18	4.50	0
	World Series Record											
1996 New York		A.L.	1	2	0	0	.000	0	2	5	22.50	0
2006 Detroit		A.L.	1	8	1	0	1.000	5	3	2	0.00	0
World Series Totals			2	10	1	0	1.000	5	5	7	4.50	0

a On disabled list from April 12 to April 30, 1986.
b On disabled list from March 28 to April 30, 1987.
c On disabled list from March 20 to May 15, 1988.
d Pitched perfect no-hit, no-run game against California Angels, winning 4-0, July 28, 1994.
e Filed for free agency, October 19, 1994; ruled ineligible by Player Relations Committee due to insufficient service time.
f Declared restricted free agent under Major League Baseball implemented labor proposal, December 23, 1994.
g Re-signed with Texas Rangers, April 7, 1995.
h Filed for free agency, November 12, 1995. Signed with New York Yankees, December 30, 1995.
i Traded to Oakland Athletics for player to be named later, November 7, 1997. New York Yankees received infielder Scott Brosius to complete trade, November 18, 1997.
j Traded to New York Mets for outfielder Terrence Long and pitcher Leoner Vasquez, July 23, 1999.
k Filed for free agency, October 29, 1999. Signed with Texas Rangers, December 29, 1999.
l Filed for free agency, October 29, 2002. Signed with Minnesota Twins, March 12, 2003.
m Filed for free agency, October 29, 2003. Signed with Texas Rangers, January 13, 2004.
n Filed for free agency, October 28, 2005. Signed with Detroit Tigers, December 12, 2005.
o On disabled list from March 25 to June 22 and July 26 to September 5, 2007.
p Filed for free agency, October 31, 2007, re-signed with Detroit Tigers, November 30, 2007.
q Filed for free agency, November 11, 2008.

ROMERO, JUAN CARLOS (J.C.)

Born, Rio Piedras, Puerto Rico, June 4, 1976.
Bats Both. Throws Left. Height, 5 feet, 11 inches. Weight, 205 pounds.

Year	Club	Lea	G	IP	W	L	Pct	SO	BB	H	ERA	SAVES
1997 Elizabethtown		Appal.	18	24	3	2	.600	29	7	27	4.88	3
1997 Ft. Myers		Fla.St.	7	$12^1/3$	1	1	.500	9	4	11	4.38	0
1998 New Britain		Eastern	51	78	6	3	.667	79	43	48	2.19	2
1999 New Britain		Eastern	36	53	4	4	.500	53	34	51	3.40	7
1999 Salt Lake		P.C.	15	$19^2/3$	4	1	.800	20	14	18	3.20	1
1999 Minnesota		A.L.	5	$9^2/3$	0	0	.000	4	0	13	3.72	0
2000 Fort Myers		Fla.St.	2	$4^2/3$	0	0	.000	3	1	4	1.93	0
2000 Salt Lake		P.C.	17	$65^1/3$	4	2	.667	38	25	60	3.44	4
2000 Minnesota a		A.L.	12	$57^2/3$	2	7	.222	50	30	72	7.02	0
2001 Edmonton		P.C.	12	$63^2/3$	3	3	.500	55	24	67	3.68	0
2001 Minnesota		A.L.	14	65	1	4	.200	39	24	71	6.23	0
2002 Minnesota		A.L.	81	81	9	2	.818	76	36	62	1.89	1
2003 Minnesota		A.L.	73	63	2	0	1.000	50	42	66	5.00	0
2004 Rochester		Int.	3	8	0	0	.000	11	5	4	2.25	0
2004 Minnesota		A.L.	74	$74^1/3$	7	4	.636	69	38	61	3.51	1
2005 Minnesota b		A.L.	68	57	4	3	.571	48	39	50	3.47	0
2006 Los Angeles c		A.L.	65	$48^1/3$	1	2	.333	31	28	57	6.70	0
2007 Boston		A.L.	23	20	1	0	1.000	11	15	24	3.15	1
2007 Philadelphia d-e		N.L.	51	$36^1/3$	1	2	.333	31	25	15	1.24	0
2008 Philadelphia		N.L.	81	59	4	4	.500	52	38	41	2.75	1
Major League Totals ...... 10 Yrs.			547	$571^1/3$	32	28	.533	461	315	532	4.14	4
	Division Series											
2002 Minnesota		A.L.	3	$3^1/3$	0	0	.000	2	1	3	0.00	0
2003 Minnesota		A.L.	3	$3^1/3$	0	0	.000	1	2	3	0.00	0
2004 Minnesota		A.L.	2	1	0	0	.000	1	1	0	9.00	0
2007 Philadelphia		N.L.	3	2	0	1	.000	1	0	3	4.50	0
2008 Philadelphia		N.L.	1	$0^1/3$	0	0	.000	0	0	0	0.00	0
Division Series Totals			12	10	0	1	.000	5	4	9	1.80	0
	Championship Series											
2002 Minnesota		A.L.	4	2	0	1	.000	3	2	4	22.50	0
2008 Philadelphia		N.L.	3	$2^1/3$	0	0	.000	3	3	0	0.00	0
Championship Series Totals			7	$4^1/3$	0	1	.000	6	5	4	10.38	0
	World Series Record											
2008 Philadelphia		N.L.	4	$4^2/3$	2	0	1.000	4	0	2	0.00	0

a On disabled list from March 25 to May 9, 2000.

b Traded to Los Angeles Angels for infielder Alexi Casilla, December 9, 2005.
c Filed for free agency, October 28, 2006. Signed with Boston Red Sox, December 15, 2006.
d Released by Boston Red Sox, June 18, 2007. Signed with Philadelphia Phillies organization, June 22, 2007.
e Filed for free agency, October 30, 2007, re-signed with Philadelphia Phillies, November 10, 2007.

ROMO, SERGIO FRANCISCO

Born, Brawley, California, March 4, 1983.
Bats Right. Throws Right. Height, 5 feet, 11 inches. Weight, 190 pounds.

Year Club	Lea	G	IP	W	L	Pct	SO	BB	H	ERA	SAVES
2005 Salem-Keizer	Northwest	15	68²/₃	7	1	.875	65	9	70	2.75	0
2006 Augusta	So.Atl.	31	103¹/₃	10	2	.833	95	19	78	2.53	4
2007 San Jose	Calif.	41	66¹/₃	6	2	.750	106	15	35	1.36	9
2008 Connecticut	Eastern	24	27	1	3	.250	30	7	22	4.00	11
2008 Fresno	P.C.	3	6	0	0	.000	7	2	3	0.00	0
2008 San Francisco	N.L.	29	34	3	1	.750	33	8	16	2.12	0

ROWLAND-SMITH, RYAN BENJAMIN

Born, Sydney, Australia, January 26, 1983.
Bats Left. Throws Left. Height, 6 feet, 3 inches. Weight, 240 pounds.

Year Club	Lea	G	IP	W	L	Pct	SO	BB	H	ERA	SAVES
2001 Mariners	Arizona	17	33¹/₃	1	1	.500	39	9	25	2.97	5
2002 Wisconsin	Midwest	12	41¹/₃	1	2	.333	38	19	50	6.75	0
2002 Everett	Northwest	18	61²/₃	4	1	.800	58	22	58	2.77	2
2003 Inland Empire	Calif.	15	19²/₃	0	1	.000	15	8	12	3.20	0
2003 Wisconsin	Midwest	13	32¹/₃	0	0	1.000	37	14	22	1.11	1
2004 Inland Empire	Calif.	29	99²/₃	5	3	.625	119	30	107	3.79	3
2005 San Antonio a	Texas	33	122	6	7	.462	102	51	133	4.35	0
2006 Inland Empire	Calif.	7	6¹/₃	0	1	.000	9	2	8	5.68	0
2006 San Antonio	Texas	23	41¹/₃	1	3	.250	48	18	38	2.83	4
2007 Tacoma	P.C.	25	41²/₃	3	4	.429	50	22	35	3.67	1
2007 Seattle	A.L.	26	38²/₃	1	0	1.000	42	15	39	3.96	0
2008 Tacoma	P.C.	3	18²/₃	2	0	1.000	12	7	12	2.89	0
2008 Seattle	A.L.	47	118¹/₃	5	3	.625	77	48	114	3.42	2
Major League Totals	2 Yrs.	73	157	6	3	.667	119	63	153	3.55	2

a Selected by Minnesota Twins in Rule V draft, December 13, 2004. Returned to Seattle Mariners, March 25, 2005.

RUPE, JOSHUA MATTHEW (JOSH)

Born, Portsmouth, Virginia, August 18, 1982.
Bats Right. Throws Right. Height, 6 feet, 2 inches. Weight, 210 pounds.

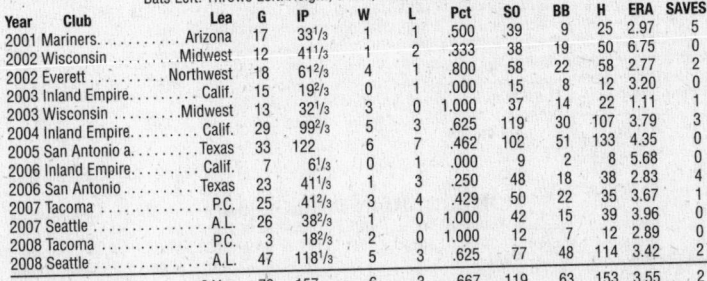

Year Club	Lea	G	IP	W	L	Pct	SO	BB	H	ERA	SAVES
2002 Bristol	Appal.	17	40²/₃	4	3	.571	41	22	41	4.87	0
2003 Clinton	Midwest	6	27²/₃	4	1	.800	23	7	29	3.90	0
2003 Kannapolis a	So.Atl.	26	65²/₃	5	5	.500	69	36	50	3.02	6
2004 Stockton	Calif.	4	18¹/₃	2	0	1.000	14	4	12	0.98	0
2004 Spokane	Northwest	4	18	2	0	1.000	19	3	14	1.50	0
2004 Frisco	Texas	7	37	2	2	.500	16	16	41	4.38	0
2005 Frisco	Texas	11	65	4	3	.571	55	26	64	3.74	0
2005 Oklahoma	P.C.	17	93²/₃	6	7	.462	62	38	116	6.25	0
2005 Texas	A.L.	4	9²/₃	1	0	1.000	6	4	7	2.79	0
2006 Frisco	Texas	6	6	0	0	.000	3	4	7	10.50	0
2006 Oklahoma	P.C.	12	13¹/₃	1	1	.500	4	6	13	3.38	2
2006 Texas b	A.L.	16	29	0	1	.000	14	9	33	3.41	0
2007 Rangers	Arizona	2	3	0	0	.000	3	1	1	0.00	0
2007 Oklahoma c	P.C.	7	37	2	2	.500	20	14	39	4.62	0
2008 Texas	A.L.	46	89¹/₃	3	1	.750	53	46	93	5.14	0
Major League Totals	3 Yrs.	66	128	4	2	.667	73	59	133	4.57	0

a Sent by Chicago White Sox to Texas Rangers as one of three players to be named later in July 1, 2003 trade for Carl Everett, July 23, 2003.
b On disabled list from March 24 to June 29, 2006.
c On disabled list from June 16 to October 15, 2007.

RUSCH, GLENDON JAMES

Born, Seattle, Washington, November 7, 1974.
Bats Left. Throws Left. Height, 6 feet, 1 inch. Weight, 225 pounds.

Year Club	Lea	G	IP	W	L	Pct	SO	BB	H	ERA	SAVES
1993 Royals	Gulf Coast	11	62	4	2	.667	48	11	43	1.60	0
1993 Rockford	Midwest	2	8	0	0	.000	8	7	10	3.38	0

Year	Club	Lea	G	IP	W	L	Pct	SO	BB	H	ERA	SAVES
1994 Rockford	Midwest		28	114	8	5	.615	122	34	111	4.66	1
1995 Wilmington	Carolina		26	165²/3	14	6	.700	147	34	110	1.74	0
1996 Omaha	A.A.		28	169²/3	11	9	.550	117	40	177	3.98	0
1997 Omaha	A.A.		1	6	0	1	.000	2	1	7	4.50	0
1997 Kansas City a	A.L.		30	170¹/3	6	9	.400	116	52	206	5.50	0
1998 Omaha	P.C.		3	14²/3	1	1	.500	14	6	20	7.98	0
1998 Kansas City b	A.L.		29	154²/3	6	15	.286	94	50	191	5.88	1
1999 Omaha	P.C.		20	114	4	7	.364	102	33	143	4.42	0
1999 Royals	Gulf Coast		2	6	0	0	.000	9	3	3	1.50	0
1999 Kansas City	A.L.		3	4	0	1	.000	4	3	7	15.75	0
1999 New York c	N.L.		1	1	0	0	.000	0	0	1	0.00	0
2000 New York	N.L.		31	190²/3	11	11	.500	157	44	196	4.01	0
2001 New York	N.L.		33	179	8	12	.400	156	43	216	4.63	0
2002 Milwaukee d	N.L.		34	210²/3	10	16	.385	140	76	227	4.70	0
2003 Milwaukee	N.L.		32	123¹/3	1	12	.077	93	45	171	6.42	1
2003 Indianapolis e	Int.		4	21	1	1	.500	20	4	17	3.86	0
2004 Iowa	P.C.		4	19	2	0	1.000	16	1	18	1.89	0
2004 Chicago f-g-h	N.L.		32	129²/3	6	2	.750	90	33	127	3.47	2
2005 Chicago	N.L.		46	145¹/3	9	8	.529	111	53	175	4.52	0
2006 Iowa	P.C.		1	4	0	0	.000	2	0	2	2.25	0
2006 Chicago i-j	N.L.		25	66¹/3	3	8	.273	59	33	86	7.46	0
2007					INJURED—Did Not Play							
2008 Colorado Springs	P.C.		7	41	1	2	.333	24	13	48	4.61	0
2008 San Diego-Colorado k-l	N.L.		35	83²/3	5	5	.500	55	25	94	5.16	0
Major League Totals	11 Yrs.		331	1458²/3	65	99	.396	1075	457	1697	5.02	4
Division Series												
2000 New York	N.L.		1	0²/3	0	0	.000	2	0	0	0.00	0
Championship Series												
2000 New York	N.L.		2	3²/3	1	0	1.000	3	0	3	0.00	0
World Series Record												
2000 New York	N.L.		3	4	0	0	.000	2	2	6	2.25	0

a On disabled list from June 16 to July 1, 1997.

b On disabled list from May 31 to June 1 and August 9 to September 4, 1998.

c Traded to New York Mets for pitcher Dan Murray, September 14, 1999.

d Traded to Milwaukee Brewers with outfielder Alex Ochoa and infielder Lenny Harris for outfielder Jeromy Burnitz, pitcher Jeff D'Amico, infielder Lou Collier, outfielder Mark Sweeney and cash, January 21, 2002.

e On disabled list from July 29 to August 22, 2003.

f Filed for free agency, October 28, 2003. Signed with Texas Rangers organization, January 20, 2004.

g Released by Texas Rangers, March 31, 2004. Signed with Chicago Cubs organization, April 1, 2004.

h Filed for free agency, October 28, 2004, re-signed with Chicago Cubs, November 20, 2004.

i On disabled list from June 17 to July 3 and August 1 to August 21, 2006.

j Released by Chicago Cubs, January 25, 2007. Signed with San Diego Padres organization, December 14, 2007.

k Filed for free agency, May 10, 2008. Signed with Colorado Rockies organization, May 16, 2008.

l Filed for free agency, November 3, 2008. Signed with Colorado Rockies organization, December 18, 2008.

RYAN, ROBERT VICTOR (B.J.)

Born, Bossier City, Louisiana, December 28, 1975.
Bats Left. Throws Left. Height, 6 feet, 6 inches. Weight, 260 pounds.

Year	Club	Lea	G	IP	W	L	Pct	SO	BB	H	ERA	SAVES
1998 Billings	Pioneer		14	18²/3	2	1	.667	25	5	15	1.93	4
1998 Chstn-WV	So.Atl.		3	4¹/3	0	0	.000	5	1	1	2.08	2
1998 Chattanooga	Southern		16	16¹/3	1	0	1.000	21	6	13	2.20	4
1999 Rochester	Int.		11	14¹/3	0	0	.000	20	4	8	2.51	1
1999 Chattanooga	Southern		35	41²/3	2	1	.667	46	17	33	2.59	6
1999 Indianapolis	Int.		11	9	1	0	1.000	12	3	9	4.00	0
1999 Cincinnati	N.L.		1	2	0	0	.000	1	1	4	4.50	0
1999 Baltimore a	A.L.		13	18¹/3	1	0	1.000	28	12	9	2.95	0
2000 Rochester	Int.		14	24²/3	0	1	.000	28	9	23	4.74	1
2000 Baltimore	A.L.		42	42²/3	2	3	.400	41	31	36	5.91	0
2001 Baltimore	A.L.		61	53	2	4	.333	54	30	47	4.25	2
2002 Baltimore	A.L.		67	57²/3	2	1	.667	56	33	51	4.68	1
2003 Baltimore	A.L.		76	50¹/3	4	1	.800	63	27	42	3.40	0
2004 Baltimore	A.L.		76	87	4	6	.400	122	35	64	2.28	3
2005 Baltimore b	A.L.		69	70¹/3	1	4	.200	100	26	54	2.43	36
2006 Toronto	A.L.		65	72¹/3	2	2	.500	86	20	42	1.37	38
2007 Toronto c	A.L.		5	4¹/3	0	2	.000	3	4	7	12.46	3
2008 Dunedin	Fla.St.		4	4	0	1	.000	5	1	2	2.25	0
2008 Toronto d	A.L.		60	58	2	4	.333	58	28	46	2.95	32
Major League Totals	10 Yrs.		535	516	20	27	.426	612	247	402	3.24	115

a Traded by Cincinnati Reds to Baltimore Orioles with pitcher Jacobo Sequea for pitcher Juan Guzman, July 31, 1999.
b Filed for free agency, October 28, 2005. Signed with Toronto Blue Jays, November 28, 2005.
c On disabled list from April 15 to November 13, 2007.
d On disabled list from March 21 to April 13, 2008.

SABATHIA, CARSTEN CHARLES (C.C.)

Born, Vallejo, California, July 21, 1980.
Bats Left. Throws Left. Height, 6 feet, 7 inches. Weight, 290 pounds.

Year	Club	Lea	G	IP	W	L	Pct	SO	BB	H	ERA	SAVES
1998	Burlington	Appal.	5	18	1	0	1.000	35	8	20	4.50	0
1999	Kinston	Carolina	7	32	3	3	.500	29	19	30	5.34	0
1999	Mahoning Valley	N.Y.-Penn.	6	19²/₃	0	0	.000	27	12	9	1.83	0
1999	Columbus a	So.Atl.	3	16²/₃	2	0	1.000	20	5	8	1.08	0
2000	Kinston	Carolina	10	56	3	2	.600	69	24	48	3.54	0
2000	Akron	Eastern	17	90¹/₃	3	7	.300	90	48	75	3.59	0
2001	Cleveland	A.L.	33	180¹/₃	17	5	.773	171	95	149	4.39	0
2002	Cleveland	A.L.	33	210	13	11	.542	149	88	198	4.37	0
2003	Cleveland	A.L.	30	197²/₃	13	9	.591	141	66	190	3.60	0
2004	Cleveland	A.L.	30	188	11	10	.524	139	72	176	4.12	0
2005	Akron	Eastern	2	9	0	1	.000	9	2	4	1.00	0
2005	Cleveland b	A.L.	31	196²/₃	15	10	.600	161	62	185	4.03	0
2006	Buffalo	Int.	1	5	1	0	1.000	5	1	6	1.80	0
2006	Cleveland c	A.L.	28	192²/₃	12	11	.522	172	44	182	3.22	0
2007	Cleveland d	A.L.	34	*241	19	7	.731	209	37	238	3.21	0
2008	Cleveland	A.L.	18	122¹/₃	6	8	.429	123	34	117	3.83	0
2008	Milwaukee e-f.	N.L.	17	130²/₃	11	2	.846	128	25	106	1.65	0
Major League Totals	8 Yrs.		254	1659¹/₃	117	73	.616	1393	523	1541	3.66	
Division Series												
2001	Cleveland	A.L.	1	6	1	0	1.000	5	5	6	3.00	0
2007	Cleveland	A.L.	1	5	1	0	1.000	5	6	4	5.40	0
2008	Milwaukee	N.L.	1	3²/₃	0	1	.000	5	4	6	12.27	0
Division Series Totals			3	14²/₃	2	1	.667	15	15	16	6.14	0
Championship Series												
2007	Cleveland	A.L.	2	10¹/₃	0	2	.000	9	7	17	10.45	0

a On disabled list from April 1 through June 20, 1999.
b On disabled list from March 25 to April 17, 2005.
c On disabled list from April 3 to May 2, 2006.
d Selected Cy Young Award Winner in American League for 2007.
e Traded to Milwaukee Brewers for outfielder Matt LaPorta, pitcher Zach Jackson, pitcher Rob Bryson and player to be named later, July 7, 2008. Cleveland Indians received outfielder Michael Brantley to complete trade, October 3, 2008.
f Filed for free agency, November 1, 2008. Signed with New York Yankees, December 18, 2008.

SAITO, TAKASHI

Born, Miyagi, Japan, February 14, 1970.
Bats Left. Throws Right. Height, 6 feet, 2 inch. Weight, 215 pounds.

Year	Club	Lea	G	IP	W	L	Pct	SO	BB	H	ERA	SAVES
1992	Yokohama	Japan Cent.	6	16	0	2	.000	21	10	18	8.44	0
1993	Yokohama	Japan Cent.	29	149	8	10	.444	125	61	127	3.81	0
1994	Yokohama	Japan Cent.	28	181	9	12	.429	169	69	175	3.13	0
1995	Yokohama	Japan Cent.	26	162	8	9	.471	132	45	166	3.94	0
1996	Yokohama	Japan Cent.	28	196²/₃	10	10	.500	206	63	157	3.29	0
1997					INJURED—Did Not Play								
1998	Yokohama	Japan Cent.	34	143²/₃	13	5	.722	101	23	131	2.94	1
1999	Yokohama	Japan Cent.	26	184²/₃	14	3	.824	125	31	178	3.95	0
2000	Yokohama	Japan Cent.	19	115²/₃	6	10	.375	97	36	123	5.52	0
2001	Yokohama	Japan Cent.	50	64²/₃	7	1	.857	60	14	51	1.67	27
2002	Yokohama	Japan Cent.	39	47²/₃	1	2	.333	46	15	37	2.45	20
2003	Yokohama	Japan Cent.	17	103¹/₃	6	7	.462	72	22	103	4.18	0
2004	Yokohama	Japan Cent.	16	44	2	5	.286	37	13	64	7.71	0
2005	Yokohama	Japan Cent.	21	106	3	4	.429	93	29	111	3.82	0
2006	Los Angeles a	N.L.	72	78¹/₃	6	2	.750	107	23	48	2.07	24
2007	Los Angeles	N.L.	63	64¹/₃	2	1	.667	78	13	33	1.40	39
2008	Los Angeles b-c	N.L.	45	47	4	4	.500	60	16	40	2.49	18
Major League Totals	3 Yrs.		180	189²/₃	12	7	.632	245	52	121	1.95	81
Division Series												
2006	Los Angeles	N.L.	2	2²/₃	0	0	.000	4	0	0	0.00	0

Year	Club	Lea	G	IP	W	L	Pct	SO	BB	H	ERA	SAVES
2008 Los Angeles	N.L.	1	0	0	0	.000	0	0	3	INF	0	
Division Series Totals		3	2²/₃	0	0	.000	4	0	3	6.75	0	

a Signed with Los Angeles Dodgers organization, February 7, 2006.
b On disabled list from July 13 to September 13, 2008.
c Not offered contract, December 12, 2008. Signed with Boston Red Sox, January 10, 2009.

SAMPSON, CHRISTOPHER KEITH (CHRIS)
Born, Pasadena, Texas, May 23, 1978.
Bats Right. Throws Right. Height, 6 feet, 1 inch. Weight, 190 pounds.

Year	Club	Lea	G	IP	W	L	Pct	SO	BB	H	ERA	SAVES
2003 Salem	Carolina	9	10²/₃	1	1	.500	6	5	14	5.91	1
2003 Lexington	So.Atl.	22	84	4	3	.571	66	14	66	1.39	1
2004 Salem	Carolina	27	151²/₃	7	11	.389	101	26	170	3.80	0
2004 Round Rock	Texas	1	2	0	0	.000	1	0	3	0.00	0
2005 Corpus Christi	Texas	32	150	4	12	.250	92	19	147	3.12	4
2006 Round Rock	P.C.	27	125²/₃	12	3	.800	68	14	110	2.51	4
2006 Houston	N.L.	12	34	2	1	.667	15	5	25	2.12	0
2007 Round Rock	P.C.	2	3	1	0	1.000	0	2	3	0.00	0
2007 Houston a	N.L.	24	121²/₃	7	8	.467	51	30	138	4.59	0
2008 Houston	N.L.	54	117¹/₃	6	4	.600	61	23	118	4.22	0
Major League Totals	3 Yrs.	90	273	15	13	.536	127	58	281	4.12	0

a On disabled list from August 1 to August 31, 2007.

SANCHEZ, DUANER
Born, Cotui, Dominican Republic, October 14, 1979.
Bats Right. Throws Right. Height, 6 feet. Weight, 210 pounds.

Year	Club	Lea	G	IP	W	L	Pct	SO	BB	H	ERA	SAVES
1997 Arizona	Dominican	21	59²/₃	4	4	.500	44	48	57	5.13	1
1998 Arizona	Dominican	14	50¹/₃	2	3	.400	44	24	36	1.79	1
1999 High Desert	Calif.	3	14¹/₃	0	0	.000	9	9	15	7.53	0
1999 Missoula	Pioneer	13	63¹/₃	5	3	.625	51	23	54	3.13	0
2000 Royals	Gulf Coast	19	28²/₃	2	2	.500	25	23	25	5.02	0
2000 South Bend	Midwest	28	165¹/₃	8	9	.471	121	54	152	3.65	0
2001 Lancaster	Calif.	10	59	2	4	.333	49	18	65	4.58	0
2001 El Paso	Texas	13	70¹/₃	3	7	.300	41	25	92	6.78	0
2002 El Paso	Texas	31	35²/₃	4	3	.571	37	13	31	3.03	13
2002 Tucson	P.C.	4	5¹/₃	1	1	.500	9	1	6	6.75	1
2002 Nashville	P.C.	20	22²/₃	0	3	.000	20	11	24	4.76	6
2002 Arizona-Pittsburgh a	N.L.	9	6	0	0	.000	6	7	6	9.00	0
2003 Nashville	P.C.	41	61	4	4	.500	34	27	63	3.69	1
2003 Pittsburgh b	N.L.	6	6	1	0	1.000	3	1	15	16.50	0
2004 Los Angeles	N.L.	67	80	3	1	.750	44	37	81	3.38	0
2005 Los Angeles	N.L.	79	82	4	7	.364	71	36	75	3.73	8
2006 New York c-d	N.L.	49	55¹/₃	5	1	.833	44	24	43	2.60	0
2007 New York e	N.L.					INJURED—Did Not Play					
2008 St. Lucie	Fla.St.	3	4	0	0	.000	6	0	6	4.50	0
2008 New Orleans	P.C.	2	2	0	0	.000	1	1	0	0.00	0
2008 New York f	N.L.	66	58¹/₃	5	1	.833	44	23	54	4.32	0
Major League Totals	6 Yrs.	276	287²/₃	18	10	.643	212	118	274	3.91	8
Division Series												
2004 Los Angeles	N.L.	2	2	0	0	.000	3	1	1	0.00	0

a Traded to Pittsburgh Pirates for pitcher Mike Fetters, July 2, 2002.
b Claimed on waivers by Los Angeles Dodgers, November 20, 2003.
c Traded to New York Mets with pitcher Steve Schmoll for pitcher Jae Seo and pitcher Tim Hamulack, January 4, 2006.
d On disabled list from July 30 to October 31, 2006.
e On disabled list from March 23 to November 6, 2007.
f On disabled list from March 27 to April 15, 2008.

SANCHEZ, JONATHAN O.
Born, Mayaguez, Puerto Rico, November 19, 1982.
Bats Left. Throws Left. Height, 6 feet, 2 inches. Weight, 190 pounds.

Year	Club	Lea	G	IP	W	L	Pct	SO	BB	H	ERA	SAVES
2004 Giants	Arizona	9	26	5	0	1.000	27	9	22	2.77	0
2004 Salem-Keizer	Northwest	6	22¹/₃	2	1	.667	34	19	16	4.84	0
2005 Augusta	So.Atl.	25	125²/₃	5	7	.417	166	39	122	4.08	0
2006 Connecticut	Eastern	13	31¹/₃	2	1	.667	46	9	14	1.15	2

Year	Club	Lea	G	IP	W	L	Pct	SO	BB	H	ERA	SAVES
2006	Fresno	P.C.	6	23⅔	2	2	.500	28	13	13	3.80	0
2006	San Francisco	N.L.	27	40	3	1	.750	33	23	39	4.95	0
2007	San Jose	Calif.	2	3	0	0	.000	5	1	0	0.00	0
2007	Fresno	P.C.	6	20⅔	0	0	.000	27	8	15	2.18	0
2007	San Francisco a	N.L.	33	52	1	5	.167	62	28	57	5.88	0
2008	San Francisco b	N.L.	29	158	9	12	.429	157	75	154	5.01	0
Major League Totals	3 Yrs.		89	250	13	18	.419	252	126	250	5.18	0

a On disabled list from June 25 to July 19, 2007.
b On disabled list from August 12 to September 1, 2008.

SANTANA, ERVIN RAMON

Born, La Romana, Dominican Republic, January 10, 1983.
Bats Right. Throws Right. Height, 6 feet, 2 inches. Weight, 185 pounds.

Year	Club	Lea	G	IP	W	L	Pct	SO	BB	H	ERA	SAVES
2001	Angels	Arizona	10	58⅔	3	2	.600	69	35	40	3.22	0
2001	Provo	Pioneer	4	18⅔	2	1	.667	22	12	19	7.71	0
2002	Cedar Rapids	Midwest	27	147	14	8	.636	146	48	133	4.16	0
2003	Rancho Cucamonga	California	20	124⅔	10	2	.833	130	36	98	2.53	0
2003	Arkansas	Texas	6	29⅔	1	1	.500	23	12	23	3.94	0
2004	Arkansas	Texas	8	43⅔	2	1	.667	48	18	41	3.30	0
2005	Arkansas	Texas	7	39	5	1	.833	32	15	34	2.31	0
2005	Salt Lake	P.C.	3	19⅓	1	0	1.000	17	2	19	4.19	0
2005	Los Angeles	A.L.	23	133⅔	12	8	.600	99	47	139	4.65	0
2006	Los Angeles	A.L.	33	204	16	8	.667	141	70	181	4.28	0
2007	Salt Lake	P.C.	5	32⅓	2	1	.667	32	10	39	5.01	0
2007	Los Angeles	A.L.	28	150	7	14	.333	126	58	174	5.76	0
2008	Los Angeles	A.L.	32	219	16	7	.696	214	47	198	3.49	0
Major League Totals	4 Yrs.		116	706⅔	51	37	.580	580	222	692	4.42	0
Division Series												
2005	Los Angeles	A.L.	1	5⅓	1	0	1.000	2	3	5	5.06	0
2007	Los Angeles	A.L.	1	2	0	0	.000	2	0	0	0.00	0
2008	Los Angeles	A.L.	1	5⅓	0	0	.000	3	0	8	8.44	0
Division Series Totals			3	12⅔	1	0	1.000	7	3	13	5.68	0
Championship Series												
2005	Los Angeles	A.L.	1	4⅓	0	1	.000	2	3	3	10.38	0

SANTANA, JOHAN ALEXANDER

Born, Tovar, Venezuela, March 13, 1979.
Bats Left. Throws Left. Height, 6 feet. Weight, 210 pounds.

Year	Club	Lea	G	IP	W	L	Pct	SO	BB	H	ERA	SAVES
1996	Houston/Bos	Dominican	23	40	4	3	.571	51	22	26	2.70	3
1997	Auburn	N.Y.-Penn.	1	4	0	0	.000	5	6	1	2.25	0
1997	Astros	Gulf Coast	9	36⅓	0	4	.000	25	18	49	7.93	0
1998	Quad City	Midwest	2	6⅔	0	1	.000	6	3	14	9.45	0
1998	Auburn	N.Y.-Penn.	15	86⅔	7	5	.583	88	21	81	4.36	0
1999	Michigan a-b	Midwest	27	160⅓	8	8	.500	150	55	162	4.66	0
2000	Minnesota	A.L.	30	86	2	3	.400	64	54	102	6.49	0
2001	Minnesota	A.L.	15	43⅔	1	0	1.000	28	16	50	4.74	0
2002	Edmonton	P.C.	11	48⅔	5	2	.714	75	27	37	3.14	0
2002	Minnesota	A.L.	27	108⅓	8	6	.571	137	49	84	2.99	1
2003	Minnesota	A.L.	45	158⅓	12	3	.800	169	47	127	3.07	0
2004	Minnesota c	A.L.	34	228	20	6	.769	*265	54	156	*2.61	0
2005	Minnesota	A.L.	33	231⅔	16	7	.696	*238	45	180	2.87	0
2006	Minnesota d	A.L.	34	*233⅔	*19	6	.760	*245	47	186	*2.77	0
2007	Minnesota	A.L.	33	219	15	13	.536	235	52	183	3.33	0
2008	New York e	N.L.	34	*234⅓	16	7	.696	206	63	206	*2.53	0
Major League Totals	9 Yrs.		285	1543	109	51	.681	1587	427	1274	3.11	1
Division Series												
2002	Minnesota	A.L.	2	3	0	0	.000	2	2	3	6.00	0
2003	Minnesota	A.L.	2	7⅔	1	0	.000	6	3	9	7.04	0
2004	Minnesota	A.L.	2	12	1	0	1.000	12	4	14	0.75	0
2006	Minnesota	A.L.	1	8	0	1	.000	8	1	5	2.25	0
Division Series Totals			7	30⅔	1	2	.333	28	10	31	3.23	0
Championship Series												
2002	Minnesota	A.L.	4	3⅓	0	1	.000	4	0	4	10.80	0

SARFATE, DENNIS SCOTT

Born, Queens, New York, April 9, 1981.
Bats Right. Throws Right. Height, 6 feet, 4 inches. Weight, 225 pounds.

Year	Club	Lea	G	IP	W	L	Pct	SO	BB	H	ERA	SAVES
2001 Ogden	Pioneer	9	23⅓	1	2	.333	32	10	20	4.63	1
2002 Brewers	Arizona	5	14	0	0	.000	22	7	6	2.57	0
2002 Ogden	Pioneer	1	1	0	0	.000	2	1	2	9.00	0
2003 Beloit	Midwest	26	139⅔	12	2	.857	140	66	114	2.84	0
2004 Huntsville	Southern	28	129	7	12	.368	113	78	128	3.98	0
2005 Nashville	P.C.	2	12	0	1	.000	10	4	6	2.25	0
2005 Huntsville	Southern	24	130	9	9	.500	110	59	120	3.88	0
2006 Nashville	P.C.	34	125	10	7	.588	117	78	125	3.67	0
2006 Milwaukee	N.L.	8	8⅓	0	0	.000	11	4	9	4.32	0
2007 Nashville	P.C.	45	61⅔	2	7	.222	68	47	61	4.52	4
2007 Houston a-b	N.L.	7	8⅓	1	0	1.000	14	1	5	1.08	0
2008 Baltimore c	A.L.	57	79⅔	4	3	.571	86	62	62	4.74	0
Major League Totals	3 Yrs.	72	96⅓	5	3	.625	111	67	76	4.39	0

SAUNDERS, JOSEPH FRANCIS (JOE)

Born, Falls Church, Virginia, June 16, 1981.
Bats Left. Throws Left. Height, 6 feet, 3 inches. Weight, 210 pounds.

Year	Club	Lea	G	IP	W	L	Pct	SO	BB	H	ERA	SAVES
2002 Cedar Rapids	Midwest	5	28⅔	3	1	.750	27	9	16	1.88	0
2002 Provo	Pioneer	8	32⅓	2	1	.667	21	11	40	3.62	0
2003 Provo a	Pioneer			INJURED—Did Not Play								
2004 Rancho Cucamonga	Calif.	19	105⅔	9	7	.563	76	23	106	3.41	0
2004 Arkansas	Texas	8	39	4	3	.571	25	14	51	5.77	0
2005 Arkansas	Texas	18	105⅔	7	4	.636	80	32	107	3.49	0
2005 Salt Lake	P.C.	9	55	3	3	.500	29	21	65	4.58	0
2005 Los Angeles	A.L.	2	9⅓	0	0	.000	4	4	10	7.71	0
2006 Salt Lake	P.C.	21	135	10	4	.714	97	38	117	2.67	0
2006 Los Angeles	A.L.	13	70⅔	7	3	.700	51	29	71	4.71	0
2007 Salt Lake	P.C.	14	86⅓	4	7	.364	84	20	89	5.11	0
2007 Los Angeles	A.L.	18	107⅓	8	5	.615	69	34	129	4.44	0
2008 Los Angeles	A.L.	31	198	17	7	.708	103	53	187	3.41	0
Major League Totals	4 Yrs.	64	385⅓	32	15	.681	227	120	397	4.04	0
Division Series												
2008 Los Angeles	A.L.	1	4⅔	0	0	.000	2	4	5	7.71	0

SCHERZER, MAXWELL M. (MAX)

Born, St. Louis, Missouri, July 27, 1984.
Bats Right. Throws Right. Height, 6 feet, 3 inches. Weight, 215 pounds.

Year	Club	Lea	G	IP	W	L	Pct	SO	BB	H	ERA	SAVES
2007 Fort Worth	Amer.Assoc.	3	16	1	0	1.000	25	4	9	0.56	0
2007 Visalia	Calif.	3	17	2	0	1.000	30	2	5	0.53	0
2007 Mobile a-b	Southern	14	73⅔	4	4	.500	76	40	64	3.91	0
2008 Tucson	P.C.	13	53	1	1	.500	79	22	35	2.72	0
2008 Arizona	N.L.	16	56	0	0	.000	66	21	48	3.05	0

SCHMIDT, JASON DAVID
Born, Lewiston, Idaho, January 29, 1973.
Bats Right. Throws Right. Height, 6 feet, 5 inches. Weight, 210 pounds.

Year Club	Lea	G	IP	W	L	Pct	SO	BB	H	ERA	SAVES
1991 Braves .... Gulf Coast	11	45⅓	3	4	.429	44	23	32	2.38	0
1992 Macon .... So. Atl.	7	24⅔	0	3	.000	33	19	31	4.01	0
1992 Pulaski............. Appal.	11	58⅓	3	4	.429	56	31	55	4.01	0
1993 Durham ....Carolina	22	116⅔	7	11	.389	110	47	128	4.94	0
1994 Greenville........ Southern	24	140⅔	8	7	.533	131	54	135	3.65	0
1995 Richmond ....Int.	19	116	8	6	.571	95	48	97	2.25	0
1995 Atlanta .... N.L.	9	25	2	2	.500	19	18	27	5.76	0
1996 Greenville........ Southern	1	2	0	0	.000	2	0	4	9.00	0
1996 Richmond ....Int.	7	45⅔	3	0	1.000	41	19	36	2.56	0
1996 Atlanta-Pittsburgh a-b ... N.L.	19	96⅓	5	6	.455	74	53	108	5.70	0
1997 Pittsburgh .... N.L.	32	187⅔	10	9	.526	136	76	193	4.60	0
1998 Pittsburgh .... N.L.	33	214⅓	11	14	.440	158	71	228	4.07	0
1999 Pittsburgh .... N.L.	33	212⅔	13	11	.542	148	85	219	4.19	0
2000 GC Pirates ...... Gulf Coast	1	4	0	0	.000	1	1	4	2.25	0
2000 Pittsburgh c .... N.L.	11	63⅓	2	5	.286	51	41	71	5.40	0
2001 Altoona............ Eastern	3	9⅓	0	1	.000	17	1	7	0.96	0
2001 Nashville .... P.C.	1	7	1	0	1.000	6	0	4	0.00	0
2001 Pittsburgh-San Fran. d-e-f N.L.	25	150⅓	13	7	.650	142	61	138	4.07	0
2002 Fresno .... P.C.	2	12	2	0	1.000	12	2	11	3.00	0
2002 San Francisco g .... N.L.	29	185⅓	13	8	.619	196	73	148	3.45	0
2003 San Francisco .... N.L.	29	207⅔	17	5	*.773	208	46	152	*2.34	0
2004 San Jose ....California	1	5	1	0	1.000	7	1	2	0.00	0
2004 San Francisco h .... N.L.	32	225	18	7	.720	251	77	165	3.20	0
2005 San Francisco i......... N.L.	29	172	12	7	.632	165	85	160	4.40	0
2006 San Francisco j........ N.L.	32	213⅓	11	9	.550	180	80	189	3.59	0
2007 Inland Empire......... Calif.	1	6	0	0	.000	7	1	2	0.00	0
2007 Los Angeles k......... N.L.	6	25⅔	1	4	.200	22	14	32	6.31	0
2008 Los Angeles l......... N.L.				INJURED—Did Not Play						
Major League Totals .... 13 Yrs.	319	1978⅔	128	94	.577	1750	780	1830	3.94	0
Division Series										
2002 San Francisco .... N.L.	1	5⅓	0	1	.000	5	4	3	6.75	0
2003 San Francisco .... N.L.	1	9	1	0	1.000	5	0	3	0.00	0
Division Series Totals	2	14⅓	1	1	.500	10	4	6	2.51	0
Championship Series										
2002 San Francisco .... N.L.	1	7⅔	1	0	1.000	8	1	4	1.17	0
World Series Record										
2002 San Francisco .... N.L.	2	10⅓	1	0	1.000	14	4	16	5.23	0

a Traded to Pittsburgh Pirates with infielder Ron Wright and outfielder Corey Pointer for pitcher Denny Neagle, August 29, 1996.
b On disabled list from July 15 to August 28, 1996.
c On disabled list from April 15 to May 1 and June 10 to November 17, 2000.
d On disabled list from March 22 to May 11, 2001.
e Traded to San Francisco Giants with outfielder John Vander Wal for outfielder Armando Rios and pitcher Ryan Vogelsong, July 30, 2001.
f Filed for free agency, November 5, 2001, re-signed with San Francisco Giants, December 14, 2001.
g On disabled list from March 21 to April 24, 2002.
h On disabled list from March 26 to April 16, 2004.
i On disabled list from May 8 to May 24, 2005.
j Filed for free agency October 29, 2006. Signed with Los Angeles Dodgers, December 8, 2006.
k On disabled list from April 15 to June 5 and June 17 to October 31, 2007.
l On disabled list from March 21 to November 4, 2008.

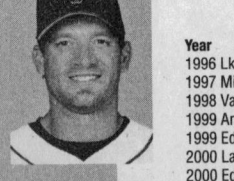

SCHOENEWEIS, SCOTT DAVID
Born, Long Branch, New Jersey, October 2, 1973.
Bats Left. Throws Left. Height, 6 feet. Weight, 190 pounds.

Year Club	Lea	G	IP	W	L	Pct	SO	BB	H	ERA	SAVES
1996 Lk Elsinore........California	14	93⅔	8	3	.727	83	27	86	3.94	0
1997 Midland .... Texas	20	113⅓	7	5	.583	94	39	145	5.96	0
1998 Vancouver .... P.C.	27	180	11	8	.579	133	59	188	4.50	0
1999 Anaheim............. A.L.	31	39⅓	1	1	.500	22	14	47	5.49	0
1999 Edmonton .... P.C.	9	35⅓	2	4	.333	29	12	58	7.64	0
2000 Lake Elsinore ......California	1	4⅔	0	0	.000	3	3	3	1.93	0
2000 Edmonton .... P.C.	1	7	0	0	.000	6	1	2	0.00	0
2000 Anaheim a .... A.L.	27	170	7	10	.412	78	67	183	5.45	0
2001 Anaheim............. A.L.	32	205⅓	10	11	.476	104	77	227	5.08	0
2002 Anaheim............. A.L.	54	118	9	8	.529	65	49	119	4.88	1

326

Year	Club	Lea	G	IP	W	L	Pct	SO	BB	H	ERA	SAVES
2003 Anaheim-Chicago b	A.L.	59	64²/₃	3	2	.600	56	19	63	4.18	0
2004 Chicago c-d	A.L.	20	112²/₃	6	9	.400	69	49	129	5.59	0
2005 Toronto	A.L.	80	57	3	4	.429	43	25	54	3.32	1
2006 Toronto	A.L.	55	37¹/₃	2	2	.500	18	16	39	6.51	1
2006 Cincinnati e-f-g	N.L.	16	14¹/₃	2	0	1.000	11	8	9	0.63	3
2007 New York	N.L.	70	59	0	2	.000	41	28	62	5.03	2
2008 New York h	N.L.	73	56²/₃	2	6	.250	34	23	55	3.34	1
Major League Totals 10 Yrs.		517	934¹/₃	45	55	.450	541	375	987	4.91	9
Division Series											
2002 Anaheim	A.L.	3	0¹/₃	0	0	.000	0	0	2	27.00	0
Championship Series											
2002 Anaheim	A.L.	1	0²/₃	0	0	.000	0	0	0	0.00	0
World Series Record											
2002 Anaheim	A.L.	2	2	0	0	.000	2	1	1	0.00	0

a On disabled list from June 17 to July 25, 2000.
b Traded to Chicago White Sox with pitcher Doug Nickle for pitcher Gary Glover, pitcher Scott Dunn and pitcher Tim Bittner, July 29, 2003.
c On disabled list from June 22 to July 7 and from August 5 to September 30, 2004.
d Not offered contract, December 20, 2004. Signed with Toronto Blue Jays, January 11, 2005.
e Traded to Cincinnati Reds for player to be named later, August 16, 2006.
f Toronto Blue Jays received infielder Trevor Lawhorn to complete trade, October 13, 2006.
g Filed for free agency, October 31, 2006. Signed with New York Mets, January 16, 2007.
h Traded to Arizona Diamondbacks for pitcher Connor Robertson, December 12, 2008.

SEAY, ROBERT MICHAEL (BOBBY)

Born, Sarasota, Florida, June 20, 1978.
Bats Left. Throws Left. Height, 6 feet, 2 inches. Weight, 235 pounds.

Year	Club	Lea	G	IP	W	L	Pct	SO	BB	H	ERA	SAVES
1997 Chston-SC	So.Atl.	13	61¹/₃	3	4	.429	64	37	56	4.55	0
1998 Chston-SC	So.Atl.	15	69	1	7	.125	74	29	59	4.30	0
1999 St. Petersburg	Fla.St.	12	57	2	6	.250	45	23	56	3.00	0
1999 Orlando	Southern	6	17	1	2	.333	16	15	22	7.94	0
2000 Orlando	Southern	24	132¹/₃	8	7	.533	106	53	132	3.88	0
2001 Orlando	Southern	15	64²/₃	2	5	.286	49	26	81	5.98	0
2001 Tampa Bay	A.L.	12	13	1	1	.500	12	5	13	6.23	0
2002 Durham	Int.	10	15	0	0	.000	14	2	15	6.00	0
2002 Orlando a	Southern	15	35²/₃	2	0	1.000	24	15	31	3.28	0
2003 Tampa Bay	A.L.	12	9	0	0	.000	5	6	7	3.00	0
2003 Durham b	Int.	25	30	3	0	1.000	29	15	23	2.10	0
2004 Durham	Int.	29	36²/₃	2	1	.667	35	9	26	1.72	1
2004 Tampa Bay	A.L.	21	22²/₃	0	0	.000	17	5	21	2.38	0
2005 Tulsa	Texas	4	5	1	0	1.000	3	0	3	1.80	1
2005 Colorado	N.L.	17	11²/₃	0	0	.000	11	8	18	8.49	0
2005 Colorado Springs c-d-e	P.C.	17	22²/₃	1	0	1.000	24	10	23	3.28	3
2006 Detroit	A.L.	14	15¹/₃	0	0	.000	12	9	14	6.46	0
2006 Toledo	Int.	24	24²/₃	1	2	.333	14	6	25	4.74	0
2007 Detroit f	A.L.	58	46¹/₃	3	0	1.000	38	15	38	2.33	1
2008 Detroit	A.L.	60	56¹/₃	1	2	.333	58	25	59	4.47	0
Major League Totals 7 Yrs.		194	174¹/₃	5	3	.625	153	73	170	4.13	1

a On disabled list from March 22 to June 3, 2002.
b On disabled list from April 24 to June 3, 2003.
c On disabled list from April 17 to June 5, 2005.
d Traded to Colorado Rockies for outfielder Reggie Taylor, April 8, 2005.
e Filed for free agency, October 3, 2005. Signed with Detroit Tigers organization, November 30, 2005.
f Filed for free agency, October 2, 2006, re-signed with Detroit Tigers organization, January 9, 2007.

SHEETS, BEN M.

Born, Baton Rouge, Louisiana, July 18, 1978.
Bats Right. Throws Right. Height, 6 feet, 1 inch. Weight, 220 pounds.

Year	Club	Lea	G	IP	W	L	Pct	SO	BB	H	ERA	SAVES
1999 Stockton	California	5	27²/₃	1	0	1.000	28	14	23	3.58	0
1999 Ogden	Pioneer	2	8	0	1	.000	12	2	15	5.63	0
2000 Indianapolis	Int.	14	81²/₃	3	5	.375	59	31	77	2.87	0
2000 Huntsville	Southern	13	72	5	3	.625	60	25	55	1.88	0
2001 Indianapolis	Int.	2	10²/₃	1	1	.500	6	3	14	3.38	0
2001 Milwaukee a	N.L.	25	151¹/₃	11	10	.524	94	48	166	4.76	0
2002 Milwaukee	N.L.	34	216²/₃	11	*16	.407	170	70	237	4.15	0

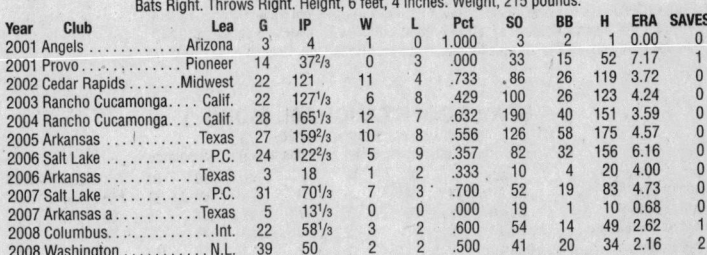

Year	Club	Lea	G	IP	W	L	Pct	SO	BB	H	ERA	SAVES
2003 Milwaukee		N.L.	34	220⅔	11	13	.458	157	43	232	4.45	0
2004 Milwaukee		N.L.	34	237	12	14	.462	264	32	201	2.70	0
2005 Milwaukee b		N.L.	22	156⅔	10	9	.526	141	25	142	3.33	0
2006 Brewers		Arizona	1	4⅓	0	0	.000	8	2	5	10.38	0
2006 Huntsville		Southern	1	2⅔	0	0	.000	5	0	4	3.38	0
2006 Nashville		P.C.	3	15	2	1	.667	15	5	9	2.40	0
2006 Milwaukee c		N.L.	17	106	6	7	.462	116	11	105	3.82	0
2007 Milwaukee d		N.L.	24	141⅓	12	5	.706	106	37	138	3.82	0
2008 Milwaukee e		N.L.	31	198⅓	13	9	.591	158	47	181	3.09	0
Major League Totals	8 Yrs.		221	1428	86	83	.509	1206	313	1402	3.72	0

a On disabled list from August 6 to September 21, 2001.
b On disabled list from April 21 to May 28 and August 27 to October 10, 2005.
c On disabled list from March 24 to April 16 and May 3 to July 25, 2006.
d On disabled list from July 15 to August 29, 2007.
e Filed for free agency, October 30, 2008.

SHELL, STEVEN DANIEL
Born, Longview, Texas, March 10, 1983.
Bats Right. Throws Right. Height, 6 feet, 4 inches. Weight, 215 pounds.

Year	Club	Lea	G	IP	W	L	Pct	SO	BB	H	ERA	SAVES
2001 Angels		Arizona	3	4	1	0	1.000	3	2	1	0.00	0
2001 Provo		Pioneer	14	37⅔	0	3	.000	33	15	52	7.17	1
2002 Cedar Rapids		Midwest	22	121	11	4	.733	86	26	119	3.72	0
2003 Rancho Cucamonga		Calif.	22	127⅓	6	8	.429	100	26	123	4.24	0
2004 Rancho Cucamonga		Calif.	28	165⅓	12	7	.632	190	40	151	3.59	0
2005 Arkansas		Texas	27	159⅔	10	8	.556	126	58	175	4.57	0
2006 Salt Lake		P.C.	24	122⅔	5	9	.357	82	32	156	6.16	0
2006 Arkansas		Texas	3	18	1	2	.333	10	4	20	4.00	0
2007 Salt Lake		P.C.	31	70⅓	7	3	.700	52	19	83	4.73	0
2007 Arkansas a		Texas	5	13⅓	0	0	.000	19	1	10	0.68	0
2008 Columbus		Int.	22	58⅓	3	2	.600	54	14	49	2.62	1
2008 Washington		N.L.	39	50	2	2	.500	41	20	34	2.16	2

a Filed for free agency from Los Angeles Angels, October 29, 2007. Signed with Washington Nationals organization, November 17, 2007.

SHERRILL, GEORGE FRIEDERICH
Born, Memphis, Tennessee, April 19, 1977.
Bats Left. Throws Left. Height, 6 feet. Weight, 225 pounds.

Year	Club	Lea	G	IP	W	L	Pct	SO	BB	H	ERA	SAVES
1999 Evansville (Ind)		Frontier	22	40	2	4	.333	33	18	40	3.15	2
2000 Evansville (Ind)		Frontier	13	75⅓	3	5	.375	61	35	71	4.66	2
2001 Sioux Falls (Ind)		Northern	48	58⅔	4	4	.500	45	14	53	2.45	2
2002 Winnipeg (Ind)		Northern	38	41	3	5	.375	61	13	35	3.07	2
2003 Winnipeg (Ind)		Northern	16	16	1	0	1.000	30	4	8	1.13	2
2003 San Antonio a		Texas	16	27⅓	3	0	1.000	31	12	19	0.33	0
2004 Tacoma		P.C.	36	50⅓	4	2	.667	62	9	42	2.32	13
2004 Seattle		A.L.	21	23⅔	2	1	.667	16	9	24	3.80	0
2005 Mariners		Arizona	3	4	0	0	.000	5	0	0	0.00	0
2005 Tacoma		P.C.	22	23⅔	1	3	.250	38	6	19	2.28	7
2005 Seattle		A.L.	29	19	4	3	.571	24	7	13	5.21	0
2006 Seattle		A.L.	72	40	2	4	.333	42	27	30	4.28	1
2007 Seattle		A.L.	73	45⅔	2	0	1.000	56	17	28	2.36	3
2008 Baltimore a-b		A.L.	57	53⅓	3	5	.375	58	33	47	4.72	31
Major League Totals	5 Yrs.		252	181⅔	13	13	.500	196	93	142	3.96	35

a Signed with Seattle Mariners, July 2, 2003.
a Traded to Baltimore Orioles with pitcher Tony Butler, outfielder Adam Jones, pitcher Kam Mickolio and pitcher Chris Tillman for pitcher Erik Bedard, February 8, 2008.
b On disabled list from August 16 to September 11, 2008.

SHIELDS, JAMES ANTHONY (JAMIE)
Born, Newhall, California, December 20, 1981.
Bats Right. Throws Right. Height, 6 feet, 4 inches. Weight, 215 pounds.

Year	Club	Lea	G	IP	W	L	Pct	SO	BB	H	ERA	SAVES
2001 Hudson Valley		N.Y.-Penn.	5	27⅓	2	1	.667	25	5	27	2.30	0
2001 Charleston-SC		So.Atl.	10	71⅓	4	5	.444	60	10	63	2.65	0
2002 Charleston-SC a						INJURED—Did Not Play						

Year	Club	Lea	G	IP	W	L	Pct	SO	BB	H	ERA	SAVES
2003	Bakersfield	Calif.	26	143²/₃	10	10	.500	119	38	161	4.45	1
2004	Bakersfield	Calif.	20	117	8	5	.615	92	33	119	4.23	0
2004	Montgomery	Southern	4	18¹/₃	0	3	.000	14	8	24	7.85	0
2005	Durham	Int.	1	6	1	0	1.000	6	3	9	6.00	0
2005	Montgomery	Southern	17	109¹/₃	7	5	.583	104	31	95	2.80	0
2006	Durham	Int.	10	61¹/₃	3	2	.600	64	6	60	2.64	0
2006	Tampa Bay	A.L.	21	124²/₃	6	8	.429	104	38	141	4.84	0
2007	Tampa Bay	A.L.	31	215	12	8	.600	184	36	202	3.85	0
2008	Tampa Bay	A.L.	33	215	14	8	.636	160	40	208	3.56	0
Major League Totals		3 Yrs.	85	554²/₃	32	24	.571	448	114	551	3.96	0
Division Series												
2008	Tampa Bay	N.L.	1	6¹/₃	1	0	1.000	4	1	6	4.26	0
Championship Series												
2008	Tampa Bay	N.L.	2	13	0	2	.000	9	5	15	3.46	0
World Series Record												
2008	Tampa Bay	N.L.	1	5²/₃	1	0	1.000	4	2	7	0.00	0

a On minor league disabled list April 4 to September 10, 2002.

SHIELDS, ROBERT SCOT (SCOT)

Born, Fort Lauderdale, Florida, July 22, 1975.
Bats Right. Throws Right. Height, 6 feet, 1 inch. Weight, 170 pounds.

Year	Club	Lea	G	IP	W	L	Pct	SO	BB	H	ERA	SAVES
1997	Boise	Northwest	30	52	7	2	.778	61	24	45	2.94	2
1998	Cedar Rapids	Midwest	58	74	6	5	.545	81	29	62	3.65	7
1999	Lake Elsinore	California	24	107¹/₃	10	3	.769	113	39	91	2.52	1
1999	Erie	Eastern	10	74²/₃	4	4	.500	81	26	57	2.89	0
2000	Edmonton	P.C.	27	163	7	13	.350	156	82	158	5.41	0
2001	Salt Lake	P.C.	21	137²/₃	6	11	.353	104	31	141	4.97	0
2001	Anaheim	A.L.	8	11	0	0	.000	7	7	8	0.00	0
2002	Salt Lake	P.C.	28	47	2	2	.500	50	6	39	3.06	1
2002	Anaheim	A.L.	29	49	5	3	.625	30	21	31	2.20	0
2003	Anaheim	A.L.	44	148¹/₃	5	6	.455	111	38	138	2.85	1
2004	Anaheim	A.L.	60	105¹/₃	8	2	.800	109	40	97	3.33	4
2005	Los Angeles	A.L.	78	91²/₃	10	11	.476	98	37	66	2.75	7
2006	Los Angeles	A.L.	74	87²/₃	7	7	.500	84	24	70	2.87	2
2007	Los Angeles	A.L.	71	77	4	5	.444	77	33	62	3.86	2
2008	Salt Lake	P.C.	1	1	0	0	.000	3	0	2	0.00	0
2008	Los Angeles a	A.L.	64	63¹/₃	6	4	.600	64	29	56	2.70	4
Major League Totals		8 Yrs.	428	633¹/₃	45	38	.542	580	229	528	2.93	20
Division Series												
2004	Anaheim	A.L.	2	3	0	0	.000	3	2	5	6.00	0
2005	Los Angeles	A.L.	4	5	1	1	.500	5	3	4	3.60	0
2007	Los Angeles	A.L.	2	4	0	0	.000	4	4	0	2.25	0
2008	Los Angeles	A.L.	4	5²/₃	0	1	.000	7	1	6	4.76	0
Division Series Totals			12	17²/₃	1	2	.333	19	10	15	4.08	0
Championship Series												
2005	Los Angeles	A.L.	4	6	0	0	.000	5	1	4	0.00	0
World Series Record												
2002	Anaheim	A.L.	1	1²/₃	0	0	.000	1	0	5	5.40	0

a On disabled list from March 21 to April 5, 2008.

SHOUSE, BRIAN DOUGLAS

Born, Effingham, Illinois, September 26, 1968.
Bats Left. Throws Left. Height, 5 feet, 11 inches. Weight, 190 pounds.

Year	Club	Lea	G	IP	W	L	Pct	SO	BB	H	ERA	SAVES
1990	Welland	N.Y.-Penn.	17	39²/₃	4	3	.571	39	7	50	5.22	2
1991	Augusta	So.Atl.	26	31	2	3	.400	32	9	22	3.19	8
1991	Salem	Carolina	17	33²/₃	2	1	.667	25	15	35	2.94	3
1992	Carolina	Southern	59	77¹/₃	5	6	.455	79	28	71	2.44	4
1993	Pittsburgh	N.L.	6	4	0	0	.000	3	2	7	9.00	0
1993	Buffalo	A.A.	48	51²/₃	1	0	1.000	25	17	54	3.83	2
1994	Buffalo	A.A.	43	52	3	4	.429	31	15	44	3.63	0
1995	Calgary	P.C.	8	39¹/₃	4	4	.500	17	7	62	6.18	0
1995	Carolina	Southern	47	114²/₃	7	6	.538	76	19	126	4.47	0
1996	Calgary	P.C.	12	12²/₃	1	0	1.000	12	4	22	10.66	0
1996	Rochester a	Int.	32	50	1	2	.333	45	16	53	4.50	2
1997	Rochester	Int.	54	71¹/₃	6	2	.750	81	21	48	2.27	9

Year	Club	Lea	G	IP	W	L	Pct	SO	BB	H	ERA	SAVES
1998 Kintetsu	Pacific		13	26	0	2	.000	20	13	40	0.00	0
1998 Boston	A.L.		7	8	0	1	.000	5	4	9	5.63	0
1998 Pawtucket b-c-d	Int.		22	31	2	0	1.000	25	7	21	2.90	6
1999 Tucson e-f	P.C.		30	44²/₃	3	4	.429	32	18	63	6.25	0
2000 Norfolk	Int.		4	3¹/₃	0	1	.000	1	2	6	13.50	0
2000 Rochester g-h	Int.		43	57²/₃	4	4	.500	52	14	63	2.81	2
2001 New Orleans i	P.C.		56	53	2	2	.500	56	15	51	2.89	1
2002 Kansas City	A.L.		23	14²/₃	0	0	.000	11	9	15	6.14	0
2002 Omaha j	P.C.		5	2¹/₃	0	0	.000	2	1	7	11.57	0
2002 New Orleans k-l	P.C.		19	21	1	0	1.000	20	3	17	3.43	0
2003 Oklahoma	P.C.		6	7¹/₃	0	1	.000	2	3	8	3.68	1
2003 Texas	A.L.		62	61	0	1	.000	40	14	62	3.10	1
2004 Oklahoma	P.C.		9	7¹/₃	0	0	.000	3	4	12	6.14	0
2004 Texas m	A.L.		53	44¹/₃	2	0	1.000	34	18	36	2.23	0
2005 Texas	A.L.		64	53¹/₃	3	2	.600	35	18	55	5.23	0
2006 Frisco	Texas		2	2	0	0	.000	1	1	2	0.00	0
2006 Oklahoma	P.C.		5	5	0	1	.000	3	4	7	5.40	0
2006 Texas n-o	A.L.		6	4¹/₃	0	0	.000	3	1	6	4.15	0
2006 Milwaukee	N.L.		59	34	1	3	.250	20	17	34	3.97	2
2007 Milwaukee	N.L.		73	47²/₃	1	1	.500	32	14	46	3.02	1
2008 Milwaukee p	N.L.		69	51¹/₃	5	1	.833	33	14	46	2.81	2
Major League Totals	9 Yrs.		422	322²/₃	12	9	.571	216	111	316	3.65	6

a Released by Pittsburgh Pirates, May 16, 1996. Signed with Baltimore Orioles organization, May 22, 1996.
b Filed for free agency October 17, 1997. Signed with Boston Red Sox organization, April 6, 1998.
c Sold to Kintetsu (Japan), June 25, 1998.
d Signed by Arizona Diamondbacks organization, November 11, 1998.
e On disabled list from September 18 to October 5, 1999.
f Filed for free agency, October 15, 1999. Signed with New York Mets organization, November 16, 1999.
g Released by New York Mets, April 14, 2000. Signed with Baltimore Orioles organization, May 13, 2000.
h Filed for free agency, October 15, 2000. Signed with Houston Astros organization, December 22, 2000.
i Filed for free agency, October 15, 2001. Signed with Kansas City Royals organization, December 8, 2001.
j On disabled list from April 28 to May 13, 2002.
k Released by Kansas City Royals, June 27, 2002. Signed with Houston Astros organization, July 16, 2002.
l Filed for free agency, October 15, 2002. Signed with Texas Rangers organization, November 13, 2002.
m On disabled list from March 27 to May 13, 2004.
n On disabled list from April 22 to May 8, 2006.
o Traded to Milwaukee Brewers for infielder Enrique Cruz and cash, May 13, 2006.
p Filed for free agency, October 30, 2008.

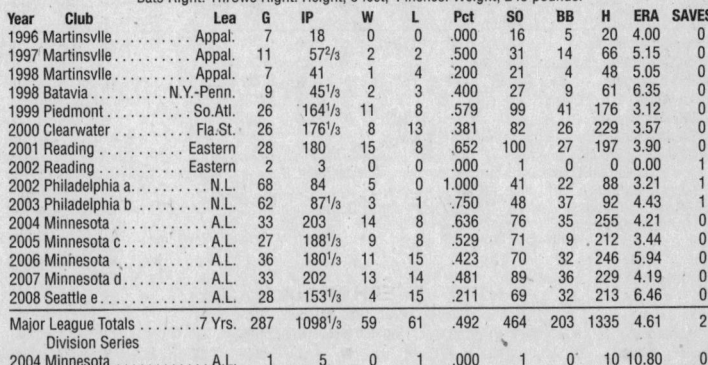

SILVA, CARLOS
Born, Bolivar, Venezuela, April 23, 1979.
Bats Right. Throws Right. Height, 6 feet, 4 inches. Weight, 245 pounds.

Year	Club	Lea	G	IP	W	L	Pct	SO	BB	H	ERA	SAVES
1996 Martinsvlle	Appal.		7	18	0	0	.000	16	5	20	4.00	0
1997 Martinsvlle	Appal.		11	57²/₃	2	2	.500	31	14	66	5.15	0
1998 Martinsvlle	Appal.		7	41	1	4	.200	21	4	48	5.05	0
1998 Batavia	N.Y.-Penn.		9	45¹/₃	2	3	.400	27	9	61	6.35	0
1999 Piedmont	So.Atl.		26	164¹/₃	11	8	.579	99	41	176	3.12	0
2000 Clearwater	Fla.St.		26	176¹/₃	8	13	.381	82	26	229	3.57	0
2001 Reading	Eastern		28	180	15	8	.652	100	27	197	3.90	0
2002 Reading	Eastern		2	3	0	0	.000	1	0	0	0.00	1
2002 Philadelphia a	N.L.		68	84	5	0	1.000	41	22	88	3.21	1
2003 Philadelphia b	N.L.		62	87¹/₃	3	1	.750	48	37	92	4.43	1
2004 Minnesota	A.L.		33	203	14	8	.636	76	35	255	4.21	0
2005 Minnesota c	A.L.		27	188¹/₃	9	8	.529	71	9	212	3.44	0
2006 Minnesota	A.L.		36	180¹/₃	11	15	.423	70	32	246	5.94	0
2007 Minnesota d	A.L.		33	202	13	14	.481	89	36	229	4.19	0
2008 Seattle e	A.L.		28	153¹/₃	4	15	.211	69	32	213	6.46	0
Major League Totals	7 Yrs.		287	1098¹/₃	59	61	.492	464	203	1335	4.61	2
Division Series												
2004 Minnesota	A.L.		1	5	0	1	.000	1	0	10	10.80	0

a On disabled list from May 27 to June 14, 2002.
b Traded to Minnesota Twins with infielder Nick Punto and player to be named later for pitcher Eric Milton, December 3, 2003. Minnesota Twins received pitcher Bobby Korecky to complete trade, December 17, 2003.
c On disabled list from April 7 to April 22, 2005.
d Not offered contract, December 2, 2007. Signed with Seattle Mariners, December 20, 2008.
e On disabled list from August 16 to September 1, 2008.

SLATEN, DOUGLAS (DOUG)

Born, Venice, California, February 4, 1980.
Bats Left. Throws Left. Height, 6 feet, 5 inches. Weight, 200 pounds.

Year	Club	Lea	G	IP	W	L	Pct	SO	BB	H	ERA	SAVES
2000 Diamondbacks	Arizona	9	9$\frac{1}{3}$	0	0	.000	7	3	7	0.96	0	
2001 Lancaster	Calif.	28	157$\frac{2}{3}$	9	8	.529	110	45	207	4.79	0	
2002 Lancaster	Calif.	8	35	1	6	.143	23	12	59	9.00	0	
2002 South Bend	Midwest	7	14$\frac{1}{3}$	0	0	.000	5	4	18	4.40	0	
2003 Lancaster	Calif.	32	119$\frac{1}{3}$	6	7	.462	78	47	156	6.03	0	
2004 South Bend	Midwest	36	44	5	2	.714	40	13	44	2.25	5	
2004 El Paso	Texas	11	9	0	1	.000	6	10	16	10.00	0	
2005 Tennessee	Southern	58	61$\frac{1}{3}$	2	2	.500	72	26	61	4.26	1	
2006 Tennessee	Southern	40	43	2	3	.400	59	15	31	1.88	8	
2006 Tucson	P.C.	18	20	2	1	.667	21	7	10	0.45	2	
2006 Arizona	N.L.	9	5$\frac{2}{3}$	0	0	.000	3	2	3	0.00	0	
2007 Arizona	N.L.	61	36$\frac{1}{3}$	3	2	.600	28	14	41	2.72	0	
2008 Tucson	P.C.	6	6$\frac{2}{3}$	0	0	.000	9	4	6	4.05	0	
2008 Arizona a	N.L.	45	32$\frac{1}{3}$	0	3	.000	20	14	33	4.73	0	
Major League Totals	3 Yrs.	115	74$\frac{1}{3}$	3	5	.375	51	30	77	3.39	0	
Championship Series												
2007 Arizona	N.L.	3	1$\frac{1}{3}$	0	0	.000	1	2	1	0.00	0	

a On disabled list from July 19 to August 13, 2008.

SLOWEY, KEVIN MICHAEL

Born, Conroe, Texas, May 4, 1984.
Bats Right. Throws Right. Height, 6 feet, 3 inches. Weight, 195 pounds.

Year	Club	Lea	G	IP	W	L	Pct	SO	BB	H	ERA	SAVES
2005 Elizabethton	Appal.	4	7$\frac{2}{3}$	0	0	.000	15	0	2	1.17	1	
2006 New Britain	Eastern	9	59$\frac{1}{3}$	4	3	.571	52	13	50	3.19	0	
2006 Fort Myers	Fla.St.	14	89$\frac{1}{3}$	4	2	.667	99	9	52	1.01	0	
2007 Rochester	Int.	20	133$\frac{2}{3}$	10	5	.667	107	18	110	1.89	0	
2007 Minnesota	A.L.	13	66$\frac{2}{3}$	4	1	.800	47	11	82	4.72	0	
2008 Fort Myers	Fla.St.	2	8	0	0	.000	10	2	1	1.13	0	
2008 Rochester	Int.	1	5	0	1	.000	9	2	3	3.60	0	
2008 Minnesota a	A.L.	27	160$\frac{1}{3}$	12	11	.522	123	24	161	3.99	0	
Major League Totals	2 Yrs.	40	227	16	12	.571	170	35	243	4.20	0	

a On disabled list from April 4 to May 7, 2008.

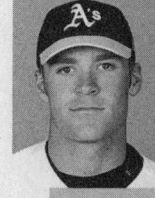

SMITH, GREGORY THOMAS (GREG)

Born, Alexandria, Louisiana, December 22, 1983.
Bats Left. Throws Left. Height, 6 feet, 2 inches. Weight, 190 pounds.

Year	Club	Lea	G	IP	W	L	Pct	SO	BB	H	ERA	SAVES
2005 Missoula	Pioneer	16	82$\frac{1}{3}$	8	5	.615	100	18	69	4.15	0	
2006 Lancaster	Calif.	13	88$\frac{1}{3}$	9	0	1.000	71	31	57	1.63	0	
2006 Tennessee	Southern	11	60	5	4	.556	38	23	65	3.90	0	
2007 Tucson	P.C.	10	52$\frac{1}{3}$	4	2	.667	34	18	61	3.78	0	
2007 Mobile a	Southern	12	69$\frac{2}{3}$	5	3	.625	62	14	64	3.36	0	
2008 Sacramento	P.C.	1	6	0	1	.000	4	1	6	3.00	0	
2008 Oakland b	A.L.	32	190$\frac{1}{3}$	7	16	.304	111	87	169	4.16	0	

a Traded by Arizona Diamondbacks to Oakland Athletics with pitcher Brett Anderson, pitcher Dana Eveland, infielder Chris Carter, outfielder Aaron Cunningham and outfielder Carlos Gonzalez for pitcher Danny Haren and pitcher Connor Robertson, December 14, 2007.
b Traded to Colorado Rockies with outfielder Carlos Gonzalez and pitcher Huston Street for outfielder Matt Holliday, November 12, 2008.

SMITH, JOSEPH MICHAEL (JOE)

Born, Cincinnati, Ohio, March 22, 1984.
Bats Right. Throws Right. Height, 6 feet, 2 inches. Weight, 215 pounds.

Year	Club	Lea	G	IP	W	L	Pct	SO	BB	H	ERA	SAVES
2006 Binghamton	Eastern	10	12$\frac{2}{3}$	0	2	.000	12	11	12	5.68	0	
2006 Brooklyn	N.Y.-Penn.	17	20	0	1	.000	28	3	10	0.45	9	
2007 New Orleans	P.C.	8	9	0	0	.000	5	4	7	2.00	2	
2007 New York	N.L.	54	44$\frac{1}{3}$	3	2	.600	45	21	48	3.45	0	
2008 New York a-b	N.L.	82	63$\frac{1}{3}$	6	3	.667	52	31	51	3.55	0	
Major League Totals	2 Yrs.	136	107$\frac{2}{3}$	9	5	.643	97	52	99	3.51	0	

a Traded to Seattle Mariners with pitcher Aaron Heilman, outfielder Endy Chavez, pitcher Jason Vargas, infielder Mike Carp, outfielder Ezequiel Carrera and pitcher Maikel Cleto for pitcher J.J. Putz, pitcher Sean Green and infielder Jeremy Reed, December 10, 2008.
b Traded to Cleveland Indians with pitcher Luis Valbuena for outfielder Franklin Gutierrez, December 10, 2008.

SMOLTZ, JOHN ANDREW

Born, Detroit, Michigan, May 15, 1967.
Bats Right. Throws Right. Height, 6 feet, 3 inches. Weight, 220 pounds.

Year Club	Lea	G	IP	W	L	Pct	SO	BB	H	ERA	SAVES
1986 Lakeland. . . . . .Fla. St.		17	96	7	8	.467	47	31	86	3.56	0
1987 Glens Falls a. . . . . . . Eastern		21	130	4	10	.286	86	81	131	5.68	0
1987 Richmond . . . . .Int.		3	16	0	1	.000	5	11	17	6.19	0
1988 Richmond . . . . .Int.		20	135⅓	10	5	.667	115	37	118	2.79	0
1988 Atlanta . . . . .N.L.		12	64	2	7	.222	37	33	74	5.48	0
1989 Atlanta . . . . .N.L.		29	208	12	11	.522	168	72	160	2.94	0
1990 Atlanta b. . . . . .N.L.		34	231⅓	14	11	.560	170	*90	206	3.85	0
1991 Atlanta c. . . . . .N.L.		36	229⅔	14	13	.519	148	77	206	3.80	0
1992 Atlanta d. . . . . .N.L.		35	246⅔	15	12	.556	*215	80	206	2.85	0
1993 Atlanta . . . . .N.L.		35	243⅔	15	11	.577	208	100	208	3.62	0
1994 Atlanta e. . . . . .N.L.		21	134⅔	6	10	.375	113	48	120	4.14	0
1995 Atlanta f. . . . . .N.L.		29	192⅔	12	7	.632	193	72	166	3.18	0
1996 Atlanta g-h. . . . . .N.L.		35	*253⅔	*24	8	*.750	*276	55	199	2.94	0
1997 Atlanta . . . . .N.L.		35	*256	15	12	.556	241	63	*234	3.02	0
1998 Greenville. . . . . Southern		3	14	0	1	.000	16	3	11	2.57	0
1998 Macon . . . . .So.Atl.		2	10	0	0	.000	14	1	7	3.60	0
1998 Atlanta i. . . . . .N.L.		26	167⅔	17	3	*.850	173	44	145	2.90	0
1999 Greenville. . . . . Southern		2	4	0	0	.000	7	1	5	4.50	0
1999 Atlanta j. . . . . .N.L.		29	186⅓	11	8	.579	156	40	168	3.19	0
2000 Atlanta k. . . . . .N.L.			INJURED—Did Not Play								
2001 Macon . . . . .So.Atl.		1	5	0	0	.000	5	0	4	1.80	0
2001 Greenville. . . . . Southern		3	6	0	0	.000	6	0	3	0.00	0
2001 Atlanta l-m. . . . . .N.L.		36	59	3	3	.500	57	10	53	3.36	10
2002 Atlanta . . . . .N.L.		75	80⅓	3	2	.600	85	24	59	3.25	*55
2003 Atlanta n. . . . . .N.L.		62	64⅓	0	2	.000	73	8	48	1.12	45
2004 Atlanta . . . . .N.L.		73	81⅔	0	1	.000	85	13	75	2.76	44
2005 Atlanta . . . . .N.L.		33	229⅔	14	7	.667	169	53	210	3.06	0
2006 Atlanta . . . . .N.L.		35	232	*16	9	.640	211	55	221	3.49	0
2007 Atlanta o. . . . . .N.L.		32	205⅔	14	8	.636	197	47	196	3.11	0
2008 Rome. . . . . .So.Atl.		2	3	0	0	.000	4	0	1	0.00	0
2008 Mississippi. . . . . . . Southern		1	1	0	0	.000	0	0	1	0.00	0
2008 Atlanta p-q. . . . . .N.L.		6	28	3	2	.600	36	8	25	2.57	0
Major League Totals . . . . . . .20 Yrs.		708	3395	210	147	.588	3011	992	2979	3.26	154
Division Series											
1995 Atlanta . . . . .N.L.		1	5⅔	0	0	.000	6	1	5	7.94	0
1996 Atlanta . . . . .N.L.		1	9	1	0	1.000	7	2	4	1.00	0
1997 Atlanta . . . . .N.L.		1	9	1	0	1.000	11	1	3	1.00	0
1998 Atlanta . . . . .N.L.		1	7⅔	1	0	1.000	6	0	5	1.17	0
1999 Atlanta . . . . .N.L.		1	7	1	0	1.000	3	3	6	5.14	0
2001 Atlanta . . . . .N.L.		3	4	0	0	.000	3	0	3	2.25	2
2002 Atlanta . . . . .N.L.		2	3⅓	0	0	.000	7	2	2	2.70	0
2003 Atlanta . . . . .N.L.		2	3	1	0	1.000	1	0	4	6.00	1
2004 Atlanta . . . . .N.L.		2	5	1	0	1.000	4	2	4	0.00	0
2005 Atlanta . . . . .N.L.		1	7	1	0	1.000	5	1	7	1.29	0
Division Series Totals		15	60⅔	7	0	1.000	53	12	43	2.52	3
Championship Series											
1991 Atlanta . . . . .N.L.		2	15⅓	2	0	1.000	15	3	14	1.76	0
1992 Atlanta . . . . .N.L.		3	20⅓	2	0	1.000	19	10	14	2.66	0
1993 Atlanta . . . . .N.L.		1	6⅓	0	1	.000	10	5	8	0.00	0
1995 Atlanta . . . . .N.L.		1	7	0	0	.000	2	2	7	2.57	0
1996 Atlanta . . . . .N.L.		2	15	2	0	1.000	12	3	12	1.20	0
1997 Atlanta . . . . .N.L.		1	6	0	1	.000	9	5	5	7.50	0
1998 Atlanta . . . . .N.L.		2	13⅔	0	0	.000	13	6	13	3.95	0
1999 Atlanta . . . . .N.L.		3	8⅔	0	0	.000	8	0	8	6.23	1
2001 Atlanta . . . . .N.L.		2	3	0	0	.000	1	0	0	0.00	0
Championship Series Totals		17	95⅓	6	2	.750	89	34	81	2.83	1
World Series Record											
1991 Atlanta . . . . .N.L.		2	14⅓	0	0	.000	11	1	13	1.26	0
1992 Atlanta . . . . .N.L.		2	13⅓	1	0	1.000	12	7	13	2.70	0
1995 Atlanta . . . . .N.L.		1	2⅓	0	0	.000	4	2	6	15.43	0
1996 Atlanta . . . . .N.L.		2	14	1	1	.500	14	8	6	0.64	0

Year	Club	Lea	G	IP	W	L	Pct	SO	BB	H	ERA	SAVES
1999 Atlanta		N.L.	1	7	0	1	.000	11	3	6	3.86	0
World Series Totals			8	51	2	2	.500	52	21	44	2.47	0

a Traded by Detroit Tigers to Atlanta Braves organization for pitcher Doyle Alexander, August 12, 1987.
b Appeared in four additional games as pinch runner.
c Appeared in two additional games as pinch runner.
d Appeared in one additional game as pinch hitter.
e Suspended eight games by National League for May 14 hitting batter with pitch, June 20 to June 28, 1994.
f Selected Cy Young Award Winner in National League for 1996.
g Filed for free agency, October 31, 1996.
h Re-signed with Atlanta Braves, November 20, 1996.
i On disabled list from March 31 to April 15 and May 24 to June 20, 1998.
j On disabled list from May 17 to June 1 and July 5 to July 24, 1999.
k On disabled list from April 2 to October 30, 2000.
l On disabled list from March 23 to May 17 and June 10 to July 22, 2001.
m Filed for free agency, November 5, 2001, re-signed with Atlanta Braves, December 2, 2001.
n On disabled list from August 24 to September 20, 2003.
o On disabled list from July 3 to July 18, 2007.
p On disabled list from March 21 to April 6 and April 28 to June 2 and June 3 to September 29, 2008.
s Filed for free agency, October 31, 2008. Signed with Boston Red Sox, January 13, 2009.

SNELL, IAN DANTE
Born, Dover, Delaware, October 30, 1981.
Bats Right. Throws Right. Height, 5 feet, 11 inches. Weight, 190 pounds.

Year	Club	Lea	G	IP	W	L	Pct	SO	BB	H	ERA	SAVES
2000 Pirates	Gulf Coast		4	7²/₃	1	0	1.000	8	1	5	2.35	0
2001 Pirates	Gulf Coast		3	19	3	0	1.000	13	5	12	0.47	0
2001 Williamsport	N.Y.-Penn.		10	64²/₃	7	0	1.000	56	10	55	1.39	0
2002 Hickory	So.Atl.		24	139²/₃	11	6	.647	149	45	127	2.71	0
2003 Lynchburg	Carolina		20	116¹/₃	10	3	.769	122	33	105	3.33	0
2003 Altoona	Eastern		6	36²/₃	4	0	1.000	23	10	36	1.96	0
2004 Altoona	Eastern		26	151	11	7	.611	142	40	147	3.16	0
2004 Pittsburgh	N.L.		3	12	0	1	.000	9	9	14	7.50	0
2005 Pittsburgh	N.L.		15	42	1	2	.333	34	24	43	5.14	0
2005 Indianapolis	Int.		18	112	11	3	.786	104	23	90	3.70	0
2006 Pittsburgh	N.L.		32	186	14	11	.560	169	74	198	4.74	0
2007 Pittsburgh	N.L.		32	208	9	12	.429	177	68	209	3.76	0
2008 Pittsburgh a	N.L.		31	164¹/₃	7	12	.368	135	89	201	5.42	0
Major League Totals	5 Yrs.		113	612¹/₃	31	38	.449	524	264	665	4.67	0

a On disabled list from June 23 to July 8, 2008.

SONNANSTINE, ANDREW MICHAEL (ANDY)
Born, Barberton, Ohio, March 18, 1983.
Bats Left. Throws Right. Height, 6 feet, 3 inches. Weight, 185 pounds.

Year	Club	Lea	G	IP	W	L	Pct	SO	BB	H	ERA	SAVES
2004 Hudson Valley	N.Y.-Penn.		9	27	3	1	.750	24	3	18	1.00	1
2004 Charleston	So.Atl.		8	30²/₃	2	0	1.000	42	7	18	0.59	0
2005 Visalia	Calif.		10	64	4	1	.800	75	7	71	3.80	0
2005 Southwest	Midwest		18	116²/₃	10	4	.714	103	11	103	2.55	0
2006 Montgomery	Southern		28	185²/₃	15	8	.652	153	34	151	2.67	0
2007 Durham	Int.		11	71	6	4	.600	66	13	60	2.66	0
2007 Tampa Bay	A.L.		22	130²/₃	6	10	.375	97	26	151	5.85	0
2008 Tampa Bay	A.L.		32	193¹/₃	13	9	.591	124	37	212	4.38	0
Major League Totals	2 Yrs.		54	324	19	19	.500	221	63	363	4.97	0
Division Series												
2008 Tampa Bay	N.L.		1	5²/₃	1	0	1.000	4	1	3	3.18	0
Championship Series												
2008 Tampa Bay	N.L.		1	7¹/₃	1	0	1.000	2	1	6	3.68	0
World Series Record												
2008 Tampa Bay	N.L.		1	4	0	1	.000	2	3	6	6.75	0

SORIA, JOAKIM AGUSTIN (RAMOS)
Born, Monclova, Mexico, May 18, 1984.
Bats Right. Throws Right. Height, 6 feet, 3 inches. Weight, 185 pounds.

Year	Club	Lea	G	IP	W	L	Pct	SO	BB	H	ERA	SAVES
2002 Dodgers	Gulf Coast		4	5	0	0	.000	6	0	6	3.60	0
2003				INJURED—Did Not Play								

Year Club	Lea	G	IP	W	L	Pct	SO	BB	H	ERA	SAVES
2004 Dodgers........Dominican		4	5⅓	0	0	.000	4	5	3	1.69	1
2005 Mexico City a.......Mexican		30	66⅓	5	0	1.000	60	31	75	4.48	0
2006 Mexico City........Mexican		39	37	0	0	.000	30	11	37	3.89	15
2006 Fort Wayne b......Midwest		7	11⅔	1	0	1.000	11	2	5	2.31	0
2007 Kansas City c.........A.L.		62	69	2	3	.400	75	19	46	2.48	17
2008 Kansas City.........A.L.		63	67⅓	2	3	.400	66	19	39	1.60	42
Major League Totals ....2 Yrs.		125	136⅓	4	6	.400	141	38	85	2.05	59

a Released by Los Angeles Dodgers, October 12, 2004. Signed with San Diego Padres organization, December 20, 2005.

b Selected by Kansas City Royals from San Diego Padres in Rule V draft, December 7, 2006.

c On disabled list from May 23 to June 7, 2007.

SOWERS, JEREMY BRYAN

Born, St. Clairsville, Ohio, May 17, 1983.
Bats Left. Throws Left. Height, 6 feet, 1 inch. Weight, 180 pounds.

Year Club	Lea	G	IP	W	L	Pct	SO	BB	H	ERA	SAVES
2005 Kinston............Carolina		13	71⅓	8	3	.727	75	19	60	2.78	0
2005 Akron.............Eastern		13	82⅓	5	1	.833	70	9	74	2.08	0
2005 Buffalo...............Int.		1	5⅔	1	0	1.000	4	1	7	1.59	0
2006 Buffalo...............Int.		15	97⅓	9	1	.900	54	29	78	1.39	0
2006 Cleveland............A.L.		14	88⅓	7	4	.636	35	20	85	3.57	0
2007 Buffalo...............Int.		15	96⅔	4	5	.444	61	24	112	4.10	0
2007 Cleveland............A.L.		13	67⅓	1	6	.143	24	21	84	6.42	0
2008 Buffalo...............Int.		10	60⅔	4	3	.571	43	17	56	2.08	0
2008 Cleveland............A.L.		22	121	4	9	.308	64	39	141	5.58	0
Major League Totals ....3 Yrs.		49	276⅔	12	19	.387	123	80	310	5.14	0

SPEIER, JUSTIN JAMES

Born, Daly City, California, November 6, 1973.
Bats Right. Throws Right. Height, 6 feet, 4 inches. Weight, 205 pounds.

Year Club	Lea	G	IP	W	L	Pct	SO	BB	H	ERA	SAVES
1995 Williamsport......N.Y.-Penn.		30	36⅓	2	1	.667	39	4	27	1.49	12
1996 Daytona............Fla.St.		33	38⅓	2	4	.333	34	19	32	3.76	13
1996 Orlando.........Southern		24	26⅓	4	1	.800	14	5	23	2.05	6
1997 Orlando.........Southern		50	78⅓	6	5	.545	63	23	77	4.48	6
1997 Iowa................A.A.		8	12⅓	2	0	1.000	9	1	5	0.00	1
1998 Iowa................P.C.		45	51⅔	3	3	.500	49	19	52	5.05	12
1998 Chicago-Florida a.......N.L.		19	20⅔	0	3	.000	17	13	27	8.71	0
1999 Richmond.............Int.		27	41⅔	2	4	.333	39	22	51	5.62	3
1999 Atlanta b-c............N.L.		19	28⅔	0	0	.000	22	13	28	5.65	0
2000 Buffalo...............Int.		13	13	0	0	.000	12	3	13	4.15	9
2000 Cleveland............A.L.		47	68⅓	5	2	.714	69	28	57	3.29	0
2001 Cleveland............A.L.		12	20⅔	2	0	1.000	15	8	24	6.97	0
2001 Colo Sprngs..........P.C.		11	12⅓	1	0	1.000	16	7	10	1.46	2
2001 Colorado d-e-f.........N.L.		42	56	4	3	.571	47	12	47	3.70	0
2002 Colorado Springs.......P.C.		12	14	2	0	1.000	14	3	20	3.86	2
2002 Colorado............N.L.		63	62⅓	5	1	.833	47	19	51	4.33	1
2003 Colorado h...........N.L.		72	73⅓	3	1	.750	66	23	73	4.05	9
2004 Dunedin.............Fla.St.		2	2	0	0	.000	2	0	3	4.50	0
2004 Toronto i............A.L.		62	69	3	8	.273	52	25	61	3.91	7
2005 Toronto.............A.L.		65	66⅔	3	2	.600	56	15	48	2.57	0
2006 Toronto j-k...........A.L.		58	51⅓	2	0	1.000	55	21	47	2.98	0
2007 Azl Angels........Arizona		2	3	0	0	.000	3	0	1	0.00	0
2007 Rancho Cucamonga....Calif.		8	9	1	0	1.000	7	5	10	3.00	0
2007 Los Angeles l.........A.L.		50	50	2	3	.400	47	12	36	2.88	0
2008 Los Angeles..........A.L.		62	68	2	8	.200	56	27	69	5.03	0
Major League Totals ....11 Yrs.		572	635	31	31	.500	549	216	568	4.04	17
Division Series											
2007 Los Angeles..........A.L.		2	1⅔	0	1	.000	0	1	4	27.00	0

a Traded to Florida Marlins with infielder Kevin Orie and pitcher Todd Noel for pitcher Felix Heredia and infielder Steve Hoff, July 31, 1998.

b Traded to Atlanta Braves for player to be named later, April 1, 1999. Atlanta Braves received pitcher Matt Targac to complete trade, June 11, 1999.

c Claimed on waivers by Cleveland Indians, November 23, 1999.

d Traded to New York Mets for player to be named later, May 19, 2001.

e Cleveland Indians received pitcher Brian Jenkins to complete trade, May 21, 2001.

f Claimed on waivers by Colorado Rockies, May 29, 2001.

g On disabled list from March 31 to May 6, 2002.
h Traded to Toronto Blue Jays for pitcher Joe Kennedy and player to be named later, December 14, 2003. Colorado Rockies received pitcher Sandy Nin to complete trade, December 15, 2003.
i On disabled list from May 11 to June 8, 2004.
j On disabled list from August 9 to September 10, 2006.
k Filed for free agency, October 28, 2006. Signed with Los Angeles Angels, November 19, 2006.
l On disabled list from May 1 to July 13, 2007.

SPEIER, RYAN ANDREW

Born, Frankfort, Kentucky, July 24, 1979.
Bats Right. Throws Right. Height, 6 feet, 7 inches. Weight, 210 pounds.

Year	Club	Lea	G	IP	W	L	Pct	SO	BB	H	ERA	SAVES
2001	Casper	Pioneer	17	25²/₃	1	2	.333	24	9	19	3.16	1
2002	Salem	Carolina	24	32	2	2	.500	33	11	35	3.94	4
2002	Asheville	So.Atl.	28	36²/₃	3	1	.750	39	13	32	3.93	1
2003	Visalia	Calif.	56	58²/₃	4	2	.667	73	17	50	1.53	18
2004	Tulsa	Texas	61	61²/₃	3	1	.750	71	26	33	2.04	37
2005	Colorado Springs	P.C.	45	52¹/₃	2	2	.500	45	18	70	4.99	6
2005	Colorado	N.L.	22	24²/₃	2	1	.667	10	13	26	3.65	0
2006 a				INJURED—Did Not Play								
2007	Colorado Springs	P.C.	50	49¹/₃	1	4	.200	40	23	47	4.38	33
2007	Colorado	N.L.	20	18	3	1	.750	13	8	20	4.00	0
2008	Asheville	So.Atl.	2	1²/₃	0	0	.000	3	2	1	10.80	0
2008	Colorado Springs	P.C.	11	13¹/₃	1	0	1.000	9	4	10	2.03	5
2008	Colorado b	N.L.	43	51	2	1	.667	33	18	52	4.06	0
Major League Totals		3 Yrs.	85	93²/₃	7	3	.700	56	39	98	3.94	0
Division Series												
2007	Colorado	N.L.	1	1¹/₃	0	0	.000	0	0	1	0.00	0
Championship Series												
2007	Colorado	N.L.	1	1	0	0	.000	1	0	0	0.00	1
World Series Record												
2007	Colorado	N.L.	1	0	0	0	.000	0	3	0	INF	0

a On minor league disabled list from April 1 to September 30, 2006.
b On disabled list from May 12 to June 3, 2008.

SPRINGER, RUSSELL PAUL (RUSS)

Born, Alexandria, Louisiana, November 7, 1968.
Bats Right. Throws Right. Height, 6 feet, 4 inches. Weight, 215 pounds.

Year	Club	Lea	G	IP	W	L	Pct	SO	BB	H	ERA	SAVES
1989	Yankees	Gulf Coast	6	24	3	0	1.000	34	10	14	1.50	0
1990	Yankees	Gulf Coast	4	15	0	2	.000	17	4	10	1.20	0
1990	Greensboro	So.Atl.	10	56¹/₃	2	3	.400	51	31	51	3.67	0
1991	Ft.Lauderdale	Fla.St.	25	152¹/₃	5	9	.357	139	62	118	3.49	0
1991	Albany	Eastern	2	15	1	0	1.000	16	6	9	1.80	0
1992	Columbus	Int.	20	123²/₃	8	5	.615	95	54	89	2.69	0
1992	New York a	A.L.	14	16	0	0	.000	12	10	18	6.19	0
1993	Vancouver	P.C.	11	59	5	4	.556	40	33	58	4.27	0
1993	California	A.L.	14	60	1	6	.143	31	32	73	7.20	0
1994	Vancouver	P.C.	12	83	7	4	.636	58	19	77	3.04	0
1994	California	A.L.	18	45²/₃	2	2	.500	28	14	53	5.52	2
1995	California	A.L.	19	51²/₃	1	2	.333	38	25	60	6.10	1
1995	Vancouver	P.C.	6	34	2	0	1.000	23	23	24	3.44	0
1995	Philadelphia b-c	N.L.	14	26²/₃	0	0	.000	32	10	22	3.71	0
1996	Philadelphia	N.L.	51	96²/₃	3	10	.231	94	38	106	4.66	0
1997	Jackson	Texas	1	1	0	0	.000	2	0	2	9.00	0
1997	Houston d-e	N.L.	54	55¹/₃	3	3	.500	74	27	48	4.23	3
1998	Arizona-Atlanta f-g	N.L.	48	52²/₃	5	4	.556	56	30	51	4.10	0
1999	Richmond	Int.	11	15¹/₃	1	0	1.000	13	1	9	1.17	2
1999	Atlanta h-i	N.L.	49	47¹/₃	2	1	.667	49	22	31	3.42	1
2000	Arizona	N.L.	52	62	2	4	.333	59	34	63	5.08	0
2001	Arizona	N.L.	18	17²/₃	0	0	.000	12	14	20	7.13	1
2001	Tucson j	P.C.	7	7¹/₃	0	0	.000	6	3	7	4.91	0
2002				Did Not Play								
2003	St. Louis	N.L.	17	17¹/₃	1	1	.500	11	6	19	8.31	0
2003	Memphis k-l	P.C.	7	6¹/₃	0	0	.000	5	4	2	1.42	0
2004	New Orleans	P.C.	26	31	1	2	.333	33	14	31	3.48	6
2004	Houston m-n	N.L.	16	13²/₃	0	1	.000	9	6	15	2.63	0
2005	Houston o	N.L.	62	59	4	4	.500	54	21	49	4.73	0
2006	Houston p	N.L.	72	59²/₃	1	1	.500	46	16	46	3.47	0

Year	Club	Lea	G	IP	W	L	Pct	SO	BB	H	ERA	SAVES
2007 St. Louis		N.L.	76	66	8	1	.889	66	19	41	2.18	0
2008 St. Louis q-r		N.L.	70	50⅓	2	1	.667	45	18	39	2.32	0
Major League Totals	16 Yrs.		664	797⅔	35	41	.461	716	332	754	4.55	8
Division Series												
1997 Houston		N.L.	2	1⅔	0	0	.000	3	1	2	5.40	0
1999 Atlanta		N.L.	1	1	0	0	.000	1	1	2	0.00	0
2004 Houston		N.L.	2	2	0	1	.000	5	1	3	18.00	0
2005 Houston		N.L.	2	2⅓	0	0	.000	1	1	5	3.86	0
Division Series Totals			7	7	0	1	.000	10	4	12	7.71	0
Championship Series												
1999 Atlanta		N.L.	2	2	1	0	1.000	1	1	0	0.00	0
2005 Houston		N.L.	1	1	0	0	.000	1	1	0	0.00	0
Championship Series Totals			3	3	1	0	1.000	2	2	0	0.00	0
World Series Record												
1999 Atlanta		N.L.	2	2⅓	0	0	.000	1	0	1	0.00	0
2005 Houston		N.L.	2	2	0	0	.000	1	0	2	4.50	0
World Series Totals			4	4⅓	0	0	.000	2	0	3	2.08	0

a Traded to California Angels with infielder J.T. Snow and pitcher Jerry Neilsen for pitcher Jim Abbott, December 6, 1992.
b Kevin Flora was traded to Philadelphia Phillies with player to be named later for outfielder Dave Gallagher, August 9, 1995. Philadelphia Phillies received pitcher Russ Springer to complete trade, August 15, 1995.
c Released by Philadelphia Phillies, December 20, 1996. Signed with Houston Astros, December 30, 1996.
d On disabled list from June 17 to July 10, 1997.
e Selected in expansion draft by Arizona Diamondbacks, November 18, 1997.
f On disabled list from August 6 to August 21, 1998.
g Traded to Atlanta Braves for pitcher Alan Embree, June 22, 1998.
h On disabled list from April 3 to May 17, 1999.
i Filed for free agency, November 2, 1999. Signed with Arizona Diamondbacks, November 23, 1999.
j On disabled list from May 23 to November 7, 2001.
k Filed for free agency, November 7, 2001. Signed with St. Louis Cardinals organization, January 3, 2003.
l On disabled list from May 1 to August 30, 2003.
m Filed for free agency, October 28, 2003. Signed with Houston Astros organization, June 29, 2004.
n Filed for free agency, November 4, 2004. Re-signed with Houston Astros organization, December 7, 2004.
o Filed for free agency, November 10, 2005, re-signed with Houston Astros, December 2, 2005.
p Filed for free agency, October 30, 2006. Signed with St. Louis Cardinals, December 8, 2006.
q On disabled list from April 5 to April 21, 2008.
r Filed for free agency, October 30, 2008.

STREET, HUSTON LOWELL
Born, Austin, Texas, August 2, 1983.
Bats Right. Throws Right. Height, 6 feet. Weight, 190 pounds.

Year	Club	Lea	G	IP	W	L	Pct	SO	BB	H	ERA	SAVES
2004 Kane County		Midwest	9	10⅔	0	1	.000	14	5	9	1.69	4
2004 Sacramento		P.C.	2	2	0	0	.000	2	0	2	0.00	1
2004 Midland		Texas	10	13⅓	1	0	1.000	14	3	10	1.35	3
2005 Oakland a		A.L.	67	78⅓	5	1	.833	72	26	53	1.72	23
2006 Oakland b		A.L.	69	70⅔	4	4	.500	67	13	64	3.31	37
2007 Sacramento		P.C.	1	1	0	0	.000	2	0	1	0.00	0
2007 Oakland c		A.L.	48	50	5	2	.714	63	12	35	2.88	16
2008 Oakland d		A.L.	63	70	7	5	.583	69	27	58	3.73	18
Major League Totals	4 Yrs.		247	269	21	12	.636	271	78	210	2.88	94
Division Series												
2006 Oakland		A.L.	3	3	0	0	.000	1	1	4	3.00	2
Championship Series												
2006 Oakland		A.L.	2	3⅓	0	1	.000	3	0	4	10.80	0

a Selected Rookie of the Year in American League for 2005.
b On disabled list from August 19 to September 8, 2006.
c On disabled list from May 13 to July 23, 2007.
d Traded to Colorado Rockies with outfielder Carlos Gonzalez and pitcher Greg Smith for outfielder Matt Holliday, November 12, 2008.

SUPPAN, JEFFREY SCOT (JEFF)
Born, Oklahoma City, Oklahoma, January 2, 1975.
Bats Right. Throws Right. Height, 6 feet, 2 inch. Weight, 235 pounds.

Year	Club	Lea	G	IP	W	L	Pct	SO	BB	H	ERA	SAVES
1993 Red Sox		Gulf Coast	10	57⅔	4	3	.571	64	16	52	2.18	0
1994 Sarasota		Fla. St.	27	174	13	7	.650	173	50	153	3.26	0

Year	Club	Lea	G	IP	W	L	Pct	SO	BB	H	ERA	SAVES
1995	Trenton...........	Eastern	15	99	6	2	.750	88	26	86	2.36	0
1995	Pawtucket	Int.	7	45⅔	2	3	.400	32	9	50	5.32	0
1995	Boston	A.L.	8	22⅔	1	2	.333	19	5	29	5.96	0
1996	Pawtucket	Int.	22	145⅓	10	6	.625	142	25	130	3.22	0
1996	Boston a.	A.L.	8	22⅔	1	1	.500	13	13	29	7.54	0
1997	Pawtucket	Int.	9	60⅔	5	1	.833	40	15	51	3.71	0
1997	Boston b	A.L.	23	112⅓	7	3	.700	67	36	140	5.69	0
1998	Arizona..............	N.L.	13	66	1	7	.125	39	21	82	6.68	0
1998	Tucson c.	P.C.	13	67	4	3	.571	62	17	75	3.63	0
1998	Kansas City	A.L.	4	12⅓	0	0	.000	12	1	9	0.71	0
1999	Kansas City	A.L.	32	208⅔	10	12	.455	103	62	222	4.53	0
2000	Kansas City	A.L.	35	217	10	9	.526	128	84	240	4.94	0
2001	Kansas City	A.L.	34	218⅓	10	14	.417	120	74	227	4.37	0
2002	Kansas City d	A.L.	33	208	9	16	.360	109	68	229	5.32	0
2003	Pittsburgh	N.L.	21	141	10	7	.588	78	31	147	3.57	0
2003	Boston e-f	A.L.	11	63	3	4	.429	32	20	70	5.57	0
2004	St. Louis..............	N.L.	31	188	16	9	.640	110	65	192	4.16	0
2005	St. Louis..............	N.L.	32	194⅓	16	10	.615	114	63	206	3.57	0
2006	St. Louis g	N.L.	32	190	12	7	.632	104	69	207	4.12	0
2007	Milwaukee	N.L.	34	206⅔	12	12	.500	114	68	243	4.62	0
2008	Milwaukee h..........	N.L.	31	177⅔	10	10	.500	90	67	207	4.96	0
Major League Totals	**14 Yrs.**		**382**	**2249**	**128**	**123**	**.510**	**1252**	**747**	**2479**	**4.63**	**0**
Division Series												
2004	St. Louis..............	N.L.	1	7	1	0	1.000	2	3	2	2.57	0
2006	St. Louis..............	N.L.	1	4⅓	0	1	.000	3	3	6	6.23	0
2008	Milwaukee	N.L.	1	3	0	1	.000	3	2	6	15.00	0
Division Series Totals			**3**	**14⅓**	**1**	**2**	**.333**	**8**	**8**	**14**	**6.28**	**0**
Championship Series												
2004	St. Louis..............	N.L.	2	12	1	1	.500	9	4	8	3.00	0
2005	St. Louis..............	N.L.	1	5	0	0	.000	5	3	3	1.80	0
2006	St. Louis..............	N.L.	2	15	1	0	1.000	6	6	5	0.60	0
Championship Series Totals			**5**	**32**	**2**	**1**	**.667**	**20**	**13**	**16**	**1.69**	**0**
World Series Record												
2004	St. Louis..............	N.L.	1	4⅔	0	1	.000	4	1	8	7.71	0
2006	St. Louis..............	N.L.	1	6	0	0	.000	4	2	8	4.50	0
World Series Totals.............			**2**	**10⅔**	**0**	**1**	**.000**	**8**	**3**	**16**	**5.91**	**0**

a On disabled list from August 25 to September 30, 1996.
b Selected in expansion draft by Arizona Diamondbacks, November 18, 1997.
c Sold to Kansas City Royals, September 3, 1998.
d Not offered contract, December 20, 2002. Signed with Pittsburgh Pirates, January 29, 2003.
e Traded to Boston Red Sox with pitcher Brandon Lyon and pitcher Anastacio Martinez for infielder Freddy Sanchez, pitcher Mike Gonzalez and cash, July 31, 2003.
f Filed for free agency, October 27, 2003. Signed with St. Louis Cardinals, December 16, 2003.
g Filed for free agency, November 1, 2006. Signed with Milwaukee Brewers, December 24, 2006.
h On disabled list from July 7 to July 22, 2008.

TALLET, BRIAN CURTIS

Born, Midwest City, Oklahoma, September 21, 1977.
Bats Left. Throws Left. Height, 6 feet, 7 inches. Weight, 220 pounds.

Year	Club	Lea	G	IP	W	L	Pct	SO	BB	H	ERA	SAVES
2000	Mahoning Valley...	N.Y.-Penn.	6	15⅔	0	0	.000	20	3	10	1.15	0
2001	Kinston............	Carolina	27	160	9	7	.563	164	38	134	3.04	0
2002	Akron............	Eastern	18	102⅓	10	1	.909	73	32	93	3.08	0
2002	Buffalo...............	Int.	8	44	2	3	.400	25	16	47	3.07	0
2002	Cleveland.............	A.L.	2	12	1	0	1.000	5	4	9	1.50	0
2003	Buffalo...............	Int.	15	84	4	4	.500	67	34	89	5.14	0
2003	Cleveland.............	A.L.	5	19	0	2	.000	9	8	23	4.74	0
2004	Akron.............	Eastern	14	22⅔	1	1	.500	24	13	26	5.56	1
2004	Buffalo...............	Int.	5	8⅔	0	0	.000	7	3	7	4.15	0
2004	Mahoning Valley...	N.Y.-Penn.	2	2⅔	0	0	.000	2	0	3	0.00	0
2004	Lake County a	So.Atl.	2	2	0	0	.000	1	0	1	0.00	0
2005	Cleveland.............	A.L.	2	4⅔	0	0	.000	2	3	6	7.71	0
2005	Buffalo...............	Int.	22	97⅔	6	5	.545	61	25	98	4.05	0
2006	Syracuse	Int.	20	25⅓	1	2	.333	21	10	32	5.68	3
2006	Toronto b	A.L.	44	54⅓	3	0	1.000	37	31	45	3.81	0
2007	Syracuse	Int.	7	6⅔	0	0	.000	11	3	4	1.35	0
2007	Toronto	A.L.	48	62⅓	2	4	.333	54	28	49	3.47	0
2008	Syracuse	Int.	2	2	0	0	.000	1	1	2	4.50	0

Year Club	Lea	G	IP	W	L	Pct	SO	BB	H	ERA	SAVES
2008 Toronto c . . . . A.L.		51	56⅓	1	2	.333	47	22	52	2.88	0
Major League Totals . . . . .6 Yrs.		152	208⅔	7	8	.467	154	96	184	3.49	0

a On disabled list from April 1 to July 26, 2004.
b Traded to Toronto Blue Jays for pitcher Bubbie Buzachero, January 17, 2006.
c On disabled list from July 26 to August 16, 2008.

TASCHNER, JACK GERARD
Born, Milwaukee, Wisconsin, April 21, 1978.
Bats Left. Throws Left. Height, 6 feet, 3 inches. Weight, 210 pounds.

Year Club	Lea	G	IP	W	L	Pct	SO	BB	H	ERA	SAVES
1999 Salem-Keizer . . . . . Northwest		7	28⅔	3	2	.600	36	10	26	2.51	0
2000 San Jose . . . . Calif.		10	26⅓	2	2	.500	22	17	23	4.10	1
2001 San Jose . . . . Calif.		14	65⅔	4	4	.500	72	29	62	4.11	0
2002						INJURED—Did Not Play					
2003 Norwich . . . . Eastern		34	75⅔	0	6	.000	46	45	78	5.71	0
2004 Norwich . . . . Eastern		14	58	3	1	.750	55	16	47	2.48	0
2004 Fresno . . . . P.C.		18	53⅓	4	7	.364	44	32	71	9.28	0
2005 Fresno . . . . P.C.		44	49⅓	3	0	1.000	62	24	30	1.64	10
2005 San Francisco . . . . N.L.		24	22⅔	2	0	1.000	19	13	15	1.59	0
2006 Fresno . . . . P.C.		45	49⅓	6	7	.462	68	17	49	3.65	14
2006 San Francisco . . . . N.L.		24	19⅓	0	1	.000	15	7	31	8.38	0
2007 San Francisco . . . . N.L.		63	50	3	1	.750	51	29	44	5.40	0
2008 San Francisco . . . . N.L.		67	48	3	2	.600	39	24	57	4.88	0
Major League Totals . . . . .4 Yrs.		178	140	8	4	.667	124	73	147	5.01	0

TAVAREZ (CARMEN), JULIAN
Born, Santiago, Dominican Republic, May 22, 1973.
Bats Left. Throws Right. Height, 6 feet, 2 inches. Weight, 195 pounds.

Year Club	Lea	G	IP	W	L	Pct	SO	BB	H	ERA	SAVES
1990 Cleveland . . . . Dominican		2	4⅔	0	1	.000	1	7	6	11.57	0
1991 Cleveland . . . . Dominican		19	121⅓	8	2	.800	75	28	95	2.67	0
1992 Burlington . . . . Appal.		14	87⅓	6	3	.667	69	12	86	2.68	0
1993 Kinston . . . . Carolina		18	119	11	5	.688	107	28	102	2.42	0
1993 Canton-Akron . . . . . . Eastern		3	19	2	1	.667	11	1	14	0.95	0
1993 Cleveland . . . . A.L.		8	37	2	2	.500	19	13	53	6.57	0
1994 Cleveland . . . . A.L.		1	1⅔	0	1	.000	0	1	6	21.60	0
1994 Charlotte . . . . .Int.		26	176	15	6	.714	102	43	167	3.48	0
1995 Cleveland . . . . A.L.		57	85	10	2	.833	68	21	76	2.44	0
1996 Buffalo . . . . A.A.		2	14	1	0	1.000	10	3	10	1.29	0
1996 Cleveland a-b . . . . A.L.		51	80⅔	4	7	.364	46	22	101	5.36	0
1997 San Francisco . . . . N.L.		89	88⅓	6	4	.600	38	34	91	3.87	0
1998 Fresno . . . . P.C.		1	2⅓	0	0	.000	1	0	6	19.29	0
1998 San Francisco c . . . . N.L.		60	85⅓	5	3	.625	52	36	96	3.80	1
1999 Fresno . . . . P.C.		4	8	0	0	.000	9	3	3	2.25	0
1999 San Jose . . . . .California		1	4	0	0	.000	3	1	1	0.00	0
1999 San Francisco d-e . . . . . . N.L.		47	54⅔	2	0	1.000	33	25	65	5.93	0
2000 Colorado f . . . . N.L.		51	120	11	5	.688	62	53	124	4.42	1
2001 Chicago . . . . N.L.		34	161⅓	10	9	.526	107	69	172	4.52	0
2002 Florida g-h-i . . . . N.L.		29	153⅔	10	12	.455	67	74	188	5.39	0
2003 Pittsburgh j . . . . N.L.		64	83⅔	3	3	.500	39	27	75	3.66	11
2004 St. Louis . . . . N.L.		77	64⅓	7	4	.636	48	19	57	2.38	4
2005 St. Louis k . . . . N.L.		74	65⅔	2	3	.400	47	19	68	3.43	4
2006 Boston . . . . A.L.		58	98⅔	5	4	.556	56	44	110	4.47	1
2007 Boston . . . . A.L.		34	134⅔	7	11	.389	77	51	151	5.15	0
2008 Boston . . . . A.L.		9	12⅔	0	1	.000	6	9	18	6.39	0
2008 Milwaukee-Atlanta l-m-n . N.L.		43	42	1	4	.200	45	19	55	4.71	0
Major League Totals . . . . . . .16 Yrs.		786	1369⅓	85	75	.531	810	536	1506	4.45	22
Division Series											
1995 Cleveland . . . . A.L.		3	2⅔	0	0	.000	3	0	5	6.75	0
1996 Cleveland . . . . A.L.		2	1⅓	0	0	.000	1	2	1	0.00	0
1997 San Francisco . . . . N.L.		3	4	0	1	.000	0	2	4	4.50	0
2004 St. Louis . . . . N.L.		2	2⅓	0	0	.000	3	0	2	0.00	0
2005 St. Louis . . . . N.L.		2	1⅓	0	0	.000	0	1	4	13.50	0
Division Series Totals		12	11⅔	0	1	.000	7	5	16	4.63	0
Championship Series											
1995 Cleveland . . . . A.L.		4	3⅓	0	1	.000	2	1	3	2.70	0

Year	Club	Lea	G	IP	W	L	Pct	SO	BB	H	ERA	SAVES
2004 St. Louis............	N.L.	5	6	2	1	.667	3	2	3	3.00	0	
2005 St. Louis............	N.L.	3	3¹/₃	0	0	.000	2	0	5	5.40	0	
Championship Series Totals		12	12²/₃	2	2	.500	7	3	11	3.55	0	
World Series Record												
1995 Cleveland	A.L.	5	4¹/₃	0	0	.000	1	2	3	0.00	0	
2004 St. Louis.............	N.L.	2	2	0	1	.000	1	0	1	4.50	0	
World Series Totals............		7	6¹/₃	0	1	.000	2	2	4	1.42	0	

a Traded to San Francisco Giants with infielder Jeff Kent, infielder Jose Vizcaino and player to be named later for infielder Matt Williams and player to be named later, November 13, 1996.

b Cleveland Indians received outfielder Trenidad Hubbard and San Francisco Giants received pitcher Joe Roa to complete trade, December 16, 1996.

c On disabled list from July 13 to August 7, 1998.

d On disabled list from May 1 to June 1, 1999.

e Claimed on waivers by Colorado Rockies, November 16, 1999.

f Filed for free agency, October 31, 2000. Signed with Chicago Cubs, November 16, 2000.

g Traded to Florida Marlins with pitcher Jose Cueto, pitcher Dontrelle Willis and catcher Ryan Jorgensen for pitcher Antonio Alfonseca and pitcher Matt Clement, March 27, 2002.

h On disabled list from April 17 to May 11, 2002.

i Filed for free agency, October 28, 2002. Signed with Pittsburgh Pirates organization, January 28, 2003.

j Filed for free agency, November 2, 2003. Signed with St. Louis Cardinals, January 9, 2004.

k Filed for free agency, October 28, 2005. Signed with Boston Red Sox, January 18, 2006.

l Filed for free agency, May 20, 2008. Signed with Milwaukee Brewers, May 27, 2008.

m Released by Milwaukee Brewers, June 24, 2008. Signed with Atlanta Braves, July 8, 2008.

n Filed for free agency, October 30, 2008.

THOMPSON, BRADLEY JOSEPH (BRAD)

Born, Las Vegas, Nevada, January 31, 1982.
Bats Right. Throws Right. Height, 6 feet, 1 inch. Weight, 190 pounds.

Year	Club	Lea	G	IP	W	L	Pct	SO	BB	H	ERA	SAVES
2003 Palm Beach	Fla.St.	2	6	1	0	1.000	4	0	3	0.00	0	
2003 Peoria............	Midwest	30	65	5	3	.625	43	10	70	2.91	0	
2004 Memphis	P.C.	3	14²/₃	1	0	1.000	10	3	20	5.52	0	
2004 Tennessee	Southern	13	72¹/₃	8	2	.800	57	11	56	2.36	0	
2005 Memphis	P.C.	9	13²/₃	2	1	.667	11	7	12	3.29	0	
2005 St. Louis.............	N.L.	40	55	4	0	1.000	29	15	46	2.95	1	
2006 Memphis	P.C.	14	42²/₃	2	0	1.000	33	6	36	2.11	0	
2006 St. Louis.............	N.L.	43	56²/₃	1	2	.333	32	20	58	3.34	0	
2007 Memphis	P.C.	2	8¹/₃	0	0	.000	2	1	8	4.32	0	
2007 St. Louis.............	N.L.	44	129¹/₃	8	6	.571	53	40	157	4.73	0	
2008 Memphis	P.C.	3	12²/₃	1	1	.500	4	2	22	7.82	0	
2008 St. Louis a	N.L.	26	64²/₃	6	3	.667	32	19	72	5.15	0	
Major League Totals ....4 Yrs.		153	305²/₃	19	11	.633	146	94	333	4.24	1	
Division Series												
2005 St. Louis.............	N.L.	2	1¹/₃	0	0	.000	1	0	3	13.50	0	
2006 St. Louis.............	N.L.	1	0²/₃	0	0	.000	1	1	0	0.00	0	
Division Series Totals		3	2	0	0	.000	2	1	3	9.00	0	
Championship Series												
2005 St. Louis.............	N.L.	2	1	0	0	.000	0	0	2	0.00	0	
2006 St. Louis.............	N.L.	2	0²/₃	0	1	.000	1	0	3	27.00	0	
Championship Series Totals		4	1²/₃	0	1	.000	1	0	5	10.80	0	
World Series Record												
2006 St. Louis.............	N.L.	1	0²/₃	0	0	.000	1	0	0	0.00	0	

a On disabled list from April 23 to June 19, 2008.

THORNTON, MATTHEW J. (MATT)

Born, Three Rivers, Michigan, September 15, 1976.
Bats Left. Throws Left. Height, 6 feet, 6 inches. Weight, 235 pounds.

Year	Club	Lea	G	IP	W	L	Pct	SO	BB	H	ERA	SAVES
1998 Everett	Northwest	2	1¹/₃	0	0	.000	0	3	1	27.00	0	
1999 Wisconsin	Midwest	25	29¹/₃	0	0	.000	34	25	39	4.91	1	
2000 Wisconsin	Midwest	26	103¹/₃	6	9	.400	88	72	94	4.01	0	
2001 San Bernardino	California	27	157	14	7	.667	192	60	126	2.52	0	
2002 San Antonio	Texas	12	62	1	5	.167	44	29	52	3.63	0	
2003 Inland Empire......	California	2	9	0	0	.000	14	4	9	4.00	0	
2003 Tacoma	P.C.	2	9	0	2	.000	5	3	14	8.00	0	
2003 San Antonio	Texas	4	25¹/₃	3	0	1.000	18	9	8	0.36	0	

Year	Club	Lea	G	IP	W	L	Pct	SO	BB	H	ERA	SAVES
2004 Tacoma	..............P.C.		16	83	7	5	.583	74	63	85	5.20	0
2004 Seattle	................A.L.		19	32²/₃	1	2	.333	30	25	30	4.13	0
2005 Seattle	...............A.L.		55	57	0	4	.000	57	42	54	5.21	0
2006 Chicago a	............A.L.		63	54	5	3	.625	49	21	46	3.33	2
2007 Chicago	..............A.L.		68	56¹/₃	4	4	.500	55	26	59	4.79	2
2008 Chicago	..............A.L.		74	67¹/₃	5	3	.625	77	19	48	2.67	1
Major League Totals	.......5 Yrs.		279	267¹/₃	15	16	.484	268	133	237	3.97	5
Division Series												
2008 Chicago	..............A.L.		3	3¹/₃	0	0	.000	2	2	2	0.00	0

a Traded to Chicago White Sox for outfielder Joe Borchard, March 20, 2006.

TIMLIN, MICHAEL AUGUST (MIKE)

Born, Midland, Texas, March 10, 1966.
Bats Right. Throws Right. Height, 6 feet, 4 inches. Weight, 210 pounds.

Year	Club	Lea	G	IP	W	L	Pct	SO	BB	H	ERA	SAVES
1987 Medicine Hat	.......Pioneer		13	75¹/₃	4	8	.333	66	26	79	5.14	0
1988 Myrtle Beach	.......So. Atl.		35	151	10	6	.625	106	77	119	2.86	0
1989 Dunedin	............Fla. St.		33	88²/₃	5	8	.385	64	36	90	3.25	7
1990 Dunedin	............Fla. St.		42	50¹/₃	7	2	.778	46	16	36	1.43	22
1990 Knoxville	.......Southern		17	26	1	2	.333	21	7	20	1.73	8
1991 Toronto a	...............A.L.		63	108¹/₃	11	6	.647	85	50	94	3.16	3
1992 Dunedin	............Fla. St.		6	10	0	0	.000	7	2	9	0.90	1
1992 Syracuse	...............Int.		7	11¹/₃	0	1	.000	7	5	15	8.74	3
1992 Toronto b	..............A.L.		26	43²/₃	0	2	.000	35	20	45	4.12	1
1993 Dunedin	............Fla. St.		4	9	0	0	.000	8	0	4	1.00	1
1993 Toronto	...............A.L.		54	55²/₃	4	2	.667	49	27	63	4.69	1
1994 Toronto c	..............A.L.		34	40	0	1	.000	38	20	41	5.17	2
1995 Syracuse	...............Int.		8	17¹/₃	1	1	.500	13	4	13	1.04	0
1995 Toronto d	..............A.L.		31	42	4	3	.571	36	17	38	2.14	5
1996 Toronto	...............A.L.		59	56²/₃	1	6	.143	52	18	47	3.65	31
1997 Toronto-Seattle e	.......A.L.		64	72²/₃	6	4	.600	45	20	69	3.22	10
1998 Seattle f	..............A.L.		70	79¹/₃	3	3	.500	60	16	78	2.95	19
1999 Baltimore	...............A.L.		62	63	3	9	.250	50	23	51	3.57	27
2000 Baltimore g	...........A.L.		37	35	2	3	.400	26	15	37	4.89	11
2000 St. Louis h	..............N.L.		25	29²/₃	3	1	.750	26	20	30	3.34	1
2001 St. Louis i	..............N.L.		67	72²/₃	4	5	.444	47	19	78	4.09	3
2002 St. Louis-Philadelphia j-k	N.L.		72	96²/₃	4	6	.400	50	14	75	2.98	0
2003 Boston l	................A.L.		72	83²/₃	6	4	.600	65	9	77	3.55	2
2004 Boston	................A.L.		76	76¹/₃	5	4	.556	56	19	75	4.13	1
2005 Boston	................A.L.		*81	80¹/₃	7	3	.700	59	20	86	2.24	13
2006 Boston m	..............A.L.		68	64	6	6	.500	30	16	78	4.36	9
2007 Pawtucket	...............Int.		8	8²/₃	0	0	.000	3	3	9	4.15	0
2007 Boston n-o	............A.L.		50	55¹/₃	2	1	.667	31	14	46	3.42	1
2008 Pawtucket	...............Int.		5	5	0	0	.000	4	0	2	0.00	0
2008 Boston p-q	..............A.L.		47	49¹/₃	4	4	.500	32	20	60	5.66	1
Major League Totals	.......18 Yrs.		1058	1204¹/₃	75	73	.507	872	377	1168	3.63	141
Division Series												
1997 Seattle	................A.L.		1	0²/₃	0	0	.000	1	1	3	54.00	0
2000 St. Louis	...............N.L.		2	1²/₃	0	0	.000	2	1	5	10.80	0
2001 St. Louis	................N.L.		1	1¹/₃	0	0	.000	0	0	1	0.00	0
2003 Boston	................A.L.		3	4¹/₃	0	0	.000	5	0	0	0.00	0
2004 Boston	................A.L.		3	3	0	0	.000	5	1	3	9.00	0
2005 Boston	................A.L.		1	1	0	0	.000	1	0	1	9.00	0
Division Series Totals	....		11	12	0	0	.000	14	3	13	7.50	0
Championship Series												
1991 Toronto	...............A.L.		4	5²/₃	0	1	.000	5	2	5	3.18	0
1992 Toronto	...............A.L.		2	1¹/₃	0	0	.000	1	0	4	6.75	0
1993 Toronto	...............A.L.		1	2¹/₃	0	0	.000	2	0	3	3.86	0
2000 St. Louis	...............N.L.		3	3¹/₃	0	1	.000	0	2	1	0.00	0
2003 Boston	................A.L.		5	5¹/₃	0	0	.000	6	2	1	0.00	0
2004 Boston	................A.L.		5	5²/₃	0	0	.000	2	5	10	4.76	0
2007 Boston	................A.L.		3	3¹/₃	0	0	.000	3	0	1	0.00	0
2008 Boston	................A.L.		2	2²/₃	0	1	.000	0	4	2	10.13	0
Championship Series Totals	......		25	29²/₃	0	3	.000	19	15	27	3.03	0
World Series Record												
1992 Toronto	...............A.L.		2	1¹/₃	0	0	.000	0	0	0	0.00	1
1993 Toronto	...............A.L.		2	2¹/₃	0	0	.000	4	0	2	0.00	0
2004 Boston	................A.L.		3	3	0	0	.000	0	1	2	6.00	0

Year	Club	Lea	G	IP	W	L	Pct	SO	BB	H	ERA	SAVES
2007 Boston	A.L.	3	2$^1/_3$	0	0	.000	4	0	2	7.71	0	
World Series Totals		10	9	0	0	.000	8	1	6	4.00	1	

a On disabled list from August 1 to August 15, 1991.
b On disabled list from March 27 to June 12, 1992.
c On disabled list from May 25 to June 9, 1994.
d On disabled list from June 22 to August 18, 1995.
e Traded to Seattle Mariners with pitcher Paul Spoljaric for outfielder Jose Cruz Jr., July 31, 1997.
f Filed for free agency, October 22, 1998. Signed with Baltimore Orioles, November 13, 1998.
g On disabled list from April 2 to April 16, 2000.
h Traded to St. Louis Cardinals for outfielder Chris Richard and pitcher Mark Nussbeck, July 29, 2000.
i On disabled list from July 26 to August 17, 2001.
j Traded to Philadelphia Phillies with infielder Placido Polanco and pitcher Bud Smith for infielder Scott Rolen and pitcher Doug Nickle, July 29, 2002.
k Filed for free agency, October 28, 2002. Signed with Boston Red Sox, December 24, 2002.
l Filed for free agency, October 28, 2003, re-signed with Boston Red Sox, November 17, 2003.
m On disabled list from May 26 to June 13, 2006.
n On disabled list from March 23 to April 10 and May 3 to June 9, 2007.
o Filed for free agency, November 6, 2007, re-signed with Boston Red Sox, December 7, 2007.
p On disabled list from March 20 to April 11 and June 17 to July 3, 2008.
q Filed for free agency, November 4, 2008.

TORRES, SALOMON (RAMIREZ)

Born, San Pedro de Macoris, Dominican Republic, March 11, 1972.
Bats Right. Throws Right. Height, 5 feet, 11 inches. Weight, 210 pounds.

Year	Club	Lea	G	IP	W	L	Pct	SO	BB	H	ERA	SAVES
1990 San Fran.	Dominican	13	90	11	1	.917	101	27	44	0.50	0	
1991 Clinton	Midwest	28	210$^1/_3$	16	5	.762	214	47	148	1.41	0	
1992 Shreveport	Texas	25	162$^1/_3$	6	10	.375	151	34	167	4.21	0	
1993 Shreveport	Texas	12	83$^1/_3$	7	4	.636	67	12	67	2.70	0	
1993 Phoenix	P.C.	14	105$^1/_3$	7	4	.636	99	27	105	3.50	0	
1993 San Francisco	N.L.	8	44$^2/_3$	3	5	.375	23	27	37	4.03	0	
1994 San Francisco	N.L.	16	84$^1/_3$	2	8	.200	42	34	95	5.44	0	
1994 Phoenix	P.C.	13	79	5	6	.455	64	31	85	4.22	0	
1995 San Francisco	N.L.	4	8	0	1	.000	2	7	13	9.00	0	
1995 Phoenix	P.C.	1	2	0	0	.000	5	0	2	0.00	0	
1995 Tacoma	P.C.	5	28	1	1	.500	19	13	20	3.21	0	
1995 Seattle a.............	A.L.	16	72	3	8	.273	45	42	87	6.00	0	
1996 Tacoma	P.C.	22	134$^1/_3$	7	10	.412	121	52	150	5.29	0	
1996 Seattle	A.L.	10	49	3	3	.500	36	23	44	4.59	0	
1997 Seattle	A.L.	2	3$^1/_3$	0	0	.000	0	3	7	27.00	0	
1997 Montreal.	N.L.	12	22$^1/_3$	0	0	.000	11	12	25	7.25	0	
1997 Ottawa b..............	Int.	2	5	0	0	.000	2	2	7	5.40	0	
1998-2000				Voluntarily Retired								
2001 Samsung c-d-e	Korea	2	5$^1/_3$	0	2	.000	5	10	8	20.25	0	
2002 Nashville	P.C.	26	162$^1/_3$	8	5	.615	136	39	169	3.83	0	
2002 Pittsburgh f	N.L.	5	30	2	1	.667	12	13	28	2.70	0	
2003 Nashville	P.C.	1	5	1	0	1.000	4	1	2	1.80	0	
2003 Pittsburgh g	N.L.	41	121	7	5	.583	84	42	128	4.76	2	
2004 Pittsburgh	N.L.	84	92	7	7	.500	62	22	87	2.64	0	
2005 Pittsburgh	N.L.	78	94$^2/_3$	5	5	.500	55	36	76	2.76	3	
2006 Pittsburgh	N.L.	*94	93$^1/_3$	3	6	.333	72	38	98	3.28	12	
2007 Pirates	Gulf Coast	2	3	0	0	.000	4	0	2	0.00	0	
2007 Indianapolis	Int.	1	1$^1/_3$	0	0	.000	3	0	1	0.00	0	
2007 Pittsburgh h-i.	N.L.	56	52$^2/_3$	2	4	.333	45	17	57	5.47	12	
2008 Milwaukee j	N.L.	71	80	7	5	.583	51	33	75	3.49	28	
Major League Totals	12 Yrs.	497	847$^1/_3$	44	58	.431	540	349	857	4.31	57	
Division Series												
2008 Milwaukee	N.L.	2	2$^1/_3$	0	0	.000	1	0	4	0.00	1	

a Traded to Seattle Mariners for pitcher Shawn Estes and infielder Wilson Delgado, May 20, 1995.
b Claimed on waivers by Montreal Expos, April 18, 1997.
c Voluntarily retired, August 1, 1997 though January 29, 2001.
d Released by Montreal Expos, January 29, 2001. Signed with Samsung (Korea) for 2001.
e Signed with Pittsburgh Pirates organization, December 30, 2001.
f On disabled list from July 2 to 15, 2002.
g On disabled list from August 6 to August 29, 2003.
h On disabled list from June 9 to July 15 and August 22 to September 11, 2007.
i Traded to Milwaukee Brewers for pitcher Marino Salas and pitcher Kevin Roberts, December 7, 2007.
j Announced retirement, November 11, 2008.

VALVERDE, JOSE RAFAEL

Born, San Pedro de Macoris, Dominican Republic, July 24, 1979.
Bats Right. Throws Right. Height, 6 feet, 4 inches. Weight, 255 pounds.

Year Club	Lea	G	IP	W	L	Pct	SO	BB	H	ERA	SAVES
1997 Arizona	Dominican	14	18⅔	0	0	.000	19	13	20	5.30	0
1998 Arizona	Dominican	23	51⅓	1	3	.250	56	22	31	1.75	7
1999 Diamondbacks	Arizona	20	28⅔	1	2	.333	47	10	34	4.08	8
1999 South Bend	Midwest	2	2⅔	0	0	.000	3	2	2	0.00	0
2000 South Bend	Midwest	31	31⅔	0	5	.000	39	25	31	5.40	14
2000 Missoula	Pioneer	12	11⅔	1	0	1.000	24	4	3	0.00	4
2001 El Paso	Texas	39	41⅓	2	2	.500	72	27	36	3.92	13
2002 Tucson	P.C.	49	47⅔	2	4	.333	65	23	45	5.85	5
2003 Tucson	P.C.	22	29	1	1	.500	26	14	26	3.10	5
2003 Arizona	N.L.	54	50⅓	2	1	.667	71	26	24	2.15	10
2004 Arizona	N.L.	29	29⅔	1	2	.333	38	17	23	4.25	8
2004 Tucson a	P.C.	10	10⅔	1	1	.500	5	5	9	4.22	3
2005 Tucson	P.C.	2	2	0	0	.000	3	1	1	0.00	0
2005 Arizona b	N.L.	61	66⅓	3	4	.429	75	20	51	2.44	15
2006 Tucson	P.C.	15	17⅔	1	0	1.000	18	10	13	3.06	3
2006 Arizona	N.L.	44	49⅓	2	3	.400	69	22	50	5.84	18
2007 Arizona c	N.L.	65	64⅓	1	4	.200	78	26	46	2.66	*47
2008 Houston	N.L.	74	72	6	3	.667	83	23	62	3.38	*44
Major League Totals	6 Yrs.	327	332	15	17	.469	414	134	256	3.31	142
Division Series											
2007 Arizona	N.L.	3	3	0	0	.000	6	1	1	0.00	1
Championship Series											
2007 Arizona	N.L.	1	1⅔	0	1	.000	2	3	1	5.40	0

a On disabled list from June 14 to October 4, 2004.
b On disabled list from March 25 to May 2, 2005.
c Traded to Houston Astros for pitcher Chad Qualls, pitcher Juan Gutierrez and outfielder Chris Burke, December 14, 2007.

VAZQUEZ, JAVIER CARLOS

Born, Ponce, Puerto Rico, June 25, 1976.
Bats Right. Throws Right. Height, 6 feet, 2 inches. Weight, 215 pounds.

Year Club	Lea	G	IP	W	L	Pct	SO	BB	H	ERA	SAVES
1994 Expos	Gulf Coast	15	67⅔	5	2	.714	56	15	37	2.53	0
1995 Albany	So.Atl.	21	102⅔	6	6	.500	87	47	109	5.08	0
1996 Delmarva	So.Atl.	27	164⅓	14	3	.824	173	57	138	2.68	0
1997 Wst Plm Bch	Fla.St.	19	112⅔	6	3	.667	100	28	98	2.16	0
1997 Harrisburg	Eastern	6	42	4	0	1.000	47	12	15	1.07	0
1998 Montreal	N.L.	33	172⅓	5	15	.250	139	68	196	6.06	0
1999 Ottawa	Int.	7	42⅔	4	2	.667	46	16	45	4.85	0
1999 Montreal	N.L.	26	154⅔	9	8	.529	113	52	154	5.00	0
2000 Montreal	N.L.	33	217⅔	11	9	.550	196	61	247	4.05	0
2001 Montreal	N.L.	32	223⅔	16	11	.593	208	44	197	3.42	0
2002 Montreal	N.L.	34	230⅓	10	13	.435	179	49	*243	3.91	0
2003 Montreal a	N.L.	34	230⅔	13	12	.520	241	57	198	3.24	0
2004 New York b	A.L.	32	198	14	10	.583	150	60	195	4.91	0
2005 Arizona c	N.L.	33	215⅔	11	15	.423	192	46	223	4.42	0
2006 Chicago	A.L.	33	202⅔	11	12	.478	184	56	206	4.84	0
2007 Chicago	A.L.	32	216⅔	15	8	.652	213	50	197	3.74	0
2008 Chicago d	A.L.	33	208⅓	12	16	.429	200	61	214	4.67	0
Major League Totals	11 Yrs.	355	2270⅔	127	129	.496	2015	604	2270	4.32	0
Division Series											
2004 New York	A.L.	1	5	0	0	.000	6	2	7	9.00	0
2008 Chicago	A.L.	1	4⅓	0	1	.000	6	1	8	12.46	0
Division Series Totals		2	9⅓	0	1	.000	12	3	15	10.61	0
Championship Series											
2004 New York	A.L.	2	6⅓	1	0	1.000	6	7	9	9.95	0

a Traded to New York Yankees for infielder Nick Johnson, outfielder Juan Rivera and pitcher Randy Choate, December 4, 2003.
b Traded to Arizona Diamondbacks with pitcher Brad Halsey, catcher Dioner Navarro and cash for pitcher Randy Johnson, January 11, 2005.
c Traded to Chicago White Sox for pitcher Orlando Hernandez, pitcher Luis Vizcaino and outfielder Chris Young, December 20, 2005.
d Traded to Atlanta Braves with pitcher Boone Logan for catcher Tyler Flowers, infielder Jonathan Gilmore, infielder Brent Lillibridge and pitcher Santos Rodriguez, December 4, 2008.

VERAS, JOSE ENGER

Born, Santo Domingo, Dominican Republic, October 20, 1980.
Bats Right. Throws Right. Height, 6 feet, 5 inches. Weight, 235 pounds.

Year	Club	Lea	G	IP	W	L	Pct	SO	BB	H	ERA	SAVES
1998	Devil Rays	Gulf Coast	5	16	1	1	.500	19	12	19	6.75	0
1999	Princeton	Appal.	14	60²/₃	3	5	.375	48	50	74	7.12	0
2000	Charleston-SC	So.Atl.	20	106²/₃	8	8	.500	102	41	125	4.81	0
2001	Bakersfield	Calif.	27	153	9	8	.529	138	55	163	4.53	0
2002	Bakersfield	Calif.	11	59	3	4	.429	57	30	77	5.34	0
2002	Hudson Valley	N.Y.-Penn.	2	7	0	0	.000	7	5	2	0.00	0
2003	Durham	Int.	3	5¹/₃	0	0	.000	3	1	9	8.44	0
2003	Orlando	Southern	27	130¹/₃	6	9	.400	118	53	108	3.45	0
2004	Durham	Int.	30	84¹/₃	6	5	.545	63	33	101	5.23	0
2004	Montgomery a	Southern	3	10	1	0	1.000	6	7	10	6.30	0
2005	Oklahoma b	P.C.	57	61²/₃	3	5	.375	72	33	63	3.79	24
2006	Columbus	Int.	50	59²/₃	5	3	.625	68	19	49	2.41	21
2006	New York	A.L.	12	11	0	0	.000	6	5	8	4.09	1
2007	Yankees	Gulf Coast	2	2	0	0	.000	1	0	2	0.00	0
2007	Tampa	Fla.St.	2	3	0	0	.000	5	2	0	0.00	0
2007	Scranton-WB	Int.	12	16	2	0	1.000	17	7	17	4.50	4
2007	New York c	A.L.	9	9¹/₃	0	0	.000	7	7	6	5.79	2
2008	Scranton-WB	Int.	13	13	0	0	.000	21	4	8	1.38	9
2008	New York	A.L.	60	57²/₃	5	3	.625	63	29	52	3.59	0
Major League Totals	3 Yrs.		81	78	5	3	.625	76	41	66	3.92	3
Division Series												
2007	New York	A.L.	2	0²/₃	0	0	.000	1	1	1	0.00	0

a Filed for free agency from Tampa Bay Devil Rays, October 15, 2004. Signed with Texas Rangers organization, November 15, 2004.
b Filed for free agency, October 15, 2005. Signed with New York Yankees organization, December 12, 2005.
c On disabled list from March 23 to August 14, 2007.

VERLANDER, JUSTIN BROOKS

Born, Manakin Sabot, Virginia, February 20, 1983.
Bats Right. Throws Right. Height, 6 feet, 5 inches. Weight, 200 pounds.

Year	Club	Lea	G	IP	W	L	Pct	SO	BB	H	ERA	SAVES
2005	Lakeland	Fla.St.	13	86	9	2	.818	104	19	70	1.67	0
2005	Erie	Eastern	7	32²/₃	2	0	1.000	32	7	11	0.28	0
2005	Detroit	A.L.	2	11¹/₃	0	2	.000	7	5	15	7.15	0
2006	Detroit a	A.L.	30	186	17	9	.654	124	60	187	3.63	0
2007	Detroit b	A.L.	32	201²/₃	18	6	*.750	183	67	181	3.66	0
2008	Detroit	A.L.	33	201	11	*17	.393	163	87	195	4.84	0
Major League Totals	4 Yrs.		97	600	46	34	.575	477	219	578	4.11	0
Division Series												
2006	Detroit	A.L.	1	5¹/₃	0	0	.000	5	4	7	5.06	0
Championship Series												
2006	Detroit	A.L.	1	5¹/₃	1	0	1.000	6	1	7	6.75	0
World Series Record												
2006	Detroit	A.L.	2	11	0	2	.000	12	5	12	5.73	0

a Selected Rookie of the Year in American League for 2006.
b Pitched no-hit, no-run game against Milwaukee Brewers, June 12, 2007.

VILLANUEVA, CARLOS MANUEL

Born, Santiago, Dominican Republic, November 28, 1983.
Bats Right. Throws Right. Height, 6 feet, 2 inches. Weight, 215 pounds.

Year	Club	Lea	G	IP	W	L	Pct	SO	BB	H	ERA	SAVES
2002	Giants	Arizona	19	30¹/₃	4	0	1.000	23	3	24	0.59	3
2003	Giants	Arizona	12	59	3	6	.333	67	13	64	3.97	0
2004	Beloit a	Midwest	25	114²/₃	8	8	.500	113	30	102	3.77	1
2005	Brevard County	Fla.St.	21	112¹/₃	8	1	.889	124	32	78	2.32	0
2005	Huntsville	Southern	4	20²/₃	1	3	.250	14	9	21	7.40	0
2006	Huntsville	Southern	11	62¹/₃	4	5	.444	59	14	60	3.75	0
2006	Nashville	P.C.	11	66¹/₃	7	1	.875	61	26	42	2.71	0
2006	Milwaukee	N.L.	10	53²/₃	2	2	.500	39	11	43	3.69	0
2007	Nashville	P.C.	2	8¹/₃	0	0	.000	9	1	3	3.24	0
2007	Milwaukee	N.L.	59	114¹/₃	8	5	.615	99	53	101	3.94	1
2008	Milwaukee	N.L.	47	108¹/₃	4	7	.364	93	30	112	4.07	1
Major League Totals	3 Yrs.		116	276¹/₃	14	14	.500	231	94	256	3.94	2

Year Club	Lea	G	IP	W	L	Pct	SO	BB	H	ERA	SAVES
Division Series											
2008 Milwaukee	N.L.	2	3²/₃	0	0	.000	3	0	0	0.00	0

a Traded to Milwaukee Brewers by San Francisco Giants with pitcher Glenn Woolard for pitcher Wayne Franklin and pitcher Leo Estrella, March 30, 2004.

VILLONE, RONALD THOMAS (RON)
Born, Englewood, New Jersey, January 16, 1970.
Bats Left. Throws Left. Height, 6 feet, 3 inches. Weight, 245 pounds.

Year Club	Lea	G	IP	W	L	Pct	SO	BB	H	ERA	SAVES
1993 Riverside	California	16	83¹/₃	7	4	.636	82	62	74	4.21	0
1993 Jacksonville	Southern	11	63²/₃	3	4	.429	66	41	49	4.38	0
1994 Jacksonville	Southern	41	79¹/₃	6	7	.462	94	68	56	3.86	8
1995 Seattle	A.L.	19	19¹/₃	0	2	.000	26	23	20	7.91	0
1995 Tacoma	P.C.	22	29²/₃	1	0	1.000	43	19	9	0.61	13
1995 San Diego a	N.L.	19	25²/₃	2	1	.667	37	11	24	4.21	1
1996 Las Vegas.	P.C.	23	22	2	1	.667	29	9	13	1.64	3
1996 San Diego	N.L.	21	18¹/₃	1	1	.500	19	7	17	2.95	0
1996 Milwaukee b	A.L.	23	24²/₃	0	0	.000	19	18	14	3.28	2
1997 Milwaukee c	A.L.	50	52²/₃	1	0	1.000	40	36	54	3.42	0
1998 Buffalo	Int.	23	22¹/₃	2	2	.500	28	11	20	2.01	7
1998 Cleveland d	A.L.	25	27	0	0	.000	15	22	30	6.00	0
1999 Indianapolis	Int.	18	19	2	0	1.000	23	13	9	1.42	1
1999 Cincinnati	N.L.	29	142²/₃	9	7	.563	97	73	114	4.23	2
2000 Cincinnati e	N.L.	35	141	10	10	.500	77	78	154	5.43	0
2001 Colorado-Houston f-g ...	N.L.	53	114²/₃	6	10	.375	113	53	133	5.89	0
2002 Pittsburgh h-i	N.L.	45	93	4	6	.400	55	34	95	5.81	0
2003 Tucson	P.C.	15	25¹/₃	1	1	.500	22	12	20	3.55	1
2003 New Orleans.	P.C.	5	29¹/₃	3	1	.750	18	10	24	1.23	0
2003 Houston j-k	N.L.	19	106²/₃	6	6	.500	91	48	91	4.13	0
2004 Seattle l	A.L.	56	117	8	6	.571	86	64	102	4.08	0
2005 Seattle	A.L.	52	40¹/₃	2	3	.400	41	23	33	2.45	1
2005 Florida m-n	N.L.	27	23²/₃	3	2	.600	29	12	24	6.85	0
2006 New York o.	N.L.	70	80¹/₃	3	3	.500	72	51	75	5.04	0
2007 Scranton-WB	Int.	17	23²/₃	0	1	.000	27	10	21	1.90	1
2007 New York p-q	A.L.	37	42¹/₃	0	0	.000	25	18	36	4.25	0
2008 St. Louis r	N.L.	74	50	1	2	.333	50	37	45	4.68	1
Major League Totals ....14 Yrs.		654	1119¹/₃	56	59	.487	892	608	1061	4.75	7
Division Series											
2001 Houston	N.L.	1	0²/₃	0	0	.000	0	0	0	0.00	0
2006 New York	A.L.	1	1	0	0	.000	1	1	1	0.00	0
2007 New York	A.L.	1	0¹/₃	0	0	.000	0	0	0	0.00	0
Division Series Totals		3	2	0	0	.000	1	1	1	0.00	0

a Traded to San Diego Padres with outfielder Marc Newfield for pitcher Andy Benes and a player to be named later, July 31, 1995. Mariners received pitcher Greg Keagle to complete trade, September 16, 1995.

b Traded to Milwaukee Brewers with pitcher Bryce Florie and outfielder Marc Newfield for outfielder Greg Vaughn and a player to be named later, July 31, 1996. Padres received outfielder Jerry Parent to complete trade, September 16, 1996.

c Traded to Cleveland Indians with pitcher Mike Fetters and pitcher Ben McDonald for pitcher Jeff Juden and outfielder Marquis Grissom, December 8, 1997.

d Released by Cleveland Indians, April 2, 1999. Signed with Cincinnati Reds organization, April 5, 1999.

e Traded to Colorado Rockies for two players to be named later, November 8, 2000. Cincinnati Reds received pitcher Jeff Tahlienti and pitcher Justin Carter to complete trade, December 20, 2000.

f Traded to Houston Astros with cash for pitcher Jay Powell, June 27, 2001.

g Filed for free agency, November 5, 2001. Signed with Pittsburgh Pirates organization, February 12, 2002.

h On disabled list from August 15 to September 1, 2002.

i Filed for free agency, October 29, 2002. Signed with Arizona Diamondbacks organization, January 29, 2003.

j Released by Arizona Diamondbacks, May 15, 2003. Signed with Houston Astros organization, May 18, 2003.

k Filed for free agency, November 2, 2003, re-signed with Seattle Mariners, December 19, 2004.

l Filed for free agency, October 28, 2004.

m Traded to Florida Marlins for pitcher Yorman Bazardo and pitcher Michael Flannery, July 31, 2005.

n Traded to New York Yankees for pitcher Ben Julianel, December 16, 2005.

o Filed for free agency, October 31, 2006. Signed with New York Yankees organization, February 13, 2007.

p On disabled list from August 22 to September 6, 2007.

q Filed for free agency, October 31, 2007. Signed with St. Louis Cardinals organization, February 19, 2008.

r Filed for free agency, October 30, 2008.

VOLQUEZ, EDINSON

Born, Santo Domingo, Dominican Republic, July 3, 1983.
Bats Right. Throws Right. Height, 6 feet, 1 inch. Weight, 200 pounds.

Year	Club	Lea	G	IP	W	L	Pct	SO	BB	H	ERA	SAVES
2003	Rangers	Arizona	10	27	2	1	.667	28	11	24	4.00	1
2004	Stockton	Calif.	8	39²/₃	4	1	.800	34	14	31	2.95	0
2004	Clinton	Midwest	22	91	4	4	.500	77	30	83	4.05	3
2005	Bakersfield	Calif.	11	66²/₃	5	4	.556	77	12	64	4.18	0
2005	Rangers	Arizona	1	2	0	0	.000	2	0	2	0.00	0
2005	Frisco	Texas	10	58²/₃	1	5	.167	49	17	58	4.14	0
2005	Texas	A.L.	6	12²/₃	0	4	.000	11	10	25	14.21	0
2006	Oklahoma	P.C.	21	120²/₃	6	6	.500	130	72	86	3.21	0
2006	Texas	A.L.	8	33¹/₃	1	6	.143	15	17	52	7.29	0
2007	Bakersfield	Calif.	7	35¹/₃	0	4	.000	38	20	27	7.13	0
2007	Frisco	Texas	11	58¹/₃	8	1	.889	62	19	46	3.55	0
2007	Oklahoma	P.C.	8	51	6	1	.857	66	21	25	1.41	0
2007	Texas a	A.L.	6	34	2	1	.667	29	15	34	4.50	0
2008	Cincinnati	N.L.	33	196	17	6	.739	206	93	167	3.21	0
Major League Totals	4 Yrs.		53	276	20	17	.541	261	135	278	4.37	

a Traded to Cincinnati Reds with pitcher Danny Herrera for outfielder Josh Hamilton, December 21, 2007.

VOLSTAD, CHRISTOPHER KENNETH (CHRIS)

Born, Palm Beach Gardens, Florida, September 23, 1986.
Bats Right. Throws Right. Height, 6 feet, 8 inches. Weight, 225 pounds.

Year	Club	Lea	G	IP	W	L	Pct	SO	BB	H	ERA	SAVES
2005	Marlins	Gulf Coast	6	27	1	1	.500	26	4	25	2.33	0
2005	Jamestown	N.Y.-Penn.	7	38	3	2	.600	29	11	43	2.13	0
2006	Greensboro	So.Atl.	26	152	11	8	.579	99	36	161	3.08	0
2007	Jupiter	Fla.St.	21	126	8	9	.471	93	37	152	4.50	0
2007	Carolina	Southern	7	42²/₃	4	2	.667	25	10	41	3.16	0
2008	Carolina	Southern	15	91	4	4	.500	56	30	86	3.36	0
2008	Florida	N.L.	15	84¹/₃	6	4	.600	52	36	76	2.88	0

WADE, CORY NATHANIEL

Born, Indianapolis, Indiana, May 28, 1983.
Bats Right. Throws Right. Height, 6 feet, 2 inches. Weight, 185 pounds.

Year	Club	Lea	G	IP	W	L	Pct	SO	BB	H	ERA	SAVES
2004	Dodgers	Gulf Coast	11	32²/₃	2	1	.667	26	1	28	3.03	1
2004	Ogden	Pioneer	8	14	1	2	.333	19	4	24	5.14	0
2005	Ogden	Pioneer	16	72¹/₃	2	3	.400	60	19	81	4.35	0
2005	Columbus	So.Atl.	12	20	0	2	.000	14	10	29	4.05	2
2006	Vero Beach	Fla.St.	7	39¹/₃	2	4	.333	32	13	52	8.24	0
2006	Columbus	So.Atl.	23	94¹/₃	6	5	.545	94	11	101	4.96	2
2007	Inland Empire	Calif.	25	66	7	0	1.000	67	17	50	2.45	6
2007	Jacksonville	Southern	14	33	0	1	.000	33	11	22	1.36	0
2008	Great Lakes	Midwest	1	1	0	0	.000	0	0	1	0.00	0
2008	Jacksonville	Southern	6	14²/₃	0	0	.000	13	1	14	4.30	1
2008	Los Angeles a	N.L.	55	71¹/₃	2	1	.667	51	15	51	2.27	0
Division Series												
2008	Los Angeles	N.L.	3	3²/₃	0	0	.000	2	0	3	2.45	0
Championship Series												
2008	Los Angeles	N.L.	4	3²/₃	0	0	.000	2	0	3	4.91	0

a On disabled list from August 9 to August 28, 2008.

WAECHTER, DOUGLAS MICHAEL (DOUG)

Born, St.Petersburg, Florida, January 28, 1981.
Bats Right. Throws Right. Height, 6 feet, 4 inches. Weight, 210 pounds.

Year	Club	Lea	G	IP	W	L	Pct	SO	BB	H	ERA	SAVES
1999	Princeton	Appal.	11	35	0	5	.000	38	35	46	9.77	0
2000	Hudson Valley	N.Y.-Penn.	14	72²/₃	4	4	.500	58	37	53	2.35	0
2001	Charleston-SC	So.Atl.	26	153¹/₃	8	11	.421	107	38	179	4.34	0
2002	Bakersfield	Calif.	17	108¹/₃	6	3	.667	101	29	114	2.66	0
2002	Charleston-SC	So.Atl.	7	36¹/₃	3	3	.500	36	16	39	3.47	0
2002	Orlando	Southern	4	18	1	3	.250	18	13	27	9.00	0
2003	Orlando	Southern	13	76¹/₃	5	3	.625	45	19	74	4.13	0
2003	Durham	Int.	10	51¹/₃	3	3	.500	35	12	51	3.33	0

Year	Club	Lea	G	IP	W	L	Pct	SO	BB	H	ERA	SAVES
2003 Tampa Bay	A.L.	6	35¹/₃	3	2	.600	29	15	29	3.31	0
2004 Durham	Int.	8	29¹/₃	0	2	.000	22	17	33	6.75	0
2004 Tampa Bay a	A.L.	14	70¹/₃	5	7	.417	36	33	68	6.01	0
2005 Durham	Int.	3	13²/₃	0	2	.000	16	5	17	9.22	0
2005 Tampa Bay b	A.L.	29	157	5	12	.294	87	38	191	5.62	0
2006 Tampa Bay	A.L.	11	53	1	4	.200	25	19	67	6.62	0
2006 Durham c	Int.	17	79	1	12	.077	45	24	129	8.32	0
2007 Vero Beach	Fla.St.	9	43²/₃	4	4	.500	34	5	53	4.74	0
2007 Hudson Valley d	N.Y.-Penn.	4	19	2	1	.667	12	0	16	1.42	0
2008 Marlins	Gulf Coast	1	1	0	0	.000	2	0	1	0.00	0
2008 Jupiter	Fla.St.	2	1²/₃	0	0	.000	2	0	3	5.40	0
2008 Albuquerque	P.C.	2	10²/₃	1	0	1.000	4	2	17	4.22	0
2008 Florida e-f.	N.L.	48	63¹/₃	4	2	.667	46	21	63	3.69	0
Major League Totals ....5 Yrs.		108	379	18	27	.400	223	126	418	5.30	0

a On disabled list from June 9 to September 6, 2004.
b On disabled list from June 29 to July 25, 2005.
c Released by Tampa Bay Devil Rays, November 20, 2006, re-signed by Tampa Bay Devil Rays organization, December 22, 2006.
d Filed for free agency October 29, 2007. Signed with Florida Marlins, November 27, 2007.
e On disabled list from August 11 to August 26, 2008.
f Filed for free agency, October 1, 2008. Signed with Kansas City Royals, December 11, 2008.

WAGNER, WILLIAM EDWARD (BILLY)
Born, Tannersville, Virginia, July 25, 1971.
Bats Left. Throws Left. Height, 5 feet, 11 inches. Weight, 205 pounds.

Year	Club	Lea	G	IP	W	L	Pct	SO	BB	H	ERA	SAVES
1993 Auburn	N.Y.-Penn.	7	28²/₃	1	3	.250	31	25	25	4.08	0
1994 Quad City	Midwest	26	153	8	9	.471	204	91	99	3.29	0
1995 Jackson	Texas	12	70	2	2	.500	77	36	49	2.57	0
1995 Tucson	P.C.	13	76¹/₃	5	3	.625	80	32	70	3.18	0
1995 Houston	N.L.	1	0¹/₃	0	0	.000	0	0	0	0.00	0
1996 Tucson	P.C.	12	74	6	2	.750	86	33	62	3.28	0
1996 Houston a	N.L.	37	51²/₃	2	2	.500	67	30	28	2.44	9
1997 Houston	N.L.	62	66¹/₃	7	8	.467	106	30	49	2.85	23
1998 Jackson	Texas	3	3	0	0	.000	7	0	1	0.00	0
1998 Houston b	N.L.	58	60	4	3	.571	97	25	46	2.70	30
1999 Houston	N.L.	66	74²/₃	4	1	.800	124	23	35	1.57	39
2000 Houston c	N.L.	28	27²/₃	2	4	.333	28	18	28	6.18	6
2001 Round Rock	Texas	1	1	0	0	.000	2	0	0	0.00	0
2001 Houston d	N.L.	64	62²/₃	2	5	.286	79	20	44	2.73	39
2002 Houston	N.L.	70	75	4	2	.667	88	22	51	2.52	35
2003 Houston e	N.L.	78	86	1	4	.200	105	23	52	1.78	44
2004 Reading	Eastern	1	1	0	0	.000	2	0	1	0.00	0
2004 Philadelphia f	N.L.	45	48¹/₃	4	0	1.000	59	6	31	2.42	21
2005 Philadelphia g	N.L.	75	77²/₃	4	3	.571	87	20	45	1.51	38
2006 New York	N.L.	70	72¹/₃	3	2	.600	94	21	59	2.24	40
2007 New York	N.L.	66	68¹/₃	2	2	.500	80	22	55	2.63	34
2008 Binghamton	Eastern	1	1	0	0	.000	2	0	0	0.00	0
2008 New York h	N.L.	45	47	0	1	.000	52	10	32	2.30	27
Major League Totals ....14 Yrs.		765	818	39	37	.513	1066	270	555	2.40	385
Division Series											
1997 Houston	N.L.	1	1	0	0	.000	2	0	3	18.00	0
1998 Houston	N.L.	1	1	1	0	1.000	1	0	4	18.00	0
1999 Houston	N.L.	1	1	0	0	.000	1	0	0	0.00	0
2001 Houston	N.L.	2	1²/₃	0	0	.000	3	0	1	5.40	0
2006 New York	N.L.	3	3	0	0	.000	4	0	3	3.00	2
Division Series Totals		8	7²/₃	1	0	1.000	11	0	11	7.04	2
Championship Series											
2006 New York	N.L.	3	2²/₃	0	1	.000	0	1	7	16.88	1

a On disabled list from August 23 to September 7, 1996.
b On disabled list from July 16 to August 7, 1998.
c On disabled list from June 18 to November 5, 2000.
d On disabled list from June 4 to June 19, 2001.
e Traded to Philadelphia Phillies for pitcher Brandon Duckworth, pitcher Taylor Buchholz and pitcher Ezequiel Astacio, November 3, 2003.
f On disabled list from May 8 to June 8 and from July 22 to September 4, 2004.
g Filed for free agency, October 27, 2005. Signed with New York Mets, November 29, 2005.
h On disabled list from August 3 to October 9, 2008.

WAINWRIGHT, ADAM PARRISH

Born, Brunswick, Georgia, August 30, 1981.
Bats Right. Throws Right. Height, 6 feet, 7 inches. Weight, 205 pounds.

Year	Club	Lea	G	IP	W	L	Pct	SO	BB	H	ERA	SAVES
2000 Danville	Appal.		6	29⅓	2	2	.500	39	2	28	3.68	0
2000 Braves	Gulf Coast		7	32	4	0	1.000	42	10	15	1.13	0
2001 Macon	So.Atl.		28	164⅔	10	10	.500	184	48	144	3.77	0
2002 Myrtle Beach	Carolina		28	163⅓	9	6	.600	167	66	149	3.31	0
2003 Greenville a	Southern		27	149⅔	10	8	.556	128	37	133	3.37	0
2004 Memphis	P.C.		12	63⅔	4	4	.500	64	28	68	5.37	0
2005 Memphis	P.C.		29	182	10	10	.500	147	51	204	4.40	0
2005 St. Louis	N.L.		2	2	0	0	.000	0	1	2	13.50	0
2006 St. Louis	N.L.		61	75	2	1	.667	72	22	64	3.12	3
2007 St. Louis	N.L.		32	202	14	12	.538	136	70	212	3.70	0
2008 Springfield	Texas		1	4⅔	0	0	.000	7	0	4	0.00	0
2008 Memphis	P.C.		2	3⅔	0	1	.000	3	2	8	12.27	0
2008 St. Louis b	N.L.		20	132	11	3	.786	91	34	122	3.20	0
Major League Totals	4 Yrs.		115	411	27	16	.628	299	127	400	3.48	3
Division Series												
2006 St. Louis	N.L.		3	3⅔	0	0	.000	6	0	3	0.00	1
Championship Series												
2006 St. Louis	N.L.		3	3	0	0	.000	4	1	2	0.00	2
World Series Record												
2006 St. Louis	N.L.		3	3	1	0	1.000	5	1	2	0.00	1

a Traded by Atlanta Braves to St. Louis Cardinals with pitcher Jason Marquis and pitcher Ray King for catcher Eli
Marrero and outfielder J.D. Drew, December 13, 2003.
b On disabled list from June 8 to August 22, 2008.

WAKEFIELD, TIMOTHY STEPHEN (TIM)

Born, Melborne, Florida, August 2, 1966.
Bats Right. Throws Right. Height, 6 feet, 2 inches. Weight, 230 pounds.

Year	Club	Lea	G	IP	W	L	Pct	SO	BB	H	ERA	SAVES
1989 Welland	N.Y.-Penn.		18	39⅔	1	1	.500	42	21	30	3.40	2
1990 Salem	Carolina		28	190⅓	10	14	.417	127	85	187	4.73	0
1991 Buffalo	A.A.		1	4⅔	0	1	.000	4	1	8	11.57	0
1991 Carolina	Southern		26	183	15	8	.652	123	51	155	2.90	0
1992 Buffalo	A.A.		20	135⅓	10	3	.769	71	51	122	3.06	0
1992 Pittsburgh	N.L.		13	92	8	1	.889	51	35	76	2.15	0
1993 Carolina	Southern		9	56⅔	3	5	.375	36	22	68	6.99	0
1993 Pittsburgh	N.L.		24	128⅓	6	11	.353	59	75	145	5.61	0
1994 Buffalo	A.A.		30	175⅔	5	15	.250	83	98	197	5.84	0
1995 Pawtucket	Int.		4	25	2	1	.667	14	9	23	2.52	0
1995 Boston a-b	A.L.		27	195⅓	16	8	.667	119	68	163	2.95	0
1996 Boston	A.L.		32	211⅔	14	13	.519	140	90	238	5.14	0
1997 Boston c	A.L.		35	201⅓	12	*15	.444	151	87	193	4.25	0
1998 Boston	A.L.		36	216	17	8	.680	146	79	211	4.58	0
1999 Boston	A.L.		49	140	6	11	.353	104	72	146	5.08	15
2000 Boston d	A.L.		51	159⅓	6	10	.375	102	65	170	5.48	0
2001 Boston	A.L.		45	168⅔	9	12	.429	148	73	160	3.90	3
2002 Boston	A.L.		45	163⅓	11	5	.688	134	51	121	2.81	3
2003 Boston	A.L.		35	202⅓	11	7	.611	169	71	193	4.09	1
2004 Boston	A.L.		32	188⅓	12	10	.545	116	63	197	4.87	0
2005 Boston	A.L.		33	225⅓	16	12	.571	151	68	210	4.15	0
2006 Boston e	A.L.		23	140	7	11	.389	90	51	135	4.63	0
2007 Boston	A.L.		31	189	17	12	.586	110	64	191	4.76	0
2008 Boston f	A.L.		30	181	10	11	.476	117	60	154	4.13	0
Major League Totals	16 Yrs.		541	2802	178	157	.531	1907	1072	2699	4.32	22
Division Series												
1995 Boston	A.L.		1	5⅓	0	1	.000	4	5	5	11.81	0
1998 Boston	A.L.		1	1⅓	0	1	.000	1	2	3	33.75	0
1999 Boston	A.L.		2	2	0	0	.000	4	4	3	13.50	0
2003 Boston	A.L.		2	7⅔	0	1	.000	7	3	6	3.52	0
2005 Boston	A.L.		1	5⅓	0	1	.000	4	1	6	6.75	0
Division Series Totals			7	21⅔	0	4	.000	20	15	23	9.14	0
Championship Series												
1992 Pittsburgh	N.L.		2	18	2	0	1.000	7	5	14	3.00	0
2003 Boston	A.L.		3	14	2	1	.667	10	6	8	2.57	0
2004 Boston	A.L.		3	7⅓	1	0	1.000	6	3	9	8.59	0
2007 Boston	A.L.		1	4⅔	0	1	.000	7	2	5	9.64	0

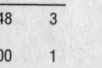

Year Club	Lea	G	IP	W	L	Pct	SO	BB	H	ERA	SAVES
2008 Boston .... A.L.		1	2²/₃	0	1	.000	2	2	6	16.88	0
Championship Series Totals		10	46²/₃	5	3	.625	32	18	42	5.21	
World Series Record											
2004 Boston .... A.L.		1	3²/₃	0	0	.000	2	5	3	12.27	0

a Released by Pittsburgh Pirates, April 20, 1995.
b Signed by Boston Red Sox, April 27, 1995.
c On disabled list from April 15 to May 6, 1997.
d Filed for free agency, October 31, 2000, re-signed with Boston Red Sox, December 7, 2000.
e On disabled list from July 18 to September 13, 2006.
f On disabled list from August 7 to August 26, 2008.

WALKER, JAMES ROSS (JAMIE)
Born, McMinnville, Tennessee, July 1, 1971.
Bats Left. Throws Left. Height, 6 feet, 2 inches. Weight, 185 pounds.

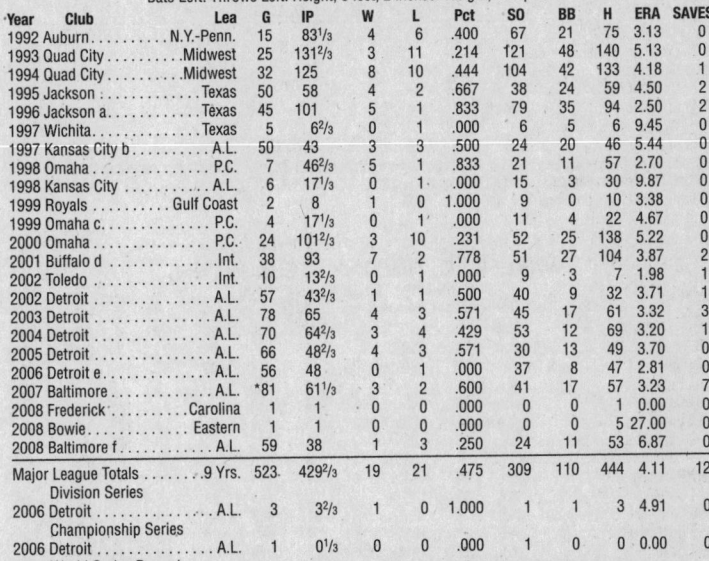

Year Club	Lea	G	IP	W	L	Pct	SO	BB	H	ERA	SAVES
1992 Auburn .... N.Y.-Penn.		15	83¹/₃	4	6	.400	67	21	75	3.13	0
1993 Quad City .... Midwest		25	131²/₃	3	11	.214	121	48	140	5.13	0
1994 Quad City .... Midwest		32	125	8	10	.444	104	42	133	4.18	1
1995 Jackson .... Texas		50	58	4	2	.667	38	24	59	4.50	2
1996 Jackson a........... Texas		45	101	5	1	.833	79	35	94	2.50	2
1997 Wichita............. Texas		5	6²/₃	0	1	.000	6	5	6	9.45	0
1997 Kansas City b......... A.L.		50	43	3	3	.500	24	20	46	5.44	0
1998 Omaha .... P.C.		7	46²/₃	5	1	.833	21	11	57	2.70	0
1998 Kansas City .... A.L.		6	17¹/₃	0	1	.000	15	3	30	9.87	0
1999 Royals .... Gulf Coast		2	8	1	0	1.000	9	0	10	3.38	0
1999 Omaha c............. P.C.		4	17¹/₃	0	1	.000	11	4	22	4.67	0
2000 Omaha .... P.C.		24	101²/₃	3	10	.231	52	25	138	5.22	0
2001 Buffalo d .... Int.		38	93	7	2	.778	51	27	104	3.87	2
2002 Toledo .... Int.		10	13²/₃	0	1	.000	9	3	7	1.98	1
2002 Detroit .... A.L.		57	43²/₃	1	1	.500	40	9	32	3.71	1
2003 Detroit .... A.L.		78	65	4	3	.571	45	17	61	3.32	3
2004 Detroit .... A.L.		70	64²/₃	3	4	.429	53	12	69	3.20	1
2005 Detroit .... A.L.		66	48²/₃	4	3	.571	30	13	49	3.70	0
2006 Detroit e............. A.L.		56	48	0	1	.000	37	8	47	2.81	0
2007 Baltimore .... A.L.		*81	61¹/₃	3	2	.600	41	17	57	3.23	7
2008 Frederick .... Carolina		1	1	0	0	.000	0	0	1	0.00	0
2008 Bowie............. Eastern		1	1	0	0	.000	0	0	5	27.00	0
2008 Baltimore f........... A.L.		59	38	1	3	.250	24	11	53	6.87	0
Major League Totals ....9 Yrs.		523	429²/₃	19	21	.475	309	110	444	4.11	12
Division Series											
2006 Detroit .... A.L.		3	3²/₃	1	0	1.000	1	1	3	4.91	0
Championship Series											
2006 Detroit .... A.L.		1	0¹/₃	0	0	.000	1	0	0	0.00	0
World Series Record											
2006 Detroit .... A.L.		1	0¹/₃	0	0	.000	1	0	0	0.00	0

a Selected by Atlanta Braves from Houston Astros in Rule V draft, December 9, 1996.
b Traded to Kansas City Royals with outfielder Jermaine Dye for infielder Keith Lockhart and outfielder Michael Tucker, March 27, 1997.
c Filed for free agency, December 19, 1998, re-signed with Kansas City Royals, January 28, 1999.
d Filed for free agency, October 15, 2001. Signed with Detroit Tigers organization, November 6, 2001.
e Filed for free agency, October 30, 2006. Signed with Baltimore Orioles, November 21, 2006.
f On disabled list from June 26 to July 28, 2008.

WALKER, TYLER LANIER
Born, San Francisco, California, May 15, 1976.
Bats Right. Throws Right. Height, 6 feet, 3 inches. Weight, 275 pounds.

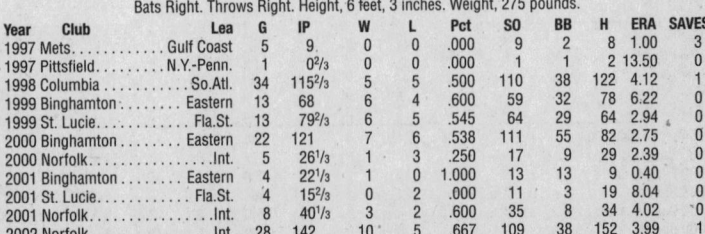

Year Club	Lea	G	IP	W	L	Pct	SO	BB	H	ERA	SAVES
1997 Mets........... Gulf Coast		5	9	0	0	.000	9	2	8	1.00	3
1997 Pittsfield......... N.Y.-Penn.		1	0²/₃	0	0	.000	1	1	2	13.50	0
1998 Columbia .... So.Atl.		34	115²/₃	5	5	.500	110	38	122	4.12	1
1999 Binghamton .... Eastern		13	68	6	4	.600	59	32	78	6.22	0
1999 St. Lucie........... Fla.St.		13	79²/₃	6	5	.545	64	29	64	2.94	0
2000 Binghamton .... Eastern		22	121	7	6	.538	111	55	82	2.75	0
2000 Norfolk.............. Int.		5	26¹/₃	1	3	.250	17	9	29	2.39	0
2001 Binghamton .... Eastern		4	22¹/₃	1	0	1.000	13	13	9	0.40	0
2001 St. Lucie........... Fla.St.		4	15²/₃	0	2	.000	11	3	19	8.04	0
2001 Norfolk.............. Int.		8	40¹/₃	3	2	.600	35	8	34	4.02	0
2002 Norfolk.............. Int.		28	142	10	5	.667	109	38	152	3.99	1

Year	Club	Lea	G	IP	W	L	Pct	SO	BB	H	ERA	SAVES
2002 New York		N.L.	5	10²/3	1	0	1.000	7	5	11	5.91	0
2003 Toledo a-b		Int.	26	131¹/3	2	9	.182	117	47	139	4.45	0
2004 Fresno		P.C.	9	15²/3	1	1	.500	15	2	16	1.72	0
2004 San Francisco		N.L.	52	63²/3	5	1	.833	48	24	69	4.24	1
2005 San Francisco c		N.L.	67	61²/3	6	4	.600	54	27	68	4.23	23
2006 San Francisco		N.L.	6	5¹/3	0	1	.000	3	5	9	15.19	0
2006 Tampa Bay d-e-f		A.L.	20	20	1	3	.250	16	7	18	4.95	10
2007 San Jose		Calif.	10	10¹/3	0	0	.000	15	2	9	1.74	3
2007 Fresno		P.C.	20	23	1	2	.333	23	10	25	4.70	7
2007 San Francisco		N.L.	15	14¹/3	2	0	1.000	9	4	12	1.26	0
2008 San Francisco g		N.L.	65	53¹/3	5	8	.385	49	21	47	4.56	0
Major League Totals	6 Yrs.		230	229	20	17	.541	186	93	234	4.52	34

a Claimed on waivers by Detroit Tigers, April 3, 2003.
b Filed for free agency, October 15, 2003. Signed with San Francisco Giants organization, November 25, 2003.
c On disabled list from August 20 to September 7, 2005.
d Traded to Tampa Bay Devil Rays for pitcher Carlos Hines, April 27, 2006.
e On disabled list from June 13 to September 9, 2006.
f Released by Tampa Bay Devil Rays, November 9, 2006. Signed with San Francisco Giants organization, December 11, 2006.
g Filed for free agency, October 16, 2008. Signed with Seattle Mariners, January 6, 2009.

WANG, CHIEN-MING

Born, Tainan City, Taiwan, March 31, 1980.
Bats Right. Throws Right. Height, 6 feet, 3 inches. Weight, 220 pounds.

Year	Club	Lea	G	IP	W	L	Pct	SO	BB	H	ERA	SAVES
2000 Staten Island		N.Y.-Penn.	14	87	4	4	.500	75	21	77	2.48	0
2001 Staten Island a		N.Y.-Penn.				INJURED—Did Not Play						
2002 Staten Island		N.Y.-Penn.	13	78¹/3	6	1	.857	64	14	63	1.72	0
2003 Trenton		Eastern	21	122	7	6	.538	84	32	143	4.65	0
2003 Yankees		Gulf Coast	1	3	0	0	.000	2	0	2	0.00	0
2004 Trenton		Eastern	18	109	6	5	.545	90	26	112	4.05	0
2004 Columbus		Int.	6	40¹/3	5	1	.833	35	8	31	2.01	0
2005 Columbus		Int.	6	34	2	1	.667	21	6	40	4.24	0
2005 New York b		A.L.	18	116¹/3	8	5	.615	47	32	113	4.02	0
2006 New York		A.L.	34	218	*19	6	.760	76	52	233	3.63	1
2007 Tampa		Fla.St.	1	5	0	0	.000	4	1	5	5.40	0
2007 New York c		A.L.	30	199¹/3	19	7	.731	104	59	199	3.70	0
2008 New York d		A.L.	15	95	8	2	.800	54	35	90	4.07	0
Major League Totals	4 Yrs.		97	628²/3	54	20	.730	281	178	635	3.79	1
Division Series												
2005 New York		A.L.	1	6²/3	0	1	.000	1	0	6	1.35	0
2006 New York		A.L.	1	6²/3	1	0	1.000	4	1	8	4.05	0
2007 New York		A.L.	2	5²/3	0	2	.000	2	4	14	19.06	0
Division Series Totals			4	19	1	3	.250	7	5	28	7.58	0

a On minor league disabled list from April 5 to September 15, 2001.
b On disabled list from July 9 to September 6, 2005.
c On disabled list from March 23 to April 24, 2007.
d On disabled list from June 16 to November 14, 2008.

WASHBURN, JARROD MICHAEL

Born, LaCrosse, Wisconsin, August 13, 1974.
Bats Left. Throws Left. Height, 6 feet, 1 inch. Weight, 190 pounds.

Year	Club	Lea	G	IP	W	L	Pct	SO	BB	H	ERA	SAVES
1995 Boise		Northwest	8	46	3	2	.600	54	14	35	3.33	0
1995 Cedar Rapids		Midwest	3	18¹/3	0	1	.000	20	7	17	3.44	0
1996 Lake Elsinore		California	14	92²/3	6	3	.667	93	33	79	3.30	0
1996 Vancouver		P.C.	2	8¹/3	0	2	.000	5	12	12	10.80	0
1996 Midland		Texas	13	88	5	6	.455	58	25	77	4.40	0
1997 Midland		Texas	29	189¹/3	15	12	.556	146	65	211	4.80	0
1997 Vancouver		P.C.	1	5	0	0	.000	6	1	4	3.60	0
1998 Midland		Texas	1	8²/3	0	1	.000	8	2	13	6.23	0
1998 Vancouver		P.C.	14	91²/3	4	5	.444	66	43	91	4.32	0
1998 Anaheim		A.L.	15	74	6	3	.667	48	27	70	4.62	0
1999 Edmonton		P.C.	11	59	1	5	.167	55	17	50	4.73	0
1999 Anaheim		A.L.	16	61²/3	4	5	.444	39	26	61	5.25	0
2000 Lake Elsinore		California	1	3	0	0	.000	7	2	3	6.00	0
2000 Edmonton		P.C.	5	30²/3	3	0	1.000	20	13	35	3.52	0

Year	Club	Lea	G	IP	W	L	Pct	SO	BB	H	ERA	SAVES
2000 Anaheim a	A.L.	14	84⅓	7	2	.778	49	37	64	3.74	0
2001 Salt Lake	P.C.	1	7⅔	0	1	.000	5	1	9	5.87	0
2001 Anaheim b	A.L.	30	193⅓	11	10	.524	126	54	196	3.77	0
2002 Anaheim	A.L.	32	206	18	6	.750	139	59	183	3.15	0
2003 Anaheim	A.L.	32	207⅓	10	15	.400	118	54	205	4.43	0
2004 Rancho Cucamonga	Calif.	1	4	0	0	.000	5	3	4	2.25	0
2004 Anaheim c	A.L.	25	149⅓	11	8	.579	86	40	159	4.64	0
2005 Los Angeles d-e	A.L.	29	177⅓	8	8	.500	94	51	184	3.20	0
2006 Seattle	A.L.	31	187	8	14	.364	103	55	198	4.67	0
2007 Seattle	A.L.	32	193⅔	10	15	.400	114	67	201	4.32	0
2008 Seattle	A.L.	28	153⅔	5	14	.263	87	50	174	4.69	1
Major League Totals	11 Yrs.	284	1687⅔	98	100	.495	1003	520	1695	4.13	1
Division Series											
2002 Anaheim	A.L.	2	12	1	0	1.000	4	3	12	3.75	0
2004 Anaheim	A.L.	2	3⅓	0	1	.000	3	3	6	10.80	0
Division Series Totals		4	15⅓	1	1	.500	7	6	18	5.28	0
Championship Series											
2002 Anaheim	A.L.	1	7	0	0	.000	7	0	6	1.29	0
2005 Los Angeles	A.L.	1	4⅔	0	0	.000	1	1	4	0.00	0
Championship Series Totals		2	11⅔	0	0	.000	8	1	10	0.77	0
World Series Record											
2002 Anaheim	A.L.	2	9⅔	0	2	.000	6	7	12	9.31	0

a On disabled list from March 25 to April 8 and July 22 to August 6 and August 8 to October 1, 2000.
b On disabled list from March 23 to April 16, 2001.
c On disabled list from July 21 to September 2, 2004.
d On disabled list from July 25 to August 12, 2005.
e Filed for free agency, October 28, 2005. Signed with Seattle Mariners, December 22, 2005.

WEATHERS, JOHN DAVID
Born, Lawrenceburg, Tennessee, September 25, 1969.
Bats Right. Throws Right. Height, 6 feet, 3 inches. Weight, 230 pounds.

Year	Club	Lea	G	IP	W	L	Pct	SO	BB	H	ERA	SAVES
1988 St. Catharines	N.Y.-Penn.	15	62⅔	4	4	.500	36	26	58	3.02	0
1989 Myrtle Beach	So. Atl.	31	172⅔	11	*13	.458	111	86	163	3.86	0
1990 Dunedin	Fla. St.	27	158	10	7	.588	96	59	158	3.70	0
1991 Knoxville	Southern	24	139⅓	10	7	.588	114	49	121	2.45	0
1991 Toronto	A.L.	15	14⅔	1	0	1.000	13	17	15	4.91	0
1992 Syracuse a	Int.	12	48⅓	1	4	.200	30	21	48	4.66	0
1992 Toronto b	A.L.	2	3⅓	0	0	.000	3	2	5	8.10	0
1993 Edmonton	P.C.	22	141	11	4	.733	117	47	150	3.83	0
1993 Florida	N.L.	14	45⅔	2	3	.400	34	13	57	5.12	0
1994 Florida c	N.L.	24	135	8	12	.400	72	59	166	5.27	0
1995 Brevard City	Fla. St.	1	4	0	0	.000	3	1	4	0.00	0
1995 Charlotte	Int.	1	5	0	1	.000	0	5	10	9.00	0
1995 Florida d	N.L.	28	90⅓	4	5	.444	60	52	104	5.98	0
1996 Charlotte	Int.	1	2⅓	0	0	.000	0	3	5	7.71	0
1996 Florida e	N.L.	31	71⅓	2	2	.500	40	28	85	4.54	0
1996 Columbus	Int.	3	16⅔	0	2	.000	7	5	20	5.40	0
1996 New York	A.L.	11	17⅓	0	2	.000	13	14	23	9.35	0
1997 Columbus	Int.	5	36⅔	2	2	.500	35	7	35	3.19	0
1997 Buffalo f-g	A.A.	11	68⅔	4	3	.571	51	17	71	3.15	0
1997 New York-Cleveland h	A.L.	19	25⅔	1	3	.250	18	15	38	8.42	0
1998 Cincinnati-Milwaukee i	N.L.	44	110	6	5	.545	94	41	130	4.91	0
1999 Milwaukee j	N.L.	63	93	7	4	.636	74	38	102	4.65	2
2000 Milwaukee k	N.L.	69	76⅓	3	5	.375	50	32	73	3.07	1
2001 Milwaukee l-m	N.L.	80	86	4	5	.444	66	34	65	2.41	0
2002 New York	N.L.	71	77⅓	6	3	.667	61	36	69	2.91	0
2003 New York	N.L.	77	87⅔	1	6	.143	75	40	87	3.08	7
2004 N.Y.-Houston-Florida n-o-p	N.L.	66	82⅓	7	7	.500	61	35	85	4.15	0
2005 Cincinnati	N.L.	73	77⅔	7	4	.636	61	29	71	3.94	15
2006 Cincinnati q	N.L.	67	73⅔	4	4	.500	50	34	61	3.54	12
2007 Cincinnati	N.L.	70	77⅔	2	6	.250	48	27	67	3.59	33
2008 Dayton	Midwest	2	2	0	0	.000	3	0	0	0.00	0
2008 Louisville	Int.	1	0	0	0	.000	1	0	0	0.00	0
2008 Cincinnati r-s	N.L.	72	69⅓	4	6	.400	46	30	76	3.25	0
Major League Totals	18 Yrs.	896	1314⅓	69	82	.457	939	576	1379	4.27	74
Division Series											
1996 New York	A.L.	2	5	1	0	1.000	5	0	1	0.00	0

Year	Club	Lea	G	IP	W	L	Pct	SO	BB	H	ERA	SAVES
	Championship Series											
1996 New York	. . . .	A.L.	2	3	1	0	1.000	0	0	3	0.00	0
	World Series Record											
1996 New York	. . . .	A.L.	3	3	0	0	.000	3	3	2	3.00	0

a On disabled list from May 11 to July 31, 1992.
b Selected by Florida Marlins in expansion draft, November 17, 1992.
c Appeared in two additional games as pinch runner.
d On disabled list from June 26 to July 13, 1995.
e Traded to New York Yankees for pitcher Mark Hutton, July 31, 1996.
f Traded to Cleveland Indians for outfielder Chad Curtis, June 9, 1997.
g Released by Cleveland Indians, December 15, 1997.
h Signed as free agent with Cincinnati Reds, December 19, 1997.
i Claimed on waivers by Milwaukee Brewers, June 24, 1998.
j Filed for free agency, October 29, 1999, re-signed with Milwaukee Brewers, December 2, 1999.
k On disabled list from August 2 to August 21, 2000.
l Traded to Chicago Cubs with pitcher Roberto Miniel for pitcher Ruben Quevedo and outfielder Peter Zoccolillo, July 30, 2001.
m Filed for free agency, November 5, 2001. Signed with New York Mets, December 13, 2001.
n Traded to Houston Astros with pitcher Jeremy Griffiths for outfielder Richard Hidalgo, June 17, 2004.
o Waived by Houston Astros, September 7, 2004. Signed with Florida Marlins, September 8, 2004.
p Filed for free agency, November 1, 2004. Signed with Cincinnati Reds, December 15, 2004.
q Filed for free agency, October 28, 2006, re-signed with Cincinnati Reds, December 12, 2006.
r On disabled list from April 20 to May 5, 2008.
s Filed for free agency, November 1, 2008. Accepted arbitration, December 7, 2008.

WEAVER, JERED DAVID

Born, Northridge, California, October 4, 1982.
Bats Right. Throws Right. Height, 6 feet, 7 inches. Weight, 205 pounds.

Year	Club	Lea	G	IP	W	L	Pct	SO	BB	H	ERA	SAVES
2005 Arkansas	. . . .	Texas	8	43	3	3	.500	46	19	43	3.98	0
2006 Salt Lake	. . . .	P.C.	12	77	6	1	.857	93	10	63	2.10	0
2006 Los Angeles	. . . .	A.L.	19	123	11	2	.846	105	33	94	2.56	0
2007 Rancho Cucamonga	. . . .	Calif.	2	11	1	0	1.000	12	3	5	0.82	0
2007 Los Angeles a	. . . .	A.L.	28	161	13	7	.650	115	45	178	3.91	0
2008 Nashville	. . . .	P.C.	9	55	2	4	.333	37	20	64	6.22	0
2008 Buffalo	. . . .	Int.	13	29²/₃	2	2	.500	22	10	38	6.07	0
2008 Los Angeles	. . . .	A.L.	30	176²/₃	11	10	.524	152	54	173	4.33	0
Major League Totals	. . . .	3 Yrs.	77	460²/₃	35	19	.648	372	132	445	3.71	0
	Division Series											
2007 Los Angeles	. . . .	A.L.	1	5	0	1	.000	5	3	4	3.60	0
2008 Los Angeles	. . . .	A.L.	1	2	1	0	1.000	3	1	1	0.00	0
Division Series Totals	. . . .		2	7	1	1	.500	8	4	5	2.57	0

a On disabled list from March 23 to April 17, 2007.

WEBB, BRANDON TYLER

Born, Ashland, Kentucky, May 9, 1979.
Bats Right. Throws Right. Height, 6 feet, 3 inches. Weight, 230 pounds.

Year	Club	Lea	G	IP	W	L	Pct	SO	BB	H	ERA	SAVES
2000 Diamondbacks	. . . . . .	Arizona	1	1	0	0	.000	3	0	2	9.00	0
2000 South Bend	. . . .	Midwest	12	16²/₃	0	0	.000	18	9	10	3.24	2
2001 Lancaster	. . . .	California	29	162¹/₃	6	10	.375	158	44	174	3.99	0
2002 El Paso	. . . .	Texas	26	152	10	6	.625	122	59	141	3.14	0
2002 Tucson	. . . .	P.C.	1	7	0	1	.000	5	4	5	3.86	0
2003 Tucson	. . . .	P.C.	3	18	1	1	.500	17	9	18	6.00	0
2003 Arizona a	. . . .	N.L.	29	180²/₃	10	9	.526	172	68	140	2.84	0
2004 Arizona	. . . .	N.L.	35	208	7	*16	.304	164	*119	194	3.59	0
2005 Arizona	. . . .	N.L.	33	229	14	12	.538	172	59	229	3.54	0
2006 Arizona b	. . . .	N.L.	33	235	*16	8	.667	178	50	216	3.10	0
2007 Arizona	. . . .	N.L.	34	*236¹/₃	18	10	.643	194	72	209	3.01	0
2008 Arizona	. . . .	N.L.	34	226²/₃	*22	7	.759	183	65	206	3.30	0
Major League Totals	. . . .	6 Yrs.	198	1315²/₃	87	62	.584	1063	433	1194	3.24	0
	Division Series											
2007 Arizona	. . . .	N.L.	1	7	1	0	1.000	9	3	4	1.29	0
	Championship Series											
2007 Arizona	. . . .	N.L.	1	6	0	1	.000	4	2	7	6.00	0

a On disabled list from May 24 to June 8, 2003.
b Selected Cy Young Award Winner in National League for 2006.

WELLEMEYER, TODD ALLEN

Born, Louisville, Kentucky, August 30, 1978.
Bats Right. Throws Right. Height, 6 feet, 3 inches. Weight, 225 pounds.

Year Club	Lea	G	IP	W	L	Pct	SO	BB	H	ERA	SAVES
2000 Eugene.........	Northwest	15	76	4	4	.500	85	33	62	3.67	0
2001 Lansing	Midwest	27	147	13	9	.591	167	74	165	4.16	0
2002 Daytona	Fla.St.	14	73²/₃	2	4	.333	87	19	63	3.79	0
2002 West Tenn	Southern	8	46	3	3	.500	37	18	33	4.70	0
2003 West Tenn	Southern	4	21¹/₃	1	1	.500	34	10	19	5.48	0
2003 Iowa................	P.C.	13	66	5	5	.500	56	33	68	5.18	0
2003 Chicago	N.L.	15	27²/₃	1	1	.500	30	19	25	6.51	1
2004 Chicago	N.L.	20	24¹/₃	2	1	.667	30	20	27	5.92	0
2004 Iowa a	P.C.	14	23	1	1	.500	22	11	23	3.91	0
2005 Iowa	P.C.	12	53²/₃	3	2	.600	48	25	47	3.02	0
2005 Chicago	N.L.	22	32¹/₃	2	1	.667	32	22	32	6.12	1
2006 Florida b..........	N.L.	18	21¹/₃	0	2	.000	17	13	20	5.48	0
2006 Kansas City c	A.L.	28	57	1	2	.333	37	37	48	3.63	1
2007 Springfield	Texas	1	1	0	0	.000	2	1	3	0.00	0
2007 Kansas City	A.L.	12	15²/₃	0	1	.000	9	11	25	10.34	0
2007 St. Louis d-e	N.L.	20	63²/₃	3	2	.600	51	29	52	3.11	0
2008 St. Louis...........	N.L.	32	191²/₃	13	9	.591	134	62	178	3.71	0
Major League Totals ....6 Yrs.		167	433²/₃	22	19	.537	340	213	407	4.42	3

a On disabled list from May 22 to July 16, 2004.
b Traded to Florida Marlins for pitcher Lincoln Holdzkom and pitcher Zach McCormack, March 28, 2006.
c Claimed on waivers by Kansas City Royals, June 9, 2006.
d Claimed on waivers by St. Louis Cardinals, May 15, 2007.
e On disabled list from July 9 to August 24, 2007.

WESTBROOK, JACOB CAUTHEN (JAKE)

Born, Athens, Georgia, September 29, 1977.
Bats Right. Throws Right. Height, 6 feet, 3 inches. Weight, 215 pounds.

Year Club	Lea	G	IP	W	L	Pct	SO	BB	H	ERA	SAVES
1996 Rockies	Arizona	11	62²/₃	4	2	.667	57	14	66	2.87	0
1996 Portland	Northwest	4	24¹/₃	1	1	.500	19	5	22	2.55	0
1997 Asheville a	So.Atl.	28	170	14	11	.560	92	55	176	4.29	0
1998 Jupiter	Fla.St.	27	171	11	6	.647	79	60	169	3.26	0
1999 Harrisburg b........	Eastern	27	174²/₃	11	5	.688	90	63	180	3.92	0
2000 Columbus	Int.	16	89	5	7	.417	61	38	94	4.65	0
2000 New York c-d-e-f	A.L.	3	6²/₃	0	2	.000	1	4	15	13.50	0
2001 Buffalo.................	Int.	12	64²/₃	8	1	.889	45	23	60	3.20	0
2001 Cleveland	A.L.	23	64²/₃	4	4	.500	48	22	79	5.85	0
2002 Akron.............	Eastern	3	15	0	1	.000	8	1	13	4.80	0
2002 Buffalo................	Int.	1	6	1	0	1.000	2	0	8	6.00	0
2002 Cleveland g	A.L.	11	41²/₃	1	3	.250	20	12	50	5.83	0
2003 Buffalo	Int.	2	10	1	0	1.000	7	4	0	0.00	0
2003 Cleveland	A.L.	34	133	7	10	.412	58	56	142	4.33	0
2004 Cleveland	A.L.	33	215²/₃	14	9	.609	116	61	208	3.38	0
2005 Cleveland	A.L.	34	210²/₃	15	15	.500	119	56	218	4.49	0
2006 Cleveland..........	A.L.	32	211¹/₃	15	10	.600	109	55	*247	4.17	0
2007 Lake County.........	So.Atl.	1	5	0	1	.000	5	0	6	7.20	0
2007 Akron.............	Eastern	1	2¹/₃	0	1	.000	1	3	5	15.43	0
2007 Buffalo............	Int.	2	5¹/₃	0	1	.000	5	5	9	8.44	0
2007 Cleveland h	A.L.	25	152	6	9	.400	93	55	159	4.32	0
2008 Lake County.........	So.Atl.	1	3²/₃	0	0	.000	4	1	3	2.45	0
2008 Akron	Eastern	1	6	0	0	.000	2	4	3	0.00	0
2008 Cleveland i	A.L.	5	34²/₃	1	2	.333	19	7	33	3.12	0
Major League Totals ....9 Yrs.		200	1070¹/₃	63	64	.496	583	328	1151	4.31	0
Division Series											
2007 Cleveland	A.L.	1	5	0	1	.000	1	0	9	10.80	0
Championship Series											
2007 Cleveland	A.L.	2	12²/₃	1	1	.500	7	4	16	3.55	0

a Traded to Montreal Expos by Colorado Rockies with pitcher John Nicholson and outfielder Mike Hamlin for infielder Mike Lansing, November 18, 1997.
b Traded to New York Yankees with two players to be named later for pitcher Hideki Irabu, December 22, 1999. Pitchers Ted Lilly and Christian Parker were sent to New York Yankees to complete trade, March 17 and March 22, 2000.
c On disabled list from May 5 to 23, 2000.
d Sent to Cleveland Indians by New York Yankees with pitcher Zach Day to complete trade for outfielder David Justice, July 24, 2000.
e On disabled list from July 25 to September 1, 2000.
f On disabled list from September 1 to October 31, 2000.

g On disabled list from March 30 to July 11 and August 26 to November 4, 2002.
h On disabled list from May 3 to June 24, 2007.
i On disabled list from April 20 to May 28 and May 29 to November 13, 2008.

WHEELER, DANIEL MICHAEL (DAN)

Born, Providence, Rhode Island, December 10, 1977.
Bats Right. Throws Right. Height, 6 feet, 3 inches. Weight, 220 pounds.

Year	Club	Lea	G	IP	W	L	Pct	SO	BB	H	ERA	SAVES
1997 Hudson Valley	....N.Y.-Penn.		15	84	6	7	.462	81	17	75	3.00	0
1998 Chston-SC	.........So.Atl.		29	181	12	14	.462	136	29	206	4.43	0
1999 Orlando	.........Southern		9	58	3	0	1.000	53	8	56	3.26	0
1999 Durham	...............Int.		14	82 1/3	7	5	.583	58	25	103	4.92	0
1999 Tampa Bay	............A.L.		6	30 2/3	0	4	.000	32	13	35	5.87	0
2000 Tampa Bay	............A.L.		11	23	1	1	.500	17	11	29	5.48	0
2000 Durham	...............Int.		26	150 1/3	5	11	.313	91	42	183	5.63	0
2001 Durham	...............Int.		18	65 1/3	3	5	.375	39	11	72	5.23	0
2001 Tampa Bay	............A.L.		13	17 2/3	1	0	1.000	12	5	30	8.66	0
2001 Orlando	.........Southern		3	16	0	2	.000	12	6	15	2.81	0
2002 Richmond a	............Int.		27	155	9	6	.600	110	42	163	4.65	0
2003 Norfolk b	.............Int.		22	45 2/3	4	2	.667	44	16	48	3.94	4
2003 New York	.............N.L.		35	51	1	3	.250	35	17	49	3.71	2
2004 Norfolk	.............Int.		5	7 1/3	1	0	1.000	10	2	8	2.45	0
2004 New York-Houston c	....N.L.		46	65	3	1	.750	55	20	76	4.29	0
2005 Houston	.............N.L.		71	73 1/3	2	3	.400	69	19	53	2.21	3
2006 Houston	.............N.L.		75	71 1/3	3	5	.375	68	24	58	2.52	9
2007 Houston	.............N.L.		45	49 2/3	1	4	.200	56	13	46	5.07	11
2007 Tampa Bay d	.........A.L.		25	25	0	5	.000	26	10	28	5.76	0
2008 Tampa Bay	............A.L.		70	66 1/3	5	6	.455	53	22	44	3.12	13
Major League Totals	.......9 Yrs.		397	473	17	32	.347	423	154	448	3.96	38
Division Series												
2004 Houston	.............N.L.		1	1	0	0	.000	0	0	0	0.00	0
2005 Houston	.............N.L.		3	4 1/3	0	0	.000	5	3	4	2.08	0
2008 Tampa Bay	............N.L.		1	1	0	0	.000	1	0	1	9.00	1
Division Series Totals	....		5	6 1/3	0	0	.000	6	3	5	2.84	1
Championship Series												
2004 Houston	.............N.L.		4	7	1	0	1.000	9	0	4	0.00	0
2005 Houston	.............N.L.		3	2 2/3	0	0	.000	2	0	2	0.00	0
2008 Tampa Bay	............N.L.		3	5	0	0	.000	5	3	5	5.40	0
Championship Series Totals	......		10	14 2/3	1	0	1.000	16	3	11	1.84	0
World Series Record												
2005 Houston	.............N.L.		2	2	0	0	.000	1	1	2	13.50	0
2008 Tampa Bay	............N.L.		3	2 2/3	0	0	.000	3	1	3	6.75	0
World Series Totals	....		5	4 2/3	0	0	.000	4	2	5	9.64	0

a Released by Tampa Bay Devil Rays, December 13, 2001. Signed with Atlanta Braves organization, January 20, 2002.
b Filed for free agency, October 15, 2002. Signed with New York Mets organization, January 27, 2003.
c Traded to Houston Astros for outfielder Adam Seuss, August 27, 2004.
d Traded to Tampa Bay Devil Rays for infielder Ty Wigginton, July 28, 2007.

WILLIS, DONTRELLE WAYNE

Born, Oakland, California, January 12, 1982.
Bats Left. Throws Left. Height, 6 feet, 4 inches. Weight, 225 pounds.

Year	Club	Lea	G	IP	W	L	Pct	SO	BB	H	ERA	SAVES
2000 Cubs	.............Arizona		9	28	3	1	.750	22	8	26	3.86	0
2001 Boise	.............Northwest		15	93 2/3	8	2	.800	77	19	76	2.98	0
2002 Kane County	.......Midwest		19	127 2/3	10	2	.833	101	21	91	1.83	0
2002 Jupiter a	...........Fla.St.		5	30	2	0	1.000	27	3	24	1.80	0
2003 Carolina	.........Southern		9	36 1/3	4	0	1.000	32	9	24	1.49	0
2003 Florida b	.............N.L.		27	160 2/3	14	6	.700	142	58	148	3.30	0
2004 Florida	.............N.L.		32	197	10	11	.476	139	61	210	4.02	0
2005 Florida	.............N.L.		34	236 1/3	*22	10	.688	170	55	213	2.63	0
2006 Florida	.............N.L.		34	223 1/3	12	12	.500	160	83	234	3.87	0
2007 Florida c	.............N.L.		35	205 1/3	10	15	.400	146	87	241	5.17	0
2008 Lakeland	............Fla.St.		6	28	0	3	.000	18	11	30	4.50	0
2008 Toledo	...............Int.		6	28 1/3	3	1	.750	20	14	34	4.45	0
2008 Detroit d	............A.L.		8	24	0	2	.000	18	35	18	9.38	0
Major League Totals	........6 Yrs.		170	1046 2/3	68	56	.548	775	379	1064	3.91	0

Year	Club	Lea	G	IP	W	L	Pct	SO	BB	H	ERA	SAVES
	Division Series											
2003 Florida	N.L.	2	5²/₃	0	0	.000	3	2	7	7.94	0
	Championship Series											
2003 Florida	N.L.	2	3¹/₃	0	1	.000	4	6	4	18.90	0
	World Series Record											
2003 Florida	N.L.	3	3²/₃	0	0	.000	3	2	4	0.00	0

a Traded by Chicago Cubs to Florida Marlins with pitcher Julian Tavarez, pitcher Jose Cueto and catcher Ryan Jorgensen for pitcher Antonio Alfonseca and pitcher Matt Clement, March 27, 2002.

b Selected Rookie of the Year in National League for 2003.

c Traded to Detroit Tigers with infielder Miguel Cabrera for pitcher Burke Badenhop, pitcher Eulogio De La Cruz, pitcher Andrew Miller, catcher Mike Rabelo and outfielder Cameron Maybin, December 5, 2007.

d On disabled list from April 12 to May 21, 2008.

WILSON, BRIAN PATRICK

Born, Londonderry, New Hampshire, March 16, 1982.
Bats Right. Throws Right. Height, 6 feet, 1 inch. Weight, 205 pounds.

Year	Club	Lea	G	IP	W	L	Pct	SO	BB	H	ERA	SAVES
2004 Hagerstown	So.Atl.	23	57¹/₃	2	5	.286	41	22	63	5.34	3
2005 Norwich	Eastern	15	15²/₃	0	0	.000	22	5	6	0.57	8
2005 Fresno	P.C.	9	11¹/₃	1	1	.500	13	8	8	3.97	0
2005 Augusta	So.Atl.	26	33	5	1	.833	30	7	23	0.82	13
2006 San Jose	Calif.	1	1	0	0	.000	1	1	1	9.00	0
2006 Fresno	P.C.	24	28	1	3	.250	30	14	20	2.89	7
2006 San Francisco	N.L.	31	30	2	3	.400	23	21	32	5.40	1
2007 San Jose	Calif.	3	3	0	0	.000	6	0	1	0.00	2
2007 Fresno	P.C.	31	34¹/₃	1	2	.333	37	24	24	2.10	11
2007 San Francisco	N.L.	24	23²/₃	1	2	.333	18	7	16	2.28	6
2008 San Francisco	N.L.	63	62¹/₃	3	2	.600	67	28	62	4.62	41
Major League Totals .... 3 Yrs.		118	116	6	7	.462	108	56	110	4.34	48

WILSON, CHRISTOPHER JOHN (C.J.)

Born, Newport Beach, California, November 18, 1980.
Bats Left. Throws Left. Height, 6 feet, 2 inches. Weight, 215 pounds.

Year	Club	Lea	G	IP	W	L	Pct	SO	BB	H	ERA	SAVES
2001 Pulaski............	Appal.	8	37²/₃	1	0	1.000	49	9	24	0.96	0
2001 Savannah...........	So.Atl.	5	34	1	2	.333	26	9	30	3.18	0
2002 Charlotte..........	Fla.St.	26	106	10	2	.833	76	41	86	3.06	1
2002 Tulsa	Texas	5	30	1	0	1.000	17	12	23	1.80	0
2003 Frisco	Texas	22	123	6	9	.400	89	38	135	5.05	0
2004				INJURED—Did Not Play							
2005 Bakersfield........	Calif.	4	13²/₃	0	1	.000	14	4	10	3.29	0
2005 Frisco.............	Texas	12	44²/₃	0	4	.000	43	14	51	4.43	0
2005 Texas	A.L.	24	48	1	7	.125	30	18	63	6.94	1
2006 Frisco.............	Texas	4	3¹/₃	0	0	.000	6	2	3	2.70	0
2006 Oklahoma..........	P.C.	9	11	1	0	1.000	17	5	10	2.45	2
2006 Texas a............	A.L.	44	44¹/₃	2	4	.333	43	18	39	4.06	1
2007 Texas	A.L.	66	68¹/₃	2	1	.667	63	33	50	3.03	12
2008 Texas b............	A.L.	50	46¹/₃	2	2	.500	41	27	49	6.02	24
Major League Totals .... 4 Yrs.		184	207	7	14	.333	177	96	201	4.83	38

a On disabled list from March 24 to April 14, 2006.

b On disabled list from August 6 to October 2, 2008.

WOLF, RANDALL CHRISTOPHER (RANDY)

Born, Canoga Park, California, August 22, 1976.
Bats Left. Throws Left. Height, 6 feet. Weight, 205 pounds.

Year	Club	Lea	G	IP	W	L	Pct	SO	BB	H	ERA	SAVES
1997 Batavia..........	N.Y.-Penn.	7	40	4	0	1.000	53	8	29	1.58	0
1998 Reading	Eastern	4	25	2	0	1.000	33	4	15	1.44	0
1998 Scranton-WB..........	Int.	24	148	9	7	.563	118	48	167	4.62	0
1999 Scranton-WB..........	Int.	12	77¹/₃	4	5	.444	72	29	73	3.61	0
1999 Philadelphia	N.L.	22	121²/₃	6	9	.400	116	67	126	5.55	0
2000 Philadelphia	N.L.	32	206¹/₃	11	9	.550	160	83	210	4.36	0
2001 Scranton-WB..........	Int.	2	9	0	1	.000	7	5	10	5.00	0
2001 Reading	Eastern	1	6	0	0	.000	7	2	5	4.50	0
2001 Philadelphia a.......	N.L.	28	163	10	11	.476	152	51	150	3.70	0
2002 Clearwater	Fla.St.	1	5	0	0	.000	8	1	1	0.00	0

Year Club	Lea	G	IP	W	L	Pct	SO	BB	H	ERA	SAVES
2002 Philadelphia b	N.L.	31	210²/₃	11	9	.550	172	63	172	3.20	0
2003 Philadelphia	N.L.	33	200	16	10	.615	177	78	176	4.23	0
2004 Reading	Eastern	1	4	0	0	.000	4	0	5	2.25	0
2004 Philadelphia c.........	N.L.	23	136²/₃	5	8	.385	89	36	145	4.28	0
2005 Philadelphia d	N.L.	13	80	6	4	.600	61	26	87	4.39	0
2006 Clearwater	Fla.St.	2	5²/₃	0	0	.000	4	4	6	0.00	0
2006 Reading	Eastern	3	12	1	1	.500	11	7	15	6.75	0
2006 Lakewood	So.Atl.	2	8	0	0	.000	7	3	2	1.13	0
2006 Philadelphia e-f	N.L.	12	56²/₃	4	0	1.000	44	33	63	5.56	0
2007 Inland Empire........	Calif.	1	4	0	0	.000	4	1	6	6.75	0
2007 Los Angeles g-h	N.L.	18	102²/₃	9	6	.600	94	39	110	4.73	0
2008 San Diego-Houston i-j ...	N.L.	33	190¹/₃	12	12	.500	162	71	191	4.30	0
Major League Totals ....10 Yrs.		245	1468	90	78	.536	1227	547	1430	4.26	0

a On disabled list from August 2 to September 1, 2001.
b On disabled list from March 25 to April 12, 2002.
c On disabled list from June 3 to June 26 and August 29 to October 8, 2004.
d On disabled list from June 12 to November 1, 2005.
e On disabled list from March 24 to July 30, 2006.
f Filed for free agency, October 28, 2006. Signed with Los Angeles Dodgers, November 28, 2006.
g On disabled list from July 4 to October 31, 2007.
h Filed for free agency, November 9, 2007. Signed with San Diego Padres, December 10, 2007.
i Traded to Houston Astros for pitcher Chad Reineke, July 22, 2008.
j Filed for free agency, October 31, 2008.

WOOD, KERRY LEE

Born, Irving, Texas, June 16, 1977.
Bats Right. Throws Right. Height, 6 feet, 5 inches. Weight, 210 pounds.

Year Club	Lea	G	IP	W	L	Pct	SO	BB	H	ERA	SAVES
1995 Cubs.	Gulf Coast	1	3	0	0	.000	2	1	0	0.00	0
1995 Williamsport.	N.Y.-Penn.	2	4¹/₃	0	0	.000	5	5	5	10.38	0
1996 Daytona a..........	Fla.St.	22	114¹/₃	10	2	.833	136	70	72	2.91	0
1997 Orlando	Southern	19	94	6	7	.462	106	79	58	4.50	0
1997 Iowa................	A.A.	10	57²/₃	4	2	.667	80	52	35	4.68	0
1998 Iowa................	P.C.	1	5	1	0	1.000	11	2	1	0.00	0
1998 Chicago b..........	N.L.	26	166²/₃	13	6	.684	233	85	117	3.40	0
1999 Chicago c..........	N.L.	INJURED—Did Not Play									
2000 Daytona	Fla.St.	2	12	2	0	1.000	17	5	3	1.50	0
2000 Iowa...............	P.C.	1	7	0	0	.000	7	4	4	2.57	0
2000 Chicago d..........	N.L.	23	137	8	7	.533	132	87	112	4.80	0
2001 Chicago e..........	N.L.	28	174¹/₃	12	6	.667	217	92	127	3.36	0
2002 Chicago	N.L.	33	213²/₃	12	11	.522	217	97	169	3.66	0
2003 Chicago	N.L.	32	211	14	11	.560	*266	100	152	3.20	0
2004 Iowa................	P.C.	1	5	1	0	1.000	4	1	2	0.00	0
2004 Chicago f..........	N.L.	22	140¹/₃	8	9	.471	144	51	127	3.72	0
2005 Peoria............	Midwest	2	2¹/₃	0	0	.000	5	0	1	0.00	0
2005 Iowa...............	P.C.	3	12²/₃	0	0	.000	18	6	11	2.84	0
2005 Chicago g..........	N.L.	21	66	3	4	.429	77	26	52	4.23	0
2006 Peoria............	Midwest	1	5	0	0	.000	12	1	1	0.00	0
2006 Iowa...............	P.C.	1	5	0	1	.000	3	2	5	1.80	0
2006 Chicago h-i........	N.L.	4	19²/₃	1	2	.333	13	8	19	4.12	0
2007 Azl Cubs..........	Arizona	4	4	0	1	.000	5	1	4	2.25	0
2007 Peoria............	Midwest	3	3	1	0	1.000	3	1	1	0.00	0
2007 Tennessee	Southern	1	1²/₃	0	0	.000	1	1	0	0.00	0
2007 Chicago j-k........	N.L.	22	24¹/₃	1	1	.500	24	13	18	3.33	0
2008 Chicago l-m........	N.L.	65	66¹/₃	5	4	.556	84	18	54	3.26	34
Major League Totals ....10 Yrs.		276	1219¹/₃	77	61	.558	1407	577	947	3.65	34
Division Series											
1998 Chicago	N.L.	1	5	0	1	.000	5	4	3	1.80	0
2003 Chicago	N.L.	2	15¹/₃	2	0	1.000	18	7	7	1.76	0
2007 Chicago	N.L.	2	3	0	0	.000	2	0	3	3.00	0
2008 Chicago	N.L.	1	1	0	0	.000	0	0	2	0.00	0
Division Series Totals		6	24¹/₃	2	1	.667	25	11	15	1.85	0
Championship Series											
2003 Chicago	N.L.	2	12¹/₃	0	1	.000	13	7	14	7.30	0

a On disabled list from May 24 to June 19, 1996.
b Selected Rookie of the Year in National League for 1998.
c On disabled list from March 31 to November 2, 1999.
d On disabled list from March 25 to May 1 and July 30 to August 21, 2000.
e On disabled list from August 4 to September 7, 2001.

f On disabled list from May 12 to July 11, 2004.
g On disabled list from May 1 to June 29 and July 21 to August 5 and August 30 to October 31, 2005.
h On disabled list from March 27 to May 18 and June 7 to October 29, 2006.
i Filed for free agency, October 29, 2006, re-signed with Chicago Cubs, November 15, 2006.
j On disabled list from March 29 to August 3, 2007.
k Filed for free agency, October 29, 2007, re-signed with Chicago Cubs, November 28, 2007.
l On disabled list from July 14 to August 5, 2008.
m Filed for free agency, October 31, 2008. Signed with Cleveland Indians, December 13, 2008.

WRIGHT, DEQUAM LA WESLEY (WESLEY)
Born, Montgomery, Alabama, January 28, 1985.
Bats Right. Throws Left. Height, 5 feet, 11 inches. Weight, 160 pounds.

Year	Club	Lea	G	IP	W	L	Pct	SO	BB	H	ERA	SAVES
2003 Dodgers	Gulf Coast	14	37²/₃	3	1	.750	26	19	37	3.58	0
2004 Ogden	Pioneer	17	44¹/₃	3	3	.500	66	23	56	6.29	0
2005 Vero Beach	Fla.St.	6	6²/₃	0	0	.000	8	10	8	9.45	0
2005 Columbus	So.Atl.	30	60²/₃	1	5	.167	68	33	38	1.93	1
2006 Vero Beach	Fla.St.	26	42¹/₃	3	3	.500	51	23	29	1.49	0
2006 Jacksonville	Southern	15	21¹/₃	1	1	.500	28	11	14	4.64	1
2007 Las Vegas	P.C.	14	16²/₃	1	2	.333	18	18	28	9.18	0
2007 Jacksonville a	Southern	30	61¹/₃	6	2	.750	68	31	45	2.49	2
2008 Houston	N.L.	71	55²/₃	4	3	.571	57	34	45	5.01	1

a Selected by Houston Astros from Los Angeles Dodgers in Rule V draft, December 6, 2007.

WRIGHT, JAMEY ALAN
Born, Oklahoma City, Oklahoma, December 24, 1974.
Bats Right. Throws Right. Height, 6 feet, 6 inches. Weight, 235 pounds.

Year	Club	Lea	G	IP	W	L	Pct	SO	BB	H	ERA	SAVES
1993 Rockies	Arizona	8	36	1	3	.250	26	9	35	4.00	0
1994 Asheville	So.Atl.	28	143¹/₃	7	14	.333	103	59	188	5.97	0
1995 Salem	Carolina	26	171	10	8	.556	95	72	160	2.47	0
1995 New Haven	Eastern	1	3	0	1	.000	0	3	6	9.00	0
1996 New Haven	Eastern	7	44²/₃	5	1	.833	54	12	27	0.81	0
1996 Colorado Springs	P.C.	9	59²/₃	4	2	.667	40	22	53	2.72	0
1996 Colorado	N.L.	16	91¹/₃	4	4	.500	45	41	105	4.93	0
1997 Salem	Carolina	1	1	0	1	.000	1	1	1	9.00	0
1997 Colorado Springs	P.C.	2	11	1	0	1.000	11	5	9	1.64	0
1997 Colorado a	N.L.	26	149²/₃	8	12	.400	59	71	198	6.25	0
1998 Colorado	N.L.	34	206¹/₃	9	14	.391	86	95	235	5.67	0
1999 Colorado	N.L.	16	94¹/₃	4	3	.571	49	54	110	4.87	0
1999 Colorado Springs b	P.C.	17	100¹/₃	5	7	.417	75	38	133	6.46	0
2000 Huntsville	Southern	2	12¹/₃	2	0	1.000	10	5	7	0.00	0
2000 Indianapolis	Int.	1	5	0	0	.000	7	3	8	1.80	0
2000 Milwaukee c	N.L.	26	164²/₃	7	9	.438	96	88	157	4.10	0
2001 Milwaukee d	N.L.	33	194²/₃	11	12	.478	129	98	201	4.90	0
2002 Indianapolis	Int.	3	15¹/₃	1	1	.500	13	5	16	4.11	0
2002 Milwaukee-St. Louis e-f-g	N.L.	23	129¹/₃	7	13	.350	77	75	130	5.29	0
2003 Indianapolis	Int.	7	22	1	3	.250	17	10	32	7.36	0
2003 Oklahoma	P.C.	7	39¹/₃	2	1	.667	40	21	38	4.12	0
2003 Omaha	P.C.	13	76²/₃	3	5	.375	65	38	70	3.64	0
2003 Kansas City h-i-j-k-l	A.L.	4	25¹/₃	1	2	.333	19	11	23	4.26	0
2004 Omaha	P.C.	18	104²/₃	8	6	.571	70	35	111	4.21	0
2004 Colorado m	N.L.	14	78²/₃	2	3	.400	41	45	82	4.12	0
2005 Colorado n	N.L.	34	171¹/₃	8	16	.333	101	81	201	5.46	0
2006 San Francisco o	N.L.	34	156	6	10	.375	79	64	167	5.19	0
2007 Frisco	Texas	1	4	0	0	.000	2	0	6	4.50	0
2007 Oklahoma	P.C.	3	16¹/₃	2	1	.667	11	3	21	4.41	0
2007 Texas p-q	A.L.	20	77	4	5	.444	39	41	72	3.62	0
2008 Texas r	A.L.	75	84¹/₃	8	7	.533	60	35	93	5.12	0
Major League Totals	13 Yrs.	355	1623	79	110	.418	880	799	1774	5.06	0

a On disabled list from May 15 to June 8, 1997.
b Traded to Milwaukee Brewers with catcher Henry Blanco and pitcher Justin Miller for infielder Jeff Cirillo and pitcher Scott Karl, December 13, 1999.
c On disabled list from March 28 to May 22, 2000.
d On disabled list from May 21 to June 10, 2001.
e On disabled list from April 5 to May 24, 2002.
f Traded to St. Louis Cardinals with cash for outfielder Chris Morris and player to be named later, August 29, 2002.
g Milwaukee Brewers received pitcher Mike Matthews to complete trade, September 11, 2002.
h Filed for free agency, November 1, 2002. Signed with Seattle Mariners organization, January 24, 2003.

i Released by Seattle Mariners, March 18, 2003. Signed with Milwaukee Brewers organization, March 23, 2003.
j Released by Milwaukee Brewers, April 28, 2003. Signed with Texas Rangers organization, May 5, 2003.
k Released by Texas Rangers, June 16, 2003. Signed with Kansas City Royals organization, June 24, 2003.
l Filed for free agency, October 30, 2003. Signed with Chicago Cubs organization, December 18, 2003. Released by Chicago Cubs March 26, 2004. Signed with Kansas City Royals organization, March 29, 2004.
m Filed for free agency, November 1, 2004, re-signed with Colorado Rockies, December 21, 2004.
n Filed for free agency, November 2, 2005. Signed with San Francisco Giants organization, January 17, 2006.
o Filed for free agency, November 2, 2006. Signed with Texas Rangers organization, January 25, 2007.
p On disabled list from April 11 to June 16, 2007.
q Filed for free agency, November 12, 2007. Signed with Texas Rangers organization, January 11, 2008.
r Filed for free agency, October 30, 2008.

WUERTZ, MICHAEL JAMES

Born, Austin, Minnesota, December 15, 1978.
Bats Right. Throws Right. Height, 6 feet, 3 inches. Weight, 205 pounds.

Year	Club	Lea	G	IP	W	L	Pct	SO	BB	H	ERA	SAVES
1998 Williamsport	N.Y.-Penn.		14	86⅓	7	5	.583	59	19	79	3.44	0
1999 Lansing	Midwest		28	161⅓	11	12	.478	127	44	191	4.80	0
2000 Daytona	Fla.St.		28	171⅓	12	7	.632	142	64	166	3.78	0
2001 West Tenn	Southern		27	160	4	9	.308	135	58	160	3.99	0
2002 Iowa	P.C.		28	154	9	5	.643	131	69	185	5.55	0
2003 Iowa	P.C.		43	124	3	9	.250	92	35	140	4.57	1
2004 Chicago	N.L.		31	29	1	0	1.000	30	17	22	4.34	1
2004 Iowa	P.C.		37	44⅔	1	1	.500	59	15	30	2.42	19
2005 Chicago	N.L.		75	75⅔	6	2	.750	89	40	60	3.81	0
2006 Iowa	P.C.		30	41⅔	6	0	1.000	67	9	30	1.73	10
2006 Chicago	N.L.		41	40⅔	3	1	.750	42	16	35	2.66	0
2007 Chicago	N.L.		73	72⅓	2	3	.400	79	35	64	3.48	0
2008 Iowa	P.C.		17	20	0	1	.000	29	14	13	3.60	4
2008 Chicago	N.L.		45	44⅔	1	1	.500	30	20	44	3.63	0
Major League Totals	5 Yrs.		265	262⅓	13	7	.650	270	128	225	3.57	1
Division Series												
2007 Chicago	N.L.		2	1⅔	0	0	.000	2	1	0	0.00	0

YABU, KEIICHI

Born, Mie, Japan, September 28, 1968.
Bats Right. Throws Right. Height, 6 feet. Weight, 230 pounds.

Year	Club	Lea	G	IP	W	L	Pct	SO	BB	H	ERA	SAVES
1994 Hanshin	Japan Cent.		26	18⅓	9	9	.500	110	42	174	3.18	0
1995 Hanshin	Japan Cent.		27	19	7	13	.350	118	50	185	2.98	0
1996 Hanshin	Japan Cent.		30	19⅓	11	14	.440	145	51	204	4.01	0
1997 Hanshin	Japan Cent.		29	18	10	12	.417	111	62	172	3.59	0
1998 Hanshin	Japan Cent.		24	16	11	10	.524	90	51	159	3.51	0
1999 Hanshin	Japan Cent.		28	17⅓	6	16	.500	95	57	175	3.95	0
2000 Hanshin	Japan Cent.		25	15	6	10	.375	95	30	162	4.17	0
2001 Hanshin	Japan Cent.		17	9	0	4	.000	26	33	55	4.09	0
2002 Hanshin	Japan Cent.		20	13⅔	10	6	.625	97	30	118	3.14	0
2003 Hanshin	Japan Cent.		23	9⅔	8	3	.727	67	27	97	3.96	0
2004 Hanshin	Japan Cent.		19	11⅓	6	9	.400	75	36	108	3.02	0
2005 Oakland a	A.L.		40	58	4	0	1.000	44	26	64	4.50	1
2006 b					INJURED—Did Not Play							
2007 c					INJURED—Did Not Play							
2008 Fresno	P.C.		3	5	0	0	.000	7	6	4	1.80	0
2008 San Francisco d	N.L.		60	68	3	6	.333	48	32	63	3.57	0
Major League Totals	2 Yrs.		100	126	7	6	.538	92	58	127	4.00	1

a Signed with Oakland Athletics, January 12, 2005.
b Filed for free agency, October 15 2005. Signed with Colorado Rockies organization, January 18, 2006.
c Released by Colorado Rockies, March 20, 2006. Signed with San Francisco Giants organization, December 26, 2007.
d On disabled list from July 20 to August 6, 2008.

YATES, TYLER KALI

Born, Lihue, Hawaii, August 7, 1977.
Bats Right. Throws Right. Height, 6 feet, 4 inches. Weight, 240 pounds.

Year	Club	Lea	G	IP	W	L	Pct	SO	BB	H	ERA	SAVES
1998 Athletics	Arizona		15	23	0	0	.000	20	14	28	3.91	2
1998 Sou Oregon	Northwest		2	2⅓	0	0	.000	1	0	2	0.00	1

357

Year	Club	Lea	G	IP	W	L	Pct	SO	BB	H	ERA	SAVES
1999 Visalia	Calif.	47	$82\frac{1}{3}$	2	5	.286	74	35	98	5.47	4	
2000 Modesto	Calif.	30	$56\frac{2}{3}$	4	2	.667	61	23	50	2.86	1	
2000 Midland	Texas	22	$26\frac{1}{3}$	1	1	.500	24	15	28	6.15	0	
2001 Sacramento	P.C.	4	$5\frac{1}{3}$	1	0	1.000	3	1	3	0.00	1	
2001 Midland a	Texas	56	$62\frac{2}{3}$	4	6	.400	61	27	66	4.31	17	
2002 Norfolk	Int.	24	34	2	2	.500	34	13	29	1.32	6	
2003 Binghamton	Eastern	8	$39\frac{1}{3}$	1	2	.333	36	17	33	4.35	0	
2003 St. Lucie	Fla.St.	14	48	1	2	.333	49	24	41	4.31	0	
2003 Norfolk b	Int.	4	20	1	2	.333	15	9	22	4.05	0	
2004 New York	N.L.	21	$46\frac{2}{3}$	2	4	.333	35	25	61	6.36	0	
2004 Norfolk	Int.	30	$39\frac{2}{3}$	6	2	.750	43	22	28	3.18	4	
2005 New York c	N.L				INJURED—Did Not Play							
2006 Richmond	Int.	7	$8\frac{1}{3}$	0	0	.000	10	3	6	2.16	0	
2006 Atlanta d-e	N.L.	56	50	2	5	.286	46	31	42	3.96	1	
2007 Atlanta	N.L.	75	66	2	3	.400	69	31	64	5.18	2	
2008 Pittsburgh f	N.L.	72	$73\frac{1}{3}$	6	3	.667	63	41	72	4.66	1	
Major League Totals	4 Yrs.	224	236	12	15	.444	213	128	239	5.00	4	

a Traded by Oakland Athletics to New York Mets with outfielder Mark Guthrie for outfielder David Justice and cash, December 14, 2001.
b On disabled list from March 21 to April 5, 2003.
c On disabled list from March 15 to October 31, 2005.
d Not offered contract, December 21, 2005. Signed with Baltimore Orioles organization, January 24, 2006.
e Released by Baltimore Orioles, March 31, 2006. Signed with Atlanta Braves organization, May 3, 2006.
f Traded to Pittsburgh Pirates for pitcher Todd Redmond, March 26, 2008.

YOUNG, CHRISTOPHER RYAN (CHRIS)

Born, Dallas, Texas, May 25, 1979.
Bats Right. Throws Right. Height, 6 feet, 10 inches. Weight, 280 pounds.

Year	Club	Lea	G	IP	W	L	Pct	SO	BB	H	ERA	SAVES
2001 Hickory	So.Atl.	12	$74\frac{1}{3}$	5	3	.625	72	20	79	4.12	0	
2002 Hickory a	So.Atl.	26	$144\frac{2}{3}$	11	9	.550	136	34	127	3.11	0	
2003 Harrisburg	Eastern	15	83	4	4	.500	64	22	83	4.01	0	
2003 Brevard County	Fla.St.	8	50	5	2	.714	39	5	26	1.62	0	
2004 Frisco	Texas	18	$88\frac{1}{3}$	6	5	.545	75	31	94	4.48	0	
2004 Oklahoma	P.C.	5	$30\frac{1}{3}$	3	0	1.000	34	9	20	1.48	0	
2004 Texas b	A.L.	7	$36\frac{1}{3}$	3	2	.600	27	10	36	4.71	0	
2005 Lynchburg	Carolina	10	15	0	1	.000	14	5	9	3.00	2	
2005 Tulsa	Texas	35	53	3	2	.600	35	17	53	4.75	1	
2005 Texas c-d	A.L.	31	$164\frac{2}{3}$	12	7	.632	137	45	162	4.26	0	
2006 San Diego	N.L.	31	$179\frac{1}{3}$	11	5	.688	164	69	134	3.46	0	
2007 San Diego e	N.L.	30	173	9	8	.529	167	72	118	3.12	0	
2008 Lake Elsinore	Calif.	2	$8\frac{2}{3}$	0	1	.000	7	1	5	3.12	0	
2008 San Diego f	N.L.	18	$102\frac{1}{3}$	7	6	.538	93	48	84	3.96	0	
Major League Totals	5 Yrs.	117	$655\frac{2}{3}$	42	28	.600	588	244	534	3.72	0	
Division Series												
2006 San Diego	N.L.	1	$6\frac{2}{3}$	1	0	1.000	9	2	4	0.00	0	

a Traded by Pittsburgh Pirates to Montreal Expos with pitcher Jon Searles for pitcher Matt Herges, December 20, 2002.
b Traded to Texas Rangers with catcher Josh McKinley for catcher Einar Diaz, April 3, 2004.
c Traded to Arizona Diamondbacks with pitcher Orlando Hernandez and pitcher Luis Vizcaino for pitcher Javier Vazquez, December 20, 2005.
d Traded to San Diego Padres with infielder Adrian Gonzalez and outfielder Terrmel Sledge for pitcher Adam Eaton, pitcher Akinori Otsuka and catcher Billy Killian, January 4, 2006.
e On disabled list from July 25 to August 9, 2007.
f On disabled list from May 22 to July 29 and August 11 to September 1, 2008.

ZAMBRANO, CARLOS ALBERTO

Born, Puerto Cabello, Venezuela, June 1, 1981.
Bats Both. Throws Right. Height, 6 feet, 5 inches. Weight, 255 pounds.

Year	Club	Lea	G	IP	W	L	Pct	SO	BB	H	ERA	SAVES
1998 Cubs	Arizona	14	40	0	1	.000	36	25	39	3.15	1	
1999 Lansing	Midwest	27	$153\frac{1}{3}$	13	7	.650	98	62	150	4.17	0	
2000 Iowa	P.C.	34	$56\frac{2}{3}$	2	5	.286	46	40	54	3.97	6	
2000 West Tenn	Southern	9	$60\frac{1}{3}$	3	1	.750	43	21	39	1.34	0	
2001 Iowa	P.C.	26	$150\frac{2}{3}$	10	5	.667	155	68	124	3.88	0	
2001 Chicago	N.L.	6	$7\frac{2}{3}$	1	2	.333	4	8	11	15.26	0	
2002 Iowa	P.C.	3	9	0	0	.000	11	6	2	0.00	0	